Ref 920 Cu 2005

Current biography yearbook.

Current Biography Yearbook 2005

EDITOR
Clifford Thompson

THE H. W. WILSON COMPANY
NEW YORK   DUBLIN

SIXTY-SIXTH ANNUAL CUMULATION—2005

PRINTED IN THE UNITED STATES OF AMERICA

International Standard Serial No. (0084-9499)

International Standard Book No. (0-8242-1056-5)

Library of Congress Catalog Card No. (40-27432)

Table of Contents

PREFACE

The aim of *Current Biography Yearbook 2005*, like that of the preceding volumes in this series of annual dictionaries of contemporary biography, now in its seventh decade of publication, is to provide reference librarians, students, and researchers with objective, accurate, and well-documented biographical articles about living leaders in all fields of human accomplishment. Whenever feasible, obituary notices appear for persons whose biographies have been published in *Current Biography*.

Current Biography Yearbook 2005 carries on the policy of including new and updated biographical profiles that supersede earlier articles. Profiles have been made as accurate and objective as possible through careful researching of newspapers, magazines, the World Wide Web, authoritative reference books, and news releases of both government and private agencies. Immediately after they are published in the 11 monthly issues, articles are submitted to biographees to give them an opportunity to suggest additions and corrections in time for publication of the *Current Biography Yearbook*. To take account of major changes in the careers of biographees, articles are revised before they are included in the yearbook.

Classification by Profession—2005 and *2001–2005 Index* are at the end of this volume. *Current Biography Cumulated Index 1940–2000* cumulates and supersedes all previous indexes.

For their assistance in preparing *Current Biography Yearbook 2005*, I thank the staff of *Current Biography* and other members of The H. W. Wilson Company's General Reference Department, and also the staffs of the company's Computer and Manufacturing departments.

Current Biography welcomes comments and suggestions. Please send your comments to: The Editor, *Current Biography*, The H. W. Wilson Company, 950 University Ave., Bronx, NY 10452; fax: 718-590-4566; E-mail: cthompson@hwwilson.com.

Clifford Thompson

List of Biographical Sketches

ix

Current Biography Yearbook 2005

AC/DC

Music group

Young, Malcolm
Jan. 6, 1953– Rhythm guitarist

Young, Angus
Mar. 31, 1959– Lead guitarist

Johnson, Brian
Oct. 5, 1947– Vocalist

Williams, Cliff
Dec. 14, 1949– Bassist

Rudd, Phil
May 19, 1954– Drummer

Address: c/o Epic Records, 550 Madison Ave., New York, NY 10022

Throughout its decades-long career, the rock band AC/DC has consistently written dynamic, gritty music with lyrics that often feature mischievously sexual and raucous imagery. The combination has resulted in sales of more than 80 million records in the United States alone, which may explain why the band has never altered its formula. Writing for the *Chicago Tribune* (January 20, 1991), Greg Kot noted, "AC/DC keeps coming back every few years with what sounds like the same album: a series of songs consisting of three ear-shattering guitar chords, a piston-pumping drum beat and a gravel-voiced banshee screaming about sex, booze and/or damnation." Angus Young, the band's lead guitarist, agreed, telling James Rotondi for *Guitar Player* (February 1993), "With AC/DC you know what you're getting. We've been this way ever since we started, and we've kept that raw approach. We don't go out there to take your temperature down— we go out there to take it up." Through the years members of AC/DC have left or died, but the core of the group—Angus Young and his brother, the guitarist Malcolm Young—has remained the same. Brian Johnson, the band's lead singer since 1980, said of the brothers to Kot, "They're basically two quiet fellows who have taken boogie-woogie, the blues of B.B. King and Muddy Waters, and electrified it. It's great, timeless stuff. The kids may not know it's coming from B.B. and Muddy, but they're tapping their feet to it just the same."

Malcolm Young, the sixth of the nine children of William and Margaret Young, was born on January 6, 1953 in Glasgow, Scotland. Angus was born there on March 31, 1959. (Some sources have different dates.) A working-class family, the Youngs moved to Australia in 1963, during a period of recession in Great Britain. At the time Australia was still experiencing the economic boom that began after World War II, and the Australian government encouraged immigration through a program that enabled those seeking entry to sail to the nation for £10 (less than $30) per person. In Australia one of the Young siblings, George, who also showed musical talent, became a star with the Easybeats, a popular group of the 1960s.

As youths, Angus and Malcolm Young read *DownBeat* magazine to learn about their favorite Chicago blues and rock idols, among them Chuck Berry, Muddy Waters, and Buddy Guy. "That transformed me," Angus Young told Greg Kot for the *Chicago Tribune* (March 8, 1996). "I'm in awe of those guys still." Malcolm Young left school at the age of 15 and began working as a machine maintenance engineer for a company that manufactured brassieres. Angus also quit school at 15; he went to work as a printer for the pornographic magazine *Ribald*. For a while the two brothers, who had both learned guitar, performed in separate bands in their leisure time. In 1973, after Malcolm Young's group broke up, the brothers decided to play together. Their older sister Margaret, whose collection of rock-and-roll albums had strongly influenced her brothers, suggested the name AC/DC after seeing the acronyms (which stand for "alternating current" and "direct current") on the back of a vacuum cleaner. She also suggested that Angus wear his school uniform on stage; he has continued to do so ever since. "It really has that Jekyll and Hyde thing about it," he told James Rotondi. "If you met me, normally you'd say, 'Jeez this guy's a right wallflower.' I'm shy and very quiet. But as soon as I put on that suit, I become an extrovert." The band held its first concert on December 31, 1973 at Chequers, a pub in Sydney, Australia; their program consisted mostly of covers of Chuck Berry, the Beatles, and the Rolling Stones. Angus Young described the band's early audiences to Kot as "a very hard-drinking crowd, people who, when they went to a bar, went to a bar for one reason only. And you had to entertain them in a way that would enable them to still enjoy drinking. You had to give them some blood. Otherwise they had sub-

Getty Images
AC/DC (left to right): Brian Johnson, Phil Rudd, Angus Young, Malcolm Young, Cliff Williams

tle ways of letting you know you weren't, and you better be quick to get out of the way. That's where I learned my act." Along with their lead singer, Dave Evans, whom the brothers had recruited through an ad in the *Sydney Morning Herald*, the band cut its first single, "Can I Sit Next to You," produced by their brother George and another former Easybeat member, Harry Vanda. The single became a minor regional hit in the Australian cities of Perth and Adelaide. In the band's early days, AC/DC played in any venue that would hire them, occasionally performing up to six times a day. In 1974 the group moved to Melbourne, Australia, and after a succession of bassists and drummers came and went, settled on the drummer Phil Rudd (born on May 19, 1954 in Melbourne) and the bassist Mark Evans (born on March 2, 1956, also in Melbourne). After Dave Evans refused to go on stage at one concert, the band replaced him with their chauffeur, Bon Scott (born Ronald Belford on July 9, 1946 in Kirriemuir, Scotland). Scott had previously served as drummer with the Australian pop bands Fraternity and the Valentines; he had also been convicted several times on minor criminal offenses and had been rejected by the Australian Army on the grounds that he was socially maladjusted.

In early 1975 the band released their first album, *High Voltage*, in Australia. They followed with *TNT* in December of that year. *TNT* peaked at the number-two position on the Australian charts, while the band's version of the blues standard "Baby Please Don't Go" reached number 10. "We'd been in local bands before AC/DC, and the one thing missing out there was that toughness— toughness with a blues influence," Angus Young

told Greg Kot. "So we'd play stuff like 'Baby, Please Don't Go' at 100 miles an hour and tear the audience apart." In January 1976 the band signed a contract with Atlantic Records and moved to England. On their earliest tours of that country, they were accompanied by a vice squad, which tried unsuccessfully to stop the performers from swearing or dropping their pants to moon audiences. AC/DC's first recording to be released in Great Britain (in April 1976) and the U.S. (in October 1976) was a version of *High Voltage* containing material from their first two Australian albums. Writing for the *All Music Guide* (on-line), Steve Huey called it "a stripped-down collection of loud, raw, rude rockers, mostly odes to rock & roll and its attendant hard-partying lifestyle." Huey also noted that Angus Young's "manic guitar solos overlaid a series of simple, basic boogie grooves delivered with ferocious power and volume." Although their singles and albums did not sell in sufficient numbers to reach any charts in either country, the single "It's a Long Way to the Top (If You Wanna Rock 'n' Roll)" climbed to the number-five position on the Australian charts. The group released another disk, *Dirty Deeds Done Dirt Cheap,* in England at the end of 1976 (it was released in the U.S. in 1981 to much success); it included a rare rhythmic blues ballad by the group, "Ride On." In October 1976 the band performed for the first time in the United States.

In 1977 Mark Evans left AC/DC, after reportedly having difficulties with Angus Young and complaining that he was tired of touring. His replacement was Cliff Williams (born on December 14, 1949 in Rumford, England). Williams played for the band's next album, *Let There Be Rock* (1977), which was their first to appear on charts in the U.S.

(at number 154) and Great Britain (at number 75). According to Steve Huey, *Let There Be Rock* is a "bracing hard rock record of blasting guitar and basic, aggressive grooves. . . . While the music still meanders on occasion, the songwriting is overall a bit more memorable." AC/DC followed with *Powerage* (1978), which Angus Young has called his favorite in the group's discography. The record rose to number 133 on U.S. charts and made it to number 26 in Great Britain. It also contained the band's first single to appear on a British chart— "Rock 'N' Roll Damnation," which peaked at number 24. By this point the band had become a top concert draw, known for frantic performances led by Angus Young, who leapt around on stage and sometimes even played the guitar while lying down. "For me," Angus told James Rotondi, "the physical element of performing actually comes from the guitar. I'm a pretty small guy . . . and I've got very little fingers. I'm not saying that being small is a disability, but when a guy of average height bends a string, his fingers bend the string, whereas I have to put my whole arm into it!" The band's live act was captured on *If You Want Blood You've Got It*, recorded in Glasgow. That album hit number 113 on the U.S. charts and number 13 in the U.K.

AC/DC hired Robert John "Mutt" Lange to produce their next record. The result was the band's commercial breakthrough, *Highway to Hell* (1979), which sold over a million copies and made it to number 17 on the U.S. charts and number eight in Great Britain. *Highway to Hell* offers "a series of songs about drink, lust and depravity that rocked with a fury not heard since Aerosmith's mid-'70s landmark, *Rocks*," Greg Kot wrote. The title track was not a big hit when it was released, but it has since become known as a hard-rock classic. "It's not just a snotty, nihilistic party anthem," Steve Huey wrote, "but a moment of unrepentant self-recognition from a rowdy ruffian (Bon Scott) who, for better or worse, exulted in what he was." The lyrics proclaim, "Hey Satan, paid my dues, / playing in a rockin' band. / Hey Mama, look at me. / I'm on my way to the promised land."

The band's second hit single in Great Britain was "Much Too Much," released in January 1980. One night during the next month, Scott consumed a great deal of alcohol while watching other bands with a friend. He fell asleep in the car afterward, and his friend left him there. The next morning the friend found him still in the car, unconscious, and took him to the hospital. Scott was pronounced dead on February 20, 1980. (Most sources list his actual date of death as February 19.) The official coroner's report stated that he had "drunk himself to death." "At first I didn't really believe it, but in the morning it finally dawned on me," Angus Young said, as quoted on *AC/DC Riff Raff* (on-line). "It's just like losing a member of your family, that's the only way to describe it. Maybe even a bit worse, [because] we all had a lot of respect for Bon as a person, even though he did like to drink and have

a bit of a crazy time, [because] he was always there when you needed him to do his job and things."

Despite the tragedy, AC/DC continued to perform, with Brian Johnson (born on October 5, 1947 in Newcastle upon Tyne, England), whose voice resembled Scott's, as Scott's successor. "We hit it off right away, instant magic," Johnson told Greg Kot in 1991. "We came from the same backgrounds, working-class guys who left school at 15. No talk of college or big universities, just go to work and make some money." Johnson wrote the lyrics for *Back in Black*, which AC/DC released in 1980. The album sold more than 16 million copies in the United States alone, and reached number four on U.S. charts. In Great Britain it topped the charts. In *Rolling Stone* (on-line), David Fricke hailed it as "not only the best of AC/DC's six American albums, it's the apex of heavy-metal art: the first LP since *Led Zeppelin II* that captures all the blood, sweat and arrogance of the genre." Similarly, Kurt Loder wrote for *Rolling Stone* (on-line) that the record was "AC/DC's best album," on which "the case for the band's talents is finally made with undeniable force and clarity." The recording featured three hit singles: the title track, "You Shook Me All Night Long," and "Rock 'N' Roll Ain't Noise Pollution." The band returned following year with *For Those About to Rock We Salute You*, which topped the charts in the United States and hit number three in England. The title track, with cannon-like sound effects, was a hit single in England, as was "Let's Get It Up." Nevertheless, in the opinion of Steve Huey, "it became apparent" from that album "that the group really did miss Scott more than it initially indicated. Brian Johnson's lyrics started to seem more calculated and a bit cliched, lacking Scott's devil-may-care sense of humor. And the band itself slows down the tempo frequently, sounding less aggressive and inspired." AC/DC was also criticized for what many perceived as sexist lyrics, but the group did not make apologies for them. "All the anti-sexist women in the world can't change what a man thinks," Brian Johnson told Greg Kot. "Men lust after women. They always have and they always will. But I think most people have come to realize our lyrics are just tongue-in-cheek stuff."

AC/DC toured Japan in 1981 and again in 1982. The following year Rudd quit the group; he had been having drug problems and had not been getting along with Malcolm Young. Simon Wright (born on June 19, 1963 in Alden, England) took his place. The band's next release, *Flick of the Switch* (1983), represented their return to more up-tempo music. The record made it to number four on the British charts and number 15 in the U.S. In addition, it spawned two top-40 British hits, "Guns for Hire" and "Nervous Shakedown." In January 1985 the band performed as headliners at the Rock in Rio Festival, in Rio de Janeiro, Brazil, in front of 342,000 fans. AC/DC's next album, *Fly on the Wall*, arrived later that year. The record rose to number seven on the British charts but only to number 32 in the United States and contained only one top-40 single in Great Britain—"Shake Your Foundations." Steve Huey faulted it for continuing AC/DC's "descent into cookie-cutter mediocrity, with the leering humor of past glories seeming forced and uninspired, and the music remaining somewhat underdeveloped and directionless."

AC/DC fared better with *Who Made Who* (1986), a greatest-hits compilation with a new track that was produced for use in the Stephen King movie *Maximum Overdrive* (1986). The album sold well and earned the group new fans. Returning to the studio with George Young and Harry Vanda, the band next released *Blow Up Your Video* (1988). The album climbed up the charts to number 12 in the U.S. and number two in Great Britain, where it spawned two hit singles, "Heatseeker" and "That's The Way I Wanna Rock 'n' Roll." "The album pounds out material as brutal as the band's best, but there are subtle shifts along the way," Jim Farber wrote for *Rolling Stone* (on-line). "In general, there are more fast numbers than usual and more cuts featuring hooks based on single-note progressions rather than a succession of solid chords." Because of exhaustion, Malcolm Young did not perform with the band on their subsequent tour; his nephew Stevie Young stepped in for him. The following year Simon left the band and Chris Slade (born on October 30, 1946 in Pontypridd, Wales) came on board.

AC/DC's next album, *The Razor's Edge* (1990), was praised by many critics as their best album since *Back in Black*. In a year dominated by pop albums, *The Razor's Edge* became one of the few hard-rock efforts to place high on the U.S. charts as well as charts in the U.K. When "Moneytalks" peaked, at number 24, it became the first AC/DC single in 10 years to make the top-40 in the U.S. The album also contained the hit British single "Thunderstruck." In 1992 the band released *AC/DC Live* in both one- and two-CD versions. The group returned in 1995 with *Ballbreaker*, recorded with the legendary producer Rick Rubin. Angus and Malcolm Young wrote the lyrics for *Ballbreaker*, because, as Brian Johnson later told Kot, "To be quite honest, I dried up on lyrics. You can only write so much on a certain theme." "Throughout the album," Stephen Thomas Erlewine wrote for the *All Music Guide* (on-line), "the band sounds committed and professional, making *Ballbreaker* the best late-period AC/DC album to date." The album marked a reunion with the band's original drummer, Phil Rudd. The British rock magazine *NME* named *Ballbreaker* among the top 50 albums of the year. The band released the studio album *Stiff Upper Lip* in 2000. That work struck Erlewine as a "simple, addictive, hard album, bursting with bold riffs and bolstered by a crunching, thrillingly visceral sound. Sure, there are absolutely no new ideas, but that's the point. . . . Each song has a riff so catchy, it feels like you've heard it for years." The band has also released occasional multi-CD compilations of their music, including a 17-CD set

called *AC/DC* (2002). Many bootleg AC/DC albums, made clandestinely by fans during performances, are in circulation.

In 1998 the Australian postal service produced a stamp bearing an image of AC/DC, as part of a series depicting rock legends. In 2003 the group was inducted into the Rock and Roll Hall of Fame, in Cleveland, Ohio. The following year a street in Melbourne was officially renamed AC/DC Lane. (A street in Madrid, Spain, is also said to bear the band's name.) AC/DC was recently certified by the Recording Industry Association of America (RIAA) as the fifth-best-selling band in U.S. history, behind the Beatles, Led Zeppelin, Pink Floyd, and the Eagles. The "DualDisc" *Back in Black*, released in February 2005, contains the original *Back in Black*, a stereo version, and a DVD with interviews, archival footage, in-studio performances, and the film *The Story of Back in Black*. *Family Jewels*, a DVD of select AC/DC performances from the mid-1970s to the mid-1990s, was released in March 2005. Reviews were mostly positive, and by the end of April 2005, the DVD had reached number one on *Billboard*'s video charts; it remained among the top-10–selling videos in the U.S. until the last week in September of the same year.

—G.O.

Suggested Reading: ACDCrocks.com; *Chicago Tribune* XIII p6+ Jan. 20, 1991, with photos, Mar. 8, 1996, with photos; *Guitar Player* p23+ Feb. 1993, with photos, p81+ Dec. 1995, with photos

Selected Albums: *High Voltage*, 1976; *Let There Be Rock*, 1977; *Powerage*, 1978; *If You Want Blood You've Got It*, 1978; *Highway to Hell*, 1979; *Back in Black*, 1980; *For Those About to Rock We Salute You*, 1981; *Dirty Deeds Done Cheap*, 1981; *Flick of the Switch*, 1983; *Fly on the Wall*, 1985; *Who Made Who*, 1986; *Blow Up Your Video*, 1988; *The Razor's Edge*, 1990; *AC/DC Live*, 1992; *Ballbreaker*, 1995; *Stiff Upper Lip*, 2000; *Back in Black*, 2005

Selected Videos or DVDs: *Family Jewels*, 2005

Anderson, Ray C.

July 28, 1934– Businessman; environmental activist

Address: Interface Inc., 2859 Paces Ferry Rd., S.E., Suite 2000, Atlanta, GA 30339-6216

Once dubbed the "carpet king," because his company is the world's largest producer of commercial carpeting, Ray C. Anderson has become known as one of the nation's greenest—that is, most environmentally conscious—businessmen. An industrial engineer, Anderson worked for another carpet

Courtesy of Interface

Ray C. Anderson

manufacturer before founding his own company, Interface, in 1973. For more than a quarter of a century, Anderson never considered the destructive effects on the environment of the processes and materials used in the production of carpets. Then, in the early 1990s, spurred in part by concerns about pollutants mentioned by some of his clients, he read *The Ecology of Commerce: A Declaration of Sustainability* (1993), in which the author, Paul Hawken, urged businesses in the developed world to reduce their consumption of fuels and other resources by 80 percent, with the goal of becoming ecologically and environmentally sustainable before the year 2050. Sustainability, as Anderson explained to Monica Elliot for *Industrial Engineer* (September 2003), "means taking nothing from the Earth that's not renewable by the Earth naturally and rapidly, and doing no harm to the biosphere: Taking nothing, doing no harm." "By the time I got one-third of the way through the book, I felt like I got a spear in my chest," Anderson recalled to Ernest Holsendolph for the *Atlanta Journal–Constitution* (August 15, 1999), "because I realized what we were doing to contribute to the decline of the biosphere." In a single year at that time, Interface was consuming more that 500 million pounds of raw materials, releasing more than 900 tons of pollutants into the air and 600 million gallons of waste into waterways, and discarding 10,000 tons of solid trash. "Hawken talks about 'the death of birth,'" Anderson told Keith Dunnavant for *Atlanta Magazine* (December 2001). "Can you imagine? The whole system just collapses. The death of birth! . . . I stood convicted as a plunderer of the earth, convinced that in the future, people like me will go to jail."

Anderson's realization—which he has labeled an epiphany—led him to make a "mid-course correction" in his life, as he recalled to an interviewer for *Engineering Enterprise* (Spring 2004), and he began to read extensively on the subject of sustainability. He pledged that he would make Interface completely sustainable by 2020; it would use no petroleum, a nonrenewable resource, and would create no nonbiodegradable or dangerous solid wastes or harmful gaseous emissions. "Part cheerleader, part scold, part dreamer, Ray Anderson wants to be the man to reconcile them all—left and right, ecologist and oil baron . . . ," Gwen Kinkead wrote for *Fortune* (May 24, 1999). "Drawing on his Baptist roots and his engineer's head for facts, he has spread the gospel of sustainability: Unless we as a species stop bickering and do something, he says, the end—our end—is imminent." "This is a crisis: It is a funeral march to the grave, if someone or something doesn't do something to reverse the deadly decline," Anderson told Kinkead. "Business and industry—the largest, wealthiest, most powerful, most pervasive institutions on earth, and the ones doing the most damage—must take the lead. Once one understands this crisis, no thinking person can stand idly by and do nothing. When you get past denial, you must do whatever you can. Conscience demands it."

In the past decade, according to its Web site, Interface "has reduced its environmental footprint by over one-third," by undertaking more than 400 "sustainability initiatives." To make greater use of renewable sources of energy (the sun and wind), Interface engineers have invented new technologies and redesiged processes. In addition, they have reformulated products, to some extent by increasing the proportions of renewable materials in them. By 2004 Interface had reduced waste by 80 percent and water intake by 78 percent. The company's emissions of greenhouse gases had been cut by 46 percent, its energy consumption by 31 percent, and its use of petroleum-based materials by 28 percent. Those decreases saved Interface more than $230 million without hurting profits—evidence that corporate responsibility and profitability can coexist. In addition to carpet tiles, the firm now manufactures broadloom carpeting, specialty fabrics, and other products in facilities on four continents, and it has clients in some 110 countries. "You have to do well in this business of doing good," Anderson told Monica Elliot. "We're out to prove there's a better model that does do well and do good." For about three years when Bill Clinton occupied the White House, Anderson served as the co-chairman of the President's Council on Sustainable Development. Since he relinquished the posts of chief executive officer and president of Interface, in 2001, he has held the title of chairman. Among his many honors are the inaugural Millennium Award from Global Green USA (1996); the George and Cynthia Mitchell International Prize for Sustainable Development (2001), administered by the National Academy of Sciences; a Leadership Award from the U.S. Green Building Council (2002); and the National Wildlife Federation's Conservation Achievement Award for Corporate Leadership (2002).

Ray C. Anderson was born on July 28, 1934 in West Point, Georgia, where he grew up. His father was a postmaster, his mother a teacher. Anderson was smart and athletic, and in high school he excelled at football. The former college baseball star Carlton Lewis coached his high school's football team and served as a mentor and inspiration to him. Lewis "taught me to compete and made the team better than it wanted to be," Anderson told Kathryn Woestendiek for *Industrial Management* (March 13, 1998). Anderson attended Lewis's alma mater, the Georgia Institute of Technology, in Atlanta, where he played quarterback for the Yellow Jackets under the legendary football coach Bobby Dodd, whom he has cited as another of his role models. He majored in industrial engineering and earned a B.S. degree with highest honors in 1956.

After his graduation Anderson got a job in Atlanta with Procter & Gamble, as an industrial engineer in the firm's Buckeye division (now known as Procter & Gamble Cellulose), which operated cottonseed-oil and soybean-oil mills. In 1959 he joined the Callaway Mills Co., which produced cotton textiles in LaGrange, Georgia. He advanced steadily through the ranks, eventually being promoted to vice president. One of the company's owners, Fuller Callaway Jr., who became another of his advisers, instilled in him the desire to own his own business. In 1968 Callaway Mills was sold to Milliken & Co. Inc., a leading manufacturer of textiles. The next year Anderson's new managers sent him to Great Britain to learn about the latest developments in carpet technology. One of the companies he visited was Carpets International, which manufactured carpet tiles. Such tiles are square (usually at least 17 inches on a side), making them easier to install and remove than traditional broadloom carpets, which are manufactured in 6-foot or 12-foot widths and must be cut to fit a room or passageway. Since individual tiles can also be replaced easily when they get worn, and their use can expedite the redecoration of offices whose layouts are changed, many companies prefer them to traditional carpeting, even though the initial cost of a square yard of carpet squares is about 30 percent more than that of a square yard of broadloom. Anderson was impressed with what he observed overseas and returned to the States to build a carpet-tile business for Milliken.

Although many people in the industry disparaged tiles as an inferior form of carpeting, Anderson was certain that there was a large potential market for them. In 1973 he resigned from Milliken, and with $50,000 (his total savings) plus $450,000 he had raised from friends in his hometown, he approached Carpets International to propose a joint venture. The company was eager to enter the U.S. market and gave him $750,000 for a 50 percent stake in his enterprise. When he began to

set up operations, in LaGrange, the U.S. was in a recession, and the economic outlook was bleak: oil-producing Arab nations had declared an embargo on oil sold to the U.S., and at the same time had quadrupled the price of oil and other petrochemicals, which are vital ingredients in the manufacture of synthetic yarns, glues, and other materials used to make carpets. Anderson, who had sunk his whole nest egg into an undertaking that seemed in danger of failing, told Alyssa A. Lappen for *Forbes* (April 17, 1989) that it was the "scariest time of my life." He had some advantages over his competitors, however; for instance, the cutting-edge technology that he had obtained from Carpets International reduced his yarn costs by 10 percent. Other technology from Carpets International helped Interface (as Anderson had named his company) develop equipment that produced a backing that made gluing for installation unnecessary.

Interface performed poorly during its first year; in 1974, the company racked up $400,000 in losses on little more than $800,000 in sales. Then, in 1975, business started to improve, following a nationwide spurt in office construction. Sales grew an average of 70 percent annually for the next five years. "In 1982, we woke up to the fact that we had developed something the world needed," Anderson told Shelley A. Lee for *Business Atlanta* (October 1992). "Through the European technology we acquired, we improved it over and over, and during the mid-'80s, we were making better products than anyone ever had." Anderson's British partners were not faring well, however, because the United Kingdom was being flooded with inexpensive broadloom carpets from abroad. Anderson began buying equity in Interface until he gained full control of it, in 1983. He acquired Carpets International as well. By 1985 Interface had become the leading producer of carpet tile in the U.S., and it had gained a significant share of the overseas market.

With the goal of diversifying and attracting additional markets, Interface acquired a small research company that had developed a germ-killing agent known as Intersept. Adding Intersept to carpet tiles made them resistant to bacteria and fungi and the odor and discoloration that such microorganisms cause, thus increasing their appeal to hospitals, schools, and other potential customers. In 1986 Interface acquired Guilford Industries, which manufactured fabrics for office furniture, cubicle dividers, walls, and ceilings. Later, Interface began applying Intersept to those materials as well. In 1989 Interface purchased its largest competitor, the Dutch company Heuga Holding B.V., which had a bigger share of the European, Canadian, and Asian markets than Interface. Anderson's company thereby became the world's leading manufacturer of carpet tiles, with an estimated 40 to 45 percent of the market. That year sales reached $581.8 million.

During the next few years, Anderson became aware of questions about the environmental hazards of his company's production processes and about health hazards of toxic substances that evaporate from new carpeting. Anderson, who had previously had no interest in or knowledge of ecology or environmental conservation or restoration, set up a task force to study the matter. When its members asked him to present to them an outline of Interface's environmental vision, he was at a loss. During the process of coming up with a philosophy, he received a copy of Paul Hawken's book *The Ecology of Commerce*. In that book and elsewhere, Hawken, a successful entrepreneur, described the many ways in which commercial activities have harmed or destroyed the environment. Corporations, he wrote, may enjoy success as it is usually defined, but "business as we know it" has "failed in one critical and thoughtless way: It did not honor the myriad forms of life that secure and connect its own breath and skin and heart to the breath and skin and heart of our earth." "We may have already surpassed the point at which we can sustainably support the world's population using present standards of production and consumption," he wrote. "That disturbing possibility should impel us to seek, as sensibly and quickly as possible, an integration of our wants and needs as expressed and served by commerce, with the capacity of the earth, water, forests, and fields to meet them. Thus, this book proposes three approaches, all guided by the example of nature. The first is to obey the waste-equals-food principle and entirely eliminate waste from our industrial production. . . . The second principle is to change from an economy based on carbon to one based on hydrogen and sunshine. . . . Third, we must create systems of feedback and accountability that support and strengthen restorative behavior, whether they are in resource utilities, green fees on agricultural chemicals, or reliance on local production and distribution. . . . All three recommendations have a single purpose: to reduce substantially the impact that each of us has upon our environment."

Meanwhile, several days after he had completed reading Hawken's book, Anderson had called a meeting of Interface managers, at which he described and condemned Interface's ecologically unsound practices. By his own account, reading *The Ecology of Commerce* had brought Anderson to the point of tears; his words sparked the same reaction in his managers, some of whom actually wept. "It was the most stunning experience," he told Gwen Kinkead. "The feeling was, 'We've been doing it wrong all these years.' You can call it guilt." He immediately resolved to act upon Hawken's recommendations. First, he recruited a group of advisers, among them Hawken himself; the environmental activist David Brower, who founded such conservation organizations as the Sierra Club and Friends of the Earth; the architect William McDonough, a "sustainability guru" who specializes in "green" designs; and the physicist Amory Lovins, who co-founded the Rocky Mountain Institute, "an entrepreneurial nonprofit organization that fosters the efficient and restorative use of natural, human and other capital to make the world more secure, just, prosperous, and life-sustaining," according to its Web site. Anderson also set about reeducating Interface's employees. "It's not easy to get 6,000 associates to accept a role in a cause," he told a reporter for the *Georgia Tech Alumni Magazine* (Summer 1997). "I cannot dictate, nor can anyone else, what someone will believe in his or her heart. It's just basically our internally focused effort to do what's right."

In 1995 Interface introduced a fabric produced entirely from recycled polyethylene terephthalate (PET), which is widely used in making containers for beverages and other liquids. In 2002, in another first for the industry, it began producing a carpet made from polylactic acid (PLA); derived from corn, PLA is a renewable and biodegradable alternative to traditional petroleum-based products. Earlier, Anderson had launched a program called QUEST (Quality Utilizing Employee Suggestions and Teamwork), to encourage workers to redesign products or procedures with the goal of reducing and eventually eradicating waste—the waste of time as well as resources, so as to cut production costs. "The sustainability initiative has made Ray a better executive because it has expanded his thinking about the ways a company should do business," Daniel T. Hendrix, who was named Interface's president and CEO in 2001, told Monica Elliot. "[He] has become more in touch with our associates and the work they are doing, and he has created an atmosphere of wanting to do better for the world." In 1997 and 1998 *Fortune* named Interface one of the "100 Best Companies to Work for."

At present there is no substitute for the petrochemical adhesive required to link nylon strands, so Interface redesigned a new generation of carpet tiles that contain 25 percent less nylon than earlier tiles. The elimination of petroleum from the carpet-production process is one of Anderson's main goals; it is also among the most difficult to achieve. In 1998 Interface installed a $1 million photovoltaic grid, one of the largest in use in manufacturing, to power Interface looms in California. Photovoltaics, which use sunlight (rather than the sun's heat) to create electricity, are more expensive than fossil fuels, but only because the prices of the latter do not reflect their costs to the environment. "We need a tax shift to raise the price of oil to reflect the externalities ignored by the market, such as . . . the cost of [the U.S.'s] military presence in the Middle East," Anderson told Kinkead. "I really do believe the earth cries out for a carbon tax to make renewables more competitive." According to the terms of a deal that Interface negotiated with British Petroleum (BP), whenever a company car refuels at a BP station, Interface receives a rebate of four cents per gallon. The accumulated rebates are used to plant trees, which absorb carbon dioxide produced by the burning of fossil fuels. With its "Trees for Travel" program, Interface plants one tree in a rainforest for every 4,000 miles flown by employees.

Anderson's environmental initiatives have helped boost Interface's bottom line. Between 1994 and 1999, the value of the company's stock rose 70 percent, profits increased 81 percent, and annual sales grew 77 percent. "We're trying to be successful according to conventional standards, because we have that kind of responsibility to our shareholders," Anderson told a reporter for the *Maine Times* (October 12, 2000). "But we're achieving conventional success through unconventional methods. It's good business to be environmentally responsible, to be good stewards. The marketplace, more and more, is demanding that kind of responsibility." According to PR Newswire (February 23, 2005, on-line), Interface's sales in 2004 reached $881.7 million, an increase of 15 percent over the previous year's total.

Anderson has written or co-written three books: *The Journey from There to Here—The Eco-Odyssey of a CEO* (1995); *Face It: A Spiritual Journey of Leadership* (1996), co-written with Charlie Eitel and J. Zink; and *Mid-Course Correction: Toward a Sustainable Enterprise: The Interface Model* (1999). With his earnings from the last-named book, he set up the Interface Environmental Foundation, whose mission, according to the Interface Sustainability Web site, is "to inspire and financially support the creation of the next industrial revolution and to ensure a sustainable society." Anderson frequently delivers speeches to business leaders on the topic of sustainability. "I believe this effort to reform the way we work is vitally important," he told Ernest Holsendolph, "and all industries, not just mine, must begin to think about ways to change and become more sustainable. Then we need to convince our customers and other countries to adopt the same priorities." "Our long-term objective is to move beyond sustainability to become restorative through the power of influence," Anderson told Woestendiek. "If we can influence just one other company to move toward sustainability, that's when we become restorative. Changing the world is an intimidating proposition. . . . It's presumptuous to even use the expression 'changing the world.' The best I can do is change myself and change my company and hope that others follow suit." In the conviction that future leaders of industry must become more environmentally aware, in 2000 Anderson endowed the Anderson/Interface Chair of Natural Systems at the School of Industrial and Systems Engineering at the Georgia Institute of Technology. "The objective is to have someone in the school . . . thinking about natural systems and nature's organizing principles," he told Monica Elliot. "You look at nature and there's enormous abundance; it's waste-free and non-polluting. Now that's an ideal industrial system: abundance, waste-free, and benign. Hopefully, we'll begin to get that new kind of thinking injected into designing industrial systems."

Anderson was prominently featured, in a positive light, in the award-winning documentary *The Corporation* (2003), which was based on Joel Barkan's book *The Corporation: The Pathological Pursuit of Profit and Power*. Directed by Jennifer Abbott and Mark Achbar, the film "focuses attention on the corporation as an insatiable machine for turning human and natural resources into commodities and profit," as Lawrence Daressa wrote for *Cineaste* (Fall 2004). "If the film has a controlling metaphor, it is that the corporation has become a psychopathic entity with a distinct social etiology." Anderson serves on the boards of the Natural Step USA; the Georgia Conservancy; the Upper Chattahoochee Riverkeeper; the Ida Cason Callaway Foundation; the Rocky Mountain Institute; Business for Social Responsibility; and the University of Texas Center for Sustainable Development, among other entities. He has received honorary doctorates from Northland College, LaGrange College, and North Carolina State University.

Anderson's commitment to the environment extends to his personal life; after his epiphany, he gave up driving a Bentley in favor of a Toyota Prius, a gas-electric hybrid, which emits far less gaseous pollution than ordinary cars. He and his second wife, Pat, have built an "eco-friendly" log home (one that causes as little damage to the environment as possible) in the Appalachian Mountains near Highlands, North Carolina. He has two children from his first marriage and half a dozen grandchildren. Anderson has often said that thinking about the world in which his grandchildren will spend their lives motivates him as an environmental activist. "What we're doing is incredibly difficult," he told Kinkead. "My executives may be right—it may be several generations. But I hold out this hope of living to see it."

—J.C.

Suggested Reading: *Architectural Record* p232 June 2001; *Atlanta Magazine* p74+ Dec. 2001; *BusinessWeek* p60+ July 19, 2004; *Industrial Engineer* p28+ Sep. 2003; *U.S. News & World Report* p51 Dec. 28, 1998–Jan. 4, 1999; *Waste News* p1 Jan. 2001;

Selected Books: *The Journey from There to Here—The Eco-Odyssey of a CEO*, 1995; *Face It: A Spiritual Journey of Leadership* (with Charlie Eitel and J. Zink), 1996; *Mid-Course Correction: Toward a Sustainable Enterprise: The Interface Model*, 1999

Steve Liss/Time-Life Pictures/Getty Images

Angell, Marcia

(ANG-el)

Apr. 20, 1939– Medical doctor; writer

Address: Harvard Medical School, Dept. of Social Medicine, 641 Huntington Ave., Boston, MA 02115

"It pays to listen to Dr. Marcia Angell," *Time* magazine (April 21, 1997) declared in 1997, the year its editors named Angell one of the 25 most influential Americans. She received that recognition largely as a result of the impact of her 1996 book, *Science on Trial: The Clash of Medical Evidence and the Law in the Breast Implant Case*, on popular opinion regarding the federal government's ban of silicon breast implants—a ban that Angell claimed was without basis in scientific fact. Those who attacked Angell in the wake of that book's publication as a stooge of medical-product manufacturers were silenced in 2004 by the appearance of *The Truth About the Drug Companies: How They Deceive Us and What to Do About It*. Angell argued in that book that the high cost of health care in the U.S. can be attributed to a focus on marketing and profit, rather than research, on the part of drug companies. As a result, "we certainly are in a health care crisis," Angell told an interviewer for the Web site of the television program *Healthcare Crisis* in 2000. "If we had set out to design the worst system that we could imagine, we couldn't have imagined one as bad as we have."

From 1979 until 2000 Angell, a graduate of Boston University Medical School, served as an editor of the prestigious *New England Journal of Medi-*

cine, a post in which she exercised considerable influence on the medical field. During her tenure there George Annas, a professor at Boston University who specializes in medical ethics, told Thomas Maier for New York *Newsday* (March 18, 1997) that Angell is "one of the most powerful women in medicine. She's broadened the journal's agenda to examine social policies, medical ethics and how doctors impact on society—rather than just printing what's the new drug." While with the *New England Journal of Medicine*, Angell voiced her opinions on a wide array of controversial medical issues, ranging from her opposition to weight-loss programs to her advocacy of government-sponsored universal health care for all citizens. Her prestige in the medical community is noted even by her opponents; David Kessler, the former head of the Food and Drug Administration (FDA) who enacted the ban on silicon breast implants, told Thomas Maier, "She's pretty gutsy. . . . She's not always right, but she's done medicine a service."

Marcia Angell was born on April 20, 1939 in Knoxville, Tennessee, to Lester and Florence Angell. Six years later the family moved to Arlington, Virginia, where her father worked as a civil engineer with the U.S. Army Corps of Engineers. When Angell was a child, her parents and older brother instilled in her a sense of the importance of hard work, to which she has attributed her decision to enter the field of medicine. "I was brought up by Puritans," she told Ellen Ruppel Shell for the *Boston Globe* (May 2, 1999), "and science was hard, so I figured it must be good for me." In 1960 she graduated from Madison College (now James Madison University), in Harrisonburg, Virginia, where she had double-majored in chemistry and mathematics and minored in biology. After she earned her bachelor's degree, she received a Fulbright grant, given to accomplished students to allow them to pursue their academic interests abroad. She spent a year in Germany, then returned to the U.S., where she entered medical school at Boston University, in Massachusetts. "I know it sounds really corny," she told Thomas Maier, "but I wanted to help people. I was firmly convinced that taking care of people was an unmitigatedly good thing."

Angell, a self-described feminist, has been vocal about the prejudice she faced as a woman in medical school. She told Anne Saita for *Montpelier* (Winter 1998), the magazine of James Madison University, "There was tremendous bias against women in medicine. The very first day at school a classmate—a male classmate—came up to me and said, 'Why don't you become a nurse?' And I said, 'I don't want to be a nurse. If I wanted to be a nurse, I would have been a nurse.'" The prejudice was not limited to remarks from fellow classmates. "Even scientifically," she told Saita, "there was a lot of what can only be described as old wives' tales being taught in medical school as though they were true. I was taught by a psychiatrist at Boston University School of Medicine that morning sickness was a woman's attempt to reject her feminine role. . . . And I was taught this by people who, if they wanted to know about dysmenorrhea, could have asked me."

While in Boston Angell fell under the tutelage of Stanley Robbins, the author of one of the most influential medical texts of all time, *Textbook of Pathology* (1957). Robbins chose Angell as a test reader for new editions of the book. "Even as a student, I saw in her actions and in her words a woman of extraordinary intelligence who had a great capacity to distill the complex into a few clear and relevant words," he told Ellen Ruppel Shell. "She never tried to please; she pursued her own ideas, no matter what I thought of them. But she was never bull-headed; she was always willing to listen." Robbins also credited the politically aware Angell, who attended rallies during those years to protest the Vietnam War, with increasing his "awareness of many things."

After graduating from medical school, Angell began a residency in internal medicine at the University Hospital in Boston in 1968. At the end of her first year there, she married the medical physicist Michael Goitein and soon conceived a child. Her daughter, Lara, was born with health problems, prompting Angell to take a leave of absence from her residency. "Motherhood was extremely important to me, so being forced to stay home with Lara was not a great blow," she told Ellen Ruppel Shell. A year later, Angell gave birth to a second daughter, Liza; she was subsequently expelled from the residency program. "That was the end of it," she told Shell. "The chief of medicine told me: 'That's the last time I hire a woman.' I accepted that, because I thought I'd done something wrong by getting pregnant."

While staying at home full-time with her daughters, Angell remained involved with medicine, co-authoring the textbook *Basic Pathology* (1971) with Stanley Robbins. The book was widely read and brought Angell recognition in the medical community. Returning to the field full-time, she began a second residency in pathology (the study of the nature of illness) at the New England Deaconess Hospital in Boston. Toward the end of her residency, she wrote to another of her mentors from medical school, Arnold Relman, who had recently been made editor in chief of the *New England Journal of Medicine*. The *Journal* had been one of the most prestigious medical publications in the world since its inception, in 1812, often setting trends in medical opinion. "I said 'OK, congratulations on being the editor of the journal,'" Angell recalled to Jonathan Bor for the Baltimore *Sun* (October 26, 1997). "'I'm now a resident in pathology. This is how medicine looks to me.'" Following a trial period, Relman offered Angell a position in 1980 as the journal's assistant deputy editor. Angell excelled at the job. "She was a quick learner, had a very disciplined mind, a wonderful sense of style and wrote well," Relman told Jonathan Bor. He recalled to Ellen Ruppel Shell, "Basically, I had

to get out of her way. I just stood back and let this phenomenal talent grow."

Angell rose through the ranks of the *New England Journal of Medicine*, writing editorials on a wide array of hotly contested medical issues. In 1982 she criticized doctors in hospitals for denying pain-relieving narcotics to their patients. Several years later she attacked the commonly held notion that a positive state of mind can help heal terminally ill patients, writing that recent medical literature contained "very few scientifically sound studies of the reaction, if there is one, between mental state and disease. . . . We have been too ready to accept the venerable belief that mental state is an important factor in the cause and cure of disease," as quoted by Sandy Rovner in the *Washington Post* (June 26, 1985). Particularly significant for Angell was the issue of doctor-assisted suicide for terminally ill patients; her father, Lester Angell, had shot himself to death after a long battle with prostate cancer. "If physician-assisted suicide had been available, I have no doubt that my father would have chosen it," Angell wrote, as quoted by Thomas Maier. "I don't think people should have to do that—be driven to [commit suicide alone]," she told Thomas Maier, explaining that her father's death "strengthened my conviction that [physician-assisted suicide] is simply a part of good medical care—something to be done reluctantly and sadly, as a last resort, but done nonetheless." Angell's outlook was also influenced by her experiences as a resident in pathology, a position in which she had to examine the corpses of those who had died in hospitals. One of the ways in which the practice of medicine had changed between her first residency and her second, she explained to Jonathan Bor, was that there was now a "refusal to let patients die. Patients, dead patients, would come to me more like they had come out of [the Nazi concentration camp] Buchenwald than out of a hospital. Their charts would make your hair curl, the horrible things these patients had been put through before they died."

In 1988 Angell became executive editor of the *New England Journal of Medicine*. Three years later Arnold Relman retired as editor in chief, leading many to speculate that Angell would be chosen by the journal's publishers, the Massachusetts Medical Society, as his successor. The job went instead to Jerome Kassirer, a professor from Tufts University Medical School. Angell announced that she was uncertain as to whether she would remain in her current position after being overlooked; one of Kassirer's first concerns at the helm of the journal was to make sure that Angell stayed. "I knew I needed her," he told Ellen Ruppel Shell. "She's a first-class editor, and she knew the business of running a world-class journal. I didn't." Angell chose to stay with the journal. "I wanted the job [of editor in chief]," she told Shell, "and I was disappointed not to get it. But I felt I already had a plum job. I had all the input I wanted in the best medical journal in the world. There was nothing lacking."

By the 1990s the issue of health-care reform was becoming increasingly important to Angell, who was an advocate for a government-sponsored universal health-care system. In 1993 she criticized the newly elected president, Bill Clinton, for what she saw as his lack of action on the issue. "Like many people, I gave Clinton a chance on health care," she told Derrick Z. Jackson for the *Boston Globe* (June 20, 1993). "But now many people are sufficiently discouraged with his indecision. With health care costs skyrocketing, no decision is a decision." (Later in the year Clinton unveiled a proposal for a universal health-care plan—the product of months of work by the Task Force on National Health Care Reform, led by the president's wife, Hillary Rodham Clinton. For a variety of reasons, the proposal did not garner sufficient support to become law, and it was later abandoned.) According to Angell, "It is time to acknowledge that market forces are simply not suited to distributing health care efficiently according to medical need, no matter how successful the market may be in distributing toothpaste or computers. If we regard health care as a social good rather than as a commodity, as other Western countries do, we could devise a more rational system for delivering it."

In 1996 Angell took what became her most controversial stand yet, with the publication of her book *Science on Trial: The Clash of Medical Evidence and the Law in the Breast Implant Case* (1996). In the book Angell argued against the federal government's 1992 ban on silicon breast implants. David Kessler, then-commissioner of the FDA, had banned the implants on the grounds that they had been said to cause connective-tissue disease and other ailments. At the time that the ban went into effect, more than one million women already had the implants, leading to a massive rush to have them removed. The issue led to lawsuits and forced implant manufacturers to agree to "the largest class-action settlement in the annals of American law," as Angell wrote in her book, quoted in the *Anchorage Daily News* (November 16, 1997). Angell was initially drawn to the subject after Kessler wrote an article for the *New England Journal of Medicine* explaining his reasons for the ban. "The article was important and we were happy to publish it," she wrote in her book. "Still I was troubled by the likely consequences of Kessler's action, as well as by some of his arguments. He seemed disdainful of women who wanted breast implants for purely cosmetic reasons, and his decision, though welcomed by many women, struck me as a little patronizing. More important, how would the sudden ban strike the million or so women who already had implants? Would they accept Kessler's legalistic argument that he was simply responding to the lack of evidence adduced by the manufacturers? I thought not. Far more likely, they would see the FDA ban as proof that the implants were extremely dangerous. And that is exactly what happened."

Kessler, in an interview with Thomas Maier, said that he had put the ban in place after reading documents provided by the implant manufacturers that reported problems with the product. "When I read these documents I couldn't allow these devices to be further implanted," he said. According to Angell, however, "At the time the FDA made its decision to ban them, we knew next to nothing. Incredibly, there had been no systemic studies of the effects of breast implants." When those studies were conducted, however, first by the Mayo Clinic School of Medicine and later by other researchers, almost no evidence arose, according to Angell, that linked the implants with any of the ailments they had been said to cause. Angell's book was a scathing attack on what she called "the growing gap between scientific reality and what passes for it in the courtroom," as quoted by William M. Sage in *Health Affairs* (Winter 1996). Specifically, Angell criticized the use of emotional arguments in courtrooms and on television talk shows about such issues as breast implants, saying that they were based on scientifically unproven premises. "I'd like Marcia to sit down with me, or come live in my body," Martha Carney, a cancer patient who had her implants removed after "a number of unexplained ailments," told Michael Kenney for the *Boston Globe* (July 3, 1996). Angell responded by telling Kenney, "Passion, claims, anecdotes won't settle this issue. It's a scientific issue and it will be settled by science." In the excerpt of her book published in the *Anchorage Daily News*, she wrote, "Plaintiffs' attorneys, consumer advocates, implant manufacturers and scientists can debate the point as loudly and insistently as they like, but the noise of the debate should not be allowed to obscure the basic truth that the question has an answer and the answer lies in nature. . . . Does this mean that breast implants do not contribute to connective-tissue disease? Not exactly. No study can absolutely prove that; all it can do is tell us how likely or unlikely it is. Each study that fails to find a link adds to the evidence that there is none." David Kessler told Thomas Maier about Angell, "She's enormously bright and talented, but I think there's been one essential fact that she's been blind to—that we have a system of regulation that places the responsibility for efficacy and safety squarely on the manufacturers."

In a review of *Science on Trial*, Richard Bernstein wrote for the *New York Times* (July 1, 1996), "Dr. Angell is not an exciting writer. Her book includes no courtroom drama, no inside glimpses of boardrooms, no interviews with plaintiffs. . . . But her presentation is convincing and her conclusions well substantiated: a combination of greed, media-sensationalism, judicial gullibility and the cleverness of lawyers triumphed so totally over science that we have to doubt society's commitment to such things as evidence and scientific logic." For her contribution to the debate over breast implants, and for her work at the *New England Journal of Medicine*, Angell was ranked by *Time* magazine as one of the 25 most influential Americans.

In September 1997 Angell turned her attention to the clinical testing of AIDS drugs in Africa, where in recent years the disease had been killing some two million people every year. In her article "The Ethics of Clinical Research in the Third World," published in the *New England Journal of Medicine*, Angell criticized the use of placebos in testing cheaper alternatives to the drug AZT, which was unaffordable in poor countries. AZT was designed to prevent the transmission of AIDS by pregnant women to their unborn children; Angell charged that scientists, by giving the women fake drugs, were endangering the lives of the children for the sake of the experiment. Her article drew criticism from scientists who said that the experiments were performed on women who would otherwise have received no treatment at all. In February 1998 the scientists performing the experiments, who were affiliated with the U.S. government and the Centers for Disease Control and Prevention, announced that they had found an alternative drug and that the testing had ceased. "I'm delighted," Angell was quoted as saying by Sheryl Gay Stolberg in the *New York Times* (February 19, 1998). "Better late than never."

The following year Angell drew fire when she and Jerome Kassirer co-wrote for the *New England Journal of Medicine* the article "Losing Weight—An Ill Fated New Year's Resolution," which argued that too much emphasis has been placed by Americans on losing weight and eliminating obesity. "Until we have better data about the risks of being overweight and the benefits and risks of trying to lose weight," they wrote, as quoted in the *AAP Newsfeed* (January 1, 1998), "we should remember that the cure for obesity may be worse than the condition. . . . We simply do not know whether a person who loses 20 pounds will thereby acquire the same reduced risk as a person who started out 20 pounds lighter. . . . Since many people cannot lose much weight no matter how hard they try, and promptly regain whatever they do lose, the vast amounts of money spent on diet clubs, special foods and over-the-counter remedies, estimated to be on the order of $ US30 billion to $ US50 billion . . . yearly, is wasted." C. Everett Koop, a former U.S. surgeon general, was quoted by the PR Newswire (January 6, 1998) as saying that the article "trivializes [obesity,] the second leading cause of preventable death in the United States."

In July 1999 it was announced that Jerome Kassirer had been relieved of his position as editor in chief of the *New England Journal of Medicine* after disputes with the Massachusetts Medical Society over the journal's marketing. Angell was appointed interim editor in chief on September 1, after receiving word that she would have total editorial independence. Angell's brief tenure in the post was marred by a controversy in which the authors of 19 reviews of medical products were found to have had ties with the companies that manufactured the products, violating the journal's conflict-of-interest policy. "This is the most serious mistake for which we have had to apologize," Angell told Lawrence K. Altman for the *New York Times* (February 24, 2000), saying that the incident had resulted from "poor coordination among the editors and carelessness within the office. It was a mistake, to put it as bluntly as possible."

Several months later Angell removed her name from the list of those being considered as editor in chief of the journal, announcing that she would resign to devote her full attention to writing a book about the United States' health-care system. (In May 2000 Jeffrey M. Drazen of Brigham and Women's Hospital was chosen as the new editor in chief of the journal.)

After her departure from the *New England Journal of Medicine*, Angell began publicly lamenting the fact that health-care costs were increasingly being placed on working Americans. "Coverage is shrinking, as more employers decide to cap their contributions to health insurance plans and workers find they cannot pay their rapidly expanding share . . . ," she wrote in an op-ed article for the *New York Times* (October 13, 2002). "When health care becomes a commodity, the criterion for receiving it is ability to pay, not medical need." Angell's proposed solution was what she referred to as "a national single-payer system that would eliminate unnecessary administrative costs, duplication and profits. In many ways, this would be tantamount to extending Medicare to the entire population. . . . Many people believe a single-payer system is a good idea, but that we can't afford it. The truth is that we can no longer afford not to have such a system."

In 2004 Angell laid out her case against the current health-care system in *The Truth About the Drug Companies: How They Deceive Us and What to Do About It* (2004). In the book she placed the blame for high health-care costs on prescription-drug companies, contending that they keep drug prices artificially high, spending minimal time and money on researching cures for illnesses and focusing their energies, instead, primarily on marketing drugs to people who do not actually need them. "Once upon a time, drug companies promoted drugs to treat diseases," she wrote in the book, as quoted by Janet Maslin in the *New York Times* (September 6, 2004). "Now it is often the opposite. They promote diseases to fit their drugs." "The truth is that [drug companies] spend . . . relatively little on research and development. Far less than they spend on marketing and administration. And they have so much left afterwards that they are year after year the most profitable industry in the United States," Angell told Ann Curry during an interview for the *Today* show, as quoted by *NBC News Transcripts* (September 2, 2004).

Angell was criticized, particularly by conservatives, for her denouncement of the influence of big business on medicine. For the *National Review* (September 8, 2004), Elizabeth M. Whelan wrote,

"Why are pharmaceuticals not like other consumer products? Housing and food are essential for life—is it the right of everyone to have these at below-market prices? What entitles people to expensive pharmaceuticals?" Other reviews were more positive. Janet Maslin wrote, "Over all, Dr. Angell's case is tough, persuasive and troubling. . . . Her readers will be galvanized to look at the drug industry with closer scrutiny."

Marcia Angell lives in Boston, where she is a senior lecturer in the Department of Social Medicine at Harvard Medical School. Her daughter Liza is a pianist (Angell herself played the piano before arthritis in her hands forced her to stop); her other daughter, Lara, is a physician. Angell is divorced. She continues to write for professional journals about the medical industry, frequently focusing on the disparity in the health-care industry between efforts to help patients and efforts to make profits—and on the necessity for doctors to choose between the two. "A doctor who takes good care of his patients can lose his job for doing that," she told Thomas Meier. "And a doctor who doesn't can lose his soul."

—R.E.

Suggested Reading: *Newsday* B p23 Mar. 18, 1997; *Boston Globe* p14 May 2, 1999

Selected Books: *Science on Trial: The Clash of Medical Evidence and the Law in the Breast Implant Case*, 1996; *The Truth About the Drug Companies: How They Deceive Us and What to Do About It*, 2004

Brian Bahr/Getty Images

Anthony, Carmelo

May 29, 1984– Basketball player

Address: Denver Nuggets, 1000 Chopper Circle, Denver, CO 80204

In 2002 Carmelo Anthony led his high-school basketball team to a 32–1 record and a top-five national ranking. As a college freshman in 2003, he led the Syracuse University Orangemen to their first National Collegiate Athletic Association (NCAA) championship. In 2004 Anthony led the Denver Nuggets to their first National Basketball Association (NBA) play-off appearance in nine years. The results may all be similar, but the dramatic step up in competition, pressure, and media exposure with each new stage in his evolving career has meant the difference between the proverbial frying pan and the fire. Yet Anthony, while under the age of 21, rose to every new challenge. His game is equal parts finesse and muscle; he has the speed, ball-handling skills, and outside touch of a shooting guard, while his solid six-foot eight-inch, 220-pound build makes him a rebounding threat around the boards as a small forward, his natural position. In other words, his greatest asset as a player is that he creates matchup problems against other players who are either too small or too slow to cover him. He plays with a poise and grace appropriate in light of his nickname, Melo (pronounced "mellow"). "He's really stepped it up. . . . Carmelo continues to grow in terms of his confidence, in terms of his development, in terms of his overall knowledge of the game," Nuggets coach Jeff Bzdelik told Adam Thompson for the *Denver Post* (March 16, 2004). "He's growing daily. You can just see it."

Carmelo Kyan Anthony was born on May 29, 1984 in the New York City borough of Brooklyn. The youngest of five siblings by some 10 years, he has two brothers, Robert and Wilford, a sister, Michelle, and a half-sister, Daphne. When Carmelo was two years old, his father, Carmelo Iriarte, a native of Puerto Rico, died of liver failure. By the time Carmelo was eight, his mother, Mary Anthony, had moved with him to a west side neighborhood in Baltimore, Maryland, known by the epithet "The Pharmacy" for its local narcotics trade and high crime rate. (The neighborhood is the setting for HBO's dramatic crime series *The Wire*.) Mary Anthony worked as a housekeeper at the University of Baltimore, earning enough to enable Carmelo to attend Towson Catholic High School. As a youth Carmelo enjoyed basketball to the extent that the loss of playing privileges was among his mother's most effective disciplinary tools. Still, he did not begin taking the sport seriously until, as a six-foot-tall freshman, he was dropped from the Towson Catholic varsity-squad roster. Shortly thereafter he began practicing in earnest, aided by a growth spurt that added five inches to his frame over the next year. He built a local reputation for his court skills. "As a good player in the inner city, you're always hearing people saying you're better than you really are and that you don't have to do things like everybody else," Anthony told Ian Thomsen for *Sports Illustrated* (November 17, 2003). "When I was in Baltimore I took all that talk and ran with it. It distracted me from my schoolwork. I started getting suspended." Despite his mounting troubles in the classroom, he attracted the attention of Syracuse University's head basketball coach, Jim Boeheim, and during his junior year he made a commitment to play for Syracuse. "He was basically a regional recruit," Syracuse assistant coach Troy Weaver told Tim Layden for *Sports Illustrated* (December 23, 2002). "But then in the summer he just blew up nationally."

Following his junior year of high school, Anthony rededicated himself to academics and basketball. After he performed remarkably well in a handful of summer camps and tournaments that tested his court savvy against some of the nation's best high-school basketball talent, he decided that he would attend college rather than moving directly into the NBA. To make good on his commitment to Syracuse, however, he needed to improve his standardized-test scores. Because of his inattentiveness to his studies during the previous three years, his test scores made him academically ineligible to play in the NCAA. To improve his chances, he transferred to the Oak Hill Academy, a Baptist boarding school in rural Virginia. Oak Hill has produced many future NBA players, among them Jerry Stackhouse and Ron Mercer, and routinely has one of the country's top prep teams. The academy also emphasizes rigorous coursework and strict discipline: all students wear uniforms, must stay on campus unless given permission to leave, attend socials that are heavily chaperoned, and must be in bed by 10:30 p.m. Moreover, Oak Hill demanded that Anthony attend five weeks of summer school at the academy to prepare him for the coming year. "He would go to classes from 7 am to noon, six days a week, and then at 2 pm each day he had to meet me in the gym," the Oak Hill basketball coach, Steve Smith, told Thomsen. "It would be 100 degrees, with no air-conditioning, and we would work him out for two hours, all by himself. Then he would have study hall." By the end of the summer, Anthony had added 20 pounds of muscle to his then six-foot, seven-inch physique. During the ensuing season he averaged 21.7 points and 7.4 rebounds per game and led the Oak Hill Academy to a 32–1 record and number-three ranking in *USA Today*'s assessment of national high-school basketball teams. Anthony was subsequently named a first-team All-American by *USA Today* and *Parade* and was voted to the McDonald's All-America Team. On the academic front, he took the ACT

(American College Test) entrance exam five or six times until, in April 2002, he scored 19, one point more than he needed to play for Syracuse University.

Jim Boeheim, who is among the most successful college-basketball coaches of all time, is renowned for his gruffness and unusually high standards. His effusive praise of Anthony was thus uncharacteristic. He described Anthony to Ian Thomsen as "the best player I've ever coached" and said, "There was never a problem with him. In the admissions office they're always looking for that kid who acts like he's from the suburbs, nice and well-mannered, but when it comes to basketball [we] want him to be tough as hell and banging people. Carmelo is all of those things." Beginning with a 27-point, 11-rebound performance in a season-opening loss to the University of Memphis, Anthony started at small forward for Syracuse throughout his freshman season (2002–03). On the way to a 30–5 record and the school's first NCAA men's basketball championship, he led the Orangemen in minutes played, with an average of 36.4 per game, as well as in scoring and rebounding, with averages of 22.2 and 10 per game, respectively. Showing remarkable court presence and maturity, Anthony performed especially well on college basketball's biggest stage: in a Final Four face-off against a talented and senior-laden University of Texas team, he earned 33 points and made 14 rebounds. Days later he put in a more complete performance in the championship game against another gifted veteran team, the University of Kansas, with 20 points, 10 rebounds, and seven assists. Syracuse took the 2003 NCAA championship, and Anthony was named the Final Four's most valuable player.

Then, having packed what for many would have been an entire college-basketball career's worth of achievements into a single season, Anthony declared himself eligible for the 2003 NBA draft. He was drafted third overall by the Denver Nuggets. A franchise that had fallen on hard times, the Nuggets had not reached the NBA play-offs since 1995 and had tied the Cleveland Cavaliers in the 2002–03 season for a league-worst 17–65 record. Anthony's presence immediately paid dividends. Fan attendance for home games rose 15.6 percent as Anthony took over as the Nuggets' starting small forward and became the focal point of their offense. As he had in Syracuse, he started every game for the Nuggets, leading them in scoring with an average of 21 points per game, thus becoming the most productive rookie in the NBA since Tim Duncan averaged 21.1 points per game for the San Antonio Spurs in the 1997–98 season. Anthony's more than six rebounds per game, on average, also contributed to the Nuggets' renaissance, which included a 43–39 record and an appearance in the 2004 NBA play-offs. The Minnesota Timberwolves outmatched the Nuggets in the first round of the play-offs, taking the best-of-seven series 4–1, but Anthony proved his mettle in the Nuggets' lone victory, in game three, with a series-high 24 points. Anthony received all six Rookie of the Month awards for the Western Conference, joining David Robinson, Tim Duncan, and his Eastern Conference counterpart LeBron James of the Cleveland Cavaliers as the only rookies to have done so in NBA history. (One major honor failed to come his way: the NBA Rookie of the Year award, which went to James.)

Because he is half Puerto Rican, Anthony was eligible to play in the 2004 Olympics for Puerto Rico's senior national basketball team, and he received an invitation to do so. If he had accepted, he would have had to play for Puerto Rico throughout his Olympic career, since international regulations do not allow athletes to switch allegiances. In the hope that he would someday receive an invitation to join the U.S. Olympic team, he turned down Puerto Rico's offer. As it turned out, after a number of NBA veterans declined to play for the U.S. in 2004, Anthony was tapped for the team. The composition of the hurriedly assembled team led many observers to express doubts about U.S. prospects in the Games. One reason was that unlike the so-called Dream Team of 1992 (the year that the Olympics were opened to professional athletes), which included the basketball veterans Charles Barkley, Larry Bird, Patrick Ewing, Magic Johnson, and Michael Jordan, the 2004 squad contained a large number of young, inexperienced players, and the team's head coach, Larry Brown, was notoriously hard on such athletes. In addition, the crew lacked a consistent, outstanding long-range shooter—a glaring weakness in international basketball, which relies on the outside jump shot because of the tightly packed zone defenses that international rules encourage. Moreover, the team had mere weeks to prepare, while most other international squads practice and play together for months, if not years.

Such misgivings proved to be well founded. The U.S. team rebounded from a first-round, 92–73 beating at the hands of perennial also-ran Puerto Rico and a 94–90 defeat to Lithuania (the first two American losses in Olympic basketball since 1992) to make it into the medal round. There they survived a quarterfinal battle with Spain, only to come up short against the eventual gold-medal winner, Argentina. They secured third place by defeating Lithuania, 104–96, in the bronze-medal game. Anthony took the brunt of Brown's frustrations. Perceiving little evidence of team spirit in Anthony, which he viewed as selfishness, the coach gave him little opportunity to play: Anthony averaged a team-low 6.7 minutes per game in the tournament. "He is a hell of a coach," Anthony told Marc J. Spears for the Denver Post (September 3, 2004). "But at the same time, . . . he still makes mistakes. He ain't perfect. . . . There are just some things you can't approach the same. We weren't the Detroit Pistons. We didn't have 90 games to play together. We had two weeks." Brown did not comment publicly when questioned about his clashes with Anthony, though word of their conflicts and Anthony's perceived selfishness leaked to the press, which reported on the matter widely. Anthony told Adrian Dater for the Denver Post (October 5, 2004) that his experience at the Olympics "just motivated me to come back here and try to prove people wrong, that I'm not the person that they portrayed me to be. . . . Everybody knows that I like to win, and I'm going to do what it takes. Everybody has a little adversity, and it's good that I went through it at the beginning of my career. I grew up a lot from the end of August until now."

Questions regarding Anthony's character resurfaced on October 15, 2004, when he was issued a summons at Denver International Airport for possession of approximately one ounce of marijuana. The illegal substance was found in his backpack before he boarded a team plane headed to Milwaukee, Wisconsin, for a preseason game. The charge was dropped a month later, after one of Anthony's friends, James Cunningham, signed an affidavit claiming ownership of the marijuana and responsibility for its placement in Anthony's bag. "He passed every drug test with the Nuggets because he does not take illegal drugs," Anthony's lawyer, Daniel Recht, said, according to an Associated Press article posted on ESPN's Web site (November 18, 2004). "The case has upset Carmelo a great deal because he does not want his fans, especially the kids, to get the wrong impression of him." Around the time of Anthony's exoneration from the marijuana-possession charge, however, a DVD, titled Stop Snitching, was being distributed in Baltimore, apparently to intimidate would-be police informants, and Anthony appears briefly on screen. Upon learning of the DVD, Anthony denounced the video's message and denied any knowledge of its making. In February 2005 he agreed to participate in a Maryland campaign against drugs and violence. "I'm completely against drugs and violence—that's not me," he told the Washington Post, as quoted on ESPN's Web site (February 1, 2005). "I just want to get the word out. I've lost friends to violence. I would never support anybody harming anyone. . . . I just want to help."

Four games into the NBA's 2005–06 preseason, Anthony had an average of 21.5 points and 5.5 rebounds in four starts. He is currently the spokesperson and the cover athlete, along with Tony Parker of the San Antonio Spurs and Pau Gasol of the Memphis Grizzlies, for NBA Live 2005, which has the distinction of being the all-time best-selling basketball video game. While images of Parker and Gasol are slated to appear on the covers in their respective homelands (France and Spain), Anthony's photo will be on the packaging and other forms of merchandising in North America.

With Greg Brown, Anthony wrote an autobiography, It's Just the Beginning (2004), aimed at young adults. "It sounds crazy . . . to write a book about my life before I turn 21," Anthony said, as quoted on the Denver Nuggets Web site. "But so much has happened to me so quickly, there's a lot to tell. I've written this book to share with you my life story because a lot of kids are going through situations similar to mine. Everyone will have bumps in the road, so you need to stay focused. I'm here to tell you to stay strong. Don't give up. No matter what, today is a new chance."

Anthony has been engaged to Alani "La La" Vasquez, a video jockey with the music-television channel MTV, since Christmas 2004; as of October 2005, no wedding date had been set.

—T.J.F.

Suggested Reading: Carmelo Anthony Web site; Denver Nuggets Web site; *Esquire* p76+ Jan. 2005; *Sports Illustrated* p46+ Dec. 23, 2002, with photos, p64+ Nov. 17, 2003, with photos, p54+ Mar. 15, 2004, p50+ Apr. 26, 2004, p66+ Apr. 11, 2005; *Vibe* p14+ Nov. 2004; Anthony, Carmelo, and Greg Brown. *It's Just the Beginning*, 2004

Courtesy of Benihana

Aoki, Rocky

(ah-oh-kee)

Oct. 9, 1938– Restaurateur; sportsman; philanthropist

Address: Benihana Inc., 8685 N.W. 53d Terr., Miami, FL 33166

"One of the world's most colorful entrepreneurs," as *Pacific Business News* (April 7, 1986) described him, Rocky Aoki is the founder of Benihana, a chain of Japanese restaurants that feature knife-flipping, shrimp-tossing hibachi chefs. With the opening of his first restaurant, in New York City in 1964, Aoki pioneered a concept that he dubbed

"eatertainment." He has also been widely credited with introducing Americans to Japanese cuisine. Indeed, as Ko Kodaira, then the Japanese consul general in Miami, Florida, told Elaine Walker for the *Bradenton (Florida) Herald* (July 15, 2003), he "put Japanese food on the world map and helped bring Japanese culture into the mainstream." Aoki "has always had the right ingredients for success," Elaine D'Aurizio wrote for the Bergen County, New Jersey, *Record* (February 14, 2002). "He's high energy, a hard worker, a risk-taker, smart, and imaginative. It doesn't hurt that he's warm, witty, and outgoing, too." Aoki has made his mark as an athlete and sportsman as well: he is a champion wrestler, a record-making hot-air balloonist, and a world-class racecar and speedboat driver; in addition, he has devoted himself to many philanthropic causes and maintains his own charitable foundation. He is the subject of the book *Making It in America: The Life and Times of Rocky Aoki, Benihana's Pioneer* (1985), by Jack McCallum, and the Japanese nonfiction *manga* (comic book) *Mr. Benihana: The Rocky Aoki Story* (1997), by Takahashi Miyuki. His own book, *Sake: Water from Heaven* (2003), about the Japanese national drink, a wine made from rice, has an introduction by the internationally renowned chef and restaurateur Nobu Matsuhisa.

The eldest of the four sons of Yunosuke Aoki, a vaudeville entertainer and a descendant of samurai, and his wife, Katsu, Aoki was born on October 9, 1938 in Tokyo, Japan, with the given name Hiroaki (hee-roh-ah-kee). A few years after the end of World War II, his parents opened a small coffeehouse in Tokyo. They named it Benihana, meaning "red flower" (a reference to a variety of safflower that grew wild in their neighborhood). The café soon became popular and profitable, partly because its food was cooked with real sugar. (Sugar was a rarity in Japan during the lean postwar years; Yunosuke's source was more than 20 miles distant by bike.) Hiroaki and his brothers (one of whom currently owns several restaurants in the U.S.) spent much of their time in the café, which in time grew into a full-fledged restaurant. Its success, they recognized as they got older, stemmed not only from its cuisine—good food prepared with fresh ingredients and fine cooking tools in a clean kitchen—but from their father's flair for theatrics.

As a youngster, Aoki told Tom Jory for the Associated Press (May 30, 1977), he dreamed of becoming a doctor or a lawyer. Even at an early age, he said, "I was a trouble solver. . . . If I'm in trouble, I can come up with new ideas all the time." In high school he earned money as a musician, performing at local American military bases. According to his Benihana.com biography, he graduated from college in Japan. Meanwhile, he had become a top wrestler in his country, and he earned a spot on the Japanese Olympic wrestling team that competed in the 1960 Olympic Games, in Rome, Italy. In 1959, en route to the Games, Aoki visited New York City for the first time. He promptly decided that New

York would be his future home; as he explained to Elaine D'Aurizio, "It excited me more than any other city."

In 1960 Aoki returned to New York. He told people that his first name was Rocky (as one of his non-Japanese girlfriends had nicknamed him), since it was easier for Americans to pronounce than his real given name. He took courses in English at Columbia University and supported himself by working as a parking-lot attendant and a chauffeur for Japanese tourists. His mother, by then widowed, moved into a studio apartment with him; she helped out with the bills by waitressing. After briefly attending Springfield College in Springfield, Massachusetts, and Cornell University, in Ithaca, New York, Aoki decided that he wanted to open a restaurant. Toward that end he took night classes in restaurant management at New York City Community College (later renamed New York City College of Technology). He also made "a systematic analysis of the U.S. restaurant market," as he called it, according to W. Earl Sasser Jr.'s book *Service Management Course* (1991). (That book contains details of an in-depth study of the Benihana chain and of Aoki's philosophy and modus operandi, conducted in 1972 by Sasser and John R. Klug of the Harvard Business School. In April 2005 the pertinent chapter of the book was posted on Amazon.com.)

In the summer of 1963, Aoki rented an ice-cream truck for $25 a day, and for 13 hours daily, he sold ice cream on the streets of the Harlem section of the New York borough of Manhattan. His business thrived, thanks in part to his inventive idea of inserting Japanese-made cocktail umbrellas into the ice cream. He also became the prey of criminals. "During that time, I was stabbed two times in the leg, mugged several times, beaten up and robbed. It was a real challenge to my spirit," he told Tamra Orr for *Hepatitis Magazine* (April–June 2003, online). "I'm only 5 [feet] 4 [inches] but I am one pretty good street fighter." Within just a few months, he had saved $10,000. In 1964, with the addition of a $20,000 loan, he opened his first restaurant, with only four tables, on West 56th Street, near New York City's theater district.

Drawing on an approach that his father had suggested (or adopted himself, according to some sources), Aoki had designed the restaurant so that food would be prepared teppan-yaki style, on gas-fired grills built into the patrons' tables. (In Japanese, "teppan" means "steel grill" and "yaki" means "broiled." In the U.S. the term is "hibachi-style.") His father had told him that "Americans love to be entertained," as he recalled to Cynthia Kilian for the *New York Post* (August 18, 1999), and he himself wanted an air of drama to pervade the restaurant. He hired chefs who had completed three-year apprenticeships in Japan and who, in New York, were trained to perform such tricks as flinging their knives in the air and catching them, flipping the food they grilled directly onto diners' plates, and tossing shrimps so that they landed on

their hats. For a while the restaurant, named Benihana of Tokyo, drew only a few customers a day; to pay their expenses, Aoki and his mother took additional jobs at other restaurants. After Clementine Paddleford, a prominent food writer for the venerable (and now defunct) *New York Herald Tribune*, gave Benihana a glowing review, the restaurant quickly became a smashing success, attracting more customers than could fit inside at any one time. Within six months the restaurant had paid for itself, and Aoki opened a second Benihana of Tokyo, a few blocks from the first. The second Benihana enjoyed similar popularity. Four years later Aoki opened a third restaurant, in Chicago, Illinois; before long that Benihana was generating higher profits than both of its predecessors combined. By the age of 31, Aoki had opened a dozen additional restaurants; he later expanded the chain into Thailand, Japan, Turkey, Peru, Canada, and Russia, among other places. Now located at more than 100 addresses, Benihana has become one of the best-recognized restaurants in the world. Aoki also launched a chain of sushi restaurants, called Doraku, and in late 1999 he purchased a majority share in Haru, a small chain of New York sushi restaurants. He also began dabbling in the stock market. "Slow down means no money," he said to Kevin Maney for *USA Today* (March 3, 1994). "I can slow down when I'm dead."

Earlier, in 1983, Aoki had split *his restaurant* business, keeping part of it private and going public with Benihana National, of which he owned 51 percent. Two years later he introduced a line of frozen Asian food; by 1987 he had lost $13 million on that endeavor and ended it. During the same period he opened a Miami seafood restaurant, Big Splash; it, too, failed. He invested $35 million in the Benihana Hotel and Casino in Atlantic City, New Jersey, but it was never completed. In 1999 Aoki stepped down as chairman and chief executive officer of Benihana National, after he learned that he was being investigated on suspicion of insider trading. Aoki pleaded guilty to the charge, admitting that he had profited from a tip that Spectrum Information Technologies, in which he owned stock, was about to hire the former Apple Computer chairman John Sculley. He paid a $500,000 fine and served three years' probation. In retrospect, he told Elaine Walker in 2003, he wished he had fought the charge. "It's my mistake and I have to eat it," he said. "But now I have a new life."

While engaged in his various business ventures, Aoki remained active in sports, both as a participant and a promoter. As a wrestler with the New York Athletic Club, he won U.S. flyweight championships in 1962, 1963, and 1964. In 1995 he was inducted into the National Wrestling Hall of Fame. Meanwhile, he also became a prominent backgammon competitor. In 1974 he took up powerboat racing and, in less than five years, had won at least six major races (and sponsored the Benihana Grand Prix, a 208-mile race off the coast of New Jersey). Between 1979 and 1982 he was involved in three serious boating accidents, including a near-fatal crash that left him with a lacerated liver, a ruptured aorta, and injuries to his left leg and right arm. "I always say, you afraid of dying, you afraid of living also. Death and life are next to each other anyways," he told Alexander Wolff for *Sports Illustrated* (July 26, 1982). Aoki next took up hot-air-balloon racing—by his own account, as a way of combating his fear of heights. In 1981 he was a member of the crew of the longest successful balloon flight up to that date: a flight across the Pacific Ocean. The four-day trip, from Japan to California, was described in a *National Geographic* cover story, in April 1982, and in a novel by Ray Nelson, *Flight of the Pacific Eagle* (1985). Aoki also drove racecars and amassed a collection that, at its largest, included 40 cars. In 1987 he won a 1,300-mile road rally, driving a vintage 1959 Rolls Royce Silver Wraith from Milan, Italy, to Moscow, Russia, in eight days. In the capacity of promoter, Aoki brought heavyweight boxing to Japan in 1971; in the first match held in that nation, Muhammad Ali won in a 15-round contest with Mac Foster. Aoki later took the Japanese national tennis team to the United States to participate in U.S. competitions.

In the late 1990s Aoki set up the Rocky Aoki Foundation, whose motto is "One Planet, One People." The foundation supports medical research, amateur-sports education, environmental protection, and programs in the arts. In 1997 Aoki established the Aoki Foundation House, a townhouse on New York's Upper East Side, where his foundation hosts fund-raising events for charities (in the form of auctions, gallery shows, dinners, and cocktail parties). He has supported the work of the Juvenile Diabetes Foundation, the National Foundation for Cancer Research, the Leukemia Foundation, and the Liver Foundation, among others. When Aoki learned that Benihana restaurants in the U.S. consumed 50 trees' worth of disposable wooden chopsticks every day, he immediately began ordering chopsticks made from bamboo, a more easily renewable resource.

In the early 1980s, probably through a blood transfusion administered after one of his boating accidents, Aoki contracted hepatitis C, an incurable disease that often leads to serious, permanent liver damage and, in some cases, death. In order to stay fit, he exercises and takes 70 vitamin pills daily and gets vitamin C intravenously once or twice a week. He runs (albeit slowly) a few miles a week and participates in ballooning festivals whenever he can. From his first two marriages (both of which ended in divorce) and several extramarital affairs, Aoki has seven children: Grace, Kevin (Benihana's vice president for marketing), Steven, Kyle, Echo, Kana, and Devon. He married his first wife, a Japanese woman, both to please his father and for practical reasons, as he confessed to Joyce Wadler for the *New York Times* (March 23, 2000). "It was mainly a business decision," he told Wadler. "I needed her help as a Japanese hostess." His second wife, Pamela Hilberger, is a German-English jewel-

ry designer. Aoki married his third wife, Keiko, in 2002. With Keiko, Aoki recently founded the RKA Sake Club, which aims to educate the public about sake by holding sake tastings, among other activities. He and his wife maintain homes in Japan and New York.

"People tend to measure success with money, possessions and power. I've made a certain amount of money, so I'm considered successful," Aoki told Jean Penn for *Playboy* (January 1985). "But success is a journey. If you stop satisfying yourself, that's the end of life. You've got to keep trying to achieve. For me, making money is not the only success. It's also personal freedom and the ability to say 'To hell with what other people think.' Success means being able to do anything I want, and that includes making world and national records. I want to make history." "I will challenge myself until I die," Aoki told Tamra Orr. "I work hard and I work smart. You win only if you are not afraid to lose."

—K.J.E.

Suggested Reading: Benihana.com; (Bergen County, New Jersey) *Record* I p1 Feb. 14, 2002; *Bradenton (Florida) Herald* p4 July 15, 2003; *Forbes* p80+ Mar. 20, 1989, with photo; *Hepatitis Magazine* (on-line) Apr.–June 2003; *New York Times* B p2 Mar. 23, 2000; McCallum, Jack. *Making It in America: The Life and Times of Rocky Aoki, Benihana's Pioneer*, 1985; Miyuki, Takahashi. *Mr. Benihana: The Rocky Aoki Story*, 1997

Selected Books: *Sake: Water from Heaven*, 2003

Arnold, Eve

Apr. 21, 1913– Photojournalist

Address: c/o Magnum Photos, 5 Old St., London EC1V 9HL, England

"I don't just hate having my picture taken, I absolutely abhor it," Eve Arnold, one of the first women to enter the field of photojournalism, told Jan Moir for the London *Guardian* (October 28, 1992). Having her own finger on the shutter button is another matter, however, and since the middle of the 20th century, Arnold has captured on film roughly 750,000 photos of others in far-flung parts of the world: migratory potato pickers in New York State; black protesters of racial inequality in Virginia; veiled members of a harem in Dubai; impoverished Afghans and Chinese; centenarians in the Soviet satellite republic of Georgia; newborn babies; royalty; U.S. and other political leaders; wives of American presidents; artists; dancers; and dozens of Hollywood stars (among them Marlene Dietrich, James Cagney, Orson Welles, Clark Gable, Paul Newman, Vanessa Redgrave, and Elizabeth Tay-

Courtesy of Bloomsbury USA

Eve Arnold

lor), whom she photographed unposed, at work (on the sets of *Patton, A Man for All Seasons, Alien,* and more than three dozen other movies) and at leisure. "Her work has been celebrated for portraying the extraordinary nature of ordinary lives, and the mundanity of extraordinary lives," as the Web site of the National Museum of Photography, Film & Television (nmpft.org.uk), in Bradford, West Yorkshire, England, put it. In the *Austin-American Statesman* (May 13, 1996), a Texas daily, Sarah Glinsmann wrote, "Arnold captures the same human vulnerability in an image of a woman in a Haitian insane asylum that is evident in a candid portrait of Marilyn Monroe."

The story of Arnold's life and career, according to a writer for the BBC (on-line), amounts to "a history of photojournalism in the 20th century." The photographer became a member of Magnum Photos, a renowned cooperative agency, shortly after its founding, in 1947, and was a frequent contributor of pictures to such high-circulation publications as *Look, Life,* and the magazine of the London *Sunday Times.* Since the mid-1970s she has also published a dozen books of her photographs, the most recent ones after she turned 90. Her work has been included in many solo and group exhibitions, in such places as the Brooklyn Museum of Art and the International Center of Photography (ICP), both in New York City; the Menil Collection, in Houston, Texas; and the National Portrait Gallery, in London, England. In 1980 Arnold earned the Lifetime Achievement Award of the American Society of Magazine Photographers. In 1995 the ICP designated her a master photographer, one of the most prestigious honors in the profession; also that year she was named a fellow of the Royal Photographic

Society of Great Britain, that organization's highest distinction. In a brief biography of her written in 2004 for the Web site of the Southeast Museum of Photography, in Daytona Beach, Florida, the renowned documentary photographer Susan Meiselas offered the following quote of Arnold's: "If the photographer cares about the people before the lens and is compassionate, much is given. It is the photographer, not the camera, that is the instrument."

Arnold was born Eve Cohen on April 21, 1913 in Philadelphia, Pennsylvania. She was one of the nine children of William Cohen, a rabbi, and his wife, Bessie, both of whom had immigrated to the U.S. from Odessa, in the Ukraine (which was then part of Russia). "It was a love match between my mother and father," Arnold told Jan Moir. "We were loved and cosseted and looked after, within the framework of what was possible." Her parents encouraged her to pursue a career. "My mother had had just enough training to write a laundry list," she recalled to Dana Thomas for the *New York Times* (August 18, 2002). "My father wanted more than this for me." After she completed high school, Arnold worked at a real-estate management firm. At night she took courses toward a degree in medicine.

When Arnold was 28 years old, she moved to New York City, because, as she told Thomas, "that's where the boys were." In New York a boyfriend of hers gave her a camera, hoping that it might inspire her to share his passion for photography. "If I wanted to keep the boyfriend, I had to take up photography," she told Thomas. Her first photo showed a derelict sleeping on the New York City waterfront. She soon became so excited by her new hobby that she gave up medicine to concentrate on taking photos. "Photography was more expressive, more interesting, less closed and freer," she explained to Thomas. "I never thought I'd make it as a doctor." She learned more about technical aspects of photography after she found a job in a photo-finishing plant, in 1946. For the most part she acquired knowledge and skills on her own. "Being self-taught gives you a chance to develop an originality and personality because you're not bound by conventions, so you can find other ways of approaching problems," she told Elana Roston for *New Times Los Angeles* (January 10, 2002, on-line). In her memoir *Eve Arnold: In Retrospect,* as quoted by Patricia C. Johnson in the *Houston Chronicle* (March 3, 1996), she wrote, "I learned by doing. I began to understand how to approach a subject, how to get close to a subject and how to search out and try to record the essence of a subject in the 125th part of a second." According to Dana Thomas, Arnold once described photography as "a combination of high adventure and low comedy, of meticulous planning and absolute change, of infinite patience and quick reflexes."

In 1948 Cohen married Arnold Arnold, an industrial designer. Later that year she gave birth to a son. At around that time her husband encouraged her to enroll in a six-week photography course at the New School for Social Research (now called simply the New School), in New York City, taught by the renowned Alexei Brodovitch, who was then the art director of *Harper's Bazaar*. "I took a course, then the course took me," she told Roston. "I never had any cognizance of myself as a pioneer—I felt it was a wonderful craft, I loved it and I was going to learn it." The first night the class met, one of Arnold's friends gave Brodovitch a photo of Arnold's to critique. "I felt flayed alive," Arnold wrote in her book *The Unretouched Woman*, as quoted by Thomas. "But what came through to me was important. I learned more that night about the meaning of a photograph than I have learned from anyone since." After Brodovitch assigned the students to produce a fashion story, Arnold found out from her son's baby sitter that informal fashion shows were sometimes staged in churches, bars, and other places in the Harlem section of Manhattan, and she took a series of photos of such a show in a Harlem church. Brodovitch was impressed by the images, which, unlike most fashion photography of the day, were not staged. He suggested that Arnold take additional photos in Harlem and build a portfolio of samples of her work. After she completed that project, which occupied her for a year, her husband, who had spent some time in Great Britain, sent a selection of her images to the popular British magazine *Picture Post*. (He knew that at that time a photo essay featuring African-Americans stood little chance of being published in any general-interest U.S. magazine.) *Picture Post* editors used some of the photos to compose an eight-page cover article called "The Harlem Story." "Although I had taken extreme care to report the facts accurately and to present the captioned pictures fairly, when the article appeared . . . the text was changed and the tone was snide . . . ," Arnold wrote in *In Retrospect*. "It took years until I had sufficient clout and sufficient reputation to insist upon being consulted if my text was to be altered."

On the strength of her *Picture Post* photos, in 1951 Arnold received an invitation to sell her work through Magnum Photos, a cooperative agency for freelance photographers founded in 1947 by Robert Capa, Henri Cartier-Bresson, George Rodger, and David Seymour (better known as Chim). Magnum photographers own the copyrights to all their photos, so the images cannot be printed anywhere without the photographers' permission (as Arnold's "Harlem Story" photos were, in several European periodicals in addition to *Picture Post*). The first woman to become affiliated with the New York division of Magnum, Arnold became a full-fledged member of the agency in 1955. During that period Magnum's roster of photographers grew to include such masters of the genre as Werner Bischof, Ernst Haas, Erich Hartmann, Erich Lessing, and Marc Riboud. "From Henri Cartier-Bresson I learned . . . to tell an entire story in a single, definitive image," Arnold wrote in *In Retrospect*, as quoted by Johnson. "From Robert Capa I

learned to dare. . . . I almost hear his injunction—'If your pictures aren't good enough, you aren't close enough.' From Erich Hartmann I learned technical restraint and discipline." While she felt annoyed that members of the then all-male New York office of Magnum occasionally treated her with condescension, she enjoyed almost total freedom as a professional. "I usually worked on my own ideas . . . ," she told Glinsmann. "I preferred being a one-man band." Cartier-Bresson and Capa, in particular, she once wrote, as quoted on nmpft.org.uk, "created a heady atmosphere in which the rest of us could develop. In the beginning this was particularly true because photojournalism had not yet solidified and become institutionalised. Daily we created our own rules and improvised."

As one of only a few female photojournalists in the 1950s, Arnold "had a much easier time" than her male peers "because I was a woman," as she told Jan Moir. "[Male subjects] are more relaxed with [female photographers] and no matter how old or ugly you are, it always becomes a personal thing, sometimes almost like a flirtation. And women like to be photographed by other women. Legend has it that [male photographers] go to bed with every starlet, movie star, personality they ever photographed—all of which I think is a lot of braggadocio—but it does set up an atmosphere I never had to battle with." In *In Retrospect* she wrote, "I didn't want to be a 'woman photographer.' That would limit me. I wanted to be a photographer who was a woman, with all the world open to my camera. What I wanted was to use my female insights and personality to interpret what I photographed."

In one of her first major assignments, Arnold recorded events at the 1952 Republican National Convention, during which the World War II general Dwight D. Eisenhower earned the presidential nomination and chose Senator Richard M. Nixon of California as his running mate. Also in the early 1950s, she aimed her camera at Republican senator Joseph McCarthy of Wisconsin, who became notorious as the instigator of government efforts to flush out suspected members of the Communist Party or Communist sympathizers from within the federal government. She chose as another of her subjects the first five minutes of babies' lives—a theme she was to revisit often. "I photographed more deliveries than most doctors have delivered babies," she told Regina Weinreich for the *New York Times* (January 21, 1996), to whom she revealed that she had lost a child herself once; taking pictures of newborns, she said, was "the only way I could lay that pain to rest."

Along with some of her Magnum colleagues, Arnold was among the first to take candid pictures of Hollywood stars; previously, images of actors and actresses for public consumption had been limited almost entirely to posed, often retouched studio portraits or stills from films. With the photos she took of such luminaries of the silver screen as Marlene Dietrich (on an assignment for Columbia Records in 1952) and Joan Crawford (for the *Woman's Home Companion* in 1959), as Dana Thomas wrote, "Arnold gave birth to the celebrity portfolio as we know it today. . . . Arnold's photography took movie-star fanaticism to a broader audience and by doing so nurtured today's insatiable hunger for celebrity trivia and the disrobing of public figures." In working with movie stars, Arnold built a reputation for respectfulness and discretion; the trust she inspired enabled her to illuminate aspects of her subjects' real personalities not usually seen. "Be concerned about the people [you're] photographing," Arnold advised aspiring photographers during her conversation with Sarah Glinsmann. "When somebody lends you their face and their body, you owe it to them not to savage them." Over a span of five decades, Arnold took pictures on the sets of more than 40 films.

Arnold is perhaps best known for the many photos she took of Marilyn Monroe from 1954, when the actress was a starlet rather than a star, until shortly before Monroe's death, in 1962. At first, Arnold told Weinreich, "I didn't quite know what I was doing and she didn't know what she was doing and it formed a bond between us." In addition to five other brief or long sessions with Monroe, Arnold devoted two months to documenting Monroe's activities on the set of the film *The Misfits* and elsewhere in 1961, before the end of the actress's marriage to the playwright Arthur Miller (the screenwriter of *The Misfits*). Dozens of Arnold's photos of the actress appear in her book *Marilyn Monroe: An Appreciation* (1987; reissued with additional pictures in 2005), and they have been included in many shows of Arnold's work. In an assessment of an exhibition at the Gallery of Photography in Dublin, Ireland, in 1998, Lynsey Muir wrote for *Source* (on-line), a quarterly magazine of contemporary photography published in Belfast, Northern Ireland, "What is special about Arnold's portraits is that they are not set-up or engineered. All are captured in the moment and Arnold appears to have the ability to relax her subjects to the point where they are completely at ease. As a result the photographs that she produces capture very private and intimate moments. . . . The photographs of Monroe show a depth of understanding between photographer and subject that is rare. . . . Arnold shows us another side to Monroe, the star as a real person, with feelings, thoughts and fears just like everyone else."

Commissioned by *Life* magazine to take pictures of Malcolm X in about 1959, when he was a leader of the black separatist Nation of Islam, Arnold spent many months and $1,000 negotiating with one of Malcolm X's representatives before she succeeded in gaining access to him. In one photo, taken in 1960, which various sources have labeled "iconic," Malcolm X stands at a podium at a Nation of Islam gathering in Washington, D.C., soliciting donations from those present; in mid-2005 the photo appeared on the Web site of the National Galleries of Scotland, which own a copy of it. One

day when Arnold was photographing a Nation of Islam rally in Harlem, some of the participants spat on her and yelled "Kill the white bitch!," as she recalled to Dana Thomas. When she came home she discovered cigarette burns on the back of her dress. "Luckily, my dress was wool jersey, and wool just smolders, it doesn't burn," she told Thomas. *Life* magazine declined to publish her Malcolm X photos; instead, the pictures appeared in *Esquire* and in several magazines overseas.

In 1961 the photographer and her husband moved to England, so as to remain close to their son, whom they had enrolled in the same boarding school that Arnold Arnold had attended. The London *Sunday Times* became one of the main buyers of Eve Arnold's photos after it launched a color magazine, in the early 1960s. The magazine provided "a wonderful playground for artists and writers . . . ," as Arnold told Regina Weinreich. "We had carte blanche. I'd call up [my *Sunday Times* editor] and say, 'I want to work in Afghanistan.' [He] would never say, 'How much will it cost?' He'd say, 'Make sure you're home for the Christmas party.' I was the top woman photographer in those years. Represented by Magnum, I could work anywhere"—including the Soviet Union and Cuba, which were usually off-limits to photographers from other countries at that time. "Anywhere" did not include North or South Vietnam during the Vietnam War, however: Arnold failed in her repeated attempts to get an assignment to take pictures there, because, without exception, editors told her that covering the war on location would be too onerous and dangerous for a woman.

Along with work by Richard Avedon and 15 other respected photographers, six of Arnold's images were published in the book *For God's Sake Care* (1967), a pictorial depiction of social work published as a fund-raising project by the Salvation Army. Two years later, on commission from the BBC, Arnold made her only motion picture, *Behind the Veil*, for which she had obtained permission to record daily activities of a harem in Dubai, an emirate on the Arabian Peninsula. The medium of film did not suit her; as she explained to Glinsmann, "I found it was so much easier to pick up a few rolls of film and grab a camera, one that would fit in your bag." A four-month assignment in South Africa in 1973 left her feeling so ill that, after she returned to England, doctors wondered whether she had suffered a heart attack. "It took a long time before I realised there was nothing physically wrong with me at all," she recalled to Moir in 1992. Rather, she simply felt "heartsick," as she put it, over the repression and exploitation of black South Africans under the system of apartheid then reigning in South Africa and the dreadful working and living conditions that blacks were forced to endure. "What I had seen had bitten into my mind to such a degree that I haven't shaken it yet," she added.

Arnold's first book of photographs was *The Unretouched Woman* (1976), a collection of candid images of both famous and uncelebrated women. Her next book, *Flashback! The 50's*, was published two years later. "[This] is sharp-eyed, unpretentious photojournalism at its best," Charles Michener wrote of *Flashback!* for the *New Republic* (December 16, 1978). "Arnold's pictures of the decade . . . literally tell stories: the bright-eyed simplicity of television in those days is caught in her shot of Alastair Cooke gazing serenely into a CBS camera, cigarette in hand; the polarization of America is summed up ironically in her picture of George Lincoln Rockwell and two henchmen . . . [wearing] swastikas on their sleeves, at a Black Muslim meeting. The impact of such pictures is not easy or ephemeral: they stick because Arnold seems to have been just as surprised at what she was shooting as we are when we see them two decades later." Also in 1978 Arnold exhibited her work in a private gallery (Castelli Graphics, in New York City) for the first time. To counter what she regarded as the elitism of such galleries, she set a maximum price of $50 for each photo; she also signed purchased photos upon request.

After waiting for more than 10 years for the required visa, Arnold visited China twice in 1979; she traveled a total of more than 40,000 miles within that country, much of the time in regions normally restricted to foreigners, such as areas near China's borders with the Soviet Union and Tibet. Her subjects ranged from peasants, factory workers, oil drillers, cooks, rug weavers, and Mongolian horsemen and horsewomen to high government and Communist Party officials. "Studying her remarkable series of portraits that look their subjects straight in the eye, a reader comes away with the feeling that the nearly 1 billion people living under Communist Chinese rule remain individuals . . . ," Gordon N. Converse wrote for the *Christian Science Monitor* (December 8, 1980). "The spirit of China's people . . . radiates from these wonderful photos." A selection of Arnold's photos of China and its people were exhibited at the Brooklyn Museum (now the Brooklyn Museum of Art) in 1980, in her first major solo show.

In 1981 Arnold returned to the U.S. and began what became a two-year project: photographing her native land. From the vantage point of an expatriate who had lived abroad for much of the previous two decades, she viewed the U.S. as "the most exotic country I had ever been in," as she wrote in her book *In America* (1983), according to Byron Dobell in the *New York Times Book Review* (December 4, 1983). Dobell, who was then the editor of *American Heritage* magazine, praised the book as "a work of great charm and strength, capturing the incredible diversity of our people in all their humor, beauty, dignity, pain and optimism." He also noted the "excellence of [Arnold's] text."

Photos that Arnold shot on the set of a movie starring the dancers Mikhail Baryshnikov and Gregory Hines appear in her book *Portrait of a Film: The Making of White Nights* (1985). Later, during 13 months in 1986 and 1987, she and the Canadian dance critic John Fraser documented the activities of the New York City–based American Ballet Theatre, for which Baryshnikov served as artistic director. *Private View: Inside Baryshnikov's American Ballet Theatre* (1988), with Fraser's text and Arnold's photos, offers a behind-the-scenes look at the workings of a major dance troupe. In *Newsday* (December 4, 1988), the dance reviewer Janice Berman wrote that Arnold's "stunning backstage and rehearsal photographs . . . give the reader the feeling of being right there in the wings or next to the barre." In her next book, *All in a Day's Work* (1989), Arnold "shows us the human condition through the prism of our labor," as Douglas Balz wrote for the *Chicago Tribune* (December 3, 1989). Balz added, "This 35-year project is like a one-woman 'Family of Man'"—a reference to a famous exhibition of more than 500 photographs by 273 photographers from 68 countries, which was mounted at the Museum of Modern Art, in New York City, in 1955. As of late August 2005, more than 100 of the photos in *All in a Day's Work* were posted on Magnum's Web site.

Arnold selected images from the many she took in the United Kingdom for *The Great British* (1991), which Robert LaRouche, in the *St. Louis (Missouri) Post-Dispatch* (December 1, 1991), described as "a judicious, incisive view of her adopted country. . . . Arnold treats her subjects with dignity, a journalist's sense of timing and a delicate balance in constructing her images." Ninety-five photos gleaned from her vast body of work appear in *Eve Arnold: In Retrospect* (1995). That book earned the 1996 Kraszna-Krausz Book Award, given by the foundation set up by Andor Kraszna-Krausz (1904–89), who published 1,200 books on the art and craft of photography.

While Arnold stopped accepting or seeking assignments in the late 1990s, her work continues to be available to public view in exhibitions and recent photographic anthologies, and she has published additional books. *Film Journal* (2002), which contains pictures of Hollywood stars at moments between sessions in front of the movie camera, stirred a reviewer for bookmunch.co.uk to write that Arnold "seems to have survived a lifetime in and around the movie business with her humility intact. Openness, generosity and diplomacy are clearly important traits for a film star photographer to have, and Eve Arnold has them in spades." *Handbook (with Footnotes)* (2004) is a collection of almost 200 pictures of her subjects' hands (and, in two dozen cases, feet), taken as the final frames of her photo shoots. "Brought together, they offer a poignant portrayal of a diverse but shared humanity," according to a writer for the London *Times* (October 9, 2004).

In 2003 Arnold was awarded an honorary OBE (Order of the British Empire) by the British government. She has received several honorary degrees, from schools including the University of St. Andrews, in Scotland, and Staffordshire University, in England. Her negatives, prints, letters, manuscripts, and other materials will be stored permanently in the Beinecke Library, at Yale University, in New Haven, Connecticut, where part of her archive has been held since 2003. Divorced several decades ago, she has lived in England for most of the past half-century; her apartment is near Grosvenor Square, in the City of Westminster, a London borough. Also living in England are her son, Francis (called Frank), a surgeon, who has often helped her select images for her books; in addition, she has several grandchildren. According to Sarah Glinsmann, Arnold always sent prints of her photos to each person portrayed in them (if she had the individual's address), and even in her 80s, she could "take one glance at any photo she has taken and remember the subject's name and correct spelling." She was the subject of a 1996 BBC documentary filmed by Beeban Kidron.

—G.O.

Suggested Reading: *Austin-American Statesman* E p1 May 13, 1996, with photos; *Houston Chronicle* (Zest section) p11 Mar. 3, 1996, with photos; (London) *Guardian* p8+ Oct. 28, 1992, with photo; *New Times Los Angeles* Jan. 10, 2002; *New York Times* XIII (Long Island) p13 Jan. 21, 1996, with photos, Fashions of The Times p72 Aug. 18, 2002, with photos; *Newsweek* p106+ Sep. 25, 1978, with photos; Arnold, Eve. *Eve Arnold: In Retrospect*, 1995, *Film Journal*, 2002

Selected Books: *The Unretouched Woman*, 1976; *Flashback!: The 50's*, 1978; *In China*, 1980; *In America*, 1983; *Portrait of a Film*, 1985; *The Fifties: Photos of America*, 1985; *Marilyn Monroe: An Appreciation*, 1987; *Private View: Inside Baryshnikov's American Ballet Theatre*, 1988; *All in a Day's Work*, 1989; *The Great British*, 1991; *Eve Arnold: In Retrospect*, 1995; *Film Journal*, 2002; *Handbook (with Footnotes)*, 2004

Baldwin, Tammy

Feb. 11, 1962– U.S. representative from Wisconsin (Democrat)

Address: 1022 Longworth House Office Bldg., Washington, DC 20515; 10 E. Doty St., Suite 405, Madison, WI 53703

Democratic U.S. congresswoman Tammy Baldwin of Wisconsin has remained an unabashed leftist in an era when many politicians in her party take pains to distance themselves from any label other than "centrist" or "moderate." Referring to Democratic Party "spin doctors," as she called them, she told Frank A. Aukofer for the *Milwaukee Journal Sentinel* (February 4, 1999), "I'm their worst nightmare! Liberal-lesbian-lawyer-left wing . . . they're thinking LOSER!" Despite being considered virtually unelectable, in November 1998 Baldwin became the first woman from her state to win a seat in Congress. She is currently serving her fourth term as the representative for Wisconsin's Second Congressional District, advocating for the interests of her constituents in Columbia, Green, and Dane counties and parts of Sauk, Jefferson, and Rock counties. In the national arena she has broadened her constituency to include the poor, the elderly, members of minority groups, homosexuals, and others who she believes have been short-changed politically, socially, or economically. Since her arrival in the nation's capital, she has strongly opposed many policies associated with the administration of President George W. Bush. In 2001 she voted against the Patriot Act, which in her view sacrifices civil liberties in the name of security, and in 2003 she voted against giving the president

Courtesy of Tammy Baldwin

the authority to invade Iraq. One of her primary goals in Congress has been the passage of legislation that would ensure the provision of health care to all Americans. She has also fought to maintain or initiate affirmative-action programs for people of color and has pushed for the legalization of gay marriage. Baldwin has served on the House Budget and Judiciary Committees and currently sits on the Committee on Energy and Commerce. She is a member of the Congressional Caucus for Women's Issues, the Congressional Human Rights Caucus, and the Congressional Progressive Caucus. Earlier in her career, she served several terms on the Dane County Board of Supervisors and three in the Wisconsin state Legislature.

More often than not, articles about Baldwin in newspapers and magazines introduce her as either the first lesbian to hold a seat in the U.S. House of Representatives or the first openly gay first-time candidate to win a congressional election. (According to a CNN report [November 3, 1998, online], four gay men have served in the House, but they did not make their sexual orientations public until after their elections.) Baldwin has never shied away from discussing her sexuality, telling Pat Schneider for the Madison, Wisconsin, *Capital Times* (October 10, 1998), "It's just incredibly important to me on a personal level to know that I've been honest. Who wants to go through life feeling there's something you've not been candid about, especially if you're in the public eye?" Although the subject of homosexuals' rights remains highly controversial in the U.S. and thus has the potential to define campaigns, Baldwin has avoided being tagged a one-issue candidate. "People took her as Tammy Baldwin—legislator from Madison . . . ," the Democratic Wisconsin state representative Rebecca Young told a *Wisconsin State Journal* (October 11, 1998) reporter. "You dealt with Tammy Baldwin—not 'Tammy Baldwin, first openly lesbian member of the Legislature.'" According to an editorial (October 28, 2003) in which the *Wisconsin State Journal* endorsed Baldwin's reelection, Baldwin has "a knack for finding common ground with folks who disagree with her" and "a reputation as a soft-spoken but tenacious advocate on social justice issues."

Tammy Suzanne Green Baldwin was born on February 11, 1962 in Madison, Wisconsin, the state capital and biggest city in Dane County. She has traced some of her ancestors to a neighboring county in the mid-1800s. Her parents separated when she was two months old, and she was raised by her mother and her maternal grandparents. "My grandmother was a costume designer for my first six years but also worked full time in the home, and I remember growing up believing that I needed to be all of those roles; I needed to be the career success that my grandfather was as a university professor, and also the success that my grandmother was as a person who kept the home running perfectly," Baldwin told Kathy Maeglin for the *Capital Times* (December 31, 1998). "It took me well into adulthood to realize, well, wait a second, there were two human beings there, combining their forces to have all that come together, and if you're doing it alone, it's going to be impossible to do. The message yet for so many women is that you have to do all of that [alone]. It was a personal struggle for me to move beyond that."

Baldwin's mother, Pam Bin-Rella, an antiwar protester and civil rights activist during the 1960s, instilled a strong sense of political commitment in her daughter. Baldwin became a member of her middle school's student council and was active in raising money for a school in Wisconsin's "sister state," Managua, Nicaragua, after Managua suffered an earthquake. She and her fellow council members also worked toward improving relations between her school and residents of its surrounding neighborhood. Once, the students installed a fence around the garden of a woman whose flowers were being trampled by students crossing through her yard; on another occasion, they petitioned the school board to install a muffler on the noisy air exchanger in the school's industrial-arts wing. As a teenager Baldwin "learned that the actions of a small group of people could make a meaningful difference in the lives of others," as she wrote for her congressional Web site. After she graduated, first in her class, from Madison West High School, in 1980, Baldwin enrolled at Smith College, in Northampton, Massachusetts, where she majored in mathematics and government. She graduated with a B.A. degree in 1984 and then began an internship in the office of the governor of Wisconsin, Tony Earl, researching differences in earnings of men and women in the same jobs. In 1986 she briefly filled a vacancy on the Madison City Council. Later that year, at age 24, she was elected to the Dane County Board of Supervisors (which at that time had two other openly gay members); concurrently, she studied law at the University of Wisconsin, where she earned a J.D. degree in 1989. As a member of the county board, Baldwin promoted a socially liberal political agenda, crusading for abortion rights, the legalization of gay marriage, and universal health care. She vigorously rejected charges by local Republicans that Dane County was allocating a disproportionately large part of its budget to welfare.

In 1992 Baldwin ran for a seat in the Wisconsin state Legislature. Her sexual orientation became an issue during her campaign; news reporters often noted that she was a lesbian without mentioning her positions on issues. Baldwin believed that the best way to combat stereotypes was to be open about her sexuality. "As we hide the fact that there are gay men or lesbians," she told Kim Schneider for the *Wisconsin State Journal* (September 10, 1992), "the only thing people can judge the gay and lesbian community by is images they have of us, however they got them. Even if they do paint a single issue profile of me—Tammy Baldwin, lesbian candidate—I am still presenting an alternative to negative stereotypes as an elected official, attorney, articulate woman." Baldwin's positions on most issues resembled those of her chief opponent in the race, Mary Kay Baum, a member of the progressive Labor-Farm Party. One of their major differences was that Baum opposed the dominance of the Democratic and Republican parties in American politics, and her platform emphasized campaign-finance reform. "Conservative Democrats run the Assembly," Baum said, as quoted by the *Capital Times* (October 8, 1992). "I won't be bound by party loyalty to keep quiet when the party bosses stonewall us." The Republican candidate, Patricia Hevenor, was a social liberal and fiscal conservative. Baldwin defeated both of her opponents, registering a two-to-one margin of victory over Baum, the runner-up. "To have a voice in the state Legislature hopefully will challenge stereotypes people have about gays and lesbians," Baldwin said after her election, as quoted by Kim Schneider in the *Wisconsin State Journal* (November 4, 1992). Baldwin served her first term in the Legislature and her fourth and final term on the Dane County Board of Supervisors concurrently. She won reelection to the state Legislature twice, serving there until January 1999.

Earlier, in 1993, Baldwin applauded President Bill Clinton's controversial decision to allow homosexuals to serve openly in the military. Then, after much pressure, Clinton backed away from his original stance and instead ruled that gays could serve in the military "only if they refrain from all homosexual activity"—a policy that became known as "don't ask, don't tell." "While the compromise is politically pragmatic, it is a concession to bigotry," Baldwin told Arthur L. Srb for the Associated Press, as quoted in the *Capital Times* (July 20, 1993). "It shows how far we still have to go to eradicate irrational prejudices and homophobia." Later that year Baldwin proposed legislation to make homosexual marriage legal in Wisconsin, although she knew such a law had no chance of passing in the foreseeable future. Rather, she hoped to stir discussion about the issue. "I think we'll have to have a dialogue for quite some time before anything happens," she told Todd Moore for the *Capital Times* (December 1, 1993). In June 1994 Baldwin traveled to New York City to take part in the 25th anniversary of the Stonewall riots, in Greenwich Village, in which gay and lesbian protesters had overpowered police who had raided the Stonewall Bar on moral grounds. The riots, Baldwin said in an interview with the *Capital Times* (June 20, 1994), "are broadly agreed to be the starting point of the contemporary gay and lesbian rights movement. . . . We're often thinking about how far we have to go, without taking the time to really take in how far we've come." Baldwin played in the volleyball competition of the fourth quadrennial Gay Games, held in conjunction with the Stonewall anniversary celebrations.

In January 1995 the American Civil Liberties Union (ACLU) of Wisconsin presented Baldwin with its Special Recognition Award for her work to strengthen civil rights in the U.S. Later that year Ralph Ovadel, the director of a group called Wisconsin Christians United—in what some interpreted as a way to gain attention and donations for the organization—challenged Baldwin to a debate on homosexuality. "Since your actions and lifestyle place you in violation of the oath you took to uphold and support the U.S. Constitution as well as the Constitution of the state of Wisconsin, I would suggest you consider stepping down from the office you now hold," Ovadel wrote, according to the *Capital Times* (December 7, 1995). Baldwin turned him down, stating, as quoted in the same article, "I am too busy representing my constituents in the state legislature to debate you at this time." As for Ovadel's reference to her homosexual "lifestyle," Baldwin responded, "Tending to the health care needs of my 89-year-old grandmother. That . . . is my lifestyle. I suspect it is more similar than dissimilar to yours." In 1996 Baldwin and her like-minded colleagues in the state Legislature successfully fought plans to reinstate capital punishment in Wisconsin. "Why do we kill people who kill people to show people killing is wrong? I get the idea of wanting revenge. I do not believe it is the role of the state to carry out my anger or my outrage or the outrage of people in this state," she told Dave Newbart for the *Capital Times* (February 28, 1996). Also in 1996 she attempted, without success, to repeal state caps on the funding of home health care for disabled people.

In 1997 Scott Klug, the Republican congressman for Wisconsin's Second District, announced that he would not seek another term. Baldwin declared her intention to run for the Democratic nomination. In an editorial for the *Capital Times* (February 25, 1997), John Nichols wrote that while Baldwin was considered an underdog, she had significant strengths: "Baldwin . . . has had the guts to get out front on criminal justice, civil rights and First Amendment issues that most Democrats only back behind closed doors. And her commitment to international human rights is rare and refreshing." In a subsequent editorial for the *Capital Times* (May 15, 1997), Nichols wrote, "There are those who say she cannot win unless she raises her 'comfort level' by de-emphasizing causes like the fight against homophobic bigotry, the campaign to permit the medicinal use of marijuana, and the movement to reform a criminal justice system that has become a vehicle for warehousing poor kids whom society would rather jail than employ. Baldwin has refused to submit to the image consultants who have warped our politics into the sterile lie that they are today. As such, she has taken a bold risk. She is gambling her political future on the notion that the voters aren't as dumb as most politicians think."

Baldwin defeated former Dane County executive Rick Phelps and state senator Joe Wineke to capture the Democratic nomination. Her Republican opponent was Josephine Musser, who had served as the state insurance commissioner. Musser ran as a pro-choice moderate and made no mention of Baldwin's sexual orientation during her campaign. Her most vehement criticisms of Baldwin centered on the legislator's alignment with the Democratic Party at a time when its leader, President Bill Clinton, faced impeachment for lying under oath. Baldwin, for her part, remained staunchly partisan and most of the time refused to discuss anything except the issues. Still, as Election Day neared, both Baldwin's and Musser's advertisements became increasingly negative. One Democratic ad accused Musser of taking bribes from insurance companies while she was state insurance commissioner, while a Republican ad showed a couple being splashed with mud from a television set that bellowed Baldwin's name. On November 3, 1998 the electorate of Wisconsin's Second Congressional District chose Baldwin to represent them, thus making her the first woman from Wisconsin and the first openly homosexual nonincumbent to win election to Congress. "Through our activism and hopefulness we . . . made a bit of history," she said in her victory speech, as quoted by Jeff Mayers for the *Wisconsin State Journal* (November 4, 1998). Baldwin said in an interview with Ruth Conniff for the *Progressive* (January 1999), "Throughout my political career, I've always been dealing with the skeptics and the cynics, who say, 'This isn't going to be our best candidate to win the primary.' And, you know, 'She's too progressive, she's too young, she's a woman, she's a lesbian.' You hear that, and what was important for us to communicate was just that simple reminder: Hey folks, this is a democracy, and in a democracy the cynics don't decide who's elected to office unless you let them—unless they're the only ones who vote. We decide. And that's a message that pervaded the entire campaign—stop listening to those people who say 'you can't, you shouldn't, it won't work,' and start deciding that we can do it. It was great to watch that build.'"

Baldwin's first priority in Congress was to initiate debate on legislation that would provide universal health care. She told Conniff that she raised the issue because "we have [an] extraordinary number of people who are uninsured in this nation—over 43 million—almost 16 percent. . . . How to do it? I think one works both within the institution of Congress as well as outside. I think what you do inside is start asking the sort of bold, goal-oriented questions: are you for universal health care or not? If you are, let's talk about how to get there. If you're not, let's talk more explicitly about who we're leaving behind and why." Baldwin used her first opportunity to speak on the floor of the House to support a proposed patients' bill of rights; the Democrats' proposed bill sought to lessen the role of insurance companies in medical decisions. Baldwin's first direct attempt to promote her vision of health-care reform ended in failure; her multifaceted health-care amendment to the House Budget Committee's spending plan for 2000 was rejected in a committee vote that fell exactly along party lines.

Early in her first term, Baldwin supported the bombing by North Atlantic Treaty Organization (NATO) forces of Serbian fighters in the former Yugoslavia, where the Serbian president, Slobodan Milosevic, had been engaged for years in what became known as ethnic cleansing: the attempt to forcibly rid large areas of ethnic Croats, Albanians, and Muslims. Recently he had intensified his attacks on Albanian insurgents in the province of Kosovo. "I have concluded that a sustained campaign

of targeted air strikes is the best of many bad options," Baldwin said, as quoted by Elizabeth Hurt for the States News Service (March 25, 1999). "[Not acting] could result in a more serious conflict in the future." Her opinion later changed, and in April 1999 she voted against the continuation of NATO attacks. "As the weeks passed, and as the bombing escalated to include the civilian infrastructure of Yugoslavia, I saw that the bombing was not helping the refugees, nor was it weakening support among civilian Serbs for Slobodan Milosevic," she wrote for the *Capital Times* (May 20, 1999), after returning from a trip to Kosovo with a bipartisan congressional delegation. "In fact, I saw more and more of our resources going into the military campaign and not enough going to refugee relief." Also during her first term, Baldwin worked with midwestern Republicans in Congress to help dairy farmers financially.

In her effort to win reelection in 2000, Baldwin faced the Republican John Sharpless, a University of Wisconsin professor of history. Sharpless, whose war chest was one-third the size of Baldwin's, fiercely criticized her for raising about 60 percent of her total from contributors outside Wisconsin. Baldwin countered that soliciting funds from out-of-staters was legal—and necessary, too, because she was being forced to combat negative stereotypes invoked by her Republican challengers. In November she narrowly defeated Sharpless, with 51.4 percent of the vote. The American political landscape during Baldwin's second term was dominated by foreign policy after the September 11, 2001 terrorist attacks on New York and Washington. Baldwin supported retaliation for the attacks but noted to Scott Milfred for the *Wisconsin State Journal* (September 19, 2001), "Unlike our attackers, we must spare innocent life." Baldwin opposed the passage of the USA Patriot Act, which, among other provisions, allows the federal government access to medical records, financial information, and library transactions in its efforts to root out terrorist cells. Along with many others, she criticized the bill for sacrificing civil liberties in favor of closer monitoring of terrorist activities. Craig Gilbert quoted her in the *Milwaukee Journal Sentinel* (September 25, 2001) as saying that the bill did not measure up to Congress's "dual task of protecting American lives and the American way of life." After approval in the Senate by a vote of 98–1 and in the House by 357–66, President George W. Bush signed the bill into law, on October 26, 2001. Baldwin has since worked to monitor potential civil rights encroachments linked to provisions of the Patriot Act.

In 2002 Ron Greer, an outspoken evangelical Christian pastor, won the Republican primary to challenge Baldwin for her seat in Congress. A major point of contention between Baldwin and Greer was President Bush's proposed war in Iraq, which Greer supported and Baldwin opposed. According to the Associated Press (September 15, 2002), Baldwin stated, "It is high time that the president recognizes the importance of the U.N. and the international community in addressing the situation in Iraq. Actions that could lead to war and global instability should not be taken lightly." On Election Day, November 5, Baldwin defeated Greer decisively, capturing two-thirds of the votes. She entered her third term continuing her strong opposition to the Bush administration's policies on Iraq, in particular its willingness to act unilaterally; she voted against giving the president authorization to use force against the Iraqi dictator Saddam Hussein. "In our efforts to combat terrorism, we rely very heavily on the international community and our allies around the world," she told Lib Sander for the *Capital Times* (March 18, 2003). "Because the international community has been rebuffed in our dealings with the situation in Iraq, I am concerned that that weakens our hand in combating terrorism." After the start of the war, she pledged to support the troops and proposed legislation that would increase monetary and medical assistance for American soldiers returning from Iraq.

The debate over gay marriage was raised again in 2004, with a Republican proposal that the United States Constitution be amended to ban gay marriage. On the February 29, 2004 broadcast of the television news program *Face the Nation*, Baldwin clashed with Republican senator Rick Santorum of Pennsylvania. According to Chuck Nowlen in the *Capital Times* (March 1, 2004), Santorum suggested on the program that "same-sex couples are behind the erosion of the American family" and that "same-sex marriage would open the legal doors" to polygamy. "Senator, this should be a respectful debate. And I think the words and logic you're using right now are nonsense," Baldwin responded. "To make these false associations—to imply that same-sex couples are somehow to blame for some of these problems in society—is harmful. The reality is that same-sex couples are raising children in a very wonderful environment, and we ought to be *protecting* those couples and [treating] those children fairly."

Later that year Baldwin gained additional national exposure when she appeared briefly in the filmmaker Michael Moore's controversial documentary *Fahrenheit 9/11*, which criticized most of the Bush administration's antiterrorism policies. She also appeared in support of the 2004 Democratic presidential nominee, Senator John Kerry of Massachusetts, at a rally in Madison during her campaign for her fourth term in Congress. In that contest she was pitted against Republican Dave Magnum, the owner of a broadcast company, who repeatedly reminded voters of his business experience and promised a common-sense approach to governance. Running on the strength of her record, which included her success in fighting for $64 million in federal funding for her district, Baldwin captured 64 percent of the votes cast to handily defeat Magnum.

Baldwin voted against the bankruptcy-reform bill, which President Bush signed into law in April 2005. "Knowing that about half of all personal bankruptcy cases involve medical debt, knowing that many national guardsmen and reservists sent overseas face financial collapse at home because of that service, and knowing that every 30 seconds an American files for bankruptcy after experiencing a health crisis, I cannot condone a bill that deliberately punishes those in such dire circumstances in order to feather the nests of the very profitable credit card and banking industries," she said, as quoted on the Web site of Project Vote Smart. Also in 2005 she criticized the president's proposed budget, decrying cuts in funds for such educational services as after-school programs, college scholarships, and vocational classes; increases in the out-of-pocket costs of health care for veterans; and the retention of tax cuts for the wealthiest Americans despite the huge, growing federal deficit. In March 2005 she voted against an emergency appropriations bill that provided additional funds for continuing military operations in Afghanistan and Iraq. In a statement posted on the Project Vote Smart Web site, she explained, "Time and again, the President has requested money to fund the war in Iraq while refusing to answer our questions about this war and provide a comprehensive strategy for bringing our troops home. In our democracy, the Congress controls the purse strings. Before allocating additional funds, we must insist that the administration articulate the conditions necessary to bring our troops home, and push them to do that as soon as possible. The administration's refusal to address that is quite astounding to me and should be of great concern to all Americans who believe in principles of accountability and checks and balances. . . . Emergency supplemental spending should be reserved for true emergencies, those instances in which the need for expenditures is unforeseen or unforeseeable. The vast majority of funds in this supplemental fail to meet that criterion. Both last year and this year, the Administration excluded Iraq costs from their budget requests, although most of the costs could be estimated. Shortfalls or additional needs then could have been funded through a supplemental. That is the proper way to manage taxpayer funds." She added, "My vote against this spending bill should not be characterized as a rejection of [people in the armed forces] or the resources they need to carry out their duties. If this bill had been defeated yesterday, funds would have continued to flow to Iraq tomorrow and over the next few months." She has also vowed to try to prevent the Bush administration's attempts to privatize Social Security. In July 2005 Baldwin secured $750,000 in funds, allocated by the Transportation Reauthorization bill, for the preliminary design phase of a commuter railroad that would run between Middleton and Madison, Wisconsin.

Baldwin's honors include a NOW (National Organization for Women) Women of Power Award, in 1993; a Nature Conservancy Leadership Award, in 2003; the Uncommon Woman of the Year Award, in 2003, from the Uncommon Legacy Foundation; a BSSD (Bay State Stonewall Democrats) Award (known as a Barney, for Congressman Barney Frank of Massachusetts), in 2004; and several National Gay and Lesbian Task Force Leadership Awards. She lives in Madison with her partner, Lauren Azar, an environmental lawyer. The couple are currently restoring their 19th-century home. In her increasingly scarce leisure time, Baldwin enjoys sewing and playing volleyball.

—R.E.

Suggested Reading: *Advocate* (on-line) p32 Aug. 15, 2000, p26+ June 8, 2004; *Lesbian News* p26+ June 1999; (Madison, Wisconsin) *Capital Times* F p1+ Dec. 31, 1998, with photo; *Milwaukee Journal Sentinel* p1+ Nov. 6, 1998, with photo, p4 Feb. 4, 1999, with photo; Tammy Baldwin's congressional Web site; *Wisonsin State Journal* F p1+ Oct. 11, 1998, with photos

Barris, Chuck

June 3, 1929– Television producer; writer

Address: c/o Carroll & Graf Publishers, 245 W. 17th St., 11th Fl., New York, NY 10011-5300

Chuck Barris rose to fame in 1965 as the creator of *The Dating Game*, a wildly popular game show in which a contestant questioned three hidden players of the opposite sex to determine which one to date. Barris followed that success a year later with *The Newlywed Game*, which placed four recently married couples in a competition to see which husband and wife knew the most about each other. But Barris is probably best remembered for his manic introductions of hordes of show-business hopefuls who sang badly, delivered wincingly unfunny jokes, and generally made fools of themselves on his 1970s hit creation *The Gong Show*. By making the contestants' lives part of the games' drama, his programs were the progenitors of such contemporary reality game shows as *Survivor* and *The Apprentice,* and they earned Barris the moniker "godfather of reality TV." "The day *The Dating Game* went on the air, the *Chicago Tribune* had a story that said television had hit an all-time low," Chuck Barris recalled in an interview with B. J. Sigesmund for *Newsweek* (February 13, 2003, on-line). "From that point on, I was the guy the critics seemed to love to hate. I was called the 'king of schlock.' The difference is, today these [reality game] shows are accepted. These shows aren't seen as lowering any bars. These are simply entertainment today."

Barris has claimed that at the same time that he was making television history with his trademark over-the-top programming, he was also altering world history—as an assassin for the Central Intelligence Agency (CIA). In his memoir *Confessions of a Dangerous Mind* (1984), Barris maintained that he killed more than 30 people in the 1960s and '70s for the United States government. The CIA has dismissed such assertions, as has Barris himself from time to time. However, since the release of the film adaptation of the book, in late 2002, Barris has remained tight-lipped about his claimed CIA exploits. He has usually responded to direct questions about them with a shrug that neither confirms nor denies the veracity of his tales, leading many to wonder if the master showman is simply presenting one more bravado performance.

Charles Hirsch Barris was born in Philadelphia, Pennsylvania, on June 3, 1929. (Various accounts written by Barris have also placed his birthday in 1930 and 1932.) His father was a dentist; his mother, a homemaker. Little has been written about his childhood, though it is known that when he was young, his father died of a stroke, leaving the family (which also included Barris's younger sister) with little money. Barris drifted from college to college, six in all, before he graduated from Drexel University, in Philadelphia, in 1953. For a while he worked at U.S. Steel, then tried his hand at such vocations as, among others, film editor, prizefight promoter, TelePrompTer salesman, and book salesman. During that period he moved to New York City and became a page at NBC headquarters. In 1955 he was promoted to management trainee. According to Barris, he conned his way into the trainee program by forging letters of recommendation from board members of RCA, then the parent company of NBC. At around the same time, he married his first wife, Lyn Levy, a niece of William Paley, then head of CBS Television.

After 18 months as a management trainee, Barris left NBC (accounts of his life differ about whether he quit or was laid off) and held a series of jobs. In 1959, after traveling in Europe for six months, he was hired by the U.S. Information Agency in Washington, D.C. Shortly before he was to start there, he received a telegram from ABC Television in Philadelphia offering him temporary work: his assignment was to keep an eye on Dick Clark, the host of the pop-music television show *American Bandstand*, to make sure that he was not involved in payola. Since Clark had a stake in a number of music ventures, including record labels, publishing companies, and even record-pressing plants, the network suspected that he might have been paid by record-company executives to promote certain songs on the show. ABC executives asked Clark to sell off his competing business interests and allow Barris to shadow him on the set. Barris wrote a daily memo detailing what went on during the staging of *American Bandstand* and offering personal observations and jokes. Eventually, a 500-page compilation of his memos was brought before a U.S.

Chuck Barris

House of Representatives subcommittee that was investigating payola, and it helped clear Dick Clark's name.

Barris's work on *American Bandstand* had two immediate benefits: he gained a lifelong friend in Dick Clark, and ABC offered him a position as the director of daytime television programs for its West Coast division. "ABC gave me $700 and a plane ticket; I was supposed to prove I could set up all the show ideas on the West Coast for ABC. I checked in at a small hotel and made like hundreds of phone calls to producers. Nobody ever called back," Barris recalled in an interview with Joan Barthel for *Life* (October 10, 1969). "I called the Beverly Hills Hotel and asked how much a bungalow cost. They said $100 a day. I moved in with my wife and baby and spent $3,500 in a week. Everybody returned my calls. It was the best investment I ever made in my life." Barris soon ran against convention by penning a song, "Palisades Park," which was recorded by a friend of Dick Clark's, Freddie "Boom Boom" Cannon; in 1962 Cannon's version of it shot to number three on the pop charts. ABC, fearing another payola scandal, ordered Barris to stop writing songs. After setting up an office in Los Angeles, Barris further angered ABC executives by shortening his title to the "Duke of Daytime" and developing a pilot for a game show called "The People Pickers" (in some sources called "People Poker"), in which 15 people sat together in their street clothes and contestants had to guess their professions. In the pilot Barris used five strippers, five stewardesses, and five policewomen. The show did not sell, and Barris began to chafe under what he viewed as ABC's culture of conservatism. After being reprimanded by ABC executives for attending a civil rights march in Selma, Alabama, he left the company, in May 1965, to pursue a career as an independent producer.

In five months Barris had burned through all of his savings, which primarily consisted of the residuals he had received from "Palisades Park." Some years earlier his mother had married a wealthy man, and when Barris was down to his last $72, he appealed to his mother and stepfather for help. Barris borrowed $20,000 from his stepfather to develop *The Dating Game*, which he sold to ABC. *The Dating Game* began broadcasting in December 1965 and became Barris's first smash hit. Before long the show was running in prime time as well as during the day, making it one of the first programs to do well in both time slots. On each installment, a single woman (referred to as a bachelorette on the show) would ask three prospective suitors questions and, based on their answers, choose one to go out with on a date; occasionally, roles were reversed, with one bachelor asking three bachelorettes questions. The questions were often odd, sometimes even mildly sexually suggestive, and were intended to generate interesting responses from the contestants and laughter from the audience. Unlike the prizes on modern game shows, those given away on *The Dating Game* were modest—a dinner at an expensive restaurant or a weekend getaway (chaperoned by a staff member from the show). And unlike the contestants on such current dating shows as *The Bachelor*, the participants on each installment of *The Dating Game* were strictly segregated by race, reflecting the mores of the time. If there had been any hint of blacks and whites mixing, "southern stations, and for that matter stations all across the country, would drop the show," as Barris explained to Barthel in 1969. "We're not even supposed to mix up Orientals and Puerto Ricans with whites, although we do. But when it comes right down to a black guy with a white girl, or vice versa, it would be just suicidal. We're restricted in a purely corporate, national way—I don't know how else you would say it."

The Newlywed Game, Barris's next game show, premiered in 1966. In it four couples who had been married less than two years each vied for appliances and other prizes by independently answering questions about their spouses' likes and dislikes. When one spouse's answer matched the other's, the couple earned points. Most viewers looked forward to watching the arguments that often ensued when a couple's answers disagreed. The questions were playfully intimate and often involved the host asking couples about "whoopee," as the show referred to sex—a word that broadcasters were not allowed to say on air in the 1960s. Like its predecessor, *The Newlywed Game* became a tremendous hit and was shown in prime time as well as during the day.

Critics across the country panned Barris's productions as catering to the lowest common denominator in terms of taste. Barris admitted that the shows were fairly insipid but also noted that millions of people across the country were tuning in to watch them. "It's the bargain basement of the arts. Daytime TV does not make meaningful statements. You begin and end with the banal," he said to Dwight Whitney for *TV Guide* (March 29, 1975). In the same interview he also noted that certain key elements made his brand of game shows work: "Emotions and tensions. You must bring out those hidden hostilities in your contestants. You can actually watch them temporarily lose their sanity on the air. We prompt them to do that. Thus audiences are being entertained either in awe or shock or horror or joy over someone going bananas in public."

In 1968 Barris scored another success as a producer, with *Operation: Entertainment*, a variety-show special showcasing Cass Elliot (of the group the Mamas and the Papas), which was filmed at military bases across the country. In his next game show, *The Game Game*, a panel of psychologists would come up with the best solution to a problem while a contestant and three celebrities would guess what that solution was. The show, which debuted in 1969, did not last the season, but it gave Barris a valuable insight into the workings of game shows: the simpler it is, the more likely it is to become a hit. By the early 1970s, he had earned more than $8 million through producing hit game shows. In 1975 his personal wealth was estimated at between $20 million and $40 million.

Inspired to try his hand at fiction after reading the novel *Love Story*, Barris wrote *You and Me, Babe* over the course of five months. After getting rejection slips from 14 publishers during the next two years, he found an approving editor at Harper's Magazine Press, which published the book in 1974. A semiautobiographical work about a young, struggling television producer who marries a rich woman and later suffers through a divorce, the novel became a best-seller in both hardcover and paperback (with combined sales of nearly one million copies) but received mixed reviews. Various critics agreed with Martin Levin, who wrote in his assessment for the *New York Times Book Review* (April 28, 1974), "Chauffeured Rolls-Royces, lots of conspicuous consumption, and an inevitable drifting apart. It's an old, old story, peculiarly American, and I can't say Mr. Barris tells it particularly well. He is a rudimentary writer with a limited command of word magic. Only when he describes the selling of a TV pilot does the novel crackle with communicable emotion." An expanded version of the novel was published in August 2005 by Carrol & Graf.

After *The Newlywed Game* ended its first run on TV, in 1974 (a version of the show was revived several times in the next decades and ran until 2000), many television insiders wondered if Barris's brand of lowbrow entertainment was becoming obsolete. The answer was no, as Barris showed with his next production, *The Gong Show*. When it premiered, in 1976, even many hardened television critics were taken aback by its real-life oddballs and misfits. The show's concept was simple: it was a spoof of old-time amateur shows, but with a twist: instead of trying to present the best acts, it tried to display the worst. Forty-five seconds after a performer had started his or her act, Barris and his panel of B-list celebrities could choose to ring a huge gong, to end it. If a performer completed the full 90 seconds allotted, each celebrity panelist would rate him or her on a scale from zero to 10. Whoever got the highest score received a gong-shaped trophy and a check for $516.32. The only problem during the pilot phase of *The Gong Show* was with its host, John Barbour, who seemed out of place. Representatives of NBC, who had expressed interest in the program, told Barris that unless he acted as its host, they would not buy it. Given that ultimatum, Barris spent the next four seasons moving frenetically on the stage, clapping madly, and pointing and squinting at the audience from beneath a floppy hat. Various commentators labeled him sadistic for putting obviously untalented people on national television as objects of derision for viewers apparently in search of the visceral thrill of watching ordinary people do extraordinarily embarrassing things, but Barris expressed his belief that the show had merit. "What it's doing is fulfilling some kind of fantasy that these people can live on for a long time," he told Jonathan Steele for the Manchester (now London) *Guardian* (January 3, 1979). "They are going to be seen coast-to-coast." Indeed, the series never ran out of willing contestants. It even endowed some of them—Gene Gene the Dancing Machine, a heavyset man with a hyperkinetic dance style, for example, and the Unknown Comic, whose jokes were so corny he wore a paper bag over his head—with ephemeral celebrity.

The daytime version of *The Gong Show* captured up to 78 percent of viewers ages 18 to 49—a highly desirable demographic for advertisers—which led the network to produce a nighttime version. Barris became a household name, recognized wherever he went. *The Gong Show*'s success gave him enough industry clout to produce more entertainments, including *The Chuck Barris Rah-Rah Show*, a variety hour featuring an odd mix of old-time performers and amateurs that lasted six weeks in 1978; *The $1.98 Beauty Show* (1978–80), which presented winners with a bouquet of rotting carrots and a check for $1.98; and *Three's a Crowd* (1979), a series in which a businessman stood offstage while the show's host peppered the man's wife and secretary with questions to see which of them knew him better.

By the late 1970s Chuck Barris Productions had become hugely successful. At the same time Barris was growing tired of what had become a grind for him. In March 1980 he canceled production of all of his still-lucrative game shows to focus on writing, directing, producing, and starring in *The Gong Show Movie* (1980), a seriocomic look behind what the public saw on TV. The film received a critical drubbing and earned little money at the box office. The cancellation of all of his television shows made Barris something of a mystery to his fellow television producers, to whom ending so many profitable ventures in one swoop seemed unimaginable. In an interview with Peter Brown for *Parade* (July 6, 1980), Barris offered an explanation for his action: "Lately, I've been wondering how history will judge me. If I never did anything else—then my legacy of game shows would paint a terribly bleak picture of me. So I've got to stop it and hope I can shake the image I have. I only hope I can do something in the time I have left."

In December 1980 it was reported that Barris had married his long-time girlfriend, Robin "Red" Altman, the previous month. (It is unclear when he and his first wife divorced.) Over the next few years, Barris sold off various parts of his business enterprises (reportedly for a total of $100 million) and began to write his first autobiography, *Confessions of a Dangerous Mind* (1984). Unlike many celebrity biographies that supposedly "reveal" star secrets that have already been hinted at in the press, Barris's book delivered a bombshell: while he worked as a television producer in the 1960s and 1970s, he moonlighted as a trained assassin for the CIA. The book was largely ignored. In 1986 Barris and his wife moved to the south of France, and for a number of years afterward, he remained out of the public eye. In 1993 he published a second autobiography, *The Game Show King*, which did not mention the CIA. Currently, Barris tells people to ignore the second autobiography, and he has refused to say whether or not *Confessions* was an out-and-out fabrication. While publicizing the film adaptation of *Confessions of a Dangerous Mind* (written by Charlie Kaufman, directed by George Clooney, and starring Sam Rockwell as Barris), which was released in late 2002, Barris told a reporter for *Time* (January 13, 2003), "People forget the point of the book. Here I was getting crucified by critics for entertaining people and getting medals for killing them. That just didn't seem logical." At the time of the film's release, a CIA spokesman denied Barris's claims. As a response of sorts, Barris wrote a third memoir, *Bad Grass Never Dies: More Confessions of a Dangerous Mind* (2004), in which he asserted that he had continued to kill people at the behest of the American government after moving to France. "Barris is a skilled storyteller," Vicki Cameron wrote for the *East Bay Express* (July 28, 2004), "and in this marriage of *Spy vs. Spy* and *Entertainment Tonight*, the CIA, Hollywood wunderkind, and stuffy NYC publishing types all get gonged with equal relish."

In recent years Barris has suffered enormous losses. In 1998 his only child, Della (who had often appeared with him on *The Gong Show*), died of a drug overdose after a long struggle with mental illness and substance abuse. In 1999 he and his second wife divorced. In 2000 he lost part of a lung to cancer. Barris has said that he has thought about writing a book about his daughter. "I just don't want to do it because it's so depressing," he said in an interview with Karen Valby for *Entertainment Weekly* (January 10, 2003). "I don't know, I don't know. It's a book that should be written, but I don't know if I want to write it." Barris plans to write a detective story, tentatively titled "Who Killed Art Deco?" He and his third wife, Mary, live in New York City.

—C.M.

Suggested Reading: *Entertainment Weekly* p28+ Jan. 10, 2003, with photos; *Forbes* p116+ Nov. 27, 1978, with photos; *Life* p116+ Oct. 10, 1968, with photos; *Newsday* II p2 May 26, 2004, with photos; *Parade* p6+ July 6, 1980, with photos; *Salon* (on-line) Mar. 6, 2001, with photo

Selected Television Shows: *The Dating Game*; *The Newlywed Game*; *The Game Game*; *The Gong Show*; *Three's a Crowd*

Selected Books: *You and Me, Babe*, 1974, 2005; *Confessions of a Dangerous Mind*, 1984; *The Game Show King*, 1993; *Bad Grass Never Dies*, 2004

Bateman, Jason

Jan. 14, 1969– Actor

Address: Attn: Fox Broadcasting Publicity Dept., Arrested Development, P.O. Box 900, Beverly Hills, CA 90213-0900

The actor Jason Bateman is one of the rare child stars who has successfully reinvented himself as a performer in adulthood. At age 11 he made his debut as a regular on a television series, *Little House on the Prairie*; his status quickly progressed from child actor to teenage heartthrob with his role on the sitcom *Silver Spoons*. TV viewers may remember him best for his portrayal of the teenage wise guy David Hogan in the late-1980s NBC comedy *Valerie*, which turned him into a bona fide star of the small screen. Currently, after more than 10 years away from the spotlight, he is enjoying newfound popularity in the role of Michael Bluth, a man who finds himself in charge of his family's fortunes after his father is jailed for fraudulent accounting practices, on the Fox television network's critically acclaimed comedy *Arrested Development*. In January 2005 Bateman's comedic timing and nonchalant air earned him a Golden Globe Award for outstanding performance by an actor in a television comedy or musical. "I notice that my style changes as I get a little bit older," Bateman told Robert Lloyd for the *Los Angeles Times* (April 3, 2005), "and generally that means I do less acting. . . . The less you can do the better off you are. The audience wants to see just enough. They don't want to be told a lot of things or shown a lot of things; they want to try to find it."

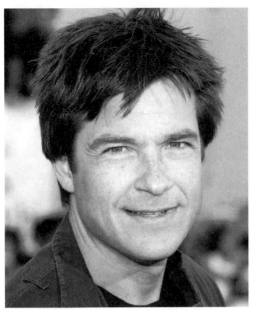

Vince Bucci/Getty Images

Jason Bateman

The second child of Kent Bateman, a director and producer of educational films and television shows, and his wife, Victoria, a flight attendant, Jason Kent Bateman was born in Rye, New York, on January 14, 1969. His older sister, Justine, is an actress; as a teenager she had a starring role in the popular television show *Family Ties*. When Jason and Justine were children, the family changed addresses several times, moving to such places as Winchester, Massachusetts, and Salt Lake City, Utah. The Batemans ultimately settled in California's San Fernando Valley in 1981; Bateman once told an interviewer that he considered himself a "real California boy." He told Bart Mills for the *Chicago Tribune* (March 9, 1994) that he did not have a "normal childhood" because he had acted from an early age. Despite the unusual circumstances of their upbringing, both he and his sister have credited their parents for providing a positive environment in which to grow up. Bateman recalled that his father would whisk him off to the movies rather than to a park for a game of catch, as a way of bonding with the boy. "Another kid might want to play football to impress his dad," he told Tom Gliatto for *People* (November 23, 2002). "I wanted to be an actor." At age 10 he accompanied a friend to an audition for an educational film; at the request of the director, Bateman himself read for the part and won it.

Endowed with what are described as "wholesome looks," Bateman soon acquired an agent and landed parts in a string of television commercials, for such products or services as Cheerios, Coca-Cola, and McDonald's. At 11 he was cast in a recurring role on the long-running NBC drama *Little House on the Prairie*, based on the autobiographi-

cal series of books in which Laura Ingalls Wilder described how she and her sisters grew up on the American frontier during the late 19th century. For two seasons, in 1981 and 1982, Bateman depicted an orphaned boy, James Cooper, whom the Ingalls family adopted. Next, in the fall of 1982, he was cast as the charming but calculating Derek Taylor on NBC's lighthearted hit family comedy *Silver Spoons*. Derek served as friend and foil to the leading character, Ricky Stratton (played by Ricky Schroder), the son of a feckless millionaire. During the show's first season, Bateman exhibited a penchant for stealing the spotlight from Schroder, which created a rift between the two young actors. "Jason was starting to get a lot of mail," the show's co-writer Ron Leavitt recalled to Andrea Darvi for *TV Guide* (February 9, 1985). "The girls liked him because he had a sexy quality." (The animosity between Schroder and Bateman reportedly ended in 1997, after the two unexpectedly encountered each other at a car race.) Bateman's popularity led television executives to create a series around him; the humor and tone of the show, which was called *It's Your Move*, were more subtle than those of *Silver Spoons*. The show's premise centered on the relationship between Bateman's character, the 14-year old prankster Matt Burton, and his nemesis—his mother's new boyfriend, Norman Lamb (played by David Garrison). *It's Your Move* received lukewarm praise from critics and was cancelled after its second season.

Bateman next appeared in the television comedy *Valerie*, which originally aired on NBC in March 1986 and was named for the actress cast in the lead role, Valerie Harper. Shortly after the beginning of the third season, Harper and the producers of the series engaged in a highly publicized dispute that led to her leaving the show; Harper's character was written out of the story, by having her die suddenly, and in 1988 the name of the show was changed to *The Hogan Family*. Throughout the series' run Bateman played David, the girl-crazy older brother of a pair of fraternal twins, Mark and Willie (Jeremy Licht and Danny Ponce), and he himself became the idol of large numbers of girls. "When he comes out and 150 girls [in the studio audience] scream, I think he likes it because he's human," the show's executive producer, Tom Miller, told Susan Toepfer for *People* (May 16, 1988), "but it also makes him uncomfortable. Jason doesn't find being cute a negative in his life, but he also wants to be taken seriously." At the end of its fifth season, NBC cancelled *The Hogan Family*; it was picked up by CBS and was broadcast for one more season.

After *The Hogan Family* went off the air, Bateman's career stalled for a decade, during which he appeared in a string of pilots that were never developed into series. "I was basically doing a pilot every year and not that interested in working the other 10 months," he recalled to Lloyd. "I would tell my agents to stop sending me feature scripts, because they would sit there winking at me on my coffee table, and they'd ultimately be turned into coasters. . . . I was so set on playing as hard as I had been working up until '91 . . . which would mean everything you think it might. Luckily, it didn't take some incarceration to make me figure out that I'd caught up."

Bateman's current show, *Arrested Development,* which is set in Southern California, debuted on the Fox television network in November 2003. Bateman plays Michael Bluth, the son of a dishonest real-estate mogul. Described as "the most sane" of the Bluth family on the sitcom's official Web site, Bateman's character is "persuaded by the rest of his family to stay in California and run the business while his father is in jail." Noting his "pleasantly good-looking . . . rumpled, sleepy charm" and "wry, laconic tone," Robert Lloyd praised Bateman's ability "to preserve his boyishness in a way that makes his maturity more attractive." Lloyd added of Bateman's revived celebrity: "This is not a comeback for him, really, so much as a happy collusion of maturity and opportunity that has brought him to a new level of public consciousness, as if the essential Jason Bateman had been hiding in plain sight all these years." In addition to winning a Golden Globe Award, Bateman was nominated for a 2005 Emmy Award for best actor on a comedy series. He has also earned the respect of his fellow cast members for his work on *Arrested Development.* "He lets the people around him shine, then he has his moment and he just kills," Jeffrey Tambor, a fellow cast member, explained to Gliatto. For its quirky nature, innovative dialogue, and talented ensemble cast, which includes such veteran television actors as Will Arnett, David Cross, and Portia de Rossi in addition to Bateman and Tambor, the show has enjoyed widespread critical success, including the 2004 Emmy Award for best comedy. Rumors that it would be cancelled to the contrary, in May 2005 *Arrested Development* was renewed for a third season.

In 1984 Bateman made his feature-length debut in the made-for-TV movie *Just a Little More Love.* The following year he portrayed Joe Kennedy III in a CBS miniseries entitled *Robert Kennedy and His Times.* In 1987 he co-starred with his sister, Justine, in the NBC made-for-television drama *Can You Feel Me Dancing?,* a production for which his father served as supervising producer. That year he also starred for the first time on the big screen, in *Teen Wolf Too,* the critically panned and commercially disappointing sequel to a hit movie that had starred Michael J. Fox. In 2002 Bateman's feature-film career rebounded with his critically applauded performance in the romantic comedy *The Sweetest Thing* (2002), which also starred Cameron Diaz, Christina Applegate, and Selma Blair. In 2004 he was featured as a sports commentator in the box-office hit comedy *Dodgeball: A True Underdog Story* (2004), which starred Vince Vaughn and Ben Stiller. Earlier that year, he had played a villainous associate of Vaughn's in the feature film *Starsky and Hutch,* based on the 1970s TV show.

He is currently working on a film scheduled for release in 2006, *The Heartbreak Kid.* A remake of the same-titled 1972 movie, which starred Charles Grodin, the film will co-star *Saturday Night Live's* Amy Poehler and will be directed by James Bobin, who is a contributing writer to the HBO sketch comedy *Da Ali G Show.* In the film Bateman's character encounters the woman of his dreams while on his honeymoon with Poehler's character.

Behind the camera Bateman directed an episode of *The Hogan Family* that aired on December 2, 1988, becoming the youngest person (age 19) at the time to have ever directed a network telecast. He has since served as director for his current show, *Arrested Development,* and for other television programs, including *Family Matters* and the short-lived ABC comedy *Two of a Kind.*

Bateman met his wife, Amanda Anka, who is one of the singer-songwriter Paul Anka's five daughters and a successful commercial and voice-over actress, at a Los Angeles Kings hockey game in 1988. They married 13 years later. "Like everybody else, I just want to get married once. I had found that I got bored or tired of girlfriends, but never bored or tired of friends, so I reasoned that I should give it a go if I was attracted to a female friend," he told Eirik Knutzen of the Copley News Service (November 10, 2003). The couple live in Los Angeles.

Regarding future endeavors, Bateman has said that the success of *Arrested Development* will give him the comfort to choose his next film project freely. "You could be capable, qualified and worthy of doing *Hamlet,* but there's a right time for that," he told Lloyd, "and to me there's nothing more annoying than a performer jumping three steps forward when they should have just taken one."

—D.F.

Suggested Reading: *Chicago Tribune* V p3 Mar. 9, 1994, with photos; *Los Angeles Times Magazine* p15 Apr. 3, 2005, with photos; *People* p101+ May 16, 1988, with photos, p121+ Dec. 8, 2003, with photos; *TV Guide* p38+ Feb. 9, 1985, with photos, p4+ Apr. 22, 1989, with photos; *USA Weekend* (on-line) June 13, 2004

Selected Films: *Teen Wolf Too,* 1987; *Necessary Roughness,* 1991; *The Sweetest Thing,* 2002; *Starsky & Hutch,* 2004; *Dodgeball: A True Underdog Story,* 2004

Selected Television Shows: *Little House on the Prairie,* 1981; *Silver Spoons,* 1982; *Valerie,* 1986–87; *Valerie's Family,* 1987; *The Hogan Family,* 1988–91; *Arrested Development,* 2003–

Christian Petersen/Getty Images

Beane, Billy

Mar. 29, 1962– General manager of the Oakland Athletics

Address: Oakland Athletics, McAfee Coliseum, 7000 Coliseum Way, Oakland, CA 94621

"The math works," Billy Beane told Keith H. Hammonds for *Fast Company* (May 2003), speaking about how he handles his job as vice president and general manager of the Oakland Athletics baseball team. "Over the course of a season, there's some predictability to baseball. When you play 162 games, you eliminate a lot of random outcomes. There's so much data that you can predict individual players' performances and also the odds that certain strategies will pay off." Since 1997, when Beane assumed his current position, the Athletics have become one of the best teams in professional baseball. Defying conventional wisdom, Beane and his front-office colleagues have hired players whose abilities were not fully recognized by other ball clubs. Unlike the Atlanta Braves, the Los Angeles Dodgers, and other affluent teams, whose lucrative cable-television and non–cable-network contracts provide them with the money to acquire the best players, executives with teams like the Athletics have to wheel and deal to get the best among the players remaining on the market. As of the 2003 season, Oakland's player payroll totaled $49 million, only a third of the New York Yankees'. The Athletics' home city has a population of only 410,000 (New York's is over eight million; Los Angeles', over 3.8 million), and in 2002 an average of fewer than 27,000 people attended home games, leaving some 23,000 seats vacant in the Coliseum,

the team's ballpark. With the goal of winning more games, and thus possibly attracting more people to home games, Beane has relied on sabermetrics—a system for analzying baseball statistics—to procure the best players available with his limited budget. Sabermetrics was especially attractive to Beane because he had been mistakenly considered an excellent prospect himself when he was drafted, so he knew that the traditional ways of evaluating players were flawed. Beane and the Athletics are the subjects of Michael Lewis's book *Moneyball: The Art of Winning an Unfair Game* (2003).

William Lamar Beane was born on March 29, 1962 in Orlando, Florida, and raised in San Diego, California, where his father, who made his career in the U.S. Navy, was then stationed. As a student at Mount Carmel High School in the late 1970s, Beane attracted the attention of Major League Baseball scouts. Standing six feet four inches and weighing 195 pounds, he was both a fast runner and a power hitter. On June 3, 1980 he was drafted by the New York Mets in the first round of the amateur draft. (He was the 23d draft pick overall.) During his years in the minor leagues (1981–84), scouts often commented on his athletic physique and good looks, and many in the Mets organization viewed him as the future "face" of the franchise. Although he occasionally made a phenomenal play or a key hit in a clutch situation, his performance was generally mediocre, primarily, according to various observers, because he overanalyzed his actions and became overly emotional when he made errors. Nevertheless, the Mets called him up to the majors toward the end of the 1984 season, and he participated in five games. In the two games in which he played with the Mets in the 1985 season, he did not display the skills needed to succeed at the major-league level. On January 16, 1986 the Mets traded him (along with Joe Klink and Bill Latham) to the Minnesota Twins, in exchange for Tim Teufel and Pat Crosby, a minor leaguer.

Beane fared somewhat better with the Twins; in 1986 he played in 80 games as a reserve outfielder. But with a batting average of .213, with three home runs and 15 runs batted in, he did not live up to his supposed potential. In 1987 he appeared in only 12 major-league games; the rest of the time, he tried to polish his skills in the team's farm system. On March 28, 1988 the Twins traded Beane to the Detroit Tigers for Balvino Galvez. Beane performed poorly in the six major-league games in which he played that year. After being granted free agency in October 1988, he signed with the Oakland Athletics, who included him in the lineup for only 37 games. By the season's end Beane had amassed a career total of only 301 at-bats, with a six-year batting average of .219, 80 strikeouts, and 11 walks. At that point he surprised the Athletics' front office by telling them that he wanted to quit being a player and instead work in the organization as a scout. The managers accepted his decision and sent him on the road to evaluate up-and-coming players.

As a scout Beane used his own experiences to assess how a particular player had helped his team in the previous season and as a way to predict how that player might perform in the coming season. Instead of focusing on the person's physique and power, as had the scouts who had evaluated Beane, he adopted sabermetrics, a technique invented and advanced by the baseball statistician Bill James in the 1970s. (The term "sabermetrics" comes from SABR, the acronym of the Society of American Baseball Research.) In the belief that many of the statistics used to judge players' abilities were woefully inadequate, James had searched for statistics that would provide more reliable indicators. He came up with some that had largely been ignored by professional baseball players, owners, scouts, and managers. For example, he found that batting average—traditionally used to gauge the effectiveness of a player's hitting—was actually a limited tool, because it gave no hint of a team's rate of success in scoring runs. A batting average did not account for the walks a batter earned, even though, more often than not, a walk helps the team at bat. James also criticized the use of the statistic for runs batted in (RBIs) to appraise a player's hitting. He noted that often a player can accumulate RBIs simply by being on a team whose members produce a large number of runs—an opportunity unavailable to a player of a similar caliber who plays for a less productive team. Among other formulas, James devised one that would measure "runs created." Based on limited information about a player's performance, the formula may be used to predict a player's run production as a member of a particular team. James suggested that teams put greater emphasis on getting walks and extra base hits, both of which may lead to greater run production. James made his theories available to the public in his text *The Baseball Abstract*, which was issued annually from 1977 through 1988. Many baseball experts greeted his ideas with skepticism; in recent years, though, increasing numbers of professionals have started to adopt sabermetrics. (James remains active in his field. In 2002 he was named special adviser to the Boston Red Sox, who won the World Series two years later—their first championship since 1918.)

In 1993 Beane was promoted to assistant to Sandy Alderson, who was then in his 11th year as the Athletics' general manager. As a staffer in the front office, Beane made suggestions based on what he had learned on the road, especially in connection with the application of sabermetrics. His ideas appealed to Alderson, who had once practiced law and was not hobbled by the many preconceived notions held by professional baseball players and scouts regarding players' abilities. When Beane succeeded Alderson as general manager, on October 17, 1997, he hired Paul DePodesta, a Harvard University graduate who had majored in economics, to apply his computer skills to analyze players' statistics as a means of predicting their performances in a coming season. (According to some reports, DePodesta did so without ever seeing any of the players on the field.) Next, Beane began enforcing a strict adherence to sabermetrics throughout the Athletics organization. By the beginning of the 1999 season, the A's had begun assembling a new team.

In 1997, the year Beane became general manager, Oakland's payroll was smaller than those of all but three of the 14 teams in the American League, but the Athletics were fifth in wins in the American League for the season. In 2000 and 2001 Oakland ranked 12th in terms of size of payroll and second in wins. In 2002 their payroll again ranked 12th, but the team won more games than any other in the major leagues except for the Yankees, who won an equal number (103). Between 1999 and 2002 the A's total win–loss record was second only to that of the Yankees, whose payroll was triple that of the Athletics'. Even more remarkable is that Oakland had lost three of the team's best players between the 2001 and 2002 seasons. (The players who had become free agents wanted larger salaries than the Athletics could pay them.) In terms of statistics, their replacements were more or less their equivalents.

In 2003 the writer Michael Lewis published *Moneyball: The Art of Winning an Unfair Game*, about Beane, the A's organization, and their approach to player evaluation. To research the book, Lewis had intended to spend most of the 2002 season investigating how major-league teams signed players, but before long he had shifted his focus to Beane. In *Moneyball* Lewis described how Beane and his staff, armed with reams of statistics but little money, acquired nearly every prospect they wanted in the June draft, and how they also captured a much-needed left-handed relief pitcher. Notable among players who joined the team during that period were Jeremy Brown, Chad Bradford, and Scott Hattenberg. Brown was an overweight college catcher when Beane chose him as a first-round draft pick, despite the predictions made by many that he would be a 15th-round pick. Bradford came from the Chicago White Sox's farm system and became a key set-up pitcher for the Athletics. And Hattenberg was a onetime catcher who was transformed into a first baseman. As Lewis noted in *Moneyball*, Beane's success at putting together winning teams despite his small budget proved to be something of an embarrassment to Bud Selig, the commissioner of baseball, and other people who remained skeptical about the merits of sabermetrics. Many of them, as well as baseball commentators and columnists, criticized Beane for sitting for the flattering portrait that Lewis drew of him, one in which he appeared as something of a genius. As Michael Lewis wrote for *Sports Illustrated* (March 1, 2004), "For the six months of the 2003 baseball season the sun did not set without some professional blowhard spouting off about Beane's outsized ego. To catalog the scorn heaped on the poor man, whose only crime was not throwing me out of his office often enough, would take even longer if I had to include the countless examples of front office executives who condemned Beane anonymously to their friendly local columnists. . . . [Beane had simply] had the nerve to seize upon ideas rejected, or at least not taken too seriously, by his fellow Club members, and put them into practice. But I'd never thought of Beane as a genius. He was more like a gifted Wall Street trader with no talent for research."

One criticism lobbed at Beane and the A's organization has been that despite having maintained a consistently winning record since 1999, the team has yet to advance in the postseason. (The team clinched the American League West division title three times, in 2000, 2002, and 2003, and secured the American League Wildcard spot in 2001.) Beane told Keith H. Hammonds, "Getting to the play-offs isn't random: Over 162 [regular season] games, if you have the right team, the odds work out. But once you get to the postseason, everything becomes random. In a 5-game series, you can flip a coin five times, and you might come up tails five times. In our market and many others, we can't build a team that's specifically geared for 162 games and also for a 5-game play-off. That I don't think we'll ever overcome." Another criticism fired at Beane stems from the fact that once players become free agents and are available for contract arbitration, the A's cannot keep them because of their limited finances. This has resulted in an annual exodus of top talent, which year after year has forced Beane and his co-managers to come up with creative ways to fill the resulting gaps.

Coming into the 2005 season, the Athletics had amassed a 483–326 win–loss record over the past five seasons, second only to the New York Yankees, who had won 487 games and lost 319 over the same period. At the end of the 2004 season, the club had posted its sixth straight winning season, with 90 or more victories each year. In 2005 they placed second in their division, with 88 wins and 74 losses. During the eight seasons the A's have been under Beane's general management, the team has won more than half—644—of the games played (1,133), producing a ratio of .568. On April 1, 2005 Lewis Wolff, an owner of the Athletics, announced that he had extended Beane's contract with the team through the end of the 2012 season. The team's president, Michael Crowley, had his contract extended through 2008, and both men became part owners in the team, along with Wolff, his son, Keith, Steve Schott, and John Fisher.

Despite the criticisms that have been leveled against Beane, his approach to the game has consistently produced winning results. Oakland's ownership has shown confidence in Beane's management style, and many sportswriters are beginning to reassess his contributions to the game. Suggesting that Beane may be one of the few general managers who deserve to enter the Baseball Hall of Fame solely on those contributions, Rob Neyer argued in an article for ESPN.com, "It's pretty clear that Billy Beane is the most successful general

manager in the game today, based purely on what his teams have accomplished relative to their financial resources. In fact, Beane has been so successful that he makes other baseball executives nervous. He makes the Commissioner's Office nervous because he proves that competitive balance is about far more than just payrolls. And he makes other general managers nervous. How can they complain about not having enough money when that #@&%$ out in Oakland is winning division titles with less money than just about anybody?"

Beane and his wife, Tara, live in San Ramon, California. Their daughter, Casey, is in her early teens.

—C.M.

Suggested Reading: baseball-reference.com; *Fast Company* p84+ May 2003; *Michigan Law Review* p1390+ May 1, 2004; MLB.com; Oakland Athletics (on-line); *Pensions and Investments* p1+ Sep. 15, 2003; *Sports Illustrated* p66+ Mar. 1, 2004, p100 Apr. 4, 2005; *Sports Illustrated* (on-line) June 25, 2003

Courtesy of Ruth Behar

Behar, Ruth

(BAY-har)

Nov. 12, 1956– Anthropologist; poet; filmmaker

Address: Dept. of Anthropology, University of Michigan, 1020 LSA Bldg., Ann Arbor, MI 48109

After she won a MacArthur Fellowship, in 1988, and thereby firmly established herself as a scholar, the anthropologist Ruth Behar began working with experimental forms of ethnography, incorporating autobiographical material into her texts. Her innovative approach, exemplified in her books *Translated Woman: Crossing the Border with Esperanza's Story* and *The Vulnerable Observer: Anthropology that Breaks Your Heart*, has received both praise and criticism. "Behar . . . is a champion of a relatively new form of anthropology that seems to be driving the fuddy-duddies in academia nuts," Sally Eckhoff wrote for the on-line magazine *Salon* (January 28, 1997). "Combine traditional fieldwork with a researcher's personal experience, she asserts, and you come up with a mode of study that informs the intellect as it grips the emotions— without smashing the delicate subject(s) flat, the way conventional research often does. It takes an extremely clear-eyed and self-critical writer to get an enterprise like this off the ground, and Behar is one of the very few who can swing it." A professor at the University of Michigan, Behar has edited two anthologies—*Bridges to Cuba/Puente a Cuba* (1995), a collection of works by Cuban and Cuban-American writers and artists, and *Women Writing Culture* (1995), which attempts to redefine anthropology from feminist and multicultural perspectives. "What is drawing me and, I believe, other scholars to write personally is a desire to abandon the alienating 'metalanguage' that closes, rather than opens, the doors of academe to all those who wish to enter," Behar wrote for the *Chronicle of Higher Education* (June 29, 1994). "Personal writing represents a sustained effort to democratize the academy. Indeed, it emerges from the struggles of those traditionally excluded from the academy, such as women and members of minority groups, to find a voice that acknowledges both their sense of difference and their belated arrival on the scholarly scene."

Ruth Behar was born in Havana, Cuba, on November 12, 1956, during the brutal dictatorship of Fulgencio Batista. Her mother, Rebecca (Glinsky) Behar, was the daughter of Ashkenazi Jews who had immigrated to Cuba from Poland and Russia; her father, Alberto Behar, was the son of Sephardic Jews who had immigrated to Cuba from Turkey and traced their roots to 15th-century Spain. In 1492 the Spanish monarchy, in what has been described as religious zeal, forcibly expelled virtually all of the country's Jews. Many of those who fled, like Behar's ancestors, resettled in the Balkans, the Near East, or Turkey, where, despite their exile, they retained aspects of Spanish culture. By the mid-1920s, because of rising Turkish nationalism and the economic upheaval caused by World War I, many in the Sephardic community began to fear for their safety. Behar's paternal grandparents fled to Havana, where her grandfather became a peddler.

In Cuba Behar's father worked as an accountant. Her mother occasionally helped out at her parents' lace shop but mostly stayed home to care for her children—Ruth and her younger brother, Maurice

(nicknamed Mori), who is now a jazz musician and teacher. On January 1, 1959 guerrillas led by Fidel Castro toppled the Batista regime, and Castro turned Cuba into a Communist state. "My parents were very supportive of the revolution because they were in a position to benefit, at least initially," Behar told *Current Biography*, "but as the revolution went on they started to feel threatened because afterwards properties were nationalized, and so . . . my grandparents lost their store." In 1961 the Behar family left Cuba. They lived for a year on a kibbutz in Israel before moving to a Jewish section of the New York City borough of Queens. Many of their neighbors assumed that the Behars were Puerto Rican, because they spoke Spanish, and people often asked young Ruth how someone could be both Cuban and Jewish. After a while a small Jewish Cuban community developed in Queens and an adjoining part of Brooklyn; Cuban friends of Behar's parents settled there, as did Behar's maternal grandparents, aunts, uncles, and cousins. "They were all Cuban, they all spoke Spanish, they all loved Cuban food, they all danced to Cuban music—but at the same time they were Jewish, and it was hard to find that combination anywhere else except among themselves," Behar told *Current Biography*. "My parents' friends actually came to call themselves 'El Grupo,' the group."

When Behar was nine she broke a leg in a car accident; she was encased in a full-body cast (to prevent the uninjured leg from growing longer than the damaged one) and was confined to bed for a year. During that time a private tutor, sent by her school, gave her lessons at home. "The tutor filled my bed with English storybooks and I read voraciously," Behar wrote in *The Vulnerable Observer*. "When I returned to school I was no longer a Spanish-speaking child struggling with English, but among the more gifted kids who would be steered toward 'Special Progress' . . . classes in junior high school." As with many immigrant children, Behar picked up English more quickly than her parents and served as their translator. "I think that experience really made a mark on me and made me think a lot about being a translator between cultures and languages," Behar told *Current Biography*. As a high-school student, she set her sights on gaining entrance to an elite, private university. Her father, however, wanted her to attend Queens College, a division of the City University of New York, so that she could live at home until she married. She found an ally in her mother, who surreptitiously paid the application fee for Wesleyan University, in Middletown, Connecticut. Behar was accepted and became a freshman in the school's College of Letters in 1974.

At Wesleyan Behar felt insecure, as if she had to prove that her admittance had not hinged on her minority status. She turned down a room in university housing where Latino culture was promoted and for a brief period affected a British accent. "Maybe I hadn't just gotten off the boat, but the world of the academy . . . was a world for which my immigrant milieu had not prepared me," she wrote in *Translated Woman*. "No one in our Grupo of sales clerks, accountants, and engineers turned owners of shoe stores and envelope factories could understand what this College of Letters . . . was about, and they all thought I was wasting my time." Aware that the costs of her education placed a financial strain on her parents, Behar arranged her course load so as to graduate within three years. She spent one semester studying abroad, in Madrid, Spain. At the end of her sophomore year, as required, she took Wesleyan's comprehensive examinations, but she had not studied for them, immersing herself instead in the production of a play by Federico García Lorca. The middling grade she earned shook her confidence. Her spirits lifted when she took a course in anthropology the next semester. "I was in the wilderness then, so the insight that all products of culture, great books included, were social constructions, not timeless monuments that spoke in a universal language, fell upon me like manna," she wrote in *Translated Woman*. "In anthropology I felt I had found an intellectual home. Here, the little shelf of great books was seen for what it was: just one little shelf."

Behar graduated from Wesleyan with a B.A. degree cum laude in 1977. She then entered the graduate program in anthropology at Princeton University, in New Jersey, from which she earned an M.A. degree in 1981. At the suggestion of James Fernandez, the chairman of her department, she studied the tiny, rural town of Santa María del Monte, in the province of León, Spain, for her doctoral thesis. Her research materials included land records, parish registers, and other historical documents as well as her observations of and conversations with people who lived there. "I was really amazed because I didn't know anything about that aspect of Spain. I didn't know that there was still a part of Spain that was very traditional, that still farmed the land in very traditional ways with cows, and they raised sheep, and they kept their animals right in their own houses . . . ," Behar told *Current Biography*. "People were very protective of me . . . and they treated me as a kind of granddaughter. Most of the people I worked with at the time were old or in late middle age. They . . . took me in and taught me what they could about their life." The November 1985 issue of *Natural History* included an article by Behar about Santa María del Monte, accompanied by photos she had taken. In 1986 Princeton University Press published her dissertation, with the title *Santa María del Monte: The Presence of the Past in a Spanish Village* and with illustrations by her husband, David Frye, whom she had married in 1982. (The book was reprinted in 1991 with the title and subtitle reversed.) "Behar captures well the sense of the past and its presence in village life, and her attention to the role of the written word is uncommon in cultural anthropology studies of this kind," Joan W. Gartland wrote in a *Library Journal* (July 1986) review. Peter Sahlins,

in the *Journal of Social History* (Winter 1987), described *Santa María del Monte* as "an innovative methodological contribution to a long espoused but seldom practiced marriage of ethnography and history in Europe."

Behar received a Ph.D. in anthropology in 1983. Some months earlier she and her husband, an anthropologist and translator, had moved to Mexiquitic, a small Mexican town. For the next two years, Behar conducted research in Mexico on women who had been accused of witchcraft during the Mexican inquisition (the victims of which were primarily people believed to be practicing Judaism, and which extended from the early 1500s to the early 1800s). For several years after that, she worked alternately in Mexico and the U.S., as a postdoctoral fellow at Johns Hopkins University, in Baltimore, Maryland. She next entered the Michigan Society of Fellows postdoctoral program, at the University of Michigan at Ann Arbor, where she taught part-time as an assistant professor. When her fellowship was nearing its end, she applied for a full-time University of Michigan teaching position open only to members of minority groups, but she was turned down. "Apparently I was not an authentic enough Latina because my four grandparents had been European Jewish immigrants to Cuba," she wrote in *Translated Woman*. "An extensive genealogy was put together, not unlike the . . . writs of the Inquisition that sought to determine 'purity of blood,' and it was decided that 'my race' wasn't pure Cuban because I had European blood in my veins."

Behar had returned to Mexico, to work on what became *Translated Woman*, when, in 1988, she received word that she had won a MacArthur Fellowship. Commonly known as the "genius" grant, the fellowship is highly prestigious and includes a substantial monetary stipend, paid in five annual installments. Immediately after she learned about the grant, the University of Michigan offered her an associate professorship. She accepted when the university gave her tenure as well. For several months afterward, she suffered from severe panic attacks and agoraphobia, which, according to the University of Michigan News Service (January 28, 1997, on-line), she has attributed to previously buried memories connected with her year in bed. Meanwhile, as she recalled in the *Chronicle of Higher Education* (November 4, 1992), she had "vowed that I'd use the aura conferred upon me by the MacArthur award to take big risks in my writing and in the way I practice anthropology. I began to search for ways to explore the intersection of the analytical voice that years of education had drilled into me and the personal voice that I had been taught to leave out of my scholarship." *Translated Woman* blurs genres by combining autobiography with the first-person narrative of a Mexican peddler whom Behar called Esperanza (not her real name). Shortly after she had arrived in Mexquitic, Behar had begun to hear talk about the peddler; the townspeople suspected that she was a *bruja* (witch), because she had cursed her philandering, abusive husband, and a short time later he had mysteriously become blind. "Hearing rumors about Esperanza, I was fascinated by the way they echoed the documents I had begun to read from the colonial Mexican inquisition," Behar wrote in *Translated Woman*. "While these colonial women were desperately seeking relief from abusive male dominance, the cultural assignment of mystic powers to women also made them vulnerable to charges of witchcraft, sometimes by the very men who had hurt or shamed them. . . . To hear about Esperanza, a woman living in the present, within the context of these inquisitorial stories, I felt as though history had come alive."

Behar met Esperanza for the first time on the Day of the Dead (actually, two days, November 1 and 2) in 1983, in a local cemetery. Grudgingly, Esperanza allowed Behar to photograph her. They spoke again the next month and slowly became close. At Esperanza's request, Behar and Frye became the godparents of the cake for her daughter Norberta's *quinceañera*, a coming-of-age party that marks a girl's 15th birthday, and she later asked them to serve as the godparents of her *niño Dios*, a doll that represents the baby Jesus in Christmas festivities. Behar and Esperanza were now *comadres*. Such traditional relationships are common in rural Mexico between people of different socioeconomic classes. Behar would provide financial assistance to Esperanza, while Esperanza would give Behar produce or flowers from her garden and show extreme courtesy to Behar when they met in town. Esperanza eagerly shared stories of her life with Behar and became Behar's most valuable informant.

Translated Woman: Crossing the Border with Esperanza's Story (1993) was pieced together from Behar's recordings and is told largely in Esperanza's voice. In what many critics hailed as a vivid, nuanced recounting, Esperanza emerges as a strong, defiant woman, despite the suffering she endured at the hands of her abusive father and her adulterous husband, and the pain of having to bury many of her children. In an autobiographical chapter at the end of the book, Behar attempted to "articulate the connections between who [Esperanza] is as a visibly invisible Indian street peddler and who I am as an academic woman with a certain measure of power and privilege," as she wrote. She also drew parallels between Esperanza's life and her own and discussed her struggles to come to terms with her Cuban-American identity and to secure her position in academia.

Critics greeted the chapters in *Translated Woman* that focus on Esperanza as an impressive example of ethnography, and some also praised the chapter in which Behar herself is the subject. "This is postmodernist writing at its best," the anthropologist Louise Lamphere wrote for the *Women's Review of Books* (May 1993). "The difficulties of articulating the connections between the American woman academic and Mexican female street ped-

dler, the sense of contradictions in tension, and the lack of an easy resolution are perhaps, paradoxically, the most satisfying aspects of Behar's book. In the end she asks us to embrace dissonance, to get beyond the self/other division that has marked Western thinking." Others found fault with the final chapter. In the *Nation* (September 20, 1993), for example, the journalist Victor Perera, a Guatemalan-born Jew, wrote, "The closing section of *Translated Woman* could stand as a set piece in a larger autobiographical work. For this reader, what is most interesting in it is the balancing of polarities between the university investigator and the poet/essayist, the 'mestizo' Jew and the Cuban Chicana. But does this polemical self-portrait belong in a book about a Mexican peddler? Something rings false in Behar's comparing herself to her comadre as fellow literary wetbacks and victims of the patriarchy. It is disingenuous to compare the suffering Mexican village society inflicts on Esperanza for rebelling against its strictures with the ordeal of having to accept tenure at a prominent university. Esperanza's betrayal of her Mexican mores is not comparable to Behar's determination to be an 'academic traitor.'" Perera concluded, "The final section may make for feisty and innovative feminist anthropology, but it shifts the book's gravitational center in a wrenching way that detracts from more than it contributes to an otherwise powerful and brilliant study." Behar wrote for the *Chronicle of Higher Education* (June 29, 1994) that such criticism notwithstanding, "I continue to receive letters from women and men who say that my relating my own story made the book whole for them. A Chicana anthropology student in Los Angeles told me that the book's importance to her was twofold: She could see her mother in Esperanza and herself in me."

Behar's next book was *Women Writing Culture* (1995), a collection of essays by some of the most prominent women in anthropology and ethnography, among them Lila Abu-Lughod, Aihwa Ong, Ellen Lewin, and Barbara Tedlock. Behar co-edited the book with Deborah A. Gordon, who teaches courses in women's studies and postmodernism in anthropology at Wichita State University, in Kansas. *Women Writing Culture* "redefines anthropology through feminist and multicultural eyes," according to the medical writer Francesca Coltrera in a review for Amazon.com. Coltrera also wrote, "At its heart is the 'poetics and politics' of ethnography, an uneasy marriage of art and science that attempts to distill the essence of another person's culture." In a review for *Contemporary Sociology* (January 1997), Sharon Hays, a professor of sociology at the University of Virginia, wrote, "A provocative and often compelling volume, *Women Writing Culture* is a self-conscious attempt to revise the anthropological cannon, include the multiplicity of women's voices, and counter the claim made by James Clifford in the seminal anthology *Writing Culture* (1986), that feminists have not 'produced either unconventional forms of writing or a developed reflection on ethnographic textuality as such.'"

Earlier, in 1979, Behar had traveled to Cuba with a group of students and professors from Princeton. During her next visit, in 1991, she began to establish relationships with Cubans. After she returned to the U.S., she started networking with Cuban Americans in New York, Boston, and Chicago. Behar made several subsequent trips to Cuba. The year 1995 saw the publication of *Bridges to Cuba/Puentes a Cuba*, an anthology co-edited by Behar and Juan Leon, a Cuban-American who teaches English at the University of Michigan. In the introduction to the book, Behar described it as a forum in which Cubans could "openly define themselves and dismantle, once and for all, the hurtful stereotypes of the islander as a brainwashed cog of a Marxist state and the immigrant as a soulless worm lacking any concern for social justice." By her own account, editing the book also served as a way for Behar to "re-engage and connect with Cuba as an adult," as she said in an interview posted on the Fathom Knowledge Network Web site.

Behar's next book, *The Vulnerable Observer* (1996), is a collection of essays that blend memoir and ethnography. "No one objects to autobiography, as such, as a genre in its own right," Behar wrote in one essay. "What bothers critics is the insertion of personal stories into what we have been taught to think of as the analysis of impersonal social facts. Throughout most of the twentieth century, in scholarly fields ranging from literary criticism to anthropology to law, the reigning paradigms have traditionally called for distance, objectivity, and abstraction. The worst sin was to be 'too personal.' . . . The charge that all variants of vulnerable writing that have blossomed in the last two decades are self-serving and superficial, full of unnecessary guilt or excessive bravado, stems from an unwillingness to even consider the possibility that a personal voice, if creatively used, can lead the reader, not into miniature bubbles of navelgazing, but into the enormous sea of serious social issues." *The Vulnerable Observer* earned mixed reviews. "Behar proves that anthropology can make you cry, but changing her delicate science from a self/other exploration into a self/self trip sometimes strains logic," Sally Eckhoff wrote for *Salon* (on-line). Judith Bolton-Fasman, by contrast, wrote for the *Jerusalem Report* (May 1, 1997), "That insistent looking back is what makes Ruth Behar's vision of anthropology so compelling. Memories do not vanish; they recede and leave traces. The anthropologist who makes herself vulnerable to these indications makes the world a more intelligible and hopeful place."

Behar perceives herself as someone who has always existed in a sort of borderland, caught between different cultures and cultural identities. That is one reason why, as she told *Current Biography*, she is "interested in creating these . . . new kinds of combinations. You sort of find that in all

kinds of human creativity, including cooking. We're always used to cooking chicken with onion and pepper, but suddenly you add mango and it adds another sort of flavor. It's sort of the same for me with ethnography. . . . Just all by itself, for me, it's not a sufficiently exciting genre—so I add autobiography or I make it poetic because I like poetry also. I do things to make these genres more exciting, less predictable, more vivid."

In 1999 Behar began making a documentary that followed her as she visited what remains of the Sephardic community in Cuba (which shrank when many Jews emigrated after the Communist revolution); in Miami, Florida, where some Cuban Jews settled; and in New York, with members of her family. In 2002 the New York City–based organization Women Make Movies began distributing the film, entitled *Adio Kerida* (*Goodbye Dear Love*). Narrated by the Cuban-American actress Elizabeth Peña, the film had a mixed reception. "*Adio Kerida* . . . at times is moving and informative, but unfortunately becomes too much of a personal quest to be engaging," Marta Barber wrote for the *Miami Herald* (January 25, 2002). "Behar's love for her abandoned past is clear, but she doesn't know how to engage the rest of us in that personal quest." Robert J. Rosenthal, writing for the *Jewish Bulletin* (November 8, 2002), reacted differently: "Behar . . . puts herself in the film and records many of her own emotional reactions to her exploration. As a postmodern anthropologist trained to avoid cultural exploitation, she brings a refreshing honesty to the current bumper crop of Cuban cultural exports." *Adio Kerida* has won awards at the Latino Film Festival of the San Francisco Bay Area and the San Antonio CineFestival.

Behar has published several collections of her poetry, in handmade, mimeographed, bilingual chapbooks produced by Ediciones Vigía in Matanzas, Cuba, in editions of no more than 200. Currently, she is writing "Nightgowns from Cuba," a novel told from the perspective of an Afro-Cuban woman, whom Behar has based on the woman who served as her nanny when she was an infant in Cuba. "If writing this novel brought me to a place where I write novels for the rest of my life, I would be delighted," she told Michelle Adam for the *Hispanic Outlook in Higher Education* (February 26, 2001). "It would be a wonderful ending to the story."

In addition to the MacArthur Fellowship, Behar's honors include a John Simon Guggenheim Memorial Foundation Award, a Hunting Family Faculty Fellowship from the Institute for the Humanities at the University of Michigan, a Harry Frank Guggenheim Foundation Career Development Award, a Rockefeller Residence Fellowship in the Humanities, the Distinguished Alumna Award in Recognition of Outstanding Achievement and Service from Wesleyan University, a Lucius N. Littauer Foundation grant, and the Special Recognition Award from the American Psychological Association. *Latina* magazine named her one of the 50 Latinas who made history in the 20th century.

Behar and her husband live in Ann Arbor. Their son, Gabriel Frye-Behar, is studying filmmaking at New York University.

—J.C.

Suggested Reading: *Chronicle of Higher Education* A p44 Nov. 4, 1992; *Kenyon Review* p5+ Winter 1997; Ruth Behar Web site; *Salon* (on-line) Jan. 28, 1997; Behar, Ruth. *The Vulnerable Observer: Anthropology That Breaks Your Heart*, 1996

Selected Books: as writer—*Translated Woman: Crossing the Border with Esperanza's Story*, 1993; *The Vulnerable Observer: Anthropology That Breaks Your Heart*, 1996; as co-editor (with Juan Leon)—*Bridges to Cuba/Puentes a Cuba*, 1995

Patrick Hertzog/AFP/Getty Images

Benedict XVI

Apr. 16, 1927– Supreme Pontiff of the Roman Catholic Church; Sovereign of the State of Vatican City

Address: Apostolic Palace, 00120 Vatican City State

Following the death of Pope John Paul II, in April 2005, the College of Cardinals convened in Vatican City to elect the 265th pontiff of the Roman Catholic Church. They selected Joseph Cardinal Ratzinger, who had presided over the deliberations as dean of the college. In accepting their decision Ratzinger took the name Benedict XVI. Ratzinger had previously served, since 1981, as the prefect of the Sacred Congregation for the Doctrine of the Faith (CDF), the Vatican office that protects and promotes doctrinal purity. Under Ratzinger's leadership, and with his papal predecessor John Paul II's blessing, the CDF tripled its workload, disciplining at least a dozen Catholic theologians, bishops, and priests, and expanded beyond its investigative capacity to issue broad policy statements on moral and theological matters. As the church became increasingly intolerant of dissent during John Paul's pontificate, observers noted that the CDF became the most important department in the Vatican. "Cardinal Ratzinger is a singular figure in the history of his office and perhaps the church," Gianni Baget Bozzo, a theologian who specializes in the Vatican, told Daniel Williams for the *Washington Post* (November 5, 2004). "He takes the initiative on a wide range of subjects in a way that is usually reserved to the pope. That's not to say he acts against the pope. He is trusted. But he is a kind of vice pope." While Ratzinger was often singled out for criticism or praise for the church's hard-line positions (the Italian press dubbed him the "Panzer-Kardinal," after the German tank), Father Joseph Fessip, who studied under Ratzinger in what was then West Germany, told Russell Chandler for the *Los Angeles Times* (November 7, 1986), "There isn't a single issue of church and theology the Pope and Ratzinger would disagree on." Yet Ratzinger's visibility frequently drew criticism away from the pontiff. "Ratzinger's job is a thankless one," a high Vatican official told Chandler. "It's inevitable that he would be seen as the 'fall guy.' And general civility within the church would avoid an overly blunt, personal attack on the Pope." Although many observers have predicted that Ratzinger will continue to embrace conservative positions as Pope Benedict XVI, others have suggested that his views might be more moderate than expected. "Experience shows that the papacy in the Catholic Church today is such a challenge that it can change anyone: someone who went into the conclave a progressive cardinal can emerge as a conservative pope," the priest and theologian Hans Küng, whom Ratzinger disciplined while CDF prefect, wrote for the BBC News (April 26, 2005, on-line); he went on to cite the example of Cardinal Montini, who became Pope Paul VI. Referring to Cardinal Roncalli, who became Pope John XXIII, Küng added, "Someone who went into the conclave a conservative cardinal can emerge as a progressive pope."

Benedict's belief in an unwavering church stems, some say, from his childhood in Nazi Germany. "Having seen fascism in action, Ratzinger today believes that the best antidote to political totalitarianism is ecclesial totalitarianism," the journalist and Ratzinger biographer John L. Allen Jr. wrote, according to Williams. "In other words, he believes the Catholic Church serves the cause of human freedom by restricting freedom in its internal life, thereby remaining clear about what it teaches and believes." Benedict's philosophy is squarely opposed to relativism, the belief that there are no moral or theological absolutes. That belief, in Benedict's view, presents the greatest danger to the church today; he sees it embedded in modern society and in the work of some contemporary Catholic theologians. Although he was a supporter of the progressive reforms of Vatican Council II in the 1960s, Ratzinger's experience with Marxism in German universities later that decade changed his views and convinced him that the essential truths of theology and morality cannot be debated publicly without resulting damage to the church. Benedict perceives "two cities: city of God and city of man," Avery Cardinal Dulles told reporters for *Time* (May 2, 2005). "He sees a world very much in conflict."

The youngest son of Joseph Ratzinger, a policeman, and his wife, Maria (née Peintner), a hotel cook, Joseph Alois Ratzinger (some sources spell his middle name Aloysius) was born in the Bavarian town of Marktyl am Inn, near the German border with Czechoslovakia, on April 16, 1927. His family were devout Catholics. Ratzinger's older brother George became a priest and later conducted the famous choir at the Regensburg Cathedral. His sister Maria became his longtime secretary. Ratzinger later recalled in his memoir *Milestones* (1998) that his childhood was a happy one of nature walks and learning to play the piano. He also found a mystical resonance in the Catholic Mass conducted in Latin, as it was everywhere pre–Vatican II. "Here I was encountering a reality that no one had simply thought up, a reality that no official authority or great individual had created," he wrote, according to the reporters for *Time*. "It was much more than a product of human history." In 1937 Joseph Ratzinger retired and moved his family to Traunstein, in Bavaria. There, Ratzinger attended the city's humanistic gymnasium, a grammar school now called the Chiemgau School, and also attended St. Michael's Catholic Seminary.

Growing up in Hitler's Germany, Ratzinger was prevented from embracing Nazism, he said, by his faith in Roman Catholicism, which he called in *Milestones* "a citadel of truth and righteousness against the realm of atheism and deceit," according to Daniel J. Wakin for the *New York Times* (April 20, 2005). Ratzinger joined the Hitler Youth at age 14, as was required of young Germans at the time. His participation was less than enthusiastic. His father had conflicts with the regime, leading him to move his family frequently. When Ratzinger was 14 Nazis killed his cousin who suffered from Down syndrome as part of their systematic extermination of the mentally ill. Ratzinger's seminary studies were interrupted when he was drafted into an antiaircraft unit in Munich, in 1943. However, an infected finger prevented him from learning how to shoot. He later joined a unit protecting a Bavarian Motor Works (BMW) factory that produced aircraft engines, and in 1944 he set tank traps near the Ger-

man borders with Czechoslovakia, Austria, and Hungary. As the war drew to a close, Ratzinger deserted the German army and was briefly held as a prisoner of war by American forces, in 1945.

After the war Ratzinger returned to his studies with the goal of becoming a professor of theology. While studying at the University of Munich, he was drawn to the priesthood. He was ordained in 1951. "I was convinced—I myself don't know how—that God wanted something from me," he told E. J. Dionne Jr. for the *New York Times Magazine* (November 24, 1985), "something which could be accomplished only by becoming a priest." Ratzinger began teaching theology at the University of Freising. Considered something of a wunderkind, he moved on to professorships at the universities of Bonn (1958), Münster (1963), Tübingen (1966), and Regensburg (1969), all in Germany. "He fascinated all of us with his wonderful, angelic voice, his clear language, his deep intellect and powerful faith," Max Seckler, a theology professor at Bonn, told reporters for *Newsweek* (May 2, 2005). At the same time, he wrote books on Christology, patrology, church history, liturgy, homiletics, and other aspects of Catholic doctrine and practice. "From the very beginning, I had a big need to communicate," Ratzinger explained to Dionne. "I wasn't able to keep for myself the knowledge which seemed to be so important to me. The beautiful thing in it was the possibility of giving it to others."

At Vatican Council II (1962–65), the historic conclave of the international episcopate convened by Pope John XXIII for the announced purpose of renewing the church spiritually and reassessing its position in the contemporary world, Ratzinger was theological adviser to Joseph Cardinal Frings of Germany. Frings, encouraged by Ratzinger, joined with French bishops and other German bishops in resisting the efforts of the Roman Curia to block reform. Ratzinger had come to believe that liberalizing reforms were necessary because the church had become too restrictive and stagnant. With the Jesuit theologian Karl Rahner, Ratzinger wrote draft documents replacing those emanating from the Holy Office, the forerunner of the CDF, and he collaborated in the writing of the speech in which the German cardinal Julius Dopfner sharply criticized the Holy Office for "methods and behavior [that] do not conform to the modern era and are a source of scandal to the world," as quoted by Dionne. Ratzinger himself described the Holy Office as being "detrimental to the faith," according to *Time* (December 14, 1981), and he was a founding member of the Concilium, an international board of Catholic scholars, many of whom he would later count among the "aggressive polemical forces" undermining the Catholic faith, as reported by *Newsweek* (December 31, 1984).

As the dean of faculty at Tübingen, Ratzinger began to have doubts about the liberal movement in the Roman Catholic Church. A student assembly there attacked the Gospel as a "mass deception" aimed at maintaining capitalism and called the cross of Jesus "an expression of the sadomasochistic glorification of pain," according to the 2005 article in *Newsweek*. Many of the protests had underpinnings of Marxist theory. Ratzinger told Dionne that he began to see such theories as hypocritical, "if one only compared them with the praxis," which revealed them to be "a radical attack on human freedom and dignity." An incident in which students aggressively interrupted his class seems to have particularly affected him. "That experience made it clear to me that the abuse of faith had to be resisted precisely," he later wrote, according to the BBC News (April 19, 2005, on-line). By the mid-1970s Ratzinger was openly expressing his concern over the direction the church was taking, a drift toward the "fashionable" left that he had unwittingly helped to set in motion. In 1975 he characterized the decade since Vatican II as "a period of ecclesiastical decadence in which the people who started it became incapable of stopping the avalanche," as quoted by the reporter for *Time* in 1981.

Pope Paul VI named Ratzinger archbishop of Munich and Freising in 1977. At a synod of bishops that year, Ratzinger met a like-minded prelate, Karol Cardinal Wojtyla, the archbishop of Krakow, Poland, and the future John Paul II. "I was particularly impressed by his human warmth and the deep inner rooting in God which appeared so clearly," he told Dionne. "And then, of course, I was also impressed by his philosophical education, his acuteness as a thinker and his ability to communicate his knowledge." Tempered in the crucible of totalitarianism, Cardinal Wojtyla shared Ratzinger's chagrin over what they saw as the spiritual disarray of Catholicism, his urgent sense that the permissiveness and heterodoxy rampant in the church since Vatican II had gone far enough, and his belief in the need for a "restoration" of orthodoxy in faith and discipline.

Following the deaths of Pope Paul VI, in August 1978, and his immediate successor, Pope John Paul I, one month later, Cardinal Wojtyla was elected pontiff, in October 1978. As Pope John Paul II, Wojtyla set a conservative course, reaffirming the church's traditional teachings on birth control, abortion, and divorce; shortening the leash on religious orders; and approving a partial revival of the tridentine Latin Mass, which had been replaced by revised Masses in the vernacular after Vatican II. Pope John Paul II named Cardinal Ratzinger the prefect of the Sacred Congregation for the Doctrine of the Faith in November 1981. Previously known successively as the Congregation of the Roman and Universal Inquisition (not related to the infamous Spanish Inquisition, which lasted from 1478 to 1834), and as the Holy Office, the CDF has been operating under its current name since 1965. Joaquin Navarro Valls, a Vatican spokesman, told Dionne that John Paul's selection of Ratzinger was "one the most personal choices of his Pontificate." According to Navarro and others, at first Ratzinger did not want the job, arguably the toughest in the Vatican.

Like Ratzinger, Pope John Paul II was especially concerned over Marxist infiltration of the church in the guise of liberation theology, which holds that the fundamental mission of the church is to enact social change, even to the extent of fostering revolution. During the 1970s and early 1980s, the writings of liberation theologians became extremely popular among Roman Catholics throughout Latin America. In Brazil alone 70,000 groups headed by liberation-theology–inspired church people sprang up, usually outside the ecclesiastically approved parochial structure. Ratzinger claimed that liberation theology came dangerously close to the idea that Christ's kingdom can be fully realized in this world through social action, which contradicted his understanding of Christian belief and, he thought, could easily lead to the rise of false political utopias such as Nazi Germany. In response to some liberal theologians in Latin America who had argued that all baptized Catholics are priests, in 1983 the CDF released a document, written by Ratzinger, reaffirming the church's rule that only priests can say Mass and consecrate the Eucharist. In April 1984, at the first press conference ever held by a head of the CDF, Ratzinger denounced theologies that "reduce the faith to a duty apart, and use Marxist analysis to interpret not only history and the life of society but also the very Bible and the Christian message," according to Marjorie Hyer in the *Washington Post* (June 25, 1984). In September 1984 he presented to the press the "Instruction on the Theology of Liberation," a Sacred Congregation document warning of the dangers to faith and Christian living posed by certain forms of liberation theology. Soon afterward, Ratzinger and his Sacred Congregation colleagues forbade the Brazilian liberation theologian and Dominican friar Leonardo Boff from publicly speaking or writing about his work for one year. After a second silencing, in 1992, Boff left the Dominican order. At a meeting chaired by Ratzinger in October 1984, 44 of Peru's 52 bishops voted to endorse the principles contained in the Sacred Congregation document condemning liberation theology. The Vatican considered the vote "symbolically important," because the liberation-theology movement had been born in Peru and dominated rank-and-file clerical and religious activity in that country. An April 1986 Sacred Congregation document signed by Ratzinger and titled "Instruction on Christian Freedom and Liberation" was slightly more conciliatory to liberation movements than past statements from the Vatican. It noted that serving the poor through charity and working to change oppressive political and economic structures must be priorities for Christians and that armed struggle may be justified "as a last resort" in "the extreme case." However, it noted, "those who discredit the path of reform and favor the myth of revolution . . . encourage the setting up of totalitarian regimes" leading to "merely a change of masters." By the end of the 1980s, liberation theology was no longer a powerful movement within the Roman Catholic Church.

In addition to liberation theology, Ratzinger's targets in the early 1980s included the hedonism and materialism of many American Catholics, the "disenchanted" Catholicism common in Western Europe, the influence of "liberal-radical" theologians, and the hegemony of national bishops' conferences. The last mentioned, viewed widely as a vehicle of democratic collegiality, was considered by Ratzinger to be a bureaucratic innovation that discourages some bishops from properly shepherding their own flocks. In an extensive interview, later expanded into the book *The Ratzinger Report* (1985), the cardinal explained that the "restoration" of the church under Pope John Paul II was not a return to outmoded structures but the search for "a new balance" for a church threatened by adaptation to "an agnostic and atheistic world," according to Joseph A. Komonchak in the *New York Times* (December 22, 1985). And, as Robert Di Veroli reported for the *San Diego Union-Tribune* (September 21, 1985), Ratzinger criticized many Catholic theologians for believing the "spirit of the council" meant that "everything which is new will always, no matter what, be better than that which was or that which is."

In the spirit of restoration of the church, the CDF disciplined many clergymen. It ordered Archbishop Peter Gerety of Newark, New Jersey, to withdraw his imprimatur from *Christ Among Us: A Modern Presentation of the Catholic Faith*, a book it deemed doctrinally defective. On another occasion it ordered Archbishop Raymond Hunthausen of Seattle, Washington, to withdraw his imprimatur from two books, and it relieved him of pastoral responsibility in several areas. In 1988 the CDF silenced the Dominican priest Matthew Fox for one year for his religiously pluralistic teaching and hiring practices at his Institute in Culture and Creation Spirituality, in Oakland, California. An editorial in the *National Catholic Reporter*, quoted by Rich Cartiere for the Associated Press (October 20, 1988), called the silencing "a fruitless exercise" and opined, "People cannot be told to stop thinking or recording their thoughts. Silencing efforts come from another time." In March 1993 the Dominican Order expelled Fox, who believes the order acted under pressure from Ratzinger.

Ratzinger did not penalize only liberal theologians. In July 1988 he excommunicated the conservative archbishop Marcel Lefebvre, who had opposed Vatican Council II, for consecrating four bishops against Vatican orders. The consecration marked the first schism in the Roman Catholic Church in over a century. In June 1989 Ratzinger released a 7,500-word "instruction" for theologians and bishops designed to quell public dissent from official church teachings. The document asserts that the church is by nature and divine inspiration a hierarchical institution that demands obedience to central authority personified by the Pope. It also stated that, even though a papal teaching may not be declared "infallible," it is divinely inspired and must be obeyed.

One of Ratzinger's most controversial decisions was his order, in August 1986, that the prominent moral theologian Charles E. Curran would "no longer be considered suitable or eligible to exercise the function of a professor of Catholic theology," as a result of his refusal to disavow his belief that the Vatican's positions on divorce, artificial contraception, sterilization, abortion, and homosexual acts are not among the church's "infallible" teachings and therefore should not be considered absolute. Curran, who had been a faculty member at the papally chartered Catholic University of America, in Washington, D.C., has since been barred from teaching at any Catholic institution of higher education.

In January 1997 Ratzinger ordered the excommunication of the Sri Lankan priest Tissa Balasuriya for expressing views that clashed with Roman Catholic tenets of original sin, the Immaculate Conception, and baptism. The excommunication was lifted in January 1998, when Balasuriya agreed to sign a profession of faith, although he did not recant any of his views. In April 2001 Ratzinger barred another priest, Roger Haight, from teaching, after his book *Jesus Symbol of God* was found to contradict church teachings in examining the possibility that non-Christians can get to heaven without belief in Christ.

In an effort to clearly state the beliefs of the Roman Catholic Church, in 1992 the Vatican released the church's first universal catechism since 1566. The catechism was drafted by a council of 12 cardinals and bishops headed by Ratzinger. In addition to outlining many positions that had already been defined, the catechism contained definitions of modern sins, such as driving while intoxicated, paying unjustly low wages, and evading taxes. It stated, among other things, that women priests— approved in 1992 by the Church of England— would not be allowed in the Catholic Church. Ratzinger signed a CDF proclamation in 1996 that the church's position on women priests was infallible. On July 22, 2001 Ratzinger excommunicated seven women who claimed to be priests after they failed to retract their assertions.

Ratzinger also sparked controversy among adherents of other faiths. In a 1997 interview with the French weekly *L'Express*, Ratzinger offended many Buddhists when he said that their religion is attractive to many only "because it suggests that by belonging to it you can touch the infinite, and you can have joy without concrete religious obligations"; he also called the faith "spiritually self-indulgent eroticism," according to David O'Reilly, writing for the *Philadelphia Inquirer* (April 23, 2005). Although the Catholic Church had abandoned its former belief that Judaism finds its completion in Christianity, Ratzinger told a writer for the Italian weekly *Il Sabato* in 1988 that "the faith of Abraham finds its fulfillment" in Jesus Christ, as Ari L. Goldman reported for the *New York Times* (November 18, 1987). Although the Vatican said that his words had been misconstrued, Jewish leaders reacted with anger. Ratzinger later eased tensions between the Catholic Church and Jews when he reaffirmed, at a public gathering in Jerusalem in 1994, the Catholic belief that Jews have no collective guilt for Christ's death. In January 2002 Ratzinger released the treatise "The Jewish People and the Holy Scriptures in the Christian Bible." In it he argued that Jews and Christians both are waiting for the Messiah, although Jews are waiting for the first coming and Christians for the second. "The Jewish wait for the Messiah is not in vain," Ratzinger stated in the document, according to Melinda Henneberger in the New York Times (January 18, 2002). The Vatican announced that the work was now part of church doctrine. Rabbi Alberto Piattelli, a professor and leader of the Jewish community in Rome, Italy, told Henneberger that the work "recognizes the value of the Jewish position regarding the wait for the Messiah, changes the whole exegesis of biblical studies and restores our biblical passages to their original meaning."

In September 2000 the CDF released a dictum on religious pluralism entitled "On the Unity and Salvific Universality of Jesus Christ and the Church," in which Ratzinger stated that Christ's church "continues to exist fully and only through the Catholic Church," according to Facts on File World News Digest (September 5, 2000). The document allows that non-Catholics could achieve salvation only if their faith shared the Catholic ecclesiastical structure and understanding of the Eucharist. It condemned "relativistic theories" of religious pluralism and described other faiths as "gravely deficient." Although not a change in doctrine, the document angered many non-Catholics who had been in dialogue with the Roman Catholic Church. "It's a jump backwards in terms of ecumenism and with dialogues with other religions," the Reverend Valdo Benecchi, president of the Methodist Evangelical Churches of Italy, told Jeffrey Smith for the Washington Post (September 6, 2000). "There is nothing new about this, but we had hoped they had taken another road. This is a return to the past."

In an expansion of its previous role, the CDF began issuing proclamations in the 1980s on a wide range of moral issues. In an October 1986 letter, Ratzinger urged church leaders to minister to homosexual Catholics and to condemn any violence committed against them. However, he recommended the withdrawal of support from "any organizations which seek to undermine the teaching of the church" regarding homosexuality as immoral, including allowing such groups access to church property, according to Bruce Buursma in the Chicago Tribune (October 31, 1986). In July 1999 the CDF finished a 12-year investigation of an American outreach program for Roman Catholic homosexuals and ordered it to stop ministering to gays and lesbians. Although the two leaders of the program had encouraged gays to remain in the church and held workshops to combat homophobia and cultivate compassion, the church's investi-

gation concluded that they had failed to comply with its teaching on the "intrinsic evil of homosexual acts." Ratzinger also took a conservative line on artificial birth control and abortion, believing that sexuality without parenthood detaches humans from nature and leaves them to view each other as objects. At a 1991 meeting of cardinals he said that abortion and birth control had caused "a hidden bloodbath," as reported by the Orlando Sentinel (April 5, 1991). In a March 1987 document on bioethics, he declared that surrogate motherhood, test-tube baby production, most methods of artificial insemination, and human cloning techniques were "morally illicit."

In the late 1990s and early 2000s, after several Roman Catholic priests in the United States were publicly accused of pedophilia, many American Catholics demanded a response from the Vatican. According to some estimates, the church had spent more than $1 billion in court judgments and out-of-court settlements in the United States by 2002. In a January 2002 letter, Ratzinger released new rules for dealing with accusations of pedophilia, including a mandate that individual churches open an investigation into any charge of abuse by resident clergy and immediately notify the Vatican. Accusers also had to lodge their charges within 10 years of their turning 18. Controversially, the rules had secretly been released to parishes the year before and did not require churches to notify lawenforcement officials if priests were found guilty. Ratzinger later told Jeff Israely for Time (December 16, 2002) that the pedophilia scandal is an "intentional, manipulated . . . desire to discredit the church" by the media.

In July and August 2003, the Vatican began a campaign against gay marriage, then a burgeoning issue in the United States. In August 2003 the CDF released the treatise "Considerations Regarding Proposals to Give Legal Recognition to Unions Between Homosexual Persons." The document called homosexual marriage "a legalization of evil," which Catholic politicians have a "moral duty" to oppose. The document also stated that recognizing gay marriage "could actually encourage a person with a homosexual orientation to declare his homosexuality or even seek a partner in order to exploit the provisions of the law."

In August 2004, as many Catholics in the United States debated whether the Democratic presidential candidate John F. Kerry, a Roman Catholic, should be allowed to receive communion despite his position in favor of legal abortions, Ratzinger confirmed, in a letter to Theodore E. Cardinal McCarrick of Washington, D.C., that was leaked to the press, that communion must be denied to those who publicly support the pro-choice positions on abortion and euthanasia. However, Ratzinger also stated in the letter that Catholics could vote for someone who was pro-choice on the abortion issue as long as the decision to vote for that person was based on other issues. In another political statement that year, Ratzinger told the French newspaper *Le Figaro* that Turkey, a predominantly Muslim country, should be denied entry into the European Union on the grounds that European culture has been formed by Christianity.

As Pope John Paul II's health worsened in late November 2004, many observers began to put Ratzinger's name forward as a possible successor to the pontiff. According to Daniel Williams, writing for the *Washington Post* (November 5, 2004), one Vatican watcher, Sandro Magister, wrote for *L'Espresso* magazine, "Some look at him as if he were already de facto pope." As the Pope's condition grew dire in early 2005, Ratzinger and three other cardinals assumed broad day-to-day authority in the management of the church. John Paul chose Ratzinger to compose the meditations to be read aloud during the Good Friday procession in March 2005 as well as to lead the Easter vigil, two of the most sacred and solemn events on the Catholic calendar.

John Paul II died on April 2, 2005, and Ratzinger gave the homily at his funeral. Shortly before eligible cardinals began voting for a new Pope, Ratzinger addressed his fellow cardinals at St. Peter's Basilica and delivered a withering attack on relativism, warning of the need to preserve traditional Catholic beliefs against modern trends. Some saw the address as amounting to a campaign speech for the papacy, although a number of reports indicated that Ratzinger did not want the position. In past years he had sometimes seemed exhausted and in ill health. He often spoke of his wish to retire and dedicate himself to writing books. On April 19, 2005, on the fourth ballot, Ratzinger received a majority of votes among the 115 cardinals in the conclave, surprising many who had thought that his advanced years would prevent his election. "When the majority was reached, 77 or 78 votes, there was a gasp all round, and everyone clapped," Cormac Murphy Cardinal O'Connor of Westminster, England, told reporters for *Newsweek* in 2005. "[Ratzinger] had his head down. I think he must have said a prayer, but I didn't see his face."

Ratzinger's ascent to the papacy upset liberal Catholics, some of whom were seen to leave the Vatican angrily after Ratzinger's election was announced. "The election of Cardinal Joseph Ratzinger as pope is an enormous disappointment for all those who hoped for a reformist and pastoral pope," Hans Küng, a Catholic priest whose authority to teach theology was rescinded by the Vatican in 1979, wrote for the BBC News. By contrast, a traditional Catholic, Sam Gregg of the Acton Institute for the Study of Religion and Liberty, in Rome, wrote for the BBC News (April 26, 2005, on-line) that Ratzinger "will continue the authentic interpretation of Vatican II that John Paul pioneered. There will be a clear, strong intellectual proposition in defence of Catholic orthodoxy. There will be an attention to the Christian unity that can only be founded upon the truth and there will be a continued critique of moral relativism and the type of secular fundamentalism that we find rearing its head in the EU and the UN." Ratzinger took the

name Benedict XVI, reflecting his devotion to historic Catholic figures who had guided the church in times of secular chaos.

At age 78 Benedict XVI is the oldest Pope chosen since Clement XII, who became pontiff in 1730 (at 78 and three months). His age has led to some speculation that his fellow cardinals chose him as a trusted figure for a period of transition. However, most observers believe that Benedict will be a powerful leader. "This man is not just going to mind the store," George Weigel, an American scholar, told Laurie Goodstein for the *New York Times* (April 20, 2005, on-line). "He is going to take re-evangelization, especially of Europe, very seriously. I think this represents a recognition on the part of the cardinals that the great battle in the world remains inside the heads of human beings—that it's a battle of ideas." Writing for the *American Spectator* (May 19, 2005), Roger A. McCaffrey opined that the tone of Benedict's papacy after 30 days "varies from the expectations of both left and right," including his appointment of a moderate cardinal to succeed him as prefect of the CDF.

In October 2005 Pope Benedict presided over the Synod of Bishops, a three-week-long gathering of 250 Catholic bishops. Prominent among the issues discussed was the crisis facing the priesthood in the wake of the sexual-abuse scandal in the United States. (According to news reports, the Vatican planned to announce publicly in November 2005 that all homosexuals will be banned from seminaries.) At the conclusion of the synod, the church reaffirmed its position on the importance of celibacy among the clergy, despite calls for reevaluating the doctrine in light of the worldwide shortage of priests. The synod also addressed the issue of lay Catholics' holding views that oppose the teachings of the church, and it indicated that there could be no "dichotomy" between a Catholic's beliefs and his or her everyday life. The synod also agreed that church officials needed to decide on a case-by-case basis whether they should deny communion to Catholic politicians who support laws that approve abortion, the imposition of the death penalty, or other actions that are contrary to Catholic teachings.

Aside from *The Ratzinger Report*, Benedict's best-known work in translation is *Introduction to Christianity* (1969). He has published dozens of books, many in English. In 1999 he published *Many Religions, One Covenant: Israel, the Church, and the World*, which focuses on reconciliation between Jews and Christians. He is also the author of *Truth and Tolerance* (2004), which addresses the issue of religious pluralism. Many of his beliefs are detailed in *Salt of the Earth: Christianity and the Catholic Church at the End of the Millennium* (1997). His theological work is highly regarded even among those who disagree with him, and he is known as an expert on Martin Luther (1483–1546), the priest who began the Protestant Reformation. "When you read his books, you can see that he writes at the highest level of theology,"

Karl-Joseph Hummel, director of research at the Commission for Contemporary History, in Bonn, told the writers for the *New York Times* in 2005. "He looks at politics as ethics; he looks at literature, and the whole of human possibilities, and I don't think he's narrow." Within two days of his election to the papacy, Benedict's writings had displaced J. K. Rowling's latest Harry Potter novel at the top of a German best-seller list.

Pope Benedict is known as a hardworking, shy, soft-spoken man who is self-effacing. "No senior churchman gave up more of himself to serve John Paul II," Weigel wrote for *Newsweek* (May 2, 2005). "Abandoning any hope of pursuing his major theological projects, he stayed in Rome for more than 20 years, serving a pope who refused his resignation on at least two occasions." As a cardinal, he was known to inspire a great deal of loyalty in his staff. "I've never known him to be angry or vindictive," Thomas Herron, a priest who worked on Ratzinger's staff, told Dionne. "He's one of the most even-tempered people I've ever met." Even his theological opponents have said that they like him personally. The eighth German to become Pope, Benedict speaks 10 languages. He is known as an accomplished pianist with a preference for Beethoven and Mozart. Weigel noted, "[Ratzinger] is one of only two men I know who, in answering a question, pauses, reflects—and then speaks in complete paragraphs (in his fourth language)."

—G.O.

Suggested Reading: Associated Press Apr. 4, 1991; *Los Angeles Times* p1 Nov. 7, 1986, with photo; *New York Times* p40 Nov. 24, 1985, with photos, A p8 Jan. 18, 2002, A p1 Apr. 20, 2005, with photos, A p1 Apr. 20, 2005, with photos, IV p4 Apr. 24, 2005; *Newsweek* p63 Dec. 31, 1984, with photos, p40 May 2, 2005, with photos, p48 May 2, 2005, with photo; *Philadelphia Inquirer* Apr. 23, 2005; *San Diego Union-Tribune* A p7 Sep. 21, 1985; *Time* p38 May 2, 2005, with photos; *Washington Post* A p13 Sep. 6, 2000; Allen, John L. Jr. *Cardinal Ratzinger: The Vatican's Enforcer of the Faith*, 2000; Nichols, Aidan. *Theology of Joseph Ratzinger: An Introductory Study*, 1988; Tobin, Gregg. *Holy Father: Pope Benedict XVI: Pontiff for a New Era*, 2005

Selected Books: *Christian Brotherhood*, 1966; *Introduction to Christianity*, 1969; *Faith and the Future*, 1971; *Theology and History in St. Bonaventure*, 1971; *God of Jesus Christ: Meditations on God in the Trinity*, 1979; *Daughter Zion: Meditations on the Church's Marian Belief*, 1983; *Dogma and Preaching*, 1985; *Behold the Pierced One: An Approach to a Spiritual Christology*, 1986; *Seek That Which Is Above: Meditations Through the Year*, 1986; *Principles of Catholic Theology: Building Stones for a Fundamental Theology*, 1987; *Church, Ecumenism, and Politics: New Essays in Ecclesiology*, 1988; *Ministers of Your Joy: Scriptural Meditations on Priestly Spirituality*, 1989; *In the Beginning: A Catholic Understanding of the Story of Creation and the Fall*, 1990; *Turning Point for Europe?: The Church in the Modern World: Assessment and Forecast*, 1994; *The Nature and Mission of Theology: Essays to Orient Theology in Today's Debates*, 1995; *Called to Communion: Understanding the Church Today*, 1996; *New Song for the Lord: Faith in Christ and Liturgy Today*, 1996; *Salt of the Earth: Christianity and the Catholic Church at the End of the Millennium*, 1997; *Gospel, Catechesis, Catechism: Sidelights on the Catechism of the Catholic Church*, 1997; *Milestones: Memoirs, 1927-1977*, 1998; *Many Religions, One Covenant: Israel, the Church, and the World*, 1999; *God and the World: Believing and Living in Our Time*, 2002; *On the Way to Jesus Christ*, 2004; *Truth and Tolerance: Christian Belief and World Religions*, 2004; *Fellowship of Faith: The Church as Communion*, 2005; *Let God's Light Shine Forth: The Spiritual Vision of Pope Benedict XVI*, 2005; *On Conscience*, 2005

Bittman, Mark

Feb. 17, 1950– Food columnist; cookbook writer

Address: New York Times, *229 W. 43d St., New York, NY 10036*

The food columnist and cookbook writer Mark Bittman has "a single goal," Amy Traverso wrote for *Yankee* (July/August 2004, on-line): "to prove time and again that food needn't be complicated to be interesting and delicious." According to Traverso, who is *Yankee*'s food editor, Bittman has become famous "because he is a master at creating menus that can be thrown together at the last minute, without sacrificing an ounce of flavor or pleasure. He takes an iconoclast's delight in staring down food-world pretensions: the assumption that everyone has endless time to cook multi-layered dishes, the insistence on formal training, the insensitivity to cost and availability of ingredients." Jean-Georges Vongerichten, an internationally acclaimed chef and restaurateur, has described Bittman as "the best home cook I know," and Bittman's guide *How to Cook Everything: Simple Recipes for Great Food* as "the best basic cookbook I've seen." Vongerichten, a classically trained chef who epitomizes the highest standards of French cooking, collaborated with the largely self-taught Bittman in writing two cookbooks: *Jean-Georges: Cooking at Home with a Four-Star Chef* and *Simple to Spectacular: How to Take One Basic Recipe to Four Levels of Sophistication*. "Jean-Georges is always looking to make dishes more worthy of a four-star res-

Courtesy of the *Houston Chronicle*

Mark Bittman

taurant, and I to make them simple enough to prepare by a single cook in a minimally equipped kitchen," Bittman wrote in *Simple to Spectacular*, as quoted by Marilyn Wright Ford in her food column "Cravings," on littleyellowhouse.com (April/May 2001).

Bittman himself has written a dozen cookbooks in addition to the award-winning *How to Cook Everything: Simple Recipes for Great Food.* Since 1997 he has also written a weekly column, called "The Minimalist," for the "Dining" section of the *New York Times.* The column is based on Bittman's conviction, as he wrote in his book *The Minimalist Cooks at Home: Recipes That Give You More Flavor from Fewer Ingredients in Less Time,* that "a disproportionate amount of space and time in food magazines, newspapers, cookbooks, and television shows is devoted to needlessly and sometimes outrageously complex recipes." In another of his books, *How to Cook Everything: The Basics: Simple Recipes Anyone Can Cook,* Bittman assured readers that "home-cooked food can be easy and fast [to make], and is almost always better for you than anything you buy prepared." He continued, "We are blessed with supermarket food of reasonably high quality, and an incomparable variety—including important ingredients that were once found only at the swankiest shops—at prices so low that visitors from other countries are frequently shocked. Even as a novice home cook, you have the opportunity to create, simply and with minimal effort, a variety of food unparalleled in the history of the world. . . . And, contrary to what many beginners believe, there are no 'secrets' to cooking—only good guidance combined with experience." Articles by Bittman about food, cook-

ing, and recommended places to eat in the U.S. and abroad have appeared in *Bon Appetit, Travel Holiday, Redbook, Gentlemen's Quarterly, American Health,* the *New York Times Magazine,* and *Working Woman,* among other publications. Bittman has also served as the executive editor of *Cook's Illustrated,* a magazine linked to the television series *America's Test Kitchen.* He has appeared on TV many times, conducting interviews and giving cooking demonstrations on the *Today* show and on CNN, the Food Network, QVC, and Lifetime Television. He has also shared cooking tips on the National Public Radio program *All Things Considered.*

Mark Bittman was born to Murray and Gertrude Bittman on February 17, 1950. He grew up in New York City. According to Amy Traverso, at one time he worked as a community organizer. By his own account, he has never attended a cooking school or any formal cooking classes and never worked in a restaurant. (Since he has become well-known, though, he has learned much from celebrated chefs who have accepted his invitations to cook with him.) In the 1980s he wrote on a wide variety of topics for several magazines. His articles from that period include "Insulate the Outside to Cut Heat Loss through Foundation Walls" and other advice for do-it-yourselfers, published in *Popular Science* (February 1983); "Comparable Worth Is Put to the Test at Yale," about a strike of employees at that university, for *BusinessWeek* (November 26, 1984); "Health Plans May Leave Retirees Out in the Cold," also for *BusinessWeek* (December 17, 1984); "Finding a New Front Door for Your Home," for the *Family Handyman* (September 1985); and "Buyer's Guide to Personal Copiers," for *Family & Home Office Computing* (January 1988). "What I really wanted to write about was politics because, after all, I knew how to fix everything," he told Traverso. "But, for some reason, no one wanted to listen to me."

In the 1990s Bittman began to write about food, cooking, and restaurants. "It was all sort of an immediate success," he told Traverso of his food-related writing. Many of his articles appeared in *American Health* magazine. Among the first was "Taming the Bistro" (March 1991), which reported that, contrary to popular belief, meals prepared in the French style are often "direct, honest, unpretentious—and in many cases healthful"; recipes accompanying the article served as examples. In subsequent *American Health* pieces, Bittman's topics included the basics of healthful cooking; techniques for eating healthfully in restaurants; low-fat, low-calorie sandwiches and picnic foods; nontraditional Thanksgiving dinners, with duck, goose, capon, or Cornish game hen rather than turkey; olive oil and its uses; homemade breads; and barbecue sauces. For the *New York Times,* Bittman wrote about fruits and vegetables as antioxidants; for the *New York Times Magazine,* he offered suggestions for cooking shrimp and for avoiding "food fights" with children at mealtimes. In an article for

Bon Appetit (June 1999), he wrote about arugula, a plant in the mustard family that is native to the Mediterranean region, and gave instructions for making an arugula salad and risotto (a rice dish) with arugula and shrimp. In the November 2002 issue of *Bon Appetit*, he discussed the herb thyme and provided recipes for cabbage soup with apples and thyme; leg of lamb with thyme and orange; a thyme and garlic cheese dip; and red snapper with thyme, tomatoes, and olives. The November 2003 issue of *Bon Appetit* contained Bittman's discussion of aperitifs (alcoholic drinks, such as vermouth and sherry, that are served as appetizers, before meals). In various articles that appeared in the monthly magazine *Travel Holiday*, he recommended places to eat in New York City; Washington, D.C.; San Francisco, California; Paris, France; Istanbul, Turkey; Berlin, Germany; London, England; Rome, Italy; and the coast of the Italian region of Liguria, sometimes called the Italian Riviera. Also for *Travel Holiday* he wrote about Stockholm, Sweden, at Christmastime, and about foods associated with the Basque region of Spain.

Bittman's first cookbook was *Fish: The Complete Guide to Buying and Cooking* (1994), which won the Julia Child Cookbook Award (now known as the IACP [International Association of Culinary Professionals] Award) for best cookbook on a single subject. Illustrated with color photos, *Fish* contains detailed information on 70 types of fish and shellfish, the health benefits of fish, buying tips, and more than 500 recipes. A reviewer for *Library Journal* (June 15, 1994) described *Fish* as "a very user-friendly guide to what is still an unknown area for many home cooks. . . . The recipes . . . are simple, varied, and unintimidating." In the *Christian Science Monitor* (December 1, 1994), Jennifer Wolcott wrote, "It's this easy: Buy it right, cook it simply, [Bittman] writes in this hefty guidebook, which demystifies the often intimidating task of cooking fish at home. . . . Unencumbered by esoteric ingredients, [the recipes] include plenty of alternatives, and appear to average a mere 20 minutes."

Leafy Greens (1995), Bittman's second book, is subtitled *An A-to-Z Guide to 30 Types of Greens Plus 200 Delicious Recipes*. It was followed by *How to Cook Everything: Simple Recipes for Great Food* (1998), which won both the Julia Child (IACP) and James Beard Awards for general cookbooks the year it was published; to date it has sold more than 1.7 million copies and been reprinted half a dozen times. "I wanted to create a book that would make anyone who picked it up want to go into the kitchen, a cookbook with something for everyone, even the most inexperienced cook . . . ," Bittman explained in an interview that appeared on the Web site starchefs.com. "I wanted to convey the simplicity and joy I bring to cooking. . . . *How to Cook Everything* can take anyone to the level of a really fine home cook. It cannot make you into a chef—nor does it try." (The word "chef" is short for "chef de cuisine," a French term that means "head of the

kitchen." A chef is thus someone who cooks professionally and manages the kitchen of a restaurant, club, or other large establishment.) *How to Cook Everything: Simple Recipes for Great Food* is more than 900 pages long and contains upwards of 1,500 recipes, along with detailed, illustrated descriptions of culinary techniques, an exhaustive glossary, and a menu-suggestion section. It offers many recipes that can be prepared in less than an hour, and many more that require less than 30 minutes. In a review of the book for Amazon.com, the food writer Schuyler Ingle declared, "This isn't just the big top of cookbooks: it's the entire three-ring circus. This isn't just how to cook everything: it's how to cook everything you have ever wanted to have in your mouth. And then some. . . . Every inch of the way the reader finds Bittman's calm, helpful, encouraging voice." "Sometimes all the things that a particular person does best come together in a burst of synergy, and the result is truly marvelous," the chef Chris Schlesinger and John Willoughby, co-authors of *License to Grill*, wrote in their assessment, as quoted on Amazon.com. "This book is just such an instance. Mark Bittman is not only the best home cook we know, he is also a born teacher, a gifted writer, and a canny kitchen tactician who combines great taste with eminent practicality." As of October 2005, 271 owners of the book had commented on it for the Amazon Web site, most of them favorably. The remarks of a woman from Texas are typical: "I have owned this cookbook for at least four years," she wrote. "When I first got it, I hardly cooked anything that didn't come from a box, can, or jar. I was afraid to deviate from the recipe and found most cookbook recipes too complicated, with too many ingredients. This book changed all that. . . . Every section explains the basics of [a particular] type of cooking, then tells you how to expand on [it]. . . . My copy is falling out of its binding now from so much use (and many of the pages are a bit sticky)!" Another ordinary reader wrote, "I bought this book several years ago and the cashier at Border's laughed at me. In a snide tone she said something like, 'Does it really teach you how to cook everything?' The answer is, yes (with very, very few exceptions). Mark Bittman's book explains how to boil an egg on one page and makes the idea of homemade puff pastry sound appealing on another. . . . [Whatever you pay for] this book is some of the best money you will ever spend because it will improve the quality of your life."

How to Cook Everything: Simple Recipes for Great Food is the first in a series of same-titled cookbooks by Bittman. Those published in 2003 bear the subtitles *Easy Weekend Cooking*; *Holiday Cooking*; *Quick Cooking*; *The Basics: Simple Recipes Anyone Can Cook*; and *Vegetarian Cooking*. *How to Cook Everything: Mark Bittman Takes on America's Chefs* was published in conjunction with a public-television series that debuted in April 2005. In each installment of the show, a famous chef prepares a special dish, and then Bittman demonstrates a much simpler way to make something comparable. Jean-Georges Vongerichten, for example, produced his apple tart tartin (a type of pastry) with tart apple ice cream; Bittman's alternative was skillet tart tartin.

Bittman and Vongerichten took the reverse approach in their book *Simple to Spectacular: How to Take One Basic Recipe to Four Levels of Sophistication* (2000). (Earlier, the men had teamed up to write *Jean-Georges: Cooking at Home with a Four-Star Chef* [1998].) In *Simple to Spectacular*, uncomplicated recipes for roast chicken, pasta with saffron oil, scrambled eggs, and butternut squash soup with herbed cheese dumplings, to cite just a few, are each followed by four progressively more-sophisticated variations. "Mastery of basic recipes and an idea of how to vary them lead to almost limitless options," the book advises, as quoted by Marilyn Wright Ford. Variations on a recipe for chicken breasts in foil with olive oil and rosemary include chicken breasts with tomatoes, olives, and Parmesan cheese; with mushrooms, shallots, and sherry; with foie gras and porcini mushrooms; and chicken breasts with Thai spices. "In hands other than the authors', the dishes could be banal or overwrought," the food writer Arthur Boehm noted in an Amazon.com review. "Vongerichten and Bittman triumph, however, presenting richly imagined yet straightforward fare whose preparation almost all cooks can manage." A reviewer for *Publishers Weekly* (September 18, 2000) wrote, "Clean, pared-down prose, helpful 'Keys to Success' sidebars and clear recipe instructions ably guide both novice and seasoned cooks. With a masterful understanding of today's global pantry, the authors have produced a modern classic."

Bittman's first "Minimalist" column for the *New York Times*, entitled "Every Day, a Red Pepper Day," appeared on September 17, 1997; it offered a recipe for a puree made with roasted red peppers. Since then the *Times* has published more than 350 of his "Minimalist" pieces, on such subjects as clam chowder; corn chowder; curry blends; pasta with spinach sauce; pasta with cauliflower; fish and chips; vinaigrettes; grilled asparagus with a lemon dressing; rosemary-lemon bean puree; pork stew; pork and onions with amontillado sherry; salmon burgers; strawberries with balsamic vinegar; strawberry shortcake; beef pancakes; scallion pancakes; Italian sausages on a bed of grapes; chicken salad; chicken with ginger; braised squid with artichokes; sautéed red snapper with rhubarb sauce; adding raw beets to salads; cooking with coconut milk; beef wrapped in lettuce leaves, Korean style; a streamlined cassoulet (a casserole made with white beans, herbs, and meat); a creamy horseradish sauce; pot roast with cranberries; kale, sausage, and mushroom stew; roasted tomatoes; crunchy stuffing; Asian-inspired leeks with ginger and shrimp; Turkish-inspired carrot, spinach, and rice stew; watermelon and tomato salad; stir-fried chicken with creamed corn; rice pudding, with some exotic variations; churros (cruller-like strips

of crisp fried dough); "meatless, but not joyless" vegetarian meals; raita, a yogurt salad of Indian origin that can be used as a relish, dip, or side dish; and uses of tahini paste (made from ground sesame seeds) as a condiment.

In his January 5, 2005 "Minimalist" column, Bittman offered a recipe for a sweet-and-sour sauce of his own creation, made with dried figs and served with chicken, duck, pork, lamb, or game (deer or other usually wild animals). In addition to chopped figs, the ingredients included a very dry white wine; lightly caramelized honey; the zest and juice of an orange; and coriander seeds. "None of these ingredient choices were self-evident," Bittman wrote. "But once I had the sauce at a place I liked, I found there was yet another choice to make, and this one was the most difficult. Though I'm not a chef, I've spent enough time with chefs that I sometimes think automatically that sauces should be smooth. For elegance, I thought I should finish the sauce as a chef might: strain it then reheat it while adding . . . lemon juice and probably a lump of butter for glossiness, thickness and smoothness. That's what I did at first. But in my heart I really prefer the sauce as it is, with its irregular texture: the chunky figs, which absorb scads of flavor from the honey and orange; the crunchy coriander seeds; the chewy orange zest. I spoon the thin liquid over the chicken, then serve the solids on the side, as a kind of relish. It isn't elegant, but it's really good." Bittman's "Minimalist" recipes have been collected in three books: *The Minimalist Cooks at Home: Recipes That Give You More Flavor from Fewer Ingredients in Less Time* (2000); *The Minimalist Cooks Dinner: More than 100 Recipes for Fast Weeknight Meals and Casual Entertaining* (2001); and *The Minimalist Entertains: Forty Seasonal Menus for Dinner Parties, Cocktail Parties, Barbecues, and More* (2003).

In October 2005 Bittman published *Best Recipes in the World: More than 1,000 International Dishes to Cook at Home*. As it is in the first *How to Cook Everything*, Bittman's approach in his latest book is encyclopedic, covering food from 44 countries in 11 chapters, and like those in his "Minimalist" columns and books, the recipes are all designed to be prepared in fewer than 30 minutes. Though Bittman drew from cuisines as diverse as Scandinavian and Malaysian, he organized *Best Recipes in the World* by course or main ingredient (appetizer or meat, for example) first, and then by method of preparation (cold appetizers versus hot, or braised meat versus sautéed), so as to draw connections among various regions' or cultures' foods.

Bittman has been described as down-to-earth and witty. When an interviewer for starchefs.com asked him to name the five items that he considers essential in a kitchen pantry, he replied, "Olive oil: you can use it as an all-purpose fat and it's delicious and healthful; pasta: no one ever gets sick of it; good vinegar: when a dish tastes flat, it's often because it lacks acidity—a few drops of vinegar (or lemon juice) usually does the trick; soy sauce: the most distinctive flavor of Asia; garlic: can't live without it; peanut butter: that makes six, but sorry—I'm an addict." Bittman lives with his wife and two daughters, Emma and Kate, in Woodbridge, Connecticut. He told Linda Richards for *January Magazine* (August 2000, on-line) that he has "a very weird life. I have complete privacy when I'm at home. No one ever comes to visit me, because it's a schlep. I have a terrible kitchen. It's one of the worst kitchens ever. It just doesn't bother me. If I wanted to spend $30,000 on something, it wouldn't be on that."

—C.F.T.

Suggested Reading: eGullet (on-line) May 12, 2003; *January Magazine* (on-line), Jan. 2000, Aug. 2000, with photo; starchefs.com

Selected Books: *Fish: The Complete Guide to Buying and Cooking*, 1994; *Leafy Greens*, 1995; *How to Cook Everything: Simple Recipes for Great Food*, 1998; *The Minimalist Cooks at Home: Recipes that Give You More Flavor from Fewer Ingredients in Less Time*, 2000; *The Minimalist Cooks Dinner: More than 100 Recipes for Fast Weeknight Meals and Casual Entertaining*, 2001; *How to Cook Everything: Easy Weekend Cooking*, 2003; *How to Cook Everything: Holiday Cooking*, 2003; *How to Cook Everything: Quick Cooking*, 2003; *How to Cook Everything: The Basics: Simple Recipes Anyone Can Cook*, 2003; *How to Cook Everything: Vegetarian Cooking*, 2003; *The Minimalist Entertains: Forty Seasonal Menus for Dinner Parties, Cocktail Parties, Barbecues, and More*, 2003; *Best Recipes in the World: More than 1,000 International Dishes to Cook at Home*, 2005; *How to Cook Everything: Mark Bittman Takes on America's Chefs*, 2005; with Vongerichten, Jean-Georges—*Jean-Georges: Cooking at Home with a Four-Star Chef*, 1998; *Simple to Spectacular: How to Take One Basic Recipe to Four Levels of Sophistication*, 2000

Boulud, Daniel

(boo-LOO, dan-YEL)

Mar. 25, 1955– Chef; restaurant owner; cookbook writer

Address: Daniel, 60 E. 65th St., New York, NY 10021

Daniel Boulud is often called a "celebrity chef," meaning one who is as well-known—and considered as glamorous—as the famous patrons he or she serves. Born and raised in France, Boulud spent over a decade honing his culinary artistry there and elsewhere in Europe. He made his name in the United States when he served as executive chef of the legendary restaurant Le Cirque, in New York City, beginning in 1986. In a profile of Boulud for the *New York Times Magazine* (April 5, 1992), written about six years later, Molly O'Neill wrote, "Half of Boulud is a big-city executive; the other half is a shy, fastidious Frenchman who cooked his way off his family's farm to the apex of his craft." In 1993 Boulud opened his own upscale restaurant, Daniel, in New York City. There, according to Ruth Reichl, the editor of *Gourmet* magazine, as quoted by John Tanasychuk in the Fort Lauderdale, Florida, *Sun-Sentinel* (June 5, 2003), Boulud has taken "everything that's so good about being French and everything that's good about being American and combined them"—"good" referring both to food that is superlatively prepared and served and to an unusually warm, friendly atmosphere. Daniel, which serves French cuisine and dishes that are variations on its themes, is one of only a handful of restaurants to have received the

Courtesy of P. Medilek

New York Times's highest rating—four stars; the *International Herald Tribune* has ranked it among the 10 finest restaurants in the world, and, year after year, other sources have listed it among the 10 best restaurants in New York City as well as the rest of the U.S. Boulud himself has also won many honors, among them the James Beard Foundation's Outstanding Chef of the Year Award, in 1994. In the *New York Times* (March 14, 2001), William Grimes, the paper's longtime food critic, wrote after having a meal at Daniel, "Mr. Boulud has both feet planted in the rich gastronomic soil of the Lyonnais region [of France], an area known for its robust, no-holds-barred cuisine. . . . Rarely have I experienced so much distress in ordering dinner, or witnessed so much around-the-table envy once the food arrived. Mr. Boulud's go-for-broke menu inspires greed. You want it all." Building on his success, Boulud has become the head of a growing culinary empire. In addition to Daniel, he now owns two Cafés Boulud (one in New York City and another in Florida) and DB Bistro Moderne (in New York City); from 1997 to 2000 he co-owned Payard Patisserie & Bistro (in New York City). He also co-owns the catering division of Daniel, called Feast & Fêtes, and he has written several cookbooks. Daniel Boulud Kitchen (or DBK), a professional line of cookware, cutlery, and kitchen tools designed by Boulud and a team of industrial designers, has been on sale since 2004.

Boulud "has a perfect command of technique, and that leads to depth of flavor," Susan Spicer, the chef and owner of the restaurant Bayona, in New Orleans, Louisiana, told Peter Kaminsky for *New York* (December 14, 1998, on-line). "Sometimes he extracts flavor, sometimes he infuses it, but the techniques, the way he roasts bones to make a stock, the way he caramelizes vegetables, the way he makes a broth of salmon, all show an understanding of what you do with ingredients to get the most out of them." "What makes [Boulud] different from every other chef who says that his food is based on fresh local ingredients and regional fare is technique," Dorothy Cann Hamilton, the founder of the French Culinary Institute, told Kaminsky. "The flavors are precise, identifiable, and at their peak." Boulud himself told Kaminsky, "It's not even so much about technique as it is about understanding the connecting wire of the recipe and being sensitive to how each ingredient hangs off that wire." According to his wife, Micky, Boulud "thinks about food deeply and all the time."

One of the five children of Julien and Marie Boulud, Daniel Boulud was born on March 25, 1955 near Lyon, France. He grew up on the Boulud family farm, in the small town of St.-Pierre-de-Chandieu, outside Lyon. His parents and other relatives grew vegetables and transported them by truck to local markets to sell. The Bouluds also raised turkeys, lambs, and chickens for meat and livestock for milk and cheese, and they ran a roadside café, founded by Boulud's great-grandparents, whose clientele consisted mainly of their neighbors. "It was the rendezvous point for generations of townsfolk," Boulud wrote in the introduction to his book *Daniel Boulud's Café Boulud Cookbook*, as quoted on the WNYC Web site. His paternal grandmother, Francine Boulud, cooked most of the family's meals. Boulud has fondly recalled omelets that she prepared with fresh morels (edible fungi) and wild asparagus.

In 1969, at age 14, Boulud left his family to apprentice at Nandron, a restaurant in Lyon, owned by Gérard Nandron, that had received two stars in the *Michelin Guide*. (Three stars is the highest rating conferred by Michelin, whose guide to restaurants is considered the most influential in Europe. The vast majority of eating places get no stars.) Boulud's working conditions were very difficult, and he earned a pittance for 13-hour days. "No one asked if you were happy with the arrangement," he told O'Neill. Nevertheless, he knew that he was lucky to have the chance to learn at Nandron, not least because while there he became acquainted with a few of France's outstanding chefs. In 1972 he was named among the finalists for the title "best culinary apprentice in France." Soon afterward, in 1973, Boulud took a job as first cook at La Mère Blanc, a three-star restaurant in Vonnas, France, owned by Georges Blanc (who was also its executive chef), where he further polished his skills. (A first cook performs general cooking and/or baking tasks under supervision.) Blanc later changed the name of the restaurant to Georges Blanc. According to Peter Kaminsky, "Blanc opened Boulud's eyes to the possibilities of adding elegance to basic country ingredients."

In 1974 Boulud left Blanc to work at Le Moulin de Mougins, in the town of Mougins, under the renowned chef Roger Vergé, as first cook and then as chef de partie. (Chef de partie is the fourth-ranking position in a restaurant kitchen, after the executive chef, who is the administrator of the kitchen; the chef de cuisine, or head cook; and the sous chef, who is second in command after the head chef and takes over when the head chef is absent. A chef de partie is in charge of particular sections of the kitchen, such as the pastry section or the soup section.) Vergé told Kaminsky that Boulud demonstrated "a mastery of the simplest ingredients" and the instincts of an outstanding *saucier* (maker of sauces). Boulud, for his part, told Kaminsky that Vergé introduced him to a "sunnier" cuisine than Blanc's, one that was "much more complex in its sauces and much more vegetable-oriented." He told O'Neill that Vergé had transmitted to him "an energy, a spirit of adventure."

Boulud and Vergé remained in touch after Boulud took a job, in 1976, as the sous chef in the four-star Plaza Hotel restaurant in Copenhagen, Denmark, for which Vergé served as a consultant. In Denmark Boulud experimented with ingredients that were new to him, such as elk meat, lingonberries (also called mountain cranberries), and many kinds of fish. "With the known, you are in control," he noted to O'Neill. "With the unknown, you have no choice but to trust your instincts and just cook." Boulud next worked, as chef de partie, with the highly regarded chef Michel Guérard in Les Prés d'Eugénie, a three-star restaurant in southern France. In 1980 he returned to Denmark to serve as the sous chef at the Plaza Hotel. Later that year, also in Copenhagen, he cooked for Les Etoiles, which that year had been voted the number-one restaurant in Denmark. For a short time toward the end of 1980, he cooked for a wealthy Saudi Arabian in Mougins. In 1981 he moved to Washington,

D.C., where he became the private chef for Roland de Kergorlay, who then headed the U.S.-posted delegation from the European Commission.

In 1982 Boulud relocated to New York City, where, for about two years, he managed, and served as co-chef at, the Westbury Hotel's restaurant, the Polo Lounge—a position he secured, as he told Peter Kaminsky, by preparing a 15-course lunch for those who interviewed him. Then, for another two years or so, he worked as the executive chef at Le Régence, at the Plaza-Athenée Hotel. During that period, according to O'Neill, Boulud gained a reputation for the "vivid modernity" of his cuisine. His skills impressed the Italian-born Sirio Maccioni, the charismatic owner of Le Cirque; located on East 65th Street in Manhattan, Le Cirque had become a choice place to dine among the rich, famous, and powerful—everyone from First Lady Nancy Reagan to the musician Frank Zappa. As quoted on the Le Cirque Web site, the food writer and critic James Villas, in an article for Town & Country, once described the restaurant as a "gastronomic mecca" and "premier social dining room" and noted that it had come to "symbolize all that is so cosmopolitan, so kinetic, so thrilling about New York." In 1986 Boulud became Le Cirque's executive chef. From Maccioni, according to Peter Kaminsky, Boulud "learned how to work the front of the house, how to make guests feel pampered, loved, special." Boulud developed an easy rapport with Le Cirque's clientele, which, as William Grimes described it to John Tanasychuk, was made up of "exclusive, very well-to-do, Upper East Side New Yorkers who are very clubby." "He's very much a part of the community that his restaurants cater to," Grimes said.

Boulud's noteworthy diplomacy and tact notwithstanding, "something in the set of his Lyonnais jaw," according to O'Neill, "belies the warm, easygoing smile that [Boulud] flashes for the cameras of food and society magazines." Rather, she wrote, he is "easily bored" and "relentlessly demanding." But in displaying the latter characteristic, Boulud is no different from the executive chef or chef de cuisine of any top-tier restaurant. As Patricia B. Dailey wrote for Restaurants and Institutions (March 1, 2004), "Chefs are driven by attitude and moxie. They're loath to accept mediocrity. . . . Chefs understand with absolute certainty the importance of paying attention to everything— the big picture as well as the smallest detail. A single thing can bring down the house—even one bad clam or a bunch of unwashed green onions." On any given day there were often as many as 20 specials on Le Cirque's menu: for example, fresh crab claws on a confetti of julienned mango, chayote, and almonds, seasoned with lime and coriander; roast duck in a bacon jacket; and roasted pig's feet with fresh morels and Chinese pea shoots. With Boulud in the kitchen, Le Cirque reached the pinnacle of its popularity.

Regarding that time in his life, Boulud recalled to Cynthia Steffe for the Palm Beach, Florida, Post (December 31, 2003), "I was tossing between where I had come from and where I [was then]. It had taken me 10 years to prove to New York that I could do something. OK, now I've done that. So do I go home [that is, back to France] or stay and make a success of my own here?" In 1992 Boulud took steps toward opening a restaurant of his own in Manhattan. "Le Cirque is a very stressful job," he told Florence Fabricant for the New York Times (June 23, 1992), "and I didn't want to wait to leave until I was burned out." When he told Maccioni about his plans, he offered to remain at Le Cirque for six more months, but Maccioni insisted that he leave immediately.

With the help of a $2 million investment from Joel Smilow, the former chairman and CEO of Playtex, in May 1993 Boulud opened Daniel, on the ground floor of the Surrey Hotel, on East 76th Street. Soon after it opened, Marion Burros, who was then the New York Times's lead restaurant reviewer, criticized aspects of the setting and the service and awarded Daniel only two stars; in response, Boulud increased Daniel's service staff by 50 percent. After dining at Daniel again in early November 1993, Burros upped the restaurant's rating to four stars. (The New York Times's assessments of restaurants carry considerable weight among in-the-know gourmands and restaurant lovers. Among the thousands of restaurants that were or are in business in New York City, the only others that have received four stars from the New York Times are Bouley Bakery, Lespinasse, Le Cirque 2000, Jean Georges, and Le Bernardin.) In 1998 Boulud relocated Daniel to the site of what had been the Mayfair Hotel, on Park Avenue, and had it decorated in the style of the Venetian Renaissance (in 16th-century Italy). After it reopened, in January 1999, William Grimes downgraded it to three stars, complaining, as he recalled in the New York Times (March 14, 2001), that there were "too many dull dishes"; he disliked the new decor, too, which he described as "stodgy and awkward, the lighting harsh." By the end of 1999, Grimes had restored the restaurant to its exalted status as a four-star establishment. Boulud's struggle to achieve near-perfection at the reopened Daniel is the subject of Leslie Brenner's book The Fourth Star: Dispatches from Inside Daniel Boulud's Celebrated New York Restaurant (2002). Brenner was impressed by what she saw as Boulud's lack of pretensions, despite the glitz and glamour with which he has been identified, as well as the varied aspects of his personality. "The minute he crossed the door into the kitchen," she told Tanasychuk, "he turned into a different person. He seems like a very gentle and kind person when you talk to him in the dining room. And maybe he is. But when he crosses the threshold into the kitchen, when he goes through those swinging doors, he gets very sort of military. He's like a general who just sort of galvanizes everyone with his presence."

In the *New York Times* (March 14, 2001), Grimes praised Daniel for its "soothing atmosphere . . . a warmth usually associated with small neighborhood restaurants." Grimes declared that that special ambience emanated from Boulud himself: "His personality, as a proprietor, has been shaped by the little restaurant that his parents once ran, and if he does not actually stand outside on the sidewalk greeting guests, there is an unmistakable spirit of generosity hovering over the dining room that makes Daniel unique." Since its reopening Daniel has received *Gourmet* magazine's Top Table Award. In late 2003 Daniel was also honored with both *Wine Spectator*'s Grand Award for restaurants and top ratings for cuisine, service, and decor in the Zagat Survey, a trusted and influential guide to restaurants nationwide. In addition, *Bon Appetit* magazine named Boulud chef of the year in 1999.

One of Boulud's favorite recipes, inspired by his recollections of his grandmother's cooking, is for what he calls lamb chops Champvallon: braised lamb chops with onions and potatoes, flavored with fresh thyme. (Champvallon, an actual or fictional figure, according to differing sources, was a mistress of King Louis XIV who prepared the dish as a way to win the king's favor.) Boulud has served the dish to heads of state and to his family during Sunday dinners. Typical appetizers offered at Daniel include chilled Charentais melon velouté (a French canteloupe in a white sauce with Carolina shrimp, opal basil, lemongrass, and lime); cold curried green-asparagus soup with sweet red pepper chutney and a crab spring roll; and gingered lobster with carrots, sugar snap beans and a "peashoot emulsion." Typical main courses include roasted skate with arugula, "heirloom" tomatoes, black olives, saffron potatoes, and a fennel-tomato emulsion, and roasted rack of lamb with a lemon-rosemary crust, grilled radiccio, honey-glazed eggplant, and a sweet garlic panisses (the latter resembling a giant French fry made with chickpea puree). More than 1,600 wines are stored in Daniel's wine cellar. Prices for Daniel's Thanksgiving dinner in 2004 were $110 for an adult and $55 for a child age 12 or under.

In 1998 Boulud opened Café Boulud on New York City's tony Upper East Side. (The name is that of the café run by his family in France.) Specializing, like Daniel, in French cuisine, Café Boulud offers diners a less formal and less expensive alternative to Daniel. In 2001 Boulud opened the doors of his third restaurant in New York City, DB Bistro Moderne. It is described on Boulud's Web site (Danielnyc.com) as a "casual and contemporary restaurant" that serves "updated bistro cooking rooted in French tradition." In 2002–04 Boulud served the cruise-ship operator Cunard as a culinary adviser for the legendary ship the *Queen Mary II*, which has 10 restaurants on board and can accommodate more than 2,500 passengers at once. In 2003 Boulud opened the doors of a second Café Boulud, this one housed in the Brazilian Court Hotel in Palm Beach, Florida. Boulud provides 24-hour room service at the hotel and handles private dining and catering functions on the premises. In April 2005 Boulud opened Daniel Boulud Brasserie, one of 18 restaurants forming part of the new multibillion-dollar casino Wynn Las Vegas. Later that year Boulud hired the famed wine steward Daniel Johnnes to oversee the wine selection in his five New York restaurants; the two have also made plans to open a wine bar in New York in 2006.

Boulud has published several books, including *Cooking with Daniel Boulud* (1993), *Daniel Boulud's Café Boulud Cookbook: French-American Recipes for the Home Cook* (1999), *Daniel's Dish: Entertaining at Home with a Four-Star Chef* (2003), and *Letters to a Young Chef* (2003). He pens a bimonthly column, titled "Daniel's Dish," for *Elle Decor* magazine. He regularly lectures at cooking schools and universities, among them the Culinary Institute of America and the French Culinary Institute. Through his Web site, Boulud answers readers' questions concerning culinary matters.

Boulud has appeared on such television programs as *Fox Five Live*, *Charlie Rose*, *Late Show with David Letterman*, *Live with Regis and Kathie Lee*, and *Today*. He appears in the documentary film *Eat This New York*, which premiered on the Sundance cable channel in 2003. Boulud follows the time-honored tradition of giving his employees and their families a meal free of charge once a year, and he has donated his time and resources to many charitable causes, among them City Meals on Wheels, the American Heart Association, the American Cancer Society, March of Dimes Birth Defects Foundation, PBS Channel 13, the Tourette Syndrome Fund, and the Children's Center for Therapy and Learning. After the September 11, 2001 terrorist attacks on the World Trade Center, he was among the first people to organize and prepare meals for the rescue workers.

Boulud, his wife, and their teenage daughter, Alix, live above Daniel in an apartment with a tiny kitchen. In an interview with Amy Barrett for the *New York Times Magazine* (February 9, 2003), he talked about many of his habits (he gets a massage every week, for example) and revealed the names of his favorite restaurant, favorite cooking show on television, favorite cookbook, and other personal preferences.

—C.F.T.

Suggested Reading: Danielnyc.com; *Gourmet* p286+ Oct. 2000, with photo, p69+ Dec. 2001, with photos; *New York* (on-line) p26+ Dec. 14, 1998; *New York Times* B p2 June 23, 1992, F p1 Mar. 14, 2001, with photo; *New York Times Magazine* p59+ Apr. 5, 1992, with photo; Brenner, Leslie. *The Fourth Star: Dispatches from Inside Daniel Boulud's Celebrated New York Restaurant*, 2002; Dornenberg, Andrew and Karen Page. *Becoming a Chef: With Recipes and Reflections from America's Leading Chefs*, 1995

Selected Books: *Cooking with Daniel Boulud*, 1993; *Daniel Boulud's Café Boulud Cookbook*, 1999; *Daniel's Dish: Entertaining at Home with a Four-Star Chef*, 2003; *Letters to a Young Chef*, 2003

Evan Agostini/Getty Images

Branch, Michelle

July 2, 1983– Singer/songwriter

Address: c/o Maverick Records, 9348 Civic Center Dr., Beverly Hills, CA 90210-3606

A self-described singer/songwriter in the pop/rock/folk tradition, Michelle Branch has pursued stardom with uncommon determination since her early teens. She achieved her goal at the age of 18, with the release of her album *The Spirit Room*. In a highly enthusiastic review of that record, which has sold more than two million copies, Liana Jonas wrote for the *All Music Guide* (online), "The 11-track set showcases this precocious artist on guitar (electric and acoustic) and a substantial vocal presence that blends innocence, passion, vulnerability, yearning, intensity, and tenderness all in one voice. She also has a knack for crafting melodic vocal leads, which further define her infectious sound. However, what truly shines through are the young musician's lyrics . . . which are some of the most open, simple, and idealistic ruminations on love to drop in 2001." Branch has since recorded a Grammy Award–winning song with the renowned guitarist and bandleader Carlos Santana; performed with the Dixie Chicks and Sheryl Crow and on the show preceding the 2003

Super Bowl broadcast; concertized on three continents; and released a second successful album, *Hotel Paper*. She has also been the focus of intense media attention, which has both boosted her career tremendously and subjected her to the sometimes unreachable expectations and other pressures that arise from overnight celebrity in the entertainment industry. In a capsule biography of her for the *All Music Guide*, Greg Prato wrote, "Although she lists such classic rock acts as Led Zeppelin, the Beatles, and Jimi Hendrix as prime influences, Branch's music is more akin to such modern-day female artists as Lisa Loeb, Alanis Morissette, and Melissa Etheridge"; Christine Ho, writing for the Happy Girls Archives (on-line), advised, "Think of Branch as a cross between the pop likeability of Britney Spears and the stark rawness of . . . Morissette." In an interview with Aaron Cummins for the MTV Web site in 2002, Branch said, "I'm having so much fun. I learn something new every day. . . . That's why people like Aerosmith and the Rolling Stones are still putting out records. Because every time you pick up the guitar you learn something, and you can write something that didn't exist five minutes ago."

The second of three children, Michelle Jacquet DeSevren Branch was born prematurely on July 2, 1983 in Phoenix, Arizona. According to the Eurasian Nation Web site, she is of mixed Irish, Dutch, French, and Indonesian descent; other Web sites have listed Spanish-Mexicans, too, among her antecedents. Her father, David Branch, worked as a plumbing contractor; her mother, Peggy, managed a restaurant. She and her family, which includes her older brother, David, and younger sister, Nicole, lived in Flagstaff, Arizona, until she was 11. Recorded or broadcast music was ever-present in the Branch home, and "as far [back] as she can remember, songs have always danced around in her head," as an unsigned article in the Malaysian publication *New Straits Times* (June 29, 2003, on-line) reported. As a three-year-old, she used her parents' karaoke equipment to make a recording of Beatles songs for her grandmother. She loved to watch such movie musicals as *Oklahoma!* and *The Sound of Music*; she memorized their songs and would perform them for her relatives, sometimes in little shows that she and her sister mounted at home. Her goal of becoming a Broadway star changed after she attended a concert by the band New Kids on the Block (NKOTB). "When I saw them live and witnessed how the music touched people, I was in awe," she recalled for michellebranch.net, as quoted on collectedsounds.com and other Web sites. The following day she saw one of the NKOTB musicians, along with ecstatic admirers, in the hotel in which both she and the band had been staying. "I knew at that moment that I no longer wanted to be singing show tunes," she reported. "I wanted to be a pop star."

Branch took voice lessons at Northern Arizona University, in Flagstaff, for three years beginning when she was eight. After her family moved to Sedona, Arizona, she studied voice privately with Gina Bettum. "It was the best thing I've ever done," Branch wrote for michellebranch.net. "Gina has been in the music industry so she was the perfect mentor. She also started teaching me about singing from your heart with a lot of soul. . . . She helped me find my own voice." At her own request, for her 14th birthday Branch received a guitar—an "heirloom," as she has labeled it, that had belonged to one of her uncles. That day she began teaching herself how to play. "The next few months I was basically living in my room playing guitar and writing songs all day long," she wrote for michellebranch.net. Speaking of songwriting years later in an interview with Melissa Glassman for *YM* (2003, on-line), she said, "Finding a melody for the words is the easiest part for me. If someone comes to me and has a couple cool chords that they are playing, I can find a melody for it in two seconds. It is my favorite ting to do. It's always the lyrics that are the hard part for me."

For a while when she was 15, Branch studied guitar with Bettum's husband, Gary; she reportedly stopped taking lessons because she felt that she was focusing on technique at the expense of spontaneity and emotion. While growing up she also learned to play the piano. Meanwhile, as a freshman at Red Rock High School, in Sedona, she had begun to perform at restaurants, fairs, art shows, and other venues, at times with, among others, her sister on drums and her friend and occasional songwriting collaborator Jenifer Hagio. During her sophomore year, certain that her Red Rock classes would not help her achieve her career goal, Branch dropped out of high school; she completed her secondary-school requirements by means of home schooling, with her mother as her teacher.

One afternoon when she was 16 and at home with her sister, a family friend called to urge her to bring a demo tape and a photo of herself to the friend's workplace immediately, to give to one of the woman's clients, Jeff Rabhan, a music manager and former *Rolling Stone* writer. Lacking access to a car, Branch took a neighbor's golf cart and drove with her sister the three miles to the friend's office, where she met Rabhan. Two months later, after she had almost given up hope of hearing from him, Rabhan contacted her, and after talking with her parents, he became her manager. Within months he had helped her record, in eight days, an independent CD called *Broken Bracelet*, which she distributed at local concerts. The disk included 10 songs written by Branch, among them "If She Only Knew," "Sweet Misery," "I'd Rather Be in Love," and "Goodbye to You" (all of which she re-recorded for her first mainstream album, *The Spirit Room*). Partly on the strength of *Broken Bracelet*, in 2000 Branch secured two gigs as the opening act for the musical group Hanson (the brothers Isaac, Taylor, and Zachary Hanson) during their tour promoting *This Time Around*. A representative from Maverick Recording Co., a subsidiary of Warner Bros., saw her perform at one of those concerts, and

she soon signed with that label. (Others in Maverick's stable of more than two dozen soloists and groups are Alanis Morissette, Madonna, the Deftones, Goldfinger, and American Hi-Fi.)

Branch began to record *The Spirit Room* in January 2001, when she was 17; it arrived in stores in mid-August of that year. "Mostly my album is just love songs, because I think it's the one thing that everybody in the world can relate to, no matter how old they are or where they live," she told Linda Wertheimer for the National Public Radio program *All Things Considered* (August 14, 2001, on-line). *The Spirit Room* was produced by John Shanks, a top rock and pop writer/producer who had been recruited to work with Branch by Danny Strick, an A&R (artists and repertoire) executive at Maverick. "Michelle and I got together, and in the first hour we wrote 'You Set Me Free,' which ended up making the album," Shanks told Dale Kawashima in an undated interview for *Songwriter Universe Magazine* (on-line). "I quickly realized that she's a great writer and a great person. . . . She was a breath of fresh air with her attitude and ability." Branch had written the album's first track, "Everywhere," before she met Shanks; when he heard it, he told Kawashima, he thought it sounded "close" to being finished but "needed a fresh approach and a re-write." The reworked "Everywhere," the first song on the album to be released as a single, climbed to number 12 on *Billboard*'s Hot 100 chart. "It's no surprise that . . . the lively and heartfelt 'Everywhere'—with its electric-guitar power chords, spirited vocal delivery, and catchy chorus—spread like wildfire on the radio," Liana Jonas wrote for the *All Music Guide*. In *Entertainment Weekly* (September 7, 2001), Laura Morgan wrote, "'Everywhere' is as great a song as you could hope to hear on the radio: Its swoony sentiment and poppy power chords are irresistible. And, miraculously, the TRL kids"—a reference to the MTV program *Total Request Live*, which broadcasts music videos—"have embraced it. (Could it be that a girl who can actually sing and has no use for back-up tracks and dancers has a shot in this musical climate?)." Morgan concluded, in a nod to Nirvana's rock anthem "Smells Like Teen Spirit," "Branch's talent may not be fully developed, . . . but she sure smells more authentic than the current brand of teen spirit." In writing five additional songs on *The Spirit Room*, among them "You Get Me," "Something to Sleep to," and "Drop in the Ocean," Branch worked with Shanks and/or others. Of the remainder of the 11 songs on *The Spirit Room*, all of which were written solely by Branch, "All You Wanted" and "Goodbye to You" became hit singles. The video for "Everywhere" won the Viewer's Choice Award at the 2002 MTV Music Video Awards ceremony.

To date, *The Spirit Room* has reportedly sold more than two million copies. According to the Asian Music Source and other Web sites, it remained on *Billboard*'s Top 100 chart for 82 weeks. Its popularity notwithstanding, some reviewers expressed reservations in their assessments of it. Among them was David Sinclair, who wrote for the London *Times* (April 12, 2002, on-line) that Branch "is every inch a product of the modern music world, a place where kids . . . [learn] how to strike all the approved, pop-literate poses, while displaying little command of emotional nuance and even less originality of approach. It's not that there is anything intrinsically wrong with *The Spirit Room*. Indeed as an example of the modern young American singer-songwriter's craft it is pretty near faultless. . . . It's just that the package as a whole is so predictable. . . . If [Branch] has ever entertained a thought about something other than her romantic feelings towards various boyfriends, we are certainly none the wiser as to what it might have been after listening to these 11 tracks." Sona Charaipotra, in *People* (October 15, 2001, on-line), complained, "When you call yourself a singer-songwriter, your words should stand on their own. And on some overly earnest tracks, Branch is still studying for her lyrical learner's permit. She flails through metaphors both weird . . . and tired. . . . Joni Mitchell she ain't. Bottom Line: Room to grow."

The renowned musician Carlos Santana, by contrast, was impressed enough by Branch's work to invite her to provide the vocals for his song "Game of Love," a cut on his album *Shaman* (2002). (Others among his collaborators on *Shaman* were the renowned tenor Placido Domingo, the singer/songwriter Macy Gray, and the band Ozomatli.) As a single from the album, "Game of Love" reached *Billboard*'s top five. It also earned Branch a nomination for a 2002 Grammy Award in the category "best new artist"; at the ceremony in which the National Academy of Recording Arts and Sciences named the winners, she and Santana won the award for best pop collaboration with vocals. The honor greatly enhanced Branch's name recognition and gave her career a huge boost.

For about two years following the release of *The Spirit Room*, Branch performed in many locations in the U.S., Europe, and Asia. She also provided the opening acts for other artists, among them Sheryl Crow, at the Oneida Casino, in Green Bay, Wisconsin, in September 2002; that same month she also performed alone and with Crow at the Reno Hilton Outdoor Amphitheatre, in Nevada. While on the road she continued writing music and lyrics. "I realized that [my next] record had already been written in hotel rooms around the world, hence the name *Hotel Paper*," she told an interviewer, as quoted on the Asian Music Source Web site. *Hotel Paper* was released in June 2003, one week after Branch began a seven-week stint as the opening act for the Dixie Chicks' *Tour of the World* concert series. John Shanks produced *Hotel Paper* and co-wrote four of its 13 tracks: "Love Me Like That" (a duet with Sheryl Crow), "Breathe," "'Til I get Over You," and "Are You Happy Now?" (sung with Dave Navarro), the last of which earned Branch a Grammy Award nomination for "best female rock vocal performance."

Stephen Thomas Erlewine's lukewarm review of *Hotel Paper* for the *All Music Guide* was representative of most other critics': "Part of the appeal of Michelle Branch on . . . *The Spirit Room* was that she came across as a spirited normal girl with an enthusiasm for music," Erlewine wrote. "She wasn't teasingly sexy like Britney Spears, nor was she a brat like the then-unknown Avril Lavigne; she felt like a real teenager, something that was enhanced by her direct songs and earnest vocals, which were the furthest thing from flashy. . . . *Hotel Paper* finds Branch two years older and a whole lot more 'mature,' in the sense that . . . she positions herself as a serious singer/songwriter in the adult alternative vein. Branch remains appealing—her blend of pop and mild roots rock sounds good and she has a nice, plainspoken charm and straight-ahead voice—but she's buried beneath the slick veneer of *Hotel Paper*'s production . . . and does not help herself with her compositions, which . . . rarely rise above the generic level. All of it is too self-consciously serious. . . . Taken on the surface, *Hotel Paper* is fine . . . but without that infectious spirit she displayed on *The Spirit Room* or songs as catchy as 'Everywhere,' the album doesn't have the detail of character that made Michelle Branch so appealing the first time out." Within the first year of its release, *Hotel Paper* had sold more than a million copies.

Branch's avoidance of "teasingly sexy" clothing, behavior, and publicity photos, which had led some observers to label her the "anti-Britney," seemed to end when an image of her wearing only a bikini bottom appeared on the cover of the January 2004 issue of *Maxim*; on half a dozen pages inside the magazine, which is geared toward men, there were pictures of her in similar states of undress. Later in 2004 Branch headlined the "Virgin College MegaTour," accompanied by the band Rooney and the singer/songwriters Gavin DeGraw and Tyler Hilton, among others. In March 2005 she joined a 23-city tour to promote the WB television network show *One Tree Hill*. Branch and the singer/songwriter Jessica Harp, a longtime friend of hers, performed as a duo called the Wreckers. An album that she and Harp recorded together, titled "Stand Still, Look Pretty," is expected to be released in 2006.

Branch's songs "Everywhere," "You Get Me," and "You Set Me Free" are on the soundtracks of the movies *American Pie 2* (2001), *Girl Fever* (2002), and *What a Girl Wants* (2003), respectively. She has appeared on television on *The Sharon Osbourne Show*, *The Chris Isaak Show*, *The Tonight Show with Jay Leno*, and *Late Night with Conan O'Brien*, and played herself in installments of such series as *Charmed* and *Buffy the Vampire Slayer*, and she portrayed the singer Lesley Gore on the show *American Dreams*. For a short while in 2004, she appeared in ads for Flirt cosmetics, made by Estée Lauder.

Branch, with Harp and Santana, recorded the song "I'm Feeling You" for Santana's album *All That I Am*, which was scheduled to reach stores in November 2005. The trio performed the song, which Branch wrote with John Shanks and Kara DioGuardi, at the National Football League kickoff game and the World Music Awards ceremony, both in September 2005, and on *The Tonight Show with Jay Leno* in October 2005.

In May 2004 Branch married Ted Landau, a bassist in her backup band. She and Landau, who is 19 years her senior, became the parents of a daughter, Owen Isabelle, on August 3, 2005.

—H.T.

Suggested Reading: *All Music Guide* (on-line); *Kansas City Star* E p8 Aug. 9, 2002; (London) *Times* Features p10 Apr. 12, 2002; michellebranch.com; michellebranch.net; MTV.com May 22, 2003; *Phoenix (Arizona) New Times* Arts & Music Nov. 1, 2001; VH1.com Oct. 11, 2001

Selected Albums: *Broken Bracelet*, 2000; *The Spirit Room*, 2001; *Hotel Paper*, 2003

Courtesy of Rock Brynner

Brynner, Rock

Dec. 23, 1946– Writer; historian

Address: Quaker Hill Rd., Pawling, NY 12564

During a 1976 dress rehearsal for a production of the musical *The King and I* in Indianapolis, Indiana, the voice of Yul Brynner, who became famous in the title role, emerged as little more than a rasp, because of damaged vocal cords. Rock Brynner, whose voice sounded remarkably like his father's, offered to stand in the orchestra pit and speak the king's lines while Yul lip-synched. "It was the most presumptuous, audacious and outrageous idea [Yul] had ever heard of and it put an angry scowl across his face," Rock recalled, according to S. Plant in the *Herald* (February 16, 1990), an Australian publication. Yul acquiesced, though, and for one night father and son shared the role of king.

Such moments were rare for the two Brynners, as Rock related in his best-selling book *Yul: The Man Who Would Be King: A Memoir of Father and Son* (1989). As a young man Rock had difficulty meeting his father's expectations, and after an early battle with alcohol and drug addiction, he held a variety of jobs, including street busker, restaurateur, bodyguard for the boxer Muhammad Ali, road manager for Bob Dylan and the Band, and computer programmer. He has since settled into the roles of acclaimed author and historian. In addition to his memoir, he has written two novels, *The Ballad of Habit and Accident* (1981) and *The Doomsday Report* (1998), and co-authored the medical and social history *Dark Remedy: The Impact of Thalidomide and Its Revival as a Vital Medicine* (2001). His Ph.D. dissertation, "'Fire Beneath Our Feet': The Constitutional Impact of Shays' Rebellion" (1993), has become a valuable resource for scholars. The history of Russia and of his own family are the subjects of his latest book, which has the working title "Empire and Exile: The Brynners in Far East Russia and Beyond" and is scheduled for publication in early 2006 by Steerforth Press.

Yul Brynner Jr. was born on December 23, 1946, the only child of Yul Brynner and his first wife, the stage and screen actress Virginia Gilmore. He has two half-sisters—Lark, who was born out of wedlock in 1958, and Victoria, who was born in 1962, the product of his father's second marriage, to Doris Kleiner—and two Vietnamese-born sisters, Mia and Melody, whom Yul Brynner adopted with his third wife, Jacqueline de Croisset, in the mid-1970s. As a boy Yul Jr. was nicknamed Rock, after the champion middleweight prizefighter Rocky Graziano. The actor kept his son with him whenever possible, taking him along when touring the world in various productions of *The King and I*. (All theatrical productions and movies of *The King and I* are banned in Thailand, on the grounds that they are historically inaccurate and their depictions of King Mongkut, also known as Rama IV, who reigned in the mid-1800s, when the country was called Siam, are distorted and demeaning.) Brynner felt closer to his father than to his mother until he learned from his mother "her spiritual values, compassion and her Christian beliefs, something my father didn't have," as he told Judi Hunt for the *Seattle Post-Intelligencer* (February 12, 1991). Rock Brynner's youth was one of privilege and excess in such places as New York, Paris, and Switzerland, where he socialized with his father's high-profile friends, among them the heiress Gloria Vanderbilt, the playwright and Nobel laureate Samuel Beckett, and Rat Pack members—the entertainers Sammy Davis Jr., Dean Martin, and Frank Sinatra. By his own admission, he became thoroughly spoiled and insufferable. "I had my first car when I was 10, with a chauffeur," he told Helen Oldfield for the London *Guardian* (November 11, 1989). "We'd go out on the town, hit a few cocktail parties, go dancing, and I'd drop a few hundred quid on a weekend."

Brynner attended the International School of Geneva, in Switzerland. He then studied briefly at Yale University, in New Haven, Connecticut, before transferring to Trinity College, in Dublin, Ireland, on the advice of Samuel Beckett, a Trinity alumnus whom Brynner had met in Paris. He had begun drinking as an adolescent, and by the time he graduated with an M.A. in philosophy from Trinity, in the 1960s, Brynner had become an alcoholic. During the 1960s he also began experimenting with a variety of drugs, including cocaine, which he used heavily. In 1970 Brynner appeared on Broadway (with his first name spelled "Roc") in *Opium*, a one-man play he translated and adapted from the writer and director Jean Cocteau's notebooks about his struggle to overcome addiction. In a review for the *New York Times* (October 6, 1970), Clive Barnes described the play as "a strange and curious entertainment" and wrote that he had been "impressed" by Brynner's "sensitively observed portrait of the artist as a young addict." George Oppenheimer, a *Newsday* (October 6, 1970) critic, found the play "strange and fascinating" and wrote that Brynner had "style and grace and, above all, a voice that is resonant even when he whispers. What's more," Oppenheimer continued, "he creates a genuine character that is tortured by his addiction, deviate in his tastes, an exhibitionist and a genius. . . . *Opium* . . . has wit and imagery and, at times, a dramatic power without the usual habiliments of drama. It is hard to describe but, for me, easy and rewarding to see and hear, thanks largely to [Brynner's] bravura yet altogether natural and convincing performance." When the play closed, after only eight performances, Brynner admitted to his own addiction and realized that he could not support himself. "Alcohol did me the greatest favour, which is that it brought me down to earth. I was otherwise condemned to be a Hollywood brat," he told Helen Oldfield.

Brynner next moved to Europe, where, he told Oldfield, he "travelled among the street people" and supported himself as Red Hat the clown (named for a battered red fedora he wore). "I learned a thousand crafts," he told Oldfield. "I have a hundred different ways to earn a living."

Among Brynner's myriad short-lived careers, he helped establish the original Hard Rock Cafés in London and New York; served as road manager for Bob Dylan and the Band and as a roadie with the Rolling Stones; and worked in computer programming for Bank of America. In 1971 Brynner toured with the Rolling Stones and, while in Zurich, Switzerland, met a man who wanted the boxer Muhammad Ali to stage a fight there. The man did not speak English, so he sent Brynner to negotiate for him. Brynner and Ali quickly became friends. While they talked, a man tried to attack Ali; as a professional boxer, Ali was forbidden to fight outside the ring, on pain of losing his license. "When I saw this man punching Ali, I grabbed his hand and broke two of his fingers, sending him to the ground," Brynner told Olga Liakhovich for the *Moscow News* (July 7, 2004). "And then Muhammad turned to me and said: 'Who would ever have thought that the son of the Pharaoh of all Egypt [one of Yul Brynner's roles] would be protecting a little black boy from Louisville?' So for the next three years whenever he had a fight, I got a plane ticket and a hotel room, and stayed by his side."

Brynner is best known not as Muhammad Ali's bodyguard, however, but as a writer. His first book, a fictionalization of his life entitled *The Ballad of Habit and Accident*, was published in 1981. It focuses on a young man from age 19 to 30, detailing his travels (often while he was inebriated), his drug-related experiences, and his days as a vagabond clown. In a review for the *Wall Street Journal* (January 26, 1981), Edmund Fuller wrote that the book's "flaws are commensurate with its merits, both being considerable," adding that the "candor, the self-castigating humor in the midst of horror, and the testimony of a salvaged life justify the aspects of unsparing ugliness." In about 1988, three years after his father's death, Brynner began writing what would become his most recognized title, *Yul: The Man Who Would Be King: A Memoir of Father and Son*. In it he traced the arc of his father's life, recounting his trajectory from troupe performer to movie star and sex symbol to once-great performer locked into the role of the greatly fictionalized king of Siam, both onstage and off. Brynner wrote about his father's temper, emotional bullying, and tough-love tactics; his love affairs with women including Judy Garland, Marlene Dietrich, Marilyn Monroe, and Joan Crawford; his string of failed marriages; and his longstanding career playing King Mongkut. Above all, the younger Brynner hoped some good might come from making public his father's agonizing death from lung cancer. "I want others who still smoke to know how this strong, powerful human being suffered," he explained to Judi Hunt, "even though it was terrible to experience his death twice, the second time for this book." (Brynner's mother also died of a smoking-related disease, emphysema, in 1986, one year after Yul Brynner's death.) In his book Brynner revealed that his father had effectively disowned all his children by leaving his entire estate to his 28-

year-old fourth wife, Kathy Lee, a dancer. "This book is not 'Daddy Dearest,'" Barbara Shulgasser wrote in her review for the *New York Times* (November 12, 1989), referring to the infamous tell-all memoir *Mommy Dearest*, written by Christina Crawford about her adoptive mother, the actress Joan Crawford; "the son seems to love his father with as much energy as he despises him. But when he calls [Yul] Brynner 'an established sex symbol, the masculine counterpart to Marilyn Monroe,' you wonder if this is meant as a compliment or a recognition that his father's macho exploits . . . teetered on the verge of self-parody."

Following the publication of *Yul*, Brynner pursued a Ph.D. in history, with a specialization in colonial America, at Columbia University, in New York City; he completed his doctorate in 1993. His next book, the novel *The Doomsday Report* (1998), is about a scientist who publishes findings that predict the extinction of the human race in less than half a century. As a result of the scientist's conclusions, a fatalistic malaise descends on the public. A summer blockbuster, *The Doomsday Report* received mixed reviews. Writing for *Newsday* (July 1, 1998), Liz Smith declared that the book kept her "riveted," terming it "a shattering thriller about global warming." Louis Bayard wrote for the *Washington Post* (June 29, 1998) that Brynner's book "overflows with absurdities, but perhaps the most endearing nonsense is the notion that a book, in these post-literate days, could generate planet-wide dystopia." *The Doomsday Report* was reportedly optioned as a made-for-television movie, but the project has yet to come to fruition.

In *Dark Remedy: The Impact of Thalidomide and Its Revival as a Vital Medicine* (2001), Brynner and his co-author, Trent Stephens, a professor of anatomy and embryology at Idaho State University who had studied thalidomide for a quarter-century, examined the historic and social impacts of a drug that was once touted as the world's first safe sedative but turned out to be extremely harmful to fetuses during the first three months of their development; it also caused very painful, irreversible nerve damage in some adults. In nearly 50 countries in Europe, Asia, Africa, Australia, and South America in the 1950s and '60s, thalidomide was available over the counter, and many pregnant women took it to combat morning sickness. The drug caused tens of thousands of miscarriages and, in tens of thousands of babies, horrendous birth defects—deafness, blindness, cleft palate, malformed internal organs, and severely malformed limbs; an estimated 40 percent of babies affected by thalidomide did not survive their first year. In Australia and Europe, reports began to surface of unusually large numbers of birth defects that most doctors had rarely if ever seen before, and some physicians discovered that the mothers of the babies with those rare defects had taken thalidomide early in pregnancy. For years, though, the German company Chemie Grünenthal, the original manufacturer of the drug, vigorously denied any connection between the defects and thalidomide, and, as Thomas Dormandy wrote in a review of *Dark Remedy* for *Nature* (March 22, 2001), "a barrage of slander, innuendo and threats of legal action were mounted against those who tried to sound the alarm." Similarly, the Distillers Co., a British distributor of the drug, claimed that it was perfectly safe, and "for years," as Dormandy wrote, "Distillers indignantly refused to acknowledge responsibility, let alone try to compensate their victims." He noted, "No complicitous chairman, director of research or head of advertising in any country was ever held to account" for their criminal actions, the motive for which, he declared, "was greed." In the United States, the drug company Richardson-Merrell had manufactured 10 million thalidomide tablets and was awaiting U.S. Food and Drug Administration (FDA) permission to begin distributing them. But Frances O. Kelsey, a middle-level, middle-aged FDA pharmacologist whose job was to evaluate applications for new drugs from pharmaceutical companies, had serious misgivings about the validity and adequacy of the evidence presented to show thalidomide's safety. Thanks to her strenuous efforts to prevent approval of thalidomide, despite enormous pressure from the drug industry and her superior's threats of dismissal, the drug did not become available in the U.S. Since its ban in the 1960s, thalidomide has been seen as symbolic of the dangers of unfettered or insufficiently tested medical developments. Recently, however, doctors have discovered valuable uses for thalidomide, and Brynner himself has benefitted from such research. For five years he suffered from pyoderma gangrenosum, a rare autoimmune disorder in which wounds would appear on his legs, grow larger, and fail to heal. He had taken a variety of medications to no avail and was contemplating suicide when his dermatologist mentioned that thalidomide might be a viable treatment. He began taking it in 1998, and his disorder went into remission. The drug is now being tested as a possible treatment for dozens of forms of cancer and autoimmune diseases. In the United States thalidomide is currently approved only for treating leprosy. In a review of *Dark Remedy* for the *New England Journal of Medicine* (July 19, 2001), as reprinted on Amazon.com, E. M. Tansey of University College London wrote, "Together, contributing their different skills and knowledge, [the authors] have told a compelling story decisively, with style and clarity. *Dark Remedy* deserves to be widely read." After labeling the book "brilliant," Thomas Dormandy declared that something like the thalidomide tragedy could "surely" happen again, for various reasons. "If there is hope," he concluded, "it lies in meticulously researched books such as *Dark Remedy* to remind us of the perils that pave the way to pharmacological utopia." In September 2001 the editors of *Scientific American* named *Dark Remedy* among three books that they recommended that month to readers of the magazine.

Rock Brynner has lived in Pawling, New York, since the 1970s. A sought-after lecturer, he has taught at Bard College, in Annandale-on-Hudson, New York; Marist College, in Poughkeepsie, New York; and within the State University of New York system. From 2003 to 2005 he made five lecture tours of Russia, speaking at universities and other institutions on behalf of the U.S. State Department's Speakers Tour; his subjects ranged from the ideological origins of the U.S. Constitution, to the social and political impacts of rock and roll, to the effects of global warming. His tour coincided with the publication in Russian of his book *Yul: The Man Who Would Be King* and a festival of Yul Brynner's films in the Far Eastern city of Vladivostok, which was founded by his Swiss-born great-grandfather Juli Bryner and where his father was born. While in Russia in 2005, Brynner toured with the film director Olivier Gaborsek and the cameraman Gleb Teleshov, with whom Brynner is collaborating to film a documentary, tentatively titled "Full Circle," about his family's history. He also visited his girlfriend, Olya Vigorskaya, whom he has been dating since 2003. Speaking of his forthcoming book, he told *Current Biography*, "My history of Russia and the Brynner family, and my return to Vladivostok, will probably be the work I am best remembered for."

—K.J.E.

Suggested Reading: (Australia) *Herald* p11 Feb. 16, 1990; (London) *Guardian* Nov. 11, 1989; *Moscow News* (on-line) July 7, 2004; *Seattle Post-Intelligencer* C p1 Feb. 12, 1991; *Washington Post* X p1 June 19, 1994; Brynner, Rock. Y*ul: The Man Who Would Be King: A Memoir of Father and Son*, 1989

Selected Books: *The Ballad of Habit and Accident*, 1981; *Yul: The Man Who Would Be King: A Memoir of Father and Son*, 1989; *The Doomsday Report*, 1998; *Dark Remedy: The Impact of Thalidomide and Its Revival as a Vital Medicine*, 2001

Burstyn, Mike

July 1, 1945– Actor; singer

Address: c/o Folksbiene Yiddish Theater, 45 E. 33d St., Third Fl., New York, NY 10016

"Good humor and professionalism radiate from veteran musical actor Mike Burstyn, brightening any stage on which he appears," Jeanne Lieberman wrote for the *New York Law Journal* (June 26, 1998). A multitalented actor and singer, Burstyn has appeared in Broadway musicals, one-man shows, films, and television productions, and he has recorded more than 20 albums. Hailing from a famous family of Yiddish actors, Burstyn is currently recognized as one of the leading lights of Yiddish theater, an art form that its proponents are struggling to revive. (Spoken by the majority of Jews in Eastern Europe before World War II, Yiddish is derived largely from German and Hebrew. Today it is taught in universities; as a primary language, it is used by only a small number of Jews.) Burstyn has performed most recently in the acclaimed Off-Broadway production *On Second Avenue*, a musical revue based on songs from the heyday of Yiddish entertainment, during the early part of the 20th century, when theaters lined a stretch of New York City's Second Avenue, and tickets could be purchased for well under a dollar—a boon to recent immigrants eager for entertainment after a hard week of work and for reminders of their native lands.

Mike Burstyn's father, Pesach (sometimes spelled Pesach'ke) Burstein (1896–1986), ran away from his deeply religious Polish family during his teens to join a traveling acting troupe. He immigrat-

Courtesy of Mike Burstyn

ed to the United States in 1924 and found success in the flourishing Yiddish-theater scene of New York City's Lower East Side. Burstyn's mother, the actress Lillian Lux, who was 22 years younger than her husband, appeared in ingenue roles in Second Avenue theaters. Pesach and Lillian devised an act and began touring together, performing for Jewish communities all over the world; they were married during a stint in Buenos Aires, Argentina, in the 1930s. They frequently enacted a dramatic piece by Pesach called *Kasene in Shtetl* (A Village Wedding), which remains one of their best-known works. In 1939, while touring Europe, they narrowly escaped Poland after German troops invaded, by promising to entertain passengers on the ship that brought them to safety.

Burstyn was born Michael Burstein on July 1, 1945 in the New York City borough of the Bronx. He has a twin sister, Susan. He made his first appearance on stage at the age of three, during his parents' act. "They put a beard and a top hat on me and it stopped the show," he told Blake Green for New York *Newsday* (July 25, 1990). At age seven Burstyn and his sister, using the stage names Motele and Zisele, began appearing regularly with their parents. "I was very lucky growing up in Yiddish theater," Burstyn told Green. "It gave me the tools to work in every facet of the entertainment business—nightclubs, production, directing, films, theater. You had to learn a little bit of everything." In time Burstyn surpassed his parents as an audience favorite. Growing up on the road took its toll, however. "I had no roots, no room, no friends," Burstyn told Enid Nemy for the *New York Times* (March 16, 1990). "For my bar mitzvah [a rite of passage that occurs when a Jewish boy is 13], we rented a theater and put on a show. My father invited his friends, like [the actors] Zero Mostel and Maurice Schwartz. The proceeds went to the family, and I still have the I.O.U. my father gave me."

Burstyn graduated from the High School of Music and Art (now known as the Fiorello H. La-Guardia High School of Music & Art and Performing Arts), in New York City. Shortly afterward, in 1962, he moved to Israel with his parents and sister. In 1963 his sister, who had been billed as the youngest professional ventriloquist in the world, abruptly quit show business to marry. (On the day of her wedding, Burstyn and his parents were obligated to give an evening performance, so the ceremony was held at midnight.) At around that time Burstyn began to work solo, much to his parents' dismay. Pesach and Lillian were left to perform on their own to dwindling audiences. "Slowly the older generation died out and [Yiddish] started disappearing, so I switched to the Israeli, Hebrew stage and film and television and went off on my own," Burstyn told Frank Magiera for the *Worcester (Massachusetts) Telegram & Gazette* (October 16, 1998). He told an interviewer for the *Forward* (April 5, 20002, on-line), "My parents really thought I was a traitor. They used all sorts of ways to convince me to change my mind—particularly guilt trips. . . . In the end I had to support them financially. I felt it was the result of my betrayal." The family's life together was the subject of the Israeli film *Der Komediant* (The Comedian), which was released in 1999 and won an Israeli Academy Award as best documentary. *What a Life! The Autobiography of Pesach'ke Burstein, Yiddish Matinee Idol*, co-authored by Lillian Lux Burstein, was published in 2003.

In 1964 Burstyn had a small part in the satiric Israeli film *Sallah Shabati*, which was nominated for an Academy Award as best foreign film and won a Golden Globe Award in the same category. (The film, about a shiftless immigrant from Morocco who settles in Israel shortly after its founding, starred the popular actor Topol.) In 1965 Burstyn was cast in in *Shabbat Hamalka* (The Sabbath Queen). In 1966 he took on a dual role in *Schnei Kuni Leml* (released in the U.S. as *The Flying Matchmaker*), a farcical film inspired by William Shakespeare's play *A Comedy of Errors*. Burstyn won a best-actor award from the Israeli Film Academy for his portrayal of a village idiot and a tutor who look alike. "[The film] turned me overnight into a household name in Israel," he told Michael Grossberg for the *Columbus (Ohio) Dispatch* (June 24, 2004). "To this day, Israelis come up to me and say, 'We grew up on you.'"

Burstyn served in the entertainment division of the Israeli Army during the Six Day War, in 1967, and performed for the troops on the front lines. (He has since performed several times for Israeli troops.) He next appeared in the Israeli film *The Dybbuk* (1968). (In Jewish folklore, a dybbuk is a demon.) He returned to the U.S. later that year to make his debut on Broadway, in the Yiddish musical *The Megillah of Itzik Manger*. During the late 1960s he also starred in Israel's first television variety show.

In 1970 Burstyn returned to Broadway to play the prosecuting attorney Roy Cohn in the short-lived play *Inquest*, based on the real-life trial of Ethel and Julius Rosenberg, an American Jewish couple who were executed after being convicted of spying for the Soviet Union in the 1950s. In 1976 he was cast in a sequel to *Schnei Kuni Leml* called *Kuni Lemel Be' Tel Aviv* (*Kuni Leml in Tel Aviv*). In that film an elderly man (Burstyn) offers his two grandsons $1 million to marry Jewish women and move from Brooklyn to Israel. The following year Burstyn won a best-actor award from the Israeli Film Academy for his work in *Hershele*, in which he starred as the title character, an educated European immigrant in Israel who gives music lessons to the children in his poor neighborhood.

In 1978 Burstyn hosted a special program about Israel for Dutch TV. Its success led to his having his own series in the Netherlands, *The Mike Burstyn Show*, a variety program that aired monthly until 1981. Following a guest appearance on the show, the actress Chita Rivera recommended him to succeed Jim Dale as the star of the Broadway musical *Barnum*. Dale, who had performed in the circus early in his career, had won a Tony Award for best actor in the role of the circus founder and showman P. T. Barnum. Burstyn had reservations about auditioning for the part. "I called Cy Coleman—the show's composer—and put it very frankly," Burstyn told Jay Sharbutt for the Associated Press (October 14, 1981). "I said, 'I'll come in with great pleasure, at my own expense and audition for you. But please be honest with me. Are you looking for a [big] name? Because, if you are, what good is it, my coming?' And Cy told me, 'If we find that you are what we're looking for, we'll make [you] that [big] name.'" Burstyn was hired and trained for six weeks for the role at the Big Apple Circus, learning how to walk a high wire, juggle, and use a trampoline. "The first week in the role I never thought I'd make it. I was fighting for breath for 30 minutes in the first act; there was no pause long enough for me to take a deep breath," he told Evelyn Renold for the New York *Daily News* (December 29, 1981). He told Sharbutt, "In a way, this is the fourth time I've begun a new career. First the Yiddish theater, then Hebrew theater and films in Israel, then television in Holland. And now *Barnum*." During the Broadway run of *Barnum*, Burstyn suffered two sprained ankles, torn ligaments in both arms, a shoulder wound, and a severely skinned hand, among other injuries. He reprised his role in 1989 in a Dutch-language production of *Barnum* that toured Holland.

Burstyn played Mike, a piano player who begins a romantic liaison with a teenage girl, in the Dutch film *Sabine* (1982). The following year he appeared in *Kuni Leml B'Kahir* (*Kuni Leml in Cairo*), in which his popular characters arrive in the Egyptian capital to deliver a Torah (a scroll containing the first five books of the Hebrew Bible) for a Jewish community, in return for antique coins. It was the first Israeli film to contain scenes shot in Egypt. The movie earned mixed reviews, while Burstyn was nominated as best actor by the Israeli Film Academy.

In 1990 Burstyn returned to New York to act in a revival of the 1970 show *The Rothschilds*, mounted at the American Jewish Theater. He portrayed the family patriarch, Mayer Amschel Rothschild, in the play, which focuses on the beginnings of the Rothschild financial dynasty in 18th-century Frankfurt, Germany. In the *New York Times* (February 26, 1990), Stephen Holden called Burstyn's performance "riveting" and wrote, "Burstyn creates a huge, vibrant portrait of a relentlessly determined salesman, deal maker and empire builder who seems at moments almost consumed by his own unquenchable self-confidence. Mr. Burstyn's performance doesn't soften the character's demonic edge. Conducting business, he flashes obsequious crocodile smiles, and you can almost feel the gears whir behind his glinting eyes as he calculates his odds." Burstyn received a Drama Desk Award nomination for his performance.

Burstyn starred in a one-man show of Yiddish music and humor, *Rozhinkes Mit Mandlen [Raisins and Almonds] and Other Great Yiddish Songs*, in New York City in 1992. Aileen Jacobson, writing for New York *Newsday* (January 9, 1992), described Burstyn as a "master showman" with the ability to sing sentimental standards with "absolute sincerity"; she bristled, though, at certain traditional Yiddish-theater jokes that she felt were stale and misogynistic. In 1992 Burstyn also toured with the Yiddish-English musical *Those Were the*

Days. In the *Washington Post* (April 11, 1992), Jeanne Cooper wrote that while the title of the play "may suggest indulgent nostalgia for a world largely disappeared, the experience is more rejuvenating than memorializing," and she praised Burstyn's "classic vaudeville timing."

The next year Burstyn starred as the famed film and theater producer Mike Todd in the Broadway production of *Ain't Broadway Grand*. Michael Kuchwara wrote for the Associated Press (April 18, 1993) that while "Burstyn sings well, he doesn't have the star power to illuminate the brash producer or galvanize the musical." Ward Morehouse III, by contrast, in his review for the *Christian Science Monitor* (April 23, 1993), wrote that Burstyn "ably captures the swagger and drive" of Todd in "a dazzling and nostalgic trip down Broadway of an earlier era." Burstyn's performance won an Outer Critics Circle Award.

In 1995 Burstyn starred as Nick, a lawyer, in *Circus Life* at the Kaufman Theater in New York City. In the play Nick and his law partner, who is also his brother in-law, are seduced by the same woman. Later in the year Burstyn starred as Nathan Detroit alongside Vic Damone in a revival of *Guys and Dolls* at the Westbury Theater, in Westbury, New York. Steve Parks wrote for New York *Newsday* (October 12, 1995) that Burstyn "holds the fabric of *Guys and Dolls* together with a fine sense of perpetual exasperation combined with indefatigable Noo Yawk moxie."

To celebrate what would have been his father's 100th birthday, in 1996, Burstyn mounted an Israeli production of *Kasene in Shtetl*, with his mother reprising her original role and Burstyn in Pesach's. In 1997 Burstyn appeared in the straight-to-video thriller *Dog Watch*, filmed in California. That year he was cast in the romantic thriller *Minotaur* (also released under the title *Mossad*, the name of Israel's foreign-intelligence agency), and he starred as Tevye in a revival of the musical *Fiddler on the Roof* at the Westchester Broadway Theater in Elmsford, New York. In a review for the *New York Times* (June 15, 1997), Arthur Klein complained that Burstyn was "somehow more a showman from Atlantic City than a milkman from Anatevka," the fictional village in Russia in which the musical takes place.

At the Jewish Repertory Theater in New York City in 1998, Burstyn played Boris Fishkin, an aging matinee idol, in *The Fishkin Touch*, which earned favorable reviews. He next took on the title role in the musical *Jolson*, which toured the U.S. in 1998 and 1999. (Burstyn's father had worked with Al Jolson when the singer was a superstar, in the early 1920s.) "My dream has come true," Burstyn told Frank Magiera. "I've always loved Jolson. I've listened to Jolson since I was a child. I knew all his songs by heart." In his review for the *Boston Herald* (October 23, 1998), Terry Byren wrote, "Burstyn himself has a lot of charisma as Jolson, but he opens the show with his energy level on 10, and leaves him[self] no room for improvement. Although he does a credible job putting over songs Jolson made famous . . . he's so busy mimicking some image of Jolson, he never makes the part his own." "Obviously, vocally I'm trying to get close to what he sounded like," Burstyn told Magiera, "but I'm not mimicking him at all. I really want to try to bring him back to life in the spirit. I'm fortunate in that physically I'm about the same height and I have a background in the musical theater." While earlier productions of the play in England had emphasized Jolson's arrogance and occasional ruthlessness, Burstyn opted for a more complex approach. "What I wanted to do is at least make clear why he was the way he was. . . . My Jolson is a scared little boy who never lost that fear," he told Julia M. Klein for the *Philadelphia Inquirer* (January 3, 1999). In the American production of the show, unlike the British version, Jolson was never depicted in blackface, an integral part of his act in the 1920s, when such racial stereotyping was common. "The last thing we want to do is offend anyone, and it really does not affect any part of the musical," Burstyn told Marianne Evett for the *Cleveland Plain Dealer* (October 4, 1998). Bowing to critical pressure, however, while the show toured Burstyn opted to wear blackface for one scene, in which Jolson applies it and then quickly removes it before a performance.

In 2003 Burstyn joined the touring company of Charles Busch's popular play *The Tale of the Allergist's Wife*, in the role of the husband of the title character (depicted by Valerie Harper), a wealthy denizen of New York City's Upper West Side who experiences a midlife crisis of epic proportions. In 2004 he starred in the Florida Stage's production of *Miklat* ("Refuge" in Hebrew), a drama set in Israel during the Gulf War of 1991. The protagonists in *Miklat* are the Kleinmans, who are culturally Jewish but have little interest in organized religion. They are shocked to discover that their son has become ultra-Orthodox. In the *Palm Beach Post* (October 26, 2004), Charles Passy wrote that Burstyn's "natural, warmhearted turn as Howard [the father] . . . is the show's most affecting performance. He could play the role just for its Neil Simon-esque laughs and get by, but he's willing to add a layer of paternal wisdom that frames the production beautifully."

In 2005 Burstyn starred in *On Second Avenue*, a revue of Yiddish songs and comedy produced by the Folksbiene Yiddish Theatre—currently, the only Yiddish theater company in the United States. Referring to such giants of the Yiddish stage as Mollie Picon, Menashe Skolnik, and Moishe Oysher, he told a writer for *Voice of America News* (March 28, 2005), "All these people we sing about in *On Second Avenue*, I remember them as if they were aunts and uncles." His performance earned him a nomination for a Drama Desk Award in the category of outstanding actor in a musical.

Burstyn's credits include appearances on the American television shows *Law & Order* and *The Cosby Mysteries*. He has performed in Off-

Broadway productions of *The Prisoner of Second Avenue* at the American Jewish Theater, *Fiorello* at Encores/City Center, and *The Prince of Grand Street* at the Jewish Repertory Theater. He has served as the host and narrator for the 92nd Street Y's renowned Lyrics & Lyricists series in New York City. His many albums include *Rozhinkes Mit Mandlen* (1998), a collection of traditional Yiddish songs; *Live* (2001), a recorded concert performance; and *Tomorrow* (2002), for which he sang pop tunes. Burstyn mounted an extensive concert tour throughout Israel to mark his 50th year in show business. He has performed for various presidents and prime ministers of Israel as well as other heads of state and royalty. In addition to Yiddish, Hebrew, English, and Dutch, he is fluent in German, Spanish, and French and has given performances in all those languages. He has been an honorary board member of Gilda's Club, a trustee of the American Friends of the Hebrew University, and honorary president of the Cystic Fibrosis Foundation of Israel.

Burstyn has two sons from his first marriage, which ended with the death of his wife, Idit. He married the former Cyona Warech in 1998. He recently moved to Los Angeles to focus on television and film projects.

—G.O.

Suggested Reading: Associated Press Oct. 12, 1981; Mike Burstyn's Web site; (New York) *Newsday* II p3 July 25, 1990, II p72 Jan. 9, 1992; *New York Times* C p25 Sep. 9, 1981, C p16 Feb. 26, 1990; *Philadelphia Inquirer* F p1 Jan. 3, 1999; *Voice of America News* (on-line) Mar. 28, 2005; *Washington Post* G p7 Apr. 11, 1992

Selected Films: *Shabbat Hamalka* (The Sabbath Queen), 1965; *Schnei Kuni Leml* (*The Flying Matchmaker*), 1966; *The Dybbuk* (*The Demon*), 1968; *Hershele*, 1977; *Sabine*, 1982; *Dog Watch*, 1997

Selected Plays: *Barnum*, 1981, 1989; *The Rothschilds*, 1990; *Rozhinkes Mit Mandlen* [Raisins and Almonds] and Other Great Yiddish Songs, 1992; *Ain't Broadway Grand*, 1993; *Circus Life*, 1995; *Guys and Dolls*, 1995; *Fiddler on the Roof*, 1997; *The Fishkin Touch*, 1998; *Jolson*, 1998–99; *The Tale of the Allergist's Wife*, 2003; *On Second Avenue*, 2005

Selected Television Shows: *The Mike Burstyn Show*, 1978–81

Courtesy of Kurt Busiek

Busiek, Kurt

(BYOO-sik)

Sep. 16, 1960– Comic-book writer

Address: c/o Nat Gertler, About Comics, 217 Red Oak Ln., Thousand Oaks, CA 91320

"I am simply interested in comics as a storytelling form," the comic-book writer Kurt Busiek told Alan David Doane for the Comic Book Galaxy Web site (2000). "I didn't get into comics because I had one particular kind of story I wanted to tell. I got into comics because I love the comics form, and I want to do all kinds of things with it." Since the early 1990s, when his miniseries *Marvels* appeared, Busiek has built a reputation as a sophisticated creator of dramatic plots, sympathetic characters, and evocative settings—notably those depicted in his series *Astro City*—that are simultaneously recognizable and yet more magical and wondrous than real ones. He has also written enormously popular tales about long-established characters from superhero series published by Marvel and DC Comics. Reminiscent of stories produced during what is often called the golden age of comics (the 1930s through the 1950s), his works appeal to many readers who consider comic books to be a legitimate art form. According to an interviewer for *Ninth Art* (March 7, 2005), an on-line journal about comics, Busiek writes "timeless stories of awesome wonder." Busiek has collaborated with such prominent comic-book artists as Brent Eric Anderson, Sean Chen, Carlos Pacheco, George Perez, and Alex Ross. "Comics is a beautiful medium—elegant, powerful and subtle by turns, or all

at once," he told Christy Kallies for *Sequential Tart* (April 1999, on-line), a comics-industry publication. "I can't imagine ever not doing comics."

Kurt Busiek was born on September 16, 1960 in Boston, Massachusetts. He has four sisters. His mother is a librarian and "an inveterate reader," as he told Ray Mescallado for the *Comics Journal* (2002, on-line). "She instilled a love of books into all her kids," Busiek said. "We weren't allowed to watch TV, except for a minimal number of shows that were preapproved by my parents, so we got into the habit of reading books as our primary recreation." He continued, "Comics, on the other hand, were another matter. My parents lived through the comics witch-hunt of the '50s, and had been left with the impression that comics were bad for kids, so we weren't allowed to have comics in the house." (In 1954 Fredric Wertham, a New York psychiatrist, published the book *Seduction of the Innocent*, which linked children's reading of comic books with juvenile delinquency. Wertham lectured and even testified before a U.S. Senate subcommittee about his theory, which he presented without empirical evidence. At the time, many comic books really did contain scenes of extreme brutality and sadistic violence, but Wertham did not distinguish among the different genres available. His crusade against comic books led to the demise of many publishers and the establishment by others of a censorship body called the Comics Code Authority.) As Busiek told Christy Kallies, his parents did not ban European comics or newspaper strips, "so we had *Pogo*, *Peanuts* and *Dennis The Menace* books, and they brought home *Asterix* and *Tintin* books in English, French and other languages in the hopes of getting my sisters and me interested in languages."

Busiek told the *Ninth Art* interviewer that his interest in reading became a passion after his third-grade teacher, Mrs. Renzi, read aloud to the class E. L. Konigsberg's book *From the Mixed-up Files of Mrs. Basil E. Frankweiler.* Afterward, he recalled, "I tore through the kids' library looking for more good books for the next few years, reading anything and everything I could find." He added that Renzi "was also very encouraging of creativity, and I can't help but think that had a factor in turning my vague desire to be a writer, some kind of writer, someday into an actual ambition." As a youngster he would read comic books that he found in his friends' houses. One day he read a stack of *Sad Sack* comics, which focused on the tribulations of a hapless military man. Aimed at an older readership, those comics did not appeal to him much, but they increased his interest in the art form. He was also especially intrigued by issues of the Marvel Comics superhero titles *The Defenders* and *The X-Men.* As he developed a more discriminating eye, he became enamored of other works published by Marvel, which include *The Amazing Spider-Man*, *The Incredible Hulk*, and *The Avengers* series. Marvel's characters, as created by the writer Stan Lee and the artist Jack Kirby in the early 1960s, were not simply noble or iconic figures like Superman and Batman, whose adventures appeared in publications of Marvel's chief rival, DC Comics; rather, a Marvel protagonist was likely to face the same everyday problems as his readers. Often, to keep his comic-book reading secret from his parents, Busiek would hide whatever he had bought under a rock or in other places out-of-doors.

As he became familiar with increasing numbers of comic books, Busiek entertained the notion of writing one himself. "I've wanted to be a writer for as long as I can remember," he told Marv Wolfman (a fellow comic-book writer) for *Silver Bullet Comic Books* (2004, on-line), "but I always found the prospect of writing an entire novel or an entire screenplay, only to find out that I sucked, to be intimidating. So I'd start stuff and not get very far into it. I stumbled into the idea of writing comics—I hadn't read them on a regular basis until I was 14, and sometime early on, I realized that real people wrote and drew these things, and they made a living doing it. That seemed like a lot of fun to me, and besides, they were only 17 pages long! If I sucked at it, I'd find out soon enough."

With his friend Scott McCloud serving as artist, Busiek began writing what he envisioned as a 16-page story about a group of already-existing Marvel Comics characters. But, as he recalled to David Doane, "by the time [it was finished,] we'd gotten 60 pages of stuff done, [and] we'd progressed from absolutely, horribly awful to having some idea of craft and storytelling and pacing." After the three years they took to complete their project, Busiek felt certain that he could succeed as a comic-book writer. (McCloud went on to become a renowned figure in the comic-book world, as the author of the serious studies *Understanding Comics: The Invisible Art* [1993] and *Reinventing Comics: How Imagination and Technology Are Revolutionizing an Art Form* [2000].)

Busiek attended the University of Syracuse, in New York State, where he majored in English literature. He also took courses in creative writing, mythology, playwriting, and magazine publishing, feeling that all of them would be useful to him as an aspiring comic-book writer. In his senior year the teacher of his magazine-publishing class assigned him to interview the publisher of a mass-market magazine. He chose Dick Giordano, then editor in chief of DC Comics. During the interview he mentioned his career goal, and Giordano invited him to submit sample scripts directly to his attention. Throughout that spring Busiek worked on a number of filler scripts—stand-alone stories that can be used during the run of a series whose creative team does not meet a deadline. Giordano passed the scripts to Ernie Colon, who oversaw the *Flash* and the *Green Lantern* series and who suggested that Busiek pitch a filler story for *Tales of the Green Lantern Corps*, a backup series for *Green Lantern* comics. Busiek's story, "The Price You Pay," was included in number 162 of that series and became his first published work.

Busiek graduated from college in 1982. He continued to sell stories to Colon until assignments tapered off; then he began pitching ideas to editors at Marvel Comics. Denny O'Neill purchased one of his filler scripts for *Power Man/Iron Fist* (which was then in transition between creative teams) and began to solicit more stories. With assignments coming his way steadily, Busiek felt that he had established himself in the business. That source of income dried up soon afterward, however, when O'Neill decided to move *Power Man/Iron Fist* in a different creative direction to help boost sales.

In an effort to find work, Busiek left Syracuse and settled in New York City. For the next decade he made a living as a freelance writer, mostly coming up with stories for *Tales of the Green Lantern Corps* and *Justice League of America* (also known as *JLA*), a series about a superhero team made up of the major DC characters. In 1985 he wrote the *Red Tornado* miniseries (illustrated by Carmine Infantino), about an android with red skin, who had been a minor DC character for decades. Busiek also worked as a freelance assistant editor for *Marvel Age* magazine, which was devoted to news and features of interest to Marvel fans. In addition, he wrote for fanzines—magazines written by and for comic-book aficionados. He explained to Wolfman, "Doing whatever you can to get your name known—in a positive context—can't hurt. Writing articles for the fan press, helping organize a convention, putting together an in-store newsletter at your local store—things like this are a way to come in contact with the business and to show you can do something well. . . . And looking for where the opportunities are, rather than wishing that the door you most want to open would suddenly open, is far more constructive."

Although Busiek was supporting himself as a freelance writer, he had yet to establish himself as someone whose name readers would remember and whose work they would seek out. A turning point came in 1993, when Marvel editors tapped him to write *Marvels*, a four-issue miniseries. An immediate best-seller, the issues were compiled as a trade paperback in 1994; the book has been in print continually since then. (Often, a series that is issued in monthly or bimonthly installments is later collected for sale in one volume, partly for readers who missed one or more issues.) *Marvels* represented a departure from traditional comic books. It features elaborate watercolor paintings by Alex Ross instead of filled-in ink drawings, and it seeks to depict what life would be like for an ordinary person living in a world populated by superheroes. The story chronicles events of the Marvel universe beginning in 1939, when Marvel, then known as Timely Comics, introduced its first superheroes: the Sub-Mariner, a prince of the undersea kingdom of Atlantis, and the Human Torch, a synthetic man with the ability to burst into flame. The series, told from the perspective of a photojournalist for the *Daily Bugle*, continued with a second generation of heroes—among them the Fantastic Four, Spider-

Man, the Hulk, and the Avengers—all of whom came to prominence in the 1960s.

"*Marvels* turned out to be the perfect project at the perfect time—Alex's stunning artwork got readers to pick it up, while the stories gave them something they weren't expecting, something they couldn't get anywhere else," Busiek told Wolfman. "And they liked it. Apparently, we brought the experience of that world, that context, to life in a way that hadn't really been done before—giving the heroes feet of clay was of course the Marvel revolution [in the 1960s], but we put them back as figures of wonder, without losing a sense of humanity. We didn't do it out of calculation—it's simply where Alex's and my interests crossed, where we thought we had a good story to tell." A 10th-anniversary edition of *Marvels* was published in 2004.

Following *Marvels*, Busiek began work on *Astro City: Life in the Big City*, a six-issue miniseries that was collected as a paperback in 1996. Like *Marvels*, *Astro City* centers on the lives of superheroes as seen through the eyes of everyday people. The six stories are connected, but each can stand alone. With paintings by Alex Ross on the covers and interior art by Brent Eric Anderson, the series portrays superheroes as larger-than-life, noble figures worthy of admiration. Unlike *Marvels,* in which he used preexisting characters, Busiek created new heroes to populate Astro City. The main "character" of the series is Astro City itself, a place where powerful beings hurtle through the sky, saving lives and fighting criminals every day. Busiek's other *Astro City* series include *Astro City: Family Album*, *Astro City: Confession*, and *Astro City: The Tarnished Angel*, the first of which appeared as a single-volume paperback in 1997 and the next two in 2000. (The infrequency with which *Astro City* was published was due in part to Busiek's chronic sinus infection, which often limited his ability to work. His health has reportedly improved in recent years.)

Astro City was reminiscent of comic-book writing before the 1980s, a decade when some superheroes began to be portrayed as malevolent and vindictive. In Frank Miller's *The Dark Knight Returns*, for example, a middle-aged Batman comes out of retirement to punish a world gone wrong; in Alan Moore's *Watchmen*, the superheroes are alcoholics, rapists, murderers, and political opportunists. Busiek had originally been impressed by such series, feeling that they brought a welcome diversity to comic-book characters. To his dismay, however, mainstream comics publishers soon began churning out second-rate imitations of Miller's and Moore's work, apparently with the aim of boosting sales. As Busiek told Mescallado, "I think there's room in the industry—and even in the superhero genre—for a full range of tones, from sunny to grim, and from hyper-realistic to utter fantasy. [But] as long as the majority of editors and creators all rush off in the same direction as soon as something turns out to be popular, . . . we'll have that pendulum ruling the industry, because there's no

sense of proportion. Or at least, it seems that way." Busiek has said that *Marvels* and *Astro City* were indirect responses to stories about deeply flawed superheroes.

By the mid-1990s Marvel and DC Comics had come to consider Busiek a hot commodity. At Marvel he worked steadily on several series, notably *Thunderbolts* (1997–2003), which follows a group of super-villains, known as the Masters of Evil, who masquerade as superheroes, and *Untold Tales of Spider Man* (1995–97), which fills in gaps between issues produced by Stan Lee and Steve Ditko in the early 1960s and fleshes out the relationships between Spider-Man and individuals in the supporting cast of characters. Busiek's reputation enabled him to take on more high-profile projects, including *Iron Man* for Marvel and *Shockrockets,* a six-issue miniseries for Gorilla Comics, a small publishing company (now defunct) founded by Busiek, Tom Grummett, Joe Kelly, Barry Kitson, and other comic-book writers and artists.

Busiek's writing for *The Avengers* is arguably his most celebrated work on a continuing series. Published continually since its debut, *The Avengers* is about Marvel's preeminent superhero group, whose members include Captain America, Thor, and Iron Man, among others. Busiek and the artist George Perez collaborated on it from 1999 until 2002; in January of that year, Busiek left Marvel to write *The Power Company* for DC Comics. The last *Avengers* installment in which his work appears is number 55.

Along with Perez, Busiek was invited by both DC and Marvel to produce a four-issue crossover miniseries, in which DC's greatest heroes join forces with Marvel's to combat a cosmic threat to their universes. Featuring both the Avengers and the JLA, the series *JLA/Avengers* was launched in 2003, with installments published alternately by each company. It proved to be a commercial and critical success. Busiek's next project was the highly popular, six-issue *Arrowsmith* miniseries, published in 2003 by the DC imprint Wildstorm. In it Busiek, working with the artist Carlos Pacheco, recast world history, making magic develop along with technology; thus World War I is fought not only with guns, bombs, and mustard gas but also with mystical spells. The central character, Fletcher Arrowsmith, is a young wizard; eager to help the war effort, he gives himself the power of flight. The year 2003 also saw the publication as a paperback of Busiek's nine-issue series *The Liberty Project* (1997), about a group of former super-villains forced to fight for good as a condition of their probation.

Along with Fabian Nicienza, Busiek is currently writing for the series *Conan*, published since early 2004 by Dark Horse Comics and illustrated by Cary Nord. The hero is based on a character created by Robert E. Howard in the 1930s. By turns an adventurer, thief, pirate, mercenary, and then king, Conan lived thousands of years before the dawn of recorded history. "One of the things I like most about Conan is the grand sweep of his life—the way he changes and grows and does different things over time," Busiek told an interviewer for the Dark Horse Comics Web site (July 29, 2005).

When John Babos, writing for the pop-culture Web site 411mania (August 12, 2003), asked Busiek if he preferred to write original stories or tales related to existing DC or Marvel comics, Busiek replied, "I like 'em both. There's a similarity, in that in both cases it's a matter of presenting an interesting, complex, fleshed-out world, but in doing a Marvel or DC book it's a matter of doing the research to get the references and make the world seem 'right,' and in doing something like *Arrowsmith* or *Astro City* it's a matter of making it up. But in both cases, the story has to stand on its own—the world may be cool, but if the story doesn't work, it's like having a great background painting and nothing to put in front of it."

Kurt Busiek and his wife, Ann Huntington Busiek, live in the Pacific Northwest with their children. Ann Busiek edited *Astro City: Life in the Big City*, which won a Harvey Award (a comic-

book industry honor) in 1997 for best graphic album of previously published material. Busiek and his work have won a total of eight Harveys, including one for best writer, in 1998, for his body of work in the previous year.

—C.M.

Suggested Reading: 411mania Web site Aug. 12, 2003; Comic Book Galaxy (on-line) 2000; *Comics Journal* (on-line) 2002; comiXtreme.com July 25, 2003; *Daily Oklahoman* B p16 Feb. 15, 2002, D p21 Aug. 16, 2002, D p16 Sep. 12, 2003; *Ninth Art* (on-line) Mar. 7, 2005; *Sequential Tart* (on-line) Apr. 1999; *Silver Bullet Comic Books* (on-line) 2004

Selected Comic Books: *Marvels*, 1994; *Astro City: Life in the Big City*, 1996; *Astro City: Family Album*, 1997; *Astro City: Confession*, 2000; *Astro City: The Tarnished Angel*, 2000; *Avengers: Ultron Unlimited*, 2001; *Avengers: Clear and Present Dangers*, 2001; *Thunderbolts: Justice Like Lightning*, 2001

Canada, Geoffrey

Jan. 13, 1952– President and CEO of the Harlem Children's Zone

Address: Harlem Children's Zone, 35 E. 125th St., New York, NY 10035

"We are in a state of war in the inner cities," the educator, author, and public advocate Geoffrey Canada told David Holmstrom for the *Christian Science Monitor* (June 5, 1995). "I call it American's secret war against itself, . . . and the war's chief victims are children." For nearly three decades Canada, the president and chief executive officer of the Harlem Children's Zone (HCZ), has worked to help urban children escape violence and poverty. Raised in the South Bronx, Canada understands firsthand the effect poor urban areas have on the children who grow up in them. Through HCZ, a nonprofit community-based organization, Canada has instituted innovative new programs and services that address a variety of problems faced by impoverished families and children. Among the resources HCZ offers are community-organizing services, after-school programs, training for new parents, family counseling, and, as of the fall of 2004, a new charter school called the HCZ Promise Academy. By providing smaller class sizes, longer instruction time, and basic health-care services, the academy seeks to create an environment in which poor urban youngsters have the chance to perform well in school and in life. "There may be some in this country who think being poor is a matter of lack of values and determination. But I know it to be something different," Canada said during his

Courtesy of Geoffrey Canada

speech to accept the Heinz Award, in January 1995. "You can work hard all of your life, have impeccable values and still be poor."

The third of four brothers, Geoffrey Canada was born on January 13, 1952 in New York City. The marriage of his father, McAlister Canada, and mother, Mary Canada, ended when Geoffrey was four; afterward, his father did not contribute to the support of his children, and they rarely saw him. Geoffrey and his brothers (Daniel, John, and the youngest, Reuben) were raised by their mother in the South Bronx, a section of New York City that has long symbolized urban decay. In the 1950s white residents of the South Bronx began fleeing the area as low-income blacks and Hispanics moved there in growing numbers. Thus, the Canadas and their neighbors had "little contact with whites and black middle-class families . . . ," as Canada recalled in an essay for *Daedalus* (Winter 1999). "We [grew] up poor, segregated from other races, ethnic groups, and economic classes." During Canada's boyhood his mother worked at odd jobs; at times she relied on welfare and donations of food from charities. "We were too poor to dress properly," Canada recalled to Michelle Green for *People* (April 10, 1995). "I had thin socks, thin pants, no sweaters and no boots. It wasn't until years later that I found out you could remain warm in the winter if you had the right clothes." When Canada gave his acceptance speech for the Heinz Award, he said that he and his brothers "hated being poor. . . . And though there was much love in our family, being poor strained our loving bonds. We had to blame someone for our condition, and our mother was our only target. And here she was giving all she had for us." Canada has expressed gratitude toward his mother for imparting to him and his brothers solid values, including the belief that one is responsible for one's actions. She also emphasized the importance of a good education and encouraged them to read; she herself later earned bachelor's and master's degrees and became a substance-abuse counselor. Another big influence in his life was his first-grade teacher, who introduced him to *The Cat and the Hat* and other books by the author and illustrator Dr. Seuss. "Poetry saved my life," Canada said in a speech at Syracuse University, as quoted by Jean Stevens in the college's student newspaper, the *Daily Orange* (January 20, 2004, on-line). By the time he was nine years old, he told Felicia R. Lee for the *New York Times* (January 9, 2000, on-line), he had resolved that some day he would help inner-city youngsters like himself. "It was simply being very aware of how unjust the world was for poor children," he said.

As a means of ensuring his survival in his tough, crime-ridden neighborhood, the adolescent Canada became a sort of mascot for a teenager named Mike. From Mike, and through careful observation, he learned the "codes of conduct," or unspoken rules and hierarchies, that prevailed among the youths in his neighborhood; he learned how to fight with his fists most effectively, how to hide feelings of weakness and the importance of doing so, and other ways of being street smart. Mike, he wrote in his memoir *Fist Stick Knife Gun* (1995), "rescued me when I was a small, helpless boy, confused and scared. . . . [He] was like a knight in shining armor." Later Canada took to carrying a knife, which made him feel bolder and less vulnerable to attack. One day he accidentally sliced his right index finger to the bone with the knife; know-

ing that his mother would confiscate the weapon if he came to her for help, he treated the cut himself. Within days he reinjured it while playing basketball, and the finger healed with the last joint at an angle. He has never had surgery to straighten it because, as he wrote in *Fist Stick Knife Gun*, "the finger keeps the urgency of the work my colleagues and I do with children at the forefront of my mind. The slight deformity is such a small price to have paid for growing up in the South Bronx. . . . I don't want to forget what life was like [there]. . . . Fear and the struggle to survive were ever-present realities. The finger is my reminder of what young people are willing to do for protection."

When Canada was in his mid-teens, his mother sent him to live with her parents in Freeport, on Long Island, New York. His grandmother, he said in his Heinz Award acceptance speech, "cooled my hot temper and anger over being poor and showed me there was dignity, even in poverty. . . . She taught me how one could have a deep, spiritual love of life that was not tied to material things." Canada attended the nearby, nearly all-black Wyandanch Memorial High School. He earned good grades, and as a senior he won a scholarship from the Fraternal Order of Masons. In the fall of 1970, he enrolled at Bowdoin College, a small liberal-arts school in Brunswick, Maine, where—since he had never been there before—he was shocked to learn that the student body was all male (it became co-ed the next year) and 95 percent Caucasian. His grave misgivings about how he would fare in such an environment soon faded; indeed, he discovered, as he wrote for *Daedalus*, "Bowdoin was my kind of place." One reason, he explained, was "its academic excellence"; another was that "people cared about one another. Students would go out of their way to help you if you needed it. The longer we were at the school, the more we felt responsible for those who followed us. The faculty seemed to feel the same way." In his senior year he enjoyed many private discussions with his professors about the issues of the day and his personal goals; he also earned high honors in all his classes. "My success was less a testament to my brilliance than a tribute to the hard work of professors and students who believed in me, challenged me, molded me, and finally sent me out into the world to do what I had to do," he wrote for *Daedalus*. Canada majored in psychology and sociology and took many courses in education. He graduated from Bowdoin with a B.A. in 1974. The next year he completed a master's degree in education at the Harvard Graduate School of Education, in Cambridge, Massachusetts.

In the summer of 1975, Canada supervised a program for children with emotional problems at Camp Freedom, in Ossipee, New Hampshire. Later that year he joined the staff of the Robert White School, a private day school for what were labeled "emotionally disturbed adolescents." "Really, the school was the last stop before jail or a locked psychiatric hospital for teenagers from Boston slums,"

Canada wrote in *Fist Stick Knife Gun*. Although the White School's students were Caucasian, "by and large [they were] just like the kids I had grown up with in the Bronx. They were poor, angry, estranged from society . . . [and] preoccupied with violence." Canada soon became recognized for his skill in handling the most angry and violent of the students. In 1976 he was named associate director of the school; he became its director the next year.

In 1983 Canada left the Robert White School to assume the post of educational director and director of the truancy-prevention program at the Rheedlen Centers for Children and Families, in New York City. Founded in 1970 by Richard L. Murphy, Rheedlen provided after-school programs and anti-violence training for urban youths. In 1990 Canada was named president and CEO of Rheedlen, after Murphy left to become commissioner of the New York Department of Youth Services. Although the program grew significantly during the 1990s, with the number of children served rising from 1,500 to 7,000 and the annual budget increasing from $2.5 million to $15 million, Canada knew that the needs of many neighborhood children were not being met; one Rheedlen after-school program, for example, had far more applicants than available spots. "We've got to really do something radically different if we're going to save these kids," he told Paul Tough for the *New York Times Magazine* (June 10, 2004), referring to both those in Rheedlen's programs and those left out. "If we keep fooling around on the fringes, I know 10 years will go by, and instead of 75 percent of the kids in Harlem scoring below grade level on their reading scores, maybe it will be 70 percent, or maybe it will be 65 percent. People will say, 'Oh, we're making progress.' But that to me is not progress. This is much more urgent than that."

Canada became determined to prove that, if given proper preparation and equal opportunities, all inner-city children—not only the most motivated or intellectual or those from the most stable, supportive families—could perform as well in school as average white American children. With that goal in mind, in the late 1990s he proposed to Rheedlen's board that the organization adopt a radically new, far more expensive, holistic approach to helping children and families. To remake the board into a stronger fund-raising entity, Canada and a new board member, Stanley Druckenmiller—a 1975 Bowdoin alumnus, billionaire hedge-fund manager, and skilled fundraiser—"politely deposed" the board's chairman, as Tough put it. Druckenmiller took his place. Canada, Druckenmiller, and a representative from the Edna McConnell Clark Foundation (a longtime Rheedlen sponsor) then devised a business plan that called for an initial outlay of $6 million, with annual budgets increasing to a maximum of $46 million over the course of nine years. (The current fiscal year's budget is $24.6 million.) By structuring the proposed program like a business rather than a nonprofit,

and backed by a sympathetic board, Canada no longer had to spend valuable time seeking short-term grants; instead, he could devote much of his attention to the initiatives he planned to offer. He chose to implement his program in a 24-block area in central Harlem whose residents included some 3,400 children under the age of 18, the majority of them living below the poverty line and scoring below grade level on state reading and math tests. Canada dubbed the area, which he expanded in 2004 to encompass 60 city blocks, the Harlem Children's Zone and launched an array of programs that offered educational, social, and medical services to residents of the zone. "The objective," Tough wrote, was "to create a safety net woven so tightly that children in the neighborhood just can't slip through."

The Harlem Children's Zone employs more than 650 people, who work on about 20 different programs. Initiatives include Harlem Gems, a program for prekindergarten students; the Family Support Center, which provides family counseling; Baby College, a class for new parents; and the after-school program Truce, which is an acronym for The Renaissance University for Community Education. Within the original 24-block zone, 88 percent of the children have participated in at least one of Canada's programs. The HCZ Promise Academy, a charter school, is the newest and most ambitious of Canada's projects. The academy opened its doors to 100 kindergarteners and 100 sixth-graders in the fall of 2004, with plans to add 200 new students each year until grades kindergarten through 12 are filled. As a charter school, HCZ Promise Academy is a self-governing public school that is free from some city and state education regulations, freeing its teachers and administrators to use innovative techniques that they feel best serve their students. The school, whose classes are significantly smaller than those of area public schools, runs five days a week from 8:00 a.m. to 4:00 p.m., which is an hour and a half longer per day than most New York schools. After-school programs operate until 6:00 p.m., and their school year contains 210 instructional days, extending into August, as opposed to the 180 instructional days mandated by New York State.

In April 2004 Canada held a lottery to randomly select, from among the 359 applications submitted, the children to be admitted to the HCZ Promise Academy's first kindergarten and sixth-grade classes. The United Federation of Teachers union is skeptical of Canada's expectations of the teachers he hires and his alliance with New York City mayor Michael Bloomberg and the city's schools chancellor, Joel I. Klein, both of whom the union perceives as adversaries. Further antagonizing the teachers' union is Canada's stated long-term goal of taking over existing neighborhood public schools and converting them into charter schools, either under the academy's banner or modeled after it. Canada remains convinced that such drastic measures are necessary to ensure that disadvantaged

Harlem youngsters have a chance to break the cycle of violence and poverty they are born into. "In communities where children are failing . . . you have to go in and change the way teaching and learning happen inside these buildings," he told Karen Matthews of the Associated Press (September 5, 2004). "And teachers have to be in those buildings for more hours and more days if these kids are ever going to catch up."

As of late 2005, all of the HCZ programs have reported progress among their enrollees. A majority of Baby College graduates have said that they read and sing to their children and make certain that the youngsters' immunizations are kept up to date. A full 100 percent of the children in the past three Harlem Gems prekindergarten classes were found to be "school-ready." And although only 11 percent of the 100 kindergarteners who entered the Promise Academy in 2004 had initially tested above grade level, 80 percent had done so by the end of the school year. The progress was not as pronounced among older students, but test scores improved nonetheless; of the 100 sixth-graders who enrolled in the Promise Academy in 2004, only 10 percent had tested at or above grade level, but by the end of the year, 19 percent had reached the appropriate level in math and 39 percent in English. Though the older children might require a greater investment of time and effort than their younger, more impressionable counterparts, Canada has expressed his conviction that, after the students have spent a few years in the HCZ school system, "it will be clear we can save them," as he told Deborah A. Pines for *U.S. News & World Report* (October 31, 2005). He also said that he hopes to add another 31 blocks to the Harlem Children's Zone by 2007. He told Pines, "The only thing that really worries me is that we won't get a chance to really do this completely before I don't have the stamina to continue at this pace." Great leaders, he continued, "have to be indefatigable. The ability to work long hours, under stressful conditions, for many years, is a requirement—and it's something people often overlook."

Canada has written extensively about his experiences, both as a child and as a community organizer, in depressed urban neighborhoods. His first book, *Fist Stick Knife Gun: A Personal History of Violence in America* (1995), was widely hailed as what Jim Bencivenga termed, in the *Christian Science Monitor* (June 5, 1995), "an urban coming-of-age story. Part memoir, part social reform advocacy, it contrasts the mean streets of the author's South Bronx youth in the 1960s to the drug-and-gun culture afflicting today's urban youth." Canada's next book, *Reaching Up for Manhood: Transforming the Lives of Boys in America* (1998), is a broader overview of the trials boys face in urban cultures, specifically the rampant misconceptions that abound about what it means to "be a man" and the need for stronger father-son relationships. When Canada was young, he told David Gergen in an interview for the Public Broadcasting System

(PBS) program *NewsHour with Jim Lehrer* (January 20, 1998, on-line), he received the message that "if you want to be a man, you have to learn how to take it, learn how to make sure that you never cried, and you didn't go to your mother, and you were willing to fight. We thought that meant being a man! We thought being promiscuous meant that you were a man. We thought if you could drink a bottle of wine, that you were a man." Canada maintains that there are even fewer positive male role models for boys today than there were when he was growing up. He told Gergen, "Young boys are getting messages constantly about sex, alcohol, tobacco, clothing, sneakers, stuff that means absolutely nothing when we really look at what it means to be a caring, responsible father, a real responsible adult in today's society." To that end, Canada insists that following the current trend of simply advocating safe sex or abstinence is not enough, and that boys must be taught that nurturing children is not a sign of weakness or compromised masculinity.

In January 1995 Canada was honored as one of the first six individuals to receive the Heinz Award, which carries a prize of $250,000. The Heinz Awards are annual grants created in honor of the late Senator John Heinz by his widow, Teresa Heinz (now Teresa Heinz Kerry). Much like the recipients of the MacArthur "genius" grants, the Heinz Awards honorees receive their grants without prior knowledge of their candidacies. The grants have no strings attached and beneficiaries may apply the money wherever they consider it best used. Canada's numerous other awards include the Robin Hood Foundation's 1992 Heroes of the Year Award, the 1993 Spirit of the City Award from the Cathedral of St. John the Divine, Bowdoin College's 1993 Common Good Award, a Children's Champion Award from *Child* magazine, and the 2004 Harold W. McGraw Jr. Prize in Education. He holds honorary degrees from Harvard University, in Cambridge, Massachusetts; Williams College, in Williamstown, Massachusetts; the Meadville Lombard Theological Seminary, in Chicago, Illinois; the Bank Street College of Education, in New York City; and the John Jay College of Criminal Justice, in New York City. Canada contributed to the essay collection *The Culture of Violence* (2002) and is a frequent public speaker. He hosted a 1994 PBS special entitled *Jobs: A Way Out?* and often appears on such television programs as *Good Morning America*, *Today*, and *Nightline*.

In 1983 Canada founded the Chang Moo Kwan Martial Arts School, where he is chief instructor. In addition to teaching students the principles and techniques of Tai Kwon Do, Canada, a third-degree black belt, instructs his pupils in violence-prevention methods, and the school is a nationally recognized model for its efforts. Canada has taught at the school, which offers lessons free of charge, two nights a week for 21 years.

Geoffrey Canada is the father of four children. From his first marriage, to Joyce Henderson, he has a daughter, Melina, age 35, and a son, Jerry, 32. He and his second wife, Yvonne Grant, have two sons: Bruce, 28, and Geoffrey Jr., seven.

—K.J.E.

Suggested Reading: *Christian Science Monitor* p13 June 5, 1995; *Daedalus* p121+ Winter 1999; Harlem Children's Zone Web site; *Mother Jones* p75+ Sep./Oct. 1995; *New York Times Magazine* p44+ June 6, 2004, with photos; *People* p67+ Apr. 10, 1995, with photos; *Philanthropy News Digest* (on-line) Oct. 17, 2002; Canada, Geoffrey. *Fist Stick Knife Gun: A Personal History of Violence in America*, 1995

Selected Books: *Fist Stick Knife Gun: A Personal History of Violence in America*, 1995; *Reaching Up for Manhood: Transforming the Lives of Boys in America*, 1998

Tim Matsui/Getty Images

Cantwell, Maria

Oct. 13, 1958– U.S. senator from Washington State (Democrat)

Address: U.S. Senate, 717 Hart Senate Office Bldg., Washington, DC 20510-0514

On November 7, 2000 Maria Cantwell, a Democrat, defeated the three-term Republican incumbent Slade Gorton to win a seat from Washington State in the U.S. Senate. A native of Indiana, Cantwell settled in Washington State four years after she graduated from college, after helping in the unsuccessful attempt of Senator Alan Cranston of California to win the 1980 Democratic presidential nomination. While working in the private sector in the field of public relations, she served for six years in the Washington House of Representatives, where she earned a reputation as an effective bipartisan leader. In 1992, at age 36, Cantwell was elected to the U.S. House of Representatives from Washington State's First Congressional District. Along with 33 other congressional Democrats, she failed in her bid for reelection in 1994, a victim, to some extent, of widespread public dissatisfaction with the administration of President Bill Clinton, which enabled Republicans to gain control of the House for the first time in 40 years and of the Senate for the first time in eight years. When her term ended she joined a newly launched high-tech company, later renamed RealNetworks; it became enormously successful, and by the end of the 1990s, on the strength of her RealNetworks stock, she had become a multimillionaire. She used her wealth to underwrite her campaign for election to the U.S. Senate, portraying herself as a business-savvy social liberal whose financial independence would enable her to remain impervious to the pressures of lobbyists and other special-interest groups. Popular in Washington State's urban centers and among union members, environmentalists, and Indian tribes, Cantwell captured a Senate seat with less than .09 percent more votes than the total cast for Gorton—the narrowest margin in any senatorial race in 2000. She subsequently found herself the target of sharp criticism, when a precipitous drop in the value of her RealNetworks stock left her with a huge campaign debt, and the Democratic Party and various politicians (who themselves had received contributions from special-interest groups) raised money to help pay it off. Described as "an intelligent, hard-working politician" by the *Economist* (April 28, 2001), she has concentrated on efforts to improve Washington State's economy as well as measures to protect the environment; prevent attempts by corporations to manipulate the energy market and thus defraud governments, individuals, and businesses; reduce energy consumption; and make the U.S. more energy-independent.

The second of the five children of Paul and Rose Cantwell, Maria E. Cantwell was born on October 13, 1958 in Beach Grove, Indiana, and grew up in a working-class Irish neighborhood on the south side of Indianapolis. Her mother, an administrative assistant, described Maria to Richard Jerome for *People* (May 21, 2001) as "definitely the dominant personality among the children." Both of Cantwell's parents were active in local Democratic Party politics. Her father, a one-time construction worker, served as a Democratic county commissioner, a city councilman, and a state legislator. "Maria was the child he really connected with," her sister Carey told Richard Jerome. "She was Daddy's girl." At their father's bidding, every Election Day the Cantwell children would go door-to-door to urge people to vote. In her early years Maria Cantwell dreamed of becoming the first female astronaut. She attended a Roman Catholic grammar school and then Emmerich Manual High School, an Indianapolis public school. In 1976 she enrolled at Miami University, in Oxford, Ohio; she majored in public administration, taking courses in government organization and the formulation and implementation of public policy. She paid her tuition with loans, grants, and her earnings from temporary jobs. Among other extracurricular activities, she headed the university's Democratic club. When she received a B.A., in 1981, she became the first member of her family to graduate from college.

In 1982 Cantwell served as the deputy field director for Jerry Springer's failed bid for the governorship of Ohio. (Springer, who later became the host of the controversial television talk show that bears his name, had stepped down as mayor of Cincinnati to run for governor; he remains a major figure in Ohio Democratic circles.) Two years later she came to Washington State to aid another ultimately unsuccessful campaign—that of U.S. senator Alan Cranston of California for the Democratic presidential nomination. She decided to remain in Washington State and moved to the Seattle suburb of Mountlake Terrace. Soon afterward she organized a successful effort to win approval for the construction of a new library in that town. Concurrently, she launched a public-relations consulting firm, Cantwell & Associates; according to the Web site of WITI (Women in Technology International), she remained in the public-relations field for eight years. After she settled in Seattle, in the mid-1980s, she worked out of her home. At around that time, according to Richard Jerome, friends of hers suggested that she seek a seat in the Washington state Legislature. At first she ruled out taking such a step, because, as she told Jerome, she had long planned to marry and raise a family before she sought an elective post. But after some reflection, she threw her hat into the ring. By her own account, she knocked on innumerable doors to introduce herself to voters. On November 4, 1986 she was elected to the Washington House of Representatives from what was then District 44, which included parts of Seattle; at 28, she was the youngest woman ever elected to that body. She was reelected in 1988 and 1990. In a widely quoted comment made years later, Joe King, a former Washington State House Speaker, told an interviewer, "Maria is still the best legislator I ever served with. She understands every facet of the game of politics and legislating."

One of Cantwell's greatest accomplishments as a state legislator was the formulation and passage, in two parts, in 1990 and 1991, of Washington's Growth Management Act, which, according to her U.S. Senate Web site, she "shepherded through a marathon 65-day session" of the Legislature. The act spelled out, in the words of lawmakers, "common goals expressing the public's interest in the conservation and wise use" of land, and was designed to end "uncoordinated and unplanned growth, . . . [which] pose[d] a threat to the envi-

ronment, sustainable economic development, and the health, safety, and high quality of life enjoyed by residents of this state." On other fronts, she helped to create the Student Transportation Safety Task Force, the Transportation Improvement Board, and the Nursing Home Ombudsman Program. She also pushed effectively for measures to aid the biotechnology industry. In her second term as a state representative, she was named chairperson of the Trade and Economic Development Committee, an influential House panel. According to the WITI Web site, in a poll conducted during Cantwell's tenure in which Washingtonians ranked the 98 state representatives, she placed fourth.

In 1992 Cantwell declared her candidacy for the Democratic nomination in Washington State's First Congressional District, the site of many high-tech corporations, among them Microsoft and McCaw Cellular Communications, as well as such industry giants as Boeing and Nintendo. The district had been represented by Republicans for more than 40 years, the last eight by John Miller, who planned to retire. In the primary race, held in September 1992, Cantwell captured 52 percent of the vote, far more than any of her five opponents. (At that time what were known as blanket primary elections took place in Washington State. [The Supreme Court has since ruled blanket primaries unconstitutional.] In such primaries, all voters were permitted to cast ballots for any of the candidates competing for a particular office, regardless of party; the top vote-getter then faced, in a runoff election, whoever among those affiliated with other parties had gotten the most votes.) In the general election Cantwell faced the runner-up in the primary—Gary Nelson, a Republican who had served in the Washington Legislature for 20 years—as well as two minor-party candidates. During the ensuing campaign, in which she outspent Nelson by more than five to one, Cantwell reminded voters of Nelson's opposition to abortion and his conservative stances on other social issues. Describing herself as a pro-business Democrat, she emphasized her efforts on behalf of women and labor unions and called for health-care reforms and massive cuts in defense spending. Despite Nelson's efforts to sow doubts about her in voters' minds because of her youthfulness and out-of-state roots and her status as both a single woman and a renter (rather than a wife, mother, and homeowner), Cantwell won the general election, capturing 148,844 votes to Nelson's 118,897. She was sworn in to office on January 3, 1993.

With the help of Representative Thomas S. Foley of Washington State, who was then the Speaker of the House, Cantwell got a seat on the Public Works and Transportation Committee. She also became a member of the Democratic Steering and Policy Committee, a plum assignment for a newly elected congresswoman, and the Foreign Affairs and the Merchant Marine and Fisheries Committees. She supported the Brady Bill (a section of the 1994 Crime Bill, which, among other provisions, required a five-day waiting period for handgun purchases and background checks to determine whether a buyer has a criminal record) and the Family and Medical Leave Act (which required most employers whose payrolls include at least 50 people to approve 12 weeks of unpaid leave to workers under certain specified circumstances). She also backed President Bill Clinton's deficit-reduction plan but opposed the Clinton administration's push for the so-called clipper chip, which would have enabled the federal government to record private electronic communications. After nearly a year in Congress, Cantwell told Elaine S. Povich for the *Chicago Tribune* (November 28, 1993), "Sometimes you bump up against something and get disappointed. The bottom line is I'd like things to change more quickly than they are." The virtual absence of female legislators in positions of power also struck her. "I came from a state legislature where women chaired important committees," she told Lois Romano for the *Washington Post* (March 24, 1993).

According to the left-leaning, all-volunteer, Seattle-based *Washington Free Press* (October/November 1994, on-line), which endorsed her reelection, Cantwell "compiled a strong labor, civil liberties, and pro-choice record" but was "a little shaky" on environmental issues. Their opinion of her environmental record was a minority one, though. The League of Conservation Voters, for example, gave her a 100 percent rating based on her votes on environment-related legislation. In the 1994 general election, Cantwell's Republican opponent was Rick White, an attorney, who, like nearly all Republicans running for election or reelection to Congress that year, had signed the "Contract for America," in which each signatory promised to push for measures long advocated by Republicans, among them a huge increase in defense spending, a constitutional amendment mandating a balanced federal budget, tax cuts for individuals, and a decrease in the capital-gains tax, all within 100 days of taking office. White also opposed all forms of gun control and disapproved of most pro-abortion measures. On Election Day, November 8, 1994, Cantwell was among the many Democratic victims of the Republican sweep of Congress (Republicans won a majority of seats in both the House of Representatives and the U.S. Senate for the first time in four decades); she was defeated with 48.3 percent of the vote to White's 51.6 percent. "I went crazy," she told Jerome. "For three weeks I did nothing but get up, install software and surf the Web."

In 1995 Cantwell joined Progressive Networks (later renamed RealNetworks), a newly launched Seattle firm specializing in the then-novel technology of Internet-based audio and visual software, which enables people to hear music and watch movies via their computers. "It was like being pioneers in the first days of radio," she told Jerome. As RealNetworks' senior vice president of consumer products, according to the senator's Web site, she

helped create 1,000 new jobs in Washington State. The company quickly became enormously profitable. By late 1999 the estimated worth of Cantwell's RealNetworks stock had risen to about $40 million.

At about that time Cantwell made public her intention to seek the seat in the U.S. Senate held by the Slade Gorton, a Republican, who had represented Washington State in the Senate from 1981 to 1987 and since 1989. "I guess I really was motivated [to run] by the fact that I think the government doesn't move as fast as our world in the new economy is moving and does need to reinvent itself," Cantwell told Dana Greenlee in an undated interview for the WebTalkGuys Radio Show. In the September 19, 2000 senatorial primary, which included four Democrats, four Republicans, and one Libertarian, the winners were Cantwell, among the Democrats; Gorton, among the Republicans; and Jeff Jared, the Libertarian Party candidate.

During the ensuing battle to win votes, Gorton (whose ancestors founded the fish-products company Gorton's of Gloucester) reminded Washingtonians of his seniority in Congress, thus implying that he could help them far more than a first-term senator. He depicted Cantwell as a typical liberal who, as a U.S. representative, had voted to raise taxes, and, according to the Web site of the Annenberg Public Policy Center (APPC) of the University of Pennsylvania, he warned voters that she would "put state bureaucrats in charge of healthcare." For her part, Cantwell campaigned with the slogan "Your time for a change." In her previous campaigns for public office, she had accepted contributions from PACs (political action committees, through which corporations, trade unions, organizations, and other groups support political candidates financially), but in her bid for a Senate seat, she emphasized her commitment to finance reform. She asserted that because she was using her own money (some $10 million, including bank loans secured with her RealNetworks stock as collateral) to pay for her campaign, she would not be beholden to special interests; Gorton, by contrast, was getting a substantial portion of his funds from PACs linked to timber, mining, and energy companies, among others. Thirty years younger than Gorton, Cantwell also stressed her intimate familiarity with and knowledge of the high-tech industry, an increasingly important sector of Washington State's economy. In addition, she pointed to her efforts on behalf of organized labor, and she was backed by many unions. She also received the endorsements of environmental organizations and Indian tribes, groups that strongly opposed Gorton, and of various newspapers. One of them, the *Seattle Post-Intelligencer*, declared in an editorial (October 29, 2000, on-line), "She has an excellent grasp of the concerns of ordinary citizens. . . . As a multimillionaire high-tech executive, Cantwell is well qualified to carry out her promises to shape badly needed federal legislation on consumer cyberspace privacy and to facilitate urgently needed expansion of the digital economy to this state's depressed rural areas."

As the race between Cantwell and Gorton neared its end, it became increasingly close; indeed, Cantwell was not declared the winner until November 27, 2000, nearly three weeks after Election Day; her victory did not become official until the completion, on December 7, of a mandated machine recount. The recount showed Cantwell with a total of 1,199,437 votes (48.73 percent of the total), Gorton with 1,197,208 (48.64 percent), and Jared with 64,734 (2.63 percent). Thus, she defeated Gorton by only 2,229 votes, or less than .09 percent of the 2,461,379 votes cast. Moreover, she secured a majority of the votes in only five of Washington's 39 counties, but one of them was the most populous: King County, which encompasses Seattle and its suburbs and whose residents include one-third of the state's voters. (The other counties she won were Thurston, the site of the state's capital, Olympia; San Juan; Snohomish; and Jefferson.) When she was sworn in as a U.S. senator, on January 3, 2001, Cantwell became one of 13 women serving in the Senate, and Washington became the third state, after California and Maine, to have two female senators serving concurrently. (Washington's other senator is Patty Murray, a Democrat, who was elected to a third term in 2004.)

Within two months of Election Day, the value of Cantwell's RealNetworks stock had plummeted to less than $9 per share, down from a high of $93 a year earlier. The loss left Cantwell with a campaign debt of between $3 million and $4 million, far more than she could repay by herself. In addition to renegotiating a new loan, she began raising money through Democratic colleagues of hers, among them Senator Hillary Rodham Clinton of New York State and former president Clinton, each of whom hosted benefits held on her behalf. According to the *Almanac of American Politics* (2004, on-line), "Washington lobbyists" also came to her aid. Because she had made her independence from contributors and her dedication to campaign-finance reform a central theme of her campaign, Cantwell drew a great deal of negative publicity. The chairman of the Washington State Republican Party, Christopher Vance, for example, charged on the state GOP's Web site, "Cantwell spent the whole 2000 campaign bragging that she'd never be beholden to special interests. She trashed her opponent for being a tool of lobbyists and other special interests. Now she's relying on these very same groups to pay off her personal campaign debt. Her entire campaign was a lie." The *Seattle Times*, which had endorsed her, published an editorial (January 30, 2002, on-line) questioning the propriety of "enlist[ing] Bill Clinton to drum up donations," in light of his being "a morally compromised man, not only for his philandering with a woman who was not his wife, but by his last-minute issuing of presidential pardons to the family members of donors" (a reference to people who had either contributed toward his own campaigns

or helped to defray his personal legal bills); Cantwell, the editorial concluded, had approached "the wrong bank." As of April 11, 2005, almost four and a half years after the 2000 election, Cantwell's campaign committee remained $2.4 million in debt—the heaviest campaign liability of any sitting member of Congress, according to *CongressDaily* (September 15, 2005). (Fund-raising for her 2006 campaign, however, has been very successful, with Cantwell raising close to $5 million in the first nine months of 2005.) The controversy surrounding her fund-raising efforts notwithstanding, Cantwell pushed for the passage of the McCain-Feingold campaign-finance-reform bill (named for Senator John S. McCain of Arizona, a Republican, and Russ Feingold of Wisconsin, a Democrat); a weakened version of McCain and Feingold's original bill (proposed in 1996) became law in March 2002.

In the Senate, Cantwell currently serves on the Committee on Small Business and Entrepreneurship; the Committee on Indian Affairs; the Committee on Energy and Natural Resources and three of its subcommittees (Energy; Water and Power; and Public Lands and Forests); and the Committee on Science, Commerce, and Transportation and five of its subcommittees (Aviation; Disaster Prevention and Prediction; Fisheries and the Coast Guard; National Ocean Policy Study; and Trade, Tourism, and Economic Development). In the previous Congress, she served on all of those committees except the last named, and also on the Judiciary Committee and four of its subcommittees (Antitrust, Business Rights and Competition; Crime and Drugs; Immigration; Technology, Terrorism and Government Information).

Cantwell has been described as the Democratic point-person on electricity-grid reliability. She introduced the Electric Reliability Act of 2004, which would hold companies more accountable and reduce the threat of major power outages (such as the one that temporarily shut down much of the Northeast in the summer of 2003). She has also worked to ensure that consumers are protected from price gouging by sometimes unscrupulous energy companies. She was instrumental in defeating President George W. Bush's energy bill, which was widely referred to by opponents as the "Hooters and Polluters" Act. (One of the provisions of the bill, which included generous subsidies for large energy companies, called for taxpayer funding of a riverfront development in Louisiana that would feature a restaurant named Hooters, part of a popular chain famous for its buxom waitresses.) Cantwell and Senator Patti Murray co-sponsored an addition to the 2002 Farm Bill that allocated $94 million in emergency payments to Washington State's apple growers. She has traveled on trade missions to Mexico, helping to open the market for her state's potatoes and apples, as well as to Cuba, where she opened the market to Washington State peas. She has also helped promote Washington State wines to major buyers from other countries. Cantwell has introduced legislation to close a loophole in the regulations governing animal-feed production, thereby reducing the risk of bovine spongiform encephalopathy (also known as mad cow disease) to consumers. (In December 2003 a cow in Mabton, Washington, was found to have the disease.) Cantwell was responsible for both the Lewis and Clark National Historic Park Dedication Act and the Mount Rainier National Park Boundary Adjustment Act. In August 2005 President Bush signed into law a bill that Cantwell had introduced in the Senate with the goal of protecting part of the White Salmon River. The legislation names the river and one of its tributaries, Cascade Creek, as components of the National Wild and Scenic River System. As such, according to what is known as the Wild and Scenic Rivers Act, they "shall be preserved in free-flowing condition, and . . . they and their immediate environments shall be protected for the benefit and enjoyment of present and future generations."

Additionally, Cantwell, who is known for her willingness to work with Republicans on major issues, has sponsored or co-sponsored bills to reauthorize and revise the Renewable Energy Production Incentive program; fund the creation of so-called national digital school districts, in which schools would be made technologically up-to-date; broaden certain eligibility requirements for federal Pell Grants (in response to an attempt by the Bush administration to remove $1.3 billion from that federal student-loan program); and prevent identity theft and lessen the harm to victims of such theft. To date, none of those bills has become law. Cantwell also co-sponsored the Debbie Smith Act, which would fund training for hospital workers who attend to victims of sexual assault; introduce standardized evidence-collection kits to speed the processing of DNA evidence in rapes; and require states to complete analyses of DNA evidence within 10 days of receipt. (Currently, it takes government agencies an average of a year and a half to process DNA evidence and identify rapists.)

Cantwell often works 16-hour days. She shares a ranch house in Edmonds, Washington, with her mother, and also maintains an apartment in Washington, D.C. According to the *Almanac of American Politics*, she has "never shown much interest in an affluent lifestyle." As she promised during her campaign, she visits each Washington State county every year.

—K.E.D.

Suggested Reading: *Chicago Tribune* I p1+ Nov. 28, 1993, with photo; *Economist* Apr. 28, 2001; *New York Times* A p1+ Sep. 22, 2000; *People* p179+ May 21, 2001; *Seattle Post-Intelligencer* (on-line) Oct. 29, 2000; Senator Maria Cantwell's Web site; *Time* p42 Oct. 30, 2000; *Washington Post* A p12 Mar. 15, 2001; *Working Woman* p20+ Apr. 2001

Capa, Cornell

(CAP-ah)

Apr. 10, 1918– Photographer; founder and former executive director of the International Center of Photography

Address: c/o International Center of Photography, 1133 Ave. of the Americas, New York, NY 10036

Cornell Capa has been perhaps the single most important figure in achieving recognition for documentary photography as an art form. As he told Diana Loercher for the *Christian Science Monitor* (October 10, 1974), "No other graphic art form deals with reality like photographs do, a visual image with or without commentary that can inform man about himself. Through the commitment, courage, devotion required in eye-witness photography, we can bring back images we wouldn't otherwise of both political and social content." As a photographer, Capa used his camera not simply to capture images but also to focus attention on important issues, such as mental retardation, old age in America, poverty and politics in Latin America, and the campaigns of major U.S. political figures, including Adlai E. Stevenson, Barry Goldwater, John F. Kennedy, and Robert F. Kennedy. His 1967 book, *The Concerned Photographer*, offers descriptions of photographers who have aspired to go beyond recording events, intending for their photographs to serve as catalysts for change; collections of Capa's own photographs have been published to acclaim. The principle of "concerned photography" led Capa to found the International Center of Photography (ICP), which he served for 20 years as executive director. As Capa told Charles Hagen for the *New York Times* (May 27, 1993), "I don't like the gallery art of photography as I see it now. The photography I'm interested in is urgent. It's humanistic and concerned." Under Capa's leadership, the center has immortalized the works of documentary and commercial photographers from around the globe. It has also earned a reputation as one of the foremost photographic institutions, attracting more than 250,000 people to its programs each year.

Cornell Capa was born Cornell Friedmann on April 10, 1918 in Budapest, Hungary, into a Jewish, middle-class family. His parents, David and Julia Friedmann, owned a tailoring business. While Capa was growing up, his father inspired the vagabond lifestyle that Cornell and his older brother, Andre, would later embrace. "My mother did most of the work. Papa liked to play cards and travel. Mother didn't like that much. But the free, gypsy

Courtesy of Michael O'Neill

Cornell Capa

spirit of my brother and me came from Papa," Capa told Jack Robbins for the *New York Post* (September 30, 1974).

The person with the greatest influence on Capa, however, was his brother. In 1936 Cornell moved to Paris, France, where he served as a printer for Andre—who by then, under the name Robert Capa, had passed himself off as a rich American photojournalist. The ruse was successful, and Andre's photos began commanding higher fees, which had been his aim in changing his name; he continued to work under the name Robert Capa even after the hoax was uncovered. That same year, Cornell, who at the time was referred to as "le petit Capa," took the reins of his brother's Paris operation after Robert was assigned to document the Spanish Civil War. That assignment resulted in Robert's most famous photograph, "The Falling Soldier," which captured the image of a Spanish Loyalist fighter at the moment of death and is one of the most enduring of 20th-century war images; Robert's up-close-and-personal style serves as the archetype for the modern photojournalist. In 1937 the Capa brothers relocated to New York, where Robert shot photographs and Cornell worked in the darkroom, first at the now-defunct Pix photo agency and then at *Life* magazine.

Cornell Capa's first notable success came when his pictures of the 1939 New York World's Fair were published in the British magazine *Picture Post*. In 1940 he married a fellow Hungarian, Edith Schwartz; in the following year he became a naturalized U.S. citizen and adopted his brother's new last name as his own. Also in 1941 he served stateside as a member of the photo-intelligence unit in the U.S. Air Force, first as an aerial-photo inter-

preter and then as a public-relations photographer. In 1946, after the end of World War II, Capa joined *Life* as a staff photographer—three years after his brother had done so. The events he covered for the magazine over the following two decades ranged from a baby-crawling race to a Miss America contest, and from the folk painter Grandma Moses's 100th birthday celebration, in 1960, to the presidential campaigns of Adlai E. Stevenson and John F. Kennedy and Robert F. Kennedy's senatorial campaign. In a review of the book *Cornell Capa: Photographs*, containing pictures taken from 1946 to 1974, Nachman Spiegel wrote for the *Jerusalem Post* (May 21, 1993) about the appeal of Capa's work: "Part of his ability to engage the viewer must be attributed to his constant use of spontaneity. . . . This is the photo journalist's forte and what most distinguishes him from the portrait photographer." A classic example of Capa's work is "Harlem, 1949," a black-and-white photograph of the shoes of people lining a Harlem street curb as they await the funeral procession for the legendary dancer Bill "Bojangles" Robinson.

From 1950 until 1952, on assignment in London, England, Capa produced photo essays for *Life* depicting everyday scenes in that country, including shots of a private boys' school, soldiers of the Queen's Guard, and people in Hyde Park. Capa also made the first of several trips to Latin America in the mid-1950s, taking pictures that helped to illuminate such events and issues as the dethroning of Juan Perón in Argentina and the destruction of indigenous cultures by the modern world. He recalled his coverage of the 1956 murder of five missionaries by Auca Indians in Ecuador as his most memorable assignment. "I boarded a plane in New York in a white button-down shirt," Capa told *People* magazine (June 27, 1977), "and within 24 hours I was walking through the jungle, having buried the missionaries. Suddenly I touched my button-down collar and realized that I had gone back a thousand years in one day. I had lived an entire lifetime in just a few hours. And photography had allowed me to do it." The images from his travels, which lasted until the 1970s, produced three books, the most famous being *Farewell to Eden* (1964), his study of the Amahuaca tribe in the jungles of Peru.

On May 24, 1954 Capa resigned as a staff photographer at *Life*, following the tragic death of his brother, Robert, who, while on assignment in Indochina for the magazine, had stepped on a land mine. (Robert Capa was the first American correspondent to die in what would become the Vietnam War.) Werner Bischof, Robert's colleague and close friend, died on the same day, when his jeep plunged off a cliff and into a gorge in the Peruvian Andes. "On that awful day," Capa recalled for *People*, "I realized how a man can give a lifetime being a witness to great and historic events, but leave nothing in tangible form for the next generation. I could not let their work perish with them." At his late brother's request, while rejoining *Life* in the role of contributing photographer from 1955 until 1967, Capa joined Magnum Photos, an international photo agency co-founded in 1947 by Robert Capa and fellow photographers Henri Cartier-Bresson, George Rodger, William Vandivert, and David "Chim" Seymour. Magnum Photos was the first worldwide cooperative agency for photographers and is the world's preeminent agency employing documentary photographers; its members retain the rights to their images for future publications. After Seymour's death in the Suez War between Egypt and Israel in 1956, Capa assumed the role of president of Magnum Photos, holding the post until 1960. During his years at Magnum, he traveled to the Soviet Union and also covered the Six-Day War, but his most extensive projects focused on U.S. politicians, including Stevenson and Goldwater.

In 1966 Capa established the International Fund for Concerned Photography for the express purpose of preserving and honoring the work of photojournalists killed in action, including Robert Capa, Seymour, Bischof, and Dan Weiner. The fund acted as a floating museum, supporting documentary photography and mounting traveling exhibitions at various art institutions in New York and abroad. The following year Capa used $5,000 of his own money to fund and co-curate The Concerned Photographer, an exhibit at Riverside Museum, in Manhattan, featuring the images taken by Robert Capa, Leonard Freed, André Kertész, Bischof, Weiner, and Seymour. In describing the traits shared by those photographers, Capa told Jack Robbins, "It seemed to me that what united their work was their concern for mankind."

Capa put his camera down for good in 1974—the same year he founded the International Center of Photography, an outgrowth of the International Fund for Concerned Photography, whose mission was the same: to preserve and make public the works of documentary photographers. Under Capa's guidance the center has become one of the leading photographic institutions in the world, presenting over 450 exhibitions in its former location, the former Willard Straight mansion, on the Upper East Side of Manhattan, and at its current Midtown location, on West 43d Street; the center's 27,000-square-foot campus is located across the street. To date the center has showcased the work of more than 2,500 photographers and other artists in one-person and group exhibitions. It houses a collection of approximately 45,000 original photographic prints, representing 600 photographers, among them Robert Capa, Cartier-Bresson, Seymour, Roman Vishniac, Elliott Erwitt, and Harold Edgerton. In keeping with its roots, the museum has mounted thought-provoking exhibitions on topics such as Los Angeles street gangs and the U.S.-led war in Iraq. In the U.S. in 2003, the center held its first Triennial, which included contemporary art photographs and videos from around the world. ICP now incorporates conceptual art into its regular exhibits, which change four or five times a year.

In June 1994, at the age of 76, Capa retired after two decades as executive director of ICP. Willis "Buzz" Hartshorn, who had previously worked at the center as the deputy director for programs and director of exhibitions, was named his successor; he continues to hold the post. Capa, who currently lives in New York City, remains involved in operations at the center, where, as founding director emeritus, he still has an office. According to the center's on-line annual report, the staff totals 151, including interns and volunteers. Over the last several years, the International Center of Photography has expanded its involvement in art photography, staging several exhibitions that were considered provocative, including a Helmut Newton show in 2001 that featured highly sexual portraits of mostly naked women and a 2004 exhibit of photos taken by American guards at the Abu Ghraib prison in Iraq, the scene of abuse of prisoners by U.S. military personnel.

Capa's 1957 book *Retarded Children Can Be Helped* was the product of his pioneering study of mentally retarded children in 1954. His stirring photos documenting the work of missionaries in South America and the daily lives of Amahuaca Indians of the Amazon and the poor of El Salvador and Honduras have been included in three books: *Savage My Kinsman* (1961), *Farewell to Eden* (1964), and *Margin of Life* (1974). Capa immortalized the works of documentary photojournalists—many of whom were also Magnum agency members—in his books *The Concerned Photographer* (1968) and *The Concerned Photographer 2* (1972). In 1992 a retrospective collection of his work, *Cornell Capa: Photographs*, was published in the United States. Capa not only served as editor for his brother's book, *Children of War, Children of Peace* (1991), but also wrote an essay for *Robert Capa: Photographs* (1996), a collection of his brother's most dramatic war photographs, and the foreword to his brother's World War II memoir, *Slightly Out of Focus* (2001). His most recent book, *JFK for President: Photographs* (2004), is a photographic portrayal of John F. Kennedy's campaign for the presidency in 1960 and of the first 100 days of his administration.

More than 70 pictures from Capa's coverage of Kennedy's presidential campaign appeared in a 2004 exhibition at the International Center of Photography. Looking at Life, another show at the center that made its debut at the same time, included Robert Capa's D-Day photos among other pictures taken by *Life* staff photographers. In 2005 more than 160 photographs by Cornell and Robert Capa were featured at Tokyo's Fuji Art Museum in an exhibition entitled Capa Brothers and the World of the Child.

Despite his retirement, Capa remains one of the photographic community's most respected figures. His accolades have included the Honor Award (1975) from and honorary membership (1995) in the American Society of Magazine Photographers; the Joseph A. Sprague Lifetime Achievement

Award (1976); and the City of New York Mayor's Award of Honor for Arts and Culture (1978). He was also the recipient of the Distinguished Career in Photography Award from Friends in Photography (1995) and the Lifetime Achievement Award in Photography from the Aperture Foundation (1999). In 2004 he received the Visionary Award at the second annual Lucie Awards, which honors the greatest achievements in photography by legendary and emerging photographers. Each year the International Center of Photography presents an award named after its founder. But Capa seems content to downplay his impact on the medium of photography. In the preface to his book *Photographs*, Capa wrote, "I am not an artist, and I never intended to be one. I hope that I have made some good photographs, but what I really hope is that I have done some good photo stories with memorable images that make a point, and perhaps even make a difference."

Capa's wife, Edith Schwartz Capa, died on November 24, 2001 at the couple's Midtown Manhattan home. She had organized and maintained the negatives and archives of Capa and his brother, Robert. Cornell and Edith Capa had no children.
—B.M.

Suggested Reading: International Center of Photography Web site; *New York Post* p43 May 23, 1966, with photo, p33 Sep. 30, 1974, with photo; *New York Times* II p31 Nov. 14, 982, with photo, C p13+ May 27, 1993, with photo, C p1 Sep. 16, 1994; *People* p65+ June 27, 1977, with photos

Selected Books: *Retarded Children Can Be Helped*, 1957; *Savage My Kinsman*, 1961; *Farewell to Eden* (with Matthew Huxley), 1964; *The Concerned Photographer*, 1968; *The Concerned Photographer 2*, 1972; *Margin of Life*, 1974; *Capa & Capa: Brothers in Photography*, 1990; *Cornell Capa: Photographs*, 1992; *Cornell Capa*, 2002; *Robert Capa, Obra Fotografica*, 2002; *JFK for President: Photographs*, 2004; as editor—*Children of War, Children of Peace* (by Robert Capa), 1991

Cave, Nick

Sep. 22, 1957– Singer; songwriter

Address: c/o Mute Records, 429 Harrow Rd., London W10 4RE, England

To the casual listener, Nick Cave's musical career might seem to represent a journey from the profane to the sacred, but closer examination reveals that his songs have long balanced images of violence with lyrics that celebrate a firm spiritual belief. In the late 1970s, during the anarchistic postpunk era, Cave co-founded the gothic rock group Birthday Party, whose songs combined bleak themes with a wildly dissonant sound. After that group disbanded, in the early 1980s, Cave formed the Bad Seeds, the act with which he continues to perform and record. By the following decade Cave had become as well known for his piano ballads and spiritual lyrics as he was for his raucous songs about violence and chaos; for example, he followed *Murder Ballads* (1996), a collection of songs about senseless killings, with *The Boatman's Call* (1997), an album of tender love songs with religious overtones. Cave is known for his booming baritone voice, tall, thin frame, pale skin, and dark clothing. Karen Schoemer wrote for the *New York Times* (July 31, 1992), "In the wide-screen, supersonic, Technicolor world of rock-and-roll, Nick Cave is film noir. His grim persona comes complete with a curl of cigarette smoke; his vision is bleak and whisky-soaked, and his music screeches and crashes like an unclean getaway." Writing for the *All Music Guide* (on-line), in a review of the 2001 album *And No More Shall We Part*, Thom Jurek

Patrick Riviere/Getty Images

provided a later assessment of Cave's career and persona: "Lyrically, and as a vocalist, Cave has undergone a startling, profound metamorphosis. Gone is the angry, humorous cynic whose venom and bile touched even his lighter moments. His deep taunting ambivalence about Jesus Christ and Christianity in general is gone, vanished into a maturity that ponders spiritual things contemplatively."

Nicholas Edward Cave was born on September 22, 1957 in the small Australian town of Warracknabeal, the third of four children; his father was a schoolteacher and his mother a librarian. Cave was a rambunctious youth who frequently got into trouble and began drinking alcohol regularly at the age of 12. As a young man he often found himself in facilities for juvenile delinquents, usually for the use of alcohol and other drugs. He and his friends "were the archetypal bored Australian teenagers with nothing to do but get drunk and take drugs and smash phone booths," he told Ben Thompson for the London *Independent* (April 17, 1994). His behavior was not, however, as wild as some have reported, according to John Nelson, one of Cave's high-school teachers. "People wonder if he was shooting up behind the shelter shed at school. That's not true," Nelson told the Australia *Sunday Herald* (July 15, 1990). "He was just a run of the mill boy with exceptional creative talent." He even sang in a choir and attended Sunday school, "attracted not so much by religious zeal as by the wild stories in the Bible," as Lindsay Baker reported in the London *Guardian* (February 1, 2003).

When Cave was 19 years old, his father was killed in a car accident. Cave later recalled that the tragedy froze his emotional development. "The things I love, the things I hate, the things that really affect me—I felt those things forming, right down to the type of music and literature I liked," Cave told Lindsay Baker. "I don't feel that they've progressed particularly since that time, and that was pretty much the time my father died, and I think that's not coincidental." Baker quoted Cave as writing that "a great gaping hole was blasted out of my world" by the death of his father, and that "the way I learned to fill this hole, this void, was to write." Cave also taught himself the basics of playing the piano, so that he could compose simple melodies for his words. (He has played piano on recordings made with the Bad Seeds.)

While the sound of Cave's songs from the late 1970s owed much to the aggressive edge of the punk and postpunk groups of the period, their lyrics showed the influences of such singer/songwriters as Bob Dylan, Johnny Cash, and Leonard Cohen, whose songs were narratives about murder and other actions connected with dark aspects of human nature. Cave was also influenced by the British rock musician Alex Harvey; when he was young, Cave told John Williamson for the Glasgow *Herald* (April 28, 1992), he was "hooked on [Harvey's] interpretive skills as a singer. He was also a genuinely demented singer and person. An utter hero."

While in high school Cave had met Mick Harvey, who played guitar, bass, drums and piano; with the bassist Tracy Pew and the drummer Phil Calvert, the two teens formed a band, the Boys Next Door, which played a loud, raucous style of rock music. After performing several shows and signing with an independent Australian record label, the group added the guitarist and songwriter Rowland S. Howard to their ranks and recorded an album, *Door, Door,* which they later felt was too pop-oriented. In the belief that they had achieved as much success as was possible in Australia, they changed their name to the Birthday Party and moved to London, England, where they felt their music could be heard more widely.

After the group changed their name, their sound moved in a decidedly dark direction, turning toward the chaos of the postpunk landscape that was popular at the time and becoming known for its atonal quality and discordant chord progressions. Cave's songs tended to have violent lyrics, such as, "Last night she kissed me / but then death was upon her." Many critics did not know what to make of the Birthday Party, and reviews of their two albums, *Prayers on Fire* (1981) and *Junkyard* (1982), consisted largely of puzzlement and disgust. "The Birthday Party's music was practically unlistenable," Karen Schoemer later wrote for the *New York Times* (June 24, 1990). "The guitars crackled and spat like a live wire, and Mr. Cave unleashed an animalistic roar that had little to do with actual singing." The band's live performances were intended to unsettle audiences; in an interview with Jim Sullivan for the *Boston Globe* (February 8, 1989), Cave said, "When we went on stage it was to become something quite frightening for people, like a car accident, some sort of terrible event that people were drawn towards and they could look on and cross themselves and look away. We wanted to be completely, irresponsibly violent towards the audience."

The Birthday Party broke up because of disagreements between Cave and Howard over who would write the group's songs and because, as Cave later told Ben Thompson, "When we finally started to get acclaim, we really didn't know how to respond to it." Cave and Harvey then enlisted the bassist Barry Adamson, from the group Magazine, and the guitarist Blixa Bargeld, from the influential industrial band Einsturzende Neubauten, to form the Bad Seeds. The group released their first album, *From Her to Eternity,* on Mute Records in 1984. While proving to be somewhat difficult for average listeners to digest, as the Birthday Party's music had been, *From Her to Eternity* nonetheless marked for Cave a step toward a more melodic sound. Ned Raggett wrote in a review for the *All Music Guide,* "*From Her to Eternity* is crammed with any number of doom-laden songs, with Cave the understandable center of attention, his commanding vocals turning the blues and rural music into theatrical exhibitionism unmatched since Jim Morrison stalked stages." The album featured two cover songs that demonstrated Cave's interest in a more lyrically driven approach to music: Leonard Cohen's "Avalanche" and "In the Ghetto," a song made famous by Elvis Presley. Cave's interest in Presley and the American South informed the band's second album, *The Firstborn Is Dead* (1985). The album's title was a reference to Presley's still-born twin brother, Jesse Garon Presley, who was the focus of the record's central track, "Tupelo." The South provided the setting for Cave's first (and to date only) novel, *And the Ass Saw the Angel*, written over the course of the 1980s and published in 1989. The novel centers on Euchrid Eucrow, a mute and social outcast who is accused of murdering a young prostitute. The book is filled with the brutal violence and religious imagery that had come to permeate Cave's music.

Meanwhile, in 1988, Cave and the Bad Seeds released *Tender Prey*, an album that featured driving rhythms and showcased Cave's maturing capabilities as a storyteller, particularly on the opening track, "The Mercy Seat." A song written from the point of view of a death-row inmate who is being led to the electric chair, "The Mercy Seat" was almost unanimously hailed by critics as a masterpiece of narrative songwriting. (In 2000 one of Cave's heroes, Johnny Cash, covered "The Mercy Seat" on his album *American III: Solitary Man*.)

In the same year that *Tender Prey* appeared, Cave was arrested in London for possession of heroin. Knowing that a prison sentence was likely, in light of his history of drug arrests, he sought rehabilitation to show the courts that he wanted to end his addiction to the drug. By 1990 Cave had given up drugs, gotten married, fathered a child, and moved to São Paulo, Brazil. He told Georgina Safe for the *Weekend Australian* (March 3, 2001), explaining his change of lifestyle, "I looked around at everybody else and I looked around at my lifestyle and I knew I had a certain amount of time and it was all going to go horribly wrong." Cave's time in Brazil resulted in *The Good Son* (1990), a Bad Seeds album, whose tracks—such as "The Weeping Song"—balanced Cave's penchant for telling stories in his lyrics with the listenable quality of pop music. "We wanted to do a very sad, very beautiful album," Cave told Bill Reynolds for the *Toronto Star* (September 25, 1990). "We'd just [spent] some time in Brazil before we actually decided to record, and I thought it was the most incredible place that I've ever been to. Sao Paulo itself is such a big, dirty, nasty city, very inspiring." Karen Schoemer wrote for the *New York Times* (June 24, 1990), "The change from [Cave's] early work is marked. His ferocious, wild-eyed howls and garbled groans have become a smooth, rich croon." While *The Good Son* featured a more accessible sound than his previous efforts, Cave insisted that its stories and themes were not a departure from his previous work. He told Bill Reynolds, "It's not a shift in my fundamental ideas about things, or my relationship with the world."

The album *Henry's Dream* (1992) represented a return to a more aggressive sound, coupling stories about murderers, convicts, and drifters with love songs such as "Straight to You." *Let Love In* (1994) continued in that vein, mixing songs such as "Jangling Jack," about a senseless killing, with the tender "Nobody's Baby Now," a song that Cave considers to be his first unironic love song. *Let Love In* continued Cave's streak of critical successes.

Whereas Cave's romantic ballads, like his harsh stories of violent death, had previously been presented as fictional narratives, the lyrics on *Let Love In* were intensely personal. He later told Elysa Gardner for the *Los Angeles Times* (March 24, 1996), "My state of mind was quite bad at that time. And the songs I was writing reflected that. But I wanted to push that approach to one side and write a record where I didn't have any emotional attachment—a series of songs about invented characters." That record, *Murder Ballads*, would prove to be Cave's most controversial. The album fully embraced the dark side of Cave's writing, combining detailed stories of brutal murders with a melodic, catchy musical backing. Many reviewers of *Murder Ballads*, searching for a moral or message in the songs' grim tales, responded in disgust at the seeming lack of either. Other critics, however, praised Cave's storytelling. Parry Gettelman, for example, wrote for the *Orlando Sentinel* (March 22, 1996), "Nick Cave has never made a grimmer album—or one more beautiful. Cave's 10 somber melodies have an epic grandeur. . . . *Murder Ballads* is not for the faint of heart, but as a story teller, Cave has never been more masterful."

Cave followed *Murder Ballads* with *The Boatman's Call* (1997), an album that, composed of love songs infused with religious imagery, was the polar opposite of its predecessor. *The Boatman's Call* has proved to be Cave's best-reviewed album to date. Matt Diehl, writing for *Rolling Stone* (March 20, 1997), called it "Cave's most romantic and positive work yet, doing away with his tortured-goth image. He has almost completely stripped his lyrics of the literary excess that has held him back before, resulting in narratives that are more emotionally direct. All is not sweetness and light, however, as his twisted worldview is still clear in the first lines of the opening track, 'Into My Arms.'" In an interview with Leigh Paatsch for the Queensland, Australia, *Courier Mail* (March 6, 1997), Cave said about that song, "I do remember writing that opening line 'I don't believe in an interventionist God' and thinking that it was going to be difficult to get away with it. But I just did it anyway." In an interview about the album, the Bad Seeds' longtime guitarist, Blixa Bargeld, told Louise Gray for the London *Guardian* (January 18, 1997) that the material explored on *The Boatman's Call* did not actually represent a great divergence from Cave's earlier work. "The Birthday Party had an obvious strain of deep human feeling; you could probably call it romantic in an 18th-century sense," he told Gray. "It was never a pose, never empty; there was this deep element, this aesthetic quality. *The Boatman's Call* shares this."

The Boatman's Call represented for Cave a culmination of many aspects of his career, bringing together the different themes of his writing. He told Richard Jinman for the *Australian* (January 7, 1997), "I think this is a record I've always wanted to make. . . . It's a record of personal songs rather than fictitious narratives—a place I've been heading for a long time. I don't really know where to go after this." The latter statement was perhaps not made lightly, as it would be four years before he released another album. Cave found his personal life changing once more; following a divorce, he had gotten remarried, to the model Susie Bick, moved to London, and fathered twins. The happiness he found in his personal life apparently did not provide him with musical inspiration; for the first time since his career had begun, more than a year passed without his releasing a new album. He told John Dingwall for the *Daily Record* (April 27, 2001), "After doing *The Boatman's Call*, I hit a brick wall, fell into some kind of creative slump." To inspire himself to write, Cave rented an office near his house and began keeping regular work hours there, from 9 a.m. to 5 p.m. That move was emblematic of a new image he was presenting, that of a disciplined family man, which was a surprise to many—fans and detractors alike—who had expected him to succumb to a drug addiction 20 years earlier. As for his new schedule, Cave told John Dingwall, "The way that I used to write songs, which was to have a pad or something and to write down a line here and a line there, it wasn't working anymore, so I had to really apply myself and do it as a job really."

Cave's newfound peace ultimately manifested itself in his music. As he told Georgina Safe, "I do find, obliquely, a cruel aspect to the world, it's just there. But I don't need to document it anymore, I'm not particularly concerned with that." In 2001 Cave released *And No More Shall We Part*, a collection of spiritual love songs that was even softer in tone and more introspective than *The Boatman's Call*. He told Sean O'Hagan for the London *Observer* (March 18, 2001), "As you get older, rock and roll has the potential to be a really embarrassing, even humiliating, way to make a living. I really think the music I make now is adult music. There isn't any other word for it. And I really feel that the music I made when I was young is very different. It's a place I can't go back to, even if I wanted to, which I don't. I guess I just feel differently towards the world these days. I think it's called maturity."

Cave followed with *Nocturama,* an uneven collection of songs whose slapdash quality was intended partially as a response to his most recent work, as Cave explained to Thomas Bartlett for *Salon* (November 18, 2004, on-line): "*Boatman's Call* is a hugely important record. The two records after that are living very much under its shadow. *Nocturama* was a record that was supposed to be made quickly in every possible way. Write the lyrics fast, write the music fast, record it quickly. Everything was done in a casual way—the cover, even the title. And that was because we felt a need to get away from the solemnity of [*And No More Shall We Part*]. . . . Everything we do seems to come from a need to remedy certain things that happened on the last record." *Nocturama* was widely panned by critics.

The period after the release of *Nocturama* saw a significant change in the lineup of the Bad Seeds. Bargeld left the band, finding that his musical interests no longer mirrored Cave's. At the same time, the violinist Warren Ellis, who also plays regularly with the Australian group the Dirty Three, was becoming more of a presence in Cave's music. Cave had collaborated with Ellis since the mid-1990s, when Ellis's distinctive style of playing had begun to add a new flavor to the Bad Seeds' sound. In 2004 the new lineup of the Bad Seeds put out a double album, *Abbatoir Blues/The Lyre of Orpheus*. The collection of songs was widely considered to be Cave's first work of note since *The Boatman's Call*. Thom Jurek, writing for *All Music Guide*, called it "a true high point in a long career that is ever looking forward."

Cave lives in London with his wife and twin children; his two other children live in Australia. He told John Dingwall in 2001, "It's a good period. Things are going really well. I have a whole brood of beautiful children. I'm very much in love with my wife, I'm working well and these are really the things that are most important to me. I even have a small collection of friends."

—R.E.

Suggested Reading: *Boston Globe* Arts & Film p70 Feb. 8, 1989; (London) *Guardian* Weekend Pages p56 Feb. 1, 2003; (London) *Independent* Sunday Review Page p25 Apr. 19, 1994; *Los Angeles Times* p70 Mar. 24, 1996; *New York Times* II p25 June 24, 1990; *Scottish Daily Record & Sunday Mail* Features p8+ Apr. 27, 2001

Selected Recordings: *From Her to Eternity*, 1984; *The Firstborn Is Dead*, 1985; *Tender Prey*, 1988; *The Good Son*, 1990; *Henry's Dream*, 1992; *Let Love In*, 1994; *Murder Ballads*, 1996; *The Boatman's Call*, 1997; *And No More Shall We Part*, 2001; *Nocturama*, 2003; *Abbatoir Blues/The Lyre of Orpheus*, 2004

Celmins, Vija

(SELL-mins, VEE-ya)

Oct. 25, 1939– Artist

Address: c/o McKee Gallery, 745 Fifth Ave., New York, NY 10151

"Think of Vija Celmins and you think of immense space and an almost compulsive intricacy at once," Cherry Smyth wrote for *Art Monthly* (September 1999). "You think of contemplation, of the emptiness of mind and then of myriad systems of thought." Celmins, a New York–based, Latvian-born painter, printmaker, and draftswoman, has been an important contributor to the American art

Vija Celmins

scene since the mid-1960s. Throughout her more than 30-year career, Celmins has repeatedly drawn inspiration from everyday objects, photographs of war, and images of nature. The last-named have sparked her best-known creations: working from photographs, Celmins uses meticulous brush or pencil strokes to create detailed expanses of ocean waves, desert sands, and night skies. Her horizonless sea, land, and skyscapes evoke thoughts of infinity while also addressing the themes of desolation, loss, search, and transcendence. "The beauty and power of Celmins' art," Mary Abbe wrote in the Minneapolis *Star-Tribune* (June 10, 1993), "is in her ability to make much of little—to find an infinity of time, space and loneliness in a field of sand." While Celmins belongs to the generation of artists that includes the West Coast pop artist Edward Ruscha, the photorealist Chuck Close, and the abstractionist Brice Marden, her work defies easy categorization or placement within any particular art movement. Whereas other artists are preoccupied with expressing feeling or emotion through their work, or with attempting to portray people, places, and things within certain contexts, Celmins's primary interest lies in the formal and conceptual process of rendering the three-dimensional world onto a two-dimensional surface. "Her work does not fall in with any movement or trend, and yet it manages to succeed by all the standards of painting—abstract, realist and formal," Susan Morgan wrote for the *Los Angeles Times* (December 12, 1993). "What is essential in Celmins' work is essential to art itself: She is able to translate observation through the hand and produce a stunning visual record."

Vija Celmins was born in Riga, the capital of Latvia, on October 25, 1939, less than two months after England, France, Australia, and New Zealand had declared war on Nazi Germany, signaling the start of World War II. As part of a nonaggression pact signed the same year by Germany and what was then the Soviet Union, whereby the two governments divided the Baltic States into "spheres of influence," Latvia fell under Soviet jurisdiction. Within months of the signing of the pact, the Soviet army invaded the country, and by 1940 Latvia, Lithuania, and Estonia were declared republics of the USSR. Conditions under the Soviet occupation were grim: according to one estimate, 35,000 Latvians were killed, deported, or fled the country. In 1941 Germany invaded the Soviet Union and subsequently occupied Latvia. When the USSR began to reclaim the country as its own in 1944, many people, including the five-year-old Celmins, her parents, and her older sister, fled to Germany, where the Celmins family spent four years in a Latvian refugee community in Esslingen. There, as Susan Morgan reported, Celmins often played hooky from school, preferring to search for treasures at sites of recent bombings. "I generally think of my childhood as being full of excitement and magic, and terror, too—bombs, fires, fear, escape—very eventful," the *Los Angeles Times* (December 12, 1993) quoted her as saying. "It wasn't till I was 10 years old and living in the United States that I realized living with these images was not everyone's experience."

In 1948, with the help of a U.S.-based refugee-assistance organization called Church World Service, Celmins and her family resettled in the U.S. For four months they lived in a hotel in the New York City borough of Manhattan. Celmins's treasure-hunting continued in New York; one day she discovered stacks of comic books selling for two cents each outside a shop, and she persuaded her father to buy some of them for her. "I couldn't read them but how I loved them, loved them," Celmins recalled to Morgan. "I thought that comic books were one of the great things that came with living in America." Later in 1948 her family settled in Indianapolis, Indiana. "It was very hard for my parents," Celmins said to Morgan. "They were in their 40s and didn't speak English, but they were extremely hopeful about America. I didn't know anything, I just went outside and played—I was a great player."

When Celmins began her schooling in the U.S., at age nine, she herself did not speak English. As a result she spent much of her time in class drawing; she continued to draw and paint throughout her school years. Her art classes sometimes took trips to museums in Chicago and New York, where she encountered the work of abstract expressionists, who experimented in their work with uses of form and color. After graduating from high school, Celmins spent five years studying at the John Herron School of Art, in Indianapolis, graduating with a B.F.A. degree in 1962. The year before she graduated, she spent a summer participating in Yale University's summer session in Norfolk, Connecticut, through a fellowship. It was there that she decided to become a painter; as she recalled to Susan Morgan, "It was an amazing time for me, a real eye-opener. I met talented, competitive people"—among them Chuck Close and Brice Marden—"and I realized that painting was something that I could do for my whole life."

In 1962 Celmins, having won a scholarship to pursue graduate studies at the University of California (UC), moved to Los Angeles, where she would spend the next 18 years. Because the university did not provide its graduate students with work spaces, Celmins rented a storefront studio in the city's Venice Beach area. After graduating, with an M.F.A. degree, in 1965, Celmins spent a year teaching painting and drawing at the University of California's Los Angeles campus. Between 1967 and 1972 she taught at UC Irvine, and during 1976 and 1977 she taught at the California Institute of the Arts in Valencia. By the time Celmins moved to California, she had rejected abstract expressionism and other influences of the New York art scene. She instead wanted to let her subject matter itself, rather than any school of thought, dictate the content of her work. To that end she painted everyday objects she found in her studio—for example, an electric heater, a television, and a gun. She attached no emotional, political, or symbolic meaning to the objects she painted, but saw them simply as material entities existing in time and space. Celmins made the process of observing and depicting the three-dimensional her only concern; she concentrated on looking at objects and rendering those objects onto canvas. "I came up with a lot of rules and tried to break them in my own way," Celmins explained to Morgan. "I wanted to find a way of painting that would be more authentic to me. . . . I started all over, really looking at everything. " In addition to the still-life oil paintings she created during her early years in California, she painted enormous images of hand-held objects, such as gently worn pink erasers and a tortoiseshell comb. Celmins next began to create works in layers of gray paint, based on photographs from World War II; many of the photos were of military planes and bombing sites. Critics have commented that these works hark back to the terrifying days of her childhood, yet keep that terror at a distance. One piece, for example, depicts a television tuned to an image of a World War II bomber plane breaking apart in mid-air. "This is an art in which hurts, where present, are never paraded . . . ," the art critic John Russell wrote for a *New York Times* review (July 27, 1980) of Celmins's 1980 solo exhibition at the Hudson River Museum, in Yonkers, New York. "But in these paintings they come to us at one or more removes, as if in an old newsreel that is not quite in focus and is being run at slightly the wrong speed . . . dread speaks in a whisper."

In the late 1960s and early 1970s, Celmins began spending time observing the desert landscapes of California, northern Arizona, and New Mexico. She subsequently renounced painting, color, and form in favor of making charcoal and graphite drawings from photographs of nature. The photographs from which she worked, which she usually took herself, showed seemingly infinite expanses of ocean waves, desert sands, and starry skies. From one photograph, Celmins would create several prints, with varying degrees of density, tone, distance, and scale, each comprising a vast pattern of marks. Her drawings did not emphasize the traditional visual elements of line, shape, color, form, and texture, but focused almost exclusively on use of of space. Christopher Knight described her approach in a *Los Angeles Times* review of a 1993 exhibition (December 21, 1993): "In her drawings . . . Celmins fuses the surface of the perceivable world with the surface of a piece of paper or cloth. The result is a conceptual space of quiet tension and peculiar vastness, in which surface membranes are an ideal vehicle for journeys into profound depth." "I wanted to purge myself of style," Celmins told Morgan. "I had given up on color. I had given up on gestures and strokes. All I had left to work with was the image, so I had to use the image to create a different kind of space."

Celmins showed her work for the first time in a 1969 exhibition at the Riko Mizuno Gallery, one of Los Angeles's preeminent showrooms for new artists; the show consisted of graphite drawings of oceans and the moon. Soon thereafter she gained public attention through her association with the group known as the California Light and Space artists; these individuals, who also included James Turrell and Doug Wheeler, were known for their minimalist approach to art as well as their use of the natural environment to explore the elements of light and space.

Celmins held her first East Coast solo exhibition in the summer of 1980. The show, mounted at the Hudson River Museum and then the Corcoran Gallery, in Washington, D.C. consisted of paintings, drawings, and constructions created between 1964 and 1977, including still lifes, sculptures, World War II–inspired paintings, and nature prints. Celmins's work, particularly the prints, met with rave reviews. John Russell of the *New York Times* (July 27, 1980), remarking on the different media and styles presented in the show, wrote, "What holds these apparently disparate groups of work together is a shared intensity, a shared awareness of what can still be done in art, and an elemental will to do well." Paul Richard, in the *Washington Post* (September 25, 1980), noted that "in these astonishingly meticulous drawings, in the patience of their making, [there is] something close to prayer." He also wrote, "These are not works about art theory. Anyone who's spent hours in observing sunsets, grazing deer, or wind moving on water, has sensed within such sights a beauty beyond art. That nonhuman beauty is the subject of these shows."

In 1981 Celmins moved to New York City. She told Susan Morgan that she had felt too isolated in Los Angeles: "New York was more of a community, and I could be in touch with more painters. So many people there look at art, I found it more hopeful." During the 1980s Celmins exhibited her work only twice, in 1983 and 1988; both shows were held at the McKee Gallery, in Manhattan. Celmins, however, was not idle during this period: she had begun to work with oil and canvas again, using the same images of sea, land, and sky as her subjects. The artist exhibited her new work for the first time in 1992, again at the McKee Gallery. The centerpiece of the show consisted of five paintings of the night sky. There were subtle yet profound differences among the pieces: one, for example, was suffused with a translucent gray haze, while another was merely a series of flat gray and white dots covering a black matte canvas, and a third depicted a black sky with glowing stars. As Roberta Smith wrote for the *New York Times* (March 6, 1992), "One feels that every molecule of Ms. Celmins's painted surface has been attended to. Her images are more built than rendered, her surfaces more condensed, or rubbed down, than painted, and it is this sense of obdurate physicality that gives her art its power."

From 1992 to 1994 a retrospective of Celmins's work, organized by the Institute of Contemporary Art in Philadelphia, Pennsylvania, traveled to some of the country's most important galleries and museums, including the Walker Art Center in Minneapolis, Minnesota, the Whitney Museum of Art, in Manhattan, and the Museum of Contemporary Art in Los Angeles. One of the works on display, entitled *To Fix the Image in Memory*, consisted of 11 bronze and acrylic "rocks" she had created in the years 1977 to 1982. The pieces had been modeled on 11 real rocks she had collected. The finished works of art were virtually indistinguishable from the originals, and most viewers could not tell the real rocks from the copies. Celmins said the piece was meant to challenge viewers. As she explained to Mary Abbe, "The point is not to fool the eye, but to open it up. This is an instigation to look, to open up your eyes and look and look more. It's a piece that says, 'Looking is one of the answers.' . . . It's not some sort of trick. When you see that it is invented, you should get a little spark of joy and wonder." The retrospective brought Celmins once more to the attention of the art world, and was subsequently featured on the covers of *Artforum* and *Art in America*. In 1996 and 1997 the artist's work traveled for the first time to Europe, where it was exhibited at the Institute of Contemporary Art, in London, England, the Museo Nacional de Arte Reina Sofia, in Madrid, Spain, and the Museum für Moderne Kunst, in Frankfurt, Germany.

Celmins's 2001 exhibit of new work at the McKee Gallery featured prints and oil paintings, among them two images of spiderwebs, the artist's first new subject matter in years. The web paintings consisted of close-up views of spiderwebs, rendered in varying shades of gray paint with loose strokes. Some critics noted that the presence of the artist could be felt more in these works than in her previous ones; as Carol Kino wrote for *Art in America* (December 1, 2001), "In place of Celmins's usual seamlessly finished surfaces—made by finely sanding each carefully applied layer of paint—all the paintings here combine smoothly finished areas with passages in which the brushwork or even the canvas or linen ground is evident." "Celmins' spiderwebs amount to self-portraying symbols of her spirit as an artist," Peter Schjeldahl wrote for the *New Yorker* (June 4, 2001). "Embedding ghostly gray lines in dirty black grounds, they pay tribute to creatures that, like painters, toil in two dimensions. That she paints them from reproduced photographs minimizes any sentimental guff about nature's splendor. She divorces the subject from experience, then returns it to experience as painting." From October 15 to December 29, 2002, an exhibit titled The Prints of Vija Celmins appeared at the Metropolitan Museum of Art, in New York. The following year her work was featured in a show at the Mori Art Museum, in Tokyo, Japan, and she is one of the artists to have work displayed in The Undiscovered Country, a show at the UCLA Hammer Museum, in Los Angeles, which ran from October 3, 2004 to January 16, 2005. In October 2005 the Museum of Modern Art added to its small collection of works by Celmins 18 pieces donated by the Los Angeles real-estate developer Edward R. Broida. Noteworthy among the three paintings, three sculptures, eight drawings, and four prints are her illustration from the 1960s of a gun being discharged and a spiderweb painting executed in 2002.

Celmins has received fellowships from the National Endowment for the Arts, the Guggenheim Foundation, and the MacArthur Foundation. Her work has been featured in retrospectives at the Whitney Museum of American Art and the Metropolitan Museum of Art, both in New York City, and at the Museum of Contemporary Art in Los Angeles; it is also in the permanent collections of the Art Institute of Chicago, the National Gallery of Art in Washington, D.C., the Walker Art Center, in Minneapolis, Minnesota, and the Whitney, the Metropolitan, and the Museum of Modern Art, in New York.

Throughout her career, Celmins has consistently shunned the limelight, preferring to work privately at her art. Her concern with technical perfection—which has been called an obsession—has resulted in a small output of work, with one painting taking as long as a year to complete. That dedication to the work of making art has made her, in the words of one critic, an artist's artist. "Celmins's images are both homeless and universal," Adrian Searle wrote for the London *Guardian* (November 12, 1996). "She has mapped the beyond with the means closest to hand—pencil and paper, paint and canvas. How often we forget, these days, that making art is still the work of the hand and the eye.

The long and lonesome business, day after day in the studio, rarely impinges on our consciousness as we rush after the next big thing."

—H.T.

Suggested Reading: *Art in America* p102+ Oct. 1993, with photo; *Art Monthly* p40+ Sep. 1999; *Los Angeles Times* Calendar p4+ Dec. 12, 1993, with photos; *New Yorker* p85+ June 4, 2001; *New York Times* C p19+ Sep. 17, 1993, with photo; Minneapolis *Star Tribune* E p1 + June 10, 1993, with photo

starbulletin.com

Chapman, Duane

Feb. 2, 1952– Bounty hunter

Address: P.O. Box 22537, Honolulu, HI 96823

In June 2003 the dramatic capture in Mexico of Andrew Luster, a fugitive rapist and heir to the Max Factor cosmetics fortune, was reported widely in the media. Most accounts mentioned a shadowy American bounty hunter who had tracked down and apprehended Luster in order to bring him to justice. That captor was Duane "Dog" Chapman, a reformed ex-convict who calls himself the "greatest bounty hunter in the world." In his singular career on the fringes of law enforcement, Chapman has claimed, he has captured 6,000 fugitives, mostly so-called bail jumpers—those indicted for felonies (serious crimes including rape, murder, drug offenses, and robbery) who flee either before their cases go to trial or during their trials. Chapman, who for the last two television seasons has been the

subject of the A&E reality series *Dog the Bounty Hunter*, will track down anyone with a warrant out for his or her arrest, including those on the FBI's most-wanted list. He has said, as quoted on the A&E Web site, "I don't care if [a fugitive] went into hell. I'll find him."

The oldest of four children, Duane Chapman was born on February 2, 1952. He grew up in Denver, Colorado. His father, Wesley, was a welder in the U.S. Navy; his mother, Barbara, was a minister in the First Assemblies of God. In an autobiographical profile posted on his Web site (dogthebounty-hunter.com), Chapman described his father as verbally and emotionally abusive. (The two grew closer before the older man's death.) During his youth Chapman lived in Texas and other parts of the U.S. and pursued a life of crime. According to his Web site, as an adolescent he was arrested 18 times for armed robbery. In Texas he joined a motorcycle gang called the Devil's Disciples. In 1976 he and a number of other members of the Devil's Disciples were arrested for the murder of a local pimp and drug dealer. Although Chapman insisted that a fellow gang member had acted alone in killing the man, he was found guilty for his alleged role in the murder, and in 1977 a Texas court sentenced him to five years of hard labor. By his own account, while serving time in a Texas state penitentiary, Chapman found God (he has said that his nickname comes from the word "God" spelled backward) and vowed to reform his life. He was paroled in 1979. He has often pointed to his prison experience as a motivation for his work, in which, as he has often described it, he enables lawbreakers to arrive at a point in their lives at which they will be inspired to "go straight"—that is, give up their old ways and adopt a more principled and moral life style. "It's why I hunt men—fugitives of the law," Chapman wrote for his Web site. "I am what rehabilitation stands for."

Before his arrest Chapman had fathered at least one child, and after his release from prison, he still owed child support to the mother. According to Chapman, the judge presiding over the child-support case agreed to pay $200 toward the debt if Chapman caught a fugitive for him. Chapman earned his first bounty, he has said, by tying the wanted man up with his belt. He thereby launched his career. Soon, his Web site reported, he was capturing as many as four fugitives a week.

Bounty hunters are also known as bail enforcement agents (BEAs) or fugitive recovery agents—terms that Chapman dislikes. A BEA is an individual (or group of individuals—an agency, for example) who, in exchange for payment, apprehends people who have failed to appear as ordered while on bond or bail and surrenders them to the presiding authorities. Bail entails the temporary release of a suspect or prisoner in a criminal case in exchange for money or other collateral—usually a bond or formal guarantee provided on the suspect's behalf by a bail agent—meant to ensure that prisoner's eventual return to hear the case against him or her in court. Every year many people "jump," or flee, while free on bail, traveling to other states or countries or otherwise attempting to hide from the authorities. Such individuals represent the majority of the fugitives Chapman and those in his line of work track and capture.

According to Chapman's Web site, every year bounty hunters and BEAs capture an estimated 30,000 to 40,000 people who have jumped bail. Stephen Kreimer, the executive director of Professional Bail Agents of the United States (PBUS), told *Current Biography* that there are approximately 1,100 BEAs in the United States. Chapman's Web site puts the number at 8,000. That discrepancy has arisen in part because there is no standard system for regulating or licensing BEAs or bounty hunters; regulations on BEAs vary from state to state, with some states maintaining rigorous licensing and training requirements and others exerting little control. (There is broad concern within law-enforcement communities about the activities of bounty hunters—their capturing of fugitives, though ostensibly acts of justice, has been likened to kidnapping—and legislation calling for better regulation of the profession has been introduced in the U.S. Congress.) The legal precedent for bounty hunters in the U.S. was set in the 1872 U.S. Supreme Court case *Taylor v. Taintor*; that ruling gave bounty hunters broad authority in carrying out their duties. A growing number of states, however, have since legally restricted the activities of bounty hunters; for example, some have required them to undergo background checks and sanctioned training, or have prohibited their use of firearms.

In the profile of his life and work posted on his Web site, Chapman stated that he did not want to be simply an informer who tracks a fugitive and tells the authorities of his whereabouts; rather, he wanted to be the one to physically apprehend the fugitive, "to look the guy in the face when I brought him in and see the entire process through." On his Web site he has posted lists of his past captures and pictures of the most-wanted fugitives still at large. In trying to track down those who have fled the law, Chapman seeks, in his words, "relatives [of the fugitives], friends, anyone who might be willing to help bring the fugitive in. . . . Seventy percent of all my captures happen because some good ole American has turned them in by giving me information." Among the high-profile fugitives Chapman has singlehandedly captured or helped to apprehend are Quinton Wortham, a man convicted of rape in Washington, D.C.; Wayne Williams, a child murderer from Atlanta; and William Scatarie, a white supremacist and murderer. (The captures and escapades Chapman described on his Web site have not all been independently verified.) "Dog's a genius at the practical side of humanity, especially when it comes to understanding the criminal mind," the well-known author and motivational speaker Anthony Robbins is quoted as saying of Chapman on the latter's Web site. "He's

the best in the world at what he does." (Robbins wrote of Chapman in his book *Awaken the Giant Within* [1991].)

On his Web site Chapman cautioned that many fugitives are armed and dangerous. "I like to hear that God goes before us, because he is the biggest bulletproof vest of all," he once wrote. (As a former felon, he is not allowed to carry a gun.) Chapman has admitted that he has often showered a just-captured fugitive with choice expletives, a habit that is part of what he euphemistically refers to on his Web site as "holding court in the street." He has told many of them, as quoted on the A&E Web site, "Twelve men can judge you or six men can carry you. You decide." As tough as he appears to be, Chapman is not impervious to fear. "I'm a normal guy," he acknowledged on his Web site. "I'm scared all the time." As an example, he recalled one particular capture in which he and a number of his small children duped a dangerous heroin dealer into surrendering without a fight. Chapman and his children had shined flashlights into the cabin in the Colorado mountains in which the criminal was hiding out, leading the fugitive to believe that he was surrounded by many armed federal agents. The man was furious at having been fooled. "When [the suspect] said that he was going to kill me, well, that shook me up for a pretty long time," Chapman wrote.

As payment for their efforts, bounty hunters are often promised between 10 and 15 percent of the bail set for a given fugitive. Chapman has estimated that he has been paid for fewer than half of the more than 6,000 fugitives he has captured, because bondsmen do not always have the required cash on hand. (Chapman has said that he has been offered watches, old trucks, and, once, even a puppy in lieu of money.) Indeed, despite certain stereotypes to the contrary, making a living as a bounty hunter is not easy; Stephen Kreimer told *Current Biography* that only a small percentage of bounty hunters can support themselves by practicing the trade.

Chapman made headlines for his involvement in the case of Andrew Luster, a great-grandson of Max Factor, who had built a cosmetics empire in the 1920s. On January 3, 2003, while on trial in California for drugging and raping three women, Luster fled during a court recess. (He was convicted in absentia of the crimes.) In June of that year, Chapman, his brother, and one of his sons tracked Luster to Puerto Vallarta, on Mexico's Pacific coast, and took him into custody. Chapman has offered no detailed accounts of how they restrained Luster; a bystander reported a scuffle to the police, who then arrested Chapman and the others working with him. (Bounty hunting is illegal in Mexico.) In late June Luster was deported by Mexican authorities to the U.S. and was taken into custody by FBI agents. Shortly afterward, Chapman and his helpers returned from Mexico as well. While some observers viewed Chapman as a hero and an enforcer of justice, the episode highlighted the murky legal territory in which bounty hunters operate. Although he estimated that he was owed about $350,000 for the capture, Chapman was denied payment of a percentage of Luster's bail. "[Chapman] went to Mexico and failed to comply with the law," California Superior Court judge Edward Brodie said, as quoted on CBSNews.com (August 6, 2003). "I cannot condone vigilante justice." Chapman accepted the ruling but has rejected the notion that he and other bounty hunters are vigilantes who obstruct the work of official law-enforcement agencies.

Chapman owns several bail-bonding businesses in Hawaii, where he settled in the late 1980s, and Colorado. According to Stephen Kreimer and PBUS, there are 14,000 licensed or appointed bail agents in the country (half of whom are women). As described by Kreimer for *Current Biography*, bail bondsmen operate somewhat like insurance agents, ensuring courts and local authorities that prisoners or suspects will appear at the appropriate time to face the charges against them. (Thus, BEAs and bounty hunters are hired by bail bondsmen.) In the belief that bounty hunters are a dying breed, Chapman runs a training course in Hawaii. He also offers his services as a motivational speaker to schools, prisons, and other institutions.

A reality show documenting Chapman's professional exploits and family life—*Dog The Bounty Hunter*—premiered on A&E in August 2004. In addition to Chapman, the show features several of his fellow bounty hunters, including his son Leland; his young nephew, Justin Bihag; and a longtime friend, Tim Chapman (to whom he is not related). Beth Smith, Chapman's fourth wife and business partner, also figures prominently in the program. In a review for *Entertainment Weekly* (September 10, 2004), the critic Ken Tucker wrote that *Dog the Bounty Hunter* "shows you how a sly hunter captures his prey." "It's fascinating," Tucker added, "to watch a guy who looks like a middle-aged Hell's Angel trap evildoers by sweet-talking the suspects' relatives on the phone (Chapman's a natural actor with an array of voices) and then racing to ambush the thugs." With an average weekly audience of 1.6 million people in the U.S., surging at times to three million, *Dog the Bounty Hunter* has become the highest-rated show in A&E's history, according to Tim Ryan in the *Honolulu Star-Bulletin* (October 10, 2005). *Dog the Bounty Hunter* is also broadcast in other countries, and in Australia, Canada, the Netherlands, and Great Britain, it has become, as Tsai Michael wrote for the *Honolulu Advertiser* (April 12, 2005), "a cultural phenomenon." Chapman has claimed that the show has also served indirectly to help some of the people he hunted. "Half the people we caught in our first season have jobs and are trying to be responsible now," he told Michael. "The other half is doing time. I was there and I think everybody deserves a second chance." In August 2005 Chapman published his autobiography, *You Can Run But You Can't Hide: The Life and Times of Dog the Bounty Hunter*, and in October of that year he was said to

be negotiating with A&E for a third season of his series.

Chapman is a muscular man with blue eyes and a mane of long blond hair. He often wears tight sleeveless T-shirts, boots, and armbands. According to his Web site, he and Smith, along with seven of their 12 children, live together in Honolulu, Hawaii. Chapman has said that the natural beauty of the Hawaiian islands helps to keep him sane. On his Web site he declared, "For me, Hawaii is like decompression."

—C.F.T.

Suggested Reading: A&E Web site; Dakinebailbonds.com; dogthebountyhunter (online); *Honolulu (Hawaii) Advertiser* E p1+ Apr. 12, 2005; Professional Bail Agents of the United States Web site

Selected Books: *You Can Run But You Can't Hide: The Life and Times of Dog the Bounty Hunter*, 2005

Selected Television Shows: *Dog the Bounty Hunter*, 2004–

Charles, Michael Ray

1967– Artist

Address: University of Texas, Dept. of Art & Art History, 1 University Station D1300, Austin, TX 78712

The painter Michael Ray Charles uses visual stereotypes of African-Americans, particularly as they have evolved in advertising, to demonstrate links between the past and present. For example, Charles often juxtaposes racist historical images, including those of oversized lips, bulging eyes, and unruly hair, with modern images culled from such venues as jazz lounges, basketball courts, and circuses. In doing so he suggests that society's representations of African-Americans have remained the same in essence, in that they continue to imply that the talents and value of blacks are limited to the entertainment and sports industries. The resultant paintings are often incendiary. "Of course, it is precisely because Charles is African-American that he can paint the pictures he does," Patricia C. Johnson wrote for the *Houston Chronicle* (June 6, 1997). "They are savagely ironic. No non-black could get away with them." Charles himself explained to Michael Ennis for *Texas Monthly* (June 1997), "My work attempts to bring about change. In that sense I'm a political artist. But I've never said I'm angry. And I'm not." He elaborated to Anne Price for the Baton Rouge, Louisiana, *Advocate* (October 26, 1997), "My work is about the state of humanity, of racism and how we under-

Michael Ray Charles

stand information. Racism is only one facet. My work is more about communication."

Michael Ray Charles was born in 1967 in Lafayette, Louisiana, and was raised in St. Martinsville, where his father worked for a community action agency and was a town councilman. His tiny hometown was "a good, safe place. When you played sports and wore the uniform that represented the town, the whole town was behind you," Charles explained to Ennis. "But after graduation, blacks went to one side of the railroad track and whites to the other. The businesses were all owned by whites. There were boundaries blacks were not supposed to cross." Growing up, Charles looked up to his father and grandfather, who "was a gentleman," as he told Ennis. "He couldn't read or write, but he'd get up and go to work every day, work hard. He was a master carpenter who could build, wire, and plumb entire houses." As an activist and public official, his father was also a builder—of communities. "I remember my father clashing with the powers that be in this small town," he recalled to Ennis. "I remember the pain and stress on his face, trying to figure out how to work things out and still stand up and be a man. I can't say I'm the kind of person to get up on a soapbox and speak out. But my dad was. He still is."

Even as a youngster Charles was interested in art, and he has recalled being a compulsive sketcher. He also loved playing basketball, and hoped to win an athletic scholarship to college; instead, McNeese State University, in Lake Charles, Louisiana, offered him a $500 art scholarship, which he accepted. As an undergraduate Charles majored in advertising and played on the university's basketball team. He would have transferred to another

school on a basketball scholarship but for his father's refusal to sign the necessary consent form. While at McNeese Charles had the opportunity to see, for the first time in his life, works produced by other black artists. Upon his graduation, in 1985, during an economic recession, he was unable to secure a position in advertising or public relations (though he did land a job as a personnel counselor, placing other people in jobs), so he enrolled in the graduate fine-arts program at the University of Houston, in Texas, in 1990.

During Charles's first year as a graduate student, his friend Sean Thorton gave him an antique figurine of Little Black Sambo. (Sambo was a common stereotype—a cartoonish representation of an African-American man or boy, drawn with inky black skin, oversized red lips, bulging eyes, and a mop of black hair and often used in early American advertisements. *Little Black Sambo* was the title of a children's book written by Helen Bannerman in 1899, and the word "Sambo" was often used as a derogatory term for African-Americans throughout the early and middle 20th century.) Having forgotten about the figurine for a time, Charles rediscovered it while cleaning up his studio. He then became obsessed with it, drawing the figure over and over again, casting it in plaster, and researching the history of Sambo. He also began collecting similar memorabilia and old advertisements featuring the Sambo and mammy characters. (Mammies were typically caricatures of large, smiling, matriarchal black women sporting head kerchiefs and aprons, also frequently used in advertising.) "He was searching for something," Michelle Barnes, the director of Houston's Community Artists Collective and the first gallery owner to display Charles's images, told Shaila Dewan for the *Houston Press* (June 12, 1997, on-line). "Because I knew Michael, I understood that he was on a true search." Through his research, Charles "discovered how the Sambo image developed out of the black minstrel shows, how the minstrel shows evolved into Barnum and Bailey and into the entertainment industry, how sports have become a form of the entertainment industry," he told Michael Ennis. "I started to see the similarities between the present and the past, how those images have been repackaged and recast. People say those stereotypes don't exist anymore. But the image is more sophisticated now, just as discrimination is more sophisticated now. We're not looking at grotesque caricatures anymore. We're looking at [the football player] Deion Sanders smiling next to a Pepsi can."

Among other pieces that Charles's search inspired him to create was a series of 50 clay baby carriages and replicas of the Little Black Sambo, featured in a 1992 exhibition at the Houston Public Library. The installation proved to be controversial, but despite several complaints, the library refused to remove the piece. Charles recalled in an interview for the televised PBS series *Art in the Twenty-First Century* (on-line), "It was the first time I got a sense of not only the seriousness involved with the use of these images, but also the emotion, the emotional presence of the past. People began to knock over the glass case and, on many occasions, condemned the presence of such imagery." Such reactions convinced Charles that he was addressing issues of significance. He continued to work with the same themes, painting black men dressed as menacing clowns, circus performers dressed like prison inmates, and mammies reoutfitted as Wonder Woman and Marilyn Monroe. Also in 1992 Charles created his signature, a Lincoln penny glued to the canvas. He chose the penny because it generally looks darker than other coins. When he entered the University of Houston, Charles was the only African-American attending the program, and one black professor told him that he would not make it to graduation. Contrary to the professor's prediction, in 1993 Charles became only the second African-American ever to receive an M.F.A. degree from the university. He accepted a one-year contract to teach studio art at the University of Texas at Austin, which less than a year later offered him a tenure-track appointment.

Many of Charles's paintings have been designed to look like advertising posters from an earlier era. To achieve an old-fashioned feel, Charles used dated fonts in the images and distressed his canvases so that they appeared bent, torn, or otherwise damaged from age. References to entertainment or sports feature prominently in his works, because he believes that black individuals have been commodified and promised fame and fortune, but only in those two industries. "We have too many African American youths who want to grow up and go into basketball," he told Jeanne Claire van Ryzin for the *Austin (Texas) American-Statesman* (April 13, 2003). "This is the only thing that America is telling them they can do and do well." Similarly, he lamented to Arthur Hirsch for the *Baltimore Sun* (March 2, 2002) that the "most predominant form of cultural distribution is film" and that African-Americans have little clout as a group in the industry.

Charles's first major solo exhibition, entitled *Michael Ray Charles, 1989–1997: An American Artist's Work*, was held at the University of Houston's Blaffer Gallery in 1997. The gallery director, Don Bacigalupi, was told by colleagues that the racially oriented show would be "too hot to handle," as he told Dewan. "Why else would I want to be a curator? To show pretty pictures?" The show proved as controversial as Bacigalupi's colleagues had feared, but it exposed Charles to a wider audience than before and attracted more devotees as well. "Raw, edgy and confrontational almost to a fault, his works exceed all boundaries of good taste and appear to be a mockery of his own race," Janet Kutner wrote for the *Dallas Morning News* (December 6, 1996). "But what he's really ridiculing is a society that tolerates prejudice, and the power of his message is inescapable, given the poster-style format in which it is presented." Recently, both the D. Berman Gallery, in Austin, and the Weatherspoon Art Museum, in Winston-Salem, North Carolina, hosted small exhibits of Charles's basketball-themed work, the series "The Property of . . . ," which features 20 mock basketball jerseys constructed of burlap coffee-bean bags with logos painted on them with black shoe polish. The exhibits (staged in 2003 and 2004, respectively) attacked preconceptions about the athletic prowess of black males, specifically with regard to basketball (which, Charles has noted, he still enjoys playing). "Blackness is always linked to the body in American society," he told Tom Patterson for the *Winston-Salem Journal* (March 21, 2004). "Anything that has to do with intellect is not considered to be part of black culture."

With a catalogue of works filled with such charged imagery, Charles has faced his share of criticism. "I get a lot of flak from black people who don't know what I'm doing," Charles told Peter Donald for the *Palm Beach (Florida) Post* (January 27, 1999). "They say: 'Brother, what are you doing? You're selling out.'" Ed Golson, president of the African American Cultural Arts Organization of West Palm Beach, complained to Donald that Charles is "commercializing painful images." African-Americans have not been the sole objectors to the artist's work, however. "There were people of all backgrounds that despised the work," Bacigalupi told Hirsch. Many people, Bacigalupi continued, felt that the works were "taking us back to a period of time we don't want to look at again." While Bacigalupi is a supporter of Charles, he admits to understanding some of the complaints leveled against Charles's work. "In some cases," he told Dewan, "he's not doing enough violence to [the stereotypes] to make it clear and unambiguous what his relation to the images is." Similarly, although she considered Charles "adept" as an artist, praising his "considerable graphic talent and a penchant for biting social satire," the art critic Roberta Smith found something lacking in Charles's paintings, writing in a review for the *New York Times* (October 3, 1997), "These images can cause double takes, so full are they of traditional illustrational flourishes and carefully induced signs of age—and this is a bad sign. All that really distinguishes Mr. Charles's images from their sources is his subject matter. Ultimately, this is not enough to raise them above the level of clever, stylish calculation."

Despite such criticism Charles has attracted a following that includes many prominent figures, including the film director Penny Marshall and the actors David Alan Grier, Matt Dillon, Whoopi Goldberg, and Dennis Hopper. Perhaps Charles's most visible patron is the director Spike Lee, who commissioned a painting for *4 Little Girls*, his 1997 documentary about the 1963 bombing of a church in Birmingham, Alabama. Lee also hired Charles as a creative consultant for the 2000 film *Bamboozled*. In fact, it has been conjectured that the film was titled after one of Charles's paintings, which Lee owns. Though Lee has denied borrowing the title of the artwork, "I like to think [I inspired him],"

Charles told Kendra Hamilton for *Black Issues in Higher Education* (January 2, 2003). "After all, there was no *Bamboozled* before my work." In an introduction to the exhibition catalogue for Charles's 1997 show at the Blaffer Gallery (as quoted by Patricia C. Johnson), Lee pronounced Charles "a major artist," adding, "Please take notice I didn't say African-American artist."

Charles's paintings have been exhibited throughout Europe and the United States, including successful solo shows in New York City, France, and Belgium. Reproductions of his works can be found in three books: *Michael Ray Charles, 1989–1997: An American Artist's Work* (1997), *Michael Ray Charles: Paintings* (1997), and *Michael Ray Charles* (1998). He, his wife, Renee, and their two sons live in Austin, where Charles is an associate professor of studio art at the University of Texas.

—K.J.E.

Suggested Reading: *Austin (Texas) American-Statesman* K p1 Apr. 13, 2003; *Baltimore (Maryland) Sun* D p1 Mar. 2, 2002; *Houston (Texas) Chronicle* p1 June 6, 1997; *Houston Press* (on-line) June 12, 1997; *New York Times* p35 Oct. 3, 1997; *Palm Beach (Florida) Post* C p1 Jan. 27, 1999; *Texas Monthly* p88 June 1997

Chertoff, Michael

Nov. 28, 1953– Secretary of the Department of Homeland Security

Address: U.S. Department of Homeland Security, Washington, DC 20528

Michael Chertoff "has shown a deep commitment to the cause of justice and an unwavering determination to protect the American people," President George W. Bush told an audience at the White House on January 11, 2005, announcing Chertoff as his nominee for the post of secretary of the Department of Homeland Security (DHS), as quoted in a press release posted on the White House Web site. Replacing former secretary Tom Ridge, Chertoff has assumed a wide range of responsibilities, including managing airport security and immigration policy and safeguarding the nation's infrastructure, while overseeing the efforts of almost two dozen federal agencies, from the Federal Emergency Management Agency (FEMA) to the U.S. Coast Guard. Chertoff, a conservative Republican, has won supporters on both ends of the political spectrum, and as a result he was easily confirmed by the Senate in February. "In both private practice and public service, . . . Chertoff has earned the respect of his peers and adversaries in a long and distinguished career," Democratic senator Jon Corzine asserted in an interview with Amy Klein for

Alex Wong/Getty Images

the Bergen County, New Jersey, *Record* (January 12, 2005). Chertoff's noted ambition and intelligence led him to a position as one of the youngest United States attorneys (U.S. attorneys represent the federal government in the U.S. district courts);

in addition he has served as assistant U.S. attorney general and has held a coveted spot as a U.S. Appeals Court judge.

Chertoff developed a reputation for toughness as a criminal prosecutor during the 1980s, attracting national attention for securing convictions of the bosses of New York City's major organized-crime families. As assistant attorney general, under the direction of Attorney General John Ashcroft, Chertoff helped craft the legal strategy for the aggressive pursuit of terrorists after the September 11, 2001 attacks against the United States. Chertoff has come under fire from critics who charge that his forceful tactics sometimes override civil liberties; he helped draft the controversial USA Patriot Act, which expanded federal surveillance powers, and directed the investigation that led to the incarceration of hundreds of Arab and Muslim illegal immigrants—a roundup that drew criticism from the Justice Department's inspector general, who reported that many prisoners had been held for overly long periods, prevented from contacting lawyers or family, and subjected to mistreatment. Chertoff has defended his hard-nosed approach; at George Washington University, in his first major address since he assumed his new position, he remarked, "To be blunt, we have forced terrorists to spend more time worrying about how to defend themselves against death and capture, leaving them less time to plot how to get by our own defenses," as quoted in a report in *Congressional Quarterly* (March 16, 2005). "That strategy pays enormous dividends in terms of diminishing the threat. First, the intelligence we gain is a major tool in disrupting the threat. Second, by taking the fight to our enemies, we keep them on the run [and] limit their abilities to plan, train and act."

Chertoff faced his first major test as head of DHS in late August 2005, when Hurricane Katrina decimated portions of the Gulf Coast in what has been called the largest natural disaster in American history; New Orleans, Louisiana, took the worst hit—the city not only incurred significant damage from the storm, but the levees surrounding the low-lying city were unable to hold back the rising storm waters, and much of the area was flooded. Although the mayor had issued a mandatory evacuation in the days before the hurricane arrived, about 100,000 residents (roughly a fifth of New Orleans's population) remained behind. As the water rose as high as 20 feet in some areas, stranded individuals sought safety on rooftops while thousands of others massed at the New Orleans Superdome and Convention Center. Although rescue operations began immediately, days passed before the majority could be removed to safety; in the meantime, images in the media depicted desperation and near-anarchy as people suffered from lack of food and water while local and state officials pleaded for help. Criticism over the slow response was directed at authorities at all levels, but DHS, which oversees FEMA and is responsible for coordinating the federal response to natural disasters, came in for

particularly heavy vituperation. Chertoff infuriated many when he praised the relief effort in its early days while the media portrayed an increasingly dire situation, and some critics pointed out that he had no emergency-management experience. "The system broke," Susan Cutter, director of the Hazards Research Lab at the University of South Carolina told Amanda Ripley for *Time* (September 12, 2005). "A system that cannot airlift water and food to a community that's desperate for it is a system that is broken." Ripley noted that the failure to enact a swift and successful relief operation had generated doubts about the agency's preparedness for future attacks: "After all the post-9/11 vows, are we still not well enough armed for the next big one?"

Michael Chertoff was born on November 28, 1953 in Elizabeth, New Jersey. His father, Gershon B. Chertoff, was a prominent rabbi at Temple B'nai Israel (which served the towns of Elizabeth and Millburn), and his mother, Livia Chertoff, was a homemaker, former flight attendant for Israel's El Al Airlines, and onetime owner of an art gallery in Elizabeth. Though Chertoff has seldom spoken about his childhood, he told Brian Bennet in an interview for *Time* (March 28, 2005), "My parents always taught me two things: Do the difficult and unpleasant things first, and always admit your mistakes if you make them. Don't try to shave the truth. You are much better off if you come out up front and say, 'Hey, I messed up.'" Chertoff attended the Pingry School, a preparatory academy near Elizabeth. Chertoff was managing editor of the school newspaper and wrote editorials. He went on to attend Harvard University, in Cambridge, Massachusetts, graduating magna cum laude with a bachelor's degree in history in 1975. Despite having "no burning desire to do so," as he told Gay Jervey for the American Lawyer News Service, as reported in the *New Jersey Law Journal* (October 5, 1972), Chertoff enrolled at Harvard Law School, where he edited the *Harvard Law Review*. "It just seemed like a logical step," he told Jervey. Chertoff attained a J.D. degree magna cum laude in 1978. With a reputation as a brilliant student, Chertoff served as the inspiration for two characters in *One L*, a fictionalized memoir written in 1977 by his Harvard Law School classmate Scott Turow. Chertoff, Turow recalled, would engage in marathon debates with one of their professors, Duncan Kennedy—and would usually win.

The summer after graduating from law school, Chertoff joined the law firm of Miller, Cassidy, Larroca & Lewin, based in Washington, D.C., as a summer associate; by the fall of 1978, he had secured a position as a law clerk for Murray Gurfein, a judge in the U.S. Court of Appeals, Second Circuit. The following year Chertoff took another job as a law clerk, this time to William J. Brennan Jr., a justice on the U.S. Supreme Court. From 1980 to 1983, Chertoff worked in private practice as an associate at the Washington, D.C., offices of Latham & Watkins, but he ultimately yearned to try cases, particularly criminal cases, himself. The opportunity came in 1983, when he was hired as an assistant U.S. attorney for the Southern District of New York, working under then–U.S. attorney Rudolph Giuliani. He soon earned a reputation for being a hard-hitting and dogged prosecutor. "In the courtroom, he was self-confident, precise, relentless, intimidating and well-prepared," Mary Jo Patterson wrote for the Newhouse News Service (January 12, 2005). "When questioning witnesses, Chertoff could be withering. But he was also courteous and capable of great charm." Chertoff took over from Giuliani as the lead prosecutor in the noted "Mafia Commission" trial of the late 1980s, in which the bosses of several organized-crime families in New York were tried together as members of a commission; Chertoff successfully convicted the bosses Anthony "Fat Tony" Salerno, Carmine "Junior" Persico, and Anthony "Tony Ducks" Corallo. His fervor and skill at getting results landed the 32-year-old Chertoff a cover story in *Time* magazine. Giuliani praised Chertoff in an interview with R. H. Melton for the *Washington Post* (April 8, 1996), commending his "sense of anger and injustice that drives him to work harder."

Chertoff's next career move was across the Hudson River to Newark, New Jersey, where he served as a first assistant U.S. attorney for three years. He upheld his reputation for taking down Mafia figures by convicting Louis "Bobby" Manna for attempting to assassinate rival crime boss John Gotti. In 1990 Chertoff was appointed U.S. attorney for the district; sources note that he distinguished himself with the amount of personal attention he brought to many prosecution cases. During that period Chertoff obtained several convictions, including that of the New York State chief judge Sol Wachtler for the harassment and attempted extortion of a former lover; the kidnappers and murderers of Exxon International president Sidney Reso; Eddie Antar, the founder of the consumer-electronics chain Crazy Eddie, for racketeering; and the former Jersey City mayor Gerald McCann for corruption. Chertoff was reportedly the only Republican U.S. attorney that Bill Clinton, upon assuming the presidency in 1993, allowed to remain in place, due in part to the recommendation of the Democratic senator Bill Bradley of New Jersey.

After four years as U.S. attorney, Chertoff returned to private practice, joining the Newark office of Latham & Watkins as a partner. He focused on criminal defense; in one prominent case, he defended Michael Francis, the former head of the New Jersey Sports and Exposition Authority. When Francis was indicted for allegedly abusing his position to aid his private business, he had immediately sought Chertoff's counsel. When the case went to trial, in 2000, Chertoff promptly secured his client a full acquittal—the presiding judge dismissed the charges midway through the trial due to a lack of evidence. "That was a very satisfying case," Chertoff recollected in an interview with Christopher Mumma for the *Record* (June 19,

2000). "Of course, the most satisfying cases are where you avert somebody being indicted."

Also in 1994 Chertoff was named special counsel to the Senate Whitewater Committee, which had been convened to investigate the involvement of President Clinton and his wife, Hillary Rodham Clinton, in a failed 1970s Arkansas real-estate venture by the Whitewater Development Corp., in which the Clintons were partners. Chertoff unearthed obscure documents and questioned witnesses—for hours, when necessary—to assemble a case for the prosecution. The investigation took two years to complete, but Chertoff remained steadfast in his involvement. "My personality is such that having taken on that question, I'm absolutely dead set about seeing it through to the end," he told R. H. Melton. "I don't know what the end will be, and I can't say I've always been successful. But I can tell you I've never left an investigation without exhausting every avenue available." Ultimately, the Clintons were not charged with any wrongdoing, though friends of the Clintons who were involved in the deal, Susan and James McDougal, and Clinton's successor as governor of Arkansas, Jim Guy Tucker, were all convicted of fraud. Chertoff's participation in the Whitewater investigation led him to join the campaign of the Republican presidential candidate Bob Dole. (Dole lost the 1996 election to Clinton.)

In 2000 Chertoff, who had developed a million-dollar criminal-defense practice at Latham & Watkins, signed on as pro bono counsel to a New Jersey legislative probe to investigate alleged racial profiling by the state police, ultimately donating more than 1,000 hours of his time to the cause. "I have a love for public service," he explained to Jim Oliphant for the *New Jersey Law Journal* (July 16, 2001). "I like to contribute to an organization." Upon finding evidence suggesting that former state attorney general Peter Verniero knew that some New Jersey police were targeting minority motorists, Chertoff called for Verniero's dismissal from the state Supreme Court, where he had since become a justice. Despite Chertoff's efforts, Verniero was allowed to remain on the bench.

Chertoff returned to full-time public service in 2001 when he took over the U.S. Department of Justice's criminal division as assistant attorney general under Attorney General John Ashcroft. Chertoff became known for his participation in the Enron probe, which investigated allegations of accounting fraud and conspiracy within the energy company and its accounting firm, Arthur Anderson. Chertoff helped facilitate the cooperation of David Duncan, an executive with Arthur Anderson who proved a useful witness in testifying against the accounting firm. Chertoff was also one of the key legal strategists in the "war on terror" launched by President George W. Bush following the September 11, 2001 attacks on the World Trade Center and the Pentagon. Chertoff helped draft the USA Patriot Act, which increased the FBI's authority to conduct domestic surveillance and improved information sharing between federal agencies; the legislation also allowed for the interviewing of thousands of Middle Easterners (primarily recent immigrants) to determine their involvement, if any, in the attacks, and the use of certain immigration regulations and warrants to detain suspected terrorists. Chertoff was involved in the prosecution of the Al Qaeda member Zacarias Moussaoui, who was charged with participating in planning the attacks of September 11, and the American Taliban fighter John Walker Lindh. Some critics have alleged that Chertoff's tactics are extreme. "Chertoff has bought into a very simplistic rationale for an egregious assault on civil liberties," Laura Murphy, the director of the national office of the American Civil Liberties Union (ACLU), in Washington, D.C., told Toni Locy and Kevin Johnson for *USA Today* (August 14, 2002). "He's not as flashy or prone to hyperbole as Ashcroft, but he still embraces a very scary 'damn the Bill of Rights' attitude." Chertoff once defended his approach at a Senate hearing as a necessary reaction to a shifting reality: "Are we being aggressive and hard-nosed? You bet. In the aftermath of Sept. 11, how could we not be?" he said, as quoted by Deborah Orin in the *New York Post* (January 12, 2005).

Despite the criticism, politicians from both sides of the congressional aisle commended Chertoff's dedication, and when President Bush nominated Chertoff for a seat on the U.S. Court of Appeals, Third Circuit (in Philadelphia, Pennsylvania), his appointment carried by a vote of 88 to one. (The one dissenting vote was cast by Senator Hillary Clinton.) Chertoff was confirmed in June 2003. "Everything he said both publicly and privately indicated that he was enjoying" his spot on the bench, Chertoff's friend and fellow lawyer Walter Timpone told Chris Mondics for the *Philadelphia Inquirer* (January 12, 2005). "The only thing he missed was the day-to-day contact with people."

Lack of contact with others is unlikely to be a problem for Chertoff in his newest position; after New York Police Commissioner Bernard Kerik withdrew his nomination as head of DHS because of an immigration issue involving a former housekeeper, President Bush asked Chertoff to head the department, which coordinates the efforts of 22 agencies and their 180,000 employees. The department was established in November 2002, in response to heightened concerns about terrorism after the attacks of September 11. Broadly conceived as an organization whose goal is to prevent U.S. citizens and property from harm, it was formed through the consolidation of several divisions of the executive branch of government into a single agency—the largest government reorganization in more than 50 years; the head of the department is a Cabinet member, reporting directly to the president.

Chertoff's nomination came as a surprise to most, as he was not known to have been under consideration. Despite his comfortable lifetime appointment to the Third Court of Appeals, Chertoff accepted Bush's offer. "There is no question I left behind a very enviable professional situation," Chertoff told Brian Bennet. "But for me, after living through 9/11, I really think [securing our country] is the most important challenge of my generation." When the president publicly announced his nomination of Chertoff on January 11, 2005, he praised him as a "talented and experienced public servant" with a "stellar career." "Mike has also been a key leader in the war on terror," Bush asserted in his speech, as reproduced on the White House Web site. Chertoff pledged "to devote all my energy to promoting our homeland security, and as important, to preserving our fundamental liberties."

Some critics voiced displeasure with President Bush's selection; Timothy Edgar, the legislative counsel for the ACLU, complained to Robert Timberg and David L. Greene for the *Baltimore Sun* (January 12, 2005) that Chertoff was "one of the architects of many of the policies to abridge civil rights and civil liberties adopted after 9/11." Lawrence W. Lustberg, a criminal-defense lawyer and friend of Chertoff, disagreed with such assessments: "It's one thing to react to an immediate crisis," Lustberg told Amy Klein. "Mike is going to do an excellent job in balancing the security interests of the nation with the civil liberties of people." (Some have noted that Chertoff has criticized Bush and Defense Secretary Donald Rumsfeld for permitting the indefinite detention of prisoners at the U.S. military facility in Guantanamo Bay, Cuba.) Other observers expressed concerns that unlike the previous head of DHS, Tom Ridge, who had formerly served as a governor, Chertoff lacked managerial experience. Chertoff "is a brilliant lawyer," Clark Kent Ervin, the former DHS inspector general, told Michael Hedges for the *Houston Chronicle* (January 12, 2005). "That said, he does not have the management experience of running a vast federal agency. That will be a challenge for him. The most important ingredient in running DHS is management expertise, and Judge Chertoff lacks that." Despite such qualms, Chertoff was easily confirmed as secretary of homeland security on February 15, 2005. Even Senator Clinton voiced her approval of Chertoff's appointment. In his speech on March 15 at George Washington University, Chertoff told listeners, "We win the war against terror by rejecting terror as a tool of intimidation, and we triumph when we take account of real risks and threats but do not become hypersensitive or overly responsive to them," as reported by Frank Davies for the *Miami Herald* (March 17, 2005). "We want to live mindfully but do not want to live fearfully," he said.

Chertoff's reputation suffered a significant blow in late August, when he and his agency weathered a barrage of criticism over the exiguous federal response to Hurricane Katrina. The Category Four hurricane made landfall on the morning of August 29, not far from New Orleans. When levees surrounding the city, which is largely below sea level, were breached, as much as 80 percent of the city was flooded, leaving many individuals stranded for days before they could be airlifted or bussed to safety. Echoing the sentiments of many, an editorial for the New York *Daily News* (September 3, 2005) opined, "As for Chertoff, if this is the best his department can do, the homeland is not very secure at all. It is absolutely outrageous that the United States of America could not send help to tens of thousands of forlorn, frightened, sick and hungry human beings at least 24 hours before it did, arguably longer than that. . . . What is already more than clear is that the nation's disaster-preparedness mechanisms do not appear to be in the hands of officials who know how to run them."

Chertoff defended the agency's response in an interview with Tim Russert on NBC's *Meet the Press* (September 4, 2005), insisting that the levee breach "really caught everybody by surprise." Tim Naftali, however, writing for *Slate* (September 6, 2005, on-line), wondered, "What has DHS been doing if not readying itself and its subcomponents for a likely disaster? The collapse of a New Orleans levee has long led a list of worst-case urban crisis scenarios." Robert Novak, a columnist for the *Chicago Sun-Times* (September 8, 2005), denounced Chertoff for his "political deafness" and "lawyerly evasion," adding, "Chertoff's miserable performance on the air reflected a fiasco at all levels of government." The aftermath of Hurricane Katrina is likely to have dramatic consequences for the future of DHS; several legislators (including Senator Clinton) have called for FEMA to be removed from the agency's umbrella and reestablished as an independent organization reporting to the president. In his interview with Russert, Chertoff insisted that while rescue operations were continuing, his job was to stay focused on resolving the emergency: "I promise you we will go back and review the lessons that we have to learn, what went right and what went wrong. But I will tell you now we will be making a huge mistake if we spend the time in the immediate future looking back instead of dealing with, as you point out, what's going on now and what may yet come." On September 9 Chertoff removed the director of FEMA, Michael D. Brown, from management of the on-site hurricane-relief operation, placing Coast Guard vice admiral Thad W. Allen in his stead. Brown resigned his post three days later.

On October 24, 2005 Hurricane Wilma, a Category Three hurricane, swept over southern Florida, leaving millions without water, gas, and electricity. As with Hurricane Katrina, many were frustrated with what they perceived to be a slow response from the federal government. Chertoff responded to such complaints, telling a reporter for the Associated Press (October 26, 2005), "I have to say, in honesty, patience will be required for everybody. Under the best circumstances, even in the best planning, you still confront the physical reality of a destructive storm."

Chertoff and his wife, the former Meryl Sali Justin, were married in 1988. Like her husband, Meryl Chertoff is a Harvard Law School graduate and lawyer. During the 1990s she served as the co-chair of the regional Anti-Defamation League's civil rights committee. She resigned from her position as a lobbyist with the Trenton, New Jersey–based firm Nancy H. Becker Associates following her husband's homeland-security appointment. The Chertoffs have two children, Emily and Philip. For recreation, Chertoff enjoys kayaking, running, and reading true-crime books, particularly if they concern cases in which he had some involvement.

"Some people don't like Mike because he is so intense and driven," a former colleague of Chertoff's in the U.S. attorney's office for the Southern District of New York said in an interview with Gay Jervey. Chertoff "doesn't see anything else other than what he's doing, but after a while you see that it's not mean-spirited. And in a weird way it becomes kind of endearing." The colleague continued, "It's just that in a very cerebral way, Michael has no slow gear." Chertoff himself has admitted to being single-minded and relentless. "My experience . . . has led me to respect most people," Chertoff told Gay Jervey. "But I also know that there is a minority of people who do not deserve respect because they will not conform to the natural order of things. And I want to lock them up." —K.J.E.

Suggested Reading: (Bergen County, New Jersey) *Record* A p1 Jan. 12, 2005; CNN.com Sep. 5, 2005; *New Jersey Law Journal* p4 Oct. 5, 1992; *New York Times* p55 Feb. 21, 1988; *Washington Post* A p19 Apr. 8, 1996

Clarkson, Patricia

Dec. 29, 1959– Actress

Address: c/o Gersh Agency, 41 Madison Ave., 33d Fl., New York, NY 10010

Patricia Clarkson's career is unusual in a couple of ways. Unlike many other celebrated film actresses, who reach the peak of their success and exposure as early as their mid-20s, Clarkson did not achieve widespread recognition until she was almost 40 years old. Additionally, she has seldom played parts in big-budget pictures from major Hollywood studios, tending instead to star in smaller, independent pictures. She told Christian Toto for the *Washington Times* (March 7, 2003), "Great parts for women in studio films are few and far between. That's the system, and you can't really fight it. The independent film world doesn't have to play by those specific rules." In an interview with Faith Dawson for *New Orleans Magazine* (December 1, 2004, on-line), Clarkson—a veteran of dozens of

Evan Agostini/Getty Images

Patricia Clarkson

television and feature films—said, "I always have been attracted to characters that are challenging, characters that require many facets of you, of your personality, of your psyche, of your temperament. I think if you look back at most of my work, there is a common thread that emerges. I think I've played a lot of women on the edge, women on the outskirts that are bold or different or in very dramatic situations." Clarkson has won acclaim, as well as an Emmy Award and an Oscar nomination, for portraying such women, in television productions and movies including *High Art, Far from Heaven, Pieces of April, The Station Agent,* and *Miracle.*

Patricia Clarkson was born on December 29, 1959 in New Orleans, Louisiana, the youngest of the five children of Arthur and Jacqueline Brechtel Clarkson, who is now a city councilwoman. Clarkson has said that her family was very close-knit during her childhood. "It's funny how I'm always playing someone from a troubled family, because that is the exact opposite of how I grew up . . . ," she told Richard Ouzounian for the *Toronto Star* (September 7, 2003). "Maybe that's why I'm good at understanding people who aren't so happy. I know what I have and I know how sad it would be not to have it." Clarkson was barely a teenager when she realized how she wanted to spend her life. "I always knew I wanted to be an actress," she told Mervyn Rothstein for the *New York Times* (November 25, 1988). "I knew from the time I was 13. Something about acting has always consumed me. . . . For me, it's just confronting fear dead on. It's the fear of failing, of disappointment. But I really can't imagine doing anything else." As a girl Clarkson was active in theater, winning a citywide

competition with her performance of a monologue from *Our Town* when she was 14.

Clarkson began college at Louisiana State University. In her junior year she moved to New York City, where she attended Fordham University. "The moment I got here, it felt like home," she told Randee Dawn for the *Hollywood Reporter* (June 29, 2004). "I am most happy in New York." She earned a bachelor's degree in liberal arts from Fordham, then completed a master of fine arts degree at the Yale School of Drama, in New Haven, Connecticut. "It was the biggest transformation," Clarkson told Jan Stuart for *Newsday* (October 12, 2003) of the transition from Fordham to Yale. "As an undergraduate at Fordham, I was doing first leading lady. . . . At Yale, they purposely cast you against type. I was doing all this wild character stuff: an 8-year-old murderer, a 200-pound Cajun mama with an Afro and a muumuu. I had to sing and tap-dance. Yale made me locate character, find power and fulfillment in being something other."

Clarkson soon landed roles in Broadway and Off-Broadway plays in New York, where she gained notice, thanks in part to her unusual voice—whose "distinctively deep" quality is "so at odds with her porcelain beauty," as David Cuthbert wrote for the Newhouse News Service (May 7, 2004). Clarkson told Ann Hornaday for the *Washington Post* (May 9, 2004), "I've had this voice since I was 5," adding that her voice was "troublesome when I first got out of Yale . . . I would walk in, you know, blond, pretty, whatever. But then I'd open my voice and they'd say, 'Hmmm.'" Still, Clarkson credits the combination of voice and appearance with catching the attention of the director Brian de Palma, who cast her as the wife of the federal agent Eliot Ness (played by Kevin Costner) in his hit film *The Untouchables* (1987). On the strength of her appearance in that film, she soon won roles in several others, including the 1988 movies *Everybody's All-American*; *Rocket Gibraltar*, in which she performed with the screen legend Burt Lancaster (in one of his last movies); and *The Dead Pool*, the final installment of the *Dirty Harry* movies, starring Clint Eastwood.

Clarkson spent the next few years working in television, appearing in a number of series, including *Law & Order, Murder One, Tales from the Crypt,* and *Frasier,* and made-for-TV movies, among them *Legacy of Lies* (1992), *Queen* (1993), and *Caught in the Act* (1993). She also had small roles in such major motion pictures as *Tune in Tomorrow* (1990), *Jumanji* (1995), and *Pharaoh's Army* (1995). The real turning point in her career, however, came with her role in Lisa Cholodenko's 1998 film, *High Art.* In it Ally Sheedy starred as Lucy Berliner, an award-winning photographer who falls in love with Syd, a young, female magazine editor played by Radha Mitchell. Clarkson co-starred as Greta, formerly an actress in films by the German director Rainer Werner Fassbinder and Lucy's drug-addicted lover. When Lucy and Syd start to fall in love, Greta does everything she can to keep them apart. *High Art* received very positive reviews, most of which singled out Clarkson's performance. In a representative review, Roger Ebert wrote for the *Chicago Sun-Times* (July 3, 1998), "Patricia Clarkson succeeds in creating a complete, complex character without ever overplaying the stoned behavior." Clarkson explained to David Germain for the Australian *Cairns Post* (October 27, 2003) what her role in *High Art* meant to her career: "I went through a lull in my early 30s, oddly, but hey, in my late 30s, things took off. Every day, I wake up and I have a little thank you to Lisa Cholodenko for casting me in her movie. Because it changed everything for me. It is a cliché, but sometimes it is just one part that opens people's minds and eyes. And I think also, I needed to get older. There was a part of me that needed to kind of grow into my voice and my face and my body." The critical success of *High Art* led to an influx of offers of roles for Clarkson, who appeared in the following years in TV and feature films including *The Green Mile* (1999), *Joe Gould's Secret* (2000), *Falling Like This (2000), The Pledge* (2001), and *The Safety of Objects* (2001). Her appearance on the cable-television program *Six Feet Under* earned her an Emmy Award in 2002 for outstanding guest actress in a drama series.

In 2002 Clarkson played a supporting role in Todd Haynes's film *Far from Heaven*, which explores the mores and taboos—particularly those against homosexuality and interracial romance—of America in the 1950s. Clarkson played a bigot in the film, which led her to consider elements of her youth in Louisiana. "There's a connection between that character and the women I knew in the South," she told Kevin Maynard for the *Los Angeles Times* (October 8, 2002). "It crosses the Mason-Dixon line. In high school, we would have to have slumber parties at my house because some of the white girls' parents would not allow blacks to sleep in their house. I saw a lot more prejudice there than I care to remember." Also in 2002 Clarkson was seen in *The Baroness and the Pig, Heartbreak Hospital, Welcome to Collinwood*, and *Carrie*, a made-for-TV remake of the 1976 film based on Stephen King's novel.

The year 2003 was significant for Clarkson, as she starred in four films—*Dogville, All the Real Girls, The Station Agent*, and *Pieces of April*—that premiered at the prestigious Sundance Film Festival. Together, the films led to a considerable buzz about Clarkson in the press. Two of the movies were particularly important to Clarkson. "My focus is on *Pieces of April* and *The Station Agent*," she told Richard Ouzounian, "two films that are very dear to me, more so than almost anything I've done in this business so far." In *The Station Agent* Clarkson played Olivia Harris, whose young son has recently died and whose marriage is falling apart. Olivia befriends the film's central character, a dwarf named Finbar McBride (played by Peter Dinklage). The role allowed her to explore aspects of her personality that, she said, other films have left

untapped. "So often when women hit their late 30s, 40s, into their 50s [on the screen] we become either asexual or predatory, it's never just a real day-in, day-out existence," she told Moira Macdonald for the *Seattle Times* (October 16, 2003). "What is most alluring about this part is that [the director Thomas McCarthy] got a real sensuality and sexuality." Ann Hornaday, reviewing the film for the *Washington Post* (October 17, 2003), wrote that Clarkson, "with her porcelain delicacy and tinkling, musical voice, is at once heartbreaking and sharply funny."

Clarkson's other major critical success in 2003 was *Pieces of April*, in which she played Joy, a terminally ill cancer patient who spends what is probably her last Thanksgiving with her estranged daughter, portrayed by Katie Holmes. The film met with rave reviews. Rene Rodriguez wrote for the *Miami Herald* (October 30, 2003, on-line), "The movie is buoyed by strong performances, especially Clarkson's, who effortlessly conveys the inner resolve of a terminally ill woman who has made peace with her fate and must now tolerate the overreactions of her family, who worry about her every sneeze." Even the few negative reviews of the film, such as Jamie Russell's for the BBC (February 18, 2004, on-line), pointed to Clarkson's work as one of the stronger elements in the movie: "There's a typically electric performance from Patricia Clarkson as April's ailing Mom . . . to keep the interest up." Many critics noted Clarkson's decision to embrace her character's weaknesses in addition to making her sympathetic. Peter Hedges, the film's director, told Stephen Witty for the Newhouse News Service (October 6, 2003), "Patricia Clarkson is a national treasure. A lot of actors are so worried about always being likable that they take shortcuts. They're afraid of making the ugly choice, or risk having the audience reject them. Patty's absolutely fearless." For her performance in *Pieces of April*, Clarkson was nominated for an Academy Award for best supporting actress.

In the film *Miracle* (2004), Clarkson portrayed the wife of Herb Brooks, the real-life coach who led the United States hockey team to victory against the Russian team in the 1980 Olympic Games. Also in 2004 she made stage history as the first woman from New Orleans (where the play is set) to take on the role of Blanche DuBois in a major production of Tennessee Williams's *A Streetcar Named Desire*. While the production, at the Kennedy Center, in Washington, D.C., received mixed reviews, most critics praised Clarkson's work. "Clarkson's Blanche is the most compelling element in the strange yet ordinary production," Linda Winer wrote for *Newsday* (May 18, 2004).

Clarkson played the role of Shirley Wershba in *Good Night, and Good Luck* (2005), directed by George Clooney. The film focuses on the role of the journalist Edward R. Murrow in the downfall of Senator Joseph McCarthy, the instigator of what many have referred to as a "Communist witch-hunt" in the 1950s. Wershba, who has referred to

McCarthy's tactics as "psychological terrorism," as quoted on participate.net, was a broadcast journalist who at one time worked for CBS, Murrow's employer. Clarkson's next film, *The Dying Gaul*, which was shown at film festivals in June 2005 and co-stars Campell Scott, was scheduled for release in November 2005. Clarkson was also cast in the upcoming films *The Woods*, *All the King's Men*, and *Conquistadora*.

Patricia Clarkson lives in New York City with her dog, Beau. She is reportedly in a long-term relationship with Campbell Scott.

—R.E.

Suggested Reading: *Los Angeles Times* VI p1+ Oct. 8, 2002, with photos; *New Orleans Magazine* (on-line) Dec. 1, 2004; *Newsday* D p10 Oct. 12, 2003, with photos; Newhouse News Service May 7, 2004; *Toronto Star* D p3 Sep. 7, 2003, with photo; *Washington Post* N p1+ May 9, 2004, with photos

Selected Films: *The Untouchables*, 1987; *High Art*, 1998; *Far from Heaven*, 2002; *The Station Agent*, 2003; *Pieces of April*, 2003; *Miracle*, 2004; *Good Night, and Good Luck*, 2005

Thos Robinson/Getty Images

Coddington, Grace

1941– Fashion director of Vogue

Address: c/o Condé Nast, 4 Times Square, New York, NY 10036

Grace Coddington "is easily the world's most influential fashion editor, famous for transforming photographic spreads into narratives, a signature she pioneered in the 1970s at British *Vogue*," Nadia Mustafa wrote for *Time* (September 8, 2003). For the last three decades, Coddington has worked all over the world with the fashion industry's top models and photographers to create memorable fashion images. After a successful career as a model in London, England, during the 1960s, Coddington spent 19 years at the British edition of *Vogue*, a glossy fashion magazine based in London, where in time she became its creative director. Since 1988

she has held the title of fashion (or creative) director of the U.S. edition of *Vogue*. According to Mustafa, Coddington's signature aesthetic style is marked by a "witty, modern romanticism that makes readers feel they are flipping through a picture book instead of just looking at shots of models in pretty clothing." The designer Karl Lagerfeld told Sarah Mower for style.com, the on-line home of *Vogue* and *W*, that Coddington "has the highest taste of modernity. She never, ever fell for a cheap trend." Anna Wintour, the editor of U.S. *Vogue*, told Colin McDowell for the London *Sunday Times* (August 4, 2002), "Grace has a body of work unmatched by any other fashion editor, because she has the best eye in the business. She can sense a trend before the designers have an inkling of what's going on." "I like fairy tales, and I like dreaming," Coddington told Nadia Mustafa. "I try to weave the reality into a dream. When readers pick up *Vogue*, I want them to smile. Everything should be a little tongue in cheek, a little dare-to-go-there." Coddington's honors include the 2002 Lifetime Achievement Award of the Council of Fashion Designers of America.

Pamela Rosalind Grace Coddington was born in Wales in 1941 and raised on the remote Welsh island of Anglesey, where her parents ran a small hotel. She had at least one sibling, a sister. As a youngster, one of her teachers wrote of her, as quoted by Colin McDowell, "Grace has a sweet way of getting her own will." During her early years she read British *Vogue*, which she would order from the local store in her hometown. "For me, the magazine represented an amazing fantasy world of sophistication and grown-ups," she recalled to Mark Holgate for the *New York* magazine Web site newyorkmetro.com. "I dreamt of getting away from the tiny place I was raised." When Coddington was 18 she moved to London, which, she told Holgate, she imagined "would be full of these amazing-looking women. . . . I remember thinking that if I ever got to be one of those women, it would change everything. *That* was my dream—it was always my desire to be an incredibly elegant woman."

For a while Coddington supported herself as a waitress. She also took classes at a modeling school run by Cherry Marshall, a former model, where she was told that she had little chance of success in that field, because she did not have blond hair and was "not very pretty," as she recalled to Holgate. Nevertheless, in 1959 (1960, according to one source) she won first prize in the category "Young Idea" in a modeling contest sponsored by British *Vogue*. The contest brought her to the attention of the photographer Norman Parkinson, who was described on staleywise.com as "the preeminent fashion photographer in Great Britain from the late 30s until his death in 1990," and thanks to his help, she soon found herself in demand as a model. Along with such icons of 1960s fashion as Jean Shrimpton and Twiggy, she became a fixture of the celebrity and fashion jet set of the time, whose members included the Beatles, the Rolling Stones, Vidal Sassoon, and Mary Quant. Anna Wintour recalled to Holgate that Coddington was a "huge celebrity in that world, an incredible beauty. I was in awe of her." According to Coddington herself, although she was "never pretty," as she put it to Colin McDowell, she became popular because in those days, models had to supply their own shoes, belts, jewelry, and other accessories (as well as style their own hair and apply their own makeup), and she had "good accessories. I was always nosy about fashion and wanted to have the newest thing." The hairstylist Vidal Sassoon told Holgate that "with Coddington's bone structure, and that sense of herself, she had something beyond beauty." The late fashion editor Liz Tilberis, who worked with Coddington as a young *Vogue* intern, wrote in her memoir, *No Time to Die* (1998), "I can say without the prejudice of friendship that she was one of the greats, not in terms of mere beauty but because of the interpretive powers that enabled her to engage in the photographs on a level few models ever reach. Her face and posture could reflect haughty insolence, mischievous decadence, or serene come-hitherness, and her chameleon looks had expressed the myriad phases of fashion so successfully, you often had to look twice at a photo to check whether or not it was her." Coddington's looks were marred temporarily during the early 1960s, when she was involved in a car accident that left her with a severed eyelid. Plastic surgery successfully repaired the damage.

In 1969 Coddington was recruited to join the staff of British *Vogue* as a junior fashion editor. In the conviction that she needed a change in her life, she abandoned modeling and quickly established herself as both capable and creative in the photographic side of print journalism. Norman Parkinson again served as her mentor. In 1976 she was named senior fashion editor, and in the early 1980s, fashion director. Among other tasks, a fashion director's job entails making many of a magazine's fashion and story decisions jointly with the publication's chief editor, selecting the photographer and models for specific layouts, and then, while acting as a kind of producer and inspirational guide during the actual photo shoots, ensuring that the photographer expresses in his or her photos the magazine's fashion ideas. Like film and theater, fashion photography is a collaborative effort, in this case between the fashion director, the photographer, the stylists, the models, and the hair and makeup artists, among others. While at British *Vogue* Coddington developed a fashion-spread style that was to become her trademark: the narrative epic, in which the photographs tell a story and are often set in vast open locales, such as cornfields, deserts, and bodies of water. Vicki Goldberg, in the *New York Times* (November 14, 1993), wrote that Coddington's work was informed by a "mild dose of poetic lyricism and so strong a devotion to good photographs that the picture occasionally upstages the clothes." "She is especially partial to gardens," Goldberg added. Glenn Belverio wrote for the fashion magazine *Hint* (Summer 2002, on-line) that Coddington's style "veers from bucolic Puritanism (models schlepping hay in Amish fields) to pop posturing (a stripped-to-the-waist Puff Daddy leering at a couture-clad Kate Moss)." Regarding her job as creative director, Coddington told Holgate, "Of course, choosing the clothes to shoot is part of it, but it's also much more than that. It's playing with everyone's personalities and making sure that everything is jelling. When I'm on top of a mountain with a photographer who doesn't want to shoot something because it doesn't look sexy, and the magazine wants it in the issue—at that point, I'm the one who has to keep everyone motivated."

During her nearly two decades at British *Vogue*, Coddington helped to coordinate fashion shoots with such well-known photographers as David Bailey, Helmut Newton, Sarah Moon, Arthur Elgort, and Guy Bourdin. She was renowned for her perfectionism and her vision, to which she typically held fast. Her refusal to compromise, she told Holgate, is "the secret to my career: If you give in, you don't get perfection. I don't get close to perfection now, really," she continued, "but if you give in, then you'll never get anywhere *near* it." She also became famous for her ability to anticipate the next fashion trend. As Liz Tilberis wrote, "She could transform her personal style thoroughly and instantaneously—flowing robes would be replaced almost overnight by sculptural Yves Saint Laurent pantsuits, her long red hair suddenly chopped off and dyed punk blond—and it was guaranteed that any new look, no matter how radical and unimaginable, was a premonition of the next fashion wave, that a year down the road, everyone would be wearing it."

The designer Calvin Klein told Holgate that Coddington was the "first European fashion editor to appreciate American design." In 1986 Klein asked Coddington to work with him. She accepted his offer, and in 1987 she moved to the U.S., where she served as a design director for Klein for a year. Coddington told Holgate, "He taught me so much about living in America. But I missed being all over the place"—that is, on location for photo shoots—"and seeing a lot of different people." "In the end," Klein told Holgate, "her passion was for working with photographers and doing her stories."

In 1988 Anna Wintour, the newly appointed editor of U.S. *Vogue*, hired Coddington as the magazine's creative director. (The two had worked together at British *Vogue*, and while they sometimes clashed, they shared a deep respect for each other's talents.) "I was over the moon when she came to the magazine," Wintour told Holgate. "Her vision was and is very close to mine." Before every photo shoot, Coddington told Holgate, "[we] have this game of pushing each other as far as we can. I do say, 'Why do we have to go through this every time?' But it's crucial to do it; it's that process which makes a story work really well." Tilberis summed up what she termed the "classic dilemma" between the two: "Grace was always going for the look, and Anna was always [going] for the reader."

In 1993 a photographic retrospective of Coddington's work, titled "Short Stories: 25 Years of *Vogue* Fashion by Grace Coddington," was held at the James Danziger Gallery in New York City. The exhibit included 375 pictures by 30 photographers. In a review for the *New York Times* (November 14, 1993) entitled "Fashion Imagery That Can Upstage the Clothes," Vicki Goldberg noted that the show, apparently the first of its kind, "[paid] tribute to a fashion director's influence not just on fashion but on photography." "Nothing could be better" for a "behind the scenes view of a fashion editor at work," Cathy Horyn wrote of the exhibit for the *Washington Post* (November 21, 1993).

Coddington and her work are the subjects of *Grace: Thirty Years of Fashion at Vogue* (2002), which had a list price of $120 and sold out within months of its publication. Weighing over 10 pounds and measuring 14.5 x 11.2 x 2.5 inches, the 408-page book was edited by Coddington and Michael Roberts (the *New Yorker*'s fashion editor), both of whom served as art directors for the project, and offers forewords by Anna Wintour and Karl Lagerfeld. *Grace* includes pictures taken by many of the photographers with whom Coddington collaborated, among them David Bailey, Helmut Newton, Cecil Beaton, Sarah Moon, Sheila Metzner, Herb Ritts, Mario Testino, Annie Leibovitz, Ellen von Unwerth, and Bruce Weber. Sarah Mower wrote that the book is a "record of [Coddington's] working life" and tells "stories about the love affair between clothes, girls and the camera."

"Coddington is quiet and reserved," according to Michael Holgate, "her cool demeanor shot through with a dry wit and a self-deprecating sense of humor. . . . Yet she's also blessed with what her friend Michael Roberts . . . called 'the personality of a Brontë heroine; she has this absolute will, a quiet determination.'" In 1998 Tilberis wrote, "To outsiders, Grace was and still is an enigma—elusive, severe, silent. If she rates you as someone

who understands fashion, the beautiful statue becomes animated, and you are drowned in an eloquent runaway monologue about the color purple or a pinstripe. But if Grace dismisses you as unworthy of her commentary, you might as well be part of the wallpaper. This air of detachment and the impact of her presence as a fashion icon make her terrifying, even to this day." "With her mane of red hair, pallid complexion and pale eyes, there is something of the medieval penitent about Coddington," Colin McDowell wrote. Said to love "all things feline," in Holgate's words, she has four Chartreux cats. Her marriages to the restaurateur Michael Chow and the photographer Willie Christie ended in divorce. For some years in the 1970s and early 1980s, she raised her nephew Tristan, after the death of his mother, her sister Rosemary. She lives with her partner, the hairstylist Didier Malige, and maintains homes in New York City and Wainscott, New York, on Long Island.

—C.F.T.

Suggested Reading: *Hint* (on-line) Summer 2002; *New York* p126+ Aug. 26–Sep. 2, 2002, with photos; *New York Times* II p39+ Nov. 14, 1993, with photos; *Time* (on-line) Sep. 9, 2003, with photo; *Vogue* p190+ Nov. 1993, with photo, p638+ Sep. 2002, with photo; Coddington, Grace, and Roberts, Michael, eds. *Grace: Thirty Years of Fashion at Vogue*, 2002

Selected Books: Coddington, Grace, and Roberts, Michael, eds. *Grace: Thirty Years of Fashion at Vogue*, 2002

Colbert, Gregory

(kohl-BEHR)

1960– Photographer

Address: Bianimale Foundation, 210 E. Fifth St., New York, NY 10003

"People's sense of wonder has atrophied so much," the photographer Gregory Colbert told Rachel Sklar for the Montreal, Canada, *Gazette* (March 6, 2005). "We need to be inspired by nature." In a project that he launched in 1992 and, by his own account, intends to continue for the rest of his working life, Colbert has tried through photography "to dissolve the boundaries between man and other species, between art and nature, between now and forever," as a writer for *Smithsonian* magazine (June 2005) put it. "When you collaborate across the species and break down those barriers, extraordinary things happen," Colbert told Sklar. He has captured on film many celebrated images of animals—including elephants, sperm whales, leopards, baboons, seals, zebras, manatees, gyrfalcons, caracals, and elands—sitting, standing, or

Courtesy of Gregory Colbert

Gregory Colbert

flying next to or near Buddhist monks, African tribespeople, and so-called trance dancers, among other humans, in such far-flung locales as Burma, Namibia, and Dominica. Among his pictures are those of a boy reading to an elephant that reclines a few feet away from him; a meerkat perching atop a girl's head; a boy resting his head on the paw of a recumbent cheetah; an old woman cradling a wild cat; and an eagle soaring inches above a dancing woman. Many of his photographs feature children, because youngsters have the "capacity to treat animals as equals," as he told Donna Nebenzahl for the Toronto, Canada, *National Post* (March 8, 2005). Colbert takes pride in the fact that, while he focuses on deliberate juxtapositions of people and animals, he directs but does not pose his human subjects and does not digitally or in any other way manipulate his photos. "I have invented nothing," he told Alan Riding for the *New York Times* (April 22, 2002). "I have simply documented a magical alchemy that I want to share." Colbert prints his photos on handmade Japanese paper as large as six feet by 10 feet; the finished works have sold for as much as $500,000 apiece. The photographer has used his earnings to finance both his expeditions and his Bianimale Foundation, which supports conservation initiatives and the work of other artists, among other projects. Speaking of the Canadian-born Colbert to Grania Litwin for the *Ottawa (Canada) Citizen* (March 7, 2005), Pamela Wallin, a journalist and currently the Canadian consul general to New York, said that he "communicates the intelligence of animals more effectively than anyone I've ever known, as well as their grace, beauty and elegance. And in every way his own principles are absolutely firm. He is highly ethical,

passionate, intense, with a genius and creativity that are larger than life."

The second of the two children of Brad and Joan Colbert, Gregory Colbert was born in 1960 in Rosedale, an upscale section of Toronto, in the Canadian province of Ontario. While he was quite young, his family moved to the city of Brantford, about an hour's drive from Toronto. By his own account, since his early years he has felt a strong affinity for animals, particularly elephants. "As a kid I was always called an elephant because my ears stuck out," Colbert recalled in his interview with Alan Riding. "My mother was worried that I'd be traumatized, and she had my ears fixed"—that is, surgically pinned closer to his head. Young Gregory was also fascinated by nature and mysticism. Those interests were encouraged by his weekday babysitter, Joyce, a Native American who would often take the boy and his sister, Laurie, to the Six Nations Reserve, where the children became acquainted with Joyce's father, a chief. Laurie Colbert, who is now a professional filmmaker, told Peter Goddard for the *Toronto Star* (February 19, 2005), "A lot of what's in [my brother] springs from that experience. It was magnificent being there. . . . It was a very mystical environment, very quiet. It was like going back 100 years." She also told Goddard that she has always thought of her brother as "a bit of a tree-hugger. But he's also a relatively fearless man. That's how he negotiates his way through life." As a youngster Gregory Colbert disliked school and earned only average grades, but he enjoyed reading and spent a lot of time in the local library.

After he graduated from high school in Brantford, in about 1978, Colbert worked at an assortment of jobs. According to Laura McCandlish, writing for the Columbia University News Service (March 1, 2005, on-line), he also took classes in film and comparative literature at a college but did not earn a degree. At age 21, thinking that he might become a writer, he moved to Paris, France. There he joined a group of 30 artists from various countries who planned to promote French culture after they returned to their native lands. Under their influence, Colbert began making documentaries reflecting social consciousness, on such subjects as rape and the ways that artists confront death. An insurance company provided funds for the production of his film *On the Brink*, about AIDS. When the company objected to footage of two men kissing and demanded that the scene be cut, Colbert vowed never again to seek corporate sponsorship. He also ruled out applying for government support after the Canadian Council for the Arts, a grant-making agency, turned down his request for financial aid for one of his projects.

While in Europe Colbert began taking still photographs and experimenting with ways to print them. In 1992 he held his first photography exhibit, Timewaves, at the Musée de l'Élysée in Lausanne, Switzerland. The same exhibit was mounted at the Parco Galleries, in Japan. Later, judging many of the pictures he had displayed to be inferior, he destroyed most of them. Nevertheless, with the 1992 show he gained ardent admirers, some of whom have since financed his work. Their support made possible the nearly three dozen photographic trips he has made to date, to countries including Egypt, Kenya, Namibia, Somalia, Ethiopia, South Africa, Sri Lanka, Burma, and India, in each of which he took hundreds of photographs of animals and individuals native to the area. He has also spent many months photographing and swimming with sperm whales off the coasts of Tonga (a group of islands in the South Pacific), Dominica (an island in the Caribbean), and the Azores (nine islands in the mid–Atlantic Ocean). The material on which Colbert prints his photographs is a "cloth-like parchment," as Jeff Schewe described it for *Photoshop News* (April 8, 2005, on-line), made by the Japanese firm Hiromi Paper, which uses a technique that reportedly dates from the 13th century. Colbert has so far refused to divulge the process that he uses to make the prints, each of which is covered with a thin coating of beeswax. "The cynical eye is trained to assume trickery in images such as these, is resistant to the idea that they could represent the actual and the possible, but these images owe nothing to Photoshop, photo manipulation, montage, artificial lighting, or special effects," according to a writer for bookLA.com (New Life Issue 2003).

For about 10 years beginning in 1992, Colbert devoted himself almost exclusively to work in the field. After he tried in vain to find someone who would swim with sperm whales, he decided to serve as a subject himself; he hired Kogi Nakamura, an underwater photographer, to take photos of him with the 30-to-40-foot animals. To avoid irritating the whales with air bubbles from scuba gear, he dived without an oxygen tank. He made so many dives during a two-and-a-half-year period that he developed an enlarged heart—a consequence that, as he told Sklar, did not faze him. "I would hang off a cliff with my fingernails to get a shot of a cheetah or leopard if I had to," he told her. Colbert has never been seriously injured, and none of his crew members or subjects have been hurt, during his photo shoots.

In 2002 an exhibition of about 200 of Colbert's photos was mounted at the Venice Arsenale, in Italy. Entitled Ashes and Snow, the show did not include captions, "because it matters little how or when or where the photographs were taken," as Alan Riding wrote. "They are simply windows to a world in which silence and patience govern time." Riding also wrote, "The power of the images comes less from their formal beauty than from the way they envelope the viewer in their mood." The exhibit struck Jordan Baldwin, the associate curator of photographs at the Getty Museum in Los Angeles, as "brilliant," as he described it to Grania Litwin. "[Colbert's] work is romantic, majestic, tranquil, with a wonderful poetic grace, simplicity and purity," Baldwin said. "He is an extraordinary person who isolates his work in space so it looks like a cosmological event. There are no others like him." The photos impressed Patrick Heiniger, the head of the Swiss watch company Rolex, to such a degree that he arranged for Rolex to buy all of them, with the intention not only of keeping them together in a single collection but also of making them available for public viewing in different parts of the world. With Rolex, the businessman and philanthropist George Soros, and others funding the creation of such a traveling installation, Colbert commissioned the Japanese architect Shigeru Ban to design a building that could be easily assembled and then dismantled and transported to different sites. Ban came up with the idea of stacking steel cargo containers—the kind that tractor-trailers pull—for the outside walls of the building; a few dozen of them also serve as the containers in which Colbert's photos are shipped from one location to another. (The balance of the necessary containers are borrowed at each exhibition site.) Specially made, two-foot-thick cardboard tubes, fashioned from recycled materials, provide the structure's internal supports. On either side of a long wooden walkway bordered to the left and the right by smooth white stones, Colbert's photos are suspended on wires hanging from a tin ceiling. Also suspended overhead is a curtain made from a million humidity-damaged teabags from Sri Lanka, which Colbert purchased from a supplier; he then had his assistants dry them, empty them of their contents, glue them together, and cover them in beeswax. Sepia lighting and tranquil music composed for the show by David Darling contribute to what a commentator identified as Lingual X, writing for fervidus.typepad.com (March 19, 2005), described as a "fully integrated environment." At the end of the walkway, a continuously playing one-hour film—edited by the two-time Academy Award winner Pietro Scalia and narrated by the actor Laurence Fishburne—shows the photographer swimming with whales and otherwise engaged in his work and features still images of his subjects. Also present is a store, which sells posters, monographs, and books, among them a handmade exhibition catalog priced at $130 and Colbert's 36-page *Ashes and Snow: A Novel in Letters*, in which, in the last of the 365 letters that his fictional hero writes to his wife, the origin of the show's title is revealed.

The Bianimale Foundation, a nonprofit organization that aims to protect animals in their natural habitats, organized the Ashes and Snow exhibit; both the Rolex company and the Canadian consulate promoted it, placing ads in magazines and subway cars and on 8,000 banners throughout New York City. The show opened in the minimally heated, 45,000-square-foot, 672-foot-long "nomadic museum" in March 2005 on the West Side of New York City, on a Hudson River pier. The exhibit attracted tens of thousands of visitors and a great deal of praise. According to the bookLA writer, for example, Colbert "has taken the medium of the instantaneous and turned it into something slow, expansive, epic. You could be looking at a moment that occurred yesterday, or three hundred years ago. The effect is uncanny. You feel as if you are in the presence of a dream, a myth, a fairy tale." Those who found fault with the show included a critic for the *Creative Review* (April 6, 2005), who deemed Colbert's photos to be "somewhat overwrought," and Roberta Smith, an art critic for the *New York Times* (March 12, 2005), who labeled the exhibit a "vanity production." "Colbert's efforts form an exercise in conspicuous narcissism that is off the charts," Smith complained. "The exhibition pulls out all the stops to sensitize us to the natural world, but mainly it reveals that selfless sincerity is often close to overweening egomania and that the path between them is unconsciousness." The exhibit closed in New York in June 2005. Its next stops will include Los Angeles, California; Beijing, China; Tokyo, Japan; and Vatican City, Italy. Colbert is particularly proud of the upcoming Vatican show, because, as he told Peter Goddard, Ashes and Snow will be "the first non-religious exhibition [there] in 2,000 years."

"For all the contemplative mood of [his] images, Mr. Colbert does not come across as a New Age dreamer," Alan Riding wrote. "An athletic-looking man with a pony tail, he has down-to-earth views and a self-deprecating sense of humor. He may be in awe of nature, for instance, yet he mocks what he regards as the naivete of militant ecologists." Colbert's father told Litwin that Colbert "is focused on opportunities, not problems, and he is very disciplined. He always maintains a high level of fitness—never drinking, never smoking, never taking drugs—and while he has many natural abilities, like an Olympic athlete he has worked on them to become world class." The elder Colbert also told Litwin, "When he sees a window of opportunity Greg jumps in. He is a risk-taker, willing to go into a venture, even if he doesn't have the money to finish it." Colbert maintains studios in Paris, New York, and Scotland. "I'd love to have a family, but I am trying to fit this [work] all into one lifetime and while the grace of nature is infinite, time is finite," he told Litwin, explaining why he remains unmarried. The photographer said to Rachel Sklar, "It's wonderful to have enthusiasm expressed for what I'm doing, but for me the privilege is to do the work. I have no social aspirations, no intention of dying rich, and I don't allow my images to be used for commercial purposes." In future trips Colbert hopes to photograph penguins in Antarctica, orangutans in Borneo, and jaguars in Belize or Brazil.

—K.J.E.

Suggested Reading: ashesandsnow.org; (London) *Guardian* p10 Mar. 2, 2005; (Montreal) Gazette B p1 Mar. 6, 2005; *Ottawa Citizen* B p1 Mar. 7, 2005; *New York Times* E p1 Apr. 22, 2002; *Toronto Star* H p1 Feb. 19, 2005

Cometbus, Aaron

1968– Writer; zine publisher; drummer

Address: P.O. Box 4726, Berkeley, CA 94704

An icon in both the punk scene and the world of independent publishing, Aaron Cometbus is one of America's most prolific and well-known underground authors. Deliberately elusive about his real identity, Cometbus avoids cameras and has not publicly revealed his true surname. (Several news sources have identified it as Elliot, most frequently in connection with his side career as a drummer for various punk-rock bands.) The surname that has become his nom de plume doubles as the unofficial title of his zine, a periodical collection of autobiographical pieces, essays, interviews, drawings, collages, and other materials that he has been publishing in various incarnations since 1981. Bearing the full title *Ride the Wohl Whip Cometbus*, a nonsensical phrase invented by one of his friends, *Cometbus* has evolved over the years from a photocopied pamphlet about punk-rock music into a professionally printed, perfect-bound, softcover booklet of writings about Cometbus's own life and the ethos of punk. In recent years, for occasional "contributor issues," Cometbus has gathered friends and acquaintances to engage in concentrated explorations of various themes or issues. For Cometbus, writing a zine is above all a way of connecting with others, especially fellow members of the punk community. "A lot of people say they do their fanzines for themselves first," he told John Marr during an interview for the *San Francisco Bay Guardian* (February 26, 1997, on-line). "Well, I'm not. I'm doing it for other people."

Although Cometbus no longer hand-collates individual issues of his publication, a task he performed for years before he acquired the resources to hire a professional printer, his commitment to punk's "do-it-yourself" (DIY) ethic is evident on each of the zine's meticulously hand-lettered pages. Acutely aware of the popular misconception that the punk movement is based exclusively "on rejection, youthful rebellion and a certain kind of rage," in the words of Alec Hanley Bemis in *LA Weekly* (November 10, 2000), Cometbus has devoted the bulk of his writing to stories and first-person essays that reveal unknown aspects of the moral and intellectual framework and cooperative spirit of punk. "Punk rock is like a religion," he wrote for *Cometbus* #29. "It's got a set of morals, it's got a collective consciousness, and a feeling of community. But most of all, it's a personal feeling, a way of thinking, a driving force within your head, within your life." Using anecdotes and personal accounts of mundane occurrences as springboards to discussions of philosophical issues, Cometbus frequently takes on such themes as community, identity, alienation, and prejudice, with the individual's role in society considered central to each. "The idea is you take something very simple and focus

CHICAGO
STORIES
aaron cometbus

Cover art: Megan Kelso. World Wide Web
Partial cover of a Cometbus *collection.*

on it and you may get a higher, larger truth," he explained to John Marr. "Despite his first-person narrative style," Mark Athitakis wrote for *SF Weekly* (May 29, 2002), "Cometbus is no navel-gazer. He questions what community is, over and over, in different ways—angrily or jokingly, but always with a sober and informed wit."

Priced at $2.00 an issue or $2.50 by mail, *Cometbus* has never been a particularly lucrative enterprise. Cometbus keeps the cost of the zine low in order to ensure that it remains affordable for all those who want to read it, particularly other members of the punk community who, like him, choose to pursue a low-budget lifestyle. Lacking a source of steady income, he lives frugally, "scavenging, scamming, and occasionally being a welfare bum," as he wrote for *Cometbus* #29. "I'm living off the excesses of our excessive society, taking advantage of a system that's trying to take advantage of me." Because he objects on principle to participating in the U.S. labor system, which he regards as restrictive, demeaning, and exploitative, he survives mainly on proceeds from sales of *Cometbus* and his record albums and engages in more conventional forms of employment for only a few months at a time. Explaining his decision to pursue a life of voluntary poverty, he wrote for *Cometbus* #29, "I'm not opposed to working. I suppose I'd work if we had maybe a 2 day work week, workers owned the means of production, wealth was distributed equally and professions equally respected, everyone who *wanted* to work could work, there was socialized medicine . . . Well, you get the idea, and it sure isn't that way now."

Many journalists have compared Cometbus to the Beat writer Jack Kerouac, a fellow Californian famed for his writings about life on the move and at the fringes of society. Like Kerouac, Cometbus has pursued an itinerant lifestyle since he was a teenager, spending much of his time on the road and periodically settling down for several months in one location before moving on to another. His wanderings through the U.S., Canada, and Europe have brought him into contact with people from many walks of life, and, by his own account, those interactions have significantly contributed to his evolving perception of both the world and his place in it. "People are always saying that it doesn't matter where you go because everywhere is the same and what counts is what's inside you. I disagree," he wrote for *Cometbus* #31. "I think people live differently, talk differently, and think differently in different places, and being exposed to that helps you gain perspective on yourself." Because he tends to travel without concrete plans for lodging or transportation, Cometbus has long relied on luck and the kindness of others to see him through difficult times. For the most part, his experiences in this regard have been rewarding. "I always operate under the premise that if I throw myself into unknown or sketchy situations, and take [the] risk of being stranded and miserable, that things will work out," he wrote for *Cometbus* #27. "Usually taking a risk totally pays off in unexpected and spontaneous ways."

Cometbus approaches both punk and self-publishing from a historical perspective, methodically documenting the narratives of two subcultures in the pages of his zine. In a series of articles that appeared over the course of several issues of *Cometbus*, he explored the history of underground publishing (also known as "samizdat," a figurative term referring to government-suppressed literature distributed clandestinely in the Soviet Union). *Cometbus* #24 included an examination of high-school underground newspapers, #34 included histories of street flyers and the 1960s underground press in Berkeley, California, and #40 included an article about the *Rat*, a late-1960s underground newspaper based in New York City. *Cometbus* #29 1/2, a collection of reproduced clippings from punk fanzines dating from 1977 to 1983, was another issue dedicated to the recording of punk and samizdat history. "There's tons of old bands reforming and old albums being reissued, but no one does old zine reissues or reforms old zines. Except me, I guess," Cometbus wrote in his introduction. In addition to republishing the works of others, he has reprinted selections from early issues of his own zine (*Cometbus* #33), as well as flyers for punk shows dating from the late 1980s (*Cometbus* #35 1/2) and a collection of press and publicity materials documenting the history of the Gilman Street Project, a Berkeley concert venue central to the East Bay punk scene (*Cometbus* #38 1/2). "As you get older, you realize that punk is folklore and oral tradition and myths," Cometbus remarked during an interview for the Zinebook Web site. Writing in issue #34 of the zine, he explained, "I want to take what we have and add it all up."

Aaron Cometbus was born in 1968 and raised in Berkeley, California. His mother was the daughter of Russian Jewish immigrants; his father, who was not Jewish, spent two years in the army after completing graduate school and then became a university professor. (Both of his parents are deceased.) He has a brother, Jeremy, who is five years his junior. Although Cometbus's interests and activities during his adolescence are fairly well documented, both in Cometbus and in the mainstream press, little has been written about his childhood, which, as he wrote in issue #43 of his zine, "was unimportant except for two events. My dad taught me to ride a bike . . . and once me and my brother called the neighbor kid 'egghead.' My parents got so mad that they lectured us for half an hour about [Senator Joseph] McCarthy and why you shouldn't make fun of people for being intellectuals."

Cometbus began his career in self-publishing in July 1981, the year he was bar mitzvahed. Inspired by Berkeley's burgeoning punk-rock scene and the many independent publications to which it gave rise, he and his friend Jesse Michaels, who was later the frontman for the influential ska-punk band Operation Ivy, created a fanzine called Rip It Up. Named after a song by the Adolescents, a hardcore punk band from Orange County, California, the publication focused on punk music and reports on the Bay Area punk scene. Every week for the rest of the summer, Cometbus and Michaels published a new issue with a new title. On August 21, 1981 Cometbus interviewed Johnny Ramone, the guitarist and co-founder of the seminal punk band the Ramones, having managed to track him down as he was leaving a radio studio; parts of that interview appeared in the zine.

Michaels moved away from Berkeley, in the autumn of 1981, after collaborating with Cometbus on a total of six issues of their publication, and from then on, Cometbus continued to produce zines on his own. In October 1981 he published Decay, the first issue of the zine that would eventually come to be called Cometbus, by printing 500 pamphlets on a copy machine at a friend's workplace after hours. Like the six issues that Cometbus had created with Michaels, Decay consisted mostly of news about bands and concerts. Cometbus continued to rename his publication with each successive issue, adopting such titles as Impending Doom, Outlash, and Sick Society. Issue #15, Yogi Cometbus, marked his first use of the name by which both he and his publication have since come to be known. The names of subsequent issues were variations on the "Cometbus" theme, including Liberace Piano Cometbus, Pleasures of the Cometbus Harbor, Bee That Cometbus Bracero, and Free the Cometbus 5000. Ride the Wohl Whip Cometbus, which later became the zine's official name, made its first appearance in 1986, as the title of issue #22.

Cometbus produced a total of 23 issues of his zine between 1981 and 1986. In addition to his own writings, which continued to focus on punk music and culture, he began to include "contributor" materials, some of which he obtained without securing the express permission of the authors. "I used to steal English papers and rip things out of people's journals and just print them without asking," he recalled to John Marr. "That's how you end up with columnists." Since that time, Cometbus has regularly gone out of his way to persuade friends to submit writing and artwork to the zine, which he has always regarded as a forum for members of the punk community to share their ideas.

In 1982 Cometbus entered Berkeley High School as a freshman. That same year he and several of his friends started a band, writing songs with lyrics that, like Cometbus's later work, interspersed material about the minutiae of everyday life with commentary on larger issues. "Since we were acne-ridden adolescents," he wrote for Cometbus #43, "we had songs about insecurities, homework, and Ms. Pac Man. Since we were kids of professors, we also had songs about [the political theorist Karl] Marx." Already committed to ideals of freedom and self-determination, Cometbus became frustrated with his teachers and the school administration, whom he perceived to be unnecessarily rigid and unmindful of students' needs. In 1984 he co-founded an underground school newspaper called the Berkeley High Editorial, whose main purpose was to criticize the school's policies and administrators' attitudes toward students. The paper folded when Cometbus and his friends realized that none of their classmates seemed to take the subject as seriously as they did. "By tenth grade," Cometbus wrote for Cometbus #41, "school had crushed any desire I'd had to read or write, and was even working away at my desire to draw." Nevertheless, he continued to publish Cometbus throughout high school, keeping it hidden from his teachers and, for years, his parents. His mother and father learned about its existence only when parents of classmates of his happened to mention how much they enjoyed it.

After he graduated from Berkeley High School, in 1986, Cometbus took a job working the overnight shift at a local copy shop, which gave him both the time and the means to continue publishing his zine. He abandoned the position a few months later, leaving Berkeley to tour the country with his band. After two weeks half the band members quit, leaving Cometbus and one other musician stranded in Florida with no equipment, no means of transportation, and very little money. Nevertheless, Cometbus and his friend continued their travels, scraping by and eventually making it back to California with the help of strangers who offered them rides, shelter, food, and other resources.

From 1986 to 1989 Cometbus took a break from publishing his zine. He worked instead as a contributor to other zines and as a reporter on the

Northern California punk scene for *Maximum RockNRoll* (*MRR*), a widely read underground publication based in Berkeley. Around that time he co-founded the band Crimpshrine, taking the roles of drummer and lyricist. Along with Operation Ivy, Crimpshrine quickly became one of the East Bay's most popular and influential punk groups. Known for their "sincere, authentic, intelligent punk," in the words of Adam Bregman in *LA Weekly* (December 4, 1998), the members of Crimpshrine wrote and played music that, like most of Cometbus's writing, was "more personal than political, occasionally negative, but more often relentlessly hopeful." The band's first LP, *Lame Gig Contest*, was released in 1988 by Musical Tragedies, a German record label. Later albums, including *Duct Tape Soup* (1992) and *The Sound of a New World Being Born* (1998), appeared on Lookout!, a popular East Bay record label.

In 1989 Cometbus moved into a warehouse in a semi-industrial Bay Area neighborhood. The rent was low, but there was little to do in the area and public transportation was limited. (Cometbus has never learned to drive.) Seeking activities to occupy himself, he revived the zine that he had set aside three years earlier. This time around, however, he decided to create a publication devoted to the ideas and ideals that united Bay Area punks, rather than individual bands and punk shows. He began work on *Cometbus* #24 in September 1989, finishing and publishing it early in 1990. The newly formulated zine still contained some writing by and interviews with punk musicians, but the emphasis had shifted away from the music to discussions of the musicians' ideas and experiences. "How can it be a punk zine without covering bands, records, or 'the scene'?" Cometbus wrote in his introduction to the issue. "Because all those things are temporary, and covered enough anyway. More important is taking the lifestyle, perspective, and attitude of punk and applying it to *real life*. I think a lot of people have problems applying it all to the world outside of our little scene, and that's what I hope to do."

On June 19, 1990 Cometbus embarked on a cross-country tour as a roadie for the pop-punk band Green Day, which became commercially successful when it signed to the Warner Bros. record label several years later. In early August the band dropped him off in Minneapolis, Minnesota, where he settled down for the next several months. He had somehow managed to support himself for the previous year and a half without a job; now he once again found himself working the overnight shift at a copy shop. In December 1990 he published *Cometbus* #25, an issue entirely by and about people from the Minneapolis area. He then hit the road again, traveling around the country for a brief period and touching down in Arcata, California, about six hours north of San Francisco. He lived in Arcata for three months, working on *Cometbus* #26 and trying to start a band that he hoped to call Pinhead Gunpowder (the name of a highly

caffeinated green tea). Creative disagreements, several months of unproductive rehearsals, and one unsuccessful show left Cometbus and the other musicians frustrated, and they disbanded before ever agreeing on the band's official name.

Cometbus moved back to the Bay Area, where he tried again to assemble a band under the name Pinhead Gunpowder. This time he persuaded a small group of established punk musicians to join the band as a side project. Considered a "supergroup" by many music journalists and punk fans, Pinhead Gunpowder featured Billie Joe Armstrong, Green Day's frontman, on vocals and guitar; Bill Schneider, of the band Monsula, on bass and vocals; Mike Kirsch, of the band Fuel, on guitar; and Cometbus on drums. Between 1991 and 1993 Pinhead Gunpowder released several EPs and compilation tracks on various record labels. In 1994 Jason White, a member of Chino Horde and the Influents, replaced Kirsch on guitar. That same year, Lookout! released *Jump Salty*, a compilation of Pinhead Gunpowder's earlier recordings, followed by the EP *Carry the Banner* (1995) and the full-length album *Goodbye Ellston Avenue* (1997). In 1999 Adeline Records, an Oakland, California–based label, released *Shoot the Moon*, a seven-song EP. The members of Pinhead Gunpowder continue to play together on occasion; their latest EP, *Compulsive Disclosure*, was released on the Lookout! label in October 2003.

In addition to Crimpshrine and Pinhead Gunpowder, Cometbus has played the drums for a number of other punk bands, among them Cleveland Bound Death Sentence, Redmond Shooting Stars, Shotwell Coho, and S.A.G. (of which Jesse Michaels was also a member). He continues to publish his zine regularly and to travel often, maintaining the peripatetic, low-budget existence that many of his friends from the punk community relinquished years ago. Still faithful to the ideals that prompted him to pursue his way of life in the first place, he has expressed disappointment with those who gave up or compromised their antiestablishment principles for the sake of convenience, and especially with those who have gone so far as to criticize his perpetual wanderings as a form of escapism. "Leaving is putting something in your past and moving on. I had never done that," he once wrote, as quoted by Darby Romeo in the *Village Voice* (October 20, 1998). "I'd come back to the same people and places and things over and over again. I was sick of people always thinking I was leaving, when really they were the ones who were always looking to leave, secretly waiting to get married or make some other huge change in their life to break with the past."

In 2002 Last Gasp, an independent firm based in San Francisco, published *Despite Everything: A Cometbus Omnibus*, a collection of *Cometbus* excerpts. The 608-page book contains interviews, essays, drawings, and short pieces by Cometbus and a handful of contributors written over a period of two decades. The following year Last Gasp published *Double Duce*, a book-format reprint of *Cometbus* #42, which had been published in 1997 or 1998. Jeff Stark, writing in *SF Weekly* (July 1, 1998), described the original #42, which is essentially a full-length novel about a group of young people living together at a collective in Berkeley, as "possibly one of the most ambitious zines in micropublishing history." Like Cometbus himself, the characters in *Double Duce* "ponder life's mundane questions—how to get by on no money, where to scam free photocopies, and the finer points of dumpster diving—with the seriousness of ancient philosophers," according to the Last Gasp Web site. *Double Duce* also includes the "WDH Stories," a collection of excerpts from *Cometbus* #32 through #45. Some of the most recent issues of the zine, which Cometbus described to *Current Biography* as "anthropological study issues," consist largely of interviews with members of Northern California's fringe communities. Issue #46 focuses on employees and patrons of the Dead End, a collectively owned café in Berkeley; issue #48, titled "Back to the Land," spotlights children of "back-to-the-landers"—hippies who, during the 1970s, moved to the countryside in hopes of building communities there. Cometbus published his second novel, *Lanky*, a love story composed of short fragments, as *Cometbus* #47, late in 2001; it was the first perfect-bound issue of the zine. In 2004 he published *Chicago Stories*, a pocket-size collection of pieces from Cometbus issues #35, #37, #38, #41, and #45.

When not on the road, Aaron Cometbus lives in Berkeley, where a post-office box number serves as his only permanent address. He continues to think critically about both the punk movement and his own beliefs, offering new ideas and revisiting old ones when he deems it necessary. In what may be considered a victory for an author who has always valued community over exclusivity, over the years his readership has grown beyond the parameters of the punk subculture to include people with a wide range of lifestyles and interests. As he wrote in *Despite Everything*, "It's counterproductive to call our scene, our culture, our very existence 'underground,' 'subterranean,' or 'fringe.' . . . The truth is, there's no mainstream, just one body of water we're all part of, with many different tributaries."

—L.W.

Suggested Reading: *LA Weekly* p54+ Nov, 10, 2000; *San Francisco Bay Guardian* (on-line) Feb. 26, 1997; *SF Weekly* May 29, 2002

Selected Books: *Lanky*, 2001; *Despite Everything: A Cometbus Omnibus*, 2002; *Double Duce*, 2003; *Chicago Stories*, 2004

Cromwell, James

Jan. 27, 1940– Actor

Address: c/o SDB Partners Inc., 1801 Ave. of the Stars, Los Angeles, CA 90067

"I'm not the sort of personality that people stare at and then ask for an autograph," the actor James Cromwell said to Philip Wuntch for the *Dallas Morning News* (June 8, 2002). "People just come up to me and say, 'I like your work.' And that's what I like to hear." Cromwell has appeared in films and on television since the 1970s and has consistently earned plaudits for his portrayals of characters ranging from insidious lowlifes to wise, empathetic old men. His memorable roles include those of Stretch Cunningham on the television series *All in the Family* and Mr. Skolnick in four *Revenge of the Nerds* films. He is best known for his work in the movie *Babe* (1995), about a pig (the title character) and a host of other talking animals, in which he played an Australian farmer named Arthur Hoggett, a performance that earned him an Academy Award nomination for best supporting actor. "Andy Warhol said everybody gets their 15 minutes of fame," Cromwell said after learning of the nomination, as quoted in the Plymouth, England, *Evening Herald* (September 7, 2004). "And if this is mine, I couldn't imagine a better 15 minutes." "I

Carlo Allegri/Getty Images

owe an incredible debt to the wonderful pig . . . who gave me my career, which I didn't have until then," he told Scott Murdoch for the Queensland, Australia, *Courier Mail* (December 22, 2004). Before *Babe*, he said to Mark Olsen for the *Los Angeles Times* (August 1, 2004), "I had what I call a 'careen,' where you bounce like a pinball from one thing to another." In the decade since the release of *Babe*, Cromwell has had parts in such films as *The People vs. Larry Flynt*, *Star Trek: First Contact*, *The General's Daughter*, *The Green Mile*, and *The Longest Yard* and in the popular TV series *Six Feet Under*.

James Cromwell was born John Oliver Cromwell on January 27, 1940 in Los Angeles, California. Readily available sources do not indicate when he changed his given name. His mother was the actress Kay Johnson, who made her silver-screen debut in 1929, as the star of *Dynamite*, the director Cecil B. DeMille's first film with audible dialogue; she had a supporting role in *Of Human Bondage* (1934), which starred Leslie Howard and Bette Davis and was directed by John Cromwell, Cromwell's father. John Cromwell, who was 52 when James was born, was an acclaimed stage actor—he won a Tony Award for his work in the play *Point of No Return* (1952)—as well as a prolific, highly respected film director who worked with some of Hollywood's leading actors and actresses. The elder Cromwell and Johnson divorced when James was six years old, and the boy moved to Waterford, Connecticut, with his mother and brother. (His father later remarried three times.) As a child Cromwell occasionally visited his father at work; by his own account, he particularly enjoyed being on the set of *Anna and the King of Siam* (1946), which starred Irene Dunne and Rex Harrison. After he completed high school—the private Hill School, in Pottstown, Pennsylvania—in 1958, he enrolled at Middlebury College, in Middlebury, Vermont, with the goal of becoming a mechanical engineer. He spent the summer of 1960 in Sweden, on the set of a film (*A Matter of Morals*) that his father was directing. "I thought, 'Damn, this is the life!'" he recalled to Michael A. Lipton and Jeanne Gordon for *People* (March 25, 1996). Shortly thereafter he left Middlebury College and enrolled as a theater major at the Carnegie Institute of Technology (since renamed Carnegie Mellon University), in Pittsburgh, Pennsylvania. A year later he quit school "in a huff," in his words; as he explained to Lipton and Gordon, "Institutions and I get on each other's nerves something fierce."

Cromwell spent the next decade acting in and directing a variety of productions in regional theaters, prominent among them the Mark Taper Forum, in Los Angeles, California. In 1974 he began working in television, with roles in the series *The Rockford Files*, *Maude*, and *All in the Family*. In the last-named show, he appeared in three installments, in October and November 1974, as Stretch Cunningham, a buddy of the main character, the cantankerous Archie Bunker, played by Carroll O'Connor. At around that time O'Connor requested a pay raise that the show's producers considered exorbitant; for a while they considered killing off Archie and replacing him with Stretch. Then

O'Connor reached an agreement with the producers, and he returned to the set. "When Carroll came back, he had to feed me all the straight lines—I had all the jokes—and that was the end of Stretch Cunningham," Cromwell told Eirik Knutzen for the *Washington Times* (November 1, 2001). He told Jim Slotek for the *Toronto Sun* (May 17, 2002), "Carroll O'Connor saved my life. He thought Stretch was getting too many laughs and he refused to let me be a regular character. If he had, the character might have become like Fonzie and it would have been the end of my career." (He was referring to the character played by Henry Winkler for 10 years on the TV series *Happy Days*. Winkler's career suffered because of the public's close identification of him with Fonzie.) In 1975 Cromwell was cast as a lead in the TV sitcom *Hot L Baltimore*, which was soon cancelled. The following year he landed his first film role, playing the part of a French manservant in the comedy/mystery *Murder by Death*, whose screenplay was written by Neil Simon.

Although Cromwell was seldom cast as a leading man, he did not lack jobs. During the next two decades, he had parts in some 40 movies for the big and small screens and in more than 50 episodes of various TV series. He appeared in such silver-screen motion pictures as *Oh God! You Devil* (1984), *Pink Cadillac* (1989), and *Romeo Is Bleeding* (1993); made-for-television movies including *Barefoot in the Park* (1981), *Alison's Demise* (1987), and *The Shaggy Dog* (1994); and such television series as the *Nancy Walker Show* (1976), *Born to the Wind* (1982), and *China Beach* (1988). His better-known roles include that of Mr. Skolnick, the father of one of the title characters, in the films *Revenge of the Nerds* (1984) and *Revenge of the Nerds II: Nerds in Paradise* (1987), as well as the televised sequels *Revenge of the Nerds III* and *IV*, which had the subtitles *The Next Generation* (1992) and *Nerds in Love* (1994). (He is credited in those films, and a few others, as Jamie Cromwell.)

When Cromwell was offered the part of Arthur Hoggett, a kindly, laconic Australian sheep farmer, in a movie about a talking pig who wants to be a shepherd, he had misgivings about the film. But he was facing a period without work, and as he told Eleanor Ringel Gillespie for the *Atlanta Journal-Constitution* (May 31, 2002), he decided to take the advice of an actor friend, who had told him to accept the role. "You don't carry the picture," the friend said. "The pig carries the picture. If it flops, it's his fault." "When we saw James, we just saw Hoggett," Chris Noonan, who directed *Babe*, told Michael A. Lipton and Jeanne Gordon. "It was a difficult job," Noonan continued. "Hoggett is very withdrawn. I kept [telling Cromwell], 'Do less, don't smile, don't give anything away.' James was brilliant." *Babe* was the surprise hit of 1995, popular not only with its intended audience—children—but adults as well. "*Babe* is a movie made with charm and wit, and unlike some family movies it does not condescend, not for a second,"

Roger Ebert wrote for the *Chicago Sun-Times* (August 4, 1995). "It believes it is OK to use words a child might not know, and to have performances that are the best available." He added, "James Cromwell, as the farmer, and Magda Szubanski, as his wife, are always convincing." In the Salt Lake City, Utah, *Deseret News* (August 4, 1995), Chris Hicks, echoing many other reviewers, described Cromwell's performance as "wonderfully deadpan."

Cromwell was nominated for a 1995 Oscar for best supporting actor for his depiction of Farmer Hoggett. Although he did not win (the award went to Kevin Spacey, for his work in *The Usual Suspects*), he soon felt the effects of the publicity that followed his recognition by the Academy of Motion Picture Arts and Sciences. With his status as an actor at a new high, he began to be offered roles that were more prominent and more substantial than nearly all those that had preceded that of Hoggett. "As an older character actor, you have to accept a lot of junk or go unemployed for long periods of time—both options drive me crazy," he told Eirik Knutzen. "Fortunately, the cute Australian pig in *Babe* changed all that and gave me a legitimate screen career for the first time." Cromwell next appeared in, among other films, *The People vs. Larry Flynt*, (1996), as the real-life banker and antipornography activist Charles Keating; *Star Trek: First Contact* 1996), as the often drunk, brilliantly inventive, rock-and-roll–loving engineer Zefram Cochrane (who is reportedly the only character ever to utter the words "star trek" in any TV installment or film in that long-running series); *L.A. Confidential* (1997), as a sharp-tongued, crafty police captain; and *The General's Daughter* (1999), as a general with vice-presidential ambitions whose daughter has been murdered. Also in 1999 he played a judge in *Snow Falling on Cedars* and a prison warden in *The Green Mile*. He has since appeared on the silver screen in *The Sum of All Fears* (2002), *I, Robot* (2004), and *The Longest Yard* (2005). Also among his screen credits are the independent films *The Education of Little Tree* (1997) and *The Snow Walker* (2003), both of which deal with issues relevant to Native Americans—matters in which Cromwell has long had a special interest. Some years ago he founded Hecel Oyakapi (which means "They do it this way" in the Lakota Indian language), an organization whose goal was to help the Lakota tribespeople of South Dakota preserve their heritage, language, and culture through traditional arts.

Meanwhile, on television, Cromwell portrayed the newspaper magnate William Randolph Hearst in the film *RKO 281* (1999), and the following year he appeared in a remake of the movie *Fail Safe*. In 2001 Cromwell starred in his own series, *Citizen Baines*, about a former U.S. senator who is trying to reconnect with his three adult daughters. The show received mixed reviews, with most critics writing approvingly of Cromwell's portrayal but disparagingly of the daughter characters, and it was canceled later the same year. In 2002 Cromwell was cast in a new version of Orson Welles's 1942 film *The Magnificent Ambersons*. He also had a role in the highly lauded 2003 miniseries adaptation, for HBO, of Tony Kushner's play *Angels in America*. In 2004–05 he starred in the darkly comedic series *Six Feet Under*. "One of the reasons I was excited about doing *Six Feet Under* is [that] I've been [acting for] 40 years now and I've never gotten the girl," he explained to Mark Olsen. On *Six Feet Under* he played George Sibley, the new husband of the widowed Ruth, the matriarch of the Fishers, who own a funeral home. As the sixth, and final, season of *Six Feet Under* began, in June 2005, George was descending into madness—a turn of events that angered Cromwell. "They didn't tell me what was going to happen to [Sibley]—all of a sudden, he started to fall to pieces, and I had no idea," he complained to Bruce Fretts for *TV Guide* (June 12, 2005). "I'm not used to working this way. I like to know when I'm being led somewhere. . . . I've been doing this for 40 years. I'm not a goof. It doesn't add any more life to keep actors out of the loop." Since the conclusion of *Six Feet Under*, Cromwell has worked in the film *The Queen* and the television movie *Pope John Paul II*, both of which were in production in the latter half of 2005.

Cromwell has always tried to remain true to his real-life values in his work as an actor. "I have turned down [projects] that I thought were exploitative of any number of issues: women, violence, insensitive in terms of race and class," he told Laura Weinert for *Adweek* (May 6, 2004). "Mostly my career is directed by my intention to be of service. There are always two options: You choose things that you like and exemplify what you stand for, and then there are jobs that you simply do because you've got to pay rent. You don't want to do something in paying rent that compromises what you stand for, that limits your ability to speak out and be effective." Cromwell has believed in the importance of speaking out since his childhood, when, in the early 1950s, during the witchhunt for supposed Communists in government and elsewhere that was sparked by Republican senator Joseph McCarthy of Wisconsin, Cromwell's father was falsely accused of harboring Communist sympathies; his failure to testify to the satisfaction of the House Un-American Activities Committee led to his blacklisting by Hollywood. Like his father, James Cromwell is an active member of the Screen Actors Guild. "Early in my career, people used to tell me to keep my mouth shut. But now nobody cares as long as you don't violate the unspoken rule of not messing up the movie," he told Philip Wuntch.

Cromwell has actively supported causes connected with non–acting-related issues as well. (He told Laura Weinert, "Neither film nor theatre causes revolutions. People don't run out of the theatre and overthrow governments.") He has traced his passion to make a positive difference in the world in part to a "series of assassinations of people I respected and revered and loved and had hopes for"—President John F. Kennedy, in 1963, and the Reverend Martin Luther King Jr. and U.S. senator and presidential aspirant Robert F Kennedy, in 1968. "[Those] hopes were shattered," he told Laura Weinert. In the mid-1960s, a few years after the efforts by the so-called Freedom Riders, in 1961, to test the effectiveness of the 1960 Supreme Court ruling outlawing segregation in all interstate public facilities, Cromwell toured the South with an acting troupe called the Free Southern Theater. During the summer of 1964, at about the time that three civil rights workers (James Earl Chaney, Michael Schwerner, and Andrew Goodman) were murdered in Meridian, Mississippi, Cromwell took part in the Free Southern Theater's integrated production of *Waiting for Godot*, in which he wore blackface and the African-American actors wore whiteface. Cromwell recollected to Laura Weinert that, following one of the performances, the civil rights activist Fanny Lou Hamer spoke to the audience, telling them, "I want you people to take this play seriously because unlike the two characters in this play, we're not waiting for anything. We're on the road. We're taking charge. We're taking control. So you learn what happens to people who wait for somebody else to bring them freedom." In the late 1960s Cromwell joined the Committee to Defend the Panthers, a group that supported the release of 13 leaders of the Black Panther Party who had been jailed on conspiracy charges. During that period he was arrested for participating in a protest against the Vietnam War outside the White House. With his acting career seemingly stalled, he briefly held a job as a counselor at a Connecticut school for juvenile delinquents—work that he described to Philip Wuntch as "an eye-opening and disillusioning experience." "The school was basically a profit-making endeavor at the expense of the kids, all of whom had committed crimes because of their backgrounds," he told Wuntch. "The people in charge didn't care about the kids. The school was just a warehouse to keep the kids in. It provided practically the same environment as the streets."

Cromwell has also been a longtime supporter of animal rights. He gave up eating red meat years ago, after riding his motorcycle through stockyards in Texas during a cross-country trip. "It seemed like the whole day. It just went on and on. There were pens on both sides," he recalled to Nora Fraser for the *Pet Press* (2000, on-line). "And the smell was horrible. The sense of doom and [the cattle's] awareness—being able to project and feel that kind of terror of what is coming. I never ate red meat again!" After filming *Babe* Cromwell adopted veganism (eliminating all animal flesh and animal by-products from his diet). In 2001 he was arrested for demonstrating at a Wendy's fast-food restaurant in Virginia, where he had gone at the request of the organization People for the Ethical Treatment of Animals (PETA). A PETA representative had asked him if he "wanted to commit this civil disobedience," as he explained to Philip Wuntch. "I

thought, 'Hey, I haven't been arrested in a while, so why not?' But we were successful. Wendy's changed their farming practices to suit PETA." Cromwell, who has adopted Thanksgiving turkeys rather than eaten them, said to Scott Murdoch that he is trying to prevent "that creature [from being] reduced to an object which has no more value than the sum of its parts."

Cromwell's nine-year marriage to Ann Ulvestad ended in divorce in 1986; the actor retained custody of the couple's three children, Kate, John, and Colin. Later that year Cromwell married the actress Julie Cobb, whose father was the actor Lee J. Cobb and who has a daughter, Rosemary, from a previous marriage. In October 2004 Cromwell and Cobb separated, and Cromwell has since filed a petition for divorce.

—K.J.E.

Suggested Reading: *Adweek* May 6, 2004; *Dallas Morning News* June 8, 2002; Internet Movie Database (on-line); *Los Angeles Times* E p3 Aug. 1, 2004; *People* p105 Mar. 25, 1996; *Washington Times* B p5 Nov. 1, 2001

Selected Television Series or Movies: *The Rockford Files*, 1974; *All in the Family*, 1974; *Maude*, 1974, 1978; *Hot L Baltimore*, 1975; *The Nancy Walker Show*, 1976; *Barefoot in the Park*, 1981; *Born to the Wind*, 1982; *The Last Precinct*, 1986; *Easy Street*, 1986; *Alison's Demise*, 1987; *China Beach*, 1988; *Matlock: Nowhere to Turn*, 1990; *Revenge of the Nerds III: The Next Generation*, 1992; *Revenge of the Nerds IV: Nerds in Love*, 1994; *The Shaggy Dog*, 1994; *RKO 281*, 1999; *Fail Safe*, 2000; *Citizen Baines*, 2001; *The Magnificent Ambersons*, 2002; *RFK*, 2002; *Angels in America*, 2003; *Salem's Lot*, 2004; *Six Feet Under*, 2004–05

Selected Films: *Murder by Death*, 1976; *The Cheap Detective*, 1978; *The Man with Two Brains*, 1983; *Revenge of the Nerds*, 1984; *Oh God! You Devil*, 1984; *A Fine Mess*, 1986; *Revenge of the Nerds II: Nerds in Paradise*, 1987; *Pink Cadillac*, 1989; *The Babe*, 1992; *Romeo Is Bleeding*, 1993; *Babe*, 1995; *Eraser*, 1996; *The People vs. Larry Flynt*, 1996; *Star Trek: First Contact*, 1996; *L.A. Confidential*, 1997; *The Education of Little Tree*, 1997; *Deep Impact*, 1998; *Babe: Pig in the City*, 1998; *The General's Daughter*, 1999; *Snow Falling on Cedars*, 1999; *The Green Mile*, 1999; *Space Cowboys*, 2000; *The Sum of All Fears*, 2002; *The Snow Walker*, 2003; *I, Robot*, 2004; *The Longest Yard*, 2005

Craig Schwartz, courtesy of Mark Taper Forum

Davidson, Gordon

May 7, 1933– Former artistic director of the Mark Taper Forum

Address: Ahmanson Theatre/Mark Taper Forum, Center Theatre Group, Music Center Annex, 601 W. Temple St., Los Angeles, CA 90012

"Gordon Davidson and the Mark Taper Forum represent everything that is important and good about the American theater," Zelda Fichandler, the producing director of the Arena Stage, in Washington, D.C., told Daniel B. Wood for the *Christian Science Monitor* (April 8, 1987). Davidson was the artistic director of the Mark Taper Forum of the Los Angeles County Music Center, one of the finest regional theaters in the United States, for almost four decades, until September 2005, and artistic director/producer of the Ahmanson Theatre since 1989. Both the Mark Taper Forum and the Ahmanson Theatre function under the auspices of the Center Theatre Group (CTG), a nonprofit regional theater company. According to Fichandler, both Davidson and the Mark Taper Forum boast "high artistry, a conscience, awareness of the world they inhabit, and always motion toward the achievement of their artistic goals." In an interview with Thomas Thompson for the *New York Times Magazine* (March 11, 1979), the legendary composer and conductor Leonard Bernstein called Davidson "a real artist, not just a theater man. . . . He's one of the rare people of the world. I would trust him not only with my work but with my life." The producer Emanuel Azenberg has called Davidson a "genius," the actress Joyce Van Patten has called him "cute," and the drama critic Sandra Kreiswirth seemed to

be speaking for many when she described him to Bernard Weinraub for the *New York Times* (May 14, 1992) as "L.A.'s Mr. Theater. . . . Nothing happens [at the Mark Taper Forum] without Gordon's input. . . . He loves actors and directors and playwrights, his whole heart is in it, and there would be no Mark Taper Forum if it wasn't for him."

Davidson was not always as well loved as he seems to be today. Indeed, controversy has long been his forte: his early productions at the Taper triggered protests from the Catholic Church and were watched with some suspicion by the FBI. Nevertheless, Davidson is best known for having produced some of the most highly regarded theatrical pieces of the last several decades, including the Tony Award– and Pulitzer Prize–winning play *Angels in America*, a two-part drama about love, loss, politics, history, and the effects of AIDs, written by Tony Kushner. In the eyes of many critics and fans, Davidson's departure from the Mark Taper Forum spells the end of an era; many have wondered what will become of West Coast theater in his absence.

Gordon Davidson was born on May 7, 1933 in the New York City borough of Brooklyn. His father, Joe Davidson, was a professor of theater at Brooklyn College for 46 years, and his mother, Alice Davidson, was a concert pianist who relinquished her career to raise her children. As Davidson recalled to Tom Tugend for the *Jewish Journal* (March 3, 2000, on-line), he and his younger brothers, Michael and Robert, grew up in a neighborhood composed of "Jews, Irish Catholics, Italian Catholics and one Protestant." Davidson's own family was, as he explained to Tugend, a "prototypical American Jewish family." In terms of Judaism, his grandfather was Orthodox, and his father Conservative, while Davidson himself is Reform. Davidson was valedictorian of Brooklyn Technical High School, and he gained admittance to Cornell University, in Ithaca, New York, with a number of scholarships, including one from the Telluride Association, as an engineering student. While attending Cornell, Davidson met Judith Swiller, a student at Vassar College, whom he married shortly thereafter. He changed his major to drama before receiving his B.A. degree from Cornell, in 1956. The following year he earned an M.A. degree in directing for the theater from Case Western Reserve University, in Cleveland, Ohio.

Davidson began his career in theater in 1958, as an apprentice stage manager at the American Shakespeare Festival in Stratford, Connecticut, earning $40 a week. In 1959 he took a job on Broadway, as stage manager of the Phoenix Theater, working on plays that included a revival of *The Great God Brown*; *Peer Gynt*; and *Henry IV, Part One*. Also on Broadway, he stage-managed *From the Second City* and the Martha Graham Dance Company in 1961. Recalling those early days to Sue Reilly for *People* (November 3, 1980), Davidson's wife, Judith, who was then working for the now-defunct magazine *Charm* for $45 a week, maintained that she and her husband, despite their meager earnings, "didn't know we were starving. We were just two kids from Brooklyn who thought we had it made—[because] we lived in Manhattan." In 1964 the couple's situation improved tremendously, when the director, producer, and playwright John Houseman hired Davidson to assist him on a production of Shakespeare's play *King Lear* at the University of California at Los Angeles (UCLA). Davidson and his wife moved to Los Angeles, and Davidson eventually succeeded Houseman as managing director of the Theatre Group at UCLA. During a two-and-a-half-year period, Davidson and the UCLA troupe staged 11 productions, including *The Deputy*, by Rolf Hochhuth, and Leonard Bernstein's *Candide* (a theatrical version of Voltaire's famous 18th-century novel), which Davidson directed. Davidson was excited by what he saw as a general willingness in the Los Angeles theater world to mount productions of daring and controversial plays, and as managing director of a theater group he benefitted from "a tremendous talent pool that wanted to work in the theater and had no outlet for it," as he told Arthur Unger for the *Christian Science Monitor* (March 15, 1984).

In 1967 Dorothy "Buffy" Chandler, chair of the board of governors for the Music Center of Los Angeles County, persuaded Davidson to become the first artistic director of the new Mark Taper Forum in Los Angeles. The Taper is part of the nonprofit Center Theatre Group (formerly the Theatre Group at UCLA), which was funded by subscription and single-ticket sales, as well as grants from the Ford Foundation, the Rockefeller Foundation, and the new National Endowment for the Arts, among others. The Taper's reliable income enabled the theater to create, in addition to its usual five to seven plays per season, a special program of untried, unconventional new plays. As artistic director of the Taper, Davidson faced the challenge of trying to foster a new theater scene in a city famous for its movie industry. "When Gordon arrived, the town was indifferent, if not hostile, to the theater, and he has nurtured a very loyal audience in a place downtown where people said it was not possible," the *Orange County (California) Register* theater critic Thomas O'Connor told Weinraub.

Davidson immediately created controversy by staging, as the theater's inaugural production, *The Devils*, a play by John Whiting based on a book by Aldous Huxley—and a true incident in 17th-century France—about a promiscuous priest and the sexual fantasies of a nun. (In the resulting hysteria in the 1600s, two offenders were burned at the stake.) Both the Catholic Archdiocese and Davidson's superiors on the County Board of Supervisors were livid and, had it not been for the intercessions of Dorothy Chandler and the Hollywood mogul and CTG board president Lew Wasserman, would have succeeded in having the production canceled. "I'll never forget it," Davidson told Daniel B. Wood. "We thought [the Taper] was over before it began." In response to the incident, the County Board of Supervisors formed a committee to over-

see all creative choices at the Music Center. Davidson was not cowed, however, and held fast to his artistic vision. "Theatre has many purposes," he told Viola Hegyi Swisher for *After Dark* (April 1969). "But the purpose of my theatre is the open meeting and confrontation of people with society. I don't aim our plays at any particular age group or income level. What I do try for is to find plays that challenge the overly acquiescent outlook, wherever it occurs." He continued to do just that throughout his tenure as artistic director. In 1969 he staged *In the Matter of J. Robert Oppenheimer*, which told the true story of how Oppenheimer, a brilliant physicist who directed the Manhattan Project, the U.S. government's program to develop the atomic bomb during World War II, was torn between his loyalty to the government and his moral conscience. *Oppenheimer* opened at Lincoln Center later that same year, marking Davidson's New York City directorial debut.

Perhaps the most colorful story concerning a Davidson production involves *The Trial of the Catonsville Nine*, an anti–Vietnam War drama written by Daniel Berrigan, a Roman Catholic priest, which was staged at the Taper in 1971. At that time Berrigan was wanted by the FBI for illegal, nonviolent protests against the war, and Davidson claimed that government agents had tapped his home phone line and hassled one of the actors in his troupe. Berrigan chose not to attend the opening-night performance of *The Trial of the Catonsville Nine*. Recalling to Steven Leigh Morris for *LA Weekly* (April 25–May 1, 2003, on-line) the events of that night, Davidson said that he "had contacted Dan [Berrigan] and said it's usual to have a playwright present for the opening, please send a message. So the house goes to half [lighting], and over the sound system, there's an announcement: 'Good evening, this is Dan Berrigan speaking to you from the underground.' Suddenly, some people in the front of the theater jumped up and moved forward. They were obviously the FBI looking for him." In spite of the somewhat tense atmosphere at the Taper, the play was well received. Davidson won an Obie Award for best director and received a Tony Award nomination. (In 1972 he made a rare foray into film to direct a movie version of *The Trial of the Catonsville Nine*, produced by Gregory Peck.)

In 1977 Davidson won a Tony Award for best director for the Taper's production of *The Shadow Box*, a Pulitzer Prize–winning play by Michael Cristofer, about three groups of people, all at the same large hospital, who are trying to come to terms with the death of a loved one and the process of dying. That same year Davidson and the Taper won the coveted Tony Award for best regional theater. In 1980 he was again nominated for the Tony Award for best director for his staging of *Children of a Lesser God*, a drama about a speech teacher at a school for the deaf who falls in love with one of his students. Though Davidson did not win the award for best director, the production won the

Tony Award for best play, while John Rubinstein and Phyllis Frelich, the two lead performers in Davidson's production, won the awards for best actor and best actress, respectively. When Frelich accepted her award, she praised Davidson for his sensitivity and courage.

Running a theater in Los Angeles rather than New York, which has traditionally been regarded as the theater capital of the country, was often challenging for Davidson. "We have a hard job getting new plays," he told Lewis Funke for the *New York Times* (March 6, 1969). "We should be generating new material. We can't simply exist as repositories for revivals. It's the playwright's agent who frequently is the villain, advising his client to keep his eye on Broadway [New York]." Facing the inevitable comparisons between the two cities, Davidson told Weinraub 23 years later, "New York will always be a great city . . . but it doesn't have the only baseball team, it doesn't have the only symphony, and it certainly doesn't have the only theater." Another challenge for theater in general, whether in New York, Los Angeles, or elsewhere, is the dearth of recognizable star power. As Davidson told Kathleen O'Steen for *Variety* (December 12, 1994), "Today's stars don't come from the stage and there are very few actors anymore who regularly pay their dues [in theater]." In addition, because the Taper is a nonprofit theater, Davidson has had to contend with budget cuts and grant reductions while facing ever-increasing pressure to produce more mainstream entertainment in order to attract larger audiences. He has had to come to terms with the business demands that impinge upon the artistic side of the theater world. Davidson told Funke, "If I do a play that pleases 80 to 85 per cent of an audience, that in itself makes the undertaking valid. No one judges the success of a symphony by the number of people who've heard it. A painting is not evaluated on the basis of how many people come to a museum to see it. The trouble is that the theater is equated with show business, which is judged by financial success." Despite such conflicts and difficulties, the Taper now boasts an annual attendance of more than 250,000 people, and the theater's regular subscription season attracts more than 25,000 subscribers.

In addition to continuing his award-winning work at the Taper, in 1989 Davidson took the post of artistic director/producer of the Ahmanson Theatre, the other home venue of the Center Theatre Group. After supervising the renovation of the theater, in 1995 Davidson reopened the Ahmanson with a revival of his successful Theatre Group at UCLA production of Leonard Bernstein's musical *Candide*, as the first event on the new stage.

Davidson's success continued into the 1990s as Tony Kushner's extraordinary two-part drama, *Angels in America*, premiered at the Taper before moving to Broadway. Both *Part One, Millennium Approaches*, and *Part Two, Perestroika*, won the Tony Award for best play, in 1993 and 1994, respectively. (For *Millennium Approaches* Kushner

also took home a Pulitzer Prize. *Angels in America* was later made into an HBO movie starring Al Pacino, Meryl Streep, and Emma Thompson and directed by Mike Nichols.) In 1993 Davidson also produced at the Taper the Pulitzer Prize–winning play *The Kentucky Cycle*, by Robert Schenkkan, which had been developed in part by the Taper and made its stage debut in Seattle. A series of nine plays, *The Kentucky Cycle* focuses on three intertwined families in rural Kentucky as they grow, suffer, and change over the course of 200 years. Three of the four nominees for the 1994 Tony Award for best play were staged at the Taper: *Angels in America: Part Two, Perestroika*; *The Kentucky Cycle*; and Anna Deveare Smith's *Twilight: Los Angeles, 1992*, which had been a Taper commission.

In recent years some critics have complained that the Taper's repertoire has become less politicized, less challenging of the status quo. Attempting to explain that perception, Davidson told Steven Leigh Morris, "We live in a different world now. *Catonsville* was providing a forum for a discussion about the war in Vietnam before there was much discussion in the press or in the media. Now you get an overdose of that. The question of what the performing arts can do is not as clear. That doesn't mean there isn't a desire" to present socially important work. He told Weinraub, "Yesterday's cutting edge is tomorrow's left of center and the next day's conservatism. Is focusing on the socially relevant really criticism? I don't know. I do believe that's one of the functions of the theater." He added that he also likes to laugh, and so he tries "for a mixture in what we do." Other original plays or musicals directed or produced by Davidson include *Zoot Suit* (1979), a landmark Latino play written by Luis Valdez and starring Edward James Olmos; *I Ought to Be in Pictures* (1981), by the legendary playwright Neil Simon, about a young girl who dreams of becoming a movie star; *Burn This* (1987), a searing love story by the acclaimed playwright Lanford Wilson; *Jelly's Last Jam* (1992), a musical that starred the dancer and actor Gregory Hines; *Smokey Joe's Café* (1995), a musical nominated for seven Tony Awards; and *QED* (2001), a world premiere developed by the Taper about the Nobel Prize–winning physicist Richard Feynman. *QED* went on to Lincoln Center for a run at the Vivian Beaumont Theater.

Additionally, Davidson has directed the operas *Harriet: The Woman Called Moses* for the Virginia Opera, *A Midsummer Night's Dream* with the L.A. Philharmonic, *Così Fan Tutte* and *La Bohème* for the Corpus Christi Symphony, and *Il Trovatore* for the Houston Grand Opera. In 1971 he directed the world premiere of Leonard Bernstein's *Mass*, as the opening event at the newly built John F. Kennedy Center for the Performing Arts, in Washington, D.C.

In 2004, after nearly four decades of overseeing programming at the Taper, Davidson decided to retire, although he himself views the change differently. "I'm not retiring, I'm moving on," he told Leigh Morris. His exit has led to questions concerning the future of theater in Los Angeles. Indeed, Davidson himself wondered the same fairly early on: "I think we've created the possibility of a legacy," he told Hilary DeVries for the *Christian Science Monitor* (June 30, 1987), "but there is some serious question about how to pass it on." In September 2005 Davidson stepped down; he was succeeded by Michael Ritchie, whose 25-year career in theater includes serving as the producer of the Williamstown Theater Festival.

In addition to his other honors, Davidson won the Governor's Award for the Arts (1990), an L.A. Stage Alliance Ovation Award for long-term commitment and contributions to the Los Angeles theater scene (1992), and a Casting Society of America's Lifetime Achievement Award (1993). He received a Career Achievement Ovation Award from the L.A. Stage Alliance (2003), and he won an *L.A. Weekly* Queen of the Angels Award (2004). The Los Angeles Drama Critics Circle has honored Davidson with three Distinguished Direction Awards and a special award in recognition of his outstanding contributions to American playwrights, as well as a Lifetime Achievement Award in 2005. A member of the American Academy of Arts and Sciences, Davidson was appointed to the National Council on the Arts by former president Bill Clinton and was inducted into the Theatre Hall of Fame on Broadway in 2002. He has been awarded honorary doctorates from the California Institute of the Arts, the Claremont University Consortium, Occidental College, and the University of Judaism, all of which are located in California, as well as Brooklyn College, in New York.

Davidson has sat on the advisory boards and panels of various organizations, including the National Endowment for the Arts, the Fund for New American Plays, the Cornell Center for the Performing Arts, and the National Foundation for Jewish Culture. He formerly presided over the Theatre Communications Group and the League of Resident Theatres. Davidson and his wife have two children, Adam and Rachel, and a granddaughter, Arielle.

—K.J.E.

Suggested Reading: *After Dark* p24+ Apr. 1969; Center Theatre Group Web site; *LA Weekly* (online) Apr. 25–May 1, 2003; *New York Times* p36 Mar. 6, 1969, p1+ Jan. 9, 1972, C p17 May 14, 1992; *People* p45+ Nov. 3, 1980

Selected Plays: *The Devils*, 1967; *In the Matter of J. Robert Oppenheimer*, 1969; *The Trial of the Catonsville Nine*, 1971; *The Shadow Box*, 1977; *Children of a Lesser God*, 1980; *Burn This*, 1987; *Angels in America: Millennium Approaches*, 1993; *The Kentucky Cycle*, 1993; *Angels in America: Perestroika*, 1994; *Smokey Joe's Cafe*, 1995; *QED*, 2001

Courtesy of Purdue University

de Branges, Louis

(de brawnzh)

Aug. 21, 1932– Mathematician

Address: Mathematics Dept., Rm. 800, 1395 Mathematics Bldg., Purdue University, Lafayette, IN 47907-1395

Louis de Branges, the Edward C. Elliott Distinguished Professor of Mathematics at Purdue University, in West Lafayette, Indiana, is among the most famous figures in the international community of mathematicians—and one of its most belittled as well. De Branges's unconventional approaches to determining the truth of mathematical propositions enabled him to complete, in 1984, a proof of the so-called Bieberbach conjecture, thus solving a problem that had stumped mathematicians for nearly seven decades. Although de Branges's proof of the conjecture, described by many mathematicians as "the Holy Grail of mathematics," is widely regarded as one of the greatest achievements in the recent history of mathematics, de Branges is "considered a crank by nearly all of his colleagues," in the words of Eric Wolff, writing for the *New York Sun* (June 18, 2003). That assessment may be attributed to some extent to de Branges's personal eccentricities, such as his unwillingness to explain his calculations to those who lack expertise in the particular mathematical topics on which he works, and his reputation for being "brusque, obsessive and stubborn," as Karl Sabbagh wrote for the British magazine *Prospect* (January 2002, on-line). For the most the part, though, it stems from what many of his colleagues regard as acts of unforgivable hubris: his premature claims to have produced solutions to other mathematical problems—solutions that were later found to have fatal errors. In 2004 de Branges announced that he had proved another notoriously difficult mathematical proposition, known as the Riemann hypothesis, which had confounded mathematicians ever since its formulation, in 1859. That proof has yet to be verified by other mathematicians, but if and when it is, de Branges will be able to claim a $1,000,000 prize for his feat.

De Branges has written several mathematical monographs and many research articles. Referring to the hundreds of mathematics journals currently being published, with such titles as *Annals of Combinatorics, Journal of Integer Sequences, Linear and Multilinear Algebra, Random Operators and Stochastic Equations, Research in Nondestructive Evaluation*, and *Journal of Symplectic Geometry*, de Branges wrote in his "Apology for the Proof of the Riemann Hypothesis" ("apology" here means an argument to support an assertion), as posted on the Purdue University Web site (December 17, 2004), "The structure of mathematical journals creates the impression that mathematics is fragmented into unrelated disciplines. The underlying unity of mathematics is however maintained by problems which span these disciplines."

Louis de Branges de Bourcia was born in Paris, France, on August 21, 1932 to a member of the French aristocracy and an American-born mother, whose maiden name was Diane McDonald. He lived in Paris until 1941, when the occupation of the city by German forces during World War II prompted his mother to bring him and his two sisters to live in the United States. (De Branges's father remained in France.) The family settled in a seaside cottage in Rehoboth Beach, Delaware, not far from de Branges's maternal grandparents' home, in Wilmington. As a child de Branges enjoyed solving cryptogram puzzles published in the *Philadelphia Inquirer*. "The mystery of wartime secrecy stimulated logical thought," he explained in his "Apology for the Proof of the Riemann Hypothesis." "Deciphering coded messages was part of the general effort for survival." Having already learned the rudiments of the English language during summer visits to the United States to see his mother's parents, de Branges quickly became accustomed to his new surroundings and excelled in school. His academic success enabled him to skip the seventh grade, and at the age of 12, he enrolled at Saint Andrew's School, a Christian high school in Middletown, Delaware, where he boarded. His mother sold the house at Rehoboth Beach and moved in with her parents, and from then on de Branges spent all his school vacations at his grandparents' home.

De Branges has credited his maternal grandfather, Ellice McDonald, with persuading him to take his studies seriously. McDonald was a distinguished surgeon, cancer researcher, and university lecturer and the director of the Biochemical Research Foundation, in Delaware. He was a friend of Irénée DuPont, a former president of the DuPont Corp. (some years earlier the DuPonts had bought property in France that had been owned by the de Branges family), and as a young teenager Louis de Branges spent many Sunday mornings in the company of his grandfather and Iréneé DuPont, serving as a caddy during their golf games. One morning DuPont, who had noticed de Branges's interest in mathematics, posed a very difficult math problem to him: find positive integers a, b, and c such that $a^3 + b^3 = 22c^3$. De Branges spent a year working on the equation, conducting independent research at the libraries of Saint Andrew's, the Biochemical Research Foundation, and the University of Delaware. He arrived at a solution in which the values of a, b, and c are five or six digits in length. Years later, in the "Apology for the Proof of the Riemann Hypothesis," de Branges described his achievement as "comparable to my doctoral thesis written ten years later."

Impressed by his grandson's progress as a mathematician, McDonald agreed to help pay for de Branges's college education. (According to de Branges, DuPont may have supplied the funds in secret.) In 1949 de Branges enrolled at the Massachusetts Institute of Technology (MIT), in Cambridge, where he pursued a double major in chemistry and mathematics. "The aim of my undergraduate education," he wrote in the "Apology for the Proof of the Riemann Hypothesis," "was . . . not to prepare for a career in [pure] mathematics, but to acquire knowledge of value in applications to science." However, he soon realized that his "talents [lay] in theory rather than applications," and partly to distinguish his work from that of his grandfather as a practical scientist, he resolved to devote his career to mathematical study.

De Branges graduated from MIT in 1953. That same year he gained admittance as a doctoral student of mathematics at Cornell University, in Ithaca, New York, where his thesis adviser was Harry Pollard, who later taught mathematics at Purdue. De Branges immersed himself in number theory (which concerns questions about and properties of numbers, usually whole numbers) and developed an interest in the Riemann hypothesis (RH). The RH soon became central to his research; his dissertation, titled "Local Operators on Fourier Transforms," began with a discussion of it. De Branges was awarded his Ph.D. degree in mathematics in 1957. For the next five years, he conducted postdoctoral research on the theory of Hilbert spaces, a subject in which he is now considered one of the world's foremost authorities. His work was published in 1968 under the title *Hilbert Spaces of Entire Functions*. Also during that period he taught at Lafayette College, in Easton, Pennsylvania, and Bryn Mawr College, also in Pennsylvania. In 1962 he joined the Mathematics Department at Purdue as an associate professor; the following year he was promoted to full professorship. From 1963 to 1966 he was an Alfred P. Sloan Fellow.

In 1964 de Branges publicly declared that he had proven "the existence of invariant subspace for continuous transformations in Hilbert spaces," as he put it to Sabbagh. His inability to support his claim, then and later, caused many of his peers to lose respect for him. That is the main reason, he believes, why the mathematical community has continued to ostracize him. "I declared something to be true which I was not able to substantiate," he admitted to Sabbagh. "And the fact that I did that destroyed my career. My colleagues have never forgiven it." Nevertheless, in 1967 de Branges was awarded a prestigious Guggenheim fellowship.

When de Branges published his proof of the Bieberbach conjecture, in 1984, even his detractors were obliged to acknowledge the significance of his achievement. The problem had posed a challenge to mathematicians ever since its formulation, in 1916, by Ludwig Bieberbach, a German mathematician known for his active involvement in the Nazi Party, and over the years had spurred many unsuccessful attempts to prove it. De Branges's proof involved the use of two branches of mathematics—operator theory and special functions—neither of which had been pinpointed by other mathematicians as a likely source for the solution. "It's a stunning feat of intellectual mountain climbing—like conquering Everest," Allen H. Clark, then the dean of Purdue's School of Science, told a reporter for the Purdue News Service (August 28, 1984), as quoted on the Purdue University Web site. "Undoubtedly it's the best piece of mathematical work to come out of Purdue." Joseph Lipman, then the acting head of Purdue's Mathematics Department, commented, "Experts on the subject are astounded by the brevity and ingenuity of de Branges' solution."

The Bieberbach conjecture, according to the Purdue News Service, is "a statement about the coefficients of power series for a function of a complex variable with certain properties" that "concerns certain transformations of the unit disc (i.e. the region bounded by a circle whose radius is one unit of length) into other planar regions." It can be expressed by the sentence "The nth coefficient in the power series of a univalent function can be no greater than n." Thus, $f(z) = a_0 + a_1z + a_2z^2 + \ldots + a_nz^n + \ldots$ Although the conjecture relates to all coefficients of the power series, Bieberbach himself verified it for only the second coefficient. In 1923 the Czech mathematician Charles Loewner verified it for the third coefficient by using a special differential equation, now known as the Loewner differential equation. The conjecture was verified for the fourth coefficient in 1955 by Paul R. Garabedian and Menachem Schiffer; for the sixth coefficient, in 1968 and 1969, respectively, by Roger N. Pederson and Mitsuru Ozawa; for the fifth coefficient, in 1972, by Pederson and Schiffer.

In February 1984 de Branges collaborated with Walter Gautschi, a professor of computer science at Purdue, to test the validity of Bieberbach's equation using a Cyber-205 supercomputer; he succeeded in verifying it for the first 30 coefficients (that is, through $a_{30}z^{30}$). This information provided him with enough material to arrive at the general solution to the conjecture the next month. In doing so, he first proved the so-called Milin conjecture, formulated in 1971 by the Soviet mathematician I. M. Milin; he then showed that the Milin conjecture implied the correctness of an earlier, 1936 conjecture by M. S. Robertson, which, in turn, implied the correctness of the Bieberbach conjecture. In developing his proof de Branges also made use of other work by his predecessors, notably Loewner's differential equation and an inequality involving functions that had been established in 1976 by Richard Askey and George Gasper.

De Branges's proof, which filled 350 pages of manuscript, at first elicited skepticism. In the past many mathematicians had offered proofs of the Bieberbach conjecture that were found to be erroneous, and "it was the general expectation that some subtle error would be found in the present argument," according to the Purdue News Bulletin. "Everyone has been very suspicious of him," Felix Browder, a mathematician at the University of Chicago, in Illinois, told an interviewer for *Science* magazine (September 7, 1984). Furthermore, at the age of 52, de Branges was considered too old to have made such a significant discovery. (According to conventional wisdom, mathematicians tend to do their best work before they reach their 30th birthdays.) Acceptance of the proof by the mathematical community was further forestalled by the unwillingness of any of the U.S. mathematicians to whom de Branges sent his manuscript to take the time and effort to examine it closely; another obstacle was the discovery of errors early on in the calculations by the few experts who had begun to read the proof. Ultimately, however, none of those errors affected the accuracy of the proof.

Coincidentally, de Branges had already scheduled a visit to the V. A. Steklov Mathematical Institute, in St. Petersburg (then known as Leningrad), in what was then the Soviet Union, from April to June 1984, under an exchange agreement between the U.S. and Soviet academies of sciences. When he learned that Milin would be there at the same time, de Branges arranged to give five lectures, in which he presented his proof of the Bieberbach conjecture to Milin and several other mathematicians. After the lecture series ended, Milin and another attendee, E. V. Emelianov, each wrote a report attesting to the merits of de Branges's proof. In July 1984 de Branges presented his proof at universities in Würzburg and Hanover, in Germany, and in Amsterdam, in the Netherlands. It produced a sensation within the international mathematical community, and soon many additional mathematicians reviewed and confirmed Milin's and Emelianov's favorable assessments of de Branges's work. De Branges's article "A Proof of the Bieberbach Conjecture" appeared in *Acta Mathematica* (published by the Royal Swedish Academy of Sciences) in 1985. His accomplishment earned de Branges an

Alexander von Humboldt Prize, Germany's highest award for senior U.S. scientists and scholars in all disciplines, in 1989; the Alexander Ostrowski Prize, awarded every other year by an international jury from five overseas universities or scientific academies, also in 1989; and a Leroy P. Steele Prize, from the American Mathematical Society, in 1993.

In 2000 a group of leading mathematicians joined the privately funded Clay Mathematics Institute (founded by a Boston businessman in 1998), in Cambridge, Massachusetts, in offering $1,000,000 to anyone who could solve at least one of seven so-called "millennium problems," generally regarded as the world's greatest unsolved mathematical problems. Among them was the Riemann hypothesis, formulated by the German mathematician Georg Friedrich Bernhard Riemann. (In an indication of its importance to mathematicians, Marcus du Sautoy, a professor at Oxford University, in England, told Tim Radford for the London *Guardian Weekly* [September 17–23, 2004], "Most mathematicians would trade their soul with Mephistopheles for a proof.") Based on a complex mathematical expression known as the Riemann zeta function, the RH states that "the non-trivial zeros of the Riemann zeta function all have real part equal to H [one-half]," according to Karl Sabbagh in his illuminating article for *Prospect*. If proven, the RH would provide a mathematical explanation for the apparently random distribution of prime numbers—whole numbers (integers) that are divisible only by themselves and one. Since the time of Euclid, who lived about 2,300 years ago, mathematicians have known that the number of prime numbers is infinite—a fact that many people find counterintuitive. Thanks to high-speed supercomputers, mathematicians have thus far identified prime numbers that have as many as a million digits. Some primes differ from those closest to them by only two (17 and 19; 857 and 859; 3,767 and 3,769); the difference separating others is greater and seemingly random: in the series of primes 7,841, 7,853, 7,867, 7,873, 7,877, 7,879, 7,883, 2,901, 7,907, 7,919, for example, the differences are 12, 14, 6, 4, 2, 4, 18, 6, and 12. Among much higher numbers, the differences may be in the hundreds or even thousands. The nearest prime number after 1,693,182,318,746,371 (1.693 trillion), for example, appears after another 1,132 integers.

According to Karl Sabbagh in *Prospect*, "A proof of the Riemann Hypothesis would be far more significant than providing one piece in a jigsaw puzzle. It would form the final piece for hundreds of puzzles, all incomplete." That is because many mathematicians since Riemann have taken the RH as a given—that is, they have assumed that it is true. As Sabbagh explained, "Number theory . . . is full of conjectures that start, 'if the Riemann hypothesis is true, then . . .'" Thus, many mathematicians have based their work on a hypothesis whose accuracy has yet to be verified. "The condition of mathematics before the proof of the Rie-

mann hypothesis," de Branges wrote in his "Apology for the Proof of the Riemann Hypothesis," "is comparable to the condition of American democracy before the abolition of slavery. Mathematics without the Riemann hypothesis abounds in good intentions which are unfulfilled."

On June 8, 2004 de Branges issued a press release announcing that he had proven the Riemann hypothesis. Due to intense competition surrounding the race for a proof, he decided to broadcast his work as soon as it was completed, posting the paper detailing his solution on the Purdue Web site instead of making a formal announcement in a scientific journal or at a conference. "I invite other mathematicians to examine my efforts," he wrote, as reported by David Whitehouse for the BBC News (June 10, 2004, on-line). "While I will eventually submit my proof for formal publication, due to the circumstances I felt it necessary to post the work on the internet immediately."

In order for it to earn full recognition by the international mathematics community, an abbreviated version of de Brange's 124-page proof must first be accepted by a scientific journal. Then, after a two-year waiting period, it must be approved by a panel of expert mathematicians appointed by the Clay institute. But the mathematics that de Branges used to arrive at his proof is so difficult and abstruse that the verification process has not yet begun. "Because de Branges's proof uses mathematical tools in which he is one of the few experts," Sabbagh explained, "the amount of study required even to become familiar with those tools before embarking on reading the paper seems too great for anyone to commit the time." Furthermore, de Branges's reputation for erroneous claims has led many of his colleagues reflexively to ignore or dismiss his work, and others are convinced that a satisfactory proof of the RH could not possibly have been achieved using his particular methods—even in light of the fact that similar doubts about his proof of the Bieberbach conjecture were laid to rest. "It may be," Sabbagh wrote, "that a possible solution of one of the most important problems in mathematics is never investigated because no one likes the solution's author." Nikolai Nikolski, a Russian mathematician who helped to verify the accuracy of de Branges's proof of the Bieberbach conjecture, told Karl Sabbagh for the *London Review of Books* (*LRB*, July 22, 2004, on-line), "The Riemann Hypothesis is much more complicated than the Bieberbach Conjecture. So you have to be more enthusiastic if you want to validate the proof. You need to have a team of really enthusiastic high-level people. De Branges found in the middle of the 1980s the only place in the world where there were some curious people who just love to solve complicated problems and who were ready to spend a half a year on it. He has asked me several times if it's possible to organise some people to do the same thing with the Riemann Hypothesis. I love him, so I said to him: 'Yes, if you have a very huge grant.'"

If confirmed, de Branges's proof of the Riemann hypothesis will qualify as a major mathematical breakthrough. De Branges told Karl Sabbagh for the *LRB* that the proof is "just part of a longer paper on the zeta functions. That's the important work. It's a theory that could lead to a new understanding of quantum physics, for example, since the way I approach the subject uses a type of mathematics—spectral theory—that seems to underlie the behaviour of atoms." Ironically, de Branges's proof might lead to serious problems in a seemingly unrelated area: commerce conducted over the Internet. Because Internet cryptography is based on prime numbers, with such confidential information as credit-card and bank-account numbers kept secret by way of a coding system that depends on "the extreme difficulty of factoring huge numbers that are the product of very large primes," according to Jeffrey Marsh, writing for the *Washington Times* (October 12, 2003), de Branges's proof could conceivably result in a breakdown in on-line security systems. As du Sautoy explained to Tim Radford, "The whole of e-commerce depends on prime numbers. . . . If the Riemann hypothesis is true, it . . . should give us more understanding of how the primes work, and therefore the proof might be translated into something that might . . . bring the whole of e-commerce to its knees, overnight. So there are very big implications." Still, the extreme complexity of both the Riemann hypothesis and de Branges's proof makes it unlikely that hackers would be able to use his findings to crack prime-number–based codes anytime in the near future.

According to Sabbagh in the *LRB*, de Branges "may not be a crank, but he is cranky. . . . And he does seem to have left a trail of disgruntled, irritated and even contemptuous colleagues behind him." "My relationships with my colleagues are disastrous," de Branges told Sabbagh. Sabbagh also wrote that de Branges is "a person of strict routine" and is "disarmingly honest," sometimes about his past or his personal characteristics, including what others might consider flaws. De Branges mentioned to Sabbagh that he is "very musical," has a good singing voice, and likes to whistle tunes when he walks.

De Branges's first marriage ended in divorce. Since 1989 he has spent his summers in an apartment outside Paris with his second wife, devoting much of his free time to mathematical inquiry. He has suggested that if he is awarded the million-dollar Clay Mathematics Institute prize for his proof of the Riemann hypothesis, he will use the money to restore his family's ancestral castle in France and convert it into a mathematical research institute.

—L.W.

Suggested Reading: *Indianapolis Star* A p1+ June 28, 2004; (London) *Guardian* Oct. 11, 1984; (London) *Guardian Weekly* p21+ Sep. 1723, 2004; *London Review of Books* (on-line) July 22, 2004; *New York Sun* p14+ June 18, 2003; *Purdue News* (on-line) Mar. 17, 1989, June 8, 2004; *Science* p1006+ Sep. 7, 1984;

Delilah

Feb. 15, 1960– Radio music-and-talk-show host

Address: c/o Public Relations Coordinator, Premiere Radio Networks, 15260 Ventura Blvd., Suite 500, Sherman Oaks, CA 91403

Delilah Luke, known simply by her first name to legions of fans, hosts one of the most popular radio programs in the nation. *Delilah After Dark*, a syndicated call-in show broadcast from Seattle, Washington, airs six nights a week and is carried by more than 200 radio stations across the country. More than eight million people tune in to Delilah's engaging mix of soft rock and relationship advice each evening. The show reportedly served as the inspiration for the hit film *Sleepless in Seattle* (1993), in which the young son of a recent widower (played by Tom Hanks) calls a radio talk show to reveal his father's loneliness and find him a new mate.

The success of *Delilah After Dark* has been attributed largely to its host, who draws on her own troubled childhood, addiction struggles, failed marriages, and parenting challenges to help her listeners. "People are people," she told Jo Thomas for the *New York Times* (January 19, 1999). "Even though you can fax someone across the world, and they can E-mail you, it seems communication is less and less effective. I try to encourage people to form relationships. If you're a parent, love your children. If you're married, honor your spouse instead of looking on the Internet for love in all the wrong places. I'm talking about real relationships, not false intimacies. To show love for people, that's what the whole show is about."

The second of Dick and Wilma Luke's four children, Delilah Rene Luke was born on February 15, 1960 in Reedsport, Oregon. Her father, who worked as an engineer, was, by most accounts, an emotionally and physically abusive alcoholic; Delilah has described her mother, a homemaker, in many interviews as a "classic co-dependent." In retrospect, she has come to believe that "the school of hard knocks is a lot more valuable than any college degree," as she told Adrian McCoy for the *Pittsburgh (Pennsylvania) Post-Gazette* (February 16, 1997). In junior high school Delilah won a speech contest for her recitation of President Abraham Lincoln's Gettysburg Address. The judges of

Courtesy of Premiere Radio Networks

Delilah

the contest, who owned an AM radio station, were so impressed with her voice and speaking skills that they offered her a part-time job reporting school news. Thereafter she spent most of her free time in the studio.

On the day of Delilah's high-school graduation, she left home and moved to Eugene, Oregon. (Some sources say her father kicked her out for coming home an hour late.) There she won a scholarship to study at a community college and earned an associate's degree in broadcasting. In 1981 she moved to Seattle, where she landed a job at a radio station. "I did traffic, weather, soft rock, hard rock," she told Suelain Moy for *Good Housekeeping* (September 1999). "But my real thing was the calls. I loved the contact with listeners."

In 1983 Delilah married an African-American man. When the couple visited her parents' house at Christmas, according to one often-quoted tale, her father chased them from the porch with a shotgun. She and her father did not speak again until shortly before his death, in 1993. Delilah and her husband became the parents of a son, Isaiah, who is known by the nickname Sonny.

In 1985 Delilah's brother and his wife died in an airplane crash. (According to some sources, they had been on their way to Sonny's christening.) Later that same year her husband left her for another woman. In the wake of those events, Delilah developed an eating disorder and became addicted to diet pills. In 1986 she lost her job after the radio station that employed her changed its format. She became severely depressed. "My brother was a born-again Christian," she told Judy Harrison for the *Bangor (Maine) Daily News* (June 2, 1997). "He'd tried to talk to me, but I hadn't wanted to lis-

ten. One day I just said I need help. I hurt. I can't do this anymore. Lord, if you're up there, please let me know. That afternoon I found a small Bible on my windshield. Inside the cover was written, 'Jesus loves you.'" After that, Delilah began attending church and going to meetings of Al-Anon, the self-help program for relatives and friends of alcoholics. She found a job working for an oldies station in Seattle; later, she quit and moved east. She worked at various radio stations in Boston, Massachusetts; Philadelphia, Pennsylvania; and Rochester, New York. In 1993 she married her second husband, Doug Ortega, with whom she had another son and a daughter. (She and Ortega divorced in 2002.)

In February 1996, while in Rochester, she launched her current show, *Delilah After Dark*. In December of that year, the show went into syndication, and by January 1997 it could be heard on 12 stations. Initially, radio executives were reluctant to give Delilah airtime. "Delilah broke all the rules," Jim LaMarca, the director of the syndication company, explained to Jo Thomas. "[Station managers] told me: 'I spend all day making the program consistent, run the same 200 songs. Now she's going to talk two to three minutes at a time and then play a song I don't know?'" Despite such skepticism, the format proved popular—particularly with women between the ages of 25 and 54, the target audience for many advertisers—and by the end of 1997, *Delilah After Dark* was being aired on 70 stations. The show continued to grow in popularity and is currently carried on more than 200 stations. An estimated eight million listeners tune in each night between the hours of 7:00 p.m. and midnight to hear it. (The show is broadcast from Seattle, where Delilah settled soon after its syndication. In other time zones, later portions of the previous evening's broadcast air at the beginning of the time slot.) Delilah explained her broad appeal to Adrian McCoy: "People are hungry for intimacy. They want to connect with other people. They want human contact. They can hear hits anywhere. They want to hear something inspirational."

Unlike many other radio programs that offer advice and dedicate songs to particular listeners, *Delilah After Dark* tries to reach a far wider audience than only people who are in love or who are nursing broken hearts. "The show is more than just a romantic show," Delilah told Jessica Marshall for the *Wichita (Kansas) Eagle* (February 14, 2000). "It's also for families and friends. People call in because they want to brag or complain about their marriage or their kids, they want to cry because they've lost someone they love. All they really want is a friend to listen." *Delilah After Dark* receives, on average, 100,000 calls a night; about 30 of the callers get air time. Delilah typically listens to a caller's story, commiserates with him or her, and then plays a song whose lyrics apply to the caller's situation. When a man phoned in to relate narrowly escaping a house fire, for example, she played Toni Braxton's "Breathe Again." When a mother called to express gratitude that her son's life had been saved after an auto accident, Delilah played "Angels Among Us" by the band Alabama, to honor the boy's rescuers. Although she has sometimes been described as a cross between the soft-spoken Fred Rogers, the late host of a children's television series, and the radio therapist Laura Schlesinger, Delilah has often reminded listeners that she is not a trained therapist. "[Playing] a three-minute song is not going to fix things," she told Christina Lee Knauss for the Columbia, South Carolina, *State* (February 14, 2001). "We frequently refer people to professional counseling or psychologists. There are plenty of times when I tell them, go directly to professional help."

Delilah is the co-author, with Dave Newton, of *Love Someone Today: Encouragement and Inspiration for the Times of Our Lives* (2001). She has re-leased several CD compilations of her favorite songs. In addition to her three biological offspring, she has four adopted children. Many articles about her have emphasized her devotion to her children, who on occasion call her on-air to discuss homework or domestic concerns. About 10 years ago Delilah founded PointHope, a ministry and relief organization that operates both in the U.S. and overseas. Its activities, which have aided thousands of people, are described on the Web site pointhope.org.

—H.T.

Suggested Reading: *New York Times* E p2 Jan. 19, 1999; *People* p153+ Oct. 7, 2002; *Pittsburgh Post-Gazette* F p3 Feb. 16, 1997; pointhope.org; radiodelilah.com; *Wichita (Kansas) Eagle* B p1 Feb. 14, 2000;

Evan Agostini/Getty Images

Diaz, Cameron

Aug. 30, 1972– Actress

Address: c/o International Creative Management, 8942 Wilshire Blvd., Beverly Hills, CA 90211

A combination of talent, beauty, and serendipity have been the keys to success for the actress Cameron Diaz. In 1993, after working as a professional fashion model for five years and having neither experience nor training in acting, she won a major role in the movie *The Mask*, starring Jim Carrey. The film was extremely popular, and Diaz held her own beside the frenetic Carrey. Unlike many young actresses who have starred in a smash-hit movie and seek roles in other big-budget films, Diaz honed her craft by starring in several low-budget independent films, among them *The Last Supper*, *She's the One*, and *Feeling Minnesota*. In 1997 she returned to mainstream cinema, in *My Best Friend's Wedding,* a showcase for both Julia Roberts and Rupert Everett, in which, in a supporting role, she acquitted herself admirably. Her skills were put on full display in *There's Something About Mary* (1998), a slapstick comedy directed by Peter and Bobby Farrelly. A frizzy brown wig, brown contact lenses, and frumpy costumes failed to hide her charms in her turn as a quirky pet-shop worker in the bizarre comedy *Being John Malkovich* (1999), while her role in *Charlie's Angels* (2002) gave her a chance to show off her knack for balancing glamour with nonsense. In the computer-animated *Shrek* (2001) and its sequel, *Shrek 2* (2004), she lent her voice to great effect as the character Fiona. Diaz has also impressed critics in serious roles, in such movies as Oliver Stone's *Any Given Sunday* (1999), Cameron Crowe's *Vanilla Sky* (2001), and Martin Scorsese's *Gangs of New York* (2002). Thanks to Diaz's looks, screen presence, and ability to portray a wide variety of characters, she has become one of the highest-paid actresses in Hollywood. According to Gary Arnold, who reviews films for the *Washington Times* (December 13, 2001), "Miss Diaz is peerless when it comes to immediate radiance and impact." Many of her colleagues in Hollywood have been similarly impressed. "She's funny and fearless and tough and romantic," the director Cameron Crowe has said, as quoted in *Premiere* (October 2001). Referring to a famous 1930s Hollywood comedian, Crowe added, "She reminds me of Carole Lombard with her extraordinary accessibility and great sense of humor."

Cameron Michelle Diaz was born on August 30, 1972 in Long Beach, California, where she grew up with her older sister, Chimene. Her father, Emilio, a foreman at an oil company, is of Cuban heritage. Her mother, Billie, an import broker, is of mixed German, English, and Native American ancestry. "I had a very normal upbringing in a California beach town," Diaz told Michael Kilian for the *Chicago Tribune* (September 15, 1996). "I was blessed with an incredible family with whom I'm very close. I was raised healthy and loved." Her parents were supportive of their daughters' interests and gave them free rein to develop their own styles. Cameron and her sister were fans of heavy-metal music, and when they clamored to attend a Van Halen concert at the Los Angeles Forum, their mother drove them there and then waited for them in the parking lot, where she worked on a needlepoint project for the duration of the show. "I was the tough kid with the jeans, the concert shirt with the flannel over it, the comb in the back pocket, the feathered hair," Diaz told Jancee Dunn for *Rolling Stone* (August 22, 1996). "It was frightening."

With the help of a photographer whom she met at a party, Diaz secured a contract with the Elite modeling agency when she was 16 years old. The following summer she accepted an assignment in Japan, where she shared an apartment with a fellow model, a 15-year-old friend of hers. Once, at age 18, while she was in Australia on a photo shoot for a Coca-Cola commercial, she drank a nearly fatal amount of alcohol. (Approximately as many people die from overdoses of alcohol as from overdoses of illegal drugs in the U.S.) Although she worked full-time as a model during those years, she reportedly earned a diploma from Long Beach Polytechnic High School in 1990.

Diaz's foray into acting began in 1993, when she noticed the script for *The Mask* on the desk of her modeling agent. "I said, 'What's this?'" the actress recalled to Dunn. "She said, 'A movie. Do you think you can handle it?' I said, 'Sure, no problem.' I was joking. She wasn't." Diaz went to the audition thinking that she would try out for the small role of a reporter. Instead, she was tested for the female lead, opposite the star of the film, Jim Carrey, and returned for readings a dozen times. By her own account, she felt so rattled during the process that she had difficulty sleeping and even eating. In *The Mask*, directed by Chuck Russell, Diaz was cast as Tina Carlyle, a sultry nightclub singer who wins the heart of Stanley Ipkiss (Carrey), a mild-mannered bank clerk who becomes a human dynamo when he dons a magical mask. Diaz was so nervous before the first day of shooting that she nearly threw up on the way to the studio. "I had a hundred model friends who were trying to be actresses," she told Christa D'Souza for *Esquire* (February 1995). "They had to work so hard. At the time, I just wanted to spend the spring in Paris!" *The Mask* was one of the most commercially successful motion pictures of 1994. While much of the critics' praise went to Carrey and the special-effects team,

Diaz earned kudos, too. Leonard Klady, in *Variety* (August 17, 1994), described her as "a real find as the femme fatale who's just looking for the decent thing to do." Her screen persona reminded Jack Mathews, a *New York Newsday* (July 29, 1994) critic, of "a live-action version of Jessica Rabbit"—a reference to the sexy cartoon character in the movie *Who Framed Roger Rabbit?*

For her second movie role, a leading part, Diaz chose to portray a graduate student in the black comedy *The Last Supper* (1995), an independent film that did not find a large audience. She next appeared as Heather, the lover of a married man, in Ed Burns's *She's the One* (1996). In the *Chicago Sun-Times* (August 8, 1996), Roger Ebert wrote that *She's the One* disappointed him, but that Diaz struck him as "a real actress, in addition to being one of the most beautiful women in the movies." "It is interesting how she lets Heather maintain a certain privacy and reserve, so that we can't make easy assumptions about her," Ebert wrote. In 1996 Diaz co-starred with Keanu Reeves and Vincent D'Onofrio in Steven Baigelman's *Feeling Minnesota* (1996) and with Harvey Keitel, Craig Sheffer, and Billy Zane in Jim Wilson's *Head Above Water* (1996). In 1997 she was featured with Ewan MacGregor in Danny Boyle's *A Life Less Ordinary* (1997) and had a supporting role in Leslie Greif's *Keys to Tulsa* (1997). None of those four films was particularly well received.

A turning point for Diaz came when she was cast in the box-office hit *My Best Friend's Wedding* (1997), directed by P. J. Hogan (the writer and director of *Muriel's Wedding*). The screwball comedy starred Julia Roberts as Julianne, a food writer who is determined to prevent the marriage of her closest pal, Michael (Dermot Mulroney), to an heiress, Kimmy (Diaz). Diaz's performance, along with those of Roberts and Rupert Everett (who played a gay man who poses as Julianne's fiancé), received enthusiastic praise. "Cameron Diaz is delightfully daffy as Kimmy, the angelic debutante . . . ," Kevin Maynard wrote for Mr. Showbiz (on-line). "When Julianne tries to break down the differences between them by telling Kimmy that she's crème brulée when Michael might be more comfortable with good old reliable Jell-O, Diaz cries, 'Then I have to be Jell-O!' We believe her sincerity, and that makes her a great comic character. The actress's screechy rendition of the Burt Bacharach–Hal David song 'I Just Don't Know What to Do with Myself' at a karaoke bar brings the house down."

Diaz's next major starring role was in *There's Something About Mary* (1998*)*, directed by two of the most prominent creators of over-the-top cinematic humor, Peter and Bobby Farrelly. In this lowbrow romantic comedy, Ted (played by Ben Stiller) is a nerdy man who still obsesses over an unfortunate accident with the zipper of his tuxedo trousers that prevented him from taking Mary (Diaz) to their high-school prom a dozen years earlier. After he hires a sleazy private detective (Matt Dillon) to track her down, Ted finds himself competing with the detective, among others, for Mary's affection. In the *New York Times* (July 15, 1998), Janet Maslin noted that Diaz portrayed Mary "with a blithe comic style that makes her as funny as she is dazzling." In *Time* (July 20, 1998), Richard Corliss wrote, "There's surely something about Cameron Diaz; everyone's crazy about her. Maybe it's the throaty laugh, the sinewy silhouette, the radiant smile that seems to wonder at the edges if you really think she's all that gorgeous. Well, she is—and a fine comic actress too. In *My Best Friend's Wedding*, she outdazzled and outcuted Julia Roberts, no contest. . . . But for those who park their sense and sensibility at the 'plex door, there's plenty to enjoy in the performances, the rowdy innocence of the whole thing, the closing sing-along of 'Build Me Up Buttercup'—and the vision of Cameron Diaz in giggly, gangly bloom."

In another of Diaz's highly acclaimed comedic performances, she played Lotte, a shy, dowdy pet-shop employee who is married to an unemployed master puppeteer named Craig (John Cusack), in the highly imaginative film *Being John Malkovich* (1999), written by Charlie Kaufman and directed by Spike Jonze. After Craig gets a job as a file clerk, he discovers a portal that allows him to spend 15 minutes in the actor John Malkovich's mind before being tossed onto the New Jersey Turnpike. Craig develops a crush on his sexy, brittle co-worker Maxine (Catherine Keener), who sets about turning the portal into a money maker; Maxine, meanwhile, falls for Lotte when Lotte is in Malkovich's brain and thus becomes, in effect, a man. The work of Diaz and Keener in *Being John Malkovich* earned them both Golden Globe nominations.

In Diaz's next major role, she portrayed Natalie, one of a trio of undercover agents, in the 2000 film version of the popular 1970s television program *Charlie's Angels*. The film, directed by Joseph McGinty Nichol (known as McG), takes a more tongue-in-cheek approach to the concept than the TV show did, poking fun at the idea that three gorgeous women (Diaz, Drew Barrymore, and Lucy Liu) are also expert crime-fighting spies. "As she did in *There's Something About Mary* and *Being John Malkovich*, Ms. Diaz plays against her own sexiness, emphasizing Natalie's gawky cluelessness to good comic effect," A. O. Scott wrote for the *New York Times* (November 3, 2000). "In one scene, her love interest (Luke Wilson) takes her on a date to a taping of *Soul Train*, and Natalie bumps and grinds to Sir Mix-A-Lot's 'Baby Got Back.' The joke, about as subtle as they come in this movie, is that Ms. Diaz hardly conforms to the steatopygous ideal of female beauty the song celebrates, but Natalie is too goofily naive to notice or care." The film spawned a sequel, *Charlie's Angels: Full Throttle* (2003), in which the trio battles a former Angel gone bad (Demi Moore). Although the sequel did not match the critical success of the first *Charlie's Angels*, it proved to be nearly as popular as its well-attended predecessor.

In 2001 Diaz supplied the voice of Fiona, a fairy-tale princess in need of rescuing from a castle guarded by a dragon, in the animated film *Shrek*; with pop-culture references and riffs on various classic fairy tales, *Shrek* appealed to adults as well as children. Mike Myers provided the voice of Shrek, and Eddie Murphy that of Shrek's sidekick, Donkey. After Diaz saw the film, she told an Associated Press (June 1, 2001) interviewer, "I couldn't believe what I was seeing. It was this . . . person that didn't look anything like me, but it shared the same gestures and movements and voice, and sort of the essence, like the light behind the eyes in the character." Desson Howe wrote for the *Washington Post* (May 18, 2001) that Diaz "makes a funny, earthy princess," while Todd McCarthy wrote for *Variety* (May 7, 2001), "Diaz's readings are energetic and willful, making Fiona a medieval *Charlie's Angels* candidate." The actress won a Nickelodeon Kids' Choice Award for "best burp," for a belch that Fiona emits.

Many people lauded *Shrek* (which is based, extremely loosely, on a children's book by William Steig) for offering the idea that beauty is more than skin deep; indeed, some thought it ironic that a woman as attractive as Diaz was speaking the lines of Fiona, who turns out to be a female ogre. The actress is said to eat unusually heartily, and she engages in strength training several times weekly. Speaking of her physical appearance, she told an interviewer for *People* (May 13, 2002), "It's not about what you weigh. Your body just has to be strong. Anyone who is strong will look good as well." Diaz reprised the role of Fiona in *Shrek 2* (2004), which was another critical and commercial hit. As of February 2005 the sequel, which received an Oscar nomination for best animated feature film, was the highest-grossing animated movie of all time and in the top five among all movies.

Diaz has had prominent roles in several serious films: as the aggressive co-owner of a football team, in Oliver Stone's *Any Given Sunday* (1999), opposite Al Pacino and a bevy of other major stars; as the mentally unstable girlfriend of a playboy (Tom Cruise) who gets disfigured in an accident, in Cameron Crowe's *Vanilla Sky* (2001); and as a savvy pickpocket who becomes the love interest of a young man (Leonardo DiCaprio) seeking revenge for the murder of his father, in Martin Scorsese's *Gangs of New York* (2002), set in New York City in the mid-19th century. In *Any Given Sunday*, Jack Mathews wrote for the New York *Daily News* (December 22, 1999), Diaz was "surprisingly convincing" in a part quite different from any of her previous ones; according to Bob Longino in the *Atlanta Journal-Constitution* (December 24, 1999), she portrayed her character with "venomous verve." Her performance in *Vanilla Sky*, a remake of the Spanish film *Abre los ojos* (Open Your Eyes, 1997), earned Diaz awards for best actress from the New York Film Critics Circle and best supporting actress from the Boston Society of Film Critics.

Among Diaz's other films are Peter Berg's *Very Bad Things* (1998), Cameron Pearson's *Man Woman Film* (1999), Adam Brooks's *The Invisible Circus* (2001), and Roger Kumble's *The Sweetest Thing* (2002). In 2005 she appeared in *In Her Shoes*, directed by Curtis Hanson and co-starring Toni Collette, with Shirley MacLaine in a supporting role. Diaz is signed to star in *Shrek 3* and *W.A.S.P.S.*

A natural blond with bright blue eyes, Diaz is five feet nine inches tall. She has been linked romantically with, sequentially, the video producer Carlos De La Torre, the actors Matt Dillon and Jared Leto, and the singer Justin Timberlake. Interviewers have reported that she talks readily and lovingly about her pet cats.

—C.M.

Suggested Reading: *Biography Magazine* p74+ Apr. 2000; *Chicago Tribune* p12 Sep. 15, 1996, with photos; *Deseret News* E p15 May 27, 1998; *Details* p110+ Aug. 1998, with photos;

Entertainment Weekly p23 Mar. 25, 1994, with photo, p28+ June 20, 2003, with photos; *Nation* p50+ July 21–28, 2003; *New York Times* (on-line) May 18, 2004; *People* p51+ Aug. 22, 1994, with photos; *Premiere* p60+ Oct. 2001; *Rolling Stone* p112+ Aug. 22, 1996, with photos; *Salon* (on-line) Dec. 20, 2002; *Washington Post* p45 May 21, 2004

Selected Films: *The Mask*, 1994; *The Last Supper*, 1995; *Feeling Minnesota*, 1996; *Head Above Water*, 1996; *She's the One*, 1996; *Keys to Tulsa*, 1997; *A Life Less Ordinary*, 1997; *My Best Friend's Wedding*, 1997; *Fear and Loathing in Las Vegas*, 1998; *There's Something About Mary*, 1998; *Very Bad Things*, 1998; *Being John Malkovich*, 1999; *Any Given Sunday*, 1999; *Charlie's Angels*, 2000; *Shrek*, 2001; *Vanilla Sky*, 2001; *The Sweetest Thing*, 2002; *Gangs of New York*, 2002; *Charlie's Angels: Full Throttle*, 2003; *Shrek 2*, 2004; *In Her Shoes*, 2005

Domini, Amy

(DAHM-ih-nee)

Jan. 25, 1950– Investment manager

Address: Domini Social Investments, 536 Broadway, Seventh Fl., New York, NY 10012

"I would certainly lose interest in finance were it not for activism," Amy Domini told an interviewer for the *Women's Review of Books* (July 2001, on-line). "Finance is a fascinating three-dimensional chessboard, but it is the root cause of much that's going wrong in the world." Domini is the founder and CEO of Domini Social Investments and a founder of KLD Research & Analytics, which specializes in corporate-accountability research. Over the last 20 years, her passionate belief in the good that the global financial industry can do, along with her sharp, politically sensitive analyses of the industry's real-life effects on people around the world, has helped make her an influential if somewhat controversial player in the U.S. investment community, criticized by investors of all political stripes for her ideas about what makes one economic activity acceptable to her and her companies while another is not. A pioneer in the field of socially responsible investing and perhaps its most recognizable figure, Domini has disproved what had long been a common notion about investments made with social and political factors in mind: that they inevitably paid investors poor returns. The tool that Domini and her partners developed some 15 years ago, called the Domini 400 Social Index, has demonstrated that, in decisions about what stock to purchase, evaluating a company in terms

Courtesy of Domini Social Investments

of the public good can turn out to be at least as profitable for investors as focusing on only its bottom line. "Without the index, I think we'd still be fighting the battle that socially responsible investing means we're not getting any performance," Francis G. Coleman, then vice president of socially responsible investing for Christian Brothers Investment Services, told Miriam Hill for the *Philadelphia Inquirer* (June 20, 2000). "This is where [Domini's] vision really played out. She knew that. That was the single most difficult point to overcome in people's minds."

Amy Lee Domini was born on January 25, 1950 in New York City. Her father, Enzo Vice Domini, was a native of the southern Italian coastal city of Naples; his father supported the principles of socialism. In the 1930s, as a teenager, Enzo joined the Italian resistance to the country's fascist rulers. After World War II ended, in 1945, he and a group of college friends helped children orphaned by the war. Through their makeshift orphanage, he met Domini's mother, born Margot Cabot Colt, a socially well-connected and solidly left-wing New Yorker (with family ties in Boston, Massachusetts, as well) who had come to Italy to help rebuild the country after the devastation caused by the war. The couple later settled in Newtown, Connecticut, where Enzo worked in various capacities in the food business and Margot taught elementary school. "My father's war years had convinced him there was no God," Domini told Alison Maitland for the London *Financial Times* (July 15, 2002); her mother, on the other hand, she said, took Domini and her younger brother, John (who is now a writer), to a local Episcopal church every Sunday "because my mother, like all 1950s mothers, thought it was the thing to do." Domini remains a practicing Episcopalian; she is a member of the board of the church pension fund of the Episcopal Church in America.

While still a child, Domini received her first lessons in high finance from her mother's father. A New York reporter turned stockbroker, her grandfather taught her how to read the financial statements in companies' annual reports; she has often cited him as a strong influence in her choice of career. Domini has credited her political sensibilities to her coming of age in the 1960s and early 1970s, when the civil rights movement was achieving significant victories, environmental awareness was broadening, and the effects of a new wave of feminist activism were being felt. At the same time, Domini told Kathie O'Donnell for the Bloomberg News (March 26, 2000), "you had the Vietnam War, which meant that my friends were in a lottery to see whether they'd die. That's a pretty powerful introduction to the military industrial complex." Still, she has generally denied having a strong political agenda before she became involved in the financial industry. "It was socially responsible investing that made me an activist," Domini told Maitland. "The cart pushed the horse." After taking a year's break from college and quitting smoking on Earth Day 1970, Domini graduated from Boston University in 1973 with a B.A. degree in international and comparative studies. She then went to work as a copy clerk for the brokerage firm Tucker Anthony in Cambridge, Massachusetts. In 1975 she was promoted to stockbroker, a position she held for the next five years.

During that period Domini's ideas about socially responsible investing began to take form. She has traced them partly to her clients. One client refused to buy tobacco stocks, for example, while another, an enthusiastic birdwatcher, asked Domini not to invest in a company that the client had heard was using a pesticide that was endangering wildlife. By her own account, an additional push toward a change in her thinking came one morning in 1978, when, during the daily announcements of Tucker Anthony's stock recommendations, an analyst mentioned a company that seemed poised to win a government weapons contract. The analyst "made a really good case" for buying the stock, Domini told Jennifer Openshaw for CBS MarketWatch.com (September 3, 2001). "I was taking notes, thinking who might like it. And then, I thought, 'Wait a minute. How far have you fallen? You want to call people you're fond of and tell them about a company that kills people?'"

Not long afterward Domini had a meeting with representatives of the Episcopal chaplaincy at Harvard University, in Cambridge, Massachusetts. She looked over their stock portfolio and began to question how well it reflected their church's values. Why were there stocks in the defense contractor Lockheed Martin? Why had they bought government bonds? (Domini considered the bonds a way of directly supporting a military that was already unnecessarily powerful; she still refuses to buy them.) At the end of their discussion, a chaplain condescendingly told Domini that she should write a book on ethical investing. "I said to myself, 'Ok, wise guy, I will,'" Domini told Openshaw.

In 1980 Domini bought her first home and married Peter D. Kinder, a lawyer and writer who had worked in the Ohio attorney general's office. That same year Domini left Tucker Anthony to take a job at Moseley Securities, another brokerage firm based in Cambridge; she also began teaching a class on ethical investing at the Cambridge Center for Adult Education. When the school's course catalogue was distributed, a Boston-area book editor noticed the class and called Domini to suggest that she expand its contents into a book. *Ethical Investing*, written with Kinder, was published in 1984, the same year that the couple's second child was born. (Their first was born in 1982.)

In *Ethical Investing*, Domini and Kinder provided readers with strategies for learning about nonpublicized activities of the companies in which they had invested. At the time even Domini had her doubts about the potential effectiveness of this approach. As she told the *Women's Review of Books*, "The first book was called *Ethical Investing* and not Socially Responsible Investing because at that time I didn't want to imply that you could make a difference. I felt that you should be able to invest in a more holistic way, but I didn't want to falsely advertise it as some kind of a solution."

Domini's views on ethical investing continued to evolve, thanks particularly to the success of widespread boycotts against companies with business interests in South Africa, where the black majority had long suffered the brutal oppression and racial segregation institutionalized by the white minority through the nation's apartheid laws. When apartheid ended, in 1993, the anti-apartheid leader and later South African president Nelson Mandela credited the change in part to the boycotts. In the experience of South Africa, Domini saw what she has characterized as a "clear-cut" case of socially responsible investment practices producing real and significant changes. Years later, in 2001, she told the *Women's Review of Books*, "I now feel that the social investor is motivated by making a difference in the world more than by personal concerns."

Still, the idea of ethical investing met with criticism, not least because it violated what amounted to a fundamental rule of investing: investors should buy and sell stocks based only on companies' expected financial performance. The consideration of social and political factors, it was believed, would diminish an investor's returns. When Domini offered proof that those assumptions were misguided, she encountered skepticism. "Amy would come back from making presentations to investors just in a fury," Kinder told Hill, "because the first question out of the audience was, 'Well, your performance numbers are interesting, but where are your real numbers?'—implying . . . that the numbers are somehow cooked." Driven by what Kinder characterized as her "intense frustration," Domini worked for several years with Kinder and their partner Steven Lydenberg to develop a formal, objective measure of the success of ethical investing. They compiled a list of stocks that represented what a typical investor might buy if the investor screened each stock according to a set of political or ethical principles. Like the more rudimentary ethical-investment methods that some had been applying for decades, the criteria Domini and her colleagues used at first were essentially negative: firms were removed from consideration if they earned profits from proscribed sources, particularly gambling, tobacco, and alcohol (or, colloquially, "betting, butts, and booze"). Companies that derived more than 2 percent of their revenues from defense contracts were also screened out, as were companies with revenues from the sale of nuclear power or with poor records of labor relations or environmental practices. As it developed, Domini's list (referred to as an index) also included positive screens: for example, a company's willingness to end disapproved practices or its actions toward increasing diversity among its workers.

The Domini 400 Index, as it was named, was intended to imitate the financial industry's benchmark, Standard and Poor's 500-stock index (S. & P. 500). Unlike the Standard & Poor's index, which tracks 500 stocks, all from large companies, the Domini index follows 400 stocks, most for large companies but some for mid-size or small ones as well. Like the S. & P. 500, the Domini 400 is used to measure how the stock market as a whole is performing. In other words, the value of the Domini 400 should rise when the values of stocks traded in the New York Stock Exchange have generally increased and fall when they have decreased. Also like the S. & P. 500, the Domini 400 is a weighted index. Unlike a price index such as the Dow Jones Industrial Average, which measures fluctuations in the price of individual shares of the companies on the index, a weighted stock index reflects changes in the prices of indexed companies' shares relative to the companies' overall presence in the marketplace, a relationship that is referred to as its capitalization weight. The more shares a company has available on the market and the more valuable they are, the greater the proportion of the index they take up.

The Domini 400 was formally launched in May 1990 by Kinder, Lydenberg, Domini, and Co. (KLD), which the trio founded with the intention of licensing the index to other investment companies, which they hoped would be attracted to the sort of diverse and relatively reliable holdings that the index listed. When no one came forward with a sufficiently attractive licensing fee, Domini and her partners created their own mutual fund, the Domini Social Index Trust, in August 1990. They then began to seek investments in the fund—enough to fulfill its primary goal: to hold stocks in all 400 of the companies on the Domini index in exact proportion to their weight on the index. It is this exact replication of an already established set of stocks that makes what is now called the Domini Social Equity Fund an index fund. They reached their goal in about 1995, when investments topped $30 million.

Earlier, in 1985, Domini had resigned from Moseley Securities to become a portfolio manager at Franklin Research and Development Corp., an investment firm, founded in 1982, that followed socially responsible investing principles. (It is now called Trillium Asset Management.) In 1987 she left Franklin to become a private trustee at Loring, Wolcott, and Coolidge, where she has worked ever since, offering socially responsible investing advice to clients who, in the main, are very wealthy. In 1988 she published a second book, *The Challenges of Wealth: Mastering the Personal and Financial Conflicts* (co-written with Dennis Pearne, a wealth counselor and consultant, and Sharon L. Rich), and in 1992 a third, *The Social Investment Almanac: A Comprehensive Guide to Socially Responsible Investing* (co-written with Kinder and Lydenberg). Her next two books are *Investing for Good: Making Money While Being Socially Responsible* (1993), co-written with Kinder and Lydenberg, and *Socially Responsible Investing: Making a Difference in Making Money* (2001).

In 1991 the first Gulf War (which followed the invasion of Kuwait by Iraq and the subsequent attack on Iraq by a coalition of forces from the U.S. and some of its allies) caused the values of defense and oil-related stocks to rise, leading Domini and her partners to worry about the survival of their new product. Even so, the Domini index beat the S. & P. 500 in its first year. In 1993 and 1994

Domini's index fell slightly behind the S. & P. 500; in 1995 it surpassed the S. & P. 500, and it stayed ahead for the next four years. Meanwhile, the fund had kept growing. By late 1995 its assets totaled more than $60 million. A year later it held $100 million, and over the course of 1997, its assets more than doubled. The most impressive gains, though, came after a 1998 Department of Labor ruling that allowed the pension planners to invest in socially responsible funds such as Domini's. Up until then pension planners had worried that making the fund available to their companies' employees might be a breach of their legally mandated responsibilities, since those types of funds did not have a proven track record. But the consistently strong returns enjoyed by Domini's and similar funds served as evidence that socially responsible firms presented no greater risks than any others. The result was that Domini went from controlling $100 million in 1996 to controlling almost 20 times that amount by July 2000, with most of the money coming from retirement accounts.

The growing popularity of the fund was also spurred by the largely enthusiastic response of the business media. Profiles of Domini appeared in the business sections of newspapers from Boston to Los Angeles. In January 2000 the business magazine *Barron's*, which in 1994 had called socially responsible funds "a lot of New Age mumbojumbo," included Amy Domini in its "All-Century Team of All Stars" in an article subtitled "The Fund World's Heaviest Hitters." In 2003 *SmartMoney* magazine called Domini one of the 30 most influential people in investing, and in 2000 *Time* named her one of the country's top 100 innovators, describing her as "a capitalist tool from a different mold." In April 2005 *Time* included her along with only one other person from the world of finance on its list of the 100 most influential people in the world.

Those honors notwithstanding, Domini's ideas about what makes one company socially responsible and another irresponsible have been questioned by people and organizations from all parts of the political spectrum. Some religious groups, for example, have objected to Domini's support for companies that extend benefits to same-sex partners; some on the left have criticized Domini's heavy holdings in the fast-food company McDonald's, which they blame for helping cause an epidemic of obesity among Americans. After the September 11, 2001 terrorist attacks on the U.S., some socially responsible investment companies of long standing began to ask themselves whether avoiding investments in the defense industry was really the most responsible way of guaranteeing the welfare of other Americans.

Domini has often responded to these types of criticism by emphasizing that she seeks to define socially responsible investment in the way that best suits her clients' needs. She buys shares in the best available companies, she says, which is not the same as choosing companies that are unquestionably benevolent. When Debora Vrana, writing for the *Los Angeles Times* (February 25, 1997), asked Domini whether she believed there is "truly such a thing as an ethical company," Domini answered with a categorical no. "I think there are model companies that come as close as you can come," she said. As an example, she cited Coca-Cola, which exists to make money and to give people something to drink. "If you think of delivering soft drinks as one circle and making money as another circle, there are places where the two intersect. The goal of socially responsible investing is to become an important enough voice to make a difference in where those circles intersect."

Indeed, as Domini's business has grown and diversified (a socially responsible bond fund was added in 2000), its influence has grown as well. Domini has attributed policy changes regarding overseas sweatshops by both McDonald's and the Gap to negotiations she and her colleagues conducted with the companies over the course of several years. Similarly, in 2000, as a result of Domini's activism, the home-improvement retail chain Home Depot agreed to stop buying lumber made from old-growth trees. More broadly, Domini was directly responsible for causing the U.S. Securities and Exchange Commission (SEC) to issue new rules in 2003 requiring mutual-fund companies such as Domini's to reveal to their investors how the funds had used their voting rights in companies in which they held stock. Until then, virtually all mutual funds other than Domini's had wielded their considerable influence behind closed doors, so that investors had no way of knowing whether their decisions favored managers rather than workers, customers, or fellow citizens. In September 2005 Domini Social Investments announced the formation of a new fund, the Domini European Social Equity Fund, which will trade in stocks of European companies that fulfill Domini's criteria for socially responsible policies and operations.

Domini has two adult sons, John and Jotham. In 2001 she and Kinder divorced after several years of legal separation; in interviews she has indicated that their marriage ended in part became of the demands of her work. She now owns more than three-quarters of Domini Social Investments, while Kinder has given up his share in the company; she no longer has a financial stake in KLD. Domini commutes between her company's offices in New York and the offices of Loring, Wolcott and Coolidge in Boston. She told Openshaw, "I have a desire, a passion to work until the day I die, to use what skills I have to build the world of environmental sustainability and human and economic justice."

—D.R.

Suggested Reading: CBS MarketWatch (on-line) Sep. 3, 2001; Domini Social Investments Web site; *Los Angeles Times* D p4 Feb. 25, 1997; *Philadelphia Inquirer* (on-line) June 20, 2000;

Women's Review of Books (on-line) p14+ July
2001

Selected Books: *Ethical Investing* (with Peter D.
Kinder), 1984; *The Challenges of Wealth:
Mastering the Personal and Financial Conflicts*
(with Dennis Pearne and Sharon L. Rich), 1988;
The Social Investment Almanac (with Peter D.
Kinder and Steven D. Lydenberg), 1992;
*Investing for Good: Making Money While Being
Socially Responsible* (with Peter D. Kinder and
Steven D. Lydenberg), 1993; *Socially Responsible
Investing: Making a Difference in Making Money*,
2001

Alex Wong/Getty Images

Donald, Arnold W.

*Dec. 17, 1954– Chairman and former CEO of
Merisant*

*Address: c/o Merisant, 1 North Brentwood, Suite
510, St. Louis, MO 63105*

"I've never focused on a title; I've never focused on
trying to please a boss; and I've never focused on
trying to network with certain people," Arnold W.
Donald told Ronald E. Childs for *Black Enterprise*
(May 2003). "What I did was to focus on 'What's
the result? How am I maximizing my return to
shareholders over the life of the firm?' Simply stated, I've always looked for jobs and opportunities,
which gave me experiences that trained me well
for that task." That approach seems to have worked
well for Donald, who emerged from humble origins
to become a top executive at Monsanto and then,

in 2000, formed Merisant, a maker of tabletop
sweetener products—such as Equal—sold in more
than 100 countries. Donald has made a point of
supporting causes in which he believes, in the
hope that he may help other African-Americans to
fulfill their dreams, in part through his own example. While acknowledging the relatively low number of blacks in high-level corporate positions, he
said to Beverly Schuch on the CNN television
show *Business Unusual* (December 28, 2000), "I
think the opportunities are certainly there—case in
point, myself—for African-Americans, and other
minorities to ascend to CEO-type positions." Andrew Bursky, a Connecticut-based businessman
and a college friend of Donald's, said about him in
a conversation with Thomas Lee for the *St. Louis
Post-Dispatch* (January 13, 2002), "He is a general
who leads from the front. He's not the big bureaucratic type. He gets the best out of everybody." Another businessman, Leonard Guarraia, told Lee
about Donald, "He is an honest person. You may
not like what he has to say, but he will say it. . . .
But he really does care about people."

Arnold W. Donald was born on December 17,
1954 in New Orleans, Louisiana, to Hilda and Warren Donald. Neither of his parents had graduated
from high school. Donald grew up in the city's
poor, rough Desire neighborhood, living with four
older siblings and some 27 foster children in a
house built by his father, a carpenter. "We were
poor, but I was blessed with a loving and nurturing
family," he told Cassandra Hayes for *Black Enterprise* (September 30, 1997). "My parents did whatever they could to make life good for us." Thanks
to his family's support, "I really believed that I
could do whatever I wanted," Donald said to Nancy Rotenier for *Forbes* (May 22, 1995). A bright
child, Donald learned how to read, write, and do
basic math under the tutelage of his sister Yvonne
before he even entered kindergarten. Donald attended the primarily black Catholic boys' school
St. Augustine, in New Orleans, which had a reputation for producing excellent athletes as well as
high achievers in academics. He also took summer
courses at prep schools in Exeter, New Hampshire,
and Andover, Massachusetts, and benefited from
the informal mentoring of successful St. Augustine
alumni. Donald was a driven student, as a St. Augustine faculty member, Edwin Hampton, who led
the marching band in which Donald was saxophone line captain, told Allen Powell II for the
New Orleans *Times-Picayune* (August 10, 2001).
"He was just No. 1, a gentleman and scholar,"
Hampton said. "He learned his craft, and always
strived for perfection." By his junior year of high
school, Donald had decided what he wanted his
career to be, as he told Cassandra Hayes: "I wanted
to be a general manager at a science-based company whose products would make a difference in the
world."

In order to work in the realms of both science
and business, Donald felt that he would need to
study economics and mechanical engineering and

earn an M.B.A. degree. As a graduating senior in 1972, Donald turned down offers to attend Yale University, Stanford University, and West Point in favor of Carleton College, a small liberal-arts school in Northfield, Minnesota. He graduated in 1976 with a B.A. degree in economics, then earned a second bachelor's degree, this one a B.S. in engineering, from Washington University, in St. Louis, Missouri. Upon his graduation, in 1977, Donald took a job in industrial chemical sales with the Monsanto Co., a St. Louis-based maker of agricultural products such as pesticides, animal-food supplements, and lawn and garden products. Meanwhile, he also attended the University of Chicago, where he received his master's degree in business administration with a concentration in finance and international business in 1980. "My strategy was always to maximize the probabilities," he explained to Cassandra Hayes. "Although I had no desire to work in finance, I thought that knowing it would be important to general management, so I immersed myself in it."

At Monsanto Donald was quickly pegged as a rising star and promoted successively to the posts of senior market analyst, U.S. product director of RoundUp herbicide, vice president of the residential-products division, and vice president and general manager of the crop-protection products division. In the latter position he was one of the more vocal advocates for the development of crops enhanced through the use of biotechnology. Talking with Laurie Kretchmar for *Fortune* (September 9, 1991), Donald revealed his guiding principle for maintaining what he called a "high-performance organization": "Have three people do five jobs but pay them like four." Donald was noted not only for his managerial skills but for his success in promoting RoundUp, an environmentally friendly weed killer that, with Donald's help, became the best-selling herbicide in the world. In 1988 he was named lawn and garden director for the company's industrial and residential business unit, and in four years in that position, he brought about a five-fold increase in retail revenues. He became Monsanto's group vice president of North America in 1993 and president of the company's agricultural sector in 1995. In the latter capacity he was responsible for the department that, through the sale of crop, industrial, and turf agricultural products throughout the U.S., Canada, and Latin America, accounted for half of Monsanto's operating profits. As president of the agricultural sector, Donald worked closely with the Environmental Protection Agency and the U.S. Department of Agriculture to ensure that all Monsanto products would adhere to guidelines set to protect the environment. The National Agri-Marketing Association named Donald Agri-Marketer of the Year for 1997, the same year that *Black Enterprise* singled him out as its Corporate Executive of the Year. In 1998 he became senior vice president of the company and president of its Consumer and Nutrition Sector, responsible for worldwide growth and technology initiatives.

When the Monsanto Co. decided to sell its ownership of more than 20 brands of what the industry calls "low-calorie, high-intensity" sweeteners, including Equal and its European counterpart, Canderel, Donald concluded that it would be a wise business decision to assemble a group of investors and buy the sweetener division. Urged by a friend from his engineering-school days at Washington University, Andrew Bursky, Donald successfully pitched the idea to investors such as the private-equity firm Pegasus Capital Advisors (with which Bursky was associated); MSD Capital LP, an investment fund affiliated with Michael Dell, chairman of Dell Computer Corp.; and the Brener International Group. In 2000 Donald left Monsanto, and he and his fellow investors created the privately held Merisant Co., which bought the tabletop sweeteners from Monsanto for $570 million. "I was really happy at Monsanto," he told Thomas Lee. "Even when I chose to do this, I was really enjoying my Monsanto experience. But I have to tell you, as wonderful as that was, it pales in comparison to this." Donald became chairman and CEO of the newly formed company, which counted among its executives six former Monsanto employees. One of them, Merisant's vice president of communications, Karl Sestak, told a writer for the *St. Louis Commerce Magazine* (April 1, 2002), "People love to work with Arnold." Kevin Eichner, former CEO and president of the GenAmerica Financial Corp. (on whose board Donald sits), described Donald for the same article as "very bright, very gracious. He has an accommodating style. He's the type of person who is an excellent leader . . . that smart combination of strength and empathy that I think resonates with many people."

By acquiring Equal, Canderel, and other sugar substitutes, which accounted for over a third of the global market share of tabletop sweeteners, Donald immediately became head of a $400 million business. "All of us are excited about our shift from a company division to a stand-alone business," Donald announced to Joe Ruklick for the *Chicago Defender* (March 21, 2000). "The company is the undisputed leader in the tabletop sweetener market, and there are huge opportunities in foreign countries." In order to increase sales of Equal, Merisant's best-known product in the U.S., Donald wanted to both strengthen its hold in the tabletop market as a sweetener for coffee and tea and promote its uses in baking. "Equal should be a household staple," he told Thomas Lee. "People who don't even use ketchup have ketchup in their homes. Why? For friends who come to visit, for guests. It's a staple." Donald actively promoted Equal in local restaurants, too. "If I'm in a restaurant that doesn't serve Equal," he told *St. Louis Commerce Magazine*, "I'll ask to speak to the manager or owner. Almost always by just asking and explaining the benefits, they'll make the switch and carry the brand." (He also reportedly rearranges sweetener packets on restaurant tables to give prominence to Equal.) One of the first actions

Donald took as head of the company was to announce the formation of the Equal Foundation, a nonprofit organization dedicated to combating diabetes, which Donald described to the *Los Angeles Sentinel* (June 13, 2001) as "a health threat of enormous proportions in the African American community." He added, "The rate of increase in diabetes cases among African American adults is at an all time high—and more than one-third of those afflicted with the disease don't even know they have it." In 2002 *Fortune* magazine identified Donald as one of the 50 most powerful black executives in America. In 2003 Donald resigned as CEO of Merisant while retaining his post as chairman, turning over many of his previous duties to Etienne Veber, the former chief operating officer of the company.

Donald's dedication to scientific advances is such that he still lists as the proudest moment of his career an occurrence at Monsanto. "I was standing in a rice field in Indonesia, and this group of women in a small village came up to me with tears in their eyes. They thanked me for transforming their quality of life," he told Ronald E. Childs. "[To grow] rice, they would flood the fields, and then they'd work the field with bull oxen. It's backbreaking work. We had come up with an agricultural practice that eliminated the need to flood the fields, [so] where they used to produce two crops per year, now they [can] grow three. We dramatically increased their earnings and changed their everyday quality of life, because they [can now] grow their yield in less time and with less labor than before. I felt great to be a part of all of that."

Donald married his wife, Hazel, when both were sophomores at Carleton College; they had met on the school's campus when each was a visiting high-school student. The couple have three children, Radiah, Alicia, and Stephen Zachary. The Donalds live in Town and Country, Missouri, with their son; their daughters live in Chicago. Donald credits affirmative action with providing him with many opportunities when he was a young man; he and his wife, who are ardent supporters of educational causes, created the Donald Scholars Program, which provides scholarships for two students per year from St. Augustine or Xavier University Preparatory School to attend the Donalds' alma mater, Carleton. They also were the founders and original sponsors of a summer program through which 50 African-American high-school juniors spend a week at Carleton, expense-free, and they have served as co-chairs of the Charmaine Chapman Society, which recognizes African-Americans who give $1,000 or more to the annual United Way campaign in St. Louis. Donald recalled for the Carleton College Web site (March 1, 2001) that, when he and his wife attended the university, they were two of but a few black students. Some of their white classmates "would ask to touch our hair. . . . They hadn't had any exposure to African Americans and it was honest curiosity on their part. The campus was inviting and warm, but there was still a lot of [racial] separation."

Through their donations to and other support of the college, Donald and his wife have sought to diversify the student body in the hopes of adding to the quality of the educational experience for all students at Carleton.

Interviews with Donald appeared in the film *The Director's Dilemmas* (2005), which was co-developed by professors at Washington University, in St. Louis, Missouri, in conjunction with a St. Louis law firm. The film, created mainly for teaching purposes, examines questions of ethics that face the heads of major corporations, by interspersing a story about the dilemmas of a fictional company with insights from actual CEOs.

Donald sits on the boards of numerous institutions, including Carleton College; Dillard University; Washington University; the Dean's Council for Harvard University's Kennedy School of Government; the United Way of Greater St. Louis; the St. Louis Art Museum; the Missouri Botanical Garden; the Opera Theatre of St. Louis; the St. Louis Science Center; the St. Louis Regional Commerce and Growth Association; BJC Hospital System; Russell Athletic; Crown Cork & Seal Co., Inc.; the Oil-Dri Corp. of America; Belden, Inc.; Carnival Corp.; Laclede Group; the Scotts Co.; and the St. Louis Sports Commission. Additionally, he serves on the National Advisory Council for Washington University School of Engineering. He was appointed to serve on the President's Export Council for international trade in November 1998 and reappointed in 2003, and in November 2001 the governor of Missouri appointed Donald to the Missouri Life Sciences Research Committee. He is a past president of the Leadership Center of Greater St. Louis and previously served on the boards of other organizations, such as the Keck Graduate Institute of Applied Life Science; the US-Russia Business Council; the Eurasia Foundation; the British-American Project; the FFA; and 4-H. Donald has also won a number of awards, among them the Washington University Distinguished Alumni Award (1998), the Eagle Award from the National Eagle Leadership Institute (1999), and the Black Engineers President's Award (2000).

—K.J.E.

Suggested Reading: *Black Enterprise* p107 Sep. 30, 1997; *Los Angeles Sentinel* p10 June 13, 2001; merisant.com; *St. Louis (Missouri) Post-Dispatch* E p1 Jan. 13, 2002

Michael Marsland/Courtesy of Yale University

Doudna, Jennifer

(DOWD-nuh)

Feb. 19, 1964– Biochemist

*Address: University of California at Berkeley,
Dept. of Chemistry, 301B Hildebrand Hall #3206,
Berkeley, CA 94720-3206*

Jennifer Doudna, a professor of biochemistry and molecular biology at the University of California at Berkeley, has done groundbreaking research into the nature and function of ribonucleic acid, known as RNA. In the 1980s scientists discovered that RNA, previously thought to be simply a passive carrier of genetic material (a determinant of, among other traits, the color of one's eyes and one's height), also functioned at times like an enzyme. (Enzymes act as organic catalysts, speeding up various biochemical reactions in an organism. Enzymes are at work, for example, in human digestion and in the ripening of fruit.) Doudna is investigating the structure of ribozymes—RNA with enzymatic properties—and how they affect biochemical processes, including the spread of damaged or viral cells, as happens in cases of cancer and AIDS. Her RNA research, which has been characterized as among the most important in her field in recent years, may help scientists develop treatments for those diseases. While the possible applications could be of enormous importance, Doudna told Melissa Marino in an article for the *Proceedings of the National Academy of Sciences* (December 7, 2004) that her interest in RNA is more basic. "For me, the bigger question is, 'Can we get enough information so that we can understand the chemical

basis for RNA's many biological functions?'" she said. "It will be exciting to make meaningful comparisons between the chemistry of ribozyme reactions and what happens in protein enzymes that carry out similar reactions." Scientists have hypothesized that early life forms may have been based largely on RNA (or a related molecule), and if Doudna discovers many similarities between the structures and functions of RNA and proteins, that hypothesis will gain credence. "Obviously, until we build a time machine, we can't really go back and look at that," Doudna told Marino; thus, such an idea can never truly be tested. But, she added, "I think the idea that RNA might have played a critical role" in the development of early life forms "is very tantalizing."

Jennifer Doudna was born on February 19, 1964 and raised in Hawaii. Her parents both worked in academia. Although their professional focus was on the humanities, they were interested in astronomy and geology, among other subjects, and encouraged Doudna to pursue her own passions. In high school Doudna took her first chemistry class. She became fully hooked on science after reading *The Double Helix: A Personal Account of the Discovery of the Structure of DNA* (1968), by James D. Watson, who had done his seminal work with Francis Crick in the 1950s. Doudna's parents were friends of Don Hemmes, a mycologist and professor of biology at the University of Hawaii at Hilo, and they arranged for her to work in Hemmes's lab for a summer, studying mushrooms.

After high school Doudna enrolled at Pomona College, in California, where she studied French and medieval history in addition to science. At Pomona she worked in the chemistry lab of Sharon Panasenko, who was her faculty adviser. Doudna has described Panasenko as being a strong female role model—a rarity in the male-dominated sciences. Doudna earned a bachelor's degree in chemistry in 1985 and then entered Harvard University, in Cambridge, Massachusetts, to pursue a doctoral degree in biochemistry, which she earned in 1989. At Harvard Doudna studied with Jack Szostak, who was doing exciting research on RNA. Doudna remained at Harvard as a postdoctoral fellow until 1991. While in Cambridge Doudna also served as a research fellow at Massachusetts General Hospital and Harvard Medical School.

After she left Harvard, in 1991, Doudna continued her RNA research as a Lucille P. Markey scholar and postdoctoral fellow at the University of Colorado. There she worked in the laboratory of the biochemist Thomas Cech, a pioneer in the study of RNA. Cech, along with the biochemist Sidney Altman, had documented the existence of ribozymes in the early 1980s. Their research, which won them the Nobel Prize in chemistry in 1989, proved that RNA was not merely a passive transportation device for an organism's genetic code, as had previously been believed, but also acted as an enzyme that stimulated chemical reactions leading to the growth of new cells. In Cech's lab Doudna began working on mapping the three-dimensional chemical structure of a portion of the *Tetrahymena thermophila* ribozyme. (*Tetrahymena thermophila* is the single-celled pond organism that Cech and Altman had used earlier to prove the existence of ribozymes.)

In 1994 Doudna joined the faculty of Yale University, in New Haven, Connecticut, as a professor of biochemistry and biophysics. At Yale Doudna continued to try to better understand the molecular structure of RNA. Her research was funded in part by the National Institutes of Health and various federal grants. Cech continued to collaborate with Doudna as well as with her Yale colleagues. The first task facing them was to grow in crystal form the *Tetrahymena thermophila* ribozymes they had isolated, so that they could examine the ribozymes' atomic structure. To grow the crystals, the researchers used salt compounds, which counteracted the ribozyme molecules' tendency to repel one another rather than crystallize. It was a difficult and time-consuming process. Once Doudna and her colleagues had grown a ribozyme crystal that was large enough, they placed it in an X-ray crystallography machine. The X-rays the machine fired at the crystals produced reflections of the ribozymes' structure, which Doudna and her team studied and copied; eventually, in about 1996, they were able to build a three-dimensional model of a portion of the ribozyme's molecular structure. Though Doudna and her colleagues had mapped only about half of their subject, the model they created represented a tremendous advance. The structural model "showed us how RNA is able to pack helices together to form a three-dimensional shape," Doudna explained to Marino, "which is much more reminiscent of what we see in proteins than anybody had been previously aware of for RNA." In further studies Doudna and her colleagues found that a portion of the ribozyme folded in upon itself, a phenomenon similar to that observed in proteins. For this work Doudna won the Johnson Foundation Prize for Innovative Research, the Beckman Young Investigator Award, the Searle Scholar Award, and the David and Lucille Packard Foundation Fellow Award.

In the October 8, 1998 issue of the journal *Nature,* Doudna and her collaborators reported that they had found an RNA enzyme in a human pathogen—a scientific first. In particular, they described the crystal structure of a ribozyme that contributes to the replication of the hepatitis delta virus, which can cause a potentially fatal secondary infection; such infections occur most frequently among people living in developing nations. In the October 9, 1998 issue of *Science,* Cech described the three-dimensional structure of the *Tetrahymena thermophila* ribozyme. Later in 1998 Doudna was granted tenure at Yale. (Tenure affords a professor greater respect, and in practical terms, means that he or she cannot be fired summarily.) She was named Henry Ford II Professor of Molecular Biophysics and Biochemistry in 2000.

In 2003 Doudna joined the faculty of the University of California at Berkeley as a professor of biochemistry and molecular biology. The move allowed her, her husband, and their preschool son to be closer to members of their extended family. It also gave Doudna easy access to the synchrotron (an apparatus that imparts high speed to charged particles using magnetic and electric fields of varying frequencies) at the Lawrence Berkeley National Laboratory. Much of her most recent work concerns viral RNA and its functions, in particular a section of viral RNA called the internal ribosome entry site (IRES). (Ribosomes, a component of cells, synthesize proteins.) Doudna described IRES to Marino as a "pretty amazing structure that's basically able to grab the ribosomes of infected cells and hijack them for making viral proteins." She continued, "I think this is the project in the lab that has the greatest potential to lead to something that might have an impact on human health." The practical applications of her work include the creation of ribozyme-based drug therapies to stop the spread of mutated cells. Pharmaceutical companies began putting Doudna's structural model to use soon after she and her team created it. As reported by David Fletcher for the *Yale Daily News* (September 26, 1996), researchers working for such companies as Innovir (which was founded by Sydney Altman) sought to use Doudna's model to learn how to manipulate cells affected by various genetic diseases, including cystic fibrosis and sickle-cell anemia.

Doudna is a member of the editorial boards of *Current Biology* and the *Journal of Molecular Biology.* She has authored or co-authored more than 70 monographs and papers on her research. In 2000 Doudna became the third woman ever to be honored with the prestigious Alan T. Waterman Award from the National Science Foundation; the award included a grant of $500,000 over the course of three years. Joan Steitz, one of Doudna's former colleagues in Yale's Biochemistry Department, who recommended Doudna for the award, told a reporter for AScribe Newswire (April 18, 2000) that Doudna possesses a "particular constellation of qualities as a scientist. She knows a lot of biochemistry. . . . And she has all sorts of guts and determination, and that's the reason why she tackled what was a very, very hard problem. . . . There can be no question that her pioneering accomplishments have changed the way the scientific community thinks about RNA molecules." In addition to her teaching responsibilities at the University of California at Berkeley, Doudna is an investigator at the Howard Hughes Medical Institute, in Chevy Chase, Maryland, a post she has held since 1997. She has been elected to the American Academy of Arts and Sciences and the National Academy of Sciences, honors usually reserved for older scientists with longer careers.

—C.F.T.

Suggested Reading: AScribe Newswire Apr. 18, 2000; Howard Hughes Medical Institute Web site; National Science Foundation Web site; *Proceedings of the National Academy of Sciences* p16987+ Dec. 7, 2004; University of California at Berkeley Web site

---

Drake, James

Sep. 12, 1946– Artist

Address: c/o Adair Margo Gallery, 415 E. Yandell, Suite 10-B, El Paso, TX 79902

For nearly 40 years the American artist James Drake has explored the concept of borders, expressing his ideas in a variety of media, ranging from sculpture and charcoal drawing to video. "I have always been a mixed-media person," Drake told *Current Biography*. "I always tried to use the media that seemed most appropriate or defined the concept in a visually clear, dramatic, and thought-provoking manner." The border he has perhaps explored most often in his work is the real one shared by Mexico and the United States. But as Drake presents them, borders are conceptual as well as physical entities and often reveal themselves to be permeable or unstable. Indeed, his work, it could be argued, illustrates their permeability; as Paul Richard wrote for the *Washington Post* (October 9, 1990), Drake "makes Latino-gringo art" that breaks down the divisions separating the two cultures that infuse the American Southwest. This aspect of his work suggests that Drake is not as interested in borders themselves as he is in humanity's simultaneous need to build and tear them down to fashion a better world. As the artist explained to *Current Biography*, "All of my work is based on communication and the desperate desire people have to communicate."

Born on September 12, 1946 in Lubbock, Texas, James Drake grew up straddling the cultures of Latin America and the United States. His family moved to Guatemala when he was about two and lived there for four or five years. His first language was Spanish. Political turmoil in Guatemala forced the family to return to Lubbock, and "because of the nature of the west Texas town," Drake told *Current Biography*, "I either forgot or refused to speak Spanish." In 1960 he moved with his mother and sister, Pi, to El Paso, Texas, across the border from Juarez, Mexico; afterward he relearned Spanish, which he then spoke with a Texas accent. Drake's artistic talents emerged early. While he was in the seventh grade and still living in Lubbock, he entered a fire-prevention poster contest and won first place in the city's competition and ninth place in the state's. His mother—who had founded a weaving and crafts business, called Mayatex, in Guatemala in 1944 (it is still operating in El Paso, under

Pi's management)—did all that she could to encourage his interest in art, and he resolved to become an artist. At his mother's suggestion, when he was 14 he took a trip to Mexico City by himself to see murals painted by such giants of Mexican art as Diego Rivera, José Clemente Orozco, and David Alfaro Siqueiros. "That trip had a profound impact on me and the future direction of my work," he told *Current Biography*. After high school Drake attended Texas Tech University, in Lubbock, for two semesters and then transferred to the Art Center College of Design, in Los Angeles, California, where he earned a bachelor of fine arts degree, in 1969, and a master's degree, also in fine arts, in 1970. He then returned to Texas and settled in El Paso, where he remained until the late 1990s.

Drake began exhibiting his work professionally while he was an undergraduate. In 1967 he participated in the Annual Sun Carnival Exhibition, at the El Paso Museum of Art. The following year the Butler Institute of Art, in Ohio, included his work in another group exhibit, and in 1971 the Pavilion Art Gallery, in Arizona, mounted Drake's first solo exhibition. During that period Drake focused on painting and drawing, which he had studied in college. While on a trip to Europe in 1972, he saw Theodore Géricault's *Raft of the Medusa* (1819) and was so awestruck that he gave up painting. "I didn't think I could do anything to equal that," he told Steven Henry Madoff for the *New York Times* (February 6, 2005), "and I never painted again—I just started drawing." Throughout the 1970s Drake refined his drawing techniques and also began to explore other artistic mediums. Later his drawings came to serve as studies for the large steel sculptures that he produced—works such as those appearing in *Trophy Room II*, an installation that was exhibited in the Third Western States Exhibition, in the Brooklyn Museum, in New York City, in 1986. "Everything in the work is made of blackish steel," Michael Brenson explained in the *New York Times* (June 15, 1986). "Walking into the metal room, we are surrounded by trophies of a skull, antlers and a huge angry boar. There is also a metal bow and arrow, a big, blustery gun and a display case filled with knives." Drake has also incorporated his drawings in sculptural pieces. For example, the pieces he exhibited at the Fendrick Gallery in Washington, D.C., in 1987 "pair free-standing sculptural elements with large charcoal and conté drawings hung on the wall behind them," as Jo Ann Lewis wrote for the *Washington Post* (November 6, 1987). (So-called conté crayons are comparable to colored chalk.) Drake soon became known more for his sculptures than for his other work. Indeed, so famous had his sculptures become that when he began exhibiting drawings without sculptural elements, in 2004, Doug MacCash—ignoring Drake's earlier drawing projects—wrote for the Arthur Roger Gallery Web site, "Drake could have ridden his popular welded-steel wave forever. . . . He says he always began his sculptural projects with drawings. These days he's letting the drawings themselves come to the fore."

James Drake with a sketch made in preparation for his sculpture Police-Dog Attack

Drake also became known as a politically inspired artist. "Profound political and humanitarian messages underlie the work of James Drake," Deloris Tarzan Ament wrote for the *Seattle Times* (January 17, 1990). "Drawing in charcoal, Drake appropriates images from famous historical paintings of suffering such as the *Raft of the Medusa*, mounting them with panels of black steel. He attaches welded guns, to make the point that the death, starvation and suffering they depict are urgent current events." An installation called *Juarez/El Paso* (1986–89), which was exhibited in 1989, memorialized 18 Mexicans who died as they attempted to cross the border into the U.S. in an airtight refrigerated boxcar; the work paid "homage to the lost lives in a tone shifting from elegy to anger, irony to anguish," according to a reviewer for the *Los Angeles Times* (February 3, 1989). In each of the installation's pieces, Drake paired large charcoal drawings with sculptures and sometimes text. In *Boxcar*, for example (which was later included in an exhibition called The Passionate Adventure of the Real: Collage, Assemblage and the Object in 20th Century Art, at Houston's Museum of Fine Arts), Drake "combined a large charcoal drawing of a boxcar with real railroad spikes and crowbar, embedded in a mound of charcoal on the floor . . . ," as Patricia C. Johnson wrote for the *Houston Chronicle* (October 25, 2003). "Evoking the Nazi use of boxcars as conveyances of death, it also reminds that trains and trucks continue to become coffins for many seeking escape."

Having become well known for creating large, politically motivated sculptures, Drake was commissioned in the early 1990s to work on a memorial for those who suffered while fighting for civil rights during the 1963 demonstrations in Kelly Ingram Park, in Birmingham, Alabama. To fulfill the commission, he fashioned three large sculptures: *Children's March* (1992), *Police-Dog Attack* (1993), and *Fire Hosing of Demonstrators* (1993). Those sculptures invite viewers to place themselves in the position of the civil rights activists, by drawing them into the art and the struggle it memorializes. *Police-Dog Attack*, for instance, features, as Roy Williams wrote for the *Birmingham News* (May 31, 1993), "several sculpted dogs that appear to be leaping toward walkers as they pass through a pathway in the park leading toward the Birmingham Civil Rights Institute." The other sculptures, Anne Whitehouse wrote for the *Los Angeles Times* (April 11, 1993), "are dark, brooding works in steel and bronze whose static drama reenacts the violence of the park's past. One depicts two youths standing in a doorway. Across the path from them is a wall of prison bars commemorating the marching children who were imprisoned. Another sculpture shows two young people flung against a wall by the imagined jets of water issuing from the monitor guns mounted on tripods behind them."

For his next major project, Drake collaborated with his friend Terry Allen, a Lubbock-born artist whom Drake knew as a child. "We started fooling around in Terry's studio one day, just making these drawings and putting things together," Drake told Johnson for the *Houston Chronicle* (August 31, 1994). "We thought it'd be interesting to see what would happen to the drawings if we made them into rugs." The men hired weavers in Oaxaca, Mexico, to transform their pastel, ink, and charcoal creations into rugs, which "then became the inspiration for . . . two sculptures and five tableaux," as Frances Colpitt wrote for *Art in America* (October 1994). The sculptures and tableaux formed the exhibition Poison/Amor (1994). "The works are rooted in *la frontera*, the border with Mexico," Johnson wrote. The physical reality of that setting is portrayed in such pieces as *Frontera*, "a packing-cratelike hut on a dirt floor," as Colpitt explained. "Visible through a window was a crouching child-sized figure with his hands to his ears, in front of a small television set." The exhibit also included symbolic representations of the border. *Dream Dog*, for example, as Johnson observed, "consists of a large, rectangular cage with no ceiling, into which a blindfolded figure is dropping head first, a rope tied to one foot. A live dog in the cage completes this frightening, loaded tableau. It insinuates itself at several levels, from unspeakably cruel situations to the chain-link fences we build around us, including those on the border."

In the year in which Poison/Amor was mounted, Drake saw several women standing outside the walls of an El Paso prison. The women were moving their arms and bodies as they looked up at the prison walls. He initially thought they were dancing but discovered later that they were conversing with their imprisoned husbands and boyfriends with the help of a sign language that "combines American Sign Language with gang signals," as Andrew Patner wrote for the *Chicago Sun-Times* (July 16, 1997). Drake became fascinated with the women, and after gaining the trust of gang members, both inside and outside the prison, he worked with the women and the prisoners, videotaping them as they communicated their own messages through sign language, along with poems by William Shakespeare, Jorge Luis Borges, and other writers. Using those tapes he produced three multi-work solo exhibitions: Tongue-Cut Sparrows (1996), Conversation: Inside/Outside (1996–97), and A Thousand Tongues Burn and Sing (1998). Tongue-Cut Sparrows juxtaposes a video installation of the women's movements with charcoal drawings of hands in the act of forming signs. The drawings, Kenneth Baker wrote for the *San Francisco Chronicle* (August 21, 1997), "are graphically powerful whether we know their significance or not. . . . We may also be meant to see the make-shift sign language as a metaphor for Drake's own work. Taking it as a subject, he turns his art into a set of signals to us that may call our attention to social walls separating us that we do not acknowledge." Alan G. Artner, writing for the *Chicago Tribune* (August 8, 1997), had a different reaction: Viewers' inability to know what the signs mean without reading Drake's explanatory material led him to complain, "Drake's words and images should be yoked together, equal in strength; otherwise, his introduction of literature to the signing process has meaning only as a concept apart from visual impact." Conversation: Inside/Outside contains a series of still photos of couples conversing interspersed with pages of text. In the piece, Alice

Thorson wrote for the *Kansas City Star* (March 28, 1999), Drake succeeded in portraying the couples "without sentimentality; nor does he use their experience to convey a moral lesson. Rather, what he offers us is a view into their world." Experiencing the piece, Holly Willis wrote for *Artweek* (March 31, 2000), is "like viewing a strip of movie footage, but in this case, the strip stretches out across the wall, stopping the temporal flow while maintaining a sense of both separation and proximity." A Thousand Tongues Burn and Sing contains three diptychs, each of which is composed of large photographs of the prisoners' world—one of the prison's interior, one of its exterior, and one of the men silhouetted in a window—and large drawings of perhaps 100 tongues placed in a rocklike configuration that forms, as Teresa Annas described them for the *Virginian-Pilot* (February 28, 1998), "a constellation of concentric circles. The allusion to a Stonehenge-type rock formation is a reminder of the ritualistic aspect of the girls' communication." In the view of Michael Plante, writing for *Art in America* (March 1, 1999), the three series taken together represent "problems of the inner city, El Paso's in this instance, without offering the viewer a privileged position or pat solution. The uninitiated onlooker—in El Paso or in the museum—is left to puzzle at the language while marveling at its grace."

Throughout the 1990s Drake also documented the activities of transvestite and transsexual prostitutes working along the Juarez–El Paso border, photographing and videotaping them at work. The photographs were gathered to produce *Que Linda la Brisa (How Lovely the Breeze)*, 1999), a multi-piece work that was included in the Whitney Museum's 2000 Biennial exhibition, in New York City. The Biennial's co-curator Michael Auping told Michael Ennis for *Texas Monthly* (February 2000) that Drake's "is an art about borders. In this case it's not just geographical borders but gender borders. But instead of stridently protesting social injustice, these pictures record a certain element of beauty and melancholy." In the *Houston Chronicle* (May 4, 2000) Patricia C. Johnson called the images "cheesy and sentimental but also oddly powerful." Drake's video, which was included in Natural Deceits (2000), an exhibition at the Modern Art Museum of Fort Worth, "personifies" the idea that "art is attractive because it is a beautiful lie," as Janet Kutner wrote for the *Dallas Morning News* (May 14, 2000). Kutner went on to write about the video: "A glamorous transvestite [Zona Mariscal] who sells her body on the El Paso-Juarez border ponders the precarious nature of her pretense in poetic terms while applying makeup."

More recently, Drake took his art in a different direction. He began working with Murray Gell-Mann, the 1969 winner of the Nobel Prize for Physics. Fascinated by Gell-Mann's work, Drake "asked him to develop an equation for a hummingbird, whose ability to propel itself for extended periods and in multiple directions has never been explained by science," according to the *El Paso Times* (July 14, 2002). Drake used what Gell-Mann came up with to create *Hummingbird's Equation* (2001), which Ken Johnson of the *New York Times* (February 15, 2002) described as "wispy watercolor pictures of hummingbirds, captioned with penciled mathematical equations."

Drake's latest work is *City of Tells* (2004), the idea for which came to him while he was chatting with the novelist Cormac McCarthy in 2001. "What I remember most," Drake told Steven Henry Madoff for the *New York Times* (February 6, 2005), "is talking about the past. . . . I was thinking, 'Who are the really important people in my life?' You know, relatives, friends, the living and the dead who have influenced my art. And I said out loud that it would be interesting to make a picture like that, a banquet, a gathering, like the old court painters made." For the next two and half years, Drake re-created such a banquet in charcoal, producing a 12-by-32-foot drawing that portrays members of Drake's family; his friends, among them McCarthy and Gell-Mann; such historical figures as Dante, Michelangelo, and Goya; himself as a child; and a snake. *City of Tells* also includes a three-part video series, which focuses on a banquet table Drake set up in the middle of a wooded area to see which animals would visit the site. "It was interesting," Drake told Doug MacCash for the New Orleans *Times-Picayune* (October 15, 2004), "because certain animals did come to the table, birds and feral hogs. There was the element of chance, just like poker." Indeed, poker ties the two sides of

the piece together, for a "tell," in poker parlance, is an unconscious mannerism that reveals someone's intentions. "Drake investigates both animal and human nature through two very different mediums," Max Beckmann wrote for *Art in America* (August 1, 2003). "With a banquet table as their shared motif, the two monumental works—a three-panel video projection and a drawing—reference biblical tales and cultural mythology."

Since 1998 Drake and his wife, the artist Colleen Cassidy Drake, have divided their time between New York City and Santa Fe, New Mexico. James Drake is currently focusing his energies on drawings and "plans to make more drawings on the scale of *City of Tells*," as Elizabeth Cook-Romero reported for the Santa Fe *New Mexican* (February 11, 2005). He told her that he "had fun" drawing *City of Tells*. "I was happy," he said, "and being happy is difficult to come by. I'm even happy thinking about the next big drawings I'm going to do." Nonetheless, he told *Current Biography*, "if offered a commission and the concept seemed appropriate, I would gladly make more sculpture or video."

—A.R.

Suggested Reading: *Artweek* Mar. 2000; *Houston Chronicle* p1 Aug. 31, 1994; *Los Angeles Times* B p23 Feb. 3, 1989; (New Orleans) *Times-Picayune* p17 Oct. 15, 2004; *New York Times* p36 Feb. 6, 2005; (Santa Fe) *New Mexican* A p56 Feb. 11, 2005; *Washington Post* N p51 Nov. 6, 1987, E p3 Oct. 9, 1990

Ehlers, Vernon J.

Feb. 6, 1934– U.S. representative from Michigan (Republican); former research physicist

Address: 1714 Longworth House Office Bldg., Washington, DC 20515; 110 Michigan St., N.W., Grand Rapids, MI 49503

Republican congressman Vernon J. Ehlers has served Michigan's traditionally Republican Third District in the U.S. House of Representatives since 1994, and he has been reelected by a wide margin six times. A former professor of physics and the first research physicist to serve in Congress, he spent eight years on the Kent County, Michigan, Board of Commissioners and 11 years in the Michigan state Legislature before arriving in Washington. Throughout his career in public service, Ehlers has been recognized as a leader on issues concerning the environment, education, and public health. He has built a reputation as the foremost congressional authority on scientific and technological matters and is a relentless champion of scientific causes, from elementary-school education

to research and development. As he wrote in the November 1998 issue of the *MRS Bulletin* (a publication of the Materials Research Society), "The scientific and technology enterprise is critical to bringing about advances in understanding that can help ensure that we can maintain our national defense, keep people healthy, and bring about prosperity. . . . A vigorous and sustainable U.S. science and technology enterprise may be our most important legacy to future generations." A devout member of the Christian Reformed Church, Ehlers brings to his work a combination of religious faith and scientific training that has resulted in "a middle-of-the-House voting record," according to the *Almanac of American Politics*; the *Congressional Quarterly Daily Monitor* (June 24, 2003) reported that "the *Basic Dictionary of Science* and the Holy Bible sit side-by-side on his office shelf." During his 11 years as a congressman, he has introduced various acts aimed at reforming education in science, technology, engineering, and mathematics (four disciplines known collectively by the acronym STEM), as well as legislation to end funding for the National Endowment for the Arts (NEA) in favor of other arts programs and to make permanent the ban on human cloning.

Courtesy of the Office of Congressman Vernon J. Ehlers

Vernon J. Ehlers

Ehlers is a member of the House Science Committee, for which he serves as chairman of the Subcommittee on Environment, Technology and Standards. Despite a number of successes in reforming the nation's science policies, he regards his efforts to secure funding for science-related programs as an uphill battle. During an acceptance speech for a Public Service Award, sponsored by the American Physical Society (APS), the American Astronomical Society (AAS), and the American Mathematical Society (AMS), according to the *APS News* Web site (May 16, 2001), he remarked, "There is precious little reward in Congress for pursuing science policy and the advancement of science. We don't get positive feedback from fellow Congressmen or constituents, or from the scientific community, since scientists tend to be apolitical."

In addition to chairing the Subcommittee on Environment, Technology and Standards, Ehlers holds positions on the Education and the Workforce Committee, the House Administration Committee, and the Joint Committee on the Library of Congress. As a member of the Transportation and Infrastructure Committee, he has led efforts to secure a fair funding formula and more money for Michigan's roads, highways, and transit systems.

A staunch environmentalist, Ehlers has served as the chairman of the National Conference of State Legislatures' Environment Committee and as a member of the Federal Clean Air Act Advisory Committee. His commitment to the environment, which has won him an endorsement from the Sierra Club, among other groups, has led him to cross party lines on several occasions. For example, unlike most other Republican congressmen, he has opposed appropriations-bill riders that would undercut the ability of the Environmental Protection Agency (EPA) to enforce various environmental and public-health laws; supported the National Biological Survey; and opposed setting aside part of the Mojave Natural Reserve for hunting. His amendment to the 1996 Safe Drinking Water Act converted from voluntary to mandatory the Great Lakes Water Quality Initiative standards, and during the 107th Congress he led the formulation of the Great Lakes Legacy Act, which authorized spending $270 million to clean up sediments in the Great Lakes. On April 30, 2002 the House passed a bill Ehlers had designed to ensure the soundness of the EPA's scientific standards; according to a news release from his office (April 30, 2002), Ehlers commented, "If the EPA does not have a fundamental understanding of science in its work of establishing rules and priorities for clean land, air, and water then we are putting ourselves at risk." In 2003, together with Republican representative Wayne Gilchrest of Maryland, Ehlers introduced the National Aquatic Invasive Species Act and the Aquatic Invasive Species Research Act, a pair of bills dedicated to determining how invasive species enter U.S. waterways and then developing a plan to prevent their spread.

Vernon James Ehlers was born in Pipestone, Minnesota, on February 6, 1934. One of four children, he is the son of John Ehlers, a Christian Reformed minister, and Alice Doorn Ehlers. He enrolled at Calvin College, a Christian liberal-arts school in Grand Rapids, Michigan, in 1952 and remained there until 1955, when he transferred to the University of California (UC) at Berkeley. Soon after UC–Berkeley awarded him an A.B. degree in physics, in 1956, he began working for the university as a research assistant. In 1960 Ehlers received a Ph.D. in nuclear physics from UC–Berkeley. During the next six years he held the position of lecturer in physics there. He also worked at the Lawrence Berkeley National Laboratory, a U.S. Department of Energy facility managed by the University of California. Meanwhile, in 1961, he won a two-year North Atlantic Treaty Organization postdoctoral research fellowship, with which he devoted himself to physical research at the University of Heidelberg, in what was then West Germany.

In 1966 Ehlers returned to Calvin College to join its faculty as a physics professor, a position he held until 1983. The organization Outstanding Educators of America named him an outstanding educator in 1970 and 1973. In 1977 he became chairman of Calvin's Physics and Astronomy Department. Concurrently, in 1974, concerned about local waste management, he announced his candidacy for a seat on the Board of Commissioners of Kent County, which encompasses Grand Rapids. He won the election and served as a Kent County commissioner from 1975 to 1982, including three years as the board's chairman.

Meanwhile, in 1978, as a member of the Christian Reformed Synodical Task Force on World Hunger, Ehlers co-authored his first book, *And He Had Compassion on Them: The Christian and World Hunger.* In 1979 he collaborated with the same task force to produce a second book, *For My Neighbor's Good: World Hunger and Structural Change.* He co-authored his third book with several other fellows of Calvin College's 1977-78 Calvin Center for Christian Scholarship. Entitled *Earthkeeping: Christian Stewardship of Natural Resources* (1980), the book is a guide to environmental management from a Christian perspective. Also with fellows of the Calvin Center for Christian Scholarship, he co-wrote *Earthkeeping in the '90s: Stewardship of Creation* (1991) .

Ehlers began his full-time political career in 1983, when he was elected to the Michigan House of Representatives and was promptly appointed assistant Republican floor leader. During his years as a state representative, he served on the House Committee on Colleges and Universities, helped to institute Michigan's 911 emergency telephone system, and drew up legislation that allocated funds for early preventive medical screening tests for newborns. In 1985 he entered the race to fill a vacant seat in the Michigan state Senate in a special election against Stephen V. Monsma, a former Democratic Michigan state lawmaker who, like Ehlers, was a Christian Reformed Church elder and a former professor. Ehlers won the race and served Michigan as a state senator from 1986 to 1993, during which time he was a member of the Senate Appropriations subcommittee overseeing aspects of higher education. From 1990 to 1993 he held the post of president pro tempore of the state Senate.

After U.S. congressman Paul Henry of Michigan died, in July 1993, Ehlers ran to succeed him. (He had succeeded Henry in both houses of the state Legislature.) He won the November 1993 Republican primary with 33 percent of the vote; 25 percent went to Ken Sikkema, 19 percent to state commerce official Marge Byington, and 16 percent to a local furniture manufacturer. A month later, at the special December 7 election, Ehlers defeated the Democratic candidate by a landslide, 67 percent to 23 percent, winning the seat in Congress for Michigan's Third District.

At the time of Ehlers's election, the U.S. House Republicans were about to enter their 40th year in the minority. Ehlers was sworn in to the 103d Congress on January 25, 1994, when Congress reconvened after its holiday recess, and was immediately elected by his peers to serve as the Midwest regional vice president of the freshman Republican representatives. During his first month in office, Ehlers was appointed to two major committees: the Transportation and Infrastructure Committee and the Science Committee. As a member of the latter, he called for substantial federal support of scientific research and a strengthening of STEM education in public schools. His background in science and his extensive knowledge of science-related issues earned him the respect of fellow committee members, and it was not long before he ascended to the position of vice chairman of the committee. In September 1998 he produced the report "Unlocking Our Future: Toward a New National Science Policy," the first major discussion of federal support of science and technology since 1945. The report, which called for "stable and substantial" funding of scientific research by the federal government and proposed permanent tax credits for private companies' research-and-development expenditures, was approved by the House on October 8, 1998. While many Republicans praised the study, George Brown, a Democrat from California, criticized it as overly vague regarding its aims: "When we use public resources to support science and technology, we should clearly identify the public purposes that we desire to achieve," he said, according to Vincent Kiernan for *Laser Focus World* (November 1, 1998).

Ehlers retained his seats on the Science Committee and the Transportation and Infrastructure Committee after he was elected to Congress for his first full term, in 1994. He soon assumed further responsibilities, because Republican victories in many states produced a Republican majority in the House, and the new House Speaker, Congressman Newt Gingrich of Georgia, named Ehlers to his transition team. At that time Gingrich also appointed him to the House Administration Committee, a special task force dedicated to reviewing computerization in the House of Representatives. Ehlers was put in charge of revamping the House computer system and connecting members of Congress to the Internet; he also spearheaded an effort to make House vote tallies and transcripts, bills, and other documents available to the public online. In an article by Robert Pear for the *New York Times* (November 19, 1994), Ehlers was quoted as calling his various technology projects for Congress "a movement toward electronic democracy."

In the 1996 congressional race, Ehlers ran against the Democratic candidate Betsy J. Flory and won 69 percent of the vote to her 29 percent. That same year he received a National Association of Children's Hospitals Award for his leadership in advocacy for children's health, as well as a Distinguished Alumni Award from Calvin College. He was sworn into office for his second full congressional term on January 7, 1997. Later that year, in recognition of his leadership in promoting science education in Congress, he received a Science Coalition Award from the Science Coalition, a group of more than 400 science-related organizations.

During the first session of the 105th Congress, Ehlers introduced one piece of legislation to ban the cloning of humans and another to withhold federal money from human-cloning experiments. Justifying his position on the cloning issue, he cited concerns about the potential of heightened susceptibility to disease among cloned humans and negative social and biological effects arising from reductions in genetic variety. "What if in the cloning process you produce someone with two heads and three arms?" he asked rhetorically, according to an article for the *New York Times* (March 6, 1997). "Are you simply going to euthanize and dispose of that person? The answer is no. We're talking about a human life." In an essay for the *Hofstra Law Review* (Spring 1999), Ehlers declared, "When a human being is created through cloning, we have crossed the line from experimentation and legitimate scientific work to an activity with profound moral and social repercussions." Despite his strong opposition to human cloning, as a scientist Ehlers was eager to ensure that research on animal cloning could proceed with as few restrictions as possible. He argued that animal cloning might produce substantial human-health and agricultural benefits and that if Congress did not ban human cloning in particular immediately, it might make the lamentable decision to ban cloning altogether later on. In a press release from his office (January 14, 1998), Ehlers maintained, "It is important that we continue to explore and experiment with various nonhuman subjects to learn all we can about this development, but it is imperative that scientists refrain from crossing the line into research on cloning humans."

In 1997 Ehlers worked with other House Republicans to advance a new formula for government funding of the arts that would have eliminated the National Endowment for the Arts, a federal agency whose awarding of grants to some controversial artists, such as the photographer Robert Mapplethorpe, has outraged conservatives. The so-called Ehlers amendment proposed replacing grants for individual artists with block grants that would be sent directly to the states for local arts projects and arts education, thus doing away with the need for a federal arts agency. NEA supporters strenuously opposed the amendment, which was defeated in the House, 271 to 155.

In 1998 Ehlers led a task force to investigate voter fraud in the 1996 election of Representative Loretta Sanchez of California, who had defeated Republican Robert K. Dornan by 984 votes. The task force uncovered "substantial voter fraud," but it was unable to prove that there were enough illegal votes to overturn the election and ultimately recommended that the House dismiss Dornan's vote challenge. Ehlers ran unopposed in the 1998 Republican primary and won the general election against Democrat John Ferguson Jr. with 73 percent of the vote. In 1999 he joined the Education and the Workforce Committee. That year he was the only Republican member of Congress to vote against the deployment of a National Missile Defense (NMD), a component of what is known colloquially as "Star Wars," a land-based system designed to defend U.S. territory against long-range ballistic missiles. Also in 1999 Ehlers was honored by the National Parks and Conservation Association with a Friend of the National Parks Award for his voting record on national parks and related public-lands issues in the 105th Congress.

In April 2000 Ehlers introduced a trio of legislative proposals aimed at improving science and math education nationwide. The National Science Education Incentive Act proposed the creation of tax credits to help prospective teachers pay for a portion of their undergraduate college education. The National Science Education Enhancement Act focused on improving and expanding the activities of the Department of Education that concentrate on science, math, engineering, and technology. The National Science Education Act, or NSEA, called for the allocation of federal funds to schools for the training of teachers and the ordering and maintaining of science-teaching equipment. The NSEA originally had 16 co-sponsors, a number that grew to include 62 Republicans and 45 Democrats by September 2000, when it was brought out of committee and to the full House. On October 23, 2000, the day before the House was scheduled to vote on the bill, a Democratic congressional aide noticed a funding provision in it that allows federal monies to be given to schools, including private and parochial institutions, to hire "master teachers" to oversee their science programs. According to the *APS News* Web site (February 2001), *Science* magazine quoted the aide as recalling, "We were sitting around during a lull in [unrelated] negotiations when I saw the language and said, 'Whoa! There's a church-state entanglement here.'"

The National Education Association, the American Association of School Administrators, and several other influential teachers' organizations were alerted, and they immediately began to petition Democratic House members not to allow the bill to pass. On October 24 many of the NSEA's original supporters, including 30 of the 45 Democratic sponsors and 114 others among the 187 House Democrats, voted against it. Ehlers continued to stand by his proposal, however, telling *Science*, "I don't see any reason to modify my position, and I resent the last-minute effort to dismantle [the bill]." The NSEA, with the controversial provision, finally passed in the House on July 30, 2001, and on December 14, 2001 the House of Representatives approved the No Child Left Behind Act, which included a section drafted by Ehlers allocating federal resources to improve math and science teaching in public grade and high schools.

On January 7, 2003 Ehlers was sworn in to the 108th Congress, to serve his fifth full congressional term. In June of that year he was one of only nine Republicans to vote against an $82 billion tax-cut bill to increase child tax credits for both low-income and hgh-income families; the bill did not include any taxes or fees to offset the loss of government income. Regarding the question of whether to authorize military action in Iraq, as requested by President George W. Bush, he wavered before voting in favor of using force if diplomacy failed. According to *USA Today*, Ehlers, who has called himself "slightly pacifist by nature," expressed the opinion that a preemptive strike against Iraq would be "contrary to our nature as a nation." In the 2004 election Ehlers handily defeated his Democratic challenger, Pete Hickey, with 67 percent of the vote.

In 2005 Ehlers and other members on the House Committee on Science, responding to a report by the National Academy of Sciences regarding the increased threat of global competition facing the United States, proposed an increase in federal funding for scientific research and development and for education through high school. On other fronts, Ehlers and House Science Committee chairman Sherwood Boehlert urged the Election Assistance Commission and the National Institute of Standards and Technology to institute procedures for improving the security and reliability of voting equipment in the U.S. Ehlers also introduced a measure, which was passed by the House and was under consideration by the Senate, to create an 11-person panel to determine how to increase the number of workers in the science, engineering, and aerospace industries and to coordinate aerospace career education and training programs with industry, organized labor, academia, and state governments. According to various specialists, the

aerospace industry is in jeopardy of losing more than one in four workers to retirement before 2009.

Congressman Ehlers lives in Grand Rapids, Michigan, where he is a member and former elder of Eastern Avenue Christian Reformed Church. He and his wife, the former Johanna Meulink, who married in 1958, have four adult children: Heidi, Brian, Marla, and Todd. They also have three grandchildren and a great-granddaughter.

—L.W.

Suggested Reading: *APS News* (on-line) Feb. 2001; *Hofstra Law Review* Spring 1999; *MRS Bulletin* (on-line) Nov. 1998; *New York Times* B p12 Mar. 6, 1997

Selected Books: as co-author—*And He Had Compassion on Them: The Christian and World Hunger*, 1978; *For My Neighbor's Good: World Hunger and Structural Change*, 1979; *Earthkeeping: Christian Stewardship of Natural Resources*, 1980; *Earthkeeping in the '90s: Stewardship of Creation*, 1991

Elling, Kurt

Nov. 2, 1967– Jazz vocalist

Address: c/o Blue Note Records (EMI Music), 150 Fifth Ave., New York, NY 10011

"In an era when bona fide young jazz singers are in perilously short supply," the critic Howard Reich wrote for the *Chicago Tribune* (February 28, 2001), "the under-40 Elling seems hellbent on rewriting the definition of what jazz singing is all about." Kurt Elling is one of the most innovative and adventurous of contemporary jazz vocalists and is perhaps the best-known among today's young male jazz singers. Acclaimed for singing classic jazz with flair, he is also highly regarded for his scatting and his improvisational lyrics, which he calls "poetry on the fly." Inspired by Beat poetry and vocalese—the writing of lyrics over the transcription of a recorded instrumental solo—and influenced as well by such jazz poets as Mark Murphy and John Hendricks, Elling has blurred the boundary between music and the written word, by reading poems by the likes of Edgar Allan Poe, St. John of the Cross, and Rainer Maria Rilke during his performances of jazz standards. While his records have not sold in great numbers outside of the Chicago, Illinois, area, from which he hails, his work has led to critical accolades and several Grammy Award nominations. "Elling manages to express love or convey pain without sounding emasculated," Mathew Bahl wrote for *All About Jazz* (on-line). "He submerges himself into each song's story to such a degree that he is able to paraphrase a lyric without

Courtesy of Jeff Sciortino

disrupting its conversational flow. His interpretations avoid both the shallowness of irony and the self-absorption of melodrama in search of a genuine connection with the material."

While his performances on record have drawn acclaim, it is during his live concerts that Elling really shines. Reviewing a show for the *Winnipeg Sun* (June 28, 1999, on-line), Anna Lazowski noted that he is "equal parts comedian, old-school jazz

cat, beatnik and showman. . . . He also showcased his voice as an instrument, creating a medley
of sounds and a fine didgeridoo impression." In addition to his performances as a jazz vocalist, Elling
has written and staged several performance-art
pieces that have received enthusiastic notices. In
his review of one of those shows, Howard Reich
commented, "Someone, somewhere ought to give
Elling the means to take this stage work, or any of
his others, and bring them to fruition through a
longer engagement. With that opportunity, Elling
truly might be able to change the way audiences
think about jazz, poetry and life in America."

Kurt Elling was born on November 2, 1967 in
Chicago, Illinois. As a child he studied violin and
French horn and sang in the church where his father was the organist and choirmaster. The senior
Elling also taught in high schools in the Chicago
area. "I learned a lot from him about the positive
effects of music, how to put on a show, the corporate side of music, and how to translate elements
of the human experience into beautiful, dignified,
moving, musical experiences," Elling told Mike
Metheny for *Jazz Ambassadors Magazine* (Febru-
ary/March 2000, on-line). Elling also told Metheny
that he was influenced by the church, "where music is so integral to the forwarding of the ritual experience. And I think I got a sense from that of what
could happen in any kind of musical setting, if you
chose to have it go that way." Elling attended Gus-
tavus Adolphus College, in Saint Peter, Minnesota,
where he studied history and religion. It was there
that a friend in his dormitory introduced him to
jazz, including the music of the tenor saxophonist
Dexter Gordon, the pianist Dave Brubeck, and the
fusion pianist Herbie Hancock. "It seemed like a
natural thing to start singing that music," Elling
said for *All About Jazz*. "I turned to Ella [Fitzger-
ald] right away because she was really swinging
and because with her scat-singing, she went beyond the usual boring pattern of singer/horn
solo/singer." Elling started sitting in with a student
jazz combo and also joined the college's jazz orchestra.

After receiving his bachelor's degree, in 1989,
Elling attended the University of Chicago's Divinity School, with the goal of becoming a professor of
religion. He was unable to concentrate on his
studies, however, and spent three years trying to
complete the one-year master's program before
dropping out in 1992. He is still one language-
credit short of his degree. "I know now that what
I really wanted was to be a very well-read and
philosophical poet," he told *All About Jazz*. "Unfortunately, they don't teach courses in that!" Elling performed as a vocalist at jazz clubs in Chicago
and became a regular performer at the saxophonist
Ed Petersen's Monday-night jam sessions at the
Green Mill, which the gangster Al Capone had
once made his hangout. There, Elling became noted for both his scatting and his improvised lyrics.
He recalled for *All About Jazz* that Petersen once
told him, "I dig what you're doing, the scat stuff is

cool, but when it comes to improvising, I'm still
heavier than you. There are a lot of guys heavier
than you, and every musician out there can tell
that's not your strength." In response, Elling began
to focus on improvising lyrics. He also found a
good friend and musical collaborator in Petersen's
pianist, Laurence Hobgood. Hobgood introduced
Elling to his bandmates in Trio New—bassist Eric
Hochberg and drummer Paul Wertico—and the trio
began playing with Elling at his performances.

While continuing to improve his vocal skills, Elling borrowed money from friends to record a
demo tape in a studio. He later sent the tape to the
manager of a friend and fellow jazz musician, to get
the manager's opinion of it. The manager was so
taken by the recording that he decided to represent
Elling and began shopping his tape around to various record labels. One day Elling was surprised to
receive a phone call from Bruce Lundvall, the president of the legendary jazz label Blue Note. "He
had just read an article about me in the *Chicago
Tribune* a few days earlier," Elling was quoted as
saying on *All About Jazz*. "So now he gets this tape,
and the name is fresh in his mind. He pops it in on
the way to his dentist, and three days later calls me
from his car phone and says he wants to sign me."
Elling signed with Blue Note, and his first album—
Close Your Eyes—was released in the spring of
1995, with Laurence Hobgood as musical director,
pianist, and co-producer. "We did everything here
in Chicago," Elling told *All About Jazz*. "Blue Note
bought the album we made here: they changed
nothing, not the concept, not the players." The album was released to rave reviews and opened the
way for Elling's concerts at Carnegie Hall, in New
York; his appearances at several major jazz festivals; and a Grammy Award nomination for best
jazz vocal performance. Writing for *All Music
Guide* (on-line), Michael J. Nastos noted, "Acting
much like a tenor saxophonist, Elling can wail and
shout, expound on social themes, and scat like a
demon. . . . This is as auspicious a vocal jazz debut as the world has heard." On one song on *Close
Your Eyes*, "These Clouds Are Heavy, You Dig?,"
Elling set a poem by Rainer Maria Rilke to Paul
Desmond's saxophone solo from the Dave Brubeck
recording of "Balcony Rock." Elling also impressed
many with the scatting and Beat poetry on his debut record, referring to Chicago on the track "Dolo-
res Dream," for example, as "fat frying, spluttering
rank Chicago smeltering along, smothered in hot
wooly sweat."

Elling's success led to performances around the
world, in cities ranging from Tel Aviv, Israel, to
Los Angeles, California. In 1997 he spent a month
performing in New York City, then recorded his
second album, *The Messenger*, which earned him
a second Grammy nomination. He was also noted
as a "talent deserving wider recognition" by the
Down Beat International Critics Poll, won the Prix
Billie Holiday from the Academic du Jazz, in Paris,
and got the prize for "jazz record of the year" at the
Chicago Music Awards ceremony. Remarking on

awards in general, and the Grammys in particular, Elling commented to Mike Metheny, "Art justifies itself. And an award, or a nomination for an award, is just the icing on the cake. And the cake already exists, because the artist made that first." In 1998 Elling released *This Time It's Love*, for which he focused on ballads and standards. Although the album was nominated for a Grammy Award and reached number 25 on the *Billboard* jazz album charts, it received mixed reviews. Elling himself noted that his shift on the album toward a more relaxed, romantic style was perhaps related to his having turned 30 and gotten married; a writer for *Centerstage Chicago* (on-line) offered a different take, writing that Blue Note "seemed to be trying to make him into a Harry Connick, Jr.-style crooner," with the result that the album was "probably the weakest of his recordings." On the other hand, Tim Sheridan wrote for the *All Music Guide* that the album's track "Freddie's Yen for Jen" was "a stellar jazz experience that comes pretty damn close to committing the pure emotion of love to tape," and the *Jazz Times* Readers Poll voted Elling the best male vocalist of 1998.

In 1999 Elling was commissioned by Chicago's mayor, Richard M. Daley, to organize a musical extravaganza for the city's end-of-the-millennium celebrations. Elling later expanded on the idea to include all forms of art and media. At the festivities, dubbed "This Is Our Music, These Are Our People," Elling and his band performed, as did the blues music legend Buddy Guy, a 90-voice gospel choir, the jazz saxophonist Von Freeman, the writer Studs Terkel, the spoken-word artist Ken Nordine, the poet Gwendolyn Brooks, and members of the Joffrey Ballet; in addition, there was an exhibition of visual art by Ed Paschke and Tony Fitzpatrick. Writing for the *Chicago Tribune* (December 31, 1999), Carl Kozlowski called the performances "stirring." In 2000 Elling released the album *Live in Chicago*, which was recorded at the Green Mill. Among its notable tracks was a 12-minute version of the standard "My Foolish Heart," along with Elling's reading of a poem by St. John of the Cross. The singer also read a poem by Pablo Neruda to Vince Mendoza's "Esperança." In his review of the album for *Jazz 52nd Street* (on-line), Michael Colby called the version of "My Foolish Heart" an "excellent demonstration of how Elling can bend and stretch the melody, harmony and rhythm of a phrase while managing to leave shadows of the original, like a palimpsest." Reviewing the record for the *Washington Post* (March 17, 2000), Geoffrey Himes wrote, "The further Elling gets away from pop crooning and the closer he gets to jazz, the better he sounds."

Elling's fourth studio album, *Flirting with Twilight*, was released in 2001 to strong reviews. "It's different from our other records in that it isn't as much of a roller coaster ride. It's more of a true, composed exercise in luxury," Elling told Steve Frisbie for *On Tour with Shure* (on-line). Mathew Bahl wrote that the record is "a beautiful, deeply involving, smartly paced album built around a core of standard ballads," and that it "is both Elling's most cohesive musical statement and his most accessible CD yet. For the first time on record, he has set aside the poetic rants, the surreal vocalese excursions and the scatting to focus exclusively on his role as a singer of songs." The album reached the number-12 position on *Billboard*'s jazz-album charts.

In 2003 Elling's sixth album, *Man in the Air*, appeared. Its 12 tracks include "The More I Have You," which Elling composed; he also wrote eight of the other songs, including the title track. "After spending years attempting to court a broad, mainstream audience that had scant interest in him—preferring, instead, the saccharine crooning of Harry Connick Jr., Norah Jones, Diana Krall and their ilk—Elling belatedly has gone back to putting music first, commercial aspirations second," Howard Reich wrote for the *Chicago Tribune* (October 12, 2003). "You can hear it in virtually every track of *Man in the Air* . . . , the Chicago jazz singer's first great release since his recording debut of eight years ago, *Close Your Eyes*. If Elling's freshman recording announced the arrival of a technically brilliant, artistically fearless vocalist who might re-energize the rarefied art of male jazz singing, *Man in the Air* . . . finally delivers on the promise of that stunning debut. Moreover, it shows how much Elling has learned about life, love and music in the years that have passed, and how much it has enriched his work." *Man in the Air* was nominated for a Grammy Award.

Among the concert highlights of Elling's career have been his opening for Herbie Hancock in France, appearing at the JVC Jazz Festival at Bryant Park, in New York, and giving a seldom-offered repeat performance at the Montreaux Festival, in Switzerland. In addition to his jazz singing, Elling has been commissioned by the famous Steppenwolf Theater, in Chicago, to write and stage several performance pieces. Among those was a 1998 examination of the life and work of the Beat poet Allen Ginsberg. While celebrating the work of Ginsberg and other key figures in the Beat movement, Elling also explored the possibly negative effects of their influence on culture in the U.S., resulting in what Howard Reich, writing for the *Chicago Tribune* (January 14, 1998), called a "bold, if somewhat flawed" show. Reich noted that "Elling's [treatment] turned a fairly predictable survey of Beat Literature into a more balanced view of a key chapter in American cultural history. Here was an evening of poetry and music informed by a sense of morality, as well as an aversion to politically correct points of view." The show was later performed at the Kennedy Center in Washington, D.C., the Annenberg Center in Philadelphia, and at the Galway Festival, in Ireland. In 1999 another of Elling's works—*The Best Things Happen While You're Dancing*—fused jazz and modern dance in a series of performances that featured his wife, the professional dancer Jennifer C. Elling, and other members of the Tyego Dance Project. In February 2001 Elling unveiled a work for the Steppenwolf Theater, LA/CHI/NY, in which one poet and one musician each from Los Angeles, Chicago, and New York performed together. The piece featured the poets Kamau Daa'ood, Elling, and Tracie Moore fronting a jazz group consisting of the guitarist Charlie Hunter, the drummer Herb Graham Jr., and the saxophonist Mars Williams. In his review for the *Chicago Sun-Times* (February 28, 2001), Lloyd Sachs wrote that the performance "was less about geographical connections than spiritual ones. But it radiated such a good vibe, you can only hope that plans to take it east and west come to fruition."

Despite his extensive activity, Elling told an interviewer for *Jazz Online*, "I worry about going dry—I suppose that's valid but grace comes and there is always more. As long as you are actively engaged in the creative exploration of music, you won't go dry because there is always more music and you are called by the music to do more. It just never ends." "I still want to be the best possible version of this jazz singing thing that I can muster," Elling told Mathew Bahl. "I want to continue to grow. I hope that in thirty years, I look at my [current] self not with regret, but with [the realization that] I've learned a lot since then. I sort of expect the longer I go, the less hip I will have been in my own mind." While Elling long ago put aside his plan to become a professor of religion, he told the interviewer for *Jazz Online*, "I grew up with metaphysical ideas and music. They are very closely aligned. They speak to a lot of the same issues with two different languages. It would be bad of me to leave that behind because it is so much the fiber of myself. I really want both of the trees to grow up inside of me as tall and as strong as they can." Elling is a national trustee of the Recording Academy and serves on the board of governors of the academy's Chicago chapter. In addition, he is a member of the Visiting Committee of the Divinity School at the University of Chicago. He and his wife, the former Jennifer Carney, have been married since 1997.

—G.O.

Suggested Reading: All About Jazz Web site; *Jam* (on-line) Feb./Mar. 2000; *Jazz Online*; *On Tour with Shure* (on-line) Summer 2002; *University of Chicago Magazine* (on-line), June 1997, with photo

Selected Recordings: *Close Your Eyes*, 1995; *The Messenger*, 1997; *This Time It's Love*, 1998; *Live in Chicago*, 2000; *Flirting with Twilight*, 2001; *Man in the Air*, 2003

Everett, Rupert

May 29, 1959– Actor

Address: c/o ICM, 8942 Wilshire Blvd., Beverly Hills, CA 90211; c/o ICM, 76 Oxford St., London W1N 0AX, England

In 1982, the year he turned 23, Rupert Everett gained much positive attention in London, England, when he portrayed a homosexual student in the debut production of the highly lauded play *Another Country*. His depiction of the same character in the movie version of *Another Country*, released two years later, earned similar praise. Everett's greatest silver-screen success to date came in 1997, in the comedy *My Best Friend's Wedding*, in which he was cast as the gay friend and editor of the main character, a food critic named Julianne; in a comment that appeared in many reviews, he "stole the movie" from the actress who played Julianne: the superstar Julia Roberts. "A lot of dramatic actors turn their noses up at light comedy," he told an interviewer for *Entertainment Weekly* (June 25–July 2, 1999). "I feel it's what I do best." The British-born Everett revealed his homosexuality to the media in 1989, and according to many sources, he is Hollywood's first openly gay leading man. The actor himself told Chuck Arnold for *People* (July 5, 1999), "To me [my sexuality] is really not an issue.

Brenda Chase/Getty Images

From my point of view, if I had to wear a banner across my chest and write something on it, I wouldn't write 'gay,' I'd write 'actor.' My being out is not about anything for me other than I can't both-

EVERETT

er to be in." In more than 60 roles in a career that now spans nearly 25 years, Everett has portrayed far more heterosexuals than gay characters, in motion pictures including *Dance with a Stranger*, *The Madness of King George*, and *Stage Beauty*; plays including George Bernard Shaw's *Heartbreak House*, Tennessee Williams's *The Milk Train Doesn't Stop Here Anymore* (in which he was cast as the female lead), Oscar Wilde's *Picture of Dorian Gray*, and Noël Coward's *Private Lives*; and such TV movies or miniseries as *The Far Pavilions*, *Arthur the King*, and *Les Liaisons dangereuses*. "His appeal is that he looks incredible in whatever he is wearing, and you know he would probably look equally as good without it," the actress Minnie Driver, who co-starred with Everett in the film *An Ideal Husband*, told a reporter for *People* (May 8, 2000), in an issue in which he was listed among the world's 50 most beautiful people. "Rupert is a perfect example of a person who doesn't project sexuality, he projects sensuality."

Rupert James Hector Everett was born on May 29, 1959 in Norfolk, England. His father was a British army officer, his mother a homemaker. As a youngster, he told Michael Giltz for the *Advocate* (November 9, 2004), he was "a seasoned crossdresser." "I used to be taken out on these very macho things like hunting, and I would just be dreaming of going home and trying on my mother's nightdress." During his teens and early 20s, he told Marina Cantacuzino for *Attitude* (April 1999, online), he felt drawn not only to males but also to females (though not sexually: "Everything isn't only about sex," he remarked); that feeling "just faded away," and he became "certain," as he put it, of his homosexuality.

Everett had a strict Catholic upbringing. At age seven he began attending a Roman Catholic boarding school, Ampleforth College (near York), where he was taught by Benedictine monks. "The moment you have to leave your family is very heartbreaking," he told Mark Miller for *Newsweek* (July 12, 1999). "I had a good time at school, but I think there is something that happens to English people when they are sent away. There is something in your heart that kind of calcifies. . . . That's the thing I possibly regret." In other interviews, he has recalled feeling bored and like a "misfit" at Ampleforth. While at boarding school Everett studied classical piano. At 15 he left Ampleforth and enrolled at the Central School of Speech and Drama, in London. Two years later he was expelled for what various sources have labeled "insolence," "insubordination," or "subversion." Shortly afterward he became an apprentice actor at the avant-garde Citizens' Theatre, in Glasgow, Scotland, where the director Philip Prowse became his mentor. (On the theater's Web site, its name appears both with and without an apostrophe after the "s" in "Citizens.") As Michael Coveney reported in his book *Citz: 21 Years of the Glasgow Citizens Theatre* (1990), Everett appreciated Prowse's encouraging actors to share their ideas with him, which

made productions truly collaborative endeavors. Everett appeared in the Citizens' 1980 mounting of Molière's *Don Juan*. For about two years around that time, he has said, he supplemented his meager income through prostitution—working as a "rent boy," in British slang. He "sort of fell into" that role, he has told interviewers, after a stranger propositioned him on the street one day. "This guy offered me such a massive amount of money—it was like a year-and-a-half's pocket money—and it just came in real handy," he told Marina Cantacuzino.

Everett's luck changed in 1982, when he was cast in a starring role in Julian Mitchell's drama *Another Country*, which had a long run in a London West End theater. *Another Country* is set in 1930s England, at an elite, private, all-boys secondary school, of the sort that graduated the poet and critic Stephen Spender and other well-known real-life socialist intellectuals as well as the infamous Guy Burgess, who spied for the Soviet Union while serving in the British intelligence service before and during World War II (and who later defected to Russia). Everett portrayed a student named Guy Bennett (based on Burgess), whose homosexuality costs him a coveted leadership position at the school; that crushing disappointment, Mitchell's story suggests, leads him to embrace the Marxist philosophy spouted by another student, his friend Tom Judd (originally portrayed by Kenneth Branagh). The London *Evening Standard* named Everett "best newcomer" for his work in *Another Country*. Also in 1982 he was seen in a made-for-television movie (*Soft Targets*) and two big-screen motion pictures (*A Shocking Accident* and *Dead on Time*). In 1983 he appeared in the TV film *Princess Daisy* and the theatrical release *Real Life*; the next year he portrayed the character George Garforth in the TV miniseries *The Far Pavilions*.

Everett reprised the role of Guy Bennett in the film version of *Another Country* (1984), directed by Malek Kanievska from Julian Mitchell's screenplay; Colin Firth, one of Everett's successors in the role of Bennett in the staged production, played Tom Judd. In the film, according to Mark Englehart on KillerMovies.com (2004), Everett portrayed Bennett "with a vigor, flair, and smoldering appeal that was rarely seen onscreen in the early '80s." Everett's performance earned him a "best newcomer" award nomination from BAFTA (the British Academy of Film and Television Arts).

In productions mounted by the Glasgow Citizens' Theatre Company, Everett appeared as Flamineo in John Webster's play *The White Devil* (1984) and as Randall Utterwood in George Bernard Shaw's *Heartbreak House* (1985). After attending a performance of the former, Michael Ratcliffe wrote for the London *Observer* (February 5, 1984, on-line), "When he stops speaking great chunks of his part through clenched teeth or delivering them out of the side of his mouth . . . , [Everett] speaks clearly and well, taking us to the murderously poetic heart of what is here clearly seen to be a great play and to the particular desperation of the career-courier's life." Ratcliffe also wondered whether Everett would "grow out of" his reliance on such mannerisms as a "cracked nursery laugh" and "Byronic pout" "as he takes on the big classical parts he is so gifted by wit, intelligence and good looks to play." Michael Coveney, who reviewed *Heartbreak House* for the London *Financial Times* (August 31, 1985, on-line), had no such reservations about Everett's technique; rather, Coveney described the actor's portrayal of Utterwood as "definitive."

For several months during the first half of the 1980s, Everett worked with the American filmmaker and actor Orson Welles on a project that never came to fruition: an autobiographical film about the controversy surrounding Welles's staging of Marc Blitzstein's pro-union drama *Cradle Will Rock* in the late 1930s. Everett had a leading role in the British film *Dance with a Stranger* (1985), directed by Mike Newell from a screenplay by Shelagh Delaney, about the real-life Ruth Ellis (played by Miranda Richardson), who murdered her lover after he left her; Ellis was the last woman to be hanged in England. Although her lover, a wealthy race-car driver (Everett), abused her both emotionally and physically, she much preferred him to the decent businessman (Ian Holm) who genuinely loved her. Critics were sharply divided as to the movie's merits and Everett's performance. In 1986 Everett appeared, along with Julie Andrews, Alan Bates, and Max von Sydow, in Andrei Konchalovsky's little-noticed film *Duet for One*.

For the next few years, Everett, who is fluent in French and Italian as well as English, worked primarily in France and Italy. He modeled in Milan and, in 1987, had prominent roles in two Italian-language motion pictures: *Cronaca di una morte annunciata*, an adaptation of Gabriel García Márquez's novel *Chronicle of a Death Foretold*, and *Gli Occhiali d'oro* (The Gold-Rimmed Glasses), about anti-Semitism and homophobia in 1930s Italy. According to some accounts, he remained in Europe because he had developed a reputation in Great Britain for arrogance and rudeness: for example, he would abruptly end interviews that to his mind were not proceeding satisfactorily, and once he mailed a snippet of his pubic hair to a woman who had written to him to criticize one of his performances. Everett, who has insisted that he was not avoiding his native land and simply preferred living in Europe at that time, has attributed his offensive behavior to feelings of insecurity. "When you start out you feel so threatened by everybody," he told a *New York Times* (September 20, 1992) interviewer. "The older you get, the longer you do it, you realize you can sort of slip into it and work in it and forget your own ego."

Everett made his American film debut as a musician in the poorly received *Hearts of Fire* (1987), which starred the singer/songwriter Bob Dylan. In 1988 he played the drug-addicted Nicky in a Glasgow Citizens' Theatre production of Noël Coward's *The Vortex*. He headed the cast of the French film *Tolérance* the following year. In 1990 he co-starred, along with Natasha Richardson, Christopher Walken, and Helen Mirren, in the creepy thriller *The Comfort of Strangers*, which Paul Shrader directed. The screenplay, adapted by Harold Pinter from a novel by Ian McEwen, focuses on an English couple who become the victims of a stalker. Everett next appeared in the poorly received movie *Inside Monkey Zetterland* (1992). In a Citizens' Theatre staging of Oscar Wilde's *Picture of Dorian Gray* in 1993, he was acclaimed for his portrayal of Lord Henry Wotton, Gray's cynical, hedonistic "tempter and mentor," in the words of Timothy Ramsden, who, in *Plays & Players* (April 1993, on-line), described Everett's performance as "absorbing." In 1994 Everett appeared in the Glasgow company's productions of Noël Coward's *Private Lives* and Tennessee Williams's *The Milk Train Doesn't Stop Here Anymore*. In the latter he wore a dress and heavy makeup to play the main character, Flora Goforth, a rich, elderly, hypochondriacal alcoholic who has survived four husbands and is nearing the end of her life. In a review of *Milk Train* for the London *Independent* (November 8, 1994, on-line), Richard Loup-Nolan wrote, "Everett gives a virtuoso performance of considerable grotesquerie and some pathos, sweeping across the stage like some transvestite cardinal." In the London *Observer* (November 6, 1994, on-line), Michael Coveney wrote, "Everett's remarkable performance crumbles from grand, drug-fuelled hauteur to quivering fear and self-doubt: this palpably AIDS-age disintegration is exactly comparable to his picturesque fate as a dowager Henry Wotton in *The Picture of Dorian Gray* last year."

In 1994 Everett starred in the Russian science-fiction film *Strelyayushchiye angely* (Shooting Angels) and the French-Italian horror/comedy *Dellamorte Dellamore* (*Cemetery Man*); had a small role in the director Robert Altman's *Prêt-à-Porter* (also called *Ready to Wear*); and received positive notices for his small but memorable turn as the Prince of Wales in *The Madness of King George*. In 1996 he appeared with Faye Dunaway and Jason Alexander in the film comedy *Dunston Checks In* (1996), in which all the actors were upstaged by a chimpanzee.

In *My Best Friend's Wedding* (1997), Everett played George Downes, a gay editor, whose friend and client Julianne (Julia Roberts) enlists him to pretend to be her boyfriend, in a failed attempt to derail the wedding plans of her onetime lover Michael (Dermot Mulroney), with the aim of leading Michael to jilt the beautiful heiress (Cameron Diaz) to whom he is betrothed and marry her instead. A high point in the film comes during a pre-wedding meal at a restaurant, when George spontaneously begins singing Burt Bacharach and Hal David's "I Say a Little Prayer for You"; soon, nearly every diner joins in. Everett's portrayal of George so delighted the director, P. J. Hogan, that the part was significantly expanded as shooting proceeded. Although critics' reactions to the film were mixed, virtually all extolled Everett's portrayal, and many declared that he "stole" every scene in which he appeared. For his work in *My Best Friend's Wedding,* Everett received Blockbuster Entertainment and London Film Critics Awards as well as Golden Globe and BAFTA award nominations for best supporting actor.

Next, Everett appeared in the role of a junkie in the drama *B. Monkey* (1998) and had a small, uncredited part as the playwright Christopher Marlowe in *Shakespeare in Love* (1998). He received a Golden Globe nomination for his portrayal of the roguish bachelor Lord Goring in *An Ideal Husband,* Oliver Parker's 1999 adaptation for the big screen of Oscar Wilde's same-titled play. "Cast as Wilde's (heterosexual) stand-in, Everett gets all the good lines, but he's daring enough to deliver them gently, with a knowing touch of rue," Owen Gleiberman wrote for *Entertainment Weekly* (June 18, 1999). Stanley Kauffmann, in the *New Republic* (July 19–26, 1999, on-line), expressed a similar view: "Everett . . . quite evidently enjoys the part immensely but . . . (unlike the man who played the role on Broadway a few years ago) restrains his pleasure so that we can enjoy it too. Excellent, airily precise acting." "I admire Wilde, I must say," Everett said after the film was released, as quoted by Bridgette White for the Web site The Movie Club. "He means a lot to me on many levels. I'm immensely pleased to be doing one of his plays a hundred years after he died, as a mark of respect. And I do see the suffering he went through for being gay as just one of the most moving things."

Everett portrayed Oberon in Michael Hoffman's screen adaptation of Shakespeare's *A Midsummer Night's Dream,* whose star-studded cast included Kevin Kline, Michelle Pfeiffer, Stanley Tucci, Bill Irwin, and Roger Rees. He provided the voice of Dr. Claw, the evil nemesis of the title character, in *Inspector Gadget* (1999), based on the long-running TV cartoon series of the same name (a cartoon parody of the 1960s television spy parody *Get Smart*). Everett narrated Robert Epstein and Jeffrey Friedman's documentary *Paragraph 175* (2001), about the persecution and murder of homosexual men in Nazi Germany. In John Schlesinger's widely panned movie *The Next Best Thing,* he played the gay best friend of a single woman (portrayed by Madonna), whom he accidentally impregnates during their single sexual encounter, following a mutual bout of heavy drinking; the two raise their child in platonic harmony for several years, until the woman, having met a man she decides to marry (Benjamin Bratt), sues for sole custody. When A. J. Claire, who interviewed Everett for Dr.Drew.com (2001, on-line), asked him how he felt about his romantic sequences with Madonna, he responded, "People always think love scenes are the worst thing to do. I don't. I think they are the easiest thing to do. . . . I don't find it embarrassing or difficult."

In 2002 Everett appeared in another Oliver Parker adaptation for the silver screen of an Oscar Wilde play—*The Importance of Being Earnest.* He and Colin Firth played the male protagonists, the eligible bachelors Algernon (Everett) and Jack (Firth), opposite Reese Witherspoon, Judi Dench, and Frances O'Connor. "Everett, whose scenes with Firth are a droll delight, nails every sly laugh," Peter Travers wrote in a review of the film for *Rolling Stone* (May 6, 2002). In P. J. Hogan's comedy/thriller *Unconditional Love* (2002), which premiered on cable TV in the U.S., he played a man tracking down the killer of his lover, a pop star, with the help of the singer's biggest fan (Kathy Bates). In *To Kill a King* (2003) he played King Charles I of England, who struggles to regain his crown from Oliver Cromwell (played by Tim Roth). Also that year he appeared as Valmont in a TV miniseries remake of *Les Liaisons dangereuses,* which co-starred Catherine Deneuve. In *Mr. Ambassador,* a TV sitcom that was to debut on NBC in 2003, Everett was cast as the title character, a newly appointed British ambassador to the U.S.; to date the show has not aired. His credits in 2004 include the feature films *Stage Beauty,* starring Billy Crudup and Claire Danes, about the ending, in the 17th century, of the prohibition against females in theatrical productions in Great Britain, in which he was cast as King Charles II; *A Different Loyalty,* with Sharon Stone, in which he played a fictionalized version of the notorious Kim Philby, an Englishman who spied for and then defected to Russia; and the French-language comedy *People.* Also in 2004 he provided the voice of the character Prince Charming in the animated film *Shrek 2.* In the drama *Separate Lies* (2005), Everett played an English aristocrat, recently returned from the U.S., who gets involved with a high-powered London barrister and his wife.

Everett has published two comic novels: *Hello Darling, Are You Working?* (1991), which is partly autobiographical, and *The Hairdressers of San Tropez* (1995). He has also tried his hand at singing; in the late 1980s he released two virtually forgotten pop albums. He contributed backup vocals on Madonna's remake of "American Pie" and sang a duet with the British pop star Robbie Williams on a remake of "They Can't Take That Away from Me." For about four years beginning in 1995, he appeared in ads for Yves Saint Laurent's aftershave Opium. The six-foot four-inch actor won the 1999 VH1 Vogue Fashion Award for most fashionable male celebrity.

Everett has homes in Los Angeles and New York City. His beloved black labrador, Mo, who appeared in *The Next Best Thing,* died in 2004. When Michael Glitz, writing for the *Advocate* (November 9, 2004, on-line), asked him whether he planned to get another dog, he answered, "No, I want a human being next." "I never stay long enough in one place to have [a boyfriend] . . . ," he told Glitz. "Once you get into that rhythm of moving all the time, then you're moving all the time, and it's difficult to break it. And I want to break it, because I'd definitely like to be in a relationship." By his own account, Everett no longer adheres to Catholicism.

—K.E.D.

Suggested Reading: *Advocate* (on-line) p46+ Nov. 9, 2004; *Biography* p16+ Apr. 2001, with photo; celebritztrendz.com; *Citzsite* Web site; *Entertainment Weekly* p30+ July 11, 1997, with photos; *Los Angeles Magazine* p68+ Apr. 2000, with photos; Movie Thing Web site, with photo; *Vogue* p228+ Feb. 1998, with photos, p125+ Dec. 1999, with photo;

Selected Films: *The Manhood of Edward Robinson*, 1981; *Soft Targets*, 1982; *A Shocking Accident*, 1982; *Dead on Time*, 1982; *Princess Daisy*, 1983; *Real Life*, 1983; *Another Country*, 1984; *Dance with a Stranger*, 1985; *Duet for One*, 1986; *Cronaca di una morte annunciata*, 1987; *The Right Hand Man*, 1987; *Gli Occhiali d'oro* (The Gold-Rimmed Glasses), 1987; *Hearts of Fire*, 1987; *Tolerance*, 1989; *The Comfort of Strangers*, 1990; *Inside Monkey Zetterland*, 1992; *Strelyayushchiye angely* (Shooting Angels), 1994; *Dellamorte Dellamore* (Cemetery Man), 1994; *Prêt-à-Porter*, 1994; *The Madness of King Geroge*,

1994; *Remembrance of Things Fast: True Stories Visual Lies*, 1994; *Dunston Checks In*, 1996; *My Best Friend's Wedding*, 1997; *B. Monkey*, 1998; *Shakespeare in Love*, 1998; *An Ideal Husband*, 1999; *A Midsummer Night's Dream*, 1999; *Inspector Gadget*, 1999; *The Next Best Thing*, 2000; *South Kensington*, 2001; *The Importance of Being Earnest*, 2002; *Unconditional Love*, 2002; *The Wild Thornberrys Movie*, 2002; *To Kill a King*, 2003; *A Different Loyalty*, 2004; *Stage Beauty*, 2004; *Shrek 2*, 2004; *Separate Lies*, 2005

Selected Television Movies or Miniseries: *The Far Pavilions*, 1984; *Arthur the King*, 1985; *Les Liaisons dangereuses*, 2003; *Boston Legal*, 2005; *Sherlock Holmes: The Case of the Silk Stockings*, 2005

Selected Books: *Hello Darling, Are You Working?*, 1991; *The Hairdressers of San Tropez*, 1995

Fadiman, Anne

Aug. 7, 1953– Author; journalist; editor

Address: Dept. of English, Yale University, P.O. Box 208302, New Haven, CT 06520-8302

Anne Fadiman has had a distinguished literary career, as an essayist, editor, award-winning journalist, and author of two well-received nonfiction books: *The Spirit Catches You and You Fall Down* (1997), about a family of Laotian refugees and the culture clash between the parents and the American doctors who tried to help one of the children, a girl with severe epilepsy; and *Ex Libris: Confessions of a Common Reader* (1998), a collection of essays that celebrate reading and books. A review of the latter in the *New Yorker*, as quoted on the book's back cover, noted that each essay "speaks volumes about the author's appreciation for people as well as books." From 1998 to 2004 Fadiman served as the editor of the quarterly literary journal *American Scholar*. She is also the editor of *The Best American Essays 2003* and *Rereadings: Seventeen Writers Revisit Books They Love.*

"If I were to rank life's pleasures," Fadiman wrote in the acknowledgments section of *Ex Libris*, "talking about books with my brother and my parents would be close to the top." Anne Fadiman was born in Connecticut on August 7, 1953 into a literary family: her father, Clifton Fadiman, was a book editor and literary critic as well as the host of the radio quiz show *Information Please*, and her mother, Annalee Whitmore Jacoby Fadiman, was a World War II correspondent for *Time* magazine and co-author, with Theodore H. White, of the 1946 book *Thunder Out of China*, about the victory

Courtesy of Farrar, Straus & Giroux

of the Communists led by Mao Zedong over the nationalist followers of Chiang Kai-Shek. "My mother and father . . . ," Fadiman wrote in her *Ex Libris* acknowledgments, "read tens of thousands of pages aloud to me when I was a child, transmitting with every syllable their own passion for books. Because they are both writers, it would have been easy for them to squash my literary hopes under the weight of their unmatchable achievements, but somehow they managed to do the opposite." For the first eight years of Anne's life, the Fadimans lived in Connecticut; for the next eight, in Los Angeles, California. The family's home contained more than 7,000 books. Before she could read, Anne Fadiman has recalled, she used her father's collection of books by Anthony Trollope as toy building blocks, and after she began reading, her favorite book was *The Lion, the Witch, and the Wardrobe*, by C. S. Lewis. Fadiman, her older brother, Kim (who became a naturalist and hiking guide), and their parents would spend Sunday afternoons watching the television quiz show *General Electric College Bowl*, on which teams of students from two universities competed against each other. Calling themselves "Fadiman U.," the family (which, as Fadiman explained in *Ex Libris*, "viewed all forms of intellectual competition as a sacrament"), would shout answers to the questions. Over the course of "five or six years of competition, we lost only to Brandeis and Colorado College," Fadiman proudly announced in an interview with Christopher Lehmann-Haupt for the *New York Times* (October 15, 1998). She and her brother competed, too, to see who could discover the longest words (her brother won with *paradimethylaminobenzaldehyde*, the name of a chemical). The family were what Fadiman described to Lehmann-Haupt as "compulsive proofreaders," who looked for mistakes in published texts and even menus. Despite Fadiman's early immersion in the world of books, and the example set by her parents, she did not initially lean toward a career as a writer. Some people, she explained to Laura T. Ryan for the Syracuse *Post-Standard* (April 4, 2002), "assume it would be as easy as falling off a log . . . that is, one would simply, naturally surrender to the family's business. . . . But, in fact, it actually is quite difficult. In many ways, I think it's harder to become a writer or an actor or even a mortician if both of your parents have done it and done it well."

Fadiman attended Harvard University, in Cambridge, Massachusetts, where she attempted to write fiction and poetry but was displeased with the results of her efforts. She found, however, that she had an inclination for journalism, and as an undergraduate she wrote for the school's alumni magazine. After she graduated, in 1975, her interests leaned toward the outdoors as well as journalism, and she got a job as a wilderness instructor at the National Outdoor Leadership School, based in Lander, Wyoming. Later, in 1978, she combined her love of the written word with her fondness for the outdoors as a nature writer for *Life* magazine. She subsequently worked as a staff writer for the magazine's science and medical section; a story she wrote in 1987 about suicide among the elderly earned *Life* a National Magazine Award.

Seeking to advance her writing career further, Fadiman pitched several story ideas to Robert Gottlieb, who was then editor of the *New Yorker*. Of those she mentioned, as Fadiman told Michael Kenney for the *Boston Globe* (December 2, 1997), Fadiman was most interested in the one having to

do with a topic "about which both he and I were the least knowledgeable"—an idea she had gotten from her brother's freshman roommate, Bill Selvidge. Selvidge, the chief resident for family practice at the Merced Community Medical Center, in Merced, California, had complained to her about his "difficult" patients, a group of Hmong (pronounced "mong") immigrants who distrusted modern American medical practices. (The Hmong, which translates as "free people," are an ethnic group who have lived in scattered parts of Southeast Asia; some fought, primarily as guerrillas, alongside U.S. troops in the Vietnam War. After the Communist victory, in 1975, the government of the newly united Vietnam began a genocide campaign against the remaining Hmong and their families, many of whom fled to the U.S. About 12,000 Hmong immigrants settled in the agricultural community of Merced.) The case of one Hmong family in particular, the Lees, piqued Fadiman's interest. When Gottlieb asked her to write a three-part, 35,000-word article for the *New Yorker*, she quit her job at *Life* and, in 1988, moved to California to research the story of Lia Lee and her family.

In 1979 Nao Kao Lee, his wife, Foua, and their eight surviving children were among a group of 400 villagers who fled Vietnam and spent the next two years in a Thai refugee camp before settling in Merced. On October 24, 1982 the Lees' infant daughter Lia had a seizure shortly after her sister Yer slammed a door. Her parents surmised that the slammed door had frightened their baby's soul out of her body. The Lees rushed Lia to the Merced Community Medical Center, where doctors attempted to help the baby but were hindered by their inability to communicate with her parents, who spoke no English. (At that time there was no Hmong translator among the hospital staff.) After examining Lia, who was no longer suffering from the seizure, medical personnel determined that she had a bronchial infection, prescribed an antibiotic, and sent the child home with her parents. On November 11 Lia had another seizure and received the same diagnosis and treatment. When Lia returned to the same hospital after another episode on March 3, 1983, her illness was correctly diagnosed as epilepsy. The Hmong refer to that disease as *qaug dab peg*, which translates as "the spirit catches you and you fall down." With the help of an English-speaking relative, the Lees were told to give their daughter anticonvulsants. "That was the beginning of many years of tragic misunderstanding," Fadiman told Ron Hogan for the on-line publication *Beatrice* (1997).

Whereas doctors attributed Lia's condition to a misfiring of cerebral neurons, her family remained convinced that it was caused by her wandering soul. "The Hmong don't make the same divisions as we do," Fadiman explained to James S. Howard for the *Fresno* (California) *Bee* (September 28, 1997, on-line). "In our culture, religion and health care are separate. For the Hmong, illness can be caused by many things. The most common is soul loss. There is a huge degree of concern for the whole person in Hmong healing arts." During the next four years, Lia continued to have seizures, resulting in 16 trips to the hospital and 23 changes in medication. While her doctors attempted to determine which prescriptions and dosages would best treat Lia's epilepsy, her parents tried such traditional Hmong remedies as animal sacrifices in an effort to bring her soul back. Medical personnel were dismayed to find that the Lees were trying to help Lia in their own fashion and were often unable or unwilling to administer their daughter's medications properly. (Fadiman noted to Michael Kenney that sometimes Hmong patients would refuse to take pills if they were "inauspicious" in color.) Lia's health continued to deteriorate until the Merced County Department of Child Protective Services took Lia from her parents, whom the department deemed to be neglectful, and placed her in a foster home. Fadiman explained to Ron Hogan, "They knew that the Lees weren't child abusers according to any standard American definition. They were loving parents, but they declined to give Lia her antidepression pills because they were under the impression that the pills were making their daughter sick, not curing her sickness. That's not as crazy as it sounds, because her medication did include a number of drugs with discernible side effects. The drugs *were* making her sick; from the doctors' point of view, it was a minor sickness outweighed by the major sickness that was being cured. The Lees didn't see it that way." When Lia was placed in foster care, her mother became so distraught that she considered committing suicide. Lia's foster family recognized the Lees' devotion to their daughter and not only allowed them to spend time with their daughter but also lobbied to allow Lia to be sent back home. A few months after Lia returned to her parents, she suffered a grand mal seizure that left her effectively brain-dead. Doctors, anticipating that Lia would soon die, allowed her parents to remove her from the hospital. The Lees took Lia home, where she has lived in a semi-comatose state ever since. Her family continues to treat Lia with meticulous, loving care; her mother sings to her, keeps her spotlessly clean, and dresses her (Lia evidently reacts by moving her eyes when her mother sings), and her parents still periodically sacrifice a pig in the hope of reuniting Lia's soul with her body. It's "a wonderful community to have a disabled child in," Fadiman told Michael Kenney.

After completing her research Fadiman wrote, and was paid for, a 100-page manuscript for the *New Yorker*. By the time she had finished it, however, Robert Gottlieb had been replaced as editor of the *New Yorker* by Tina Brown, who was not interested in including Fadiman's lengthy article in the magazine. The manuscript languished on Fadiman's desk at home. "I found that I was too attached to the material to let it die," she told Jean Peerenboom for the *Green Bay (Wisconsin) Press-Gazette* (November 19, 2001). "So I turned it into

a book." Meanwhile, Fadiman and her family endured several medical crises of their own. During the writing of *The Spirit Catches You and You Fall Down*, Fadiman's father suffered from colon cancer and lost his eyesight; her husband contracted meningitis; her infant daughter, Susannah, was diagnosed with a prolapsed rectum; and Fadiman herself endured two miscarriages before giving birth to her second child, Henry, in 1995.

Earlier, just after she had finished college, Fadiman had shared a memorable lunch with Jonathan Galassi, then an editor at the book publisher Houghton Mifflin; Galassi had invited Fadiman and her brother to send him the first books they wrote. After nearly a decade of intermittent research and writing, Fadiman completed *The Spirit Catches You and You Fall Down: A Hmong Child, Her American Doctors, and the Collision of Two Cultures*. She contacted Galassi, and the company to which he had moved by that time, Farrar, Straus & Giroux, published her book, in 1997. *The Spirit Catches You and You Fall Down* was very well received and won the National Book Critics Circle Award for general nonfiction, the *Los Angeles Times* Book Prize for current interest nonfiction, the *Salon* Book Award for nonfiction, and the *Boston Book Review*'s Ann Rea Jewell Award for nonfiction. Fadiman's Hmong interpreter, May Ying Xiong, told James S. Howard that Fadiman's book was "more than accurate. Through her research and her stories, she has come to know more than I will ever know, even as a Hmong." In another article for the *Fresno Bee* (September 28, 1997), James S. Howard called the book "stunning" in its blend of "impressive reporting, brilliant writing and great compassion." The "power of this book," he wrote, "cannot be overstated. In beautiful and insightful prose, Anne Fadiman explores two cultures and a tragedy that occurred when they were unable to communicate."

In December 1997, after the publication of her first book, Fadiman was asked by the Phi Beta Kappa Society to become editor of the quarterly journal it has published since 1932, the *American Scholar*. The choice was controversial. Fadiman would replace Joseph Epstein, who had been the journal's editor for 22 years; while the Phi Beta Kappa Society objected to what was described as Epstein's conservatism, many readers worried that Fadiman's appointment would push the publication too far to the left in the political and cultural spectrum. With Fadiman as editor, "we're going to get feely-goody, multi-culti stuff, and we've got plenty of that elsewhere," Sheldon Penman, a professor emeritus of biology at the Massachusetts Institute of Technology, predicted to Jennifer K. Ruark for the *Chronicle of Higher Education* (November 28, 1997). "What [Epstein] brings in, which I doubt Anne Fadiman can do, is this whole middle-European tradition—the underpinning of our culture." For her part, Fadiman explained to Ruark that she hoped to keep cultural politics out of the journal entirely and had no intention of eliminating the traditional

European influences on the publication. "I'm not as [informed about] people who are writing about Africa and Asia and so on," she told Ruark. "If I find out about wonderful writers about, and of, those cultures, I would love to run them in the *Scholar*. But the people in my Rolodex are much more likely to be writing about Jane Austen." During her tenure at the *American Scholar*, Fadiman garnered much praise, especially in her efforts to recruit, and help launch the careers of, new writers—among them Mark Oppenheimer, Paul DePalma, Jonathan Rosen, and Adam Kirsch. Under her stewardship the *American Scholar* won three National Magazine Awards and was nominated for eight others. Todd Gitlin, a professor of journalism and sociology at Columbia University, told David Carr for the *New York Times* (September 11, 2004) that Fadiman was a "very discerning, very inspired all-around editor who was able to work with a great range of writers and was a masterful editor." In 2004, following a dispute between the Phi Beta Kappa Society and Fadiman over budget cuts, Fadiman was fired from her post. Twenty contributing editors and board members resigned in protest of the decision. Even Fadiman's successor, Robert S. Wilson, expressed his appreciation for her work, telling David Carr, "It is absolutely indisputable that Anne Fadiman did a great job" as the journal's editor.

Meanwhile, in 1998, one year after the publication of *The Spirit Catches You and You Fall Down*, Fadiman had published a second book. *Ex Libris: Confessions of a Common Reader* is a compilation of 18 columns about books and reading that Fadiman had written for *Civilization*, the now-defunct magazine of the Library of Congress. (Fadiman had worked as a columnist and editor-at-large for *Civilization* from 1994 to 1998.) In *Ex Libris* she touched on topics such as the difference between "courtly lovers" and "carnal lovers" of books, "the courtly lover being the platonic lover who wants to keep the book in a very chaste state, and the carnal lover who loves the book to pieces physically," as Dan Cryer paraphrased her in *Newsday* (November 1, 1998). *Ex Libris* also provides readers with Fadiman's opinions about electronic books and other on-line texts. "The e-book as an addition to our lives is something I'm 100% for," she told David Colker for the *Los Angeles Times* (November 2, 2000). "As a replacement, I'm 100% against." She elaborated to Dan Cryer, "I want something I can write on. I want something I can put a bookmark in. You never want to cuddle up in bed with a computer." Reviews of *Ex Libris* were generally good, though critics had minor complaints. "The chief flaw here," Merle Rubin wrote about the book for the *Christian Science Monitor* (November 12, 1998), "is the author's tendency to lapse into a precious, self-satisfied tone." In the *Chicago Tribune* (October 25, 1998), Lucia Perillo wrote, "*Ex Libris* is pleasant reading, but like most collections of columns it scratches wide and not deep. Perhaps what is does best is make a case for reading as a social

act. In an era when most families turn to the TV because we assume that video can be enjoyed collectively while books are best experienced in isolation, Fadiman asks us to reconsider. With breezy, self-effacing humor and dollops of literary trivia, the essays in *Ex Libris* try to cajole us into restoring books to the heart of family life."

Fadiman's essays have appeared in a variety of publications, including the *New Yorker*, *Esquire*, *Life*, the *Washington Post*, and the *New York Times*, and her work has helped to win National Magazine Awards. Her topics have included medical matters (the disease anorexia, for example), gender bias, animals (among them Koko, a gorilla who learned to communicate with humans using a modified form of American sign language), and the lives of individuals. From 1991 to 1992 Fadiman was a John S. Knight Fellow at Stanford University, in California, and from 2000 to 2002 she was a visiting lecturer at Smith College, in Northampton, Massachusetts. She recently began an appointment as the first Francis Writer in Residence at Yale University, in New Haven, Connecticut. Fadiman edited the 2003 edition of *Best American Essays*. Another book that she edited, *Rereadings: Seventeen Writers Revisit Books They Love*, was published in 2005. Its contributors include Vivian Gornick, Phillip Lopate, Sven Birkerts, Allegra Goodman, Pico Iyer, Patricia Hampl, and Luc Sante.

Fadiman is married to the nonfiction writer George Howe Colt, whose most recent book, *The Big House: A Century in the Life of an American Summer Home*, was among the *New York Times*'s choices of most notable books of 2003. Colt was two years behind his future wife at Harvard; the two did not meet until they were both working at *Life*. When Colt traveled to California to visit Fadiman, who was researching Lia Lee's story at the time, Lia's mother, evidently with Fadiman's marriageability in mind, dressed Fadiman in the clothing traditionally worn by Hmong brides. Fadiman told Michael Kenney that Colt was "stunned" by her appearance, adding that the ensemble "must in some way have had the intended effect, because a week later George asked me to marry him." The couple and their two children, Susannah and Henry, live in Whately, in western Massachusetts. Fadiman credits her experience with the Lees with teaching her a great deal about the importance of family. She told Ron Hogan, "I learned how to be a good mother from watching Hmong with their children. They are the warmest parents in the world. I saw those loving, happy, tumbling extended families and said to myself, 'This is a better way to be.' I'm sure that it's influenced the kind of mother that I've tried to become."

—K.J.E.

Suggested Reading: *Chicago Tribune* p4 Oct. 25, 1998; *Chronicle of Higher Education* A p15 Nov. 28, 1997; *Fresno (California) Bee* E p1 Sep. 28, 1997; *Green Bay Press-Gazette* D p1 Nov. 19, 2001; *New York Times* p14 Sep. 11, 2004

FAIRPORT CONVENTION

Selected Books: *The Spirit Catches You and You Fall Down: A Hmong Child, Her American Doctors, and the Collision of Two Cultures,* 1997; *Ex Libris: Confessions of a Common Reader,* 1998; as editor—*The Best American Essays 2003,* 2004; *Rereadings: Seventeen Writers Revisit Books They Love,* 2005

Fairport Convention

Music group

Nicol, Simon
Oct. 13, 1950– Vocalist; guitarist

Leslie, Chris
Dec. 15, 1956– Vocalist; fiddler; songwriter

Conway, Gerry
Sep. 11, 1947– Drummer

Pegg, Dave
Nov. 2, 1947– Bassist

Sanders, Ric
Dec. 8, 1952– Fiddler

Address: 6 Stonehouse Business Centre, Market Sq., Chipping Norton, Oxfordshire OX7 5NA, England

Widely considered the most important British folk-rock band of the late 1960s, Fairport Convention has over the course of almost four decades redefined modern folk—through both original compositions and rearrangements of British folk music from as long ago as the Middle Ages. Combining acoustic and electric instruments and furious rock drumming, Fairport Convention was among the first British bands to play traditional folk songs in a rock context. The band has influenced generations of folk-rock, pop, and progressive-rock artists and has been a stepping stone for several renowned musicians, among them the guitarist Richard Thompson, who has been dubbed the "John Coltrane of the guitar"; the vocalist Sandy Denny, regarded by many fans and critics as the best British folk-rock vocalist; and the acclaimed fiddle player Dave Swarbrick.

Despite many changes in personnel, and periods in which it virtually vanished, Fairport Convention has become one of the most successful folk-rock concert draws. Each August they headline Fairport's Cropredy Convention, a three-day music festival held in England. Attracting some 18,000 people a year, Copredy is known as the best and largest folk-rock festival in Europe. "Most other bands probably consider things like airplay or whether the record company will like it," Dave Pegg, the band's current bassist, told Anil Prasad

for *Innerviews* (on-line). "Those aspects have never been a priority for Fairport right from the start of the band's career. We've been lucky enough to do what we want without being pressured by what's popular or fashionable. It's the way people do their best work—playing stuff they really want to play. We just hope our audience likes it." Ric Sanders, the band's fiddler, told Prasad, "I think we're a real people's band. . . . A Fairport concert is like a meeting of friends. There's no big security wall around us. It's kind of how music should be."

The group that became Fairport Convention was initially called the Muswell Hillbillies. It was formed in London, England, in 1966 by the bassist Ashley Hutchings (born on January 26, 1945 in Southgate, England), the guitarist Simon Nicol (born on October 13, 1950), the guitarist Richard Thompson (born on April 3, 1949 in London), the drummer Martin Lamble (born on August 28, 1949), and the guitarist Ian Matthews (born on June 16, 1946 in Lincolnshire, England). They played a style of music that was inspired by such California folk-rock bands as the Byrds, the Mamas and the Papas, and Ian & Sylvia. Soon after their first live performance, they were joined by the vocalist Judy Dyble (born on February 13, 1949), who became the group's main singer. In 1968, having renamed themselves Fairport Convention after Nicol's mother's home (the Fairport Lodge), where the band practiced, the group became prominent in the London underground folk-rock scene, and was soon signed by an American record producer.

In that same year, Fairport Convention released its eponymous debut record; it featured two Joni Mitchell covers and was generally deemed respectable, if unspectacular. In May 1968 Dyble was asked to leave the band; she was replaced by the more powerful and evocative vocalist Sandy Denny (January 6, 1947–April 21, 1978), whose unique, haunting vocals have won her acclaim as the greatest British folk-rock singer ever. A former nursing student, Denny had previously recorded solo as well as with the folk-rock band the Strawbs on the album *Sandy Denny & the Strawbs* (1968). She helped Fairport Convention dig further back into the roots of the folk-rock sound. "When Sandy joined, she was already a knowledgeable, schooled singer of traditional British folk songs," Nicol recalled to Greg Kot for the *Chicago Tribune* (May 5, 1989). "We were always interested in this type of music, but up till then only as listeners. She was the catalyst."

In January 1969 Fairport Convention released *What We Did on Our Holidays*, which was followed in July of that year by *Unhalfbricking*. Both albums included covers of songs by Joni Mitchell and Bob Dylan as well as strong original material and recordings of traditional British folk music with modern arrangements. Among the band's most noted songs from those two albums are Denny's "Fotheringay" (a tribute to Mary, Queen of Scots) and "Who Knows Where the Time Goes"; Richard Thompson's "Meet on the Ledge," which

Iconic Music & Media

Fairport Convention (left to right): back row—Chris Leslie, Simon Nicol, Dave Pegg; front row—Ric Sanders, Gerry Conway

has become Fairport Convention's unofficial anthem; and the mesmerizing "A Sailor's Life," which William Ruhlmann and Bruce Eder lauded in their review for the All Music Guide Web site as "one of the great[est] English folk-rock showcases ever recorded."

Ian Matthews left the group in January 1969 for a successful career as the leader of several folk-rock and acoustic-rock bands. (He scored a number-one single in the U.K. in 1970 with his band Matthews Southern Comfort.) The following May, as the band was returning from a concert in Birmingham, England, their van crashed on the M1 highway, killing both Martin Lamble and Richard Thompson's girlfriend. Fairport Convention soldiered on, adding the drummer Dave Mattacks (born in 1948) and the renowned fiddle player Dave Swarbrick (born on April 5, 1947), who had played with the Ian Campbell Folk Group. In December 1969 the band exceeded expectations with the release of the acclaimed *Liege & Lief*. Focusing almost entirely on rearranged traditional English folk songs, the album included only one original song. Among its most popular tracks were "Matty Groves" and "Crazy Man Michael." Bruce Eder and Richie Unterberger wrote for the All Music Guide Web site that the album was "ornamented with gorgeous harmonies and striking instrumental virtuosity."

In 1970 Ashley Hutchings left Fairport Convention to join Steeleye Span, a folk-rock band devoted to playing only traditional British folk music. She later recorded both solo and with the Albion Band. In another blow to the group, Sandy Denny quit that year to help form the folk-rock group Fotheringay. In addition to recording with that band,

Denny recorded several solo albums in the early 1970s and contributed memorable vocals as a guest artist on Led Zeppelin's "The Battle for Evermore," from *Led Zeppelin IV* (1971).

To fill the spaces left by their two most prominent members, Fairport Convention added the bassist Dave Pegg (born on November 2, 1947) to their lineup. Deciding to refocus on folk-rock music, with only occasional traditional material, the band released *Full House* (1970), their first album recorded without a female vocalist. Among the record's highlights were "Walk Awhile" and the nine-minute "Sloth," which continues to be a concert favorite.

Richard Thompson parted ways with Fairport Convention in January 1971, leaving Nicol as the band's last original member. Thompson began a solo career and later, after marrying the singer Linda Peters, started recording with her. Thompson's recordings, guitar playing, and songwriting are considered by some to be among the best in rock music. After Thompson's departure Swarbrick assumed the leadership of the group, writing much of its material. Their first album following the guitarist's departure was *Angel Delight* (1971), whose title came from the former pub where the band lived commune-style with their families. The title track told the true story of a truck's crashing into Swarbrick's bedroom. In the opinion of Rob Beattie, writing for the British magazine *Q* (on-line), "The album travels hopefully but never arrives." *Angel Delight* brought the band unprecedented commercial success, however: it reached number eight on the British charts, the highest charting of the band's career, and became the first Fairport

FAIRPORT CONVENTION

Convention album to reach *Billboard*'s U.S. album chart, squeaking in at number 200.

In November 1971 Fairport Convention released their only concept album, *Babbacombe Lee*, about a real-life individual who, in the late 1800s, was accused of murder and was hanged three times without being killed. All but one of the songs were originals. On the All Music Guide Web site, Bruce Eder noted, "Some of the songs are beautiful—but a few are lugubrious, and as with most other concept albums, the fit between the songs and the larger subject ultimately isn't entirely comfortable for the listener." The record sold poorly in England. Not long after its release Nicol left the band. He was replaced first by Roger Hill, then David Rea, then Jerry Donahue, all in fairly quick succession. In August 1972 the band was augmented by Sandy Denny's husband, the guitarist and vocalist Trevor Lucas.

After a two-year recording hiatus, Fairport Convention released *Rosie* (1973), which found the band leaning toward a more modern sound. Later that year they made the album *Nine*. Sandy Denny returned to tour with the band; some of those performances are documented on the live-concert album *A Fairport Live Convention* (1974). Denny returned to the band full-time in 1975 to record *Rising for the Moon*, to which she contributed seven of the album's 11 songs. The drummer, Dave Mattacks, quit halfway through the recording and was replaced first by Paul Warren and then by Bruce Rowland. Produced by the rock-oriented Glyn Johns, the record exhibited a renewed emphasis on guitar work. It was also the band's first studio album that did not feature any traditional music. *Rising for the Moon* also marked, in the words of Bruce Eder, "the last time Fairport Convention would present itself to the public as a contemporary rock group. . . . Beyond this point, they became part of the folk revival circuit, albeit with a huge audience."

Sandy Denny, Trevor Lucas, and Jerry Donahue left Fairport Convention in December 1975 to work on their own projects. Denny, who suffered from drug and alcohol addiction, died in 1978. With the band in disarray but under contractual obligation to record another album, Dave Swarbrick, Dave Pegg, and Bruce Rowland returned to the studio with several session musicians to record *Gottle O'Geer* (1976), which was credited as Fairport Featuring Dave Swarbrick. "As you might expect, it's fairly listless," William Ruhlmann wrote for the All Music Guide Web site.

In September 1976 Nicol rejoined Fairport Convention. With him the band released *Bonny Bunch of Roses* (1977) and *Tippler's Tale* (1978), both of which featured rock-tinged traditional English folk songs along with several originals. Remarking on those two records, Nicol told Anil Prasad, "They have very strong material, but sonically, they're quite compromised. They aren't very well recorded."

After *Tippler's Tale* the group did not record a studio album for seven years. In 1979, having resolved to disband permanently, they released the live album *Farewell, Farewell*. "We'd worked so hard slogging around touring for years because we never, ever sold any records so the only way the group could exist was to tour nonstop," Dave Pegg told Jim Washburn for the *Los Angeles Times* (April 26, 1989). "And . . . Dave Swarbrick had this hearing problem that couldn't tolerate the noise levels we made on stage and he just wanted it to stop. Nobody wanted to carry on, so it just disintegrated. . . . And the musical climate at the time wasn't exactly inducing [us] to go out and attempt to play songs and stuff. It was the height of the punk era, which we obviously never quite fit into."

Mattacks, Nicol, Pegg, and Swarbrick reunited in August 1980 for a one-time performance. The musicians began to repeat the event every year, and it soon evolved into the Cropredy Festival, an annual event that has become one of the most famous and respected British folk festivals. In 1985 Pegg, Nicol, and Mattacks regrouped in the studio for the first time since 1978 to record *Gladys' Leap*. Swarbrick was invited to participate in the recording, but declined due to his work with his acoustic band, Whippersnapper. The musicians then turned to Ric Sanders (born on December 8, 1952), formerly of the Albion Band and Soft Machine, who joined them on fiddle and keyboards; he later became an official member of Fairport Convention. The first Fairport studio album to be released on their own Woodworm label, *Gladys' Leap* featured three songs written by the modern British folk composer Ralph McTell. It was the first of several Fairport Convention albums that featured prominent synthesizers and fuller arrangements.

Shortly after recording *Gladys' Leap*, Fairport Convention was joined by the guitarist and keyboardist Maartin Allcock (born in 1957). In 1986 the band released *Expletive Delighted*—their only all-instrumental album—and began touring in support of the progressive-rock band Jethro Tull, for which Pegg played bass from 1979 to 1995. Fairport Convention followed in 1988 with *Red & Gold*. Reviewing the record for the All Music Guide Web site, Richard Foss wrote, "Simon Nicol's vocal on the title cut is worth the price of the album by itself; it's as sure and passionate a track as he's ever cut, a sorrowful account of a great battle as seen by a peasant farmer who doesn't understand why it's happening." As Pegg later commented, the song was about the battle of Cropredy Bridge, which occurred on the site of the folk festival.

In 1990 Fairport Convention released *The Five Seasons*. In 1995 they completed *The Jewel in the Crown*, which featured songs by Clive Gregson and Leonard Cohen in addition to more traditional music. The band's first entirely acoustic album, *Old-New-Borrowed-Blue*, recorded both live and in the studio, followed in 1996. After that release, Allcock left the group and was replaced by the former Albion Band member Chris Leslie (born on December 15, 1956) on guitar and fiddle. A prolific songwriter, Leslie ended the need for outside writers, whom the band had used regularly since 1985. Leslie also sang lead vocals on a number of songs—a change of pace for the band, for whom Nicol had been the sole lead vocalist for some 15 years. "It's worked out brilliantly because not only does it give me a chance to sit back and listen to his really wonderful and enjoyable singing, but it gives us two bites at songs that come along," Nicol told Prasad. "If it doesn't work for me it might for him. It gives us a bigger range of keys to go with because we sing in totally different, yet complementary registers." The band's first record with Leslie was *Who Knows Where the Time Goes?* (1997), which, as evidenced by "Spanish Main" and "Dangerous," was a more rock-oriented album than any they had recorded in some time.

Mattacks left the group once again in 1998, this time to be replaced by Gerry Conway (born on September 11, 1947), who had briefly drummed with the band in the early 1970s. In 2000, making a shift toward acoustic pop, Fairport Convention released *The Wood and the Wire*. For that album Leslie cowrote some lyrics with Nigel Stonier. Writing about the record for the *Washington Post* (November 3, 2000), Geoffrey Himes noted, "Leslie has a genuine gift for melody. Tunes such as 'Wandering Man,' 'Banbury Fair,' and the title track are so infectious that they seem destined to inspire singalongs in pubs throughout England. His lyrics . . . are full of colorful British mythology—the traveling troubadour spellbound by 'The Wood & the Wire' of his guitar, the pirate haunted by his victim's chess pieces, the land-bound wife aching for her sailor husband. Unfortunately, Leslie has a weakness for sunny romanticism that gives many of these songs a cloying sweetness."

In 2002, for the 35th anniversary of their first concert, Fairport Convention issued *XXXV*, which continued in the vein of *The Wood and the Wire*. Remarking on the album's mixed reception from critics, Leslie told Prasad, "You're never going to please all the people all the time. There will always be people who look back and have their favorite period of the band, and favorite band members who may no longer be there. That's really as it should be. It's human nature." Leslie told Prasad that to his mind *XXXV* "is a very consistent album. I listen [to] it from start to finish and think there's an overall sound and there's an identity as a band again." *XXXV* also proved controversial among fans because of its covers of songs from earlier Fairport albums. "The reason we recorded older material on the new album is because we've been playing it in the set," Conway told Prasad. "Obviously the first version you hear, be it a piece of Fairport or classical music, is the one that sticks with you. But with the line-up changes over the years, we felt it was valid to present those songs with the new line-up. . . . We also benefit from using newer technologies, sounds and all those things."

In 2004 the group released *Over the Next Hill*, for their own new label, Compass. Chris Nickson, reviewing the album for the All Music Guide, discerned "a new attitude to the music, with a slightly rawer, more rocking feel, as on 'Wait for the Tide to Come In,' where Simon Nicol's electric guitar work simply sparkles." Nickson noted that the album merged the present with the past by including a reprise of the band's 1969 hit "Si Tu Dois Partir," which made use of an earlier recording of a percussion break from the original drummer, Martin Lamble. "Elsewhere the songs are of a consistently high standard," Nickson continued, "with Chris Leslie's 'I'm Already There' a standout. In a couple of places the music veers toward that comfortable middle of the road space Fairport's carved out over the last few years, but they seem to jerk themselves away before becoming too complacent about the music. . . . So what does this say about Fairport for the future? Other than that they'll still be there, and that they're in the process of taking a long hard look at themselves, not a great deal. But if this new attitude and grit persists, there'll be plenty of excellent music ahead." Fairport Convention's most recent album is *Who Knows? The Woodworm Archives Series, Vol. 1* (2005), a recording of a 1975 concert.

Fairport Convention recently received the BBC Radio Lifetime Achievement Award. Regarding the band's consistently shifting personnel, Nicol told Prasad, "Fairport is a family and when you lose someone in your family they don't go away. It's nice to have had partnerships and associations, but if we were a small office, over a 35-year period, you'd expect people to come and go, and some to fall off the perch. You just get on with it." The band continues to headline the Cropredy Festival every August, occasionally joined by past members. "At our concerts we hopefully cheer people up," Pegg told Lindsay Walker for the *Arizona Daily Wildcat* (October 3, 2002, on-line). "Our main thing is to do live gigs; we really enjoy those more than doing the actual recordings, you know. We want people to have a really good time, and we want to get them to feel happy. But we also have songs that make people think." Nicol has recorded a pair of solo albums and provided the music to the video *Singing Games for Children* (1990). Sanders has also recorded a couple of solo records and has recorded with the vocalist Vikki Clayton and the jazz bassist Fred Thelonious Baker. He has a new group known as the Ric Sanders Trio.

—G.O.

Suggested Reading: All Music Guide Web site; *Arizona Daily Wildcat* (on-line) Oct. 3, 2002; Associated Press June 27, 1989; *Chicago Tribune* Tempo p3 May 5, 1989, with photo; *Innerviews* (on-line), with photos; *Los Angeles Times* VI p8 Apr. 26, 1989, with photo

Selected Recordings: *Fairport Convention*, 1968; *What We Did on Our Holidays*, 1969; *Unhalfbricking*, 1969; *Liege & Lief*, 1969; *Full House*, 1970; *Angel Delight*, 1971; *Babbacombe Lee*, 1971; *Rosie*, 1973; *Nine*, 1973; *Rising for the Moon*, 1975; *Gladys' Leap*, 1985; *Expletive Delighted*, 1986; *Red & Gold*, 1988; *Old-New-Borrowed-Blue*, 1996; *Who Knows Where the Time Goes?*, 1997; *The Wood and the Wire*, 2000; *XXXV*, 2002; *Over the Next Hill*, 2004; *Who Knows? The Woodworm Archives Series, Vol. 1*, 2005

John Foraste, courtesy of Brown University

Fausto-Sterling, Anne

July 30, 1944– Developmental biologist; writer

Address: Brown University, Box G-160J, Providence, RI 02912

When European imperialism was at its height, in the 19th century, scholars measured skull circumference, height, and other physical characteristics of humans to distinguish among races and justify the domination of one race over another. Some scientists went so far as to argue that the various races were actually separate species and that Africans were the closest taxonomically to apes. Today virtually all scientists acknowledge that there are greater physical variations within racial categories than among them, indicating that biologically the concept of race among humans is both "arbitrary and subjective," as the Web site of the American Anthropological Association put it. "Historical research has shown that the idea of 'race' has always

carried more meanings than mere physical differences," the association declared; "indeed, physical variations in the human species have no meaning except the social ones that humans put on them." Anne Fausto-Sterling, a developmental biologist and professor of biology and women's studies at Brown University, in Providence, Rhode Island, sees parallels between the ways the scientific community once viewed race and the ways it continues to view gender. Thus, for instance, scientific inquiry into brain anatomy has long been guided by the assumption—or even attempts to prove—that women are incapable of performing as well as men in math and science. In her landmark book *Myths of Gender*, she scrutinized the work of other scientists to show how cultural notions of gender influence scientific research. Although she wrote in that book that "to be scientific is to be unsentimental, rational, straight-thinking, correct, rigorous, exact," she told Michael Bronski in an interview for *Z Magazine* (March 2000), "There is no 'pure science.' Science is a particular kind of cultural activity and the nature of science is rules—providing empirical evidence, etc. The point is not to eliminate culture from science—which would be impossible—but to understand what is going on so we can make appropriate use of science in our social decisions such as how we allocate money, and on choosing research topics." Fausto-Sterling has also challenged the notion that there are two discrete sexes, arguing in her second book, *Sexing the Body*, that sexuality exists on a continuum. "Anne Fausto-Sterling is one of the leading theorists on science, sexuality, and gender . . . ," Bronski wrote. "But through all of Fausto-Sterling's writing her underlying concern is how social attitudes, biases, and prejudices—particularly about issues of sex, sexuality, and gender—inform and influence scientific research, theory, and practice: the social construction of science."

Fausto-Sterling was born Anne Sterling on July 30, 1944 in New York City and raised in Sunnyside, in the city's borough of Queens. Her father, Philip Sterling, was a caseworker for the New York Emergency Home Relief Bureau as well as a print and broadcast journalist and editor. In 1971 he won the Christopher Book Award for his young-adult volume *Sea and Earth: The Life of Rachel Carson*. He also wrote other nonfiction books for young readers, including *Polio Pioneers* (1951), which he co-authored with his wife, Dorothy Sterling (nee Dannenberg), as well as for adults. Fausto-Sterling's mother also wrote a handful of nonfiction books for adults, but she is best known for her many young-adult titles—particularly her nonfiction books about science and her biographies of African-American heroes and heroines. Marxists and social activists, Philip and Dorothy Sterling encouraged Fausto-Sterling and her older brother, Peter (now a neurophysiologist), to value the scientific method and oppose social injustice. In her early teens Fausto-Sterling began participating in the civil rights, peace, and women's liberation movements.

After she completed high school, Fausto-Sterling attended the University of Wisconsin at Madison and graduated with a bachelor's degree in zoology in 1965. In December of that year, she married a fellow scientist, Nelson Fausto, and went with him to Brown University, in Providence, Rhode Island, where he had accepted a position as a teacher of pathology. Fausto-Sterling studied developmental genetics at Brown and earned a Ph.D. there in 1970. In 1971 she became an assistant professor at Brown; she has remained on the school's faculty ever since. Initially Fausto-Sterling taught embryology—the study of the development of embryos—and her research focused on the role of genes in the embryological development of fruit flies. She later began to integrate her interest in the women's movement into her work, teaching courses on the biology of gender (the expression of gender and its evolution throughout the animal and plant kingdoms) and on social issues in biology, which included the historical attempts to codify racist doctrines by means of science.

During the 1970s Fausto-Sterling started to notice a trend in her conversations with colleagues. Whenever the topic of feminism arose, they would frequently cite studies that indicated that male rats were more aggressive than female rats. Fausto-Sterling began to wonder whether that difference really existed, and if so, whether it was valid to use studies of rats to draw conclusions about human behavior. "Up until then most feminist thinking about women and science was about the discrimination women faced in the field," she told Michael Bronski. "Not many people were conceptualizing or talking about how to bring feminist ideas into the lab, or applying them to how science was done. And I realized that I was trained and had the tools to do that, to look at how preconceptions about gender affected scientific research."

In 1985 Fausto-Sterling published *Myths of Gender: Biological Theories About Women and Men*. In that landmark book she wrote about the dearth of solid evidence behind some of the assumptions that scientists had long made about the biology of men and women. For centuries scientists had either taken for granted or attempted to prove that behavioral differences between men and women—and their respective social positions—could be traced to biologically based differences. Examining a broad range of studies that ostensibly connected behavioral differences to biology, Fausto-Sterling found that the investigations were almost invariably riddled with procedural errors. For example, many scientists drew conclusions about sex differences after studying only men or studying men and women in one narrow segment of the population (usually middle-class whites). Some researchers had also focused so single-mindedly on biology that they had completely disregarded social factors in their analyses. In one of many examples, Fausto-Sterling noted their repeated attempts to link men's higher test scores in math to differences in the physiology of men's and women's brains.

Many such studies, she pointed out, failed to acknowledge the social pressures that led female high-school students to take fewer math classes, on average, than males.

Fausto-Sterling also rejected what she saw as the simplistic approaches to the nature-versus-nurture debates that dominated biology at the time, promoting instead a more complex analysis of the influence on people's development of social and environmental factors (nurture, considered in a broad sense), on the one hand, and genetic and biological factors (nature) on the other. "Biology may in some manner condition behavior, but behavior in turn can alter one's physiology . . . ," she wrote. "The question, 'What fraction of our behavior is biologically based,' is impossible—even in theory—to answer, and unanswerable questions drop out of the realm of science altogether, entering instead that of philosophy and morality."

Fausto-Sterling acknowledged in *Myths of Gender* that the book was both a "scientific statement *and* a political statement." As such, it inevitably drew complaints of bias from some reviewers, but overall it inspired praise. "Mrs. Fausto-Sterling's book is neither muckraking in tone nor shrill in argument, yet she is sometimes given to dubious pronouncements," Daniel J. Kevles, a historian of science, wrote for the *New York Times* (December 29, 1985). "She violates her own standards of responsible discourse by declaring offhandedly, without evidence, that many studies of menstruation and menopause 'express deep hatred and fear of women.' . . . But never mind the missteps: Mrs. Fausto-Sterling has, for the most part, given us a temperate, judiciously argued book that makes its complicated subjects accessible in clear and uncomplicated prose. She has also provided an excellent primer of the methodological and epistemological issues that must be considered in any scientific treatment of human behavior, whether sexually specific or not." *Myths of Gender* was quickly deemed to be a classic in the gender-studies field and is still used in many women's-studies courses throughout the country.

In the years following the publication of *Myths of Gender*, whenever the results of a new gender-related study were announced, Fausto-Sterling—much to her displeasure—was inundated with calls from reporters who wanted her reaction. As she explained in the preface to the second edition of *Myths of Gender* (1992), "The question of sex differences in cognition was one I considered *in extenso* in the first edition of this book, and thus to see it leap once more to the forefront of public discussion made me weary. Second, I knew that the public debate was really about the question of social equity. . . . Having fought such battles for several decades, I did not relish having once more to leap into the fray. But as one of a handful of scientists equipped to fight this particular battle, I felt that I had no choice."

In 1990 Fausto-Sterling began analyzing how differing environmental factors and methods of reproduction influence the regenerative capabilities of flatworms. (There are some 20,000 species of flatworms, primitive worms that can reproduce both sexually and asexually.) She also became interested in intersexuals (more commonly known as hermaphrodites)—people who are born with ambiguous genitalia. "I was interested in a theoretical question that was circulating around feminist studies at that time," she told Claudia Dreifus for the *New York Times* (January 2, 2001). "I wanted to know, What is meant when we say, 'The body is a social construction'? At the time, social scientists were looking into how our ideas about the human body were shaped by politics and culture. That inquiry led me to a lot of the medical literature on intersexuality."

In 1993 Fausto-Sterling published an article about intersexuals in the March/April issue of the *Sciences* (a bimonthly journal, now defunct, published by the New York Academy of Sciences). Titled "The Five Sexes," the article opens with the tale of Levi Suydam, a Salisbury, Connecticut, resident who in 1843 requested that the town validate his right to vote in a highly contentious local election. Members of the opposing political party were insisting that Suydam was more female than male and—like all other women at the time—was thus not entitled to vote. A doctor was called in to settle the dispute, and upon observing that Suydam possessed a penis, ruled that he was indeed male. Then, a few days later, Suydam began menstruating. "Western culture is deeply committed to the idea that there are only two sexes . . . ," Fausto-Sterling wrote. "But if the state and the legal system have an interest in maintaining a two-party sexual system, they are in defiance of nature." In the article Fausto-Sterling argued that gender encompasses "many gradations running from male to female," and "depending on how one calls the shots, one can argue that along that spectrum lie at least five sexes and perhaps even more." She offered labels for three additional sexes: herms (hermaphrodites who possess one testis and one ovary), merms (male pseudohermaphrodites who have testes and some elements of female genitalia but no ovaries), and ferms (female pseudohermaphrodites who have ovaries and some elements of male genitalia but lack testes). Intersexuals often undergo surgery and hormonal treatments shortly after birth that transform them into males or females. Fausto-Sterling, however, believed that intersexuals should be viewed not as aberrations but as individuals of genders other than male or female. She also suggested that if intersexuals could gain the acceptance they needed to live openly, then "the prize might be a society in which sexuality is something to be celebrated for its subtleties and not something to be feared and ridiculed." "The Five Sexes" received honorable mention in *The Best American Essays of 1994* and was reprinted in many publications. It also stirred up a great deal of controversy, drawing angry responses from conservative members of the scientific community and right-wing religious groups. The Catholic League for Religious and Civil Rights took out an ad in the *New York Times* that denounced "radical individualism" and specifically cited Fausto-Sterling's article as an example. "It is maddening to listen to discussions of 'five genders' when every sane person knows there are but two sexes, both of which are rooted in nature," the ad declared, as quoted on pbs.org. Seven years later Fausto-Sterling revisited the controversy in another article for the *Sciences* (July/August 2000): "Clearly, I had struck a nerve," she wrote. "The fact that so many people could get riled up by my proposal to revamp our sex and gender system suggested that change—as well as resistance to it—might be in the offing. Indeed, a lot has changed since 1993, and I like to think that my article was an important stimulus."

Fausto-Sterling gave a more detailed account of intersexuals, and the medical community's efforts to correct them, in *Sexing the Body: Gender Politics and the Construction of Sexuality* (2000). In that book she returned to the notion that science is never "pure" and should not be accepted without examination. She argued that the existence of intersexuals challenges cultural notions about sexuality; for that reason, she wrote, medical practitioners insist on assigning the intersexed to one of the two accepted sexes by surgically modifying their bodies, even though such operations may have negative effects on the patients' health. "I begin [the book] here because this is a fairly obvious example of how our ideas about gender affect science and medical practice," Fausto-Sterling told Bronski. "But I wanted a more complicated example. . . . So I started exploring the history of how what are usually called 'sex hormones' were discovered, named, and how they work in the body. What I found was that before they were ever even identified both estrogen and testosterone were conceived of as being 'female' and 'male' and pertaining to, quite discretely, male or female bodies. When it turned out—through increasingly sophisticated research—that all hormones are found in both sexes, scientists were quite distressed."

Sexing the Body won the Distinguished Publication Award from the Association for Women in Psychology and the Robert K. Merton Award of the American Sociological Association's Section on Science, Knowledge and Technology. Reviewers lauded the book for both its intellectual rigor and its engaging style. "Fausto-Sterling's cogent use of concrete historical examples, her simple language and personal anecdotes keep this complex synthesis accessible," Jeff Zaleski and Paul Gediman wrote for *Publishers Weekly* (January 3, 2000). "Her insightful work offers profound challenges to scientific research, the creation of social policy and the future of feminist and gender theory." In his review for the *New England Journal of Medicine* (August 31, 2000), the neuroscientist S. Marc Breedlove wrote, "Fausto-Sterling is not above rhetoric. It is plain that she disagrees with certain writers, and she unabashedly declares her hopes for our political future. . . . However, Fausto-Sterling also takes pains to present at least two sides of every story, and she never fails to credit the intelligence and good intentions of others, even if, in hindsight, they have made dreadful mistakes. As physicians, scientists, and other citizens continue to take stock of ideas about men and women, and boys and girls, in this new century, Fausto-Sterling's careful and insightful book offers us the chance to question past assumptions and to dream of new formulations nearly as radical as allowing women to vote."

While Fausto-Sterling was finishing her work on *Sexing the Body*, she grew interested in the theory of dynamical systems—an area of mathematics used to describe the behavior of complex systems (such as the motions of falling bodies, colliding billiard balls, or the planets) by employing a set of coupled differential equations—and its application to the study of human development. On her Web site Fausto-Sterling explained that the theory "permits us to understand how *cultural* difference becomes *bodily* difference." She is currently examining sex differences in bone development.

Fausto-Sterling has served as a visiting professor of biology, medical science, gender studies, and science studies at various institutions in the United States and abroad. She has contributed articles to *Contemporary Sociology, Bioscience, Developmental Biology, Genetics, Journal of Experimental Zoology, Radical Teacher, Signs and Symptoms, Women's Review of Books, Women's Studies International Quarterly, Women's Studies Quarter-*ly, and *Women's Studies Newsletter*, among other publications. She has received many grants and fellowships, including a National Science Foundation grant, an American Association for the Advancement of Science fellowship, and a Mellon fellowship from the Wellesley Center for Research on Women. She is a member of the International Association of Developmental Biology, the Society of Developmental Biology, the Genetics Society of America, the National Women's Studies Association, and the History of Science Society. In 1995 she won the Women of Distinction Award from the City University of New York.

Fausto-Sterling and her husband separated in 1988 and later divorced. Shortly after the separation, Fausto-Sterling started dating the playwright Paula Vogel. The two women married in September 2004 in Massachusetts, where such services were then legal for homosexual couples. Vogel is a professor of creative writing at Brown; she won the 1998 Pulitzer Prize for her play *How I Learned to Drive*. "Paula and I are working on the same intellectual and social issues about gender, sex, and politics," Fausto-Sterling told Bronksi. "She does it onstage and with literature; I do it through testing and evaluating how science works."

—J.C.

Suggested Reading: *Advocate* Mar. 14, 2000; *New Republic* p37 Feb. 3, 1986; *New York Times* VII p12 Dec. 29, 1985, with photo, F p3 Jan. 2, 2001; *Z Magazine* (on-line) Mar. 2000

Selected Books: *Myths of Gender*, 1985; *Sexing the Body*, 2000

Felt, W. Mark

Aug. 17, 1913– Former FBI official; informant

Address: c/o PublicAffairs Books, 250 W. 57th St., Suite 1321, New York, NY 10107

Who was Deep Throat? For more than 30 years, journalists, conspiracy theorists, and average Americans pondered that question, eager to know the identity of the high-level government informant who helped the *Washington Post* reporters Bob Woodward and Carl Bernstein expose the plot behind the infamous 1972 burglary of the Democratic National Committee headquarters at the Watergate complex, in Washington, D.C. The Watergate scandal, as it came to be known, led not only to the imprisonment of many of President Richard Nixon's loyalists but to the resignation of the president himself, an event unique in U.S. history. For decades afterward Woodward and Bernstein, as well as their editor, Ben Bradlee, were regularly peppered with questions about Deep Throat, whose identity they vowed not to reveal until the informant's death. The mystery surrounding Deep Throat, played by the actor Hal Holbrook in the 1976 film version of Woodward and Bernstein's book *All the President's Men*, heightened the sense of wonder that characterized the Watergate affair—whose continuing power to fascinate stems in part from the idea that one clandestine source and two intrepid reporters could end the career of the most powerful man in the free world.

As portrayed in the book and film, Deep Throat was an enigmatic figure whose reasons for passing along and corroborating information were as shrouded in darkness as his name. Deep Throat's identity—if not his motive—came to light on May 31, 2005, when the frail, 91-year-old W. Mark Felt, once the number-two official at the Federal Bureau of Investigation (FBI), revealed that he had been Woodward and Bernstein's informant. While Felt had often been mentioned as one of the people who might possibly have been Deep Throat, Felt himself had always strenuously denied it. Later that day, Woodward, Bernstein, and Bradlee, feeling that they were no longer bound by their pledge,

Justin Sullivan/Getty Images

W. Mark Felt

confirmed that Felt had indeed been their source. With that Watergate mystery at an end, new questions have emerged in the public consciousness, chief among them: who is W. Mark Felt, and why did he become Deep Throat?

The son of Mark Earl Felt, a carpenter and building contractor, and the former Rose Dygert, William Mark Felt was born in Twin Falls, Idaho, on August 17, 1913 into a family of modest means. (Contrary to some rumors, the family was not of Jewish descent.) As a child he enjoyed playing sports; he also took piano lessons, at his mother's urging. When his father's business floundered during the Great Depression, Felt took a number of odd jobs—everything from waiting tables to stoking furnaces—so he could attend the University of Idaho, where he became president of his fraternity, Beta Theta Phi. He graduated in 1935 with a bachelor's degree, only to find, as did many young people of that era, few prospects for gainful employment. He then began to search for a job that would enable him to pay his tuition at law school. As Felt noted in his autobiography, *The FBI Pyramid from the Inside* (1979), he heard that government jobs were available in Washington, D.C., and contacted U.S. senator James P. Pope of Idaho in the hope of landing such a position. To Felt's "great good fortune," as he wrote, he became a correspondence clerk on Pope's staff.

From five to seven in the evenings, after spending long hours at Pope's office, Felt attended George Washington University Law School. He received his J.D. degree in 1940 and was admitted to the District of Columbia bar a year later. His first job after law school was with the Federal Trade Commission (FTC), where he was initially as-

signed to determine whether or not Red Cross toilet paper had an unfair competitive advantage because consumers might think it was associated with, or recommended by, the American Red Cross. Finding his work at the FTC to be mind-numbing, in November 1941 Felt applied for a position with the Federal Bureau of Investigation, then at the height of its power under the leadership of its longtime director J. Edgar Hoover. In his autobiography he noted that he was "well aware that J. Edgar Hoover was a tough disciplinarian, that the work was demanding, and that the Bureau imposed strict conformity. But I was looking for a career of more substance than interviewing reluctant consumers. Europe was at war and I wanted to be involved in work that would be significantly helpful to my country."

Felt joined the bureau on January 16, 1942 and then completed 16 weeks of training, starting at the FBI Academy in Quantico, Virginia. The early stages of Felt's career reflected Hoover's belief in moving his agents around, so that they would get a great deal of experience. He first did field work in Texas, spending six months in Houston and San Antonio. When he returned to Washington, he was assigned to the agency's Espionage Section and learned counterintelligence techniques intended to combat Nazi spies and saboteurs during World War II. After the German surrender, in May 1945, the Espionage Section was dismantled, and Felt again found himself doing field work, this time in Seattle, Washington. After two years he was promoted from special agent to supervisor. Following the establishment of the Atomic Energy Commission (AEC), which took over the production of nuclear warheads from the military, Felt oversaw the background checks of people who worked at the Hanford plutonium plant, near Richland, Washington. He wrote that he was in charge of as many as 1,500 cases at once, as part of what he called "a tremendous burden for the FBI."

In 1954, feeling that he was ready to move up in the bureau's ranks, Felt set up an appointment with Hoover, telling the FBI director of his ambition to become a special agent in charge, or an agent who heads an FBI field office. During the meeting Felt also discussed with Hoover ways to make the clearance investigations at the AEC more efficient, and suggested that the routine checks be handled by the Civil Service Commission, leaving only clearance for the top positions as the responsibility of the FBI. Hoover seemed to agree with those suggestions and promised to keep Felt in mind for a promotion. Six days later, in Seattle, Felt received a letter from Hoover transferring him to Washington, D.C., a move that included a promotion to inspector's aide. Within two months he was back in the field, this time as assistant special agent in charge of the New Orleans, Louisiana, field office. A little more than a year later, he took over operations of the Los Angeles field office, another step up the promotional ladder, as the Los Angeles office was the second largest, after the New York City office.

In 1956 Felt received a promotion to special agent in charge and was again transferred, this time to Salt Lake City, Utah, where he oversaw the bureau's first investigations into the Mafia's involvement with the gambling casinos in Reno and Las Vegas, Nevada. In February 1958 he continued his investigations of organized crime at the FBI field office in Kansas City, Missouri. Four years later Felt returned to the FBI's main office, in Washington, D.C., where he was assigned to be second-in-command of the bureau's Training Division. In that position he also oversaw the FBI Academy. According to John D. O'Connor's article about Felt for *Vanity Fair* (May 31, 2005, on-line), "Felt mastered the art of succinct, just-the-facts-ma'am memo writing, which appealed to the meticulous Hoover, who made him one of his closest protégés." In 1964 the FBI director promoted Felt to chief inspector, a position that put him in charge of the Inspection Division, with responsibility for ensuring internal compliance with the bureau's regulations and for conducting internal investigations. (During the same period Felt also served as an unpaid technical adviser for *The F.B.I.*, a popular dramatic television series starring Efrem Zimbalist Jr.) "My transfer to the Inspection Division marked a great change in my relationship with Hoover," Felt wrote. "Prior to that time . . . I saw him once a year for no more than thirty minutes. During my tenure in the Training Division, I saw him only a few times. Now all that changed. He would call me on the intercom and I saw him with increasing frequency for personal conferences."

As head of the Inspection Division, Felt exercised a great deal of power. He reported directly to Hoover and had the ability to request an investigation of anyone or into any matter. He also understood that this power came with considerable responsibility, noting in his autobiography: "During my movement up the FBI pyramid I had learned that there was a major difference between constructive and destructive criticism. I was determined to be as constructive as possible, and I think it is fair to say that during my six years as FBI Chief Inspector I lived up to that resolve. I tried to achieve a balance between the rigid demands of Hoover and what I felt were the best interests of the Bureau and its personnel."

In July 1971 Hoover promoted Felt to deputy associate director, charged with assisting the FBI's associate director, Clive A. Tolson, Hoover's longtime second-in-command. As Tolson was in declining health and often unable to attend to his duties, Felt often served as Hoover's right-hand man. According to several sources, Hoover promoted Felt because he wanted someone he trusted to keep William C. Sullivan, the head of domestic intelligence, in check; Hoover suspected—correctly, as it turned out—that Sullivan was secretly passing information about the bureau's workings to the administration of the Republican president Richard Nixon. Though Hoover maintained extensive files on people in the highest offices of the U.S. government, he wanted to keep the FBI pure of political machinations and had spent years trying to keep various presidential administrations from politicizing the bureau for their own ends. (In his autobiography Felt devoted much space to Hoover's battles with the administration of President John F. Kennedy, which, the director believed, saw the FBI as "an adjunct of the Kennedy wing of the Democratic Party rather than as a nonpolitical investigative force," in Felt's words.) Relations between the Nixon White House and the FBI had also been strained for some time.

In 1971 President Nixon's aides asked Felt to come to the White House because they suspected that someone inside the government was leaking details about the administration's plans for upcoming arms talks with the Soviet Union. During that meeting the White House staff urged Felt to do what was necessary, such as using wiretaps or forcing people to submit to lie-detector tests, to find those who were leaking information. As the meeting ended without Felt's agreeing to the request, the White House began hiring former government agents, nicknamed the Plumbers, to stop the leaks. (One such unit, working inside the White House, would play a key role in the Watergate break-in.) Felt, like Hoover, believed that the Nixon administration was attempting to use the FBI and its parent agency, the Justice Department, for political purposes. In the *Washington Post* (June 20, 2005), Michael Dobbs wrote: "As a protege and ardent supporter of J. Edgar Hoover . . . Felt was determined to perpetuate Hoover's vision of the bureau as an almost autonomous institution, feared by criminals and politicians alike."

After Hoover died in his sleep, on May 2, 1972, Nixon named L. Patrick Gray, a longtime Nixon supporter, as acting director of the FBI. Tolson subsequently resigned, and Felt took over his position as associate director. According to several sources, Felt—who had viewed himself as Hoover's heir apparent—had conflicted feelings about Gray's appointment. He thought Gray to be hardworking but questioned the interim director's decision to leave Felt himself in charge of the bureau's day-to-day operations. Felt wrote, "What Gray never understood was that his impact on the FBI would be minimal if he spent so much of his time away from actively directing Bureau activities while he traveled the land making speeches." Felt also worried that Gray, as a Nixon loyalist, would report back to the White House about everything going on at the FBI, thereby impeding the bureau's independent investigative capacity. Felt's concerns proved to be well founded, as Gray soon began reporting to Nixon about the power struggles going on at the highest levels of the FBI (though he resisted the president's entreaties to polygraph FBI employees about the leaks). But Gray also implicitly trusted Felt as his deputy, in part because Felt had discreetly investigated (at Hoover's request) a homosexuality scandal earlier in the year involving the White House aides H. R. Haldeman and John D. Ehrlichman.

On June 17, 1972 five men were arrested after attempting to break into the offices of the Democratic National Committee at the Watergate complex. The men were caught carrying photographic and eavesdropping equipment and a large amount of money. One of the burglars, as first reported by Woodward and Bernstein in the *Washington Post*, was James W. McCord Jr., the security coordinator for the Committee to Re-Elect the President (CREEP), Nixon's 1972 campaign organization. In the address books of two of the burglars, the name E. Howard Hunt, that of a former Central Intelligence Agency (CIA) operative, appeared next to the notation "W. H." or "W. House."

Under Felt's authority the FBI began investigating the Watergate break-in. The bureau soon traced the money found in the burglars' pockets to a bank in Mexico City—a link Bernstein made separately in his investigative reporting for the *Washington Post*. The investigation initiated by Felt produced copies of Mexican checks in amounts totaling $89,000 as well as a $25,000 check deposited in the account of one of the burglars, Bernard L. Barker, which was directly tied to the president's campaign: the check was made out to CREEP. At that point the White House, through Gray, began trying to block the investigation. Gray told Felt to call off interviews in Mexico City, as they might compromise a CIA operation there. Felt protested the decision, arguing that the reputation of the bureau was at stake. He also complained that John Dean, a special adviser to the president, and the reelection committee were not cooperating with the FBI. Ultimately, Felt was able to persuade Gray not to go along with the White House's stonewalling.

At the same time that Felt was investigating the break-in, convinced that someone high up in the White House had played a role in it, he received a telephone call from Bob Woodward. Woodward and Felt had met two years earlier, in 1970, while the former was a navy lieutenant delivering documents to the White House. Since that time they had maintained contact, and on previous occasions, including the May 1972 shooting of the Alabama governor and presidential candidate George C. Wallace, Woodward had called Felt, asking him to serve as an unnamed source for his story. This time Woodward contacted Felt as part of his own investigations into the Watergate affair. Knowing that the name E. Howard Hunt had been found in the address books of the burglars, Woodward had placed a call to Hunt at the White House. Though he did not reach Hunt, he was able to confirm that Hunt sometimes worked at the office of Nixon's special counsel, Charles W. Colson, and also worked at a public-relations firm. When Woodward called Hunt at that firm and asked him why his name had been in the burglars' address books, Hunt abruptly hung up.

When he spoke to Felt, Woodward wanted to understand the links connecting Colson, the White House, and the CIA. As Woodward recalled in an article for the *Washington Post* (June 2, 2005): "Felt

sounded nervous. He said off the record—meaning I could not use the information—that Hunt was a prime suspect in the burglary at the Watergate for many reasons beyond the address books. So reporting the connections forcefully would not be unfair."

Following that phone call, Bernstein turned up the connection between the burglars' money and the reelection committee. On August 1, 1972 the story Woodward and Bernstein published in the *Post* indicated that the money had come from a campaign check given to Maurice H. Stans, the president's fund-raiser, on a golf course in Florida—the first time the Nixon administration was directly implicated in the Watergate break-in. Soon afterward Woodward made several attempts to contact Felt by telephone before showing up at his home in Fairfax, Virginia. There, Felt told him that there could no longer be any telephone contact between them, as Felt feared that his phones were likely bugged; he would have to meet Woodward in person, clandestinely. To that end Felt and Woodward developed a system for contacting each other. "I said that I had a red cloth flag, less than a foot square . . . that a girlfriend had found on the street. She had stuck it in an empty flowerpot on my apartment balcony," Woodward explained in his *Post* article. "Felt and I agreed that I would move the flowerpot with the flag, which usually was in the front near the railing, to the rear of the balcony if I urgently needed a meeting. This would have to be important and rare, he said sternly. The signal, he said, would mean we would meet that same night about 2 a.m. on the bottom level of an underground garage just over the Key Bridge in Rosslyn." If Felt needed to contact Woodward, he would do so by drawing on page 20 of Woodward's home-delivered copy of the *New York Times* a clock face indicating the time of the meeting. In the first meetings, Felt simply corroborated Woodward and Bernstein's conclusions or told them if their investigation was heading toward a dead end. Later he also supplied them with some information; for example, in October 1972 Felt told Woodward that the break-in was part of a coordinated effort to spy on the Democrats and that Haldeman, Nixon's chief of staff, had secured the funds to finance it.

Woodward and Bernstein's reporting in the *Washington Post* was only the beginning of the media's fascination with Watergate. Soon, other media outlets began picking up on the story and discussing it at length. Nixon began to suspect a number of government officials of being the source. Felt, in order to cover his own tracks, demanded leak investigations into the *Washington Post* stories, which had suggested that the unnamed source was a member of the FBI. A tape-recorded conversation between Nixon and Haldeman on October 19, 1972 pointed the finger at Felt, though neither man felt certain or ready to confront the FBI official. (Haldeman erroneously told Nixon that Felt was Jewish.)

Despite the *Washington Post's* persistent reporting, the Watergate story did little to upset Nixon's reelection campaign. In November 1972 he defeated the Democratic nominee, Senator George McGovern of South Dakota, in an unprecedented landslide. The affair began to loom larger in the public consciousness, however, in early 1973, when the Watergate burglars as well as Hunt and G. Gordon Liddy, the masterminds of the break-in, were convicted. In April Woodward again met with Felt, who informed him that the conspiracy went higher than just Hunt and Liddy: White House special counsel Charles Colson and Nixon's campaign chair, John Mitchell, had participated in meetings arranged to plan and cover up the break-in. He also notified them that Gray, then still in confirmation hearings with the Senate, had destroyed files from Hunt's White House safe at the behest of members of the administration. After the story was confirmed and published, Gray resigned from the FBI, on April 27, 1973. In his autobiography Felt recalled that he again had hopes of being named FBI director, only to have those hopes dashed a few hours later, when Nixon announced that William D. Ruckelshaus, the chief of the Environmental Protection Agency (EPA), would replace Gray. On April 30 Haldeman, Ehrlichman, and Attorney General Richard Kleindienst, acting on Nixon's request, resigned over the Watergate scandal. On the same day the president discharged John Dean, who had begun cooperating with the FBI investigation. In May the Senate opened hearings into the Watergate affair.

Meanwhile, at the FBI, a conflict raged between Felt and Ruckelshaus. Felt blamed Ruckelshaus for giving in to all of the White House's demands; Ruckelshaus, in turn, believed Felt was the source of the leaks, a charge Felt forcefully denied. In June, around the time that Dean was testifying before the Senate about discussing with Nixon a cover-up of the break-in, Felt retired from the FBI, though he maintained contacts within the government. (His retirement had an unintended benefit for Felt: after subsequent leaks Nixon stopped suspecting him of being the informant, believing that he no longer had access to the necessary information.) Felt's departure coincided with the revelation that President Nixon had a secret taping system in the Oval Office. In July Nixon refused to turn the tapes over to the special prosecutor or the Senate Watergate Committee, as each had requested.

After his retirement Felt met with his *Washington Post* contacts once more, in November 1973. During that meeting he revealed to Woodward and Bernstein that the Nixon tapes contained deliberate erasures. On July 24, 1974 the U.S. Supreme Court ruled that Nixon had to relinquish the tapes. Three days later Congress passed the first of three articles of impeachment against the president. Now facing charges, among them obstruction of justice, Nixon resigned, on August 9, 1974. He received a full pardon from his successor, President Gerald R. Ford, about a month later.

In 1974 Woodward and Bernstein published their book *All the President's Men*, which detailed their relationships with many of their sources, among them Felt, whom they called Deep Throat. (The name Deep Throat had been coined by Howard Simons, then the *Post's* managing editor, and was both a play on the term "deep background," used by journalists to indicate sources who cannot be directly named or quoted, and the name of a pornographic movie.) Immediately upon the publication of *All the President's Men*, the American public became intrigued by the mystery surrounding Deep Throat, which was made more tantalizing by Hal Holbrook's portrayal of the character in the same-titled film version of the book. In the years between the book's publication and Felt's 2005 revelation, there was much speculation about Deep Throat's identity. Many famous names were bandied about as possible suspects, including the CIA officials Cord Meyer Jr. and William Colby and even such high-placed government figures as Henry Kissinger, Alexander Haig, and future president George H. W. Bush.

By the time Jimmy Carter was elected president, in 1976, the country had grown weary of corruption at the highest levels of government and wanted elected leaders to follow strict rules of honesty and accountability. In that spirit Carter and Attorney General Griffin Bell pursued lawbreakers in government, partly in an attempt to show the American people that no one was above the law. In 1977 Felt and several other former FBI officials, including Edward S. Miller, were indicted on charges of having authorized illegal break-ins in the early 1970s. At that time the FBI had been pursuing members of the Weather Underground, a radical left-wing group that had planted bombs around Washington, D.C. Felt and Miller had ordered FBI agents to search the homes of family members and friends of the Weather Underground, in unsuccessful attempts to discover the group's whereabouts. Felt, who had lived quietly in the years since the Watergate affair, publicly admitted that he had ordered the break-ins, stating on the CBS television program *Face the Nation* that the searches had been justified and that he would authorize them again under the same circumstances. An ironic twist of fate came in November 1980, when former president Nixon appeared as a witness at Felt's trial. Nixon testified that he believed Felt had acted properly in his pursuit of the Weather Underground. Despite Nixon's assertions, and the support of hundreds of FBI colleagues who rallied outside the courthouse, Felt and Miller were convicted of violating the civil rights of their fellow Americans and received fines. Then, in April 1981, President Ronald Reagan pardoned Felt and Miller, asserting his belief that the two had acted in good faith in pursuing an organization hostile to the United States government.

In 1979 Felt published his little-noticed autobiography, *The FBI Pyramid from the Inside*, in which he discussed his 31-year career with the bureau and made a point of denying that he had been Deep Throat. In 1990 the widowed Felt moved from Alexandria, Virginia, to Santa Rosa, California, to live with his daughter, Joan. According to O'Connor's *Vanity Fair* article, he suffered a stroke in 2001, which impaired his mental faculties somewhat.

Though Felt had long been out of the public eye, the mystery of Deep Throat remained. In 1999 a report surfaced that Jacob Bernstein, the son of Carl Bernstein and the screenwriter Nora Ephron, had told his friend Chase Culeman-Beckman during the summer of 1988 that Felt was Deep Throat. Both Carl Bernstein and Ephron publicly denied at the time that that was true, with Bernstein maintaining that he had never told Ephron Deep Throat's identity. Felt also dismissed the allegation. Around the same time, Woodward began visiting Felt at his home and asking his daughter about his health.

According to O'Connor's article, Felt had in recent years shared his secret with his family, who urged him to reveal the truth to the public. While they believed that he had been a hero who helped to bring a corrupt administration to justice, Felt himself was more ambivalent about his acts, feeling that by going behind the backs of his superiors he had breached the FBI code of ethics. In order to help persuade him to reveal the truth, Joan Felt asked O'Connor, a California lawyer, to talk to her father. O'Connor began by offering legal advice and ultimately wrote the *Vanity Fair* story that revealed Deep Throat's identity. In the article O'Connor wrote that Felt's children, Joan and Mark, took him to a restaurant to argue their case for disclosure: "They explained that they wanted their father's legacy to be heroic and permanent, not anonymous. And beyond their main motive—posterity— they thought that there might eventually be some profit in it. 'Bob Woodward's gonna get all the glory for this, but we could make at least enough money to pay some bills, like the debt I've run up for the kids' education,' Joan recalls saying. 'Let's do it for the family.' With that, both children remember, [W. Mark Felt] finally agreed."

When the story broke, on May 31, 2005, Woodward, Bernstein, Ben Bradlee, and the current *Washington Post* management were caught by surprise. Though Woodward had been in contact with the Felt family and had even discussed revealing the secret along with them, no past or current *Post* staff members expected the revelation to come without notice. After some initial consultation and public denials, Woodward, Bernstein, Bradlee and the management of the *Post* agreed that the newspaper had been released from its obligation and acknowledged that Felt had been their secret source in the Watergate affair. "Felt's role in all this can be overstated," Bernstein told David Von Drehle for the *Washington Post* (June 1, 2005). "When we wrote the book, we didn't think his role would achieve such mythical dimensions. You see there that Felt/Deep Throat largely confirmed information we had already gotten from other sources."

Public and media reactions to the revelation of Deep Throat's identity, and judgments of Felt's actions, were split. A writer for the *Economist* (June 4, 2005) asked: "Why did Mr. Felt reveal the information? At the time of the Watergate break-in there was a power-struggle inside the FBI between new Nixon political appointees and career bureaucrats who had worked for J. Edgar Hoover and wished to uphold the agency's independence. Turning to the press was the only way that Mr. Felt could make public the information crossing his desk that pointed to corruption at the highest levels of government, yet was being culled or changed by Nixon's people. . . . Pat Buchanan, a former Nixon speechwriter, called Mr. Felt a 'snake' this week. Other men in power at the time have said that Mr. Felt should have worked through proper channels. That view is surely wrong. 'Watergate is not one thing,' Mr. Woodward once said, 'it's a mindset.' That justice was in this instance served we have Mr. Felt to thank."

Taking a different view, James Bowman argued in the *American Spectator* (June 7, 2005): "Felt did what he did and in the way that he did it because he himself was ashamed of his actions—either because he was conscious of having disreputable motives (he was said to be resentful about not getting the top job at the FBI) or just because anyone who has ever been a part of an organization like the FBI instinctively feels the shame of being thought by his colleagues to be a rat. That's obviously what he meant by saying that he had been silent for so long because of his fear that he would 'bring dishonor on his family.' For him now to have allowed himself to be browbeaten by his revolting family into thinking, quite falsely, that what he did was honorable just so that they could cash in on his fame—or notoriety—before he dies is pitiable. Yet we can't help feeling that there is also something appropriate about it. Judas only really becomes Judas when he finally accepts the 30 pieces of silver."

In his article for the *Washington Post*, Woodward wrote, "Felt believed he was protecting the bureau by finding a way, clandestine as it was, to push some of the information from the FBI interviews and files out to the public, to help build public and political pressure to make Nixon and his people answerable." Woodward's book *The Secret Man: The Story of Watergate's Deep Throat* was published in July 2005.

W. Mark Felt married Audrey Robinson, his classmate at the University of Idaho, in 1938 in Washington, D.C. Their daughter, Joan, is a professor of Spanish; their son, Mark, is an airline pilot and former lieutenant colonel in the United States Air Force. Audrey Felt died in 1984.

On June 16, 2005 the *Washington Post* reported that Felt's family had chosen PublicAffairs Books to publish a combination biography and autobiography of Felt. Felt's story was also optioned as a movie, to be developed by Playtone, the production company of the actor Tom Hanks.

—C.M.

Suggested Reading: *American Spectator* (on-line) June 7, 2005; BBC News (on-line) June 1, 2005; *Economist* p54 Apr. 15, 1978, p37 Apr. 25, 1981; *Economist* (on-line) June 4, 2005; *Newsweek* p35 Dec. 19, 1977, p35 Apr. 24, 1978, p46 Apr. 27, 1981; *Time* p81 Aug. 9, 1999, p30 June 13, 2005; *U.S. News & World Report* p11 Apr. 27, 1981, p26 June 13, 2005; *Vanity Fair* (on-line) July 2005; *Washington Post* A p1+ June 1, 2005, A p1+ June 2, 2005, C p1+ June 16, 2005, A p1+ June 20, 2005; Felt, W. Mark. *The FBI Pyramid from the Inside*, 1979; Woodward, Bob. *The Secret Man: The Story of Watergate's Deep Throat*, 2005

Selected Books: *The FBI Pyramid from the Inside*, 1979

Yoshikazu Tsuno/AFP/Getty Images

Fields, Mark

Jan. 1961– President, North and South American Divisions, and executive vice president, Ford Motor Co.

Address: Ford Motor Co., P.O. Box 685, Dearborn, MI 48126-0685

Mark Fields, a New Yorker who mastered the subtleties of Japanese culture during his nearly four years as president and chief executive officer (CEO) of Mazda Motor Corp., has served since mid-2002 as an executive with Ford Motor Co., which owns a controlling minority interest in Mazda. Fields held jobs at Ford for half a dozen years before he took the reins at Mazda, Japan's fifth-largest

carmaker, in 1999, when he was 38 years old. At the time, industry insiders expressed doubts about his capacity to pull the beleaguered company out of debt; reinforcing those misgivings was his inability to speak Japanese and his reliance on a translator at meetings at Mazda's headquarters, in Hiroshima, Japan. "When [Japanese] people look at me, they see a foreigner and a young person," Fields told Alex Taylor III for *Fortune* (May 14, 2001), during his second year as Mazda's head. "I've had to balance the process of consensus building with the need for urgency." Fields directed a restructuring of the company and worked to bring a coherent look to Mazda's vehicles; in the process he saw the firm's financial health improve significantly. "Since Mark has been at Mazda, the business has turned around dramatically," William Clay Ford Jr., the chairman of the board and CEO of Ford Motor Co., said, as quoted on the Web site PR Newswire (April 19, 2002), when he announced Fields's appointment as group vice president, Premier Automotive Group. "He has led a significant revival and repositioning of the brand and the development of a whole new generation of cars." In the spring of 2004, Fields earned a new title: executive vice president, Ford of Europe and Premier Automotive Group. Only a little more than a year later, he was promoted again, this time to the post of president of Ford's North and South American divisions.

Mark Fields was born in January 1961 in the New York City borough of Brooklyn. He worked his way through Rutgers, the state university of New Jersey, where he earned a B.A. in economics in 1983. He received an MBA from Harvard University's School of Business in 1989. In 1993, after working in marketing and sales at IBM, he began his career at Ford Motor Co., as a regional marketing manager. He was named president of Ford Argentina in 1997; the unit was rebuilding at that time, as a consequence of the ending of Ford's alliance with Volkswagen in that country. Among other responsibilities and activities, Fields oversaw the construction of two assembly lines, started production of an economy car and a pickup truck, and reorganized the company's network of dealerships in Argentina. "It was like starting a new company," he told Alex Taylor. In just 15 months he turned the debt-burdened Ford Argentina into a profitable enterprise.

In 1998 Fields left Ford Argentina to join the marketing team at Mazda, in which, in 1996, Ford had acquired 33 percent of shares and thus had taken a controlling minority stake. He became a member of the board of Mazda in 1999. As senior managing director for sales, marketing, and customer service—a title he assumed that year—Fields spent much of his time trying to improve the company's worldwide distribution networks and its brand identity; for the latter task, he teamed up with the product-development staff to try to ensure that new models fit the "personality" of the Mazda brand. On November 25, 1999 he was named representative director and executive vice president.

When Fields was named president and CEO of Mazda, on December 15, 1999, most observers were surprised, as was Fields himself. "If someone would have told me 15 months ago that I'd either be president of Mazda or the first man on Mars, I probably would have said I'd be the first man on Mars," he said, as James B. Treece reported for *Automotive News* (December 20, 1999). A month shy of his 39th birthday, Fields had become the youngest president of a Japanese car company and the youngest person in the industry to hold the title of president. Since, in Japan, greater age implies greater wisdom (and greater youth implies less wisdom), Mazda's Japanese executives were very mindful of his new status. As Fields recalled to Gary Witzenburg, when one of his new Japanese colleagues would say to him, "I have a son your age," he would reply, "I have a dad your age"—a response that, as Fields said, "kind of broke the ice."

In his new position, Fields was charged with cutting costs and increasing efficiency. Although Mazda had just recorded a profit for the first time since the early 1990s, its financial well-being was by no means assured. "There's no finish line in our business," Fields told Mark Rechtin for *Automotive News* (January 24, 2000). "Mazda has made tremendous progress, but we can't stop and declare victory. If we don't change, we'll start to deteriorate." Maintaining the approach of his predecessor, James Miller, Fields continued to aim for $1 billion in cash-flow improvements, in part by buying parts from Europe rather than Japan. He led the management team that developed Mazda's so-called Millennium Plan, a business blueprint that was made public in November 2000. In the conviction that too many Mazda models lacked the distinctive features and appearance of the Mazda brand, Fields delayed further production of vehicles so that engineers could change designs to conform to a particular brand image. For more than 12 months, including the entire fiscal year that ended on March 31, 2002, Mazda unveiled no new models. In addition to the expenses entailed in the redesigns, sales suffered; to prevent even greater losses, the company released a small number of limited-edition vehicles. Also, in March 2001, to increase customer satisfaction and reduce inventory costs, Mazda launched a trial Internet ordering system that enabled purchasers to customize their cars in certain ways before delivery—something not possible with cars awaiting buyers at dealerships.

Meanwhile, Fields had persuaded Mazda workers to accept sweeping changes. In February 2001, with the hope that its workforce in Japan would be reduced by 1,800, or 9 percent, Mazda offered employees an early-retirement package. A total of 2,213 employees took advantage of the offer, among them almost 550 workers in their 30s. In addition, the salaries of 20 percent of the firm's white-collar workers were reduced by 20 percent, while those of Fields and 24 other officials were cut by 10 percent. To try to prevent employees' morale from suffering, Fields ate lunch with Mazda factory workers once a month, to give them the opportunity to air their ideas for improving productivity and working conditions. In mid-2001 Fields announced a plan to dramatically increase the number of women in management positions at Mazda, not least because 50 percent of Mazda customers were women. Among other measures, the plan called for flexible hours and on-site day care. Fields recalled to Dorothee Ostle for *Automotive News* (June 15, 2002), "I was shocked when I first came to Japan and saw that most women in the company were relegated to menial administrative tasks." At the time, fewer than 10 percent of Mazda managers were women; if the plan meets its goals, within the next decade 30 to 35 percent will be women. (At present, women hold only about 11 percent of management positions in all Fortune 500 companies and only about 7.4 percent in Mazda's parent company, Ford.)

In January 2002 Fields anounced that Mazda intended to introduce 16 new products in Japan, 11 in North America, and nine in Europe during the period beginning in the summer of 2002 and ending in March 2005. Some analysts pointed out that another, similarly ambitious move had led to Mazda's recent financial woes—specifically, when Mazda had doubled its offerings during 18 months beginning in 1989, just as the world economy had entered a major recession. Fields countered by explaining that the company's troubles during that time stemmed in part from lack of communication between engineers and product managers, which had led to the absence of a distinct Mazda image. "Our brand strategy is matched to our product portfolio," he told Mark Rechtin for *Automotive News* (March 26, 2001). "Before, no one could tell if all those cars were Mazdas. Now, from 50 feet away, people are going to see the design cues and know it's a Mazda. . . . The cars should build on one another, rather than being points in time. I think we have one of the clearest brand-building plans in the industry." "We are the guardians of an 81-year-old Japanese company with a heritage of innovation," he also told Rechtin. "We need to revive that image." In 2001 Mazda unveiled the Atenza (Mazda 6), which it labeled "the first of our new generation of cars that fully embody the company's revitalized brand and product DNA, alongside the production design model of the unique RX-8, that heralds the return of the rotary engine in a new market proposition—a four-door sports car," as described in a company press release (April 4, 2004, on-line). The Atenza went on sale in May 2003, 11 months after Fields's departure; in November 2003 the nonprofit Automotive Researchers' & Journalists' Conference of Japan (RJC) judged it to be superior to 22 other new models in styling, handling, and comfort, among other features, and named it the car of the year.

Mazda posted an operating profit of $214.3 million for the fiscal year ending March 31, 2002, a sharp contrast to the company's net loss of $1.165 billion the previous year. "Mark Fields is responsible for a significant transformation at Mazda," Kazuhide Watanabe, Mazda's chairman, said in a company news release issued on April 19, 2002. "Our forecast record financial turnaround in 2001 is a tribute to his leadership."

In June 2002 Fields left Mazda to become group vice president of the Premier Automotive Group (PAG)—Ford's "prime thoroughbreds," as the company calls them: Volvo, Land Rover, Jaguar, and Aston Martin. According to Ford, the company oversees those brands' "sales, marketing, communications, franchise development, parts, distribution, and customer service" but not their manufacture. PAG's main office is in England; a second office is located in Irvine, California. "I'm still getting educated into luxury," Fields told Mark Rechtin for *Automotive News* (October 14, 2002). He told David Kiley for *USA Today* (Feburary 10, 2003), "It's not a question of whether we can do better; it's, 'Are we learning?'" Fields has encouraged innovation in PAG's product line; for example, he supported the development of a Volvo model designed chiefly by women, so as to attract female buyers. Although many men at the 2003 Geneva Motor Show, in Switzerland, snickered at some of the car's features—including gull-wing doors (which open vertically rather than horizontally), to enable women to get in and out of the car more easily, and fold-down rear seats to facilitate the storage of shopping bags—Fields told Mark Landler for the *New York Times* (March 6, 2004), "This is not just a token gesture. What we're really testing is a list of options." One of Fields's next challenges is to revive Jaguar's sagging image. Once considered one of the most exciting, sexy cars on the road, Jaguar has not competed successfully in recent years with more-modern sportscars outfitted with up-to-the-minute electronics. "Jaguar has passion," Fields said to Mark Rechtin for *Automotive News* (October 18, 2004), "but passion alone won't pay the bills."

By the end of his first year leading the PAG, Fields was able to report a 17 percent increase in global sales. That news prompted John Casesa, the auto analyst for Merrill Lynch in New York, to remark, according to Bradford Wernle in *Automotive News* (April 19, 2004), "If Mark can deliver in this assignment, he's got a chance of running Ford Motor Co. some day." In March 2004 Fields was promoted to executive vice president, Ford of Europe and PAG. At the 2005 Geneva Motor Show, he reported that in 2004, despite a highly competitive market, adverse exchange rates, and increases in the prices of raw materials and parts, Ford of Europe had turned a profit, and Ford had increased its share of the European market by 0.1 percent over its share in 2003, to 8.7 percent. In addition, overall customer satisfaction had increased, and Ford of Europe had succeeded in cutting costs by

$900 million, a record amount. According to a summary of Fields's presentation at the motor show, a "$1.2 billion turnaround in profitability at Ford of Europe" was partially offset by an overall loss at PAG, "although performance among the luxury brands varied widely." A box on the summary of Fields's presentation read, as posted on the Ford Web site, "Some progress made, but much still to do."

In September 2005 Ford's chief executive officer, William Clay Ford Jr, surprised industry observers by appointing Fields the head of the company's operations in North and South America—only 16 months after another executive had taken the position covering North America. According to Daniel Howes in the *Detroit News* (September 14, 2005), Fields's top priorities at his new position included reducing the costs of parts, by purchasing them from "low-cost countries," and heightening the company's brand identity among consumers. Only a few weeks after Fields's appointment, two top Ford executives resigned, opening up the company's leadership ranks and also causing some industry analysts to question whether Ford's leadership lacked adequate experience. Fields, however, seemed optimistic. According to Amy Wilson in *Automotive News* (October 17, 2005), he said in a prepared statement that he had asked the company's chief executive officer and chief operating officer "for not only the best and brightest leaders in our company, but for the kind of people who can work as one team on one agenda. That agenda is to turn around our North American operation with a team that knows how to win, an innovative product lineup that wins in the marketplace and a brand that has strong emotional appeal."

Fields is married and has two young sons. He and his wife maintain homes in Dearborn, Michigan, and London, England. In his leisure time he enjoys jogging and cycling.

—K.E.D.

Suggested Reading: *Automotive Industries* p24 Nov. 1, 2004; *Automotive News* p8 Dec. 20, 1999, with photo, p1 Jan. 24, 2000, with photo, p46 Mar. 26, 2001, with photo, p27 Apr. 29, 2002, with photo, p25 July 15, 2002, p4 Oct. 14, 2002, with photo; *Fortune* p140+ May 14, 2001, with photos; PR Newswire Apr. 19, 2002; *Time* p21 July 1, 2002, with photo; *USA Today* B p4 Feb. 10, 2003 with photos

Bruce Bennett/Getty Images

Forsberg, Peter

July 20, 1973– Hockey player

Address: Philadelphia Flyers, Wachovia Center, 3601 S. Broad St., Philadelphia, PA 19148

In 1994, when the then-21-year-old Peter Forsberg came to North America from his native Sweden to play in the National Hockey League (NHL), he was already an accomplished player—having made an impressive performance for Sweden in the World Junior Championships in 1993 and scored the gold-medal–winning point for his country in the 1994 Olympic Games. In the years since then, playing center, he has only added to his achievements. Forsberg began his NHL career by winning rookie-of-the-year honors with the Quebec Nordiques, which moved to Colorado in 1995 to become the Avalanche. He helped lead that team to two Stanley Cup victories, in 1996 and 2001, along the way winning the most-valuable-player and top-scorer awards as well as berths in five All-Star Games, three of them as a starter. In the summer of 2005, after 10 years with the Avalanche (including the lockout-eclipsed 2004-05 season), Forsberg signed a lucrative contract with the Philadelphia Flyers.

Peter Forsberg was born on July 20, 1973 in Ornskoldsvik, Sweden, a seaport city 300 miles north of Stockholm. The younger son of Kent Forsberg, a hockey coach, and Gudrun Forsberg, he grew up competing constantly with his brother, Roger, who is two years older. Both boys began playing hockey at an early age. "[Roger] was a good player, so it was pretty natural for me to follow along," he explained to Adrian Dater for the *Denver Post* (October 6, 1995). "He was better than me in everything

in the beginning, but we were pretty even after awhile." By his early teens Forsberg was better at hockey than nearly everyone else in his hometown of 60,000, where the sport was extremely popular. When he was 15 he helped his junior-league team, which was coached by his father, to win Ornskoldsvik's local hockey tournament. Forsberg attended the ice-hockey academy at Nolaskolan, a high school in Ornskoldsvik, which combined standard academic subjects with hockey instruction and regular on-ice practice. "It's great competition," he told ASAPsports.com (January 17, 1998) about the academy. "Every practice was hard. . . . It's like a war every practice. I think it helped us a lot." He entered Sweden's junior hockey league in 1989, playing for MoDo, a team named for the pulp and paper company that sponsored it; he made 15 goals and 12 assists in 30 games that season. During the 1990–91 season, when Forsberg was just 17, he began to show signs of becoming a world-class player, scoring 38 goals and making 64 assists in only 39 games. Continuing to play for MoDo, he was promoted in November 1990 to the Swedish Elite League, in which he scored seven goals and made 10 assists in 23 games. He played for Sweden in the 1991 European Junior Championships. In late 1991 his father, Kent, became coach of the MoDo team.

Despite his early successes, Forsberg planned to study economics after finishing high school rather than play hockey full-time. Though at 18 he was selected in the first round of the 1991 National Hockey League draft—sixth overall—by the Philadelphia Flyers, he chose to remain in Sweden and continue playing for MoDo, instead of moving to North America, where he might find himself relegated to the NHL's minor-league system. "I didn't feel mature enough to go and play 84 games," he told Adrian Dater, "and I just wanted to stay home. And I had school to finish there." In the 1991–92 season he scored nine goals and made 18 assists and continued his aggressive skating style, which was regarded as out of step with the less physical European style of play. "Peter always played with older guys," Kent Forsberg told Austin Murphy for *Sports Illustrated* (December 9, 1996), "and he wanted to show them he could give a hit and take a hit. Sometimes, he was a little too physical." In 1992 Forsberg played for the Swedish national team in the World Championships. Sweden won the tournament, with Forsberg contributing four goals and two assists.

In the 1992-93 season Forsberg helped MoDo reach the play-offs of the Elite League; in the regular season he had 23 goals and 24 assists in 39 games, the best showing of his career up to that time, and he added four goals and an assist in three play-off games. He won the Elite League's Most Valuable player trophy, beating Hakan Loob, an NHL veteran, for the honor. In January 1993 he participated in the World Junior Championships and astonished NHL scouts by scoring seven goals and making 24 assists over the course of the seven-game tournament, with 10 points (including goals and assists) in Sweden's 20–1 victory over Japan. (Sweden finished in second place after losing one game to Canada.) Forsberg also helped the Swedish team to win the silver medal in the 1993 World Championships. In 1993–94, his final full season with MoDo, he scored 18 goals and made 26 assists during the 39-game schedule.

In 1994 Forsberg was part of the gold-medal–winning Swedish team at that year's Olympic Games, held in Lillehammer, Norway. In eight games he made six assists and two goals, one of them in the final contest, against Canada. After the teams had played to a 2–2 tie and gone into over-time, the game was decided by a sudden-death penalty shootout. Forsberg made a goal one-on-one against the Canadian goalie, Corey Hirsch, while the Swedish goalie, Tommy Salo, blocked a shot by the Canadian forward Paul Kariya. Forsberg's goal lifted the Swedes to a 3–2 victory and added to his popularity at home. "I don't know if it made me a star, but I got pretty famous after we won," he told Brendan Hanrahan for the *Chicago Tribune* (April 18, 1995). The Forsberg-Hirsch matchup was commemorated on a Swedish postage stamp in 1995. (Hirsch's name was removed from the stamp after he protested.) A number of sportswriters commented on Forsberg's modesty during that period. "God forbid you pay Forsberg a compliment in his presence," Johnette Howard wrote for the *Washington Post* (February 16, 1994). "Suddenly he seems ready to run off and hide in a team equipment trunk." His modesty notwithstanding, the hockey luminary Wayne Gretsky—as quoted in numerous publications in the mid-1990s—called Forsberg the best young hockey player in the world.

Meanwhile, in the NHL, the Flyers had acquired the sought-after player Eric Lindros by trading several others, as well as the rights to Forsberg, to the Quebec Nordiques. After finishing the 1993–94 season with the Swedish Elite League, Forsberg headed to Quebec, having signed a three-year, $4 million contract prior to the Winter Olympics. "It's everybody's dream to play in the NHL. The older I get the more I think about that and want to be here," he told Brendan Hanrahan. "But I'm glad I stayed to play for Sweden; I don't know if I'll have that opportunity again." Forsberg's first season with the Nordiques, 1994–95, was shortened by the 104-day NHL lockout, which began in October; but in 47 games he scored 15 goals and made 35 assists, enough to capture the Calder Memorial Trophy for the best rookie performance in the NHL. To stay in shape during the NHL dispute, he appeared in 11 games in Sweden with MoDo, making five goals and nine assists during his brief stay. The Nordiques made it to the play-offs as the top seed in the Eastern Conference, but were beaten in the first round by the eighth-seeded New York Rangers.

In the summer of 1995, the Quebec Nordiques, receiving little fan support in a small market and overshadowed by the Montreal Canadiens, moved to Denver and became the Colorado Avalanche. In 1995–96, Forsberg's first full NHL season, he amassed an outstanding 116 points (30 goals and 86 assists), the fifth-highest total in the NHL. Even so, some expressed the wish that he would score more goals rather than making assists. In his interview with Brendan Hanrahan, Forsberg said, "I try to be a goal scorer, but it's easier to pass the puck." The Avalanche's then-coach, Marc Crawford, had a different explanation for Forsberg's style of play, telling Michael Farber for *Sports Illustrated* (June 17, 1996), "He's one of those people who think shooting is like cheating." Pushed to score more goals, Forsberg had his first NHL hat trick (three goals in one game) on February 11, 1996. He was selected to play in the 1996 NHL All-Star Game. In the play-offs, during which the Avalanche faced and defeated Vancouver, Chicago, and Detroit to emerge as the Western Conference champions, Forsberg scored 10 goals. Pitted against the less experienced Florida Panthers in the Stanley Cup Finals, Colorado won handily, finishing the best-of-seven series in a four-game sweep. The 1996–97 season saw Forsberg team with the center Joe Sakic for a potent offensive line; Forsberg scored 28 goals and made 58 assists during 65 games of the regular season. (He missed approximately three weeks of the regular season, as well as the opportunity to play in the 1997 NHL All-Star Game, due to a leg injury.) In 14 games of the play-offs, Forsberg contributed five goals and 12 assists; Colorado beat Chicago and Edmonton in the preliminary rounds before falling to perennial power Detroit in the Western Conference finals. Early in 1997 Forsberg signed a new three-year contract with the Avalanche, worth $12.8 million.

During the 1997–98 season Forsberg had 25 goals and 66 assists over 72 games. In the 1998 NHL All-Star Game, he was elected to his first start, and he kept busy during the NHL's Olympic break, skating with the Swedish national team at the 1998 Winter Games, in Nagano, Japan. (The Swedish team, who had won the gold in 1994, had a disappointing tournament, playing four games and ending their run with a loss to Finland.) In the spring of 1998, the Avalanche appeared in the play-offs for the third time in as many seasons. They were eliminated in the first round by the Edmonton Oilers in a seven-game contest, in which Forsberg contributed six goals and five assists. Forsberg made a second appearance that year as a member of the Swedish national team, helping his fellow players, who were coached by his father, to victory over Finland in the World Championships.

Forsberg continued his outstanding play in his fifth NHL season, 1998–99, racking up 30 goals and 67 assists for 97 points and leading Colorado in scoring. He was named a starter in the NHL All-Star Game for the second straight year. He saved his best performances for the play-offs, however, accumulating 24 points (eight goals and 16 assists) in only 19 games. "I like the play-offs," he told Michael Farber for *Sports Illustrated* (June 3, 2002). "It's all about the hockey, winning the Stanley Cup. Yes, you play as hard as you can in the regular season, but the playoffs are when it really counts, when you have to be really good." Seeded second in the Western Conference, the Avalanche defeated San Jose and Detroit before succumbing to Dallas, the eventual Stanley Cup champions, in the Western Conference Finals. Forsberg was out for 23 games in the 1999–2000 year after undergoing shoulder surgery and missed the All-Star Game due to a concussion. Still, he made 14 goals and 37 assists in the 49 games he played and was again a powerhouse in the play-offs, scoring seven goals and adding eight assists, as the Avalanche defeated Phoenix and Detroit before falling to the Dallas Stars in the Western Conference Finals.

In the 2000-01 season Forsberg's numbers were consistent with those of previous years—27 goals and 62 assists in 73 games—and he was elected to start in the 2001 NHL All-Star Game. The Avalanche began the play-offs with a four-game sweep of Vancouver, then moved on to defeat the Los Angeles Kings in seven games. During those 11 games Forsberg had four goals and 10 assists. Colorado faced the St. Louis Blues without him; a hit in Game Seven against the Kings caused Forsberg's spleen to rupture, necessitating emergency surgery. He was benched for the remainder of the play-offs, in which the Avalanche defeated the Blues to win the Western Conference title and then beat the New Jersey Devils to win their second Stanley Cup in six seasons. After recuperating from his injuries, Forsberg asked for a leave of absence, so that he could return to form and allow his chronically injured ankles to heal. "I'm not retiring . . . ," he said in a news conference, as reported by the *Washington Post* (September 16, 2001). "I just feel that right now, in my current frame of mind, I can't go out and play at the level I expect out of myself. Over the last few years, the numerous injuries and recent surgeries made me come to this decision. I think I need to sit back and listen to my body." He planned to return to the ice in January 2002, until an examination revealed a damaged tendon in his foot. Following surgery, he sat out for the rest of the 2001–02 regular season. He was able to participate in the 2002 play-offs, however, and returned to the rough-and-tumble playing style he had cultivated during his career. "I had a few injuries throughout my career, but I think it's the way hockey is played nowadays. You have to play physical every game," he told Kevin Allen for *USA Today* (May 22, 2002). "You go out and play as hard as you can, and if injury happens, it happens." Forsberg had his best showing in the play-offs up to that time, amassing 27 points in 20 games. In his June 3, 2002 *Sports Illustrated* article, Michael Farber noted: "Forsberg, who has never scored more than 30 goals in any of his seven regular seasons, qualifies as the top playoff performer among active NHL players with at least 100 postseason games." Nonetheless, after defeating the Kings and the Sharks, the Avalanche lost to Detroit in the Western Conference Finals, in a mara-

thon contest in which several of the seven games went into overtime. In the weeks following the end of the 2002 season, Forsberg signed a one-year, $9.5 million contract extension.

For the 2002–03 regular season, Forsberg led the NHL in points, with 106 (29 goals and 77 assists). The Avalanche made it to the play-offs, losing in seven games to the Minnesota Wild. Forsberg took home that year's Hart Trophy, given to the NHL's most valuable player, as well as the Art Ross Trophy, presented to the league's top scorer. That season he was also selected once again as a starter in the All-Star Game. Plagued with injuries in 2003–04, Forsberg fell short of his stats from the previous year, playing in only 39 games for 18 goals and 37 assists; the Avalanche made it past round one of the play-offs, besting the Dallas Stars in five games, only to fall to the San Jose Sharks in six. Forsberg helped the Swedish national team to win a silver medal at the 2004 World Championships, held in Prague, in the Czech Republic, and also represented Sweden in that year's World Cup of Hockey. With the 2004–05 NHL season canceled by the 301-day lockout, Forsberg returned to Sweden to play again for MoDo, until he was sidelined once more by physical problems, including a concussion (his fourth over the course of his career) and a wrist ailment that required surgery.

In early August 2005 Bob Clarke, the general manager of the Philadelphia Flyers (the team that had drafted Forsberg in 1991), learned that Forsberg had not re-signed with Colorado, which had salary caps for the team. Clarke immediately contacted Forsberg's agent with an offer of a two-year, $11.5 million contract, and the hockey star accepted the deal. "I wanted to go to the East Coast because it would be more respectful to Colorado," Forsberg said, as quoted by Michael Farber in *Sports Illustrated* (August 22, 2005). "I didn't want to have to play against them. Plus Clarkie wants to win. And the team is tough. It's good having big guys on your side."

Forsberg divides his time between Sweden and the U.S. He enjoys fishing and playing golf, particularly in the midnight sun of a Swedish summer.

—K.S.

Suggested Reading: *Chicago Tribune* VII p7 Apr. 18, 1995, with photo; *Sports Illustrated* p108 Feb. 7, 1994, with photo, p50+ Dec. 9, 1996, with photos, p52 Aug. 22, 2005, with photos; *Washington Post* F p7 Feb. 16, 1994, with photo

Courtesy of Sprint Nextel

Forsee, Gary D.

Apr. 10, 1950– Telecommunications executive

Address: Sprint Nextel Corp., 2001 Edmund Halley Dr., Reston, VA 20191

Over the past two decades, Gary D. Forsee has emerged as one of the most sought-after executives in the telecommunications industry. He served as the chairman and chief executive officer (CEO) of the Sprint Corp. until August 2005, when the company's merger with the wireless telephone carrier Nextel Communications became official. Sprint and Nextel, whose combined worth is estimated at $35 billion, now form the third-largest wireless carrier in the United States, with more than 39 million customers in their combined subscriber bases; only Cingular, which in October 2004 acquired AT&T Wireless, and Verizon have more wireless subscribers than the newly formed Sprint Nextel—which is the country's largest wireless company with no ties to a traditional phone-service provider. Foresee is president and CEO of the combined company.

As many have noted, Forsee's advice and leadership are prized in his field in part because he is perhaps uniquely experienced with all three of the industry's major services: long-distance, local, and wireless. "He's the full package," John Hodulik, a telecommunications analyst with UBS Warburg, told the *New York Times* (May 26, 2003). Prior to accepting Sprint's top position, in March 2003, Forsee served as vice chairman of BellSouth Corp., where he was responsible for all of that company's domestic operations; in addition, he was chairman of Cingular, then a wireless subsidiary BellSouth

operated with SBC Communications. Regarded as a decisive, goal-driven manager, Forsee has risen to the top of his field through a philosophy of team-building and a belief in seeking and valuing the counsel of those working under him.

Readily available sources reveal little about the early years of Gary D. Forsee, who was born on April 10, 1950 in Kansas City, Missouri. He graduated from the University of Missouri at Rolla (UMR) in 1972 with a bachelor's degree in civil engineering. He has described the curriculum at UMR as difficult and has said that his studies there prepared him for the demands he would face later in life. He told the *UMR News* (January 28, 2004, on-line): "Sometimes I wish I'd have worked harder, looking back at some of those challenges. But I think the campus life prepared you to understand how important working with teams is." While in college Forsee joined the Kappa Sigma fraternity, which "really helped me understand the importance of getting along with people, a big group of people who are diverse in their backgrounds," he told the *UMR News*. "Also, from the leadership standpoint, [I learned] how to make that diverse group of people work together for a common interest." Also during college he worked as a civil engineer for the Missouri State Highway Department, and during his junior and senior years, he interned with Procter & Gamble in Cape Girardeau, Missouri, at a plant where the company made Charmin tissue paper. "As a result of those experiences, I focused my energy, when I was looking for places to work after college . . . on companies giving me a broad-based use of the engineering discipline," he told the *UMR News*.

In 1972 Forsee joined the Southwestern Bell telephone company and participated in its management training program; Southwestern Bell was one of several arms of the AT&T–owned Bell telephone company, which, together, provided local service to most of the U.S. In 1980 Forsee moved to AT&T. In an agreement with the United States Department of Justice, in 1984 AT&T divested itself of the Bell operating companies, which formed seven separate businesses. Forsee remained with AT&T, where in 1987 he was named vice president in charge of the company's $12 billion, Washington, D.C.–based FTS-2000 program, a long-distance telecommunications service for the U.S. federal government. Toward the end of 1989, Forsee accepted a similar position at Sprint, which was running the FTS-2000 network jointly with AT&T. AT&T then sought a temporary restraining order from a federal judge in Virginia to stop Forsee from joining Sprint, arguing that Forsee would inevitably disclose its trade secrets to Sprint if the move was allowed. The judge denied the restraining order, and within weeks Forsee had joined Sprint.

Sprint's roots can be traced back more than 100 years, to the town of Abilene, Kansas, where a small manual switchboard company, United Telecom, was founded in 1899 by Cleyson L. Brown and his father, Jacob Brown. United Telecom made it possible for homes in the surrounding rural areas to be connected with Western Union or the town hall. The Brown Telephone Co., as United Telecom was soon called, installed its first long-distance circuit in 1900. By the late 1920s the company, then known as United Telephone and Electric, had operations in Kansas, Pennsylvania, Indiana, Ohio, and Illinois. By the 1950s the company—United Utilities at that time—had become the second-largest non-Bell telephone company in the U.S. Its domestic long-distance service was launched in 1986, by which time the company was known as Sprint.

Upon joining Sprint, Forsee was named a vice president of the company and president of its government-systems division. Shortly before his arrival, the company had won the authority to bid for 40 percent of a 10-year, $25 billion federal contract; two years later Sprint acquired 53 percent of the government's business, edging out AT&T. In 1991 Forsee was named president of Sprint's business-services group. From 1995 to 1998 he served as Sprint's interim chief executive for the company's venture into wireless service. In 1995 he led Sprint and its cable partners in a purchase of personal communications service (PCS) wireless licenses in 29 major markets, which together were valued at $2.1 billion and remain one of Sprint's most valuable assets. (Through PCS, mobile-phone users' signals are picked up by local antennae and linked to the wired network; PCS reportedly allows greater user mobility than does cellular service.) Later that same year, Forsee was named president and chief operating officer (COO) of Sprint's long-distance unit, which then accounted for most of the company's revenues; Sprint's long-distance profits later outpaced those of AT&T and MCI. Television commercials featuring the actress Candice Bergen during those years had made Sprint known to most Americans.

In February 1998 Forsee was appointed by Sprint to bring profitability to Global One, which had been formed in January 1996 by Sprint, France Telecom (FT), and Deutsche Telekom (DT) to provide communication services to companies that do business globally. Working in Brussels, Belgium, Forsee replaced Viesturs Vucins as president of Global One, which, despite having increased its profits to $1.1 billion in the years before Forsee took over, had grown more slowly than predicted. While Forsee himself was able to boost profits during his year in the position, the venture soon failed. Nonetheless, Forsee "was very well liked and very well respected by Sprint employees and by DT and FT employees," a former Global One employee explained to Suzanne King for the *Kansas City Star* (April 1, 2003).

Forsee left Sprint in 1999 to become chief staff officer at the BellSouth corporation. In 2000 he was promoted to vice chairman of BellSouth and president and chief executive officer of BellSouth International. In the latter post Forsee oversaw the company's digital wireless and voice-data services, which at the time operated in 11 countries in Latin America. In its January 1, 2002 edition, *Foreign Policy* reported that the company's affiliates in Colombia, Ecuador, Peru, and Venezuela had together averaged a 46 percent annual customer growth over a five-year period. "That growth is mainly a reflection of three key factors," Forsee explained to *Foreign Policy*. "First, low landline penetration, which often resulted from insufficient facilities; second, a regulatory framework known as 'Calling Party Pays,' whereby the person who makes the call to or from a cellular number pays for the call. This eliminated the burden on the cellular subscriber of having to pay for incoming calls, which has been a deterrent to growth in 'Mobile Party Pays' environments, such as the United States; and third, the launch and subsequent popularity of prepaid service, which opened new market segments by making cellular more affordable to lower income levels. In fact, prepaid has been the main driver for customer growth in Colombia and Venezuela."

In October 2001 BellSouth named Forsee vice chairman for domestic operations, a move that seemed to signal, according to some observers, that BellSouth was grooming him to become the company's next chief executive officer. In the new position Forsee oversaw BellSouth's domestic advertising, customer markets, network services, and regulatory affairs. By that time Forsee was also serving as BellSouth's chairman of Cingular Wireless, then the nation's second-largest mobile-phone company, based in Atlanta, Georgia. BellSouth owned 40 percent of Cingular Wireless; the remaining 60 percent was owned by SBC Communications.

Less than a year after Forsee's promotion within BellSouth, Sprint offered him a position as its chairman and chief executive officer. The offer from Sprint set off an extended legal battle between the two telecommunications giants. For its part, Sprint was looking to replace its COO and CEO—Ronald T. LeMay and William T. Esrey, respectively—who each generated national headlines when an independent board revealed that they had created personal tax shelters to avoid paying taxes on more than $100 million each in stock-option gains. In early 2003 both LeMay and Esrey were asked by Sprint's board to step down from their positions. "At the time," Yuki Noguchi wrote for the *Washington Post* (June 6, 2005), "Sprint was in desperate need of leadership that knew its business, and nearly every division of the company's operations was in disarray. Customers were unhappy with its cellular-phone service and its long-distance business was in rapid decline." Adding to the complications surrounding Forsee's possible defection to Sprint, his contract with BellSouth mandated that he not work for a competitor for 18 months after leaving the company. BellSouth argued, as quoted by the *Fulton County Daily Report* (March 7, 2003), that Forsee's move to Sprint "would be like the

CEO of Coca-Cola defecting to PepsiCo, taking with him the company's marketing strategies and secret product formula." Soon after learning of Forsee's intentions, BellSouth won a temporary restraining order that prevented Forsee from taking the job at Sprint. In addition, BellSouth sued Sprint in Georgia state court, claiming that Sprint's hiring of Forsee would breach the non-compete clauses in his contract and would inevitably result in BellSouth's professional secrets being revealed.

On March 18, 2003 a court-appointed arbitrator, William H. Webster, ruled that Forsee could rejoin Sprint, but placed restrictions on his hiring. To protect BellSouth, Webster prohibited Forsee from discussing mergers or sales of Sprint's assets for a 12-month period. In addition, Forsee was barred for the same duration from planning strategy for marketing combinations of wireless and land-line services in regions served by BellSouth. "I certainly didn't go into the process [of joining Sprint] with the understanding that it would have turned into the kind of feeding frenzy of the press at that point in time," Forsee told *UMR News*. "First of all, BellSouth is a great company. I had a very good three years there and worked with a lot of fine people. Sprint had a . . . very complicated and unfortunate circumstance that caused the board to conclude that they had to go outside for their next CEO. They looked at my familiarity [with the company]. . . . I had a pretty good familiarity with the board, so I guess from their standpoint there was a comfort level with me. . . . So it was one of those things that was a good match."

In December 2004 Sprint and Nextel Communications announced a merger that was valued at approximately $35 billion. The deal, which became official in August 2005, makes Sprint Nextel the nation's largest independent wireless carrier. Sprint further redefined its long-term future in June 2005, when Forsee announced that the company was focusing its energy on its wireless division and moving its corporate headquarters from Overland Park, Kansas, to Reston, Virginia. As part of the company's new strategy, Sprint-Nextel will align itself with cable companies to market "a megabundle of entertainment and communications services," according to the *Washington Post*, including "Internet-based phone service, high-speed Internet connections, and television, music and entertainment viewable on a cellular phone." "We had to think about whether we wanted our number one and number two competitors to be twice as big as us," Forsee explained to Noguchi about the impetus for the Sprint-Nextel merger. "At the same time, our strategy was to be an enabler of the cable companies." As of late 2005, Sprint-Nextel planned to shed Sprint's local telephone operations. Forsee indicated that he expected Sprint-Nextel's new wireless division to generate most of the company's income.

The business press and others have depicted Forsee as a subdued but focused leader. Noguchi observed that Forsee "speaks in a friendly but businesslike manner, breezing past jokes or small talk to get to the point." Forsee described for *UMR News* what he sees as requirements for leadership: "First, you have to be able to understand the issues. . . . There is no substitute for being able to go deep on issues and at the same time be able to understand which things are important. So prioritization is very important. There are so many things going on in any company, so many issues—certainly in a company as broad as Sprint—that you could drown trying to cover all those. So understanding what all the priorities are and being sure the plans are put in place to focus on those is very important. Probably another aspect of my style is focus. Having a clear agenda and putting that in motion and staying on point for that agenda is [an] important part of a manager's leadership style." "He's got a good style about him; people respect him and he gives respect back to people," Timothy M. Donahue, chief executive of Nextel and executive chairman of the combined company, told Yuki Noguchi about Forsee. "He doesn't motivate with a stick and we share the desire to be number one."

In May 2004 Forsee was appointed by President George W. Bush to the National Security Telecommunications Advisory Committee (NSTAC), a group of up to 30 communications, technology, finance, and aerospace industry chief executives. The NSTAC addresses a wide range of policy and technical issues. Forsee also serves on the board of directors of the Goodyear Tire & Rubber Co. and previously served as the chairman of the national board of trustees for the March of Dimes. He currently serves on the University of Missouri-Rolla board of trustees and is a member of the Business Roundtable, through which he is active in such groups as the Committee to Encourage Corporate Philanthropy and the Kansas City Civic Council. With his wife, Sherry, he has two adult children, Melanie and Kara.

—D.F.

Suggested Reading: *Fulton County Daily Report* Mar. 7, 2003; *Kansas City Star* D p1 Apr. 1, 2003, with photo; *New York Times* C p1 May 26, 2003, with photo; *New York Times* (on-line) Dec. 15, 2004; Sprint Corp. Web site; University of Missouri–Rolla *News* Web site, with photo; *Washington Post* D p1 June 6, 2005

Catherine Eldridge

Fortey, Richard

Feb. 15, 1946– Paleontologist; science writer

*Address: Department of Palaeontology, The
Natural History Museum, Cromwell Road,
London SW7 5BD, England*

"I wish to charm and cajole readers into sharing the
same delight with natural history . . . that has sustained me for a lifetime," the British-born paleontologist and science writer Richard Fortey told an
interviewer for *Something About the Author*
(2000). Judging from comments about his books by
laypeople as well as from reviews by professionals
in scientific journals and large-circulation newspapers and magazines, Fortey has often seen his wish
come true. As Christine Barker wrote for the *Birmingham (England) Post* (June 24, 2000), his books
"draw unbridled praise from the scientists and the
ordinary reader alike. He has the rare talent to turn
history that goes back more than half a billion years
into something special and exciting for the computer age." In a critique of Fortey's most recent
book, *Earth: An Intimate History*, for *American
Scientist* (July/August 2005), for example, the paleontologist Michael Novacek, a curator at the
American Museum of Natural History, wrote, "If
Fortey's narrative has a fault, it's that it left me
wanting more. . . . Fortey tells a story of the Earth
that is scientific, poetic . . . and certainly passionate. The book is a fitting tribute to our restless
home." In an assessment for *Science* (June 18,
2004, on-line), the University of Houston geologist
Kevin Burke noted that Fortey has "an easy familiarity with history, literature, art, and anthropology" as well as with earth science, that his writing

is both "elegant and entertaining," and that he "has
gifts for the happy phrase and the unexpected vision." Similarly, *Earth: An Intimate History* inspired Anton G. Hardy, a psychologist, to charac-
terize it for Amazon.com as "an ode to the imagination, flowing equally into scientific and literary
channels." "Endlessly instructive regarding the geology of the earth, it is also a pure literary delight,"
Hardy declared. "Fortey rivals such other nature
writers as [Henry David] Thoreau and [John] Muir
in his ability to depict nature in a manner that
weds descriptive power with evocative expression." And in an assessment of Fortey's book *Trilobite! Eyewitness to Evolution*, Marina Benjamin
wrote for the London *Evening Standard* (June 12,
2000), "Fortey's books are always a treat. It's not
just that they are beautifully written. . . . Unlike
some of his peers, Fortey doesn't believe in evolutionary science's swagger and strut. What he
values more than science's claims to truth is the
honest scientist and the kinship he feels with colleagues and predecessors dead and alive. His vision is wonderfully humane. And you can't say
that for many science writers."

Fortey has worked since 1970 at the Natural History Museum in London, England, where he is currently a senior paleontologist and merit researcher.
He has identified dozens of trilobites previously
unknown to science. In 1996 the Geological Society of London, Great Britain's national society for
geosciences, honored Fortey with the Lyell Medal,
which recognizes people "who have made a significant contribution to [the geological sciences] by
means of a substantial body of research," according
to the society's Web site. In addition to *Earth* and
Trilobite!, Fortey has written such books of popular science as *Fossils: The Key to the Past*; *Dinosaurs' Alphabet*, a collection of poems for children;
*The Hidden Landscape: A Journey into the Geolog-
ical Past*; and *Life: An Unauthorized Biography*. In
2005 Rockefeller University, in New York City, a
center for basic scientific research, awarded Fortey
the 2004 Lewis Thomas Prize for his books and
other writings. "If I could write a science book with
the gripping power of a novel," Fortey told an interviewer for *American Scientist* (November 19,
2004, on-line), "I would regard my life as well
spent."

Richard A. Fortey was born on February 15,
1946 to Frank A. Fortey and the former Margaret
Wilshin in London, England. He grew up in the
London borough of Ealing. His father was an avid
and skilled avocational fly-fisherman who fished
as often as he could, usually with young Richard
in tow. "Most of my childhood was spent wandering round on riverbanks," Fortey recalled to Marek
Kohn for the London *Independent* (February 27,
2004, on-line). His father, he told Kohn, "was a
very good naturalist, because fly-fishermen have to
be." "What [my father] gave me, I think," he said,
"was an awareness of the interconnectedness of
things" in nature. From an early age Fortey, too, became enamored of natural history. "I was one of

those small children who was a natural natural historian, so I went through various phases, as children do, starting with birds, then flowers, and then I got into fungi," he told an interviewer for HarperCollins.com. Fortey attended the Ealing Grammar School for Boys. He has traced his career choice in part to a trip he took with his class to London's Natural History Museum, where he learned, much to his delight, that some of the museum's employees worked with fossils full-time. Another influence was a book of essays called *Possible Worlds*, by the great science writer J.B.S. Haldane, who was among the first to merge aspects of genetics, evolutionary biology, and morphology (the study of the form and structure of organisms). The "spirit of experimental adventure" in that book, Fortey wrote in *Trilobite!*, encouraged him "to speculate upon the many mysteries of the world, and how unravelling one or two small ones might be the best thing to do with a life."

One day when Fortey was 14, while searching for fossils in rocks along the coast of Wales, he came across a fossilized trilobite—his first such find. In a very rare bit of luck, the rock in which the trilobite was embedded, as Fortey wrote in *Trilobite!*, "simply parted around the animal, like some sort of revelation. . . . I was left holding two pieces of rock. . . . Surely what I held was the textbook come alive. . . . The long thin eyes of the trilobite regarded me and I returned the gaze. More compelling than any pair of blue eyes, there was a shiver of recognition across 500 million years." As he progressed into his teens, Fortey wrote in *Trilobite!*, "while others discovered girls, I discovered trilobites." By his own account, he felt an "immediate affinity" with the fossilized creatures and became "enthralled" by them. Trilobites began to flourish beginning about 542 million years ago, during the geological period known as the Cambrian. Crustacean-like animals with no direct contemporary descendants (their closest living relative is the horseshoe crab), they became extremely diversified, with some 15,000 species ranging in length from under a millimeter to more than a foot and a half. Many species had eyes; unique in the animal kingdom then as well as now, their eyes were composed of multiple "elongate prisms," in Fortey's words, made of crystallized calcite, a common mineral that usually has many impurities but in the trilobites' lenses was clear. The last trilobites died out during the Permian period, some 300 million years after the first of them appeared on the planet. (By comparison, the dinosaurs survived for about 160 million years before the last ones perished, about 65 million years ago. As far as is known, Homo sapiens—the scientific name for modern human beings—have probably populated Earth for fewer than 200,000 years, a fraction of 1 percent of the duration of the trilobites' reign on our planet.)

In about 1964 Fortey entered King's College, a division of Cambridge University, in England. As an undergraduate, in 1967, he searched for fossils in Spitsbergen, a Norwegian archipelago that lies north of the Arctic Circle. In *Trilobite!*, he wrote that he spent most of his two months on Spitsbergen "bashing hard rocks with a geological hammer, until they were in small pieces on which fragments of trilobite could be seen. . . . I loved it. All discomfort in the harsh climate was set aside in the inspiriting warmth of discovery." Fortuitously, as he told the interviewer for HarperCollins, "whole new series of fossils were being quarried" at that time, and they later became the subject of his Ph.D. thesis. Back at Cambridge, in the university's Sedgwick Museum, Fortey spent many months manipulating a tool called a percussion needle, painstakingly removing the rock in which the trilobites— or, far more commonly, trilobite fragments—were embedded. Fortey earned a B.A. degree in geology in 1968. He then entered Cambridge's graduate program in paleontology, where his adviser was the eminent invertebrate paleontologist Harry Whittington, a world expert on trilobites. Fortey earned an M.A. degree in 1970; that same year he began working as a research fellow at the Natural History Museum. He earned a Ph.D. in 1971. In 1973 he was promoted to senior scientific officer at the museum; in 1978, to principal scientific officer; in 1986, to senior principal scientific officer, and in 1991, to merit researcher. Currently, he also holds the title of senior paleontologist.

According to Marek Kohn, it is obvious that Fortey "writes for love of writing." For a decade after he began his professional life, Fortey confined his writing mostly to the preparation of papers for scientific journals. He also wrote poetry (which, according to Kohn, he tried in vain to get published in a Cambridge University magazine) and two books of humor, both of which were published in 1981: *The Roderick Masters Book of Money-Making Schemes*, for which he used the name in the title as his pseudonym, and *Not Another Cube Book!* (written in response to the brief craze generated by Rubik's cube, a three-dimensional puzzle), which he co-wrote under the name W. C. Bindweed.

In 1982 the Natural History Museum published Fortey's book *Fossils: The Key to the Past*; in the U.S. the book appeared in the same year under the imprint of the scientific publisher Van Nostrand Reinhold. (In 1991 Harvard University Press published the second edition of *Fossils*, and in 2002 the Smithsonian Institution Press published the third.) But according to Kohn, it was not until Fortey was commissioned to write a book about the geology of Great Britain that he discovered his forte as an author. *The Hidden Landscape: A Journey into the Geological Past* (1993), written for laypeople in his spare time, describes the connections between the flora of the British Isles and the underlying rocks, and, with the author in the role of an entertaining guide and companion on a virtual field trip, shows how landscape can illuminate geological history. In 1993 the Wildlife Trusts, a British umbrella organization, named *The Hidden Land-*

scape the Natural World Book of the Year. Later, in his book *Trilobite!*, Fortey wrote, "The truth of the artist can recombine the facts of the world in the service of creation, but the scientist has a different duty, to discover the truth lying behind the façade of appearance. Both processes may be equally imaginative." He also wrote that the literature of science "never really goes out of date. . . . When new discoveries are made, we re-write historical 'facts.' The job of the paleontologist is to reinvent the past. There could be no task more demanding of the scientific imagination."

Referring to the subtitle of his next book, *Life: An Unauthorized Biography* (1997), Fortey told a reporter for the London *Independent* (August 1, 1997), "Any biography is an interpretation. What we think of as the truth about someone changes over time. . . . The complexity of life's story is such that it allows for an infinite variety of tellings." The way that Fortey chose to tell it in *Life* appealed greatly to Andrew H. Knoll, a professor of natural history at Harvard University, who wrote in a review of the book for *Nature* (August 21, 1997) that Fortey "authoritatively serves up the facts that lend substance to scientific debate about evolution, but in doing so he never loses sight of the fact that the evolutionary history assembled from fossils and comparative biology remains a story, and a darn good one at that. The result is the best account of life's history that I know, an engaging narrative that succeeds as literature as well as science." Fortey's history of life on Earth, Knoll continued, "is nearly eclipsed by a second narrative woven contrapuntally about the first. Fortey's subsidiary theme concerns palaeontology as a way of knowing, illustrated honestly, and sometimes hilariously, by scenes from the life of Richard Fortey, palaeontologist." Knoll concluded, "Perhaps the greatest pleasure of reading Fortey's book is provided by the prose itself. His style is conversational, literate, and relaxed. . . . A page that begins with the biology of sponges might proceed to a rumination on the use of animal names as insults . . . and end with an attempt to rehabilitate the epithet 'slime.' Patience is rewarded—as often as not Fortey's digressions fold back on the main narrative to reveal it from a new perspective." In the *Boston Globe* (April 12, 1998), the science writer Chet Raymo declared that *Life* is "capacious, jammed with marvelous treasures, and thoroughly Victorian in its wide-eyed wonder at the diversity and prodigiousness of life." Published with the subtitle *A Natural History of the First Four Billion Years of Life on Earth* in 1998, *Life* was shortlisted for the Rhône Poulenc Science Book Prize. It was named one of the 10 best books of 1998 by the editors of the *New York Times Book Review*.

Fortey chose *Eyewitness to Evolution* as the subtitle of his next book, *Trilobite!* (2000), because those long-extinct marine invertebrates were present (and thus could be thought of as silent observers) during most of the Paleozoic era (543 million to 248 million years ago), which en-

compassed six geologic periods, beginning with the Cambrian and ending with the Permian. At the beginning of the Paleozoic, there were six major continental land masses on Earth, all concentrated in the Southern Hemisphere. During the next 295 million years, as the continents drifted closer together, the diversity of multicelled animals increased stupendously, and plants and fungi made their appearances. By the end of the Paleozoic, the planet's land masses had fused into a supercontinent known as Pangaea, and approximately 90 percent of the species of plants and animals that had existed—among them the trilobites—had become extinct. (The fossil record indicates that five mass extinctions have occurred on Earth.) As Allison R. Palmer wrote for *Science* (October 6, 2000, on-line) in her laudatory review of Fortey's book, "Trilobites surpass the dinosaurs in their contribution to evolutionary theory. They were abundant, they were taxonomically and morphologically diverse, and their communities changed rapidly throughout their . . . history. Their fossil record provides evidence of evolutionary continuity . . . [and provides] key evidence to show the original continuity of now widely separated parts of [the Paleozoic] world." She also wrote that the book "is written with style, humor, and a distinctly British accent that add to its charm. . . . The personal joys and hazards of collecting around the world are evoked with elegant descriptions of collecting sites that would be the envy of any travel writer." In the London *Times* (June 7, 2000), the artist and marine-science specialist Richard Ellis wrote of *Trilobite!*, "This is the way science should be written: so engagingly that it makes you forget that you're actually learning something, and carrying you swiftly from page to page so that before you know it, . . . you're at the end, where the 'suggested reading' list shows you that Fortey has read practically everything about trilobites so that he could condense it here for you." The BBC shortlisted *Trilobite!* for its Samuel Johnson Prize for nonfiction in 2001.

Fortey's *Earth: An Intimate History* (2004) was shortlisted for the Aventis Prize for Science Books General Prize. (That award is managed by the Royal Society, Great Britain's national academy of science.) In *Canadian Geographic* (May/June 2005), Marq de Villiers included *Earth* among his choices of "the most influential green books of the past decade." "The single-sentence blurb on the back cover of my edition says that 'this book will change the way you view the world—permanently,' and for once, I think it is literally true," de Villiers wrote. "It is not so much that Fortey is an amiable guide to the planet or that he writes as well as some of the best travel writers or that he has managed to make the discipline of paleogeology exciting, a heroic accomplishment. It is his long timeline that is so vertiginous. He shows us the world far beyond the busy scurryings of humans, with their messy ways, and even far beyond our most distant protozoan ancestors. He demonstrates how restless the planet itself is, how mutable the mountain chains, how changeable the continents, how the seas come and go in endless cycles as the planet's crust writhes and contorts. . . . Fortey's great achievement is that he shows how everything—life itself, the most ancient of human cultures, the most current of civilizations—is all ultimately dependent on processes which go on deep beneath our feet. . . . *Earth* gives us a window into a world that otherwise we see only through fissures and vents, earthquakes and the rumblings of volcanoes."

In reviews of books by others, Fortey has written about the toll that the activities of humans is taking on Earth's environments and their flora and fauna. "The story of man's dominion over nature and his subsequent abuse of power cannot be told too often," he wrote in a critique for the *New York Times Book Review* (August 9, 1998) of *Life in the Balance: Humanity and the Biodiversity Crisis*, by Niles Eldredge. In the same piece he wrote, "There is hardly any part of the world that has avoided degradation. For now manunkind (as E. E. Cummings called him) carries destruction of habitat and extinction of species to every wilderness." In a review for the London *Times* (October 23, 2004) of Richard Ellis's books *The Empty Ocean* and *No Turning Back: The Life and Death of Animal Species*, Fortey wrote, "If we carry on as we are, it cannot be much longer before the ocean, two thirds of the planet, becomes a biological desert. . . . Everybody ought to be aware of the 'sixth mass extinction'—an extinction as great as when the dinosaurs died out—the one that our own, prolific species is inflicting on a world that has taken four billion years to evolve."

In 1968 Fortey married Bridget Elizabeth Thomas, with whom he had one son, Dominic; the couple divorced in 1975. From his second marriage, in 1977, to Jacqueline Francis, he has two daughters—Rebecca and Julia—and a son, Leo. The family lives in Henley-on-Thames, from which Fortey commutes to his job at the Natural History Museum. His recreational interests include writing poetry and humorous pieces and studying fungi.

—R.E.

Suggested Reading: *Contemporary Authors Online*, 2004; HarperCollins Web site; (London) *Independent* (on-line) Feb. 27, 2004; (London) *Times Higher Education Supplement* p22+ Mar. 5, 2004; Fortey, Richard. *Trilobite! Eyewitness to Evolution*, 2000; *Something About the Author* Vol. 109, 2000

Selected Books: *Fossils: The Key to the Past*, 1982; *The Dinosaur's Alphabet*, 1990; *The Hidden Landscape: A Journey into the Geological Past*, 1993; *Life: A Natural History of the First Four Billion Years of Life on Earth*, 1998; *Trilobite! Eyewitness to Evolution*, 2000; *The Earth: An Intimate History*, 2004; as co-editor: *Arthropod Relationships* (with Richard H. Thomas), 1997

Courtesy of Virgin Atlantic GlobalFlyer

Fossett, Steve

Apr. 22, 1944– Businessman; adventurer

Address: c/o Brian Spaeth, Marathon Racing Inc./Steve Fossett Challenges, 401 S. La Salle, Suite 200, Chicago, IL 60605

"What a day!" Steve Fossett exclaimed, according to PR Newswire (February 6, 2003), after he and his co-pilot made the first nonmilitary airplane flight across North America to be completed in less than three hours. Such days are not rare for Fossett: during the past several decades, he has broken many world records for speed and distance, traveling by balloon, plane, boat, and even on foot. In 2002 he attracted international attention when he became the first person ever to circumnavigate Earth solo in a hot-air balloon. In March 2005 he accomplished what he termed a "major ambition"— becoming the first person to fly around the world in an airplane alone and without refueling. In his custom-built jet, the *Virgin Atlantic GlobalFlyer*, Fossett circled the planet in 67 hours; he kept alert by drinking a dozen chocolate diet shakes and taking catnaps lasting only one to three minutes. "Believe me, it's great to be back on the ground," Fossett told reporters after emerging from the *GlobalFlyer*'s cramped cockpit, as quoted by John Milburn for the Associated Press (March 4, 2005). "It's one of the hardest things I've ever done."

Fossett made his fortune as a commodities trader before embarking on a life of adventure. He is renowned in the world of speed sailing: between 1993 and 2004 he set 23 official world records in sailing (13 of which still stand). He has competed in the 1,100-mile Iditarod (Alaska's famous dogsled race), France's 24-hour Le Mans sportscar race, and Hawaii's Ironman Triathalon, and he has climbed six of the world's tallest peaks. "The things I do are things that a lot of people would like to do," Fossett told a writer for *21st Century Online* (June 21, 2001). "So I go out and take on an interesting project, like driving a race car or swimming the English Channel. What's unusual is that I actually go out and do them." "Business is much easier for me," Fossett told Jim Spencer for the *Chicago Tribune* (August 24, 1987). "Sports is often very humiliating, because there are so many better athletes in these events. I would like to be the best in everything, but that's not possible. I risk humiliation because I have a genuine interest in participating." In 1998 *Penthouse* dubbed him "The Most Extreme Man on Earth," but Fossett has insisted that to label him "extreme" is "nonsense," as he put it to Charles Laurence for *Saga* (March 2005, on-line). "Riding roller-coasters? Bungee jumping? I am not the least bit interested in thrill-seeking. I am not drawn to risk—I do an enormous amount of planning to reduce the risks." He added, "I don't participate in a sport for pleasure. . . . I do it to achieve something. I take considerable pride in being licensed to pilot a jet solo. And I take pride in being able to deal with the solitude when I have to—14 days alone up there on the solo balloon record—but there's no pleasure in flying a balloon. Oh no, there is not."

J. Stephen Fossett was born on April 22, 1944 to Charalee and Dick Fossett. Some sources list his birthplace as Jackson, Tennessee. He grew up with an older brother and a younger sister in Garden Grove, California, where his father worked for Procter & Gamble. As a child he was fascinated by such great explorers as Fridtjof Nansen and Ernest Shackleton, famous for their daring attempts to reach the North and South Poles, respectively, and Edmund Hillary, who in 1953 became the first man from the Western world to reach the peak of Mount Everest. Fossett has traced the development of his adventuresomeness and ambition to his early involvement with the Boy Scouts. "I learnt my values in the Boy Scouts, and I am proud of that," he told Charles Laurence. "I went right through the Scouts when I was growing up. . . . It was in the Scouts that I climbed my first mountain, and where I learnt my leadership skills between the ages of 11 and 18."

In 1966 Fossett earned a bachelor's degree in economics and philosophy from Stanford University, in California. After his graduation he traveled to Turkey to swim the Dardanelles (the narrow strait between Asiatic Turkey and Europe), in the tradition of Lord Byron and the mythological Greek hero Leander. After he returned to the United States, he enrolled at Washington University, in St. Louis, Missouri, where he received a master's degree in business administration.

For the next few years, Fossett worked as a commodities broker in Chicago, Illinois. He soon set up his own brokerage firm, which grew rapidly. In 1980 he formed Lakota Trading, an options-trading firm, whose profits made him a multimillionaire. Once his business was firmly established, Fossett set out to fulfill many of his childhood fantasies. He drove on the Formula-Atlantic racecar circuit, trained with the U.S. Olympic luge team, skied cross-country, and ran in the 26-mile Boston Marathon. In 1985, after four abortive attempts, he swam across the English Channel, from England to France, in 22 hours (the record for the slowest swim across that waterway that year, according to some sources). During the last five hours, he battled a rough current, and when he reached the shore of France, he was barely conscious, hoarse from the effects of the salt water, and on the verge of hypothermia.

In 1992 Fossett competed in the Iditarod, finishing 47th. In 1993 he drove a Porsche in the Le Mans race. He also made two separate unsuccessful attempts to scale Mount Everest. In January 1994 he received a hot-air-balloon pilot's license; he spent most of the next decade breaking various speed and distance records in hot-air balloons. In August 1994 he became the first person to cross the Atlantic Ocean solo in a balloon, sailing from St. John's Island, Canada, to Hamburg, Germany.

By February 1995 Fossett had added to his record book the first solo balloon flight across the Pacific Ocean: about five days after departing from Seoul, South Korea, he had touched down in a field outside Leader, in western Saskatchewan, Canada. (He had planned to land in San Francisco, California, but winds took him off course.) The flight, which covered 5,435 statute miles (the same as miles on land, as opposed to nautical miles, which measure air as well as ocean travel), also broke the solo-balloonist distance record by more than 200 miles. While piloting the gondola, Fossett had had to endure temperatures as low as 10 degrees Fahrenheit below zero, because shortly after takeoff, his two propane heaters had stopped functioning. In addition, a burner (used to heat the air that keeps the balloon aloft) had failed during his first night out, and his balloon had started to lose altitude. In reigniting the burner, he had spilled some fuel, which had caught on fire and partially burned the balloon. "There was quite a lot that went wrong on this flight," he told a reporter for the Associated Press, as reprinted in the *New York Times* (February 26, 1995). Referring to the people who had helped him prepare for the flight, he added, "We were out on the edge of the technology. We were trying new things."

In January 1996 Fossett announced his intention to become the first balloonist to journey solo around Earth, in a combination hot-air and gas balloon called the *Solo Challenger*. He tried without success five times. In an interview with the reporter John Larson for the television program *Dateline NBC* (August 21, 1998), he described what occurred during the fourth attempt, in August 1998, as "the worst circumstance I could ever conceive of . . . in a balloon." After surviving a freak electrical fire early on in the flight that burned half his face, Fossett hit a vicious hailstorm two-thirds of the way into his journey. He told Larson, "With all this fire and ice, it was . . . a vision of hell." Then, when he was at an altitude of 29,000 feet, lightning struck his balloon, piercing the fabric and causing the craft to plummet at a speed of 2,500 feet (more than a third of a mile) per minute. "At first when the balloon ruptured . . . ," Fossett recalled to Jon Jeter for the *Washington Post* (August 18, 1998), "my first reaction was disappointment that I wasn't going to fly around the world, and then as I continued my descent, I realized that I was much more concerned about just living." Desperate to slow his craft's fall, Fossett decreased its weight by cutting the fuel tanks loose. Fully expecting to die, he lay down on his bunk, where he blacked out. He regained consciousness moments later to find his capsule on fire and rapidly filling with water. He quickly boarded a life raft, taking only his satellite rescue beacon with him. He spent the next 20 hours alone, without food or fresh water, floating in the Coral Sea, whose denizens include great white sharks, which are among the world's deadliest predators. The captain of the only sailing vessel close enough to respond to his distress signal turned out to be the Australian adventurer Laurie Piper, who was piloting a private yacht called the *Atlanta* in his own attempt to circumnavigate the globe. Fossett's raft had drifted into relatively shallow water; Piper risked the safety of his boat to rescue Fossett.

Despite that sobering experience, and after briefly considering giving up adventuring, in December 1998 Fossett teamed up with two of his former competitors in ballooning, Richard Branson of Great Britain (the founder of Virgin Records and Virgin Atlantic Airways) and Per Lindstrand of Sweden, in another attempt to achieve a first for humans: skippering a balloon nonstop around the world. The trio made it about half way, from Morocco to Hawaii, a distance of about 12,500 miles, but were forced down by bad weather. They planned to make a second attempt, but in 1999 the Swiss pilot Bertrand Piccard and the British ballooning instructor Brian Jones beat them to it, circling the globe in 20 days. Fossett then turned his attention to other pursuits, most notably sailing. By 1999 he had already distinguished himself as a speed sailor; he had set 14 sailing records since 1993, when he rounded Ireland in the record time of 44 hours and 42 minutes. In January 2001, sponsored by Sony, Fossett joined "The Race," a new around-the-world sailing competition that, unlike such others as the Volvo Ocean Race or the Vendée Globe, placed no specifications on the type of boat allowed. Fossett sailed in the world's biggest ocean-racing catamaran (a two-hulled watercraft), christened *PlayStation* (named for Sony's popular video-game system). Although he was one of the favorites to win, problems with the 125-foot *PlayStation*'s sails that he encountered early on forced him to withdraw from the race after two weeks.

In August 2001 Fossett attempted another around-the-world solo balloon flight—his fifth. The trip ended prematurely, when weak winds led to a crash-landing, and his balloon was dragged along the ground for more than a mile near Espantoso, Brazil. "I knew I was going to go through isolated thunderstorms, but it turned out to be a minefield of thunderstorms," Fossett recalled to Anthony Faiola for the *Washington Post* (August 18, 2001).

The next year Fossett tried again. "I suppose I had confidence in [my] other flights and I believed we were well prepared, but this time they've solved all the problems we've had in previous flights," Fossett said from the launch site of his sixth attempt, in Northam, Australia, according to Rob Griffith for the Associated Press (June 19, 2002). Sponsored by the beer company Anheuser-Busch (which backed all of his ballooning endeavors from 2002 to 2004), Fossett set off in *Spirit of Freedom* at 9:37 a.m. on June 19, 2002. By June 22 he was right on course, cruising at slightly more than 60 miles per hour at an altitude of 23,300 feet. Moving over the South Pacific, he picked up speed, to 78 miles per hour, and rose higher, to an altitude of 24,500 feet. By June 27, greatly aided by a favorable jet stream, he was traveling toward South Africa at 113 miles per hour and was more than halfway to his goal. When his journey was almost complete, Piccard and Jones congratulated him. "We are very excited that this time seems to be the good one," Piccard told Fossett, as quoted by Rob Griffith for the Associated Press (July 2, 2002). "And we hope the next 24 hours will allow you to fulfill your dream." On July 3, 2002 Fossett crossed his starting point, thus becoming the first person to fly around the world alone in a balloon. He touched down in Queensland, Australia, after being in the air for 13 days, eight hours, and 33 minutes. The total distance covered was 20,626 miles. "It's an enormous relief and satisfaction," he said in an interview aired on CNN (July 2, 2002) while still in his gondola, after reaching his goal. "I've put everything into this, all of my efforts, all of my skills, I have taken the risks associated with this over this long period of time, and finally after six flights . . . I've succeeded."

Ballooning nonstop for days on end can be extremely difficult. Because his capsule was unpressurized, Fossett had to wear an oxygen mask at all times; the device was so uncomfortable that unless he was totally exhausted, sleep eluded him. Moreover, he barely had enough room in the cramped capsule to stretch out. "It's been a progression of preparation," Fossett said on CNN about his many attempts to circle the globe. "We never appreciated how difficult it was to fly a balloon around the world solo. When I started off on this, I thought . . . maybe I might not make it the first time, but surely the second time. But then we realized that there's quite a lot of equipment that my team had to develop, basically invent. There's many more pitfalls than we had ever imagined."

For his next endeavor, just weeks later, Fossett planned to fly a modified glider from a mountain in New Zealand into Earth's upper atmosphere, more than 62,000 feet above the planet. "I'd like to hold the altitude record in gliders, which is already 49,000 feet," he told a CNN.com (July 4, 2002) interviewer. "But this also has a very genuine scientific purpose, and that's a bonus to be able to go for a record and make a contribution to the science of aeronautics at the same time." Fossett's first attempt to accomplish that goal, in August 2002, ended in failure.

Fossett next turned his attention back to the water, reclaiming his sailing record around Britain and Ireland, set in 1994 and broken by Britain's Tracy Edwards earlier in 2002. Sailing in the *Playstation*, Fossett cut a total of 55 minutes off Edwards's time. In February 2003, again in the *Playstation*, Fossett broke the east to west transatlantic sailing record, crossing from Cadiz, Spain, to the island of San Salvador, in the Bahamas, in nine days and 12 hours.

In 2004 Fossett joined another around-the-world sailing competition, the Jules Verne Trophy race, named for the 19th-century novelist who wrote the classic adventure story *Around the World in Eighty Days*. Nicknamed by some "Phileas Fossett" after Phileas Fogg, the protagonist of Verne's book, Fossett hoped to better the existing record, set by the Frenchman Bruno Peyron in 2002, of 64 days, eight hours, 37 minutes, and 24 seconds. "If we pull this off, I will be a very satisfied person to have achieved my main objective in sailing," he remarked, as quoted by Edward Gorman and Maurice Chittenden in the London *Sunday Times* (April 4, 2004). "It's a daunting endeavor. You have a less than 50-50 chance of getting the boat around the world. You might lose a mast in the Southern Ocean, which two previous attempts have done." On April 5 Fossett and his 12-person crew accomplished their mission in the catamaran *Cheyenne* (the former *PlayStation*), circling the globe in 58 days, nine hours, 32 minutes, and 45 seconds. "Everybody on this crew is absolutely delighted, this is a satisfying moment for all of us," Fossett said of the achievement, according to the Agence France Presse (April 6, 2004). Fossett's win was not officially recognized by the Jules Verne Trophy organization, however, as he had refused to pay the membership fee of 25,000 euros, about $18,000 (plus 12,000 euros annually). His record is nevertheless acknowledged by the World Sailing Speed Record Council. Fossett subsequently announced that he was ending his 11-year career in sailing, having achieved all his goals and set almost two dozen world records. "The round-the-world record has fulfilled my highest ambition in sailing," Fossett said, as quoted by the Agence France Presse (April 23, 2004). "It just seems like the right time to stop. It has been an exciting—and very fulfilling—11 years. . . . My mind is on aviation projects right now."

Next, in March 2005, Fossett set two records simultaneously: those for the fastest nonstop, non-refueled circumnavigation of the world in an aircraft and the first ever by a solo pilot. Richard Branson and Virgin Atlantic Airways financed the project for an undisclosed sum. Fossett's jet, the *Virgin Atlantic GlobalFlyer*, was crafted by Burt Rutan, the celebrated designer of the *Voyager*, which in 1986 became the first plane to circle Earth without stopping or refueling. The *GlobalFlyer*, propelled by a single jet engine, was built to carry about 18,000 pounds of fuel, an amount that would equal 80 percent of the aircraft's total weight. Branson and Fossett launched a Web site, virginatlanticglobalflyer.com, that allowed users to read about the experimental aircraft and to track Fossett's flight in real time. During the flight the site registered millions of visitors; public interest swelled on the second day, when mission control discovered that 2,600 pounds of fuel had mysteriously disappeared sometime earlier in the flight, forcing Fossett to consider abandoning his goal. As he approached Hawaii he decided to push ahead, and favorable tail winds helped to carry him over the Pacific. He landed in Salina, Kansas, where he had departed 67 hours, two minutes, and 38 seconds earlier. (The American pilot Wiley Post made the first solo around-the-world trip in 1933, taking almost eight days and stopping several times. *Voyager*, which carried two pilots, had taken nine days, three minutes, and 44 seconds.) A crowd of about 5,000 had gathered to welcome Fossett, who was in good spirits despite his fatigue; Branson offered congratulations and doused him with a bottle of champagne.

In July 2005 Fossett announced that in early 2006, in a solo voyage in the *Globalflyer*, he would attempt to break the world's distance record (29,000 miles) for a plane flying nonstop. Fossett's endeavor was again to be financed by Richard Branson. "Both pilot and plane will be tested well beyond any previous flight in history," Branson told the Associated Press (July 29, 2005), "and if successful will set a record that I suspect will never be exceeded."

Fossett retains his goal of breaking the world altitude record in a glider. Since 2002 he has broken several other gliding records, including one for duration (he remained aloft for more than eight hours in December 2002) and another for speed (in July 2003). In February 2003 he made two record-setting flights in one day, breaking the speed records for both a nonmilitary jet and for an unlimited turbo-prop aircraft.

Fossett is the president of Larkspur Securities, a Chicago-based investments company. He is a trustee of Washington University and was a recipient of the John M. Olin School of Business Distinguished Alumni Award in 1995. He serves on the national executive board of Boy Scouts of America and is a fellow of both the Royal Geographic Society and the Explorers Club. The gondola in which Fossett made his solo balloon flight in 2002 is in the collection of the National Air and Space Museum, a division of the Smithsonian Institution, in Washington, D.C.

According to Rich Roberts in yachtracing.com (February 2002), "Despite his wealth and achievements, Fossett is soft-spoken, unassuming and easily lost in a crowd." He and his wife, the former Peggy Viehland, were married in about 1968; they do not have children. The couple maintain homes in Chicago; Beaver Creek, Colorado; and Carmel, California. Speaking of his wife, Fossett told Charles Laurence, "I think she would like it if I just stayed home."

—C.M./R.E.

Suggested Reading: Associated Press June 19, 2002, June 27, 2002; *Australian* p5 July 4, 2002; BBC News (on-line) July 1, 2002; *Chicago Tribune* V p1 Aug. 24, 1987; CNN.com July 4, 2002; stevefossett.com

Frank Micelotta/Getty Images

Foxx, Jamie

Dec. 13, 1967– Actor; comedian; singer

Address: c/o William Morris Agency, One Morris Pl., Beverly Hills, CA 90212

In 2005 Jamie Foxx earned two Academy Award nominations: as best actor, for his depiction of the legendary singer Ray Charles in the highly acclaimed motion picture *Ray*, and as best supporting actor, for his portrayal of a cab driver in the crime drama *Collateral*, starring Tom Cruise. He thus became only the 10th person to be nominated in two categories in the same year. At the awards ceremony, held on February 20, 2005, Foxx won the Oscar for his work in *Ray*. That honor and others secured his status as a dramatic actor—one of the few who began their careers as comedians. Foxx got his start in stand-up comedy in the 1990s. On the strength of his side-splitting impressions of celebrities and political figures, he landed a job on the popular comedy show *In Living Color*. After starring on TV in *The Jamie Foxx Show* and appearing in *Booty Call* (1997) and other light-hearted silver-screen comedies, Foxx began to attract attention with his handling of serious roles: that of an ambitious young quarterback in Oliver Stone's *Any Given Sunday* (1999), and the troubled sidekick of the boxer Muhammad Ali, in *Ali* (2001). In a review of *Ray* for the *New York Times* (October 29, 2004), A. O. Scott wrote of Foxx, "That this erstwhile comedian possessed formidable acting chops was evident even back in the days of *In Living Color*, but it was not always clear how far he would go in developing them. It's clear now."

Foxx is well known in Hollywood for being an insatiable party animal; at the same time, his fellow actors have noted that on the set he is nothing short of professional. "I do my best work with someone who's giving more than 100 percent," Tom Cruise told Allison Samuels for *Newsweek* (August 2, 2004). "Jamie had a commitment that just forces you to go there too." Foxx is renowned for his ability to mimic anyone—a skill that was obvious in *Ray*, and one that he has claimed to use in other films to get into character. "Most comedians are brilliant men and women," Regina King, Foxx's co-star in *Ray*, told Clarissa Cruz for *Entertainment Weekly* (January 7, 2005). "So I was not surprised by the brilliance, but I was floored by his respect for the craft. When [we were] shooting, Jamie was nowhere in sight. I was working with Ray Charles. Seriously." In his review of the film, A. O. Scott observed, "There is much more than mimicry at work here. In his best big-screen performances . . . Mr. Foxx has displayed an intriguing blend of quick-wittedness, bravado and sensitivity, and his recognition of those qualities in Ray Charles is the key to his performance. You get the sense that he is not just pretending to be Ray Charles, but that he understands him completely and knows how to communicate this understanding through every word and gesture, without explaining a thing."

Jamie Foxx was born Eric Bishop on December 13, 1967 in Terrell, Texas, a small town about 30 miles east of Dallas. His parents, Louise Annette Dixon and Darrell Bishop, a stockbroker, divorced shortly after he was born. (His father later changed his name to Shaheed Abdulah, when he converted to Islam.) When he was seven months old, his mother's adoptive parents, Mark and Estelle Marie Talley, adopted Foxx as well. "Legally my mother is my sister, because the lady who adopted her in turn adopted me," Foxx explained to Michael Leshnov for *Jet* (March 24, 1997). Although his parents lived nearby, they had little contact with the boy. Estelle Marie Talley, whom he called Granny, nurtured Foxx lovingly but firmly. "[She] raised me to be a southern gentleman," Foxx told William Booth for the *Washington Post* (August 6, 2004). "We weren't rich, but we weren't poor either. Money didn't matter, couldn't replace the summers we had." Foxx's grandmother arranged for him to start taking piano lessons when he was about five. "I used to think she was a total killjoy," Foxx told Lola Ogunnaike for the *New York Times* (September 12, 2004). "I'd be like, 'Granny, everybody's going to Six Flags [an amusement park] this weekend.'" To which she would reply, "Well, you ain't." Thanks to that discipline, Foxx's pianistic skills increased quickly, and soon he was playing at his Baptist church on Sundays. In time he became a music director at another church, earning $75 a week—money that his grandmother made sure he saved. "She instilled in me the belief that I could do anything I wanted," Foxx told a reporter in 1991, as quoted by Joyce Sáenz Harris in the *Dallas Morning News* (February 27, 2005). "That failure isn't part of the equation. I live by that."

Foxx was successful academically and participated in various sports in school. He was a member of the Boy Scouts and served as the starting quarterback for Terrell High School's football team. Inspired by Prince and other musicians, he formed a band called Leather and Lace, with whom he sang. "We were hor-ri-ble," he recalled to Ogunnaike. In 1986 Foxx won a full scholarship to the United States International University (now known as the Alliant International University), in San Diego, California, where he studied classical piano and music theory.

In 1989 (some sources say 1990), while Foxx was at an open-mic night at a comedy club in Los Angeles, his girlfriend dared him to get on stage and perform; he easily won the crowd over with his impressions of such figures as Mike Tyson, Bill Cosby, and Ronald Reagan. Shortly thereafter, buoyed by his success, he dropped out of college and moved to Los Angeles, hoping to make a career as an entertainer. He began working in a shoestore during the day and, sporadically, as a stand-up comic at night. After about six months he quit his day job, to pursue his goal in show business full-time.

There were far fewer female than male performers at the comedy clubs where Foxx would try to get gigs. Referring to the lists on which all the hopeful comics would note their names each night, Foxx recalled to Michael Leshnov that the club managers "had to put all the girls on [stage] who were on the list to break up the monotony." Foxx began writing gender-neutral pseudonyms on the lists, knowing that names that seemed feminine were more apt to be noticed than an obviously male moniker like "Eric." "So when they look up and they see Tracey Green, Tracey Brown, all these unisex names I had written on the list, they picked Jamie Foxx," he recalled to Leshnov. "'Is she here?'

And I said, 'Yeah, brother, right over here man.'" After that, the name stuck.

In 1991 Foxx won the Black Bay Area Comedy Competition. That accomplishment enabled him to get an audition for the TV variety show *In Living Color*, which was created by and starred Keenan Ivory Wayans. From among more than 100 other actors who auditioned, Foxx was chosen. In addition to various impressions that he presented on the series, Foxx created the character Wanda, the Ugly Woman; dressed in drag, Foxx/Wanda would chase unsuspecting men, spouting "Haayy" or "I'll rock your world!," both of which became catch phrases. Foxx has credited *In Living Color* with launching his career. "I learned from [Wayans] that a black man can be successful," he told Alan Hughes for *Black Enterprise* (December 2004). "But I also learned from him that we have to be the best at what we do. If you're mediocre, they won't buy it." Foxx remained on the show until its cancellation, in 1994. During that period he also appeared frequently on the sitcom *Roc*, in the role of Crazy George.

Foxx had moved to California with the intention of becoming a singer. ("I was gonna be Lionel Richie," he told William Booth. "I had the hair and everything.") In 1994 he released an R&B album, *Peep This*, for which he wrote and produced the songs, sang, and played the piano. In a tour that he undertook to promote *Peep This*, Foxx offered both music and comedy. The tour got positive reviews, and the album debuted at number 12 on *Billboard*'s R&B chart.

Foxx next landed a television deal with the Warner Bros. (WB) network to star in his own program. *The Jamie Foxx Show* premiered in the fall of 1996, with Foxx playing Jamie King, a character who, much like Foxx, was a young man from Texas determined to make a name for himself as an actor in Los Angeles. The show became the WB's highest-rated series in 1996–97. It ran for five seasons, despite some critics' complaints about its crass humor and off-color dialogue.

Meanwhile, Foxx was building a film career. In 1996 he had a supporting role in *The Truth About Cats and Dogs* and appeared briefly in *The Great White Hype*. He starred in *Booty Call* (1997), a raunchy comedy that follows the sexual escapades of two couples over the course of a mishap-filled evening. In a review for the *Cincinnati Enquirer* (February 28, 1997, on-line), Margaret A. McGurk called the film "low-brow, earthy, profane, crude, shameless, sexist, irreverent, and, as it happens, pretty darn funny." According to an undated assessment for E! Online, *Booty Call* was "jam-packed with so many stereotypes, its screenwriters deserve some kind of painful award. . . . Some funny bits can't rescue what is otherwise a really bad movie, though the cast, led by comic Jamie Foxx, is extremely likable and often rises above the material." The movie, which was a modest box-office success, struck representatives of the National Association for the Advancement of Colored

People (NAACP) as offensive to African-Americans; the comedian Bill Cosby also publicly voiced disapproval of it. "There is no need for a *Booty Call*, for the stuff that shows our young people only interested in the flesh and no other depth," Cosby told Allison Samuels for *Newsweek* (March 17, 1997). He also criticized some of the African-American sitcoms on the WB network. In an interview with Neil Gladstone for the *Philadelphia City Paper* (December 25, 1997–January 1, 1998, on-line), Foxx said that he had spoken with Cosby about his complaints. "[Cosby] had good things to say and I understood where he was coming from," he told Gladstone. "But it did get under my skin a bit when he went to *Newsweek* before telling me. He didn't have to single out *Booty Call*; there were a million movies that came out [that were just as bad], but he decided to pick on that one because it was a little successful. . . . Cosby had good points: one should strive to do better things. At the same time you've got to take what you can get to get to where you want to go."

Foxx surprised many critics and filmgoers alike when he took on a serious role, that of the quarterback Willie Beaman in Oliver Stone's football drama *Any Given Sunday*, which also featured Al Pacino and Cameron Diaz. "I had very strong instincts about him right away, from the moment I met him," Stone told Soren Baker for the *Los Angeles Times* (December 25, 1999). "When Jamie appeared, it was clear as a bell that he had that quality that I was looking for in a quarterback: anger. There was an anger there, but it was leveled by humor. He was so prepared, he really is a worker and he came to the set every day prepared. He came through for me big time." In his interview with William Booth, however, Foxx recalled that Stone had expressed strong displeasure during his initial audition: "Stone is listening, then tells me I'm reading for the wrong part, tells me I can't act, that I'm a slave to TV, my acting is too broad, like I'm trying to fill in the spaces. He tells me stop acting. You're coming off as a comic." At Stone's request, Foxx made a video of himself playing football; according to Foxx, the tape convinced Stone that Foxx was right for the role. Although *Any Given Sunday* disappointed most critics, many spoke highly of Foxx's performance. Stephen Holden, in an otherwise negative review for the *New York Times* (December 22, 1999), wrote, "The movie's revelation is Mr. Foxx's Willie, who gracefully embodies the internal conflicts of a talented, insecure athlete. . . . It's a subtle performance in a movie that has nothing else subtle about it."

After starring in the largely ignored action-comedy *Bait* (2000), Foxx snared a coveted role in Michael Mann's biographical film *Ali* (2001), that of Drew "Bundini" Brown, the self-destructive cornerman for the legendary boxer Muhammad Ali (portrayed by Will Smith). Along with Ali's story, the movie depicted Bundini's struggles with alcohol and drug abuse. Mann cast Foxx because, as he told Nick Charles for *Savoy* (March 2002), he

thought the actor "could get to the depth of Bundini's despondency." Mann added, "I believed [Foxx] had the courage to bring himself to that extreme of desolation and degradation." Critics lauded Foxx's performance but their responses to the picture were lukewarm.

Foxx's busiest year to date came in 2004, when he was seen in several films that revealed the breadth and depth of his acting abilities. In the romantic comedy *Breakin' All the Rules*, written and directed by Daniel Taplitz, he played the hero, Quincy Watson, who, after his girlfriend drops him, writes a best-selling book offering advice for men who want to end relationships. In a representative review, Owen Gleiberman wrote for *Entertainment Weekly* (May 21, 2004), "The rules of good screenwriting are mostly broken, though Jamie Foxx's smash-and-grab charisma remains intact." Also that year Foxx starred in the made-for-television movie *Redemption: The Stan Tookie Williams Story*, about the founder of the Crips, a notorious Los Angeles street gang. After being sentenced to death for murder, Williams wrote a series of books designed to inspire children to steer clear of gangs. In a review for the Film Threat Web site, Tim Merrill described Foxx's performance as a "model of subtlety and strength." Robert P. Laurence wrote for the *San Diego Union-Tribune* (April 9, 2004, on-line), "The presence of Jamie Foxx, heretofore known primarily as a comic, . . . makes *Redemption* all the more interesting. But his frank, understated performance as Williams offers far more than novelty appeal. Easily worthy of an Emmy nomination, it establishes Foxx as a serious actor to reckon with."

Collateral, directed by Michael Mann, was the third film in which Foxx appeared in 2004. His portrayal of a nervous taxi driver who is forced to ferry a hitman (Tom Cruise) impressed critics, particularly those who had still thought of him as a comedian. In a review for CriticDoctor.com, for example, Peter Sobczynski wrote that "the real surprise . . . is the performance of Jamie Foxx as Max; although Mann got some interesting work out of him in *Ali*, he has spent most of his career appearing in horribly schticky comedies. . . . Here, he effortlessly nails the role of Max without ever appearing to be straining to be serious in the way that some comedians do when they attempt to play straight." Similarly, Roger Ebert wrote for the *Chicago Sun-Times* (August 6, 2004, on-line), "Foxx's work is a revelation. I've thought of him in terms of comedy, . . . but here he steps into a dramatic lead and is always convincing and involving. Now I'm looking forward to his playing Ray Charles; before, I wasn't so sure."

Foxx's portrayal of the title character of *Ray*, directed by Taylor Hackford, more than met Ebert's expectations. "Jamie Foxx suggests the complexities of Ray Charles in a great, exuberant performance . . . ," Ebert wrote for the *Chicago Sun-Times* (October 29, 2004, on-line). "Foxx so accurately reflects my own images and memories of

Charles that I abandoned thoughts of how much 'like' Charles he was and just accepted him as Charles, and got on with the story." Similarly, Joe Baltake wrote for the *Sacramento Bee* (October 29, 2004), "There's a moment, relatively early in the film, when Foxx gets so carried away by his own sound that he triumphantly throws back his head, flashes that trademark Ray Charles smile and playfully, giddily hugs himself. At that point, Jamie Foxx becomes Ray Charles."

Following Charles into his early 30s, *Ray* shows his struggles with heroin addiction, his notorious womanizing, and his development as a musician. Charles, who died in June 2004, had approved the screenplay and had lent his support to the project. He also assessed Foxx's musicianship in a sort of audition. "I met Ray and he was like, 'Oh, let me check these fingers out. Oh, you got strong fingers, oh yeah,'" Foxx recalled to Darryl Sterdan for the Ontario, Canada, *London Free Press* (November 2, 2004). "So then we sit down at dual pianos—he's playing one piano, I'm playing another. And we're singing the blues. He says, 'If you can sing the blues, Jamie, you can do anything.'" Then, when Charles began playing a complicated piece of music by the jazz pianist Thelonious Monk, Foxx "hit a wrong note. And he stopped and said, 'Now why the hell did you do that?' And he wasn't laughing. He said, 'The notes are right underneath your fingers; you just have to take time out to find them, young man.'" In the end Foxx played the piece properly. "After I got the Thelonious Monk riff, he was like, 'There it is, that's what I'm talking about.' When I finally got it, he jumped up and he slapped his thighs and he said, 'The kid's got it,' and he walked out. That's when I knew I had the role."

Foxx played the piano in the film while lip-synching the vocals to recordings made by Charles. To prepare for the role of Charles, who became blind as a boy, Foxx wore a prosthetic over his eyes during filming, rendering him sightless for 14 hours at a time. "The first two weeks, I panicked like anything. I felt claustrophobic all the time," he told Brooke Williamson for the Sydney, Australia, *Daily Telegraph* (March 1, 2005). After about six hours, he explained, "you lose the sense of how a person is physically. It was amazing to hear the little buzzing voices all around you." Foxx also shed more than 30 pounds, to look like the slimmer Charles. "It's tough when you're eating really good," he joked to Ogunnaike. "There was a period of about four days when I was like, 'What the hell is going on with my body and my mind?'"

Foxx received an unprecedented three nominations for Golden Globe Awards in 2004, and another three for Screen Actors Guild Awards, for his performances in *Ray*, *Collateral*, and *Redemption*. (In both cases he won for *Ray*.) Winning the Oscar for best actor at the Academy Awards ceremony made him the third African-American in history (after Sidney Poitier and Denzel Washington) to receive that honor. In an emotional speech Foxx gave special thanks to his recently deceased grandmoth-

er, whom he described as his first acting teacher. "She told me to stand up straight," he said, as quoted by many sources. "Put your shoulders back. Act like you got some sense."

Foxx starred in the poorly received *Stealth* (2005), a film about a maniacal computer-controlled jet fighter. Roger Ebert, in the *Chicago Sun-Times* (July 28, 2005, on-line), called the film "an offense against taste, intelligence, and the noise pollution code," while Jeremy Wheeler wrote for *All Movie Guide* (on-line), "Jamie Foxx sounds like he's still caught in Ray Charles-mode as he wraps his head around dialogue that's not quite cocky, serious, or even vaguely interesting for that matter." Foxx was cast in a major role in *Jarhead*, scheduled to be released in November 2005, and is set to star in both *Dreamgirls* and *Miami Vice* in 2006. He sang on the rapper Twista's 2004 radio single "Slow Jamz," which also featured Kanye West. His second album, *Unpredictable*, was to be released in December 2005.

Foxx lives in Tarzana, California, near Los Angeles. He is single—and likely to remain so, as he joked to Pamela K. Johnson for *Essence* (November 2004): "I'd be a great husband—in another world." He has an 11-year-old daughter, Corinne, who lives with her mother a few blocks from his house, and he spends as much time as possible with her. He told Johnson, "No matter what, me and that little girl are going to be cool. That's the most important thing."

—R.E.

Suggested Reading: *Dallas Morning News* A p1+ Feb. 27, 2005; *Essence* p160 Nov. 2004; *GQ* Feb. 2005; *New York Times* II p33 Sep. 12, 2004; *Washington Post* C p1 Aug. 6, 2004

Selected Films: *The Truth About Cats and Dogs*, 1996; *The Great White Hype*, 1996; *Booty Call*, 1997; *Any Given Sunday*, 1999; *Bait*, 2000; *Ali*, 2001; *Breakin' All the Rules*, 2004; *Redemption: The Stan Tookie Williams Story*, 2004; *Collateral*, 2004; *Ray*, 2004; *Stealth*, 2005

Selected Television Shows: *In Living Color*, 1991–94; *The Jamie Foxx Show*, 1996–2001

Selected Recordings: *Peep This*, 1994

Thos Robinson/Getty Images

Garofalo, Janeane

(guh-ROF-a-lo, juh-
NEEN)

Sep. 28, 1964– Actress; comedian; radio host

*Address: Air America Radio, 3 Park Ave., New
York, NY 10016*

"I guess I just prefer to see the dark side of things,"
Janeane Garofalo once said, as quoted on the Internet Movie Database. "The glass is always half-
empty. And cracked. And I just cut my lip on it.
And chipped a tooth." Despite such playful cynicism, or perhaps because of it, Garofalo has
achieved a measure of success and attracted many
fans, not only as an actress and comedian but also
as a writer, a radio talk-show host, and a social and
political activist. Since the early 1990s she has appeared, usually in small parts, in more than 40
movies, among them *Reality Bites* (1994), *The
Truth About Cats & Dogs* (1996), *The Cable Guy*
(1996), *Dogma* (1999), and *Steal This Movie* (2000),
and she has earned plaudits for many of her performances. Nominated several times for Emmy and
American Comedy Awards, she has co-starred in
several critically acclaimed television comedy series, including *The Ben Stiller Show* and *The Larry
Sanders Show*, and has toured the country as a
stand-up comic. Many of Garofalo's characters on
the big and small screens have closely reflected her
public persona: that of a sharp-witted, sarcastic,
somewhat jaded young woman who is blunt in her
comments about society's great inequalities. Nathan Rabin, writing for the satirical newspaper the
Onion (December 10, 2003, on-line), called Garo-

falo the "poster girl for Gen-X neuroses." (Generation X is a much-debated label for those people
born in the years from the mid-1960s to the mid-
to late 1970s who are said to reject traditional notions of success.) Stephen Holden, in the *New York
Times* (October 3, 1997), wrote that Garofalo, both
as an actress and a comedian, "conveys the attitude
of an impatient, hypercritical skeptic who can see
through anybody. If she doesn't give her trust easily, it can still be won. Once she has lowered her
storm warnings, Ms. Garofalo is capable of projecting an endearing childlike rapture. In those fitful
moments when the sun bursts through the clouds,
it blazes." An outspoken progressive activist, Garofalo currently co-hosts *The Majority Report*, a political talk show on Air America Radio, a left-
leaning network that began broadcasting in March
2004.

The middle child of three siblings, Janeane
Garofalo was born on September 28, 1964 in New-
ton, New Jersey, to Carmine Garofalo, an Exxon oil
company executive, and Joan Garofalo. "I was
very, very lucky in my upbringing," she told David
Sheff for *Rolling Stone* (May 27, 1999). During her
early years she was very close to her older brother,
Michael. "He treated me like his precious doll, and
I idolized him," she told Jennifer Wolff for *Marie
Claire* (May 2000). Her family lived in Houston,
Texas, for some years until she was nine, then
moved to Madison, New Jersey. Garofalo told Nancy Mills for the *Chicago Tribune* (January 7, 1996)
that she was a "suburban, boring, completely conservative kid. . . . I never thought about acting.
My mother was a secretary, and I wanted to be a
secretary." By contrast, she told Wolff, "My cynicism started to rear its head by the time I was 9. I
despised going to school and the day-to-day monotony. I hated getting up early. I rebelled against
any kind of organized fun. I was a lazy rebel who
questioned authority and religion. I resented having to believe that a woman [the biblical Eve] came
from the rib of a man [the biblical Adam]." By her
own account, Garofalo enjoyed her years at Madison High School and had both female and male
friends. Just before her senior year, her family returned to Houston, after another of her father's job
transfers. In Houston, she recalled to Sheff, "I got
a taste of what it was like to be the outcast—to ride
the bus with nobody letting me sit next to them. I
got hugely fat and went into a depression. I
couldn't have bought a friend. . . . I was in a John
Hughes film, with all the cruelty and cheer-
leaders"—a reference to such films as Hughes's
The Breakfast Club (1985), about the trials and tribulations of American teenagers. "When I realized
it wasn't going to be easy, I retreated into a shell of
horror." As she told Mills, she changed from being
"outspoken and outgoing to withdrawn and shy."

Meanwhile, by her own account, Garofalo had
become "obsessed with comedy," as she put it to
Wolff, after she saw Woody Allen's film *Take the
Money and Run* (1969) in the early 1970s. She
loved such TV programs as *Saturday Night Live*

and *Monty Python's Flying Circus*, and when her older brother was not home, she would spend hours playing and memorizing his George Carlin or Cheech & Chong comedy albums. During that period she also developed "a tremendous fear of sex and intimacy," as she recalled to Wolff, which she has attributed both to her shock upon seeing, as a preadolescent in the care of a babysitter, the rape scene in the movie *Lipstick* (1976), and to repeatedly hearing the warnings of her strait-laced maternal grandmother, who lived with the Garofalos for seven years. During the year she spent at James E. Taylor High School, in Houston, and her first year as an undergraduate, Garofalo told Mills, her "only joy," in her words, was watching the long-running television series *Late Show with David Letterman*. She has cited Letterman's style of acerbic humor as one of the major inspirations for her own foray into comedy.

Garofalo attended Providence College, in Rhode Island, where she majored in history and American studies. "For two years, I was a total odd man out, going to the lunchroom and having no one to sit with," she told Wolff, adding, "If I bumped into myself at that age, I would tell myself not to sweat it so badly, that it's not such a tragedy." At 20, after her junior year, Garofalo underwent a breast-reduction operation, because she had resolved to become a stand-up comic, and she feared that for a performer of her height (five feet, one inch), her large bust would be a liability. "It would be really hard to get people to pay attention to me without mocking me," she reasoned, as she recalled to Wolff. "Getting a breast reduction to prepare for my career was no different from people who work to get good grades to get into a good college to get into a good graduate school to get a good job. I went down to a B cup, and it was the best thing in the whole world, like a new lease on life." In her senior year she formed a satisfying romantic relationship for the first time. Another big morale booster was her first-place finish that year in a contest sponsored by the Showtime network, called "Funniest Person in Rhode Island," which was held in a Providence nightspot.

For a year or two after she earned a B.A. degree, in 1986, Garofalo lived in Boston, Massachusetts. She held a series of daytime jobs, among them shoe salesperson and bike messenger, and parlayed her work experiences into material for her stand-up comedy acts, presented at local venues. She then returned to Houston to be with her mother, who was ill with colon cancer and later died. "I had always been incredibly close to my mother, but her death wasn't agonizing because it wasn't sudden," she said to Wolff. "We had been very vocal about how much we loved each other. I spent a lot of time with her before she passed away." Until about 1991 Garofalo continued to work at odd jobs during the day and perform at clubs at night.

At around that time Garofalo moved to Los Angeles, where the actor Ben Stiller invited her to join the cast of his upcoming comedy and variety tele-

vision series, *The Ben Stiller Show*, which premiered on the Fox network in the fall of 1992. On the program, Stiller, Garofalo, Andy Dick, and Bob Odenkirk parodied movies, television shows, and commercials in brief sketches. Despite critical praise and an Emmy Award for outstanding writing in a variety program, the show was cancelled in 1993, after one season. Speaking of *The Ben Stiller Show*, Nathan Rabin wrote that, despite its relatively short run, the series "holds a prominent place in the 'Too Good for TV' pantheon, thanks to its scathing pop-culture satire and the auspicious careers of its gifted ensemble." As an example of the show's merits, Rabin mentioned a segment called "The Grungies," which was set in the Seattle, Washington–based grunge-rock scene of the early 1990s (as exemplified by such groups as Nirvana) and mocked the way "mass culture sells pseudo-rebellion back to the discontented at a hefty profit."

In 1994 Garofalo joined the cast of *Saturday Night Live* (*SNL*), NBC's storied, late-night sketch-comedy program. Since its debut, in 1975, *SNL* has served as a springboard for the careers of some of America's most successful comedians, among them Dan Aykroyd, Bill Murray, Chevy Chase, Eddie Murphy, Adam Sandler, and Will Ferrell. Garofalo never felt comfortable among the show's cast and crew and left after seven months. "I wasn't pleased with the material. . . . The nice, friendly atmosphere was missing," Garofalo recalled to Mills, "but if the work had been good I'd have stayed. I was a victim of bad timing."

Meanwhile, starting in 1992 and for the next half-dozen seasons, Garofalo appeared on the award-winning television series *The Larry Sanders Show*, a sardonic behind-the-scenes look at the world of a fictitious TV talk show. (The program aired on HBO until 1998.) Starring the comedian Garry Shandling, *The Larry Sanders Show* is considered by some critics to be one of the landmark television offerings of the 1990s. Reviewing a DVD release of one season's installments for CNN (February 26, 2002, on-line), Mark Harris called the series the "funniest and most poisonously accurate TV show about a TV show in history, and possibly the medium's greatest exploration of fear and loathing in the workplace." In the role of Paula, a talent booker, Garofalo further developed her signature persona of a smart, cynical woman with a sharp wit. In 1996 she was nominated for an American Comedy Award for funniest supporting female performer in a television series, and in both 1996 and 1997 she was nominated for an Emmy Award for outstanding supporting actress in a comedy series. Concurrently, in 1994–95, Garofalo was cast as a correspondent on Michael Moore's television series *TV Nation*, a humorous mock television newsmagazine that sought to expose the wrongdoings of big business and politicians. While the show had a fairly loyal following and won an Emmy Award for outstanding informational series, it was cancelled after its first season. Garofalo has made dozens of television guest appearances on *Late Show with David Letterman, Dennis Miller Live, The Daily Show, The Tonight Show with Jay Leno, The Rosie O'Donnell Show, Late Night with Conan O'Brien, The Sopranos, Law & Order, Ellen,* and *Seinfeld.* She has also lent her voice for characters on the popular animated programs *King of the Hill* and *The Simpsons.*

In the early to mid-1990s, Garofalo began to appear on the big screen. In 1994 she again teamed up with Ben Stiller, to act in his directorial debut, *Reality Bites.* Garofalo played the roommate of a young woman (Winona Ryder) who must choose between the affections of two men, one a cynical, artistic layabout (Ethan Hawke), the other a successful business executive (Ben Stiller). Though *Reality Bites* received mixed reviews, it became something of a cult classic for the college-age generation at which it had been aimed and, to the surprise of many, earned $20 million at the box office, a relatively high total for a low-budget film of its kind. In the comedy *Bye Bye, Love* (1995), which centered on the lives of three divorced men (played by Matthew Modine, Randy Quaid, and Paul Reiser), Garofalo portrayed Lucille, a difficult woman who goes on a blind date with one of the three principals. The movie did not fare well at the box office or under reviewers' scrutiny. In the *Washington Post* (March 17, 1995, on-line), Hal Hinson dismissed *Bye Bye, Love* as "little more than a warm, fuzzy commercial for traditional family values"; he was kinder toward Garofalo, whom he described as "divinely deranged." Garofalo earned another American Comedy Award nomination for her work in *Bye Bye, Love.* In 1995 she appeared in three other little-known and generally poorly reviewed movies: *I Shot a Man in Vegas, Coldblooded,* and *Now and Then.*

Garofalo was cast as a principal character for the first time in a feature film in *The Truth About Cats & Dogs* (1996), a contemporary, gender-reversed retelling of Edmund Rostand's 1897 play *Cyrano de Bergerac.* In this version, written by Audrey Wells and directed by Michael Lehmann, a handsome photographer named Brian (Ben Chaplin) becomes enamored of Abby (Garofalo), a veterinarian and radio talk-show host, after calling her show to receive advice on how to care for his dog. Insecure about her looks, Abby falsely describes herself on the air to her admirer as tall and blond. She subsequently enlists Noelle, a beautiful neighbor (Uma Thurman) who matches that physical description, to pretend to be her on dates with Brian, thus setting the stage for a comedy of mistaken identities. Regarding her role in *The Truth About Cats & Dogs,* Garofalo told Nancy Mills that it was "shocking to get such a big part in a studio movie." In the opinion of a number of critics, Garofalo carried the film. The *Chicago Tribune* (April 26, 1996) reviewer, Mark Caro, wrote that Garofalo was "sharp and soft, bookish and vibrant, intelligent and thick-skulled—in short, human. With a wry smile that conveys more amusement than bitterness at socie-

ty's unfairness, she's one of the few actresses you can praise for portraying chagrin." Roger Ebert wrote for the *Chicago Sun-Times* (April 26, 1996, on-line) that Garofalo was "so likable, so sympathetic, so revealing of her character's doubts and desires, that she carries us headlong into the story," and David Ansen wrote for *Newsweek* (April 29, 1996), "It's a tricky challenge playing a woman who must be both unglamorous and irresistible, but Garofalo, with her unforced comic timing, makes it look easy." Ideals, insecurities, and conflicts concerning feminine beauty have been a major part of Garofalo's stand-up routines as well. She has also spoken about those issues in interviews, criticizing (usually with her trademark wry humor) Hollywood's casting propensities and describing (usually self-deprecatingly) the limitations she has faced in her own acting career due to her less-than-bombshell looks. (She jokingly named her production company I Hate Myself Productions.) Garofalo told Mills that if a woman wants to be an "A-list actress, you'd better have a great body. You can fudge the hair and the face, but fat just won't make it. Men can be big [and still land leading roles], but for women it's a cardinal sin."

Also in 1996 Garofalo appeared as a disgruntled waitress in the Jim Carrey vehicle *The Cable Guy,* directed by Ben Stiller. The next year she landed a co-starring role as Marcy Tizard, a senator's aide sent to Ireland to try to find her boss's relatives, in the romantic comedy *The Matchmaker.* Marcy finds herself in a small Irish village in the middle of a matchmaking festival and tries to resist the mutual attraction she senses between her and a local man (David O'Hara). The movie received mostly middling to poor reviews. Critical reactions to Garofalo's performance in particular were mixed. Stephen Holden found that Garofalo's character in *The Matchmaker* was very similar to her stand-up persona, but that the actress's "keen intelligence demands more verbal wit than the rushed, formulaic screenplay can provide." Desson Howe, in the *Washington Post* (October 3, 1997), wrote that, although Garofalo is "likable and amusingly caustic" and has "made an art of acerbic sassiness in bit parts," she was "overexposed," having appeared too many times, on both television and in movies, playing the same general character. Garofalo's other big-screen appearances in 1997 were in *Cop Land, Romy and Michele's High School Reunion,* and *Touch.*

In 1998 Garofalo took roles in a half-dozen films, including *Permanent Midnight,* which was based on the life of the television comedy writer and one-time heroin addict Jerry Stahl; the crime drama *Thick as Thieves,* starring Alec Baldwin; and *Clay Pigeons,* a humorous mystery. In *Clay Pigeons* Joaquin Phoenix co-starred as Clay Bidwell, an unlucky small-town man suspected of several murders, including those of his former lover, her husband, and a serial killer who had befriended him (Vince Vaughn). Garofalo played a sour FBI agent with a deadpan delivery. Several critics, including

David Edelstein for the on-line publication *Slate* (October 10, 1998), felt that Garofalo's performance was a reason to see the film. Garofalo was just as busy in 1999, performing mostly small roles in six movies, among them *200 Cigarettes*, *Mystery Men*, and *Dogma*. In *Dogma*, written and directed by Kevin Smith and co-starring Matt Damon and Ben Affleck as fallen angels trying to finagle their way back into heaven, Garofalo played a worker at a Chicago abortion clinic, where the last living descendant of the Virgin Mary and Joseph is also employed. The film's humorous treatment of religious concepts created controversy, but *Dogma* nevertheless earned a respectable $30 million at the box office.

Garofalo had a fairly prominent role as the wife of Abbie Hoffman (Vincent D'Onofrio), a countercultural hero and political activist of the 1960s and '70s, in the biographical film *Steal This Movie* (2000). The picture did not attract much attention but did garner some positive critical responses. Stephen Holden, who praised it in the *New York Times* (August 18, 2000), wrote, "Garofalo gives a tender, finely shaded portrait of a woman of remarkable flexibility, strength, humor and loyalty." Since 2002 Garofalo has been cast in primarily small roles in little-seen films, among them *Martin & Orloff* (2002), *Nobody Knows Anything* (2003), *Manhood* (2003), *Ash Tuesday* (2003), and *Wonderland* (2003). In the last-named motion picture, which centered on a violent episode in the sordid life of the American pornographic film star John Holmes, she appeared alongside Val Kilmer. In 2004 Garofalo was in *Junebug and Hurricane* (2004) and *La La Wood* (2004). In 2005 she played a depressed psychotherapist in the widely panned thriller *Stay*, and she starred opposite David Schwimmer, a cast member of the long-running TV sitcom *Friends*, in *Duane Hopwood*, about a divorced father who tries to rebuild his life after a drunk-driving accident. Though the latter picture debuted as an official selection at the influential 2005 Sundance Film Festival, as of October 2005 it had yet to gain wider distribution. On the small screen Garofalo had a starring role in the film *Nadine in Dateland*, which premiered on the Oxygen cable channel in early 2005 and featured the actress as the owner of a dating service who has trouble getting a date for herself. In the spring of 2005, Garofalo appeared in *Left of the Dial*, an HBO documentary about the early days of the radio network Air America, and in the fall she took on a recurring role in the television series *The West Wing*. She has a part in the projected 2006 cinematic release "Southland Tales."

Off camera Garofalo has earned credits as a producer, on the big-screen release *Sweethearts* (1996) and the television movie *Slice O' Life* (2003), in both of which she also acted. With Ben Stiller, she co-wrote *Feel This Book: An Essential Guide to Self-Empowerment, Spiritual Supremacy, and Sexual Satisfaction* (1999), a satiric take on celebrity advice books. According to her biography on the Air America Web site, Garofalo is writing a collection of political essays, whose working title—"For Those About to Salute, We Will Rock You"—is a play on a rock song by the band AC/DC titled "For Those About to Rock (We Salute You)." (AC/DC took their title from what Roman gladiators supposedly shouted to the emperor as they entered the arena to do battle: "Hail, Caesar, those about to die salute you.")

Prior to the U.S. invasion of Iraq in April 2003, Garofalo had been a vocal opponent of the Bush administration's drive to war and had expressed her strong opinions on CNN and Fox, among other media outlets. Since March 2004 Garofalo has voiced her political and cultural opinions as co-host of *The Majority Report*, which is broadcast every weeknight on Air America Radio from 8:00 p.m. to 11:00 p.m. Established in early 2004, Air America Radio was designed as a liberal answer to the commercial-radio talk shows hosted by Rush Limbaugh, Sean Hannity, and other social and political conservatives, who greatly outnumber liberal radio commentators. Other stars of Air America Radio include the comedian and author Al Franken and the talk-radio veteran Randi Rhodes. During *The Majority Report* Garofalo and her co-host, Sam Seder, conduct interviews, report news stories, take calls from listeners, and discuss topical political and social issues. The U.S. presidential contest between the incumbent, George W. Bush, and Senator John Kerry of Massachusetts was one of the major subjects of Garofalo's on-air commentary in 2004. Beset by financial uncertainties from the beginning, Air America continues to struggle. In October 2005 announcers began soliciting money on the air, a routine occurrence on not-for-profit radio stations but highly unusual for a company that intends to turn a profit. Despite the desperation such a move seems to suggest, Air America executives have insisted that the company is financially sound. Reports of the network's ratings have varied wildly and have typically split along partisan lines, with conservatives regularly predicting Air America's imminent demise and liberals trumpeting its growing number of affiliates and consequently larger audience share. Garofalo and Sam Seder also express their political opinions on a Web log, or blog, that they post on their show's Web site.

Garofalo, who continues to perform stand-up comedy, has a number of tattoos on her body, including one on her arm that reads "Think." In 1991 she married the comedy writer Rob Cohen at a drive-in chapel. "A couple of writers from *The Ben Stiller Show* went to Las Vegas and we all got married," she told Mary Roach for *USA Weekend* (August 1, 1999, on-line). "He just happened to be my boyfriend at the time." Though the relationship ended long ago, the couple have never divorced.
—C.F.T.

Suggested Reading: Air America Radio Web site; *Chicago Tribune* XIII p6 Jan. 7, 1996, with photo; Internet Movie Database (on-line); *Majority Report* Web site; *New York Times* (on-line) Mar. 31, 2004, with photos; *USA Weekend* (on-line) Aug. 1, 1999, with photo

Selected Books: *Feel This Book: An Essential Guide to Self-Empowerment, Spiritual Supremacy, and Sexual Satisfaction* (with Ben Stiller), 1999

Selected Films: *Reality Bites*, 1994; *Suspicious*, 1994; *Bye Bye, Love*, 1995; *I Shot a Man in Vegas*, 1995; *Coldblooded*, 1995; *Now and Then*, 1995; *The Truth About Cats & Dogs*, 1996; *The Cable Guy*, 1996; *Larger Than Life*, 1996; *Sweethearts*, 1996; *Touch*, 1997; *The Matchmaker*, 1997; *Cop Land*, 1997; *Romy and*

Michele's High School Reunion, 1997; *Half Baked*, 1998; *Thick as Thieves*, 1998; *Permanent Midnight*, 1998; *Dog Park*, 1998; *Clay Pigeons*, 1998; *200 Cigarettes*, 1999; *Mystery Men*, 1999; *Dogma*, 1999; *Can't Stop Dancing*, 1999; *The Minus Man*, 1999; *The Bumblebee Flies Anyway*, 1999; *The Independent*, 2000; *Steal This Movie*, 2000; *The Search for John Gissing*, 2001; *Manhood*, 2003; *Ash Tuesday*, 2003; *Wonderland*, 2003; *Junebug and Hurricane*, 2004; *La La Wood*, 2004; *Duane Hopwood*, 2005; *Stay*, 2005

Selected Television Shows or Films: *The Ben Stiller Show*, 1992–93; *The Larry Sanders Show*, 1992–97; *Saturday Night Live*, 1994–95; *TV Nation*, 1995; *Left of the Dial*, 2005; *Nadine in Dateland*, 2005; *The West Wing*, 2005

Courtesy of Harvard Vanguard Medical Associates

Gawande, Atul

(guh-WAHN-dee, uh-TOOL)

Nov. 5, 1965– Surgeon; medical writer

Address: Brigham and Women's Hospital, ASB11-3d Fl., 75 Francis St., Boston, MA 02115

"Medicine is, I have found, a strange and in many ways disturbing business," the surgeon Atul Gawande wrote in the introduction to his essay collection, *Complications: A Surgeon's Notes on an*

Imperfect Science (2002). "The stakes are high, the liberties taken tremendous. We drug people, put needles and tubes into them, manipulate their chemistry, biology, and physics, lay them unconscious and open their bodies up to the world. We do so out of an abiding confidence in our know-how as a profession. What you find when you get in close, however—close enough to see the furrowed brows, the doubts and missteps, the failures as well as the successes—is how messy, uncertain, and also surprising medicine turns out to be." The essays in Gawande's collection, which were written while he was a resident at Brigham and Women's Hospital in Boston, Massachusetts, focus on personal anecdotes and medical case studies that highlight the risks, confusions, and complexities inherent in his discipline. Above all, they reveal doctors to be human beings capable of extraordinary achievements but subject to good days and bad, just like everyone else. *Complications* drew widespread critical praise for its candor, vivid descriptiveness, and elegant style, all of which stem not from enormous expertise but from profound curiosity. "I write as someone who got a chance as a young doctor to ask all the questions that a doctor wonders about and also a patient wonders about," Gawande told Faith McLellan for the *Lancet* (January 11, 2003, on-line). "I write as someone who is, in the end, simply a young physician and trying to make sense of things. It's been my way of sorting through all those things you wonder about—especially when you're a young doctor—but don't feel you have answers to."

Atul Atmaram Gawande was born in the New York City borough of Brooklyn on November 5, 1965 and raised in Athens, Ohio, where his father, Atmaram, a urologist, and his mother, Sushila, a pediatrician, had set up their medical practices. While becoming a physician was always a strong likelihood for Gawande, becoming an acclaimed writer as well was not. "My sister [Meeta] and I were not raised with books around us," Gawande said during his speech to Yale University Medical School graduates at their commencement in 2004. "The magazines on our living room coffee table were my parents' medical journals. My high school English classes only required us to read one book cover to cover each quarter. And that was fine with me. . . . In college I did take a fiction writing class once, but it was mainly because there was a girl taking it I had a rather keen interest in . . . and the professor half way through took me aside and suggested I find something to do other than writing." After graduating from Athens High School, in 1983, Gawande attended Stanford University, in Palo Alto, California, where he earned a bachelor's degree in 1987. He was awarded a Rhodes Scholarship and chose to study politics and philosophy at Balliol College, a division of Oxford University, in England; he received an M.A. degree there in 1989. Gawande briefly thought of pursuing a life as a philosophy professor. Then, in 1989, he moved to Washington, D.C., where his girlfriend (and future wife), Kathleen Hobson, was living; there, he worked for Congressman Jim Cooper, a Tennessee Democrat. A year later he entered Harvard Medical School, in Cambridge, Massachusetts. He took a leave of absence in 1991 to work in Little Rock, Arkansas, as a health- and social-policy adviser for the 1992 presidential campaign of Bill Clinton, who was then governor of Arkansas. For a while during President Clinton's administration, he served as an appointed senior adviser at the U.S. Department of Health and Human Services. At about this time Gawande returned to Harvard Medical School; he earned his M.D. degree in 1995. Four years later he completed a master's degree in public health, also at Harvard.

In 1997, while he was in the midst of his surgical residency at Brigham and Women's Hospital, Gawande accepted the invitation of his friend Jacob Weisberg, the chief political correspondent for *Slate*, to contribute articles about medicine for the on-line magazine. Over the next two years, he wrote approximately 30 articles, commenting on a range of topics, among them sudden infant death syndrome (SIDS), food irradiation, organ trafficking, and castration. Upon learning that an editor at the *New Yorker* was following his work, Gawande pitched a story idea to the magazine. Nine months and seven drafts later, the article was published. In 1998 Gawande became a *New Yorker* staff writer on medicine and science; he contributes four essays a year to the weekly. According to Faith McLellan, he works on each essay for three to four months and produces between five and 22 drafts before it is completed. His carefully crafted pieces have been reprinted in *Best American Science and Nature Writing 2000* and the *New Yorker* essay collection *In Sickness and in Health* (2001, on-line).

Complications: A Surgeon's Notes on an Imperfect Science contains 14 revised versions of Gawande's most memorable pieces for *Slate* and the *New Yorker* and divides them among three headings: "Fallibility," "Mystery," and "Uncertainty." Among the varied subjects they address are burnout among doctors, child abuse, why the number of autopsies performed has declined, how little physicians understand about certain phenomena (such as chronic blushing or overeating), and the successful efforts of anesthesiologists to reduce common errors. Gawande also wrote about some of his children's medical problems, ranging from relatively minor injuries, to the more severe congenital cardiac defect of his oldest child, to a life-threatening respiratory infection in his youngest child, who was born prematurely. The goal of his book, Gawande told Daniel Smith for the *Atlantic Unbound* (May 1, 2002, on-line), was to demystify medicine and debunk the myth of the infallible doctor: "We've reached a point where that myth seems to do more harm than good. It means that patients aren't asking questions, aren't getting second opinions, and that doctors are sometimes providing bad care without being questioned about it. . . . There is an art to being a patient in the same way that there is an art to being a doctor. . . . You have to know when to question and ask for second opinions and sometimes even anger your own physician, and then you also have to know when to put yourself in someone else's hands and simply trust them and go along."

Of great concern to Gawande was the impact his book might have on his professional relationships with patients and colleagues. "Talking about our mistakes makes plenty of doctors nervous," he explained to Liza Weisstuch for the *Harvard University Gazette* (May 9, 2002). "It makes me nervous about whether the public will catch on to the measured tone and aim of what I'm trying to do, and not see it simply as an exposé but something that's trying to be more constructive. But doctors and patients seem to have gotten that and that's been the most gratifying part for me." Rather than being angry with him or avoiding him for fear that he is constantly taking notes for use in future essays, neither his patients nor his colleagues have reacted negatively. "To my surprise people seem to sort of enjoy having me around," he told Rosanne Spector for the *Stanford Report* (October 20, 2004). "Other surgeons even come to me and say, Hey, I've kind of had an interest in writing—can you take a look at this piece for me?" The critical reception was equally positive. Lev Grossman took measure of *Complications* for *Time* (April 15, 2002) and declared, "Diagnosis: riveting." In the *New York Times* (April 7, 2002), the physician and writer F. Gonzales-Crussi praised the book: "*Complications* ought to earn Gawande a place of distinction among physicians who try their hand at the belles lettres. Others are perhaps more lyrical; some more poetical; still others more philosophical. . . . But none surpass Gawande in the ability to create a sense of immediacy, in his power to conjure the reality of the ward, the thrill of the moment-by-moment medical or surgical drama. *Complications* impresses for its truth and authenticity, virtues that it owes to its author being as much forceful writer as uncompromising chronicler." *Complications* was a finalist for the 2002 National Book Award.

After completing his internship and residency, in 2003, Atul Gawande remained at Brigham and Women's Hospital, joining its division of general and gastrointestinal surgery as an associate surgeon. He also holds assistant professorships at Harvard Medical School and the Harvard School of Public Health. Gawande lives in Newton, Massachusetts, with his wife, Kathleen Hobson, and their three children: Walker, Hattie, and Hunter.

—K.J.E.

Suggested Reading: *Atlantic Unbound* (on-line) May 1, 2002; *Harvard University Gazette* (on-line) May 9, 2002; Literature, Arts, and Medicine Database (on-line) May 8, 2002; Gawande, Atul. *Complications: A Surgeon's Notes on an Imperfect Science*, 2002

Selected Books: *Complications: A Surgeon's Notes on an Imperfect Science*, 2002

Alex Wong/Newsmakers

Germond, Jack W.

(jer-MON)

Jan. 30, 1928– Political commentator; columnist

Address: c/o Random House, 1745 Broadway, New York, NY 10019

The political commentator, author, and former syndicated columnist Jack W. Germond is a member of a storied, vanishing breed of journalists: a fraternity who covered elected officials and office-seekers and indulged in the trappings of the reporter's life—such as poker and whiskey—with equal fervor, and who became friendly with the politicians they wrote about, as part of their feeling that journalism "was a great way to make a living," as Germond told *People* (February 5, 2001). "It was fun." Germond began his career in the early 1950s

and started covering national politics a decade later, in the era of President John F. Kennedy; he has often been referred to as a pioneer of "horse-race journalism," whose practitioners predict winners in public elections. The column "Politics Today," which Germond co-authored with Jules Witcover, appeared five days a week in approximately 140 newspapers nationwide for about 24 years, starting in 1977. The two also co-wrote "insider" treatises on four consecutive presidential elections, beginning with their book on the 1980 race between Ronald Reagan and Jimmy Carter—volumes that are, "in many ways, the liberal equivalent of Theodore H. White's *Making of the President* series," as a *Library Journal* (September 1, 1989) reviewer wrote. Germond, who retired from the *Baltimore Sun* in 2001 after a two-decade-long association, is best known to some as a regular on the political program *The McLaughlin Group* from 1982 to 1996. More recently, Germond wrote the memoir *Fat Man in a Middle Seat: Forty Years of Covering Politics* (1999) and *Fat Man Fed Up: How American Politics Went Bad* (2004), an unsparing critique of politics and the media.

The only child of John Germond, an engineer who worked in the housing business, and Lottie (Clift) Germond, a homemaker, Jack W. Germond was born on January 30, 1928 in Newton, Massachusetts. Due to the transitory nature of his father's line of work, Germond and his family moved regularly throughout his formative years, spending a long period in the South, including parts of Mississippi and Louisiana. "I went through 11 different schools in 12 years of public school," he told Tim Russert in an interview on the NBC television program *Meet the Press* (April 2, 2005). "It made me very detached. It hardens you up a little bit." At Baton Rouge High School, in Louisiana, Germond served as co-editor of the yearbook, *The Buzzer*. Also during the 1940s he played semi-pro baseball, for a summer team in southern Louisiana. He told Jim Roberts for *World and I* (October 1, 2002), "We would go from town to town on the weekends, playing local teams in what we called 'pass the hat' baseball"—which involved passing a hat to the spectators, who would then fill it with money; the players would divide the earnings, with the pitcher receiving the largest portion. Germond told Roberts that he was a "good hitter" but was limited as a baseball player by his inability to field and run well. After graduating from high school, Germond served in the army during 1946 and 1947. He then entered the University of Missouri, an institution known for awarding the first undergraduate degrees in the field of journalism (1909) in the United States. Germond received degrees in journalism and history in 1951.

That year Germond began his newspaper career as a sports editor of the *Post-Tribune* in Jefferson City, Missouri. He quickly grew weary of covering sports, though; as he wrote in *Fat Man in a Middle Seat*, "There are only so many ways you can report a baseball game." After six months at the *Post-Tribune*, he took a job covering City Hall as a reporter for the *Evening News*, a small newspaper in Monroe, Michigan. Soon tiring of his regular visits to the city auditor's office, where he discovered nothing newsworthy at first, he frequently pleaded with his superiors at the *Evening News* to give him a more interesting assignment. "One day, though, the auditor opened his desk drawer and pulled out a confidential copy of the mayor's resignation letter," Howard Kurtz reported in the *Washington Post* (October 5, 1992). "It was a lesson Germond never forgot." In 1953 Germond left the *Evening News* to join the Gannett Co., where, serving in a variety of roles, he worked for 20 years, "climbing the career ladder," as Kurtz wrote. His first position with Gannett was at the *Times Union*, in Rochester, New York. After the Republican Nelson Rockefeller won the New York gubernatorial election, in 1958, Germond was assigned to cover the new governor closely. The two got along so well that Rockefeller offered Germond a position in his administration, which Germond declined.

In Washington, D.C., in 1961, Germond began covering national politics for Gannett. He quickly became a familiar face to such politicians as the 1964 Republican presidential nominee, Barry Goldwater; Hubert Humphrey, a U.S. senator and future vice president; and Robert F. Kennedy, the U.S. attorney general and, later, a New York senator—the latter two of whom would run for the Democratic Party's presidential nomination in 1968. That year, Germond recalled to Kurtz, he was covering Kennedy's campaign when the candidate invited him to the front of his plane. "[Kennedy] got a tumbler of Jack Daniel's, and I got a big Scotch on the rocks. We started talking about the kids we'd seen in the ghetto that day. We got pretty stiff and we talked about it the whole damn trip. He wasn't trying to plant a story; he was really interested in the subject and really affected by what he'd seen."

In 1969 Gannett newspapers promoted Germond to chief of its Washington Bureau, a role he would fill until 1973. During that period Germond and his colleagues' deeds were "immortalized," in the words of one reviewer, by Timothy Crouse's

book *The Boys on the Bus: Riding with the Campaign Press* (1973), which centered on those covering the 1972 presidential race between the incumbent, Richard Nixon, and U.S. senator George McGovern of South Dakota. That book "elevated reporters from mere spectators in the political drama to full participants," as David Shribman wrote for *Nieman Reports* (Spring 2004). In 1974 Germond joined the now-defunct *Washington Star*, serving for three years as political editor before becoming assistant managing editor and writing a column for the paper. Also in 1977, Germond and Jules Witcover, who then worked for the *Washington Post*, began working together on a syndicated column, "Politics Today," which was distributed by Tribune Media Services. Between 1977 and 2001, when the last installment appeared, the two wrote 6,912 columns, according to the *Columbia Journalism Review* (March/April 2001).

Beginning in 1982 Germond appeared regularly on the syndicated television show *The McLaughlin Group*. The program, which has been called "TV's original talkfest," features five political pundits who dissect national and foreign affairs. Found "generally lean[ing] back uncomfortably, his arms folded over his chest," according to the *New York Times* (December 16, 1992), Germond provided liberal opposition to the conservative views of Robert Novak and the show's host, John McLaughlin, among others. Germond left *The McLaughlin Group* in 1996, following a series of disputes with McLaughlin. Germond has described McLaughlin as "not very considerate," as quoted by the Associated Press (November 25, 1996), and has attributed the lengthiness of his stint on the show to financial necessity (specifically, he needed money to pay for medical school for one of his daughters).

Blue Smoke and Mirrors: How Reagan Won and Why Carter Lost the Election of 1980, co-authored by Germond and Witcover, was published in 1981. The book examines the effects of several events on the presidential election, such as key primaries, the debates, the Soviet invasion of Afghanistan, and the taking of U.S. hostages in Iran. Writing for *Library Journal* (September 1, 1981), Frank Kessler described the book as "an entertaining, anecdotal trip down the 1980 presidential campaign trail with intriguing stops in the back rooms of the party national conventions." In the book the authors discussed the vital role in national elections played by the "political technocrats" and image-makers working for the major candidates.

Wake Us When It's Over: Presidential Politics of 1984 (1985), the second book by Germond and Witcover, also examines the consequences of several events leading up to an election—this time placing emphasis on the Democratic primaries. Noting that the book revealed "an election process that appears to have little to do with a competition among different ideas and policies," John D. Fulbright, writing for the *Christian Science Monitor* (August 30, 1985), added, "Rarely, if ever, does a reader of

[*Wake Us When It's Over*] get the impression that he is observing a system that contributes to a better-informed electorate, or that encourages the best men and women to run." In a similar vein, Germond and Witcover followed *Wake Us When It's Over* with *Whose Broad Stripes and Bright Stars? The Trivial Pursuit of the Presidency 1988* (1989) and *Mad as Hell: Revolt at the Ballet Box* (1993).

Recalling his decades of writing about officeholders and the election process, the acerbic Germond next offered *Fat Man in a Middle Seat: Forty Years of Covering Politics* (1999). Giving readers glimpses of the less-seen sides of the nation's leaders, ranging from John F. Kennedy to Bill Clinton, the book received mostly favorable reviews for its conversational style and the colorful nature of its recollections. Assessing the book for the *National Review* (November 8, 1999), Robert D. Novak wrote: "I first met Jack Germond in 1959. . . . The whisky-drinking, cigarette-smoking, poker-playing Germond of 1959 loved the great game of politics, but made fun of politicians, worried not about his girth or cholesterol level, and belonged to a slightly cynical 'aw nuts!' rather than the ever-bedazzled 'gee whiz!' school of journalism. The Germond of 1999 is pretty much unchanged. Reading *Fat Man in a Middle Seat* is like sitting in a bar with Germond long after midnight, downing shots of brandy too numerous to remember after a dinner too heavy to digest, and hearing irreverent stories of a life spent chronicling the pretentious men who aspire to lead us." *Fat Man in a Middle Seat* highlighted the disparity between political reporters of the author's generation, who he claimed generally admired the politicians they were covering, and the current crop, who Germond believes typically show disdain for their subjects—and whose after-hours pursuits are healthier but, in Germond's view, less interesting than their predecessors'. Richard Hauser Costa, in *Magill Book Reviews* (November 1, 2000), wrote that the book "serves as an antidote reminding readers that politics was not always the banal creature of TV imaging." Germond wrote about, and was a part of, a generation of reporters who "liked politicians, prized chumming around with them, and warmed up to some of the worst ones. They accepted the system, abided by its rules, and sometimes had trouble standing far enough beyond the process to see, and report, its imperfections," according to an *American Journalism Review* (November 9, 1999) analysis of *Fat Man in a Middle Seat*. Germond's colleagues, each of whom covered politics nationally, included David Broder, R. W. "Johnny" Apple Jr., Jim Wooten, and Jules Witcover. (Among that group, Germond is known for having originated "The Germond Rule," which maintains that restaurant bills should be split evenly when groups of journalists dine together, regardless of the amount of food and drink each person consumes—a policy that usually worked in Germond's favor.)

Germond's most recent book, *Fat Man Fed Up: How American Politics Went Bad* (2004), contains biting criticism of the national political landscape. The book rebukes politicians for what the author views as their tendency to shape messages based on the latest poll readings rather than on steadfast principle; berates the public for its mounting apathy to national issues; and condemns the media for abetting the public's indifference by ignoring the most critical subjects. Germond wrote, as quoted in the *Charlotte Observer* (October 11, 2004), "As a newspaper reporter and columnist, I have contributed to this cheapening of the process. On more occasions than I like to remember, I have written dumb stories about issues created out of the mists that no intelligent reader should have been asked to take seriously. As a television commentator, I have too often held forth on camera about issues about which I knew enough to hum a few bars." Writing in what reviewers dubbed a curmudgeonly manner, Germond concluded that the electorate receives "what it deserves at all levels of government, up to and including the White House." "These days," Germond wrote, "because so many Americans—almost half—don't bother to vote even in presidential elections, they deserve choices like the one they were offered in 2000, between Al Gore and George W. Bush. Because so few Americans understand the political process or bother to follow it with even a modicum of attention, we elect presidents as empty as George H. W. Bush or as self-absorbed as Bill Clinton—only to be followed by a choice between a Republican obviously over his head and a Democrat too unsure of his own persona to be convincing."

With his first wife, Barbara, whom he married in 1951 and divorced in 1993, Germond fathered two children: Mandy, who died of leukemia at age 14, and Jessica, who is a pediatrician. In *Fat Man in a Middle Seat*, as quoted by Andrew Ferguson in the *Weekly Standard* (November 8, 1999), Germond wrote about his daughter's death: "The loss of a child causes a pain that has no dimension and cannot be described to those who have not shared the experience. In my case it seemed to reinforce the detachment I felt from things going on around me. Politicians might tell me something was terribly important, but I knew that, whatever it was, it didn't really matter to me." Barbara Germond died in 1995 of a heart ailment.

Germond currently resides in Charleston, West Virginia, with his second wife, the political activist Alice Travis, whom he married in 1995 and who was appointed secretary of the Democratic National Committee in May 2002. The couple share a home overlooking the Shenandoah River. Germond is known to be a member of the American Atheists' organization. An avid follower of Thoroughbred horse racing, he has frequented the racetrack since his retirement from the *Baltimore Sun*. He appeared for some time on the televised political roundtable *Inside Washington*. "You could write your . . . fingers off for 25 years and never have the same reach as television," Germond told Kurtz. "Television is just a monster. Much as we hate to admit it, what the networks play is so much more influential than what we print. We really are writing for an elite."

—D.F.

Suggested Reading: *American Journalism Review* p75 Nov. 1999; *National Review* p58+ Nov. 8, 1999; *People* p23+ Feb. 5, 2001, with photos; *Washington Post* C p1+ Oct. 5, 1992, with photos; *Wilson Quarterly* p123+ Autumn 2004

Selected Books: as author—*Fat Man in a Middle Seat: Forty Years of Covering Politics*, 1999; *Fat Man Fed Up: How American Politics Went Bad*, 2004; as co-author with Jules Witcover—*Blue Smoke and Mirrors: How Reagan Won and Why Carter Lost the Election of 1980*, 1981; *Wake Us When It's Over: Presidential Politics of 1984*, 1985; *Whose Broad Stripes and Bright Stars? The Trivial Pursuit of the Presidency 1988*, 1989; *Mad as Hell: Revolt at the Ballot Box, 1992*, 1993

Giamatti, Paul

June 6, 1967– Actor

Address: c/o Endeavor Agency, 9701 Wilshire Blvd., 10th Fl., Beverly Hills, CA 90212

"I'm interested in failure or people who perceive themselves as failures," Paul Giamatti told an interviewer for *Hollywood Reporter* (January 3, 2005, on-line). "Not losers, necessarily. I'm fascinated by what people are ashamed of and afraid of. Failure is such a no-no in this culture. Really falling on your ass—you're not supposed to do it." Ironically, Giamatti, a successful stage and screen actor, might be said to know quite a bit about failure, having made a career of playing misfits, sad sacks, cranks, and other outsiders. For years, in a variety of movies, Giamatti was cast as the quirky character slouching around the margins of the story, such as the bellboy who shares Julia Roberts's cigarette in *My Best Friend's Wedding*, the stressed-out, neurotic Todd Woods in *Duets*, or Pig Vomit, the grating radio executive in the Howard Stern vehicle *Private Parts*. More recently, Giamatti has found himself in starring roles, most notably those of the real-life comic-book author Harvey Pekar in *American Splendor* and the fictional teacher, struggling writer, and wine snob Miles Raymond in *Sideways*. "I like to find the quirkiness in ordinary things," the actor said to Paul Fischer for *Film Monthly* (October 19, 2004, on-line). "I like to find what is ordinary in quirky people. . . . There's something fascinating about ordinary."

Paul Edward Valentine Giamatti was born on June 6, 1967 to Toni Smith, a former actress, and A. Bartlett "Bart" Giamatti, a professor of Renaissance literature who became the youngest-ever president of Yale University, in New Haven, Connecticut, where Paul Giamatti grew up. Bart Giamatti was appointed in 1989 as the commissioner of Major League Baseball; in that position he was best known for banning Pete Rose from the sport for life, following charges that the Cincinnati Reds manager and all-time record holder for hits had bet on baseball games, including those of his own team. Bart Giamatti died only five months after assuming his post as commissioner. Paul Giamatti was the youngest of three children; his brother, Marcus, is also an actor, and his sister, Elena, designs jewelry. Giamatti attended Choate Rosemary Hall preparatory school, in Wallingford, Connecticut, where, he has said, creativity and self-expression were encouraged. Upon his graduation, in 1985, Giamatti enrolled at Yale, majoring in English. (As he joked to Benjamin Svetkey for *Entertainment Weekly* [July 31, 1998], "I had a *very* good in.") At the urging of a friend, Giamatti began performing in college productions. He earned a B.A. degree in English in 1989.

That degree notwithstanding, Giamatti actually wanted to pursue a career in animation. Since childhood, he had loved cartoons and felt a particular affinity for Daffy Duck, whom he considered a "genius," as he said in the *Hollywood Reporter* interview. "At first, [Daffy Duck] just laughed and bounced around on his head. But then they gave him this weird, frustrated energy that's just great. I love that." While in college Giamatti had drawn a comic book in the style of a Gothic Western and had collaborated with a friend on a short cartoon called "Flip the Chimp," which he described in an interview with Gavin Edwards for *Rolling Stone* (January 13, 2005, on-line) as containing "as much crazy violence and drug-and-sex humor as possible for five minutes." His plans to study animation following his graduation from Yale ended with the sudden death of his father from a heart attack. Giamatti fell into a deep depression and lost interest in animation; he moved to Seattle, Washington, where he began smoking marijuana and reading voraciously. Many of the books he read were culled from his late father's library; he felt that reading the books was a way of maintaining a connection to his father.

To support himself, Giamatti began performing in plays at a Seattle theater owned by a friend. He soon realized that he could make a living in the theater and, moreover, that he enjoyed acting. "I could never decide what to do and as an actor I get to be so many different things so I never had to decide to do one thing, but be an actor and be all these different things," he told Paul Fischer. After he made up his mind to become an actor, Giamatti returned to New Haven and entered the Yale School of Drama, where he earned an M.F.A. degree in 1994. (He also met his future wife, Elizabeth Co-

Evan Agostini/Getty Images

Paul Giamatti

hen, at Yale, where she had been studying to be a dramaturge.) After graduation, the couple relocated to New York City so that Giamatti could try his luck on Broadway. He soon received acclaim for his performances in productions of Tom Stoppard's *Arcadia* and David Hare's *Racing Demon*, both in 1995, Chekhov's *Three Sisters*, in 1997, and Eugene O'Neill's *The Iceman Cometh*, in which he appeared with Kevin Spacey, in 1999. For his work in that play, he earned a Drama Desk nomination for best supporting actor.

Giamatti told Ed Caesar for the London *Independent* (February 2, 2005, on-line) that he initially looked upon film acting as "a cash machine while I did plays." His movie work began with tiny roles in pictures such as *She'll Take Romance* (1990); *Singles* and *Past Midnight* (both 1992); *Mighty Aphrodite* and *Sabrina* (both 1995); *Before and After* and *Breathing Room* (both 1996); and *Donnie Brasco*, *Deconstructing Harry*, *My Best Friend's Wedding*, *A Further Gesture*, and *Arresting Gena* (all 1997). Viewers and critics found his performances in those movies to be funny and often memorable, despite their brevity, and Giamatti enjoyed exploring facets of the odd men he was playing. "I'm kind of drawn to socially and psychologically marginal characters, and even characters marginal to the story," he explained to Andrew O'Hehir for the *New York Times* (July 29, 2001). Explaining that as a boy he had always been less interested in lead actors than in such supporting performers as Peter Lorre and Sydney Greenstreet, he added, "I always wondered who the hell those guys were. They were so great and so vivid, and yet you only got little bits of them." Many of the character actors he watched as a child, he said, "were

kind of bizarre and grotesque, and that always interested me. They were physically strange. They had funny voices. There just aren't guys like that anymore. . . . The Sydney Greenstreet character interests me, the William Demarest guy interests me, the Peter Lorre guy interests me. I want to be all those guys, instead of the one guy doing the one thing."

In the 1997 movie *Private Parts*, Giamatti had his largest role up to that time, appearing as Kenny Rushton, a radio executive and the nemesis of the "shock jock" Howard Stern. Giamatti played Rushton as an apoplectic southerner so loathsome that the Stern character nicknames him Pig Vomit. His performance brought him critical praise and offers of a number of other movie roles. In 1998 alone he appeared in *The Truman Show*, *Doctor Dolittle*, *Saving Private Ryan*, *The Negotiator*, and *Safe Men*, as well as the television movies *Winchell* and *Tourist Trap*. "He reminds me of one of those character actors from the 1930s and '40s," the casting director David Rubin, who hired Giamatti for *The Negotiator*, told Benjamin Svetkey about the actor. "He has a specific, indelible look. You're always happy to see him on the screen. That's *exactly* what you're looking for when casting supporting parts."

Giamatti's next film projects included *Cradle Will Rock* and *Man on the Moon* (both 1999), *If These Walls Could Talk 2* (made for TV), *Duets*, and *Big Momma's House* (all 2000). Making the critically reviled comedy *Big Momma's House* was particularly difficult for Giamatti because, as he told Amy Kroin for *Salon* (August 12, 2003, on-line), the process was "purely about getting laughs through physical comedy, and I wanted to see if I could do that, because it's not something I feel very comfortable doing. . . . Sometimes the films that appear to be the most lowbrow choices end up being the most difficult." *Duets*, too, got negative reviews, but many critics cited Giamatti's performance as the highlight of the otherwise lackluster film. Jack Mathews wrote for the New York *Daily News* (September 15, 2000), "Whether Giamatti has the major role or is just louder than the others, *Duets* seems like his movie." The actor, Mathews wrote, "busts a gut belting out the lyrics to various karaoke numbers, when he's not otherwise occupied by throwing some of the craziest, bug-eyed fits this side of Yosemite Sam."

In 2001 Giamatti appeared in Tim Burton's remake of *Planet of the Apes* as Limbo, a slave-trader ape, and in Todd Solondz's *Storytelling* as the nerdy independent filmmaker Toby Oxman. *Storytelling* was divided into two segments, entitled "Fiction" and "Non-Fiction"; while most reviewers agreed that "Fiction" was the stronger of the two, Giamatti garnered praise for his work in "Non-Fiction." "Mr. Giamatti, playing a desperately ridiculous character who is at once Mr. Solondz's foil and his alter ego, holds the movie together with his nervous energy," A. O. Scott wrote for the *New York Times* (September 29, 2001). Giamatti then won a rare starring role as Marty Wolf, an unscrupulous Hollywood producer, in the comedy *Big Fat Liar* (2002), which was billed as a "tween" movie—or one aimed at viewers between childhood and adulthood. Though most reviewers considered *Big Fat Liar* rather tepid fare, "Giamatti deserves some credit for the way he handles such silliness," in the opinion of Damien Cave, writing for *Salon* (February 8, 2002, on-line). "He literally throws himself into the role, and when he jiggles his hips to Duran Duran's 'Hungry Like the Wolf,' it's hard not to appreciate the effort." Later the same year Giamatti appeared in the British film *Thunderpants*, followed by roles in the 2003 films *Confidence*, *Paycheck*, and the made-for-television *The Pentagon Papers*.

Giamatti's roles, even as they grew in prominence, still tended to be mainly second-banana parts. "He's a perfectly excellent actor with a stripped-wire intensity, and in a just world he'd be playing leads," M. V. Moorhead wrote for the *Dallas Observer* (September 14, 2000). The filmmakers Robert Pulcini and Shari Springer Berman evidently agreed when they cast Giamatti as the protagonist of *American Splendor* (2003). In that film Giamatti portrayed the real-life, curmudgeonly Harvey Pekar, the author of the autobiographical comic-book series of the title, which focuses on the difficulties of everyday life. (Pekar himself also appeared in the film.) Giamatti found playing Pekar to be "weirdly addictive," as he admitted to Jason Anderson for *Eye Weekly* (August 14, 2003, on-line). "I think Harvey is a romantic figure. There's a great tradition of cranky outsiders, from Socrates on down. I love that kind of angry, self-educated, outsider guy and he's the epitome of it." In a review for *Salon* (August 15, 2003, on-line), Stephanie Zacharek called Giamatti "the most perfect Pekar you could imagine—other than, of course, the real Pekar himself," and Elvis Mitchell observed for the *New York Times* (August 15, 2003, on-line), "Slumped into a posture that's a question mark with a pot belly, Mr. Giamatti is a frustrated tremor, shaking and gesticulating futilely. His performance gets some of the real Pekar notes just right." *American Splendor* won the Grand Jury Prize at the 2003 Sundance Film Festival and garnered numerous additional awards and nominations.

Following Giamatti's turn as Pekar, the director Alexander Payne offered him the role of Miles Raymond, a divorced schoolteacher, oenophile, and would-be novelist, in the 2004 comedy *Sideways*. The film co-starred Thomas Haden Church as the gregarious Jack, a third-tier actor and Miles's best friend. Together, the pair embark on a weeklong wine-tasting trip through California, where Jack, who is about to be married, pursues his last sexual flings, and Miles takes tentative steps toward a relationship with a local waitress (played by Virginia Madsen). Both the film and the actors (Giamatti, Church, Madsen, and Sandra Oh, who played one of Jack's lovers) earned plaudits. "It took courage to cast Mr. Giamatti in the central role," Manohla

Dargis wrote for the *New York Times* (October 16, 2004, on-line), "not because he isn't up to the challenge, but because he's neither pretty nor a star, two no-no's in the contemporary film industry." In a representative review of Giamatti's performance, Desson Thompson enthused in the *Washington Post* (October 29, 2004, on-line), "Giamatti is a comedic gem, a walking rain cloud of despair who steals cash from his mother and refuses, absolutely refuses, to drink the wrong wine." The film's overwhelming critical reception left Giamatti feeling both honored and daunted. "This movie has caught on way more than I expected," he told John Patterson for the London *Guardian* (January 14, 2005, on-line). "I'm comfortable in my life, and I'm just a little worried about not being comfortable anymore [with all the attention]." He also admitted to Patterson, "It'd be disingenuous to say I don't like attention—I'm an actor for God's sake—and it's flattering and all, but attention was never my big goal. I just like to work and have a good time." *Sideways* won a Screen Actors Guild (SAG) award, two Golden Globe Awards, one Academy Award (for best screenplay), and six Independent Spirit awards, including a best-actor trophy for Giamatti.

Giamatti's credits for 2005 include voice work in the animated *Robots* and the short film *The Fan and the Flower* and roles in *Cinderella Man* and the upcoming *The Hawk Is Dying*. In the fact-based *Cinderella Man*, which is set in the 1920s and 1930s and centers on the boxer James J. Braddock (played by Russell Crowe), Giamatti portrayed Joe Gould, Braddock's manager. "Mr. Giamatti does a lot of his acting with his eyebrows," Manohla Dargis wrote in her *New York Times* (June 3, 2005) review, "which doesn't make the performance any less enjoyable. Gould was as much fixer as manager, and the actor makes you see the man's every angle as cleanly as if they were drawn with a ruler and compass."

Giamatti is currently at work on six films, which are tentatively due to premiere in 2006: *The Illusionist*, *Ant Bully*, *Paper Man*, *Lady in the Water*, *Shoot 'Em Up*, and, for television, *Amazing Screw-On Head*. He lives in New York City's Lower Manhattan with his wife, the screenwriter Elizabeth Cohen, and their son, Samuel, who was born in 2001. The family share their apartment with thousands of Giamatti's books. "I buy at least one a day," he told Devin Gordon for *Newsweek* (August 11, 2003). "It's a mania. My wife has been incredibly patient about this." On the subject of his acting success, Giamatti said to the interviewer for *Hollywood Reporter*, "I'm lucky, in that I'm able to choose the things that I want to do. But if the parts that are coming to me weren't coming to me, I'd seek them out. I'd consciously try to vary it."

—K.J.E.

Suggested Reading: *Film Monthly* (on-line) Oct. 19, 2004; *Hollywood Reporter* (on-line) Jan. 3, 2005; Internet Movie Database; (London) *Guardian* (on-line) Jan. 14, 2005; *New York*

Times p30 July 29, 2001, A p16 Sep. 29, 2001; *New York Times* (on-line) Aug. 15, 2003, Oct. 16, 2004; *Salon* (on-line) Aug. 12, 2003, Aug. 15, 2003

Selected Films: *She'll Take Romance*, 1990; *Singles*, 1992; *Past Midnight*, 1992; *Mighty Aphrodite*, 1995; *Sabrina*, 1995; *Before and After*, 1996; *Breathing Room*, 1996; *Donnie Brasco*, 1997; *Deconstructing Harry*, 1997; *My Best Friend's Wedding*, 1997; *A Further Gesture*, 1997; *Arresting Gena*, 1997; *Private Parts*, 1997; *The Truman Show*, 1998; *Doctor Dolittle*, 1998;

Saving Private Ryan, 1998; *The Negotiator*, 1998; *Safe Men*, 1998; *Cradle Will Rock*, 1999; *Man on the Moon*, 1999; *Duets*, 2000; *Big Momma's House*, 2000; *Planet of the Apes*, 2001; *Storytelling*, 2001; *Big Fat Liar*, 2002; *Thunderpants*, 2002; *Confidence*, 2003; *Paycheck*, 2003; *American Splendor*, 2003; *Sideways, 2004*; *Robots*, 2005; *The Fan and the Flower*, 2005; *Cinderella Man*, 2005

Selected Television Movies: *Winchell*, 1998; *Tourist Trap*, 1998; *If These Walls Could Talk 2*, 2000; *The Pentagon Papers*, 2003

Courtesy of the *New Yorker*

Gladwell, Malcolm

Sep. 3, 1963– Author; staff writer for the New Yorker

Address: The New Yorker, 4 Times Sq., New York, NY 10036-6592

In the tradition of such famed prose stylists as E. B. White and A. J. Liebling, Malcolm Gladwell has developed a devoted following of *New Yorker* readers who appreciate his singular approach to magazine journalism. In the *Toronto Star* (June 14, 1999), Judy Stoffman proclaimed that Gladwell "may be the outstanding magazine journalist of his generation. His stories in The New Yorker, on subjects ranging from the problem of weight loss ('The Pima Paradox') to the differences between Afro-Americans and Caribbean blacks ('Black Like Them') to the meaning of men's trousers ('Listen-

ing to Khakis') to the social history of women's hair dyes ('True Colors'), arrive at profound truths through a close examination of the seemingly trivial." The *New Yorker*'s editorial director, Henry Finder, told Joseph P. Kahn for the *Boston Globe* (May 4, 2000) that Gladwell's greatest accomplishment is the invention of "a whole new genre, the Gladwell Piece," which Kahn defined as "a piece that is bound together by narrative and character but driven not just by an idea but an argument. His pieces radically reframe issues, like poverty or affirmative action, making you take a second look at things you took for granted."

With the publication of his first book, *The Tipping Point: How Little Things Can Make a Big Difference* (2000), which applied to the study of cultural phenomena theories of how diseases spread, Gladwell became especially influential as a journalist covering the business community. In his review of *The Tipping Point* for the *New York Times* (February 28, 2000), Christopher Lehmann-Haupt wrote that the implications of Gladwell's theories are powerful: "Correctly applied they could be used to run businesses more effectively, to turn products into runaway best sellers and perhaps most important to alter human behavior." Though critics were generally less impressed with his next book, *Blink: The Power of Thinking Without Thinking* (2005), it cemented his reputation as a master at exploring and conveying ideas. "There is a genuine hunger in the business world, like all aspects of Western society, for new ideas," Gladwell told Paul Wilner for the *San Francisco Chronicle* (January 30, 2005). "People are beginning to understand that there is an awful lot going on in different parts of academia and the scientific world that it makes sense to be familiar with. And that's what I am. I'm a translator of, an emissary from, other worlds."

The youngest of three sons, Malcolm Gladwell was born on September 3, 1963 in Fareham, England, to Graham M. L. Gladwell and the former Joyce Nation. His British-born father is a noted mathematician and the author or co-author of five textbooks; his Jamaican-born mother is a family therapist. When his parents met, at an English university in the 1950s, interracial couples were still quite rare and overt bigotry was commonplace. Joyce Gladwell detailed their struggle for acceptance in her autobiography, *Brown Face, Big Master* (1969). ("Big Master" refers to God.) In 1969 Graham Gladwell accepted a teaching position at the University of Waterloo, in Canada, and the family moved to Elmira, a small town near Toronto. "Elmira was a wonderful place to grow up," Gladwell told J. Timothy Hunt for the Kitchener-Waterloo, Ontario, *Record* (June 19, 1999). "It was a little bit sleepy, but it's a very close-knit, warm, genuine community." In his article "Black Like Them," written for the *New Yorker* (April 29, 1996), Gladwell recalled, "For many years, [my mother] was the only black person in town, but I cannot remember wondering or worrying, or even thinking, about this. . . . My own color was not something I ever thought much about, either, because it seemed such a stray fact." Gladwell has attributed the progressive attitudes in Elmira to the influence of the town's Mennonite population. "The example of the Mennonites is an important one: the idea that you can grow up as a group separate from the mainstream and still carry yourself with a certain dignity, tolerance and respect," he told John Congram for the *Presbyterian Record* (March 2001). "That is not a trick that many minority groups or culturally separate groups are good at carrying off. That becomes a powerful example." Terry Martin, one of his childhood friends, told J. Timothy Hunt that even in his youth, Gladwell thought about issues from multiple perspectives. "Growing up, he always liked the notion of being out of step," Martin said.

Raised in the Presbyterian faith, Gladwell started reading the Bible at age six. The Gladwells did not own a television, and young Malcolm frequently accompanied his father to Waterloo University's library, where he would spend the day immersed in the stacks. "I just remember lying around, riding my bicycle and reading books," he told Nicholas Boer for the *Contra Costa (California) Times* (April 2, 2000). "I had the quietest, least eventful childhood imaginable." He exhibited a talent for writing at an early age; when he was 12 he purchased an electric typewriter and started writing letters to car companies requesting photographs of the expensive cars that he liked. "His letters were so well written and so well presented—he signed them as though he was the boss and a secretary had typed them—that on one occasion, a car salesman came to the door and asked for Mr. Malcolm Gladwell," Joyce Gladwell told Judy Stoffman. "And I said 'Who do you want? My 12-year-old son?'" In high school he began publishing his own zine, *Ad Hominem: A Journal of Slander and Critical Opinion*, and at age 16 he won a short-story contest with an account of an "interview" with God.

After Gladwell left Elmira to attend the University of Toronto's Trinity College, in 1980, he encountered overt racism for the first time. "This was during the early nineteen-eighties, when West In-

dians were immigrating to Canada in droves, and Toronto had become second only to New York as the Jamaican expatriates' capital in North America," he wrote in "Black Like Them." "At school, in the dining hall, I was served by Jamaicans. The infamous Jane-Finch projects, in northern Toronto, were considered the Jamaican projects. The drug trade then taking off was said to be the Jamaican drug trade. In the popular imagination, Jamaicans were—and are—welfare queens and gun-toting gangsters and dissolute youths." A light-skinned man who wore his hair closely cropped most of his life, Gladwell has said that most people he meets are unaware of his Afro-Caribbean roots—and that many of them, in unguarded moments, have made bigoted comments about the Jamaican community. Though he has written about race in terms of sociological and cultural issues, he told Alex Kuczynski for the *New York Times* (March 20, 2000), he no longer wrestles with his own identity: "I don't know what I consider myself. It's too complex. There are too many ways to define yourself, and [race is] not a way I have chosen to define myself anymore."

After receiving his bachelor's degree in history, in 1984, Gladwell tried to get a job in advertising. "I applied at 14 places and got back 14 rejection letters," he told Valerie Hill for the Kitchener-Waterloo, Ontario, *Record* (November 23, 2000). He also unsuccessfully applied for editorial work at the *Toronto Star* and the *Globe and Mail*. Unable to get a job in Canada and eager to explore other cities, Gladwell accepted an internship at the *American Spectator*, in Bloomington, Indiana. He was fired from that position, perhaps because of his tendency to oversleep. Soon afterward, in 1987, he landed a job as a business reporter at the *Washington Post*. In 1990 he switched to the health beat, where one of his areas of focus was the HIV crisis. He began to see ways in which the findings of epidemiologists (who study the spread of disease) could be applied to business models. "I became interested in the dynamics of epidemics, in particular how epidemics differ from our intuition about them," he told John Congram for the *Presbyterian Record* (February 2001). "I was struck by how epidemiologists have all this wonderful specialized knowledge but did not know or never thought of sharing it outside their own medical community. It was so relevant because many of us are in the business of trying to spread a contagious idea throughout the population." This observation was the seed of his first book, *The Tipping Point*.

In 1992 Gladwell started writing "Comment" and "Talk of the Town" columns for the *New Yorker* as a freelancer. The following year he was promoted to chief of the *Washington Post*'s New York bureau. He left the newspaper in 1996, when Tina Brown, then editor in chief of the *New Yorker*, offered him a coveted position as staff writer at that weekly magazine. "Right out of the gate he started impressing the editors by taking a few relatively predictable topics they suggested and steering them in entirely unpredictable directions," Hunt wrote, "as he did in 'Conquering the Coma' (July 8, 1996), in which he turned an assignment about a tabloidy, high-profile crime victim into a piece about an important issue of medical protocol." In the article Gladwell intertwined reportage about a New York City woman who was attacked by a deranged assailant in Central Park with the story of the neurotrauma surgeon who saved her life, Jam Ghajar.

"Every piece I write must have two ingredients," Gladwell explained to Stoffman. "'The story,' which is about an event or person, and 'the idea'— some theory or organizing principle." With that approach Gladwell quickly became one of the most popular New Yorker writers. "A Gladwell piece is, or is coming to be, instantly recognizable," Joseph P. Kahn wrote. "Usually it draws upon some factual oddity or obscure scientific study to make surprising connections between micro- and macro-events, or between a little-known personage and a larger social issue. A facile, counterintuitive thinker, Gladwell is a peerless (and fearless) debunker, a writer who does not so much follow trends as perform tissue analyses on them." Gladwell has gotten many of the ideas for his articles—which have included such varied topics as the impact of the hair-coloring industry on feminism and why the television series Melrose Place was so popular among 30-something viewers—while wandering the stacks of New York University's library, browsing academic journals and books. "I see myself as an intermediary between the academic world and popular media, and if you are going to do that there is a certain amount of responsibility inherent in that," he told Vinay Menon for the Toronto Star (March 5, 2000). "And I am continually impressed by how many brilliant ideas there are that don't see the light of day beyond the world of academia."

Gladwell is not without detractors. "To fans of the author and New Yorker staff writer, Gladwell is the perfect mix of entertainer and educator, always turning them on to some cool new scientific development," Cynthia Cotts wrote for the Village Voice (September 17, 2002). "But to a handful of critics, he is a promoter of curious causes with a deceptively one-sided narrative style. One New York editor recently called Gladwell an 'intellectual tap dancer'—that is, a writer whose elite audience is so hypnotized by his performance that they don't notice the details he is leaving out." As an example, Cotts pointed to a 1997 New Yorker article in which Gladwell asserted that the oncologist Susan Love was overemphasizing the risks involved in hormone-replacement therapy for menopausal women. Love's concerns seemed to be vindicated in the summer of 2002, when a study funded by the National Institutes of Health concluded that women on such therapy did indeed run a higher risk of developing breast cancer. "I'm first and foremost a storyteller," Gladwell told Edward Nawotka for USA Today (January 25, 2005). "I'm not a trained scientist. I'm an interested amateur."

One of Gladwell's 1996 pieces for the New Yorker, "The Tipping Point," applied the principles of epidemiology to explain the falling crime rate in New York City. "Tipping point" is the epidemiological term for the moment an outbreak of a disease reaches critical mass and becomes a full-blown epidemic. Gladwell theorized that "social problems behave like infectious agents." For example, though only a few extra police officers had been added to one of the most troubled precincts in the city, crime rates dropped significantly after their arrival. The additional officers created conditions favorable to a tipping point, turning the tide toward more lawful behavior.

The publisher Little, Brown offered Gladwell an unusually large advance—$1.5 million—to turn the article into a book. In The Tipping Point: How Little Things Can Make a Big Difference, he expanded upon his thesis. "Epidemics are a function of the people who transmit the infectious agents, the infectious agent itself, and the environment in which the infectious agent is operating," Gladwell wrote in The Tipping Point. "And when an epidemic tips, when it is jolted out of equilibrium, it tips because something has happened, some change occurred in one (or two or three) of those areas." Gladwell labeled those three areas, or determinants, as "The Law of the Few," "The Stickiness Factor," and "The Power of Context." Gladwell used this theory to explain the success of Paul Revere's famous ride, in 1775, to alert the colonial militias that the British soldiers were coming. Another patriot, William Dawes, made a nearly identical ride, but he is rarely mentioned in history books. The reason for his obscurity, according to Gladwell, is that while both Dawes and Revere carried the same sensational news through towns that were equally receptive, only Revere was "gregarious and intensely social," possessing the "rare set of social skills" that allow a person to push something to the tipping point. According to "The Law of the Few," three types of people have these social skills: "Connectors" (those, like Revere, who know the right people), "Mavens" (those who know what is going on), and "Salesmen" (those who can effectively communicate information). Gladwell wrote that people who fall into one or more of these categories play an important role because "word of mouth is—even in this age of mass communications and multimillion-dollar advertising campaigns—still the most important form of communication." "Think, for a moment, about the last expensive restaurant you went to, the last expensive piece of clothing you bought, and the last movie you saw," he explained. "In how many of those cases was your decision about where to spend your money heavily influenced by the recommendation of a friend? There are plenty of advertising executives who think that precisely because of the sheer ubiquity of marketing efforts these days, word-of-mouth appeals have become the only kind of persuasion that most of us respond to anymore."

Word of mouth about Gladwell's book spread quickly throughout the business community. Starbucks's chairman and chief global strategist, Howard Schultz, has attributed his company's success to the tipping-point phenomenon explained by Gladwell, while Simmons Market Research and the public-relations agency Ketchum are both developing databases that attempt to identify the people who fit the categories in Gladwell's theory of "The Law of the Few." "No one in recent memory has slipped into the role of business thought leader as gracefully or influentially as Gladwell," Danielle Sacks wrote for *Fast Company* (January 2005). "Soon after his first book . . . fell into America's palms, Gladwell made the leap from generalist staff writer at *The New Yorker* to marketing god."

Some critics pointed out, however, that many of the concepts in the book were not new to marketers. "When he talks about mavens or connectors, in my neighborhood we call them 'gossips,'" Mario Almonte, who heads the public-relations division at Herman Associates, told Sacks. Moreover, the idea of the tipping point had been explored earlier, by the economist Thomas Schelling. Sacks suggested that Gladwell's real talent lies in his skill at repackaging for laypeople complex concepts he finds in academia. "When I was writing *The Tipping Point*," Gladwell told Sacks, "I realized that in order for people to talk about something . . . they need some way to describe and name things. So I always like to try to come up with simple, sort of catchy ways of capturing complex ideas." With *The Tipping Point*, he succeeded, judging by its popularity: the hardback edition stayed on the *New York Times* best-seller list for 28 weeks, and more than 800,000 copies of *The Tipping Point* are in print. For a time the term "the tipping point" became ubiquitous, particularly in business communications and the media. Reviews of and essays about the book appeared in an unusually wide variety of periodicals, among them *Golf Digest*, *New Statesman*, *Platt's Oilgram News*, *Business Insurance*, and *Architectural Record*.

In 2004 Gladwell figured in one of the highest-profile plagiarism cases ever to shake the theater world. The February 24, 1997 issue of the *New Yorker* had included "Damaged," Gladwell's profile of Dorothy Otnow Lewis, who studies physical and psychological aspects of the minds of murderers. Seven years later Lewis discovered that significant portions of Gladwell's piece, as well as several autobiographical descriptions in and other features of her book *Guilt by Reason of Insanity* (1998), were used by the playwright Bryony Lavery in her hit Broadway drama, *Frozen*. Lewis wanted to sue for legal compensation and asked Gladwell to assign the copyright of his article to her. He at first agreed but later changed his mind. "Lewis had told me that she 'wanted her life back,'" Gladwell wrote in his follow-up article, "Something Borrowed," for the *New Yorker* (November 22, 2004). "Yet in order to get her life back, it appeared, she

first had to acquire it from me. That seemed a little strange. Then I got a copy of the script for *Frozen*. I found it breathtaking. I realize that this isn't supposed to be a relevant consideration. And yet it was: instead of feeling that my words had been taken from me, I felt that they had become part of some grander cause. . . . Bryony Lavery had seen one of my articles, responded to what she read, and used it as she constructed a work of art. And now her reputation was in tatters. Something about that didn't seem right." As of October 2005, the dispute between Lewis and Lavery had not been settled.

A simple change in hairstyle precipitated the idea for Gladwell's second book. "When I was in my 30s, I went from having conservative, short hair to growing a wild Afro," he told Edward Nawotka. "There were some good consequences to this. Many people treated me like I was cooler and funnier. But I also started to run afoul of police all the time. I got ludicrous speeding tickets and stopped for no good reason. Then one day, I was walking on 14th Street in New York City, and a van pulled up with three police officers in it. They thought I looked like a rapist they were looking for and grilled me for 20 minutes before letting me go. It was at that moment I realized my hair was enormously relevant to how people decided who I am. I thought that, surely, this is worth some kind of examination. So in that sense, it was an important moment." Gladwell set to work on *Blink* (2005), a book about rapid cognition, the snap judgments that people make within the first few seconds of being introduced to a new person or situation. Gladwell argued that these judgments influence us more than we realize and that, though we have been taught to disregard them, in certain circumstances they are more accurate than assessments reached after far longer periods. To illustrate his point, he opened the book by describing the case of a stone kouros (a Greek statue of a naked boy) that the Getty Museum purchased for $10 million in 1983. Though the dealer provided historical documentation, and scientific tests indicated that the statue was authentic, some experts suspected at first glance that it was fake. Their immediate impressions proved to be correct.

In *Blink*, Gladwell also described a process known as "thin slicing," in which humans are able to assess accurately the entirety of a situation or thing when provided with only a small piece of information. He suggested that whatever conclusions we draw at first glance result not from intuition but from a rapid-fire rational process that likely evolved in humans as a survival mechanism. He also examined the negative social consequences of thin slicing, blaming it, for instance, for the killing by New York City police of Amadou Diallo, an unarmed immigrant who the officers thought had a gun, and for the gender bias that affects hiring for members of symphony orchestras, which with few exceptions are overwhelmingly male. Such outcomes can be avoided, he advised, with better education and training; people are inevitably influenced, consciously or subconsciously, by snap judgments, and the more that a person knows about a particular subject, the more likely it is that the person's snap judgments will be correct.

Gladwell presented his thesis at the beginning of the book; in the subsequent chapters, he offered colorfully described examples of rapid cognition at work. "Gladwell's real genius is as a storyteller," Lev Grossman wrote for *Time* (January 10, 2005). "He's like an omniscient, many-armed Hindu god of anecdotes: he plucks them from every imaginable field of human endeavor." In a review for the *New Republic* (January 24, 2005), Richard A. Posner described *Blink* as "a series of loosely connected anecdotes, rich in 'human interest' particulars but poor in analysis" and complained that Gladwell "revels in the irrelevant." "As one moves from anecdote to anecdote," Posner continued, "the reader of *Blink* quickly realizes, though its author does not, that a variety of interestingly different mental operations are being crammed unhelpfully into the 'rapid cognition' pigeonhole." On the National Public Radio program *Day to Day* (January 12, 2005), David Kipen said that while Gladwell had constructed "his arguments with the airless neatness of a statistical proof," the book's "thesis more or less boils down to 'First impressions are trustworthy except when they're not.'"

Gladwell speaks regularly before the business community, earning $40,000 per appearance, according to Sacks. Two of his articles have been adapted as screenplays: "The Dead Zone," his 1999 *New Yorker* article about the great flu pandemic of 1918, was turned into a television movie of the same title for ABC. A major motion picture based on Gladwell's 1997 *New Yorker* article "The Cool Hunt," about a scout for the sneaker manufacturer Reebok who seeks the cutting edge in foot fashion in major American cities, is currently in development.

Gladwell is single and lives in New York City. "I am fairly typical and boring . . . ," he told Vinay Menon. "I watch a lot of sports on television. I don't have any kind of great, exceptional outside interests. I'm just average. . . . I am a big believer in luck. And I think that if I look back on my life, I have had extraordinarily good luck on a number of critical occasions."

—J.C.

Suggested Reading: *Boston Globe* E p1 May 4, 2000, with photo; *Fast Company* p64+ Jan. 2005; gladwell.com; (Kitchener-Waterloo, Ontario) *Record* I p4 June 19, 1999, with photo; *New York Times Book Review* p1+ Jan. 16, 2005; *Toronto Star* June 14, 1999, with photo; *Washington Post* (on-line) May 17, 1998, with photos

Selected Books: *The Tipping Point: How Little Things Can Make a Big Difference*, 2000; *Blink: The Power of Thinking Without Thinking*, 2005

Gopnik, Adam

Aug. 24, 1956– Essayist; art critic

Address: The New Yorker, 4 Times Sq., New York, NY 10036-6592

A self-described "comic-sentimental essayist," Adam Gopnik has been writing for the *New Yorker* magazine for almost two decades. Characterized by Gersh Kuntzman in *Newsweek* (May 30, 2002) as the *New Yorker*'s "resident metaphor-maker," he is best known for his nuanced assessments of human behavior and cultural attitudes, and in particular for his writings about life in France. Although his essays, many of which are humorous, are generally grounded in current events, ranging in scale from major news stories to day-to-day personal experiences, Gopnik has a penchant for extrapolating upon concrete observations to arrive at larger conclusions about human nature and society at large. "His trick is an old one—extend the particular to the universal," Charles Bremner wrote in a review for the London *Times* (May 19, 2001). In an article for the London *Daily Telegraph* (May 19, 2001), John Lanchester lamented that Gopnik "isn't as well known in [Great Britain] as he deserves to be," adding, "He is a brilliant reporter, a wit, and he combines an innate scepticism with a taste for theory and the abstract idea—a refreshingly nonstandard combination."

In an essay for the *New Yorker* (September 24, 2001), Gopnik wrote, "It is the symbolic city that draws us here, and the real city that keeps us." He was referring to New York, but he has expressed similar sentiments about Paris, the city in which he and his family lived from 1995 to 2000. During those five years, Gopnik chronicled his daily experiences as an expatriate in a series of essays for the *New Yorker;* he later compiled his writings about the storied city into a best-selling book entitled *Paris to the Moon* (2001). In the *New York Times* (October 22, 2000), Alain de Botton attributed to Gopnik's writing a distinctly French quality, noting, "Gopnik writes essays in the French rather than the Anglo-Saxon style, by which I mean that he fuses a personal voice . . . with an essentially serious intellectual project." While many critics find Gopnik's commentary both incisive and charming, some have complained that his preoccupation with the details of everyday life is a kind of provincialism or pedantry. Chris Lehmann, writing for *Salon* (December 10, 1996, on-line), accused Gopnik of a "resolutely trivial" and "disconcertingly tiny worldview, one that accords closely with [the Austrian psychoanalyst Sigmund]

Adam Gopnik

Freud's definition of neurosis as a private religion." Nevertheless, Gopnik has no qualms about using minor events as springboards for his musings on culture, human nature, and other issues. Moreover, a professed devotee of the personal essay, he is keenly aware of the hazards of putting one's personality on the page: "It's a treacherous form," he explained to Robert Birnbaum in an interview for the Identity Theory Web site, "because the line between entertainment and egomania is particularly fine and difficult. Essayists generally—and certainly me particularly—tend to be more like performers than novelists. Novelists are like architects or builders. They are willing to sit in a room for five or six years and build something and they at some level don't give a damn what the public thinks. . . . Essayists aren't like that. At least this one isn't. You have to have a bit of the ham in you. You like to do the thing and feel that the people are reacting."

Adam Gopnik was born in Philadelphia, Pennsylvania, on August 24, 1956. One of six children, he grew up in Montreal, Canada, where both of his parents were professors at McGill University. His mother, Myrna Gopnik, was a professor of linguistics; his father, Irwin Gopnik, taught English and was the dean of students. Gopnik attended Northmount High School and Dawson College, in Montreal, before enrolling as an undergraduate at McGill, where he earned a B.A. degree in art history in 1980. He then moved to New York City to pursue a master's degree at the Institute of Fine Arts (IFA) at New York University. (He never completed the master's program.) Also in 1980, together with the Canadian author Jack Huberman, he published *Voila Carême!: The Gastronomic Adventures of*

History's Greatest Chef, a book about the 19th-century French cook Antonin Carême. After working part-time at *Gentlemen's Quarterly* (*GQ*), he got promoted to fiction editor of that magazine. In 1985 he was hired to an editorial post at Alfred A. Knopf publishers, a position that brought him into contact with some of the editors at the *New Yorker*. Gopnik had been submitting articles to that weekly since he first came to New York, but it was not until 1986 that the *New Yorker* bought one of his pieces—an article about the baseball team the Montreal Expos. The following year the magazine hired him as a writer for its "Talk of the Town" section. After some time as a columnist, he became the *New Yorker*'s art critic; later, he was named one of the magazine's editors, a position he held until his move to Paris, in 1995.

In 1990 Gopnik collaborated with Kirk Varnedoe, a former IFA professor and the chief curator of the department of painting and sculpture at the Museum of Modern Art (MoMA), in New York City, to curate a controversial exhibition at the MoMA entitled "High & Low: Modern Art and Popular Culture." The exhibition, which examined the complex and often ambivalent relationship between 20th-century "high" art and various forms of "low" art by presenting comic strips, advertisements, and graffiti alongside paintings and sculptures by celebrated artists, was met with harsh reviews from both ends of the artistic spectrum. While conservative critics condemned Varnedoe and Gopnik for elevating artifacts of popular culture to the status of art objects, liberal critics complained that the juxtaposition of "high" and "low" works undermined the validity of the latter by presenting them as "hardly more than captions below the paintings and sculptures they purportedly influenced," as Michael Kimmelman wrote for the *New York Times* (October 21, 1990). The critic Barbara Rose, writing for the *Journal of Art*, expressed frustration with Gopnik and Varnedoe's populist approach, accusing them of succumbing to "the currently 'hip' premise of the equal validity of all forms of cultural expression from Mozart to MTV," as quoted by Paul Richard in the *Washington Post* (October 7, 1990); Roberta Smith, writing for the *New York Times*, denounced the exhibition as "a disaster . . . arbitrary, peculiar and maligning," according to Robert Hughes in *Time* (October 22, 1990). By contrast, Paul Richard commended the exhibition for recognizing the importance of artists previously marginalized by the art establishment: "Varnedoe and Gopnik, unlike many of their colleagues in other art museums, here happily acknowledge that such fine comedic draftsmen as R. Crumb and Saul Steinberg, Winsor McCay and George Herriman are masters of a sort, and it is about time."

The exhibition catalogue that Gopnik and Varnedoe assembled, which bore the same title as the show, elicited more-positive reviews. While Roger Kimball, writing for the London *Guardian* (October 18, 1990), complained that the book was "full of . . . drivel," Paul Richard deemed the 460-page volume "among the most rewarding books on reading modern art to appear in many years." Robert Hughes praised the authors' "vast scholarly élan," noting that "the show reads as a set of illustrations to the book, for only in the book can the comparison of demotic source with final object be done with the necessary detail." Gopnik and Varnedoe also collaborated to edit *Modern Art and Popular Culture: Readings in High and Low*, a collection of essays related to the subject of the show.

In 2001 Gopnik published *Paris to the Moon*, a collection of articles and personal essays about his experiences living abroad. "The moral of the book," he told Robert Birnbaum, "is meant to be fairly clear. Which is that you have to take civilizations and people whole. You cannot make them be what you want them to be." Taking as his theme "the ineluctable Frenchness of the French," according to Judy Stoffman in the *Toronto Star* (November 28, 2000), he examined the differences between French and American culture by recounting his experiences as an expatriate. A Francophile and a foreigner, he expressed simultaneous enchantment and bemusement with Paris and its citizens. The city bore little resemblance to his romanticized preconceptions of it, and although he and his family were able to carve out a happy life for themselves there, they never quite felt at home. Gopnik told Robert Birnbaum, "In Paris we had . . . a genuinely beautiful existence. That is to say . . . every detail of one's daily life—from the place you go to get breakfast to how you shop for Brussels sprouts, is pleasing to the eye, pleasing to the soul. . . . But we didn't have a full life in the sense that we weren't fully connected. It wasn't home."

Paris to the Moon quickly became a *New York Times* best-seller, "a remarkable, indeed unprecedented, thing to happen to a book of reprinted journalism," according to John Lanchester. The book was also a critical success. Alain de Botton deemed it "the finest book on France in recent years"; Judy Stoffman described it as "a witty and affectionate memoir"; and Robbie Hudson, writing for the London *Sunday Times* (July 29, 2001), praised Gopnik's "frothily elegant . . . [and] beautiful fan's-eye view of Frenchness at the turn of the millennium." Even French critics were impressed with Gopnik's insights into their culture. A writer for *Le Monde*, as quoted by Robert Birnbaum, described Gopnik as a "witty and Voltairean commentator on French life," a reference to the celebrated 18th-century French writer Voltaire (the nom de plume of François-Marie Arouet).

Having established himself as something of an American authority on France with the publication of *Paris to the Moon*, Gopnik went on to pen the introductions to *The Necklace and Other Tales* (2003), a collection of Guy de Maupassant's short stories translated by Joachim Neugroschel; and *The Wrong Side of Paris* (2003), Jordan Stump's translation of Honoré de Balzac's *L'Envers de l'histoire contemporaine*. Recently, he edited a book entitled, aptly enough, *Americans in Paris: A Literary Anthology* (2004). While Gopnik's textual contributions to the book, which spans three centuries of American writing, were limited to a preface and several brief introductory essays, Janet Maslin, in the *New York Times* (April 15, 2004), ascribed "the book's sparkle . . . as much to its editor, Adam Gopnik, as to the voices that he collects." In his preface, Gopnik returned to one of the themes with which he had dealt in *Paris to the Moon*, namely, the tension between Americans' romantic ideas about Paris and their actual experiences of it. "This book is a history of the worlds Americans have made in the city where they have gone to be happy . . . ," he wrote, as quoted by Brenda Wineapple in the *Nation* (June 28, 2004). "It is in part, therefore, the history of an illusion."

Since the mid-1990s, in addition to his work for the *New Yorker*, Gopnik has contributed essays for a number of art books. In 1994 he was the author of a biographical piece about the photographer Richard Avedon that appeared in *Evidence: 1944–1994*, the catalogue for an Avedon retrospective mounted that year by the Whitney Museum of American Art, in New York City. He collaborated with the photojournalist Peter Turnley to write the text for *Parisians: Photographs by Peter Turnley* (2000), a collection of Turnley's images of Paris, and contributed an essay to *Wayne Thiebaud: A Paintings Retrospective* (2000), the catalogue for an exhibition of the same name mounted by the Fine Arts Museums of San Francisco, in California. In the latter publication, Gopnik discussed Thiebaud's paintings from a literary standpoint, comparing them to the work of such American writers as Walt Whitman, William Carlos Williams, and John Updike. Robert L. Pincus, writing for the Copley News Service (July 31, 2000), praised Gopnik's essay as "sensitive and elegantly styled," and Christine Biederman, in the *Dallas Observer* (October 5, 2000), judged it to be "intelligent and readable." In 2002 Gopnik contributed an article about the history of the elevated railway in New York City to *Joel Sternfeld: Walking the High Line*, a collection of photographs by Sternfeld. He also wrote the forewords to *Here and There* (2004), a book of photographs by Helen Levitt, and *City Art: New York's Percent for Art Program* (2005), by the art critic Eleanor Heartney.

Gopnik's first children's book, *The King in the Window*, was published in 2005. The hero is a 10-year-old American boy named Oliver, who is living unhappily in Paris, where his father devotes virtually all his time and mental energy to his work as a journalist. Oliver gets caught up in high adventure when he dons a golden paper crown that he has won on the Christian holy day known as Epiphany—Three Kings' Day—and is mistaken for the royal personage of the book's title. Reviews of the book were decidedly mixed. In *Library Journal* (September 1, 2005, on-line), Barbara Hoffert praised the book, writing that readers will "discover an entertaining, intricately plotted adventure story whose pages just keep turning." Hoffert recommended the book "highly . . . and not just for children, whatever the cover says." A critic writing for *Publishers Weekly* (September 12, 2005, on-line) was less enthusiastic, judging the story to be "ambitious, complex and overly long," and complaining that too much of it was aimed at adults, citing as examples its references to "Yoko Ono's singing, wine expert Robert Parker, [and] book royalties." "Think of this as Harry Potter for the Mensa set," the reviewer concluded, referring to the hero of J. K. Rowling's phenomenally popular series and to an organization whose members supposedly have unusually high I.Q.s. A writer for *Kirkus Reviews* (September 15, 2005, on-line) dismissed *The King in the Window* as an "overstuffed fantasy [that] is next to impossible to endure."

Gopnik's *New Yorker* writings earned the publication a National Magazine Award for essays and criticism in 1997; the following year Gopnik himself was honored with a George Polk Award for magazine reporting. His essay "The City and the Pillars," about New Yorkers' reactions to the events of September 11, 2001, was included in *The Best American Travel Writing 2002*, an anthology

edited by Frances Mayes. He is a regular broadcaster for the Canadian Broadcasting Corp. and the author of the articles about American culture in the last two editions of the *Encyclopedia Britannica*.

Adam Gopnik lives in New York City with his wife, Martha Parker, who is a filmmaker, and their two children, Luke Auden and Olivia Esmé Claire. He has attributed his keen observational faculties and cultural insights to his relationships with his children. "As long as you still have new consciousnesses in the world," he told Robert Birnbaum, "then old things never get old. As long as there are new people to see them, they remain new."

—L.W.

Suggested Reading: Identity Theory Web site; (London) *Daily Telegraph* p3+ May 19, 2001; *New York Times* VII p8+ Oct. 22, 2000; Gopnik, Adam. *Paris to the Moon*, 2001

Selected Books: *Paris to the Moon*, 2001; *The King in the Window*, 2005; as editor—*Modern Art and Popular Culture: Readings in High and Low*, 1990 (with Kirk Varnedoe); *Americans in Paris: A Literary Anthology*, 2004

Gordon, Bruce S.

Feb. 15, 1946– President and CEO of the NAACP; former telecommunications executive

Address: NAACP National HQ, 4805 Mt. Hope Dr., Baltimore, MD 21215

When a 25-year-old African-American university student was slaughtered by a trio of bouncers in New Orleans's French Quarter in the early morning hours of New Year's Day 2005, members of the National Association for the Advancement of Colored People (NAACP)—one of the oldest and largest civil rights groups in the United States—mobilized to protest the racism of proprietors of the area's businesses by organizing street demonstrations. Months later Bruce S. Gordon, the newly appointed president and CEO of the NAACP, cited that protest as an example of why the organization needs to rethink its approach to defending civil rights. "I certainly applaud the local branch for its activism. However, I would say in addition to that, we should take our dollars elsewhere," he told Kenneth Meeks for *Black Enterprise* (September 2005). "We spend money in that economy, in that community, and most of those establishments in the Quarter are not owned by African Americans. We should spend where we are respected. That, to me, is a more significant message than a protest because it has an economic impact on the offenders."

A former telecommunications executive, Gordon—who speaks of the NAACP "brand" and the need to "leverage" black buying power—was a sur-

Courtesy of Photogenic Services

prising choice for an organization that usually picks its leaders from the political or religious arena. Gordon, however, sees his appointment as in keeping with the tradition of the civil rights movement, viewing his own assent up the corporate ladder as an example of social activism. "I used to say you've got two choices," he told Vern E. Smith for *Crisis* (July/August 2005). "You can deal on the outside of an institution, whatever it is, government or corporations, and try to [effect] change by forcing that institution to behave differently. Or you can get on the inside of that institution and try to change it on the inside. . . . If you get on the inside, and you get power . . . then you get the right to make the changes yourself."

Bruce S. Gordon was born on February 15, 1946 in Camden, New Jersey. His father, Walter Gordon, was a co-founder and secretary-treasurer of the Camden chapter of the NAACP, and starting at the age of eight, Gordon accompanied his father to meetings. At the time there were fewer career opportunities available to educated African-Americans than there are today, and like many other blacks of their generation, Gordon's parents worked as educators: Walter as a school administrator, and Gordon's mother, Violet, as a teacher. Gordon expected that he, too, would teach, but as his high-school graduation approached, his parents encouraged him to take advantage of the new opportunities made available by the civil rights movement and think about entering a different profession. "They believed the world would look a lot different than it did in their generation," he told Rosalind McLymont for the *Network Journal* (January 31, 2004).

Gordon attended Gettysburg College, in Pennsylvania, where he took an interest in social sciences and played wide receiver for the football team. Although he was an undergraduate during the 1960s—a time of mass student protest on many American campuses—Gordon was neither an activist nor a protestor. "Out of the 1,800 students on campus, there were only three Blacks. I was the only Black student in my class, the 10th Black student in the history of the college," he told Vern E. Smith. "This was not about getting an NAACP chapter on Gettysburg's campus, this was just three folks. So I was at a different stage in life then. I was one of those kids who was walking through a door that civil rights activists had gotten open for me, and once I got in, I was just trying to figure out how to survive."

In 1968 Gordon earned a bachelor's degree in anthropology and sociology (liberal arts and sociology, according to some sources), and applied for a management-trainee post with the local phone company in Philadelphia, among other positions in the area. He took the position with Bell of Pennsylvania because it paid the most, but he did not intend to stay with the company for longer than a few years. "I've always been bored easily," he told Nadirah Sabir for *Black Enterprise* (May 1995). "I had this fear that if I stayed, I would be doing the same job my entire life." After he completed the training program, in 1970, Gordon accepted a job as a Bell business-office manager. In his free time he wrote a weekly column for a local suburban newspaper, *Today's Post*, addressing some of the more contentious race issues of the day. Still struggling with how he could best be of use to the civil rights movement, Gordon considered resigning

from Bell of Philadelphia to take charge of an urban Philadelphia school for academically challenged students. One Friday he turned in his resignation, only to call his boss on the following Sunday, asking to come back.

After Gordon had been the office manager for two years, a rumor started circulating that he was going to be fired. A general manager in sales, Carl Nurick, stepped in and requested that Gordon be transferred to his department. "[Nurick] was Jewish and felt that he had . . . been a victim of discrimination," Gordon told Cassandra Hayes for *Black Enterprise* (September 1998). "He liked that I was a black guy who had a lot to say about the business, and we connected on those terms." Gordon worked under Nurick for two years as a sales and marketing manager. In 1974 he became the personnel supervisor. He steadily advanced through the company, receiving a promotion roughly ever year or two.

At the time AT&T, or "Ma Bell," as it was known, enjoyed monopoly control over the government-supervised telephone industry, which was treated like a public utility. In 1974 the U.S. Department of Justice had filed an antitrust suit against Ma Bell, and when the case was settled, in the 1980s, AT&T agreed to break the Bell System into seven regional companies—"Baby Bells"—that would have to compete under market forces. In 1985 Bell of Philadelphia became the Bell Atlantic Corp., with 11 million residential and 1.2 million small-business customers in New Jersey, Delaware, Maryland, Pennsylvania, Virginia, West Virginia, and the District of Columbia.

Just after the restructuring Gordon was installed as the new general manager of marketing and sales for Bell Atlantic. With the company facing competition for customers for the first time, he developed unprecedented means of attracting subscribers. Among other measures, he set up kiosks in shopping malls and sales outlets in retail stores such as Sears. "It's important to make it easy for customers to get to you," he told Nadirah Sabir. This new foray into retail chains also gave salesmen the opportunity to pitch such add-on services as caller I.D., call forwarding, and voice messaging.

In 1987 Gordon won an Alfred T. Sloan fellowship at the Massachusetts Institute of Technology's Sloan School of Management. He earned a master's degree in management there in 1988 and was promoted to Bell Atlantic vice president of marketing that same year. Gordon received approval to change the procedures governing promotions; his announcement that all positions were open to every employee resulted in a 20 percent turnover in staff. After he was named group president of the business unit, in 1993, he opted not to have a private office, so that he could work on the same floor as most of his employees. "Information gets filtered when you're up there, and you cut yourself off," he told Nadirah Sabir.

Turning his attention to complaints from consumers about the quality of customer service, Gordon noted that only 70 percent of the phone calls at the customer call center were picked up within 20 seconds—the time a customer will typically wait for a response before hanging up. He wanted to improve the rate to 90 percent, but he could not afford to hire more employees. An investigation revealed that the problem stemmed not from an insufficient number of workers but from an unacceptably large rate of absences (center employees were frequently away at seminars) and from a failure to maintain good work ethics (too often, many people were not at their desks when they were supposed to be). In January 1994 he established new regulations for the call center. "A good number of people felt we had compromised their freedom by managing their adherence to a schedule," Gordon told Nadirah Sabir. "But they reached the '90/20' goal in two months and no one has looked back."

In 1997 Bell Atlantic merged with Nynex, the New York and New England phone system. The $26 billion deal brought millions of new customers to Bell Atlantic and made it the second-largest telecommunications company in the United States. "It was a huge merger," Gordon told Cassandra Hayes. "We had different products, prices, brands and views of the market, and had to take a very detailed and organized approach. That meant having a strong customer marketing team and plan in place to make the Bell Atlantic name appear and the name of NYNEX disappear." Gordon moved from Philadelphia to New York to lead the integration team, overseeing the change of logos on phone booths, directories, and some 28 million statements mailed to customers. The swift and successful changeover (as indicated by a rise in consumer awareness of Bell Atlantic in the new markets from 4 to 79 percent in just three weeks) led *Black Enterprise* magazine to name Gordon the executive of the year in 1998. "Thanks to his initiative during the merger, we launched what I dare say is the most successful name change and brand campaign of any company in the country," Bell Atlantic's chairman at that time, Raymond W. Smith, told Cassandra Hayes. "He is a true friend and a valuable leader at Bell Atlantic."

In 2000 Bell Atlantic merged with GTE to form the largest telecommunications company in the country. The firms jettisoned their names, and after considering as many as 8,500 others, the new entity became Verizon Communications Inc. (a combination of the Latin word *veritas*, meaning truth, and the word "horizon," implying a limitless future). Gordon was promoted to president of the retail-markets group and put in charge of corporate advertising and brand management. His first task was to familiarize the company's millions of customers with the new name and the bold red, white, and black logo. He oversaw an aggressive marketing campaign, and within a year, according to *Advertising Age* (October 8, 2001), 98 percent of the marketplace was aware of the new brand. A study conducted by the company in January 2001 found that Verizon had a higher level of brand recall (that is, more people recognized the name) than FedEx and Coca-Cola.

In 2002 *Fortune* ranked Gordon sixth on its list of the most powerful black executives. By the time he retired from Verizon, in 2003, he had been placed in charge of the largest business unit, which employed 34,000 people, served 33 million telephone and Internet customers, and recorded more than $25 billion in sales annually. Moreover, Gordon's legacy at the company extended beyond his expertise as a businessman; he was also instrumental in promoting racial diversity and fostering the advancement of African-Americans. Within the company he was involved in the Accelerated Leadership Diversity program, the Consortium of Information Technology Executives (a group of African-Americans committed to helping their colleagues succeed professionally), and the One Hundred Plus (African-Americans at the director level and above). He also started the Developmental Roundtable for Upward Mobility (DRUM), a self-help, self-mentoring group for African-American men. Every year since its founding, DRUM has presented the Bruce S. Gordon legacy award to a Verizon employee who has furthered diversity at the company. "My activism has been a function of trying to establish myself in a traditionally White environment and demonstrate that I had the same capacity to be effective and successful as my White counterparts, then use my success to get more Black folks in the door, coach and mentor and move them through the business," Gordon told Vern E. Smith. "Ultimately when I retired there were plenty of them in the position to take my place."

In December 2004 Kweisi Mfume resigned as the president of the NAACP to run for a seat in the U.S. Senate. Founded in 1909, the Baltimore, Maryland–based national organization developed a reputation for defending the civil rights of African-Americans through judicial decisions, the ballot box (by means of voter-registration campaigns), and activism at the community level. Under Mfume's leadership the NAACP had suffered from budget shortfalls that had forced the organization to dip into its reserves, as well as from allegations that Mfume favored female employees whom he dated. In addition, the Internal Revenue Service had launched an investigation into the NAACP's status as a nonprofit organization after Julian Bond, the chairman of the NAACP board, issued a sharp critique of President George W. Bush four months before the 2004 presidential election. (As of mid-2005 the NAACP had refused to cooperate with the investigation.)

Many NAACP members were surprised when, at a meeting in Atlanta, Georgia, on June 25, 2005, the association's board of directors selected Gordon to replace Mfume; Gordon would be the first president in 30 years who was neither a politician nor a clergyman, and the first businessman in nearly

100 years. Some members worried that Gordon's corporate background and approach to activism might be detrimental to the organization. "There is the concern that the N.A.A.C.P. will deviate from their historic struggle for racial justice, for voting rights, for fair housing, employment, criminal justice, all won through things like boycotts, marches, leafleting and picketing," John Brittain, chief counsel for the Lawyers Committee for Civil Rights Under Law, told James Dao for the *New York Times* (July 5, 2005). Gordon told Dao, however, that he had no plans to eschew those traditional causes or traditionally effective means of dealing with them.

According to various observers, Gordon's appointment did indeed signal a slight adjustment in the NAACP's aims and activities. "The world has changed. . . . We have a new and different set of challenges," Gordon told a reporter for the MIT Alumni Association Web site. "We will make sure that our focus and our purpose reflect the kind of issues and challenges that we see today, which in many respects are different, more subtle, more complex, than they were 40 or 50 years ago." While the battle to end legal segregation of the races may have been won, the African-American community still struggles with de facto segregation, as well as disparities in income and in the quality of housing and education. "We've got to get the right emphasis placed on economic equality," Gordon told James Dao. "I happen to think that when you have economic stability and equality that often becomes an enabler for social equality." Gordon has said that he intends to take advantage of his corporate connections to fight for increased pension funds and better jobs for African-Americans. He has also set an ambitious fund-raising goal for the NAACP's endowment, which he contends is woefully small for an organization of its size.

"For African Americans, the struggle for civil rights has always been economic, social, and political," Earl G. Graves, the founder and publisher of *Black Enterprise*, wrote for that magazine (September 2005). "Social equality and political representation without economic opportunity is an exercise in futility and frustration. That's why Gordon's goal of reframing the NAACP mission (or in his words, the NAACP 'brand') with a laser focus on building black wealth, leveraging black spending power, growing black-owned businesses, and bringing sorely needed jobs and resources to black communities, is right on point."

Gordon was officially confirmed as the 15th president and CEO of the NAACP in July 2005 at the association's 96th annual convention, in Milwaukee, Wisconsin. In his acceptance speech he vowed to help the organization "continue adapting to this new reality, and to extend its reach and influence to more of our youth, to more people of color, and to [add] more leaders in the academic, business and political worlds," as quoted in *Jet* (August 1, 2005). To increase the NAACP's membership, which has numbered about 500,000 for the past decade, Gordon wants to update electronic communications technology at the organization's more than 2,000 branches and chapters. In particular, he believes that recruiting more 20- to 35-year-olds and having their input will enable the organization to focus more productively on their priorities.

Referring to the failure of President George W. Bush to address the NAACP since his first inauguration (the last president who declined to speak before its members was Herbert Hoover, who left office in 1933), Gordon has said that he hopes to improve relations with the executive branch of the federal government. "I'm certainly disappointed that there is not a constructive relationship between the NAACP and the White House," he told Kenneth Meeks. "I don't think the NAACP and President Bush and the current administration have to agree on everything, but I have to believe that there are some things upon which we can agree. And in those cases where we disagree, we should at least give one another the opportunity to express points of view." Echoing the same philosophy that drove him in the business world, Gordon told the audience at the 2005 annual NAACP convention, according to a reporter for the Associated Press State & Local Wire (July 15, 2005), "If you had a choice to try to protest and to push and to picket against somebody to implement a policy you believe in versus sitting in the room at the table where the policy is being designed and being decided, which would you choose? I say let's go inside."

In August 2005, taking advantage of the opportunity to assuage some members' fears that he would neglect traditional civil rights issues, Gordon joined thousands of members of the NAACP and other civil rights groups to protest on the streets of Atlanta a change in Georgia law that will make access to voting sites more difficult for many people. While many states require voters to present some form of photo identification, as a means of preventing fraud at the polls, Georgia's new law—which the U.S. Justice Department approved—requires residents to present identification issued by the state's Department of Motor Vehicles. There are 159 counties in Georgia but only 56 places to obtain the required photo identification; none are in Atlanta, the state's largest city. Protestors regarded the legislation as an attempt to discourage poor African-Americans from voting and likened it to measures that had been used in the post-Reconstruction South to disenfranchise African-Americans. The Voting Rights Act of 1965, signed into law by President Lyndon B. Johnson, outlawed poll taxes, literacy tests, and other inherently unfair requirements. "By approving Georgia's onerous law requiring voters to present photo identification to vote, the Justice Department weakened one of this nation's most important voting laws," Gordon told a reporter for U.S. Newswire (August 27, 2005). "If [the law is] left unchallenged, many African Americans and other minorities in Georgia will find it difficult to cast their ballots. I will call on a coalition of civil rights groups to join us in challenging the Georgia law." The Atlanta protest also called for President Bush and the members of Congress to extend key provisions of the Voting Rights Act of 1965, which are set to expire in 2007. Gordon told Errin Haines for the Associated Press (August 6, 2005), "People need to understand if this act is not reauthorized and improved, we will lose the progress of the last 40 years."

Gordon has served as the director of the Urban League and chair of the United Negro College Fund Telethon. He has sat on the boards of directors of the Southern Co., Tyco International Ltd., Office Depot, Bartech Personnel Services, and Innroads of Philadelphia and on the boards of trustees of Gettysburg College, the Alvin Ailey Dance Foundation, and Lincoln Center. He has one grown son, Taurin, from his first marriage. Currently, Gordon lives in the Tribeca section of Manhattan with his second wife, Tawana. In his leisure time he enjoys listening to recordings by John Coltrane, the Temptations, and Luciano Pavarotti. By his own account, he is sometimes impatient, compulsive, and intense, and he has credited Hermann Hesse's novel *Siddhartha* (1922), the tale of a man's search for the meaning of life in the time of Buddha, with teaching him the need for balance in his life.

—J.C.

Suggested Reading: *Black Enterprise* p84 Sep. 1998, p184 Sep. 2005; *Crisis* July/Aug. 2005; *Ebony* p28 Sep. 2005; *Jet* p4+ July 11, 2005, p6+ Aug. 1, 2005; *New York Times* A p10 July 5, 2005; *New York Times Magazine* p15 July 10, 2005

Steve Barrett

Gordon, Ed

Aug. 17, 1960– Broadcast journalist

Address: NPR, 635 Massachusetts Ave., N.W., Washington, DC 20001

Ed Gordon is widely known as a hard-hitting broadcast journalist and a veteran of challenging, high-profile interviews. He is also African-American, and while race is a matter of significance to him, he does not feel that it ought to define him. "When you're just mentioning [someone's] job, I don't think it's important to put an African-American tag on someone, because you wouldn't say 'Caucasian anchor,'" he said to Ed Bark for the *Pittsburgh Post-Gazette* (June 26, 1996). "But when you peek into the corridors of corporate America in this country, clearly African-American men and women have not been represented in ways they should be." In the area of broadcast journalism, at least, Gordon's presence has helped to increase such representation in a number of settings. He has had two successful stints on the Black Entertainment Network (BET), hosting such shows as *Conversations with Ed Gordon* and *BET Tonight with Ed Gordon*; he has also worked for the NBC and MSNBC networks as a host or correspondent for the programs *Dateline, Internight,* and *Today.* Currently, Gordon contributes segments to the CBS show *60 Minutes Wednesday* and hosts *News & Notes*, a National Public Radio program. At *News & Notes*, "we want to be one of the leaders in saying, '[Here are] some issues that black America is talking about, needs to know about and listen to,'" as he explained to Susan Carpenter for the *Los Angeles Times* (March 8, 2005). "And we also want white America and others to understand just because there's this tag that people put on it as 'black perspective' that it doesn't mean you shouldn't listen to it or that it isn't important to you."

The younger of two sons, Edward Lansing Gordon III was born on August 17, 1960 in Detroit, Michigan. Both his mother, Jimmie, and his father, Edward Lansing Gordon Jr., were teachers at a local school, Goldberg Elementary; Edward Gordon Jr. had been a gold medalist in the long jump at the 1932 Olympic Games. Ed Gordon III, who was born when his father was 50, has admitted that he was a "daddy's boy"; when the Gordons took their youngest son with them to elementary school before he was old enough to attend it himself, the boy would invariably sneak out of his mother's classroom to tag along with his father. Edward Gordon Jr. died when his son was 11 years old. Jimmie Gordon told Rachel L. Jones for the *Detroit Free Press*

(June 7, 1996) that her son Ed dealt with the loss well, carrying on with dignity and aplomb. Young Ed "came from a winner's stock," she said. "We worked hard to try and give him a wide range of experiences, so that he wouldn't feel out of place, or wouldn't feel like he couldn't do anything. I was concerned that he would not feel he had to live in his father's shadow, but it seems he was his father's boy, and he was determined to succeed." Even as a youngster Gordon showed a penchant for journalism, as his former neighbor Fred Hudson recalled to Rachel L. Jones: "My wife and I remember [Gordon] coming to our house, and lining people up on the couch. Then he'd roll up a newspaper and pretend to interview them." Gordon attended Cass Technical High School and Western Michigan University, in Kalamazoo, where he majored in political science and minored in communications. Upon his graduation, in 1982, he faced a dilemma: whether to apply to law school or pursue a career in television journalism. "There's always a little bit of ham . . . in me," he told Roxanne Roberts for the *Washington Post* (May 20, 1993). "I'm always running my mouth. I've run my mouth since I was little. So I think that the ham part of me wanted to see what I could do."

With the help of his older brother's girlfriend, Gordon landed an unpaid internship at a Public Broadcasting System (PBS) affiliate, WTVS-TV, in Detroit. Even in that position, Gordon quickly made his presence felt at the station. "Ed Gordon was power lunching straight out of college," Alicia Nails, a former producer at the station, told Rachel L. Jones. "He already knew how to network and get himself known." In 1985 the station hired him to host the show *Detroit Black Journal*; he also freelanced for Black Entertainment Television as its Detroit correspondent. In 1988 Gordon moved to Washington, D.C., to work full-time for BET, as an anchor for *BET News* and as host of *Lead Story* (a round-table talk show in which journalists discussed topical issues) and two interview shows: *Personal Diary* and *Conversations with Ed Gordon*. The transition to what was then a small, often-ignored national network was difficult for Gordon. "Early on, it was frustrating, because people would tell me they didn't have time to do interviews for us, but then I'd see them on CNN," he told Rachel L. Jones. "I'd just get on the phone and remind them about what they said to me, and how I didn't appreciate that. They rarely did it twice." Soon Gordon acquired a reputation for hard-hitting journalism, coupled with an ability to secure interviews with a wide range of subjects, from the actor Sidney Poitier to the South African activist and statesman Nelson Mandela to the Nation of Islam leader Louis Farrakhan. Gordon was the first person to interview President George Herbert Walker Bush after the 1992 Los Angeles, California, riots, which stemmed from anger over the acquittal of four white police officers whose beating of a black man, Rodney King, had been captured on videotape. Gordon later interviewed President Bill Clin-

ton. During his tenure at BET, Gordon was best known to the public as the first person to interview the actor and former football player O. J. Simpson following Simpson's acquittal in the 1995 trial in which he had been accused of murdering his wife, Nicole Brown Simpson, and a waiter, Ronald Goldman. Some speculated that Simpson had granted Gordon the interview because the journalist, like Simpson, is black, and might treat Simpson more leniently than would a white reporter; Gordon dismissed that notion. "There were all these whispers that O. J. Simpson was going to get an easy ride from me because he was being interviewed by a black man," he said for an article in the *Miami Herald* (January 30, 1996). "With that reasoning, you could say to a white person, 'Did you pick a white interviewer because they would be easy on you?'" After the interview, which attracted three million viewers, most agreed that Gordon had done an excellent job of questioning Simpson. "Gordon struck a balance between respect and aggressiveness that some better-known network interviewers would do well to emulate," Noel Holston wrote for the Minneapolis, Minnesota, *Star Tribune* (January 25, 1996).

Although Gordon enjoyed his headlining position at BET, he periodically expressed his frustration over the limited audience the network reached. He began talking to representatives of several major television networks, whose interest in him increased significantly following the airing of the coveted Simpson interview. After eight years at BET, Gordon signed with the National Broadcasting Corp. (NBC) as a correspondent for their news show *Dateline,* a contributor to the long-running morning show *Today,* and host of the Saturday night edition of *Internight.* In his new capacity at NBC (and, later, MSNBC as well), Gordon was reaching a wider audience than ever, yet he missed the opportunity to interview the most prominent subjects, as major interviews at the network were the domain of more established anchors, such as Tom Brokaw. (Gordon's most high-profile interview was with Autumn Jackson, a woman who claimed to be the illegitimate daughter of the comedian and actor Bill Cosby.) Gordon complained to Tim Kiska for the *Detroit News* (September 19, 2000), "I think I became a little disenchanted with the fact that some of the stories that were near and dear to me, and that I thought were not only of importance to black America, but to America in general—too often [NBC executives] decided, 'Oh, well, if it's a black story it's not important to anyone other than black people.'" He continued, "I don't buy that. A story is a story. Sometimes stories impact a particular community more than another. But, particularly in the global world [that] we know today, all stories impact all people in one way, shape or form." In 2000, after three years at NBC and MSNBC, Gordon returned to BET.

Back at BET, Gordon again hosted the show *Conversations with Ed Gordon* as well as a new nightly news series, *BET Tonight with Ed Gordon.*

One of his first scoops for the latter program came about in May 2002, when he arranged an exclusive interview with the singer R. Kelly, who was then facing child-pornography charges. Another noteworthy installment of *BET Tonight with Ed Gordon,* which aired that December, found Gordon interviewing the Republican U.S. senator Trent Lott, who had recently come under criticism for what were thought to be his racially insensitive and divisive remarks at the 100th birthday celebration for his fellow Republican senator Strom Thurmond. That interview was watched by 830,000 people, approximately twice the network's usual audience. Ironically, earlier that same month, the network had canceled *BET Tonight with Ed Gordon* (along with several other programs), making the interview with Lott a bittersweet triumph for Gordon. (*Conversations with Ed Gordon,* meanwhile, was airing only sporadically.) The demise of Gordon's news show disappointed both the anchor's fans and cultural critics, who felt that the elimination of the incisive program indicated a "dumbing down" of the network. "Trent Lott knew he could connect with black folks by going on BET," the pop-culture critic Mark Anthony said, as quoted by Phil Rosenthal for the *Chicago Sun-Times* (December 18, 2002). "The irony is, when BET shuts down its news shows in a few months, where will Trent Lott go?" Rosenthal wrote, "Forget Lott. Where will those looking for an African-American perspective on news and culture go?" Another question was: Where would Ed Gordon go?

In 2004 Gordon was hired to present an unspecified number of celebrity profiles and news stories for the CBS show *60 Minutes Wednesday,* an extension of the venerated television news magazine *60 Minutes.* "So few people get invited to this party," Gordon said to Michael Starr for the *New York Post* (November 9, 2004) in regard to the show. "For years they've done such great storytelling—and I love being a part of that." His first piece, an interview of the actor Jamie Foxx, aired in November 2004. On *60 Minutes Wednesday,* Gordon explained to *Jet* magazine (December 13, 2004), "I won't solely pitch African-American issues, but I think it's important that I do [pitch some]." Later in 2004, after almost two years of negotiations, Gordon was hired by National Public Radio (NPR) to host a new show, *News & Notes,* beginning in January 2005. *News & Notes* was designed to focus on cultural trends, news, and other issues of particular importance to African-Americans. "The format of the show allows us to talk about anything from politics to pop culture, and that prospect is exciting . . . ," Gordon said, according to an NPR.org (December 21, 2004) press release, adding, "This kind of program is imperative because often these issues and voices are still, unfortunately, underreported, under-represented or overlooked altogether by most media outlets." Interviewees on the program have included Detroit's mayor, Kwame Kilpatrick; the basketball player Charles Barkley; the actress Regina King; and the Reverend Al Shar-

pton. Since *News & Notes* broadcasts every weekday from New York City, Gordon has relocated from Washington, D.C.

Gordon has received numerous awards, including an Emmy Award, the NAACP Image Award, the Communication Excellence to Black Audiences Award for Merit, Distinction and Excellence, and the National Association of Black Journalists' Journalist of the Year Award and its Excellence and Outstanding Journalistic Endeavor Award. He was also nominated for an ACE Award.

Gordon and his wife, the former Karen Haney, have one daughter, Taylor. Gordon's hobbies include playing basketball and listening to his vast collection of CDs. He is president of the Gordon Media Group, a production company. Gordon is a frequent lecturer at schools and conferences and has served as a moderator on various panels; he is actively involved in promoting community service, especially in regard to education and children.

—K.J.E.

Suggested Reading: *Chicago Sun-Times* p69 Dec. 18, 2002; *Detroit Free Press* F p1 June 7, 1996; *Sacramento (California) Observer* p2 Dec. 29, 2004; *Washington Post* D p1 May 20, 1993

Selected Television Shows: *Detroit Black Journal,* 1985-88; *Personal Diary,* 1988–91; *Today,* 1997–2000; *60 Minutes Wednesday,* 2004–

Selected Radio Shows: *News & Notes,* 2005–

Graham, Susan

July 23, 1960– Opera singer

Address: c/o Alec Treuhaft, Vocal Division Chairman, IMG Artists, 152 W. 57th St., Fifth Fl., New York, NY 10019

"Musicians are the healers of the soul," the operatic singer Susan Graham told Anne Price for the Baton Route, Louisiana, *Sunday Advocate Magazine* (October 21, 2001), a few weeks after the terrorist attacks of September 11, 2001, which killed nearly 3,000 people in the United States. "It's important to remind people there is beauty in this world and if I can help people realize that, I succeed." Judging from the views expressed by opera-loving concertgoers and CD buyers, professional reviewers, and her peers, Graham, a mezzo-soprano, has unquestionably brought beauty to the world through her performances in many productions of operas and in her solo recitals in the U.S. and abroad. According to various music critics or commentators, Graham's voice is "lustrous," "creamy," and "a marvel, enveloping in its warmth, perfectly even

Susan Graham

Courtesy of Mitch Jenkins

throughout its entire range, and amazingly supple," and it has an "alluringly full-bodied tone," "lovely timbre," and "smooth legato"; her skills and talents include the ability to reach "the extremes of her register effortlessly and without loss of color," a "lyrical sensitivity," a "fine sense of characterization," and "deft . . . comic timing." After Tim Page attended a recital by Graham at the Kennedy Center, in Washington, D.C., in 2003, he wrote for the *Washington Post* (March 26, 2003) that her performance "left no doubt that she ranks among the most capable, versatile and altogether winning mezzo-sopranos now before the public."

Distinguished also by her height (five feet, 10 inches), slender, statuesque figure, physical grace, athleticism, vivacity, and keen thespian instincts, Graham has won renown for her portrayals of a bevy of male characters, in operatic roles traditionally sung by women: Cherubino in Mozart's *The Marriage of Figaro* and Octavian in Richard Strauss's *Der Rosenkavalier*—her signature roles; the Composer in Richard Strauss's *Ariadne auf Naxos*; Ruggiero in Handel's *Alcina*; Idamante in Mozart's *Idomeneo*; the title role in Handel's *Iriodante*; and Sesto in Mozart's *La clemenza di Tito*, among others. She has also been acclaimed for the beauty of her singing and naturalistic renditions in female roles: Dido in Berlioz's *Les Troyens*; Donna Elvira in Mozart's *Don Giovanni*; Béatrice in *Béatrice et Benedict* and Marguerite in *Le Damnation de Faust*, both by Berlioz; Charlotte in Massenet's *Werther*; Iphigenie in Gluck's *Iphigenie en Tauride*; Arianna in the same-named opera by Monteverdi and Poppea in *L'Incoronazione di Poppea*, also by Monteverdi; Erika in *Vanessa*, by Samuel Barber; and Hanna Glawari in Franz Lehar's *The Merry Widow*. She has appeared in the world premieres of two operas: *The Great Gatsby*, by John Harbison, in which she was cast as Jordan Baker, and *Dead Man Walking*, which Jake Heggie wrote with her in mind and in which she played the part of Sister Helen Prejean. In the 2005–06 season of New York City's Metropolitan Opera (the Met), her "home" company, she will sing the role of Sondra Finchley in another world premiere: that of Tobias Picker's *An American Tragedy*, based on Theodore Dreiser's novel and the most famous of the films it spawned, *A Place in the Sun*. Her nonoperatic repertoire includes the mezzo part in Mozart's Mass in C minor and works by Brahms, Debussy, Ravel, Chausson, Mahler, Richard Strauss, Francis Poulenc, Alban Berg, Kurt Weill, George Gershwin, Ned Rorem, and Leonard Bernstein, among many others.

Graham first attracted attention among opera aficionados when, as a graduate student, she appeared in the title role in the U.S. premiere of Massenet's opera *Chérubin*. In 1987 she was a winner in the National Council Auditions, conducted by the Met, in which young opera singers compete for the opportunity to perform on the stage of the Met in a joint recital. Her victory, as she told Craig Smith for the *Santa Fe New Mexican* (July 17, 1998), served as "a springboard" to her career. Graham made her operatic debut at the Met during the 1991–92 season, as the Second Lady in Mozart's *The Magic Flute*. Since then she has sung in many more of the world's best-known opera houses, among them La Scala, in Milan, Italy; the Royal Opera House, in Covent Garden, England; the Vienna State Opera, in Austria; the Paris Opera, in France; and the Santa Fe Opera, in New Mexico. She has also given dozens of solo recitals in leading concert halls, with accompaniments provided by such pianists as Emmanuel Ax and Steven Blier and such orchestras as the New York Philharmonic, the Boston Symphony, the Berlin Philharmonic, the BBC Symphony Orchestra, and the Vienna Philharmonic. She has performed at many national and international music festivals and has worked with such illustrious conductors as James Levine, Georg Solti, Colin Davis, Claudio Abbado, Charles Dutoit, Seiji Ozawa, and Neville Marriner. Among other honors, in 2000 Graham was awarded a career grant from the Richard Tucker Music Foundation. In 2004 she earned the title of Commander of the Order of Arts and Letters from the French government, was selected as Vocalist of the Year by the magazine *Musical America*, and won a Grammy Award for best classical vocal performance, for her recording of songs by Charles Ives—one of nine solo albums that she has made since the late 1990s. In January 2005 millions of TV viewers saw her live as she sang the 1927 hymn "Bless This House" at the second inaugural ceremony of President George W. Bush. *Gramophone* magazine has included her among its nominations for "Artist of the Year" for 2005.

Donald Runnicles, the music director of the San Francisco Opera, told David J. Baker for *Opera World* (January 2000), "What I enjoy about Susan is that she is as fine in art song as she is on the stage. She can scale back her voice, she's careful, she's astute in the repertoire she sings, and she's a born communicator. She loves people, . . . she loves communicating in every form, and I think that it's just totally intuitive, totally instinctive within her and makes her such a magnetic personality onstage." John Nelson, the music director of the Ensemble Orchestral de Paris, told Baker, "Besides having a glorious voice and musicianship to burn, [Graham is] one of the most delightful people in the business. She's more than a professional or a star, she's a truly beautiful person inside and outside."

Susan Graham was born in Roswell, New Mexico, on July 23, 1960. When she was 13 her family—which includes her older sister, Janet, and her older brother, Alan—moved to Midland, Texas, where her father, a geophysicist, ran an oil-exploration company. The move to Texas "was such an eye opener in terms of the pride that everyone has in what they do, their ambition, and their ability to 'dream as big as Texas,'" as she told an interviewer for *Texas Monthly* (April 2004). In a conversation with Bruce Duffie for the *Opera Journal* (June 2001, on-line), Graham said that she has "always been very athletically inclined" and something of a tomboy, "climbing trees and playing kickball and throwing frisbees" beginning when she was very young. Sometimes her brother would invite her to join him and his friends in baseball games, in which "usually I had to *be* a base!," as she recalled to Duffie. "They had to run by and knock me down on their way to third!" In school, she told Martin Kettle for the London *Guardian* (December 10, 2004, on-line), "I grew up as the class clown." "I like to perform and I love to make people laugh," she added. "I like attention."

Graham was not exposed to opera as a child. Indeed, she told an interviewer for the London *Financial Times* (April 12, 2003), "There are people in my own extended family who still believe you have to weigh 400 lbs and carry a spear to be [an opera singer]. So part of what has been important for me is to dispel these myths . . . [among] people like those from my background, who don't know that opera can be hip and relevant and modern and a lot of fun." At home the young Graham was surrounded by other types of music, however, including the popular and Broadway songs that her mother, Betty Graham, played expertly by ear on the piano. Her mother made sure that Susan and her sister learned to play the piano, and for some 15 years, Graham devoted much of her musical energy to polishing her skills as a pianist.

Earlier, her mother had seen signs that Graham's real gift was for singing. "One day, when Susan was 8 or 9," Betty Graham told Vorhees, "she was singing around the house and she let out this loud trill. And I thought, 'My, she has a big voice.'" Susan Graham sang with her church and school choirs, among them the Texas all-state choir when she was a high-school student; she told Anne Price, "Without reservation I credit my life as a musician to my high school choir director, Doug Brown." She also performed in musicals, playing the female lead, Maria, in her high school's production of *The Sound of Music*.

Soon after she enrolled at Texas Tech University, in Lubbock, Graham saw her first opera, Mozart's *Cosí Fan Tutte*. "I fell in love with the . . . character of Despina," she told Craig Smith. "It made me want to do opera. She gets to dress up in all those different costumes and disguises." Her exposure to opera led her to consider the ramifications of pursuing a career as a pianist or as a singer. As she told David J. Baker, "I thought, O.K., there are two roads I can go here. Piano means sitting in a practice room for six hours a day. . . . Voice major means being very disciplined in a different way. You can't practice for six hours a day, but you have to learn all these languages, you have to learn a lot of music and all that." Graham chose voice after she had what Jeremy Eichler, writing for the *New York Times* (January 1, 2004), characterized as a "traumatic memory slip" during a piano recital she gave when she was 17. "I thought, this is my living hell right now," she told Eichler. "I knew it was not where I wanted to be. The piano is a great tool, but I'm not fully able to express myself on it." After she decided to major in voice, the work ethic instilled in her by her parents drove her to excel. "Whatever it is you do, you be the best at it you can be," they had told her, as she recalled to Baker. "So if you're going to be a voice major, you aim as high as you can. . . . I just thought, 'What is the most outrageous goal I can set my sights on? O.K., opera singer.'"

As a freshman in college, Graham sang in the chorus in a staging of Charles Gounod's opera *Faust*. "It seemed so bigger-than-life and so grand," she told Charles Ward for the *Houston Chronicle* (October 27, 2002). "There were huge emotions and huge music. I didn't even have a solo line. I think I ran onstage and found [the character] Valentine dead. I emoted and pointed. That was my operatic debut." She also said, "It was so outrageous to be doing something that was so outside the box in terms of my cultural upbringing. It seemed something that would be fun to sink my teeth into and have become a familiar part of my life."

In 1985, after earning both a B.A. degree and a master's degree in music from Texas Tech, Graham moved to New York City, where she enrolled at the Manhattan School of Music, one of the nation's preeminent private conservatories for instrumentalists and singers; as she told Deborah Voorhees for the *Dallas (Texas) Morning News* (June 18, 2000), "If I was going to be a singer there was no place else to go." Initially, Graham felt intimidated by many of her peers in New York. "I came into this profession feeling ill-equipped culturally," she told the *Financial Times* interviewer. "All my contemporaries in New York grew up steeped in opera—their mothers had taken them from age nine every Saturday to the Met—and boy, did I feel like a fish out of water. . . . By 18, some of these kids had an arsenal of Schubert songs that I still don't have." At the Manhattan School of Music, Graham felt she received excellent training in all aspects of opera. "We had the luxury of a French coach coming in three times a week," she told Michael Huebner for the *Birmingham (Alabama) News* (March 7, 2004). "We would take the libretto and read it like a play—with all the inflection, diction and expression of the spoken word. It lit the French fire for me." In 1987, while still in school, Graham performed in the U.S. premiere of Massenet's *Chérubin* and drew favorable notices. "I got an agent out of it," she told Charles Ward, "and the ball started rolling. I didn't know that I had arrived, but I knew I was on the right train."

During her years at Texas Tech, Graham's voice had still not settled comfortably into any particular vocal register (determined by the highest and lowest tones that an individual can reach). Her hope was to become an alto rather than a soprano, even though the majority of principal female roles in operas are for sopranos. "I didn't want to just sing the melody," she explained to Deborah Voorhees. "I wanted to sing harmony. The melody can get boring." When she was in her mid-20s, she and her teachers decided that her voice could reliably be characterized as mezzo-soprano, in the range just above alto. For that reason she was often cast as male characters, in what are known as trouser roles. She told Voorhees that while watching her five nephews grow into teenagers and adults, she had learned a lot about how the movements of men differ from those of women; as an example, she cited the many "subtle gestures that women do that men just don't." The physical exertion that playing male roles often entails does not faze Graham. "I've had roles where I've had to sword fight, hang from a balcony, climb ladders, scale walls—all while singing," she told Voorhees.

After she earned her second master's degree, in operatic performance, from the Manhattan School of Music, in 1987, Graham tried in vain to win an apprenticeship with the Santa Fe Opera. Later in 1987 she gained acceptance into a similar course of training, at the San Francisco Opera's Merola Program. She won the Schwabacher Award for her performance at that opera company's Schwabacher Recital Series. Soon afterward, along with 2,000 other aspirants from the U.S., she participated in the National Council Auditions, held since 1954 by the Met. Graham emerged as one of 11 regional winners (the others included the future stars of the opera world Renée Fleming and Ben Heppner), all of whom sang at the 1988 Grand Finals Concert with the Metropolitan Opera Orchestra. "I remember standing on stage awe-struck," Graham told Voorhees. "It was so big . . ." Since then Graham has worked almost continuously—learning, re-

hearsing, and performing in operatic roles and preparing for and giving solo recitals. During a 12-month period in the early 2000s, she learned new roles in five operas, for live performances and recordings; once, three years passed before she had a break in her schedule of more than a few days.

Toward the end of the 1980s, Graham began to perform in some of Europe's leading opera houses. That experience, she told David J. Baker, "was absolutely vital to my development and growth as an artist." "When I went to Europe," she explained, "I found myself in situations and in productions with directors, for instance, who demanded more of me than I thought I was able to give. . . . It's sort of the trial by fire, and it's that confidence of experience that makes all the difference." Graham has also cited as significant in her evolution as a singer her association with the Dutch conductor Edo de Waart—"a relationship that for several years was both personal and professional," according to Baker. "I pity my colleagues who haven't had a close—even a working relationship, we'll say—with a mentor-type person," Graham said to Baker. "Certainly the musical work that [de Waart and I] did together was so rich. Edo . . . lives a very artistic existence, and he taught me a lot about being an artist. He taught me that when you could begin to strip away the shell, then you could approach true artistry. He was a huge catalyst in my being able to reach that point."

In her first major role at the Met, in the 1991–92 season, Graham played Cherubino in *The Marriage of Figaro*; she has since performed in that part many times around the world. She has also frequently appeared as the title character in Massenet's *Chérubin*, a sequel of sorts to *The Marriage of Figaro*, and as Octavian in *Der Rosenkavalier*. A few years ago, as she watched a video of a Texas Tech mounting of *Der Rosenkavalier* in which she had sung the role of Octavian, she noticed, as she told the *Texas Monthly* interviewer, that "some of the instinctive physical gestures I was making I'm still using in that role." In a review of her depiction of Octavian in 2005, Jay Nordlinger wrote for the *New York Sun* (March 14, 2005), "Her singing . . . was characteristically superb. One of her chief virtues is evenness; the line is almost never out of balance. And her intonation is exemplary: You'll find her in the center of the note. As for the voice, it is pleasing up and down, but it is positively exciting in the upper register. Strauss would have loved it."

In 1997 Graham gained much wider recognition, after the release of her debut solo recording—a collection of works by Berlioz that included the song cycle *Les nuits d'été*, with the orchestra of the Royal Opera House conducted by John Nelson. According to David Mermelstein in the *New York Times* (October 1, 2000), a reviewer for the *Sunday Telegraph* of London described the album as "one of the finest recorded performances of Berlioz's evocative and haunting song cycle"; Mermelstein also quoted an assessment of the record by the famous mezzo-soprano Frederica von Stade: "my idea of sensational singing." Among Graham's other solo albums are *La Belle Époque: The Songs of Reynaldo Hahn* (1998); *Songs of Ned Rorem* (2000); *Il tenero momento: Mozart & Gluck Arias* (2001); *"C'est ca la vie, c'est ca l'amour": French Operetta Arias* (2002); and *Poèmes de l'Amour* (2005).

Graham had roles in two operas that premiered in 2000: John Harbison's *The Great Gatsby* (based on the novel by F. Scott Fitzgerald, about a group of posturing, self-centered, shallow nouveau riche Long Islanders in the 1920s) and Jake Heggie's *Dead Man Walking* (adapted from the same-titled film, which was based on the book *Dead Man Walking*, by the real-life Roman Catholic nun Helen Prejean, about her involvement with a convicted murderer on death row). "I was excited to be part of the collaboration that brings an opera to life . . . ," Graham told Mary Campbell for the Associated Press Online (March 29, 2000). "A lot of people find a new opera daunting. . . . I find it so freeing. It's brand-new. There's no one to compare you with. It's mine and the composer's and director's interpretation. It's my job to fuse those elements and breathe life into a character. To me, that's very freeing and a great adventure." While reviews of *The Great Gatsby*, which debuted at the Met, and of *Dead Man Walking*, at the San Francisco Opera, were mixed, Graham's performances drew high praise. "With her plush muscular mezzo, commanding stage presence and fearless intelligence, Graham could have been born to play Sister Helen," Joshua Kosman wrote for the *San Francisco Chronicle* (October 9, 2000, on-line). "The full, impeccably modulated stream of tone that she brought to the part, tempered by the dynamic control and flashes of subtle wit, left the listener agog."

During the run of *Dead Man Walking*, Graham's father died. "I was facing death in my personal life and having to live it out on stage at every performance," the singer recalled to Robert Wilder Blue for U.S. Opera Web (on-line). "To be able to get through it, I relied heavily on that woman I was portraying. Her words comforted me as they were coming out of my mouth." Speaking of her own emotions on another occasion, she told the *Financial Times* interviewer, "I'm not by nature a dark person. That doesn't mean, though, I don't enjoy plumbing the depths on stage, because I do, and I find that when I'm there, it gives me licence to go deeper than I ever could in my private life."

In 2003, which she described to Jeremy Eichler as "a huge transition year," Graham sang the roles of Dido in *Les Troyens* and Hanna Glawari in Franz Lehar's *The Merry Widow*. "I'm a big girl now. I'm ready for big girl parts," she told the *Financial Times* interviewer. "It is one of those things that happens as one matures and becomes a little more reflective. You know what they say about women who enter their 40s: it's a sort of coming-of-age. You're either there or you're never going to be there. In your 40s you start to embrace life." Graham's recent performances included a recital at Zellerbach Hall, in Berkeley, California, that, according to Joshua Kosman in the *San Francisco Chronicle* (April 15, 2005), underscored "her place at the very top of the current vocal pantheon." "What Graham brings to the song repertoire is a distinctive brand of diva glamour that is at once grand and intimate, and it's a combination that extends not only to her personal demeanor but to her musical delivery as well." During the 2005–06 opera season, Graham was scheduled to appear in three productions at the Metropolitan Opera, among them the world premiere of Tobias Picker's *An American Tragedy*, and in one each at the Lyric Opera of Chicago, the Houston Grand Opera, and the Opéra National de Paris.

"Even in the edgy world of opera, [Graham] seems genuinely admired as well as liked," David J. Baker wrote. Graham maintains residences in Manhattan and Santa Fe; she lives with her toy poodle, Libby, who accompanies her on concert tours and is featured on Graham's personal Web site. In her leisure time Graham enjoys rollerblading and bicycling, often in the cities where she performs. She has told interviewers that her nearly nonstop work schedule accounts for her unmarried state. "I have a wonderful network of friends and family," she told Anne Price. "After so many years in this profession, it becomes a sort of family. After a few years you develop a very warm, close relationship with other singers, a very warm and close knit family."

—M.H./R.E.

Suggested Reading: (Baton Rouge, Louisiana) *Sunday Advocate Magazine* p6 Oct. 21, 2001, with photo; *Dallas Morning News* E p1 June 18, 2000; (London) *Financial Times* p7 Apr. 12, 2003; *New York Times* II p13+ Mar. 15, 1997, p32 Oct. 1, 2000, with photo; *Opera News* p46+ Jan. 2000, p12+ June 2003; susangraham.com; *usOperaWeb.com* July 2001; *Vogue* p413+ Mar. 2002

Selected Recordings: *Hector Berlioz: Les nuits d'été and Opera Arias*, 1997; *La Belle Époque: The Songs of Reynaldo Hahn*, 1998; *Songs of Ned Rorem*, 2000; *Il tenero momento: Mozart & Gluck Arias*, 2001; *Dead Man Walking*, 2002; *"C'est ca la vie, c'est ca l'amour": French Operetta Arias*, 2002; *Susan Graham at Carnegie Hall*, 2003; *Poèmes de l'Amour*, 2005

Mike Lovett, courtesy of Brandeis University

Graves, Florence George

Mar. 12, 1946– Investigative journalist

*Address: Brandeis University Women's Studies
Research Center, 515 South St., MS079,
Waltham, MA 02454-9110*

Florence George Graves made her reputation as an
investigative reporter by going after stories that
many major American media outlets were unwilling to take on, uninterested in, or afraid to handle.
In 1980 Graves founded *Common Cause Magazine*,
which was devoted to exposing malfeasance and
abuses of power among the political and corporate
elites. One of the first and only investigative-
reporting magazines to focus solely on Washington, at its height it had 250,000 subscribers—at that
time one of the largest circulations in the country
for a political magazine. In 2004 Graves founded
the Brandeis Institute for Investigative Journalism,
the first center of its kind to be based at a university
and only the third independent reporting center in
the U.S.

Graves's work has triggered many government
probes and congressional investigations. She is
perhaps best known for her 1992 *Washington Post*
exposé of highly unprofessional conduct by then–
U.S. senator Bob Packwood, a Republican from Oregon, who was forced to resign after a historic
three-year Senate investigation into allegations
from about 20 women who said he had made inappropriate sexual advances to them. (Graves had interviewed more than 40 women who complained
about the senator's actions, but about half of them
had refused to be part of the Senate probe because
they feared reprisals.) "Doing [the Packwood] story

opened my eyes to just how large a problem sexual
harassment is and the huge toll it can take on a victim and her family," Graves said in an interview
with *Current Biography*. "I learned about women
who lost their jobs when they complained, who
moved to lower-paying jobs to escape the behavior,
or who entered therapy to try to come to terms with
the trauma or humiliation. Many people don't understand the personal and financial toll that this
kind of discrimination can create. And this situation is usually most abusive in cultures such as
Washington's where power—and often male power—is currency."

Florence George Graves was born on March 12,
1946 in Waco, Texas, halfway between Dallas and
Austin. Often called the "heart of Texas," Waco is
now a city of 100,000 people. Graves has traced her
interest in investigative journalism to her childhood, when she read the biographies of such early
20th-century muckrakers as Ida Tarbell and Nellie
Bly. Her inquisitive nature led her to question the
norms of life in Texas during the 1950s and 1960s.
She wondered why, for example, society would
not allow highly educated, accomplished women
to have professional careers. She was also greatly
troubled by racial segregation. The civil rights
movement was just beginning to spread across the
South in the mid-1950s, and there were still separate public facilities marked "colored" and
"white." Graves's close relationship with her family's housekeeper, Genner Hastings, a deeply religious black woman, enabled her to understand on
a personal level the toll that racism took on its victims. In an article for the *Columbia Journalism Review* (May/June 2001, on-line), she wrote, "Negotiating life [in Texas] helped me see just how skillfully people can operate on different, sometimes
incongruent, levels, and how difficult it can be to
figure out what is really going on. . . . Our teachers told us how lucky we were to live in America,
because everyone in a democracy is created equal
and has equal opportunities. But it was obvious to
me that there was a huge disconnect between what
we were told and what people seemed actually to
believe and do. I was constantly confused." She
continued, "I learned that a measure of truth can
be right in front of you; that to see it you sometimes
have to shift your focus or imagine yourself in
someone else's place; and that finding it involves
many types of searches, some of which take a long
time. I learned to question authority, appearances,
the majority's view, and the way things are always
done; to be aware of the dangers of generalizing
and of adhering to any fixed ideology."

Graves became a founding editor of the *Richfield
Flyer*, her high-school newspaper, and as an undergraduate at the University of Texas at Austin, she
became the editorial-page editor of the campus paper, the *Daily Texan*. In 1968 she earned a bachelor's degree in education from the University of
Texas. She then taught high-school classes in journalism, English, and other topics for several years.
She got her first newspaper job at a small daily

publication in Ohio, near Dayton, where she covered everything from the police to the court system to county government.

In 1976 Graves earned a master's degree in journalism from the University of Arizona at Tucson. She told *Current Biography*, "I was particularly influenced by two teachers—my high-school journalism teacher, Mrs. Gene Thompson, who told me I should pursue a career in journalism, and a journalism professor at the University of Arizona, Jacqueline Sharkey. After I worked with her, Professor Sharkey said to me, 'You should be doing investigative reporting in Washington!' And within one year, I was doing just that. She became a friend and has encouraged me and has given me invaluable advice ever since. She is also the journalist who most influenced me." After receiving her journalism degree Graves worked briefly as a managing editor of a magazine in Tucson, where she worked on several investigative reports, including one that turned up a prime suspect in a celebrated murder case who had been ignored by the sheriff's office. She then gained experience in Washington by working for the *Washington Journalism Review* (now called the *American Journalism Review*) and serving as editor of *Today Is Sunday*, an experimental Sunday newspaper supplement. One cover story she wrote for a 1978 issue inserted into the *New York Times* was one of the earliest pieces to suggest that the situation in Cambodia was approaching genocide. In *Today Is Sunday*, Senator George McGovern made a plea for a United Nations inspection of Cambodia.

Graves next became involved with Common Cause, a nonprofit, nonpartisan citizens' group founded in 1970 and dedicated to demanding government accountability. In 1980 she started a magazine based on the group's principles. "In 1980, when I created the magazine, women still were rarely hired to do investigative reporting at major publications," she told *Current Biography*. "I suggested the idea of creating an investigative-reporting magazine that would break major stories in the areas [in which] Common Cause was most involved, such as military spending, campaign-finance reform, and congressional-ethics reform. Many people didn't believe it was possible for a tiny group of reporters to break big stories consistently. Although it was an unconventional path, this gave me the national platform to do the kind of work I had wanted to do." The magazine's articles, which exposed corruption and blew the whistle on fraud and abuse, won numerous awards and were picked up by many of the country's major newspapers, including the *New York Times* and the *Washington Post*, as well as such television news programs as *60 Minutes* and *20/20*. While working in Washington Graves broke, among other stories, the Pentagon's practice of charging taxpayers for military contractors' lobbying and public-relations expenses. (Stopping that practice has saved the nation a large sum over the years.) She also uncovered the willingness of the U.S. Food

and Drug Administration (FDA) to approve the artificial sweetener aspartame despite serious questions about the process the agency had used to establish the substance's safety. *Common Cause Magazine*, which won the prestigious National Magazine Award for General Excellence, ceased publication in 1996, when the organization felt it could no longer maintain the cost of producing the magazine. Karen Jenkins Holt wrote for *Folio* (July 1, 2003), "If *Common Cause Magazine* threw a reunion, it would look like a convention of today's top investigative reporters. With a brand of muckraking that belonged more to the era of Ida Tarbell than [conservative media baron] Rupert Murdoch, the magazine attracted and nurtured journalists who had a zeal for exposing the abuses of the powerful."

Graves spent a decade in the nation's capital before moving with her husband, Samuel, to Massachusetts, following his hiring by Boston College for a teaching post. "I was burned out," she explained to Lynda Gorov for the *Boston Globe* (September 9, 1995). "Starting a magazine and keeping it going and doing investigative reporting day after day, year after year, well, I was ready for another challenge." After her move to Massachusetts, Graves continued to investigate abuses of power in Washington on a freelance basis. Commenting that she had attained detachment and clarity after leaving the nation's capital, Graves told *Current Biography*, "I often said to people that I could see Washington much more clearly from Boston." In the early 1990s she began investigating allegations of sexual harassment on Capitol Hill after the Senate confirmed the nomination of Clarence Thomas to the Supreme Court. During the confirmation proceedings, the Senate Judiciary Committee had heard testimony from Anita Hill, a former colleague of Thomas's. Hill had alleged that while Thomas had been the head of the Equal Employment Opportunity Commission, he had behaved inappropriately toward her. While Thomas was confirmed despite Hill's testimony, Graves felt that allegations of sexual harassment by men in power deserved further investigation, and she focused her inquires on Congress. "To me, the biggest follow-up story to the hearings was sexual harassment on Capitol Hill," Graves explained to *Current Biography*. "I assumed the major newspapers were doing that story. I waited and waited. Finally, six months later, I proposed the story to *Vanity Fair* magazine. However, they insisted I sign a contract saying effectively that I guaranteed there would be no legal action as a result of my story. I refused to sign it, saying no one could guarantee that. Eventually I was left personally financing and working on the story for several months by myself from my home."

Although initially Graves asked general questions in her investigation, she repeatedly heard references to Senator Bob Packwood. For that reason the focus of her story shifted from misconduct by men in Congress in general to Packwood's alleged misconduct in particular. "It was shocking to me that he had gotten away with the behavior for almost two decades," Graves told *Current Biography*. "Many people had heard rumors. But no one, including his hometown newspaper, the *Oregonian*, was willing to fully investigate or take him on. I felt I knew too much, and that I had a moral obligation to pursue the story. I had great difficulty getting any news organization interested. . . . By September 1992, two months before the election in which Senator Packwood was running for reelection, I had a big story but no outlet. Finally I approached the *Washington Post*, and the editor was impressed enough with the information I had gathered that he took the highly unusual step of hiring me and paying for me to commute to Washington from Boston for several months."

The *Washington Post* teamed Graves with the investigative reporter Charles E. Shepard, and together they uncovered a history of sexual misconduct on Packwood's part stretching as far back as 1969. In October 1992, after having interviewed many women, including several who had expressed willingness to go on record about the inappropriate sexual advances, Graves and Shepard traveled to Oregon to confront Packwood. Then in a tight race to keep his Senate seat, Packwood vehemently denied the allegations and tried to discredit the women who had accused him. He then contacted the editors of the *Washington Post* in an effort to kill the story. Because the issues he raised about the credibility of many of the women required additional investigating, he succeeded in delaying the publication of Graves's account until after the election that November. The story broke in the *Washington Post* on November 22, 1992 and was then picked up by news organizations all over the country.

The Senate's Ethics Committee launched a three-year investigation into the Packwood matter; this marked the first time in history that the committee had considered sexual misconduct an ethical issue, as well as the first time more than one woman had been willing to go on record about a senator's misconduct. Although the investigation was plagued by stalling tactics, including Packwood's refusal to turn over his diaries, which contained relevant evidence, in September 1995 the members of the committee voted unanimously to expel Packwood from the Senate. A day later he resigned. The Ethics Committee ruled that, besides his sexual misconduct, Packwood had intimidated witnesses, obstructed justice by altering his diaries, and linked personal financial gain to his official position by using his influence with lobbyists and businesspeople to get a job for his former wife, Georgie Packwood, so he that he could reduce his alimony payments to her. Shortly after his resignation Graves wrote for the *Washington Post* (September 10, 1995): "I find no joy in the pain Packwood and his friends must be feeling. But I keep reminding myself of the tremendous pain his behavior caused so many others over the years."

In 1998 one of Graves's reports brought to light another example of abuse of power in exclusive political circles. That one involved Kenneth W. Starr, who had been appointed to the federal post of independent counsel to continue the investigation of an investment by Bill Clinton and his wife in a real-estate venture launched by the Whitewater Development Corp. in Arkansas, made while Clinton was governor of that state. During that probe Starr broadened the scope of his inquiry by investigating various allegations of sexual misconduct by Clinton. According to Kathleen Willey, one of the accusers, Clinton had made unwelcome sexual advances when she met with him in the Oval Office to ask for a job. Starr was seeking to indict Clinton for a number of crimes, including perjury, because the president had denied under oath—falsely, as Starr correctly suspected—having had a sexual relationship with a White House intern named Monica Lewinsky. As Starr gathered his evidence, Graves wrote an extensive article for the *Nation*, published on May 17, 1999, that described ways in which he had overstepped his authority as independent counsel. Graves recalled to *Current Biography*, "My investigation, based on sealed Starr documents I obtained, established that *even Starr knew* Willey's credibility was questionable. In fact, his internal secret documents showed she had lied to his own investigators about a serious matter [on which] they had questioned her. After this story was published, he was no longer able to use Willey as a credible cudgel. It is still shocking to me that someone in Starr's position could be so reckless with the truth."

For much of her career Graves has combined journalism and academic interests. For six years she taught a course in magazine editing at George Washington University, in the nation's capital. She has had several fellowships at Harvard University, in Cambridge, Massachusetts, and since 1996 she has been a resident scholar at the Women's Studies Research Center at Brandeis University, in Waltham, Massachusetts. In her interview with *Current Biography*, Graves described the Brandeis Institute for Investigative Journalism, which she launched in 2004, as "a research institute where we will create a small newsroom of journalists doing investigative reporting and placing the work in major media outlets and/or on our own web magazine." She continued, "We will be involving students as either paid research assistants or as interns for academic credit. . . . I wanted to create a sustainable institution that was independent of the corporate media to do stories the media still don't choose to do, don't want to do, or are afraid to do. I also wanted to create a place where journalists could pass on to a new generation what many of us fear is the proud, but dying tradition of investigative reporting."

When asked by *Current Biography* what advice she would give to a young student interested in a career in investigative journalism, Graves responded, "Read, read, and read some more. Take advantage of every opportunity to learn, because as a journalist, you will likely be able to draw upon just about everything you learn. Pursue every opportunity to get experience, even if you have to work for free or almost for free in the early years. Keep an open mind; whenever you are 'sure' you know something, examine it more carefully and be willing to look at it critically from many other points of view. If being a journalist is what you feel you are 'called' to do, don't give up. And don't forget that the most valuable quality you have is your integrity. Hang onto it."

Graves and her work have received many honors, including the Investigative Reporters and Editors Award and the National Magazine Award for Excellence, the highest such recognition for magazine journalism in the United States. She has also earned the Pope Foundation Award for Investigative Journalism; two Goldsmith Research Awards from Harvard University's Joan Shorenstein Center on the Press, Politics, and Public Policy; and several research grants from the Fund for Investigative Journalism in Washington, D.C. She has also received fellowships from Harvard University's Kennedy School of Government, the Radcliffe Public Policy Institute, and the Alicia Patterson Journalism Foundation.

In January 2000 Graves and her husband adopted a child from China, whom they named Grace. "I think often about what is 'happening' to Grace as she negotiates childhood," Graves wrote for the *Columbia Journalism Review* (May/June 2003). "She asks 'why' a million times a day. And I see more clearly how naturally children—who haven't yet learned the artifices of adults—can ask surprisingly penetrating questions about aspects of life we sometimes want to hide from or soften, or don't even see. Thanks to her, I have what seems like a million new questions of my own as I make plans to write about national and international issues that I previously was blind to. Sometimes my work may overlap with Grace's inevitable search for the truth of who she is and why she is here. Whatever she does in life, someday I'll tell her what I have learned: to be true to her own experience. To be guided not by some false idea of objectivity, but by intellectual honesty and the Golden Rule."

—C.M.

Suggested Reading: *American Journalism Review* (on-line) Apr. 1998; *Boston Globe* D p1 Apr. 30, 1998; Brandeis University Web site; Common Cause Web site; *Sunday Oklahoman* A p6 Feb. 29, 2004; *Washington Post* C p1 Sep. 10, 1995

Green Day

Music group

Armstrong, Billie Joe
Feb. 17, 1972– Singer; songwriter

Dirnt, Mike
May 4, 1972– Bassist; singer

Tre Cool
Dec. 9, 1972– Drummer

Address: c/o Warner Bros. Records Inc., 3300 Warner Blvd., Burbank, CA 91505

The punk-pop trio of Billie Joe Armstrong, Mike Dirnt, and Tre Cool, known collectively as Green Day, burst onto the music scene in 1994 with their major-label debut album, *Dookie*. That recording would sell more than 10 million copies and introduce a new generation of listeners to the stylings of late-1970s punk, whose spare and abrasive sound evolved, in part, as a reaction to the musical excesses of disco and arena rock. What set Green Day apart—and made their songs more palatable to mainstream Americans than those of their punk progenitors—were their underlying pop melodies infused with catchy guitar hooks. "The whole gist of original punk was to annoy, outrage and shock people," the founder of Lookout Records, Lawrence Livermore, told Alec Foege for *Rolling Stone*

(September 22, 1994). "That's not the main thing of Green Day. They sing simple, cool love songs with lots of energy." Slumping sales of their subsequent albums and reduced radio airtime throughout the late 1990s and early 2000s removed Green Day from many rock fans' consciousness—until 2004, when their full-length release *American Idiot* won the band a new reputation as outspoken and mature social and political critics. "We just wanted to have fun, [to] push ourselves and be ambitious and make the biggest record that we've ever made as far as satisfying ourselves," Tre Cool told Corey Moss for MTV (October 1, 2004, on-line). Conceived as a rock opera in an age when inexpensive digitized music platforms have established hit singles over complete albums as the primary market force, *American Idiot* has sold more than three million copies and took the 2005 Grammy Award for best rock album. "In its musical muscle and sweeping, politically charged narrative, it's something of a masterpiece," Stephen Thomas Erlewine wrote about the album for the All Music Guide (on-line), "and one of the few—if not the *only*—records of 2004 to convey what it feels like to live in the strange, bewildering America of the early 2000s."

The youngest of six children, the guitarist, singer, and songwriter Billie Joe Armstrong was born on February 17, 1972 in Rodeo, California, a blue-collar town he called "the most unscenic place on the planet" in an interview with Jeff Gordinier for *Entertainment Weekly* (December 23, 1994). "We went to this elementary school, and they used to al-

Jo Hale/Getty Images

The members of Green Day (left to right): Billy Joe Armstrong, Tre Cool, Mike Dirnt

ways send kids home with headaches. They figured it was because of the toxins that the refineries were throwing in the air." His father was a jazz musician and truck driver, while his mother was a waitress at a local roadside café. Armstrong began singing at age five, often performing for hospital patients, and soon afterward he recorded his first song, "Looking for Love," for Fiat Records, a local company. (He wrote his first song, "Why Do You Want Him?" when he was 12.) Armstrong's father gave him his first guitar, an electric Stratocaster that Armstrong named Blue after the color of its body. (Armstrong still plays Blue and has since had several replicas made.) The elder Armstrong died of cancer of the esophagus when his youngest son was 10 years old. "Our family changed a lot because my parents had been very kid oriented," Billie Joe's sister Anna told Chris Mundy for *Rolling Stone* (January 26, 1995). "And all of a sudden, my mother withdrew and threw herself into waitressing. The family structure broke up. Then my mom remarried about a year or two afterward, and that was a big change for the negative. I'd say we were as dysfunctional as any family with the death of a father, a stepfather who no one liked and almost losing our mother at the same time."

When Armstrong was in fifth grade, he met his future band mate, the bassist Mike Dirnt, in the school cafeteria. Dirnt was born Michael Pritchard on May 4, 1972, also in Rodeo, to a heroin-addicted mother who put him up for adoption. He was adopted by a Native American woman and her white husband, who divorced when Dirnt was seven years old. Dirnt lived briefly with his adoptive father before frequent confrontations prompted him to move in with his adoptive mother in condi-

tions barely above poverty. His older sister left home at age 13. "When I was in fourth or fifth grade, my mom stayed out all night, came home the next day with a guy, and he moved in," Dirnt told Chris Mundy. "I'd never met the guy before, and all of a sudden he's my stepdad." While Dirnt and his stepfather initially did not get along, they later became very close and remained so until his stepfather died, when Dirnt was 17. As a boy Dirnt played guitar until, as he told Jonathan Herrera for *Bass Player* (September 2004), "one day my friend's brother told me that no matter how many guitar players there are in a band, there's only one bass player," which led him to switch to the bass.

Soon after Dirnt and Armstrong met, mutual friends introduced them to the music of such punk bands as the Dead Kennedys, DOA, and True Sounds of Liberty. Fascinated by the music, the pair began playing together, with Armstrong on guitar and vocals and Dirnt on bass, in part because there were few or no record stores in Rodeo. "If you wanted to hear music," Dirnt told Joel Selvin for the *San Francisco Chronicle* (February 13, 1994), "you had to play it [yourself]." Although they received no pay, they played wherever possible—in nearby cafés, at parties, and in friends' backyards. (One such gig was interrupted when Armstrong's mother phoned to tell her son to go home and finish his chores.) After eighth grade Dirnt and Armstrong decided to stop playing covers of other musicians' songs and write their own music. They then formed their first official band, Sweet Children, when both were 14. A year later, when Dirnt's mother moved out of the area, he rented a room in the Armstrongs' house rather than leave town with her. While Armstrong and Dirnt attended Pinole Valley High School, in Pinole, California, they began playing shows at all-ages clubs, and in 1987 they released a self-titled EP.

In 1989 they added drummer Al Sobrante (born John Kiffmeyer, whose stage name was a play on El Sobrante, California, his hometown) to the group and changed the band's name to Green Day. ("Green day" is a slang term for a day in which people do little more than sit around and smoke marijuana.) As high-school seniors, the newly formed trio recorded their first EP, entitled *1,000 Hours*, in two days and for only $600; it was well received by the local punk scene, and the band signed a recording deal with the local independent label Lookout Records. Green Day reportedly gave their audition performance in a rain-soaked shack, powered only by a generator, in front of an audience of 12 teenagers holding candles. The band "had that early-'60s, British Invasion kind of energy," Livermore told Gordinier. "It was just really bright and sparkly." Armstrong dropped out of school, and Dirnt, who customarily earned good grades, graduated; together, the two began squatting in Oakland, California, and concentrating primarily on their band. (Meanwhile, Dirnt completed numerous credits at a community college.) Their debut LP, *39/Smooth*, sold well without attracting widespread critical notice, as did their next EP, *Slappy*. Sobrante decided to leave the band to attend college, and at the suggestion of Lawrence Livermore, Tre Cool joined as the new drummer.

Cool was born Frank Edwin Wright III on December 9, 1972. He and his older sibling grew up in Willits, California, with their mother, Linda, a bookkeeper, and their father, Frank, a builder, bus driver, trucking-company owner, and former army helicopter pilot. Cool began playing the violin in second grade but later switched to the drums. "It was pretty noisy," Linda Wright told Steve Dougherty and Michael Small for *People* (March 20, 1995), "but a definite improvement on the violin." Livermore was well acquainted with Cool's ability: he lived adjacent to the Wrights in a house built by Frank, and Cool became the drummer for Livermore's band, the Lookouts, at age 12. "They wouldn't even let me have cymbals for a long time," Cool told Chris Mundy. "Lawrence locked them up, and after a while he would take them out one at a time and let me use them." By the time he joined Green Day, Cool, like Armstrong, had dropped out of high school, where he had been class president.

The 1992 release of *Kerplunk*, the first album featuring Cool on drums, marked Green Day's breakthrough within the underground music scene. They toured extensively in Europe and North America, sleeping on the floors of friends and fans and traveling in cramped vans with other bands. Meanwhile, sales of *Kerplunk* and *39/Smooth* steadily climbed. "I don't even know why," Dirnt told Selvin. "Sure we toured, but tons of bands have done the same thing and it didn't work for them." Touring did, however, work for

Green Day, and their growing popularity attracted the interest of several major record labels who were impressed by the band's fresh blend of the punk aesthetic with catchy melodies and clever lyrics. Realizing that the trio had outgrown the small label, Lookout Records and Green Day parted on friendly terms. The band members, accustomed to operating alone, approached involvement with the business side of the music industry with caution, but ultimately signed, for an undisclosed six-figure sum, with the Warner Bros. subsidiary Reprise Records. "They have all the elements," Warner Bros. producer and fellow musician Rob Cavallo told Dougherty and Small. "Great lyrics, great melodies, interesting influences—the Sex Pistols, the Clash, the Kinks, the Beatles."

Dookie, Green Day's first release under Reprise, appeared in 1994 and quickly became a hit, thanks in large part to MTV's frequent airing of the video for "Longview," the initial single on the album. Audiences took to the album's "slacker" complaints about boredom, girls, and getting high, all set to driving three-chord hooks and heavy basslines. Armstrong's nasal whine and occasional faux-Cockney accent, while unconventional, worked within the music's context. (Armstrong joked to Alec Foege, "I'm an American guy faking an English accent faking an American accent.") The album's second single, "Basket Case," spent five weeks at the top of the modern-rock charts, and another single, "When I Come Around," held the number-one spot on the charts for seven weeks. *Dookie* peaked at number two on the *Billboard* album chart and was ultimately certified platinum 10 times over (meaning that it sold over 10 million copies); it also furthered the sales of *Kerplunk* and *39/Smooth*, which attained platinum (indicating one million copies sold) and gold (500,000 copies sold) status, respectively. *Dookie* won the 1994 Grammy Award for best alternative music performance, and in 2003 *Rolling Stone* named it one of the 500 greatest albums of all time. Later in 1994 Green Day was invited to perform at both the Lollapalooza Festival and Woodstock '94, a massive concert commemorating the 25th anniversary of the original 1969 event. Their Woodstock gig became the stuff of legend: the band started a mud fight with the fans, and audience members flooded the stage. A security guard, mistaking the mud-caked Dirnt for an errant fan, broke several of the bassist's teeth while trying to haul him offstage. The band proved to be as loud and brash onstage as they were on recordings—and virtually single-handedly launched a punk revival.

During the summer of 1995, Green Day again topped the charts with "J.A.R.," a song they contributed to the soundtrack for the movie *Angus*. They also continued touring, consistently selling out arenas, coliseums, and other large venues. Their live shows were notorious for the band's onstage antics: Cool customarily demolished his drum kit at the end of each set, Armstrong had a habit of spitting into the crowd and mooning them, and Dirnt frequently dived from the stage into moshing fans. The spastic energy of the shows "really comes down to having fun," Armstrong explained to Matt Peiken for the *Saint Paul* (Minnesota) *Pioneer Press* (April 23, 1998). "I've even tried not to have fun on stage, just to see what it's like, to just go up and stand still. But I can't help it. When we get on stage, we act crazy again." Such craziness resulted in innumerable personal injuries, and Cool joked to Chris Mundy that the band wanted to write a book called "Insult to Injury," cataloging their various broken bones, torn ligaments, and cases of whiplash.

Green Day survived their post-*Dookie* tours to release *Insomniac*, which debuted in October 1995 and peaked at number two on *Billboard*'s album charts. The album, which went double platinum, spawned the hit singles "Geek Stink Breath" and "Brain Stew" but was not received by critics nearly as well as *Dookie* had been. In the spring of 1996, Green Day abruptly canceled a scheduled European tour, claiming exhaustion. During the remainder of the year, the band rested and wrote new material for their next album, *Nimrod*, which they released in 1997. Despite the widespread opinion among fans and critics that it was the best album of Green Day's career to date, *Nimrod* reached only the number-10 spot on the charts. In *Spin* (December 1997), Jonathan Gold announced, "*Nimrod*—saturated with acoustic numbers and swing ballads, old-fashioned hardcore and Stephen Foster-style tuneage—toys with the boundaries of pop-punk, recasting it as a thoroughly modern American music." The album also contained perhaps the most recognizable song that the band had recorded: "Good Riddance (Time of Your Life)," an unusually downtempo number for the punk trio that featured Armstrong on acoustic guitar and vocals. Greg Kot for *Rolling Stone* (October 30, 1997, on-line) called the song "a surprisingly sweet folk anthem buoyed by strings." The song was featured in the series finale of the landmark television show *Seinfeld* as well as on two episodes of the show *E.R.* The video for "Good Riddance" also won an MTV Music Video Award for best alternative video of the year.

After the exposure from *Nimrod* (which eventually earned double-platinum status) and "Good Riddance," the band virtually dropped out of sight for the next three years. In that time they hired—and subsequently fired—a new producer, Scott Litt, and began recording their 2000 release, *Warning.* Sales of that album fell far short of Green Day's customary multiplatinum, earning only gold, and it appeared that the band was in a career slump. Their next album, a 2001 compilation of previously released songs entitled *International Superhits*, reached only the 40th spot on the charts and went gold. Whereas *International Superhits* showcased Green Day's previous hit singles, its 2002 companion album, *Shenanigans*, recycled the band's lesser-known cover songs and B-sides into a compendium that, while generally regarded as enjoyable,

"never quite jells," according to Mark Kemp for *Rolling Stone* (August 22, 2002, on-line). In January 2004 Green Day re-released their pre-Reprise projects *1,000 Hours*, *39/Smooth*, and *Slappy*, which had become hard to find in record stores, as one compilation CD, entitled *1,039/Smoothed Out Slappy Hours.*

In the midst of their slump, Armstrong, Dirnt, and Cool recorded a follow-up to *Warning*, only to have their nearly completed master tapes stolen. What seemed a disaster turned into a boon, as the trio started experimenting. "One member started playing something crazy for 30 seconds," J. R. Griffin wrote for *MeanStreet* magazine (November 2004, on-line). "Then another member jammed on a totally different sound for 30 seconds, and so on and so forth. The band challenged each other to play completely different music to see how it fit—the bigger and more grandiose, the better." They came up with a track called "American Idiot" and decided to write a rock opera about an overmedicated, desensitized character unsure of what or whom to believe. "We thought, 'Wow, we're on to something here.' It was like we were finally living up to our own expectations," Armstrong told Griffin. "People always classified us as a punk-pop band, but for me, it was always the bigger, the better. It's something that we learned working on *Nimrod*, working on it with more band members and different sounds and taking a natural progression with our albums. But this was a lot more than just the normal Green Day progression. I think that we're taking the entire genre into a new place." The band immersed themselves in the project, plotting out the story they wanted to tell, pushing to make a more personal—and more political—album than they had before. "We set up shop in a really creative way with this record," Dirnt told Corey Moss. "You know, if people want to call it 'reinvention' or 'redefining' or whatever, I think it worked. I'm happy with it and hopefully all our fans like it. That's the key."

The result was Green Day's 2004 album, *American Idiot*, filled with songs—ranging from the sprawling, nine-minute "Jesus of Suburbia" to the two-and-a-half-minute jam "St. Jimmy"—that, according to Stephen Thomas Erlewine, "effectively convey the paranoia and fear of living in America in [the] days after 9/11." "Taken as a whole, [*American Idiot*] is truly a modern-day rock masterpiece which demands to be heard from beginning to end," Griffin asserted. "In pieces, it'll produce the most sonically bold—and probably most popular—Green Day singles you've ever heard." The album's unambiguous message in opposition to President George W. Bush coupled with the band's maturing musicality proved a heady—and popular—mix; *American Idiot* became Green Day's first album to hold the number-one spot on *Billboard*'s modern-rock chart. "The statement that we're making is that this is a pretty serious time. There are a lot of people living in fear, and people need something to relate to. This album is a reflection of what's going on," Armstrong told Griffin. "Maybe there aren't enough pop-punk bands taking things serious enough." "I think the problem with a lot of rock bands or pop groups or whatever is that they're so afraid of damaging their precious careers," he explained to Moss. "For me, I think it is something that can enrich mine: 'Yeah, I supported this. This meant a lot to me.'"

Throughout their decade-long career, Green Day have faced criticism that they are not a true punk band, because of their ability to switch from hardcore jams to ballads within a single album. "No matter what, we'll never fully belong in the underground, and we'll never fully belong in the mainstream," Armstrong told Matt Peiken. They first felt the backlash to their success after signing with Reprise Records, when many fans began calling them sellouts and poseurs, arguing that true punks would fight the corporations rather than align with them. "Mike and [Tre] are the people I most like to play music with," Armstrong explained to Joel Selvin. "And that's the most credibility you can have—to stay true to your music." Armstrong, perhaps himself confused by the band's versatility, once denied that Green Day was a punk band, but he later retracted his statement, telling Jonathan Gold, "I'll take that back. We are a punk band. We come from punk rock, and we don't want to bad-mouth it ever again. Punk got me out of my hick hometown. Punk was the best education I've ever had." "The beauty of the punk thing," Armstrong told Selvin, "is that everyone has their own interpretation—like the Bible."

Despite their personae as punk-rock Peter Pans, lost boys who refuse to grow up, the members of Green Day have become family men. On July 2, 1994, in a five-minute backyard ceremony, Armstrong married Adrienne Nesser, a fan whom he met on Green Day's very first tour. The day after the wedding the couple discovered that Adrienne was pregnant; they now have two sons, Joseph Marciano and Jakob Danger, born in March 1995 and September 1998, respectively. Dirnt married his longtime girlfriend Anastasia in 1996, and the couple had a daughter, Estelle Desiree, in April 1997; the two have since divorced, though they remain on friendly terms. Dirnt remarried in 2004. Cool has been married and divorced twice. With his first wife, Lisa Lyons, whom he married in March 1995, Cool had a daughter, Ramona, born earlier that year. Cool married his second wife, Claudia, in 2000; the couple had a son, Frankito, in 2001, before divorcing in 2003. All the members of Green Day still live in California: Cool and Dirnt in Oakland, and Armstrong and his family in Berkeley. Armstrong and his wife co-own Adeline Records, a small independent label, and Dirnt is a co-owner of Rudy's Can't Fail Café, in Emeryville, California. All three musicians participate in side projects with other bands: Armstrong has sung for Pinhead Gunpowder, Rancid, the Lookouts, and the Influents, among others; Dirnt has played with the Frustrators, Screeching Weasel, Crummy Musi-

cians, and Squirtgun; and Cool has played with the Lookouts, Screeching Weasel, and Samiam.

—K.J.E.

Suggested Reading: *Entertainment Weekly* p34 Dec. 23, 1994; MeanStreet (online) Nov. 2004; MTV.com Oct. 1, 2004; *People* p94 Mar. 20, 1995; *Rolling Stone* p25 Sep. 22, 1994, p40 Jan. 26, 1995; *Saint Paul (Minnesota) Pioneer Press* Apr. 23, 1998; *San Francisco Chronicle* p28 Feb. 13, 1994; *Spin* p107+ Dec. 1997, with photos

Selected Recordings: *Kerplunk*, 1992; *Dookie*, 1994; *Insomniac*, 1995; *Nimrod*, 1997; *Warning*, 2000; *International Superhits*, 2001; *Shenanigans*, 2002; *1,039/Smoothed Out Slappy Hours*, 2004; *American Idiot*, 2004

Bill Ingalls, NASA/Getty Images

Gregory, Frederick D.

Jan. 7, 1941– Deputy administrator of NASA

Address: NASA, 300 E St., S.W., Washington, DC 20546

Frederick D. Gregory became the first African-American to pilot a space shuttle when he flew *Challenger* during its seventh mission, in 1985. On his next two missions, aboard *Discovery* in 1989 and *Atlantis* in 1991, he served as the space-shuttle commander and was the first African-American to occupy that position. (Gregory was not the first African-American in space; that honor belongs to Guion Bluford, a member of *Challenger*'s flight crew on a 1983 mission.) Gregory, who joined the

National Aeronautics and Space Administration (NASA) in 1978, logged a total of 455 hours in space during his time as an astronaut. He also served in the U.S. Air Force for three decades, flying as a combat helicopter pilot and a fighter pilot and serving during the Vietnam War. Gregory retired from the air force as a colonel in 1993, after logging more than 7,000 hours in more than 50 types of aircraft. Gregory retired from active duty as an astronaut that year as well; since that time he has held several administrative positions at NASA. In 2002 he was appointed by President George W. Bush as NASA's deputy administrator, the number-two position there. In 2005 he briefly served as acting administrator while the agency sought a new chief executive to replace Sean O'Keefe, who had resigned.

In his administrative roles Gregory has helped to oversee the difficult return-to-flight program that NASA has pursued since the disaster in February 2003 in which the shuttle *Columbia* broke up during reentry, killing all on board. The return-to-flight program achieved its first success when the orbiter *Discovery* returned to space in late July 2005 and landed safely back on Earth on August 9. Gregory has also helped implement President Bush's ambitious new vision for U.S. space flight, which includes a return of humans to the moon and continued exploration of our solar system. In a speech before the U.S. House of Representatives Appropriations Committee regarding NASA's plans, Gregory said, according to a federal transcript (April 20, 2005), "A new era in space exploration begins with the return to flight of the Shuttle and the completion of the International Space Station, as we begin a journey that will take the next generation of Americans back to the Moon, to Mars, and beyond. . . . This generation inherited great legacies from the exploratory voyages and discoveries of earlier centuries. It is our responsibility to ensure that future generations inherit from our journey a similar legacy of achievement and inspiration. . . . As President George W. Bush said, 'We choose to explore space because doing so improves our lives and lifts our national spirit. So let us continue the journey.'" In September 2005 Gregory announced his intention to retire from NASA, after 31 years of service to the agency. He planned to remain in his job until Congress confirmed his replacement.

The only child of Francis Anderson Gregory and the former Nora Drew, Frederick Drew Gregory was born on January 7, 1941 in Washington, D.C. As the son of schoolteachers, Gregory developed an early and lasting appreciation of the benefits of a good education and hard work. He also developed a religious outlook, primarily thanks to his paternal grandfather, who was a minister at the family's Congregational church.

While he was growing up, Gregory witnessed the effects of racism on his family. His father, despite having been trained as an electrical engineer, was unable to find work in his chosen field. His un-

cle Charles Richard Drew, a surgeon who gained fame through his pioneering work in the area of blood plasma, had demonstrated that there were no differences in the blood of people of different races, but he failed to overcome the misconceptions of the day and was therefore prevented from conducting blood transfusions between races. Gregory was bussed to a town outside Washington to attend an all-black school until the eighth grade, when integration was permitted in local schools. As a student at Anacostia High School, Gregory was subjected to taunts and ridicule; at one point white students staged a boycott as a means of complaining about the presence of blacks. Despite such difficulties Gregory did well in school and graduated in 1958.

Gregory next contemplated a career in the military. He had been interested in military service since his days as a Boy Scout; he began focusing on flying after he became a member of the Junior Reserve Officers' Training Corps (JROTC) and visited Andrews Air Force Base, in Maryland. During one of his visits, he met members of the Thunderbirds (the division of the air force famous for its flying demonstrations), who informed him that the U.S. Air Force Academy (USAFA), in Colorado Springs, Colorado, would soon be opening.

When Gregory entered the USAFA, in the early 1960s, he was the only black cadet in his class. Despite the prejudices of some of his white classmates, he excelled academically. After his graduation, in 1964, he briefly considered becoming an engineer or teaching history at the academy before deciding to become a helicopter pilot. He trained at Stead Air Force Base, in Nevada, and earned his aviator's wings in 1965. In his first assignment, which extended from October 1965 to May 1966, he was a helicopter rescue pilot at Vance Air Force Base, in Oklahoma. In June 1966 he was reassigned overseas, as an H-43 combat rescue pilot in Vietnam.

During his approximately 13-month tour of duty in Vietnam, Gregory flew 550 combat missions, which were devoted primarily to fire suppression and rescue operations. He received numerous awards for his combat service, most notably two Distinguished Flying Cross awards, including one for his rescue of four Marines from a downed helicopter in 1967. When he returned to the U.S. later that year, he was assigned to the Whiteman Air Force Base, in Missouri, where he flew the missile-supporting UH-1F helicopter. In a career move uncommon for helicopter pilots, in January 1968 he retrained as a fixed-wing fighter-jet pilot at Randolph Air Force Base, in Texas, where he flew the T-38. He subsequently joined the F-4 Phantom Combat Crew Training Wing at Davis-Monthan Air Force Base, in Arizona.

Starting in September 1970 Gregory attended the United States Naval Test Pilot School at the Patuxent River Naval Air Station, in Maryland. When he completed his training, in June 1971, he was assigned to the 4950th Test Wing at Wright Patterson

Air Force Base, in Ohio, where he tested a wide variety of helicopters and jet fighters. In 1974 he worked as a research test pilot at the NASA Langley Research Center, in Virginia. His assignment in Virginia was interrupted when, in 1975, he was temporarily redeployed to Vietnam to aid in the evacuation of refugees from the American Embassy in Saigon.

While working as a test pilot, Gregory attended George Washington University, in Washington, D.C., graduating in 1977 with a master's degree in information systems. In that year NASA announced that it was recruiting new astronauts; the agency was then in the final stages of developing its space-shuttle program, which was designed to create reusable space vehicles that would ferry astronauts to a permanent space station in orbit around Earth. Gregory immediately applied for the astronaut corps, but the air force was reluctant to let him go. He was ready to resign his commission when air-force officials relented and forwarded his application. In 1978 he was among 35 applicants accepted by NASA; along with Guion Bluford and Ron McNair, he was among the first African-Americans whom the space agency trained as astronauts.

When Gordon completed his training, in August 1979, he was qualified to serve as a pilot aboard the space shuttle. Nevertheless, he had to wait almost six years before being chosen for a mission. (The inaugural launch of the first functional space shuttle, *Columbia*, occurred on April 12, 1981. NASA proceeded to build and operate four more space shuttles—*Challenger*, *Discovery*, *Atlantis*, and *Endeavour*.) In the interim Gregory served in a variety of capacities at NASA. He represented the Astronaut Office at the Kennedy Space Center during the first two space-shuttle missions; was a flight-data manager; served as the lead spacecraft communicator, known as the CAPCOM, and also as chief of operational safety at NASA headquarters, in Washington, D.C.; was chief of astronaut training; and worked as a member of the Orbiter Configuration Control Board and the Space Shuttle Program Control Board.

In his first, eight-day flight in outer space, in 1985, Gregory had the job of pilot of the space shuttle *Challenger*. (The role of the pilot is more accurately described as that of a co-pilot; the shuttle commander is the primary pilot of the vehicle. If the commander becomes incapacitated, the pilot takes over. Astronauts generally fly a few times as pilots before qualifying for the position of commander.) As part of the flight's Spacelab 3 mission, Gregory, along with the six other members of the crew (Robert Overmyer, Norman Thagard, William Thornton, Don Lind, Taylor Wang, and Lodewijk Vandenberg), conducted medical and materials-processing experiments. The crew also launched several satellites, including the Northern Utah Satellite. According to J. Alfred Phelps in his book *They Had a Dream: The Story of African-American Astronauts* (1994), as quoted by Ed Decker in *Contemporary Black Biography* (1994), Gregory's first space flight moved him deeply: "When you're in space and you're looking down at earth and you see this perfect globe beneath you and you see the organization and non chaos, you have to feel, as I did, that there was one great Being—one great force that made this happen," Gregory said.

On January 28, 1986 Gregory served as the CAPCOM during *Challenger*'s last mission, when the shuttle exploded a little more than a minute after takeoff. During a tribute in 2005 to the 17 American astronauts who had been killed during the performance of their duties, Gregory had difficulty suppressing his emotions when he recalled that fateful day. "It is still painful to think about those moments when we lost contact with the crew and our worst fears were realized," he said, as quoted by a Reuters reporter in the *Los Angeles Times* (February 18, 2005). "It was my intent that day at that moment to press the transmit button as I saw the *Challenger* break up and say, 'Godspeed, *Challenger*.' I didn't—and I should have."

On the evening of November 22, 1989, Gregory made his second flight into outer space, this time as commander of the space shuttle *Discovery*. In doing so he became the first black astronaut to command a space-shuttle mission. Also on board the flight were the astronauts Manley Carter, F. Story Musgrave, and Kathryn Thornton. Because the mission was classified as secret, little is known about it other than that it involved Department of Defense payloads. After five days in orbit, Gregory piloted *Discovery* to a perfect landing at Edwards Air Force Base, in California.

Gregory returned to space aboard the orbiter *Atlantis* in November 1991. As commander of the mission, his last, he oversaw the deployment of the Defense Support Program missile-warning system and conducted a number of other military operations, including the Military Man in Space study, which evaluated the potential for an orbiting observer to gather intelligence about ground operations and conduct other military activities. Along with his crew members Tom Hendricks, F. Story Musgrave, Jim Voss, Mario Runco Jr., and Tom Hennen, Gregory performed experiments designed to counteract the physical stress of long-duration space flight.

Gregory piloted the *Atlantis* to a landing at Edwards Air Force Base on December 1, 1991; by that time he had amassed some 455 hours in orbit. In April 1992 he joined NASA's Office of Safety Management and Mission Assurance, in Washington, D.C., as its associate administrator. In 1993 he left both the astronaut corps and the air force to devote himself to his new administrative duties. In December 2001 he became NASA's associate administrator for space flight. He held that position until August 2002, when he was nominated by President George W. Bush to become NASA's new deputy administrator. He was confirmed by the U.S. Senate and assumed his new duties that month.

On February 1, 2003 the space shuttle *Columbia*, returning to Earth after a successful launch and mission, broke up upon reentry. Its disintegration caused the deaths of all seven crew members. In the wake of the tragedy, NASA postponed indefinitely its plans for future space-shuttle missions. An investigation concluded that the leading edge of *Columbia*'s left wing had been hit by a piece of foam debris from one of the vehicle's external booster rockets during takeoff. The impact created a hole in the wing that allowed superheated gases to get underneath the ship's protective skin and in essence destroy it from the inside out. Following a lengthy study, the Columbia Accident Investigation Board condemned NASA for its lapses in "safety culture" and charged that the agency had done little to improve the safety of manned space flight in the 17 years since the *Challenger* explosion.

After the findings were made public, the space agency announced plans to improve the shuttle fleet by redesigning the vehicles' fuel tanks and setting up new camera systems that would film each shuttle during liftoff. New procedures were developed to permit the repair of a ship's protective outer hull while in orbit. In the event that a shuttle proved to be irreparable, NASA formulated contingency procedures that would enable the crew to either take refuge in the International Space Station or stay in orbit until a second shuttle could retrieve them.

In January 2004, with the intention of reinvigorating the space agency, President Bush gave a speech at NASA headquarters in which he described a new vision for space exploration. Responding to critics who had complained that human space flight had been confined to low Earth orbits since the last manned moon landing, in 1972, Bush called on NASA to "gain a new foothold on the moon and to prepare for new journeys to the worlds beyond our own," as quoted on NASA's Web site. His plan would require that NASA complete its commitment to the International Space Station and then retire the space-shuttle fleet by 2010. During the same period the agency would develop and test a new Crew Exploration Vehicle (CEV), to be completed by 2008, which could be used to resupply the space station and ferry astronauts to the moon. Bush's plan also called for another exploration of the moon with robotic probes before 2008, lengthy human missions to the moon by no later than 2014, and the creation of permanent colonies on the lunar surface by 2020. "With the experience and knowledge gained on the moon," Bush declared, "we will then be ready to take the next steps of space exploration: human missions to Mars and to worlds beyond."

The funding necessary to carry out those plans was estimated at approximately $12 billion over the next five years. Most of the money—some $11 billion—is to be reallocated from the agency's current five-year budget. Since Bush's speech, NASA has received additional funds from Congress—the first in what many observers anticipate as a series of budget increases for the space agency.

In February 2005, as NASA was readying itself for its return to flight after a two-year investigation and upgrade of the space-shuttle fleet, the space agency announced that Gregory was to be named acting administrator, a temporary position to replace Sean O'Keefe, who had spent three years at his post. During his brief time as the head of NASA, while the agency searched for a permanent administrator, Gregory oversaw the last phases of NASA's overhaul of the space shuttle and launch protocols as the agency prepared to launch its first shuttle since the *Columbia* disaster. In March 2005 President Bush nominated Michael D. Griffin of Johns Hopkins University to serve as administrator of NASA. Griffin, a longtime proponent of human space exploration, assumed the position on April 14, 2005. Less than five months later, Gregory made public his plans to retire from NASA as soon as his successor is confirmed by Congress.

For service to his country as an air-force pilot, Gregory received the Legion of Merit, the Defense Superior Service Medal, two Distinguished Flying Crosses, 16 Air Medals, the Defense Meritorious Service Medal, the Air Force Meritorious Service Medal, and the Air Force Commendation Medal. During his time with NASA, he has been presented with three Space Flight Medals, two Outstanding Leadership Medals, and the Distinguished Service Medal. His other honors include the U.S. Air Force Academy Distinguished Graduate Award, the Air Force Association Ira Eaker Award, the National Intelligence Medal, the National Society of Black Engineers Distinguished National Scientist Award, the George Washington University Distinguished Alumni Award, the President's Medal, and the President's Medal from Charles R. Drew University of Medicine and Science. In 2003 he earned the Presidential Rank Award for Distinguished Executives. In 2004 and 2005 he was named one of the 50 most important blacks in technology by the editors of *U.S. Black Engineer and Information Technology* magazine.

Gregory has been married to the former Barbara Ann Archer since June 3, 1964. They have two grown children, Frederick D. Gregory Jr. and Heather Lynn Gregory Skeens, and four grandchildren.

—C.M.

Suggested Reading: *Aviation Week & Space Technology* p43 Aug. 2, 2004; CNN.com Feb. 17, 2005; *Jet* p22 Dec. 1, 2003; *Los Angeles Times* A p33 Feb. 18, 2005; NASA Web site; *Washington Post* A p2 Mar. 12, 2005; *Contemporary Black Biography*, 1994

Dave Einsel/Getty Images

Griffin, Michael

Nov. 1, 1949– Administrator of NASA

Address: Public Affairs, NASA, 300 E St., S.W., Mailstop 9P39, Washington, DC 20546

"I have great confidence in the team that will carry out our nation's exciting, outward-focused, destination-oriented program," Michael Griffin, who was appointed as the administrator of the National Aeronautics and Space Administration (NASA) on April 13, 2005, said to Brian Berger for *Space News* (April 18, 2005, on-line). "I share with the agency a great sense of privilege that we have been given the wonderful opportunity to extend humanity's reach throughout the solar system." In the interview Griffin referred to the U.S. space shuttle *Columbia*, which broke apart upon reentering Earth's atmosphere on February 1, 2003 at the conclusion of a 16-day scientific mission, killing all seven crew members. "The very first issue on the plate superceding all others," he said, "is to look into return to flight, work which has gone on in the last more than two years since we lost *Columbia*, to understand . . . what the areas of concern still are." NASA's next manned flight in space, in the shuttle *Discovery*, began on July 26, 2005 and ended two weeks later. The mission was shadowed by problems with the material designed to insulate the shuttle's fuel tank—in particular, its loosening during the launch. Until that problem is solved, NASA has suspended all future shuttle launches. Griffin's plans for NASA include the introduction of the Crew Exploration Vehicle (CEV), a spacecraft that mixes design elements of the *Apollo* command capsule, used in the original moon program,

and rocket-like components designed for the space shuttle; a manned flight to Mars; and a course of action regarding the Hubble Space Telescope, which as of late October 2005 was long overdue for servicing. Regarding the difficult choices facing NASA and other government officials connected with the U.S. space program, Griffin told David E. Sanger for the *New York Times* (August 1, 2005), "What this is all about is ensuring American preeminence in space now and for the future. It is not America's place to take a back seat to other nations in the exploration of space."

As many have noted, Griffin brings extensive experience to those tasks. Prior to his appointment as NASA administrator, he was the Space Department head at the Johns Hopkins University Applied Physics Laboratory, where his team tackled space-science problems for NASA and the military. Griffin had also served as president and CEO of IN-Q-Tel Inc., a nonprofit, CIA-funded company that provides technological services in connection with the United States' national-security interests. In his first tenure with NASA, beginning in the late 1980s, he served as the chief engineer and associate administrator for exploration. Griffin was also deputy for technology at the Strategic Defense Initiative Organization, which was charged with implementing President Ronald Reagan's missile-defense program, popularly known as "Star Wars." Griffin, who holds five master's degrees as well as a doctorate, is a recipient of the NASA Exceptional Achievement Medal and the Department of Defense Distinguished Public Service Medal. "Mike is an excellent choice because of his passion for space exploration, his technical expertise and his long experience in space flight engineering," Wes Huntress, a NASA associate administrator from 1992 to 1998, said to Susan Lendroth for the Planetary Society Web site (March 11, 2005). "He resonates with the President's new vision for space and will add a down-to-earth insistence on logic and realism."

The oldest of the three children of Richard and Beryl Griffin, Michael Griffin was born on November 1, 1949 and grew up in Aberdeen, Maryland, in Harford County. His mother, who taught high-school business classes, gave him his first book on astronomy when he was five or six. "From that point on, all I ever wanted to do was be involved in space [exploration]," Griffin told a writer for the Harford County Public Schools Web site. (Referring to the same book, he noted to David E. Sanger, "Based on what we know today, everything [in it] was wrong.") Griffin was in third grade when the Soviet Union launched the first man-made, Earth-orbiting satellite, *Sputnik*, in 1957. "I was the only kid in class who knew what a satellite was," he recalled for the Web site. Griffin attended Aberdeen Elementary School until the middle of third grade, when the family moved to Woodstock, Virginia, for three years and then to Rome, Georgia, for five and a half years. The family returned to Aberdeen in 1963, and Griffin attended ninth grade at Aberdeen

High School. "Mike was very studious and an excellent student in those days, but he was small and I remember he had some trouble fitting in," Bill Loper, a former Aberdeen High School algebra teacher, said for the Harford Web site. Griffin graduated from high school in 1967, with almost straight A's; he received a C in drafting because he could not draw a straight line.

Griffin went on to study at Johns Hopkins University, in Baltimore, Maryland, where he earned a bachelor's degree in physics. He then earned a master's degree in aerospace science from the Catholic University of America, in Washington, D.C. Griffin also holds a Ph.D. degree in aerospace engineering from the University of Maryland. He has four additional master's degrees: in electrical engineering, from the University of Southern California; in applied physics, from Johns Hopkins University; in business administration, from Loyola College; and in civil engineering, from George Washington University.

In the early 1980s Griffin worked at the Applied Physics Laboratory at Johns Hopkins University, helping to design the Delta 180 series of missile-defense technology satellites for the Strategic Defense Initiative Organization. In 1986 he became the so-called deputy for technology at the organization, which oversaw the Strategic Defense Initiative (SDI)—launched by President Reagan in March 1983 to explore the feasibility of developing a defense system that would be located outside Earth's atmosphere. The overall objective of the program was to create a shield that would protect the U.S. from a nuclear attack. (The SDI has evolved into the current National Missile Defense program.) Griffin left the organization in the late 1980s to become both the chief engineer and associate administrator for exploration at NASA headquarters, in Washington, D.C. In his first stint at NASA, during the administration of President George Herbert Walker Bush, Griffin worked on the president's Space Exploration Initiative program, whose goal was to send humans to Mars. Griffin also worked on several space missions at NASA's Jet Propulsion Laboratory. Lacking congressional support, the Space Exploration Initiative was abandoned, and Griffin left NASA in 1993.

Griffin next went to work at the Orbital Sciences Corp., in Dulles, Virginia, which builds satellites and rockets; he held several leadership positions there, including chief executive officer of Orbital's subsidiary Magellan Systems Inc. Griffin then served as the president and CEO of In-Q-Tel Inc. before returning to the Applied Physics Laboratory at Johns Hopkins University in April 2004 to head the Space Department, the laboratory's second-largest department, where more than 600 specialists address space-science and engineering issues for NASA and the military. Griffin worked at the laboratory for almost a year before being nominated by President George W. Bush in March 2005 to head NASA.

On April 13, 2005 the U.S. Senate unanimously confirmed Griffin as NASA's 11th administrator. He replaced the interim administrator, Frederick Gregory, who had stepped in following the resignation of Sean O'Keefe in December 2004. As administrator Griffin has the responsibility for advancing the Vision for Space Exploration program, which was announced by President Bush in 2004. Thus, in addition to overseeing a manned shuttle mission in 2005, Griffin's focus for NASA will be on redirecting the agency's manned-space-flight program toward exploration. "If money is to be spent on space," Griffin was quoted as saying by Mike Tolson for the *Houston Chronicle* (April 14, 2005), "there is little doubt that the huge majority of Americans would prefer to spend it on an exciting, outward-focused, destination-oriented program. And that is what the president's Vision for Space Exploration is about." Griffin will also decide the future of the Hubble telescope, which orbits 375 miles above Earth to furnish scientists with views of the universe that are beyond the capabilities of ground-based telescopes. The designers of the telescope intended for it to receive periodic servicing, but the last scheduled service mission was not carried out; as a result the telescope's capabilities are thought to have been weakened and its lifespan shortened. "I believe the choice comes down between reinstating a shuttle servicing mission [to service the telescope] or possibly a very simple robotic deorbit mission," Griffin said to Brian Berger. "The decision not to execute the planned shuttle service mission was made in the immediate aftermath of the loss of *Columbia*. When we return to flight it will be with essentially a new vehicle which will have a new risk analysis associated with it."

Plans for the shuttle *Discovery* also include 28 assembly flights to help complete the International Space Station, an orbiting space-research laboratory scheduled to be fully operational in 2010. It has been suggested both that the completion date will extend beyond 2010 and that the shuttle cannot endure 28 missions. Griffin has proposed alternate methods of launching some of the space-station hardware, such as the use of expendable rockets instead of the space shuttle. "If you truly believe that the shuttle can fly all 28 planned station assembly flights between now and 2010, then it's unlikely that the switch will pay off," Griffin told Brian Berger for *Space News* (March 11, 2005), as quoted on space.com. "But if you believe that it will take until 2014 or later, then it is quite logical to ask if we could save time and money by integrating some space station assembly payloads onto larger expendables."

In any event, the space shuttle will be retired no later than 2010. Griffin's objective is to fly it as safely as possible until then. Plans are to replace the shuttle with the Crew Exploration Vehicle (CEV), a proposed spacecraft for manned missions, which is currently scheduled for a piloted launch no later than 2014. Griffin would prefer to complete a launch before that deadline. In late September 2005 Griffin unveiled NASA's $104 billion plan to build the CEV. Following up on President George W. Bush's January 2004 proposal that the U.S. space program plan another manned voyage to the moon, Griffin said that a moon mission could occur as early as 2018. He also said that he hoped such as a mission would serve as a harbinger of another, more difficult project: a manned flight to the planet Mars. According to Griffin, the new CEV will be able to carry as many as six humans to the international space station and up to 25 tons of cargo. The CEV will be wingless and weigh approximately 50 percent more than the *Apollo* spacecraft. "Think of it as Apollo on steroids," Griffin said to Warren E. Leary for the *New York Times* (September 20, 2005). Griffin and other NASA officials have expressed their conviction that space travel in the new craft will be far safer than shuttle travel.

Two teams, representing the firm Lockheed Martin and a joining of the Boeing Co. and Northrop Grumman Corp., respectively, are competing for the contract to build the CEV for NASA. "This is an area that means a lot to me," Griffin said to Brian Berger. "As a matter of what it takes to be a great nation in the 21st century, I do not believe that we wish to see a situation where the United States is dependent on any partner, reliable or unreliable, at any time for human access to space or for that matter, any access to space. We need our own capabilities." Other potential plans for the U.S.'s space program include a return to the moon by 2020, as preparation for eventual human expeditions to Mars. "It's going to be difficult, and it is going to be hectic but we are going to do it . . . ," Griffin said to Brian Berger.

The launch of the space shuttle *Discovery* in 2005 was delayed until July 26, 2005, due to problems with the external tank sensors and the thermal-protection blankets and to unfavorable weather. NASA regarded the mission as the first of two NASA flights that would permit evaluation of new safety precautions instituted in the wake of the 2003 *Columbia* disaster. Despite extensive planning and testing, during the launch a piece of foam insulation fell off the shuttle's external fuel tank. The failure of the insulation to adhere to the tank rekindled debate about the adequacy of the steps the space agency had taken to prevent such mishaps. "This was the central mistake to the loss of [*Columbia*]. It was not thought to be anything other than a maintenance and turnaround issue," Griffin told reporters at a media briefing, as quoted in the *Los Angeles Daily News* (August 10, 2005). He added, "We are learning our way. The United States has conducted 145 exactly manned spaceflights in 44 years. A student pilot has taken an airplane off the ground and landed it more times than that by the time he gets his ticket. We are at the dawn of this enterprise, not its maturity." The persisting problem led NASA to announce that all planned shuttle flights were being suspended.

Michael Griffin lives in northern Virginia with his wife and their five-year-old child; he also has three grown children. He plays golf and enjoys flying airplanes.

—L.J.

Suggested Reading: Harford County Public Schools Web site; *Houston Chronicle* A p1 Apr. 15, 2005; *Houston Chronicle* (on-line) Apr. 14, 2005; nasa.gov; *New York Times* A p10 Aug. 1, 2005, with photo, A p1+ Sep. 20, 2005, with photos; *Space News* (on-line) Mar. 11, 2005; space.com

Selected Books: *Space Vehicle Design* (with James R. French), 1991

Courtesy of www.nativethreads.com

Hall, Tex G.

Sep. 18, 1956– Tribal chairman; president of the National Congress of American Indians

Address: Three Affiliated Tribes, 404 Frontage Rd., New Town, ND 58763

"Pay attention and learn as much as you can, because someday you may have to lead your people," Tex G. Hall's grandfather told him when he was a little boy. His grandfather was a cattle rancher on the Fort Berthold Reservation, in North Dakota, the home of the Mandan, Hidatsa, and Arikara, American Indian tribes that joined as the Three Affiliated Tribes in the mid-1800s; from 1958, when Hall was two years old, to 1962, the older man also held the post of chairman of the reservation's Tribal Council. In 1998 Hall, a former high-school teacher, principal, and school superintendent, was elected to the same position, and in 2002 he became the first chairman of the council to win re-election. Concurrently, beginning in 2001, Hall has served as president of the National Congress of American Indians (NCAI); the country's oldest and largest American Indian advocacy group, the NCAI represents more than 200 of the 562 Native American tribes in the continental U.S. and Alaska. In dozens of appearances before congressional committees and in many other venues, Hall has described the huge problems with which Native Americans have been grappling for many decades: inadequate housing; widespread lack of basic utilities; badly maintained roads; deteriorating schools; extremely high rates of unemployment, poverty, alcoholism, drug abuse, crime, mental illness, and physical disease; discrimination in employment, housing, the issuing of credit, and other areas; and the many ramifications of unfair treatment and mismanagement by the Bureau of Indian Affairs and other federal and state agencies. "Unfortunately, the first Americans have been the forgotten Americans," Hall told Judy Sarasohn for the *Washington Post* (October 28, 2004). In announcing that the NCAI hoped to raise $12 million to buy its own building in Washington, D.C., where it currently rents space for its headquarters, Hall expressed the hope, as Sarasohn wrote, "that a higher visibility in Washington and increased lobbying, combined with a strong voter registration effort will help Native Americans better hold lawmakers and administration officials accountable for their Indian trust responsibilities."

One of the eight children of Leland and Audrey (Rabbithead) Hall, Tex Gerald Hall was born on September 18, 1956; he is of Mandan and Arikara ancestry. His Indian name, Ihbudah Hishi, means Red-Tipped Arrow. Hall grew up with his three brothers and four sisters on the family's cattle ranch on the Fort Berthold Reservation, located on the Missouri River in western North Dakota. According to a brief history on the Three Affiliated Tribes' Web site (mnanation.com), although the tribes have shared "cultures and histories" for many decades, each maintains its distinct clan relationships and ceremonies. As described on the Web sites of the Fargo/Grand Forks, North Dakota, newspaper the *Forum* and the Mni Sose Intertribal Water Rights Coalition (mnisose.org), the reservation is a small fraction of its original size, as delineated in the Fort Laramie Treaty of 1851. The federal government succeeded in shrinking its boundaries even before the discovery, two decades later, that Congress had never ratified the treaty, and subsequently, a series of executive orders, foreclosures, homestead acts, and other measures steadily reduced its total area. Individual members of the Mandan, Hidatsa, or Arikara tribes own 378,604 acres, or about 38 percent, of the reservation's 988,000 acres; another 8 percent, or 79,233 acres, is owned by the Three Affiliated Tribes and is man-

aged jointly by the federal Bureau of Indian Affairs and the tribal government. More than half of the remaining land is owned by non-Indians. Moreover, according to mnisose.org, in the 1940s the federal government in effect usurped 155,000 acres of "prime agricultural land" in the reservation as a consequence of its building the Garrison Dam, which created a reservoir, called Lake Sakakawea. "The reservoir . . . divided the reservation into five segments. . . . Communication between those segments is difficult because only one bridge at the northern end of the reservation crosses the lake. Central transportation is nonexistent. To reach the southern segment, one must travel over 100 miles around the lake. The overall infrastructure that was to replace the old fell short of tribal expectations and federal-tribal agreements." Of the approximately 8,400 individuals who are enrolled members of the Mandan, Hidatsa, or Arikara tribes, about 3,775 live on the reservation. The unemployment rate on the reservation in recent years has been as high as 50 percent. The majority of those who have jobs work for the tribal government, Fort Berthold Community College, the Bureau of Indian Affairs, the Indian Health Service, or the Four Bears Casino and Lodge, which opened in 1993.

Hall's father, who also served for a while as a member of the Tribal Council, earned barely enough to support his large family. Each year, according to a National Indian Gaming Association (NIGA) press release (August 27, 2003, on-line), Hall and his brothers each had to make do with only two pairs of overalls—one for wearing to school and the other for working on the ranch. Hall attended a boarding school outside the reservation whose students were both whites and Native Americans. His father, who emphasized to him and his siblings the importance of a good education, "told Hall that he would have to study hard and compete with the non-Indians in their own arena," according to the NIGA press release. The release added, "Hall said that he had been following his father's advice—to be a fighter—all his life." When Hall graduated from high school, in the mid-1970s, fewer than 40 percent of Native Americans earned high-school diplomas. He then enrolled at the University of Mary, in Bismarck, North Dakota, where he earned a B.A. degree in 1979; at that time, only 8 percent of Native Americans had completed college. (In 2000, almost 12 percent of Native Americans were college graduates; for the population of the U.S. as a whole, the figure was 24 percent.) In about 1980 Hall earned an M.A. degree in educational administration from the University of South Dakota, in Vermillion. He spent the next few years teaching at the high-school level and coaching basketball. In 1985 he became the principal of the Mandaree middle school and high school, in a town on the Fort Berthold Reservation; the students were mostly Hidatsas. He served as superintendent of the Mandaree school system from 1994 to 1996. In 1995 the North Dakota Indian Education Association named him the North Dakota Indian Educator of the Year.

In 1996 Hall won a seat on the Tribal Council (also known as the Tribal Business Council). Somewhat analogous to a state Legislature, the council consists of the chairman, who is the administrative head of the tribe and represents all members of the Three Affiliated Tribes, and six councilors, each of whom represents a different segment of the reservation. Three of the members serve as the vice chairman, the secretary, and the treasurer of the council, respectively. Hall served as a councilman until 1998, when he became the first council member to be elected chairman of the Three Affiliated Tribes in the middle of a term. Since Hall had to vacate his council seat, and the tribal constitution requires all council seats to be filled, the council voted for a replacement for him. To break a three–three tie, he voted twice, once as chairman and once as regular member. His action proved highly controversial, but he prevailed. He also denied, and surmounted, accusations that he had won the chairmanship by paying for votes. In 2002 Hall was elected to a second term as chairman.

As a councilman, Hall chaired a meeting on Indian treaty issues held in 1999 at the White House with President Bill Clinton and representatives of the Great Plains Tribes. In response to that meeting and others, in November 2000 President Clinton issued an executive order for the purpose of "ensur[ing] that all Executive departments and agencies consult with Indian tribes and respect tribal sovereignty as they develop policy on issues that impact Indian communities." (As Hall's public statements indicate, that goal has not yet been met.) Also in 1999 Hall chaired the National Steering Committee for the Reauthorization of the Indian Health Care Improvement Act (IHCIA) of 1976, which had been reauthorized four times and was scheduled to expire in 2000. In presenting its findings, the committee noted that "the unmet health needs of the American Indian people remain alarmingly severe, . . . and the health status of Indians is far below the health status of the general population of the United States." The committee reported that the death rate of American Indians from pneumonia and flu was 71 percent higher than the rate for the U.S. population as a whole; for diabetes, it was 249 percent higher; for tuberculosis, 533 percent higher; and from alcoholism, 627 percent higher. As Hall noted on February 3, 2005 in his 2005 State of the Indian Nations Address, presented at the National Press Club, in Washington, D.C., Congress has still not reauthorized the IHCIA. Currently, he reported, the federal government spends less per capita for health care for Native Americans than it does for federal prisoners, and one-third less per capita than what is spent for the average recipient of Medicaid.

Hall instituted the annual State of the Indian Nations Address in January 2003, as president of the National Congress of American Indians (NCAI). He was elected to that position in November 2001 (he had failed in his first try for the job, in 1999), and

was reelected two years later. In his 2003 address, as transcribed on ncai.org, Hall focused on three of his main concerns. The first was threats to the survival of Indian tribes as, in his words, "independent, self-governing peoples," the main threats emanating from injustices perpetuated by the federal government. One glaring example is that tribes do not have legal jurisdiction over non-Indians who commit crimes on reservations. Tribal police thus have no power to detain, say, a non-Indian who is caught driving while intoxicated or even a non-Indian who is suspected of rape. "Jurisdictional confusion," according to Hall, is "perhaps the number one issue facing tribes today." Another pertains to so-called trust responsibility. As Hall explained in his address, when the federal government confiscated Indian lands, "the U.S. gave its solemn promise to protect the rights of tribes to govern themselves, and to provide for the health, education, and well-being of tribes. That commitment, the 'trust responsibility,' is not a hand-out, but a contract—and that contract has been broken time and again by the federal government." In particular, the federal government has failed in its duties as the manager of trust money—royalties from mining, grazing, oil drilling, and other activities on Indian lands—that it has collected since the late 19th century and that are supposed to be distributed to individual Indians and tribes. "The system is such a mess that independent estimates suggest that billions of dollars that belong to individual Indian people and Indian tribes have been lost by the federal government," Hall said. Moreover, unlike the millions of Social Security checks that arrive in people's mailboxes or bank accounts according to a strict monthly schedule, Indian trust-account checks are often months late. Past efforts to fix the system have failed, Hall charged, because the proposed reforms "lacked accountability—clear standards, measurable performance goals, oversight by an independent body with power to act when those standards are not met." The problem cannot be corrected, he warned, if attempts to do so by members of the federal executive and legislative branches do not include tribal leaders as equal partners. (In June 1996 a class-action lawsuit was filed to force the federal government to account for the missing money and to permanently reform the system. Known as Cobell v. Norton, for Elouise Cobell, a member of the Blackfeet tribe in Montana, and Gale Norton, the U.S. secretary of the interior, the case has not yet been resolved. In an effort to resolve Cobell v. Norton out of court, in July 2005 Senator John S. McCain of Arizona, the chairman of the Senate's Indian Affairs Committee, and Senator Byron Dorgan of North Dakota introduced the Indian Trust Reform Act of 2005. In July 2005, at an Indian Affairs Committee hearing, Hall said, according to Congressional Quarterly (July 26, 2005), that there was "a lot" that the NCAI liked in the bill.)

The second of the concerns that Hall talked about in his 2003 State of the Indian Nations Address was "the need to move out of a century of poverty and unemployment toward meaningful development in our economies," in his words. "With more than a quarter of Indian people living in poverty, and unemployment rates on reservations more than double the population at large—13.6% on average, and over 80% in some communities—there is no group of people with a more urgent economic crisis than American Indians," he said. Moreover, neither the president nor Congress had "addresse[d] the need that exists in Indian Country for sustainable, *comprehensive* economic development." The creation of 100,000 new jobs by 2010, with the ultimate goal of producing tribal self-sufficiency by 2020, would remain illusory if, in the coming years, more than 14 percent of Native American households still had no access to electricity, nearly 24 percent still had no telephone service, and more than a third still had no indoor plumbing; if most roads on reservations remained unpaved, so that in heavy rains or snows, they became impassable; if there still were too few or no ways to "transport the employees, customers, and goods that fuel healthy economies." Moreover, Hall explained, "traditional sources of capital such as lending, banking, and bonding are all but nonexistent on reservations," and the federal bureaucracy has compounded the difficulties of would-be property owners. He himself, he said, had been waiting for two years for the Bureau of Indian Affairs to clear the title on 40 acres he had bought to expand his family's ranch. According to Hall, in 40 percent of homes in tribal communities, overcrowding and "serious physical deficiencies" made living conditions unacceptable; the comparable figure for the whole of the U.S. was 5.9 percent.

Hall's third major concern, as expressed in his 2003 State of the Indian Nations Address, was "well being and quality of life" in the realms of health, education, environmental protection, and homeland security. In illustrating the extent of deficiencies in those areas in the Indian nations, Hall noted that the dollar amount that the Bureau of Indian Affairs allotted per child in reservation schools was half the average amount allotted per child in public schools elsewhere in the U.S.; in some reservation high schools, the dropout rate was 90 percent; in some communities, the cost of maintaining schoolbuses was far greater than the amount budgeted, because of the wear and tear caused by traveling over badly maintained, rutted roads; members of at least 170 tribes lived within 50 miles of sites that the Environmental Protection Agency had classified as highly toxic; and the federal government had allocated no funds at all for homeland security on reservations, despite their international borders (a total of 260 miles) and the presence of dams and hydroelectric facilities and oil and natural-gas pipelines.

In his 2005 State of the Indian Nations Address, Hall reported that the poverty rate among Native Americans had dropped by 7 percent and that average income had increased by 33 percent. He also announced that record numbers of Indians had voted in the 2004 elections. Otherwise, little had changed, and some problems had worsened. In its 2005 budget, the Bureau of Indian Affairs had cut funds for school construction by 10 percent. Allocations for housing were smaller than they had been in five years. The Indian Tribal Justice Act of 1993, which called for additional financing of tribal court systems, had never been funded; indeed, the amounts allocated for tribal courts had actually decreased since its passage. The incidences of alcoholism, drug abuse, mental illness, and diabetes and other serious illnesses remained the highest in the U.S.; the traffic-fatality rate remained four times the national average. Once again, Hall called on Congress and the president to reauthorize the Indian Health Care Improvement Act.

In his other role, that of chairman of the Three Affiliated Tribes, Hall was instrumental in acquiring funds for a new bridge, a water project, a cultural center, a juvenile-justice facility, a health-technology task force, and the Intertribal Economic Alliance, an organization of tribal leaders that urges the launching of programs to promote economic development on reservations. According to the Institute for Tribal Government (on-line), by 2003 he had helped to create 300 new jobs on the Fort Berthold Reservation and had seen the unemployment rate there shrink from 50 percent to under 15 percent. Hall has pushed for the construction of an $81 million oil refinery on the Fort Berthold Reservation. The refinery would be the first such plant to be owned by American Indians. Using wind as one source of energy, it would produce propane, butane, gasoline, jet fuel, and diesel fuel. To date, the Department of Commerce has allocated $1.3 million and the Bureau of Indian Affairs $500,000 toward its construction. Although its design has been touted as "environmentally friendly," and Hall and others have emphasized its benefits as a potential employer of hundreds of people, some reservation residents have expressed the fear that pollution from the refinery would compound the many health problems endemic among members of their tribes.

Hall is pursuing a Ph.D. degree in education. His professional activities have included his unpaid service as secretary and treasurer of the United Tribes Technical College and chairman of the Great Plains Tribal Chairmen's Association, the Native American Bank Corp., and the 2004 Native American Basketball Invitational. In 1999 he was inducted into the North Dakota Sports College Hall of Fame, for his achievements as a high-school basketball player and his establishment of Tex Hall basketball camps in the U.S. and Canada. In 2002 he won the University of Mary Leadership Award, for his work as an educator. Hall plays basketball for the North Dakota Warriors, a team in an American Indian league. He lives and raises cattle on his family's ranch on the Fort Berthold Reservation.

—L.J.

Suggested Reading: Fort Berthold Library Web site; Institute for Tribal Government Web site; MHANation.com; mnisose.org; National Congress of American Indians Web site

Thos Robinson/Getty Images

Hallström, Lasse

(HALL-struhm, LASS-eh)

June 2, 1946– Film director

Address: c/o ICM, 8942 Wilshire Blvd., Beverly Hills, CA 90211-1934

"I find so many scripts sacrificing character for plot," the film director Lasse Hallström told Jonathan Bing for *Variety* (January 15–21, 2001). "When I get excited about a script, it always seems to have to do with character driving the story in irrational and wondrous ways, rather than plot. I just love the stories that meander with the lives of people." In his films, which often deal with emotionally charged subjects, Hallström has created realistic, unsentimental portraits of people struggling through life-altering experiences. "I think I avoid stepping into sentimentality by trying to be as truthful as possible with performances," he told Andrea Meyer for *Indie Wire* (December 8, 1999), on-line). "Just being present emotionally in the scene, truly present emotionally, should be enough to convey what should be conveyed. . . . It's just about bringing it down to reality, having that ambition. Then you can go further with sentiment." Hallström's best work is suffused with hope, de-

spite the serious problems faced by his characters, who exhibit flaws as well as redeeming qualities rather than simply stereotypical good-guy or bad-guy traits. "Sweetness per se is something that I'd shy away from and wouldn't consciously do," the director said in a conversation with David Eimer for the London *Guardian* (February 24, 2001). "But I notice that there is a lack of darkness in my movies and I don't know where that comes from. I try to be honest and truthful with the performances." Hallström first gained attention in the United States with the Swedish picture *Mitt liv som hund* (*My Life as a Dog*, 1985). Since then, he has solidified his international reputation as a premier director with such critically acclaimed American box-office hits as *What's Eating Gilbert Grape* (1993), *The Cider House Rules* (1999), and *Chocolat* (2000).

Lasse Hallström was born on June 2, 1946 in Stockholm, Sweden. His father, Nils, was a dentist and amateur filmmaker, and his mother, Karin, a poet and novelist. His father exposed him to movies when he was very young; he has recalled watching reels of Charlie Chaplin shorts on the family's home projector as a child. At age 10 Hallström borrowed his father's eight-millimeter camera and created his first short film. "It was a documentary about Gotland Island, near Stockholm—a real knockoff of my dad's work featuring tight close-ups of vegetables in the marketplace," he told Emily Eakin for the *New York Times* (December 3, 2000). "The whole thing was four minutes long, ultimately cut down to three." He has described his childhood as somewhat bohemian, since his parents socialized with members of Stockholm's artistic community. "The house was filled with painters and writers," he told Eakin. "I was up all night, mingling with the adults." Many of his films feature children as outsiders, a situation with which, he says, he can empathize. "I can't go back and label myself as an outcast because I was a pretty well-adjusted kid, but I can certainly relate to the feeling of being an outsider," Hallström said during an undated interview for the IO Film Web site. "I was shy and a bit awkward. Yeah, I can relate to that. I was sensible in a way that made me too vulnerable to rough games. I wasn't well-adjusted to the tough world of children."

A short film that Hallström made in college about a fictional band's pursuit of fame brought him to the attention of the Swedish pop group ABBA. Long before MTV, like many other bands, ABBA made music videos that they would distribute free to television stations to promote themselves. In 1972 Hallström directed all but two of their promotional clips. "We could only film two songs a day," he told Eakin. "We shot them in my living room against a gray backdrop with wrinkles that I hadn't managed to iron out. We did silly things like spin girls around in flowerpots on wheels." Hallström then shifted his focus to feature-length work, beginning with semiautobiographical comedies. "There was almost a formula for those first movies I wrote myself," he told Eakin. "They were realistic comedies about my life." They included the television projects *Ska vi gå hem till dej eller till mej eller var och en till sitt?* (*Shall We Go to My Place or Your Place or Each Go Home Alone?*, 1973), *Flyttningen* (1974), and *Semlons gröna dalar* (1977), as well as the theatrical release *En Kille och en tjej* (*A Guy and a Gal*, 1975). Hallström's collaboration with ABBA culminated in a documentary, *ABBA: The Movie* (1977), which chronicles the band's Australian tour. He added to his big-screen credits in Sweden the films *Jag är med barn* (Father to Be, 1979), *Tuppen* (The Rooster, 1981), and *Två killar och en tjej* (Happy We, 1983).

Hallström first gained attention in the United States in 1985 with *Mitt liv som hund* (*My Life as a Dog*), which received Academy Award nominations for best director and best screenplay. The film, adapted from the autobiographical novel by the Swedish author Reidar Jonsson, is set in the 1950s and tells the story of a resilient 12-year-old boy, Ingemar, whose mother is terminally ill with tuberculosis. He is sent to live with his uncle in a small country village. To cope, the boy retreats into an imaginary world and develops an obsession with the Soviet space dog Laika, who orbited Earth in *Sputnik 2* in 1957. *My Life as a Dog* won the Swedish Film Critics' award for best picture, and Anton Glanzelius, the 11-year-old star, won the award for best actor. Hallström was lauded for his ability to skillfully combine humor and pain in the film, which the New York Film Critics Circle cited as best foreign film of the year. The Hollywood Foreign Press Association likewise thought *My Life as a Dog* the year's best foreign film, awarding it a Golden Globe award.

Hallström's success led to some offers from the American film and television industries—including one to shoot a sitcom pilot for NBC and pre-production work on a movie about Peter Pan that was never filmed—but nothing panned out. His next film was a 1986 Swedish production, *Alla vi barn i Bullerbyn* (The Children of Bullerby Village), which he followed a year later with *Mer om oss barn i Bullerbyn* (More About the Children of Bullerby Village); both are based on stories by Astrid Lindgren, the creator of the character Pippi Longstocking. Not until 1991 did Hallström see the release of his first English-language film, *Once Around*, a romantic comedy starring Holly Hunter as a repressed Boston woman swept off her feet by an obnoxious millionaire salesman (played by Richard Dreyfuss). The movie received lackluster reviews and did poorly at the box office, grossing only $14.3 million.

What's Eating Gilbert Grape (1993), Hallström's second American-made film, proved to be a much stronger effort, both popularly and critically. It stars Johnny Depp as a young small-town Iowan who holds together his troubled family, which includes his mother, who is so overweight that she

has not left the house in years, and his mentally retarded younger brother, Arnie (portrayed by the then-unknown Leonardo DiCaprio). "The novel [by Peter Hodges] that *Gilbert Grape* was based on presented a challenge to me, because it did have broader and more bizarre elements," Hallström told a reporter for the London *Observer* (May 1, 1994). "It could easily have gone in a more cartoonish, John Waters–type direction," he continued, referring to the director of such cult favorites as *Pink Flamingoes* (1972). "But I really wanted to pull back from that, and make it as realistic as possible." "It's hard to describe the many eccentricities of *What's Eating Gilbert Grape* without making the film sound as if it had a case of terminal whimsy," Janet Maslin wrote in her review of the film for the *New York Times* (December 17, 1993). "Better to say that this is the work of Lasse Hallström, the Swedish director of *My Life as a Dog*, whose gentle, rueful style can accommodate vast amounts of quirkiness in enchanting ways. Mr. Hallström is also adept at viewing the world from the perspective of troubled young characters." An Oscar nomination for best supporting actor went to DiCaprio. Though it earned only $9.1 million in U.S. theaters, *Gilbert Grape* has since gained a cult following and has collected substantial receipts in video rentals and sales.

Hallström's next film, *Something to Talk About* (1995), focuses on a southerner, played by Julia Roberts, who discovers her husband (Dennis Quaid) is having an affair. The film received mixed reviews but became a box-office hit, grossing $50.8 million domestically. In the *Chicago Sun-Times* (August 4, 1995), Roger Ebert wrote, "This is an intelligent, quirky human story that finds room not only for the remarkable expanse of Julia Roberts' character but also for several other well-developed characters. . . . Hallström seems fascinated by the way dysfunctional families function: How do they accommodate the weaknesses and compulsions of their imperfect members, and still somehow endure?" In 1995 Hallström also directed a segment of *Lumière et compagnie* (Lumière and Company), for which 40 directors contributed short films shot using an original Cinématographe, a portable motion-picture camera and projector invented by the Lumière brothers in the 1890s.

In 1999 Hallström scored a major critical success with *The Cider House Rules*, which was based on John Irving's best-selling novel of the same name. Set in the early 1940s, the film stars Michael Caine, Tobey Maguire, and Charlize Theron. Caine played a physician, Wilbur Larch, the much-loved master of an orphanage in Maine who bends the rules when he sees fit, performing illegal abortions and taking ether as a narcotic. Maguire's character, Homer Wells, develops a father-son relationship with the doctor but disagrees with some of his practices and eventually leaves. Hallström was first offered the script in 1993 but turned it down, because he had difficulties with it and feared talking to Irving about them. "Just the idea of traveling to Vermont to confront this literary giant was too daunting for me," he told Bernard Weinraub for the *New York Times* (December 17, 1999). "I just couldn't do it. I wouldn't dare." Years later, after one of his other projects fell through, Hallström learned that *The Cider House Rules* was still without a director. This time he met with Irving and found him to be "a wonderful collaborator," as he told Weinraub. The film received widespread critical plaudits and earned seven Academy Award nominations, including those for best picture and best director; Caine won the Oscar for best supporting actor and Irving for best adapted screenplay. "*The Cider House Rules* is an emotionally rich experience. To call it a coming-of-age period piece is like calling Moby Dick a fish," an unidentified reviewer wrote for the IO Film Web site. "Swedish director Lasse Hallström . . . abhors cliché and prefers insinuation to confrontation. The film has what the Americans call 'a European look,' which means understatement, visual delicacy, concern for script and character, and a feeling that time will wait if you ask it nicely."

Chocolat (2000), Hallström's follow-up to *The Cider House Rules*, was inspired by Joanne Harris's novel of the same name. It stars Juliette Binoche as Vianne, a single mother who settles in a small French town in the 1950s. Vianne shakes things up by opening a chocolate shop during Lent, sparking a battle of wills between her and the town's pompous mayor and self-appointed moral guardian, Comte de Reynaud (Alfred Molina). The film also features Johnny Depp as a tinker who sets up camp along the town's riverbank and becomes Vianne's romantic interest; Lena Olin as an abused housewife whom Vianne befriends; and Judi Dench as a gruff older woman who becomes a regular at the chocolate shop. *Chocolat* won the prize for best international filmmaker at the Palm Springs International Film Festival. "*Chocolat* is a seriocomic plea for tolerance, gift-wrapped in the baby blue colors of a fairy tale and served up with a sybaritic smile," David Ansen wrote for *Newsweek* (December 18, 2000). "The moral argument may be pat and predictable, but the movie disarms you with its charm and its solid craftsmanship. In more vulgar hands, *Chocolat* could have been insufferably precious, or smug, or sentimental. But Hallström . . . has always had a delicate touch, not to mention the old-fashioned virtue of good taste." Brian D. Johnson, writing for *Maclean's* (December 25, 2000–January 1, 2001), was not as impressed, calling *Chocolat* "a sweet, pretty confection, with storybook characters that twirl like figurines under the immaculate direction of Lasse Hallström. . . . [It is] a fairy tale pitting the Roman Catholic Church against the cocoa bean. . . . But tasting more of artifice than magic, *Chocolat* . . . never quite lives up to the lovely wrapping." Despite such disparate notices, the film was popular with the public and received four Golden Globe and five Oscar nominations.

Hallström next thought about directing a film adapted from E. Annie Proulx's Pulitzer Prize– and National Book Award–winning novel, *The Shipping News* (2001). "I was taken by the novel," he told Daniel Fierman for *Entertainment Weekly* (January 11, 2002). "It mixed the dramatic, comedic, lyrical, mysterious, and trivial with this journalistic report on [Newfoundland] and this portrait of a man. But we couldn't get the script right and I left." Instead, he went to work on a family drama titled "Sebastian's Love," which was never filmed. Meanwhile, *The Shipping News* languished for five years as it passed through the hands of four screenwriters, two directors, and such actors as John Travolta, Kelly Preston, and Billy Bob Thornton. Hallström returned to head the project after Kevin Spacey agreed to take on the lead role, that of Quoyle, a born loser who returns to his native Newfoundland with his young daughter after his cheating wife's sudden death. Shortly thereafter, the noted actresses Judi Dench, Julianne Moore, and Cate Blanchett joined the cast. Such star power notwithstanding, the film received a mixed critical reception and fared poorly at the box office. "Like the best of Hallström's films, *My Life as a Dog* and *What's Eating Gilbert Grape*, it has a fresh, uncondescending appreciation of the lives of people far outside the mainstream . . . ," a reviewer wrote for *Newsweek* (December 24, 2001). "*The Shipping News* has a quiet sense of community, a wry, unsentimental sweetness, that grows on you. It's a patient movie for impatient times." Bonnie Greer, a *Sight & Sound* (March 2002) critic, wrote that the film's shortcomings stemmed from the way Proulx had handled her characters. "Unfortunately, the depth of feeling that the novel achieves has eluded Hallström and his screenwriter Robert Nelson Jacobs. This is partly because so many of the novel's concerns are internal, related to the gradual change in consciousness that Quoyle undergoes once he gets to Newfoundland. Hallström and Jacobs struggle to find visual expression for this transformation (which is exactly what Proulx's prose did so skillfully)." In his review for *Boxoffice Magazine* (online), Wade Major was more blunt: "A sloppy, meandering morass of semi-realized ideas, half-baked characters and storylines that disappear before they come to a point, *The Shipping News* is a classic example of how not to adapt a novel. . . . [It] attempts to cover far too much territory in too short a period of time, sacrificing substance for scope."

Nearly four years after the release of his last film, two of Hallström's movies debuted within weeks of each other in 2005. The first, *An Unfinished Life*, starred Jennifer Lopez, Robert Redford, and Morgan Freeman; adapted from a novel by Mark Spragg, the film told the story of a troubled widow and single mother who moves in with her estranged father-in-law in Montana. Filmed in Canada and held from release for two years after production, *An Unfinished Life* was a commercial failure that was generally attacked by critics for what they considered its clichéd and maudlin story. In a review for *Variety* (September 5–11, 2005), Leslie Felperin wrote, "Viewers will have seen too much of all this for it to feel fresh; too many better modern Westerns lauding down-home values; too many pics where a liberated animal is the symbol of redemption; too many Lasse Hallstrom middlebrow tales about misshapen or outcast folk who form makeshift families . . . ; and one too many stories where Redford co-stars with a bear . . . and [Lopez] struggles to regain audience sympathy by playing a victim of abuse . . . with perfectly coiffed hair and a decorative bruise that color-coordinates with her wardrobe." Hallström's next film, *Casanova*, premiered at the 2005 international film festival in Venice, Italy, where Hallström had spent six months of the previous year shooting the movie. Loosely based on the real-life rake, spy, and memoirist Giacomo Casanova, Hallström's film preserves Casanova's upper-class 18th-century Italian milieu while jettisoning his darker and more sexually voracious side in favor of a lighthearted comedy of tangled loves. Starring Heath Ledger and Sienna Miller, the film met with positive reviews at its festival debut. "The mind boggles at the notion of Casanova's life as family entertainment," Roderick Conway Morris wrote for the *International Herald Tribune* (September 9, 2005). "But the director, Lasse Hallstrom, and his scriptwriters have pulled it off with considerable verve by turning it into a romp."

Hallström is said to take a collaborative approach to movie making, soliciting suggestions from his casts. "I really want to have actors contribute their own ideas, with phrasings and ideas on all levels. . . . There are surprises along the way. Things might be surprisingly different than you expected," he told Andrea Meyer. "I thrive in the kind of chaos—working with kids, the chaos, ad-libbing, keeping actors on their toes, having them not know exactly what to say or do until the very last minute. That's something I appreciate. It's sort of nerve wracking for actors."

With his ex-wife, Malou, Hallström has a son, Johan, who was born in 1976. Hallström married the actress Lena Olin in 1994; their daughter, Tora, was born the following year, and their son, August, in 1998. The couple live in Bedford, New York, north of New York City, and spend summers in Sweden.

—K.E.D.

Suggested Reading: *Indie Wire* (on-line) Dec. 7, 1999; (London) *Guardian* (on-line) Feb. 24, 2001, with photo; *New York Times* E p15 Dec. 17, 1999, II p13 Dec. 3, 2000, with photo

Selected Films: *Ska vi gå hem till dej eller till mej eller var och en till sitt?* (*Shall We Go to My Place or Your Place or Each Go Home Alone?*), 1973; *Flyttningen*, 1974; *En Kille och en tjej* (*A Guy and a Gal*), 1975; *Semlons gröna dalar*, 1977; *ABBA: The Movie*, 1977; *Jag är med barn* (Father to Be), 1979; *Tuppen* (The Rooster), 1981;

Kom igen, nu'ra!, 1981; *Två killar och en tjej* (Happy We), 1983; *Mitt liv som hund* (*My Life as a Dog*), 1985; *Alla vi barn i Bullerbyn* (The Children of Bullerby Village), 1986; *Mer om oss barn i Bullerbyn* (More About the Children of Bullerby Village), 1987; *Once Around*, 1991; *What's Eating Gilbert Grape*, 1993; *Something to Talk About*, 1995; *The Cider House Rules*, 1999; *Chocolat*, 2000; *The Shipping News*, 2001; *An Unfinished Life*, 2005; *Casanova*, 2005

Evan Agostini/Getty Images

Hamilton, Laird

Mar. 2, 1964– Professional surfer

Address: c/o Oxbow U.K. and Eire Unit, 2B The Courtyard, 44 Gloucester Ave., London NW1 8JD, England

For his ingenuity and fearlessness, the surfer Laird Hamilton has earned comparisons to the renowned test pilot Chuck Yeager (the first man to break the sound barrier) and the trailblazing astronaut Neil Armstrong. Greg Noll, one of surfing's icons, has dubbed him "the best big wave rider the world has ever seen," according to Tom Tapp in *Variety* (June 7–13, 2004). Bruce Jenkins, a sports columnist for the *San Francisco Chronicle*, who considers surfing the world's most dangerous athletic pursuit, told Leslie Stahl for the CBS-TV program *60 Minutes* (February 29, 2004), during an installment featuring Hamilton, that seeing him ride a wave is "like being able to watch Willie Mays in his prime or Jim Brown running the football." The highly innovative Hamilton has opened new frontiers in the sport; his technical achievements—in particular, his role in the development of tow-in surfing—have enabled people to ride waves previously thought to be too large and fast to surf. Hamilton has sought out the most dangerous waves on the planet. His exploits at Jaws, an especially intimidating surf break in Hawaii, have won him considerable renown, and his performance at Teahupoo, Tahiti, in August 2000, when he caught perhaps the heaviest (thickest) wave ever ridden, is now part of surfing lore. ("Heavy" or "thick" refers to a wave's volume and power.)

Hamilton's feats have been documented in several movies, among them *The Endless Summer II* (1994), *Step into Liquid* (2003), and *Riding Giants* (2004), as well as in DVDs and surfing magazines; he also performed stunt work for the motion pictures *Waterworld* (1995) and *Die Another Day* (2002). His image appeared on the cover of the November 1998 issue of *National Geographic*, which contained an article about Jaws and what is dubbed extreme surfing. Recently, Hamilton formed his own company, BamMan Production, through which he hopes to develop sports-related programming for television and the silver screen. In describing the appeal of big-wave riding, Hamilton told Brendan Gallagher for the London *Daily Telegraph* (May 10, 2004), "What I love is the silent beauty of the moment. Me alone with the elements, not fighting nature but just tucking in alongside her. Riding a glassy 60ft wave, mowing up and down the face in perfect synch like it was a 6ft shore break and then just turning away and letting it go on its way untamed and unsullied." When Miki Turner, a reporter for ESPN Page 3 (July 9, 2004, on-line), asked him to "put into words what it's like to ride that big wave all the way through," he responded, "It's a sensation like if it's the fastest you've ever been driving or flying or some situation where the moment is so intense it demands so much focus that you can't see anything else. It's almost like the twilight zone where time stops for a moment and you're in a place where there is no beginning and no end. It's probably one of the truest forms of living in the moment that we have on this earthly plane."

Laird Hamilton was born Laird John Zerfas on March 2, 1964 in San Francisco, California. As part of an experiment conducted by researchers associated with the University of California Medical Center at San Francisco, Laird's mother, the former JoAnn Zyirek (various sources spell her given name differently), gave birth to him in a bathysphere, to test the benefits of lessened pressure on the baby during his delivery. Several months after the boy's birth, his biological father abandoned the family, leaving Zyirek to raise the child on her own. A surfer herself, Zyirek soon left California and settled with Laird on the North Shore of the Hawaiian island of Oahu, a mecca for surfers. When he was a few years old, Laird met Bill Hamilton, a 17-year-old professional surfer, on the beach outside Laird's house at Ehukai. Recalling their first encounter, Bill Hamilton told Leslie Stahl, "I see this little blond-haired kid just rolling around the waves and having a wonderful time. So I dove in the water, I said, 'Hey what's your name? You want to body surf?' He goes, 'Yeah.' I said, 'Hop on my back.' We just had a super connection." Laird introduced Bill to his mother; several months later JoAnn and Bill were married. Laird took his stepfather's surname and has since referred to Bill as his father. (Bill and JoAnn divorced in 1977.) In addition to competing professionally, Bill designed surfboards; not long after meeting his future stepfather, Laird fell into a barrel of the fiberglass resin Bill used to make his boards. The toddler was quickly snatched out of the noxious liquid and bathed in acetone; without such rapid measures, he might have died.

Over the next several years, the Hamiltons remained on Oahu's North Shore. In 1971, unhappy with the growth of the permanent population and numbers of visitors on the North Shore, Bill moved the family (which by then included another son, Lyon, born in 1969) to Wainiha Valley, on the island of Kauai, a secluded locale that was close to some high-quality yet relatively unknown surf breaks. Earlier, soon after Bill and Laird had met, Bill had begun teaching the boy how to surf and had instantly recognized his daredevil sensibilities. "He's been bold since day one, and hell-bent on living life to the extreme," Bill told Bucky McMahon for *Outside Magazine* (June 1994).When Laird was eight, Bill took him to Waimea Falls Park, on Oahu, where Laird insisted on hiking to the 60-foot cliff from which young men would jump, plunging into the lagoon at the bottom of the falls as a masculine rite of passage. Although he had told his stepfather that he wanted only to look, Laird leaped off the edge of the cliff. "That was in me," Laird recalled to Daniel Duane for *Men's Journal* (July 2004). "That was my personality. A proving-yourself thing, too. Trying to outdo your dad." Surrounded by the hyper-competitive surfers' culture, Laird focused his energies on matching his father's achievements. "My whole upbringing," he told McMahon, "I wanted to ride waves the way my dad could." "We had a heavy duel going, which was a driving force in spurring my stuff," he told Duane.

While Laird excelled at surfing, he had problems in school. In Kauai he was one of only a few white students, and he was subjected to racist taunts from his classmates. He often got into fights and once even punched a teacher. Surfing always interested him more than his classwork. "I'd ditch school like 45 days of a 90 day quarter to go surfing," he told Michael E. Young for the *Dallas Morning News* (August 7, 2004). One night when Laird was a young teenager, Bill spoke to the boy about his truancy and had him promise to attend school the next day. The following morning, during the 90-minute bus ride to Kapaa High School, Laird became entranced by the sight of the waves at the first surfing spot along the way and had a quick change of heart; he disembarked, went home, and returned with his surfboard. On his second run of the day, he broke his leg and was carried home by one of his father's friends. Bill drove Laird to the doctor, and as Laird recalled to Young, "I swear he purposely hit every pothole on the road, and after each one, he'd just look at me." Laird's formal education came to an end during his junior year of high school, when "somebody slammed my face in the desk and I tried to throw him out a window," as he told Duane. The principal suspended him, and he never returned to school. Such events notwithstanding, Hamilton told Miki Turner, "In a way I feel like I was fortunate that I was raised in the right place, had the right kind of background and childhood. I had the right circumstances to create who and what I am. It's almost like how it was for the big waves. To create a good wave you need all of these pieces. You need the wind from the right angle with the swell and the tide and all these variables to come together. I've been fortunate enough to be the recipient of that blessing. "

After he dropped out of school, Hamilton got work in construction. While he was at that job, an Italian fashion magazine offered him a modeling assignment. Soon afterward his image appeared in *GQ*; later, he was photographed with the actress and model Brooke Shields. In 1984 he moved to Los Angeles, where he tried to market Sunbreaker, a brand of surfwear. During the two years he spent in Los Angeles, he had little success in business. "Cities are lonely places," he told McMahon. "I felt my gills drying up. My whole youth was being wasted." While in California Hamilton discovered boardsailing, or windsurfing, a sport that he continued to enjoy after he moved back to Hawaii. In 1986 he traveled to Port-Saint-Louis, France, where he competed in a windsurfing contest, outperforming the French champion and setting a European speed record of 36 knots (about 41 miles per hour). On the strength of his exploits in France, he received a sponsorship from Neil Pryde, a windsurfing-accessories company, and spent the next two years working to raise the firm's profile by executing stunts for photographers. In 1987 Hamilton made his acting debut, in the little-noticed film *North Shore*, in a supporting role as a surfer named Lance Burkhardt. He later appeared in *The Endless Summer II* (1994) and performed stunt work for Kevin Costner's film *Waterworld* (1995) and the James Bond movie *Die Another Day* (2002).

Hamilton's stepfather had imparted to him a deep skepticism about the judged contests that dominated professional surfing. The criteria the judges had established to assess participants involved style more than skill, which both Hamiltons believed led to unwarranted subjectivity in their appraisals. Partly for that reason, the intensely competitive Laird steadfastly eschewed any professional contest. He also refused to enter contests because, as he told Duane, "I hate losing. So I just figure if you don't play you can't lose. And if you never play and never lose, then people think that

you can always win." Hamilton chose instead to work on surfing's outer fringes, performing dangerous stunts and earning a reputation for daring and ingenuity. In 1990 he paddled across the English Channel on a surfboard. He helped to develop the sport of kiteboarding—in which one surfs while harnessed to a special kite. He introduced other innovations as well: he attached foot straps to his surfboard, for example, thus enabling him to execute complete 360-degree turns while in the air. Perhaps his most transformative contribution to surfing came in 1991, when he and his friends Buzz Kerbox and Darrick Doerner used a powerboat to tow one another into oncoming waves while each towed man was strapped onto a surfboard. Finding the powerboat too slow and dangerous for their purposes, the three friends eventually chose a jet ski as the towing mechanism. This novelty greatly expanded surfers' options. To catch a wave without it, surfers must paddle until they reach a slightly greater rate of speed than that of the wave. The larger the wave, the faster it travels; since there are limits to how fast a human being can paddle, surfers could not catch waves that were above a certain height (generally agreed to be 35 feet). By employing a jet ski as a tow, a surfer can move considerably faster than he or she can by paddling and can therefore catch larger waves; indeed, theoretically, a surfer can now catch waves of any size. As with most innovations, tow-in surfing sparked criticism. Some surfing purists considered it a form of cheating, since anyone, whether expert or novice, can be towed into the largest waves; others objected to the noise and pollution generated by the jet skis. Those complaints notwithstanding, tow-in surfing has grown in popularity.

Following their development of tow-in surfing, Hamilton and his friends set their sights on finding and riding the world's largest waves. Hamilton's favorite spot for this purpose was Peahi, or Jaws, a surfing break off the northern coast of Maui. As the years progressed, pictures of Hamilton's exploits at this break appeared on the covers of many surfing magazines. Hamilton's most celebrated ride came elsewhere, however: in Teahupoo, Tahiti. Teahupoo is the site of some of the thickest waves on the planet, but the water is very shallow, making any fall potentially fatal. There, on August 17, 2000, Laird caught what many believe to be the heaviest wave ever ridden (a 25-foot face and 50-foot lip) and made surfing history. His achievement was named ESPN's Action Sports & Music Awards' Feat of 2001.

The surfing documentary *Step into Liquid* (2003) contains abundant footage that dwells on Hamilton's development of tow-in surfing. Directed by Dana Brown, the film is "an awe-inspiring survey of global surf culture," as Scott Foundas wrote for *Variety* (February 24–March 4, 2003). In 2004 Hamilton appeared prominently in and served as an executive producer of the documentary *Riding Giants* (2004), which chronicles the history of big-wave riding, from its origins in Polynesia up to the present. Directed by Stacy Peralta, *Riding Giants* opened the 2004 Sundance Film Festival and garnered considerable critical praise. According to Sara Stewart in the *New York Post* (July 4, 2004), Hamilton "really steals the show" in the movie, and "for good reason—he's constantly surpassing what anybody else thinks is humanly possible." Hamilton demonstrated his surfing prowess for such DVDs a*s The Day, Laird, Wake-Up Call*, and *Strapped*. During the mid-1990s he hosted the TV show *The Extremists*, which focused on so-called alternative sports; on various installments he was shown engaging in activities ranging from bungee jumping to extreme skateboarding. Since 1995 Hamilton's primary sponsor has been Oxbow, a company that sells surfing and other sportswear and gear.

Recently, Hamilton helped to develop a foil board, whose design is based on that of the hydrofoil. "The whole board flies above the water," he told Dawson. "It allows us to ride waves that don't break." Hamilton was honored at the Maui Film Festival, where he and Dave Kalama, another big-wave surfer, received the Beacon Award for living "beyond limits, outside fear, inside courage and inspired by wonder," as festival organizers said, according to the Associated Press Online (June 18, 2005). Hamilton and Kalama's film, *All Aboard the Crazy Train,* a documentary about surfing Jaws that "explores the 'human truth' of big wave surfing rather than the hype," as the Associated Press Online put it, premiered at the festival.

Hamilton has begun training for the 2006 Winter Olympics, to be held in Turin, Italy, where he hopes to represent Greece (his biological father's native country) in the bobsledding competition.

Hamilton married Gabrielle Reece, a professional volleyball player and world-renowned model, in 1997. Their photos appeared in the swimsuit issue of *Sports Illustrated* in 2000. The couple have a daughter, Reece, who was born in 2003. Hamilton has another daughter, Izabela, by his first wife, Maria, a Brazilian bodyboarder and clothing designer. Hamilton and Reece have homes in Malibu, California, and Maui, Hawaii. Unlike the typical male surfer, who generally possesses a relatively lithe figure, Hamilton has an imposing physique; sometimes referred to as the "uber surfer," he is six feet, three inches tall and weighs more than 200 pounds. In other ways, with his sun-bleached blond hair, bronzed skin, and jutting jaw, Hamilton resembles the stereotypical Caucasion surfer. Now over 40, Hamilton has no plans to cut back on his athletic activities. "One of my best friends, a surfer, is 72," he told Angela Dawson for BPI Entertainment News Wire (July 14, 2004). "I'm just trying to keep up with him. When I'm 60 I hope that I'll be training harder than I've ever been. . . . You can surf until you're buried."

—P.B.M.

Suggested Reading: BPI Entertainment News Wire July 14, 2004; CBS News *60 Minutes* (on-line) Feb. 29, 2004; ESPN.com Page 3 (July 9, 2004); Laird Hamilton Web site, with photo; *Los Angeles Times* A p1 Apr. 14, 2001, with photo; *Men's Journal* July 2004 (on-line), with photo; *Outside Magazine* June 1994 (on-line); Surfline Web site, with photo

Selected Films: *North Shore*, 1987; *The Endless Summer II*, 1994; *Step Into Liquid*, 2003; *Riding Giants*, 2004; *All Aboard the Crazy Train*, 2005

Courtesy of Graham Hancock

Hancock, Graham

1951– Writer

Address: c/o Penguin Books Ltd., 80 Strand, London WC2 0RL, England

"I'm somebody who explores extraordinary possibilities, not ordinary ones," Graham Hancock told Stephen Moss for the London *Guardian* (February 6, 2002). Hancock has written nonfiction books on topics ranging from the inefficacy of foreign aid, to the possible existence of life on Mars, to evidence of lost civilizations on Earth. He displays particular interest in the fields of archaeology and history, and as he has no formal training in either area, his theories often earn criticism from academic circles. Such disdain is apparently not as common among general readers: Hancock's books have sold more than five million copies and have been translated into 27 languages. Hancock told Stephen Moss, "I'm not an academic; I'm not an archaeologist. I'm a writer, communicating ideas to the public." He explained on his Web site, "I write my books to try to show that an alternative view [of history] can fruitfully be considered"; he also declared, "If you want a slavishly 'balanced' and objective account of 'both sides of the argument' then I'm the wrong author for you!" His books include *The Sign and the Seal: The Quest for the Lost Ark of the Covenant* (1992), *Fingerprints of the Gods* (1995), *Underworld: Flooded Kingdoms of the Ice Age* (2002), *Talisman: Gnostics, Freemasons, Revolutionaries, and the 2000-Year-Old Conspiracy at Work in the World Today* (2004), and *Supernatural: Meetings with the Ancient Teachers of Mankind* (2005). "Whether he is scouring the earth for evidence or simply sitting in his Cotswolds cottage making this stuff up," Gareth McLean wrote for the London *Guardian* (February 12, 2002), "Hancock is awfully good at making you want to believe in his theories, however wild they are."

An only child, Graham Hancock was born in 1951 in Edinburgh, Scotland. His father was a missionary surgeon who traveled a lot; soon after Hancock's birth, his family moved to southern India. In the Johannesburg, South Africa, *Sunday Times* (June 2, 2002), as quoted on *FarShores Ancient Mysteries News* (on-line), Brett Hilton-Barber reported that Hancock "rejected Christianity at an early age," as a "reaction against his upbringing and a consequence of his exposure to foreign cultures." During an on-line chat for the Barnes & Noble Web site, Hancock wrote that as a child he was "pretty inquisitive and was always getting into trouble. I guess nothing much has changed." Hancock attended secondary school in the city of Durham, in northern England. After he graduated he enrolled at Durham University, where in 1973 he earned a degree with first-class honors in sociology. He next launched a career in journalism, writing for such British newspapers as the London *Times*, the Manchester (now London) *Guardian*, and the London *Independent*. As a reporter for the London *Sunday Times*, he covered the war between Somalia and Ethiopia, which was being fought for control of Ogaden, a region in southeastern Ethiopia that borders Somalia. From 1976 to 1979 he co-edited the *New Internationalist* magazine, and from 1981 to 1983 he served as the East Africa correspondent for the *Economist*.

In the early 1980s Hancock decided to focus on writing books. His first, *Journey Through Pakistan* (1981), with photographs by Mohamed Amin and Duncan Willetts, was followed by *Under Ethiopian Skies* (1983), *Ethiopia: The Challenge of Hunger* (1984), and *AIDS: The Deadly Epidemic* (1986). Hancock first attracted significant recognition with his book *Lords of Poverty: The Power, Prestige and Corruption of the International Aid Business* (1989), in which he criticized UNICEF, the World Bank, UNESCO, and other relief and development agencies. He cited numerous examples of such organizations' bungling, inefficiency, and misappropriation of funds, and he characterized foreign aid to struggling nations as "nothing more than a transaction between bureaucrats and autocrats," as quoted by Thurston Clarke in the *New York Times Book Review* (November 12, 1989). Hancock wrote, "Aid is not bad . . . because it is sometimes misused, corrupt, or crass; . . . rather, it is *inherently* bad, bad to the bone, and utterly beyond reform. As a welfare dole to buy the repulsive loyalty of whining, idle and malevolent governments, or as a hidden, inefficient and inadequately regulated subsidy for Western business, it is possibly the most formidable obstacle to the productive endeavours of the poor." While many reviewers disagreed with Hancock's assertion that aid to poor countries is inherently wrong, they concurred with the writer on the need for reform of the agencies under discussion. Thurston Clarke wrote about *Lords of Poverty*, "Beneath the pumped-up language is a deadly serious book about a desperately important subject, a book that, despite its exaggerations, succeeds in standing the myth of foreign aid on its head, and demands a serious reply from the development industry." At the 1990 H. L. Mencken Awards ceremony, *Lords of Poverty* won honorable mention as an outstanding book of journalism.

The following year Hancock published *African Ark: Peoples of the Horn*, with photographs by Angela Fisher and Carol Beckwith. In 1992 he attained the status of best-selling author, with the publication of *The Sign and the Seal: The Quest for the Lost Ark of the Covenant*, an account of his search for the Ark of the Covenant—said to be the ancient, sacred, gold-lined wooden chest belonging to the ancient Hebrews; it supposedly held the stone tablets inscribed with the Ten Commandments and was thus representative of God. Hancock had been hired by the government of Ethiopia to put together a coffee-table book about the country; while there, in 1983, he encountered a religious sect claiming to be in possession of the original Ark of the Covenant, which, it is widely believed, has been lost since Nebuchadnezzar, king of Babylon, destroyed King Solomon's temple in Jerusalem, more than 2,500 years ago. Denied access to the sanctuary where it was allegedly housed, Hancock was inspired to research the history of the ark. (He has said that he was also inspired by Steven Spielberg's immensely popular movie *Raiders of the Lost Ark* [1981].) Hancock devoted two years to, and spent most of his money on, his search for the ark—which, he concluded, was kept in a sanctuary at Axum, in Ethiopia, closely guarded at all times. Since he traveled through Ethiopia during a civil war there, he placed himself in physical danger during his quest; once, he was assaulted by priests after having attempted to sneak into a temple. Although Hancock never saw the ark, his book garnered praise. In the London *Guardian* (March 21, 1992), Walter Schwarz wrote that Hancock had "invented a new genre: an intellectual whodunit by a do-it-yourself sleuth with whom we can all identify because he has no more specialist knowledge than we have."

In the same spirit, Hancock published *Fingerprints of the Gods* (1995). In it he proposed that a lost civilization that existed approximately 15,000 years ago created such famous monuments as the great pyramids and the Sphinx, in Egypt, and the Andean temples of Tiahuanaco and the Pyramids of the Sun and Moon, in Mexico. *Fingerprints of the Gods* became a number-one best-seller in the United Kingdom, ultimately selling more than 3.5 million copies. In his next work, *Keeper of Genesis* (1997), co-authored with Robert Bauval, he discussed ancient Egyptian scriptures. That book, too (published as *The Message of the Sphinx* in the United States), became a number-one best-seller. Hancock and Bauval also co-wrote *The Mars Mystery: The Secret Connection Between Earth and the Red Planet* (1999), which suggested that there had once been intelligent life on Mars and sought to establish correlations between structures on that planet and similarly shaped monuments and buildings in Egypt. In *Heaven's Mirror: Quest for the Lost Civilization* (1999), on which he collaborated with his wife, the photographer Santha Faiia, Hancock expanded on the premise of *Fingerprints of the Gods*, theorizing that certain monuments were built in accordance with astronomical principles by an ancient civilization with particular knowledge of the solar system. This book, too, reached number-one best-seller status; it also spawned a three-part British television series, *Quest for the Lost Civilization*.

While Hancock's books have consistently sold well, many scholars have noted his lack of professional credentials and questioned his unorthodox methods and, by extension, the accuracy of his conclusions. An article in the *Canberra (Australia) Times* (November 1, 2002) described Hancock as "a kind of contemporary Don Quixote, a loveable duffer at times blurring the important distinctions which might well define regions of sanity and bonkersland." The article acknowledged a "maddening point for the professionals," which is that "nobody can categorically refute his proposals." Discussing the controversies he has often stirred, Hancock told Stephen Moss, "It seems that people talk to me with a preconception about what I am, and then whatever I say or do doesn't make any difference. There are several preconceptions. One is that I'm a lunatic-fringe train-spotter with an absurd enthusiasm for something ridiculous in the past. The other is that I'm a rather sinister fellow who is misleading the public." Hancock reaped further scorn for his endorsement of works by people whom many traditional archaeologists and historians consider less than reputable, such as Michael Cremo and Richard Thompson. Hancock wrote a foreword for Cremo and Thompson's book, *The Hidden History of the Human Race* (1994), which has often been dismissed as "a religious tract dressed up in pseudo-scientific terminology," as Mikey Brass phrased it on the *Antiquity of Man* Web site. Because he has lent his support to such controversial and oft-ridiculed works, Hancock

has been accused of compromising his own credibility. In responding to criticisms of his own books, Hancock admitted to Brett Hilton-Barber in 2002 that he had been "provocative and challenging and sometimes wrong" in his early work. "Had I known the scrutiny under which *Fingerprints of the Gods* would be placed and the kind of hostility it would generate, I may have written a different book. I'm not putting it down. It was right for the time, it stirred up a hornet's nest and made people think about things they hadn't thought of before. A more balanced book might not have had the same effect."

Hancock's book *Underworld: Flooded Kingdoms of the Ice Age* (2002) earned him some newfound respect from much of the scientific community. In *Underworld* Hancock posited that a flood at the end of the last Ice Age wiped out a number of early civilizations. As evidence of this claim, Hancock mentioned what appeared to be the undersea remains of buildings off the coasts of modern-day India, Japan, and Malta. In order to study the structures, Hancock learned to scuba dive. "I'm not theorising from an armchair here," he told David Robinson for the *Scotsman* (February 16, 2002). "I've spent the last five years literally putting my life on the line. And yes, I've dived in places—Tonga and Tahiti, for example—where people told me there were structures on the seabed but which I don't think are." Despite Hancock's explorations (which were televised in Britain for the series *Underworld: Flooded Kingdoms of the Ice Age*), there has been a great deal of debate as to whether the structures in question are man-made or natural. As Hancock explained to Mary Devlin and Maki Nibayashi for the *Metropolis* Web site (July 1, 1999), "Take the case of [a site in] Yonakuni in Japan. I can give you two geologists. Both have seen it and they both have different opinions. One of them thinks it's natural, the other one thinks it's artificial. They've actually been there, they've touched it, and they can't agree." A statement from the Indian government supported Hancock's interpretations. On January 14, 2002 India's science and technology minister, Murli Manohar Joshi, announced his finding that the structures beneath the Gulf of Cambay, off the coast of India, were indeed man-made ruins and not natural formations.

Many reviewers considered *Underworld* to be a more logically constructed and cautiously written book than most of Hancock's previous works, citing its reliance on a greater number of authoritative sources and on fewer far-fetched theories. "I said things in the early 90s that I wouldn't say now," Hancock admitted to Stephen Moss. "They were done with passion, but they were also done hastily and were wrong, dead wrong. I can see that now." Hancock does not feel the need to correct his earlier publications, however. As he stated in the introduction to the 2001 edition of *Fingerprints of the Gods*, as quoted by Mikey Brass, "I don't believe in revising or 'updating' books. . . . The proper place for all this new material to come out, in my view, is in new books, not in updates to old ones. . . .

Writing new books, rather than going back to tamper with books already written, is also the way I prefer to respond to criticisms of my work."

With Robert Vauval, Hancock co-authored *Talisman: Gnostics, Freemasons, Revolutionaries, and the 2000-Year-Old Conspiracy at Work in the World Today* (2004). The book examines ancient Egyptian and Christian gnostic ideologies, known to members of secret, millennia-old societies, and what the authors consider to be the profound influence of those ideologies on the contemporary world.

Supernatural: Meetings with the Ancient Teachers of Mankind, Hancock's most recent book, was published in the United Kingdom in October 2005 and in the United States the following month. In that work Hancock discussed the possibility that some types of human behaviors, endeavors, or philosophies—for example, the belief in the supernatural, the development of ancient religions, and the desire and ability to produce art (such as prehistoric cave paintings)—may have originated with people's use of hallucinogenic substances. "A great mystery surrounds the first appearance, some time between 40,000 and 30,000 years ago, of recognisably modern behaviour," he said in an interview with the *Bath Chronicle* (October 7, 2005), a British newspaper. "It is at this time that the archaeological record begins to testify to our sudden and unexplained development—alone among animal species—of culture and religion, beliefs in life after death, in spirits, demons and angels, and the ability to create and appreciate art and manipulate symbols." In conducting research for *Supernatural*, Hancock spent time in the Amazon jungle with shamans, ingesting brews of ayahuasca, a root known as "vine of the soul," which is said to trigger hallucinations. Such hallucinations, Hancock has conjectured, may have produced visions that led disparate ancient societies to embrace strikingly similar religious or supernatural beliefs.

Hancock and his wife recently moved to Bath, in Somerset, England; according to Gareth McLean, the couple also own a home in the Cotswolds in Gloucestershire, England. Jennifer Selway noted in the *Express* (February 12, 2002) that Hancock has "the mild sheep-like face that you often find on the very, very stubborn." Hancock said, as paraphrased by Brett Hilton-Barber, that while he had renounced Christianity in his youth, "his atheism was eroded by research into ancient civilisations." Hancock also told Hilton-Barber, "I do believe there is some form of intelligent mind at work in the universe and that life is not accidental. I believe there is life after death."

—K.J.E.

Suggested Reading: grahamhancock.com; (London) *Guardian* p4 Feb. 6, 2002; *New York Times* p12 Nov. 12, 1989; world-mysteries.com

Selected Books: *Lords of Poverty*, 1989; *The Sign and the Seal: The Quest for the Lost Ark of the Covenant*, 1992; *Fingerprints of the Gods*, 1995; *Heaven's Mirror: Quest for the Lost Civilization*, 1999; *Underworld: Flooded Kingdoms of the Ice Age*, 2002; *Talisman: Gnostics, Freemasons, Revolutionaries, and the 2000-Year-Old Conspiracy at Work in the World Today*, 2004; *Supernatural: Meetings with the Ancient Teachers of Mankind*, 2005

Kevin Winter/Getty Images

Hannity, Sean

Dec. 30, 1961– Radio and television talk-show host; nonfiction writer

Address: WABC, Two Penn Plaza, 17th Fl., New York, NY 10121

In 1987 Sean Hannity was living in Santa Barbara, California, and working as a house contractor. At the time, congressional hearings investigating the Iran-Contra affair were dominating the news. It was revealed during the hearings that, despite a U.S. trade embargo on Iran, the administration of President Ronald Reagan had sold arms to the Iranian government in exchange for the release of American hostages held by Iranian sympathizers in Lebanon. Subsequently, the funds from the arms sale were diverted covertly through the National Security Council to support the Contras, a right-wing guerrilla movement in Nicaragua, which sought to violently overthrow the government of Daniel Ortega, the leader of the left-wing party known as the Sandinistas. Hannity found it hard to pull himself away from coverage of the hearings and often made calls to radio talk shows in support of the Reagan administration's actions. "Other people would call in and want to respond to me—not the on-air host," he told Michael Lipton and Jennifer Frey for *People* (February 11, 2002). "That's when I thought it was time for a career change." Shortly thereafter, Hannity became the host of an unpaid, weekly, one-hour call-in show on a radio station operated by the University of California at Santa Barbara. Earlier in 1987, the Federal Communications Commission (FCC) had overturned its fairness doctrine, which required broadcasters to air opposing viewpoints on controversial topics, so Hannity enjoyed the freedom to say nearly anything he chose. "I was terrible," he admitted to Lipton and Frey. "But I was born opinionated. I was a news junkie. Once I got behind the mike, that was the only place I wanted to be."

Hannity is now one of the most recognizable voices of American conservatism. His right-wing politics and pugnacious rhetorical style have made him a media triple threat, attracting huge audiences to his radio and television shows and impressive numbers of readers to his books. The syndicated *Sean Hannity Show* is currently heard by approximately 12 million people on some 430 radio stations nationwide, making it second in listenership only to Rush Limbaugh's program. (Limbaugh, a fellow conservative, has been broadcasting his syndicated show since 1988, and he can currently be heard on more than 600 stations.) On television Hannity plays the conservative foil to the liberal Alan Colmes on *Hannity and Colmes*, cable's top-rated debate show, which airs on the Fox News Channel. His books—*Let Freedom Ring: Winning the War of Liberty over Liberalism* (2002) and *Deliver Us from Evil: Defeating Terrorism, Despotism, and Liberalism* (2004)—were best-sellers.

Sean Hannity was born on December 30, 1961 into a conservative Catholic family on Long Island, New York. His father, Hugh Hannity, is a family-court probation officer in the New York City borough of Manhattan, and his mother, Lillian Hannity, is a homemaker. He and his three older siblings were raised in the town of Franklin Square, on Long Island, about 20 miles from New York City. Hannity attended college briefly, at two different schools over the course of two years, before a lack of funds forced him to drop out. He started his own business as a house painter in Rhode Island in 1982. By 1985 he had saved $50,000 and then spent it, touring the country; he ultimately settled in Santa Barbara.

Hannity landed his first paying radio job, at the AM station WVNN in Huntsville, Alabama, in 1991, just as Operation Desert Storm (the U.S. military response to the invasion of Kuwait by Iraq) was launched. One day three years later, after he had begun working at radio station WGST in Atlanta, Georgia, he was invited to appear as a guest on the national television-news network CNN, also based in Atlanta. While he was on the air, the ex-

football star O.J. Simpson was riding in an SUV and was being tracked by police in a low-speed chase on a California highway, after his wife and an acquaintance of hers had been found murdered. The network abandoned its regularly scheduled programming, and Hannity was allowed to stay on air to offer commentary on the chase, garnering him national exposure for the first time during a historic televised event. Other television guest spots followed, and he came to the attention of Roger Ailes, then president of the cable station CNBC and founding chairman and CEO of the Fox News Channel.

Ailes hired Hannity in 1996 to co-host one of his fledgling network's first talk shows, which was to be formatted as a debate between Hannity and a political liberal. The working title of the show was "Hannity and LTBD"—the acronym standing for "liberal to be determined"; it became *Hannity and Colmes* when the radio veteran Alan Colmes was hired as co-host. Hannity and Colmes are opposites in manner as well as politics, with the latter's calm demeanor offsetting the former's bluster. The debate partners immediately began to dent the ratings of their CNN time-slot rival, *Larry King Live*, and in October 2002 they eclipsed that popular show's ratings. (They routinely rank highest in viewership in their time slot and are currently the second-highest-rated cable news program.) Meanwhile, Hannity, who had moved back to New York, where the Fox News studios are located, was seeking a new home for his radio show. He found one at WABC, which gave him the local weekday drive-time slot. The *Sean Hannity Show* first aired in January 1998. On January 21, about two weeks into his tenure, ABC and a few other news outlets broke the story about the sexual relationship between President Bill Clinton and a young, former White House intern, Monica Lewinsky. The growing scandal provided ample fodder for Hannity's show and pushed him to the top ratings for his time slot in New York City.

Those stellar ratings held, and the ABC network began airing his program nationally on September 10, 2001. When terrorists attacked New York's World Trade Center, the next day, Hannity was among the few locally situated news broadcasters to whom radio listeners could tune for reports of the day's events. "Timing has been everything for Sean," WABC's program director Phil Boyce told Valerie Block for *Crain's New York Business* (February 17, 2003). "9/11 propelled the national show to a hit right out of the gate." According to *Talkers*, a magazine that covers the radio industry, the *Sean Hannity Show* is the fastest-growing radio program in history. Within a year it had vaulted past those of the radio-ratings stalwarts Howard Stern and Laura Schlesinger into second place nationwide, and many industry insiders have predicted that in the near future he will surpass the current top-rated radio personality, Rush Limbaugh, for whom Hannity sometimes stands in as a guest host.

Hannity is said to prepare extensively for each show by reading voraciously, and friends and opponents alike agree that he is well informed on current events and politics. His opponents are quick to point out, however, that his method of debate contains large doses of unenlightened hectoring and demagoguery. Robert B. Reich, who served as secretary of labor under President Clinton, described for the *American Prospect* (June 2004) a phone interview he had on the *Sean Hannity Show*, evidently on a day when Hannity was broadcasting before a live audience: "When I began to answer, Hannity cut me off. I tried to get a word in, but Hannity continued to rant about John Kerry [the 2004 Democratic presidential candidate] and the liberals who want to destroy the country. . . . I decided to keep talking but my words seemed to make no difference. The crowd was cheering Hannity's diatribe. One listener e-mailed me later in the day to explain that Hannity's sound engineer had apparently turned down the volume on me, in order to ensure that Hannity's voice predominated." Hannity is unapologetic about such tactics and contends that they are warranted. "The left is so wrong and the stakes are so high in a post-9/11 world that they must be defeated," he said to Richard Firstman for *TV Guide* (December 12, 2002). He also said that he has nothing against liberals on a personal level. "You can be friends with them, let your kids play with their kids," he told Firstman. "They just can't be in power."

A similar mix of research, personal anecdote, and one-sided argumentation is present in Hannity's books, and it has proven to be popular on the printed page as well as on the air. Despite limited coverage by the national press, *Let Freedom Ring: Winning the War of Liberty over Liberalism* climbed to the top of Amazon.com's sales chart a week after publication. Hannity's follow-up, *Deliver Us from Evil: Defeating Terrorism, Despotism, and Liberalism*, debuted on the *New York Times* nonfiction best-seller list at number one. A reviewer for *Publishers Weekly* (February 16, 2004) wrote of the latter, "Fans of Hannity—Christian conservatives in particular—will no doubt embrace this straightforward call to arms. Many readers, however, will find Hannity's 'irrefutable' evidence to be anything but, and his selective use of history and circular logic raises far more questions than it settles." The books' inherent merit as literature or political discourse aside, Hannity's synergistic use of media to mobilize his core following is notable. He promotes his radio show during his television program, his television program on his radio show, and his books on both. Nevertheless, he told Valerie Block, "I am not a big numbers chaser. I just try to do the best shows I can every day." In 2004 ABC Radio signed Hannity to a reported five-year, $25 million contract extension. That same year Hannity launched his Hannitization of America tour to promote his book *Deliver Us from Evil*; he visited 43 cities in six weeks, during which he hosted live shows on 30 radio stations and signed more than 100,000 copies of the book.

On the May 24, 2005 installment of *Hannity and Colmes*, Hannity claimed, reportedly in jest, that the veteran journalist Bill Moyers had referred to him as "Sean Hannity, barnstorming America, a freak show of political pornography" during the final broadcast of Moyers's PBS television program *NOW*, in 2004. (According to official transcripts from *NOW*, Moyers recalled that on the eve of Election Day 2004, when he had turned on his car radio, "What [my wife and I] instantly got was a freak show of political pornography: lies, distortions, and half-truths . . . paraded before us as informed opinion. . . . On this day alone WABC radio owned by the Walt Disney Corp. . . . would treat New Yorkers to nine straight hours of Kerry bashing.") In the *Washington Post* (December 18, 2004, on-line), Tom Shales argued that Moyers's criticism was not aimed at Hannity specifically but at the right-wing–controlled media whose televised criticisms of John Kerry, Moyers believed, unfairly influenced the 2004 election. For his part, Hannity said in response to Moyers's remarks that he had renamed his 2005 Hannitization of America tour the "Barnstorming Freak Show of Political Pornography Tour."

Hannity wrote the foreword to the book *A Deficit of Decency* (2005), by Zell Miller, a former governor of Georgia and former U.S. senator from Georgia. Through his Web site Hannity runs a dating service for politically conservative single people.

In 2003 Hannity received a Marconi Award from the National Association of Broadcasters as Network/Syndicated Personality of the Year, and in 2004 he was named Best Talk Show Host at the New York Metro AIR (Achievement in Radio) Awards. In 2005 he was named National Talk Show Host of the Year at the Annual Radio & Records Talk Radio Seminar, held in Washington, D.C.

Since 1993 Hannity has been married to Jill Rhodes, a former political columnist whom he met in Alabama; they have two children, Patrick and Merri. "I'm at peace with myself because what I talk about is the way I live," Hannity told Michael Lipton and Jennifer Frey. "I believe in faith, family and country. I really keep it that simple."

— T.J.F.

Suggested Reading: *Crain's New York Business* p1 Feb. 17, 2003, with photo; *People* p117 Feb. 11, 2002, with photos; *TV Guide* p46 Dec. 14, 2002, with photos

Selected Books: *Let Freedom Ring: Winning the War of Liberty over Liberalism*, 2002; *Deliver Us From Evil: Defeating Terrorism, Despotism and Liberalism*, 2004; *Right from the Heart: The ABC's of Reality in America* (with Phil Valentine), 2004

Frederick M. Brown/Getty Images

Harcourt, Nic

Sep. 23, 1957– Radio disc jockey

Address: c/o KCRW, 1900 Pico Blvd., Santa Monica, CA 90405

With commercial radio executives and deejays increasingly reluctant to stray from a proven programming formula, an artist such as the pianist and vocalist Norah Jones—whose sultry mix of pop, jazz, and blues does not fit the mold of manufactured teen pop—seemed unlikely to achieve major success. But Jones defied the odds, winning accolades, Grammy Awards, and multiplatinum record sales, thanks in large part to the exposure that the radio disc jockey Nic Harcourt gave her on his weekday drive-time program *Morning Becomes Eclectic*, which airs on the Los Angeles–based public radio station KCRW. "Norah Jones proves that there's an audience out there that's looking for music they're not getting to hear in traditional ways like commercial radio and MTV . . . ," Harcourt told Edward Helmore for the London *Guardian* (February 28, 2003). "[Big record companies] are so busy chasing after the same formula of breaking records that they're missing things." Harcourt has established a reputation for seeking out and publicizing artists who "fall between the cracks," or whose music is difficult to categorize and is thus considered unmarketable. "At a time in radio when D.J.'s generally possess little personality and no responsibility for choosing the music they play," Jaime Wolf wrote for the *New York Times Magazine* (June 26, 2005) about Harcourt, "he has emerged as the country's most important disc jockey and a genuine bellwether."

"What Nic can do is make people feel like they've discovered something and it's theirs," Zach Hochkeppel, the vice president for marketing at Blue Note Records, told Wolf. "And that sense of discovery is the difference between buzz and hype—they feel like they own it, and they become proselytizers on their own." Harcourt sees KCRW as being essentially a grassroots operation and believes—his efforts to attract listeners through concert promotion notwithstanding—that many of his loyal listeners are attracted by word of mouth. "A lot of people who listen to our station tell their friends about us," he told a reporter for *Billboard Radio Monitor* (July 4, 2003). "They'll say stuff like 'You're loving Norah Jones, and you're listening to it on such and such station, but if you had been listening to the station I listen to, you would've heard it a year ago.'"

Nic Harcourt was born on September 23, 1957 and raised in Birmingham, England. His father was a television journalist, and his mother worked in electrical wholesaling. Harcourt's parents had an unhappy marriage; his fondest memories from childhood are of the peaceful occasions when they played Beatles albums and danced around the living room. "My parents played the Beatles when the Beatles were still together," he told Sandra Barrera for the *Daily News of Los Angeles* (October 10, 2000). "It was an exciting time to sort of discover music. . . . To me, it's always been a passion that's been a part of my life, and I guess it's appropriate that I would end up having a career in it." His parents separated when he was seven. According to Jaime Wolf, when Harcourt's mother told him that his father had moved out, Harcourt asked, "Did he take the Beatles records?"

Harcourt drank heavily as a teenager and dropped out of high school. He supported himself by working in a factory that made plastic bags and as a production manager at a cement factory. He also performed part-time in a few unsuccessful bands. In his mid-20s he followed a girlfriend to Australia and married her shortly thereafter. In Australia he worked as a sales manager for Honeywell; he explored the local music scene in his free time, developing an affinity for the groups INXS, Men at Work, and the Hoodoo Gurus.

After his marriage ended, in 1988, Harcourt left Australia on a round-the-world airline ticket. He stopped off in Woodstock, New York, to meet a former bandmate—and ended up staying for nearly a decade. There, he joined a local chapter of Alcoholics Anonymous and overcame his drinking problem. Though Harcourt had no prior experience in radio, he took a stack of records of Aboriginal folk music to the local progressive radio station, WDST, and pitched his idea for a show on Australian music. While the station's management did not approve that idea, they later let Harcourt fill in on blues, new age, and folk shows when the regular hosts were absent. He was next hired as the station's news director, and, later, as the music director. After three years at the station, he was given his own morning drive-time show, *Nic in the Morning*. By that point in his career, Harcourt had developed a reputation for spotting future music stars ahead of everyone else; he was an early advocate of Alanis Morissette's work and is credited with the American radio premiere of the work of Moby, Garbage, Joan Osbourne, Massive Attack, and Semisonic. In his last two years at WDST, he worked as the programming director, running the entire station. "Over the years, I've learned a skill," he told John Hughes for the *Orange County Register* (April 19, 1998). "It's the first career I ever decided to focus on and get better at."

In 1997 KCRW, the Santa Monica, California–based public radio station for Los Angeles, announced that it would conduct a nationwide search for a new host for its morning drive-time music show, *Morning Becomes Eclectic*. The show has been known, since its launch in 1979, as a tastemaker, to which listeners—including Hollywood and record-company executives—tune in to hear the work of artists they cannot find on commercial radio. The show's original host, Tom Schnabel, was credited with introducing to U.S. audiences such world-music stars as King Sunny Ade of Nigeria and the Pakistani qawwali music great Nursat Fateh Ali Khan. When Schnabel left the station for more lucrative opportunities in the record industry, he was replaced by Chris Douridas, who launched the career of the platinum-selling musician Beck. The then-unknown artist had shown up at the KCRW studio to perform his stoner-rap song "Loser" on the air; a major-label bidding war broke out before the day was over. In another example of the radio program's clout, David Chase, the producer of Home Box Office's hit TV series *The Sopranos*, later chose Alabama 3's "Woke Up This Morning" as the show's theme song after hearing it on *Morning Becomes Eclectic*.

The job of hosting *Morning Becomes Eclectic* represented an exciting opportunity for a disc jockey: the show offered the chance to exert enormous influence on the national music scene without the constraints of commercial radio. (Most disc jockeys at commercial radio stations have little control over their playlists.) Still, Harcourt, who enjoyed his seven-acre mountaintop spread in Woodstock, was not sure if he wanted to move to Los Angeles. He waited a month after hearing about the position before he applied. He told Steve Hochman for the *Los Angeles Times* (April 16, 1998) that when the job was offered to him, he accepted it because he "would get to do something really creative and worthwhile on radio."

Both Harcourt and the listeners of KCRW were somewhat apprehensive about his appointment. "They made such a big deal about the search for his [Douridas's] successor," he told Sandra Barrera. "It was kind of baptism by fire when I got here." Some listeners feared that Harcourt's background in commercial radio would limit his ability to operate in public broadcasting. "He came from a station that was commercial, absolutely," KCRW's general

manager, Ruth Seymour, told Barrera. "But he grew up in a country where the preeminent form of broadcasting was public broadcasting, so he didn't come to it as if out of the blue."

Harcourt took over *Morning Becomes Eclectic*—which airs weekdays from 9 a.m. to noon—and the music programming for the station in April 1998. Listeners' worries were soon allayed: in between interviews and live sets, Harcourt plays the music of a mix of iconic and up-and-coming artists from a wide range of genres. His set lists have included such performers as Radiohead, My Bloody Valentine, Björk, Frank Sinatra, Tom Waits, the Blue Nile, Jeff Buckley, Juana Molina, Rufus Wainright, Aimee Mann, Caetano Veloso, DJ Shadow, the Eels, Petra Haden, and his old favorite, the Beatles. "I think the show is more inclusive and eclectic than it was before," Harcourt told the reporter for *Billboard Radio Monitor*. "We're embracing a more diverse range of musical styles." When the time came for station fund-raisers, listeners showed their approval of Harcourt's choices: pledges made during the airing of *Morning Becomes Eclectic* in the 1998 summer pledge drive increased significantly from the year before, and in 1999 the number of donors rose 10 percent from the previous year, with the total dollar amount from pledges increasing by 24 percent. Today, pledges called in while *Morning Becomes Eclectic* is being broadcast are the largest source of revenue for KCRW.

Harcourt also maintained KCRW's reputation for introducing new talent. "[Our] audience is attracted to something that is a little bit different that they're not going to hear anywhere else," he told Chris Morris for *Billboard* (August 21, 2004), "or maybe they're going to hear it here first." He was the first deejay in the United States to play the songs of Norah Jones and the pop band Coldplay. He spotlighted the British artists Dido, Damien Rice, and David Gray and Iceland's Sigur Rós, propelling them into the American mainstream. "He has impeccable taste," Chris Martin, the singer and songwriter for Coldplay, told Jaime Wolf. "Every time I talk to someone in L.A., whether they're a 16-year-old or a 40-year-old, if they're talking about some random band or the new Doves record, when I ask how they know about it, it's always KCRW."

Harcourt relies on a network of friends and colleagues to help him scout new talent. His British friends keep him abreast of European acts; Ariana Morgenstern, the Argentina-born producer of his show, tells him about Spanish-language rock; and his longtime girlfriend, the singer-songwriter Abba Roland, contributes her ideas as well. Harcourt was introduced to the eclectic New York City band the Brazilian Girls by his massage therapist. "You can imagine I get a lot of friends telling me something is great," Harcourt told Jaime Wolf. "And you want to love it. Ninety-nine times out of a hundred, you don't."

Although Harcourt receives approximately 400 unsolicited CDs every week, he listens to at least the first couple of tracks of each. "Within all those pieces of plastic, you find a piece of music that touches you, that makes it all worthwhile," he told Steve Carney for the *Los Angeles Times* (September 27, 2002). "You really have to retain that sense of discovery." The British singer-songwriter Jem heard *Morning Becomes Eclectic* shortly after moving to Los Angeles and immediately persuaded a friend to drive her to the station so that she could drop off her demo tape for Harcourt. After he debuted her title track in March 2002, the KCRW station was flooded with calls. Harcourt gave Jem repeated airplay, and her songs were picked up for the TV programs *The OC* and *Six Feet Under.* She also landed a job co-writing a song with Madonna and a record contract with Dave Matthews's ATO label.

"I try to be inclusive at the end of the day, the only criteria is that I have to like the music," Harcourt told Nadini D'Souza for *WWD* (November 2, 2004). "I have fairly diverse taste but I can't like everything. I'm sure there are people that wish that I would play artists that I don't." Some critics complain that Harcourt plays too much electronic music and the work of too many singer-songwriters, and that the rock he chooses does not have an "edge." While he sometimes includes songs by more rambunctious acts, such as the rock quartet Franz Ferdinand, Harcourt argues that he is trying to ease listeners into their day, and that *Morning Becomes Eclectic* is not meant to be "in your face." "We get criticized across the board," he told Chris Morris. "That's fine. I don't fret about that stuff at all. . . . The success of the music programming and the success of the various shows speaks for itself."

Though KCRW is a nonprofit station, Harcourt has had some success applying commercial principles to his music formatting. "When I first started working at WDST, it wasn't that dissimilar to KCRW in that it was pretty much a free-form station," he told the reporter for *Billboard Radio Monitor.* "Over the years, we developed a promotion and marketing angle, and I brought a little bit of that commercial world with me. A lot of people talk about how we've grown KCRW, and I think that my experience doing that kind of stuff [at WDST] has served me well. KCRW was a very successful station before, but I think we've taken it to another level." Upon arriving at KCRW, Harcourt immediately noticed that the station commanded little brand recognition beyond its loyal listenership—that is, its name was not associated in most people's minds with a particular idea. Six months into the job, he approached Ruth Seymour and convinced her that KCRW would be more visible in the community if it started presenting live shows. Harcourt began courting local venues in Los Angeles, and KCRW presented its first show, featuring the electronica band Moorcheeba, in August 1998. Having started out with a few dozen

shows a year, KCRW now averages one to two shows per week, featuring a wide range of genres, from jazz to hip-hop to the work of singer-songwriters. Lou Reed, Coldplay, Damien Rice, Polyphonic Spree, Beck, Liz Phair, Shelby Lynne, and many others have performed at KCRW shows. Unlike most concert promoters, KCRW does not receive a cut of the ticket sales. Harcourt hopes simply that the publicity from the event draws in more listeners—and more pledges. "I think a big part of the reason the station has grown in listenership and subscribers is through our concert promotion," he told *Billboard Radio Monitor.* The concerts also benefit up-and-coming artists. KCRW shows are certain to draw fans, Harcourt explained to Steve Carney for the *Los Angeles Times* (June 23, 2003), because the station's name serves as a sort of seal of approval. "It's sort of like a stamp: 'Pay attention to this artist,'" Seymour told Carney. "Especially in an age where radio is so consolidated, there's less and less diversity in music. Stations like ours have a special responsibility." In 2001 Harcourt introduced "Unsigned Indies" (later renamed "Next Up!"), an annual showcase for local bands.

In the fall of 2002, *College Music Journal* asked Harcourt to put together a KCRW-sponsored show at the Beacon Theater, in New York City, for the magazine's annual convention of college radio programmers. He curated a show featuring the Sigur Rós. "It made me realize that we had to be more active in the New York market, because we have a significant Web audience," he told *Billboard Radio Monitor.* "KCRW.com has grown and grown over the last five years, to the point that whenever I go to New York, people will tell me how they listen to the station online every day. It seemed like another opportunity to brand the station as an innovative place on the Web as well as the radio dial to hear new and independent music." *Morning Becomes Eclectic* began streaming broadcasts over its Web site in 1997 and slowly built up large fan bases in New York and San Francisco. Three years later KCRW launched *Sounds Eclectic*, a two-hour show—broadcast on National Public Radio stations throughout the country—featuring the best of *Morning Becomes Eclectic* from the previous week. The station also launched a companion Web site, through which listeners from around the world can stream current shows or explore the program's extensive archives. After the launch of *Sounds Eclectic*, Harcourt changed the name of a series of albums featuring live performances from the show, in order to raise brand recognition with the national audience. The first album was *KCRW: Morning Becomes Eclectic* (1999); the subsequent albums— *KCRW: Sounds Eclectic* (2001), *KCRW: Sounds Eclectic Too* (2002), and *KCRW: Sounds Eclectic 3* (2005)—dropped "Morning" from the title.

By the time Harcourt launched "KCRW.com Presents" for the East Coast, with a performance by the Australian singer-songwriter Butterfly Boucher at the New York City club Pianos, in June 2003, KCRW had around 1,200 paid members in the New

York metropolitan area. It had been almost unheard of in the radio industry for a station to promote shows outside its own market. "I'm not doing this to step on anyone's toes," Harcourt explained to *Billboard Radio Monitor*. "I'm doing this because there's a need for it. There are artists that we play that don't get airplay in New York, and there's an audience that listens to us online that will support those artists. I'm not going to try to present artists who are getting significant airplay on other radio stations, because they don't need our help. . . . It's basically about taking our niche and trying to build something in a very significant market."

Because TV and movie producers often turn to Harcourt's shows to fill out their soundtracks, it seems logical that they would hire him to select the tracks himself. Harcourt served as a musical consultant for the movie *Pursuit of Happiness* (2001) but did not accept any music-supervisor jobs in film until he was offered the chance to work on *Igby Goes Down* (2002), starring Kieran Culkin. "I felt that when I finally did do something where I was going to be the music supervisor, I wanted it to be a project that I felt passionately about," he told Ada Guerin for *Hollywood Reporter* (August 20, 2002). "I didn't want to do something for the sake of just doing it or for the money." He has since worked as the music supervisor for the films *Wake* (2003) and *The Dukes of Hazzard* (2005), the TV movie *Call Me: The Rise and Fall of Heidi Fleiss* (2004), and the TV series *Life As We Know It* (2004), *What About Brian* (2005), and the forthcoming *In Justice*.

Harcourt made his debut in front of the television camera on October 26, 2003, as the host of *In the Studio with Nic Harcourt*, a program that featured performances by and interviews with musicians. The A&E network aired the pilot installment, which showcased the group R.E.M. As Harcourt told *Current Biography*, the show "was made with one third of the budget required to do a weekly show of the quality" that satisfied him, and the network "decided against committing those kind of resources." That same year he appeared in the feature film *7 Songs* (2003), directed by Noah Stern. Harcourt's first book, *Music Lust: Recommended Listening for Every Mood, Moment, and Reason*, was published in September 2005.

Harcourt recognizes the irony in helping artists to get the six-figure checks he will never receive as a public-radio deejay. He has thus far, however, turned down all offers from record companies for lucrative scouting jobs. "With all due respect to people who do A.&R. for a living, they're a kind of baby sitter, and I already have two babies," Harcourt—who has two-year-old twins, Sam and Luna, with Roland—told Jaime Wolf. "I just like putting the music out there and letting other people make up their minds whether or not they like it." He lives with his family in a two-bedroom cottage in Topanga Canyon, California.

—J.C.

Suggested Reading: *Billboard* p78 Aug. 21, 2004; *Billboard Radio Monitor* July 4, 2003; *Morning Becomes Eclectic* Web site; *New York Times Magazine* (on-line) June 28, 2005; *Sounds Eclectic* Web site; *WWD* p7 Nov. 2, 2004

Selected Books: *Music Lust: Recommended Listening for Every Mood, Moment, and Reason*, 2005

Courtesy of Tim Hawkinson

Hawkinson, Tim

Oct. 1960– Artist

Address: c/o Ace Gallery Los Angeles, 5514 Wilshire Blvd., Second Fl., Los Angeles, CA 90036

Tim Hawkinson, "a maverick in this generation of mavericks," according to Michael Duncan in *Art in America* (December 1994), is known as one of the most interesting American artists working today. For almost 20 years he has been creating art out of discarded articles and other things not usually associated with fine art: extension cords, tinfoil, lightbulbs, and plastic bottles, to name a few. "By discovering incredible possibilities in banal materials," Steven Litt wrote for the Cleveland, Ohio, *Plain Dealer* (May 1, 1999), "Hawkinson has enriched the tradition of turning 'found objects' into art, started by Marcel Duchamp" in the early years of the 20th century. Hawkinson's ability to turn sundry materials into both representative and abstract sculpture and also into machines has earned him a reputation for being a supreme tinkerer, and the oddness of the sculptures and gadgets he has fashioned has led some to compare him to a creative preadolescent. "If a child had the art historical perspective, artistic range and technical know-how that Hawkinson possesses," Robert L. Pincus wrote for the *San Diego Tribune* (March 6, 2005), "he or she might produce work something like" the art that Hawkinson creates.

The artist was born Timothy Hawkinson in October 1960 in San Francisco, California. He grew up in nearby Los Altos in a church-going family. His father was an optician, his mother a homemaker. Some sources also report that his parents were antique dealers. Hawkinson's passion for making things began when he was seven. "The first time I made an object," he told Kristine McKenna for *LA Weekly* (February 19, 1999), "was after my mother read me a story about a tin soldier whose head was the end of a spoon. . . . I made a soldier out of a piece of bamboo, with arms made from bread twist ties." Thereafter, he often created his own toys. "Then I got obsessed with making musical instruments," he told Bernard Cooper for *Los Angeles Magazine* (September 1, 2001). His parents encouraged him by allowing him to turn their garage into a workshop. In high school Hawkinson became known for being an "art freak," in his words, thanks in part to an art teacher who gave him free rein in his choice of projects. Often, simply to amuse himself, he combined machines with materials most would regard as junk. "I once made a motorized tennis shoe out of Colgate toothpaste tubes," he told McKenna. He did not think about art as a profession until he enrolled at San Jose State University, in California, where his teachers included the sculptor Sam Richardson. After he earned a bachelor's degree, he entered the M.F.A. program at the University of California at Los Angeles (UCLA), studying under Charles Ray, among other artists.

Hawkinson began exhibiting his art as an undergraduate; he sold what he described to McKenna as "garish sculptures" made out of clear vinyl with what he termed "reverse painting[s]" of plants, aliens, and guts stretched over foam. In 1987, as a graduate student, he was featured in a series of exhibitions titled Young American Artists at the Mandeville Gallery in San Diego, California. In the *Los Angeles Times* (January 17, 1987), Robert McDonald called his work "enthralling" and described his vinyl sculptures as "look[ing] like contemporary versions of medieval illuminations and stained glass windows and, in their grotesquerie, like the paintings of Hieronymous Bosch, especially *The Garden of Earthly Delights*." The following year Hawkinson's work appeared with that of four other artists in an exhibition called Excavations. A sculpture of an animal tusk made from 132 snowman-shaped Jell-O molds illustrated his penchant for transforming ordinary objects into works of art while subverting the categories with which humans order their world. Thus the tusk sculpture, as Suzanne Muchnic pointed out in the *Los Angeles*

Times (December 19, 1988), recast the Jello-O molds, a symbol of "female kitsch," into something representative of "male bravado."

By 1990 Hawkinson's work was regularly being included in exhibitions and was receiving mostly positive reviews. Cathy Curtis, in the *Los Angeles Times* (May 21, 1990), while noting that "Hawkinson's peculiar little objects are bursting with high-concept ideas that sometimes seem too glib for their own good," commended his work as a whole. Some of the pieces, she argued, "retain an ineffable oddity, a cockeyed viewpoint about the imperfections and pitfalls of perception. *Untitled (White Flexing Painting)* is one of these." According to Curtis, that piece, which is connected to a motor that causes the canvas to flex, reminded the viewer of "the unfixed, shifting array of meanings an art object possesses in an era of cultural relativism." Even during this early stage of Hawkinson's career, critics commented on the difficulty of making generalizations about his work because of its great variety. Indeed, Hawkinson told Shauna Snow for the *Los Angeles Times* (July 22, 1990) that his aim was to remain "consistently inconsistent" precisely so that his work could not be easily categorized. Hunter Drohojowska-Philp later wrote for the *Los Angeles Times* (June 23, 1996), "Hawkinson considers it dishonest and boring to resort to convenient solutions. He obsessively takes on new challenges in the appearance and technique behind his work and evades the very characteristic sought by most artists: an identifiable style."

Hawkinson's reputation within the Los Angeles art scene continued to grow. In the *Los Angeles Times* (September 7, 1992), Cathy Curtis called Hawkinson "one of the most original minds to surface in recent Southern California art." Also in the *Los Angeles Times* (January 1, 1993), Curtis described Imperfect Order, a 1992 exhibition in which his work had appeared, as the highlight of the city's art season. Tim Jahns, the curator of Imperfect Order, told Zan Dubin for the *Los Angeles Times* (August 21, 1992) that he had wanted to include Hawkinson because the artist is "not into pretty pictures that duplicate what the eye sees, but [gives] us, in modified form, the things we have around us which we've become oblivious to." The following year Hawkinson had his first solo exhibition, at the Ace Galleries in Los Angeles. That show, which filled nine large galleries and spilled out into the hallways, won the Critic's Choice Award. On display were many works that critics would discuss over the next few years, among them *Signature* (1993), a machine that repeatedly signs Hawkinson's name "onto adding machine tape, then chops off the signature, dropping it into a growing pile," as Hawkinson described it, according to Michael Duncan in *Art in America* (May 1997), and *Balloon Self Portrait,* a latex cast of his body inflated to gigantic proportions and hung from the ceiling. Another piece was made with a set of large reflective disks constructed out of foil from candy and cigarette-pack wrappers.

"Hawkinson is a first-rate recycler whose efforts carry us well beyond the original significance of the materials and ideas he uses," David Pagel wrote for the *Los Angeles Times* (June 10, 1993). "His impressive array of household junk and art historical references takes us on a hallucinatory trip through the inner workings of his agile mind. Here, the absurdity of Surrealism and the irony of Dada fuse with the relentless obsessions typically given form by outsider art."

The 1993 Ace exhibition brought Hawkinson wider renown. It was reviewed in *Art in America* (January 1994), where Constance Mallinson called attention to Hawkinson's "quest to subvert the artful and elevate the mundane." "If there is a single work in this sprawling exhibition that characterizes Hawkinson's sensibility it is *Balloon Self Portrait*," she wrote. She continued, "This mannequin has the appearance of a water-logged corpse, but it is kept 'alive'—inflated—by means of a silent air compressor. The piece thus becomes a rumination on life's confounding relationship to technology." The portrait has become something of a signature piece. Discussing its appearance in the mid-career Hawkinson retrospective mounted at the Whitney Museum of American Art, in New York City, Blake Gopnik wrote for the *Washington Post* (March 6, 2005) that it "pokes fun at the old romantic notion that every work of art is really about the ego—the inflated ego—of the artist behind it, who hovers over every show he does." A similar motif is present in two other self-portraits. Hawkinson made one, *Pneuman*, of clear vinyl, by gluing the vinyl to an inflated latex mold of his body and then removing it. He created the other, *Spy Clothes* (2000), out of his work clothing. Both are inflated and impose the artist's presence "in a playful, self-mocking way," as Steve Litt wrote for the *Plain Dealer* (August 30, 1996). "You can't avoid the fact that the effigies are puffed up and full of nothing."

Hawkinson's interest in music and other sounds came to the fore in the early 1990s. One piece that revealed this interest was *Music Box (if I could save time in a bottle)*, made of a Thermos that rests inside a side table and is connected to a motor. As the Thermos revolves, screws embedded in its surface bump into the blades of a row of steak knives, producing a series of sounds that suggest, according to Curtis in the *Los Angeles Times* (March 29, 1994), "the sweet conceit of music as time made audible and stashed in a bottle, like miniature ships or secret messages." Hawkinson is also interested in merging the audible with the visual so that the two modes of expression comment on each other. For *My Favorite Things* (1992–93), he combined a sculpture with a music box. The sculpture is composed of 15 "wall-hung black disks (they look like oversized phonograph records) that track the artist's impressionistic, ink-drawn renderings of his favorite record albums," as Michael Duncan explained in *Art in America* (May 1997); the music box plays a metallic-sounding version of the song "My Favorite Things," from the musical *The Sound of Music*. "Hawkinson's synesthesia—his morphing of sound into image—is a Rimbaud-like lark," Duncan wrote, "playing off the high-school art-class experiment of 'drawing to music.'"

In 1995 the Ace Galleries mounted a solo exhibition of Hawkinson's work at its New York City location. Lilly Wei, in *Art in America* (November 1995), called it "a running commentary on the situation of art in a mechanized age," while in a review for the *New York Times* (November 3, 1995), Roberta Smith wrote, "Hawkinson is a kind of popularizer, or folk artist of avant-garde strategies, who works with a bevy of received ideas, a love and profound grasp of science and mechanics, and a pair of hands that can build anything, usually out of found materials." The exhibition brought Hawkinson an award for best show by an emerging artist from the International Association of Art Critics; it also brought him to the attention of museum curators around the U.S. One of them, Barbara Tannenbaum, of the Akron Art Museum, in Ohio, arranged to exhibit a selection of the show *Humongolous: Sculpture and Other Works* in 1996 before the complete version opened, at the Contemporary Art Center in Cincinnati, Ohio; the latter show later toured the country. The pieces that could not fit in the Akron museum were displayed in the Center for the Arts at Yerba Buena Gardens, in San Francisco.

A number of other shows dedicated to Hawkinson took place around this time. Prior to the Akron exhibit, a selection of the works seen in New York appeared at the Armory Center in Pasadena, California, in a show titled Ahi Ikmnostw, a name Hawkinson formed by alphabetizing the letters of his name—suggesting, according to Drohojowska-Philp, that "rearrangement is the simple but effective essence of his work." Hawkinson's adolescent interest in musical instruments also reemerged during this period. Drohojowska-Philp wrote about an eight-foot-tall bagpipe in Hawkinson's studio that plays 10 songs. "It's a traditional bagpipe with a chanter which plays the melody and drones, made of cardboard carpet roll tubes, which give it the wavering sound," Hawkinson told him. On display in another Hawkinson show in San Francisco were a series of clocks made of such everyday items as a manila envelope, an attaché case, a clear bulb, and a hairbrush. "Beyond their display of goofy ingenuity," Kenneth Baker wrote for the *San Francisco Chronicle* (September 24, 1996), "Hawkinson's clocks objectify our inward sense of modern experience—even of inanimate things—being pervaded by relentless time-keeping." The time motif could also be seen in *Slug* (1996), "in which a tower of turning gears is crowned by a pointer designed to spin at a rate of one revolution per 10,000 years," as Michael Duncan wrote for *Art in America* (May 1997). Explaining his fixation with the ticking of the clock, Hawkinson told Kristine McKenna, "Time tells us we're moving toward our death, but what's death? I'm not saying I'm comfortable with it, but to me it's just a passage, and although I don't believe in reincarnation, I do believe in an afterlife. I think access to that afterlife is contingent on your attitude toward God in this one. I think it starts now."

In 1997 Hawkinson collaborated with Issey Miyake, a Japanese clothes designer known for incorporating in his work images created by contemporary artists. Hawkinson became the third artist whose work graced Miyake's Pleats Please clothing line. To call attention to the line's launch, Ace Gallery put on an exhibition titled The Pneumatic Quilt, a collection of Miyake's designs and garments decorated with Hawkinson's art. The show, Susan Kandel wrote for the *Los Angeles Times* (January 2, 1998), "fails to impress. In fact, the show is less a collaboration than a gussied-up documentation of a commercial venture." Pleats Please brought Hawkinson to the attention of people outside the U.S.; in Great Britain, Andrew Lambirth wrote for the London *Independent* (February 28, 1998), "Tim Hawkinson clothes the body with representations of the body—as if you were to wear yourself somehow outside your clothes. . . . Hawkinson uses everyday materials, such as bubble-wrap and aluminium foil, in his own work, but, most important, he uses himself."

A showing of Hawkinson's work at the Ace Gallery in New York in 1999 disappointed various critics, among them Jerry Saltz, who complained in the *Village Voice* (March 16, 1999) that the artist's "vision has fragmented and dissipated; the mania has faded, replaced here by doggedness." Saltz dismissed as unimaginative *Stamtrad* (*Family Tree*) (1997), a circular genealogical chart made of Popsicle sticks, and *Untitled* (*Mobile*) (1998), a number of TV antennae molded into ship masts. But he and others had praise for other pieces, among them a bird skeleton made of Hawkinson's fingernail and toenail clippings, an egg that is made of his ground-up fingernails, and a spider web and feather that are made of his hair. Of all the works on display, *Pentecost* impressed reviewers most. Ken Johnson, in the *New York Times* (March 19, 1999), called it "the main attraction" and wrote, "It might have been built by a religiously inspired out-of-work air-conditioning installer. It is a spreading tree made of wood-grain-papered tubes with a dozen robotic figures attached here and there. Equipped with little electronically controlled hammers, the robots rap on the branches, collectively generating marvelous rhythms that reverberate throughout the room. . . . It offers an inspirational metaphor about language and community." When *Pentecost* was shown at the Whitney Museum of American Art in 2005, Blake Gopnik wrote, "The piece involves the sounds of Christian tunes and images of 12 male figures, and seems to talk about human communication. But confront the thing itself, and all you can do is gape."

The success of *Pentecost* gave Hawkinson the confidence to work on the larger-scale piece he was commissioned to create for the Massachusetts Museum of Contemporary Art (MoCA). The museum wanted him to fill a gallery the size of a football field with a single sculpture, and he responded to the challenge with *Überorgan* (2000), 12 transparent bus-size balloons reminiscent of bagpipes or bladders or other organs. Each balloon emitted air through 24-foot tubes made of cardboard and tinfoil and produced a sound similar to that of a foghorn. "The economy of filling such a large space with so much sound and form using a relatively small amount of material is impressive. *Überorgan* is definitely an experience, but the most lasting impression, as is usual with this artist, is one of boyish genius and industriousness," Roberta Smith wrote for the *New York Times* (August 11, 2000). Other critics expressed even more enthusiasm. "The work is both lovely and strange, fanciful and grounded, refined and loose, high-tech and low-. These 'bladders' are connected by a lifeline of forced air that flows from a lower floor to keep them inflated," a critic wrote for the *Pittsburgh Post-Gazette* (September 3, 2000). About six months after it was unveiled, *Überorgan* became an actual instrument, when Cynthia Hopkins collaborated with Transmission Projects to perform a rendition of the traditional spiritual "Walk that Lonesome Valley" on it.

Hawkinson has received the most praise for the pieces in which he has used his own body. In the 2002 Whitney Biennial survey of contemporary artists, he exhibited *Emoter*, a poster-size self-portrait made from a photograph of his face that has been cut up and reassembled. Each of the pieces can move, so that "every few seconds, one nostril enlarges, one segment of brow furrows, one corner of the mouth turns down in a fragment of a frown," as Ariella Budick explained for *Newsday* (March 10, 2002). "It's hard to resist trying to decipher what the picture is thinking, especially since its expressions are as enigmatic, if more extreme, than the Mona Lisa's." Other critics have called attention to the source of the stimuli producing the movement. John Zeaman, in the Bergen County, New Jersey, *Record* (February 25, 2005), for example, wrote, "The slow, seemingly random movements of the features are grotesque and artificial. The joke of the piece is that the facial expressions are controlled by light-sensitive receptors responding to the flickering images of a television set." *Emoter* thereby suggests that technological devices have the ability to animate the human form and transfigure it into an artificial object.

In 2005 the Whitney Museum mounted a Hawkinson retrospective that included a sizable portion of Hawkinson's work. The exhibit, which ran from February 11 through May 29, both delighted and dismayed critics. Blake Gopnik described it as "impressively novel. Despite its solidly old-fashioned bones, Hawkinson's art looks and feels unlike anything you've ever seen before." Clare Henry, by contrast, complained in the London *Financial Times* (March 7, 2005) that the "labour-intensive, handmade creations put together from thrift-store components and odd trinkets can create visual chaos, and Hawkinson's Whitney Museum show, which sprawls right across the fourth floor, is a confusing mixture of artist-inflicted detritus and detailed drawings, all of which could do with more explanation than the museum supplies." The show attracted members of the public—both adults and children—in unusually large numbers.

After closing in New York, Hawkinson's retrospective moved to the Los Angeles County Museum of Art, where it opened to general approval. Christopher Knight, in the *Los Angeles Times* (July 1, 2005), praised it for providing "a good overview of an artist whose work seems eccentric but is actually embedded within a larger continuum"; in *LA Weekly* (July 8, 2005), Doug Harvey greeted it as "sort of the homecoming crown atop a year of career highs for Hawkinson." The retrospective coincided with another career high for the artist, the unveiling of his first significant outdoor sculpture—a teddy-bear–shaped assemblage of eight granite boulders held together with pins, weighing over 200 tons and standing more than 20 feet high. *Bear*, as it is called, was an addition to the Stuart Collection at the University of California–San Diego, which includes such works as Elizabeth Murray's *Red Shoe* (1996) and Kiki Smith's *Standing* (1998). The inspiration for *Bear*, which rests in the courtyard of the Jacobs School of Engineering, came from Hawkinson's sometimes seeing, as he drove through the desert, "rock piles that suggest animals," as he explained to Robert L. Pincus for the *San Diego Union-Tribune* (June 12, 2005). "Different forms are suggested by seeing beautiful boulders, too, or piling rocks in the back yard," he told Pincus.

Not known for sociability, Hawkinson finds the social duties associated with being an artist very burdensome. "I'm shy and I freeze up under scrutiny," he told McKenna, "and that's one of the great things about being an artist—you get to express yourself, but there's a time delay. You say it now, and it gets heard later." Hawkinson divides his time between his studio in Los Angeles, which he moved into in the mid-1980s, and his house in Altadena, north of Pasadena, which he bought in 1998 and shares with his wife, Patty Wickman, and their young daughter, Clare. He is building a studio in his backyard, which will free him of the need to commute to work and give him a chance to spend more time with Clare, who has begun to exert an influence on his work. "Believe it or not I'm making dolls now," he told Clare Henry in 2005. "It's mind-boggling. Gentle anatomic dolls which move."

—A.R.

Suggested Reading: *Art in America* p112 May 1997; *LA Weekly* p32 Feb. 19, 1999; *Los Angeles Times* F p12 June 10, 1993; *New York Times* E p33 Feb. 11, 2005; *Newsday* B p4 Feb. 16, 2005; *San Diego Tribune* F p6 Mar. 6, 2005; *Village Voice* p143 Mar. 16, 1999; *Washington Post* G p1

Apr. 15, 2001; Desmarais, Charles. *Humongolous: Sculpture and Other Works by Tim Hawkinson*, 1996; Monk, Philip, and Laura Steward Heon. *Tim Hawkinson*, 2000; Rinder, Lawrence. *Tim Hawkinson*, 2005

Selected Books: *Tim Hawkinson: Ahi Ikmnnostw*, 1996

Courtesy of the Office of Governor Brad Henry

Henry, Brad

July 10, 1963– Governor of Oklahoma (Democrat)

Address: State Capitol Bldg., 2300 N. Lincoln Blvd., Rm. 212, Oklahoma City, OK 73105

At 39 years of age, the Democrat Brad Henry became the 26th governor of the state of Oklahoma, and the youngest governor in the U.S., when he was sworn in on January 13, 2003. A practicing lawyer and an active public servant, Henry served in the Oklahoma state Senate for 10 years, from 1992 to 2002, before running in the 2002 gubernatorial election, in which he emerged as the come-from-behind winner in one of the closest races for the governorship in state history. As governor he has focused on revitalizing Oklahoma's economy and strengthening the state's education and health-care systems; facing a nearly $700 million state-revenue shortfall when he took office, the largest in Oklahoma's history, Henry led a successful bipartisan effort to enact a balanced budget that prioritized health care and education without raising taxes. In addition to his other honors, Henry has won the Distinguished Graduate Award from the organization Leadership Oklahoma.

A third-generation Oklahoman, Brad Henry was born to Charles T. and Audre L. Henry in Shawnee, Oklahoma, on July 10, 1963. Henry was very close to his father, Charles Henry, who served in the Oklahoma House of Representatives from 1961 to 1963 and again from 1973 to 1975; the two practiced law together before Charles Henry's death, in 2001. "Oh, it was an incredible bond," Henry told Sidney K. Sperry for *Oklahoma Living* (February 14, 2003, on-line). "Dad and I were best friends, and there is not a day that goes by that I don't miss him." He also said that "growing up on a farm, in a rural area, taught me the value of hard work and discipline. Those two things, plus the leadership skills I learned from my father . . . were very instrumental in moving me toward a life in public service." (Brad's cousin Robert Henry also served in the Oklahoma House of Representatives, from 1979 to 1985.) Henry graduated from Shawnee High School in 1981, then attended the University of Oklahoma (OU) as a President's Leadership Scholar. He served as a teaching assistant in economics at OU from 1983 to 1985 and received a bachelor's degree in that subject in the latter year, when he was named Outstanding Senior Man by the university. In 1988 Henry received a juris doctorate degree from the University of Oklahoma College of Law, where he was the managing editor of the *Oklahoma Law Review* during his last year. By that time he had already started his own business, the Brad Henry Oil Co. Concurrently with the running of his fuel company, Henry also went to work as an associate attorney at the Oklahoma City law firm of Andrews, Davis, Legg, Bixler, Milsten & Price, a post he held until 1989. At that time Henry helped establish the Shawnee-based law firm Henry, Canavan & Hopkins, P.L.L.C., where he also served as managing attorney. In 1990 Henry became city attorney for Shawnee, a position he held for more than 10 years.

Henry entered politics in 1992, when, at the age of 29, he won a seat in the Oklahoma state Senate. He served in the state Senate with distinction for a decade, eventually becoming chairman of the influential Senate Judiciary Committee and vice chairman of the Economic Development Committee. Henry also served on the Appropriations, Education, and Sunset Committees.

Henry ran for the governorship of Oklahoma on a platform that included his advocacy of a state lottery, to raise money for education programs in the state, and his opposition to a plan to change from a state tax system that relies primarily on income taxes to one that would depend more heavily on sales taxes. In television commercials released by Henry's campaign team, the state senator was often shown surrounded by his young family. He embarked on a 40-city, statewide tour in a recreational vehicle and received influential and highly energetic campaign support from Barry Switzer, the well-known former coach of the University of Oklahoma football team. In the August 2002 Oklahoma Democratic gubernatorial primary, Henry

was beaten by Vince Orza, a restaurateur, who captured 44 percent of the 350,000 votes cast, compared with Henry's 28 percent. Orza's tally, however, was still short of the required majority, and a runoff election was held. In that contest Henry turned the tables on Orza, winning 52 percent of the vote and the Democratic Party's nomination for governor. In the general election, the closest gubernatorial contest in Oklahoma in 32 years, he beat both the front-runner, the Republican candidate Steve Largent, a Hall of Fame wide receiver for the Seattle Seahawks of the National Football League, and the wealthy former U.S. attorney Gary Richardson, an independent candidate; Henry bested Largent by approximately 6,000 votes out of more than one million cast. "This is just a real humbling and a tremendous experience," the governor-elect commented to Richard Benedetto for *USA Today* (November 7, 2002, on-line). Henry succeeded the Republican governor Frank Keating, who was limited to two terms in office.

In 2003 Henry balanced the state budget, despite a record revenue shortfall in Oklahoma. In the course of doing so, he led a bipartisan effort in the state Legislature to cut funding for other areas of government in order to avoid compromising the state's education and health-care systems. "The cuts we were forced to make certainly weren't painless, but I think we did do a good job of using the resources available to us," Henry said, as quoted in an Oklahoma state government press release dated May 30, 2003. The governor's other accomplishments that year included working with the state Legislature to enact measures requiring state agencies to account for every dollar they spend; restricting smoking in public places; and lowering drug costs in Oklahoma. According to the press release, Henry said, "I'm proud of the budget we enacted and the bipartisan effort that made it possible. . . . While Republicans and Democrats were fighting like cats and dogs in other states, we were pulling together in Oklahoma and addressing difficult issues."

In 2004 Governor Henry won approval from voters and legislators for measures aimed at improving education and health care. On June 9 he signed into law a pay increase for teachers, designed to raise their salaries over the next five years to the average for teachers in that region of the country; the pay raise was the first Oklahoma's teachers had received in almost four years. Meanwhile, Henry's tort-reform bill passed in the state Legislature. The new law placed limits on non-economic damages in medical malpractice cases and established penalties for frivolous lawsuits. A number of compromises were struck to enact the law, with the result that some Republicans complained that the legislation did not go far enough, and doctors contended that they are still not sufficiently protected from the kinds of lawsuits the new law seeks to end. Still, as quoted by the Associated Press (August 20, 2004), Emilee Truelove of Oklahomans for Responsible Justice said that the measure is "not pro-lawyer by any stretch." In November voters approved initiatives backed by Henry: one for an increase in the tobacco tax, designed to pay for new health-care measures; another for a state lottery to raise money for public education; and still another, granting the state government some control over the more than 80 Native American–owned casinos in Oklahoma and bringing the state a share of the profits. That money will also go toward public education.

The negotiations with Native Americans that helped bring about the changes in Oklahoma's approach to taxing tobacco have generated criticism from Republicans eager to retake the governorship in the 2006 elections. Henry is preparing for what he expects to be "a very difficult race" against a "formidable" Republican opponent, in his words, according to Nolan Gray in the *Sunday Oklahoman* (August 28, 2005). "I'm not going to take anything for granted," Henry added.

An extremely active member of his community, Henry has sat on the board of trustees of St. Gregory's University and the board of directors or advisers of Project Safe; Project for Achieving Self-Sufficiency; Youth and Family Resource Center Inc.; Gateway to Prevention and Recovery Inc.; the American, Oklahoma, and Pottawatomie County Bar Associations; the Shawnee and Norman Chambers of Commerce; the Oklahoma Academy for State Goals; Leadership Oklahoma; and the Shawnee Lions Club. In addition to his other honors, Henry was named an Outstanding Young Oklahoman by the Junior Chamber of Commerce.

Henry's wife, the former Kim Blain, teaches in Oklahoma's public-school system. The couple have three daughters, Leah, Laynie, and Baylee. Both Henry and his wife have served as Sunday-school teachers at the First Baptist Church of Shawnee, which the governor also serves as an ordained deacon.

—C.F.T.

Suggested Reading: National Governors Association Web site; *Oklahoma Living* (on-line) Feb. 14, 2003, with photos; Oklahoma State Web site; *USA Today* (on-line) Nov. 7, 2002, with photo; *Who's Who in American Politics 2001–02*

Henry, John W.

Sep. 13, 1949– Futures trader; principal owner of the Boston Red Sox

Address: John W. Henry & Co. Inc., 301 Yamato Rd., Suite 2200, Boca Raton, FL 33431

In 1980, after several years of research and trials, John W. Henry figured out a way to trace long-term trends in the notoriously unpredictable futures markets. On the strength of his system, Henry founded his own commodities-fund management company in 1981, and since then he has taken a place among the leading players in managed futures investments. When he became the principal owner of the Boston Red Sox, in 2002, he set about applying to baseball the same by-the-numbers approach that had been so effective for him as an investor. With the goal of building a winning team, he and the other members of the Red Sox front office have become devotees of sabermetrics, a system of detailed statistical analysis that is designed to measure ballplayers' abilities and true value with scientific precision. But baseball is still a game dominated by tradition and lore, and giving hard data the same status as human judgment is considered radical to some observers. The performance of the 2004 Red Sox club assembled by Henry and his baseball-operations staff strengthened his confidence in sabermetrics' merits: the team captured the World Series in dramatic fashion, bringing the championship back to Boston for the first time in 86 years.

Courtesy of John W. Henry & Co. Inc.

The son of successful corn and soybean farmers, John W. Henry was born on September 13, 1949 in Quincy, Illinois. He was raised primarily in Forrest City, Arkansas, where his parents managed 2,000 acres. He was a rabid baseball fan from an early age and regularly listened to the Hall of Fame announcer Harry Caray's broadcasts of St. Louis Cardinals games on the radio. When Henry was eight his father was diagnosed as having a brain tumor and was hospitalized in St. Louis, Missouri. The Cardinals' coach, who was staying in the same hotel as Henry's family, heard about their plight and offered the boy seats to a doubleheader. Henry sat through both games in the sun and later had to be hospitalized himself for heat stroke. The experience did not diminish his love for the game. "It was just magical. I'd been listening on the radio but I'd never seen a game," he recalled to Danny Hakim for the *New York Times* (October 26, 2000). "So my ambition in life became to move to St. Louis someday and get a job that would enable me to afford season tickets so I could go to 80 games a year." Henry suffered from a childhood respiratory ailment, and when he was 15, the family moved to Apple Valley, California, in the belief that the region's dry desert air would offer him some relief.

After he graduated from high school, Henry took classes, mostly in philosophy, at several colleges—including Victor Valley Junior College, the University of California at Los Angeles, and the University of California at Riverside—but never earned a degree.

When Henry was 25 his father died, and he took over his family's Arkansas farm. He decided to learn about trading in futures markets to hedge against crop-price changes. A futures contract is a promise to buy or sell a specific quantity of commodities, bonds, currency, or stocks at a specific price on a specific date, with the hope that the value of the futures will appreciate beyond the agreed-upon price before the contract comes due. Henry opened an account with a trader of frozen chickens, who quickly doubled Henry's initial $5,000 investment by selling contracts when they increased by a penny and buying them back when they fell by a penny. "His strategy worked pretty well," Henry told William Symonds for *BusinessWeek* (April 26, 2004), "but I looked at the long-term trend and saw that if the market went one way long enough, you'd be wiped out." Although, in 1976, he profited from hedging on his soybean crop, taking into account such factors as weather and demand, he sought a safer way to trade in futures by identifying underlying trends that drive market values over the long term. He worked on developing this new approach during a long visit to Norway with his Norwegian-born first wife in the summer of 1980. "I didn't speak the language, so I was bored quite a bit, and I started working on some ideas I'd had for a more mechanical approach to trading," he told Michael Peltz for *Institutional Investor* (August 1996). "I was so excited about what I had discovered that you could have a fairly simple philosophy of trends, and trend following, and that it worked so well."

Originally interested only in climate-sensitive agriculture trends, Henry tested his approach by examining the past performances of every market for which he could gather complete data, and he found that it worked for several types of futures. He then expanded his platform to include trading on metals, a wider range of agricultural products,

including coffee and sugar, and shares of stocks. In 1981 Henry started an investment concern, John W. Henry & Co., in Newport Beach, California. He invested only for himself and his family until 1982, when he began to accept private clients. In an industry notorious for its levels of risk, Henry was remarkably and consistently successful. It has been estimated that from 1982 through 2004 his firm generated $2.4 billion in profits for its clients.

In 1989, the same year that he moved his operations to Westport, Connecticut, Henry purchased a majority share of the Tucson Toros, the Triple-A Pacific Coast League affiliate of the Houston Astros, and also became co-owner of the West Palm Beach Tropics, of Florida's Senior League, in which retired major leaguers played. The Tropics, along with the rest of the Senior League, folded after only one season, but not before Henry had met the woman who became his second wife, who had been contracted to program the Tropics' computers. Eager to become involved in Major League Baseball, in 1992 he purchased a 1 percent stake in the New York Yankees and met George Steinbrenner, the Yankees' principal owner. "Some of the greatest times of my life were those Yankee partner meetings," he recalled to Bill Madden for the New York *Daily News* (May 23, 2002). "We had a filial relationship, like we were George's kids, and I just had so much fun."

In 1994 Henry relocated part of his investment firm to Boca Raton, Florida, and three years later relinquished his stake in the Tucson Toros. He then began negotiating with the business magnate H. Wayne Huizenga to acquire sole ownership of the Florida Marlins. In 1999 he purchased the team for approximately $150 million. Henry inherited a franchise in flux. In 1997, their fifth season, the Marlins—sooner than any other expansion club in baseball history—had captured the World Series, becoming the first wild-card team to do so. The following year, claiming that he could no longer afford the team's payroll, Huizenga traded away the veteran players largely responsible for winning the championship; in exchange, he chose less-expensive prospects, barely ready for the majors. Consequently, the 1998 Marlins finished last in their division, with a record of 54–108, 38 wins fewer than their previous year's total. Over the next three seasons Henry tried to build public and private support for a new ballpark, but fan morale was still suffering from Huizenga's course of action, and state, county, and city government support did not coalesce. "I didn't have any partners in Florida," Henry joked to Bill Madden, "primarily because as a so-called money-manager and fiduciary expert, I couldn't in good conscience ask anyone to invest in the Marlins."

Henry absorbed millions of dollars in losses on the team over three seasons and sought ways to stop the flow of red ink and pass the torch to someone who would continue the effort to build a new ballpark in South Florida. "You've been a great owner," Bud Selig, the Major League Baseball commissioner, told Henry, according to William Symonds, "and we still want you in this game." With Selig's encouragement, Henry looked for other opportunities to remain an owner in Major League Baseball. At the same time, Jeffrey Loria, the owner of the Expos, was seeking to leave the struggling Montreal market. In the winter of 2001–02, the National League collectively purchased the Montreal Expos (who later relocated to the District of Columbia and became the Washington Nationals) from Loria, who in turn bought the Marlins from Henry. Henry then called Larry Lucchino, the former San Diego Padres and Baltimore Orioles president, who was working with former Padres owner Tom Werner, former U.S. senator George Mitchell, and the ski-resort entrepreneur Les Otten on a bid to purchase the Boston Red Sox. Lucchino informed Henry that he and his partners still needed a major investor. Familiar with Lucchino's other successes, Henry eagerly joined them; he was the largest investor in the group. In March 2002 their bid was accepted, and Henry became the principal owner of the Boston Red Sox.

A team with a storied history and an avid fan base, the Red Sox presented Henry with a new set of challenges. Fenway Park, the oldest ballpark in the major leagues, was in desperate need of revitalization. Henry and his co-owners expanded the concourses, adding new seats and a new roof-box pavilion, and renovated the .406 club, an exclusive area of enclosed seating named in honor of the legendary player Ted Williams's lifetime batting record.

In addition to focusing on financial success, Henry was committed to bringing Boston its first World Championship in decades. Long a proponent of using close statistical analysis to predict variable trends and reduce risk, Henry turned to a system called sabermetrics to improve the on-field performance of the Red Sox. In the 1970s the statistician, baseball pundit, and author Bill James had conceived of an alternative method of player evaluation using arcane baseball statistics that seemed to debunk many of the game's time-honored assumptions. James called his system sabermetrics, a word whose first two syllables echo the acronym for the Society for American Baseball Research (SABR). He argued, for example, that a player's batting average is not a good assessment of how valuable he is at the plate. Instead, James favored a player's on-base percentage, which gives equal measure to how often a batter draws a walk or is hit by a pitch, since both of those events puts that batter on base as effectively as a hit. Regardless of James's findings, many fans and insiders have favored players with showy batting averages, awarding them large contracts. "There are immense inefficiencies in the market for players," James has said, according to Symonds. The few students of sabermetrics manning major-league front offices built successful teams out of inexpensive players who contributed more to their teams' success than higher-profile players might have. One such stu-

dent, the general manager Billy Beane, has kept the Oakland A's highly competitive despite its being a low-budget, small-market ball club. Indeed, one of Henry's first acts as Boston's principal owner was to try to entice Beane to jump from the A's to the Red Sox. When Beane declined, Henry turned to another believer in Bill James's theories, Theo Epstein, who became the youngest general manager in baseball history upon his appointment to the Red Sox, in 2002. Henry and Epstein immediately signed James as the team's senior baseball-operations adviser.

On James's recommendation the Red Sox shed the contracts of several highly paid veterans and trolled the free-agent market for undervalued talent: the sluggers David Ortiz and Kevin Millar, for example, who both became Red Sox stars. Boston's management "actually cut the payroll by $9 million, yet improved the team," Doug Pappas, the chair of a SABR committee, told Symonds. James also advised the Red Sox to restructure their relief pitching. If a starting pitcher gets injured, tired, or gives up too many runs, a manager will usually replace him with a long reliever, called a set-up man, to pitch for two or three innings and hold a lead until the closer—one of the team's best pitchers, who is effective for at most two innings—can be brought in to shut down opposing batters and finish the game. James considered this traditional arrangement inefficient, arguing that the team's best reliever should be used earlier in the game, especially if the score is tied. Guided by James's suggestions, the Red Sox traded their closer, Ugueth Urbina, who had racked up 40 saves during the previous season, and restructured their bullpen to a rotating system in which any reliever could be called on to close. While many of James's proposals contributed greatly to Boston's 2003 record of 95–67 and their advancement into the play-offs as a wild card, it quickly became clear that their "closer by committee" approach to relief pitching was the team's biggest weakness. During the 2003 American League Championships, while facing off against the New York Yankees, the Red Sox lost the final game of the series when the team's manager, Grady Little, who had no confidence in his bullpen, left his tiring starting ace, Pedro Martinez, on the mound in the eighth inning with a 5–2 lead. Martinez then gave up three runs, sending the game into extra innings, and the Yankees scored on a solo home run in the 11th inning to claim the championship.

While keeping the core of their formidable lineup, the Red Sox reverted to tradition in the bullpen, acquiring one of the game's top closers, Keith Foulke, in the off-season. They further shored up their pitching by signing the All-Star starter Curt Schilling, and they replaced Little with Terry Francona, who had a growing reputation as one of baseball's outstanding tacticians. In 2004 Boston posted a 98–64 record—the most wins by a Red Sox team since 1978—en route to another appearance in the play-offs as a wild-card team. After sweeping the Anaheim Angels in the Division Series, they returned to the American League Championship to challenge their arch-nemeses, the Yankees. New York took the first three games, including a 19–8 game-three drubbing of the Red Sox. The Red Sox then won the next four games and the American League Championship, thus becoming the first Major League Baseball team ever to overcome a 3–0 deficit in a play-off series. With their powerful lineup, Schilling's gritty performances on the mound despite a torn tendon in his right ankle, and Foulke's unhittable late-inning pitching, the Boston Red Sox swept the St. Louis Cardinals in four straight games to capture the 2004 World Series championship—the Red Sox's first since 1918.

Following that accomplishment, the Red Sox endured the free-agency defections in their starting pitching staff of Pedro Martinez (who joined the New York Mets) and Derek Lowe (Los Angeles Dodgers) and signed two other free agents: David Wells (who had left the New York Yankees) and Matt Clement (Chicago Cubs). Boston remained in first place in the American League East for most of the 2005 season despite injuries to their pitching staff, including the starting pitcher Curt Schilling and the closer Keith Foulke. The New York Yankees, who trailed the Red Sox by over five games on August 11, recorded 35 wins and only 12 losses afterward, capturing their eighth straight division title in a game against Boston on October 1. With

Boston's 10–1 win over the Yankees in the final game of the regular season and a loss by the Cleveland Indians, who were a game behind Boston in the wild-card standings, the Red Sox captured the American League wild card and second place in the American League East division for the eighth consecutive time, finishing the season with a 95–67 record. As winners of the wild card, the Red Sox faced the team with the best record (99–63) in the American League—the Chicago White Sox, who had not won a play-off series since 1917. The White Sox beat the Red Sox in three consecutive games, then went on to claim their first World Series crown in 88 years.

John W. Henry formerly served on the boards of directors of the National Association of Futures Trading Advisors, the Managed Futures Trade Association, and the Futures Industry Association. He also formerly served as a member of the nominating committee of the National Futures Association. He and his wife, Peggy, have one child. He divides his time between Boca Raton and Boston.

—T.J.F.

Suggested Reading: *Boston Herald* B p20 May 5, 2002, with photos; *BusinessWeek* p74 Apr. 26, 2004, with photos; *Fortune* p56 Apr. 26, 1999, with photo; *Money* p110 Apr. 2003; New York *Daily News* p80 May 23, 2002, with photos; *New York Times* C p9 Oct. 26, 2000

Hobson, Mellody

Apr. 3, 1969– Business executive

Address: Ariel Capital Management, 200 E. Randolph Dr., Suite 2900, Chicago, IL 60601

"I think money itself is generally not fully understood," Mellody Hobson said to Tricia Bisoux for *Biz Ed* (May/June 2005). "Money isn't more valuable than life or happiness, but it gives people freedom. And if you're free, you have choices. That's the best thing in the world." Hobson is president of the Chicago, Illinois–based Ariel Capital Management LLC, the first African-American-owned investment-management firm—and still one of the largest—in the U.S., with control of assets totaling more than $18 billion. As president, a post she has held since 2000, Hobson is responsible for firm-wide management and strategic planning. In 1996, while serving as Ariel's senior vice president, she began the first-ever annual survey of investment habits among blacks in the United States, the first step toward fulfilling her dream of spreading her entrepreneurial enthusiasm to the African-American community. "We want to make the stock market the subject of dinner table conversation in African American households," Hobson said to Kila Weaver for *The Hotness* (February 21, 2001,

on-line). To that end, under Hobson's leadership, the company has sponsored investment seminars around the country and has teamed with the publications *Vibe* and *Black Enterprise*, representatives of the Chicago Bulls basketball team, and a number of African-American music stars, including Jay-Z and Eve, to publicize investment opportunities at Ariel; the campaigns have involved traditional marketing as well as more innovative approaches, among them celebrity stock-picking contests. Hobson told Weaver, "The interest level has been huge." Hobson's company has also established the Ariel Community Academy, in Chicago, an institution that focuses on educating grade-school students and their parents about financial matters. "Parents and teachers have to learn these issues as well . . . ," Hobson said to Tricia Bisoux. "It's one of the most uncomfortable areas for parents to deal with—it has been documented that parents dread conversations with their kids about money more than they dread conversations about sex or drugs." Since 2000 Hobson has been featured regularly as a financial analyst on ABC's program *Good Morning America*.

Mellody Hobson was born on April 3, 1969 in Chicago, Illinois, the youngest of the six children of Dorothy Ashley, a single mother who supported her children by working as a real-estate agent. Hobson told Kila Weaver that her mother is one of the

Victor Powell, courtesy of Ariel Capital Management
Mellody Hobson

people she most admires because "she was nontraditional. She empowered us at a young age to do whatever we wanted and she instilled responsibility in us through trust." Hobson attended St. Ignatius College Preparatory School in Chicago, where her hard work and high grades earned her the opportunity for an Ivy League education: both Harvard and Princeton Universities pursued Hobson as she neared her high-school graduation. She chose Princeton, in New Jersey, beginning as a mathematics major and then, after considering the career options available to those in that field, transferring to Princeton's Woodrow Wilson School of Public and International Affairs to pursue a major in South African studies. Before she graduated, in 1991, with a B.A. degree in international relations, she had spent a summer as an intern at Ariel Capital Management Inc. The firm, founded by John W. Rogers Jr. in 1983, was the first to specialize in addressing the needs of African-American investors and the first black-run mutual fund. Since its inception, with two employees (it now has 95), it has managed so-called small-cap value portfolios, or those involving companies whose size (or market capitalization) places them in the smallest 8 percent of companies listed on the major stock exchanges; according to arielcapital.com, the firm introduced its "mid-cap value style" in 1989. As of March 31, 2005 the company was managing $21.1 billion for institutional and individual investors. Ariel performs socially conscientious investing by avoiding alcohol and tobacco stocks, which are often referred to in the company as "sin" stocks.

After graduation Hobson briefly pursued a career in journalism before returning to Ariel and joining their marketing team. "I liked the idea that the business day in this industry isn't static—I deal with so many different constituents and situations," Hobson said to Tricia Bisoux. "And I liked the fact that I'm helping to make people's lives better. The one great thing about our work is that we're helping people grow their money, which for them ultimately means a better retirement, a better house, a better inheritance to leave their children. I think that really is a noble calling." Three years later she was promoted to senior vice president and director of marketing. Hobson realized that although investment companies conducted surveys to determine how an investor's age and gender affected his or her practices and needs, no surveys existed to determine the effect of a person's race on investment. In 1996 she launched the annual survey of African-American investors, which later became a joint effort with the Wall Street brokerage firm Charles Schwab. "Every year, Ariel and Charles Schwab conduct a survey of the black community and heavily publicize the results," Hobson told Tricia Bisoux. "We want it to be a wakeup call, not just for black America but for all America. We want everyone to realize that if this issue isn't addressed, it won't just be a 'black problem'—it will be everyone's problem. After having worked to break into the middle and upper classes, we [blacks] won't be able to retire comfortably, because we didn't adequately prepare. We'll find ourselves stepping back into poverty, becoming a burden on society. We do this survey as one way to effect change." The survey is designed to identify similarities and differences between groups of potential or actual African-American and white investors; it also aims to identify factors that influence people's attitudes and behaviors in the area of finance and investment. In 2000, for example, the results of the survey showed that a majority of African-Americans "would prefer to have the choice to invest with a black-owned or managed mutual fund as part of their 401(k) or other employer-sponsored retirement plan," according to arielcapital.com. In 2004 the survey revealed that more blacks were investing in the stock market than in the previous year, but not as many as in 2002.

In 2000, less than 10 years after she joined the company, Hobson became president of Ariel Capital Management.

Over the course of her career, Hobson has seen the number of African-American investors rise, but not as much as she would like. "The stock market represents a major source of wealth creation in this country," she wrote for *Black Collegian Online* (2001). "But we've done a lot of research here, and have concluded that African-Americans have been largely left out. This is due to many factors; lack of knowledge, lack of exposure, and lack of diversity in the industry. African-American children don't grow up knowing mutual fund managers." She tries to teach people that even small investments can bring large returns over the long term. "So you should make the stock market a part of your long-term investment strategy. It doesn't take a lot of money," Hobson wrote for *Black Collegian Online*. "You can invest as little as $50 a month. So don't sit on the sidelines because you think you can't afford it. Think of the long-term benefits of compounding. Learn to ride the ups and downs of the market. You must have patience."

Based on the belief that investing should be learned at a young age, in 1996 Ariel helped start the Ariel Community Academy (ACA), a full-time public school that is part of the Chicago public-school system. The classes in ACA, which has an enrollment of 362, are smaller than those in ordinary public schools. ACA emphasizes financial literacy and oral presentation in addition to reading and writing. Ariel, in conjunction with Nuveen Investments, created and financially supported the ACA's Ariel-Nuveen Investment Program, which was developed to encourage future investors, starting at the grade-school level. The first-grade class is given $20,000 to invest; by the time the students reach the sixth grade, they manage 25 percent of the fund, and when they complete eighth grade, they give $20,000 to the incoming first-graders. Parents also learn financial skills through newsletters and seminars that discuss the basics of investing. "We wanted to do something unique and different that hadn't been done before," Hobson said to Tricia Bisoux. "We hope other organizations will be able to replicate this program at schools across the nation." Profits from the investments are used to fund academic scholarships and make charitable donations.

When asked about her vision for the economic future of African-Americans, Hobson cited the importance of stocks and bonds and overall financial stability. She believes it to be crucial "that each African American child at birth receives gifts of mutual funds and stocks that will follow them throughout his or her life," as she told Kila Weaver. "That we develop a strong sensitivity to, and comfort with, investing in the stock market. That as that child grows up he or she has a college fund, the capital to start a business after college, the money for a down payment on a home, ample resources for a comfortable retirement and money to leave to his or her children. That we become part of the economic mainstream, with the emotional and financial security that accompanies it."

Hobson's advocacy of African-American financial independence has its roots in her respect for leaders of the civil rights movement. She has described her admiration for the Reverend Jesse Jackson and for Martin Luther King Jr., who "changed the world, not just for African Americans but for all of us," Hobson told Kila Weaver. "I think he's this country's most significant political leader. The will he had was great—his will, his discipline and his legacy." Hobson has discussed her views on the subject of women in business, telling Tricia Bi-

soux, "Women want to see role models in business to show us what is possible. If traditional corporate environments can't show us that, because they lack diversity or lack women in their senior ranks, we don't want to be there. We vote with our feet. I think one reason so many women become entrepreneurs is that we see greater opportunity doing it ourselves." She also believes that having a career does not necessarily mean giving up on having a family. "I think in life you always have to make choices. Even so, there are smart ways to run your life and get things done, with or without children," Hobson said to Tricia Bisoux. "I work with women who are mothers, who are also top performers and incredibly successful here at Ariel. These women are very organized and they work hard. They haven't, from my perspective, sacrificed their careers. They've been able to achieve the best of both worlds. I'm sure it wasn't easy and I'm sure there were times certain things had to give, but they show it can be done. I don't see having a family as a reason for not achieving professional success."

In 2001 the World Economic Forum, in Davos, Switzerland, named Hobson a Global Leader of Tomorrow. *Crain's Chicago Business* magazine included Hobson in its "Top 40 under 40" list of young businesspeople. She was named one of America's "Best and Brightest" by *Esquire Magazine* in 2002 and was included on the *Wall Street Journal*'s list of 50 corporate "Women to Watch" in 2004. *Ebony Magazine* included her in its "30 Leaders of the Future" in 1992. Hobson serves on the boards of directors of three public companies—Dreamworks Animation SKG, the Estée Lauder Co., and Starbucks—and also on the boards of the Chicago Public Library, the Field Museum, and the Chicago Public Education Fund. She is also a trustee of Princeton University. In addition to sharing financial advice on *Good Morning America*, she contributes finance reports to *Minority Business Report*, a long-running television series that airs on cable channels.

Hobson wakes at 4:30 every morning and performs a physical workout before going to work. She also enjoys surfing and keeps a surfboard in her office as a memento of a memorable vacation. She has been a vegetarian since 1999.

—L.J.

Suggested Reading: *Biz Ed* p19+ May/June 2005, with photo; *Black Collegian Online* (2001); *The Hotness* (on-line) Feb. 21, 2001

Phil Cole/Getty Images

Howard, Tim

Mar. 6, 1979– Soccer player

Address: Manchester United PLC, Sir Matt Busby Way, Old Trafford, Manchester M16 0RA, England

At a very early age, Tim Howard committed himself to becoming the best soccer player he could be, and today he is one of the most successful and talented American athletes playing the game. By the age of 22, he was among the top-ranked players in Major League Soccer (MLS), the most competitive professional soccer league in the United States, and in 2003 Manchester United, the most successful team in England's Premier League, one of the top soccer leagues in the world, wooed him away from the MLS. Howard managed to win his new team's first-string goalie position—an accomplishment that is particularly extraordinary in that goalkeepers, as Ellen Hale observed in *USA Today* (January 23, 2004), "don't peak until their 30s." Among other obstacles Howard overcame to attain that level of success was the disorder known as Tourette's syndrome. He has served as a role model for others with Tourette's, not only by struggling against the symptoms of the disorder to maintain his composure on and off the field, but by talking openly about his illness and holding fund-raising events to benefit his fellow sufferers, particularly children. "God made me this way, so I have to deal with it," Howard told Hasani Pettiford and Robyn D. Clarke for *Black Enterprise* (September 30, 2001). "I've met others with the same condition, and they never let it stop them. So I knew I wouldn't let it stop me."

Tim Howard was born in North Brunswick, New Jersey, on March 6, 1979 to Matthew Howard, an African-American, and Esther Howard, a white woman born in Hungary. His parents divorced when he was three, and afterward Howard lived with his mother, a project manager for a cosmetics distributor. His father, a long-distance truck driver for a health-care firm, nonetheless maintained a presence in his life. It was his father, in fact, who was determined to get Tim and his brother, Chris, involved in sports; before they could even walk, he bought them equipment for various sports and watched them to see which games they seemed to like. Tim Howard showed a preference for basketball and soccer, activities that would help him cope with two difficulties he was forced to confront as a child. One was racism, which manifested itself most strongly when he dated a white girl whose father refused to let him in their house. The other was Tourette's syndrome, whose symptoms began to appear in Howard when he was in the fifth grade. He suffered not from the well-known form of the disease that causes one to curse randomly and unpredictably, but from a strain that made him feel compelled to touch objects and people in specific ways. For example, he would touch certain pieces of furniture in a pattern every time he arrived home or would, for no apparent reason, put his hands on his mother's shoulders or arms while he was talking with her. The disorder did not prevent his talent from emerging. Howard "was such a good athlete," Alex Yannis reported for the *New York Times* (August 19, 2001), "that he avoided being teased in school." Before he was even a teenager, Tim Mulqueen, now the goalkeeper coach for the Kansas City Wizards, saw his potential at a soccer camp Howard attended and took the boy under his wing.

In high school Howard proved a star not only in soccer, as a midfielder, but also on the basketball court, where he averaged 15 points per game and helped bring his team to the state finals in his senior year. His chief talent, however, was as a soccer player. Despite his position on his high school's team, he was better as a goalkeeper than he was in the field. Indeed, he began covering goals on U.S. youth national teams at the age of 15, when he made his international debut against Honduras on the under-17 squad. In 1997 Mulqueen became the coach of the North Jersey Imperials, a team in the Premier Development Soccer League (DSL), and served as the goalie coach for MLS's MetroStars; he immediately considered Howard for a position, and in May of that year, a month before he graduated from high school, Howard played goalie for the Imperials in his first professional game. The following year Mulqueen was instrumental in getting him on the MetroStars squad by way of Major League Soccer's Project 40, a program that lures top high-school and college players into professional soccer by giving them the chance to play for Division A teams and serve as backup players on major-league teams. Howard became the backup goalie for the MetroStars' Tony Meola, who achieved fame in the 1994 World Cup, and while he saw little play with the MetroStars in his first year, he made his Major League debut on July 15, after Meola was suspended. Howard bypassed college, for which he had won a scholarship, to participate in Project 40, and he believes that the opportunity to begin his professional career straight out of high school was beneficial to his athletic development. He told Lewis Beale for the *New York Times* (July 20, 2003), "I thought I would have taken a step back athletically [if I had gone to college]. Even if you're at a top school, you're only getting five or six games that are very competitive, and the training environment isn't that great. So over the course of four years you're getting 20 games that are meaningful. For me as a goalkeeper, I think you have to be in this environment every day, pushing yourself."

In his second year with the MetroStars, Howard had a few more starts, but he was getting the majority of his experience as a starting goalie with the U.S. under-20 national team. He helped bring the team to the 1999 World Youth Championship and played a pivotal role in advancing them to the second round of the tournament, where they were knocked out by Spain in a 3–2 loss. He also played in the Pan American Games with the U.S. under-23 team, allowing only two goals in three starts, including the bronze-medal victory over Canada. In 2000 Meola left the MetroStars and was replaced by Mike Ammann. While that change did not itself affect Howard's position on the team, Ammann's injuries soon gave Howard more starts than ever before. After Ammann suffered a back strain near the beginning of the season, Howard started in four consecutive games and allowed only one goal to be scored against him. Later in the season, with Ammann injured again, Howard took over for another four games, two of which he won. He would have been the starter at the beginning of the MetroStars' postseason run had he not won the backup-goalie position on the U.S. Olympic team. Thus, in September 2000, he went to Sydney, Australia, as a member of the squad that reached the bronze-medal game against Chile. (He did not get a chance to play.)

In 2001 the MetroStars traded Ammann and made Howard their full-time starter. "I am very excited about being the starting goalkeeper for the MetroStars during the upcoming season," Howard wrote for the team's Web site, as quoted in *Newsday* (February 18, 2001). "It is somewhat unprecedented for a 21-year-old goalkeeper to get the full-time nod." Howard performed spectacularly during the season. Playing every minute of every game, he emerged as the MLS's top goalie, stopping the highest number of goals and putting together the league's best save average and save ratio. For his efforts, he was named Pepsi MLS Best XI, the Aquifina Goalkeeper of the Year, Honda's MVP, and Defender of the Year. He was also picked for the East All-Star team and played the entire second half of the All-Star Game, in which he made 11

saves, including a penalty shot, in an exciting 6–6 draw. With the spotlight on him, Howard was exposed to the temptations that ordinarily beset rising stars. "A lot of players, especially young players, are easily led astray," Howard told Joseph D'Hippolito for *Christianity Today* (2002, on-line). "There's drinking that goes on. There's partying that goes on. You begin to see people failing. I saw players doing the same thing I was doing and not really reaching their goals or living up to their potential." To avoid such behavior, Howard renewed his commitment to Christianity and has remained a devout Christian ever since.

Off the field Howard took up a role that is perhaps more important than that of goalkeeper. In 2001 he made his struggle with Tourette's syndrome public in the hope that he could become a role model for children suffering from the disorder. "I consider myself a great example of why this condition should not hold anyone back from anything they want to accomplish," he told the *Sports Network* (October 15, 2001). "And I'd love to be able to pass that message on to children who might need some inspiring." He began doing volunteer work for the Tourette's Syndrome Association of New Jersey, giving interviews about his own experiences in order to increase the public's awareness of the disorder and participating in events for children. For instance, he hosted more than 200 children and their parents at the MetroStars' home game against the Columbus Crew on Sunday, August 19, 2001 and took part in a two-hour question-and-answer session after the game. Before the event, Howard told Christopher Lawlor for *USA Today* (August 17, 2001), "It's important for the kids to know that people live a happy, free life. I'm trying to be an inspiration but, honestly, I'm the one inspired by the kids, because I know what they are going through." He was soon made a member of the board of directors of the Tourette's Syndrome Association of New Jersey, and the MLS honored him with the 2001 Major League Soccer Humanitarian of the Year award.

In his second year as a starter for the MetroStars, Howard seemed to struggle, slipping to 10th place in the MLS goalkeeping standings by the season's end. Observers, however, pointed out that the weakness of the MetroStars' defense had put a large burden on his shoulders. "Though Howard's 1.59 goals-against average is only sixth in MLS," Jane Havsy wrote for the *Journal News* (August 3, 2002) about midway through the season, "he has faced the most shots (156) and made the most saves (115) of any goalkeeper, 25 more than second-place Nick Rimando of D.C. United. Howard stops 73.7 percent of the shots he faces, but has given up 34 goals this season, the most in the league." The MLS was sufficiently impressed by those numbers to give him a spot on the All-Star team for the second year in a row, and he was again named Pepsi MLS Best XI. The MetroStars were also happy with his performance and gave him a new four-year contract. Howard was able to negotiate the deal, one of the most lucrative in the league, reportedly because European teams were showing interest in signing him. In fact, he openly expressed his desire to play in Europe, especially in England. "England fits my style; it's the best league in the world," he told Jack Bell for the *New York Times* (December 17, 2002).

The beginning of the 2003 season found Howard training with the U.S. national team as it prepared for games against Argentina and Jamaica. He was at the goal in Kingston, Jamaica, when the U.S. beat that country for the first time in eight years. The achievement made him an even more impressive prospect for international scouts, including Tony Coton, the goalkeeping coach of the team Manchester United, of England. Coton had been impressed with Howard as early as 1999, when he took note of the goalie's performance at the Pan American Games and began monitoring Howard's progress. In July 2003 Howard signed a contract with United for $1.4 million a year, with a $1.5 million bonus if he became the club's regular starting goalie. Howard debuted with United in an exhibition game against Italy's Juventus during United's four-game U.S. summer tour. "I thought he was excellent . . . ," the Manchester United coach, Alex Ferguson, told Grant Wahl for *Sports Illustrated* (August 11, 2003) about Howard's 11 saves in a 4–1 victory over Juventus. "He showed the attributes we recognized in him. He's very agile, he's brave and he's quick, with very good spring." By the end of August, Howard had secured the starting position in Manchester, in part because he stopped two penalties in the tiebreaker with Arsenal at the Community Shield, a preseason match between the previous season's top teams. After the match with Arsenal, Howard noted, as Simon Stone reported in the *Daily Post* (August 12, 2003), "What is most important to me is to play well over a long period of time, not to do it over one or two seasons. It was a boost to be selected for such a big match but I have never been one to be over-confident. I know I have the ability but I also still have a lot to learn."

In his first season with Manchester United, Howard performed admirably, getting 14 shutouts in his first 30 starts and retaining his spot as the starting goalie for most of the season. He did have some problems, however. Manchester was knocked out of the Champions League by Porto of Portugal on March 9, 2003, and a week later the team was defeated by its cross-town rival, Manchester City. Howard was benched, and Roy Carroll, Manchester's backup goalie, took over the goalkeeping spot for six games. "It amazed me that [Ferguson] knew exactly the moment when I needed a rest and I felt better mentally and physically for it," Howard later told Ian Chadband of the *Evening Standard* (May 21, 2004). When he returned to goals, Howard was again in top form, and at the season's end he was voted the Keeper of the Year by players in the English Premier League (EPL). He also helped take Manchester into the Football As-

sociation (FA) Cup final, an event Howard called "the Super Bowl and Kentucky Derby all rolled into one" in his interview with Chadband. When Manchester defeated Milwall, 3–0, Howard became the first American member of a team that had won the FA Cup. "I never thought I would have that kind of year," he told Zack McMillin for the *Commercial Appeal* (June 27, 2004). "I know by Manchester United standards, we didn't have a great year, but I'm not going to allow the tabloids to rip apart what we did. We did win the FA Cup."

At the beginning of the 2004-05 season, Howard again lost his place to Carroll, after making a number of errors that prevented United from winning two important back-to-back games—one against Bolton in the EPL and one against Lyon in the Champions League. Howard thus became Manchester's second-string goalie. "The errors were compounded because they came back to back, and that's what killed me," Howard told Ives Galarcep for the New Jersey *Herald News* (October 19, 2004). "I could have done better, mentally I could have concentrated more, but at the same time there are other goalkeepers in the EPL who have made the same mistakes I've made and gotten away with it." In Manchester, mistakes are more visible, because the players are expected to be the best, and Howard was kept out of the goals (a sports idiom meaning "goalkeeper position") for all but 17 games in the first six months of the season. Some wondered if he would leave Manchester to play on another team, but Howard rejected the idea. "I want to stay and fight for my place," he told the *Manchester Evening News* (February 16, 2005). "I am frustrated I am not playing. If you aren't playing and you are enjoying it, then there is something wrong with you! But in terms of staying and fighting for my place, it is an easy one—I am going to fight. It would be easy to leave, but it would be a kind of cowardice." In March 2005 he took up the first-string goalie position again. He did not succeed in keeping it, however. During the summer Alex Ferguson signed Edwin van der Sar, an experienced Dutch international goalkeeper, and made him the starting goalkeeper. Still, Manchester remains committed to developing Howard's talent: the team has extended Howard's contract to keep him in Manchester until 2009. His standing on the team aside, Howard, the first American to play for the world-famous Manchester United, remains an idol among soccer enthusiasts in the U.S. In 2006 his face will adorn the cover of the video game *World Tour Soccer 2006* for PlayStation®2.

Howard divides his time between England and Germantown, a suburb of Memphis, Tennessee, where he bought a house in the summer of 2004 to be near the family of his wife, Laura, whom he married in 2003. Living in the Memphis area offers Howard some relief from the attention he receives in England, where soccer stars are among the most sought-after celebrities. In Memphis, as Zack McMillin explained, Howard "can stroll through a mall without hundreds of eyes suffocating him.

When Tim and Laura tool around town in their old Nissan Maxima, they do not encounter carloads of people pointing at them at stoplights." As Howard told McMillin during a vacation after his first season with the United, he can do in Germantown "all the stuff I can't do in England. Just hanging out, enjoying time with my family. That kind of stuff gets invaded over there."

—A.R.

Suggested Reading: (Memphis, Tennessee) *Commercial Appeal* C p1 June 27, 2004, with photo; (Liverpool) *Daily Post* p34+ Aug. 12, 2003, with photo; (London) *Evening Standard* p81 May 21, 2004; *New York Times* New Jersey edition XIV p4 July 20, 2003, with photo; *Sports Illustrated* p60 Aug. 11, 2003, with photos

Alex Wong/Getty Images

Huckabee, Mike

Aug. 24, 1955– Governor of Arkansas (Republican)

Address: Office of the Governor, State Capitol, Rm. 250, Little Rock, AR 72201-1088

Since 1874, in the midst of Reconstruction in the southern United States, Arkansas has had only three Republican governors among the 40 who have served in that post. One of the three is the state's current governor, Mike Huckabee, who assumed the position in 1996, when, as lieutenant governor, he succeeded Governor Jim Guy Tucker after Tucker's resignation. In 1998 Huckabee was elected in his own right; he won reelection four years later. (The state's 1993 term-limits law bars him from running for a third term.) Huckabee began his professional life in the Southern Baptist ministry, serving as a pastor for a total of about eight years. For two years he headed the Arkansas State Baptist Convention, which represents the largest religious denomination in the state (with upwards of 500,000 adherents). Before seeking political office he also worked in the communications industry. In his first term as governor, he persuaded Arkansans to approve a $785 million state-bond measure to generate funds for repairing the state's woefully neglected roads and highways. He has also helped to make health insurance available to tens of thousands of Arkansas's children who would otherwise lack the benefits of such coverage. He has strived, with measurable success, to improve the academic skills of schoolchildren from kindergarten through eighth grade by means of state-supported educational programs. As the chairman of the Education Commission of the States since 2004, he has stressed the vital role of the arts in the education and development of well-rounded citizens.

Huckabee is the author or co-author of four books: *Character Is the Issue: How People with Integrity Can Revolutionize America* (1997); *Living Beyond Your Lifetime: How to be Intentional About the Legacy You Leave* (2000); *Kids Who Kill: Confronting Our Culture of Violence* (1998), written after two boys, one 11 and the other 13, shot and killed four children and a teacher and wounded 10 other people at a middle school in Jonesboro, Arkansas; and *Quit Digging Your Grave with a Knife and Fork: A 12-Stop Program to End Bad Habits and Begin a Healthy Lifestyle.* Huckabee wrote the last-named book after he lost more than 100 pounds and began exercising and thus rid himself of weight-related diabetes. Once "the most prominent obese man" in Arkansas, according to National Public Radio (June 14, 2004, on-line), he has initiated statewide programs—and, as head of the National Governors Association since July 2005, promoted nationwide efforts—to improve the health of Americans. He has also joined with former Arkansas governor and U.S. president Bill Clinton in the American Heart Association's initiative to combat obesity in children. In September 2005 Ouachita Baptist University, the governor's alma mater, announced that it has tapped Huckabee to head a planned new program, the Center for Education and Public Policy, at what will be known as the Michael D. Huckabee School of Education. Huckabee will begin the job, which will be part-time, after he leaves the governor's office, in January 2007.

Michael Dale Huckabee was born on August 24, 1955 in Hope, Arkansas (the birthplace, nine years earlier, of Bill Clinton). His mother, Mae, who worked in the office of a gas company, and his father, Dorsey, a firefighter who moonlighted as an auto mechanic, raised him and his older sister, Pat, in modest circumstances. As a child, he told Richard J. Deasy for newhorizons.org (July 15, 2004, online), he was "incredibly shy" and felt "very intimidated" even to be seen in public. On the rare occasions when he attended a ball game in a stadium, for example, "I would go early and sit way up at the top so I wouldn't have to interact with anyone." He also told Deasy that such fears started to abate in junior high school, when he began to play electric guitar in bands. By his own account, as an instrumentalist and band member he also developed the discipline that countless hours of practice required, and he learned the value of teamwork.

Huckabee served on the student councils at his junior high school and at Hope High School, where he also performed in student dramatic productions. As a senior he was elected governor of Arkansas Boys State, a program that simulates the operations of local, county, and state governments. His oath of office was administered by Dale Bumpers, a Democrat who was then Arkansas's governor. Bumpers, Huckabee told Joan I. Duffy for the Memphis, Tennessee, *Commercial Appeal* (October 11, 1992), was "the first one who really encouraged me to get into politics."

Huckabee attended Ouachita Baptist University, in Arkadelphia, Arkansas, on a scholarship and earned a B.A. degree in religion, magna cum laude, in two and a half years, in 1976. Meanwhile, in 1974, he was ordained to the Southern Baptist ministry; he served as the pastor of a Baptist church in Arkadelphia in 1974 (the year he married) and 1975. In 1976 and 1977 he took classes at Southwestern Baptist Theological Seminary, in Fort Worth, Texas. During the next few years, he held jobs in television and advertising. According to *Who's Who in America*, he founded and was president of American Christian Television Systems, based in Pine Bluff, Arkansas. In 1980 he became a pastor again, this time at the Immanuel Baptist Church in Pine Bluff. He left that church in 1985 to assume the same position at the Beech Street First Baptist Church in Texarkana, Arkansas (which abuts Texarkana, Texas), in 1986. At both churches, according to the biography of him on the governor's Web site, the congregations grew under his leadership. Concurrently, from 1987 to 1992, he held the post of president of KBSC-TV, a 24-hour, ultra-high-frequency Christian family station in Texarkana. From 1989 to 1991 he was president of the Arkansas Baptist State Convention, whose purpose is to help Baptist churches carry out their evangelical missions. In 1992 Huckabee joined Cambridge Communications, a private firm in Texarkana, for which he worked until 1996.

Also in 1992, Huckabee left his position at the Beech Street church to run for the Republican nomination for the U.S. Senate seat then held by Dale Bumpers, who was up for reelection. "I almost preached myself into running for office because the thrust of my preaching ministry during all the years I've pastored churches was to say, 'If what you preach on Sunday doesn't affect the way you live on Monday, you wasted your time on Sun-

day,'" he told Joan I. Duffy. Huckabee's platform emphasized issues of government reform: term limits, the abolition of senatorial perks, and a constitutional amendment requiring a balanced federal budget. He won the Republican nomination—and widespread name recognition—but lost the general election to Bumpers, who captured 60 percent of the vote.

On December 12, 1992 Arkansas's lieutenant governor, Jim Guy Tucker, succeeded President-elect Bill Clinton as governor of Arkansas, and a special election was set to choose his successor. Traditionally, Arkansas's lieutenant governor has two primary responsibilities: to serve as acting governor whenever necessary and to moderate state legislative sessions. The post, temporarily vacated, took on added political significance before the special election, when Governor Tucker went to Washington, D.C., to attend Bill Clinton's first inauguration; during his two-day absence from Arkansas, the acting governor—the president of the Arkansas state Senate, Jerry Jewell—granted clemency to two state-prison inmates, a convicted drug dealer and a convicted murderer. Jewell's action sparked widespread public outrage and led Huckabee to announce his candidacy for the lieutenant governorship. With no other Republicans seeking the post, Huckabee ran against the Democrat, Nate Coulter, a little-known lawyer. At that time all statewide offices in Arkansas were held by Democrats; in his campaign, Huckabee spoke about the need to revive the two-party system in the state. "What's dangerous is when the only players on the field are all part of one tightly controlled group," he told the Memphis, Tennessee, *Commercial Appeal* (June 18, 1993). Targeting the religious right, he ran TV ads in which he promised to promote moral values such as "heterosexual marriages." On July 27, 1993 Huckabee captured 51 percent of the vote and the election, to become only the second Republican to serve as lieutenant governor of Arkansas in 150 years. In 1994, in a contest with Democratic state senator Charlie Cole Chaffin, he was reelected, with 59 percent of the ballots cast—the largest percentage of votes ever captured by a Republican in an Arkansas statewide election up to that date.

Huckabee was again planning a campaign for a seat in the U.S. Senate when, in August 1995, a federal grand jury indicted Governor Tucker for fraud and conspiracy in an investigation growing out of what had become known as the Whitewater scandal. The scandal involved alleged financial misdeeds related to a failed 1970s Arkansas real-estate venture in which Bill Clinton and his wife, Hillary Rodham Clinton, had been partners. On May 28, 1996 Tucker was convicted; he immediately announced that he would resign from the office of governor in seven weeks. In response, Huckabee publicly ended his bid for the Senate seat, stating at a press conference, as reported in the *New York Times* (May 31, 1996), "Duty comes ahead of personal desire. My responsibility is to lead this state as its Governor." On July 15, five minutes before his resignation was to become effective, Tucker retracted it and said that, while appealing his conviction, he would take a constitutionally legal leave of absence from the governorship. Huckabee immediately declared that if Tucker refused to step down, the legislature was duty-bound to impeach him. The state attorney general, Winston Bryant, then announced that he would file suit to force Tucker's removal from office. Within an hour Tucker agreed to resign at 6:00 p.m. that day. At 7:00 p.m. Huckabee was sworn in as Arkansas's governor, becoming the third Republican to head the state in 122 years.

In terms of average per capita income, Arkansas is the second poorest state in the union, after Mississippi. Among its residents (about 2,673,400 people in 2000), more than 17 percent live in poverty—a rate significantly higher than the national rate (about 12 percent) and greater than those of every state except New Mexico and Mississippi. The percentage of children living in poverty (about 28 percent) is also among the highest in the nation. During the nearly two years remaining before the next scheduled gubernatorial election, Huckabee signed into law a bill called ARKids First, which provides health insurance for children whose families' incomes are too high to qualify them for Medicaid but too low to enable them to afford ordinary insurance. Thanks to ARKids First, as the governor reported in his radio address of January 1, 2005 (on-line), between 1996 and 2002 "the percentage of uninsured children in Arkansas dropped from 19.4 percent to 11 percent. . . . About 50,000 more children have health insurance today than in 1996."

On another front, by obtaining funds to help welfare recipients find permanent jobs, Huckabee "reduced the welfare rolls in the state by almost 50 percent," according to his official Web site; his expanded workforce-education programs have also helped people already employed, by enabling them to improve their job-related skills and knowledge. Huckabee also obtained increases in state funds for college scholarships. He spearheaded the push for an addition to the state constitution (Amendment 75) that requires one-eighth of one percent of the money collected through the state sales tax to be dedicated to activities or projects of the state Game and Fish Commission, the Department of Parks and Tourism, the Department of Arkansas Heritage, and the Keep Arkansas Beautiful Commission.

In the 1998 campaign for the governorship, Huckabee ran against the Republican Bill Bristow, a high-profile lawyer. Bristow adopted a negative approach, claiming first that Huckabee did not believe in equal pay for women and later that he had used taxpayers' money for personal use. The governor, by contrast, maintained that he was not like other politicians. "Arkansans are weary of politics in general and of negative politics in particular. We have a positive vision for Arkansas, and that is

what I plan to focus on," he told James Jefferson for the Associated Press (November 2, 1998). Huckabee won reelection with 60 percent of the vote—a greater percentage than that of any other Republican gubernatorial candidate in state history.

During Huckabee's first full term as governor, in an action unusual for Arkansans, who had long been leery of raising money for state projects by means of government bonds, voters approved a $785 million state-bond measure to generate funds for the repair of Arkansas's roads, deemed the worst in the nation in surveys conducted by the Surface Transportation Policy Project. Huckabee also oversaw the establishment of statewide reading and math programs that aim to strengthen the reading and math skills of schoolchildren: Smart Start, for students in kindergarten through fourth grade, and Smart Steps, for those in fifth through eighth grades, respectively. According to the governor's Web site, "student scores on standardized tests have risen steadily since the creation" of the "Smart" programs. Huckabee successfully pushed for a law that would funnel the whole of Arkansas's share of the $206 billion national tobacco settlement (signed in 1998 by tobacco companies, 46 state attorneys general, and representatives of five U.S. territories) into health-related initiatives rather than into a general fund, as many other states have done. In addition, he took steps to rid the state government of corruption—in particular, the long practice of awarding state contracts without competitive bidding to businesses owned by legislators or their friends or members of their families. (In 1997, for example, the public learned that such a contract, valued at $3.3 million, for the provision of legal representation to children involved in custody cases, had been handed to a state representative, a lobbyist's wife, and a Little Rock lawyer.) Toward that end, Huckabee hired Bill Hardin, a former FBI agent, to supervise the operation of a new government hotline for reports of fraud and abuse. Within a little more than a month, the hotline had received more than 600 calls. Information gleaned from some of them led to the indictment and conviction of two former Arkansas state senators and eight other state officials on felony charges of racketeering, money laundering, and mail fraud.

Huckabee's reelection to a second full term in 2002, which many had assumed was a foregone conclusion, became far from certain after his wife, Janet Huckabee, emerged as the Republican candidate for Arkansas secretary of state. As David M. Halbfinger explained for the *New York Times* (October 31, 2002, on-line), the Arkansas secretary of state is the state's chief elections officer and is the executive who controls the use of the capitol building; as such, he or she wields considerable power. Many voters expressed uneasiness at the prospect of a husband and wife in control of so much of the state's business. Many also criticized Janet Huckabee for taking advantage of her position as the governor's wife—for example, by traveling to campaign events in a state-owned car and plane with government employees at the controls. Moreover, the governor's Democratic opponent, Jimmie Lou Fisher, a Democrat who for 22 years had served in the largely figurehead position of state treasurer, proved to be a far more formidable candidate than had been anticipated. Fisher drew many voters away from Huckabee by attacking him, in televised ads, for granting clemency to dangerous criminals (among them a rapist who allegedly committed a murder while on parole) and for failing to prevent a multimillion-dollar cost overrun on the installation of a computer system designed to link all state agencies. But on Election Day Huckabee prevailed, with 53 percent of the vote. (His wife was defeated.)

In 2003 a state court ruled that the formula used to allocate funds to Arkansas's public schools was unfair and unconstitutional and ordered the government to come up with a more equitable scheme. Despite much opposition in rural parts of Arkansas, Huckabee oversaw the consolidation of some of the state's smaller school districts, saving money that was then allocated to previously underfunded districts. (As of October 2005, the issue of inequities in school funding was again being considered in state courts.)

Also in 2003 the then–47-year-old, 280-pound Huckabee, who had been pudgy as a child and obese as an adult, learned from his physician that he had developed diabetes. The doctor warned him that if he did not lose weight and begin exercising, he would probably die before his 60th birthday. After months of restricting his intake to 800 calories daily (which included a nutritional drink) and unlimited quantities of vegetables, the five-foot 11-inch Huckabee began exercising. In his book *Quit Digging Your Grave with a Knife and Fork*, he described the steps he took to become physically fit. In March 2005 he completed the Little Rock marathon in four hours 38 minutes. His experience inspired him to launch the Healthy Arkansas program, which requires schools to determine each pupil's body-mass index and then inform the child's parents or guardians as to whether he or she is underweight, overweight, or obese or has what is considered a medically acceptable weight. In addition, Huckabee has introduced incentives for state employees to improve their health. For example, rather than having breaks for smoking, they may devote up to 30 minutes of the workday to exercising.

In the aftermath of Hurricane Katrina, in September 2005, Huckabee ordered that state funds be used to provide shelter to some 60,000 evacuees from neighboring Mississippi and Louisiana; a second wave of evacuees arrived later, from Texas, to escape another hurricane, named Rita. The governor also dispatched members of the Arkansas National Guard to help out in hurricane-devastated areas of Louisiana and Mississippi and helped to coordinate the efforts of state agencies at the Arkansas Pharmacists Association to provide free prescription drugs and access to dialysis machines to people displaced by the storms.

For his achievements in providing greater medical coverage for children and improving his state's educational systems, *Governing* named Huckabee among eight others as winners of the magazine's 2005 Public Officials of the Year Awards. Huckabee is a former chairman of the Interstate Oil and Gas Compact Commission (a 37-state coalition that proposes energy-related policies to the U.S. Congress), the Southern Governors' Association, the Southern International Trade Council, and the Council of State Governments. Currently, he is chairman of the National Governors Association, the Education Commission of the States, and the Southern Regional Education Board and state co-chairman of the Delta Regional Authority (a federal-state partnership for fostering economic development in 240 poor counties or parishes in eight states). Huckabee and his wife, the former Janet McCain, who have been married since 1974, have three adult children: John Mark, David, and Sarah. In his leisure time the governor enjoys fishing, reading, and playing bass guitar with the band Capitol Offense. The eight-member group has opened at concerts for Willie Nelson and Dionne Warwick, and they performed during Inauguration Day events for President George W. Bush in 2001 and 2005.

—H.T./M.H.

Suggested Reading: ediets.com (on-line) Oct. 12, 2005; Governor Huckabee's Web side; (Memphis, Tennessee) *Commercial Appeal* A p1+ Oct. 11, 1992, with photo; *New York Times* (on-line) Aug. 10, 2005; newhorizons.org July 15, 2004; *Runner's World* p82+ Apr. 2005; Huckabee, Mike. *Quit Digging Your Grave with a Knife and Fork*, 2005; *Who's Who in America*

Selected Books: *Kids Who Kill: Confronting Our Culture of Violence*, 1998; *Living Beyond Your Lifetime: How to be Intentional About the Legacy You Leave*, 2000; *Quit Digging Your Grave with a Knife and Fork: A 12-Stop Program to End Bad Habits and Begin a Healthy Lifestyle*, 2005

Ifill, Gwen

(EYE-ful)

Sep. 29, 1955– Broadcast journalist

Address: Washington Week, WETA-TV, 2275 South Quincy St., Arlington, VA 22206

"I always knew I wanted to be a journalist," Gwen Ifill said for the Web site of the Public Broadcasting Service (PBS), "and my first love was newspapers. But public broadcasting provides the best of both worlds—combining the depth of newspapering with the immediate impact of broadcast television." Since 1999 Ifill has served as the moderator

Courtesy of Lee Banville, editor in chief, *Online NewsHour*

Gwen Ifill

and managing editor of *Washington Week in Review*, PBS's longest-running public-affairs program, and as a senior correspondent for the *NewsHour with Jim Lehrer*, which broadcasts on the network each weeknight. In joining *Washington Week in Review*, she became the first woman and the first person of color to host the show. *Washington Week in Review* was first broadcast locally, from WETA Studios in Washington, D.C., on February 23, 1967; a few months after its debut, the show began airing over the Eastern Educational Network, a group of 14 stations located between Washington, D.C., and Maine, and in January 1969 it became the first local program to air on the newly launched PBS. Thus Ifill became the first African-American woman to host a political television talk show that reached a national audience. Prior to joining PBS, Ifill worked as a print journalist for the *Washington Post* and the *New York Times*, among other newspapers, and she served for five years beginning in 1994 as the chief congressional and political correspondent for NBC News. Ifill has been praised for projecting a mix of candor and grace on camera. "Gwen is blunt, down-to-earth and dogged. She's not a cookie-cutter journalist," the media critic Howard Kurtz told *People* (December 11, 2000). On October 5, 2004 Ifill moderated the vice-presidential debate between the incumbent, Richard B. Cheney, a Republican, and John Edwards, a Democratic U.S. senator from North Carolina.

The fifth of six children, Gwen Ifill was born in the New York City borough of Queens on September 29, 1955. Her father, O. Urcille Ifill, who emigrated from Panama, was a pastor in a succession of African Methodist Episcopal churches; in the *Washington Post* (October 1, 1999), Howard Kurtz

described him as "a black nationalist who instilled racial pride in his six children." Her mother, Eleanor Ifill, a homemaker, was born in Barbados. "They were very strict disciplinarians," Ifill told *People*. "The church was like a force in our home. My dad was the preacher, but my mom was the preacher's wife. And we were the preacher's kids. All the time." Ifill has said that her interest in journalism was rooted partially in her parents' demand that their children gather each night in front of the television to watch a national newscast; the *Huntley-Brinkley Report*, on NBC, is one of the news programs she can remember taking an interest in as a child. "We read afternoon papers in our house everyday," she said in an interview posted on the African-American Public Relations Collective (AAPRC) Web site. "We sat down and watched the evening news together every night and I lived, in my childhood, through amazing times with the assassinations of President Kennedy, Robert Kennedy and Martin Luther King as well as the Vietnam War. When you live through times like that you pay close attention." At an early age, intrigued by the news and interested in writing, Ifill decided she wanted to work for a newspaper.

Throughout Ifill's childhood, due to the transitory nature of her father's work, her family moved frequently, living in several different cities in New England and along the eastern seaboard. "We were very conscious of the fact that we didn't have any money," Ifill told Kurtz. "I make more money in a week than my father made in a year." Ifill spent her high-school years living with her family in federally subsidized housing in the Buffalo, New York, area. (Later, when she was a journalist covering the Department of Housing and Urban Development, it occurred to her that she may have been the only reporter on that assignment to have lived in public housing.)

Ifill attended Simmons College, a women's school in Boston, Massachusetts, where she majored in communications studies, receiving a B.A. degree in 1977. During that time she interned briefly for a local television station but did not have a good experience there. She told AAPRC, "No one is more shocked than me that I turned up in television in the end." While at Simmons Ifill formed a relationship with a professor, Alden Poole, who had worked for many years as a newspaperman in Boston. During classes Poole sometimes shared stories about the newsrooms where he had worked, "which to me was incredibly romantic—the idea of what happens in a newsroom and how news gets covered . . . ," as Ifill recalled for the Web site of Harvard University's School of Public Health. "And it was because of him that I had my idea of newspapering, and my love of newspapering confirmed, that this was a place where I could do this." Poole helped Ifill to land an internship at the *Boston Herald American*, where he had worked. The staff, whom Ifill described as "old white guys, frankly," had "never seen anything like me—a college-educated black woman," Ifill recalled for the

Harvard Web site. "And they didn't know how to deal with me." While interning at the *Herald American*, she received an anonymous note containing a racial slur. The newspaper's editors not only expressed outrage over the act but hired Ifill following her graduation. "And I had Alden Poole in my head saying, 'Ah, you can do it. Just go in there and show 'em, give 'em what for,'" she stated for the Harvard Web site. "And because he didn't put those limitations on me that I was talking about, and because it was always demonstrated what the possibilities were, I felt the echo throughout my career."

Ifill worked as a reporter with the *Herald American* from 1977 to 1980, covering politics extensively. "I began to appreciate . . . how the decision that's made by two squabbling lawmakers can affect whether your kid gets to go to the right school or not," she told the AAPRC interviewer. "There was always a direct connection to me between political maneuvering and people's lives and I tried never to lose sight of that." In 1981 Ifill began covering City Hall as a reporter for the *Baltimore Evening Sun*. Also during that time she made her first television appearance, on a Maryland Public Television panel show called *Maryland Newswrap*. She found herself comfortable in the format and soon became a regular on the show. In 1984 she joined the *Washington Post* as a political reporter. She stayed there for seven years, assigned at first to cover suburban Maryland politics and later promoted to the national news desk, where she wrote about the U.S. Senate. In 1988 the *Post* sent Ifill to cover her first presidential campaign. Assigned to the campaigns of the civil rights leader Jesse Jackson, who was seeking the Democratic nomination, and Pat Robertson, a former televangelist vying to become the Republican nominee, Ifill was exposed to, and reported on, a broad range of political ideologies. She told AAPRC, "The more you go out on campaigns with different kinds of candidates who attract different kinds of people, the more your presumptions [change] about what people of a certain state think and what people of a certain age think. They're all stripped away and it gives you a better sense of America."

Ifill remained in the Washington, D.C., area when she was hired by the *New York Times* in 1991 as a congressional correspondent. She had turned down a position with the *Times* a few years earlier, feeling that the offer did not represent a significant enough career advance. A year after she joined the paper, her editors gave her the opportunity to choose which candidate she would cover for the upcoming presidential election. "I had learned from previous campaigns, that if you're going to spend a lot of time on the road with somebody, it's got to be somebody who looks like they might be interesting," she told AAPRC. "I'd spent a lot of time in [1988] with Jesse Jackson who exhausted me and was so stressful to cover. I had no idea that Bill Clinton would be even more stressful. . . . I was just looking for a good story." Keeping to a "grueling" schedule, as she put it, Ifill followed Clinton, the Democratic governor of Arkansas, as he campaigned across the country. Following the election, in which Clinton defeated the incumbent, George H. W. Bush, to become the country's 42d president, Ifill became the newspaper's White House correspondent.

The new position coincided with a difficult time in Ifill's life. Having endured the loss of her father in 1991, she made frequent visits to her mother, who was diagnosed with cancer in 1993; Ifill arranged for her mother to live at an assisted-care facility in the Washington area. The strain of dealing with that situation seemed to affect her ability to cover the White House, and her editors removed her from the prestigious beat. Ifill's mother died in 1994.

Meanwhile, having made appearances on NBC's program *Meet the Press* and on the PBS show *Washington Week in Review*, Ifill had grown increasingly at ease with the medium of television and become familiar to viewers of national TV news programs. After Tim Russert, the moderator of *Meet the Press*, urged her to make a permanent switch from print to television, Ifill began meeting with a voice coach; in addition, she worked tirelessly to learn the nuances of writing news copy for broadcast. Before very long, offers poured in from each of the major television networks. "When that happened I began to think maybe God's hand is in this. When this many people come at you with the same kind of pitch, who am I to be such a coward that I don't try it?" she told AAPRC. In 1994 NBC News hired Ifill as its chief congressional and political correspondent. In that capacity she covered such subjects as the congressional budget gridlock in 1995; the so-called Whitewater investigation into alleged financial misdeeds on the part of Bill Clinton and his wife, Hillary Rodham Clinton, dating back to the former governor's time in Arkansas; and Bill Clinton's impeachment hearings, following charges that he had lied under oath about an extramarital affair. During Ifill's tenure with NBC, from 1994 to 1999, her reports appeared frequently on the *Today* show, the cable-news network MSNBC, and *NBC Nightly News*, then anchored by Tom Brokaw.

In 1999 executives at the local public broadcasting station in Washington, D.C., WETA, eager to bring to the long-running news-panel program *Washington Week in Review* a more lively exchange of opinions, offered Ifill a position as the show's moderator. Over the course of its 38-year history, the show has featured weekly appearances by such respected journalists as Gloria Borger of *U.S. News & World Report*, David Broder of the *Washington Post*, Mara Liasson of National Public Radio, Alan Murray of the *Wall Street Journal*, and Steve Roberts and Thomas L. Friedman of the *New York Times*. *Washington Week* had recently been moderated by Ken Bode, who was fired along with the show's producer in an effort to overhaul PBS's core schedule and increase its appeal to viewers.

Earlier in the year, when the position was first offered to Ifill, who had appeared intermittently on the show as a panelist beginning in 1992, she turned it down. The producers' second offer included the added title and duties of senior political correspondent for the *NewsHour with Jim Lehrer*. "If it had only been *The NewsHour* or if it had only been *Washington Week*, neither would have felt, by itself, good enough reason to leave [NBC]," she told AAPRC. "But when they said you can have your own show and be part of *The NewsHour*, it seemed like way too much candy in the jar." In accepting the position, Ifill became the first member of a minority group and the first woman to host the program as well as the first African-American woman to host a prominent, nationally televised political talk show. *Washington Week* is currently carried (on Friday evenings at 8:00 p.m. on the East Coast) by 90 percent of the 306 PBS stations around the U.S. and reaches 97 percent of U.S. television households. (Ifill agreed to appear periodically on NBC news programs for another year to cover the presidential election.)

The producers of *Washington Week in Review* designed an ad campaign for Ifill's October 1, 1999 debut that declared, "TV's Voice of Reason Has a New Face." Meanwhile, Ifill worked to avoid alienating the show's loyal viewers, who had come to appreciate *Washington Week* for the quality of its discussion. She began her first installment as host by saying, according to a PBS transcript (on-line), "We promise you three things: smart conversation, hands-on reporting and the same fair and lively analysis you've come to expect from us on Friday nights for 33 years." She quickly won critical approval for her intelligent and informed interviewing techniques and her calm and personable demeanor. Conducting extended on-air interviews and serving as a substitute anchor, Ifill also serves as a senior correspondent for the *NewsHour with Jim Lehrer*. In that position she has frequently contributed taped "Newsmaker" interviews with such world leaders as Prime Minister Tony Blair of Great Britain and Tariq Aziz, the former deputy prime minister of Iraq.

On October 5, 2004 Ifill moderated the vice-presidential debate in Cleveland, Ohio, between the incumbent, Richard B. Cheney, a Republican, and U.S. senator John Edwards of North Carolina, who was running on the Democratic ticket with Massachusetts senator John Kerry. She became the second black woman to moderate a presidential or vice-presidential debate. (On October 15, 1992 Carole Simpson of ABC News had become the first black woman to do so, moderating the "town-hall" style debate held by George H. W. Bush, Bill Clinton, and Ross Perot.) Ifill told the AAPRC interviewer, "It was a fabulous opportunity to do something that put everything I've trained to do into one place. . . . The hardest part was the weeks leading up to it as I prepared, 'cause the one thing you don't want to do is embarrass yourself in front of 45 million people." Assessments of Ifill's perfor-

mance as moderator were mixed, with some critics pointing to her failure to ask clear and relevant questions.

One of the most prominent African-American women working on television, Ifill has shared her views on the progress made in recruiting members of minority groups for positions in broadcasting. She told the AAPRC interviewer, "Sadly, I believe we are close to a failing grade, especially on the national stage. There are few of us on the air, but fewer people of color in the places where the camera does not go—making the editorial decisions in newsrooms and producing the stories on the evening newscasts. We still have a long way to go." She said to Gregory M. Lamb for the *Christian Science Monitor* (May 26, 2000), "I can't stress how important it is that young people know that anything is possible for them. . . . If it means that a little black girl sitting in her living room somewhere sees me on TV and thinks 'maybe I could do that,' then I feel like my day's work is done. I want to be that kind of example, and I'm very conscious of it and happy for it."

According to a profile of Ifill that appears on the PBS Web site, she has received more than a dozen honorary degrees. In addition, she has served as chairman of the committee for the Robert F. Kennedy Memorial Journalism Awards, which honor outstanding reporting in the area of problems of the disadvantaged. She also sits on the boards of the Harvard University Institute of Politics, the Committee to Protect Journalists, and the University of Maryland's Phillips Merrill College of Journalism and is a member of the National Association of Black Journalists.

Friends have described Ifill as an unusually competitive but friendly person. The journalist has said that nearly three decades' worth of constant pressure to meet deadlines is the main reason she is unmarried. Her Washington home is reportedly filled with African art. She is known to be an avid fan of the Washington Mystics, a team in the Women's National Basketball Association, and she frequently attends the Mystics' home games at the MCI Center, in downtown Washington. In addition, Ifill has described herself as an able dancer. A devoutly religious woman, she is a practicing African Methodist Episcopalian. Of her success, she said to Howard Kurtz, "I think God is watching out for me."

—D.F.

Suggested Reading: African-American Public Relations Collective Web site; *Current* (on-line) Mar. 8, 1999; *People* p93 Dec. 11, 2000, with photos; *Washington Post* C p1 Oct. 1, 1999

Selected Television Shows: *NBC Nightly News*, 1994–99; *The NewsHour with Jim Lehrer*, 1999– ; *Washington Week in Review*, 1999–

Courtesy of Ilitch Holdings

Ilitch, Michael

July 20, 1929– Founder of Little Caesars Pizza; owner of the Detroit Red Wings and the Detroit Tigers

Address: Little Caesars Enterprises, 2211 Woodward Ave., Detroit, MI 48201-3400

Pizza may now be a staple of the American diet, but in the late 1950s, it was viewed as little more than a snack food for teenagers. The notion of making a living, much less a fortune, selling it seemed foolish to many at the time, but Michael Ilitch ignored such critics when he opened his first Little Caesars pizzeria, in 1959. Today Little Caesars is the fourth-largest pizza chain in the United States, behind Pizza Hut, Domino's, and Papa John's; it has franchises on five continents. As chairman of Little Caesars Enterprises and its parent company, Ilitch Holdings, Ilitch was ranked 389 on the 2004 *Forbes* list of the 400 richest Americans; his net worth is reported to be $750 million. Although he was unable to fulfill his boyhood dream of playing major-league baseball, Ilitch did perhaps the next best thing in 1992, when he purchased the Detroit Tigers. Since 1982 he has also owned the Detroit Red Wings, one of the National Hockey League's most successful and popular teams. A dedicated supporter of his hometown, Detroit, Michigan, Ilitch has been a force in its revitalization, donating more than $200 million to downtown renewal projects.

Michael Ilitch was born on July 20, 1929 and grew up in Detroit. His father, Sotir, a Macedonian immigrant, was a tool-and-die worker at Chrysler. Michael's decision to pursue a career in baseball did not please him, and when the aspiring athlete broke his ankle while playing, Sotir threw him out of the house. After he persuaded a nightclub owner from Detroit's West Side to let him use the club's kitchen in return for a percentage of his sales, Ilitch spent a summer making pizzas. Shortly thereafter, his ankle having healed, he resumed playing baseball. Despite a .340 batting average, unusually high for a shortstop, Ilitch was never called up to the major leagues, and a knee injury he suffered later forced him to give up the sport. He worked for a cement company and sold dinnerware and aluminum awnings door-to-door. He then opened a thriving awning business with two partners, who later bought out his one-third share.

Meanwhile, in 1954, Ilitch had met Marian, an airline reservationist, on a blind date. The couple soon married, and they combined their $10,000 savings with a $15,000 bank loan to open a pizzeria in a strip mall in Garden City, Michigan, in 1959. Ilitch wanted to name the restaurant Pizza Treat, but Marian insisted that they use her nickname for him. "We were just married, and he was my hero, my Caesar," she recalled for *Nation's Restaurant News* (January 1995). "But he hadn't accomplished anything yet, so he was my little Caesar." As more strip malls sprang up in the area, Ilitch opened additional Little Caesars stores. Following a tip from a Texas oilman, who told him the best way to make money was to have others make it for you, Ilitch sold his first franchise (the fourth Little Caesars) in 1962. Between 1980 and 1986, the number of stores grew from 201 to 1,000, most of them franchises. Ilitch is credited with several innovations in the pizza business, including the conveyor oven, which is more suitable for making numerous pizzas than a conventional oven, and the two-for-one pizza promotion. The company's strategy is to provide enough food for a family for under $10. "When they walk out of the store, I want them to get a hernia," Ilitch, who frequently prepares new recipes in the company's test kitchen, quipped to Adam Bryant for the *New York Times* (December 6, 1992).

A humble man known as "Mr. I" among his employees, Ilitch has said that enthusiasm in a worker is more important to him than an impressive work history; half the company's vice presidents started as hourly employees, and few people on his staff have MBAs. Bryant wrote that Ilitch and his wife "still seem to act like the proprietors of a fledging mom-and-pop business" and that Ilitch has "a playful mind willing to entertain even the most ridiculous idea." Little Caesars has been voted best value in America in the quick-service category 12 times in the last 13 years, according to *Restaurants & Institutions* magazine. The company experienced difficulties in the late 1990s: in 1999 the chain closed 400 outlets that were doing poorly, and sales fell from $1.65 billion in 1998 to $1.46 billion in 1999. However, the chain has experienced double-digit increases in sales each year since 2001. In a June 24, 2002 report by *Nation's Restaurant News*, Little Caesars was ranked 36th in U.S. food-service sales.

Ilitch diversified his holdings in 1982 when he purchased the Detroit Red Wings, a National Hockey League (NHL) team, for $8 million. The team, which was struggling at the time, has won four Stanley Cups (league championships) under Ilitch's ownership. Its worth increased from $184 million in 1998 to $245 million in 2003, making it the fifth-most-valuable team in the latter year, according to Forbes. The Ilitches "are willing to put up the money to ensure they have talented teams. . . . [They] have provided the resources the Red Wings need to win on a consistent basis," the longtime NHL coach Mike Keenan wrote for the Sporting News (November 2, 1998). "They continue to reinforce the team, which shows how committed they are to winning." The Red Wings are a rarity in the NHL. Inflated player salaries, unlucrative television and radio deals, and heavy taxation of Canadian teams by Canada's government have contributed to a majority of NHL teams' operating in the red. Despite his willingness to fund one of the NHL's most expensive payrolls, Ilitch voted with the league's 29 other owners to demand acceptance of a league-wide salary cap from the players union before the start of the 2004–05 season. When the union rejected that demand, the owners locked out all of their members, thus effectively ending the season before a single game was played. The dispute ended in July 2005, when players accepted a salary cap along with a host of other changes to the league's organization. The 2005–06 season got underway on October 5 for the Red Wings with a win against the St. Louis Blues, and attendance at the games has been strong.

In 1992 Ilitch bought the Detroit Tigers baseball franchise for a reported $82 million from his business rival Tom Monaghan, founder of Domino's Pizza. (The club is currently valued at $237 million.) His dismissal of the team's chairman and CEO, Jim Campbell, and president, Bo Schembechler, caused a rift between him and the Tigers' manager, Sparky Anderson. (Anderson later retired.) In a move that was popular among fans, Ilitch also rehired the longtime Tigers' broadcaster Ernie Harwell, whose contract had lapsed in 1991. Ilitch served as president of the ball club from 1992 to 2001 and remains its owner and director. He contributed $145 million to help build a new, 40,000-seat venue for the Tigers, Comerica Park, which opened in April 2000. (The total construction cost was about $295 million.) Despite his efforts, the Tigers have remained a troubled franchise. The new ballpark has had little effect on the generally poor attendance at home games. Along with the debt incurred from construction costs, the team's relatively small income keeps their total player payroll uncompetitively low. In 2004 the Tigers, who finished fourth in the American League Central Division, well out of the play-offs, spent $46.8 million on their players; the New York Yankees, a perennial contender, spent a league-leading $184.2 million. Without a competitive team, the Tigers are unlikely to see an increase in attendance and revenue.

In 1987 the Ilitches purchased the historic Fox Theatre in downtown Detroit. The largest continually operating theater in the U.S., the Fox's physical plant had been neglected for many years. The Ilitches spent $50 million to restore the building, which has also become the site of the world headquarters of Little Caesars International and two restaurants owned by Ilitch, Tres Vite and America's Pizza Cafe. The Fox is now the top-grossing theater of its size in the country. Currently, Ilitch Holdings posts annual revenues of about $900 million. The pizza business accounts for 90 percent of the company's sales, while the remaining 10 percent comes from the sports franchises, other restaurants, and theater and arena management. Among their non–pizza-related holdings are Olympia Entertainment, which ranks among the top 10 promoters worldwide, according to Pollstar, a concert trade publication; Blue Line Distributing, a nationwide provider of restaurant equipment and supplies; Uptown Entertainment, which operates two movie theaters in Birmingham, Michigan; Hockeytown Café; the comedy club Second City-Detroit; Little Foxes, an upscale gift and china shop; and concessions in Cobo Arena (a venue for concerts and sports events), Joe Louis Arena (where the Red Wings play), and Comerica Park.

The Little Caesars Love Kitchen Foundation, which the Ilitches established in 1985, has fed more than 1.5 million needy people through its mobile pizza restaurant. The organization received a Volunteer Action Award from President Bill Clinton in 1994. Ilitch also founded Ilitch Charities for Children (ICC), a nonprofit organization dedicated to improving the lives of children in the areas of health, education, and recreation. In April 2002 ICC announced the creation of the Little Caesars AAA Hockey Scholarship program, which awards outstanding high-school athletes $5,000 scholarships to the colleges of their choice. Ilitch sponsors the Little Caesars Amateur Hockey League, the largest amateur hockey league in the United States. Ilitch Holdings sponsors the Little Caesars Amateur Baseball Federation and is a corporate partner of the Michigan High School Athletic Association, underwriting the Good Sports Are Winners! sportsmanship program. All told, more than 17,000 children currently participate in Little Caesars–sponsored sports programs in the Detroit area.

Ilitch received an Ellis Island Medal of Honor from the National Ethnic Coalition of Organizations. His wife, Marian, who is currently secretary-treasurer of Little Caesars and vice chairwoman of Ilitch Holdings, was ranked first in Working Woman magazine's 1994 "Top 50 Women in Business" list. In April 2005 Marian Ilitch acquired a majority stake in Detroit's MotorCity Casino and announced plans to develop a hotel along with a more permanent home for the casino itself. The Ilitches have seven children, three of whom work for the family business. In 2004 their daughter Denise Ilitch resigned from the company after a power struggle with her brother Christopher, who was made president and chief executive officer in July. Denise, an attorney, is now a partner in the Detroit firm of Clark Hill.

—K.E.D.

Suggested Reading: Ilitch Holdings Web site; *Nation's Restaurant News* p92 Sep. 21, 1992, with photo, p105 Jan. 1995, with photo; *New York Times* III p8 Dec. 6, 1992, with photo

---

Jackson, Michael

Mar. 7, 1942– Writer; beer connoisseur

Address: c/o DK Publishing, 375 Hudson St., New York, NY 10014

Known as the preeminent authority on beer, Michael Jackson has helped introduce many lovers of the beverage to beers whose flavors and textures he considers to be as complex and interesting as those of wine. His many books on the subject have sold over three million copies in 15 languages, and thanks in part to his efforts, what might be called "endangered" beers—such as Oatmeal Stout, Imperial Stout, cranberry lambics, and rye beers, which were previously enjoyed only among a rarefied group of connoisseurs—are being consumed in larger quantities. "I would say he is probably the singly most influential person about beer in the world," Charles Finkel, the owner of Merchant du Vin, a major importer of beer and wine, told Mitchell Landsberg for the Associated Press (May 17, 1992). Since Jackson began writing about beer, in the 1970s, the number of microbreweries in the United States has risen significantly, a development for which he takes partial credit. "He's done more to revive this industry than just about anybody," Charlie Papazian, then-president of the American Association of Brewers, told Gene Sloan for *USA Today* (November 4, 1993). While many people's idea of beer still does not extend far beyond Budweiser or Miller, there is a growing interest in the more complex beers whose 50-plus styles Jackson champions. "Remember that a beer is intended to have flavor," Jackson said, as quoted by Travis E. Poling for the *San Antonio Express-News* (June 18, 1997). "Not all beer is meant to have after you mow the lawn."

Part of what Jackson sees as his mission is to convince people that good beers are appropriate to consume with certain meals and can bring out the flavors of food, as is true of wines. "Some foods are perhaps less well suited to wine than to beer," he wrote for the *Washington Post* (November 16, 1983). "Shellfish goes well with either but sushi, for example, has a happy relationship with a light Japanese or American beer. The same is true of any spicy Oriental food. Naturally enough, smoked meats and sausages are perfectly accompanied by

German beers. Perhaps the happiest combination of all is red meat, especially roast beef, and English pale ale." Jackson, like many beer experts, is frustrated by the lack of interesting beer lists in most restaurants. He has written that beer is generally less appreciated than wine in part because it seems less exotic. As he wrote for the London *Independent* (November 29, 1997), "We drink more wine than ever, partly because it enjoys the glamour of coming from somewhere else. We drink less beer than ever, partly because it comes from here. We take it for granted."

Of Russian, Lithuanian, and Jewish descent, Michael Jackson was born on March 7, 1942 in Leeds, in Yorkshire, England. His father was a truck driver. At the age of 16 Jackson began writing for newspapers. "I've covered every type of story you could imagine," he told Sloan. Jackson worked for years as a general-news reporter and subsequently (and later concurrently) as a television journalist, covering current events in London. In the early 1970s, realizing that he had an unusually good memory for the tastes and other qualities of different beers, he began to write about the subject, inspired by the work of the wine journalist Hugh Johnson. "Journalists used to drink more and talk about it more. . . . I thought why not write about it. People wrote about wine but not beer," he told Kathy Borlik for the Indiana *South Bend Tribune* (November 10, 1994). The publication of Jackson's first articles on beer coincided with the Campaign for Real Ale, a grassroots project in England dedicated to preserving traditional beers with complex tastes in an age of mass-marketed brews. (There are dozens of varieties of beers, each with its own makeup of malt, hops, water, and yeast. Most mass-produced beers are based on the Pilsner lager style and are weaker both in flavor and alcohol content than other beers.)

Jackson's first book, *English Pub*, appeared in 1976. He followed it up the next year with *World Guide to Beer: The Brewing Styles, the Brands, the Countries*, the first well-known book to organize the world's beers according to style (for example, porter, lager, wheat, stout); a second edition of the book was published in 1982. Meanwhile, in 1978, Jackson had made his first visit to the United States, beginning his effort to convince Americans—through beer tastings and events at breweries—that beer should be considered more than an alcoholic soft drink. "Can you imagine a world of wine in which every bottle (or jug) contained a generic chablis?" he wrote in *The Good Beer Book* (1997), as quoted by Jack Schnedler for the *Arkansas Democrat-Gazette* (August 31, 1997). "Until a decade or two ago, the chablis jug wines of the beer world were everywhere. In America, scarcely anything else existed. A few discerning souls criticized the big American brewers for making bland beer, but the most famous imports were not, in truth, much different, despite the respect they received." Jackson published the *Pocket Bartender's Guide* in 1979 and the *Pocket Guide to Beer* in

Michael Jackson

Courtesy of Running Press Book Publishers

1982. That book has been published in six subsequent editions, as the *Simon and Schuster Pocket Guide to Beer* and, later, as the *Running Press Pocket Guide to Beer*. In her review for the *New York Times* (October 1, 1986) of the second edition of the book, Florence Fabricant called it "an indispensable reference for travel to such important brewing countries as England, Belgium and Germany."

The *New World Guide to Beer*, a radically altered version of Jackson's *World Guide to Beer*, appeared in 1988. In the book Jackson described the beers of 14 countries (mostly in Europe), their origins and brewing processes, and instructions for serving them, and provided histories of both famous and little-known breweries, pubs, and bars. In an article for the British magazine the *Economist* (December 24, 1988), a writer commented that the book is "refreshing. . . . By and large, Mr. Jackson eschews the fanciful pathetic fallacies of his vinous counterparts in favour of a well developed palate and great enthusiasm for the task of informing the reader." In her review for the *New York Times* (February 15, 1989), Fabricant commented, "If there is romance in beer, Michael Jackson . . . has found it." The book has sold more than one million copies and has been translated into 12 languages. Also in 1988 Jackson published *World Guide to Whisky: Scotch, Irish, Canadian, Bourbon, Tennessee Sour Mash, and the Whiskies of Japan*. Two years later came the *Complete Guide to Single Malt Scotch: a Connoisseur's Guide to the Single Malt Whiskeys of Scotland*, which has since been published in three other editions. For the book, Jackson ranked about 200 single-malt scotches on a 100-point scale. Some of Jackson's readers

were displeased that he had written about a subject other than beer. "My readers are real zealots," Jackson told Landsberg. "Some of them said, 'Have you gotten bored with beer? Are you deserting it?' And what I've said to them is, 'Look, I'm writing about beer that's been distilled.'"

The *Beer Hunter*, a six-part television series hosted by Jackson, aired on the Discovery Channel in the United States in 1990. The series took viewers around the United States and Europe in search of the best brews. The first installment focused on the beers of Belgium, which, Jackson told Calvin Ahlgren for the *San Francisco Chronicle* (August 19, 1990), is "a country that treats beer like wine." He said for the same article, "One of the things I tried to do with each film is explore what beer meant. I sort of impose my own views on it, of course, but I feel I may be able to understand it better [than the general public]." Writing about the segment on California beer, Ahlgren noted, the "production values are crisp, clear and imaginative; there are beautifully cinematographed scenes. . . . The script is knowledgeable and informative without being overbearing; Jackson is your prototypical genial host, and the whole thing rolls along as an effortless piece of info-tainment." The *Beer Hunter* won the prize for best television program at the 1991 Glenfiddich Awards, which honor works about food and drink. Jackson was also named whiskey writer of the year at the ceremony. "Jackson has an ear for dialogue and an eye for unusual juxtapositions of images," Lucy Saunders wrote about the series for the *Chicago Tribune* (July 29, 1990). "His whimsical humor infuses *The Beer Hunter* with all the sparkle of a fine ale, while his professional style enlightens the viewer on the world of beer."

Jackson's book *Great Beers of Belgium: A Complete Guide and Celebration of a Unique Culture* came out in 1992 and has since been published in two other editions. Next was *Michael Jackson's Beer Companion: The World's Great Beer Styles, Gastronomy, and Traditions* (1993), whose second edition followed four years later. For that volume Jackson categorized beers by style rather than region. "We should not look at where beer comes from, but what style it comes in," he told Alan J. Wax for *Newsday* (October 6, 1993). A critic for *Publishers Weekly*, as quoted on Amazon.com, enthused, "Jackson is excellent at combining historical detail with current information about the beers and brewers in question; his organization is logical and accessible. Beautifully photographed and designed for sustained browsing as well as authoritative reference, this book will appeal to both beer tyros and more sophisticated tipplers."

Michael Jackson's Bar & Cocktail Companion: The Connoisseur's Handbook and the *Beer Hunter* CD-ROM both became available in 1995. A guide to nearly 200 American microbrews, the CD-ROM features information on each beer as well as video and audio segments (in which background sounds from a bar environment, such as conversation, clinking glasses, and the pouring of beer, can occasionally be heard). In 1996 Jackson published *Michael Jackson's Great Beers of America*. While it is in the U.S. that Jackson has found the greatest response to his work, drinkers of artisanal beers (high-quality, unique beers usually produced by small breweries) are still a tiny minority of the beer-drinking population, even among Americans. "There's this huge misunderstanding in America where if [a beer is] not big it doesn't count," he told Susan King for the *Los Angeles Times* (August 19, 1990). "Budweiser and Pabst are well-made beers like Wonder Bread is a well-made bread. American beer lovers say beers like Budweiser are awful. They're not awful. They're very bland and not very interesting."

In 1998 Jackson published *Michael Jackson's Little Book of Beer* and *Ultimate Beer*. The latter book features brief profiles of 500 of the world's top beers, with advice on when and how to drink them. "I suppose what I'm saying [with this book] is, now we've got all of these beers and some consumers know what they are stylistically—what are you doing to do with this?" he told Lee Graves for the *Richmond Times Dispatch* (October 22, 1998). William Rice commented for the *Chicago Tribune* (December 2, 1998) that *Ultimate Beer* "is just right for the curious consumer with a thirst for experimentation." Graves wrote about the book, "The beers are photographed with such voluptuous beauty they beckon like sirens. . . . Stunning presentation is only one reason I love this book. It has succinct summaries of the making of beer and its ingredients. It describes beers for different seasons, beers for different occasions, beers for quenching thirst, beers for warming the soul, beers paired with dozens of dishes and beers to use in recipes."

Jackson followed in 2000 with the publication of the *Great Beer Guide*.

That same year the beer expert launched the Michael Jackson World Beer Tour, a service that includes a monthly delivery of 12 bottles of beer from around the world that are not available in the United States, as well as a subscription to Jackson's monthly newsletter. In 2001 Jackson published *Scotland and Its Whiskies*. "Growing taste for artisanal Scotch whisky makes this an especially useful purchase, and its exquisite Highland panoramas make it a worthwhile travel guide as well," Mark Knoblauch wrote for *Booklist* (November 15, 2001), as quoted on Amazon.com. More recently, Jackson published *Whiskey: The Definitive World Guide* (2005), which offers everything that he imagined readers might want to know about whiskey, including recipes for cocktails and a detailed survey of distilleries worldwide. The book also warns traditional whiskey makers of the rising quality of Japanese whiskey, observing that the Japanese are experimenting with various approaches to production and creating whiskeys that rival traditional favorites from such places as Scotland and Kentucky.

Jackson lives in London, England. He is not married. (One source reported that he has a lived with a female companion for a dozen years.) His four refrigerators are usually packed with bottles of more than 300 kinds of beer, sent to him from around the world. When Jackson is on the road, he tastes as many as 25 different beers in a day. In order to offset the dehydrating and intoxicating effects of the alcohol he consumes each day, he drinks a great deal of water and eats between beer tastings. "Jackson can taste more flavors in a glass of beer than most people get out of an entire meal," Landsberg wrote. Jackson told Pete Szilagyi for the *Austin (Texas) American-Statesman* (May 14, 1996), "I don't believe I have any more sensitive palate or nose than anybody else does. I think it's just the practice and also perhaps the ability to verbalize what I'm finding. The sort of words you can apply to wine [tasting] you generally can apply to beer and whiskey." When visiting the U.S., usually for about five weeks at a time, Jackson goes to as many as 100 breweries in 25 states. The public beer tastings that he hosts in the U.S. draw several hundred people each. One of his favorite American beers is Anchor Steam, brewed in California, which he described in the *Pocket Guide to Beer*, as quoted by the Associated Press (May 16, 1992), as "a beer that has some of the roundness of a lager but the fruitiness of an ale, with a characteristically high natural carbonation. It is also an all-malt beer, with a very good hoppy dryness." Although Jackson has said that any number of beers might qualify as the worst in the world, he singles out the popular Mexican brew Corona Extra for that distinction, considering it weak and overpriced. "The sight of these absurd children, sort of over-rich children dumping out large amounts of money to drink this junk, it sort of gave me a good poke to say, 'Ok, well it's Corona,'" he told Justin Bachman for the *Fort Worth (Texas) Star-Telegram* (April 13, 1998). "There are plenty of other beers as boring, as cheaply made and as overpriced as Corona. But Corona's . . . almost a sort of symbol or emblem or icon."

In addition to his books about beer and spirits, Jackson wrote much of the *American Express Pocket Guide to London*, first published in 1983, and contributed heavily to the *American Express Pocket Guide to England and Wales* in 1984. In 1994 he was awarded the Mercurius Prize, presented by Prince Philippe of Belgium, for his contributions to the popularity of Belgian beers. That occasion marked the first time that the prize, given annually by the Belgian government to two foreigners who have promoted trade between Belgium and their countries, was bestowed on a writer. In 1998 the North American Guild of Beer Writers awarded Jackson a bronze medal in the "column" category at the fourth annual Quill and Tankard Awards, for a piece he wrote for *All About Beer Magazine*. For several years Jackson penned a biweekly column on beer and whiskey for the London *Independent*, and he continues to write about fine beers for many food magazines. "There is a beer snobbery," Jackson told Bryan Miller for the *New York Times* (August 19, 1990). "I might even say that I am an unapologetic and unreconstructed beer snob myself.

It's harmless snobbery, really. If it acts to the interest of more people creating discussion and more interest in beer and wines, I'm all for it. If it serves to be a barrier against it, then I'm against it."

—G.O.

Suggested Reading:Associated Press May 17, 1992; *Beer Hunter* (on-line); *Chicago Tribune* C p8 Apr. 24, 1986, with photo; *Los Angeles Times* p82 Aug. 19, 1990, with photo; (New York) *Newsday* p63 Oct. 6, 1993, with photo; *New York Times* II p35 Aug. 19, 1990, with photo; *Richmond (Virginia) Times Dispatch* D p15 Oct. 22, 1998, with photo; *San Francisco Chronicle* Sunday Datebook p45 Aug. 19 1990, with photo; *USA Today* D p6 Nov. 4, 1993, with photo

Selected Books: *English Pub*, 1976; *World Guide to Beer*, 1977; *Pocket Guide to Beer*, 1982; *New World Guide to Beer*, 1988; *World Guide to Whisky*, 1988; *Complete Guide to Single Malt Scotch*, 1990; *Great Beers of Belgium*, 1992; *Michael Jackson's Beer Companion*, 1993; *Michael Jackson's Great Beers of America*, 1996; *Ultimate Beer*, 1998; *Great Beer Guide*, 2000; *Scotland and Its Whiskies*, 2001; *Whiskey: The Definitive World Guide*, 2005

James, LeBron

Dec. 30, 1984– Basketball player

Address: Cleveland Cavaliers, One Center Court, Cleveland, OH 44115-4001

LeBron James was only a high-school junior in his native Akron, Ohio, when, in a highly unusual occurrence, *Sports Illustrated* ran his image on the cover of its February 18, 2002 issue along with the words "The Chosen One." That designation referred to his potential to be a force in the National Basketball Association (NBA), and as a forward for the Cleveland Cavaliers, he has already begun to fulfill that promise—winning rookie-of-the-year honors at the conclusion of the 2003-04 NBA season and leading his struggling team in the following year to its first winning record since 1998. James first won national attention as the star basketball attraction at the all-male preparatory school Saint Vincent–Saint Mary's, helping the Fighting Irish to capture three state basketball championships in four years; he then joined such NBA stars as Kobe Bryant, Kevin Garnett, and Jermaine O'Neal as players who made the jump to the pros directly from high school.

Many have compared James to the legendary former Chicago Bulls shooting guard Michael Jordan, whose play has long inspired the 21-year-old. Like his idol, James is the rare player who, along with

Kevin Winter/Getty Images

his raw muscle, leaping ability, and knack for scoring from a variety of angles, shows an enthusiasm for passing the ball. In addition, his six-foot eight-inch, 240-pound frame makes him an imposing player to guard in one-on-one situations. "A lot of players know how to play the game," James explained to Grant Wahl for *Sports Illustrated* (February 18, 2002), "but they really don't know how to play the game, if you know what I mean. They can put the ball in the hoop, but I see things before they even happen. . . . That's one thing I learned from watching Jordan." Discussing James's development as a basketball player, the San Antonio Spurs' head coach, Gregg Popovich, told David DuPree for *USA Today* (February 17, 2005), "His maturity, in the sense that he really understands the responsibility he has as a big-time, money basketball player to bring it every night, is what sets him apart. I think that separates him and puts him in a category with [Michael Jordan, Larry Bird, and Earvin 'Magic' Johnson], who competed every single night like that. He just seems to know all sorts of things kids just don't know."

LeBron James was born on December 30, 1984 in Akron to Gloria James, who was six months shy of graduating from Central-Hower High School on the day she gave birth to her only son. LeBron's biological father, Anthony McClelland, who has served jail sentences for various offenses, did not contribute to his son's upbringing. The responsibility of raising LeBron became more difficult for Gloria James when her mother and grandmother, who had both helped to support the young single parent, died within 18 months of each other, before LeBron was three years old. Gloria was unable to find regular work, and she and her son, who struggled financially, were forced to move frequently. "I saw drugs, guns, killings; it was crazy," James told Grant Wahl. "But my mom kept food in my mouth and clothes on my back." While in the fourth grade, James was forced to miss an excessive number of days at school. After drifting from one unstable romantic relationship to the next, Gloria James began dating Eddie Jackson when her son was still very young. Jackson has been credited with being a father figure to LeBron, and he often took the role of the family's representative after LeBron emerged during high school as a major basketball talent.

Inspired by Michael Jordan, James found solace in sports, particularly basketball and football. (At the age of four, James excelled at slam-dunking a Nerf basketball into a tiny hoop set up in his living room.) At as young as nine, he began to show signs of being an all-around player, learning to dribble and shoot with both hands to make it easier to evade on-rushing defenders on local playgrounds. As a boy James also excelled as a receiver in pee-wee-league football, scoring 19 touchdowns in only six games in his first year.

As a consequence of his stellar play on the football field, James and his mother became close friends with LeBron's coach, Frankie Walker. Walker took notice of James's increasingly worrisome school attendance and invited the boy to live with him, his wife, Pam, and their three children. James stayed for approximately 18 months in the Walkers' home, where he was given daily chores. During that time his school attendance improved,

and afterward Gloria James again assumed the responsibility of caring for her son. Later, when she had additional financial problems, the Walkers stepped in once more to care for LeBron. "Frank and Pam were great to us," Gloria James explained to Tim Rogers for the Cleveland *Plain Dealer* (February 11, 2002). "LeBron and I were fortunate in that we always had people who looked out for us, and Frank and Pam were two of them."

LeBron James forged a close relationship with Frankie Jr., the Walkers' oldest son. The two played basketball together and were joined on the local courts by four others boys—Sian Cotton, Dru Joyce III, Willie McGee, and Romeo Travis. The group often played at the Akron Jewish Community Center, under the tutelage of Keith Drambot, a former head coach at Central Michigan University. With James as their unofficial leader, the six boys earned a local reputation for their excellent play. James became adept at playing all five of the standard basketball positions—point guard, off (or shooting) guard, small forward, power (or big) forward, and center.

Through his years as a member of the Amateur Athletic Union (AAU), from the fifth through the eighth grades, it was not uncommon for James to live with the Joyce family for extended periods. James and Dru III became very close friends and played together, with their other friends, on the Northeast Ohio Shooting Stars AAU team. Coached by Joyce's father, Dru, the Shooting Stars qualified for the under–sixth-grade AAU national competition that took place in Salt Lake City, Utah. The elder Dru Joyce explained to Tim Rogers that during that period, as later, James wanted "to act like he knows more than you do. He's coachable in the sense that when you call him out on something he's done wrong, he knows. But you'd better understand and know what you are talking about because he knows the game." Two years later, competing in the under–eighth-grade AAU national championships, the Shooting Stars advanced as far as the national finals in Orlando, Florida, before losing, 68–66, to the Southern California All-Stars, despite an exceptional performance by James.

On the advice of their parents, James and three of his close friends, Joyce, Cotton, and McGee—who were then referring to themselves as the "Fab Four," in homage to the 1992 Michigan University men's basketball team—settled on Saint Vincent–Saint Mary's High School (SVSM), a parochial school in downtown Akron. James also agreed to play football for SVSM, whose sports teams were nicknamed the "Fighting Irish." Making his debut as a freshman in the starting lineup for the varsity basketball team on December 2, 1999, James—who had by then grown to over six feet tall—quickly attracted the attention of Division I college-basketball programs and even NBA scouts. James and one of his teammates, Maverick Carter, who was then a senior, led the Fighting Irish to a perfect 27–0 record and to their first state championship since 1984. As a freshman James averaged slightly below 20 points per game (PPG) and was also among the team's leaders in many other statistical categories. Of particular interest to many scouts was James's ability to make his teammates on the court more productive players by virtue of his willingness to pass the ball, despite his own knack for scoring.

The following fall, as a sophomore, James played football for the Fighting Irish, gaining more than 700 yards receiving and scoring 14 touchdowns. For his accomplishments as a wide receiver, he was named the team's most valuable offensive player. On the basketball court as a sophomore, James became one of the hottest young prospects in the country—a position in which, normally, only upperclassmen found themselves. He led the Fighting Irish to their second consecutive state championship, averaging over 25 points per game, 7.4 rebounds, and 5.5 assists; he thus became the first sophomore in Ohio state history to be voted the state's "Mr. Basketball," an honor he would also win in his junior and senior seasons. Having grown another several inches, James began to court the attention of such college basketball enthusiasts as the ESPN commentator Dick Vitale, who included James on a list of his top five high-school sophomores in the country. In order to accommodate the large crowds that James was attracting, SVSM began to schedule some of the basketball team's home games at the University of Akron's James A. Rhodes Arena.

Between James's sophomore and junior seasons, his performance at several instructional basketball camps increased interest in him among scouts even more. Also that summer James participated with his idol, Michael Jordan, and several other NBA players in an exclusive workout session organized by Jordan. James had a brush with controversy during that time, when he said that he was considering entering the NBA draft after his junior season at SVSM. He later retracted his comments and stayed at SVSM, and on its basketball team, through his senior year.

In James's junior year the hoopla surrounding the SVSM team reached new heights. That year, for example, the shoe company Adidas became the team's official apparel sponsor. As a junior James again led SVSM to an impressive record—and to their third consecutive state championship final. Speaking to Grant Wahl, the Germantown (Pennsylvania) Academy coach Jim Fenerty, whose team played against SVSM, compared James with the former high-school phenomenon Kobe Bryant: "We played Kobe when Kobe was a senior, and LeBron is the best player we've ever played against. LeBron is physically stronger than Kobe was as a senior, and we've never had anybody shoot better against us." At year's end James was a consensus All-American performer and was named high-school basketball player of the year by such publications as *USA Today* and *Parade*. A few months after his 17th birthday, in February 2002, *Sports Illustrated* featured a photo of James on its cover,

dressed in his SVSM basketball uniform, along with the words "The Chosen One."

Prior to the start of his senior season, SVSM signed an unprecedented contract to broadcast each of the basketball team's 10 home games throughout northeastern Ohio on local pay-per-view television. The sports network ESPN2 later agreed to televise a game the team was playing in December. According to one report, approximately 1.67 million households watched the ESPN2 broadcast of a game between SVSM and Oak Hill Academy. Those developments, along with the team's busy schedule, which included games against schools as far away as California, led many to conclude that the fuss being made over James was bordering on exploitation. On the court James seemed unfazed by all the attention, leading his team to their third state championship in four years, this time on the more competitive Division II level. After the season James went on to participate in the 26th Annual McDonald's All-American High School Boys Basketball Game, a contest reserved for the U.S.'s elite high-school basketball players, and in the EA Sports Roundall Classic in Chicago, Illinois.

On April 7, 2003 James officially declared himself eligible for the National Basketball Association (NBA) draft. Soon afterward he signed a $90 million endorsement contract with the shoe company Nike. On June 26, 2003 the Cleveland Cavaliers chose James as the first player overall in the 2003 draft. Prior to the draft, James and the Cavaliers had negotiated a rookie contract valued at $18.8 million over four years. A franchise that had fallen on hard times, the Cavaliers had not reached the play-offs since 1998 and had tied the Denver Nuggets in the 2002-03 season for a league-worst 17–65 record. Despite the unusually high expectations placed upon him, James's presence immediately paid dividends. Fan attendance for home games rose by roughly 7,200 on average per home game, as James took over in the Cavaliers' starting lineup and became the focal point of their offense. Starting 79 of the Cavaliers' 81 games, James averaged 20.9 points, 5.9 assists, and 5.5 rebounds per game, contributing to the team's revitalization, which included a 35–47 record, a noticeable improvement over the previous season. James received all six rookie-of-the-month awards for the Eastern Conference, joining David Robinson, Tim Duncan, and his Western Conference counterpart Carmelo Anthony of the Denver Nuggets as the only rookies to have done so in NBA history. He was presented with the NBA's rookie-of-the-year award at the season's conclusion.

Following the 2003-04 season, after a number of NBA veterans declined to play for the United States in the 2004 Olympic Games, in Athens, Greece, James was tapped for the team. The hurriedly assembled squad included a number of young, inexperienced players, such as James, and the team's head coach, Larry Brown, was notoriously harsh on such athletes—leading many to express doubts about the U.S. team's prospects in the Games. Moreover, the team had mere weeks to prepare, while a majority of the other Olympic squads had practiced and played together as units for months, if not longer. It soon became clear that observers' misgivings were well founded. After the U.S. team endured its first two losses in Olympic basketball competition since 1992 (the first year that NBA stars played in the Olympics), it rebounded to qualify for the medal round and defeated Lithuania, 104–96, to win the bronze. Despite averaging a shade over 11 minutes per game, which was the fourth-lowest average on the team, James performed comparatively well in the Games. "The Olympic experience really helped him," Paul Silas, then the coach of the Cavaliers, told David Dupree. "What it did most was that he had to play defense in order to play at all. So that helped him be conscious of defense."

Committed to improving his long-range shooting in time for the 2004-05 season, James returned to the NBA with a renewed determination. With 2,175 points scored and an average of 27.2 points per game (third-best in the league), James finished second behind Allen Iverson of the Philadelphia 76ers for top-scorer honors. He also led the NBA in minutes played, logging 3,388 minutes (or slightly over 42 minutes per game), a high number for a second-year player, and improved his output in several other statistical categories, including assists, rebounds, and steals. In voting by fans, James was selected to start in the 2005 NBA All-Star Game, played in Denver, Colorado, on February 20. With a 42–40 record, the Cavaliers enjoyed their first winning season since 1998, even if they did not qualify for the play-offs. Over the course of the season, James set a number of personal marks. On January 20, 2005 he became the youngest player in NBA history to record a triple-double, posting double-digit figures in three important statistical categories—with 27 points, 11 rebounds, and 10 assists against the Portland Trail Blazers in a 107–101 win. Later, at 20 years and 80 days old, James eclipsed a mark held by the retired Rick Barry as the youngest player to score 50 or more points in a single NBA game. James did so by scoring 56 points on March 20, 2005 in a game that the Cavaliers lost to the Toronto Raptors, 105–98. "I had to have patience with him and teach him the fundamentals of our game," Silas explained to Pierce. "And, then, only during the first season. Now, the second season, he came back, and he had it down. He's the quickest study I've ever been around. He knows immediately when he makes a mistake, and he came back with a confidence he didn't have last year." More than halfway through the 2004-05 season, Silas was fired as the Cavaliers coach and replaced on an interim basis by Brendan Malone. Later, in the off-season, Mike Brown became the team's new head coach; the franchise also named the former Cavaliers forward Danny Ferry as its general manager.

In the months leading up to the start of the 2005-06 season, James dismissed rumors that he had demanded to be traded to the New York Knicks, the Miami Heat, or the Los Angeles Lakers. He told the Associated Press (October 4, 2005, on-line), "For the record, I am not going anywhere. I keep hearing these stories about LeBron James is not happy in Cleveland. I don't understand where these keep coming from. I'm very happy in the Cavaliers' uniform and I'm going to be wearing this uniform for a long time, OK?" As part of the team's effort to surround James with a solid supporting cast to increase its chances of getting to the NBA play-offs, the team signed the free-agent guards Larry Hughes and Damon Jones, along with the forward Donyell Marshall. "There should be no excuses for us not to get to the play-offs with the guys that we've added," James said.

James has contracts to endorse such products as Coca-Cola and Bubblicious gum. He can often be seen on television commercials for the sports drink Powerade and the soft drink Sprite, as well. The 20-year-old garnered headlines following the 2005 NBA season when he ended his association with his agent, Aaron Goodwin, who had negotiated many of James's endorsement deals. Other places to find James's image include the DC Comics series that features the basketball player competing in a clandestinely run hoops tournament.

According to USA Today (February 17, 2005), James became a father on October 6, 2004 but has guarded the identity of the child's mother from the mainstream media. He nonetheless told DuPree that becoming a father "is the best thing that ever happened to me. It has made me more humble." James often credits his mother, who raised him despite the family's small means, as being an inspiration to him. In 2005 LeBron James and his mother established the James Family Foundation, a charitable organization that sponsors events to raise money for programs that benefit Akron's youth. The James Family Foundation has arranged various events in the Akron area, including the popular "King for Kids Bike-a-Thon." James lives in a lavish home in Summit County, Ohio.

—D.F.

Suggested Reading: *Akron Beacon Journal* D p1 Nov. 26, 2000, with photo, D p1 Feb. 4, 2001, with photos; (Cleveland) *Plain Dealer* D p1 Feb. 11, 2002; *Sports Illustrated* p62+ Feb. 18, 2002, with photo, p64+ Feb. 21, 2005 with photo; *USA Today* E p1 Feb. 17, 2005, with photo; *USA Today* (on-line) Oct. 3, 2005

Kevin Winter/Getty Images

Johansson, Scarlett

(jo-HAN-son)

Nov. 22, 1984– Actress

Address: c/o William Morris Agency, 151 El Camino Dr., Beverly Hills, CA 90212

Scarlett Johansson is among the most celebrated young actresses working in film today, not only because of her classical beauty and charm, but also because of her ability to exude a maturity beyond her years. After a childhood spent studying and practicing the craft of acting, she broke into the spotlight with her appearance opposite the veteran actor Bill Murray in the award-winning film *Lost in Translation* (2003), about two alienated Americans who share a brief, tender relationship in a foreign city. Johansson gave another highly acclaimed performance later that same year as a young servant who inspires one of the painter Johannes Vermeer's masterpieces, in *Girl with a Pearl Earring*. In the wake of those successes, Johansson has found herself much in demand. Reviewing her performance in *A Love Song for Bobby Long*—one of four movies in which she appeared in 2004—the New York *Daily News* (December 29, 2004) film critic Jack Mathews wrote, "Johansson has to be the oldest 20-year-old leading lady since the studio days. The camera loves her, but she is lighted with an intelligence and confidence that comes from the inside." In a review of *Lost in Translation* for *Newsweek* (September 15, 2003), David Ansen wrote that Johansson has "always radiated a throaty gravity and projected a blunt honesty on screen. Though the native New Yorker has been

performing since . . . the age of 8, the camera never catches her Acting. She gives the impression of having arrived fully formed. She just is—like a noun that doesn't need an adjective."

Of Polish and Danish descent, Scarlett Johansson was born on November 22, 1984 in New York City. She and her twin brother, Hunter, are the youngest of Karsten and Melanie Johansson's four children. According to the Internet Movie Database, her parents separated when she was 13 and later divorced. A grandchild of the Danish screenwriter and documentary filmmaker Ejner Johansson, Scarlett was surrounded by creative people during her youth and expressed an interest in acting as early as age three. After she began taking classes at the legendary Lee Strasberg Theatre Institute for Young People, in Los Angeles, California, Johansson was brought to auditions by her mother. (Melanie Johansson later produced *A Love Song for Bobby Long* and now serves as her daughter's manager.) At age eight Johansson made her stage debut, opposite Ethan Hawke in an Off-Broadway production of the play *Sophistry*. She made her film debut when she was nine, with an appearance in *North* (1994), a Rob Reiner–directed comedy that critics panned. She next secured supporting parts in the movies *Just Cause* (1995), a thriller starring Sean Connery, and *If Lucy Fell* (1996), a romantic comedy featuring Sarah Jessica Parker and Ben Stiller.

As one of two orphaned, vagabond sisters in *Manny and Lo* (1996), Johansson received appreciative notices and a nomination for an Independent Spirit Award. (According to the Internet Movie Database, Johansson's parents, her brother, Hunter, and her sister Vanessa had small parts in the movie.) In a prescient review for the *San Francisco Chronicle* (August 9, 1996), Mick LaSalle wrote, "Finding poised child actors is difficult enough, but Johansson's peaceful aura, which takes in everything with equanimity, is something special. If she can get through puberty with that aura undisturbed, she could become an important actress." In 1997 Johansson had brief roles in *Fall* and *Home Alone 3*. Her career received a big boost when she was tapped by the renowned actor and director Robert Redford to co-star in his movie *The Horse Whisperer* (1998). In that film Johansson played Grace, the daughter of two New York professionals (Kristin Scott Thomas and Sam Neill). After Grace and her horse, Pilgrim, are severely injured in a riding accident, Grace's mother seeks out a man from Montana (Redford) who uses traditional remedies to cure horses—as well as the traumatized psyches of those who, like Grace, are afraid to ride again. Johansson told Chris Jones for *Esquire* (February 2005) that *The Horse Whisperer* "changed things for me in a lot of ways. Certainly as an actor. I went through this realization that acting, at its heart, is the ability to manipulate your own emotions. . . . It's weird to have that sort of learning process documented." Although *The Horse Whisperer* received mixed reviews, it proved to be a success at the box office, earning more than $75 million. A number of critics singled out Johansson's portrayal as the best part of the movie. Peter Howell, in the *Toronto Star* (May 15, 1998), wrote, "The standout performance is by Scarlett Johansson. . . . [The role of Grace] demands the authenticity of emotion that Johansson brings to it." For her work in *The Horse Whisperer*, Johansson was nominated for an award for most promising actress by the Chicago Film Critics Association.

In 2001 Johansson found herself on the cusp of stardom. She earned critical praise for her turns as an underage piano-playing seductress in Ethan and Joel Coen's black-and-white film *The Man Who Wasn't There* and as a young girl whose family flees 1950s-era Communist-ruled Hungary for the United States in *An American Rhapsody*. In that same year Johansson co-starred in the director Terry Zwigoff's film *Ghost World*, which was based on a novel-length comic book by Daniel Clowes. Johansson played Rebecca, who, along with her best friend, Enid (Thora Birch), struggles with life after their recent high-school graduations. Though *Ghost World* did not attract many theatergoers, it won plaudits from critics. In the *New York Times* (July 20, 2001), A. O. Scott praised *Ghost World*'s depiction of "teenage eccentricity" and its "incisive satire of the boredom and conformity that rule our thrill-seeking, individualistic land." B. Ruby Rich wrote for the *Nation* (September 3–10, 2001), "Almost without exception, *Ghost World* hits its target with a bull's-eye. It renders, nearly pitch-perfect, the tone of teenage girls' friendship—the overidentification and competition, the combined desire for and horror of boys/men, the simultaneous re-invention and rejection of femininity and the torment of succumbing to minimum-wage conformity while desperately trying to figure a way out."

Johansson graduated from the Professional Children's School in New York City in 2002. She applied to New York University's Tisch School of the Arts for the fall 2003 semester, but was rejected. That setback led her to focus on her career, which took off shortly thereafter, when *Lost in Translation*, the director Sophia Coppola's sophomore effort, made Johansson a bona fide movie star. In the film Johansson played Charlotte, a young American woman who has accompanied her photographer husband to Tokyo, Japan. Neglected by her husband, who is immersed in his work, Charlotte wanders the streets of Tokyo alone, unable to sleep and feeling isolated and uncomfortable in her own skin. At the bar of the hotel in which she and her husband are staying, she meets Bob (Bill Murray), an aging American movie actor whose career is in the doldrums and who has come to Tokyo to shoot a lucrative whiskey commercial. Like Charlotte, Bob is disenchanted with his life and unsure of how to move forward. The bond that Charlotte and Bob form becomes the central focus of the movie, which impressed audiences and crit-

ics alike. Robert W. Butler wrote for the *Kansas City Star* (September 26, 2003), "Johansson, who has quietly snuck up on moviegoers with a series of wonderful performances in little films (*American Rhapsody*, *Ghost World*, *The Man Who Wasn't There*), plays Charlotte with an enchanting blend of wistfulness and gravity. Her ability to suggest insights beyond her years is remarkable. Moreover, Johansson has been blessed with a face that at first seems average and becomes more enchanting as you watch her. By the end of this film you'll be in love with her, too." Peter Travers concurred, writing in his review for *Rolling Stone* (September 8, 2003) that Johansson "has matured into an actress of smashing loveliness and subtle grace." In his *Newsweek* review, David Ansen, too, proclaimed the young actress's virtues: "In Coppola's *Lost in Translation*, Johansson finally takes center stage and becomes an adult. . . . [She] hold[s] her own with Bill Murray at his most inspired. . . . Their brief, wondrous encounter is the soul of this subtle, funny, melancholy film." *Lost in Translation* grossed more than $40 million in box-office receipts, a remarkable total for a small-budget film. Both the movie itself and the individual actors were nominated for a slew of honors, including several Academy Awards. Johansson won a British Academy of Film and Television Arts award for best actress and took home the same prize at the Venice Film Festival. She was also nominated for best-actress awards by the Chicago Film Critics Association, the Broadcast Film Critics Association, and the Golden Globes.

Johansson next starred as the title character and fictional muse of the 17th-century Dutch painter Johannes Vermeer (Colin Firth) in *Girl with a Pearl Earring*. In the film, based on the same-titled novel by Tracy Chevalier, Johansson played Griet, an innocent yet wise servant girl who becomes the painter's assistant after Vermeer realizes that she has a rare artistic sensibility. Vermeer immortalizes Griet by making her the subject of one of his masterpieces—the portrait *A Girl with a Pearl Earring*. The remarkable expression on the sitter's face, and the knowledge that Vermeer has painted an image of their illiterate maid, throws Vermeer's wife into a jealous rage, and she banishes Griet from the house. The emotional and physical attraction that Vermeer and Griet obviously feel toward each other is never consummated. Many critics found fault with the film—in *Entertainment Weekly* (December 12, 2003), for example, Owen Gleiberman complained that "the movie's soap opera of jealousy and forbidden obsession is standard middlebrow fare"—but they were nearly unanimous in their praise for Johansson's performance. In the *Chicago Tribune* (December 26, 2003), Michael Wilmington wrote, "Johansson gives the second of two remarkable 2003 film performances. . . . As Griet, who barely says a word, Johansson creates both the portrait's image and a resilient but deeply sensitive girl, a social victim who becomes a sublime icon." In the *San Francis-*

co *Chronicle* (December 26, 2003), Ruthe Stein wrote that Johansson plays Griet "with a palpable feeling for what it's like to be on the brink of sexual awakening—'ripe as a plum,' in the words of Vermeer's lecherous art dealer. Johansson . . . shows a notable lack of vanity, going through *Girl* with no apparent makeup and her hair covered by a scarf. She bears a startling resemblance to the [real] painting's anonymous sitter."

After the release of *Girl with a Pearl Earring*, critics began to suggest that Johansson had built a niche for herself in films as a young muse for older men. In interviews Johansson suggested that she had a natural connection to older men and that she could not imagine herself dating anyone younger than 30. "Men have no aid to tell them that they're getting older," she noted in an interview with Virginia Hefferman for the *New York Times* (September 7, 2003). "They just see their bodies decaying. A young, fertile, fruitful woman can help you across that bridge." However, in her interview with Chris Jones, Johansson playfully lamented those earlier comments, saying, "It's horrible. I don't know why young men won't come up to me anymore. Seriously. . . . Now I'm stuck with the geezers."

In *A Love Song for Bobby Long* (2004), Johansson again played something of a muse, this time to an alcoholic, down-on-his-luck literature professor (John Travolta). When Johansson, as Pursy, arrives in New Orleans to claim her childhood home, which she has inherited from her estranged mother (one of the professor's former lovers), she finds the house dilapidated and occupied by ex-professor Long and his protégé and former teaching assistant (Gabriel Macht), both of whom are drowning their shared tragic past in alcohol. After Pursy insists on moving into the house with them, their lives are altered in unexpected ways. Johansson's performance, which brought her another Golden Globe nomination for best actress, was seen as one of the film's few saving graces. In the *Los Angeles Times* (December 29, 2004), Carina Chocano wrote that Johansson "brings to life the kind of teen character we rarely see on screen. She's blunt without being sarcastic, smart without being smart-alecky and confident in her own insecurity. Hovering on the edge of childhood, she (quite realistically) clings to her youth, reminding an unforgivably crass Bobby early on that, at 18, she's still just a kid. Johansson makes this look like a revelation." In the New York *Daily News* (December 29, 2004), Jack Mathews wrote, "The sole asset of *Bobby Long* is Johansson. Blossoming before our very eyes, she gives Pursy the combination of hope and determination that makes her journey worthwhile."

Johansson next appeared alongside Dennis Quaid and Topher Grace in the comedic drama *In Good Company* (2004). In that motion picture she was cast as Alex, who feels caught between her loyalty to her good-natured father, Dan, and her romantic attraction for his new boss, Carter, who is half her father's age. "Johansson is marvelous,"

Richard Schickel wrote in his review of *In Good Company* for *Time* (January 17, 2005). "Her Alex will have her way with Dan and with Carter, but she never surrenders her sweetness, her young woman's hesitancies and insecurities." Johansson's other big-screen appearances include *My Brother the Pig* (1999), *Eight Legged Freaks* (2002), *The Perfect Score* (2004), *A Good Woman* (2004), and *The Island* (2005), a science-fiction thriller. Her upcoming films include another thriller, "The Black Dahlia," based on a novel by James Ellroy, and *Match Point*, a comedy written and directed by Woody Allen. Regarding the varied roles she has chosen to play, Johansson told Chris Jones, "Different projects bring different things to you. I mean, I don't have a plan for myself, and I don't want people to see me in any particular way."

Johansson, who has worked steadily as an actress since she was 12, told Jones, "I have a hard time taking time off. Whenever I'm taking time off, all I'm thinking about is working. I feel like right now I have a one-in-a-million chance. There are so many great actors who are unemployed, and seeing them makes you wonder why everything's happening for you. It's luck. I'm just lucky. But to have this strange breakout, it's just a dream. It really is."

—C.M.

Suggested Reading: *All Movie Guide* (on-line); *Chicago Tribune* C p1 Dec. 26, 2003; *Esquire* p64+ Feb. 2005, with photos; *Interview* p22+ July 1, 2001, p188+ Sep. 1, 2003; *Kansas City Star* Sep. 26, 2003; *Los Angeles Times* E p1 Dec. 29, 2004; *Nation* p50+ Sep.3–10, 2001; (New York) *Daily News* p34 Dec. 29, 2004; *New York Times* II p39 Sep. 7, 2003, with photo; *Newsweek* p64 Sep. 15, 2003, with photo; *People* p61 Mar. 22, 2004; *San Francisco Chronicle* p15 Dec. 26, 2003; *Time* p66 Jan. 17, 2005

Selected Films: *North*, 1994; *Just Cause*, 1995; *If Lucy Fell*, 1996; *Manny and Lo*, 1996; *Home Alone 3*, 1997; *The Horse Whisperer*, 1998; *My Brother the Pig*, 1999; *An American Rhapsody*, 2001; *Ghost World*, 2001; *The Man Who Wasn't There*, 2001; *Girl with a Pearl Earring*, 2003; *Lost in Translation*, 2003; *In Good Company*, 2004; *A Love Song for Bobby Long*, 2004; *A Good Woman*, 2004; *The Island*, 2005

Peter Kramer/Getty Images

Jones, Sarah

Nov. 29, 1973– Poet; playwright; performance artist

Address: 302-A W. 12th St., #121, New York, NY 10014

The playwright, poet, and performance artist Sarah Jones was exposed early in her life to people of many different cultures, nationalities, and ethnicities, some of them in her own family. "I'm Heinz 57 sauce," she explained to Christopher John Farley for *Time* (May 15, 2000, on-line). "You get women's history month, black history month, diversity week—I'm everything." Taking advantage of the insights provided by that background, and of her gift for inhabiting a myriad of disparate characters, Jones has written and starred in four celebrated one-woman shows: *Surface Transit*, *Women Can't Wait!*, *Waking the American Dream*, and *Bridge & Tunnel*. In her works Jones has addressed themes including the experiences of immigrants in the U.S. and the difficulties faced by women around the world; her characters have ranged from an elderly Jewish woman to an African-American rapper to an accountant from Pakistan to a white racist. "I'll put myself inside their heads and say, 'I'm going to trace back. I'm a white supremacist who would do horrible things to Sarah Jones in an alley, but once upon a time I was a kid in a bassinet,'" Jones said to Jennifer Block for *Ms.* magazine (October-November 2000, on-line). As she told Dream Hampton for *BET.com* (December 3, 2001, on-line), "My work is about inclusivity."

Sarah Jones was born on November 29, 1973 in Baltimore, Maryland, the daughter of an African-American father and a white mother of European and Caribbean heritage. Her father, a medical student, served in the military; her mother was a homemaker. As her father received new assignments, the family—which came to include her younger sister, Naomi—relocated, first to Washington, D.C., and then to Boston, Massachusetts. Jones grew up in Dorchester, one of Boston's toughest neighborhoods, where her mother was often derided for being white. Intervale Street, where the family lived, "looks like Beirut," she told James Hannaham for the *Village Voice* (January 5, 1999). But, she added, "I was happy. I didn't know the reason we had all the pretty cats was to get rid of the pretty mice." As she got older she experienced what she remembers as an identity crisis. She used street slang at school but adopted a more cerebral manner at home, playing chess with her father beginning at age four and becoming immersed in literature. "I was like, Mommy, I'm fake!" she recalled to Hannaham. "I talk one way to you and another to Daddy, the kids hate me, I'm Catholic, I'm a zebra—help me!" She wrote in a piece for *Harper's Bazaar* (October 2000, on-line), "I was a very strange and inventive child. . . . In order to fit in where I wasn't fitting, I began to weave my own little worlds." The family later moved to New York, where Jones enrolled at the United Nations International School. "There were all these kids, something like 150 nationalities, and everybody had these gorgeous accents, and I would listen all day," she told Barbara Crossette for the *New York Times* (June 7, 2000). Jones perfected her mimicry skills in the student lounge of the school. "I would call up the school office and pretend to be my friends' parents," she explained to Hannaham. "I'd be like, 'Gita is very sick today . . .' They disconnected the phone in the student lounge once they figured it out." She also mimicked her teachers. "It was an easy way to hide through a very insecure adolescence," she admitted in *Harper's Bazaar*. While attending the International School, she began to consider issues of race and culture in new ways and to become aware of their complexity. "I'd see a girl with dark skin, darker than me, and she didn't identify with me, she was the premier from Sierra Leone's daughter, she was rich," Jones told Dream Hampton.

Jones enrolled at Bryn Mawr College, a women's school in Bryn Mawr, Pennsylvania. There, rather than viewing herself as multiethnic, she began to identify herself as fully African-American. ("We are a racialized society," she explained to Dream Hampton. "My mother is of European and Caribbean descent but I've never been mistaken for a White woman. I am a Black woman. Society made that clear early on.") Her earlier confusion regarding race gave way to conflicting thoughts involving gender. "At Bryn Mawr I began looking at gender, then the essence of my humanity and what was, pardon the pun, 'coloring' that," she told Dream

Hampton. "And I couldn't stomach the news . . . I felt like I was having a nervous breakdown."

Since childhood, Jones had entertained the notion of becoming a lawyer, as she explained in *Harper's Bazaar*: "I thought I wanted to be a lawyer because I knew I had a mouth on me, and from a very early age I had a profound sense of justice. I wanted to fix the fact that I felt uncomfortable when my mother and I went into certain places together. When I said, 'It's not fair!' I said it with unusual conviction. When in doubt, I could yell real loud." But when her parents' divorce and her sister's illness created financial difficulties for the family, she left Bryn Mawr and returned to New York City. While working in a restaurant (and attending Hunter College, according to some sources), she immersed herself in hip-hop music and culture, adding to her own confusion regarding gender; she frequently went to parties and caught herself singing along to songs whose lyrics she found misogynistic, and as she told James Hannaham, "You knew that when you [went to parties] . . . guys were only interested in what was in them jeans. You really had no value." During that period Jones wrote furiously about her experiences, as she explained to Jennifer Block: "I was writing in my journal the kind of where-am-I-who-am-I-where-on-earth-am-I-going-do-I-have-any-gas? poems . . . the really bad ones." Jones began to perform her work at poetry readings, which "became a character-building exercise for me," as she wrote in *Harper's Bazaar*, "to get up in front of people and sort of exorcise my demons—even though they were mostly terrible poems." She began to make regular appearances at the Nuyorican Poets Café, a well-known venue for spoken-word performances on the Lower East Side of Manhattan. In 1997 her poem "Your Revolution" won the prestigious Nuyorican Poetry Slam competition, the Holy Grail of New York's spoken-word artists; the piece, which she recorded on an album in 1999, is an inventive critique of the misogyny and commercialism of some hip-hop music, written in a style that recalls Gil Scott-Heron's 1975 poem "The Revolution Will Not Be Televised." Just as her work was beginning to be recognized, her sister, Naomi, died at 18, after experimenting with heroin. "I think I kind of really died and then started over," Jones told *Honey* magazine (October 1999, on-line). "I had all my old equipment and stuff, but she just sort of ushered me into this other place. . . . Now I'm living for two people. It's horrible and miraculous at the same time."

Also in 1997 Jones began to develop a one-woman show, *Surface Transit*, which debuted at the Nuyorican Poets Café the following year. In it Jones portrayed eight diverse characters, based on people she observed while growing up—among them a Jewish grandmother, a Russian widow raising her biracial child, a racist and homophobic policeman, and a rapper recovering from "rhyme addiction." "*Surface Transit* is tremendously personal," she explained in *Harper's Bazaar*. "It was like

I was getting paid for my own therapy. I wanted people to walk away from the show feeling quenched or refreshed or at least confused." The piece was widely praised during its first run and was revamped for the first New York Hip-Hop Theater Festival in the summer of 2000. Jones "has the clearest sense of distance; she can satirize the [hip-hop] phenomenon in ways that open it up for people who think there is something mysterious about it," D. J. R. Bruckner wrote in a review for the *New York Times* (July 28, 2000). "Ms. Jones may embody the best of hip-hop, but she makes fun." *Surface Transit* was nominated for a 2000–01 Drama Desk Award for best solo performance and won the award for best one-person show at HBO's Aspen Comedy Arts Festival in 2000. Jones performed the play at the Kennedy Center, in Washington, D.C., in 2002 and at the Berkeley Repertory Theatre, in California, in 2003.

Surface Transit created new opportunities for Jones. The film director Spike Lee became a fan of her work, and Jones appeared in a small role in his 2000 movie *Bamboozled*. She also appeared in the Off-Broadway production of Eve Ensler's *The Vagina Monologues*. After the feminist and journalist Gloria Steinem saw a performance of *Surface Transit*, she urged the international women's rights group Equality Now to commission Jones to write a stage piece. The resulting work, *Women Can't Wait!*, premiered at the June 2000 U.N. International Conference on Women's Rights. Jones portrayed eight women from all over the world and, through the characters, addressed such topics as marital rape, "honor" killings, female genital mutilation, and other practices that are demeaning, harmful, or fatal to women. Her only prop was a scarf, which she used as a head covering, a sash, a neckerchief, or a doll, depending on the character. Creating and performing *Women Can't Wait!* was a formative experience for her, she explained to Jennifer Block: "My feminist consciousness had begun developing early on, but in terms of my commitment to struggling as a woman against something that was always out there, I hadn't gotten serious. I put it on my shelf: 'I'll read about that someday.' 'I'll pay attention to that when I have time.' Equality Now made me feel I have to do it now."

Women Can't Wait! was well received, and the experience of writing and performing it deeply affected Jones's approach to her work. "I sure can't do anything that's not worthwhile anymore," she admitted to Block. "If I do, it hurts. Because I know what it's like to do something that feels like it needs to be done. I almost feel like I've redefined art for myself." Accordingly, Jones has performed regularly for the Rosewood School, a high school on New York City's prison facility Riker's Island, and teaches in dozens of high-school workshops per year. On the heels of the success of *Women Can't Wait!*, the National Immigration Forum, with financial support from the Ford Foundation, commissioned her to write a play about immigration and immigrants' rights. *Waking the American*

Dream, which premiered in 2002, included 10 separate characters and attempted to view life in the U.S. from immigrants' point of view. Jones's play also touched on the repercussions of the September 11, 2001 terrorist attacks for immigrants to the U.S.

Jones's most recent work is the one-woman show *Bridge & Tunnel*, which she conceived with Steve Colman. As with her previous works, Jones performs a wide variety of roles in the play, which is set at the annual "I Am a Poet Too" reading at the Bridge & Tunnel Café, in the New York City borough of Queens. She takes on the personas of Mohammad Ali, a Pakistani-born accountant and the reading's emcee; Rashid, a rapper from Brooklyn; Lorraine, a resident of a Long Island seniors' center whose poem is titled "No Really, Please Don't Get Up"; and nearly a dozen other characters. *Bridge & Tunnel*, produced by the actress Meryl Streep and others, opened Off-Broadway at the 45 Bleecker Street Theatre in February 2004 to much acclaim. "[Solo performance] frees gifted artists to change sex, race, age, body type and personality in an instant," Margo Jefferson wrote for the *New York Times* (February 20, 2004). "It takes great craft and generosity. Sarah Jones has both. You see this in every moment of her new show. . . . Ms. Jones's ear is flawless. So is her voice." Jefferson concluded, "What would Ms. Jones do with fewer characters and longer stories that moved us in stranger, deeper ways? She's 29, and we'll all find out. For now, I want nothing more than the uncanny accuracy with which she portrays the host of immigrants and outsiders who make up this hybrid nation." *Bridge & Tunnel* won honors including the Theatre World Award, Obie Award, and Drama League Award and was nominated for Drama Desk, Lucille Lortel, and Outer Critics Circle Awards. The play, which Jones performed at the Berkeley Repertory Theatre in early 2005, is scheduled to open on Broadway in the fall.

Jones's recording of "Your Revolution" became the center of controversy in 1999, when a listener of the Portland, Oregon, radio station KBOO-FM complained to the Federal Communications Commission (FCC) that the work was offensive. The FCC then levied a $7,000 fine for indecency against the radio station, charging that "Your Revolution" had "unmistakable patently offensive sexual references" that "appear designed to pander and shock," according to Neil Strauss in the *New York Times* (January 30, 2002). "Anyone can see it's a parody," Jones pointed out to Lynda Richardson for the July 12, 2001 edition of the same newspaper. In January 2002 Jones, with the support of the People for the American Way Foundation, filed suit against the FCC in federal district court, asking for a judgment that the song is not indecent under FCC standards; for a finding that the FCC's ruling violated her First Amendment right to free speech; and for an injunction to prevent the FCC from enforcing the $7,000 fine against KBOO-FM. In February 2003 the FCC reversed its decision and rescinded the proposed fine.

The five-foot 11-inch Sarah Jones wears long dreadlocks and "speaks rapidly, like a string of illegal firecrackers, lit at once," as Dream Hampton put it. Jones lives in Greenwich Village, in New York City, with her partner, Steve Colman.

—K.S.

Suggested Reading: *Harper's Bazaar* p260 Oct. 2000; *Ms.* p82+ Oct./Nov. 2000, with photos; *New York Times* E p1 June 7, 2000, with photos, B p2 July 12, 2001, with photo, E p1 Feb. 20, 2004, with photos; *Village Voice* p40 June 20–26, 2001, with photo; *Washington Post* C p1 Feb. 2, 2002, with photos

Selected One-Woman Shows: *Surface Transit*, 1998; *Women Can't Wait!*, 2000; *Waking the American Dream*, 2002; *Bridge & Tunnel*, 2004

Selected Films: *Bamboozled*, 2000

Sean Gallup/Getty Images

Kaufman, Charlie

Nov. 1, 1958– Screenwriter

Address: c/o United Talent Agency, 9560 Wilshire Blvd., Fifth Fl., Beverly Hills, CA 90212

Charlie Kaufman is the rare screenwriter who is able to imprint his personal vision onto films, making them recognizably his in a way that, typically, only film directors are able to do. The movies he has scripted, including *Being John Malkovich* (1999), *Adaptation* (2002), and *Eternal Sunshine of the Spotless Mind* (2004), "are founded on goofy, surrealist fantasies concerning the thwarted desires of neurotic and ineffectual characters, and all have scrambled methods of telling a story, including juggled chronologies and viewpoints," as Jonathan Rosenbaum wrote for the *Chicago Reader* (March 19, 2004, on-line). While Kaufman's screenplays have been praised for their comic brilliance and for the exquisiteness of his writing, their distinctiveness lies mainly in the premises he concocts. *Being John Malkovich*, for example, concerns a lonely puppeteer who discovers a physical passageway into the mind of the title character; in *Eternal Sunshine of the Spotless Mind*, a pair of disenchanted lovers are helped to banish their memories of each other—literally. "When you're sent a Charlie Kaufman script, the first thing you want to do is put it in a frame," the actress Kate Winslet, who starred in *Eternal Sunshine*, told Claudia Puig for the *Vancouver (British Columbia) Province* (March 19, 2004). "You just want to preserve and polish it." She added, "You watch his movies thinking, 'This shouldn't make any sense,' and yet it does. I don't know how he does it but I just want him to keep writing." Kaufman's characters "tend to be flawed, with awkward sensibilities," Elijah Wood, another performer who has worked with Kaufman, told Claudia Puig. "The things they say are not always right in every situation, which makes them immediately relatable."

Kaufman's screenplays defy easy classification. They are absurd and funny; they also focus on deeply unhappy characters and overflow with philosophical questions about the nature of identity and perception, among other issues. Are they comedies or dramas? How seriously are they supposed to be taken? Kaufman himself may have provided an answer during his interview with Moira Macdonald for the *Seattle Times* (April 7, 2002). Comedy, he said, "is based on real sadness. . . . If it isn't, it doesn't have any of that resonance. I don't think it's done a lot that way, and I don't gravitate toward movies that are called comedies for that reason. It's not funny if it's not rooted in anything."

Charles Stewart (or Stuart, according to some sources) Kaufman was born on November 1, 1958 in Massapequa, on Long Island, New York. He has said that he had a traditional Jewish upbringing and that, even as a child, he staged plays and made short films for his parents. He had a particular taste for comedy, especially the work of the Marx Brothers, Woody Allen, and, when he grew older, Lenny Bruce. In 1972 the family (which included Kaufman's older sister) relocated to West Hartford, Connecticut. Though shy and rather quiet, Kaufman was reportedly well liked at his high school, where he spent much of his time either acting in drama club or community productions or working in the TV Company, an elective course at his high school that focused on television production. Evidently a gifted actor with a flair for comedy, Kaufman landed the lead role in his high school's production of the 1969 Woody Allen play *Play It Again, Sam*, an experience Kaufman then wrote about for the

school yearbook. When Kaufman graduated, in 1976, he received the school's Diane T. Weldon Scholarship for Achievement in Dramatic Arts.

Kaufman attended Boston University, in Massachusetts, before transferring to New York University (NYU), in New York City, where he studied film. At NYU he became friends with fellow film student Paul Proch, and the two began collaborating on a variety of film scripts and plays. They also found work writing faux letters to the editor at $25 apiece for the humor magazine *National Lampoon*. After graduating from NYU Kaufman and Proch wrote a screenplay entitled "Purely Coincidental"; unsure of how to sell the piece, they sent it randomly to actors and filmmakers who they thought might be interested in it. Because the script was unsolicited, most of the recipients did not respond. Proch and Kaufman did hear back, however, from the actor, director, and writer Alan Arkin. As Kaufman told John Boonstra for the *Hartford (Connecticut) Advocate* (May 20, 2004, on-line), Arkin "wrote back this really lovely letter, which was so encouraging. He really liked it. And that somebody read it—that Alan Arkin read it—was really an enormous deal for us."

Despite that encouragement, Kaufman and Proch had little luck selling scripts or articles, and in the late 1980s the pair, who remain good friends, split up to pursue separate careers. Kaufman moved to Minneapolis, Minnesota, where he supported himself by working in the Minneapolis *Star Tribune* circulation department in the early-morning hours and at the Minneapolis Institute of Arts in the afternoon. Initially, Kaufman found the prospect of writing without Proch's feedback to be daunting, as he told John Boonstra. "My relationship with Paul is very influential in my writing, and it's incorporated into my psyche. . . . But I became dependent on [Proch's help], and when we stopped working together I didn't have that and I became very shy about my stuff, about showing it to people, and even writing it. It was important for me to get over it, and I did. I figured out a way to collaborate with myself. It's a combination of writing and distance. I'll write something and put it away, and when I read it weeks later, with fresh eyes, I'll know [how good it is]." Both Proch and Kaufman had resisted the idea of getting agents to help them secure assignments, considering it an unnecessary step. "I assumed . . . that you didn't need an agent, that we'd just write this stuff, and someone would say 'Oh my God, this is amazing!' We had that fantasy for a while," Kaufman admitted to John Boonstra. Realizing the error in his thinking, Kaufman found an agent, who advised him to move to Los Angeles, California, the center of the film and television industries. Ironically, it was after Kaufman did so, in 1991, that he received a phone call from a producer who was creating a show to be filmed in Minneapolis and who hired Kaufman after a phone interview. Then, as Kaufman was packing his belongings for the move back to Minnesota, he got a call from the producer David

Mirkin, who had read and enjoyed one of Kaufman's scripts. When Kaufman told Mirkin that he was headed back to Minneapolis, the producer told him to stay put. Shortly thereafter, Mirkin hired Kaufman as a writer for the series *Get a Life*, a sitcom about a 30-year-old paperboy living above his parents' garage. Kaufman wrote for *Get a Life* for a year and has since called it his favorite television-writing job.

Following the cancellation of *Get a Life*, in 1992, Kaufman got a job writing for another television series, *The Edge* (1992–93), a short-lived comedic skit show. He then wrote for the little-noticed series *The Trouble with Larry* (1993), which starred the comedian Bronson Pinchot. Kaufman's next job was for the series *Ned and Stacey* (1995–97), which starred Thomas Haden Church and Debra Messing as a couple who, after knowing each other for only a week, decide to get married for reasons of convenience. During that time Kaufman also wrote for the *Dana Carvey Show* (1996), a sketch-comedy program featuring the *Saturday Night Live* alumnus. While contributing to those shows, Kaufman had been working on a full-length screenplay of his own, about a puppeteer who discovers a portal that leads into the mind of the actor John Malkovich. The story, which Kaufman titled *Being John Malkovich*, was undeniably bizarre, as Kaufman acknowledged to Colin Covert for the Minneapolis *Star Tribune* (April 17, 2002): "I never thought anyone was going to make [the film]. Then Malkovich read it and liked it, which I was very happy about, and I thought that was as far as it was going to go. And it was, for a couple of years. Then it kind of came together."

The project "came together" after the fledgling filmmaker Spike Jonze expressed his interest in it. Malkovich agreed to play himself in the film. Although Jonze and Kaufman drafted a list of potential replacements for Malkovich, Kaufman was convinced that Malkovich was the perfect choice for the picture. "There's a kind of mystery to him, you never really know what's behind his eyes," Kaufman told Moira Macdonald. "And his name, it's funny." The finished film starred John Cusack as Craig, the tortured, artsy puppeteer; Cameron Diaz as Lotte, his frumpy, animal-loving wife; and Catherine Keener as Craig's colleague Maxine, with whom he is enamored. Despite, or because of, the absurd premise of the film—that Craig finds a way of allowing anyone to inhabit the actor's body for 15 minutes before being expelled on the side of the New Jersey Turnpike—the 1999 picture was a huge hit with both audiences and critics. "*Being John Malkovich* is a clever and outrageous piece of whimsical fantasy that is unique, unpredictable and more than a little strange," Kenneth Turan enthused in the *Los Angeles Times* (October 29, 1999). "It's an *Alice in Wonderland* film that slyly raises all sorts of philosophical questions about the nature of reality, identity and self, and deals with them in a genially unhinged way." The film earned three Academy Award nominations—for best di-

rector; best supporting actress (Keener); and best screenplay.

After his phenomenal success with *Being John Malkovich*, Kaufman wrote the screenplay for the 2001 film *Human Nature*, an oddball tale about a scientist (Tim Robbins), an exceptionally hirsute woman (Patricia Arquette), and a man who thinks he is an ape (Rhys Ifans). As a follow-up to his previous film, *Human Nature*, directed by Michel Gondry, was a disappointment, earning mixed reviews and limited screenings. Meanwhile, in 1999, Kaufman had accepted an offer to write a film adaptation of Susan Orlean's nonfiction book *The Orchid Thief*, about John Laroche, a devoted orchid breeder. Kaufman soon found the assignment to be much more difficult than he had anticipated. "I wanted to do it, and I thought I knew how, but I couldn't figure it out, and I just got very frustrated and decided to write about the process of my trying to write it," he explained to John DeFore for the *Austin (Texas) American-Statesman* (April 12, 2002). "But [the people who commissioned it] didn't know I was doing that—I didn't tell them, because I didn't have any other ideas at that point, and I was afraid if I said I was going to do this they'd say no. So it was a very scary several months for me." To his relief, the producers approved of his idea and the resulting screenplay, which interwove the stories of how Orlean wrote *The Orchid Thief* and how Kaufman tried to adapt the book. Orlean was also pleased with the direction Kaufman had taken, despite his having turned her character in the movie into a gun-toting, drug-snorting adulteress. "I don't need another version of exactly what I wrote," Orlean assured Moira Macdonald. "I'd rather have someone with an imagination be inspired by it and do something creative. I feel very lucky that it ended up with people who are very imaginative and passionate."

Kaufman's take on the material was nothing if not imaginative; he not only incorporated a fictionalized version of himself into the story, but gave himself a twin brother, Donald. (Nicolas Cage portrayed both characters.) He also invented an illicit relationship between Orlean and Laroche and packed the film with a variety of unexpected twists and turns. Another collaboration between Kaufman and Spike Jonze, *Adaptation* premiered in 2002 to primarily positive reviews. Some critics considered the movie an exercise in navel-gazing; in an article for the on-line magazine *Salon* (December 16, 2002), Stephanie Zacharek wrote, "Kaufman has decided he's the most interesting thing about Orlean's book, and he proceeds accordingly." Most, though, agreed with William Arnold, who wrote for the *Seattle Post-Intelligencer* (December 20, 2002, on-line) that the movie is "an occasionally brilliant, sporadically hilarious, inside-filmmaking burlesque . . . that comes excitingly close to being some kind of masterpiece of surrealism." Kaufman's film was nominated for Oscars in several categories, including best screenplay, and Chris Cooper, who portrayed Laroche, won the award for best supporting actor.

Kaufman found his next project to be less fulfilling than *Adaptation*. He wrote the screenplay for *Confessions of a Dangerous Mind*, a 2002 film based on the same-titled memoir by the television host and producer Chuck Barris, who claimed to have worked as a hit man for the CIA. The film's director and co-star, George Clooney, reportedly did not welcome Kaufman's presence on the set. "That was a very sad experience for me," Kaufman told Anthony Breznican for the Associated Press (March 16, 2004). "These things are important to me, these things I write . . . I recognize and embrace the notion of collaboration—and other people should, too." Despite that conflict, the movie version of *Confessions of a Dangerous Mind* was well received, earning praise for both Kaufman's screenplay and Clooney's direction.

The idea for Kaufman's next film came from the French artist Pierre Bismuth, who posed an unusual hypothetical question to the director Michel Gondry: What would Gondry do if he received a postcard saying that he had been erased from a friend's memory and should never again attempt to contact that friend? Gondry mentioned the question to Kaufman, who was intrigued enough to make it the basis for a screenplay. In *Eternal Sunshine of the Spotless Mind*, Kaufman told the story of Joel (Jim Carrey) and Clementine (Kate Winslet), a couple who, after seeing their relationship sour, decide to erase their memories of each other, via an invasive, high-tech procedure. (Kaufman based the character Joel loosely on his old friend and collaborator Paul Proch.) "I wanted to deal with someone's *idea* of a relationship. Because you're not seeing the relationship, you're seeing Joel's idea of the relationship," Kaufman explained in his interview with Anthony Breznican. "I was trying to figure out what a memory feels like. I think you just assume that your memory is just sort of a video playback of your experience, but it's nothing like that at all. It's a complete refabrication of an event and a lot of it is made up, because you're filling in spaces." Kaufman's second collaboration with Michel Gondry, *Eternal Sunshine of the Spotless Mind* was widely hailed as Kaufman's best movie to date. In an article for the *Washington Post* (March 19, 2004, on-line), Michael O'Sullivan raved, "Neither wholly cynical nor wholly romantic, Kaufman's story is a balance of smarts and sentiment. It's the most fully realized working out of his two favorite obsessions: the subjective nature of experience and the psychological mysteries of pair bonding." Kaufman received an Oscar for best screenplay for the film, and Winslet was nominated for best actress.

Kaufman's next film will be an as-yet-untitled horror movie to be directed by Spike Jonze. "I have no interest in making a genre horror movie, so I keep trying to make sure that's not what I'm doing, so I keep trying to figure out what's really scary, not what's scary in movies because that is too easy," Kaufman explained on his Web site. He has also said that he would like the chance to direct his own work someday, and that he is interested in writing

a novel. Kaufman is often asked how he generates his unique, often bizarre ideas. "Where does this stuff come from? I don't know. It's just the stuff I think about," he told Robert W. Butler for the *(Kansas and Missouri) Kansas City Star* (April 12, 2002). "It really doesn't seem all that odd to me. In fact I like to think that my comedies are actually serious films. They're dealing humorously with serious subjects." "Sometimes I just start writing based on a gut feeling," he told the *New Zealand Herald* (January 18, 2003). "I'm feeling tense, then I write and that's what I'm writing about. I don't really know where things come from. I just have ideas and I follow them through." His follow-through, he admitted to Anthony Breznican, can get rather intense at times. "I'm disciplined in the sense that I probably suffer from [obsessive compulsive disorder] a bit, so I can't stop thinking about things. So I go over ideas whether I want to or not—over and over and over." Kaufman explained to Claudia Puig that he never writes about the bizarre simply to be thought quirky and clever. "Weirdness just for the sake of weirdness and inside references just feels insular. The movie has to be about a human experience," he said.

Aside from having written himself into the screenplay of *Adaptation*, Kaufman generally avoids the spotlight; he has a reputation for being a shy loner. He and his wife, Denise, and their children live in Pasadena, California, where, as Kaufman told Colin Covert, "there's no sense of people looking at you to see who you are."

—K.J.E.

Suggested Reading: Associated Press Mar. 16, 2004; Being Charlie Kaufman Web site; *Hartford (Connecticut) Advocate* (on-line) May 20, 2004; Internet Movie Database; *New Zealand Herald* Jan. 18, 2003; *Seattle Times* J p7 Apr. 7, 2002; *Vancouver (British Columbia) Province* B p2 Mar. 19, 2004

Selected Television Shows: *Get a Life*, 1992; *The Edge*, 1992–93; *The Trouble with Larry*, 1993; *Ned and Stacey*, 1995–97; *The Dana Carvey Show*, 1996

Selected Films: *Being John Malkovich*, 1999; *Human Nature*, 2001; *Adaptation*, 2002; *Confessions of a Dangerous Mind*, 2002; *Eternal Sunshine of the Spotless Mind*, 2004

Courtesy of the University of California, San Francisco

Kenyon, Cynthia

Feb. 18, 1954– Geneticist; biotechnology executive

Address: Kenyon Lab, Box 2200, Dept. of Biophysics and Biochemistry, UCSF, San Francisco, CA 94143-2200

The work of the geneticist Cynthia Kenyon has helped to redefine the way that scientists understand the process of aging. "Once upon a time the study of aging was a scientific career killer right up there with cold fusion," Steven Kotler wrote in *Discover* (November 2004). "Everybody had pretty much agreed that decrepitude was the result of entropy—a seemingly inevitable increase of biological disorder. Then Cynthia Kenyon came along." Kenyon's studies of the microscopic roundworm *Caenorhabditis elegans* (known as *C. elegans*) surprised the scientific community by proving that the aging process is determined by genes, and that it is far more plastic than previously assumed; researchers in her lab have expanded the life spans of the worms they have studied by a factor of six. "People have always thought that, like a car, our body parts eventually wear out," Kenyon told Alex Crevar for *Georgia Magazine* (June 2004, on-line), a publication of the University of Georgia. "But we found that over time, when one gene was manipulated, the worm actually remained youthful—in all ways—so that age related diseases were also postponed." Kenyon's research may prove useful in the treatment of diseases associated with aging in humans, and in 2000 she co-founded Elixir Pharmaceuticals, a company whose aim is to develop drug therapies for such diseases. Kenyon is the Herbert

Boyer Distinguished Professor of Biochemistry and Biophysics, and director of the Hillblom Center for the Biology of Aging, at the University of California at San Francisco (UCSF). She has been the principal author of more than 70 publications in such prestigious scientific journals as *Cell, Nature,* and *Science.* "Kenyon is part of an elite core of researchers," Andy Evangelista wrote in *UCSF Magazine* (May 2003, on-line), "an internationally recognized pioneer who has helped thrust the science of aging to the research forefront."

The oldest of three children, Cynthia Kenyon was born on February 18, 1954 in Chicago, Illinois, where her father, James Kenyon, was attending graduate school at the University of Chicago. The family left Chicago after James Kenyon graduated, living briefly in New Jersey before settling in Athens, Georgia. Kenyon's father was appointed to the faculty in the Department of Geography at the University of Georgia; her mother, Jane Kenyon, accepted a position as an administrator in the Department of Physics. Kenyon's parents, as intellectuals and educators, encouraged their daughter's varied interests and natural curiosity. "Cynthia would keep a praying mantis on a leash and feed it from a toothpick dipped in honey," Jane Kenyon told Alex Crevar. "She liked to be outside and would go down to the river and just read all day long. She was incredibly inquisitive, and since she came from a family of teachers we never asked any of our children . . . a question that ended in a yes or no answer."

As a girl Kenyon took up the French horn, and by high school she had set her heart on a career as an orchestra musician. "I didn't know it at the time, but I was terrible at the French horn. I had almost no talent. I would miss notes and people would get mad at me. It was so unpleasant that I finally quit . . . ," Kenyon told Karen Roy for the *Chicago Tribune* (October 26, 1997). "It taught me that what you should try to find is not only something that you like, but something that you're good at. It's not enough to just work hard, you have to have some talent for it."

When Kenyon entered the University of Georgia as an undergraduate, she struggled to choose a major, vacillating among veterinary medicine, mathematics, philosophy, English, and other subjects. "Many, many different things were very interesting to me," Kenyon told *Current Biography*. "Finally, I just gave up and dropped out because I couldn't decide, and I was running out of time." Instead of returning to school for her junior year, Kenyon worked for a while on a farm, which she did not find satisfying. She discovered her calling when her mother brought home a copy of the book *Molecular Biology of the Gene* by James Watson, one of the scientists who had discovered the double helix structure of DNA. "I looked at it, and I thought: This is really cool, you know, genes getting switched on and off. And I thought: I'll study that. I loved the idea that biology was logical," Kenyon told David Ewing Duncan for *Discover* (March

2004). "A big tree seemed even more beautiful to me when I imagined thousands of tiny photosynthesis machines inside every leaf." Kenyon returned to school with renewed enthusiasm to pursue degrees in chemistry and biochemistry. "I realized that biology was sensible, that we could understand it the same way we understand electronic circuits," she told Karen Roy. "I was intrigued. This offered a way to learn about life."

After graduating—and becoming class valedictorian—in 1976, Kenyon was awarded a National Science Foundation graduate fellowship, which allowed her to pursue her doctorate in biology at the Massachusetts Institute of Technology (MIT), in Cambridge. There, she worked on a project whose purpose was to examine the response of *E. coli* bacteria to DNA-damaging agents. "That got me interested in development. You took an E. coli cell and you treated it with a DNA-damaging agent and it turned into a whole different animal," Kenyon told a reporter for the *New Scientist* (October 18, 2003). Kenyon was first exposed to *C. elegans* in the laboratory next to hers—that of H. Robert Horvitz, who won the 2002 Nobel Prize in physiology and medicine. "In Caenorhabditis elegans you have only a thousand cells and people knew where they all came from in the cell lineage, starting from the fertilized egg. It was the most amazing thing I'd seen, almost like the crystal structure of an animal . . . ," Kenyon told the *New Scientist* reporter. "And I thought, wow, that's what I want to do."

C. elegans, also known as nematodes or roundworms, are ideal for studying genes because of their short life spans; they live an average of two to three weeks, reaching maturity in just three days. The nematode's transparent body also makes it easy to study its cellular structure under a microscope. Additionally, many processes seen in nematodes have been duplicated in humans. Humans share at least 50 percent of the genes found in nematodes, including the genes that govern cell division, cell migration, cell differentiation, and tissue-pattern formation. "Everything else we know about the worm, we find happens in a similar way in humans," Kenyon told Karen Roy. "Muscles are made the same way, cells divide the same way, the body plan is set up with the same mechanism. Everything else that we thought would be different is the same."

Kenyon earned her Ph.D. degree in 1981. The following year she began working with *C. elegans*, in the course of her postdoctoral work at the Medical Research Council Laboratory of Molecular Biology, in Cambridge, England. She trained there as a developmental biologist under the Nobel laureate Sydney Bremmer, who was studying the roles of genes in the development of nematodes. It was there that Kenyon developed an interest in the subject of aging. One day she noticed an old lab dish containing sterile worms that she had forgotten to throw out. "There were all these old worms on the plate. I had never seen an old worm. I had never

even thought about an old worm," Kenyon told Nell Boyce for *U.S. News & World Report* (December 29, 2003). "I felt sorry for them. And I felt sorry for myself, 'Oh, I'm getting old, too.' And right on the heels of that, I thought, 'Oh, my gosh, you could study this.'"

In 1986 Kenyon accepted a position as an assistant professor at UCSF. Soon afterward she began to study aging in *C. elegans*. At that time the scientific community viewed the field of aging with disdain, and for that reason she forbade her colleagues from using the word "aging" on grant applications. "There was a lot of science done in that area that was not of a very high quality," Kenyon told *Current Biography*. "Plus there was a general feeling among molecular biologists that there was nothing to study. For example, one person who I worked with said, 'Be careful, Cynthia, you might fall off the end of the earth.'" Still, Kenyon believed that there was more to aging than an inevitable descent into entropy. "When I looked at it, I could see that different animals have different life spans," Kenyon told Stephen S. Hall for *Smithsonian* (March 2004). "The mouse lives two years and the bat can live 50 years and the canary lives about 15 or so years. They're all small animals. They're warmblooded. And they're not that different, really, in such a fundamental way from each other."

Convinced that genes controlled the rates and effects of aging, Kenyon searched for proof of her hypotheses in *C. elegans*. "There was already a mutant worm that was reported to live 50 percent longer. It had been isolated by Michael [Klass] 10 years earlier and been studied by Tom Johnson's lab [at the University of Colorado at Boulder]," Kenyon explained to Steven Kotler. "They thought maybe the mutant lived long because it didn't eat well or didn't reproduce well, but I thought there's a real set of dedicated genes for aging and that was the reason why. So we looked for these mutants."

Kenyon and her team shook up the scientific community when they announced in the December 1993 issue of *Nature* that they had been able—through the manipulation of a single gene, *daf-2*—to double the nematode's life span. The *daf-2* gene works as a sort of brake on the function of another gene, *daf-16*. When the nematode is faced with overcrowding or a food shortage, the *daf-16* gene causes nematode larvae to enter what is known as the dauer state—in which the larva's development is halted and it enters a period of stasis, allowing it to live for extended periods of time without any food or water. Scientists were already aware that *daf-2* and *daf-16* affected the dauer state; Kenyon and her team discovered that these genes also influenced aging, and that weakening *daf-2* in an adult worm would double its life span. Not only did the *daf-2* mutant worms live longer, but their aging processes slowed; the worms remained healthy until a few days before their deaths. A comparable development in humans would be a person's living to be 150 and having the body of a 45-year-old at the age of 90. "After two weeks, the normal worm is basically in a nursing home, or dead already. It's lying quietly, it looks old," Kenyon told Karen Roy. "In contrast, the altered worm is still active. It isn't just hanging onto life, it's out on the tennis court."

Though the results had yet to be replicated in mammals, Kenyon's discovery suggested that it might be possible to retard aging in humans as well. The *daf-2* gene encodes a hormone receptor, or a protein that allows tissues to respond to hormones. Kenyon's lab found that mutations that lower the activity of the receptor, making the tissues less responsive to the hormone, also increase life spans. "Our result told us that the normal function of these hormones was to speed up aging . . . ," Kenyon told Steven Kotler. "The same kinds of hormones are found in all animals. In people, it's insulin, which is used in food utilization, and a hormone called *IGF-1*, insulin-like growth factor." As a direct result of Kenyon's research, other scientists later determined that the same genes also regulate the aging process in flies and mice—suggesting that the mechanisms that govern aging may be universal in all species.

Philip Anderson, a professor of genetics at the University of Wisconsin at Madison, urged caution before applying those results to humans, but he also told Malcolm Ritter of the Associated Press (December 1, 1993), "When we understand how genes like daf-2 and daf-16 function, we will I think have insights into how aging works in humans, and perhaps insights that are directly applicable."

In October 1997 Kenyon was appointed the Herbert Boyer Distinguished Professor of Biochemistry and Biophysics at UCSF. The following year she made another important breakthrough in understanding the mechanism of aging. In an article published in the journal *Cell*, Kenyon and her associates announced their finding that the aging process does not occur in individual cells but is coordinated by signals exchanged by the different tissues. "Our study indicates there is a mechanism that causes all of the cells in the animal to reach a consensus," Kenyon told a reporter for *Gene Therapy Weekly* (November 2, 1998). "And that mechanism appears to be sparked into action by particular genes acting within certain types of cells." Using what is known as "mosaic" analysis, Kenyon and other researchers in her lab diminished or eliminated the *daf-2* gene—and later, the *daf-16* gene—in a variety of cells to see which affected the organism as a whole. They determined that a change in certain groups of cells, such as nerve or (as a later study indicated) intestinal cells, can affect the aging process of all cells in an organism, even those that contain the normal *daf-2* or *daf-16* gene. "In adult animals, by acting in signaling cells to control the production of a second signal, the daf-2 gene may be able to coordinate the aging process of all the cells in the animal, so that they all age together at the same rate," Kenyon told the reporter for *Gene Therapy Weekly*.

In 1999 Kenyon and her colleague Honor Hsin discovered a second hormonal pathway—in addition to the insulin receptor encoded by *daf-2*—that affects the aging process. By using a laser microbeam to remove the reproductive cells, also known as germ cells, Kenyon and Hsin extended the *C. elegans*'s life span by 60 percent. "It turns out that the germ cells do two things: they produce the next generation, the sperm and the eggs—they are the next generation in a sense—and in addition they speed up the aging of the body," Kenyon told *Current Biography*. "Let's suppose a mutation took place, or something happened to slow down the development of the germ line. What would happen? The animal would reproduce later. It would take it longer to be able to reproduce, but if you did this, the germ cells would no longer be able to speed up aging as well, and as a consequence the animal would age more slowly. . . . So it's a way of bringing the timing of reproduction into register with the aging of the body, allowing animals to reproduce in their prime, which is what you want. So my prediction is that this will turn out to be important in evolution, in the evolution of life strategies for different organisms—how fast it develops, when to reproduce."

Kenyon believes that it may be possible, once the mechanism in germ cells that controls aging has been identified, to manipulate that mechanism so as to extend the life spans of nematodes without also rendering them infertile. Nematodes whose life spans have been extended only through the manipulation of *daf-2* remain fertile. Kenyon disputes the prevailing notion that life spans can be extended only at the cost of reduced fertility or a lower metabolism. "People think that if you extend life span there has to be a trade-off, but how could that be true?" she said to Alex Crevar. "Think about it, evolution started with this little primitive animal that is one of your ancestors and that gave rise to C. elegans and then to some animal that gave rise to you. If every time you changed genes there was a trade-off, we would never be so much superior. We are amazing. If every time there was some downside, we would not live 1,000 times longer than the nematode worm . . . and we are not 1,000 times worse off."

In another research project, conducted with Javier Apfeld, Kenyon discovered that sensory perception also influences the aging process. Sensory neurons in the nematodes' heads and tails gather information about their environment, such as temperature, movement, and the presence of food. Kenyon and Apfeld found that genetic mutations that cause defects in the neurons, inhibiting sensory signals, also extend life span. "The signal affecting lifespan may be a substance that the animal can smell or taste," Apfeld and Kenyon wrote in a paper published in *Nature* (December 16, 1999). "For example, it may be a pheromone such as dauer pheromone, which reflects population density, or a compound that originates from organic material and reflects food availability." In a later study, however, Kenyon determined that the signal affecting life span was not the dauer pheromone. The results of that study, published in *Neuron* in 2004, also revealed that taking away either of two chemosensory receptors—that is, proteins that stick through the tips of the neurons and bind to odorants or substances that the worms taste—extends life span as well.

In the May 16, 2003 issue of *Science*, Kenyon published a study that addressed the question of why the elderly become susceptible to age-related diseases. For example, when the gene that causes Huntington's disease is introduced into a worm, the animal contracts Huntington's disease as it ages. By contrast, the worms with manipulated *daf-2* genes also get Huntington's disease, but not until they are older. Kenyon's lab found that those worms produced a greater number of "small heat shock proteins," also known as chaperones, which attach themselves to unfolded cellular proteins and prevent them from forming harmful aggregations that can lead to many age-related diseases, such as Alzheimer's and Parkinson's. "The chaperones also see to it that a damaged protein is either fixed or it's put into the wastebasket and degraded, making room for another protein," Kenyon told *Current Biography*. "We found that these chaperones were able to do two things: to increase life span and to delay the time of onset of Huntington's disease. So by keeping the cell's normal proteins, and also the Huntington protein, from misfolding, these chaperones may couple the normal aging process to the time of onset of this disease."

Later that year Kenyon published another study in *Nature* (June 29, 2003). Working with both normal and *daf-2* mutant nematodes, researchers in Kenyon's lab identified a large number of genes, including antioxidant, chaperone, antimicrobial, and metabolic genes, that were either more or less active in the long-lived mutants. They then used a technique known as RNA interference to disable these genes one at a time. While manipulating some genes increased life spans by only 10 to 30 percent, manipulating the *daf-2* gene can mobilize them all at once, producing a huge increase in life span. "The daf-2 gene acts as an orchestra conductor," Kenyon told Alex Crevar. "It's a very powerful regulator that brings together all the instruments in the orchestra. The cellos, for instance, are the antioxidant genes, the piccolos prevent infection, and the French horns are involved in things like fat transport. When we change the way one responds to a hormone, we know that about 100 genes turn up or down—or on or off—for a large cumulative effect."

In October 2004 the journal *Science* reported that by combining techniques—weakening the *daf-2* gene and destroying cells in the reproductive system—Kenyon, along with her colleagues Nuno Arantes-Oliveira and Jennifer Berman, had extended the lifetime of the nematode sixfold. "The thing that was so remarkable about those worms was how healthy they were. You might think they would just lie there or something—but they don't. They move around," Kenyon told *Current Biography*. "They're very healthy and very active, even when they're quite old. . . . And they look good. They're not skinny or anything. They're nice-looking worms." The equivalent in humans would be living healthy, active lives for 500 years.

Her findings notwithstanding, Kenyon does not predict that human life spans will increase dramatically in the near future. She believes that the benefits of this research will be seen, instead, in treatments for age-related diseases, such as type II diabetes, obesity, cancer, and heart disease, and perhaps in protein-aggregation disorders such as Huntington's disease. "There are lots of different age-related diseases that seem to be postponed in these long-lived animals, whether it's worms or flies or mice. . . . There's something about being biologically or physiologically older that makes you more susceptible," Kenyon told *Current Biography*. "So people traditionally have been going after this disease or that disease—cancer, osteoporosis—separately, but if you could go after aging, which is the biggest risk factor for the vast majority of all these diseases, then you might be able to delay the time of onset for many all at once."

Around 1996 Kenyon began courting venture capitalists, showing them a five-minute film about the nematodes she had studied. "I show them the movie, of worms that are normal that are about to die after two weeks, and the altered worms that are still moving," she told Stephen S. Hall. "They see it with their eyes, you know? . . . And that's really all you have to do. It speaks for itself." In 2000 Kenyon and Leonard Guarente, the Novartis Professor of Biology at MIT, founded Elixir Pharmaceuticals, a Boston, Massachusetts–based company dedicated to developing ways of extending youthfulness and improving the quality of old age. Elixir finalized an agreement with UCSF in 2003 to access discoveries made by Kenyon and her laboratory for potential drug development. "We may not have a perfect drug in 10 years, but we'll have something to build on. Potentially, we could have it sooner," Kenyon told Stephen S. Hall.

Kenyon's ability to explain science in ways that are accessible to most laypeople has made her a popular spokesperson in the media. She has appeared on the Discovery Channel and ABC News, was featured on a *Scientific American Frontiers* TV special, and has also been heard on radio specials for National Public Radio and the BBC. She is currently working on a book about aging for a general readership.

In April 2003 Kenyon was one of six speakers at the 50th-anniversary celebration of the discovery of DNA, held in in Cambridge, England, at which James Watson was also present. Kenyon is a member of the American Academy of Arts and Sciences, a member of the National Academy of the Sciences, and an Ellison Medical Foundation Senior Scholar. She has been awarded the Wiersma Visiting Professorship at the California Institute of Technology, a Searle Scholarship, a Packard Fellowship, the *Discover* Award for Innovation in Basic Research, the Award for Distinguished Research in the Biomedical Sciences from the Association of American Medical Colleges, and the King Faisal International Prize for Medicine. She served as the president of the Genetics Society of America in 2004.

In her leisure time, Kenyon still plays the French horn—as well as the guitar and Alpine horn. Taking a cue from her own research, she maintains a diet that keeps her insulin levels low. "I don't want to get old. And I don't think I'm the only person that feels that way," she told Karen Lu-

rie for *ScienCentral News* (March 26, 2004, on-line). "In fact, if you read Shakespeare's sonnets, so many of them are about the anguish of aging. People don't like to get old, they don't like to lose their abilities, their capacities. So for people who love life, like I do, what could be better?"

—J.C.

Suggested Reading: *Chicago Tribune* Womanews p3 Oct. 26, 1997, with photo; *Discover* (on-line) Nov. 2004; *Life Extension* p51+ June 2002, with photos; *Smithsonian* p56+ Mar. 2004, with photos; *UCSF Magazine* (on-line) May 2003

Courtesy of Chip Kidd

Kidd, Chip

1964– Graphic designer; editor; novelist

Address: c/o Random House, 1745 Broadway, New York, NY 10019

Originally a mere wrapping used to protect books from dust and soot, the book jacket is now regarded by many graphic designers as the last great forum for their work, and publishers now recognize it as the focal point of a book's marketing campaign. "Indeed, book jackets have evolved from the paper equivalent of trench coats into sexy boleros, elegant capes and silk dinner jackets, striving to be at once provocative, tasteful and mysterious," Mary B. W. Tabor wrote for the *New York Times* (April 24, 1995). "A bold player in this evolution is [Chip] Kidd, who is considered one of the best graphic de-

signers around." As a designer for Alfred A. Knopf, Kidd has created book jackets for the works of many of the best-selling authors in contemporary fiction and nonfiction—including John Updike, Michael Crichton, David Sedaris, Anne Rice, Oliver Sacks, and Michael Ondaatje. So many of his designs grace the covers of books on the *New York Times* best-seller lists that some authors now stipulate in their contracts that Kidd must handle their designs. Véronique Vienne noted in her monograph *Chip Kidd* (2003) that the graphic designer's lifelong interest in comics has influenced his approach to his work. Indeed, Kidd first grew interested in design as a child after examining the packaging of his favorite toys modeled on the comicbook hero Batman. Beginning with *Batman Collected*, in 1996, he has edited several coffee-table books celebrating the superhero comics and related memorabilia he enjoyed in his youth. He also serves as an editor at large for the Pantheon imprint, overseeing the publication of graphic novels by such renowned artists as Daniel Clowes and Chris Ware. After 15 years of designing the covers for other authors, Kidd got the opportunity to create one for his own book, *The Cheese Monkeys: A Novel in Two Semesters*. In 2005 he published *Chip Kidd: Book One: Work: 1986–2006*, a compendium of his covers with added material, an introduction by John Updike (a native of Kidd's hometown), and contributions by David Sedaris, Donna Tartt, and Elmore Leonard. A review at Amazon.com termed it "an important contribution to the design canon today as well as a visually dazzling and hilarious insider's look at the design and publishing process."

The second son of Ann and Tom Kidd, Charles Iacone Kidd was born in 1964 in Shillington, Pennsylvania, and raised in Reading, Pennsylvania; his parents owned a store, Annie's Balloons, in nearby Wyomissing. He was a dedicated fan of Batman by the age of two and regularly watched the live-action television series about the "caped crusader" with his father. His fascination was cemented at the age of four, when, riddled with chicken pox, he was lulled to sleep by his Batman night-light. It was then that Kidd began collecting Batman memorabilia.

In 1982 Kidd graduated from high school and enrolled at Pennsylvania State University in State College, where he studied graphic design. "I think I made a decision at some point that my strength really wasn't as a draftsman, it was more in conceptual thinking and [then] following that through visually," he told Mark Feeney for the *Boston Globe* (October 17, 2001). Kidd's favorite teacher at the school was Lanny Sommese, whose teaching method emphasized the way in which visual and verbal elements play off each other, an approach that is reflected in Kidd's later work. He was also influenced by the work of the Russian constructivists, who strove to make art more utilitarian, and the designer Alvin Lustig, who created covers for the New York book publisher James Laughlin in the 1940s and 1950s. "Coming out of college at Penn State, the most interesting designer I saw was this guy named Peter Saville, who was doing record sleeves in Britain, including all [record sleeves for the punk band New Order] for Factory Records," he told Janet Froelich for the *New York Times* (November 10, 1996). "For our generation, record sleeves were a major source of printed visual information, and all of a sudden somebody was doing it in a completely different way." Kidd is convinced that the switch from vinyl records to compact discs, which give designers a much smaller canvas, spurred the rise of interest in book-jacket art. "The book cover became the last vestige for graphic designers to have a place to play," he told Calvin Reid for *Publishers Weekly* (October 29, 2001).

In 1986, after graduating with a bachelor's degree in graphic design, Kidd moved to New York City to look for work in the field. His first cover design, a freelance job for Random House, was for Robert M. Hochheiser's *How to Work for a Jerk*. He told Philip Marchand for the *Toronto Star* (October 26, 2004), "I made the cover look like a 1950s horror comic. They thought it was very funny, but said, hey, we can't do that." A Random House editor who worked for the Alfred A. Knopf imprint happened to see Kidd's design, however, and was impressed. Soon Kidd was hired as the junior assistant to Sarah Eisenman, the art director at Knopf. "Of course, the pay was abysmal," he told Reid, "but they said you can use your office to freelance on your own time and if your jacket designs get approved, your name goes on the flap. Naive as I was, I knew that was as good as money."

Early in his career Kidd used a typographical approach to design, selecting typefaces that were evocative of the mood or the subculture described in the text. His style evolved as he worked with top-notch designers at Knopf, including Carol Carson, an innovator in the field. Traditionally, designers had used illustrations on covers of fiction books; in the 1980s Carson had begun using photographs, which sparked a sea change in the industry and influenced Kidd's work. While Kidd's use of an illustration—the silhouetted figure of a Tyrannosaurus rex—on the cover of Michael Crichton's novel *Jurassic Park* (1990) proved to be quite successful, many of his most memorable covers are those that incorporate photographs. As Vienne wrote, "Kidd stretches the visual boundaries between words and visuals by choosing pictures that appear at first glance to be non sequiturs. The jacket of David Shields' *A Handbook for Drowning* (1991) shows an upside down figure standing against a huge cloudy sky; the hardcover jacket of James Ellroy's *White Jazz* (1992) features the bullet-ridden door of a police car; the image on [Cormac] McCarthy's cover for *The Crossing* (1994) is a sepia photograph of horses' skulls. By distancing the title from the image on the cover, Kidd puts a very specific kind of pressure on readers: he asks them to bridge the gap between what they read and what they see."

When he began working with photographs, Kidd favored the practice of bisecting covers, or dividing the cover space into two rectangular, usually horizontal panes. Most often one of the panes contained the title, centered in white space, with a photograph in the pane above or below, as with Cormac McCarthy's *All the Pretty Horses* (1993); at other times a photograph occupied each pane, as with Geoff Ryman's *Was* (1992); and sometimes the cover was split into vertical panes, as with Ellen Lupton's *Mixing Messages* (1996). Vienne suggested that that technique brings to mind the panel-to-panel format of comics: "Instead of just defining a surface, his jackets define a time sequence during which the mind races between the various panels, putting together bits and pieces of visual and verbal information. His covers are successful when, upon completing this act of creation, the viewer comes away with a greater awareness of what he or she thinks the book is about."

The effectiveness of that early technique was most evident in Cormac McCarthy's Border Trilogy, which includes *All the Pretty Horses*, *The Crossing*, and *Cities of the Plain* (1999). Despite critical accolades, none of McCarthy's previous books had sold more than 2,600 copies. The frustrated author decided to switch publishers and brought *All the Pretty Horses*, a novel about a teenager crossing the U.S.-Mexican border, to Knopf. The top half of Kidd's design featured the title and author's name in a widely spaced serif font. For the lower half he selected a black-and-white extreme close-up of a horse's mane. Although he had violated one of his own cardinal rules of book design—to never be literal—by putting an image of a horse on the cover, the cropped photo of the horse's mane proved to be both elegant and evocative. Kidd often employs this technique, using partial images and obscuring detail with text, to create a sense of mystery. *All the Pretty Horses* sold half a million copies in hardcover and paperback and won the National Book Award. "I think Chip Kidd is a genius," Amanda Urban, McCarthy's agent, told Tabor. "What he is so good at—better than almost anyone—is capturing the soul of a novel."

Kidd was quickly regarded as a wunderkind in his field, and over the years that followed, he established a thriving freelance business. Though most of the more than 1,000 covers that he has designed have been for Knopf, he has also created covers for books published by HarperCollins, Doubleday, Grove Press, Penguin/Putnam, Scribner, and Columbia University Press, among others. By 1995 he was commanding freelance fees that were nearly twice what other designers were paid.

The first step in Kidd's creative process, which he terms the "magpie method," is to read the manuscript. "In any book, you have a plot, but then you usually have a subtext—that is, what the author's really talking about," he told Froelich. "Part of the designer's job is to temper these two things, and then to give form to the idea." Kidd samples elements from the work of other designers, attempting to integrate their ideas into his designs in fresh and interesting ways. For example, in preparation for designing the book jacket for William Boyd's *Brazzaville Beach* (1990), Kidd studied cigarette packages from the Third World—because the narrator of the novel smokes an obscure brand of African cigarettes. Using a logo-like title set against a bright yellow background, he evoked the impression created by those cigarette packages for the cover design.

Kidd rarely uses stock photography, preferring instead the yellowing family photographs that he purchases at flea markets. Often he will hold on to images for years before finding the right contexts in which to use them. The photo he used for Paul Golding's *The Abomination* (2000), however, fell into his lap at just the right moment. Kidd was reading the novel—the story of a child who feels alienated because of his sexual orientation—in preparation for the design process when he received in the mail a picture by the photographer Lars Kove. Kidd told Vienne that Kove's curious photograph, of a stuffed rabbit turned on its head, was "nothing I ever would have thought of using but it made perfect sense to me." Kove's photograph took on a new, unsettling meaning in Kidd's design, reflecting both the innocence and alienation of the novel's main character. Not all of Kidd's photographs are found items, however, and he has enjoyed a successful, more-than-decade-long collaboration with the photographer Geoff Spear.

Kidd often utilizes techniques such as die-cuts—irregularly cut covers—and translucent overlays. He also attempts to create the illusion of three dimensions on many of his book jackets, as with Irina Ratushinskaya's *Grey Is the Color of Hope*, a memoir about Ratushinskaya's internment in a Russian prison, where she was not allowed to write. The cover design features an image of layered strips of crumpled paper, a reference to the small pieces of paper Ratushinskaya would acquire secretly and use for writing. Kidd explained to Renee Montagne in an interview for National Public Radio's *Morning Edition* (November 28,

2003), "I wanted to give it an . . . effect of distressed paper that you could reach out and feel the folds of it and feel the tears, and [understand] how something that's so common and everyday can become so extremely precious in certain conditions."

In 2002 Kidd calculated that he had created an average of 75 book jackets a year (some sources say 50) and had designed about 1,200 covers in total. The covers are remarkably diverse, with no signature style to connect most of them. "A signature look is crippling," he told Cary L. Roberts for the *Austin Chronicle* (September 8, 2000, on-line). "Often, the simplest and most effective solutions aren't dictated by style."

Since 2000 Kidd has also served as an editor at large for Pantheon, another imprint at Random House, supervising the publication of graphic novels. Working with Pantheon's editorial director, Dan Frank, he has published the work of a variety of established and up-and-coming comics artists. "According to Dan Frank, the main credit for the success of the Pantheon graphic novel should go to Kidd because the artists he works with—Chris Ware, Daniel Clowes, Ben Katchor—trust him as an editor," Vienne wrote.

In 1996 Kidd edited and wrote the text for the coffee-table book *Batman Collected*, which includes 500 of Spear's photographs of such wide-ranging Batman memorabilia as wallpaper, bedding, lamps, toothpaste, towels, bubble bath, air fresheners, underwear, noodle soup, and a bat-shaped tortilla chip. About a third of the items pictured in the book are from Kidd's own collection; the rest belong to Joe Desris, a noted collector in Wisconsin. Kidd told Marty Crisp for the *Lancaster New Era* (December 1, 1996), "I think my book speaks to a person of my generation who is longing for a reminder of what it was like to be young and a little more innocent." Two years later Kidd edited another collection, *Batman Animated*, with text by Paul Dini. The volume features artwork from three Emmy-winning cartoons: *Batman: The Animated Adventures*, *Batman & Robin Adventures,* and *The New Batman/Superman Adventures*. Kidd also teamed up with Spear and the writer Les Daniels to produce a series of coffee-table books about Batman and some of his other favorite superheroes—*Superman, the Complete History* (1998), *Batman: The Complete History* (1999), *Wonder Woman: The Complete History* (2000), *Wonder Woman: The Golden Age* (2001), and *The Golden Age of DC Comics: 365 Days* (2004).

In 2000 Kidd got the opportunity to work on another favorite comic from his childhood. After Charles M. Schulz, the creator of the classic *Peanuts* strip, died that year, his assistant, Paige Braddock—who also happened to be a fan of Kidd's work—provided Kidd with access to Schulz's studio for a week. Kidd was thus able to do critical research for *Peanuts: The Art of Charles M. Schulz* (2001). "I was astonished at how much free rein I was given—we were hauling out originals worth tens of thousands of dollars—and I attribute that to

Paige and to [Jeannie], Schulz's wife," Kidd told Reid. Collaborating again with Spears, Kidd selected completed strips and preliminary sketches to include in the volume. His design is meant to make the reader feel as if he or she is perusing Schulz's notebook.

That same year Kidd teamed up with Art Spiegelman, the Pulitzer Prize–winning author of the graphic novel *Maus*, to publish *Jack Cole and Plastic Man: Forms Stretched to Their Limits*. The text consists of Spiegelman's previously published *New Yorker* article about the influential though little-known artist Cole. Cole drew the sort of horror and crime comics that spurred the anti-comics sentiment of the 1950s, but he was best known for *Plastic Man*, a comic book about a man who could twist and shape his body into any form imaginable. Kidd and Spiegelman's book features selected scenes from the *Plastic Man* comics and a series of Cole's drawings of voluptuous women that were originally published in *Playboy*. Though critics were delighted to see the underappreciated artist get recognition, not everyone approved of Kidd's design. In a review for the *Sunday Oregonian* (October 14, 2001), for example, Steve Duin called Kidd's design "overwrought." Many applauded Kidd, however, for reproducing the original comics with all their printing flaws in order to preserve a sense of authenticity.

In 2001 Kidd published his first novel, *The Cheese Monkeys: A Novel in Two Semesters*. For six years, on evenings and weekends, Kidd had worked on the coming-of-age story, which takes a satirical look at academia. The narrator of the book, Happy, is a freshman in the design program at a major university who hangs out with his free-spirited, whiskey-drinking friend, Himillsy Dodd. Together, the two struggle to complete the demanding and absurd assignments of Winter Sorbeck, a brilliant but abusive teacher. Sorbeck, who both tortures and enthralls his students, is based on Lanny Sommese. Reviews of Kidd's novel were positive to mixed, with many critics praising the book's humor but calling its attempts at drama unsuccessful. Kidd's second novel, *The Learners*, is tentatively slated for publication in 2006.

Kidd serves as a design consultant for the *Paris Review*, and his designs have appeared in *Vanity Fair*, the *New Republic*, *Time*, *New York*, the *New York Times*, and *ID*, among other publications. He has also written articles about graphic design for *Vogue*, the *New York Times*, the *New York Observer*, *Entertainment Weekly*, *Details*, *Arena*, *2WICE*, the *New York Post*, *ID*, *Print*, and other periodicals. He has taught at the School of Visual Arts, in New York City, and his book-jacket designs have been displayed at the Cooper-Hewitt National Design Museum, also in New York.

ID named Kidd one of the top 40 designers in the United States and honored him with the Design Distinction Award as well as two Best-of-Category Packaging Awards. He won two Eisner Awards for *Batman Animated* and the award for use of photog-raphy in graphic design from the International Center of Photography. He is a member of the Alliance Graphique Internationale.

Kidd and his partner, the poet J. D. McClatchy, are a popular couple in literary circles and often throw parties at their apartment on the Upper East Side of Manhattan, in New York City. In *Publishers Weekly* (October 29, 2001), Calvin Reid noted that Kidd is "as much in demand as a party guest, raconteur and genial wit as he is as designer and editor."

—J.C.

Suggested Reading: *Boston Globe* C p1+ Oct. 17, 2001; Identity Theory (on-line) Dec. 17, 2005; *Kansas City Star* p16+ Jan 6, 2003; *New York Times* D p9 Apr. 24, 1995, E p1 Aug. 22, 2005; Vienne, Veronique. *Chip Kidd*, 2003

Selected Books: as editor—*Superman , the Complete History*, 1998; *Batman: The Complete History*, 1999; *Wonder Woman: The Complete History*, 2000; *Wonder Woman: The Golden Age*, 2001; *Peanuts: The Art of Charles M. Schulz*, 2001; *Jack Cole and Plastic Man: Forms Stretched to Their Limits*, 2001; *Mythology: The DC Comics Art of Alex Ross*, 2003; as writer—*The Cheese Monkeys: A Novel in Two Semesters*, 2001; *Chip Kidd: Book One: Work: 1986–2006*, 2005

Knievel, Robbie

(kuh-NEEV-el)

May 7, 1962– Motorcycle stunt performer

Address: c/o Dan Zucker, Event Sales Group, 3816 Evanston Ave. N., Seattle, WA 98103-8515

"Only a lunatic would want to be an English teacher," Robbie Knievel told Franz Lidz for *Sports Illustrated* (March 17, 1986). "An accountant? Pure insanity." Many people have expressed the same thoughts about Knievel's chosen profession—including his own father, the legendary stuntman Evel Knievel, whose riding boots Robbie has filled for more than 25 years. "Robbie scares the hell out of me," the elder Knievel admitted to Lidz. "I guess I'm like any other concerned father, except that nobody else's son guns a cycle over 17 pickups without holding on to the handlebars. The greatest competitor in life is death, and here's a kid giving death the bird every time. . . . I think the little booger's nuts!" Unlike his father, whom many consider an instinctive daredevil, Robbie Knievel relies on meticulous preparation, advances in technology, and superlative riding skills. Since he began performing, at the age of eight, he has landed all of the gravity-defying jumps that his father tried—including most of the ones the older man missed—on the way

Robbie Knievel

John Gurzinski/Getty Images

to setting dozens of records of his own. But there is one record Robbie has no intention of surpassing: that for the number of bones one human being has broken. In Evel's case, that number is 433, according to the 1984 *Guinness Book of World Records*, as cited by Lidz. (Evel himself has said that 60 is closer to the truth.) "I've had eight broken bones and two knee surgeries, and they put me to sleep twice to get pavement out of my ass," Robbie Knievel told Jeff Ryan for *Sport* (June 1, 1999). "Not bad for 28 years in the business. . . . I'm doing pretty good." (He has since suffered one more fracture.)

The second of the four children of Evel and Linda Knievel, Robbie Knievel was born on May 7, 1962. He was raised on the family ranch in Butte, Montana. Robbie, the only one of the siblings to become a professional motorcyclist, began riding on the back of Evel's chopper at age two, and before long he was taking part in stunts of his own. When a local boy wanted to emulate Evel by jumping his bicycle over some playmates, for example, Robbie stretched out on the ground as the 13th child. By age seven, he was charging youngsters 50 cents a head to see him do jumps on his own minibike. A year later he was performing with his father. "Robbie's always had guts," Evel told Ryan. "It's not just the equipment. A Lear jet is a perfect piece of machinery, but just try landing it. I taught Robbie how to ride when he was six. Before long, he was flying by me, throwing rocks at me and laughing."

Robbie suffered his first serious injury during a fight with his father, who drank heavily at times to cope with chronic pain from his accidents. The injury occurred late one night when, as a teenager, he came home carrying a six-pack of beer. He and his father scuffled, and when Robbie fell to the floor, Evel kicked him, breaking Robbie's nose. (A plastic surgeon repaired the damage the next day.) "Me and him had a lot of fistfights," Robbie told Lidz, "but we always had a great father-son relationship as far as fishing and hunting." The two also bonded over their shared love of motorcycles. Still, Evel did not want his children to follow his example. "My dad would sit in the ambulance [when he got injured] and say to me and my brother, 'Look at me and promise you'll never do this,'" Robbie told Ryan. By the time he was 11, however, he knew he wanted to ride professionally.

Like his father, Robbie Knievel had several brushes with the law early in his life; twice, he stole items from music stores. Set on his course to becoming a stunt performer, he dropped out of high school. "I knew my basic math. I read and spelled really well. I knew what I wanted to do for a living. I didn't need school anymore," he told Ann Tatko for the Colorado Springs *Gazette* (July 22, 1999). "I never regretted quitting school, only because I grew up with a father who had a name and so I knew I could do this, too." Evel Knievel, also a high-school dropout, had another view of his son's choice. "Robbie never even finished reform school," he told Franz Lidz for *Sports Illustrated* (April 24, 1989). "What else was he going to do, operate on tumors?" In 1980, the same year Evel retired from jumping, Robbie hit the stunt circuit—mostly at truck and tractor shows and state fairs—wearing his father's well-known red, white, and blue leathers.

In 1986 the younger Knievel appeared before 35,000 people in Los Angeles to jump a record 13 buses. He not only succeeded, he did so using his own signature maneuver: he released the handlebars and extended his arms from his sides. Two years later Robbie cleared 22 cars and trucks in Oregon, besting his father's record by one. In April 1989 Robbie attempted his most dangerous jump to that date—over the fountains at Caesars Palace in Las Vegas. The technically difficult jump, which had put his father in a month-long coma 22 years earlier, was made even harder by new construction. "The treacherous part comes after I hit the landing ramp," Robbie told Franz Lidz in 1989. "If I sway too far left, I'll collide with a cement pillar. Drift too far right and I'll smack into a pylon. If I come up short of the ramp, I could decapitate myself." Father and son almost came to blows before the jump, because Evel persisted in giving his son unwanted advice. When Robbie safely landed, however, his father proudly greeted him. Robbie, who had planned to employ his no-hands move, apologized for abandoning it mid-flight. "Forget it, son," Evel said, according to Lidz. "The night you were conceived, I hung on to your mother with both hands too." Father and son have grown steadily closer, especially after Evel contracted hepatitis C in 1993, apparently from a blood transfusion. (The disease necessitated a liver transplant six years later.) Despite their improved relationship,

Evel told Ryan, "Robbie has a huge ego. He feels he isn't as well-known as he should be. It's tough for him being my son. It's like being the son of Muhammad Ali or Mickey Mantle or Jack Nicklaus."

Robbie Knievel has continued to shatter jumping records while keeping himself relatively intact. In 1998 he soared over 17 tractor-trailers in Green Bay, Wisconsin. Less than a year later, he cleared a 130-foot gap between two 18-story towers in Las Vegas. Months later he broke his own distance record by jumping 228 feet across a 1,500-foot-deep gorge in the Grand Canyon. Although events sponsors pay him handsomely for all of his attempts, Knievel, who refers to himself sometimes as the "Kaptain," has taken part in more overtly commercial ventures recently, including a December 2003 jump over some 10,000 plates for a dish-soap commercial.

In July 2004 Knievel cleared seven military aircraft on the deck of the *USS Intrepid*, an aircraft carrier that saw action in World War II and Vietnam and has since been docked in New York City as a maritime museum. Knievel dedicated the jump—which he successfully completed, though he landed awkwardly because of heavy crosswinds and had to ditch his bike as he slid into bales of hay—to firefighters, police officers, and military personnel. During his 2004 tour he recorded six installments for his show, *Knievel's Wild Ride*, which debuted on the Arts and Entertainment Television Network in April 2005. The remaining seven installments were shot while Knievel was on the road, during his 2005 tour.

Knievel's plans include jumping his motorcycle between two helicopters in flight and jumping over 15 Greyhound buses at King's Island, in Ohio (thus matching his father's 1974 bus-jumping record). He is said to be in negotiations with officials in Twin Falls, Idaho, to jump the quarter-mile-wide Snake River Canyon, a stunt that his father tried without success 30 years ago. Knievel told Ryan, "I'm no adrenaline junkie. I can't explain why I jump. It's in my blood. There are a lot of mouthy, overnight daredevils, and I always wanted to beat their distances and bring a little class to this sport."
—T.J.F.

Suggested Reading: (Colorado Springs) *Gazette* July 22, 1999; knieveltour.com; *New York Times* I p47 Mar. 11, 1989, with photo; *Sport* p84 June 1, 1999; *Sports Illustrated* p8 Mar. 17, 1986, with photos, p26 Apr. 24, 1989, with photos

Knipfel, Jim

(kuh-NIF-el)

June 2, 1965– Memoirist; novelist; columnist

Address: New York Press, *333 Seventh Ave., 14th Fl., New York, NY 10001*

Through his alternative weekly column, "Slackjaw," which has been a staple of the *New York Press* since 1991, Jim Knipfel has steadily built his reputation as a dark humorist and biting nonconformist. First slated to be an arts-review column, "Slackjaw" has evolved into a space for Knipfel's colorful rants and observations about his misadventures. Through the years Knipfel has had plenty of unusual experiences to share with readers: he is afflicted with a rare degenerative eye disease that rendered him legally blind by the age of 30, and he also has an inoperable brain lesion that causes severe depression, seizures, and suicidal tendencies. In writing "Slackjaw," he has never shied away from exposing his own shortcomings or from describing his most difficult challenges. Knipfel's friend Gretchen Worden told Sam Adams for the *Philadelphia City Paper* (June 1–8, 2000, on-line), "He gives you a sense of permission: It's OK to look at this stuff. I mean, my God, the self-exposure that Jim goes into—his guts are on display in his writing. . . . They're just laid out there for you to look at." In 1999 Knipfel published a memoir, also titled *Slackjaw*, which chronicles his struggles to deal

Morgan Intrieri

with his failing sight, among other topics. "If you are into the genealogy of U.S. literature, *Slackjaw* would snuggle somewhere between the gallows humour of Kurt Vonnegut and the deranged logic of Joseph Heller," Felix Cheong wrote for the Singaporean publication *Straits Times* (October 9, 1999). Knipfel's next book was *Quitting the Nairo-*

bi Trio (2000), about his six-month stay in a mental ward following a suicide attempt. His third memoir was *Ruining It for Everybody* (2004). Knipfel has also tried his hand at fiction, with *The Buzzing* (2003), a comical farce about an aging journalist on the trail of an elaborate cover-up. In a conversation with David Daley for the *Hartford (Connecticut) Courant* (April 1, 1999), he said, "After surviving 12 suicide attempts, I came to the conclusion that I simply could not be killed. It had something to do with foolish, hurtful hubris (which sounds like the sequel to *Silly Human Pride*). That sense faded very quickly as well. But suddenly I wasn't interested in killing myself anymore. So I decided I might as well deal with it. It's made me much less insufferable." "Just deal with it" is Knipfel's guiding philosophy.

Born on June 2, 1965, James M. Knipfel grew up in Green Bay, Wisconsin, where his father worked as a recruiter for the U.S. Air Force and his mother was an accountant at a local department store. He enjoyed a typical small-town childhood, with a loving family and a stable home life. However, he suffered from poor vision and started to wear glasses when he was a year old. When Knipfel was 12, an uncle who was also afflicted with failing eyesight approached him at a funeral with a prophetic warning: "You better start learning Braille now," he said, as quoted by Ellen Clegg in the *Seattle Post–Intelligencer* (March 17, 1999). Yet, as Knipfel recalled in his first memoir, *Slackjaw* (1999), "back in 1977, nobody talked about genetics much, at least not at funerals in small Wisconsin towns. And nobody then could have predicted that the world would go dark on me while I was still a reasonably young man." Knipfel did not learn the extent to which his vision would deteriorate until he was in his mid-20s, when an ophthalmologist diagnosed him with retinitis pigmentosa, a degenerative, genetically linked eye disease that causes damage in the retina. The condition has neither treatment nor cure, and Knipfel was told that he would be permanently blind by the age of 35.

Knipfel's childhood was marked by periods of severe depression. He made his first suicide attempt (by drinking bleach) before he graduated from junior high school. (He reportedly attempted suicide 12 times between the ages of 14 and 22.) After a short stay at the University of Chicago, where he studied physics, Knipfel transferred to the University of Wisconsin, Madison, and majored in philosophy. He was deeply influenced by the works of the 19th-century philosopher Friedrich Nietzsche and, with a friend nicknamed Grinch, formed a campus political party known as the Nihilist Workers Party. (The rebellious Grinch gave Knipfel the nickname Slackjaw.) The party promoted such practices as "telephone terrorism," in which its members called the same toll-free numbers repeatedly to inflate the costs to the businesses or organizations they reached. Knipfel's stunt worked so well that it earned a brief mention in *Time* magazine.

Also during his college years, Knipfel began engaging in a variety of self-destructive activities. He and Grinch spent a great deal of time drinking to excess and engaging in bar fights and petty vandalism. For a while the two performed together in a punk band known as the Pain Amplifiers, even though neither knew how to play a musical instrument. Heading to a bar with Grinch one night, Knipfel walked straight into a steel pole. The next day he was unable to move; he called an ambulance and was taken to a medical clinic. "The doctor at the clinic gave me the usual once-over," Knipfel told William R. Wineke for the *Wisconsin State Journal* (March 7, 1999), "and asked me questions and I told my usual story, this time emphasizing the blow to the head. 'Did I tell you about the steel lamp post?' 'Yes, yes, you did.' It was this doctor's conclusion that I had too much wax in my ears. He led me from his office to an examination room, pulled a giant syringe out of a drawer and flushed both ears." Knipfel later came to suspect that the blow had had much graver consequences. Some years later doctors discovered an inoperable lesion on the temporal lobe of his brain, but they could not attribute it with certainty to his collision with the pole. They linked the lesion to his overall emotional instability and his increasingly frequent fits of depression, hallucinations, seizures, and rage; those symptoms are now controlled by medications.

After earning his bachelor's degree, Knipfel enrolled in a graduate program in comparative studies in discourse and society at the University of Minnesota. At the same time he began teaching an introductory humanities course. Knipfel quickly became disillusioned with academia, particularly with the poor caliber of his students, and he was ultimately asked to leave the program. After a suicide attempt and a six-month stay in a mental institution, he followed his then-girlfriend, Laura, to Philadelphia, where she had been accepted into graduate school. (The couple later married and divorced.) He took on a series of odd jobs, including running a bar, working in a used-book store, and clerking at a pornography shop.

In about 1987 Knipfel began writing, and he sent some of his work to various small-circulation newspapers. He had been inspired by a graduate-school professor, Greg Sandow, who was also a music critic for the *Village Voice*. "I hadn't even considered [writing] before," Knipfel told Adams, "but I had this one man's opinion that maybe I was skilled at something in this world. I'd done a lot of weird things and told a lot of stories to people in bars, so I just sat down and wrote up a couple of those stories, and that's what I ended up turning in, under the guise of being a record review." In addition to targeting small New York City publications, Knipfel submitted his sample piece to Philadelphia's alternative papers; in his opinion, his writing was no worse than that of the people whose work was already being published. On the merits of his five-page review of the newest Rollins Band album, in which he mostly expounded on memories of "schizophrenics I have known," Knipfel was hired to write a column for *Welcomat* (now the *Philadelphia Weekly*). The first edition of "Slackjaw," as the column was called, featured a stinging review of a concert by the punk-rock musician Iggy Pop and appeared on October 25, 1987; in it, Knipfel declared, as quoted by Adams, "The fundamental (with emphasis on the mental) idea behind Slackjaw is . . . well, confusion. Panic. Semantic interference, that sort of thing. . . . Let's piss people off."

Knipfel was awarded a regular column, which was supposed to be devoted to arts reviews, first biweekly and then weekly. The column soon evolved into what Adams described as "an all-out assault on bourgeois values, cultural conformity, squares, would-be hipsters, sacred cows and local favorites. . . . In other words, [Knipfel] did everything he could to make people as angry as possible." The column, often chronicling Knipfel's misfortunes, was marked by dark humor and anti-establishment political leanings. At one point Knipfel urged readers to burn down outlets of the Borders Books chain; for one column printed during the Persian Gulf War, he was fired by the publisher (who soon rehired him) for voicing his support for the Iraqi dictator Saddam Hussein. Knipfel's antics produced overwhelming reader response. Beginning with his very first article, on Iggy Pop—for which he received a death threat—Knipfel's column generated more letters from readers (both complimentary and faultfinding) than anything else in *Welcomat*.

In 1993 Knipfel's column was picked up by the *New York Press*, an alternative weekly newspaper in New York City, and the young writer moved to Brooklyn with Laura. The autobiographical segments of "Slackjaw" began to grow larger. As Knipfel explained to Adams, "As time passed I was writing about myself more than the things I was supposed to be reviewing. That was unfair, I thought, so I stopped talking about other people and other things altogether, and just told stories about the adventures I'd gotten into that week." Over time, Knipfel's rants began to mellow, and he began writing about his daily struggles to adapt to life as a blind man. "You can't stay angry that long," he said, "and if you do you get real, real boring. In my case, the anger burned itself out. I couldn't do it anymore. It's like speed. I did speed for a long time, but you reach a point where your body can't handle it anymore. Your brain starts demanding that your body do things it simply cannot do: You can't move that fast. It was the same thing with [writing]. I was still angry, annoyed, bitter, but it didn't burn so hot anymore."

While writing his column for the *New York Press*, Knipfel also began working as a receptionist at the newspaper's offices; he later became a full-time columnist and staff writer. In 1998 he was approached by a publisher from Putnam to develop a book from his column. "I thought I was getting

older and crankier," he told Getta Sharma-Jensen for the *Milwaukee Journal–Sentinel* (February 15, 1999), "and I might as well do something to make my folks proud. And so I took two weeks off from the newspaper one summer and wrote it. Actually the first draft was 500 pages long. By that time, it was a collection of columns, my favorite 100 columns, and it was very, very rough. Then we bounced the manuscript back and forth, back and forth between Putnam and me. When I first wrote it, it was pretty much things that had existed already. By the time we got done, it was 60 percent fresh." When he wrote the book, Knipfel could see the print on his computer only by using large-size fonts, a magnifying glass, and a very bright light. He would rise at 6:00 a.m. each morning and work until dark, often forgoing food throughout the day. After he completed the manuscript, he told Sharma-Jensen, he wept for two days. "I had pushed myself harder than I had ever pushed myself," he said.

In *Slackjaw* (1999), Knipfel chronicled his life-long battles with disease. Unlike many other memoirs that deal with debilitating illness, *Slackjaw* presents a darkly funny version of what—on the surface—would seem to be depressing events. The book follows Knipfel from his visits to his doctor during childhood through his suicide attempts, college escapades, alcoholism, failed marriage, and eventual blindness. In the later chapters he described many of the troubles and frustrations that the loss of his vision caused; he sold his collection of books, for example, since he could no longer read them, and had to enlist the help of a "home survival trainer" to recover his independence. He wrote openly and honestly about his shortcomings and never attempted to portray himself as a stoic or a saint. Overall, *Slackjaw* received warm reviews. While some critics found the memoir lacking in direction, most praised Knipfel's sharp, black humor and exceptional knack for storytelling. Some applauded him for omitting any sort of generic epiphany and reported that they had found inspiration in his ability to look past the seriousness of his situation. "In the end, *Slackjaw* is not about being blind or about being flawed," Maureen Aitken wrote for the *Chicago Tribune* (May 23, 1999). "It's about living without excuses, questioning authority, surviving on chump change, making mistakes and moving on. In short, it's an American life coming from the edges. You'll enjoy Knipfel more than you'll pity him. After all, Knipfel has amazing talent, crazy memories and great friends. Who can feel sorry for that?" "Through it all, [Knipfel] maintains a keen sense of the absurd, that life, in its faces and phases, makes no sense, and makes nonsense of every well-laid plan," Felix Cheong wrote for the *Straits Times*. Admirers of the book included the reclusive author Thomas Pynchon, who described it, as posted on Slackjaw Online, as "an extraordinary emotional ride, through the lives and times of reader and writer alike, maniacally aglow with a born storyteller's gifts of observation, an amiably deranged sense of humor, and a heart too bounced around by his history, and ours, not to have earned Mr. Knipfel, at last, an unsentimental clarity that is generous and deep. . . . Long may he continue to astonish us."

In his next work, *Quitting the Nairobi Trio* (2000), Knipfel wrote about his six-month stay in a midwestern psychiatric ward following a suicide attempt in graduate school. In an elaborate scheme, Knipfel decided to stage his death to look like a murder committed by one of the female students in his humanities course; after that plan failed he swallowed a bottle of over-the-counter sleeping pills, washing the tablets down with a bottle of Scotch. He awakened three days later in an intensive-care unit, screaming German rhymes. After being committed to the locked-door ward, Knipfel received no medication or therapy aside from 10-minute-per-week sessions with an assigned doctor who offered little in the way of constructive treatment. He spent most days observing the unusual people he encountered, among them Gus, a patient who rode a stationary bicycle all day; the paranoid Eddie, who talked only about conspiracy theories; and his roommate, Joey, who was mysteriously taken away one night. With little else to do, Knipfel read over and over the only book he had, *Ecrits: A Selection*, by the French psychoanalyst Jacques Lacan; in one chapter of *Quitting the Nairobi Trio*, he offered an entertaining guide to understanding Lacan's work. After seeing a television special about the inventive comedian Ernie Kovacs (1919–62), Knipfel kept thinking about one of Kovacs's most famous sketches, "The Nairobi Trio." In the skit, three mechanical windup figures (actually, men in gorilla masks) gave a grotesque rendition of a musical performance; one ape used two drumsticks to hit a second ape over the head repeatedly. The skit helped Knipfel come to terms with his situation.

Like *Slackjaw*, *Quitting the Nairobi Trio* was praised for its humorous depiction of unfunny events. In the *Boston Globe* (June 2, 2000), Ellen Clegg called the book "a masterful leap forward in style and control. While some of the searing heat of *Slackjaw* is missing, Knipfel introduces more nuance and continuity. He seems to be trying to get some distance, to mediate his own life." Critics also lauded Knipfel's avoidance of self-pity in favor of candid disclosures. In one such example, Knipfel wrote, as quoted by Maureen Harrington in the *Denver Rocky Mountain News* (June 25, 2000), "I was locked away in that ward in Minneapolis because I was a self-destructive young man. Months later I left the ward a self-destructive young man. All these years later, I'm older, grumpier, too tired—and to be honest, too curious about the things going on around me—to be bothered with the effort of trying to take my life anymore." Some reviewers found flaws in Knipfel's interweaving of descriptions of real events with descriptions of his hallucinations. Clegg, for example, noted, "Knipfel doesn't need hallucinations. He is inventive and outrageous enough to make the mundane details of his real life weirdly compelling."

Knipfel next wrote *The Buzzing* (2003), a novel about a jaded, aging journalist who heads the "kook beat" at the daily *New York Sentinel*. Although he once won the Pulitzer Prize, Roscoe Baragon now covers more absurd slices of news, such as alien abductions and voodoo curses on city museums. After being exposed to so many bizarre characters, Baragon begins to believe some of their stories. When, on the same day that an earthquake hits an Alaskan town, he receives a call from a man who claims he was kidnapped "by the state of Alaska," Baragon starts tracking a story that he thinks might connect several other earthquakes, the appearance of radioactive bodies in a New York City morgue, the disappearance of an unmanned NASA satellite, and the elimination of Godzilla movies from Japanese television. "That Knipfel can coax a reader into joining this wild goose chase says a lot about this novel's unlikely charms," John Freeman wrote for the *Washington Post* (April 6, 2003). "Despite Roscoe's swirl of paranoia, Knipfel keeps the action moving with crisp dialogue and grittily familiar descriptions of newspaper rooms, immigrant-run bodegas and the grungy hangouts where Roscoe finds his sources."

The Buzzing was generally commended as an entertaining black comedy that develops into "an even blacker paranoid thriller," as Scott Eyman wrote for the *Chicago Tribune* (April 18, 2003). While several critics praised Knipfel's timely exploration of the truth behind today's news, some felt that his preposterous set-up would alienate readers. "As *The Buzzing* races toward its bizarre conclusion," Freeman observed, "Knipfel plunges Roscoe over the deep end into paranoia, making him essentially unbelievable. . . . This is an unfortunate twist in this otherwise carefully controlled farce about the elasticity of truth in today's news environment. It's hard not to feel that if Roscoe's grand conspiracy theory were even the slightest bit more believable, *The Buzzing* could speak more to a growing distrust of the news." Despite such criticism, Emily White, writing for the *New York Times* (March 30, 2003), concluded, "Knipfel knows how to pull a reader into his orbit. His writing has a hard-boiled magnetism. By the time Baragon shows signs of cracking up, you're already invested in him—he might be a lunatic but you can't be sure. It's to the author's great credit that you never quite know until late in the novel whether Baragon is simply paranoid or whether he's onto something."

In 2004 Knipfel published *Ruining It for Everybody*, a third memoir. The book's striking yellow cover and unusual square shape caused a few critics to complain that it could be mistaken for a gift or novelty publication by unwary bookstore customers. The whimsical cover belied the volume's spare, unflinching content. In it Knipfel traced his spiritual development, beginning with a childhood obsession with the crucifixion. A reviewer for *Publishers Weekly*, as quoted on Amazon.com, wrote, "What makes this book enjoyable is not

Knipfel's false opinion of just being 'a simple . . . man with psychological and neurological problems,' but rather the author's triumph in the face of often overwhelming health challenges. Witty, irreverent, and full of black humor, this is a memoir of a troubled, talented soul who can laugh at himself while refusing to throw in the towel of life."

Jim Knipfel lives in Brooklyn. Of his development as a person and a writer, Knipfel told Andrew O'Hehir for *Newsday* (March 7, 1999), "Early on, I was this enraged, suicidal animal. I quite consciously wanted to offend people. After a few years of that, I became an out-of-control drunkard. I was always out there inflicting myself on other people. Then there was a point where I stopped going out and inflicting things on the world, and through some karmic retribution, the world turned around and started inflicting itself upon me. I was just trying to lead a quiet, normal life, and things kept happening to me. That continues to this day, and I'm very lucky for it—otherwise I'd have nothing to write about." He added, "I was angry, then drunk, then hapless, then blind. Now I guess I'm a combination of all those things."

—K.A.D.

Suggested Reading: *Boston Globe* C p8 June 2, 2000, with photo; *Chicago Tribune* Tempo p2 Apr. 18, 2003; *Milwaukee Journal–Sentinel* p1 Feb. 15, 1999, with photo; *New York Times* E p7 Apr. 6, 1999, with photo, VII p4 June 25, 2000, VII p21 Mar. 30, 2003; *Philadelphia City Paper* (on-line) June 1–8, 2000, with photos; *Seattle Post–Intelligencer* E p2 Mar. 17, 1999; *Washington Post* T p10 Apr. 6, 2003; *Wisconsin State Journal* G p1 Mar. 7, 1999, with photo

Selected Books: memoirs—*Slackjaw*, 1999; *Quitting the Nairobi Trio*, 2000; *Ruining It for Everybody*, 2004; novel—*The Buzzing*, 2003

Kusturica, Emir

(KOOS-too-ree-tsa, EH-meer)

Nov. 24, 1954(?)– Film director; screenwriter; actor; musician

Address: RASTA International, Milorada Mitrovica 15, 11000 Belgrade, Serbia and Montenegro

The Yugoslavian-born Emir Kusturica is the only director to have twice won the Palme d'Or, the top honor at the Cannes Film Festival. Known for his wry sense of humor, Kusturica "is Yugoslavia's Fellini, a Balkan magic realist who makes award-winning movies," as Helena Smith Athens wrote for the London *Observer* (October 10, 1999). "Indeed, his ability to stand at a weird angle to the universe has landed Emir Kusturica more prizes (one for each of his feature films) than any other contemporary Eastern European director." When Kusturica won his first Palme d'Or, in 1985, for *When Father Was Away on Business*, Yugoslavia declared a national holiday. By the time he won his second Palme d'Or, for *Underground*, in 1995, his war-torn homeland had split into separate republics, and Kusturica—branded a traitor by many for his refusal to support Bosnian Muslim nationalists—was no longer welcome in his hometown, Sarajevo. He also found himself the target of a heated polemic launched by a noted French intellectual, who decried *Underground* as Serbian nationalist propaganda. Kusturica denied the charge and retired in frustration, but he returned to filmmaking shortly thereafter, convinced that his films—and also the music he performs with the No Smoking Orchestra—have therapeutic value for our violent and wounded world. "It takes a bit of everything to make one Emir Kusturica: a touch of Czech irony; a sense of observation . . . ; a smatter of late Italian neo-realism . . . ; a pinch of early Fellini fantasy; plenty of Balkan temper, that strange mixture between the sophistication of the West and the hot-blooded impulsiveness of the Third World," Dan Fainaru wrote for the *Jerusalem Post* (April 6, 1990). "And most of all, it takes a lot of talent, imagination and determination not to compromise, however long it may take to realize one's vision."

Emir Kusturica was born on November 24 in 1954 or 1955 in Sarajevo, in what is now Bosnia-Herzegovina. The only child of Murat Kusturica, a journalist, and Senaka Kusturica, a homemaker, he was raised in the Gorica suburbs outside Sarajevo. The Kusturicas were Muslim Bosnians but did not practice Islam. Kusturica's father had renounced his faith, as had many other Yugoslavians, when he joined the Communist Party; as a member of the party elite, he worked for the Ministry of Information of Bosnia-Herzegovina. Emir Kusturica's aversion toward Yugoslavia's ruthless dictator, Josip Broz Tito (known as Marshal Tito), and his renunciation of communism at an early age created tension within his family.

As a youth Kusturica spent much of his time with a gang of neighborhood delinquents, but he never got into serious trouble. "We were always running from the police," he told Henry Kamm for the *New York Times* (November 24, 1985). "I was glad to have had such a period in my life. I would know how to make a film about stealing wallets. I never [stole] myself, but I watched many times." While visiting a friend of his father's on the set of a feature film, Kusturica was cast in a bit part and immediately fell in love with filmmaking. As a secondary-school student, he made two short

Evan Agostini/Getty Images

Emir Kusturica

films—*A Part of the Truth* (1971) and *Autumn* (1972). At the suggestion of his parents, who were eager to sever his ties to the gang, in about 1973 he enrolled at the FAMU Academy of Performing Arts, in Prague, Czechoslovakia, the alma mater of such film luminaries as Milos Forman, Jiri Menzel (with whom Kusturica studied), and Goran Pasakaljevic.

In 1978, while at the academy, Kusturica directed the short film *Guernica*. Set in Europe in 1941, it follows a family that is ordered to report to a physician who will determine whether they are Jewish. When the father tells his son that the doctor has judged their noses to be suspiciously long, the boy cuts the noses out of every family photo and arranges them into a collage that resembles Pablo Picasso's painting *Guernica*, an anti-war masterpiece. The short garnered Kusturica his first award, at the Kalovy-Vary student film festival. Later in 1978 he directed his first TV movie, *Nevjeste dolaze* (The Brides Are Coming), and in 1980 he directed *Bife Titanic* (The Titanic Bar), also for TV. The latter picture, an adaptation of a story by the Nobel laureate Ivo Andric, won first prize at the Yugoslav television film festival at Portoz.

With his instructors' encouragement, Kusturica directed a feature film, *Sjecas li se Dolly Bell?* (Do You Remember Dolly Bell?, 1981). A coming-of-age story set in 1960s Yugoslavia, it focuses on the adolescent Dino (Slavko Stimac). "The movie also explores the social and political climate of life in the post-Stalinist [Yugoslavia]," Nina Darnton wrote for the *New York Times* (August 15, 1986). "The result is a moving, charming film that weaves universal psychological themes with specific political ones in a way that deepens our understand-

ing of both." *Sjecas li se Dolly Bell?* won the Golden Lion for best first film at the Venice Film Festival; the FIPRESCI (Fédération Internationale de la Presse Cinématographique) Award; and the São Paolo International Film Festival Critics Award.

Kusturica again offered a wry critique of Communist-era Yugoslav politics (this time set in the 1950s) in *Otac na sluzbenoh putu (When Father Was Away on Business*, 1985). Miki Manojlovic, in the first of his many roles in Kusturica's films, played Mesha, who is sent to prison for three years because he makes an offhand comment criticizing the government. The film is told mostly through the eyes of Mesha's six-year-old-son, Malik (Moreno D'E Bartolli), who believes that his father is on a business trip. "Tender as late Truffaut, slyly funny as a Kundera novel, *When Father Was Away on Business* is a family portrait that, by the end, finds the pulse of a nation . . . ," Paul Attanasio wrote for the *Washington Post* (November 1, 1985). "The mood of the movie is part magic, part knockabout farce, part political satire, part melodrama, all somehow whole." Kusturica won another FIPRESCI Award and his first Palme d'Or for *When Father Was Away on Business*. Though pleased that procuring funding for films would now be easier for him, Kusturica was troubled about his newfound celebrity. "I'm not happy about it at all," he told Henry Kamm. "I feel the person who won the prize is not the same as me. He is another man, who walks behind me, while I remain the same."

Also in 1985 Kusturica joined the No Smoking Orchestra, a punk-infused Yugoslavian band that drew on many cultural influences, including local Gypsy (Romani) music. Formed in Sarajevo in 1980, the No Smoking Orchestra adopted a style of music known as "new primitivism," which emerged from the Yugoslavian resistance movement after Tito's death, also in 1980. The band was immensely popular, selling more than 100,000 copies of their debut album, *Das ist Walter* (This Is Walter, 1984). Its members ran afoul of the government, however, by publicly criticizing Tito and appearing regularly on the TV show *Surrealist Top List*, a satire of Yugoslavian politics. Sales of the band's second album, *Dok cekas sabah sa sejtanom* (Waiting for the Sabbath with the Devil), were dismal because of government censorship, and many of the band's dozen members quit in frustration. Never one to fear political conflict, Kusturica joined the band in time to play bass on their third album, *Podzra iz zemlje safari* (Greetings from Safari Land, 1985), which sold 90,000 copies.

Kusturica left the group soon afterward to make his next film, *Dom za vesanje* (*Time of the Gypsies*, 1988), which was inspired by a newspaper article about a group of Gypsies (also known as Romas) who were arrested at the Yugoslav-Italian border. "They had crossed the border illegally for the umpteenth time in order to beg, steal and even sell the[ir] children," Kusturica told Annette Insdorf for the *New York Times* (February 4, 1990). "First, it upset me emotionally, and then I realized it could be my next film. . . . I didn't want it to be just a realistic movie. . . . I said to myself, 'If you're going to make a structure based on gypsy life, you have to change your form and explore with nonprofessionals the substance of that life.'" Toward that end, Kusturica lived with the world's largest concentration of Gypsies, in Sutka, a suburb of Skopje, Macedonia. Kusturica recruited much of his cast and derived many ideas from the local population. With his taste for magical realism, Kusturica felt comfortable with the Gypsies' ways of thinking. "They move so easily from reality to illusion to dream, like in a Gabriel García Márquez novel," he told Annette Insdorf. "*Time of the Gypsies* belongs entirely to the world of García Márquez and other Latin American writers who built art on the irrationality and poverty of their people."

In making *Time of the Gypsies*, Kusturica drew from the dissimilar styles of the Spanish director Luis Buñuel and the American filmmaker John Ford. The film is about a boy, Perhan (Davor Dujmovic), who has the power of telekinesis. The naïve child is lured away from home by the wily Uncle Ahmed (Bora Todorovic), only to discover that Ahmed is a pimp who uses Gypsy children as beggars. To build a better life for himself, Perhan resorts to criminal activities, thus losing his innocence. "Wildly ambitious, [the movie is] nearly as disorderly and spontaneous and irrepressible as its Gypsies themselves, and at times as manipulative," Sheila Benson wrote for the *Los Angeles Times* (February 9, 1990). "No matter; the sleight-of-hand holds, keeping us fascinated if not enchanted by the life and hard times of its ill-starred young hero." The film brought Kusturica the best-director award at the Cannes Film Festival and helped him to win a Roberto Rossellini Career Achievement Award.

In 1988 Kusturica moved to New York City, where Milos Forman had found him a teaching job in the graduate film division of Columbia University. When he returned to Sarajevo a year later, he found his homeland in increasing political turmoil. Yugoslavia, created in 1918, encompassed many religious and ethnic groups, and in the early 1990s the country began to split apart along ethnic lines. Those divisions dismayed Kusturica, who opposed the newly emerging ethnic/nationalistic separatist parties. "Why allow Yugoslavia to be destroyed?" he said later to Howard Feinstein for the *New York Times* (September 5, 1999). "It was very good, very multi-ethnic, very multinational. Minority rights were respected." Because he did not support the Muslim nationalist party of President Alija Izetbegovic of Bosnia and Herzegovina, Kusturica was branded a traitor by many Bosnians. The intensity of their animosity became clear in May 1990, when Kusturica came to the opening of a literary club in Sarajevo as an invited speaker. "I was going to read an Andric story on hatred in Bosnia," he told David Binder for the *New York Times* (October 25, 1992). "Before I came to it, a drunk poet

. . . started screaming, 'You traitors, Serbs, go to Belgrade! This is not Belgrade!' . . . I just lost it. I pulled him out. I hit him. I came back breathing hard while I was reciting Andric, that Andric warning against hatred. Next day those small Titoists who became democrats all of a sudden started attacking me as a Serb." Disgusted, Kusturica and his family moved to Belgrade, in the republic of Serbia; they later divided their time between Belgrade and Normandy, France, where they had bought a farmhouse.

By 1992 the Yugoslavian republics of Slovenia, Croatia, Macedonia, and Bosnia and Herzegovina had been established as independent states. Shortly thereafter, Serbia and Montenegro founded the Federal Republic of Yugoslavia, whose president, Slobodan Milosevic, instigated a brutal military campaign to unite ethnic Serbs in nearby republics under a "Greater Serbia." (Charged with committing war crimes and genocide, Milosevic was brought to trial at The Hague on February 12, 2002. As of late October 2005, the trial was continuing.) In Belgrade Kusturica continued to butt heads with nationalists; in 1993 he even challenged the leader of the ultra-nationalist Serbian Radical Party, Vojislav Seselj, to a duel. Seselj (who is also on trial at The Hague) did not accept the challenge.

That same year saw the release of a film Kusturica made in the U.S.: *Arizona Dream*, for which he used a script by David Atkins, a student whom he had met at Columbia. An absurdist comedy, *Arizona Dream* stars Johnny Depp as Axel Blackmar, a man obsessed with fish, who rather than joining the family business in Arizona has moved to New York City. After he returns to his hometown for a wedding, his uncle Leo (Jerry Lewis) again pressures him to take over his Cadillac dealership. During his visit Axel is seduced by a mother-stepdaughter duo (Faye Dunaway and Lili Taylor). Though the film received some critical acclaim and won the Silver Bear at the Berlin Film Festival, it received a tepid response from audiences during test marketing, so Warner Bros. made a shorter version for the home-video market and arranged only limited theatrical distribution in the U.S. The process embittered Kusturica toward Hollywood. "The word artistic, it's like a stinking substance to them," he told Janet Maslin for the *New York Times* (May 29, 1995). "Everybody is expecting you to be Michael Jackson. I want to be Lou Reed."

Kusturica returned to the Balkans, and in 1995 he won his second Palme d'Or, for *Underground*, a black comedy and allegorical epic about war in his homeland. Reporting from the Cannes Film Festival, Kenneth Turan wrote for the *Los Angeles Times* (May 29, 1995), "Unruly, audacious, unashamedly excessive, this emotional requiem for a dying Yugoslavia overpowered audiences here with the frenzy of a bull gone mad." Inspired by a play by Duan Kovacevic, *Underground* traces the camaraderie and conflict between two Belgradian men—Marko and Blacky (Miki Manojlovic and Lazar Ristovski)—from 1941 to 1992. The movie begins with the German invasion of Yugoslavia during World War II. When Blacky and several other people from his village are forced into hiding, Marko offers them shelter in a secret, cavernous basement under his home. The refugees turn the basement into an underground city and begin manufacturing arms for Tito's resistance forces. Marko keeps them in his basement for decades, never informing them that the war has ended, and enriches himself from their labor. Once a petty gangster, Marko becomes an intellectual and poet and serves as one of Tito's information ministers. "It's an amazing portrayal of 20th Century political insanity, so pointed and controversial that many of Kusturica's old neighbors—in besieged and bloody Sarajevo—have ostracized him for it," Michael Wilmington wrote for the *Chicago Tribune* (February 6, 1998). "Yet, *Underground*, possibly the finest film made in the old Yugoslavia, is no apologia for Serbian bloodbaths or ultra nationalism. Instead, it examines the bloody chaos and brutality of half a century with a corrosive dark humor and compassion that both exhilarate and terrify."

Underground sparked a controversy among French intellectuals, who were embroiled in a debate over the role of nationalism in contemporary Europe. In an article entitled "The Kusturica Fraud," which appeared in the French newspaper *Le Monde*, Alain Finkielkraut, a prominent philosopher and author, denounced the film—before seeing it—as blatantly pro-Serbian and scolded the Cannes jurors for awarding it the top prize. Kusturica denied that his film was pro-Serbian. "In the middle of all this total confusion, brought about by others as well as ourselves, you have leaders who are at once treacherous, charming, awful, nice, fantastic, nasty and never, ever to be trusted," he told Derek Malcolm for the London *Guardian* (June 29, 1995). "These are the people I know and the people my film is about. How can you ask me to take sides?"

Kusturica's political battles took a more violent turn in his homeland. He punched the leader of the New Serbian Right movement, Nebojsa Pajkic, and Pajkic's wife struck Kusturcia with her handbag. After Bosnia, Serbia, and Croatia initialed the Dayton Agreement, on November 21, 1995, Bosnians burned two of Kusturica's homes in Sarajevo. "They did it to people who were not following President Izetbegovic's way of doing things," he told Howard Feinstein. "Soon afterward, my father died. It was too much on my shoulders. I thought the best thing for me would be not to make movies." On December 5, 1995 he released a statement to *Liberation*, a Paris newspaper, announcing his retirement. Soon afterward Finkielkraut published an article in *Liberation* declaring that he had finally seen *Underground* and that it was worse than he had imagined. At this point another French intellectual, Andre Glucksman, came to the film's defense, declaring in an open letter to Kusturica in *Liberation* that it was a near-masterpiece.

By August 1996 Kusturica had announced his intention to return to filmmaking. In an attempt to avoid controversy, he wrote and directed a lighthearted work: *Crna macka, beli macor* (*Black Cat, White Cat*, 1998), a chaotic romp that won the Venice Film Festival's Silver Lion. The picture was inspired by an actual event: as the son and daughter of rival Gypsy families were preparing to marry, one of the patriarchs died. As guests were traveling from far and wide to attend the wedding, the family members put makeup on the dead man and propped him up at a table. "There's hardly a hint of Balkan politics in this prodigiously well-made, frantically paced comedy, which is filled to the brim with colorful characters involved in sometimes familiar but always engaging situations," David Stranton wrote for *Variety* (September 21–27, 1998). Still, some saw political implications in it, and a handful of critics accused Kusturica of presenting Gypsies in a negative light. "There is no denying the film's power. Brawls and gunfire erupt without warning—yet this sort of violence is honest and manly, Mr. Kusturica seems to be saying, in contrast to the cowardly manipulations of politicized warfare. The message is unconvincing, and the film's stereotyping of the gypsies as primitives somehow innocent to history is shameless in its condescension," a reviewer wrote for the *Economist* (April 17, 1999). "For all its visual pleasures, this is an escapist film that never manages to shake itself free of politics."

The soundtrack for *Black Cat, White Cat* was performed by the No Smoking Orchestra. The band's leader, Nele Karajilic, had moved to Belgrade and re-formed the band with younger musicians, among them Stribor Kusturica, the filmmaker's son, on drums. His son's participation induced Kusturica to rejoin the group, this time on guitar. What they chose to play, he told Helena Smith Athens, is "very much like the [Gypsy] music from my movies and that's my aim, to match two therapeutic art forms. Now that we're at the end of the twentieth century it's time to make happy endings, to help people feel good about life because in so many ways the planet's been poisoned, . . . and people are so depressed." Their album *Unza Unza Time* (2000) identifies the performers as Emir Kusturica & the No Smoking Orchestra. Kusturica directed a video clip of the band for MTV and, in 2003, a documentary, *Super8Stories*, about their behind-the-scenes antics.

Through the years, Kusturica had tested his thespian skills in minor roles, in *Strategija svrake* (The Magpie Strategy), for which he had also written the screenplay, Radomir Saranovic's *13. jul*, and many of his own movies. In 2000 he starred in a feature film: the director Patrice Leconte's *La Veuve de Saint-Pierre*, which is set in 1850 on a remote French-Canadian island. Kusturica played Neel Auguste, a man convicted of murder and condemned to death. While waiting for the guillotine to arrive, he is placed in the care of an army captain (Daniel Auteuil) and his wife (Juliette Binoche).

They grow to see goodness in Auguste, and the rest of the townspeople do as well—just before the guillotine arrives. In a *Hollywood Reporter* (May 5, 2000) review, Mark Adams wrote, "Kusturica makes an impressive move to the other side of the camera, offering a moving and very physical performance." The filmmaker later appeared as the eccentric security expert Vladimir in Neil Jordan's *The Good Thief* (2002), starring Nick Nolte.

The No Smoking Orchestra provided the soundtrack for Kusturica's next film, *Zivot Je Cudo* (*La Vie est un miracle*; *Life Is a Miracle*, 2004). A take on *Romeo and Juliet*, the tale is set in 1990s wartime and based on a real-life tale that Kusturica heard from a Serbian living in France. Slavko Stimac played Luka, a Serbian engineer whose son, Milos (Vuk Kostic), is drafted into the army and then captured. A Serbian soldier offers Luka a young Muslim woman, Sabah (Natasa Solak), as a hostage to exchange for his son. Luka falls in love with his prisoner and must eventually decide between regaining his son and keeping his mistress. "*La Vie est un miracle* has all the stunning aesthetics we expect of this most visually gifted of directors. . . . It has his unique sense of life lived out of control," John Griffin wrote for the Montreal, Canada, *Gazette* (December 3, 2004). "But this is also his most sentimental picture. Not for the insanity of war—he figured that out years ago—but for the wispy vitality of humanity. Life is a miracle, this wild, sadly hopeful film says—and it's a miracle that we haven't snuffed it out yet."

Life Is a Miracle was filmed on and around Chargan, a mountain near Serbia's border with Bosnia. Kusturica was so taken with the landscape that he moved there. Outside the Moka Gora rail station he built Eco-selo, an ecologically planned village constructed entirely with wood. As the mayor and financial backer of the town, Kusturica oversaw construction of a cinema, swimming pool, restaurant, library, and apartments in the hope of attracting tourists.

Also in 2004 the Montenegrin writer Andrej Nikolaidis wrote a commentary for the Montenegrin weekly *Monitor* in which he described Kusturica as the "media star of Milosevic's war machinery," according to Predag Milic for the Associated Press (September 20, 2004). Kusturica filed a slander suit against Nikolaidis and won damages of $6,490. Several years earlier, one of his former colleagues from Sarajevo TV had insisted to Fiacra Gibbons for the London *Guardian* (April 23, 1999) that Kusturica "is no one's puppet, least of all Milosevic's. People who say that are blind with hatred. He has always gone his own way. He has a powerful sense of humor. You know, it is so sharp it frightens, that's why he makes enemies." During 2005 Kusturica worked on a documentary in Spain.

Kusturica and his wife, Maja, have two children—Stribor and a daughter, Dunya—and recently became grandparents. His activities include the writing of short stories and plays.

—J.C.

Suggested Reading: (London) *Guardian* p10 June 29, 1995; *Los Angeles Times* F p1 Oct. 6, 1997; *New York Times* p21 Nov. 24, 1985, p7 Oct. 25, 1992; *New Yorker* p32+ Feb. 5,1996

Selected Films: *Sjecas li se Dolly Bell?* (Do You Remember Dolly Bell?), 1981; *Otac na sluzbenoh putu* (*When Father Was Away on Business*), 1985; *Dom za vesanje* (*Time of the Gypsies*), 1988; *Arizona Dream*, 1993; *Underground*, 1995; *Crna macka, beli macor* (*Black Cat, White Cat*), 1998; *Zivot Je Cudo* (*Life Is a Miracle*), 2004

Selected Recordings: Podzra iz zemlje safari (Greetings from Safari Land), 1985; Unza Unza Time, 2000

PRNewsFoto/Getty Images

Lampert, Edward S.

July 19, 1962– Professional investor; chairman of Sears Holdings Corp.

Address: ESL Investments Inc., 200 Greenwich Ave., Greenwich, CT 06830

According to a list compiled by *Alpha* magazine, Edward S. Lampert, the chief executive officer (CEO) of ESL Investments, was the highest-paid hedge-fund manager in 2004, becoming the first to take home more than $1 billion in a single year. Lampert thus unseated the billionaire George Soros, primarily because his shares in the Kmart Holding Corp.—which he had nursed back from bankruptcy in 2003—more than tripled in value when the company acquired Sears, Roebuck & Co.

to form Sears Holdings Corp., now the nation's third-largest retailer. The merger of those once-iconic retailers, each of which had struggled to stay afloat on its own, was considered by observers of the retail industry to be an audacious move. As Andrew Ross Sorkin and Riva D. Atlas noted in the *New York Times* (November 18, 2004), "The deal catapults Mr. Lampert, a virtual unknown several years ago, to one of the most powerful people in retailing and a major player on Wall Street."

Before the creation of Sears Holdings Corp., Lampert was known within the financial industry as a master of value investing, or capitalizing on companies whose stocks were undervalued. Industry observers have also noted his activism as an investor; rather than spreading his investments over a vast array of firms, he stakes out positions of influence in a handful of well-researched companies and then closely monitors their day-to-day operations. In an interview with Robert Seigel for National Public Radio's program *All Things Considered* (November 17, 2004), Andy Serwer, an editor at large of *Fortune*, said, "Lampert has a track record of going into companies, especially retailing companies, when they're down and out and providing them with capital, with money, and then helping them get back on their feet and, in the process, making a ton of money for himself and for his hedge fund."

Edward S. Lampert was born July 19, 1962 in Roslyn, on Long Island, New York. His father, Floyd M. Lampert, was a senior partner at a New York law firm, and his mother was a homemaker. Raised in privileged circumstances, Lampert played with the children of the wealthy, including the son of Fred Wilpon, who later became part owner of the New York Mets baseball team. He developed an interest in the stock market at an early age thanks to his grandmother, whom he often visited at her home in Miami Beach. "She was retired and I would sit on the bed with her going through the stock pages," he told Brett D. Fromson for the *Washington Post* (September 10, 1995). "She and I would go to the public library and look up stocks in the S&P guides to understand a little bit about the companies in the stock pages. But I really didn't know what I was doing. I was just curious."

When Lampert was 14 years old, his father died unexpectedly of a heart attack. Afterward, to help support the family, his mother went to work as a clerk at the New York store Saks Fifth Avenue. Lampert told Brett D. Fromson, "I felt a responsibility to my mother and my sister to help them get through." He found jobs in the summers and during his senior year of high school, so that he could buy a car and help pay for his college education. Lampert was accepted at Yale University, in New Haven, Connecticut, where he majored in economics and joined the Skull and Bones Society—an elite, secretive club to which many of the most powerful American men of the past century have belonged. In his sophomore year he took a seminar in investment banking taught by a partner at the

prestigious investment firm Goldman Sachs & Co., and he landed an internship there the summer before his senior year. During his three-month stint in the sales-and-training program at Goldman, he grew interested in risk arbitrage, the practice of trading the stocks of companies involved in mergers or acquisitions.

After earning his bachelor's degree in economics from Yale, in 1984, Lampert wanted to return to Goldman Sachs, but his mother urged him to apply to law school. "It was my mother's dream that I become a professional," he told Brett D. Fromson. "It represented security, a nice life, [respect] in the community. . . . She didn't know what Goldman Sachs was." Despite her wishes, and his being accepted at the prestigious Harvard and Yale law schools, in 1984 Lampert took a position as a junior research analyst in Goldman's risk-arbitrage division. "My mother thought I was a little crazy," he told Fromson. While at Goldman Sachs he worked for Robert E. Rubin, who was later appointed secretary of the U.S. Treasury Department. "I found risk arbitrage intellectually stimulating," Lampert told Fromson. "You needed to analyze the situation in a short period of time, and you needed to understand the relationship between the risks and rewards—how much money you could make and how much you could lose. . . . It appealed to me because you made the decisions. You were committing the partners' capital and could see immediately whether you were right or wrong simply by the facts. It was definite and not subject to other people's opinions."

While working in risk arbitrage, Lampert grew interested in value investing. The practice—in which the investor buys shares in companies that he or she thinks are being traded for less than they are actually worth—was made famous by the investor Warren Buffet, whom Lampert had long revered. "I liked the idea of buying something at $30 if it's worth $60 as opposed to buying it at $59 to sell at $60," he told Fromson. Goldman was not in the business of value investing, and so, with the encouragement of the investor Richard Rainwater—who years earlier had worked at Goldman himself—Lampert quit in 1988 and opened his own investment partnership, ESL Partners (later changed to ESL Investments), in Fort Worth, Texas. (E, S, and L are Lampert's initials.) Rainwater provided him with $28.8 million in financial backing for the enterprise. "[Rainwater] gave me a huge vote of faith, and I respond very well to that," Lampert told Fromson. "He really took me under his wing." ESL saw excellent returns from the beginning; the overall value of its stock went up 39 percent in 1988 and another 21 percent in 1989. Despite that promising start, Rainwater pulled his money out of ESL in 1989 due to growing conflicts with Lampert over control of the partnership. "I view my investors as partners. They are not just money," Lampert said to Fromson. "But what I have always wanted to do, and the reason I set up my own business, is to make the investment decisions in whatever areas I thought I understood and made sense. I didn't want to have to ask permission to do a deal. . . . If I was the quarterback, I didn't want the coach calling the plays."

In the early 1990s Lampert returned to the East Coast, moving the headquarters of ESL to Greenwich, Connecticut. By building substantial positions in a few heavily researched holdings, ESL has earned one of the best track records in the investment business—with returns from 1998 to 2004 averaging a 29 percent gain per year. Today Lampert manages around $10 billion, for a blue-chip roster of investors that includes the Ziff family of publishing fame, the entertainment mogul David Geffen, the Fischer family of the Gap retail chain, and Michael Dell of Dell Computers.

Lampert is often described as a private and secretive man, and despite his success, he received little coverage in the mainstream media until he was abducted at gunpoint from the parking garage of his ESL office on January 10, 2003. Four captors kept him handcuffed in a bathtub at a Days Inn motel in Hamden, New Jersey, and demanded a $5 million ransom for his release. Lampert's years of experience in negotiating on Wall Street apparently paid off: he managed to convince his abductors that he would pay them the $5 million ransom if they released him first. The abductors dropped him off at an I-95 exit ramp around 2:50 a.m. on January 12. Three of them were captured at the motel shortly thereafter (authorities were able to track them down because they had used Lampert's credit card to order a pizza, which they had delivered to the motel room); the fourth suspect was arrested in Toronto, Canada, a week later.

In May of that same year, Lampert was elected chairman of the board of the Troy, Michigan–based Kmart Holding Corp. Once an icon in American retailing, Kmart had been suffering under the competition from other "big-box" retailers, such as Wal-Mart and other very big stores. When the company filed for bankruptcy protection, in 2002, Lampert began buying its bonds, eventually purchasing a controlling share for slightly less than $1 billion. Lampert had already established a reputation for activism as an investor—he closely monitored the internal management of the companies in which he invested—and even before his appointment to chairman, he had overseen an overhaul in Kmart's management and helped the company cut costs and improve the logistics of its operations. Under his stewardship Kmart climbed out of debt, slowed the decline of its sales, and turned a $1.1 billion profit in 2004. When the company emerged from bankruptcy, in May 2003, its stock was valued at $15 per share. By November 2004 the figure had risen to $109.

Sales at Kmart were still declining, though, and most of the profit was due to the sale of some of Kmart's real estate. During the summer of 2004, the company sold 18 of its stores to Home Depot for $271 million and 54 stores to Sears for $621 million (some sources say that 50 were sold to Sears for $576 million). Some analysts on Wall Street began to wonder if Lampert actually intended to revive Kmart's sagging retail business. "Lampert is more inclined to sell off Kmart's real estate assets for his monetary purposes," Kurt Barnard, president of Barnard Retail Consulting, told Michael Rudnick for *HFN* (September 20, 2004). "Kmart has some marvelous real estate in prime markets. But does he want to make retailing a goal of his life? Probably not."

That statement notwithstanding, in 2004 Lampert masterminded the acquisition of another failing retailer, Sears, Roebuck & Co. He had begun buying shares in the company around the same time that he had begun investing in Kmart stock, eventually becoming the largest single shareholder of each company. In November 2004 Kmart announced a $12.3 billion acquisition (some sources say $11 billion) of Sears to create Sears Holdings Corp., the country's third-largest retailer—after Wal-Mart and Home Depot—with 3,800 stores in Canada and the United States and a projected $55 billion in revenue. The deal was finalized on March 24, 2005, when 69 percent of the shareholders of both companies voted to approve the deal.

Some analysts have questioned whether combining two struggling retail chains can help to salvage either of them. Lampert believes, however, that each retail chain has something to offer the other: Kmart needs more higher-margin products, such as the Craftsman tools and Kenmore appliances sold at Sears, and Sears needs to expand beyond its traditional outlets in malls to stand-alone stores. After the merger Sears Holdings announced plans to convert approximately 400 Kmart stores to a new "Sears Essentials" format over the next three years. Those midsize, stand-alone stores will stock snacks and convenience items in addition to the usual Sears offerings. "[Kmart has] this enormous store base that's not easily differentiated from Wal-Mart and Target," Lampert admitted to Becky Yerak for the *Chicago Tribune* (March 28, 2005), "but it can be by virtue of Sears services, home delivery, installation and repair, as well as the product lines that are proprietary to Sears."

Lampert set to work cutting overhead costs. Around 1,400 jobs at Kmart were eliminated or relocated, and Lampert told the remaining employees that in order to do well at the company they needed to demonstrate the commitment shown by employees at "dot-coms" and technology firms. He said to Susan Chandler for the *Chicago Tribune* (March 25, 2005), "We can't compete against the Wal-Marts, the Home Depots, the Targets, etc. without that level of passion."

As a result of the acquisition, Kmart lost market share in its stores, but profits increased. Lampert's ESL fund saw a 69 percent return in 2004—compared with the 8 percent growth that hedge funds generally saw that year—due largely to its stake in Kmart, which had tripled in value. Lampert, who earned an estimated $1.02 billion in 2004, was the highest-paid hedge-fund manager of the year, according to *Alpha* magazine. Knocking George Soros from the top of the list, Lampert became the first to pass the $1 billion mark since the list was created, four years ago. (By comparison, James Simons, second on the list, earned $607 million.) According to *Forbes* magazine, Lampert ranks as one of the world's richest people.

When Lampert announced the creation of Sears Holdings Corp., he made it clear that he would focus on the long-term profitability of the company instead of worrying about quarterly earnings reports. Unlike most retailers the company does not provide earnings forecasts or release monthly sales reports, and the posting of its first quarterly earnings report, on June 7, 2005, came without any announcement beforehand. In its first quarter Sears Holdings Corp. lost $9 million after the company was charged a $90 million after-tax fee due to its having changed accounting procedures for certain inventory costs. Before the accounting adjustment, the company's income was $81 million, compared with $91 million during the same period from the year before. Same-store sales and total sales at Kmart decreased 3.7 percent and 2.3 percent, respectively. Days before the earnings report, the investment company's stock had reached its highest levels, but it had lost nearly 10 percent of its value by the Friday after the report. Investors saw great potential for long-term investment in the company but a high level of immediate risk. "Given Mr. Lampert's track record . . . we expect a high level of success," Robert Drbul, an analyst at Lehman Brothers, told Vicki M. Young for *WWD* (June 8, 2005), adding nonetheless that Sears Holdings Corp. "remains several years away from being a formidable competitor in the industry."

Lampert reversed his position on retailing to some extent in 2005, deciding to assume personal control of marketing, merchandising, design, and on-line operations of Sears Holdings. He demoted the chief executive officer of Sears stores, Alan J. Lacy, and replaced him with Aylwin B. Lewis, who had been serving as Kmart's chief executive. (Lacy remained at Sears, as a director and vice chairman.) Lampert told shareholders that he had made the changes in order "to make the company more responsive to our customers," and he said that his new responsibilities notwithstanding, would take no salary or stock options, according to Jeff Bailey in the *New York Times* (September 9, 2005). Commenting on the reactions to Lampert's move, Sandra Guy wrote for the *Chicago Sun-Times* (September 15, 2005), "If Lampert is serious about making Sears the retailer it should have become 30 years ago, he has a funny way of showing it, the skeptical analysts say." She added, "Lampert's latest moves signal his high energy and confidence, despite the nay-sayers."

In addition to his shares of Sears Holdings Corp., Lampert is a major investor in Auto Nation, AutoZone, Payless Shoe Source, Footstar, Liz Claiborne, Deluxe Corp., and ANC Rental Corp. Lampert became a multimillionaire in his early 20s,

and by his late 20s, he co-owned the Texas Rangers baseball team with George W. Bush, the future governor of Texas and president of the United States. Despite such success, for years Lampert lived in rented apartments and drove a beat-up car; when his mother complained about the dilapidated state of her own seven-year-old automobile, Lampert responded by advising her to take better care of it. In contrast to his earlier frugality, Lampert now drives a sports car and owns a $20 million mansion in a gated community in Greenwich, Connecticut. He and his wife, Kinga Lampert, have two children.

—J.C.

Suggested Reading: Associated Press Mar. 28, 2005; *Chicago Sun-Times* p65 Sep. 15, 2005; *Chicago Tribune* Business p1 Mar. 28, 2005; *New York Times* C p1+ Sep. 9, 2005; *New York Times* (on-line) Nov. 18, 2004; *Washington Post* H p1 Sep. 10, 1995, with photos

---

Alex Wong/Getty Images

Langevin, Jim

(LAN-juh-vin)

Apr. 22, 1964– U.S. representative from Rhode Island (Democrat)

Address: 109 Cannon House Office Bldg., Washington, DC 20515

After Jim Langevin, as a teenager, suffered the accident that left him permanently without the use of his legs or hands, he was encouraged by his family and friends to become as self-reliant as possible. The independent spirit that has since driven Langevin is manifest in his political career. For example, while the Rhode Island Democrat has stood with most of his party in supporting such causes as gun control and stem-cell research, he has also, unlike many Democrats, emerged as a vocal opponent of abortion. Langevin began his career in the late 1980s, winning a seat as a state legislator before becoming Rhode Island's secretary of state, in 1994. With his election to the U.S. House of Representatives in 2000, Langevin became the first quadriplegic to serve in Congress.

One of four children, James Richard Langevin was born in Warwick, Rhode Island, on April 22, 1964. His mother, June Langevin, worked for West Bay Community Action, a local charitable group, and Travelers Aid, an international organization that helps people in need during their travels. His father, Dick Langevin, was a toolmaker and hardware-store owner. For four summers beginning in 1977, Jim Langevin trained as a Warwick police cadet, a role he took very seriously; he hoped to become a policeman and then an FBI agent. On August 22, 1980, while he was changing into his cadet uniform in the police locker room, two SWAT team officers were nearby, discussing the new .45-caliber semiautomatic handgun that one of them had recently acquired. The weapon was passed to the other officer, who, not realizing there was still a bullet in the chamber, aimed the gun at a locker and pulled the trigger. The bullet ricocheted off the locker and struck the 16-year-old Langevin in the throat, severing his spinal cord between the fifth and sixth cervical vertebrae. The policemen did what they could for Langevin, performing mouth-to-mouth resuscitation and calling a rescue crew from the fire station across the street. Langevin, drifting in and out of consciousness, was taken to Kent County Memorial Hospital in Warwick, where doctors told his parents that the teen would be permanently paralyzed from the neck down and that the medical staff could do nothing for him. When Langevin regained consciousness the following morning, he was unable to talk but indicated that he wanted to say something. As Mark Patinkin reported in the *Providence (Rhode Island) Journal-Bulletin* (February 3, 2002), Langevin's parents found a chalkboard and wrote letters on it, telling their son to blink when they pointed to the correct letters. In that fashion Langevin spelled out two sentences: "Don't be mad. It was an accident."

Langevin's parents transferred him to the spinal-cord unit at University Hospital in Boston, Massachusetts, where Langevin was told that he would never have use of his hands or legs again. Langevin was released from the hospital six months after the accident, in February 1981, and soon returned to high school. (The school was not wheelchair-accessible, so Langevin often had to be carried up and down stairs.) With his father at work and his mother taking care of her three other children, one of whom was an infant, Langevin was forced to rely on himself as much as possible—circumstances that June Langevin has credited with fostering much of her son's independence. When Langevin asked his mother to type school papers for him, for example, she would refuse, ostensibly because she needed to do other work around the house but, in truth, because she wanted her son to learn to function on his own, as he would have to do eventually. "The only way I could type my papers was to weave a pen through my fingers and peck out the words, one letter at a time," Langevin said in a 2003 address to members of TechACCESS of Rhode Island, a resource center that serves people with disabilities, according to the center's Web site. Mark Patinkin reported that when she saw her son struggle with such tasks, June Langevin would leave the room "so he wouldn't see her cry." After completing high school, in 1983, Langevin felt confused about his future. But, as he told John M. Williams for *Business Week Online* (December 13, 2000), "My inner drive would not let me sit idly by in self pity. And neither did my family and friends."

Even in the midst of his confusion, Langevin was touched by the ways in which the people of his community—including total strangers—reached out to help him, holding fund-raising events on his behalf and sending him letters of encouragement. Their efforts inspired in him a desire to serve the community himself. In 1984 he volunteered to help with the Democrat Frank Flaherty's ultimately successful campaign for mayor of Warwick; Flaherty later recalled that Langevin, despite his disability, made telephone calls and stuffed envelopes with enthusiasm. Shortly thereafter Langevin embarked on a political campaign of his own, winning a spot in 1986 as a delegate to Rhode Island's Constitutional Convention, for which he was appointed secretary. At Rhode Island College, in Providence, from which he earned a B.A. degree in public administration and political science in 1990, he was elected president of the student government. Meanwhile, in 1988, while still in college, Langevin won a seat in the Rhode Island House of Representatives. At the same time that he fulfilled his duties as a state representative, serving on the House Rules and Judiciary committees, he worked toward a master's degree in public administration from the Kennedy School of Government at Harvard University, in Cambridge, Massachusetts, which he received in 1994.

In the same year Langevin became Rhode Island's secretary of state, a position he held until 2001; he was the youngest person in the country to hold that office at the state level. In his 1998 reelection bid, he won 82 percent of the vote, the largest percentage won by any Rhode Island state official up to that time in a race with more than two candidates. During his tenure as secretary of state for Rhode Island, Langevin focused on reforming election procedures, increasing public access to government information, and making technological improvements in the previously neglected state-government offices. He acted as a driving force behind the purchase of new voting machines for Rhode Island, devices that relied on optical scans rather than the former system of flip-levers. Additionally, he supported ballots written in Braille, which would allow visually impaired individuals to vote unassisted. As part of its 2001 report on election systems in all 50 states, the U.S. House Judiciary Committee's Democratic Investigative Staff praised Langevin's efforts and recommended similar measures for other states. As quoted in an August 22, 2001 press release available on the House of Representatives Web site, Langevin expressed his pride: "We have done here in Rhode Island what many other states are struggling to do: ensure that every vote legally cast in our elections is properly counted. . . . Knowing the disastrous results of using antiquated voting machines, I pushed for, and obtained funding to purchase, state of the art equipment. I am proud to bring such recognition to the State of Rhode Island and hope that other states will look to the Ocean State as a model." As secretary of state Langevin also released "Access Denied: Chaos, Confusion and Closed Doors," a joint report conducted with the Taubman Center for Public Policy at Brown University, in Providence, Rhode Island, which listed numerous violations of the state's Open Meetings Act. (The law mandates that state government business must be conducted in an open manner, thus allowing citizens to participate in the government of their state.) While many lawmakers considered the report provocative and meddlesome, it prompted reform. In the interest of further exposing the workings of government to the people, Langevin established the Public Information Center.

After holding office for 12 years at the state level, Langevin decided to run for the United States Congress as a representative from Rhode Island. While he realized that his having limited mobility and the constant need of a wheelchair would pose difficulties if he were elected, he decided to focus on his campaign rather than worry about such matters. "I gave [God] 16 months to work out the details," Langevin told Mark Patinkin. "He came through." (So, too, did U.S. representative Patrick Kennedy, also from Rhode Island, who worked with an architect at the U.S. Capitol to ensure that it would be wheelchair-accessible for Langevin.) In 2000 Langevin was elected to represent Rhode Island's Second District in the United States Congress, beating his Republican challenger, Robert Tingle, the Green Party candidate, Dorman Hayes Jr., and Rodney Driver of the Conscience for Congress Party. When Langevin was sworn into office on January 3, 2001, he became the first quadriplegic to serve in the U.S. Congress.

Langevin quickly became well-known for his controversial stances on the topics of embryonic stem-cell research and abortion. Like most of his fellow Democrats, Langevin supported the first practice, but he held a more typically Republican view—disapproval—of the second. "As difficult as living can be for me," Langevin said to Mark Patinkin, "I have a passion for life, and I wouldn't want to deprive anybody of that experience." Just as he disapproves of abortion except in cases of rape or incest or those in which the mother's life is in danger, Langevin has said that he has struggled with the issue of stem-cell research. (His uncertainty had to do with the fact that the stem cells most useful in research into the treatment of diseases are those from human embryos, which die when stem cells are removed. Many antiabortionists oppose the creation of test-tube embryos as stem-cell sources and the "killing" of the embryos.) He ultimately reached the conclusion that it is "life-affirming" to put embryos left over from in vitro fertilization to use in helping the sick and disabled. He has therefore, in numerous letters to President George W. Bush, proposed legislation for an expanded program of stem-cell research. Despite what might be seen as a contradiction in his position, Langevin told Kathy Kiely and Mimi Hall for *USA Today* (August 7, 2001, on-line) that his decision to support stem-cell research is "very consistent with my pro-life position," since stem-cell research "has the potential of easing a great deal of pain and suffering. Not only the pain and suffering of the individuals who suffer from these ailments, but that of their families. I know just from watching what my family had to go through."

During his first term in the House, Langevin introduced legislation for the Making Health Care Available for Low-Income Workers Act, which would furnish states with as much as 50 percent of the cost of health-insurance premiums for those with low-income jobs. Similarly, he sponsored the Lifespan Respite Care Act, which would provide relief services for caregivers of disabled or elderly relatives. (Neither bill has emerged from congressional committees yet.) He also plans to introduce legislation that would make it easier and less expensive for disabled people to benefit from the technology designed to help them.

While Langevin often advocates for such causes as stem-cell research and health care, he has stated that he does not want to be seen as interested solely in topics that relate to the physically handicapped. Accordingly, Langevin has also become known for his support of stricter gun-control measures, such as mandatory seven-day waiting periods prior to the purchase of a gun and trigger locks on all guns. Following the terrorist attacks of September 11, 2001, Langevin proposed legislation that would provide for an "E-Congress" in the event of another such catastrophe; the plan would allow Congress to function on-line if members could not safely meet in the Capitol. In January 2001 Langevin was appointed to the House Armed Services Committee. During the 2001 session he did not miss a single vote, supporting such propositions as maintaining a ban on drilling for oil in the Arctic National Wildlife Refuge (the measure was defeated) and expanding the ability of law-enforcement officials to investigate suspected terrorists. (That bill passed.)

During 2002 Langevin voted for a bill to enact campaign-finance reform and a "soft money" ban, which passed, and supported the creation of an independent commission to investigate the events leading to, and responses to, the 2001 terrorist attacks, a measure that was also adopted. He opposed authorizing the United States to go to war with Iraq, a measure that passed without his support. He missed only two votes in 2002. When he ran for reelection that year, he won a landslide victory, with 76.3 percent of the votes; his two competitors, the Republican John O. Matson and the Home Protection Party candidate Dorman Hayes Jr., garnered only 22 percent and 1.4 percent of the vote, respectively. After learning of his decisive victory, Langevin announced, as quoted by Gerald M. Carbone for the *Providence Journal-Bulletin* (November 6, 2002), that it gave him "a great feeling" to win reelection. "I hope the work that we do for our constituents every day—answering mail, working on the issues that Rhode Islanders care about . . . we hope that is what led us to this victory."

In 2003 Langevin was named to the newly formed Select Committee on Homeland Security, designed to oversee the federal Department of Homeland Security. He voted in favor of giving servicemen and –women tax relief and supported the imposition of fines up to $11,000 on telemarketers who continued to phone individuals who had placed their names on the national Do Not Call list; both bills passed in the House. In 2004 Langevin voted with the majority in defeating a bill that would have reinstated the draft. At that year's Democratic National Convention, in Boston, Massachusetts, he gave a speech in which he tried to impress upon listeners the necessity of stem-cell research. Facing the largest audience he had ever addressed, he said, as quoted in a press release on his Web site (July 21, 2004, on-line), "Stem cell research holds tremendous potential to improve the lives of millions of Americans who suffer from Alzheimer's, childhood diabetes, cancer, Parkinson's and even spinal cord injuries. . . . I am hopeful that highlighting this critical issue at the Democratic National Convention will help show Americans the potential benefits of stem cell research and build support for access to additional stem cell lines." In November 2004 Langevin won a third term in Congress, with 75 percent of the vote. In 2005 he was one of more than 30 House members who sponsored the Military Readiness Enhancement Act, which would replace the "Don't ask, don't tell" policy regarding homosexuals in the military with one that would enable admittedly gay people to serve; he also voted to restore $100 million in cuts to the Corporation for Public Broadcasting for the 2006 fiscal year. (The former bill has since been referred to the House Subcommittee on Military Personnel; the latter bill won approval in the House.)

Langevin has no use of his legs or hands and very little feeling in his body below the neck. He has limited use of his arms, however (his left arm is dominant), which allows him to perform such functions as drinking coffee through a straw by holding the cup between his wrists, sending E-mail messages with his Blackberry PDA by pushing the keys with a bone in his wrist, and brushing his teeth by weaving a toothbrush between his paralyzed fingers. He also relies heavily on such devices as Dragon Dictate voice-recognition software, and he moves about by controlling a joystick on his motorized wheelchair. Langevin's health aide, Caroline, lives with him and helps him perform daily chores, including bathing, dressing, and exercising his legs, which can take up to three hours every morning. Langevin also has a special assistant, Dave Lafferty, whom he considers his "right hand," as he told Mark Patinkin. Lafferty physically carries Langevin to and from his wheelchair and is the only assistant permitted on the floor of the House of Representatives.

When not in Washington, D.C., Langevin lives in Warwick. He serves on the boards of directors of PARI Independent Living, Tech Access, the Warwick Shelter, and the Festival Ballet, among other groups. He is also a member of the Knights of Columbus, the Lions Club, and Save the Bay. In his free time Langevin enjoys playing pool (with some assistance), wine-tasting, reading about Egyptian history, and eating at restaurants. He is single and Roman Catholic.

—K.J.E.

Suggested Reading: *Business Week Online* Dec. 13, 2000; jimlangevin.com; *Providence (Rhode Island) Journal-Bulletin* A p1 Feb. 3, 2002, A p17 Nov. 6, 2002; *USA Today* (on-line) Aug. 7, 2001

Lax, Peter D.

May 1, 1926– Mathematician

Address: Courant Institute of Mathematical Sciences, NYU, 251 Mercer St., New York, NY 10012-1185

"Peter D. Lax has been described as the most versatile mathematician of his generation," the Norwegian Academy of Science and Letters declared in announcing that its members had chosen Lax as the winner of the 2005 Abel Prize—an honor equivalent to a Nobel Prize. Lax, a professor emeritus at the Courant Institute of Mathematical Sciences, at New York University (NYU), where he studied or worked for nearly half a century, "stands out in joining together pure and applied mathematics, combining a deep understanding of analysis with an extraordinary capacity to find unifying concepts," the academy stated. "He has

Peter D. Lax

had a profound influence, not only by his research, but also by his writing, his lifelong commitment to education and his generosity to younger mathematicians." Lax's discoveries have provided solutions to longstanding mathematical problems and inspired further research of enormous actual or potential usefulness. As a member of the National Science Board in the 1980s, Lax played a crucial role in impressing upon the federal government the need for state-of-the-art computers in all research facilities; thanks to the installation of such devices at many universities, he indirectly jump-started large numbers of productive mathematical research projects that would not have been possible without computerized, high-speed calculations.

The Hungarian-born Lax immigrated to the U.S. during World War II, and while still in his teens, he was recruited to assist in the top-secret project in Los Alamos, New Mexico, that led to the creation of the first atomic bomb. As a young man he was guided and inspired by such brilliant mathematicians as John von Neumann and Richard Courant, whose ideas strongly influenced the evolution of his mathematical outlook. According to an NYU press release (May 13, 2005, on-line), Lax "exemplifies the philosophy . . . that there are no real divisions between the applied and pure mathematical sciences." His name is associated with advances in "the theory and application of partial differential equations and . . . the computation of their solutions," in the words of the Norwegian academy; in that area alone, his work has had a huge impact, because such equations are ubiquitous in science, being of vital importance in fields ranging from aircraft flight simulation to computer

graphics to weather forecasting. He has also made indispensable contributions to the theory of non-linear hyperbolic systems and the allied theory of shock waves (which applies to explosions, airplanes traveling at supersonic velocities, the movement of oil in oil reservoirs, and even changing densities of cars in traffic jams); the theory of solitons (both as real, solitary waves, as in waterways, and as the solutions to mathematical problems), which applies to solid-state physics, models for biological systems, and the use of optical fibers for high-speed communications; and scattering theory, which has illuminated key aspects of high-energy physics. Discoveries and numerical methods that bear his name include Lax pairs, Lax shocks, the Lax-Phillips scattering theory, the Lax-Milgram theorem, the Lax-Richtmyer equivalence theorem, the Beurling-Lax theorem, the Lax-Friedrichs and Lax-Wendroff schemes, the Lax entropy condition, the Lax-Levermore theory, and the Lax theorem (concerning the Riemann problem). When Claudia Dreifus, a reporter for the *New York Times* (March 29, 2005), asked him, "Has mathematics become too complex for anyone to understand all of it?," Lax responded, "Compared to physics or chemistry, mathematics is a very broad subject. It is true that nobody can know it all, or even nearly all. But it is also true that as mathematics develops, things are simplified and unusual connections appear. Geometry and algebra, for instance, which were so very different 100 years ago, are intricately connected today." In 1986, at a White House ceremony hosted by President Ronald Reagan, Lax received the National Medal of Science, the U.S. government's highest honor for practitioners of mathematics and science.

Peter David Lax was born on May 1, 1926 in Budapest, Hungary. His parents, Henry Lax and Klara (Kornfeld) Lax, were physicians. During his early teens in Budapest, as he recalled in his Abel Prize acceptance speech, which he gave in Norway in May 2005, he was "helped immensely . . . by the Hungarian network of mathematicians on the lookout for talented youngsters." Among the mathematicians who nurtured him were his mother's brother Albert Korodie (born Kornfeld), Paul Turán, Rose Peter, and Dénes König. Both of Lax's parents were Jewish, and after World War II broke out, in 1939, and the Hungarian government expressed its support for Nazi Germany, his mother and father resolved to leave their native land. With the help of the American consul in Budapest, who was both a friend and a patient of Henry Lax's, the family— which included a second son—planned their escape from Europe. On December 5, 1941 they sailed from Lisbon, Portugal, on what proved to be the last passenger ship to leave the European continent for the U.S. before the conclusion of the war. Within a month of their arrival in New York City, Peter Lax had enrolled at Stuyvesant High School, an elite public school for intellectually gifted teenagers. Unlike other Stuyvesant students, he took no math courses, because, as he told Claudia Dreifus,

"I knew more [math] than most of the teachers." He added, "But I had to take English and American history, and I quickly fell in love with America." He had been in the U.S. only a short time when he received a visit by the Hungarian-born mathematical genius John von Neumann, who was conducting highly innovative work in pure and applied mathematics as one of the original staff members of the Institute for Advanced Study, in Princeton, New Jersey. Born in Budapest, von Neumann had maintained contacts with colleagues there after he came to the U.S., in 1930; from them, he learned about Lax's prodigious abilities in math. During Lax's early years in the States, he was mentored by the mathematicians Paul Erdös and Gábor Szegö.

Lax graduated from Stuyvesant in about 1943. He became a naturalized U.S. citizen in 1944, and that same year he was drafted into the U.S. Army. In 1945, after a training period of six months, he was sent to Los Alamos, New Mexico, where, in what was dubbed the Manhattan Project, the atomic bomb was being developed. Von Neumann was working there as well, as a consultant. In his Abel Prize acceptance speech, Lax said that at Los Alamos he benefited from having the "experience of working as a part of a team of scientists with different expertise and outlook." About six weeks after Lax's arrival, the scientists tested the world's first atomic bomb, in the New Mexico desert. A few weeks after that, on August 6 and 8, 1945, the U.S. dropped atomic bombs on the Japanese cities of Hiroshima and Nagasaki, respectively, killing hundreds of thousands of civilians instantly and, in the days, months, and years to come, many more thousands, who died as the result of their exposure to atomic radiation. Lax is convinced, as he told Claudia Dreifus, that dropping the bombs was necessary to bring World War II to a swift end and was therefore morally correct.

Lax received his military discharge in 1946. He then returned to New York, where in 1947 he earned a B.A. degree in math at New York University. He remained at NYU to pursue a doctoral degree, also in math. His teachers included his dissertation adviser, Kurt O. Friedrichs, and Richard Courant, who, like Lax, had been forced to leave his homeland, Germany, to escape the Nazis. Courant was in the process of building from scratch an applied-mathematics research center (later named the Courant Institute for Mathematical Sciences) at NYU that would confer advanced degrees; as a graduate student Lax profited from the presence of highly accomplished European-born instructors (among them Friedrichs) whom Courant had assisted in immigrating to the U.S. Lax completed his Ph.D. in 1949; his dissertation was entitled "Nonlinear System of Hyperbolic Partial Differential Equations in Two Independent Variables."

Lax spent the following year as a staff member of the Los Alamos scientific laboratory; most summers during the next decade, he served as a consultant there in the burgeoning new field of computer technology. In that role, he recalled in his Abel Prize speech, "I saw . . . the overwhelming importance of computation for science and the role that mathematics plays in it." "The intellectual leader [at Los Alamos] was John von Neumann, who had a vision of the role of computing in science and technology," Lax wrote for the *Newsletter* (January 1995, on-line) of the Center for Research on Parallel Computation (CRPC) at Rice University, in Houston, Texas. Von Neumann, who consulted at Los Alamos until 1955, Lax continued, was "deeply involved in the details of the science and engineering applications, the programming, and the mathematical aspects of using computers," and Lax was drawn into the same areas of study. In 1952 Los Alamos scientists completed the construction of MANIAC I, one of the earliest computers; Lax used it that year in what he termed his "first numerical experiment," which concerned one of von Neumann's research projects— "schemes for calculating flows with many interacting shocks," as Lax wrote for the CRPC newsletter.

Meanwhile, in 1951, NYU had hired Lax as an assistant professor. In 1954, thanks to von Neumann, who believed that it was critical for scientists to have access to computers, NYU opened a facility known as the AEC (Atomic Energy Commission) Computing Center (now called the Courant Mathematics and Computing Laboratory), which was equipped with an AEC-owned computer—a machine called UNIVAC, manufactured by the Remington Rand Corp. (The establishment of the center was significant enough to attract to the opening ceremony not only the chairman of Remington Rand but the famous World War II general Douglas MacArthur and General Lesley Groves, the head of the Manhattan Project, both of whom were Remington Rand board members.) The installation of a UNIVAC, Lax told the CRPC, "stimulat[ed] great interest in computing at the Courant Institute." According to Lax, as quoted by the Norwegian mathematician Helge Holden in a brief overview of Lax's contributions to mathematics for the Abel Prize Web site, high-speed computers' "impact on mathematics, both applied and pure, is comparable to the role of telescopes in astronomy and microscopes in biology"—that is, the solution of countless problems and ability to gain insights into countless phenomena were not possible until their invention. As a member of the National Science Board from 1980 to 1986, Lax successfully promoted the federal government's supplying of computers to research centers at universities.

In 1958 Lax became a full professor at NYU. From 1972 to 1980 he directed the Courant Institute, which consists of a Department of Mathematics and a Department of Computer Science. The description of the institute on its Web site also indicates the breadth of Lax's work there: it is "a center for research and advanced training in mathematics and computer science . . . [and] has long been a leader in mathematical analysis, applied mathematics, and scientific computation, with special emphasis on partial differential equations and their applications. In computer science, the Institute excels in theory, programming languages, computer graphics, and parallel computing. Mathematics and computer science are viewed as living parts of the stream of science, not as isolated specialties." One of Lax's colleagues at Courant was Louis Nirenberg, whose affiliation with the institute was concurrent with Lax's and who, like Lax, worked on the theory of partial differential equations. David W. McLaughlin, who directed the institute from 1994 to 2002, told Courtney Leatherman for the *Chronicle of Higher Education* (July 16, 1999, on-line) when Lax and Nirenberg retired, in 1999, that during their 50 years at Courant, the men had "together set a tone for the institute." "Doors are open and interaction is common and stature is not emphasized . . . ," McLaughlin explained. "It has been a style that [Lax and Nirenberg] have shaped and maintained, and one could imagine a very different place if these two very close friends had different personalities." According to the Web site of the Mathematics Genealogy Project, while at NYU Lax served as the adviser to 55 doctoral candidates in mathematics, who in turn have advised an additional 249. Thus, according to the project, he has 304 "mathematical descendants."

Lax has written or co-written half a dozen books, among them *Scattering Theory* (with Ralph S. Phillips, 1967); *Hyperbolic Systems of Conservation Laws and the Mathematical Theory of Shock Waves* (1973); *Scattering Theory for Automorphic Functions* (with Ralph S. Phillips, 1976); *Calculus with Applications and Computing* (with Samuel Burstein and Anneli Lax, 1976); *Linear Algebra*, 1997; and *Functional Analysis* (2002).

In addition to the Abel Prize and the National Medal of Science, Lax's many honors include nine honorary doctoral degrees, from universities in the U.S., France, Israel, Scotland, and China. In 1966 and 1973 he won the Lester R. Ford Award, which the Mathematical Association of America gives "to recognize authors of articles of expository excellence published in *The American Mathematical Monthly* or *Mathematics Magazine*," according to its Web site. He received the Chauvenet Prize from the same group in 1974; the Norbert Wiener Prize from the American Mathematical Society (AMS) and Society of Industrial and Applied Mathematics in 1982; the Wolf Prize, from an Israeli foundation, in 1987, and the Steele Prize, from the AMS, in 1993, both of which celebrate a lifetime of achievement; and the Distinguished Teaching Award from NYU, in 1995. He is a member of the American Academy of Arts and Sciences and half a dozen other learned societies in the U.S., Russia, Hungary, and China.

Lax, who at age 79 has a full head of curly white hair, lives in Manhattan. In 1948 he married the former Anneli Cahn, a refugee from Nazi Germany who earned a Ph.D. in math at NYU and taught there from 1961 to 1992; in addition to their book, the couple co-wrote several papers for mathematical journals. For four decades until her death, in 1999, Anneli Lax edited the New Mathematical Library series, a collection of monographs on mathematical topics for high-school and college students; the series was renamed the Anneli Lax New Mathematical Library in her honor in 2000. The union of Lax and his wife produced two sons. One, James D. Lax, is a physician who practices in New York City. The other son, John Lax, taught history at Mount Holyoke College before he was killed by a drunk driver, in 1978. The John Lax Memorial Lecture, given each year at Mount Holyoke by an eminent historian, was endowed by Peter and Anneli Lax in 1982 in his memory. Peter Lax has three grandchildren, whom he described to *Current Biography* as "charming."

—M.H./R.E.

Suggested Reading: Abel Prize Web site; BBC News (on-line) May 25, 2005; Center for Research on Parallel Computation at Rice University *Newsletter* (on-line) Jan. 1995; *Chronicle of Higher Education* (on-line) July 16, 1999; mathworld.wolfram.com; *New York Sun* p1+ Mar. 23, 2005; *New York Times* F p2 Mar. 29, 2005; New York University Office of Public Affairs press release (on-line) May 13, 2005; *Who's Who in America*

Selected Books: *Scattering Theory* (with Ralph S. Phillips), 1967; *Hyperbolic Systems of Conservation Laws and the Mathematical Theory of Shock Waves*, 1973; *Scattering Theory for Automorphic Functions* (with Ralph S. Phillips), 1976; *Calculus with Applications and Computing* (with Samuel Burstein and Anneli Lax), 1976; *Linear Algebra*, 1997; *Functional Analysis*, 2002

Lehane, Dennis

Aug. 4, 1965– Writer

Address: c/o Ann Rittenberg, 1201 Broadway, Suite 708, New York, NY 10001

Since the publication of his debut novel, *A Drink Before the War*, in 1994, Dennis Lehane has become known for creating compelling, multifaceted characters as well as gripping plots. In addition to writing the best-selling series of books featuring the detectives Patrick Kenzie and Angela Gennaro, Lehane is the author of the critically acclaimed novels *Mystic River* (2001), which was made into an Academy Award–winning movie in 2003, and *Shutter Island* (2003). Several of his novels are set in or around the Dorchester section of Boston, Massachusetts, the gritty, working-class neighborhood in which he was raised; all of them—in the opinions of many reviewers—display a keen understanding of both human psychology and the elements that make up compelling fiction. His writ-

Dennis Lehane

Scott Wintrow/Getty Images

ing, like that of the celebrated novelists Elmore Leonard and Raymond Chandler, blurs the distinction between pulp fiction and the "literary novel." Discussing the popularity of the mystery genre, Lehane noted during a *Newsweek* (February 19, 2001) interview, "We've become disillusioned with so-called literary fiction. People don't want to be told that life sucks and let's read about it for the next 250 pages. They kinda know that, that life is mundane, that life is very boring. But they're not just reading for escapism. They're reading to work stuff out, and for that they're looking for stories a little larger than life—characters going through extreme situations, grandly passionate and tragic things. And mysteries do that better than anything."

The youngest of five children, Dennis Lehane was born on August 4, 1965 and grew up in Dorchester. His parents were Catholic immigrants from County Cork, in Ireland; his mother was a school cafeteria worker, his father a warehouse foreman for the Sears retail company. In interviews Lehane has spoken with pride about his parents' struggles. "I love what I do," Lehane remarked in an interview with Louise Jones for *Publishers Weekly* (June 21, 1999), "but I'm no hero. My father worked the same job for 37 years and I don't think he loved it. That's heroism, doing the job and working toward retirement to support your family. That's awe-inspiring."

When Lehane was six years old, a new world opened up for him when his mother took him to the local public library. In a sense, reading gave him experiences he could not otherwise have had in his everyday life, and it served as a refuge from the sometimes violent conflicts in his neighborhood, which were fueled in part by racial tensions.

Those conditions, which reached their peak in the 1970s, have informed Lehane's writing since the beginning of his career.

Lehane began his college education at the University of Massachusetts, in Boston, and transferred soon afterward to Eckerd College, a small school in St. Petersburg, Florida. He received his bachelor's degree in creative writing in 1988 and immediately entered a master of fine arts program in creative writing at Florida International University, in Miami. There, he honed his craft under the tutelage of such noted writers as John Dufresne, James Hall, Les Standiford, and Lynne Barrett. (Lehane had begun writing short fiction as an undergraduate but was unwilling to send anything out for publication until his writing improved.)

During his apprenticeship Lehane often imitated the minimalist style of the famed short-story writer Raymond Carver. Later, on a lark, he wrote a mystery novel and showed it to his creative-writing teacher at Eckerd, Sterling Watson. Watson was so impressed with Lehane's novel that he showed it to his former student Ann Rittenberg, who had by that time become a literary agent. Rittenberg, in turn, agreed to represent Lehane and sent the novel to Claire Wachtel at the publishing house Harcourt Brace; it was accepted for publication there on June 17, 1993. Lehane remarked in his interview with Louise Jones: "My publishing career is such a fluke. I got to it a lot faster than I expected. I have no publishing horror stories."

The novel, *A Drink Before the War* (1994), which became a critically acclaimed best-seller, features the private detective duo Patrick Kenzie and Angela Gennaro. Patrick, who narrates the novel, and Angela bring to their work both the street smarts they honed in Dorchester, where they were childhood friends, and their personal troubles: Patrick is haunted by the abuse he suffered at the hands of his father, while Angela has to contend with a husband who occasionally beats her. In the novel they are hired by two state senators to track down an African-American cleaning woman who has stolen some sensitive documents. After finding the woman, the detectives realize that the materials she has taken point to political corruption and child prostitution. In a review of *A Drink Before the War* for *Booklist* (November 15, 1994), Emily Melton noted: "Lehane offers slick, hip, sparkling dialogue that's as good as it gets, a plot that rockets along at warp speed, and [a] wonderfully original, in-your-face crime-solving duo. . . . A terrific first novel and, one hopes, the beginning of a superb series." Writing for *Library Journal* (November 1, 1994), Rex E. Klett remarked: "Lehane's minimal use of literary references helps establish character, as do his frequent allusions to child abuse and wife battering. Rough and tumble action for a high energy, likable pair." *A Drink Before the War* won a Shamus Award from the Private Eye Writers of America.

In Lehane's second entry in the Kenzie-Gennaro mysteries, *Darkness, Take My Hand* (1996), the detectives are on the trail of a serial killer, whose crimes have left the neighborhood in shock and the police baffled. As Angela's marriage falls apart and Patrick finds love, the partners discover that the killer may have a connection to their own pasts. In *Booklist* (July 1996), Emily Melton cheered: "Lehane's latest is an explosive story that is at once gut-wrenchingly violent and achingly melancholy. . . . In a series of heart-stopping climaxes that grow ever more terrifying and bloody, Patrick and Angie lose nearly everything. Lehane's perfectly crafted plot leers, teases, taunts, and lulls, scattering bits of humor and heartbreak among the soul-chilling episodes of death and destruction. A tour de force from a truly gifted writer."

Sacred, the third Kenzie-Gennaro mystery, was published in 1997. In this outing the detectives are kidnapped by a dying billionaire named Trevor Stone, who promises them a handsome monetary reward if they help track down his missing daughter. Their investigations lead them to the cult-like Church of Truth and Revelation and to a series of murders. Ahmad Wright, in *Library Journal* (June 15, 1997), declared: "With its fast-paced plot, Lehane's . . . newest will be a winner with adventure buffs." David Pitt agreed, writing for *Booklist* (June 1–15, 1997), "This is Lehane's third novel . . . and it's devilishly twisted, a kind of Elmore-Leonard-meets-*The-Sting* in which everyone is trying to con everyone else. The characters are well drawn (especially the billionaire and his daughter, who keep revealing new things about themselves, right up until the last scene), the mystery perplexing, . . . and the conclusion deeply satisfying. *Sacred* is a first-class novel that will delight anyone who loves an intricate mystery."

The Kenzie-Gennaro series continued with *Gone, Baby, Gone* (1998), which finds the detectives on the trail of a missing four-year-old girl whose mother, a junkie and prostitute, has stolen $200,000 from a drug dealer. Patrick and Angela, meanwhile, become romantically interested in each other. When the money is recovered by the police, they offer to exchange it for the safe return of the young girl—an offer fraught with problems for everyone involved, including Kenzie and Gennaro. Pam Lambert wrote for *People* (August 10, 1998), "Lehane's evocative prose lures us into the labyrinth of this chilling, masterfully plotted tale into that dark place where men try to play God and everyone gets hurt." Reviewing the book for *Newsday* (August 4, 1998), Adam Mazmanian noted, "[Lehane's] crisp dialogue, the oddball supporting cast and the Kenzie-Gennaro romance provide much-needed lightness to what is, ultimately, a dark and harrowing tale."

In *Prayers for Rain* (1999), the most recent Kenzie-Gennaro crime novel, Patrick Kenzie and his friend Bubba Rogowski try to dissuade a man from continuing to stalk a woman; soon afterward the stalker's victim leaps naked to her death from a Boston landmark. The apparent suicide leads Patrick to turn for help to Angela, with whom he has ended his partnership and romance. In a review for *Booklist* (April 15, 1999), Wes Lukowsky wrote, "This fifth Kenzie-Gennaro novel again features well-armed heroes who exact their own brand of vigilante justice in a Boston where the police are inept and/or helpless. As in all the best hard-boiled series, each entry reveals more about the principal characters and their relationships in a violent, uncaring world. . . . Lehane has worked his way into the top echelon of crime writers." Wilda Williams, writing for *Library Journal* (June 15, 1999), was more critical, noting, "Lehane's love of Boston, its neighborhoods, and its people shines through his hard-edged prose. However, the overly convoluted plot is at times unbelievable, and the gruesome violence . . . is extreme and not for the squeamish."

Taking a break from the Kenzie-Gennaro series, Lehane penned *Mystic River* (2001). That novel, written in third person, focuses on three friends: Sean Devine, Jimmy Marcus, and Dave Boyle. One day in 1975, while the more street-smart Sean and Jimmy look on helplessly, a pair of strange men, pretending to be law-enforcement officers, order 11-year-old Dave to get into their car; Dave is then held prisoner for several days. Twenty-five years later the three friends are reunited in their old neighborhood, following the murder of Jimmy's 19-year-old daughter. That reunion—as well as the investigation into Jimmy's daughter's death—forces them to confront what happened to Dave on that day in their childhood. In the *New York Times Book Review* (February 18, 2001), Marilyn Stasio praised *Mystic River*, calling it a "powerhouse of a crime novel. . . . Lehane spares nothing in his wrenching descriptions of how a crime in the neighborhood kills the neighborhood, taking it down house by house, family by family. Although his deeply scored characterizations of the three former friends carry the soul of his story, Lehane's penetrating studies of their neighbors—including some of the strongest and saddest women you'll ever meet in this genre—are no less vital." Writing for *Newsweek* (February 19, 2001), Malcolm Jones concluded that *Mystic River* "is Lehane's best book by far. Like all his writing, it shimmers with great dialogue and a complex view of the world—what Lehane likes to call 'comic fatality'—where every hero is a little soiled and more than slightly compromised." The novel was adapted for the screen in 2003 by the actor and director Clint Eastwood; the film brought Academy Awards to Sean Penn, who was named best actor for his performance as Jimmy, and Tim Robbins, who won in the best-supporting-actor category for his portrayal of Dave.

Lehane's most recent offering, *Shutter Island* (2003), is another departure from the Kenzie-Gennaro series. The book, a historical psychological thriller, is set in 1954 on the fictional island of the title, which houses a mental hospital for criminals. As the story opens U.S. Marshall Teddy Daniels and his partner, Chuck Aule, are on their way to the island to investigate the disappearance of Rachel Solando, a woman who drowned her three children two years ago. No one knows how she got out of the hospital, a place where nothing is what it appears to be. Following on the heels of the critically acclaimed and immensely popular *Mystic River*, *Shutter Island* received mixed reviews. "Lehane's strength is dialogue and a relentless penetration into the minds of his characters. In *Shutter Island*, it is Teddy Daniels that Lehane inhabits, luring the reader to suspend belief and join him," Rob Mitchell wrote in a review for the *Boston Herald* (May 13, 2003). "Reminiscent of John Fowles' *The Magus*, *Shutter Island* envelops, encircles and floats inside-out. The ambiguous ending may disappoint some, but it is effective and cries out for a second reading to discover how and where Lehane manages his crafty manipulation." In *People* (April 21, 2003), Edward Nawotka declared, "Although Lehane's latest doesn't have the multifaceted power of his 2001 bestseller *Mystic River* . . . he has crafted a thriller as exciting as an elaborate video game (now Teddy makes his way down a craggy cliff to recover an important clue; now he's sneaking into a fort). If you like books that will make great movies, then this one is for you."

Lehane's experiences as a writing student have inspired him to teach writing classes himself, first at Tufts University and then at the Harvard Extension School. For several years, until 2004, he was a member of the faculty of the University of Southern Maine Stonecoast M.F.A. program. In interviews he has been highly critical of the "high/low" debate within the literary world, which finds some arguing that character is all-important and others

maintaining that plot is the key to a good novel. In an interview with Jillian Abbott for the *Writer* (May 2004), Lehane offered his own take on the subject: "Starting in the 1960s and continuing through the 1980s, plot became a dirty word in literary circles. Fiction lost its way. A great novel comes when there is beauty of language, illumination of character and a great plot. All three elements are necessary." He elaborated on that point in an interview with Edward Nawotka for *Publishers Weekly* (April 14, 2003): "You can't separate character—which is what the higher set champions—and plot—which is what the other side defends. They are both in service to each other. If you go to any great work of art, you talk about plot all day and then you talk about character all day. Just give me a well-written book." Lehane lives in Jamaica Plain, a suburb of Boston, with his wife, Sheila, and their dogs.

—C.M.

Suggested Reading: *Boston Herald* p46 May 13, 2003; *Chicago Tribune* V p6 Dec. 28, 1994; *Entertainment Weekly* p105+ Apr. 4, 2003; *Newsweek* p58+ Feb. 19, 2001; *People* p43 Aug. 10, 1998; *Publishers Weekly* p40+ June 21, 1999, p43+ Oct. 23, 2000, with photos, p39+ Apr. 14, 2003; *Writer* p66 Aug. 2002, with photo, p16+ May 2004, with photos

Selected Books: *A Drink Before the War*, 1994; *Darkness, Take My Hand*, 1996; *Sacred*, 1997; *Gone, Baby, Gone*, 1998; *Prayers for Rain*, 1999; *Mystic River*, 2001; *Shutter Island*, 2003

Lelyveld, Joseph

Apr. 5, 1937– Journalist; author; former executive editor of the New York Times

Address: *c/o Carl D. Brandt, 1501 Broadway, New York, NY 10036*

In his four-decade career at the *New York Times*, beginning in the early 1960s, Joseph Lelyveld rose from the position of copy boy to the newspaper's top editorial post, becoming executive editor in 1994. During his seven years at the helm, Lelyveld inspired admiration and loyalty among his colleagues while overseeing a number of changes at the paper, ranging from the introduction of color photographs to an increase in circulation to greater diversity on the staff. In 2003, when a number of crises at the paper—including a highly publicized plagiarism scandal—led to the resignation of his successor, Lelyveld came out of retirement temporarily to help restore calm, as the 152-year-old newspaper sought to repair the damage to its longstanding reputation for credibility. In addition to

his work at the *Times*, Lelyveld has penned two acclaimed books: *Move Your Shadow*, an exploration of race relations in apartheid-era South Africa, for which Lelyveld won a Pulitzer Prize in 1986, and the 2005 volume *Omaha Blues*, a memoir of his turbulent boyhood and family life. In *New York* (March 28, 2005, on-line), Stephen J. Dubner wrote, "*Omaha Blues* is a wholly eccentric and occasionally thrilling book in which Lelyveld stakes claim to the writer he was and is."

Joseph Salem Lelyveld was born on April 5, 1937 in Cincinnati, Ohio, to Arthur Joseph Lelyveld, a rabbi, and Toby (Bookholtz) Lelyveld, a former actress. The family came to include Joseph's younger brothers, David and Michael. By all accounts Arthur Lelyveld was a respected clergyman, with a congregation in Omaha, Nebraska, and then in Cleveland, Ohio. He was also an impassioned advocate for Zionism and civil rights; during the summer of 1964, when suppression of the African-American vote was still a common practice in the South, he traveled to Hattiesburg, Mississippi, to go door to door in black neighborhoods, encouraging people to vote. (A local white man re-

Courtesy of the *New York Times*

Joseph Lelyveld

sponded by attacking the rabbi with a tire iron.) As a father Arthur Lelyveld was rather distant, his son has recalled, and his marriage was a troubled one, as Joseph Lelyveld explained to Charlie Rose in an interview for the *Charlie Rose Show* (April 26, 2005): "My mother had loved the idea initially of being a rabbi's wife when she was very young. . . . But then it was not a satisfying life for her. She felt she was living in a fish bowl; everybody was commenting. She had to please in social ways so many people. And she . . . had aspirations, literary aspirations, aspirations as a scholar. Wanted to get a doctorate, wanted to write a thesis, wanted to teach. The two lives didn't flow easily together. . . . And her dissatisfaction with the life she was leading ultimately became a dissatisfaction with my dad and the whole role of rabbi's wife, and even mother for a time." Toby Lelyveld attempted suicide several times and also engaged in extramarital affairs, for which her husband always forgave her. (As an adult Lelyveld discovered that his brother Michael was not fathered by Arthur Lelyveld.) At one point during Joseph Lelyveld's childhood, his mother left the family to return to Columbia University, in New York City, where she had previously studied, to finish her doctoral work on Shakespeare. As a result of his family's turmoil, during his boyhood Lelyveld was shunted around the country, first staying with his father in Omaha, then moving into his grandparents' home in Brooklyn, New York, and ultimately finding himself with his parents again, on the Upper West Side of Manhattan, where he attended P.S. 165. He admitted to Stephen J. Dubner for the profile in *New York* that he had "the sense all my life that, at an early age, I was abandoned by my parents, that I

was incidental to what was going on in their lives." Growing up, Lelyveld told David J. Garrow for the *Chicago Tribune* (May 1, 2005), "I became guarded, pensive and . . . unusually but not happily self-sufficient."

After graduating from the Bronx High School of Science, Lelyveld enrolled at Harvard University, in Cambridge, Massachusetts. He initially aspired to become a Supreme Court justice, but by spending an hour in the Harvard law library during his junior year of college, he quickly discovered his lack of interest in the law. He graduated summa cum laude with a B.A. degree in history and English literature in 1958, then earned his master's degree in American history, also at Harvard, in 1959. After briefly contemplating a career in psychiatry, Lelyveld enrolled at Columbia University's Graduate School of Journalism, where he attained another master's degree in 1960 and won a Fulbright fellowship to Burma, to study that nation. It was while traveling throughout Burma and India that Lelyveld discovered his passion for writing, especially about foreign affairs.

In 1962 Lelyveld joined the staff of the *New York Times* as a copy boy. By the mid-1960s he had moved up to the post of foreign correspondent, based in the Congo and South Africa from 1965 to 1966, when he was expelled from the latter country for being too critical of the government in his reporting. "I found, through sheer dumb luck, that . . . news-papering suited a deep need I seemed to have to not know what was going to happen next in my life. I found that I thrived on surprise and that there were people who might pay me to cultivate this instinct," he said in a commencement speech at the Columbia University Graduate School of Journalism, as reported by June Scharf for the *Cleveland Jewish News* (August 10, 2001). He immediately became one of the *Times*'s star writers, known for what Stephen J. Dubner called his "distinctive, angular style and a surplus of attitude—a sort of cynical moralism, if such a thing were possible." His subsequent foreign posts included London, England (1966), India and Pakistan (1966–69), and Hong Kong (1973–75). He also began amassing awards for his writing, including the Page One Award for an article about the death of a 12-year-old heroin addict (in 1970), two George Polk Memorial Awards for a series of pieces about a fourth-grade class and coverage of South Africa (in 1972 and 1984, respectively), and a John Simon Guggenheim fellowship (also in 1984). By the late 1970s, Lelyveld had moved to Washington, D.C., and was writing a weekly column for the *New York Times Magazine*. At one point he wrote a piece about Oral Roberts University, a Christian institution in Tulsa, Oklahoma, which Ed Klein, then the editor of the *Times Magazine*, refused to print on the grounds that it was anti-Christian. Piqued by Klein's complaint, Lelyveld submitted the article to the *Christian Century*, a Chicago-based religious magazine, which vindicated Lelyveld by accepting his submission and contacting Klein to obtain permission to run it. A. M. "Abe" Rosenthal, the *Times*'s executive editor, told Lelyveld to retract the submission, then transferred the writer from his assignment under Klein at the *Times Magazine* to a New York City–based post as the paper's deputy foreign editor. Lelyveld discovered that he had a knack for editing and that, as he told Stephen J. Dubner, "while I might be an egocentric and difficult writer, as an editor I wasn't egocentric at all. I had a cool head and I understood the problems of writers and I could get things out of people." Still, after two years as deputy foreign editor, beginning in 1978, Lelyveld wanted to resume the life of a correspondent and returned to South Africa, where he remained until 1983.

While working as a staff writer for the *Times Magazine* and as London bureau chief, Lelyveld also spent time writing a book about his experiences in South Africa, particularly as they related to that country's rigid, brutal system of racial segregation, or apartheid. *Move Your Shadow*, published in 1985, greatly impressed critics, who consistently praised Lelyveld's immersion in the lives of black South Africans and his critical yet fair portrayals of whites and blacks alike. For the *Village Voice* (November 10, 1985), Rob Nixon wrote, "Though this is not what we would normally consider an 'inflammatory' book, almost every page resonates with the kind of commitment to understanding South Africa that should fuel international anger at apartheid's anachronistic survival. Armed only with diligent reporting, integrity, and an uncommon articulacy, Joseph Lelyveld chips away at the mountainous lies and self-deceits that shadow the land." A review in the *Economist* (April 12, 1986) dubbed the book "a strange concoction: part history, part vignettes of people and places, part argument, part prediction. It is unashamedly polemical, without being boring, and full of wit." Lelyveld's book won a number of honors, including the Sidney Hillman Award, the Cornelius P. Ryan Award, the *Los Angeles Times* Book Award and, most notably, the Pulitzer Prize.

By the end of 1986, Lelyveld had been named foreign editor of the *New York Times*. In 1989 he was designated deputy managing editor, and he became managing editor the next year. In 1994 he ascended to the paper's top post, that of executive editor. "I hope, in some small way, the paper will be a reflection of my news judgment, intuition and, if you will, my passion for news . . . ," he told Joe Deitch for *Editor & Publisher Magazine* (October 21, 1995), adding, "I do not see the paper as a personal instrument to reflect my views and ideas." During his seven-year tenure as executive editor, Lelyveld revamped the format of the paper, adding color photographs, expanding existing sections of the paper, and creating new sections. He also helped to diversify the staff and improve the *Times*'s circulation, making it available in more than 200 cities. Under Lelyveld the *Times* won 12 Pulitzer Prizes. Despite what some saw as his lack of social skills—he was known for his reserve,

awkwardness, and frequent silence—Lelyveld earned widespread respect and admiration as executive editor. The newspaper's publisher, Arthur Sulzberger Jr., told David Shaw for the *Los Angeles Times* (May 22, 2001) that Lelyveld's "contributions to the quality of our news report have been stunning." A former *Times* reporter, Gene Roberts, agreed, saying for the same article, "The entire paper has improved in every way under Joe Lelyveld." Largely because of Lelyveld's natural reticence and formality, some perceived him as a proverbial "cold fish" and perhaps undervalued his contributions; however, when Lelyveld decided to retire, in 2001, one year short of the mandatory retirement age of 65, Sulzberger again sang his praises. "Joe ran a superb newsroom, and under him we produced a superb newspaper," he told Stephen J. Dubner. "Under him we entered into the digital age, we broke circulation barriers, advertising barriers, won a plethora of awards. It was Joe who assembled the talent that's now driving the paper forward. He was a damn fine editor." Though Lelyveld favored as his successor the paper's managing editor, Bill Keller, Sulzberger instead chose Howell Raines, the editor of the paper's editorial pages. Eighteen months into Raines's leadership of the *Times*, though, significant problems became evident. Several writers and editors resigned in protest over Raines's reportedly hard-nosed policies. Moreover, a scandal broke out when it was revealed that a young *Times* reporter, Jayson Blair, had been regularly plagiarizing his stories. In the ensuing tumult, Sulzberger called for Raines's resignation—and requested that Lelyveld return as an interim editor. "I wanted two things from [Lelyveld]," Sulzberger told Stephen J. Dubner. "To help me steady the newsroom and to find his successor." Lelyveld professed reluctance to return to the paper, "but he did it as a favor to me and also because he loves the institution," Sulzberger continued. With Lelyveld at the helm, even temporarily, staffers were apparently quite relieved. "Joe established a sense of trust and respect in the top management of the newsroom and introduced a very careful approach to changing the institution," a former *Times* employee, Bill Kovach, told Mark Jurkowitz for the *Boston Globe* (June 18, 2003). "Joe's intellectual approach established a sense of confidence he would not hurt the institution. That's why [the staff was] so happy when he came back." One month later Sulzberger announced that Bill Keller would assume the position of executive editor.

In 2005 Lelyveld published his second book, the memoir *Omaha Blues: A Memory Loop*. Nine years earlier, while Arthur Lelyveld was dying, a former colleague of the rabbi's had asked Joseph if he wanted an old trunk containing the Lelyveld family's letters and photographs. Though Lelyveld felt little nostalgia for his childhood, he had the trunk shipped to his home. In about 2002 he decided that the time had come to open the trunk and begin confronting his past. He read brutally frank letters written by his mother, in which she complained about her son, and though the letters made him sad, Lelyveld managed to distance himself from them enough to see their potential as the building blocks of a book. He began researching past events and interviewing relatives and acquaintances about his family. In doing so he confirmed his own hazy memories of having been largely abandoned by his parents. Writing the book "almost became a kind of self-therapy," he told Dubner. While writing *Omaha Blues*, Lelyveld was also able to find out the fate of a former family friend, a rabbi named Ben Lowell, who had worked under Arthur Lelyveld beginning in 1948. As a boy Joseph Lelyveld had adored Lowell, who took him to baseball games and was, as Lelyveld wrote in his book, "the one adult in my life who seemed consistently and reliably available." When Arthur Lelyveld fired Lowell, the rabbi's young son was distraught; only decades later, through extensive research, did Lelyveld discover that Lowell had been dismissed for his alleged ties to the Communist Party.

Omaha Blues was published to primarily good reviews. "Mr. Lelyveld's sketches of moments from his childhood are striking and lyrical, conjuring a searing portrait of the alienation and confusion of a boy cast adrift," William Doyle wrote for the *New York Observer* (April 4, 2005). In the *Washington Monthly* (May 1, 2005), Melinda Henneberger called the book "a remarkably discreet tell-all," which, "absent the dead weight of self-justification, reads like someone's answered prayer, very much the meditation of the rabbi's son." David J. Garrow lauded it as "a vividly emotional and painfully compelling family memoir" and "an utterly unforgettable book." The *New York Times*'s current executive editor (and Lelyveld's protégé), Bill Keller, told Stephen J. Dubner, "I thought it was very brave of Joe to write this book. He's not someone who shies away from inconvenient truth, but he's also not the kind of guy who'd lean over a dinner table and say, 'Let me tell you how grim my life was.'"

Lelyveld has often been described as a devoted family man. In 1959 he married Carolyn Fox, whom he had met in high school and continued to date after he had enrolled at Harvard and she at nearby Brandeis University; the couple were married for 45 years, until Carolyn Lelyveld's death, in 2004, from complications related to breast cancer. "I think we loved each other more over time," Lelyveld told Stephen J. Dubner, "and people would see it, comment on it—because I'm this kind of squirrely character, but if Carolyn walked into a room, you could see that I would just light up, and vice versa. We were always happy to see one another." Lelyveld enjoys spending time with his grown daughters, Nita, a writer, and Amy, an architect, and his granddaughter. In his free time he exercises regularly, jogging, going to the gym, and swimming during the summer, and he is an avid reader. He owns an apartment in Manhattan and a 19th-century farmhouse in upstate New York.

—K.J.E.

Suggested Reading: *Boston Globe* E p1 June 18, 2003; *Charlie Rose Show* Apr. 26, 2005; *Chicago Tribune* C p1 May 1, 2005; *Editor & Publisher Magazine* p20 Oct. 21, 1995; *Los Angeles Times* A p10 May 22, 2001; *New York* (on-line) Mar. 28, 2005

Selected Books: *Move Your Shadow*, 1985; *Omaha Blues*, 2005

Brad Barket/Getty Images

Leon, Kenny

1955(?)– Theater director

Address: True Colors Theatre Company, 659 Auburn Ave. N.E., Apt. 257, Atlanta, GA 30312-1981

"Theater is life," the director Kenny Leon said to M. S. Mason for the *Christian Science Monitor* (November 3, 2000). "It's about connecting to other people. It's about debating and understanding ideas." Leon has devoted his professional life to introducing people to the experience of live theater, reviving classic African-American plays for the stage, and producing new works by up-and-coming as well as established playwrights. In his more than 10 years (1990–2001) as artistic director of the Alliance Theatre Company, in Atlanta, Georgia, Leon upset the status quo by adding to the company's yearly production schedules more plays written by members of minority groups and by casting actors of color in roles traditionally portrayed by whites. He succeeded in drawing many new theatergoers, often from minority communities, while attracting the interest of the national media in the company and securing many grants to support his ambitious agenda. Among the plays that he directed for the Alliance were Tennessee Williams's *The Glass Menagerie* and *A Streetcar Named Desire*; August Wilson's *Fences*, *Jitney*, and *The Piano Lesson*; and Parts I and II of Tony Kushner's *Angels in America*. Also while with the Alliance, in collaboration with Walt Disney Theatrical Productions, Leon produced the original version of the rock musical *Aida*, by Elton John and Tim Rice, which as of October 2005 was in the sixth year of its run on Broadway.

In 2002, with Jane Bishop, Leon co-founded the True Colors Theatre Company, which he serves as artistic director and which is currently based in Atlanta and Washington, D.C. According to its Web site, its name "reflects a promise to search for truth and clarity. Truth comes not from focusing on what we look like but rather from examining our true colors—who we are as a country and as individuals. By understanding our true colors, we can better understand each other and how we are to live on the planet together. Turning the traditional model for major American theatres on its head, True Colors puts Negro-American classics at its core and branches out from there, including plays and playwrights from a variety of times, cultures and perspectives." In its inaugural season, in 2003–04, the company mounted productions of August Wilson's *Fences*, Robert Harling's *Steel Magnolias*, and Langston Hughes's *Tambourines to Glory*, produced in partnership with the National Black Arts Festival. Its 2004–05 offerings included the world premiere of Samm-Art Williams's *Brass Birds Don't Sing*, presented in collaboration with the Jewish Theatre of the South; Charlie Smalls and William F. Brown's *The Wiz*, performed by young people from local schools; and Pearl Cleage's *Flyin' West*. *The Wiz* and *Flyin' West* were on the 2005–06 schedule as well. As stated on its Web site, True Colors aims to become "the anchor for an international cultural center in Atlanta that will be home to many other multi-cultural performing and visual arts groups" by 2010.

Leon has also directed works for the stage in many other locales. At the Mark Taper Forum, in Los Angeles, California, and the Huntington Theatre, in Boston, Massachusetts, he directed the premieres of August Wilson's *Gem of the Ocean* and *Radio Golf*, respectively. Leon's directorial credits also include the world premiere of the opera *Margaret Garner*, by Toni Morrison (libretto) and Richard Danielpour (music), at the Detroit Opera House, in Michigan; a Broadway revival of Lorraine Hansberry's drama *A Raisin in the Sun*; August Wilson's *The Piano Lesson*, at the San Jose Repertory Theater, in California; and Thulani Davis's *Everybody's Ruby*, at the New York Shakespeare Festival/Public Theatre. An actor as well, Leon has appeared in a half-dozen TV movies, several installments of TV serials, and, recently, *Gem of the Ocean*. "I want to be a champion of African American work, but I'm defined by more than race," Leon told Marcus Crowder for the Sacramento, California, *Bee* (September 20, 2005, online). "To see the joy of an audience watching the work and connecting to the work and understanding something about our connectedness to each other as human beings, that's immensely gratifying."

Kenny Leon was born in around 1955. According to Jonathan Mandell in the *New York Times* (February 22, 2004), Leon's mother washed sheets for a commercial laundry in St. Petersburg, Florida, and his stepfather worked as a laborer on that city's payroll. Until he was 11 Leon lived in the countryside around Tallahassee, Florida, with his grandmother Mamie Wilson, who provided him with a materially poor but loving home. Leon has recalled chopping wood for the stove every morning and "spending sleepy Sundays on the front porch, counting cars to pass the time," as Patti Hartigan wrote for the *Boston Globe* (September 10, 1993). His grandmother, who had raised 13 children and worked as a domestic for white families, impressed upon him the importance of mutual cooperation and respect. "I lived with her all those years when you get the things that make you who you are," Leon said to Hartigan. "My grandmother taught me that we're all on this planet together, and we have to figure out a way to live together, to tear down walls that keep us apart because of age or race or sex or whatever." His grandmother also sparked and nurtured his passion for acquiring knowledge by reading the newspaper aloud to him.

Leon attended Northeast High School, in St. Petersburg; as a student in the school's first racially integrated class, he "faced . . . hostility and rioting," as Jonathan Mandell reported. At 13 he enrolled in an Upward Bound program held after school and during summers for youths from low-income families who hoped to gain admission to college. As an Upward Bound participant, he read Lorraine Hansberry's play *A Raisin in the Sun*, about a poor black family in 1950s Chicago; for the first time, he identified with the characters in a play, because, as he told Mandell, they "sounded like me." Leon completed his undergraduate degree at Clark Atlanta University, a traditionally black school in Atlanta, Georgia, in 1978. He attended law school in Los Angeles, California, for less than a year before dropping out after his brother was seriously hurt in a car accident. In 1979, following his brother's recovery, he landed a job with the Atlanta Academy of Music and Theater. During his nine years with the academy, he worked mainly as an actor; he also led workshops in improvisation at schools and prisons and in facilities for homeless people. Theater attracted him as a means of bringing people of different backgrounds and races together. "I'm a people person and even in the theater I'm interested in how we deal with each other and the community as a whole," he said in an interview with Sid Smith for the *Chicago Tribune* (September 22, 1991). During that period he earned a master's degree in political science.

In 1986 Leon was one of only six aspiring young directors to win a grant from the National Endowment for the Arts and the Theatre Communications Group (TCG) for an on-the-job training program. As a TCG fellow he spent much of his time at Center Stage in Baltimore, Maryland, under the tutelage of Stan Wojewodski, an enthusiastic supporter of experimental theater who later served as the dean of the Yale School of Drama.

In 1988 Leon was hired for the position of associate artistic director of the Alliance Theatre Company, one of the 10 largest regional theaters in the United States. ("Regional theater" refers to professional theater companies outside New York City that mount several productions each year.) In 1990 the Alliance's board of directors chose Leon to succeed Fred Chappell as the company's artistic director, making him the first African-American to hold that title in a prominent regional theater.

The Alliance Theatre Company is part of the Robert W. Woodruff Arts Center, an umbrella organization that also supports the Atlanta Symphony Orchestra, the High Museum of Art, and the Atlanta College of Art. When Leon assumed his new post, nearly all of the Alliance's patrons were white. With the conviction that good theater is for people of every race and in all walks of life, he took steps to attract more customers from minority groups. "I wanted to have a model here saying that theater should serve the community," he told Kevin Sack for the New York Times (April 16, 1998). "Its doors should be open to all the community. Everyone should really feel invited. And we should go a step beyond that to make everyone really know that we want them and that it's important for them to be here. And so I tried to diversify the staff, diversify what was on stage, diversify the artists, and I tried to get blacks, whites, Asians, Hispanics to sit next to each other." According to Linda Sherbert in Atlanta Magazine (June 2001), during Leon's tenure the number of nonwhite Alliance subscribers increased from about 3 percent of all subscribers to over 20 percent.

The first play that Leon presented was David Feldshuh's Miss Evers' Boys, a drama about the U.S. government's infamous experiments at the Tuskegee Institute, in Alabama, in which many black men who were known to be infected with syphilis went untreated, some for more than 40 years. The unfounded suspicion that Leon was attempting to make the Alliance into an all-black theater unsettled a number of theatergoers—as did the subject matter of Miss Evers' Boys: during the run of the play, several dozen members of the audience reportedly fainted when the actress Carol Mitchell-Leon, who portrayed Nurse Evers, "simulated a spinal tap on a syphilis patient," as Linda Sherbert wrote. While the precipitous decline in subscriptions that occurred during his first year ended later in his tenure, the number of subscribers at the time he left the company was about one-third less than the total at the height of subscriptions (21,000, in the 1980s). On the other hand, single-ticket purchases rose from 53,500 during the 1993–94 season to 77,000 in 1996–97.

Ever on the lookout for provocative, well-written, emotionally rich plays with interesting characters, Leon mounted seven works by the Pulitzer Prize–winning playwright August Wilson at the Alliance. Among them was The Piano Lesson, one of the dramas in Wilson's highly acclaimed 10-play series, with which he aimed to illuminate the experience of blacks in the U.S. (specifically, in all but one of the plays, a section of Pittsburgh, Pennsylvania) in each decade of the 20th century. The Piano Lesson centers on an adult brother and sister in 1930s Pittsburgh who hold opposite opinions about whether to sell a family heirloom—a beautifully carved piano. The sister argues that part of the family's history would vanish if the piano were sold; the brother wants the money the sale would bring, because he wants to buy property. In the Christian Science Monitor (February 11, 1992), Tony Vellela wrote that the Alliance's 1992 Piano Lesson "captures all the values of the Broadway production, finding both humor and tragedy in the story." In 1996 the Alliance presented Pearl Cleage's Blues for an Alabama Sky, which takes place in the Harlem section of New York City in 1930, when the Great Depression was deepening. The production starred Phylicia Rashad in the role of a singer who, along with her cousin, a costume-designer, is fired from the nightclub where she worked. Left with only memories of the glittering nights in which they mingled with such African-American luminaries as the poet Langston Hughes, the cousins talk of joining Josephine Baker in Paris, knowing the futility of their dream. In a review for the Boston Herald (May 22, 1996), Iris Fanger wrote, "Credit director Kenny Leon and fine performances by the actors for making these characters so rich and complex, despite the edgy suspicion that they are figures in a medieval morality play, standing in for aspects of good and evil. Leon keeps the action humming, even as the overstuffed plot unravels into melodrama."

Blues for an Alabama Sky was one of 10 plays that debuted at the Alliance Theatre during Leon's tenure there. Leon also oversaw the world premieres of Cleage's Bourbon at the Border and Flyin' West; Sandra Deer's Gal Baby; and Alfred Uhry's The Last Night of Ballyhoo, which opened in Atlanta during the summer of 1996 and moved to Broadway in 1997, where it won a Tony Award for best play. During his stewardship of the Alliance, Leon also directed Sandra Deer's adaptation of Dickens's A Christmas Carol and her children's play The Return of Finn Macool, as well as productions for several other regional theaters, among them the Actor's Express and Theater of the Stars, in Atlanta; the Oregon Shakespeare Festival, in Ashland, Oregon; the Goodman Theatre, in Chicago, Illinois; the Indiana Repertory Theatre, in Indianapolis; the Huntington Theatre Company, in Boston; and the Arena Stage, in Washington, D.C.

In November 2000 Leon announced that he would be leaving the Alliance the following June to pursue an unnamed venture. His project turned out to be the formation of the True Colors Theatre Company, which he envisioned as a national venue for mounting the works of African-American playwrights. In an effort to ensure the success of True Colors, Leon recruited notable African-Americans to serve in advisory capacities, among them Phylicia Rashad; the actress Angela Bassett; the actor Samuel L. Jackson; the director, producer, and actor Woodie King; and the director Lloyd Richards. He also secured such corporate sponsors as Coca-Cola, Delta Airlines, and BellSouth. With the hope of establishing a presence in Washington, D.C., he and Jane Bishop, the co-founder of True Colors, negotiated an agreement to make True Colors the resident company at the Lincoln Theatre on U Street, N.W. Until the company acquires a permanent home, performances are also given at the Woodruff Center.

In early 2004 *A Raisin in the Sun*, by Lorraine Hansberry, opened on Broadway under Leon's direction. The play had not been presented on Broadway since its premiere, in 1959, in a celebrated production starring Sidney Poitier as Walter Lee Younger, a young husband and father struggling to improve his lot in life by making a business deal that will enable him to quit his chauffeuring job; Claudia McNeil, as his mother; Ruby Dee, as his wife; and Diana Sands as his sister. (The same cast appeared in the 1961 film version that Leon had seen as a boy.) In the 2004 revival, the role of Walter Lee was given to Sean Combs, a first-time actor better known as the rap musician and producer P. Diddy. The cast also included Audra McDonald, as Walter Lee's wife, and Phylicia Rashad, as his mother. Though many reviewers found little to praise in Combs's performance, Leon stood by his casting decision. "For Walter Lee Younger, you need an actor who can play someone who is trapped by his environment and wants to get out. Sean was that person," he told Allissa Hosten for *Jet* (May 17, 2004). "Once you talk to Sean and realize why he wants this, it's about wanting to do something good. It's not about another paycheck. It's about bringing a younger generation to legitimate, good, positive drama." *A Raisin in the Sun* earned four Tony Award nominations, including those for best revival of a play and three for acting. In June 2004 Rashad and McDonald each won a Tony, for the best performance by a leading actress and best performance by a featured actress in a play, respectively.

In 2005 Leon directed the world premiere of *Margaret Garner*, an opera commissioned jointly by the Michigan Opera Theatre, the Cincinnati Opera, and the Opera Company of Philadelphia. With libretto by Toni Morrison, who won the 1993 Nobel Prize for literature, and music by Richard Danielpour, the opera is based on the true story of a fugitive slave who, when faced with recapture, killed her own daughter to prevent the child's reenslave-ment. The debut performance, with Denyse Graves in the title role at the Detroit Opera House, won rave reviews for the writer and composer, the performers, and Leon.

According to Marcus Crowder, "Leon looks like a model or a movie star. He has an eye-catching physical presence, natural charisma and a vibe that says this man is living the good life." "I really *love* doing what I'm doing," Leon told Linda Sherbert in 2001. "I *love* directing for the stage. I *love* being in a relationship with the community. I *love* trying to encourage the business and political communities to put art at the top." Among other honors, Leon won the 1993–94 Connecticut Critics Circle Award, Atlanta's 1994 Abby Award, and the 1995 Boston Theater Award, all for best director; the 1994 Georgia Speaker of the Year Award, from the Barkley Forum; the 1996 Eugene McDermott Award from the Massachusetts Institute of Technology, for "creative achievement at the national level"; and the 2001 Atlanta Business League Trailblazer Award. Leon's marriage to Carol Mitchell-Leon ended in divorce. He lives in Atlanta and, in his leisure time, enjoys playing golf.

—C.M.

Suggested Reading: *Atlanta Journal-Constitution* D p1 Dec. 12, 2003, E p1 May 11, 2004, C p1 July 17, 2004; *Atlanta Magazine* p20 June 2001, with photo; *Boston Globe* Living p45 Sep. 10, 1993, with photo; *Chicago Tribune* XIII p29 Sep. 22, 1991, with photo; *Christian Science Monitor* p12 , Feb. 11, 1992, with photo, p17 Nov. 3, 2000; *Jet* p52 May 17, 2004; *New York Times* E p2 Apr. 16, 1998, E p1 Apr. 15, 2004, E p1 Apr. 27, 2004; True Colors Theatre Company Web site; *Washington Post* C p1 Sep. 18, 2002

Levine, Mel

Jan. 20, 1940– Pediatrician; educator

Address: All Kinds of Minds, 100 Europa Dr., Chapel Hill, NC 27517-2357

In public schools throughout the United States, several million children currently receive special services for the learning disabled. Mel Levine, a pediatrician who for more than three decades has studied the learning patterns of children, thinks that the vast majority of those students are not disabled. Rather, he has proposed that their problems stem from the particular ways in which their brains function—ways that in all likelihood have not been recognized by their parents or teachers. Every child has a particular, individual combination of neurological deficits and strong points, according to Levine, and thus every child learns—or has difficulty in learning—in ways that are distinctive to him or her. Through his nonprofit foundation, All

Courtesy of Gail Rubin

Mel Levine

derson Aldrich Award, named for an AAP founder and pioneer in the field of child development.

Melvin D. Levine was born on January 20, 1940 and raised on Long Island, New York. His father, Rubin Levine, who immigrated to the United States from Russia, made his career in the garment industry, beginning as a rag salesman and ending in an executive position. His mother's jobs, too, were connected with the manufacture and sale of clothing. Paraphrasing him for *Biography Magazine* (April 2001), Christina Frank wrote that as a child, Levine "ran around with his nose running, his fly open, and most of the time carrying a snake or a turtle." He was a good student but a poor athlete. "When I was a little kid, people used to figure out how not to have me on their team," he told Sumathi Reddy for the Raleigh, North Carolina, *News and Observer* (October 24, 1999). One of his favorite pastimes was reading biographies. He loved to discover how the subjects of such books achieved success, and in time he concluded that the key was specialization. By the age of eight, he told Reddy, he had decided to become a doctor.

Levine attended Brown University, in Providence, Rhode Island, where he majored in philosophy but, as he told Reddy, was "secretly pre-med." When Levine graduated, summa cum laude, with a B.A. degree from Brown in 1961, he became the first member of his family to complete college. He next enrolled at the University of Oxford, in England, as a Rhodes scholar, in which capacity he studied science and philosophy until 1963. Back in the U.S., he attended Harvard Medical School, in Cambridge, Massachusetts, where he earned an M.D. degree in 1966. Three years later, after an internship and residency at the Children's Hospital in Boston, Levine was drafted into the U.S. military. The Vietnam War was then in full swing, and he was assigned to a large U.S. Air Force base in the Philippines, where he served as a physician at a school for American servicemen's children. While there he "became fascinated with the interface between pediatricians and educat[ors]," as he told Sumathi Reddy. "They had so much to offer each other, but they weren't communicating." He began to think about how pediatricians and educators could collaborate to better understand the intellectual, emotional, and social lives of children.

Following his stint with the air force, Levine returned to the Children's Hospital, where he served for 14 years as chief of the Division of Ambulatory Pediatrics. He was also a faculty member in the Department of Pediatrics at the Harvard Medical School. In 1985 he relocated to the University of North Carolina Medical School at Chapel Hill; he has held the posts of professor of pediatrics and director of the school's Clinical Center for the Study of Development and Learning ever since.

During the course of his work with children, Levine gradually became dismayed by what he saw as the growing tendency of physicians, psychologists, and other professionals to diagnose children as suffering from a learning disorder, attention def-

Kinds of Minds, Levine offers a program called Schools Attuned, which is designed to help educators identify the nature of their pupils' problems in learning and develop ways to address them, all the while encouraging the children by recognizing their strengths and emphasizing each person's inherent worth. "It's a commitment to variation instead of deviation," Levine told Bill Lohmann for the *Richmond (Virginia) Times Dispatch* (March 1, 2005). "We believe the world needs a lot of different kinds of minds." Levine's theories and techniques gained widespread attention in 2002 and 2003, thanks to the airing of a PBS-TV special entitled *Misunderstood Minds* and his appearance on the *Oprah Winfrey Show*, respectively, and an increasing number of school districts have enrolled their teachers in Schools Attuned classes. "When you're a kid, school is your career," Levine has said, as quoted on a PBS Web site devoted to a discussion of *Misunderstood Minds*. "And if you go out of business in school, if your business goes bankrupt, if you're not having any success, you're left with almost nothing. You are poverty-stricken. Where do you go from there?" "Every student can benefit from a greater understanding of his own strengths and weaknesses along with a plan for optimizing learning and performance," Levine wrote for the All Kinds of Minds Web site. "Helping parents, teachers, and students appreciate learning differences is the first step. Helping them celebrate the differences is the goal." Levine has written a dozen books for professionals or laypeople; one of his books for the latter, *A Mind at a Time*, spent 29 weeks on the *New York Times Book Review*'s best-seller list in 2002. In 1995 the American Academy of Pediatrics (AAP) honored Levine with the C. An-

icit disorder, attention deficit hyperactivity disorder, or a behavioral disorder, among other problems. In Levine's opinion, such behavioral or learning difficulties were due to neurodevelopmental variations, or differences in the ways that children's brains were "wired." Every brain, according to Levine, has a unique blend of strengths and weaknesses. "We've never found a perfect brain," he told Richard Lee Colvin for the *Los Angeles Times* (December 15, 1999). He also said to Colvin, "Everyone has dysfunctions. It's all a question of which ones they have." After years of observation and study, Levine narrowed the activities of the brain to eight separate functions: attention, memory, temporal-sequential ordering, spatial ordering, neuromotor functions, social cognition, language, and higher-order cognition. He divided those types into subcategories, each of which may correspond to an identifiable learning difficulty. For instance, what Levine terms "saliency determination" pertains to the ability to isolate the most important information in a block of text or a set of instructions. Another subdivision, "sequential output," refers to the ability to follow directions in a particular order. Children, Levine theorized, encounter difficulties in learning depending upon their specific neurodevelopmental profiles, which are "a kind of spreadsheet of strengths and weaknesses of brain functions," as he told Bill Lohmann. To help educators to recognize their students' neurodevelopmental differences, Levine began giving lectures on his findings, suggesting techniques that teachers might use to help struggling students. In 1987 he organized his talks as Schools Attuned, a program of instructional seminars for educators.

Foremost in his Schools Attuned training courses, Levine discourages the traditional labeling of children as disordered. "Labelling oversimplifies a kid. It somehow conveys that a child has some kind of disease or deviancy," he told Elaine O'Connor for the *Vancouver (British Columbia) Province* (October 1, 2004). He also believes that, although medication may be helpful to some children, it is prescribed unnecessarily for far too many others. Levine explained to Brenda Warner Rotzoll for the *Chicago Sun-Times* (May 7, 2002), "Kids are being put on it without an adequate evaluation and without considering other possible reasons why they may be having trouble with their attention." Rather, Levine prefers to construct a child's neurodevelopmental profile and ascertain precisely in which areas the child is having difficulty. Moreover, he is convinced of the value of what he calls "demystification," the process of sharing information about children with those children so that they understand that whatever problems they are having are due not to their being defective people but to their difficulties in specific areas. Demystification helps children to avoid feelings of inadequacy, and it also enables them to learn to recognize tasks and situations that may prove troublesome, thus preparing them to deal with potential problems. For example, if Levine determines that a child has a sequencing problem, the child will be advised that in the future, when given a long set of instructions verbally, he or she should probably write them down so as not to forget in what order to execute the steps. In order to handle a fidgety child, Levine suggests that teachers keep squishy balls on hand so that the child can release his or her excess energy quietly, rather than by doing something more disruptive, such as noisily tapping a pencil on the desk. Parents and educators can help by observing children and detecting weaknesses that, once identified, can be overcome or accommodated. Other cases involve children who fear being called upon to answer questions in class. Such youngsters may not be unprepared, but may have difficulty in recalling information quickly; for them, Levine suggests that teachers give advance notice that, by the following day, they will be expected to answer questions about a particular topic. If students encounter problems in trying to master cursive handwriting, Levine encourages teachers to allow them to print or type assignments. In response to the complaint by some skeptics that offering such alternatives is a form of favoritism, Levine told Christina Frank, "We don't treat any two kids the same because some children need flexibility in one area, some in other areas," and he noted that "to treat everybody the same is not to treat them equally, because it will favor certain kids." Levine has said that he does not expect teachers to be able to tailor their curriculums, pedagogical methods, and activities to meet the needs of each student, but he thinks that it is important for instructors to make some effort to help each child. He has also said that techniques taught in the Schools Attuned program often help an entire class, rather than only one or a few students.

Another vital component of Levine's program involves praising children for their strengths, rather than focusing exclusively on their weaknesses. "Success is a vitamin that every kid must take in order to thrive during his or her school years," he wrote for his Web site. "We, as teachers and parents, must make sure that this critical learning 'supplement' is available to all students." Levine has often criticized U.S. schools for seemingly expecting students to exhibit proficiency in all subjects. While the goal of academic well-roundedness is not inherently bad, it may be impractical. "When you're an adult, you're allowed to specialize," he told Elaine O'Connor. "Part of helping kids survive is letting them know what their specialties seem to be."

In 1995, with the financial help of the brokerage-house executive Charles Schwab, who suffered from dyslexia as a child, Levine founded All Kinds of Minds, a nonprofit institute that has also received funding from the Geraldine R. Dodge Foundation. The institute administers the Schools Attuned program and finances research about the ways in which children learn and about the effectiveness of Levine's programs. It also offers what is known as the Student Success Program, through which individual students are evaluated, at an average cost of about $3,000, and their parents and teachers are provided with techniques for helping them. In 2004 All Kinds of Minds received a contract to train 20,000 New York City educators over the course of the next five years. Nationwide, by mid-2005 more than 23,000 teachers had received training in Levine's programs; after their training, the schools in which they worked reported decreases in discipline problems, in the number of students requiring special-education classes, and in the number of students who could not be promoted at the end of the school year.

In addition to *A Mind at a Time* (2002), Levine's books include *A Pediatric Approach to Learning Disorders* (1980, written with Robert Brooks and Jack P. Shonkoff); *Developmental Variation and Learning Disorders* (1987; second edition, 1993); *Keeping a Head in School: A Student's Book about Learning Abilities and Learning Disorders* (1990); *All Kinds of Minds: A Young Student's Book about Learning Abilities and Learning Disorders* (1993); *Educational Care: A System for Understanding and Helping Children with Learning Problems at Home and in School* (1994); *Jarvis Clutch: Social Spy* (2001), written for middle-school youngsters who are experiencing problems in interactions with others; *The Myth of Laziness* (2003), and *Ready or Not, Here Life Comes* (2005), in which he offered reasons why so many people in their 20s are unprepared for the responsibilities of adulthood. He co-edited the books *Developmental-Behavioral Pediatrics* (1983; third edition, 1992); *Middle Childhood: Development and Dysfunction* (1984); and *Early Adolescent Transitions* (1988). Critics of Levine's work have faulted the books he wrote for popular consumption because they contain no footnotes or appendices detailing his research methods; his detractors have also complained that no peer-reviewed studies of his findings have yet been published. "I have never really been admired by anyone who does basic research in cognition or developmental psychology," Levine told Margot Adler during an interview for the National Public Radio show *Morning Edition* (January 24, 2005). "They have a hard time with me." Levine also said that, unlike most researchers, who investigate narrow aspects of cognition, "I'm like a slob, sort of covering it all."

Levine and his wife, Barbara (known as Bambi), who married in the early 1970s, have no children. They live on Sanctuary Farm, their 30-acre spread in rural Rougemont, North Carolina, along with several hundred geese, peacocks, pheasants, swans, donkeys, dogs, and cats. Levine is a founder of both the Carolina/Virginia Pheasant and Waterfowl Society and the North Carolina branch of La Chaine des Rotisseurs, a gourmet-food club; his interests include Oriental porcelain, the poetry of Robert Frost, and metal sculpture. He feels passionate about all his endeavors. "I've never done anything without overdoing it," he told Christina

Frank. "I try to do absolutely everything in excess."
—K.J.E.

Suggested Reading: allkindsofminds.org; *Biography Magazine* p95+ Apr. 2001, with photos; *Los Angeles Times* B p2 Dec. 15, 1999; (Raleigh, North Carolina) *News & Observer* B p1 Oct. 24, 1999; *Richmond (Virginia) Times Dispatch* D p1 Mar. 1, 2005; *Vancouver (British Columbia) Province* A p19 Oct. 1, 2004

Selected Books: *Keeping a Head in School: A Student's Book about Learning Abilities and Learning Disorders*, 1990; *Developmental-Behavioral Pediatrics* (3d edition), 1992; *Developmental Variation and Learning Disorders* (second edition), 1993; *All Kinds of Minds: A Young Student's Book about Learning Abilities and Learning Disorders*, 1993; *Educational Care: A System for Understanding and Helping Children with Learning Problems at Home and in School*, 1994; *Jarvis Clutch: Social Spy*, 2001; *A Mind at a Time*, 2002; *The Myth of Laziness*, 2003; *Ready or Not, Here Life Comes*, 2005; as co-author: *A Pediatric Approach to Learning Disorders*, 1980; *Developmental-Behavioral Pediatrics*, 1983, third edition 1992); *Middle Childhood: Development and Dysfunction*, 1984; *Early Adolescent Transitions*, 1988

Lewis, Ananda

(ah-NAHN-da)

Mar. 21, 1973– Television personality

Address: c/o The Insider, Paramount Domestic Television, 5555 Melrose Ave., Hollywood, CA 90038

"Ananda is a refreshing splash of realness in the agonizingly synthetic youth market," a reporter for askmen.com wrote of the popular television personality Ananda Lewis. "Sassy . . . and unpredictable, she makes our hearts race, whether she's interviewing celebrities or tackling tough issues affecting teens. She's the celebrity sleuth with the heart of gold. [She] not only gets the stars to come clean, she does it while promoting healthy attitudes." Thanks to her refreshingly optimistic attitudes toward young people, her arresting good looks, and her dashing sense of style, Lewis has built a sizeable fan following. She served as an award-winning host on the Black Entertainment Television (BET) topical-discussion series *Teen Summit*, which dealt exclusively with issues affecting teenagers, including premarital sex, early pregnancy, and illiteracy among young people. She has also had her own, short-lived, syndicated talk program, *The Ananda Lewis Show*, which premiered in 2001. To viewers between the ages of 18

Frazer Harrison/Getty Images

Ananda Lewis

and 34, Lewis is perhaps known best as a former video jockey and featured host and interviewer for MTV. Currently she serves as the Los Angeles–based celebrity correspondent for the nationally syndicated, nightly half-hour newsmagazine *The Insider.*

The younger of two daughters, Ananda Lewis was born on March 21, 1973 in Los Angeles, California. "Ananda" means "bliss" in Sanskrit (an ancient Indic language). Her mother worked as an account manager for Pacific Bell, her father as a computer-animation specialist. Her sister, Lakshmi, is a physician. Lewis's parents divorced when Ananda was two years old, and her mother moved with her daughters to San Diego, California, to be near her own mother. Lewis has credited her mother, grandmother, and sister for providing her with a positive, supportive environment. By her own account, as she grew older she felt increasingly upset by her parents' divorce. Leaving Ananda and Lakshmi with their grandmother, the girls' mother took an extended trip to Europe "to escape the pain of her failed marriage," according to Pamela Johnson in *Essence* (October 2001). During her absence, which lasted less than a year, Lewis felt abandoned. "It was like she nurtured me and carried me in her womb and then completely left," she told Johnson. Lewis often fought with her mother while growing up and rarely saw her father, who had remarried. (In adulthood, Lewis has healed her rifts with both parents.) Her grandmother told Johnson that she and Lewis also frequently "locked horns."

Lewis struggled with a speech impediment, stuttering until she was eight years old. ("I haven't shut up since," she told Cora Daniels for *Savoy* [October 2001].) In grade school she earned a repu-

tation for outspokenness; her comments provoked her teachers' ire or, less often, their amusement. In 1981 Lewis entered herself in the Little Miss San Diego Contest, a beauty pageant, and won, despite being one of the youngest contestants. During the talent portion of the competition, Lewis performed a dance routine, which she had choreographed herself, to Stevie Wonder and Paul McCartney's ballad "Ebony and Ivory." She wore a costume with one black leg and one white leg, which she had sewed on her own, according to some sources. After her win, Lewis attracted the attention of a talent agent and began working in local theater productions and on television. As a fourth-grader she enrolled at the San Diego School of Creative and Performance Arts (SCPA), a public magnet school, where she remained for nine years. (The San Diego SCPA now enrolls only students in sixth grade or above.)

At the age of 13, Lewis began volunteering as a tutor and counselor at a Head Start facility. (Created in 1965, Head Start is a school-readiness program for preschool-age children from low-income families.) Lewis was inspired by the work and decided to become a teacher or a psychologist, with the goal of helping young people. Her family, however, urged her to follow a more lucrative career path—specifically, law. She majored in history at Howard University, a historically black, private institution in Washington, D.C., from which she graduated, cum laude, in 1995. She did not apply to law school.

Throughout college Lewis had volunteered as a mentor with the group Youth at Risk and at the Youth Leadership Institute. She was considering attending graduate school to pursue a master's degree in education when she learned that auditions were going to be held for the job of on-screen host of BET's *Teen Summit.* The children she was working with that summer "were the main ones kicking me out the door," she recalled to Johnson. "The kids said, 'You better go audition for that show. You don't have a job, and this job is almost over.'"

Lewis auditioned successfully and became the host of *Teen Summit.* For three seasons she discussed serious issues affecting teenagers for a TV audience of several million. The show's topical, debate-driven format enabled Lewis to combine skills she had acquired at the performing-arts school in San Diego with her passion for helping young people. "She had the guts to openly discuss taboo subjects without flinching. Executives knew that this kind of gumption was the right stuff for a live show host," the askmen.com reporter wrote. In 1996, on an installment of the show entitled "It Takes a Village," Lewis interviewed First Lady Hillary Rodham Clinton (currently the junior U.S. senator from New York), whose book with that title had been published earlier in the year. Also in 1996 *Teen Summit* was nominated for a CableACE Award, and the next year the National Association for the Advancement of Colored People (NAACP) presented Lewis with an Image Award for her work on BET.

Soon afterward the cable network MTV offered Lewis a position as a program host and video jockey. The thought of leaving *Teen Summit* was painful for her; indeed, several sources quoted her as recalling that she "cried for three weeks" while pondering her choices. In opting to move to MTV, the deciding factor was the possibility of greatly increasing the size of her viewing audience and, therefore, her potential for influencing America's youth.

Asking the type of pointed questions for which she had become recognized at BET, Lewis brought celebrity interviewing to a new level on a pair of regularly aired MTV shows: *Total Request Live*, a daily Top 10 video-countdown show, and *The Hot Zone*, which offered both music videos and Lewis's interviews of musicians and others. On one notable installment of *The Hot Zone*, she berated the rapper Q-Tip about the number of scantily clad dancers in one of his videos. In a reference to Lewis's broadcasting savvy, Bob Kusbit, MTV's senior vice president for production, told Douglas Century for the *New York Times* (November 21, 1999), "In the past our talent was sometimes just pretty people who could read cue cards. But when we brought Ananda to MTV, we decided we were going to do a lot more live television." MTV also called upon Lewis to host other, topical programs, including two MTV forums on violence in schools, which aired after the 1999 shootings in a Columbine, Colorado, high school (in which two students killed 13 people and wounded 21 others before turning their guns on themselves) and several memorial tributes for the singer Aaliyah, who perished in a plane crash in 2001. (Lewis and Aaliyah had been friends.) In 2001 Lewis earned another NAACP Image Award, for her hosting of the MTV special *True Life: I Am Driving While Black*.

Lewis made headlines while at MTV when she announced, in 1998, that she intended to remain celibate for at least six months. "I made the decision for selfish reasons, but I'm going public here because I realized I might be able to help other girls, too," she told Rosie Amodio for *YM* (November 1998), as quoted on the Modern Religion Web site. "I know the kind of drama that being sexually active brings to your life. I felt that if it was good for me to take a break, it might be good for other young girls, too. You see, I think I would be a whole different person if I hadn't had sex so early. Everybody was saying, 'Do it!' but nobody ever said, 'You don't *have* to do it.' I think hearing that would have made a huge difference in my life."

Also during that period Lewis became a familiar presence at celebrity-attended events in and around New York City, making her something of a socialite. "If you don't recognize the name Ananda Lewis, it may be because you're older than 23, or not a hip-hop star, or not a regular supplicant in the land of the velvet ropes," Century wrote at the height of Lewis's fame. "In the last year, Ms. Lewis has emerged as the hip-hop generation's reigning 'It Girl,' meaning she is not just an MTV personality but a woman whose looks and attitudes have made her perpetually in demand." In 2000 *People* magazine included Lewis on its list of the world's "50 Most Beautiful People."

The Ananda Lewis Show debuted on September 10, 2001, after much advance press in which Lewis was compared to Oprah Winfrey, the wildly popular talk-show host long considered to be one of the most powerful black women in television. (Intermittently for a while after the series' launch, she hosted special presentations for MTV.) Lewis's series, which was syndicated by King World Productions, targeted women between the ages of 18 and 34 by addressing such issues as domestic violence and breast cancer; it was billed as an alternative to the sensationalism and provocative offerings of Jerry Springer and Ricki Lake, whose talk shows were then dominating daytime ratings. *The Ananda Lewis Show* was cancelled after one season. "We started on a Monday and then there was the World Trade Center bombing the next day, and everything has become a mess since then," Roger King, the chairman and CEO of King World Productions and CBS Enterprises, the show's producers, told Michael Freeman for *Electronic Media* (October 15, 2001).

In 2004 Lewis became the chief correspondent on celebrity subjects for the nationally syndicated, nightly entertainment program *The Insider*, a spin-off of the popular *Entertainment Tonight*. For installments of the program in the spring of 2005, she interviewed the heiress and performer Paris Hilton; Don Cheadle and Ryan Phillippe, two of the stars of Paul Haggis's ensemble film drama *Crash*; and the veteran actress Dyan Cannon. Lewis herself has made guest appearances on several sitcoms. On radio, she currently has an hourly segment, called "Ananda's Insider Reports" and devoted to entertainment news, on *The John Smalley Block Party*, which airs from 5:30 a.m. to 10:00 a.m. on KKBT in the Los Angeles, California, area.

An avid animal lover, Lewis has served as co-host of the A&E television-network show *America's Top Dog* and as a spokesperson for the Humane Society. (She has frequently introduced her two pet chihuahuas to interviewers.) She has also been a spokesperson for Reading Is Fundamental, a nonprofit literacy group. Lewis has at various times been romantically linked in the media with several sports and music stars. She currently resides in Los Angeles and reportedly has six godchildren. She is said to be a registered member of the Muscogee (Creek Indian) Nation.

—D.F.

Suggested Reading: *Essence* p126+ Oct. 2001, with photo; *New York Times* IX p1 Nov. 21, 1999, with photos; *Savoy* p58+ Oct. 2001

Selected Television Shows: *Teen Summit*, 1994–97; *Total Request Live* 1999–2001; *The Ananda Lewis Show* 2001–02; *The Insider*, 2004–

Vince Bucci/Getty Images

Lohan, Lindsay

July 2, 1986– Actress; musician

Address: LLRocks Inc., PMB 179, 223 Wall St., Huntington, NY 11743-2060

With an onscreen persona that combines cool sophistication and approachability, Lindsay Lohan has emerged as one of the most popular actresses among "tweens"—a term developed by marketers to describe consumers and moviegoers who are on the verge of adolescence but not yet teenagers. Lohan earned the adoration of girls in that category—and many critics—with her performances in updated versions of two Walt Disney film classics, *The Parent Trap* and *Freaky Friday*. It was her starring role in *Mean Girls*, however, that established her as a bona fide box-office draw and ratcheted her salary up to $7 million per movie. Her most recent film appearance was in *Herbie: Fully Loaded*. "Lindsay Lohan is possibly the hottest young actress in America," Tom Cox wrote for the London *Times* (January 8, 2005). "With a face and voluptuous figure reminiscent of old Hollywood, she has an uncanny knack of presenting herself as a sex symbol, an angst-ridden outsider and a chummy everygirl, all at the same time."

While remaining grateful to her original fan base, which turned out in droves to purchase her debut pop album, *Speak*, Lohan hopes to transcend the label of "tween queen." "There's become this phenomenon of younger girls buying a lot of tickets," she told Robert Haskel for *W* (April 2005, on-line). "And so automatically I'm typecast as a teen actress. Other girls my age, like Evan Rachel Wood and Scarlett Johansson and even Mischa

Barton, they've done riskier roles. And, fashion-wise, they become these icons. I could do that, but people won't take me as seriously, in a way. It's hard to get around that."

Lindsay Lohan was born on July 2, 1986 and raised in an upscale neighborhood on Long Island, New York. Her father, Michael Lohan, who had inherited and sold a successful pasta business, maintained his family's comfortable lifestyle through his work as a Wall Street commodities broker, restaurateur, and entrepreneur. In his youth he had worked as a soap-opera actor, and it was on the New York acting circuit that he met his wife, Dina, a former Radio City Rockette. Lindsay Lohan is the oldest of the couple's four children. When she was only three years old, her mother took her to meet representatives of the prestigious Ford Modeling Agency and to audition for commercials. "She knew people who worked there, and they were like, 'Oh, bring her in,'" Lohan told Lynda Obst for *Interview* (June 1, 2004). "So I started by doing that, driving into the city from Long Island with my mom and auditioning for stuff—I would beg her to bring me. I was really comfortable in front of the camera, and it was fun." She soon won an assignment for a Duncan Hines commercial, and she went on to appear in more than 60 television ads, for such companies as the Gap, Pizza Hut, and Wendy's. She even made a Jell-O commercial with the comedian Bill Cosby. Encouraged by her success, her siblings—Michael, Aliann, and Dakota—also began auditioning and have landed roles in commercials and films. Lohan's mother has always managed her career, as her father was absent from the family's day-to-day life for a time; in 1990, just as his daughter was beginning to get steady work in commercials, Michael Lohan was convicted of defrauding his brokerage clients and sentenced to a four-year prison term. (Some sources state that the sentence was 36 or 37 months.)

While still in elementary school, Lohan branched out into television series, appearing on the soap opera *Guiding Light* and landing a recurring role on another daytime drama, *Another World*. Though the young girl enjoyed such typical childhood activities as playing sports and spending time with her friends, she loved the entertainment business. Inspired by her idols Ann-Margret and Jodie Foster, she longed to appear in movies. Lohan got her big break before she had even completed the sixth grade; in the spring of 1997, her agent set up an audition for the Walt Disney Co.'s remake of the 1961 film *The Parent Trap*. Though nearly 4,000 girls auditioned for the lead role of twin sisters (played by Hayley Mills in the original movie), the director of the new movie, Nancy Meyers, doubted that she would be able to find a young actress suitable for the part. "Then I saw Lindsay's tape, and I heard the lines for the first time," Meyers told Stephen Schaefer for the *Boston Herald* (July 27, 1998). "She did quirky things, made faces. She's animated. Brilliant, it turns out."

In the film Lohan portrayed Hallie and Annie, twin sisters who were separated shortly after birth by their feuding parents (played by Dennis Quaid and Natasha Richardson). When the adults parted ways, with the father moving to Napa Valley, California, and the mother returning to London, England, each took along one of the twins, intending never to speak to the other parent again. Each girl is thus unaware that she has a twin sister, until the two are accidentally reunited at summer camp. Together they hatch a scheme to switch identities and bring their parents back together. "Trading off English and American accents, and flouncing through about as many costume changes as there were in *Evita* . . . Ms. Lohan easily makes it credible that the two girls could switch places and hornswoggle their credulous parents," Janet Maslin wrote for the *New York Times* (July 29, 1998). Though many reviewers criticized the filmmakers for following the original movie too closely, almost all were united in their praise for Lohan's big-screen debut. "Little Lindsay Lohan . . . is an amazingly gifted child actress," Michael Wilmington wrote in the *Chicago Tribune* (July 29, 1998), "a natural camera performer with lots of smartness and sparkle: a welcome relief from the tousle-haired, ever-grinning cutie-pies Hollywood tends to favor."

After she had finished working on *The Parent Trap*—which had been shot over a grueling seven and a half months, on two continents—Lohan and her parents turned down an offer for her to star in another Disney movie, which was to begin filming right away. Her parents wanted her to resume a normal childhood to the extent possible, and Lohan, who had missed most of her sixth-grade year, wanted to be with her friends again. "The only thing I'm really worried about is how my friends will react," she told Steve Parks for *Newsday* (August 6, 1998). "I don't want my friends to be nice to me just because I'm in the movies. I want them to feel like they can say anything they want to me, just like before." After completing middle school Lohan attended Cold Spring Harbor High School, where she took an interest in sports, art, and math. She also was a cheerleader. After three years she dropped out of high school, because she missed acting. "I just started seeing people doing other films and thought, 'Maybe I could do that,'" she told Stephen Schaefer for the *Boston Herald* (August 4, 2003), "and I started to realize I was missing out on what I loved doing." Lohan started auditioning again and landed starring roles in two television movies for the Disney Channel, *Life-Size* (2000) and *Get a Clue* (2002). Shortly thereafter she was cast in another remake of a Disney classic, *Freaky Friday*. "We did a nationwide search, every major city in the country, and saw thousands of girls and tested a dozen of them," the writer and director Mark Waters told Stephen Schaefer for the 2003 *Boston Herald* article. "When I tested Lindsay, the way she took direction, I felt I was with an Olympic athlete. . . . She had that power and composure. There was no No. 2."

The original *Freaky Friday*, made in 1976, starred Jodie Foster. (Lohan had never seen the original film and refused to do so until she finished shooting the remake, for fear that she would be too intimidated by Foster's performance to act well.) In the new movie, Lohan portrayed a high-school student and budding rock guitarist who is at odds with her mother, a highly successful psychologist and author (played by Jamie Lee Curtis). Through a magical occurrence involving fortune cookies, the mother and daughter wake up one Friday morning to discover that they have switched bodies. Following a series of misadventures, each comes to appreciate the other's perspective. To prepare for the film, Curtis and Lohan each watched videotapes of the other's script readings, so that they could replicate one another's mannerisms. "Jamie had it easier than I did because she was a teenager," Lohan told Louis B. Hobson for the *Calgary Sun* (August 3, 2003), "but I've never been an adult so I didn't have the same kind of references." Again, critics praised Lohan's performance. "While the plot is admittedly goofy, it's flat-out fun to watch Curtis and Lohan imitating each other . . . ," Catherine Newton wrote for the *Fort Worth Star Telegram* (August 6, 2003). "Lohan is convincing and contagiously cute, both as guitar-playing, hard-rocking teen Anna and as Anna's neurotic, conservative mother." *Freaky Friday* was an enormous popular success.

While still helping to promote *Freaky Friday*, Lohan started working on her next Disney film, *Confessions of a Teenage Drama Queen*. In that "tween"-targeted film, Lohan played Mary Cep, a young Greenwich Village hipster who finds herself an outcast among her fellow high-school students after her family moves to a New Jersey suburb. Mary changes her name to Lola and invents an exotic past in order to attract friends, which works well, until her lies catch up with her. In his review for the *New York Times* (February 20, 2004), Dave Kerr predicted that the intended audience would enjoy this "modest, mildly engaging film." Most reviews of the film, however, were scathing. "After her career-making performance in *The Parent Trap*, it amounts to cruel and unusual punishment for Disney to toss Lindsay Lohan into *Confessions of a Teenage Drama Queen*, a sloppy and crass adolescent comedy," Lou Lumenick wrote in the Australian *Cairns Post/Cairns Sun* (April 28, 2004). "The premise is decent . . . but the execution is shoddy and unfunny in just about every conceivable way." While some critics felt that Lohan's charisma was the film's saving grace, others derided even her performance. "Reserved and self-contained, she's the opposite of a drama queen, and she's so serious that she weighs down what ought to be a lightweight trifle," Margaret Quamme wrote for the *Columbus Dispatch* (February 20, 2004). "The movie is designed to showcase Lohan's singing and dancing, both unremarkable."

Lohan, who completed high school through home schooling, next starred in *Mean Girls* (2004) with Tina Fey. Fey also wrote the screenplay, which was inspired by Rosalind Wiseman's book *Queen Bees & Wannabes: Helping Your Daughter Survive Cliques, Gossip, Boyfriends and Other Realities of Adolescence.* Lohan played Cady Heron, the 15-year-old daughter of zoologists who was raised in an African village. Suddenly placed for the first time in a public high school in the U.S., she is introduced to the nasty world of cliques and tormented by the Plastics, a trio of the most popular girls in school. "No one has ever filled the role of the outsider unable to grasp the subtle nuances of teen life better than this 17-year-old dynamo," Kyle Dent wrote for the *Visalia (California) Times-Delta* (May 4, 2004) about Lohan's performance. "Combining the beauty and vindictiveness of a popular girl with the shy and innocent side of the new kid on campus, she charms the viewer into loving her. *Mean Girls* is the perfect movie: A delicate mixture of morals, humor and good old-fashioned eye candy."

Audiences flocked to *Mean Girls*, and as a result Lohan received numerous offers to do other films. She starred in another Disney movie, *Herbie: Fully Loaded* (based on the 1968 movie *The Love Bug*), which opened in theaters in June 2005. Her character, Maggie Peyton, uses the $75 she receives as a college graduation present to purchase Herbie—the sentient Volkswagen Beetle at the center of the 1968 film—from an automobile junkyard. Maggie and Herbie later compete in a NASCAR race. "Ms. Lohan . . . is a genuine star who combines a tomboyish spunk with a sexy, head-turning strut, executed with minimal self-consciousness," Stephen Holden wrote about the actress's work in the movie. "Likable but never saccharine, confident but not snooty, and endowed with the natural freckled-faced beauty of an 18-year-old Everywoman, Ms. Lohan seems completely at home on the screen." *Confessions of a Broken Heart*, Lohan's next film, was scheduled to reach theaters before the end of November 2005. The actress recently finished taping a romantic film comedy, *Just My Luck*, and is currently at work on Robert Altman's movie *A Prairie Home Companion*, based on Garrison Keillor's long-running radio program. In addition, she is slated to star in the upcoming films *Fashionistas*, *Gossip Girl*, *Blindsided*, and *Dramarama*.

Lohan, who had previously recorded songs for the soundtracks to *Confessions of a Teenage Drama Queen* and *Freaky Friday*, released a solo album, *Speak*, in 2004. "A lot of the people that I looked up to, the Ann Margrets and the Marilyn Monroes, everyone was a triple threat," she told Robert Haskel. "You had to sing, dance and act, and you did it in all your movies." Lohan wrote nearly half of the songs on *Speak*, working on the album with producers and songwriters who had collaborated with Ashlee Simpson, Britney Spears, *N Sync, and Jennifer Lopez. While critics disagreed over the quality of Lohan's voice, most dismissed the album as a whole as being almost entirely derivative. "It takes a special type of self-involvement to release an album that cannibalizes the already popular work of your peers and then to declare, 'Don't want to be like every other girl,'" Glenn Gamboa wrote for *Newsday* (December 7, 2004). Despite such reviews, *Speak* debuted at number four on the pop charts, and the single "Rumors" earned gold certification.

Lohan has received nearly as much press for rumors about her offscreen behavior, and the actions of her father, as she has for her work. While Lohan remains close to her mother, her father is prohibited by court order from seeing her or the rest of their family, due to a number of criminal offenses that include assault. Lohan's mother filed for divorce in January 2005, alleging that her husband had beaten her on several occasions and threatened to take the lives of their children. The next day, Michael Lohan held a press conference to announce that he was seeking half of his wife's managerial fees and requesting that his family undergo drug and alcohol testing. Her father later offered to compromise on his demands if the family agreed to participate in a reality TV show. "The unraveling of the Lohans—carried in all the tabloids and gossip magazines—has all the outer markings of a family succumbing to the pressures of raising a child star," Samuel Bruchey and Jennifer Smith wrote for *Newsday* (February 27, 2005). "But those who know the family say Lindsay's success shone a spotlight on a relationship that had been volatile for years." Lohan denounced her father in an interview with Haskel: "He didn't do anything for my career, except go out and not come home at night and make my mom and me stay up and wonder where he was and then show up three days later. So I don't think he deserves anything. He doesn't even deserve my respect." Meanwhile, the press has also reported rumors of Lindsay Lohan's wild and frequent partying.

Lohan has said that she tries to keep in mind that many of her fans are the same age as her sister, who was born in 1994. "My little sister's always wanted to do everything I do," she told Mike Davies for the *Birmingham Post* (June 17, 2004), "and now she reads the tabloid magazines so anything that's written or made up or is true or untrue about me that she sees she usually calls me, either crying or yelling at me. . . . So I get very concerned about what I do, but I also don't want to put out an image that isn't realistic. . . . I want to be normal, I want to be like any person my age."

Lohan lives in an apartment on Sunset Boulevard, in Hollywood, California, that she co-owns with the actress Raven Symone.

—J.C.

Suggested Reading:*Entertainment Weekly* p24 Dec. 17, 2004; *Interview* p88 June 1, 2004; *Newsday* B p3 Aug. 6, 1998, A p14 Feb. 27, 2005; *Observer* p32 June 13, 2004; *W* (on-line) Apr. 2005

Selected Films: *The Parent Trap*, 1998; *Freaky Friday*, 2003; *Confessions of a Teenage Drama Queen*, 2004; *Mean Girls*, 2004; *Herbie: Fully Loaded*, 2005

Selected Recordings: *Speak*, 2004

Los Lobos

Music group

Berlin, Steve
Sep. 14, 1955– Keyboardist; saxophonist

Hidalgo, David
Oct. 6, 1954– Singer; songwriter; guitarist; accordionist

Lozano, Conrad
Mar. 21, 1951– Bassist

Rosas, Cesar
Sep. 26, 1954– Singer; guitarist

Pérez, Louie
Jan. 29, 1953– Drummer; lyricist

Address: c/o Hollywood Records, 500 S. Buena Vista St., Burbank, CA 91521

Dubbed "rock's most metaphysical party band" (the words of Greg Kot, writing for the August 18, 1999 issue of *Rolling Stone*), Los Lobos (Spanish for "The Wolves") has spent nearly three decades honing its unique blend of Mexican folk music and American rock, blues, and jazz. The group has been praised by critics for its balance of old and new elements and its poetic, often politically charged lyrics. According to Wayne Robins, writing for New York *Newsday* (November 12, 1988), "Their strength has been roots-absorbing musical prowess (Los Lobos' original songs effortlessly combine elements of every traditional strain of rock, blues, country, rhythm and blues, Cajun and Tex-Mex music), combined with English lyrics that speak passionately and poetically for the disenchanted and disenfranchised." The band has also adopted elements of norteña music, a Mexican-American musical genre of the 1930s that Robins, for *Newsday* (February 23, 1984), described as "a blend of polka rhythms, country-western music, blues and swing that ebbed and flowed across the Texas-Mexico border." Best known for their 1987 single, "La Bamba," a cover of the classic song by the 1950s Chicano rock star Ritchie Valens, Los Lobos consists of David Hidalgo on guitar, accordion, and lead vocals; Steve Berlin on keyboard and saxophone; Cesar Rosas on guitar and vocals; Conrad Lozano on bass; and Louie Pérez on drums. (Pérez is also the band's chief lyricist.) Although the band

has been lauded by critics for decades and claims many devoted fans, it has never earned a large mainstream following; "La Bamba" is its only song that has become a radio staple.

Speaking on the National Public Radio (NPR) program *All Things Considered* (June 11, 2002), David Greenberger commented, "At times Los Lobos can be dazzlingly modern, but they seem less concerned with trailblazing than with just making sure the active musical creation is fully committed and in the moment. They confidently allow centuries-old Mexican and Latin musical traditions to flourish in contemporary surroundings, and they demonstrate at every turn that these sounds are alive and vital, which means they can then grow, adapt and change." Committed to reviving elements of traditional Mexican music for contemporary, largely non-Chicano audiences, the members of Los Lobos have described their work as being not only an artistic venture but an educational one, as well. As Pérez explained during an interview for NPR (September 14, 2002), "a byproduct of our success has been . . . the opportunity to redefine a lot of the myths and stereotypes people have about our culture. . . . We can travel to Helsinki, Finland, or be in Nagoya, Japan, and people will have a certain idea of what . . . Mexican culture is about, and there might be some misunderstanding that we can . . . reconfigure when we play." "There are certain things a Chicano band is supposed to do," he told Michael Snyder during an interview for the *San Francisco Chronicle* (July 24, 1994), "and we go beyond that."

Hidalgo (born October 6, 1954), Pérez (born January 29, 1953), Lozano (born March 21, 1951), and Rosas (born September 26, 1954) grew up in the barrio of East Los Angeles, where they met as students at Garfield High School. Although Lozano and Pérez were slightly older than Hidalgo and Rosas, who had met as eighth-graders at Stevenson Junior High, also in East Los Angeles, the four future band members quickly became friends "in an art class, discussing rock & roll instead of drawing & painting," as reported by Ben Quiñones in *LA Weekly* (June 18, 2004). In 1973 they decided to form a band, adopting the name Los Lobos del Este de Los Angeles (The Wolves of East Los Angeles) and playing mostly rock-and-roll covers.

During the mid-1970s California's Chicano community experienced a flowering of artistic, cultural, and political activity. "The Mexican renaissance was happening with young people around Southern California," Pérez told Michael Pelusi for *Philadelphia Citypaper* (September 28–October 5, 2000, on-line). "Money [was] coming out of the government to support Mexican-American study departments in colleges, and there were high schools forming folkloric dance groups." Around the same time, the band began to experiment with acoustic versions of Mexican folk songs, partly to explore their ethnic heritage and partly to please their parents. "We wanted to learn about our culture through the music," Lozano explained to an

Courtesy of Scott Gries/ImageDirect

The members of Los Lobos (left to right): Cesar Rosas, Steve Berlin, Conrad Lozano, David Hidalgo, Louie Pérez

interviewer for the *Des Moines (Iowa) Register*, as quoted in the *Seattle Times* (July 16, 1998). "It started off as a hobby." Before long, however, Los Lobos del Este de Los Angeles were playing Mexican tunes on a regular basis, performing their music locally at weddings and parties, as well as at California State University, in Los Angeles, and at East Los Angeles College, which they attended. Although their parents and other older adults reacted positively to their music, "a lot of the musicians, our peers, were confused," Pérez told Pelusi. "'What are you doing that for? Why are you playing Mexican music?' [they asked]. We'd think, 'Well, why are you spending six hours a night trying to sound like a record that's on the radio? *That* sounds crazy.'" Impressed by the band's determination to revive Mexican folk music for the younger generation, producers at the Public Broadcasting System created a television special about them in 1975.

In 1976 Los Lobos del Este de Los Angeles contributed arrangements and performances to *Si Se Puede* (Yes You Can), a 10-track, Spanish-language benefit album for the United Farm Workers of America. They landed their first steady professional gig in 1978, playing traditional music at a Mexican restaurant. "It wasn't even a real Mexican restaurant, [it was] one of those tourist joints," Rosas confessed to an interviewer for *Guitar World*, as quoted on Thomson Gale's Hispanic Heritage Web site. "We were working there because we had come to a point where we had to either make more money from music or find other jobs." While employed by the restaurant, the band began to experiment with electric instruments, which lent a rock-and-

roll edge to their Tex-Mex music. Displeased with what would eventually evolve into Los Lobos' signature sound, the restaurant owners fired the band. That same year the band released their first full-length record, a self-produced EP of 12 traditional Mexican songs, titled *Del este de Los Angeles (Just Another Band from East L.A.)*.

In 1980 Los Lobos del Este de Los Angeles had their first major show (as well as their first show for a predominantly non-Chicano audience), opening for the English art-punk band Public Image Ltd. at a concert in Los Angeles. The audience reacted negatively to the band, but the gig gave the musicians their first widespread exposure. Soon afterward they began opening for such well-known punk bands as the Circle Jerks and the Clash; they also opened for the Blasters, a popular rockabilly group for which Steve Berlin (born on September 14, 1955) played saxophone. When Los Lobos del Este de Los Angeles signed a contract with Slash Records, in 1982, Berlin agreed to produce their next EP, the seven-track . . . *And a Time to Dance*, consisting of songs that fused roots-rock with norteña music. By the time that recording was released, in 1983, they had shortened their name to Los Lobos and invited Berlin to join them as a saxophonist and keyboardist. The album sold about 90,000 copies, and one of the songs, "Anselma," earned the band its first Grammy Award, for best Mexican-American performance.

In 1984 Los Lobos released their major-label debut, *How Will the Wolf Survive?*, through Warner Bros. Combining traditional Mexican songs, rock and roll, and blues, the album addressed political and social themes related to the Mexican-

American community of East Los Angeles. It was a critical success, establishing Los Lobos as an important new voice in American rock and earning them a loyal fan base. Impressed with the songs and performances he heard on *How Will the Wolf Survive?*, Paul Simon invited Los Lobos to perform on his 1986 album, *Graceland*; Elvis Costello, also a fan, featured the band on his *King of America* album, released that same year.

Los Lobos' next album, *By the Light of the Moon* (1987), reflected a more mainstream sensibility that the band hoped would allow them to reach a wider audience. Although the album was praised by critics and nominated for a Grammy, for best rock vocal group performance, it received little airplay and sold modestly. That same year, however, Los Lobos' cover of Valens's "La Bamba"—recorded for the hit movie of the same title, starring Lou Diamond Phillips—climbed the charts to become the number-one pop single in the nation. (Valens's 1958 version had reached only the 22d spot on the charts.) The *La Bamba* soundtrack won a Golden Eagle Award and earned Los Lobos two Grammy nominations (for record of the year and best pop vocal group performance), as well as an MTV Video Music Award (for best video from a film).

Defying expectations, Los Lobos chose not to build on the popular success of "La Bamba" with an easily marketable release. Instead, they released *La pistola y el corazón* (The Pistol and the Heart, 1988), an album of traditional Mexican folk music sung entirely in Spanish. Explaining the decision to an interviewer for New York *Newsday* (November 6, 1988), Pérez said, "I look at it as a responsible reaction to the success we enjoyed last year. Instead of going after a follow-up, another big hit, we're using our momentum and the attention that's on us right now to put out something that we really can be proud of, to do our part to expose this sort of music which would normally not be accessible to a lot of people." According to the Hispanic Heritage Web site, the *All Music Guide to Rock* described the album as not just "a history lesson, but a celebration of [Los Lobos'] heritage and its joyous music, which means that it's just as exciting and entertaining as their rock and roll records." *La pistola y el corazón* won the band its second Grammy Award, for best rock performance by a duo or a group.

After a two-year hiatus Los Lobos returned to the studio to record *The Neighborhood* (1990), an album that interwove traditional Mexican folk rhythms and instruments with contemporary arrangements and lyrics. Like *How Will the Wolf Survive?*, *The Neighborhood* treated political and cultural themes and was a major critical success; Stephen Thomas Erlewine described it for the *All Music Guide* (on-line) as "a varied and powerful rock & roll record that was better than anything they had released in six years." Once again, however, sales were relatively low, and the band began to question whether their music would ever achieve pop-

ular success. "We weren't sure if we had run our course," Steve Berlin told Greg Kot for the *Chicago Tribune* (June 21, 1992). "We found ourselves in this bizarre gray area, feeling sort of muddled because we thought it was a big step forward for us but everyone else was indifferent to the record."

Los Lobos' seventh album, *Kiko* (1992), has been hailed by many critics and fans as the band's best. The album built on many of the stylistic innovations introduced in *The Neighborhood*, moving toward more experimental compositions, while still featuring the band's signature blend of jazz, rock, and Mexican folk styles. Glossy studio production by the sound engineer Tchad Blake and the producer Mitchell Froom added another dimension to the sound; as Derk Richardson wrote in an article for the SFGate Web site (August 26, 1999), "What Froom and Blake brought to the mix was an arsenal of studio effects and production techniques that moved Los Lobos out of its niche as a socially conscious roots-rock band, and into the realm of self-conscious but subtly clamorous art-rock." In an article for the *New York Times* (May 17, 1992), Peter Watrous praised Los Lobos' experimental approach, writing, "*Kiko* takes spectacular songwriting and arranges it brilliantly; it is the band's breakthrough album. . . . It is an album unafraid of the possibilities of the studio, where guitars run backward and textures change rapidly." Doug Simmons, writing for the *Village Voice* (June 23, 1992), noted that despite *Kiko*'s formal complexity, "everything is still spare; for all the experimentation, for all of the elegant studio touches, the songs on *Kiko* have a lived-in feel, the stamp of a world-class working bar band." The *Los Angeles Times* and the *Chicago Tribune*, among other publications, declared *Kiko* the album of the year, and the video for the song "Kiko and the Lavender Moon" won an MTV Video Music Award, for best breakthrough video. That same year Los Lobos contributed a rendition of the song "Beautiful Maria of My Soul" to the film soundtrack of *The Mambo Kings*; the song was nominated for both a Grammy and an Academy Award, for best song from a film.

In 1993, in celebration of their 20 years together, Los Lobos released *Just Another Band from East L.A.: A Collection*, a 41-song, two-CD set featuring most of their most popular songs, as well as material from their early independent recordings, outtakes, covers of songs by other artists, and live tracks. The following year they re-recorded "Kiko and the Lavender Moon" as "Elmo and the Lavender Moon" for an album celebrating the 25th anniversary of the children's television program *Sesame Street*. Also in 1994, Pérez and Hidalgo wrote six original songs for a production of *Good Woman of Szechuan*, Tony Kushner's adaptation of a play by Bertolt Brecht, and teamed up with Blake and Froom to form the Latin Playboys, a roots band with an avant-garde sensibility. (The Latin Playboys released a self-titled album in 1994 and a second album, *Dose*, in 1999.)

In 1995 Los Lobos collaborated with the legendary musician Lalo Guerrero, widely known as the father of Chicano music, to create *Papa's Dream*, a children's record released on the Music for Little People record label. That year the band composed the bulk of the score for the film *Desperado*, and their song "Mariachi Suite" from that soundtrack won a Grammy, for best pop instrumental. Los Lobos also contributed a song to the soundtrack for the 1996 film *Feeling Minnesota*, starring Cameron Diaz and Keanu Reeves. In 1996 Los Lobos released *Colossal Head*, another collaboration with Froom and Blake and the band's seventh album on the Warner Bros. label. They recorded the songs on the album quickly in an effort to capture moments of musical inspiration. The experimental, bluesy collection was met with mixed reviews and was commercially unsuccessful. Disappointed with Los Lobos' sales, Warner Bros. decided not to sign the band on for another album.

Disheartened, the band members took a temporary break from Los Lobos to focus on side projects. In 1998 Hidalgo, Rosas, and several other musicians joined to form a group called Los Super Seven and recorded an album of the same name, produced by Steve Berlin. Hidalgo and Pérez continued to write and record with the Latin Playboys, and in 1999 Hidalgo collaborated with the blues musician Mike Halby to create Houndog, releasing a self-titled album. That year Cesar Rosas released *Soul Disguise*, a solo album that included performances by Hidalgo and Pérez.

After landing a contract with Hollywood Records, Los Lobos reconvened in 1999 to record and release *This Time*, continuing their close working relationship with Froom and Blake. Kieren Grant, writing for the *Toronto Sun* (August 12, 1999), described the album as "an artful hodge-podge of rock 'n' roll, funk 'n' soul, and diverse, non-Chicano Latin sounds culled from far-away ports such as Cuba and Colombia." The album fused the political concerns of Los Lobos' early albums with the lyrical qualities of later albums such as *Kiko* and *Colossal Head*. As Derk Richardson wrote, "On *This Time*, Los Lobos still deals with the streetcorner realities of futile ambition, squandered opportunities and broken dreams, but they do so in cryptic, poetic language over urgent rhythms. The tension between the deliberately murky instrumental colors, deep grooves, and evocative imagery is mesmerizing." In October 1999, several months after *This Time*'s release, Rosas's wife, Sandra Ann, was kidnapped and murdered by her half-brother.

In 2000 Hollywood Records re-released Los Lobos' 1978 EP, *Del este de Los Angeles (Just Another Band from East L.A.)*, and Rhino/Warner Archives released *El cancionero: Mas y mas*, a four-CD, career-retrospective boxed set. Two years later, the band came out with its 11th studio album, *Good Morning Aztlán*, on the Mammoth Records label, a subdivision of Hollywood Records. As Pérez explained during the NPR interview, "Aztlan is the name of the mythical birthplace of the indigenous peoples of Mexico, which was . . . adopted by the early Chicano movement happening in the late '60s and early '70s." Created without the studio assistance of Mitchell and Froom, *Good Morning Aztlán* is somewhat less experimental than Los Lobos' previous two albums. "We spent about 10 years [collaborating] with Froom and Blake, and I wouldn't trade a second of it. I love the records we made together," Berlin told Blake Jackson. "But it was time to do something new." Although "clearly there is still some Blake/Froom influence . . . " on the album, according to Jackson, "there's a power and passion to the performances that feels new, more akin to the way the band sounds live."

Los Lobos' album *The Ride* (2004) includes guest performances by several of the band's main musical influences—among them Tom Waits, Elvis Costello, Garth Hudson, Richard Thompson, Mavis Staples, the soul singer Bobby Womack, and the Chicano rock musician Willie Garcia, better known as Little Willie G. "We had a wish list, . . . but we weren't sure whether [anyone would] be available or interested," Pérez told Andrew Dansby for *Rolling Stone* (January 28, 2004, on-line). "We didn't anticipate that *nobody* would tell us no . . . it was a good problem to have." The album was received warmly by critics, who praised Los Lobos for incorporating performances by so many disparate musicians seamlessly into their own, unique sound. Speaking on *All Things Considered*, David Greenberger commented, "The most remarkable thing is how the music still belongs to Los Lobos. It isn't taken over by the guests; rather, they become part of the band."

In 2005 Los Lobos launched their Cancionero tour, performing acoustically for the first time in more than 15 years; they also released their first live concert recording, *Live at the Fillmore*. In explaining the band's reluctance to produce a live album, Cesar Rosas told Laura Emerick for the *Chicago Sun Times* (March 25, 2005), "We've always tried to escape that. We've always had so much other stuff that we could put out. But the timing for this one was perfect." During the tour the band also sold a disc featuring some of its recording sessions from the early 1990s. Los Lobos planned to start work on a new album in late 2005. For its annual Christmas shows, the band announced that they would perform all the songs from *Kiko*. On another front, Perez, with the help of the playwright Luis Torres, was adapting *Kiko* for the theater.

Los Lobos plays benefit concerts regularly to support charities such as Integrity House, a rehabilitation facility for people with cognitive disabilities. Over the years, the band members have remained close; Hidalgo, Pérez, Rosas, and Lozano all still live in the Los Angeles area. (Berlin lives in Seattle, Washington.) "Outside of our own immediate families, our own wives and kids, . . . everyone in this band is . . . our family . . . ," Hidalgo commented during the NPR interview. "All of our children grew up together, our wives all hung out together, so . . . it's a lot bigger than just being a band." The members of Los Lobos have passed their love of music on to their children: Lozano's son Jason plays in a blues band called the Healers, and Hidalgo's sons David Jr. and Vincent have collaborated with the hard-rock band Suicidal Tendencies. From 1991 to 2003 the Hidalgo brothers, along with Pérez's son Louie III, were also in a punk band called Los Villains, which opened for Los Lobos on several occasions.

—L.W.

Suggested Reading: *LA Weekly* p49+ June 18, 2004; *Mix* (on-line) June 1, 2002; *Philadelphia Citypaper* (on-line) Sep. 28–Oct. 5, 2000; *Rolling Stone* p87+ Mar. 26, 1987; *San Francisco Chronicle* E p1+ Oct. 15, 1990

Selected Recordings: *Del este de Los Angeles (Just Another Band from East L.A.)*, 1978; . . . *And a Time to Dance*, 1983; *How Will the Wolf Survive?*, 1984; *By the Light of the Moon*, 1987; *La pistola y el corazón*, 1988; *The Neighborhood*, 1990; *Kiko*, 1992; *Just Another Band from East L.A.: A Collection*, 1993; *Colossal Head*, 1996; *This Time*, 1999; *El cancionero: Mas y mas*, 2000; *Good Morning Aztlán*, 2002; *The Ride*, 2004; *Live at the Fillmore*, 2005

Courtesy of Creators Syndicate

Luckovich, Mike

Jan. 28, 1960– Editorial cartoonist

Address: Atlanta Journal-Constitution, 72 Marietta St., N.W., Atlanta, GA 30303

Mike Luckovich has spent the last 20 years commenting on the American cultural and political landscape through the barbed humor of his editorial cartoons. His work is distributed by the Creators Syndicate to approximately 160 newspapers across the United States, making him one of the more successful editorial cartoonists in an ever-shrinking field. (Twenty years ago there were more than 200 such full-time cartoonists; today there are about 90.) His favorite targets of ridicule include the gun lobby and racism; he has also lampooned

America's obsession with celebrity and scandal, rebuked hypocrites, and taken shots at politicians on both the left and the right. On occasion he has forsaken humor in his cartoons to comment sympathetically and touchingly on tragedies, such as the September 11, 2001 terrorist attacks on New York City and the Pentagon and the 2003 loss of the space shuttle *Columbia*. For the most part, however, Luckovich takes pleasure in using a pen to give his targets nice, sharp jabs.

"With the type of editorial cartoon I do," Mike Luckovich explained in a 1997 interview with R. C. Harvey for *Cartoon Profiles* (on-line), "people have to have a reference for it. They have to know the issues; they have to have an idea about them. And then I reflect on the issues. So I don't consider myself a reporter. I feel I definitely have something to say. And that's what is so great for me: to get my point across and to show the flaws in the other side's arguments or to show this individual to be wrong somehow, through ridicule in my cartoons. I feel that my best cartoons . . . get a point across—and are also funny. Those are the kind of cartoons that I like to read. I don't really particularly care for gag cartoons—editorial cartoons that don't make a point. I think that good editorial cartoons get the point across and are still funny."

Michael Luckovich was born on January 28, 1960 in Seattle, Washington. Because his father's career forced the family to move frequently, Luckovich often found himself in the position of having to make new friends. He discovered that a dependable way of doing so was to draw caricatures of teachers and pass them around the classroom. The popularity of the caricatures he drew in the fifth and sixth grades proved to Luckovich, who had started drawing as early as age six, that there was an audience for his kind of humor. In junior high school he became a fan of *Mad Magazine*, particularly the work of the cartoonist Mort Zucker, who was highly regarded for his caricatures of celebrities. Luckovich's interest in political cartoons did not develop until he was in high school, when he discovered the work of Mike Peters, Pat Oliphant and, most notably, Jeff MacNelly, whose drawings he would frequently cut out of the newspaper and imitate. "When I was 14 I drew my first editorial cartoon. Just some goofy thing on [President Richard M.] Nixon for my grandma," he recalled with a laugh in an interview with *JournalismJobs.com* (November 2001, on-line). "It wasn't very good."

After graduating from high school, Luckovich attended the University of Washington in Seattle, where he began publishing his cartoons in the *Washington Daily*, the college newspaper. His colleagues were surprised that the easygoing Luckovich could produce such biting political satire. As Pam McGaffin, the managing editor of the *Daily* in the early 1980s, recalled for Alansa Bates in an article for the University of Washington's Web site (September 1995), "He struck me as this wide-eyed little boy, a 'golly-gee' sort of kid, totally naive and not worldly or politically savvy at all. Then he came out with political cartoons that were pretty sophisticated. His whole persona was almost the opposite of what he was producing."

During his college days Luckovich did not stick to issues pertaining to life in and around the University of Washington. With an eye toward building a career after college, he made sure that his portfolio contained many cartoons about national and international issues. After he graduated, in 1982, he sent copies of his résumé and samples of his work to newspapers across the country but had little luck. Between 1981, the year before his graduation, and 1984, he sold a few cartoons locally, on a freelance basis, to the *Bellevue Journal American*, the *Seattle Post Intelligencer*, and the *Everett Herald*. Such work did not bring in a steady income, however, and he ended up selling life insurance door-to-door for two years. He was "miserable" during that time, as he noted during an interview with *Newsweek* (2004, on-line). He added, explaining the difficulty of finding a full-time position in his field, that political cartooning is "so much fun no one wants to leave, and when someone does, it's a big shuffling of people from one place to another."

Feeling desperate, Luckovich subscribed to *Editor & Publisher*, the newspaper-industry magazine, in the hopes of finding a steady job in editorial cartooning. In 1984 he saw an advertisement for an opening at the *Greenville News* in South Carolina and immediately sent the editors a copy of his résumé and samples of his illustrations. He landed the job and stayed there for the next nine months. "It's a good paper," he recalled in his interview with R. C. Harvey, "and the people there understood the role of a cartoonist. But I'm from a bigger town, and I wanted a bigger area, something more diverse."

Luckovich found such an opportunity with the *New Orleans Times-Picayune*, in Louisiana, where he began to work in 1985. He got the job by inundating the paper's editors with samples of his work. "Editors get stacks of stuff," he told Harvey, "so I wanted to be a little bit different. I sent them

a cartoon every day. First, I sent in a portfolio of what I thought was my best stuff and cover letter; then I sent them a cartoon daily, the ones I was doing in Greenville, so they could see the quality and consistency of my work on a daily basis. They told me it helped. They were able to see what I could do."

For the next four years, Luckovich lived and worked happily in New Orleans and felt no urge to leave his post. Then, in 1989, he was invited by editors at the *Atlanta Constitution* (now the *Atlanta Journal-Constitution*), in Georgia, to come in for an interview. Though he was not particularly interested initially in working there, he met with the editors, then went back for a second interview three weeks later. During the interview process he began to feel an appreciation for Atlanta. The newspaper offered him a job, which he accepted. As of late 2005, he was still employed there.

For many years Luckovich's work routine, as described in interviews, has remained the same: he arrives in the office at around 11:30 a.m. (he claims that his brain does not work properly in the morning), has lunch, and begins to sketch rough ideas on a pad of paper. (Unlike many cartoonists, he does not use a pencil before inking in his drawings; he prefers the smooth lines he gets from ink.) He draws and redraws the same cartoon until he is pleased with the result. He then passes the cartoon around to some of the editorial writers as well as the editorial-page editor, to make sure that it both strikes people as funny and delivers his point. "I find that I usually have an idea by around two-thirty, three o'clock," he explained to Harvey, "and I like to be done by about four-thirty, so I can beat rush hour."

At the *Journal-Constitution*, Luckovich's career has blossomed. Shortly after he arrived at the paper, his cartoons began to be syndicated in major news outlets such as *Newsweek*, and his work has since received significant recognition, including two Overseas Press Club Awards, in 1990 and 1994; a National Headliners Club Award, in 1992; and the Robert F. Kennedy Journalism Award, in 1994. Most notably, in 1995, he received a Pulitzer Prize for his editorial cartooning. One of the 20 cartoons that won him the prize concerned former Speaker of the House Newt Gingrich, a Republican from Georgia. A story had spread that Gingrich had asked his first wife for a divorce while she was lying in a hospital bed recovering from cancer. In Luckovich's cartoon, drawn at the time of the landslide Republican victory during the 1994 elections, Gingrich is portrayed in a hospital room with a pair of beautiful women identified as "D.C. highrollers," telling a sick woman named "Georgia constituents" that he wants a divorce. The cartoon infuriated Gingrich, who refused to grant interviews to Luckovich's newspaper for the next four months. (In October 1996 Luckovich revisited the setting of that cartoon by having the Republican Party, represented by an elephant, asking a bedridden Gingrich for a divorce—to show how far the

Speaker had fallen in his party's esteem.) "I prefer a politician who gets bothered by my cartoons; it means they're having an impact," Luckovich told *Newsweek*.

When the *Journal-Constitution* asked Luckovich to fly aboard Air Force One during the 1996 presidential election campaign, he was concerned about how President Bill Clinton might react to his presence, since the cartoonist had skewered Clinton in a number of cartoons. He was particularly concerned about presenting Clinton with a collection of his cartoons, *Lotsa Luckovich* (1996), whose cover drawing depicted the president reacting to the (fictional) news that the infamous bloodstained glove from the O.J. Simpson murder trial fit his wife, Hillary Rodham Clinton. To Luckovich's relief, the president laughed uproariously at the cartoon, and even allowed the cartoonist to sketch him as he spoke by telephone to German chancellor Helmut Kohl.

Following the September 11, 2001 terrorist attacks on the United States, which killed an estimated 2,800 people, Luckovich found that he had to rethink his editorial cartoons. As he explained in his interview with *JournalismJobs.com,* "Normally with my cartoons I try to use humor to get across my point. After Sept. 11th, you just couldn't use humor. The tragedy was so enormous, you couldn't be funny. It's almost like you have to come up with cartoons using a different part of your brain. I was just trying to come up with images that expressed the emotions that I was feeling and tried to focus in on different aspects of the tragedy that I thought were important." On the day of the tragedy, he drew a picture of the Statue of Liberty with a tear in one eye; the eyes also showed reflections of the hijacked passenger planes striking the twin towers of the World Trade Center, in New York City.

For a time after the terrorist attacks, Luckovich refrained from poking fun at politicians or political issues, and many of his other targets of earlier years—the National Rifle Association, celebrities, and the tobacco lobby—seemed to him unimportant in comparison with the tragedy and its many ramifications. A cartoon from January 2003, for example, shows Alan Greenspan, chairman of the Federal Reserve Board, sitting in a cave, presumably a terrorist hideout in Afghanistan; several feet away sit two bearded figures, one of them resembling Osama bin Laden, the architect of the 2001 attacks. The bin Laden figure asks, "What's he doing here?," to which the second bearded man replies, "He dissed Bush's latest tax cut scheme." Another cartoon, published the following month, is set in an airport, where a uniformed official tells people preparing to have their bags, shoes, and bodies scanned and searched, "According to plan, terrorists will leave after tiring of waiting in line." The war in Iraq, however, has been the catalyst for much of Luckovich's recent work. While his cartoons have always generated their share of hate mail, few have inspired as much as his recent, bit-

ing takes on President George W. Bush's handling of the war. In one such cartoon Luckovich alluded to the highly publicized 2003 event in which Bush, wearing a flight suit, helped pilot a military plane that landed on the deck of the U.S.S. *Abraham Lincoln*; the cartoon shows the commander in chief in a clown suit, holding a piece of paper that reads "Postwar Iraq" and thinking, "I miss my flight suit." In his interview with *Newsweek.com*, Luckovich noted that Bush had served in the National Guard during the Vietnam War, and had therefore not seen combat; he also referred to accusations that Bush's whereabouts during part of his service were unknown. "I thought the flight suit was so hypocritical," Luckovich said. "As the postwar in Iraq unfolds so badly, it looks stupider and stupider. I kept the idea of the flight suit in the back of my mind. And I wondered, 'What kind of a suit would he be wearing today?' I came up with [the clown suit] right before deadline."

A number of war-related cartoons, particularly those depicting the troops fighting in Iraq, have triggered angry responses from readers, who feel that Luckovich is too harsh in his criticism of the war. Doug Marlette, Luckovich's predecessor at the *Journal-Constitution*, defended his colleague to Mike King in an interview published in the paper on December 20, 2003: "We don't need the First Amendment to allow us to run boring, inoffensive cartoons. We need constitutional protection for our right to express unpopular views. If we can't discuss the great issues of the day on the pages of our newspapers fearlessly, where can we discuss them?"

In 2002, after the terrorist attacks on the U.S. but prior to the war in Iraq, the *Atlanta Journal-Constitution* had set up an on-line poll concerning Luckovich's cartoons, which allowed readers to vote "I like Mike" or "I don't like Mike." At that time Luckovich's anti-Bush cartoons divided readers equally, with 50 percent of responders in agreement with the cartoonist's opinions and 50 percent holding different views. With the increasingly tumultuous aftermath of the war, however, Luckovich's popularity has risen. When asked by Dave Astor for *Editor & Publisher* (February 19, 2004) if the polling has an impact on what he draws, Luckovich responded, "No, I have my own belief system and feelings about things."

Mike Luckovich and his wife, Margo, have three children: John, Mickey, and Micaela. Many interviewers have asked Luckovich if he would like to write and draw a comic strip; he has always answered that he prefers to produce five or six editorial cartoons per week.

—C.M.

Suggested Reading: *Atlanta Journal-Constitution* A p11 Dec. 2003; *Editor & Publisher* (on-line) Feb. 19, 2004; *JournalismJobs.com* Nov. 2001; *Newsweek* (on-line) 2004; University of Washington Web site; *Who's Who of Pulitzer Prize Winners*, 1999

Selected Books: *Lotsa Luckovich*, 1996

Frank Micelotta/Getty Images

Lumet, Sidney

NOTE: An earlier article about Sidney Lumet appeared in *Current Biography* in 1967.

June 25, 1924– Film director

Address: *c/o International Creative Management, 8942 Wilshire Blvd., Suite 219, Beverly Hills, CA 90211-1934*

The director Sidney Lumet is a towering figure in American film, a veteran of more than 40 movies that include such classics as *Twelve Angry Men* (1957), *The Pawnbroker* (1965), *Dog Day Afternoon* (1975), and *Network* (1976), as well as a number of other well-regarded films that focus on police corruption: *Serpico* (1973), *Prince of the City* (1981), *Q & A* (1990), and *Night Falls on Manhattan* (1997). He began his career as a stage actor, then spent time in the 1950s as a director of television and theater productions before turning his hand to feature films. Lumet's pictures have long been noted for the complexity they uncover in their examination of ethical issues and human behavior; he has said that he tries to keep his stories evenhanded—neither condemning nor excusing his complicated characters—by focusing on the way that people are often pulled simultaneously in more than one direction. "I'm not a propagandist," he told Frazier Moore for the Associated Press (January 10, 2001). "To me, it's important that I find something out about people. And if the story tells you a little bit about that person, then it's gonna tell you about that time and its issues, almost automatically. You don't have to reach." The variety of Lumet's films, and their perceived lack of concern for

visual beauty, have sometimes led to the charge that he is without the signature style thought to be the hallmark of great movie directors. What others may perceive as a shortcoming, however, is for Lumet a conscious choice. "The whole auteur nonsense is repugnant to me," he told William Wolf for *New York* (August 10, 1981). "I won't take the billing 'a Sidney Lumet film' or 'Sidney Lumet's production of.' When I go out shooting, I'm dependent on the weather, the sun, and 120 people around me knowing their work. And I don't want to settle into a particular style, because to me the style is determined by the material itself. I think this has sort of left me in a vacuum from a critical point of view. It's nothing that disturbs me a great deal." In 2005 the Academy of Motion Picture Arts and Sciences presented Lumet with its award for lifetime achievement.

Sidney Lumet was born in Philadelphia, Pennsylvania, on June 25, 1924, the only son of Baruch and Eugenia (Wermus) Lumet. His father, an actor trained in Poland, enjoyed a long and varied career in the United States, encompassing stage, radio, television, and film roles, including small parts in two of his son's motion pictures, *The Pawnbroker* and *The Group*. In 1926 the family moved to New York City, where Baruch Lumet joined Maurice Schwartz's troupe at the Yiddish Art Theater. Young Sidney made his acting debut alongside his father in the cast of a Yiddish Art Theater production when he was four years old. His first Broadway appearance was at the Belasco Theater on October 28, 1935, in *Dead End*. With his father, he appeared in *The Eternal Road* at the Manhattan Opera House in 1937, and subsequent Broadway shows in which he took part included *Sunup to Sundown* (1938), *Schoolhouse on the Lot* (1939), *My Heart's in the Highlands* (1939), and *Morning Star* (1940). In *Journey to Jerusalem* (1940) he played the starring role of Jeshua (the young Jesus). Later in the 1940–41 season he appeared in *George Washington Slept Here*, and in 1941–42 he had a role in *Brooklyn, U.S.A.* While he has indicated in other interviews that his growing-up years were spent in poor, tough New York neighborhoods, he told Philip Wuntch for the *Dallas Morning News* (May 17, 1997), "I had a great childhood." Noting that he had had the opportunity as a boy to work with the filmmaker Max Reinhardt, the composer Kurt Weill, and the playwright Sidney Kingsley, among others, he added that his early exposure to show business was "the greatest thing that could have happened to me."

Lumet attended the Professional Children's School, in New York, and during the 1941–42 academic year he remained in the city to study at Columbia University. From 1942 to 1946 he served as a radar repairman with the United States Army in the China-Burma-India theater of operations. After the war he returned to Broadway, where he succeeded Marlon Brando as David in *A Flag Is Born* (1946). In 1947 he began directing Off-Broadway and summer-stock productions, and from that point on—except for his role as Tonya in *Seeds in the Wind* at the Empire Theater, in 1948—he gave his full attention to directing. He has attributed the respect he feels for his performers to his own experiences as an actor. "I think actors feel very safe with me," Lumet told Kenneth Turan for *GQ* (September 1988). "I don't think I've ever printed the wrong take; they know I know the hot one. And in rehearsal they see I have tremendous respect for them and their craft, and that security allows them to take risks. All good work is self-revelation, and they are the most vulnerable, so I want them to feel 'I'm in my mother's arms,' without coddling them. And I do another thing: I never try and get into their heads and exploit a personal vulnerability." He is similarly respectful of film writers. "I appreciate writing and in the final analysis, if I've accepted a script and the writer and I disagree about it, and he says 'This is the way I want it,' that's the way I do it," he told James Lardner for the *Washington Post* (August 23, 1981). Lumet prefers to film scripts adapted from novels and plays, often sharing writing credits.

CBS hired Lumet as a television staff director in 1950 and assigned him first to *Danger*, a suspense and adventure series, and in 1952 to *You Are There*, a series of dramatic re-creations of significant moments in history. During the following years, known as the "golden age" of television drama, he directed more than 200 plays for CBS's *Playhouse 90*, NBC's *Kraft Television Theatre* and *Studio One*, and other dramatic shows. Many of the productions were original teleplays, and most were done live. Of this period Lumet said, according to the *New York Journal American* (February 14, 1966): "Directors such as John Frankenheimer, Delbert Mann, Bob Mulligan, Arthur Penn and myself faced only one limitation—our own competence. With fourteen hours of drama shows a week, a limited number of sets and minuscule budgets, we were able to experiment."

Another high point in Lumet's television career was *The Sacco and Vanzetti Story*, a searing vindication of the Italian immigrants and anarchists executed for murder in Massachusetts in 1927. The semidocumentary teleplay, presented on NBC in June 1960, earned Lumet a nomination for an Emmy Award. Lumet's greatest television success was probably his taped *Play of the Week* production of Eugene O'Neill's *The Iceman Cometh*, first aired in New York in November 1960. Jack Gould commented in the *New York Times* (November 16, 1960): "To television has come a moment of enrichment and excitement unequalled in the medium's thirteen years . . . a theatrical experience that remorselessly envelops the viewer in the playwright's marathon documentary on doom." Lumet received an Emmy for *The Iceman Cometh*, and O'Neill's widow, Carlotta Monterey O'Neill, was so impressed with the production that she entrusted to Lumet the future rights to all other O'Neill plays that had reverted to her control.

Lumet made his debut as a stage director with a revival of George Bernard Shaw's *The Doctor's Dilemma* at the Phoenix Theater in New York City in January 1955. The reviews were mixed, and Lumet fared even worse with the critics the following year, when *Night of the Auk*, a science-fiction propaganda vehicle by Arch Oboler, barely survived eight days. His production of the musical *Nowhere to Go But Up* also had a short run, in November 1962. The only stage production that Lumet directed and remembers positively is *Caligula*, Albert Camus's philosophical melodrama about the amoral, sadistic Roman emperor, which opened at the 54th Street Theater on Broadway on February 16, 1960.

The first motion picture directed by Lumet was *Twelve Angry Men*, an adaptation of a play by Reginald Rose that Lumet had first directed on television. It is the story of a murder-trial jury that is impeded in its rush to condemnation by a lone dissenter, a thoughtful man of conscience—played in the film by Henry Fonda—who steers the other 11 jurors, one by one, to a judgment of not guilty. Critics were unanimous in their praise of *Twelve Angry Men*, which is now considered a film classic. Lumet's *That Kind of Woman* (1959), starring Sophia Loren and Tab Hunter, was received without enthusiasm by reviewers, and Lumet himself has said that he went astray with *Stage Struck* (1958), which featured Susan Strasberg as a young woman who comes to New York to pursue her acting dreams. He was also dissatisfied with *The Fugitive Kind* (1960), his screen version of Tennessee Williams's play *Orpheus Descending*, starring Marlon Brando and Anna Magnani. Bosley Crowther in the *New York Times* (April 15, 1960), however, thought Lumet displayed "understanding of the deep-running skills of the two stars," and he particularly liked Lumet's close-ups of the stars' faces. *A View from the Bridge* (1962), Lumet's film version of Arthur Miller's play about a Brooklyn longshoreman's tragic love for his wife's niece, was generally well received by critics.

To film Eugene O'Neill's brooding and autobiographical family drama *Long Day's Journey into Night* (1962), Lumet teamed with the producer Ely Landau, with whom he had so successfully collaborated on the *Play of the Week* television series. The film was hailed by Alton Cook of the *New York World Telegram and Sun* (October 10, 1962) as "one of the great movie triumphs of all time," and Bosley Crowther in the *New York Times* (October 14, 1962) wrote, "This picture . . . conveys the substance and strength of the original where other films of O'Neill plays have failed." At the Cannes Film Festival the film's stars, Katharine Hepburn, Sir Ralph Richardson, Jason Robards Jr., and Dean Stockwell, earned top acting honors. Lumet received the 1963 Directors Guild of America Award for the movie.

Fail Safe (1964), Lumet's suspenseful film adaptation of Eugene Burdick and Harvey Wheeler's novel about the hazard of accidental nuclear warfare, suffered at the box office by following *Dr. Strangelove*, a wild farce based on a similar premise, which had been released earlier in the same year. The most controversial of Lumet's films of that period was *The Pawnbroker*, based on Edwin Lewis Wallant's novel about Sol Nazerman, the operator of a pawnshop in Spanish Harlem that is a front for a black racketeer. Nazerman, the emotion-numbed, tormented survivor of a Nazi concentration camp where his wife and children were killed, has insulated himself against painful reality with unfeeling cynicism. Some critics complained at the time that the film was too morbid, but most agreed with Bosley Crowther, who, writing for the *New York Times* (May 2, 1965), called *The Pawnbroker* "the most incisive American film so far this year." Rod Steiger won the best-actor award of the 1967 Berlin Film Festival for his performance as Nazerman.

The Hill (1965), starring Sean Connery, was lauded by some critics for its uncompromisingly stark treatment of brutality and sadism in a British military prison in North Africa during World War II. *The Group* (1966), based on Mary McCarthy's sensational, sex-filled best-selling novel about eight Vassar graduates in the 1930s, was filmed by Lumet on location in and around New York City. Most reviewers found fault with Sidney Buchman's script, either for being too faithful to McCarthy's sprawling book, and therefore unmanageable as cinematic material, or for downplaying the erotic elements just enough to render them maudlin. In *The Deadly Affair* (1967), filmed in England with James Mason in the lead, Lumet turned a mediocre story by John Le Carré into a superior spy movie. William Wolf expressed a wide consensus when he wrote for *Cue* (January 28, 1967): "Lumet makes Hitchcock seem passe. He has thoroughly mastered the art of creating suspense with a modern flair. His conception, style, choice of shots, backgrounds, and tempo add up to edge-of-the-seat thrills." Lumet next began filming an adaptation of *To an Early Grave*, a humorous novel by Wallace Markfield in which four men reminisce about their dead friend Leslie Braverman, an avant-garde writer. At the time Lumet called the project, titled *Bye Bye Braverman*, his most personal film, and said that its four post-Depression Jewish intellectuals were similar to people he had known while growing up—as well as his younger self. *Bye Bye Braverman* and Lumet's adaptation of Anton Chekhov's *The Sea Gull* were both released in 1968 to mixed reviews. Lumet followed with two disappointing films, *The Appointment*, in which a jealous husband suspects that his wife is a prostitute, and *Last of the Mobile Hot-Shots* (based on Tennessee Williams's play *Seven Descents of Myrtle*), in 1969. The following year he collaborated with Joseph L. Mankiewicz on the Oscar-nominated documentary film *King: A Film Record . . . Montgomery to Memphis*, about the slain civil rights leader Martin Luther King Jr.

Lumet's *The Anderson Tapes* (1971), a conspiracy thriller starring Sean Connery and Dyan Cannon, received modest reviews but proved to be a box-office hit, while the mystery-drama *Child's Play* (1972) was a flop both critically and commercially. In 1973 Lumet reteamed with Connery for the slow-moving character study *The Offence*, but despite Connery's strong performance the movie did not do well in theaters.

That same year, however, saw the beginning of Lumet's most successful string of films. *Serpico*, a thriller based on a true story, was the first of Lumet's celebrated studies of police corruption in New York City. Al Pacino won a Golden Globe Award for his performance as the title character, an honest policeman surrounded by crooked ones, and the picture earned two Oscar nominations. Lumet's adaptation of the Agatha Christie mystery *Murder on the Orient Express*, released in 1974, was also very successful, with critics noting not only the performances of the all-star cast (which included Albert Finney, Lauren Bacall, Sean Connery, and Ingrid Bergman), but also the beautiful photography, an area in which Lumet's films had not previously been praised. The movie earned six Oscar nominations and brought Bergman her third Academy Award. (*Lovin' Molly*, a drama about two friends who love the same woman, was released the same year but was less successful.)

The hit *Dog Day Afternoon*, which followed in 1975, details a bank robbery in New York City and featured Pacino in another standout performance—as a man seeking money for his lover's sex-change operation. It, too, earned six Academy Award nominations, including best picture, best director, and best actor, and won the best-original-screenplay trophy for Frank Pierson's script. While *Dog Day Afternoon* is generally regarded as one of Lumet's most accomplished films, he is perhaps best-known for his follow-up movie, *Network* (1976), a satire of the network-news industry that starred Faye Dunaway, William Holden, and Peter Finch and spawned the famous line, "I'm mad as hell, and I'm not going to take it anymore!" *Network* earned 10 Academy Award nominations, including those for best picture and best director, and won in four categories. Lumet won a Golden Globe Award for his direction of that film and Los Angeles Film Critics Association (LAFCA) awards for his direction of *Dog Day Afternoon* and *Network*. Both films garnered LAFCA awards for best picture as well.

Lumet's fortunes fell with his next three films. *Equus* (1977) featured Richard Burton, Joan Plowright, and Peter Firth in a screen adaptation of Peter Shaffer's Broadway drama about a psychiatrist helping a boy who has mutilated six horses. Despite the movie's lackluster box-office performance, Burton, Firth, and Shaffer's screenplay earned Oscar nominations. The fact that Lumet, who is known for completing his films ahead of schedule and under budget, went over his shooting schedule and projected costs on *The Wiz* (1978) was an early indicator of the film's problems. The adaptation of the Broadway musical (which was in turn an adaptation of *The Wizard of Oz* with an African-American cast) earned four Oscar nominations but was a critical and commercial misfire. (In it Lumet directed his former mother-in-law, Lena Horne, who portrayed Glinda the Good Witch.) *Just Tell Me What You Want* (1980), which Lumet directed and produced, was an uneven romantic comedy about the battle of the sexes that fared poorly, despite a lauded performance by Alan King.

Lumet won the New York Film Critics Circle Award for his direction of *Prince of the City* (1981), considered one of his best films. Starring Treat Williams (whom Lumet cast in the lead role after seeing him swing from a chandelier in the movie *Hair*), the multilayered film was adapted from Robert Daley's book about Bob Leuci, a New York City cop who blew the whistle on his colleagues' wrongdoing. The screenplay, by Lumet and Jay Presson Allen, earned an Academy Award nomination, while the picture, Lumet, and Williams earned Golden Globe nominations. "It is the director's most mature and restrained work, devoid of the excesses of which he is sometimes guilty," William Wolf wrote in his *New York* article. The two-hour-and-47-minute film was shot in 131 locations around New York City. Discussing his fascination with the theme of corruption, particularly among police and within the criminal-justice system, Lumet explained to Terry Diggs for the *Legal Times* (May 1, 1995), "I grew up very poor in the roughest sections in New York, and you simply become very interested in justice because you see an awful lot of injustice around." He added later in the interview, "It's not that I'm against the justice system as it exists in America. Hardly that. I not only have the greatest respect for it. . . . I think it's a miracle that it works as well as it does. But I think it has to be constantly checked. It has to be constantly questioned because it has to be kept honest."

Deathtrap (1982), Lumet's next film, was adapted from a long-running play by Ira Levin about a Broadway playwright, desperate for a hit, who plans to murder a younger writer and steal his script. The year 1982 also saw the release of the compelling courtroom drama *The Verdict*, starring Paul Newman, James Mason, Jack Warden, and Charlotte Rampling. The picture, Lumet, Newman, Mason, and David Mamet's adapted screenplay earned Academy Award nominations. The film tells the story of an alcoholic lawyer (Newman) who takes a medical-malpractice suit to trial, instead of settling out of court, in order to obtain justice for his client and redemption for himself. In a recent interview with M.S. Mason for the *Christian Science Monitor* (October 7, 2005), Lumet singled *Verdict* out as possibly his favorite among his 45 films. After *The Verdict* came the controversial drama *Daniel* (1983), an adaptation of E.L. Doctorow's novel *The Book of Daniel*, which was inspired by the story of Julius and Ethel Rosenberg,

who were executed in 1953 for spying for the Soviet Union. Timothy Hutton starred in the story of a brother and sister whose parents were executed for alleged espionage.

Lumet's reputation fell a bit with his next few films. The forgettable comedy *Garbo Talks* (1984) was followed by the thriller *The Morning After* (1986), which brought Jane Fonda an Oscar nomination (for her role as a woman who must clear her name after waking up next to a dead man with no memory of how she got there) but otherwise generated little interest. *Power* (1986), which starred Richard Gere as a cynical political campaign adviser, was equally disappointing. The director's fortunes rose again, however, with the release of *Running on Empty* (1988). The movie tells the tale of a family of four who are on the run from the FBI, routinely leaving one town for another, because the parents (played by Christine Lahti and Judd Hirsch) participated in a bomb attack on a napalm lab in 1971 as a protest against the war in Vietnam. The couple's teenage son (River Phoenix) develops a romantic relationship with a girl (Martha Plimpton) and wants to stay with her and study music at Juilliard, but knows that such a decision would destroy his family. Phoenix earned an Oscar nomination for his moving performance, Lahti won a Los Angeles Film Teachers' Association (LAFTA) award for her role, and Naomi Foner's screenplay won a Golden Globe Award and earned an Oscar nomination. The film also earned Golden Globe nominations for best picture, best director, best actress, and best actor. "Lumet is one of the best directors at work today, and his skill here is in the way he takes a melodramatic plot and makes it real by making it specific. . . . This is one of the best films of the year," Roger Ebert wrote in a review for the *Chicago Sun-Times* (September 23, 1988, online).

The disappointing gangster comedy *Family Business* was released in 1989. Next came the police thriller *Q & A* (1990). Lumet earned his first solo writing credit for that adaptation of Edwin Torres's novel, about a crooked detective (Nick Nolte) being investigated for a shooting death; Nolte and his co-stars, Timothy Hutton and Armand Assante, were praised by critics for their performances. Less well-received were *A Stranger Among Us* (1992), in which Melanie Griffith played a police detective who goes undercover among a sect of Orthodox Jews in New York to solve a murder, and the courtroom thriller *Guilty as Sin* (1993). In 1995 Lumet published a best-selling filmmaking primer. *Making Movies* (1995) eschews gossip about the actors, writers, and other film personalities he has worked with over the years while including anecdotes illuminating the ways in which a number of well-known performers approach roles. The book is a guide through all aspects of filmmaking, from the use of lighting, camera angles, and lenses to location shooting, sound mixing, and editing, as well as a reflection on the contributions of writers, art directors, and composers to movies.

The crime drama *Night Falls on Manhattan*, which Lumet adapted from Robert Daley's novel, was released in 1997. Starring Andy Garcia, Richard Dreyfuss, Lena Olin, and Ian Holm, the film is thematically similar to *Serpico*, *Prince of the City*, and *Q & A*. As with *Prince of the City*, Lumet received praise for crafting morally complex characters whose actions often fall in the gray area between right and wrong. "*Night Falls on Manhattan* is absorbing precisely because we cannot guess who is telling the truth, or what morality some of the characters possess. . . . Here intelligence is required from the characters: They're feeling their way," Ebert wrote in a May 1997 review for the *Chicago Sun-Times*. That same year Lumet released *Critical Care*. While that hospital satire was widely criticized for being heavy-handed, Rita Kempley expressed the opinion of a number of reviewers when she described the film in the *Washington Post* (November 14, 1997) as "a darkly comic meditation on the quality of life, the right to die and a peek into the afterlife" and as being "no less conscientious or entertaining than his deeper, more caustic works." Lumet's next project, *Gloria* (1999), was a remake of John Cassavetes's 1980 film of the same name, featuring Sharon Stone in the title role originated by Gena Rowlands. James Berardinelli summed up many critics' feelings when he asserted in his on-line review that the film was full of "pointless violence" and "unnecessary plot contrivances" and that it "only the deepens the question of where this film maker's talent has gone." *Gloria* made a quick exit from theaters.

In 2001 Lumet returned to television after 40 years, directing and producing the weekly courtroom drama *100 Centre Street* for the A&E cable network. The show, which took its title from the address of Manhattan's Criminal Courts Building, told the stories of prosecutors, defense attorneys, and alleged criminals and had night court as its primary setting. Lumet had begun thinking 20 years earlier of creating such a series. "The opening sequence of *Prince of the City* took place in night court, where I'd never been," he told Steve Chagollan for *Variety* (October 30–November 5, 2000). "And literally the first impression I came away with was this could be the best television series I ever made because the life of it is so extraordinary. Dramatically, you could go just about anywhere." *100 Centre Street* ended its run in 2002. In 2004 Lumet directed the film *Strip Search* for the HBO cable network and a short film, *Rachel, quand du seigneur*. His next film, tentatively titled "Find Me Guilty," based on the criminal trial of the mobster Giacomo "Fat Jack" DiNorscio and starring Vin Diesel, was scheduled for release in 2006.

Lumet, who has said that he does not read reviews of his films or watch his movies once they have been released, is critical of the present state of filmmaking in the U.S. "It's getting a lot harder," he told Jeff Craig for the *Edmonton Sun* (April 27, 1997). "It's turned into such a star-driven industry. The studios are getting out of the content-driven picture business so they can sell T-shirts and theme parks." A workaholic, Lumet keeps a pace that exceeds that of many of his younger colleagues. "Some of the happiest days of my life were in that period when I once directed three films in two years," he told Koltnow. "A lot of today's young directors, and even some directors from my generation, tend to coddle themselves. There's no such thing as a wasted film for a director. Every time you look through that lens, you learn something new." Lumet's films have received more than 50 Academy Award nominations, including four nominations for Lumet as best director (for *Twelve Angry Men*, *Dog Day Afternoon*, *Network*, and *The Verdict*), and he has also received seven Directors Guild of America Award nominations. "The whole Academy Award thing is such a fantasy," he told Larry Ratliff for the *San Antonio Express-News* (May 16, 1997) of the elusive recognition. "It's catching lightning in a bottle. None of it has much reality for me." In addition to the 2005 Academy Award for lifetime achievement, Lumet's many honors include the Directors Guild's prestigious D. W. Griffith Award, given for an unusually distinguished body of work. The Museum of Modern Art in New York honored him with a retrospective, as has virtually every major international film academy. In 1997 he was given the Billy Wilder Award for Excellence and Achievement in Film Direction from the National Board of Review as well as the Writers Guild of America's Evelyn Burkey Award for his contribution to films that have brought dignity and honor to writers. In February 2004 the actor Paul Newman presented him with the Joseph L. Mankiewicz Excellence in Film Award from the Director's View Film Festival, and in October 2005 Lumet was the subject of a documentary and a two-day-long abbreviated retrospective of his work on the cable TV channel Turner Classic Movies.

Lumet is unusual among American directors in that he has never made a picture in Hollywood; most of his films have been shot in his beloved New York City. The liberal-leaning Lumet is known as a quiet and modest man; he usually wears jeans and sneakers, whether working or relaxing. The five-foot five-inch director is credited with helping revive the historic Kaufman-Astoria Studios in the New York City borough of Queens, shooting many of his projects there. His first three marriages, to the actress Rita Gam, the heiress and designer Gloria Vanderbilt, and Gail Jones (daughter of the actress and singer Lena Horne), ended in divorce. In 1980 he married Mary Gimbel. He has two daughters, Amy and Jenny, and a son, Ed. When asked by the *New York Times Magazine* (November 23, 1997) how he wanted to "go out" when he dies, the longtime New Yorker replied, "I don't think about it. I'm not religious. . . . Burn me up and scatter my ashes over Katz's Delicatessen."

—K.E.D.

Suggested Reading: Associated Press May 16, 1997; *Edmonton Sun* (on-line) Apr. 27, 1997; *Film and Filming* p11+ Aug. 1989, with photos; *GQ* p209+ Sep. 1988, with photos; *San Antonio Express-News* H p7 May 16, 1997, with photo; *Washington Post* L p1+ Aug. 23, 1981, with photos

Selected Films: *Twelve Angry Men*, 1957; *The Fugitive Kind*, 1960; *Long Day's Journey into Night*, 1962; *Fail Safe*, 1964; *The Pawnbroker*, 1965; *The Hill*, 1965; *The Group*, 1966; *The Deadly Affair*, 1967; *Bye Bye Braverman*, 1968; *The Sea Gull*, 1968; *The Appointment*, 1969; *King: A Filmed Record . . . Montgomery to Memphis* (with Joseph L. Mankiewicz), 1970; *The Anderson Tapes*, 1971; *The Offence*, 1973;

Serpico, 1973; *Murder on the Orient Express*, 1974; *Dog Day Afternoon*, 1975; *Network*, 1976; *Equus*, 1977; *The Wiz*, 1978; *Prince of the City*, 1981; *Deathtrap*, 1982; *The Verdict*, 1982; *Daniel*, 1983; *Garbo Talks*, 1984; *The Morning After*, 1986; *Power*, 1986; *Running on Empty*, 1988; *Family Business*, 1989; *Q&A*, 1990; *Guilty as Sin*, 1993; *Night Falls on Manhattan*, 1997; *Gloria*, 1999; *Strip Search*, 2004

Selected Television Series: *Danger*, 1950; *You Are There*, 1952; *Playhouse 90*, 1956; *Mr Broadway*, 1957; *All the King's Men*, 1958; *The Sacco-Vanzetti Story*, 1959; *The Iceman Cometh*, 1960; *100 Centre Street*, 2001–02

Selected Books: *Making Movies*, 1995

Courtesy of the *New Yorker*

Mankoff, Robert

May 1, 1944– Cartoonist; cartoon editor of the New Yorker; founder of the Cartoon Bank

Address: The New Yorker, 4 Times Sq., New York, NY 10036-6592

"Humor is a valid way of thinking about the world," the *New Yorker*'s cartoon editor, Robert Mankoff, commented during an interview with Calvin Reid for *Publishers Weekly* (September 20, 2004). "It keeps people in perspective. It's like saying, 'Yeah, the big shots, they've all got suits on but they don't know what they're talking about.' Cartoonists level the playing field." A cartoonist in his

own right, Mankoff is known for creating images that poke fun at the business world and other seats of power. His trademark drawing style differs from those of many others in the field in its use of dots instead of crosshatching or ink washes to indicate shaded areas. "I guess my stipple drawing technique is idiosyncratic," he told Bob Staake for the Planet Cartoonist Web site (2001). "As a kid, I was always fascinated by the way newspaper halftones looked and was intrigued that a drawing could be created by connecting the dots." Since he began his professional career in cartooning, three decades ago, Mankoff has edited several book-length cartoon anthologies, published book-length collections of his own cartoons, and seen more than 800 of his drawings printed in the *New Yorker*, including one of the magazine's most popular cartoons ever: an image of a businessman on the phone, reviewing his calendar and saying, "No, Thursday's out. How about never—is never good for you?" In tandem with his work for the *New Yorker*, he is also a successful entrepreneur who founded the Cartoon Bank, a Web site that sells single-panel cartoons (also known as "gag cartoons") by the *New Yorker*'s contracted artists, as well as the reproduction rights to those cartoons.

One consideration that Mankoff has had to weigh in his capacity as cartoon editor is how to achieve a balance between cartoons that focus on current events and those that address broader themes. "*New Yorker* cartoons have a unique power to be both timely and timeless," he explained to Michael Kilian for the *Chicago Tribune* (December 8, 1999). In contrast to the "timeless" cartoons created by James Thurber and others who helped to define the magazine's unique aesthetic, many of the cartoons now published in the *New Yorker* are more topical, much to the expressed annoyance of some readers. Others have complained of declining standards in the quality of the drawings in the magazine; indeed, Mankoff has not hesitated to admit that he gives priority to good ideas over good draftsmanship. "The essence of cartooning, and certainly single-panel cartooning, is the idea," he told Ben Greenman for the *New Yorker*'s Web site (November 11, 2004). "Getting the idea is ninety-five percent of the battle." During an interview with Robyn Leary for the *Washington Post* (December 7, 1997), he even argued in favor of less-than-stellar draftsmanship, saying, "You need a very loose style to make certain jokes work. You don't want them drawn very well. I mean, if you have any scene, let's say, in which there's a guillotine on which someone's head is chopped off, which can be a very funny cartoon, . . . you certainly don't want it drawn very realistically—you don't want a great draftsman working on this." Nevertheless, Mankoff is far from casual about cartooning. "I'm an evangelist for the form," he told Laura T. Ryan for the Syracuse, New York, *Post-Standard* (October 24, 2004). "I believe in cartoons and cartoonists."

The son of affluent Jewish parents, Robert Mankoff was born on May 1, 1944 in the New York City borough of Queens. As a child he enjoyed drawing cartoons in the margins of his notebooks. After he graduated from the High School of Music and Art (now known as the Fiorello H. LaGuardia High School of Music & Art and Performing Arts), in Manhattan, he enrolled at Syracuse University, in upstate New York. More interested in drawing than schoolwork, he attended classes so infrequently that one of his professors had no idea who he was when he showed up to take the final examination. However, he completed all the required coursework and was awarded a B.A. degree in 1966.

A few years later Mankoff enrolled as a doctoral student of experimental psychology at the City College of New York. He dropped out in 1974 to devote himself more fully to drawing. "Actually, what happened is my pigeon died," he recalled to Jim Reisler for the *New York Times* (October 31, 1999). "I had miscalculated in a psychology experiment and the pigeon I was experimenting on didn't get enough to eat and just keeled over. I took that as a sign that I should move on." Mankoff's parents, particularly his father, disapproved of his decision, pointing out that there were already plenty of other cartoonists on the market. "Yeah, Dad. But maybe one of them will die. Maybe I'll get lucky," Mankoff joked, as he recalled to Ryan.

In 1975, after about a year of drawing full-time on his own, Mankoff sold his first cartoon. Published in the *Saturday Review*, the image showed Superman at a personnel office, handing in a résumé that lists his qualifications: "able to leap tall buildings," "faster than a speeding bullet," and so on. Unimpressed, the interviewer asks, "What, no steno?"

Mankoff sold his first cartoon to the *New Yorker* in 1977. During an interview with Craig Wilson for *USA Today* (October 2, 1997), he admitted that he was so nervous about submitting his work to the magazine that he mistook the Princeton Club, a luxurious neighboring establishment, for the *New Yorker*'s offices. "I walked in and saw all that wood and I said, 'Oh, I can't!,'" he recalled. Intimidated, he returned to his home in Brooklyn. After he realized his mistake, he went to the correct address and submitted his drawings; one was purchased for $250.

In 1980 the *New Yorker* gave Mankoff a contract, which served as an official invitation to submit work to the magazine. (It did not guarantee that his images would be published.) From then on, he joined 20 or so other contracted cartoonists each Tuesday in the office of Lee Lorenz, then the magazine's cartoon editor, to drop off cartoons for consideration. Although each artist submitted about a dozen images per week, only about 15 in total were selected for publication. "What you see in the *New Yorker* is the tippy tippy top of the iceberg," he told Bryan Miller during an interview for the *New York Times* (September 11, 1994). In 1992, confident that there must be a market for the rest of the "iceberg," he began drawing up plans for an on-line archive of cartoons for sale to private individuals and publishers of textbooks, newsletters, and advertisements, among others. He pitched the concept for what he named the Cartoon Bank—described by Staake as "a brilliantly simple, yet completely digitized, filing cabinet of sorts filled with . . . scanned, cataloged, cross-indexed and key-worded gag cartoons"—to the *New Yorker*, suggesting that, along with unpublished images by *New Yorker* cartoonists, the magazine might successfully market reprints from its collection of more than 70,000 cartoons. He received a tepid response, so he decided to start the company on his own. "At that time," he recalled to Staake, "the *New Yorker* didn't want to give me the cream of the crop, so I decided to take the crop."

In order to fund his new business venture, Mankoff obtained several small-business loans, which he supplemented with his own savings. He rented an office in Yonkers, New York; purchased a computer and scanner; and made electronic versions of about 4,000 drawings that had been rejected by the *New Yorker*, which he agreed to display on the Web site in exchange for 50 percent of the profits from each sale. He then organized the images under broad subject headings, personally contacted potential clients, and gave away a few original drawings as inducements.

Because the startup cost of the Cartoon Bank was relatively low, Mankoff began to reap profits within only a few months. As Bryan Miller wrote for the *New York Times* (September 11, 1994), "The startup company [was] a business based on a good idea and a few thousand dollars' worth of modern computer technology. And it [was] also a solution to the endemic problem faced by professional cartoonists: how to make use of—and some money on—their libraries of unpublished work." In 1994, two years after its inception, the Cartoon Bank published its first book: a collection of drawings organized around the theme of parenting. Titled *Now That You Can Walk, Go Get Me a Beer*, the book was published by Fireside Books, a division of Simon & Schuster. The Bank's second book, *This Could Be the Start of Something Stupid: A Book for Love and Laughter* (1995), dealt with romantic relationships. By the late 1990s the Bank had become such a successful business that the *New Yorker* took notice. In January 1997 the magazine purchased the Cartoon Bank from Mankoff and began scanning and indexing the thousands of cartoons that had appeared in its pages over the past 70 years. Today the Web site allows visitors to search a database of about 85,000 cartoons by keyword and buy unpublished cartoons ranging in price from $125 for matted prints to $10,000 for original pieces of artwork.

Also in 1997 Mankoff succeeded Lorenz as cartoon editor of the *New Yorker*, a position that he has described repeatedly during interviews as his "dream job." "I'm honored but not intimidated, because between us, it's just looking at cartoons," he said during an interview for the National Cartoonists Society (NCS) Web site. "You want to be careful and discriminating, but if you're a cartoonist and you've been doing this for 20 years, I have the confidence that I can distinguish funny from unfunny." Tina Brown, then the *New Yorker*'s editor in chief, explained to Ted Koppel for ABC News (December 12, 1997) why she appointed Mankoff to the post: "He's got a very edgy, very contemporary, very original, very funny, very risky kind of humor and I found I was always buying his stuff."

Each week the *New Yorker* receives thousands of cartoon submissions, including hundreds from contracted artists. Mankoff looks at each one, brings about 30 to the weekly art meeting, and, together with the magazine's other editors, selects between 15 and 20 for purchase. Over the past several years, one of his missions has been to make the cartoons even more of a signature component of the magazine. Toward that end, in December 1997 he compiled a large group of images that were published in the *New Yorker*'s first-ever Cartoon Issue—a special issue devoted almost entirely to cartoons and the subject of cartooning. Since that time, the Cartoon Issue has become an annual tradition, appearing each December. In addition, Mankoff has expressed interest in signing on more cartoonists from underrepresented demographic groups, including females and homosexuals. "I want to treasure the cartoonists that we have," he told Constance L. Hays for the *New York Times* (June 9, 1997), "but I also want to bring in new voices. . . . I want them to describe the world, the whole world. I would prefer cartoons about topics I've never even thought of."

In 2002 Mankoff published *The Naked Cartoonist: A New Way to Enhance Your Creativity*, a book detailing his thoughts on the creative process in general and cartooning in particular. Ben Greenman described it as "an odd hybrid between a psychology text—there's a lot of speculation about how the creative mind works—and a cartoon col-

lection." Recalling his days as a student of psychology to Greenman, Mankoff explained, "I have always been interested in why people think the way they do, and specifically in how ideas are generated."

In 2004 Mankoff edited *The Complete Cartoons of The New Yorker*, a coffee-table book celebrating the magazine's 80th anniversary and containing about 2,000 of the 68,647 cartoons that had appeared in the magazine since its 1925 debut. (The rest of the cartoons are included on two CDs that accompany the book.) Critics hailed the volume as not only an entertaining read but also a valuable historical document chronicling the evolution of American humor over the past eight decades. "What [Mankoff] wound up with," Joel Stein wrote for *Time* (October 11, 2004), "is not only a stand-up routine for smart people who own a coffee table but a history of American culture. You can see how confused and fascinated New Yorkers were by skyscrapers in the 1930s, how threatened and angered men were by workingwomen after World War II and how uncomfortable Americans were with the growing ubiquity of television in the '50s."

Recently, Mankoff was enlisted by the Department of Psychology at the University of Michigan to participate in a scientific examination of humor; the study will be based on various cultural products, including the *New Yorker*'s database of cartoons. "I'm going to do for humor what [the sex therapists William Howell] Masters and [Virginia Eshelman] Johnson did for sex," he told Ryan. "Humor is an important factor in what we do and how we live or else it wouldn't be completely ubiquitous."

Robert Mankoff lives in Hastings-on-Hudson, New York, with his wife, Cory Scott Whittier, who works in the direct-mail marketing business and is the vice president of the Cartoon Bank, and their grown children. When asked whether there are any openings for new cartoonists at the magazine, he has been known to reply, "Are the New York Yankees open to new hitters? Sure, they've just got to be able to hit it into the stands," as quoted by Calvin Reid. During his interview with Staake, he offered the following words of advice for young cartoonists: "Don't think ahead, don't worry about whether you can make a living, just absolutely go at cartooning. Because if you were to know what hurdles you'd face, you'd never get involved in it. You have to in some way delude yourself with optimism." Mankoff is optimistic about the future of his art. "I believe we're entering into a golden age of cartooning," he told the NCS interviewer. "I'm enthusiastic about that. . . . The best part will be nurturing the wonderful talent that we have and finding a whole new generation of people to carry it on."

—L.W.

Suggested Reading: *Chicago Tribune* p1+ Dec. 8, 1999, p1+ Oct. 20, 2004; *New York Times* III p3+ Sep. 11, 1994, D p1+ June 9, 1997; *USA Today* D p1+ Oct. 2, 1997

Selected Books: *Elementary: The Cartoonist Did It*, 1980; *Urban Bumpkins*, 1984; *Call Your Office*, 1986; *It's Lonely at the Top*, 1988; *The Naked Cartoonist: A New Way to Enhance Your Creativity*, 2002; as editor—*The New Yorker Book of Business Cartoons*, 1998; *The New Yorker Book of Money Cartoons*, 1999; *The New Yorker Book of Political Cartoons*, 2000; *The New Yorker Book of Literary Cartoons*, 2000; *The New Yorker Book of Technology Cartoons*, 2000; *The New Yorker Book of Kids Cartoons*, 2001; *The New Yorker Book of Golf Cartoons*, 2002; *The New Yorker Book of Baseball Cartoons*, 2003; *The Complete Cartoons of The New Yorker*, 2004; *The New Yorker Book of New York Cartoons*, 2004; *The New Yorker Book of Art Cartoons*, 2005

Photo by Garrett W. Ellwood/NBAE via Getty Images

Martin, Kenyon

Dec. 30, 1977– Basketball player

Address: Denver Nuggets, 1000 Chopper Circle, Denver, CO 80204

In his five years with the National Basketball Association (NBA), Kenyon Martin has established himself as one of the best power forwards in the league. Nicknamed K-mart and distinguished by his fierce facial expressions and bold tattoos, Martin is an exceptionally versatile athlete whose strengths include scoring, defending, rebounding, passing, and running the floor. The muscular, six-foot nine-inch, 240-pound Martin joined the New Jersey Nets as the first overall pick in the 2000 NBA

draft. His selection followed an outstanding four-year career with the University of Cincinnati (UC) Bearcats, during which he played with the gold-medal–winning U.S. team at the 1999 World University Games. As a senior at UC he averaged 18.9 points, 9.7 rebounds, and 3.45 blocks per game; he was recognized as perhaps the best undergraduate men's-basketball player in the U.S. that year and won a bevy of college basketball's most prestigious honors, among them the John R. Wooden Award and the Naismith Award. Writing for *Sports Illustrated* (February 7, 2000) a few months before Martin launched his career as a pro, in 2000, Grant Wahl expressed the opinion that he was "best described not as a center or a forward but rather . . . as a Cincinnati strongman. After all, his dunks are not dunks. They're detonations. He doesn't just block shots. He often catches them. More than any other player in the nation, Martin visibly frightens opposing players." Phil Ford, who, as a coach for the University of North Carolina Tar Heels, watched him in action, said of Martin to Wahl, "He gets a lot of credit for the blocks, but they haven't created a stat yet for what I call 'scares,' all the shots he makes people miss just by his presence around the basket."

Until his final season with the Nets, Martin often lost his temper during games and drew many technical or flagrant fouls for such unsportsmanlike conduct as fighting with opposing players or arguing too vehemently with referees; he has since become more disciplined on the court. Thanks in large part to Martin, as well as point guard Jason Kidd and small forward Richard Jefferson, the Nets rid themselves of the stigma of mediocrity—or outright inferiority—and became two-time Eastern Conference Champions, in 2002 and 2003. In July 2004, following the Nets' disappointing 2003–04 campaign, Martin chose to be traded to the Denver Nuggets. His seven-year contract totaled $92.5 million—a figure higher than that of any other contract in Nugget history. "Anytime you have a chance to add a player of the stature of Kenyon Martin, somebody who has been to the finals, who has been an All-Star, who plays with the ferocity that he plays with, that is an opportunity you really can't pass up," Kiki Vandeweghe, the Nuggets' general manager, said, as quoted by Chris Sheridan for the Associated Press (July 15, 2004, on-line).

Kenyon Lee Martin was born in Saginaw, Michigan, on December 30, 1977. While he was growing up, his mother, Lydia Moore—whose given name is tattooed on Martin's right shoulder—earned a meager living as a telemarketer and restaurant worker. His father, Paul Roby, who is six feet five inches tall, was an outstanding basketball player in high school and played center at the University of New Mexico in 1978–80, but never became a pro, in part because of knee problems; he had no role in Martin's upbringing. In the *Cincinnati Post* (October 26, 2000, on-line), Lonnie Wheeler wrote that Martin "has rarely talked to his father over the years." According to various sources, Martin has had only one face-to-face encounter with his father, which occurred before his adolescence. One day within the past few years, Chris Tomasson reported for the *Rocky Mountain News* (July 20, 2004), Roby attended a Nets game and asked to speak with his son, but Martin refused. Referring to that incident, Martin said to Tomasson, "I'm a grown man now. I don't need [a father now]." "My mom is my backbone," he told Tomasson. "She was my mother and my father growing up. She did the best job that she could raising me." Martin's half-sister Tamara Ridley told Marc J. Spears for the *Denver Post* (October 27, 2004, on-line) that both she and Martin have other siblings (or half-siblings), "but we were the only two that my mom reared." Although Ridley is less than four years his senior, she acted like a parent to Martin, beginning when he was still in diapers; years later, when he was applying for college, Liz Robbins wrote for the *New York Times* (July 31, 2000, on-line), he listed his sister wherever the forms called for his father's name. "I was always fussing after him," Ridley told Robbins. "I wanted him to succeed."

During his early years Martin's mother moved with him and Tamara to the Oak Cliff section of Dallas, Texas, which was then an extremely rough neighborhood, rife with gang activity, drug traffic, and violent crime. Martin was often taunted and bullied by other children, because he stuttered badly. Despite speech therapy in elementary and junior high school, the stutter remained, and he usually refused to speak in class, to avoid suffering humiliation in front of his peers. Instead, he endured whatever punishment his teachers or his mother meted out for his disobedience. His stutter "made me have a tough skin, always have a chip on my shoulder," as he told Spears. Martin, who joined the board of directors of the American Institute for Stuttering Treatment and Professional Training in 2004, also told Spears, "There is nothing I can do about [my stutter] at this time. I've been dealing with it all my life. But I've learned how to channel it and deal with it."

For a year or so in his teens, Martin attended the Tyler Street Christian Academy, near where he lived. In 1994 he represented the school as a member of the TAPPS (Texas Association of Private and Parochial Schools) All-State boys basketball team. He later transferred to a public secondary school and then to another: Bryan Adams High School, also in Dallas, where he stood out on the school's basketball team. The presence of his mother and sister at virtually every game during his high-school years strongly bolstered his morale. When he failed to complete his homework, his mother would forbid him to participate in basketball practice—the most effective way to chastise him, as she had discovered. In his senior year he averaged 18 points, 14 rebounds, and 6.5 blocked shots per game—numbers that made him a desirable prospect in the eyes of recruiters from several of the top colleges in the U.S., among them several in Texas: Texas Christian University, Baylor University, and

the University of Houston. Martin chose to accept a scholarship from an institution outside Texas: the University of Cincinnati, in Ohio. He did so despite the school's being too far away for his mother and sister to attend games, because its men's basketball program, led since 1989 by Bob Huggins, the head coach, had produced one of the most successful teams in the nation, and he believed that playing for that team, the Bearcats, would enhance his post-college prospects. When Martin entered the university, Huggins told Robbins, despite his innate talent, he "didn't have any skills" and "his mechanics were really bad"; moreover, he failed to score high enough on the SATs to play college basketball until a retest at the end of his first freshman term.

During his four years with the Bearcats (1996–2000), Martin steadily improved and, according to Huggins, gained confidence. As a freshman he averaged only 2.8 points per game, and he sank only 10 of 32 shots from the foul line, or fewer than one third; in his senior year, he averaged 18.9 points (13th-best in the nation that year) and 9.7 rebounds (eighth-best) per game, and he sank 141 of 206 foul-line shots (68.4 percent). In his sophomore year he achieved a triple double (that is, reaching numbers of 10 or more in three categories), with 24 points, 23 rebounds, and 10 blocks. "He was a hard worker and a great listener," Huggins told Chris Tomasson. "He listens better than any player that I've ever coached. He knew what every player on the court was supposed to do." In his last two years at Cincinnati, Martin unofficially helped coach his fellow players as well. He was a member of the U.S. men's team that captured a gold medal after winning all eight games at the 1999 World University Games, held in Palma de Mallorca, Spain.

Martin won an extraordinary number of college basketball awards. As a senior he was named the National Player of the Year by the Associated Press, the National Association of Basketball Coaches (NABC), and the U.S. Basketball Writers Association. He also won the two most prestigious honors in college basketball: the Naismith and Wooden Awards (named, respectively, in honor of James Naismith, who is credited with the creation of the sport of basketball, and John R. Wooden, the legendary coach of the UCLA Bruins). In addition, he was a consensus First Team All-American and the Conference USA Player of the Year, and for the third consecutive season, he was named the Conference USA Defensive Player of the Year.

Martin's—and the Bearcats'—1999–2000 season ended in disappointment, however, because on March 9, 2000, while on the court, Martin broke a fibula (the biggest bone in the lower part of the leg), leaving him unable to play in the National Collegiate Athletic Association (NCAA) tournament that year and effectively ending the team's chances for advancing to the national championship. His rehabilitation included treatment at the Kerlan-Jobe Orthopaedic Clinic, in Los Angeles, California, and several hours a day of prescribed workouts. He graduated from the University of Cincinnati in 2000 with a bachelor's degree in criminal justice.

Martin was the first overall pick in the 2000 NBA draft. According to Liz Robbins, he "dissolved in sobs" when he heard that the New Jersey Nets had chosen him. Martin was only the second number-one draft selection in Nets' franchise history. (The other was Derrick Coleman, who came on board in 1990.) A first-time coach, the former Los Angeles Lakers' star Byron Scott, led the Nets during Martin's rookie season (2000–01), and the team was hobbled by the absence (due to injuries) of two important players, Kerry Kittles and Keith Van Horn. In his first NBA game, on October 31, 2000, against the Cleveland Cavaliers, Martin scored 10 points and grabbed seven rebounds. That November he was named rookie of the month. During the season he averaged 12 points per game and led his teammates in average numbers of rebounds (7.4) and blocks (1.66) per contest. In a game against the Milwaukee Bucks in March 2001, Martin recorded the first triple double of his pro career, scoring 18 points, snatching 15 rebounds, and making 11 assists. He was the only rookie to record a triple double that season.

In a game against the Boston Celtics, in March 2001, Martin again fractured his fibula (not at the site of his earlier injury, and less severely), sidelining him for the remaining 12 games of the season. The injury occurred after Martin had been named NBA co-rookie of the month for March. He finished the season second among all NBA rookies in scoring and rebounding and first among all rookies in average number of blocks and steals per game, and he was named to the NBA All-Rookie First Team. Despite Martin's considerable contributions, the Nets won only 26 games of the season's total, 82, and missed the play-offs for the third consecutive year.

The 2001–02 season was a franchise best for the Nets, who received a huge boost from the acquisition of the All-Star point guard Jason Kidd. Martin led the team in average number of points (14.9), rebounds (5.3), and blocked shots (1.66) per game. He slammed home 108 dunks, the fourth-highest number in the NBA that season. His intense competitiveness also manifested itself in the number of technical and flagrant fouls he committed. (A flagrant foul is called when the referees deem that a foul was committed with the intention, or at too great a risk, of causing physical harm to an opposing player.) Martin's six flagrant fouls, the most in the NBA that season, earned him a reputation as a volatile and sometimes dirty player. The fines and suspensions from play that Martin incurred resulted in his losing more than $300,000 in salary. Nonetheless, with Martin and Kidd leading the team's quick, potent offense, the Nets won 52 games in the regular season, the most in the team's history, and won the Atlantic Division and the Eastern Conference Championship to reach the NBA Finals for the first time. In the Finals the Nets

proved to be no match for the formidable Lakers, who, led by superstars Kobe Bryant and Shaquille O'Neal, won four games in a row to claim their third-straight NBA crown.

Playing in a career-high 77 games during the 2002–03 season, Martin shot 47 percent from the field and set what were then career highs in average number of points (16.7), rebounds (8.4), and steals (1.27) per game. He led the Nets in rebounding and blocked shots and was second on the team in scoring. Martin again recorded the fourth-highest number of dunks in the league, with 113. In addition, he recorded both his highest-scoring game (35) and his highest number of rebounds in a game (21) as of that date. Also of note, and an important factor in his improved play, was Martin's increasing ability to control his temper. (Four other NBA players committed more technical fouls than he did in 2002–03, and he committed only two flagrant fouls.) "I've grown up a lot since last year," Martin told Skip Wood for USA Today (May 9, 2004). "I don't know what [prompted it]; it's just maturing. . . . I still play hard. I go 110% every day. I still have the same aggressiveness, I'm just trying to save my money [by not incurring fines] and stay away from the stupid things I did last year." Martin helped the Nets win their division, with a 49–33 regular-season record, and defeat both the Boston Celtics and the Detroit Pistons in the play-offs to reach the NBA Finals. The Nets performed well, but they failed to overcome the San Antonio Spurs in the championship series. Led by the All-Star big men David Robinson and Tim Duncan, the Spurs defeated the Nets for the NBA title, four games to two.

In 2003–04 the Nets won two fewer regular-season games than they had the previous year and lost to the Detroit Pistons in the hard-fought Eastern Conference semifinals, four games to three. Martin, however, had continued to excel, in both the regular season and the play-offs. He put 49 percent of his field-goal attempts in the basket and averaged 16.7 points and 9.5 rebounds per game during the regular season, all of which were career highs for him. For his performance Martin was named an NBA All-Star for the first time. In 51 career play-off games with the Nets, Martin averaged an impressive 18.1 points and 8.3 rebounds per game.

In the summer of 2004, Martin was wooed by the Atlanta Hawks and the Denver Nuggets. The Nuggets offered Martin a six-year contract worth $83 million, which included a large signing bonus. (The final contract amounted to $92.5 million for seven years.) For financial reasons, the Nets chose not to match Denver's offer and were forced to trade Martin to the Nuggets for three future first-round draft choices. Many basketball observers characterized the move as a terrible blow to the Nets' short-term prospects—as well as a big disappointment for many Nets fans. "It's an honor being here," Martin told the Associated Press (July 19, 2004) in reference to the Nuggets. "It was a great run in Jersey, but it was time for a change. I'm glad to be a part of this."

During his first season with the Nuggets, Martin maintained a high level of play despite problems with his left knee and the rocky start by his new team, which collected 25 losses and 17 wins under its interim head coach, Michael Cooper. In late January 2005 George Karl took over as head coach, and the Nuggets ended the season with a win–loss ratio of 49–33, enabling them to enter the Western Conference play-offs as the seventh seed. The team lost in the first round to the eventual NBA champions, the San Antonio Spurs. Because of the pain in his knee, Martin did not start in any of the Nuggets' five play-off games. During the regular season, he achieved the team's second-highest averages in scoring (15.6) and rebounding (7.3). He started in 67 of the 70 regular-season games and made 444 out of 907 field goals, 170 assists, 100 steals, and 78 blocks. Out of 58 attempted field goals, he made 27, as well as five blocks, five steals, and six assists. He also accumulated 17 technical fouls over the course of the year, the fourth-highest number in the NBA, and earned one flagrant foul.

In May 2005 Martin underwent surgery on his left knee, and after an almost four-month-long period in which he was forbidden to jump, he returned to the court to practice in September; by his own account, he felt better than he had since the 2002–03 season. "I can jump with no pain," he told Chris Tomasson for the Scripps Howard News Service (October 4, 2005). "When you're in pain and you're hurting, you don't work on your game. You're trying to save whatever you have for the game. Now I can work on my game and feel good while I'm working on it."

Martin married his college sweetheart, Fatimah Conley, in August 2000; the couple later divorced. In 2003 he married Heather Thompson, with whom he has three children: Kenyon Jr. (born in January 2001), Ceirra (May 2003), and Kamron (March 2005). By all accounts a devoted father, Martin has attributed the increasing gentleness of his court manner during the last few seasons to concerns about how he will be remembered after he leaves the game. "I don't want my kids to grow up and [be asked], 'Your daddy used to be in the NBA? What was his name?'" Martin told Ohm Youngmisuk for the Knight Ridder/Tribune News Service (June 7, 2003). "'Kenyon Martin? Oh, he was an —!' I don't want that for them, you know?"

When he is wearing his uniform, Martin's visible tattoos (in addition to the one that spells out his mother's name) include Chinese characters that mean "Never be satisfied" and an image of the Grim Reaper gripping a basketball. According to his biography on NBA.com, he enjoys watching movies and playing video games.

—C.F.T.

Suggested Reading: *Cincinnati Post* (on-line) October 26, 2000; *Denver Post* (on-line) Oct. 27, 2004; ESPN.com; NBA.com; *New York Times* D p1+ July 31, 2000, with photo; Nuggets Web site; *Rocky Mountain News* (on-line) July 20, 2004; *Sports Illustrated* p56+ Feb. 7, 2000, with photo, p96+ Nov. 27, 2000, with photo, p32+ Apr. 29, 2002, with photo; USA Basketball Web site; *USA Today* Cp1 May, 9, 2004, with photos

---

Martin, Kevin J.

Dec. 14, 1966– Chairman of the Federal Communications Commission

Address: Federal Communications Commission, 445 12th St., S.W., Washington, DC 20554

As the chairman of the Federal Communications Commission (FCC) since March 18, 2005, Kevin J. Martin leads the regulatory agency responsible for overseeing the activities of a broad spectrum of the businesses connected with the wide-ranging telecommunications industry. The FCC, an independent agency within the federal government, serves as an arbiter of rules and regulations that affect everything from garage-door openers to cable and satellite television to telephone service; it is also responsible for regulating the distribution of radio airwaves to commercial and public interests and the ownership of TV stations. President George W. Bush chose Martin, a Republican, to fill a seat on the FCC in 2001. In becoming its chairman, Martin succeeded Michael K. Powell, who many observers

believed lacked the necessary conciliatory skills to guide the agency to a consensus on many important issues. Martin is considered to be both a stronger proponent of deregulation and a stricter hard-liner on indecency issues than Powell. High on his agenda are rulings on three major prospective telephone-company mergers (Sprint with Nextel Communications, SBC Communications with AT&T, and Verizon Communications with MCI); a reconsideration of various FCC rules, including one that bars the owners of radio and TV stations from acquiring daily newspapers in their markets, and those that specify the maximum number of media outlets a single company can own in one geographic area; and a reexamination of decency standards for television and radio broadcasts. Martin's five-year term on the commission will end in 2006, at which time President Bush will have the option to reappoint him to the chairmanship.

Kevin Jeffrey Martin was born in Charlotte, North Carolina, on December 14, 1966 to an insurance agent and a homemaker. He was raised in Waxhaw, a small town south of Charlotte, where the family's house was on a gravel road; the street

Courtesy of the FCC
Kevin J. Martin

address was "Rural Route 3," as he recalled on June 27, 2002 at a public meeting on rural broadband access sponsored by the U.S. Department of Agriculture. "I remember when it was a long distance phone call for my mother to call her sister, who also lived in Waxhaw," Martin said. "I understand how important advanced telecommunications services are to folks living in rural and remote areas." After he graduated from high school, Martin enrolled at the University of North Carolina at Chapel Hill (UNC). As an undergraduate he was elected student-body president and president of the North Carolina Association of student governments; he also served on the university's board of trustees. He earned a bachelor's degree in political science with honors and distinction in 1989. Martin went on to study public policy at Duke University, in Durham, North Carolina; he received an M.A. degree from the school in 1990. Next, he attended the prestigious Harvard Law School, in Cambridge, Massachusetts. He received a J.D. degree cum laude in 1993.

Following a law clerkship with Judge William M. Hoeveler in the U.S. District Court in Miami, Florida, in 1993, Martin became an associate at Wiley Rein & Fielding, a Washington, D.C.–based law firm whose practice in cases involving communications was among the largest in the world. He specialized in communications, legislative, and appellate-litigation matters under the tutelage of one of the firm's partners, Richard E. Wiley, who had served as FCC chairman from 1970 to 1977 and was known as a "leading force in the effort to foster increased competition and lessened regulation in the communications field," according to the PR Newswire (September 8, 1998). Wiley told Jason

Boog for *National Law Journal* (May 2, 2005), "Martin stood out as being one of the more brilliant associates we've had. He was very politically savvy. He knows the field, but he also knows the way of Washington." In 1997, when Martin was 29, Kenneth W. Starr hired him to assist with the so-called Whitewater investigation, a highly publicized inquiry into the alleged ties of President Bill Clinton, his wife, Hillary Rodham Clinton, and others to illegalities surrounding the failure of an Arkansas savings-and-loan association in 1989 (when Clinton was Arkansas's governor) and a related land-development deal. Starr held the post of independent counsel and headed the investigation.

Also in the late 1990s, Martin served as the legal adviser to Harold W. Furchtgott-Roth, a Republican FCC commissioner who was then widely considered to be the most conservative member of the agency. In that position Martin advised the commissioner on a host of telecommunications and broadband issues. One of his first tasks, according to *Broadcasting & Cable* (May 7, 2001), was to help write a number of "stinging dissents" that criticized the FCC's management of universal telephone-service charges. He also helped to draft FCC regulations for companies that provide telecommunications services.

Next, from July 1999 through December 2000, Martin held the job of deputy general counsel on the presidential and vice-presidential campaigns, respectively, of the Republicans George W. Bush, then governor of Texas, and Richard B. Cheney, then chief executive officer of the energy company Halliburton and a former government official. According to *Broadcasting & Cable*, Martin was a "key player" in organizing the many GOP lawyers who came to Florida to observe the state's vote recount after the disputed 2000 presidential election. After the U.S. Supreme Court ruled, in December 2000, that Bush had won the presidency, Martin served as the principal technology and telecommunications adviser on Bush and Cheney's transition team. He later became the president's special assistant for economic policy and served on the staff of the National Economic Council, focusing primarily on policies related to commerce and technology. In addition, he served as the official U.S. government representative to the Digital Opportunity Task Force of the Group of Eight (informally known as the G-8: Canada, France, Germany, Italy, Japan, Russia, the United Kingdom, and the U.S.— the world's leading industrialized democracies). The mission of the task force was to identify ways in which the digital revolution can provide opportunities for developing countries. On April 30, 2001 President Bush nominated Martin as an FCC commissioner; he was sworn in on July 3, 2001.

Martin's tenure as a commissioner began shortly after Michael Powell had assumed the FCC chairmanship. With his arrival, Republicans had a 3–2 majority in the FCC for the first time since the early 1990s. In February 2003 Martin surprised conservatives by voting with the regulatory agency's Democratic minority to block a major feature of Powell's sweeping new agenda for the telecommunications industry: his attempt to further deregulate local telephone companies. The decision affirmed the right of state regulators to decide which parts of the local networks of the so-called Baby Bells (Nynex, Bell Atlantic, BellSouth, Ameritech, Southwestern Bell, U.S. West, and Pacific Telesis) should be provided to other local carriers at a discount. (According to the 1996 Telecommunications Act, when competition is threatened, long-distance carriers must be allowed discounted access to networks of rival companies. Under Powell's proposed new rules, the Baby Bells would have been relieved of having to provide competitors with access to their broadband networks.) Martin's vote caught Powell by surprise and caused a rift between the two men. According to the *Washington Monthly* (April 1, 2003), speculation arose that Martin had acted at the behest of Vice President Cheney in order to spite one of Cheney's political enemies—Colin Powell, who was then secretary of state and is Michael Powell's father.

Voting with the majority in June 2003, Martin approved sweeping changes to further deregulate the media; the changes made it possible for large media corporations to own greater numbers of TV and radio stations and other media outlets as well as a greater percentage of each in particular geographic areas. The new FCC rules sparked an uproar among many laypeople, members of the media, and various elected officials, who feared that such consolidation of media ownership might limit the public's access to diverse news coverage and cause other negative effects. Despite a threat from President Bush to veto any bill that would restore the previous cap on media ownership, in September 2003 the Senate approved a resolution, by a vote of 55–40, to repeal the new FCC rules. The vote marked only the second time in history that the Senate had used its authority to rule against a regulator or a regulatory agency.

President Bush named Martin chairman of the FCC on March 18, 2005. Because he was already a commissioner, his appointment did not require Senate confirmation. One item he intends to address is the issue of indecency in broadcasting and cable. The FCC has reported that the number of indecency complaints from the public has risen dramatically in recent years—from 111 complaints in 2000 to more than 1.4 million in 2004. Some observers have contended that the latter figure is misleading, because most of the complaints are coming from only a few sources, such as the Parents Television Council, a conservative group. At a speech made at the 21st Annual Institute on Telecommunications Policy and Regulations, as reported by the Parents Television Council (December 5, 2003, on-line), Martin told institute members, "The FCC plays an important role in protecting Americans, particularly children, from indecent

programming. We have a statutory mandate to prohibit indecency on broadcast [sic], and I take this responsibility seriously. . . . If we were implementing our statutory mandate effectively, our rules would serve as a significant deterrent to broadcasters considering the airing of obscene, indecent and profane material, and our fines would punish violators sternly. I am concerned that we are failing on both fronts. . . . I am also concerned that use of such profanity reflects a regrettable coarsening of the language and images on television today. Many observers have commented on the increase in gratuitous sexual, violent, and offensive programming on broadcast television. I have been troubled by this trend for some time now, and have been actively encouraging broadcasters and cable operators to offer more tools for parents to deal with this trend."

Recently, Martin has supported leading lawmakers in Congress, among them Senator Ted Stevens of Alaska, the chairman of the Senate Commerce Committee (which oversees the FCC), who have proposed a broad expansion of indecency rules to include cable- and satellite-television providers. He has advocated increases in the fines levied against stations that violate those rules and has proposed the implementing of new procedures that would put the licenses of those stations in jeopardy. Lawyers for cable companies have charged that such efforts to impose indecency standards on paid programming would violate the First Amendment of the Constitution. Martin has also proposed that cable operators police themselves, and he has urged broadcasters to provide at least one hour of prime-time family programming every night. "Subscribers who are interested only in programming they can enjoy with their family would finally have a way to purchase only that programming," Martin said in a speech given at a conference of fhe National Association of Television Program Executives in 2003, as quoted in *Television Week* (March 21, 2005). "Alternatively, cable and DBS [the acronym for Direct Broadcast Satellite] operators could offer programming in a more a la carte fashion."

Martin's public statements have aroused criticism from various quarters. "As an FCC commissioner since 2001, Martin has talked out of both sides of his mouth . . . ," J. Max Robins, the editor in chief of *Broadcasting & Cable*, complained in that magazine (April 11, 2005), after listening to the FCC chairman speak at the annual National Cable Television Association conference, held in April 2005. "He has supported conservative activists who want to purge prime time of edgy content and supported more-frequent and higher fines for rules violations, but then again, he has exhorted the industry to police itself. . . . After hearing from Chairman Martin in San Francisco, the industry didn't know any more about where his leadership is heading than the day he was appointed." "Martin should be busy clarifying what constitutes indecency for broadcasters and end the confusion that is causing them to unnecessarily censor themselves to the detriment of viewers," an unsigned editorial in the *Los Angeles Times* (April 7, 2005) declared, referring to such decisions as that of various ABC affiliates to cancel a showing of the film *Saving Private Ryan* in 2004 out of fear that "indecent" language in the movie would lead to FCC fines. In a statement made in 2004 and quoted by Sallie Hofmeister in the *Los Angeles Times* (April 5, 2005), Martin maintained, "Over a year ago, I urged cable and satellite operators to help us address this issue. Thus far, there has been no response. . . . Something needs to be done."

In mid-2005 Martin proposed that the FCC approve, without conditions regarding competition or restraints, the merger of SBC Communications with AT&T (a merger valued at $16 billion), and Verizon Communications with MCI (valued at $8.5 billion). The regulatory agency was expected to vote on the mergers before the end of the year. Another item remaining on the FCC's 2005 agenda, according to *TelecomWeb News Digest* (October 24, 2005), involved "an order and proposed rulemaking on the nation's emergency alert system (which may be revamped, expanded and given additional funding this year by pending legislation in the U.S. Congress)."

Martin currently serves as chairman of the Federal-State Joint Conference on Advanced Telecommunications Services and the Federal-State Joint Board on Universal Service, both of which were formed to satisfy requirements of the Telecommunications Act of 1996. The first group, made up of state public-utilities commissioners and all FCC commissioners, assists the FCC in preparing its reports to Congress on the provision of advanced telecommunications services to all Americans; the latter group consists of FCC and state utility-authority commissioners and a consumer advocate. Martin is also a member of the Florida Bar, the District of Columbia Bar, and the Federal Communications Bar Association.

Observers have described Martin's countenance as "boyish"; according to Bill McConnell, writing for *Broadcasting & Cable* (March 21, 2005), "His youthful looks belie an ambition that has driven him" to his current position. His wife, Catherine Jurgensmeyer Martin, serves as the White House deputy director of communications for policy and planning; before her husband's appointment as FCC chairman, she was Vice President Cheney's chief of staff. The couple live in Washington, D.C.

—D.F.

Suggested Reading: *Broadcasting & Cable* p38+ May 7, 2001, p11 Mar. 21, 2005; Federal Communications Comission Web site; *Los Angeles Times* C p1 Jan. 22, 2005, with photos; *National Law Journal* S p11 May 2, 2005; *Television Week* p27 Mar. 21, 2005

Martinez, Rueben

Apr. 19, 1940– Bookseller; literacy advocate

Address: Libreria Martinez Books and Art Gallery, 1110 N. Main St., Santa Ana, CA 92701

"We come into this world with nothing and leave with nothing," Rueben Martinez said to Justino Aguila for the *Orange County (California) Register* (September 28, 2004). "So why not do something with this life? I tell students, teachers and parents to take advantage of this time on earth. That's the kind of energy I like to spread." Rueben Martinez is one of 23 recipients of the 2004 MacArthur Fellowship, awarded to individuals on the basis of demonstrated creativity and intended as an investment in their future contributions to society. Such contributions have long been a priority for Martinez, the owner of Libreria Martinez Books and Art Gallery in Santa Ana, California, which had an unusual beginning: it originated on the premises of Martinez's barbershop. The store now serves as a major supplier of literature for the United States' highest concentration of urban Spanish-speaking people. (In over 66 percent of Santa Ana households, no one over 14 speaks English.) Through his visits to local schools and his work with a number of organizations, Martinez combats illiteracy and growing high-school dropout rates, seeking in particular to reach Latinos, at least one in three of whom nationwide, it has been predicted, will not complete high school. Martinez helped to establish the El Sol Science and Arts Academy of Santa Ana; with the actor Edward James Olmos, he founded the Latino Book and Family Festival, which has grown into the country's largest Spanish-language book expo. He has served as an executive board member of the California Democratic Party and treasurer of the Orange County Democratic Party and has twice been a delegate to the Democratic National Convention. "I found out my heart was in a political party that was a party of the people, for the people," Martinez said to Dennis McLellan for the *Los Angeles Times* (March 31, 1996).

A son of Mexican immigrants, Rueben R. Martinez was born on April 19, 1940 in Miami, Arizona, a mining town of 3,000 people, 80 miles east of Phoenix. His father mined copper while his mother stayed at home to take care of the couple's eight children. Martinez grew up in an environment with very few books, as there were no bookstores or libraries in Miami. The only books he had were given to him by his teachers; he eagerly accepted them. While Miami had good schools, there were not many job opportunities in the small mountainside town. "There was no future there," Martinez said to Dennis McLellan. " I had to go out and see

Courtesy of the MacArthur Foundation

Rueben Martinez

if there was anything on the other side of that mountain."

After he graduated from Miami High School, in 1957, Martinez and two friends drove to California in a 1949 Ford. "I've been here ever since. California has been very good to me," he said to Dennis McLellan. After settling in East Los Angeles, Martinez worked in a supermarket, starting as a box boy and working his way up to a position with more responsibility in the produce section. He later held jobs at firms including McDonnell Douglas and the Ford Motor Co. For a year he worked nights as a crane operator at Bethlehem Steel and spent his days learning to cut hair at Hill Street Barbers in Los Angeles. Martinez cut hair full-time for two years before opening his own shop, in 1974. In the following year he moved his business to Santa Ana.

While cutting hair, Martinez became known for inspiring his customers to keep up with current events through his discussions of news and politics. He kept newspapers and magazines at the shop for his customers to read and began lending them books written in English or Spanish. (Most of the books were not returned to the shop.) By the early 1990s Martinez had progressed to selling books that he owned between haircuts, and soon afterward, as demand grew and he began buying additional books, there were volumes spread all over the barbershop. According to Dennis McLellan, the message on the shop's answering machine announced, "The best in books and hair." David N. Ream, Santa Ana's city manager and a longtime customer of Martinez's, described Martinez as one of the most positive influences on the residents in Santa Ana, telling Dennis McLellan in 1996, "He

not only knows everybody in town and keeps up with what's going on—which is always interesting and entertaining—but he's not just a lot of talk. He's a lot of action. He really puts the efforts behind his words and ideas." Conversation is an important part of Martinez's barbering process. "Sometimes I talk too much," Martinez said to McLellan. "Some barberia customers get a kick out of it, and some of them don't. They say 'Rueben, I've got to go. Please hurry.' But they know what to expect." In the mid-1990s Martinez still made most of his income from haircuts. That did not stop him from inviting authors to speak at his 320-square-foot shop. On one occasion Isabel Allende, the famous Chilean author of novels including *The House of the Spirits* and *Daughter of Fortune*, agreed to hold a book signing at Martinez's establishment. Martinez recalled that Allende seemed surprised when she saw that the bookstore was also a barbershop. A thousand people showed up there to see her.

Martinez's book-selling business soon grew to such an extent that he moved his bookstore into a larger space, 2,800 square feet on the ground floor of a law office on Main Street. At the new site, haircutting is relegated to a back room, where there is a single chair. "I've always had that feeling that if you don't grow, you die, and the opportunity was there," Martinez said to McLellan. Twenty young volunteers from the Boys and Girls Club of Santa Ana helped Martinez to transfer his books to their new location. The new Libreria Martinez Books and Art Gallery (where new exhibits are mounted every so often) quickly became one of the largest sellers of Spanish-language books in the country. In 2000 Martinez opened a children's bookstore next door, and a third store opened in Lynwood, California, in 2003. "Every opportunity I get, I go out there and tell people buy books, rent books," Martinez said to Ben Fox for the *San Diego Union-Tribune* (October 3, 2004, on-line), "and not only will you notice growth within yourself, everyone else will, too."

Meanwhile, Martinez continued the community activity that has always been a priority for him. "You're here; you have to do something," he explained to Dennis McLellan. "I've always been this way. Some of my friends say I'm all over the place, they wonder how I get things done. I'm used to it. As far as being involved, it's just like getting a driver's license. It's a privilege to drive. It's an honor to be active, to do things. I chose a long time ago to be a giver rather than a taker." In 2001 Martinez co-founded the El Sol Science and Arts Academy of Santa Ana, a charter school for kindergarteners through eighth graders located two blocks from his bookstore. Martinez has held fund-raising events for the academy and sponsored hearing and vision clinics at the bookstore. He is also co-founder of the nationally touring Latino Book and Family Festival and, for many years, on a volunteer basis, has visited classrooms to encourage children to stay in school, going on average to one school each week.

According to the *San Diego Union Tribune* (October 3, 2004), he has appeared on a weekly, nationally broadcast Spanish-language television program, encouraging children to learn to read. He has received the Giraffe Award from the Board of Education of the Santa Ana Unified School District in recognition of his efforts. Such work is "very important because a lot of the kids drop out," Martinez said to Dennis McLellan. "Without an education, it's going to be a tough future for them." "He's so inspirational," Delia Apodaca, a teacher at Cesar Chavez High School in Santa Ana, said to McLellan about Martinez. "The students love him. He treats them like his own kids. He goes over and he hugs them and he calls them 'mijito,' which means my little son, or 'mija,' my daughter. They like that, and he's funny and very outgoing. The fact that he's Hispanic just motivates the kids to do even better."

Motivating Spanish-speaking people to value literature has won Rueben Martinez acclaim from educators and librarians across the country and, in 2004, from the MacArthur Foundation, which awarded him a fellowship consisting of $500,000, to be given over a five-year period. Often called the "genius" grant, the award is presented to a variety of individuals on the basis of previous accomplishments and as an investment in the recipients' potential to benefit society. The fellowships are given to individuals rather than institutions so that each recipient can pursue goals as he or she chooses. "Certainly, what Rueben Martinez has done to date is important and creative," Daniel J. Socolow, director of the MacArthur Fellows Program, said to Justino Aguila. "We're betting he'll continue doing great things, maybe even greater things." "I'm still stunned," Martinez said to Justino Aguila. "I'm floating and scared at the same time. But deep down inside, I think it's good." Recipients of the grant are not informed in advance that they have been considered for it, and Martinez therefore did not expect the phone call that brought him the news of the award. "I thought it was a sales rep wanting something," Martinez said to Justino Aguila. "But there was a passion in his voice that kept me listening. One quarter into the conversation he said, 'Mr. Martinez, don't hang up on me because this is the real stuff.'" In May 2005 the Latino Caucus of California's state Legislature honored Martinez in its annual tribute to people who strengthen their communities' "spirit."

Rueben Martinez has been described as gregarious and enthusiastic. He is divorced and has three adult children, all of whom have attended college. He enjoys bicycling, in-line skating, and running and has competed in five marathons. He still cuts hair in his shop, but only once or twice a week.

—L.J.

Suggested Reading: *Los Angeles Times* Life & Style E p1 Mar. 31, 1996; *Orange County (California) Register* Sep. 28, 2004; *Orange County (California) Weekly* (on-line) Oct. 1–7, 2004; *San Diego Union Tribune* (on-line) Oct. 3, 2004

Martz, Judy

July 28, 1943– Former governor of Montana (Republican)

Address: 119092 Juniper Acres Rd., Silver Bow, MT 59750

When Judy Martz, Montana's first female governor, announced in 2003 that she would not run for a second four-year term, few observers were surprised. From the beginning, Martz's tenure had been plagued by a series of alleged ethical transgressions and ill-advised off-the-cuff remarks, which, combined with a budget deficit requiring difficult spending cuts, caused her popularity to decline precipitously and made her reelection an unlikely prospect at best. In the final weeks before she left office, Martz's approval rating was only 26 percent; at its lowest, in May 2003, it had dropped to 20 percent. In the 2004 election, for the first time in 16 years, the governorship passed into the hands of a Democrat (Brian Schweitzer); Democrats assumed leadership in both chambers of the state Legislature as well.

Martz has blamed her dismal ratings on the press, which she said treated her unfairly and misrepresented her statements. At one point, her frustration was such that she took the unusual—and unpopular—step of refusing to give live interviews with certain reporters. According to some observers, Martz also suffered from comparisons with her predecessor, Marc Racicot, a fellow Republican, who had enjoyed enormous popularity among his constituents. "She had a terribly hard act to follow," Craig Wilson, the head of the Political Science Department at Montana State University–Billings, told Bob Anez for the Associated Press (December 10, 2004). A high-spirited former Olympic athlete, Martz has nevertheless maintained that her tenure was a success, pointing out that she delivered on many of her campaign promises. She cut income taxes and capital-gains taxes, aided economic development, and increased Medicaid payments to hospitals. In addition, after facing a $230 million budget deficit in 2003, the state had a projected surplus of between $190 million and $250 million (about $73 million of which came from federal relief funds) when she left office. At the start of Martz's term, Montana ranked 47th in the U.S. in per capita personal income, and the per-

Stefan Zaklin/Getty Images

Judy Martz

centage of adults working two jobs to make ends meet was the second highest in the country. By 2004 Montana was counted among the fastest-growing states in terms of gross state product, and in the past several years job growth has been among the best in the U.S., and the rate of unemployment among the lowest. "I really believe we have done what we said we'd do," Martz told Mike Dennison for the *Great Falls (Montana) Tribune* (August 2, 2004). "I just tried to concentrate on what was right and best for . . . most of the people in the state."

The fourth of six children, Martz was born Judy Helen Morstein on July 28, 1943 in Big Timber, Montana. Her parents, Joe and Dorothy Morstein, owned a cattle ranch at the time of her birth. Several years later the family moved to Butte, Montana, where Joe found work as a livestock inspector and miner. "We didn't have extravagant things, but we never went without food or clothes," Martz recalled of her childhood to Peter Johnson for the *Great Falls Tribune* (April 24, 2000). "We may have worn mended socks, but everybody else did, too." Martz began working early in life: while in grammar school she baby-sat and cleaned houses; during her teens she waited tables in the evening and assisted at a local optometrist's office.

As a youngster Martz took up speed skating and began racing competively during her grade-school years. "I was a pretty good natural skater," she told Johnson. "I had long legs, good lungs, and a desire to work." As a high-school junior, she almost won a race against Sylvia White, a national speed-skating champion. With her confidence boosted, Martz competed in the national championships in St. Paul, Minnesota, the following year; she paid

her way with money she had raised by selling raffle tickets. After she graduated from Butte High School, in 1961, Martz set her sights on the 1964 Olympics. Over the next several years, with her family's encouragement, she engaged in a grueling training regimen and conducted fund-raisers to help cover the costs of her trips to various speed-skating competitions. In 1963 Martz was named to the United States World Speed Skating Team and soon qualified to represent the U.S. in the women's 1,500-meter race at the 1964 Winter Games, in Innsbruck, Austria. Martz got off to a fast start in that race; as she circled the rink, her coach told her that she was on pace to come in first. Then, as she recalled to Johnson, "I got to thinking of winning the race and took my eyes off the goal." She slipped and fell; although she picked herself up and completed the race, she came in well out of medal contention. "I may have finished 15th," she told Johnson, "but in my heart I really won, because I gave it everything I had."

Later in 1964 Martz served as Montana's Centennial Queen during the state's celebrations of the 100th anniversary of its becoming a U.S. territory. She took a job at a Billings sporting-goods store and planned to continue her speed-skating training, with the aim of competing in the 1968 Olympics. Then, in February 1965, Martz's boyfriend, Wayne Estes, an All-American basketball player at Utah State University, died when he accidentally walked into a dangling power line and was electrocuted. His death devastated Martz, but it also gave her a new perspective and led her to abandon her pursuit of a second Olympic berth. "I realized life was not all about me and my wanting to be a world champion," she said to Johnson. "A lot of other people are hurting, and I wanted to start making a difference." Later that year Martz reconnected with a former boyfriend, Harry Martz, who was subsequently posted overseas with the military; when he returned on leave, the two were married. Harry Martz spent the following two years in Germany with the armed forces while Martz remained in Montana, where she attended Eastern Montana College (now Montana State University–Billings); she did not complete a degree.

After her husband returned to the States, in the late 1960s, the couple bought a full-service gas station; it soon went out of business, a victim of the national trend toward self-service stations. In 1971 the Martzes purchased a Butte garbage-collection firm, which they renamed Martz Disposal. Judy Martz assisted her husband in their new venture; in 1974 she left her job (at a sporting-goods store) to dedicate herself full-time to it. Martz drove the company truck and emptied trash cans. "I'd use my legs and hips to swing a 50-gallon container about four feet off the ground into the truck," she told Johnson. "You wouldn't mess with me in those days; I was buff." Martz also raised two children and served as a volunteer in her community through the Junior League, a women's organization. In addition, she coached hockey players and speed skaters.

In 1984 Martz stopped driving the garbage truck but continued to help with Martz Disposal's bookkeeping. In 1985 she was named executive director of a group of investors who were building the U.S. High Altitude Sports Center in Butte. After the center was completed, in 1989, Conrad Burns, a Montana Republican who had just been elected to the U.S. Senate, hired Martz to head his Butte field office; there, she helped constituents and served as Burns's representative in the local community. Concurrently, from 1991 to 1992, she served as president of the Butte Chamber of Commerce and vice chair of the St. James Hospital board of directors.

In 1995, during Marc Racicot's first term as governor of Montana, Lieutenant Governor Dennis Rehberg announced his candidacy for the U.S. Senate. Racicot intended to seek a second term, and at the suggestion of several of her friends, Martz told him that she was interested in becoming his running mate. "Something inside of me sparked because I thought I could do it," she told Johnson. "I prayed about it for three weeks, without telling even my husband." Racicot interviewed her twice at length before he asked her to join him; he told the press that he had based his decision on her experience and character as well as her ability to deal with complex issues. In the November 1996 elections, the Racicot-Martz ticket scored a decisive victory, and Martz became Montana's first female lieutenant governor. In her new post, Martz led the Governor's Summit on Youth/Montana's Promise and chaired a variety of committees, dealing with such matters as contingency planning in case of drought and Montana's relations with the Canadian province of Alberta, which borders three of the state's counties and part of a fourth. In addition, Martz traveled throughout the state on behalf of the governor, making speeches and meeting with constituents.

Because of Montana's term-limits laws, Racicot was not permitted to seek reelection in 2000. On July 19, 1999 Martz declared her candidacy for the governorship. She chose Karl Ohs, the Republican majority whip in the Montana House of Representatives, to be her running mate. Over the next year Martz campaigned vigorously and made her case to the voters, citing her experience in running a small business, her work ethic, and her efforts on behalf of Senator Burns and Governor Racicot. Her economic plan, unveiled on February 1, 2000, centered on the Jobs and Opportunities for a Better State (JOBS) initiative and called for $20 million in tax cuts, an easing of environmental regulations, and a five-year tax credit for high-tech companies that set up operations in Montana. With Racicot's support, Martz soundly defeated Rob Natelson, a law professor, to win the Republican primary. In the general election, she faced the Democratic Party's candidate, State Auditor Mark O'Keefe, with whom she began to exchange pointed barbs. O'Keefe attacked Racicot and Martz's economic-development record, while Martz derided her op-ponent as a "tax-and-spend liberal" who would drive business from the state. During the campaign Martz revealed her feisty side; she angered environmentalists when she autographed a shovel and mailed it to protesters demonstrating against federal land-use policies. On November 7, 2000 Martz garnered 51 percent of the vote to O'Keefe's 47 percent and captured the governorship.

Immediately after her victory, Martz began a 17-city, four-day tour of the state to thank her supporters. As her inauguration approached, Montana's fiscal situation deteriorated, leading Martz to revise the two-year budget submitted by the outgoing governor. She tabled her proposal to cut taxes by $20 million and outlined a number of cuts to social services. Further complicating the situation, Montana, like many western states, faced an energy crisis that had sparked huge price rises. During this time, Martz found herself the center of some unwanted media attention. In one interview she allegedly referred to herself as a "lap dog" for industry; she later insisted that she merely meant that she did not mind the label if it meant being willing to work with businesses to improve the economy. Then, in a January 2001 speech, she reportedly stated, "My husband has never battered me, but then again, I've never given him a reason to," as Bob Anez reported. Martz denied making the comment, telling Anez, "It gave women the perception that I didn't care if women got beaten, and I would be the first one to stand up and say that is not acceptable behavior." (One of Martz's aides was later fired after telling reporters that Martz simply could not remember having made the comment.)

Inaugurated on January 2, 2001, Martz made her first state-of-the-state address on January 25. In her speech she promised not to raise taxes and proposed initiatives to encourage logging, mining, and power-plant construction. During her first months in office, she oversaw changes to the state's environmental statutes that made it easier for businesses to gain various permits. In April, as the energy crisis continued, Martz reached a deal with the Montana Power Co. that raised 2002 energy prices by 50 percent for consumers. (Montana Power later lowered the rate hike from 50 to 20 percent.) Environmentalists and Montana Democrats complained that in easing environmental regulations, the governor had sacrificed the health of the state's resources for the benefit of out-of-state businesses. Furthermore, critics took issue with Martz's education budget, which they felt was overly frugal, as well as with certain cuts she instituted in the state's smoking-prevention program.

In June 2001 the Clark Ford Coalition, an environmental group, publicized a September 1999 land deal in which, without an independent appraisal, Martz had paid the Atlantic Richfield Co. (Arco) $24,000 for 80 acres of land adjacent to her home outside Butte. The coalition accused Martz of a conflict of interest since, as governor, she would be the state's trustee in ongoing litigation against Arco in a matter concerning the Anaconda mining company, which Arco had acquired some years earlier. (Anaconda had caused considerable environmental damage in Montana that Arco had failed to clean up.) Moreover, the litigation between the state and Arco involved the parcel purchased by Martz. The Clark Ford Coalition demanded that Martz recuse herself from any dealings with the Arco case. Martz refused, stating that the transaction would not influence how she dealt with the Arco clean-up. The following month journalists revealed that Arco had bought the parcel in question for $80,000 two years before selling it to Martz; while Martz had purchased the land with certain negative easements and no irrigation rights, many believed the price she had paid was suspiciously low. Compounding the problem, Martz had apparently failed to disclose the deal, as required, during the gubernatorial campaign. The governor denied any wrongdoing. "I don't know what Arco paid for the land, and don't care," she said, according to an account in the *Missoulian* (July 22, 2001). "I don't know what date they bought it, and don't care. We paid what they asked us. End of story." Later that summer the Democratic Party filed an ethics complaint against Martz, claiming that because of its low cost the land constituted an illegal gift and that Martz had run afoul of the law when she failed to report the purchase. During a September 2002 hearing, the state commissioner of political practices ruled in Martz's favor, concluding that there was no evidence that Arco had intended to influence the governor.

In August 2001, while intoxicated, Shane Hedges, one of Martz's chief advisers, crashed the sports utility vehicle he was driving, killing his passenger, Paul Sliter, the Republican majority leader in the Montana House. Hedges claimed that Sliter had driven the car, and the police later voiced their suspicion that Republican political operatives had tried to alter the crime scene to cover up Hedges's role in the crash. Martz became involved when she took Hedges to the governor's mansion that night, after an officer had asked him to remain at the police station. It came to light in January 2002 that the governor had then washed Hedges's clothes, an act that Martz attributed to her motherly instincts; others suggested that she may have been destroying evidence. Hedges resigned soon after the crash and pleaded guilty to negligent homicide. He was sentenced to six months in a halfway house.

In December 2001 Martz endorsed a plan, about which she had long expressed skepticism, to list the town of Libby, Montana, as a federal Superfund clean-up site. (The Superfund program was established in 1980 to provide funds to clean up abandoned or uncontrolled hazardous-waste sites.) She also announced that she would take advantage of Montana's one-time "silver-bullet" privilege, a mechanism through which the state could fast-track the clean-up and avoid a drawn-out hearing process. The site of a former vermiculite mine owned by W. R. Grace & Co., Lib-

by had been heavily contaminated with asbestos; some 200 people had died from asbestos-related illnesses, and many more were sickened. Listing Libby as a Superfund site paved the way for the Environmental Protection Agency (EPA) to begin cleaning it up. Martz had earlier suggested that private industry rather than the EPA should be charged with the task.

In March 2002 investigators reported that Martz's aides had illegally used state phones to set up fund-raisers for a conservative political organization, the Montana Majority Fund, of which Martz was honorary chair. The resulting resignation of one of Martz's aides was the latest in more than a dozen resignations or firings of Martz's staff members during her first 28 months as governor. In April 2002, after Martz had severed her ties to the Montana Majority Fund, the Associated Press reported that Tim Blixseth, a developer whose company was being sued by the state for environmental violations, had donated $40,000 to the fund (a quarter of the total raised by the group), and had spoken with Martz 25 times during the previous year. Blixseth contended that his conversations with Martz had been about environmental issues regarding one of his developments, while Martz maintained that, save for one conversation, the discussions were strictly about the Montana Majority Fund.

Martz's standing took another hit several weeks later, when reports surfaced alleging that the governor was in the process of filing a workers' compensation claim for a repetitive-stress injury to her arm caused by shaking too many hands. Martz said that she had not filed a claim but had been looking into the possibility of doing so. After inquiries, the press revealed that Martz had received $64,264 in workers' compensation in 1988 after incurring a back injury during a rough plane landing. In 1985, the public also learned, she had sued a Winnebago dealer for $298,254 for injuries to her elbow and back that she had suffered when she slipped on some ice two years earlier. In response to such unwelcome press coverage, Martz announced in May that she would no longer grant interviews to certain reporters but that she would answer, in writing, questions that they submitted to her in writing. The Associated Press refused to agree to that arrangement.

New controversies emerged in the ensuing months: in June records requested by the press showed that Martz's staff had occasionally used state E-mail accounts for fund-raising activities and that Hedges had remained a key adviser to Martz after his resignation. Martz also angered state education officials when, in praising home schooling for its low cost, she criticized public-school funding, declaring, "It shouldn't take $5,000 to $7,000 [a year] to educate a child, and it surely doesn't take a village to raise one," as Mike Dennison reported for the *Great Falls Tribune* (June 12, 2002). (*It Takes a Village* is the title of a book by Hillary Rodham Clinton, published in

1996, when she was the nation's First Lady. The title comes from the African proverb "It takes a village to raise a child.") State school officials considered the comments a polemical oversimplification and questioned Martz's commitment to public education.

In August 2002, with the state facing a $45 million budget deficit due to lower-than-expected tax revenues, despite $24 million in budget cuts that she had announced in June, Martz called the Legislature into special session. By the time it met, the deficit had grown to $57 million. Lawmakers ultimately approved $20.1 million in Martz's recommended spending cuts and $37 million in the fund transfers that she had advised. Afterward Martz complimented the Legislature for its "strong leadership and fiscal responsibility," as Bob Anez reported for the Associated Press (August 11, 2002), and she warned, "As tough as the session's been, it's just the beginning." The Democratic opposition voiced displeasure with the adopted remedies, calling the reduction in funds for education and social-welfare programs unnecessarily harsh. Polls conducted in late September 2002 showed Martz to be one of the most unpopular governors in the country.

When the Legislature convened in 2003, the budget deficit had swelled to $230 million. Despite pledges never to raise taxes, Martz reluctantly agreed to increase tax rates on cigarettes, rental cars, and overnight lodgings (items associated with the state's growing tourism industry). She succeeding in getting the Legislature to significantly lower state income taxes. (The decreases took effect in January 2005 and are expected to cost the state about $90 million over the next two years). The Legislature voted down some of her other proposals, including a proposal to borrow $90 million from Montana's coal-tax trust fund and another to forbid open containers of alcohol in cars. Martz put a positive spin on the Legislature's actions, telling a GOP officers' convention, "The session ended with all our work completed and the people of Montana spared from drastic cuts and dramatic tax increases," as Peter Johnson reported for the *Great Falls Tribune* (June 29, 2003).

Martz's relationship with Montana's Native American tribes was cordial during the first part of her term. She visited Montana's seven reservations, met with tribal leaders twice, and in June 2001 issued a proclamation supporting an equal relationship between the state government and the Native American nations and promised to work to better the quality of life on the reservations. During the 2003 legislative session, however, Martz clashed with Indian representatives and barred a tribal lobbyist from her office. She also angered tribal leaders by cutting several programs that had benefitted the state's Native Americans.

In August 2003, with her approval rating hovering around 20 percent, Martz announced that she would not seek reelection. "The poll numbers didn't curb me, nothing curbed me," she told Bob Anez for the Associated Press (August 13, 2003), explaining that she wanted to spend more time with her family. The following fall and winter were relatively quiet for Martz; the state's deficit was under control and attention shifted to the gubernatorial race. In February 2004 Martz spoke out in favor of having the Ten Commandments displayed on government property: "People who are offended by the Ten Commandments have a deeper problem than the stone that it's written on, I think," she said, as quoted in the *Chicago Tribune* (February 28, 2004).

In November 2004, although Montanans voted heavily for the Republican incumbent, George W. Bush, in the presidential election, in the race for governor a Democrat, Brian Schweitzer, defeated the Republican candidate, Bob Brown, a political veteran. Democrats also assumed control of the state Legislature for the first time in years, winning the Senate by a 27-to-23 margin and securing a 50–50 tie in the House.

As her term came to a close, Martz expressed few regrets about her time as governor, telling Mike Dennison, "I have genuinely loved this job. . . . I have appreciated the opportunity to serve, even through the bad times, even through the hard times." Regarding what she viewed as the media's unfair treatment of her, she said, "When I came into this job, [I thought] because you're honest, because you're a morally good person, because you're a hard worker, that the media will not attack you and almost try to destroy who you are. . . . I've got news for whoever's governor: It will happen to them, too." Martz advised her successor, "Suck it up and keep moving toward the goal. . . . It's more important to all of the people you serve than what's happening inside one person." Martz said that she hoped to join the lecture circuit, to talk about organ donation, her Christian faith, and her experiences competing in the Olympics, running a small business, and serving as governor. Since then she has given some lectures, filling in for Laura Bush, for example, at the Pierce County Prayer Breakfast held in the Tacoma Dome. She also joined the board of directors of the Stun-gun maker Taser International in April 2005. "I look forward to working closely with everyone at TASER International in helping to continue to provide the best equipment available to our first line responders in law enforcement that reduces injuries and saves lives everyday," Martz declared, according to the PR Newswire US (March 21, 2005).

Martz and her husband live outside Butte. Harry Martz continues to run the trash-disposal company with the help of the couple's children, Stacey and Justin. Judy and Harry Martz became grandparents on New Year's Eve 2003, when Stacey gave birth to a daughter, Remy Clair.

—P.B.M.

Suggested Reading: Associated Press Dec. 21, 2001, Aug. 11, 2002, Aug. 13, 2003; *Great Falls (Montana) Tribune* A p1 Apr. 24, 2000, with photo, A p1 Oct. 9, 2000, E p1 Nov. 5, 2000, A p1 Dec. 23, 2001, A p15 Aug. 2, 2004

Mark Hanauer, courtesy of Morphosis

Mayne, Thom

Jan. 19, 1944– Architect

Address: Morphosis Architecture, 2041 Colorado Ave., Santa Monica, CA 90404-3415

Known for his bold originality in both form and use of materials, the architect Thom Mayne has been described over the past 30 years as an "American maverick," an "iconoclast," "the bad boy and angry young man of architecture," and even a "radical." His aggressive design sensibility is "rooted in powerful physicality, with a direct, tactile sense of honest materials," in the words of Cathleen McGuigan, writing for *Newsweek* (May 23, 2005). An example is his design for the recently completed Caltrans District 7 Building, in Los Angeles, California, an expansive, 1.2 million-square-foot structure encased in material that causes the building to change in appearance throughout the day, according to the light outside—becoming opaque in bright sunlight, seemingly almost transparent at dusk, and brightly lit at night.

"The multiplicity of ideas is what I'm interested in," Mayne told Robin Pogrebin for the *New York Times* (March 21, 2005). "The hybrid in our society—where there is no singular idea of what is beautiful." In terms of recognition, his professional breakthrough came in 1999, with the design for Diamond Ranch High School, in Pomona, California,

a project that showcased his ability to connect architecture to nature. For that and other, equally impressive works, the Hyatt Foundation awarded Mayne the discipline's highest honor, the 2005 Pritzker Architecture Prize, known unofficially as "the Nobel of architecture." Hailed by the Pritzker prize committee for surpassing "the limits of modernism and postmodernism," Mayne thus became the first American in 14 years to be named a Pritzker laureate. Mayne is a co-founder of the Southern California Institute of Architecture and of the Santa Monica, California–based firm Morphosis. In a description of his work, the Pritzker jury's chairman, Lord Palumbo, celebrated Mayne's unique architectural sensibility: "Every now and then an architect appears on the international scene, who teaches us to look at the art of architecture with fresh eyes, and whose work marks him out as a man apart in the originality and exuberance of its vocabulary, the richness and diversity of its palette, the risks undertaken with confidence and brio, the seamless fusion of art and technology. Thom Mayne is such an artist. He fulfills admirably the words of the great Chicago architect, Mies van der Rohe, who said, 'Architecture is the will of an epoch translated into space, living, changing, new.'"

The older of two sons, Thom Mayne was born to Walter Mayne and the former Bernice M. Gornall on January 19, 1944 in Waterbury, Connecticut. When he was an infant, his parents moved the family to Gary, Indiana, where they subsequently divorced. (Mayne has said that he underwent psychoanalysis as an adult to try to come to terms with his parents' divorce.) Afterward, to bring her children closer to her own mother, Mayne's mother moved with him and his brother to Whittier, California, a few miles southeast of Los Angeles. As quoted in a press release made available through the Pritzker Award Web site, Mayne described Whittier as "the middle of nowhere with orange groves and avocado trees." He described his mother, a former pianist, as "completely cultured," adding, "I grew up on classical music, and reproductions of great art. As a result, I grew up as a city-kid in the suburbs, not an athlete, not a joiner." According to the press release, the artistic sensibility Mayne developed in those years left him "completely out of place . . . kind of a loner, and aloof" among his peers. Mayne's family struggled financially during that period, while his mother, who "was not equipped to support a family," as he recalled, worked various jobs.

In high school Mayne won a competition in his architectural drafting class with his design for a house. He was quoted in the press release as saying, "I had an attraction to the field of architecture . . . but not much of a clue what it meant to practice." Mayne attended the University of Southern California (USC) in Los Angeles, where he studied architecture under Craig Ellwood, Gregory Ain, Ray Kappe, and Ralph Knowles, among others. At USC Mayne felt, for the first time, that he was at home in his environment; he also embraced the counterculture movement that had taken hold at USC and on other college campuses around the nation during that era.

After graduating from USC with a bachelor's degree in architecture in 1968, Mayne worked as an urban planner for the renowned architect Victor Gruen—known primarily for his revolutionary design of shopping centers. (Gruen has been credited with inventing the concept of the mall.) In 1971 Mayne began teaching at California State Polytechnic University, in Pomona, only to be fired a short time later along with six of his colleagues, including his former mentor Ray Kappe, because their ideas were considered unacceptably radical. Committed to helping revolutionize architecture, Mayne and his colleagues decided to open their own school, with the aim of bringing to Los Angeles the questioning approach to the field then in vogue at institutions in New York City and London, England. In 1972 the group founded the Southern California Institute of Architecture (SCI-Arc), which is still in operation and has long been considered among the leading experimental architectural schools in the country. "We made no money, we worked for nothing," Mayne was quoted as saying in the Pritzker press release, adding that he found consulting work and lived frugally to make ends meet. Shortly thereafter he and Michael Rotondi formed the architectural firm Morphosis, based in a studio in downtown Los Angeles. In 1974 the firm won its first of many Progressive Architecture (PA) awards (given by *Architecture* magazine) for designing the Sequoyah Educational Research Center. "That was the beginning . . . ," Mayne explained, as quoted in the Pritzker press release. "Suddenly we had an existence."

In 1977 Mayne entered a one-year architectural graduate program at Harvard University, in Cambridge, Massachusetts, where he "began to mold his signature approach, mixing the progressive ideals of early Modernist architects with his admiration for defiant '60s-style activism," as Christopher Hawthorne wrote for the *Los Angeles Times* (March 21, 2005). Mayne received a master's degree from Harvard in 1978. Following his return to Los Angeles, after working on relatively light remodeling projects in the Venice area, his firm began to win awards for its designs of several Los Angeles–area restaurants. Mayne and Rotondi designed the Comprehensive Cancer Center at Cedars-Sinai Medical Center, which opened early in 1988. Morphosis's breakthrough design was for the Diamond Ranch High School, in Pomona, which features two rows of fragmented buildings intersected by a long central sidewalk and thus "blurs the distinction between building and landscape," according to the Pritzker press release.

In recent years Mayne's projects have reflected the thought he has devoted to certain themes, such as human interactivity and urban interconnectedness. An example is the Caltrans District 7 Building, whose mechanized exterior changes according

to natural light. The building, completed in 2004, houses the headquarters of the California Transportation Department; it contains a four-story, 328-foot "outdoor" lobby, an underground parking garage, and elevators that skip stops—fostering human interaction by making it necessary for employees to walk between floors. "The design is all about connectivity," Mayne told Christopher Hawthorne. In *Los Angeles Magazine* (October 31, 2004), Greg Goldin noted that the building is "concerned with energy efficiency, civic interaction, fraternal workspaces, and chance encounter." The building represents Mayne's first multistory, government-commissioned project in the United States.

Mayne's reputation as an architectural outsider has diminished of late, thanks in part to his firm's newfound worldwide prominence. Among its other projects in foreign countries, Morphosis designed the ASE Design and Visitors Center in Taipei, Taiwan, which was completed in 1997; a retail office building in Seoul, South Korea, called the Sun Tower; a movable stage set for the Charleroi Dance Group at the Netherlands Architecture Institute; and a 250,000-square-foot office, retail, and parking facility in Klagenfurt, Austria, which also houses a kindergarten facility. His firm is also scheduled to complete the Palenque at JVC, a 6,250-seat, open-air arena in Guadalajara, Mexico, in 2007, a project that local residents hope will help revitalize that city, and a block of public-housing units in Madrid, Spain.

Mayne's firm was recently commissioned by the U.S. General Services Administration to design a glass federal office building in San Francisco, California, a federal courthouse in Eugene, Oregon, and a satellite facility, to include 16 antennae, for the National Oceanic and Atmospheric Administration, outside Washington, D.C. In addition, Morphosis has been assigned two major projects in New York City: a nine-story art and engineering building to house the Albert Nerken School of Engineering for Cooper Union, in Manhattan, which will feature a central atrium crisscrossed by sky bridges, and a multipurpose residential waterfront structure in Hunter's Point, Queens. Morphosis's multipurpose Student Recreation Center at the University of Cincinnati, which includes athletic and food facilities, classroom space, and student housing, is scheduled to be completed in the spring of 2007. "It is the most complicated building I have done in my life," Mayne told Sara Pearce for the *Cincinnati Enquirer* (June 5, 2005). "It's really five buildings pushed into one. It is full of surprises. Because it is so large-scale and intricate there are things that happen [such as] collisions and intersections. My work is full of that. I call them 'purposeful accidents.'"

Telling Cathleen McGuigan for the *Newsweek* article that his design interests lie in "the process, the evolution of the thing as a creative idea," Mayne described his work as "alluding to the development of cities over time." Indeed, his designs were noted in *Art in America* (May 1, 2005) for their "severe, variously angular or curving asymmetrical features that charge into space, giving his buildings a futuristic sense of motion." Throughout his career Mayne has emphasized the importance of architecture's social aspects, claiming that his building designs foster "connectivity." Morphosis's method is "highly intuitive and reflexive," according to the firm's official profile, which goes on to state, "We understand our arena of operation to be one marked by contradiction, conflict, change, and dynamism. And to that end we are interested in producing work that contributes to the conversation, that adds yet another strain to what some may hear as the cacophony of modern life." Assessing Mayne's career in *Architecture* (April 2005), C. C. Sullivan wrote: "In his work, [Mayne] positions himself as a node in a pulsating network of 'silent collisions' . . . among thinkers, artists, and experts. Rather than wrapping his energy around a Grand Unified Theory of architecture, he operates as a nexus of many ideas and inputs, deftly prioritizing and assimilating them per project needs. He carefully instigates change through guerrillalike tactics, cognizant that perfection is impractical. And the 'finished product'—the diagram, building or detail—is neither faultless nor final, but rather the most elegant, most remarkable solution available in time and space."

On May 31, 2005 Mayne received the Pritzker Architecture Prize, in Chicago, Illinois, at the ceremony that marked the opening of the Millennium Park's Jay Pritzker Pavilion. The Pritzker family, who oversee the Hyatt hotel chain, began in the late 1970s to honor excellence in architecture. Mayne became the 29th recipient of the Pritzker Prize and the first American in 14 years to win the honor. (Robert Venturi won the prize in 1991.) The Pritzker Prize brought with it a bronze medallion and a $100,000 award. Mayne has garnered a number of other prestigious honors, including 25 Progressive Architecture awards, 54 American Institute of Architects (AIA) awards, the Rome prize fellowship from the American Academy of Design in Rome in 1987, a gold medal in architecture in 2000 from the American Institute of Architects, the alumnus of the year award from his alma mater, USC, in 1992, and a "member elect" distinction from the American Academy of Arts and Letters in 1992.

The six-foot five-inch, wiry Thom Mayne is an accomplished lecturer and essayist; he has written several academic essays describing the theories behind his innovative designs and is currently a tenured professor of architecture at the University of California at Los Angeles (UCLA). Over the course of his career he has taught courses at such renowned American institutions as Columbia University, in New York City; Harvard University; and Yale University, in New Haven, Connecticut. In addition, he has taught overseas, at the Berlage Institute, in the Netherlands, and the Bartlett School of Architecture, in London. Mayne is currently a member of the board of directors at the Southern California Institute of Architecture. At his firm, which is now based in Santa Monica, California, and employs close to 40 architects and designers, Mayne sits among his staff rather than in a private office. He feels that this arrangement helps to establish a sense of "collective enterprise" among his employees. In addition to its work on buildings, the firm produces a wide range of other designs, for such items as wristwatches and teapots.

While he was known for much of his career for having a contentious personality, Mayne has reportedly developed a more easygoing manner. With his first wife, Susan Burnham, whom he married in 1964 and divorced in 1970, he has a son, Richard. Mayne married his second wife, Alison, in 1981; together they have two children, Sam and Cooper. Describing his home life as "lovely," Mayne was quoted as saying in the Pritzker press release: "My wife is so, really luscious. She really knows me, and understands completely that I can be an extremely self-critical person because of all the challenges in my life. We both get that the self-critical part is also the engine that drives the creativity." He and his family live in Southern California.

In the Pritzker press release, Mayne is quoted as saying, "An architect operates, finally, more as a director does than as a painter or a sculptor. They have to focus the energy of a large group of people on a common obsession. The architect has to know a little bit about everything . . . it's a generalist discipline not a discipline for the specialist."

—D.F.

Suggested Reading: *Architectural Record* p120+ Jan. 1, 2005, with photos; *Los Angeles Times* A p1 Mar. 21, 2005, with photos; *New York Times* E p1 Mar. 21, 2005, with photos; *Newsweek* p58+ May 23, 2005, with photo; Pritzker Architecture Prize on-line media kit

Selected Works: Sequoyah Educational Research Center, Santa Monica, California, 1974; Cedars-Sinai Comprehensive Cancer Center, Los Angeles, 1988; Salick Health Care Office Building 8201, Los Angeles, California, 1991; Diamond Ranch High School, Pomona, California, 1999; International Elementary School, Long Beach, California, 1999; Calantras District 7 Headquarters, Los Angeles, California, 2004

Courtesy of Starcom MediaVest Group

McCann, Renetta

1957– CEO of the Americas of Starcom MediaVest Group

Address: Starcom MediaVest Group, 35 W. Wacker Dr., Chicago, IL 60601

Before Renetta McCann was named the 2002 Adwoman of the Year by the Women's Advertising Club of Chicago, the 24-year ad-industry veteran had been nominated for the award several times earlier without a win. Indeed, McCann had taken to calling herself "the Susan Lucci of the Women's Advertising Club of Chicago"—a reference to the soap-opera actress who became famous for her 19 consecutive, fruitless Daytime Emmy nominations. "One look at me and you can only imagine the boundaries I've had to negotiate, the challenges I've had to traverse," McCann said during her acceptance speech, as quoted by Sonia Alleyne for *Black Enterprise* (September 2002). Knowing that audience members would assume that she was speaking of obstacles familiar to African-American women in the business world, she delivered her punch line: "Such are the trials of being a short person." McCann likes to defy expectations. Beginning with her participation in a ground-floor training program at a major advertising firm, she rose through industry ranks to become, in August 2004, the chief executive officer (CEO) of the Americas for Starcom MediaVest Group (SMG). In that post she oversees all media properties in the Western Hemisphere owned by the Publicis Groupe, the Paris-based media consultancy conglomerate that controls SMG. In his announcement of McCann's promotion, SMG Worldwide CEO Jack Klues said,

as quoted by Aaron Baar in *Adweek* (August 3, 2004), "Renetta has consistently demonstrated a keen ability to run an effective organization while aggressively stewarding her clients' brands and championing innovation and results in consumer contact."

In a single year (2000), as the newly minted CEO of Starcom North America, McCann attracted more than $700 million worth of new business, with such iconic American brands as Hallmark, Polaroid, McDonald's, and Sara Lee. For years her workforce of 600 in the U.S. and Canada—half of whom were hired under her watch—has had the lowest employee-turnover rate in advertising, indicating her remarkable ability to inspire loyalty in a notoriously volatile industry. "I developed my personal brand over time," she explained to Charmon Parker Williams for *Black MBA Magazine* (Fall 2004, on-line). "As a woman of color, the rules of how I play the game are different. . . . My clients want to know how my presence will enhance their bottom line. And, in somewhat of a Pavlovian manner, I have developed a style that works with clients as well as works internally with employees." In her new position McCann assumed responsibility for Latin America, SMG's fastest-growing region, and her workforce tripled. She is now in line to succeed Jack Klues at the helm of SMG Worldwide.

The eldest of five children, Renetta E. McCann was born in Chicago, Illinois, in 1957. According to Matthew Jones in diversityinbusiness.com (September 2004), her mother is a teacher and has earned two master's degrees. In 1978 McCann graduated from Northwestern University, in Evanston, Illinois, with a degree in communication studies. She wanted to work in the advertising industry, but as she told Laurie Freeman for *Advertising Age* (February 15, 1999), "I knew, coming out of school, that I needed skills and more training." Shortly after she completed college, she was accepted into a training program at Leo Burnett Worldwide Inc., a top advertising agency that created marketing campaigns for such companies as McDonald's and Kellogg's. "I felt confident that Burnett had the program to teach me the next set of things I knew I needed to know," McCann continued to Freeman. She began as an assistant in Burnett's media department, which was responsible for placing clients' advertisements in newspapers and magazines, on radio, and on television. She became a media supervisor in 1982. McCann has credited much of her success to her mentor at Burnett, Chuck Quarnstrom, who was serving as a vice president when she began her career. "Mentoring is very personal and Chuck trained a lot of people who are now media directors," she said to Freeman. "I don't think he treated me any different than other trainees, but he set a great example professionally—and the way I operate today is very much the way Chuck would do things." "He instilled . . . things such as listening to clients," she told Jennifer Derryberry for *Business Marketing* (August 1, 1995), "turning over rocks and stones to find different answers, and the beauty of doing good work."

In 1986 the professional development organization Design and Art Direction (D&AD) recognized McCann by awarding her its prestigious Black Pencil, which honors people in advertising who produce groundbreaking work or redefine the field. She was the first Black Pencil honoree from a media department. That same year Leo Burnett promoted her to assistant media director. By 1988 she had been named vice president, and one year later she became media director. McCann subsequently took the lead in pitching for business from several high-profile clients, winning virtually all, including Sony's Consumer Electronics, in 1991; Fruit of the Loom, in 1992; Disney World, in 1994; and Johnny Walker whiskey, in 1995. In 1997, as the media department increasingly took control of the company's advertising campaigns' strategies, Burnett spun it off into a separate company, Starcom Media Services, which would also track market trends. McCann, who had accepted a promotion to senior vice president at Leo Burnett Worldwide in 1995, was appointed managing director of Starcom North America in 1999; in 2000 she took over as CEO.

Through a series of mergers and acquisitions, Starcom became part of the Starcom MediaVest Group, which in turn joined forces with other U.S. advertising and media properties to form the media group Bcom3. In 2002 the global-communications conglomerate Publicis Groupe purchased Bcom3, placing Starcom under its aegis. Throughout this period McCann maintained her title and Starcom flourished, even as the media industry grappled with reduced advertising and cuts in spending, first because of the bursting of the late-1990s dot-com stock-market bubble, and then because of the terrorist attacks of September 11, 2001. Key to McCann's success was her reputation as a strategist and media thinker, which led Disney to hand over responsibility for its corporate brand management to Starcom North America. "We were able to take the clues that they gave us and put it into a story that was coherent for them as a company," McCann told Alleyne. "Everybody talks about the Disney account as if it is one thing, but we picked up 16 pieces of business [with Disney]."

In August 2004 McCann was again promoted, this time to CEO of the Americas for SMG. "This was probably a little bit of an overdue announcement," Jack Klues said regarding McCann's advancement, according to Media Daily News (August 4, 2004, on-line). "In terms of recognition for Renetta, it's more external recognition because she's always been a trusted advisor to me, and certainly a big contributor to the SMG board at large." McCann's job encompasses oversight of SMG's four principal units: Starcom, MediaVest, StarLink, and GM Planworks, the last of which develops media strategies for General Motors. Collectively, SMG controls nearly $13 billion in ad dollars spent in the U.S., Canada, and Latin America—

16 percent of the total expended on advertising in the Western Hemisphere—making SMG the largest media buyer in the Americas.

A highly sought-after speaker at advertising and media-industry conferences, McCann serves as chair of the American Association for Advertising Agencies' Media Policy Committee; as a member of the advisory board of Northwestern University's Media Management Center; as a member of the American Advertising Federation's Business Practices Leadership Council; and as a board member of the Audit Bureau of Circulations and of Chicago United, a coalition of senior executives who advocate for racial diversity among business leaders. Her trophy collection includes several Effies, presented by the New York American Marketing Association to the creators of each year's most effective advertising campaigns, and Cannes Lions, awarded annually at the International Advertising Festival. McCann was given the Black Expo President's Award in 2000. The following year she was named a "Media Maven" by Advertising Age. In 2002 Ebony included as among "57 Most Intriguing Blacks," and Black Enterprise chose her as "Corporate Executive of the Year." In 2003 Essence listed her among "50 Women Who Are Changing the World," and the Women's Leadership Exchange presented her with its Compass Award, for her contributions in changing perceptions of women as leaders. Her other honors include a BusinessWeek Media Strategies Award and the Chicago Magazine Association's Vanguard Award.

McCann lives in Chicago, Illinois, with Kevin, her husband of 20 years, and their children, Ella and Alexander. Kevin McCann owns Glenn Poor Chicago, an electronics salon.

—R.E.

Suggested Reading: Advertising Age S p10 Feb. 15, 1999, with photo; Black Enterprise p90 Sep. 2002, with photos; Black MBA Magazine (on-line) p2+ Fall 2004, with photo; diversityinbusiness.com Sep. 2004

McCurry, Steve

Apr. 23, 1950– Photojournalist

Address: Steve McCurry Studios, 2 Fifth Ave., New York NY 10011

"Sometimes you can see the character of a whole culture in one face," the photojournalist Steve McCurry told Peter Popham for the London *Independent* (August 15, 1999). McCurry's more than 25-year-long career as a photojournalist is widely associated with a single portrait, taken in a refugee camp for Afghans in Pakistan: that of an adolescent girl, whose expression and brilliant, piercing green eyes reflect toughness, sensitivity, and pain.

Ringo H. W. Chiu/Getty Images

Steve McCurry

Known as "Afghan Girl," the photo appeared on the cover of the June 1985 issue of *National Geographic*; it has since become one of the most widely recognized pictures in the world. In the opinion of William Allen, who served as the editor in chief of *National Geographic* for 10 years, the photo was "certainly the most memorable image that we have ever published," as he told Gregg Zoroya for *USA Today* (March 13, 2002). The picture generated such widespread interest in the girl herself that, shortly before McCurry met her again, 17 years later, as he told Lloyd Grove for the *Washington Post* (November 1, 2001), "Practically daily, people have wanted to send money, adopt her, marry her. Someone tattooed her on his arm."

When the face of the Afghan girl became known to millions of readers of *National Geographic*, McCurry's career as a photojournalist was already well established. Indeed, in 1980, less than three years after he began taking pictures as a freelance photographer, he won a major prize from the Overseas Press Club for his work in Afghanistan both before and after the invasion of that country by troops from what was then the Soviet Union. His first assignment from *National Geographic* came soon afterward. McCurry has traveled to more than 80 countries, visiting India at least 50 times and Nepal more than 15. His photos have appeared in the *New York Times*, *Life*, *Time*, and many other magazines and newspapers as well as books, including six of his own: *The Imperial Way*; *Monsoon*; *South Southeast*; *Portraits*; *The Path to Buddha: A Tibetan Pilgrimage*; and *Sanctuary: The Temples of Angkor*. When McCurry became a member of Magnum, one of the world's premier photo agencies, he joined an elite group of master

photojournalists, among them Cornell Capa, Eve Arnold, Marc Riboud, and Susan Meiselas and, until their deaths, Robert Capa, Werner Bischof, W. Eugene Smith, and Henri Cartier-Bresson. By his own account, McCurry is dedicated to the documentary tradition as epitomized in the work of Cartier-Bresson, who, as he told T. J. Sony for *India Abroad* (March 15, 2002), "was never out to make art, he was looking at life and reacting to it." McCurry has photographed brutal conflicts in countries including Lebanon, Cambodia, the Philippines, Kashmir, Sri Lanka, Burma, Iran, and Iraq, and while on assignment he has been arrested, robbed at gunpoint, shot at by Russian helicopters, and left to drown after a plane crash in a Slovenian lake. On September 11, 2001, although he had returned from months of work in Asia only hours before, McCurry went to the site of the World Trade Center almost immediately after its destruction by terrorists and spent the next two days taking photos of the devastation. His experiences in witnessing and photographing large-scale violence notwithstanding, he considers his work to be primarily about individuals. "Most of my images are grounded in people," he wrote for his Web site, "and I try to convey what it is like to be that person, a person caught in a broader landscape, that you could call the human condition."

Steve McCurry was born in Philadelphia, Pennsylvania, on April 23, 1950 and grew up in the Philadelphia suburb of Newtown Square. The youngest of the three children of an electrical engineer and his wife, a homemaker, McCurry has described his upbringing as relatively uneventful. "The biggest trips we made when I was a kid were to visit relatives in South Carolina"—people who "lived a very suburban life—so they were pretty tame as far as trips went," McCurry told Sean Newson for the London *Sunday Times* (June 20, 1999). He barely graduated from Marple Newtown High because of poor grades, and, not feeling drawn to any particular academic subject or profession, he did not immediately pursue a college education. Instead, he took a job in the mailroom of a major pharmaceutical company. "Suddenly, I was surrounded by letters coming in from all over the world," he told Newson. "That's when I became aware of what was out there."

On his first trip abroad, McCurry traveled through Europe for a year, surviving on little money. "Seeing how different people live," he told Newson, "and do different things, how the architecture was different—I absolutely loved it." After he returned to the U.S., McCurry sought a way to earn his living while traveling. With that objective, he took classes at a small private college to improve his academic record and then transferred to Pennsylvania State University, in State College, to study cinematography and history. His interest in film led him to take pictures for the campus newspaper and to enroll in two photography courses. "Those two classes were probably as important to me as any part of my education," he told Lini S. Kadaba for the *Philadelphia Inquirer* (September 12, 2000). "It struck right to the core of my soul. This is what I want to do." Gerald Lang, one of McCurry's professors, told Jeremy R. Cooke for the Pennsylvania State *Daily Collegian* that McCurry's characteristic approach to photography was evident early on. "As a student, he wasn't afraid to take risks," Lang said. "If he had an idea, he would go for it."

By the time he graduated, with a B.A. degree, cum laude, in 1974, McCurry had traveled in Israel, Egypt, Uganda, and the Sudan and had hitchhiked from South Carolina to Panama and back; meanwhile, his desire to become a filmmaker had faded. Instead, he took a job as a photographer with *Today's Post*, a newspaper that covered suburban communities not far from his home in Newtown Square; he earned $5 per assignment. His first, as he recalled to Michelle Cazzulino for the Sydney *Daily Telegraph* (February 19, 2000), was to take photos at the scene of a car crash in which four people had been killed. "It was just so gruesome and terrible," he said, "that I couldn't actually look at it, except through my camera." For the most part, though, McCurry's work was routine, and the local happenings at which he took pictures were too dull to enable him to build an arresting portfolio with which to secure a job with a major newspaper. Frustrated, McCurry quit *Today's Post* in 1978 and headed to India to work as a freelance photographer. The strength of the American dollar and his willingness to live simply allowed him to get by on the occasional income he received from magazines and newspapers. He extended his trip into a roughly two-year odyssey through India, stopping to work in the Indian states of Goa, Ladakh (sometimes called Little Tibet), and Rajasthan, and venturing into Nepal as well.

By May 1979 McCurry had made his way to the North-West Frontier Province of Pakistan, where he met refugees from the neighboring Afghan province of Nuristan. For more than a year, Afghanistan had been in a state of continual internal conflict, following a bloody Communist coup and the establishment of an increasingly autocratic government. The refugees saw in McCurry a means for bringing international attention to their nation's situation. Although the danger of traveling illegally in a war-torn country at first deeply frightened him, he spent two weeks in Afghanistan, traveling in disguise and using only the most basic photo equipment to take pictures of war. When a severe case of amoebic dysentery forced him to leave, he smuggled his rolls of film back into Pakistan by sewing them into his clothes.

In September 1979 McCurry returned to Afghanistan to take more photos. A few months later, on December 24, 1979, military units from the Soviet Union took control of Kabul, Afghanistan's capital city, under the pretext of having been invited as part of a recently signed treaty between the two countries. In the context of the ongoing Cold War between the Soviet Union (and its allies in Eastern Europe) and the United States (and its allies in Western Europe), the arrival of large numbers of Soviet troops in what had only recently been an independent and relatively democratic nation became a major news story. But so few Westerners had traveled in or were then in Afghanistan that images of the Soviet invasion and its effects on ordinary people were extremely scarce. McCurry's photos were thus much in demand among newspapers and magazines worldwide. Within weeks of the invasion, McCurry was receiving assignments from *Time*, and his career as a documentary photographer had been launched. As McCurry told Al Hunter Jr. for the *Philadelphia Daily News* (September 11, 2000), "I went from [being] a shuffling, anonymous photographer to someone whose name kept appearing in magazines."

McCurry's photos of Afghanistan earned him the 1980 Robert Capa Gold Medal for best photographic reporting from abroad, an honor with which the Overseas Press Club recognizes demonstrations of "exceptional courage and enterprise." Also on the strength of his work in Afghanistan, McCurry received two assignments from *National Geographic*, thereby beginning his long association with the magazine. For documentary photographers, *National Geographic* is in many ways the ideal employer. Its high circulation (currently estimated at more than nine million copies per month) means wide public exposure, while its willingness to support photographers for weeks or even months in the field gives them the opportunity to develop closer relationships with, and a deeper understanding of, their subjects. It also enables them to take many photos—sometimes thousands—out of which only a few will be chosen for publication. *National Geographic* editors "spare no expense to get the best stories and pictures," McCurry told Gary Schwan for the *Palm Beach (Florida) Post* (June 27, 2004). "But, in turn, you have to perform at the highest level."

For one of his early *National Geographic* assignments, in about 1983, McCurry focused on people on trains and in train stations in India. His photos, along with text by Paul Theroux, filled 48 pages of the magazine's June 1984 issue; the following year an expanded version of the photo essay appeared in a book, *The Imperial Way: By Rail from Peshawar to Chittagong*. His India photos and others led the National Press Photographers' Association to name him magazine photographer of the year in 1984. It was also in 1984 that McCurry, while on assignment for *National Geographic*, shot his celebrated portrait of a young Afghan girl. While working in the Nasir Bagh refugee camp in Peshawar, Pakistan, near the border with Afghanistan, he noticed the girl in a tent set up as a makeshift school. "There was something in her eyes that was unsettling," he told Stuart Wavell for the London *Sunday Times* (March 17, 2002). "They held an ambiguity: she was poor yet she was proud, yet she had also clearly been traumatized." McCurry learned from her teacher that the girl was from the

Afghan province of Kondoz and that her parents had been killed years earlier, shortly after the Soviet occupation had begun. She had recently spent two weeks traveling to the camp through the mountains along with her grandmother, two sisters, and a brother. McCurry estimated the age of the girl to be 12; later, he found out that she did not know exactly how old she was. He spent only a few minutes with her and did not learn her name. "I didn't think the photograph of the girl would be different from anything else I shot that day," he told Cathy Newman for *National Geographic* (April 1, 2002). It was only after he returned to the U.S. and had his film developed that he realized how special the portrait was. The image appeared on the cover of the June 1985 issue of *National Geographic*.

By 1986 McCurry had joined the famed photo agency Magnum Photos and had won four first prizes in the World Press Photo contest, which is conducted by an independent, nonprofit organization based in the Netherlands. He had also earned an Olivier Rebbot Award, from the Overseas Press Club of America, for his photos of the widespread citizens' rebellion against the autocratic leader of the Philippines, Ferdinand Marcos. In 1987 he received an Award of Excellence from the National Press Photographers' Association for his photographs of the land and people of the Sahel, an environmentally unstable but culturally vital section of sub-Saharan Africa that extends east from Mauritania, on the coast of the Atlantic Ocean, to Chad.

In 1988 McCurry published *Monsoon*, another book based on a *National Geographic* assignment dating from 1983. Though technically a monsoon denotes only a shift in wind patterns, the phenomenon has become closely associated with the massive annual rains that occur along with the shift. Monsoons simultaneously threaten and revitalize many parts of South Asia every year, and they are occasions of "amazing drama," as McCurry told Jane Gottlieb for *Photo District News* (July 2004). "You had the drama of whether there is too much or not enough rain; it's rarely perfect. There's flooding, there's drought. There's all this incredible anticipation and disappointment and disaster and an incredible amount of emotion."

A series of McCurry's photos focusing on the aftermath of the 1991 Gulf War in Iraq and Kuwait earned him a second Olivier Rebbot Award and moved the National Press Photographers Association to once again name him magazine photographer of the year. Pennsylvania State University gave him its Arts and Architecture Distinguished Alumni Award in 1996 and named him a lifetime fellow in 1999. He earned one of the most prestigious honors in photojournalism—*Life*'s Alfred Eisenstadt Award for magazine photography—in 1998, for an image that appeared in the May 1997 issue of *National Geographic*. Taken in India, it showed the face of a young boy painted a striking red during an annual religious festival, at a place where, a year earlier, McCurry had almost

drowned when a group of celebrants pushed him into the water of the river in which he was standing with his camera.

In 1999 McCurry published what was to become his most widely sold book: *Portraits*, a collection of some 220 photos of people from around the world, with a heavy emphasis on South and Southeast Asia. Never primarily a portraitist, he assembled the photos at the urging of his publisher, the highly respected visual-arts press Phaidon. "It was all in my archives waiting for someone to recognize it," he told Gottlieb. For many of the selected images, McCurry cropped photos to isolate the face of a single person looking directly into the camera. According to Peter Popham in his 1999 London *Independent* article, "in these photographs that which Samuel Beckett calls 'the wealth of filthy circumstance' is stripped away. The familiar stigmata of poverty or war are absent. Colours and props are few, the background is often no more than a black void or a darkish blur or a framing window. And this stripping-away of cliche heightens intensity: these strangers speak to us with a directness from which we flinch. The strength of Steve McCurry's portraits lies in their simplicity and their minimalism." *Portraits* has sold hundreds of thousands of copies.

In 2000 McCurry brought together more than 100 photos taken in Asia, particularly India, for *South Southeast*, which won the National Press Photographers Book of the Year Award. His fascination with that part of the planet stems in part, as he wrote in the introduction to the book, from the region's distinctive combination of "colour and life and light." Although, according to McCurry, color is the most important of those elements, "colour alone, or structure for structure's sake, are not for me what finally make a good picture. What makes for a powerful image—much like Asia itself—is the confluence of all these elements within the rude stream of life. It is colour and structure all subordinated into the sacred right then of the only-offered-once."

McCurry became better known to the general public in 2001, thanks to the publication of two books. The first, *New York September 11*, contains photos documenting the events of September 11, taken by a number of Magnum photographers. The ones by McCurry include shots that he took from the roof of his office building, in Lower Manhattan, of the World Trade Center's twin towers after terrorists flew airplanes into them; one series of photos shows the south tower as it fell. The photos were widely reproduced and exhibited publicly. McCurry's photo "Afghan Girl" adorns the cover of the second book, *National Geographic, the Photographs*, a collection of what *National Geographic* editors considered the 100 best photos from the thousands published in the magazine since its founding, in 1888. After the American-led bombing and invasion of Afghanistan, which followed the September 11 terrorist attacks, the portrait of the girl came to represent, for many, the human face of a country that seemed so foreign and re- mote. McCurry later told Bob Faw on the *Today* show (March 13, 2002), on NBC-TV, "I think she's certainly an icon. I think she's emblematic of the Afghan spirit, the Afghan people, and . . . the for- titude of these people, . . . the will to survive."

From time to time during assignments that had taken him to Afghanistan, McCurry had tried in vain to find the Afghan girl. The public's growing interest in her identity in the final months of 2001 prompted National Geographic Television to send a team to Afghanistan to search for her. After a se- ries of false leads, the team returned to the refugee camp in Pakistan where McCurry had photo- graphed her. There they met a man who recognized her from the photo and said that his family and hers had been neighbors in Afghanistan long ago. After traveling back into the mountainous area where they had lived, the man returned with a woman who resembled the girl in McCurry's pho- to. Within days McCurry was reunited with his most famous subject, whose name is Sharbat Gula. Although her face bore evidence of the passage of 17 years, during which she had endured poor health, harsh living conditions, four pregnancies, and the death of one of her babies, McCurry felt sure that she was the same person—a conclusion that an analysis of the tissue patterns in her irises later confirmed. Gula remembered McCurry, too, largely because he was the only person ever to have taken her picture. Their reunion became the sub- ject of newspaper, radio, and television stories around the world, and McCurry's images of the older Gula were published widely; one appeared on the cover of the April 2002 issue of *National Geographic* and another on the back cover of the book *National Geographic, the Photographs.*

Since then McCurry has published two addi- tional collections of his photos: *Sanctuary: The Temples of Angkor* (2002), which focuses on an ex- traordinary religious and historical site in Cambo- dia that dates from the 11th century, and *The Path to Buddha: A Tibetan Pilgrimage* (2003). Also in 2003 the George Eastman House, in Rochester, New York, mounted a retrospective of McCurry's work. Called Face of Asia, the exhibition presented 100 photos taken in Afghanistan, Cambodia, India, and Tibet, along with articles related to McCurry's career, such as his passport, and some of the many paintings, letters, photos of sidewalk murals, and other items he received from people in reaction to the dissemination of "Afghan Girl." The exhibition has since traveled to sites in Edinburgh, Scotland; London, England; and San Diego, California.

In 2005 McCurry auctioned off the camera he used to photograph the older Sharbat Gula and do- nated to charity the $25,000 it brought— specifically, to relief efforts in South Asia, where a tsunami killed hundreds of thousands of people in December 2004. Also in 2005 the American So- ciety of Magazine Editors selected the *National Geographic* cover on which McCurry's photo of the young Sharbat Gula appeared as one of the 10 best

magazine covers produced in the last 40 years. Mc- Curry has often characterized as the ideal by- product of his work the clear and meaningful change for the good spurred by the publication of one or more of his photos. In a portion of his Web site labeled "Journey," he wrote that after *National Geographic* printed his photo of an Indian tailor carrying his ruined sewing machine through chin- deep floodwaters in 1985, the manufacturer of the machine sent the man a new one. "We photogra- phers say that we 'take' a picture," he wrote, "and in a certain sense that is true. We take something from people's lives, but in doing so, we tell their story. In this case, I took his picture, others saw it, were moved, and reached out to help the man. That is the best possible result."

Anthony Bannon's 74-page illustrated mono- graph about the photographer and his work, titled *Steve McCurry*, was published in July 2005. Mc- Curry, who is unmarried, lives in Manhattan.

—D.R.

Suggested Reading: (Glasgow) *Herald* p14 Apr. 6, 2002; *India Abroad* p7 Mar. 15, 2002, with photo; *Petersen's Photographic* p52+ Mar. 2002, with photos; *Philadelphia Daily News* p47 Sep. 11, 2000, with photos; *Philadelphia Inquirer* D p1, with photo; *Photo District News* p44 July 2004, with photo; *RPS Journal* p248+ July–Aug. 2002, with photos; Steve McCurry Web site; *USA Today* A p10 Mar. 13, 2002

Selected Books: *The Imperial Way*, 1985 (with text by Paul Theroux); *Monsoon*, 1988; *Portraits*, 1999; *South Southeast*, 2000; *Sanctuary: The Temples of Angkor*, 2002; *The Path to Buddha: A Tibetan Pilgrimage*, 2003; as contributor—*In Our Time*, 1989; *Magnum Landscape*, 1996; *The Human Collection*, 1997; *Photobook*, 1997; *Time Frames*, 1998; *Waterproof*, 1998; *New York September 11, 2001*

McGrath, Judy

1952– Chairperson and CEO of MTV Networks

Address: MTV Networks, 1515 Broadway, 28th Fl., New York, NY 10036

When Judy McGrath was named chairperson and chief executive officer (CEO) of MTV Networks in July 2004, she took the reins of the fastest-growing division of Viacom International, the global media company that also owns CBS, Infinity Broadcast- ing, and Simon & Schuster, among other entities. McGrath, who is now one of the most powerful women in the entertainment industry, consistently draws praise from others in the field; in *Variety* (July 21, 2004), John Dempsey and Denise Martin quoted an unnamed cable-television executive as

Matthew Peyton/Getty Images

Judy McGrath

saying, "Judy has a true programming vision that gets wrapped and marketed and sold brilliantly to the world." One network writer told John Seabrook for the *New Yorker* (October 10, 1994, on-line), "Judy would be the heart of MTV, if MTV had a heart." Seabrook, who wrote about McGrath when she was the creative head of the station, noted that although she was older than not only MTV's target audience but also most of its employees, she possessed "the ability to create an environment where people feel comfortable creatively misbehaving. She's like the ideal much older sister, who lets you get away with things your parents wouldn't but nevertheless looks out for you."

MTV Networks owns and operates the channels MTV; MTV2; VH1; MTVU; Nickelodeon; Nick at Nite; Comedy Central; TV Land; Spike TV; CMT; Noggin; Logo; MTVN International; and the Digital Suite from MTV Networks, a package of 13 digital services trademarked by MTV. In total, MTV Networks reaches appoximately 400 million viewers in 164 countries and broadcasts in 18 languages. (MTV Networks also has mobile distribution arrangements with numerous digital and cellular providers, which allows MTV's contents to be broadcast onto mobile phones.) MTV, the original station, whose acronym stands for Music Television, had its genesis when two media executives, John Lack and Bob Pittman, conceived of an outlet that, 24 hours a day, would air music videos, which at that time were used mainly by record companies for promotional purposes. MTV was launched at 12:01 a.m. on August 1, 1981. The first video that the fledgling network broadcast was, appropriately enough, "Video Killed the Radio Star," by the Buggles. Since then, MTV has been alter-

nately praised and vilified for changing the face of the television industry. (Some critics complain that the channel's content is overtly sexual and violent and claim that the frenetic pace and frequent cuts of most of the aired clips have helped to shorten the attention spans of young viewers.)

Born in 1952, Judy McGrath was raised in Scranton, Pennsylvania. She has traced her feminist values to her mother, a teacher, and has credited her father, a social worker, with instilling in her a passion for music. She has recalled that when she was a little girl, she would often stand on a chair and conduct an imaginary orchestra. In her teens, she and her friends fantasized about marrying the members of the Beatles. McGrath attended Catholic schools and then entered Cedar Crest College, a women's school in Allentown, Pennsylvania; she graduated with a bachelor's degree in English in 1974. McGrath's dream at the time was to write for the music magazine *Rolling Stone*; instead, she took successive jobs as a copywriter for an ad agency in Philadephia, a copy chief at the Condé Nast magazine *Mademoiselle*, and a senior writer for *Glamour*, also published by Condé Nast. When she left *Glamour* to work for MTV, several months after its launch, in 1981, her magazine colleagues criticized the move, calling cable television "tacky" and predicting that MTV would be a temporary fad. "At Condé Nast the staff had degrees from Ivy League schools," McGrath told Lee Alan Hill for *Television Week* (June 21, 2004). "At MTV no one had degrees. Many were refugees from radio. Some just seemed like refugees. But the one thing we had in common was our passion for music. We felt that rock had the ability to change lives."

McGrath's first position with MTV was copywriter in the promotions department. She soon came up with such successful promotional spots as "Devo Goes Hawaii," featuring a new-wave band that was popular in the 1980s, and "Win a One-Night Stand with Pat Benatar," centered on a female rocker whose videos were played in heavy rotation during the station's early years. By 1987 McGrath had been made director of on-air promotions; she later rose through the ranks to become editorial director. In 1991 she became an executive vice president and creative director. In 1994 McGrath was named president of the MTV Group and chairman of Interactive Music, providing leadership for MTV; MTV2, a spin-off station; and MTVi, the Internet component of MTV. In June 2003 McGrath was promoted to co-president of MTV Networks, along with Herb Scannell, president of Nickelodeon (which is aimed at children), Nick at Nite (which airs reruns of classic shows from past decades), Spike TV (which is geared toward a male audience), and TV Land (which specializes in nostalgic programming, much of it from the 1970s). By July of the following year, Tom Freston, the co-president and chief operating officer of Viacom, promoted McGrath to his former position of chair and CEO of MTV Networks, the position she currently holds.

To the dismay of some viewers, McGrath has helped to change MTV from being solely a music channel to one that includes a variety of programming genres. She has had a hand in creating some of MTV's best-known and most iconic original programming, notably *Beavis and Butt-head*, a cartoon that frequently featured scatological humor; the acoustic *MTV Unplugged*; the *Tom Green Show*, a comic talk format; *The Real World* and *The Osbournes*, reality shows; *MTV News*; and such programs as the *MTV Video Music Awards* and *MTV Movie Awards*. She has used the newly expanded channel to highlight social issues, spearheading such campaigns as "Choose or Lose," which encouraged young people to vote; "Fight for Your Rights: Take a Stand Against Violence"; and "Fight for Your Rights: Protect Yourself," which dealt with AIDS awareness. "MTV Networks [believes] that young people should be encouraged to express their opinions about critical social issues, and be included in the international dialogue about our world," McGrath said in an article posted on the Global Kids Web site (2002). "They deserve to be informed, respected and recognized for their place in our society, now and in the future."

Periodically, McGrath has found herself in the midst of controversy. The 2004 Super Bowl half-time show (which was staged by MTV) caused a massive uproar, for example, when, at the conclusion of a musical performance by the singers Justin Timberlake and Janet Jackson, Timberlake tore off part of Jackson's bustier, so that her breast was exposed briefly. Supposedly, a red lace undergarment should have remained under the torn cup, but, in what was described as a "wardrobe malfunction," Timberlake tore both layers of fabric. While many viewers found the incident humorous, dubbing it "Nipplegate," others were appalled. Although MTV and CBS officials denied foreknowledge of the stunt, and both Jackson and Timberlake claimed that they had acted independently of the network, the Federal Communications Commission (FCC), after reportedly receiving more than 500,000 complaints, fined Viacom a total of $550,000. Some called for McGrath's dismissal after the fiasco. Although McGrath continued to support Timberlake and Jackson as performers, she said, according to an Associated Press article printed in the *Toronto Star* (February 4, 2004), "I don't appreciate someone who doesn't communicate what [his] plans are. I think it was a misguided move on their parts." Another tempest stemmed from MTV Networks' launch, on February 17, 2005, of Logo, a 24-hour cable channel designed for the lesbian, gay, bisexual, and transgender communities.

McGrath, who is in her early 50s, has disputed the charge that she has outgrown MTV. She maintained in an interview with Bill Carter for the *New York Times* (July 26, 2004) that she is "in touch with my inner teen. . . . I think having an inner teen means idealism." She is still passionate about music and is always on the lookout for innovative bands and new trends. "I still care about who the next Nirvana is," she told John Seabrook, referring to a popular band of the 1990s. "And I don't know why. I am still trying to understand what the feeling I get from this stuff means. What are the young people saying? I just want to know."

In 2002 Global Kids, an educational program for urban youth, honored McGrath for her leadership skills and her commitment to children. In 2003 the T. J. Martell Foundation, which funds research for cancer and AIDS, named her humanitarian of the year. Also in 2003 the editors of *Fortune* listed her among the 50 most powerful women in American business.

McGrath is married to a former systems analyst who is now a stay-at-home dad; the couple have a daughter, Anna. Referring to the benefits of tracking Anna's tastes in music and television, McGrath told a writer for *Hollywood Reporter* (December 7, 2004, on-line), "She's one hidden advantage to doing my job." The family lives on the Upper West Side of New York City.

—K.J.E.

Suggested Reading: *New York Times* E p1 July 26, 2004; *New Yorker* (on-line) Oct. 10, 1994; *Television Week* p16 June 21, 2004; *Variety* A p24 Nov. 12, 2003, p1 July 21, 2004

McLurkin, James

1972– Computer engineer; roboticist; inventor

Address: MIT Computer Science and Artificial Intelligence Lab, The Stata Center, Bldg. 32, Rm. G585, 32 Vassar St., Cambridge, MA 02139

"I have always loved building things," the computer engineer and inventor James McLurkin said to a reporter for *Nova Science Now*, as quoted on the PBS Web site (December 16, 2004, on-line). "I love making things work. I love being able to write software and then watch that software make the robots move and make the lights blink and the speakers go and things like that. Robotics is the highest form of that art, the art of electromechanical software systems." McLurkin designs and creates robots that are based on biological organisms, specifically ants and bees, and that perform complex functions. He has been an adviser for many mechanical, computer, and engineering projects for such clients as Walt Disney Imagineering, which is responsible for creating the equipment at Disney theme parks, and Sensable Technologies, "a leading provider of 3D touch-enabled digital solutions" for research, product design, the development of commercial software, and the creation of digital content, according to its Web site. McLurkin created his first interactive group of robots in 1995, while doing undergraduate work at the Massachusetts Institute

Courtesy of the Lemelson-MIT Program

James McLurkin

of Technology (MIT); those small, robotic "ants" were capable of working together in simple activities. "They could move towards one another. They could move away from one another. They could pick up food," McLurkin explained to a reporter for *Nova Science Now.* "They could play some fun games like tag and manhunt." After the "ants," McLurkin worked on a bee-like "swarm" of robots for the company iRobot. Communicating with each other via infrared light to function as a group, they could also perform independent actions. "The whole advantage of the swarm is that failures of individual robots do not affect the output of the group," McLurkin explained to *Nova Science Now.* McLurkin has been a guest speaker at events for colleges as well as organizations including Interval Research Inc., Lego Advanced Design Center, and the Association of Science-Technology Centers. He has taught high-school classes in subjects ranging from physics to civil engineering. In 2003 he was included on *Black Enterprise* magazine's "Hot List" of the "Best and Brightest Under 40" and was recognized by *Time* as one of five leading robotics engineers. Also in 2003 McLurkin was the recipient of the $30,000 Lemelson-MIT Student Prize for inventiveness. "A lot of us have worked on insect-robot things," Rodney Brooks, the director of MIT's artificial-intelligence lab, said to Carolina A. Miranda for *Time* (June 8, 2004, on-line). "But James has taken the technology further than anyone else."

James Dwight McLurkin IV was born on Long Island, New York, in 1972. His parents divorced while McLurkin was very young. His mother worked as a speech therapist; his father, who had studied electronics, later became a business man-

ager for the telecommunications giant AT&T. By the time McLurkin was eight, he had earned a reputation for causing trouble at school. "School was always awful and it still is," McLurkin said to Elizabeth J. Sherman for the Lemelson Center Web site. "Every report card said 'not working up to potential,' and even though I was in the gifted programs and got A's in science, the rest of my grades were usually pretty bad." His mother moved several times, trying to find the best schools for her son. McLurkin's father encouraged him to spend more time studying and less time with what he considered toys—the objects making up the building projects that consumed James McLurkin's attention. McLurkin explained to Elizabeth J. Sherman, "Mostly I was trying to build better toys than those you get in stores, which are always lamer than what you really want. My first memory is of building an erector set, and I was always getting into things. I hoarded broken bits, made messes, built things, burnt up bathrooms." In 1978 his parents indulged his penchant for building by giving him an extensive set of Lego toys, which McLurkin described to Sherman as "the key to life." In sixth grade he discovered the world of computers while spending Christmas with an older cousin. He read a book on the fundamentals of programming and began writing his own video-game programs. McLurkin soon persuaded his father to buy him a computer of his own, an Atari 800 XL with a 1050 disc drive and 64 kilobytes of memory. When McLurkin was in ninth grade, as Sherman reported, he requested placement in his school's honors program in mathematics; he excelled in the program and became a better all-around student.

Meanwhile, McLurkin continued to experiment with programming. He also developed an interest in mechanics, sparked by the gift of a BMX bicycle. While he enjoyed the bike's maneuverability, he began to envision ways that he could increase its speed. McLurkin recalled to Sherman, "I was putting thirty miles on it every weekend and knew that if I could add two gears, I could go much faster. I was told it couldn't be done—but if there is one thing I'm grateful for in my personality, it's that I don't listen to those who are older and wiser." His experiences with his bike further encouraged his creativity. "I was particularly irked the time an extra sprocket came off and I crashed at 30 mph," McLurkin explained to Sherman, "because someone else had welded the sprocket on for me. This taught me three things: that the forces I was dealing with were really big; that metal is not as strong as it looks; and that if I wanted it done right I should do it myself." He later learned about electronics from his cousin and built his first robot when he was 15, successfully writing its program and building it from parts including a casing from a remote-control car. The robot, which he named Rover, featured a squirt gun. Rover was followed by Stomper, McLurkin's first very small robot, and Tracker, the first all-metal robot he built without recycled parts. Tracker, the transporter for Stomper, had a docking bay in which Stomper could be stored. Each of the robots was equipped with an internal minicomputer and an infrared communications system that allowed it to track the other robot's location. (McLurkin began work on the robots in high school and completed them while attending college.)

McLurkin enrolled at MIT, where he earned a bachelor's degree in electrical engineering. In 1992, as a sophomore, while working at the Undergraduate Research Opportunities Program at MIT's Artificial Intelligence (AI) Lab, he created the Dwarves—palm-sized robots, created for the purpose of studying cooperative construction in a small robot community. Those robots, designed to use their interchangeable bulldozer and backhoe pieces for sand-construction endeavors, were not fully successful at functioning as a group. The following year, at the AI Lab, McLurkin built Goliath, a robot measuring one inch per side and powered by motors of the kind that were used for the vibration feature in pagers; Goliath's features included bump sensors and light detectors. In the mid-1990s McLurkin's fascination with tiny robots led to the "ants." He was inspired by an ant colony that he kept on his desk at MIT. McLurkin explained to the reporter for *Nova Science Now*, "You see how nature has solved certain hard problems, and what problems nature simply hasn't solved because they are not worth solving. For example, ants don't worry about avoiding each other. They simply walk over each other. Ants don't worry about getting lost and dropping things. As long as most ants are doing the right things most of the time, they'll all get to the common goal." McLurkin applied his observations of ants to his work in artificial intelligence. While working on his thesis project as an undergraduate at MIT, McLurkin designed and built 12 "ant" robots, which had photoreceptors and "feelers" in their 17 sensors, designed to help them detect and maneuver around obstacles as well as move toward light. Each robot measured approximately an inch on each side and was powered by a tiny, internal computer that ran its three motors. Two of the motors were for driving, while the third controlled the robot's "mandibles," used to pick up "food" in the form of brass-foil balls. That feature captured the interest of the Explosive Ordinance Disposal Branch of the Defense Advanced Research Projects Agency (DARPA), which then funded areas of McLurkin's research; DARPA is a division of the U.S. Department of Defense that selects research and technology projects that will potentially result in military advances. While the ants themselves do not currently have a practical application, future uses of the technology may include detection of nuclear, biological, and chemical threats, covert surveillance, and the exploration of other planets.

Beginning in 1999 McLurkin served as the lead research scientist for the Swarm project at iRobot, a Boston, Massachusetts–based robotics company. The 4.5-inch micro robots that make up the Swarm can break into smaller groups, explore new territo-

ry, and coordinate with one another, mimicking similar actions by bees. McLurkin explained to the reporter from *Nova Science Now* that the Swarm robots "have the same kind of physical limitations" as bees, "especially in terms of their communication with each other. Bees don't have cell phones. They don't have GPS. They are not sending e-mail to each other. They are only communicating to nearby bees. And the robots have the same kind of communication constraints, same kind of mobility. Bees pretty much live in a two-dimensional world. They do fly but they don't fly to 40,000 feet. They stay pretty close to the surface of the Earth, so you can imagine that they look kind of like a bunch of robots rolling around on the ground." Each robot has the ability to work in a group as well as independently. The robots are also able to recharge themselves. They communicate through infrared light, in much the same way that a remote control communicates with a television set. Each robot has three large spherical lights that can blink. "Information is encoded in the blinking pattern so you know what each robot is doing," McLurkin explained to a reporter for *Black Enterprise* (May 2005), adding that he gives thought to the robots' form as well as their function. "I care very much how things look and the feelings they engender," he said.

Future applications for swarms potentially lie in military and other government-related areas. "The government is very, very interested in swarms of robots that can be deployed into bad places looking for bad people doing bad things with bad chemicals. Imagine a swarm of robots that you could infiltrate a city with . . . ," McLurkin said to the reporter for *Nova Science Now*. Referring to the mastermind of the September 11, 2001 terrorist attacks against the U.S., McLurkin added, "You might be able to find Osama [bin Laden]. The government is very interested in stuff like that, and, no, it's not all science fiction." Despite government interest in robotic swarms, McLurkin is less interested in military applications than in the potential for robot-performed research. He told *Nova Science Now,* "I'd love to go to Mars with robots. Right now we have two robots on Mars. What if we had 2,000? We could cover a much larger area. But we can't communicate with 2,000 robots from Earth. It takes too long to get a signal to Mars. So they would have to be autonomous. They would have to work on their own and cooperate and communicate. But nobody has any idea how to program 2,000 robots right now. So I'm in an area where I can make a lot of strides." McLurkin has said that he envisions the creation of robots that would serve as self-directing rescue teams to be used after such disasters as earthquakes.

McLurkin is currently working toward his Ph.D. degree at MIT. He still enjoys riding his BMX bicycle and also rides a motorcycle. Elizabeth J. Sherman described him as "good-looking and engaging."

—L.J.

Suggested Reading: *Black Enterprise* p110 May 2005; Lemelson Center Web site; pbs.org; MIT Computer Science and Intelligence Laboratory (on-line)

Tom Pidgeon/Getty Images

McNair, Steve

Feb. 14, 1973– Football player

Address: Tennessee Titans, 460 Great Circle Rd., Nashville, TN 37228

"Pressure is what you make of it," the Tennessee Titans star quarterback, Steve McNair, once told Thomas George for the *New York Times* (August 28, 1994). "It makes me play harder. Something comes over your body, you just say to yourself, 'this is what I want.' Then you go get it." The pressure McNair has faced over the course of his career includes entering the National Football League (NFL) in 1995 from a small school, Alcorn State University, that was relatively obscure in football circles, and playing a position that had traditionally been difficult for African-Americans to obtain in the pros. McNair overcame a rocky start in the NFL to lead the Titans to the Super Bowl in the 1999 season and to postseason play in three of the following five years. Along the way he was named the league's co-MVP (Most Valuable Player) in 2003; emerged as one of five players in NFL history to have passed for 20,000 yards and rushed for 3,000 yards; and became, in 2000, the first black quarterback to pilot an American Football Conference (AFC) team to the Super Bowl. As quoted on the Tennessee Titans Web site, the Philadelphia Eagles

quarterback Donovan McNabb said, "Steve has defined how a quarterback can suffer through adversity and overcome it."

Steve Latreal McNair was born on February 14, 1973 in the tiny rural town of Mount Olive, Mississippi. His father, Selma McNair, who worked on an off-shore oil rig, separated from McNair's mother, Lucille, when the boy was eight years old. Lucille McNair, left to bring up five sons alone, worked 14-hour shifts at a chicken hatchery and, later, at an electronic-component factory. McNair helped out at home by picking peas every morning before school and working in the garden after school when needed. For his less helpful antics in the front-yard cherry tree, McNair earned the nickname "Monk," as his mother explained to Tim Crothers for *Sports Illustrated* (August 30, 1993). "When he was escaping a whupping, Steve could climb that tree faster than any monkey I've ever seen," she said, "so we just started calling him Monk."

McNair also displayed his athleticism on what was called Mount Pleasant Arena, a small, weedy field near his house where the local children came to play football. The first big star at Mount Pleasant Arena was Fred McNair, Steve's older brother, who went on to become a star quarterback for Alcorn State University, in nearby Lorman, Mississippi, and enjoyed a brief stay in the NFL before moving on to the Canadian Football League. Fred McNair had a huge influence on his little brother. He helped raise McNair and even lent him his on-field persona: Fred, as a star at Mount Olive High School, became known as "Air McNair," while Steve initially settled for "Air II." Soon, though, Steve McNair would supplant his brother as the sole owner of the moniker. At Mount Olive High School, McNair played both quarterback and safety while leading his team to a state championship. He was also scouted by the Seattle Mariners baseball team, but his brother advised him against leaving school. McNair listened to his big brother, as he would in making several other key decisions.

McNair has often emphasized the influence his older brother has had on him. "Fred has taught me absolutely everything I know," he told Crothers. "I can't thank him enough for giving me a map and then showing me how to take the short road when he's taken the longer one." Because of his athletic prowess, many major universities courted McNair, but most were interested in making him a safety rather than a quarterback. (He had 30 interceptions as a safety at Mount Olive High School.) Even though his brother had encouraged him to follow his dream of becoming a quarterback, McNair decided on the University of Southern Mississippi in Hattiesburg, where he was to play safety. The night before he signed on, though, McNair had a change of heart. Like his brother before him, he would go to Alcorn State, where he could be the leader of the team as quarterback, the position he had always loved.

Cardell Jones, the Alcorn head coach, was immediately rewarded for giving McNair the chance to play quarterback. During a 1991 game against their arch-rival, Grambling, Alcorn got nowhere with their first few possessions—and then someone suggested putting in McNair, who was just another freshman sitting on the bench. McNair went in and threw for over 200 yards and three touchdowns to lead Alcorn to victory, 27–22. By McNair's sophomore year there was no doubt in Jones's mind that he had a future star on his hands. Playing Grambling again, McNair was carried off the field at halftime with a severely sprained ankle. The quarterback not only returned but threw three touchdowns in the second half and limped across the goal line with a minute left to seal the victory, 35–33. (One of McNair's prime receivers was his older brother, Tim.) By the end of his senior year, McNair had broken every game, season, and career passing and total-offense record at Alcorn. He also broke the National Collegiate Athletics Association (NCAA) career-yardage record, with 16,823 yards in total offense. His average yardage per game (400.55) was also an NCAA record. His career passing statistics were impressive as well: 928 completions on 1,673 attempts for a total of 14,496 yards, 119 touchdowns, and 58 interceptions. With those numbers, McNair became a unanimous choice for All-America. "Steve has the intelligence of a [Joe] Montana, the release of a [Dan] Marino, the scrambling ability of [John] Elway," Alcorn's offensive coordinator, Rickey Taylor, said to S. L. Price for *Sports Illustrated* (September 26, 1994). "He's got all that like I've never seen in an athlete before. This is my 19th year, and I've seen a lot of great players. . . . I haven't seen anybody yet I can compare this kid with."

That assessment notwithstanding, when it came time for journalists to pick the winner of the prestigious Heisman Trophy, many said that McNair was not at the level of the best players in the NCAA—and that he had not encountered serious competition while playing at his small southern college. Many others felt that McNair's race played a part in such conclusions. The Heisman Trophy balloting is determined largely by players' exposure in the national media; Alcorn State, an all-black Division I-AA college, was unable to get any of the bigger Division I teams to play them, a fact that has itself been attributed to racism.

At his brother's suggestion, McNair passed up an opportunity to join the NFL after his junior year, so that he could continue to perfect his game and earn his bachelor's degree, in recreation, in 1994. (In the NFL there was still some resistance to the idea that African-Americans could play quarterback. Fred McNair, whose time in the NFL had been filled with difficulties, maintained that he was given fewer chances to play quarterback because of his race; he warned his younger brother to give critics little room for accusations, both on and off the field.) In 1995 McNair was picked third in the NFL draft by the Houston Oilers, who signed him for a seven-year, $28.4 million contract. Soon afterward McNair purchased a 640-acre ranch near Mount Olive and had a large house built for his mother. (As a boy he had slept in a bunk bed in a small room with three of his brothers, until he grew so large that one day he crashed through the top bunk onto an unfortunate sibling.) On the field, McNair's adjustment to pro football was more difficult. For one thing, he saw less playing time initially than he had in college; because the Oilers already had a talented quarterback in Chris Chandler when McNair arrived, the plan from the beginning was to cultivate McNair's talents slowly. For another, the quarterback position in the NFL is extremely demanding, as McNair discovered in his first exhibition game, against the Arizona Cardinals—a contest in which he was blitzed constantly, resulting in three sacks, a fumble, and a safety. Finally, he had trouble at first earning the respect of his fellow players. When he filled in for an ailing Chandler against the Detroit Lions later that season, McNair made an attempt at establishing a tone of leadership and camaraderie in the huddle. The response from one of his linemen was, "Shut . . . up, rookie, and call the play."

McNair did not call many plays his rookie season. He played in only six games and threw only 80 passes. During the off-season he came into the Oilers practice facility nearly every day to work and study with the offensive coordinator, Jerry Rhome. As Rhome told Dennis Dillon for the *Sporting News* (August 12, 1996), "For a whole month, [McNair] struggled. He'd get back some tests that looked like they had been painted in red, because I mark things with a red pen. He'd just look at it and say, 'I've got to do better, huh?' And he'd keep hammering away." In his second season, McNair started four times and played in nine games, increasing his pass attempts to 143 and completing 61.5 percent. Though the Oilers coaches had hoped that their starting quarterback, Chris Chandler, would help tutor McNair, the relationship between the two was tense. Chandler made little attempt to speak with McNair at all, and eventually the decision was made to trade Chandler. The Oiler guard Kevin Donnalley expressed his approval of the decision to Michael Silver for *Sports Illustrated* (September 1, 1997). "It's better for everybody that we traded Chris," he said. "Steve handled that whole thing in a first-class manner and never once complained. He came out of it smelling like a rose."

In 1997, McNair's third season, he became a starter. That year the team moved from Houston to Nashville, Tennessee, changing their name to the Tennessee Oilers. McNair performed well over the course of 16 games. He helped the Oilers set a team record for the fewest interceptions in a season (13) and had the most rushing touchdowns on the team, with eight. With 674 yards rushing, he attained the third-highest season total ever by an NFL quarterback, and his rushing average of 6.7 yards per carry led all NFL rushers that year. McNair proved to be the rare quarterback who could pass with accuracy in the pocket and also scramble under pressure to keep the defense off-balance. In 1998 McNair continued to improve. Once again, he broke the team record for fewest interceptions, this time with only 10. He became the youngest quarterback in franchise history to reach 3,000 yards passing, amassing 3,228 yards for the season. And he continued to astound fans with his running prowess, leading all quarterbacks with 559 rushing yards that year. In Tampa Bay on November 8, he turned a broken play into a 71-yard touchdown run to seal the victory. His completion average was a very respectable 58.7 percent, with 289 completions in 492 attempts, leading fans to vote him the most-improved NFL player in an ESPN poll.

The 1999 season was a break-out year for McNair and his team, which changed its name to the Tennessee Titans that year. For the season opener, against the Cincinnati Bengals, McNair threw three touchdown passes and racked up 341 passing yards to win the game, 36–35. In the next game he suffered a ruptured disk, which required back surgery; in spite of that, McNair missed only five games. In the meantime, the team's backup quarterback, Neil O'Donnell, had done a good job, winning four games and losing only one. McNair picked up where he had left off and went 7–2 for the rest of the season, thus securing a wildcard play-off berth for the Titans. The team's first play-off game was a January 8, 2000 nail-biter against the Buffalo Bills—a defensive battle that Buffalo appeared to have won when they kicked a 41-yard field goal to take a 16–15 lead, with little time remaining. But on the following kickoff, with three seconds left on the clock, the Titans' tight end Frank Wycheck lateraled the ball to Kevin Dyson, who ran it 75 yards into the end zone for a stunning victory. The play was surrounded by controversy, with many commentators saying that Wycheck's lateral was actually an illegal forward pass that should have been called a penalty. The Titans nonetheless walked away with a win, with McNair completing 13 of 24 passes for 76 yards and rushing for 19 yards on six carries.

For the American Football Conference final, the Titans faced the favored Indiana Colts, led by another young star quarterback, Peyton Manning. At halftime the Titans were down 9–6 in a game that was, like the contest with the Bills, a defensive battle. Then, in the second half, McNair made six straight completions, producing 13 points, and the Titans held on to beat the Colts, 19–16. In the game McNair had 13 completions on 24 passing attempts for 112 yards and also ran for 35 yards on seven carries, including a 29-yard run that led to a field goal. Though his numbers were not particularly high, McNair was doing exactly what coach Jeff Fisher wanted: he was playing smart football, eating up time on offense, not turning the ball over, and letting the Titans' formidable defense do its job. After the game, Frank Wycheck said to Jim Wyatt for the *Tennessean* (January 17, 2000), "Steve

was our leader today—he pumped us up. He handled himself great."

McNair continued to pump up the Titans in the 1999 Super Bowl, in which they faced the heavily favored St. Louis Rams. McNair kept the Titans even with the Rams, until St. Louis scored in the fourth quarter on a 73-yard pass to take a 23–16 lead. With less than two minutes left, McNair came onto the field determined to lead an 88-yard drive. He completed five of his first six passes, rushing for 12 yards on one play and then breaking two tackles to complete a clutch 16-yard pass, which set up the final play. With seconds left, McNair dropped back and looked to the end zone, but no one was open. He then fired the ball to Kevin Dyson, who caught it on the five-yard line and seemed to have a relatively clear path to the end zone. But the Rams' Mike Jones hit Dyson near the goal line and knocked him back a yard shy of it, to clinch the game for his team. McNair had come a yard short of leading what would have been one of the best clutch drives in Super Bowl history. As it stood, his 22 completions on 36 attempts for 214 yards, along with his 64 rushing yards, proved once and for all that he was a force to be reckoned with in the NFL.

In the 2000 season McNair, working with a new offensive coordinator, Mike Heimerdinger, led the Titans to a league-best 13–3 record. Among their wins was a come-from-behind victory on November 5 against the Pittsburgh Steelers, who had led 7–6 with just over two minutes remaining; McNair and the wide receiver Derrick Mason then made a 17-yard completion, helping to put Al Del Greco in position to kick a 29-yard field goal and win the game, 9-7. The Titans fell in the postseason, however, losing to Baltimore on January 7, 2001. McNair made 248 completions on 396 attempts that year and accumulated 2,847 yards.

The 2001 season was a dismal one for the Titans, who won only seven games and lost nine. For a time in 2002 things looked even worse, as the team won its first game of the season, against Philadelphia, and then proceeded to lose the next four. At that point head coach Jeff Fisher, Heimerdinger, and McNair changed tactics, having McNair, who had been the league's leading rusher among quarterbacks for several seasons, focus less on running and more on passing. The plan worked, and the Titans amassed an 11–5 regular-season record, which included five straight wins in December alone—a feat that was all the more impressive since McNair, with toe, rib, and back injuries, could not even make practice that month. The Titans followed a hard-fought, 34–31 victory over Pittsburgh on January 11 with a 24–41 loss to Oakland on January 19. For the season McNair racked up a career-best 301 completions on 492 attempts and amassed 3,387 yards, another career high.

The McNair-led Titans had another winning season in 2003, with 12 victories in the regular season against four losses. In a postseason game against the Baltimore Ravens on January 3, 2004,

McNair and the star running back Eddie George "delivered a clinic on resiliency," as Damon Hack put it in the *New York Times* (January 4, 2004); following a series of Titan errors that left the game tied at 17, with two minutes left to play, the two men led a drive that allowed Gary Anderson to kick a 46-yard field goal to win the game. On January 10, though, the Titans lost to the year's eventual Super Bowl champions, the New England Patriots, 17 to 14. McNair's statistics for the season included 250 completions on 400 attempts with 3,215 yards gained.

McNair shared the NFL's 2003 MVP award that year with Peyton Manning, becoming only the second Oilers/Titans player to win the award (the first was Earl Campbell, in 1979) and the first black quarterback to be so honored. In his acceptance speech, on January 2, 2004, as quoted on the Titans' Web site, McNair acknowledged the trail blazed by African-American quarterbacks who had preceded him in the NFL. "First and foremost," he said, "I'd like to thank the guys who paved the way for myself and a lot of other guys. The Warren Moons, the Doug Williamses, the Randall Cunninghams. Those guys paved the way for us as black quarterbacks to come in this league and be successful." That season McNair was also named the *Sports Illustrated* Player of the Year. At the end of the 2004–05 season, the Titans' record was five wins and 11 losses, with McNair's play having been hampered by injuries during the season. The beginning of the 2005–06 season was equally dismal for the Titans. As of October the team had two wins and five losses, and the threat that injuries would compromise McNair's effectiveness for the rest of the season had become a concern for the Titans' coach, Jeff Fisher. McNair was forced to sit out the Titans' game against the Arizona Cardinals because of a sore back, and the media began speculating that he would soon retire. But McNair, who had thrown for 1,375 yards with an impressive pass-completion percentage of 65.2 in the six games in which he had played, worked hard to become fit to play.

Steve McNair is six feet two inches tall and weighs 235 pounds. On June 21, 1997 he married his longtime girlfriend, Mechelle, in Mount Olive, as 1,200 guests looked on. He has four sons. The McNairs divide their time between Nashville, Tennessee, and their ranch in Mount Olive. Since 2001 the quarterback has hosted the annual Steve McNair Golf Classic, in Gulfport, Mississippi, which benefits Boys & Girls Clubs in that state and Tennessee and provides scholarships for McNair's football camps in the two states.

—P.G.H./C.T.

Suggested Reading: *New York Times* B p11+ Sep. 28, 1994, with photos, VIII p8+ Aug. 28, 1994, with photo, VIII p3+ Aug. 10, 1997, with photo, VIII p1 Jan. 4, 2004; *People* p103+ Dec. 5, 1994, with photos; *Sporting News* p42+ Aug. 12, 1996, with photos, p14+ Nov. 24, 2003; *Sports Illustrated* p76+ Aug. 30, 1993, with photos, p42+ Sep. 26, 1994, with photos; Tennessee Titans Web site

---

Meiselas, Susan

(my-ZELL-iss)

June 21, 1948– Photographer

Address: c/o Magnum Photos, 151 W. 25th St., New York, NY 10001-7204

Susan Meiselas is an award-winning documentary photographer best known for her work in Central America. Her photographs of politically turbulent events in Nicaragua and El Salvador during the late 1970s and 1980s were published in international newspapers and magazines, earning her professional recognition worldwide. Her first monograph, *Carnival Strippers*, appeared in 1976. Self-taught in the art of photography, she was a pioneer who worked with color film when most photojournalists were still using black-and-white. Meiselas creates distinctive images with a "saturated, almost otherworldly look," according to a reporter for the *New York Times* (June 6, 1996). In addition to her work in Nicaragua and El Salvador, Meiselas has worked on projects in India, Chile, Iraq, and Afghanistan, among other countries.

A member of the prestigious international cooperative Magnum Photos, Meiselas has dedicated herself to uncovering the stories of the people and places that she has captured on film. At times she also engages in extensive research, gathering texts to accompany her images and those that she collects in the role of visual historian. Whether in rural South Carolina or Kurdistan, she has demonstrated a sense of moral obligation toward her subjects, which manifests itself in a desire to represent them accurately and sensitively. "Photography involves ethics in the deepest way, right from the beginning," she said during a lecture at the University of Oregon at Eugene, according to Mike Viera on the Flash Online Web site (Summer 1999). "I see my work as a bridge between cultures—coming from one, understanding my own specific perspective, inviting others to contribute their perspectives." In 2005 the International Center for Photography honored Meiselas with the Cornell Capa Infinity Award for her distinguished achievements in her field.

Susan Clay Meiselas was born on June 21, 1948 in Baltimore, Maryland, to Leonard and Murrayl Groh Meiselas. She attended Sarah Lawrence College, in Bronxville, New York, graduating with a

Maximilian Lamy/Getty Images

Susan Meiselas

B.A. degree in 1970. In 1971 she earned a master's degree in visual education from Harvard University, in Cambridge, Massachusetts. Since then she has been awarded honorary doctor of fine arts degrees by the Parsons School of Design, in New York City (1988); the Art Institute of Boston, in Massachusetts (1996); and Trinity College, in Hartford, Connecticut (1999).

In 1971, just after leaving Harvard, Meiselas worked as an assistant film editor on the documentary *Basic Training*, about a U.S. Army training center in Fort Knox, Kentucky. (The film was directed by Frederick Wiseman, who is generally acknowledged to be one of the most important documentary filmmakers of his generation; he is perhaps best known for *Titicut Follies* [1967], which focuses on a Massachusetts institution for the criminally insane.) From 1972 to 1974 Meiselas ran photography workshops for teachers and children in the South Bronx, then a blighted area of New York City, while simultaneously working as a freelance photographer. One of her first professional assignments was for a 1973 article in *Harper's Bazaar* about an artist who made clothing out of food. "I shot this young woman wearing nothing but an asparagus vest and salami necklace," Meiselas recalled to a reporter for the *New York Times* (June 9, 1996). "I think there were some scallions involved, too." Between 1972 and 1975 Meiselas spent three summers following traveling striptease shows around New England, taking photographs and conducting interviews with strippers, managers, and customers. The project, which served as the basis for her black-and-white photographic essay *Carnival Strippers* (1976), was the first of many in which Meiselas sought to establish a personal relationship with her subjects, creating a bond of trust that she believes to be an essential prerequisite for ethical documentary photography. Through her work on *Carnival Strippers*, according to Mike Viera, Meiselas "learned the necessity of crossing lines to enter the culture of the women she was photographing."

Meiselas was an artist-in-residence at the South Carolina Arts Commission, in Columbia, South Carolina, from 1974 to 1975, during which time she helped to establish film and photography programs at rural schools. In 1975 she taught photography at the New School (now the New School University), in New York City. The next year, on the strength of the photographs in *Carnival Strippers,* Magnum photographers nominated her to join their agency. (Magnum was established by a group of photographers as a cooperative in 1947; it differed from other agencies in that the photographers themselves owned the agency and fought to control the copyrights to their images, rather than have those copyrights rest with the magazines that published them.) Since then Meiselas has worked consistently as a freelance photographer with Magnum, which, according to Abigail Foerstner in the *Chicago Tribune* (March 30, 1990), "provides an extended family . . . for a modern breed of nomads." Meiselas became an associate of Magnum Photos in 1977 and a full member in 1980; from 1986 to 1991 she served as the vice president of the agency's New York office.

Between 1978 and 1983 Meiselas lived in Central America for up to 10 months a year, working on self-assigned projects; her photos and commentaries later appeared in domestic and foreign publications. She visited Nicaragua for the first time in 1978, traveling alone and learning Spanish, which she did not speak at all until then. Her earliest pictures of the country document the activities of the popular resistance against the dictator Anastasio Somoza, who was overthrown by the revolutionary Sandinistas in 1979. As events in Nicaragua began to attract international attention, newspapers and magazines contacted Magnum with requests for photographs, and before long Meiselas's images were appearing in the *New York Times*, the *Washington Post, Time, Rolling Stone*, and several European publications. Although such periodicals still carry her work, Meiselas does not consider herself strictly a photojournalist. She has insisted that she is documenting historic processes rather than individual events for magazines and newspapers. "I think it has to do with whom you make pictures for," she told Foerstner. "Even if my photographs are in the magazines, I don't think of myself as conceptualizing them for magazines."

In 1979 the Overseas Press Club presented Meiselas with a Robert Capa Gold Medal Award (named for one of the founders of Magnum) for her coverage of the insurrection in Nicaragua. In 1981 Meiselas published *Nicaragua: June 1978–July 1979*, a collection of 72 color photographs chronicling the Sandinista revolution. In 1982 she received the Leica Award for Excellence and was named photojournalist of the year by the American Society of Media Photographers (ASMP).

Meiselas was awarded a National Endowment for the Arts (NEA) grant in 1987. That same year she participated in a group photography show at the Museum of Contemporary Photography at Columbia College, in Chicago, Illinois. Entitled This and Other Worlds, the exhibition featured work by several Magnum photographers (Gilles Peress, Eugene Richards, and Alex Webb) and included images by Meiselas of El Salvador and Nicaragua.

In July 1989 Meiselas returned to Nicaragua to shoot a film inspired by a young man who had approached her in the capital city, Managua, and identified himself as one of the people who appeared masked in a photograph of hers that had been published in a revolutionary newspaper. After that encounter Meiselas began to seek out subjects and return to locales of other photographs she had taken during the Sandinista insurrection; she documented her experiences all the while. The resulting film, *Pictures of a Revolution* (1991), was met with critical acclaim. Vincent Canby, writing for the *New York Times* (May 30, 1992), described it as "a somber meditation on what sometimes looks like the futility of all social struggle" and praised Meiselas for her "serious and moving film reportage."

In 1990 the Art Institute of Chicago mounted an exhibition of Meiselas's work. The show, called Crossings, featured photographs of political turbulence in Nicaragua and El Salvador, interspersed with panoramic pictures of Latin Americans caught by immigration patrols while they were trying to flee to the United States. During the interview with Foerstner, Meiselas explained that while she was taking those pictures, she had been especially struck by the border patrols' matter-of-fact treatment of terror-stricken would-be refugees. "I went on what they call a ride-along with the [U.S. Immigration and Naturalization Service]," she said. "The first image that just landed on me was seeing a family coming across a dirt field. . . . The searchlight and the vehicle kind of swung around and they hit the ground and of course [the officer] saw the movement and pulled them in. . . . And what was going on in my head was . . . 'Who are they? Where do they come from?'"

After the Persian Gulf War ended, in April 1991, Meiselas traveled to northern Iraq, where she visited villages from which thousands of Kurdish refugees were fleeing the Iraqi leader Saddam Hussein's military forces. "I had never witnessed such a complete and systematic destruction of village life," she wrote in an article for the *Western Mail* (May 16, 2003), a Welsh newspaper, "even in 10 years of covering the conflicts in Central America." Her interest in the Kurds persisted. In 1992, with the help of the money (a so-called genius grant) she received as a MacArthur Foundation Fellow, she spent more than six years compiling the images and documents that would appear in her book *Kur-*

distan: In the Shadow of History (1997). The book, a visual history of the Kurds, was widely recognized as an important record of the world's largest stateless ethnic group. To tell the story of those marginalized people, Meiselas presented several different forms of documentation, including photographs from the past 100 years, oral histories, diaries, letters, newspapers, memoirs, and British and American government documents. Karl E. Meyer, writing for the *New York Times* (February 22, 1998), described *Kurdistan* as "a superb and enriching book" that "speaks movingly to the fate of all marginal peoples." Akos Ostor, in a review for *American Anthropologist* (December 2000), praised Meiselas's complex interweaving of texts and images, writing, "It is the multi-vocal, multi-layered approach that sets this book apart."

Although the *Kurdistan* project was arguably Meiselas's most ambitious research endeavor to date, it was far from the first expression of her interest in investigating and recording local histories. During the 1970s, for example, Meiselas spent several months in Lando, a South Carolina mill town, documenting the stories of the families who lived there. As she told Molly Metz during an interview for the *Progressive* (April 1998), "The idea was to do an oral genealogy of the town, and complement it with a photographic genealogy." The investigation culminated in a bicentennial exhibition entitled A Photographic Genealogy: The History of Lando. Meiselas's interest in storytelling developed further during her time in El Salvador, Chile, and especially Nicaragua, where she conducted interviews and used other collaborative methods as well, in addition to taking photographs.

In 1994 Meiselas was awarded the Maria Moors Cabot Prize by the trustees of Columbia University, in New York City, for promoting press freedom and inter-American understanding. That same year she was awarded a Hasselblad Foundation prize for exceptional photographic achievement. She was further honored in 1995 with a Rockefeller Foundation Fellowship to develop a Web site dedicated to the history and culture of Kurdistan; called www.akaKURDISTAN.com, it contains contributions from Kurds, historians, travelers, and archivists.

On February 28, 2002 Meiselas participated in the *A Day in the Life of Africa* book project, for which nearly 100 photojournalists spent the same 24 hours documenting various aspects of Africa—from its cities and citizens to its geography and wildlife. For the first time in her professional career, she made use of a digital camera, a technology that she has since integrated into her photographic toolbox.

Meiselas's *Pandora's Box* (2002) is a book of photographs documenting the upscale Manhattan sex club of the same name. (Special signed copies of the book have sold for over $600.) Her most recent book is *Encounters with the Dani* (2003), which explores the impact of Western exposure on the Dani, an indigenous people of the West Papuan highlands in New Guinea. Meiselas has had one-woman shows in New York, Chicago, London, and Paris, among other major cities. Besides producing her own photographic monographs, she has served as the editor or co-editor of several volumes, including *Learn to See* (1974), a book for teachers that aims to bring photography into the classroom; *El Salvador: Work of 30 Photographers* (1983), a collection of images by El Salvadoran artists and photojournalists; and *Chile: From Within* (1990), a pictorial record of Chile during Augusto Pinochet's military regime.

Together with the filmmakers Richard P. Rogers and Alfred Guzzetti, Meiselas has co-produced and co-directed two films: *Living at Risk* (1986), a documentary about a Nicaraguan family, and *Pictures from a Revolution* (1991), a documentary about the protagonists of her photographs from the 1978–79 Sandinista insurrection. She collaborated with the British director Marc Karlin to make *Voyages*, a reflective exploration of her life as a photographer; that film was produced as part of a series of four films about Nicaragua for Channel 4, on British TV.

Since 1995 Meiselas has served on the board of directors of the Three Guineas Fund, a philanthropic foundation dedicated to investing in economic opportunities for women and girls. When she is not traveling in connection with her work, she lives in New York City. Because of her professional interests, she has opted not to become a mother. As she explained to Foerstner, "I can't imagine how I could have a family. . . . I wouldn't take those risks in the same way if I had a child."

—L.W.

Suggested Reading: *Chicago Tribune* VII p83 Mar. 30, 1990; Magnum Photos Web site; *New York Times* VII p33 Feb. 22, 1998; *Progressive* Apr. 1998

Selected Books: *Carnival Strippers*, 1976; *Nicaragua: June 1978–July 1979*, 1981; *Kurdistan: In the Shadow of History*, 1997; *Pandora's Box*, 2002; *Encounters with the Dani*, 2003

Meron, Theodor

(mah-RONE)

Apr. 28, 1930– International humanitarian-law scholar; president of the International Criminal Tribunal for the Former Yugoslavia

Address: New York University Law School, Vanderbilt Hall, 40 Washington Square S., Rm. 304, New York, NY 10012-1099

The common proverb "All's fair in love and war" has been around since the 16th century. Its longevity is surprising, since it has always been, at best, only half true: certain activities are *not* considered fair in war, and actions deemed appropriate and just in battle have been agreed upon and codified. War and military conduct have been scrutinized for millennia. The sixth-century B.C.E. Chinese philosopher Sun Tzu discussed in his writings ideas of proper conduct in war. Four hundred years later the Hindu Code of Manu addressed the topic. During medieval times, European warriors were expected to abide by the chivalric code, an unwritten agreement among the nobility to grant one another mercy in battle in return for sizable ransoms. As technology made weapons more effective and lethal, conflicts increasingly became faceless long-distance events; the gentlemen's battleground agreement became less relevant, and the need to have written laws governing armed struggle grew. King Richard II of England filled this need in 1385 with the Ordinances of War, which King Henry V renewed in 1419. (Among the limits they placed on soldierly conduct, the Ordinances

Hrvoje Polan/AFP Photo

declared rape a war crime punishable by death.) Today, most people think of the rules of war as a 20th-century creation, dating to the post–World War II Nuremberg and Tokyo trials, at which international tribunals prosecuted German and Japanese leaders and combatants, respectively, for war crimes. Our modern conception of the rules of war has also been largely influenced by the Geneva Conventions of 1949, which attempt to regulate the wartime behavior of soldiers and leaders toward one another and toward noncombatants and were signed by nearly every nation in existence at that time.

Despite the establishment of the Geneva Conventions and the world's renewed interest in war crimes following World War II, military regimes in many parts of the world continued to commit atrocities and crimes during armed conflict. Other 20th-century governments seemed reluctant to stop them or bring them to any measure of justice. Perhaps most notoriously, in the late 1970s the Cambodian Communist government known as the Khmer Rouge slaughtered an estimated 1.7 million of its own citizens with impunity. The international community responded quickly and decisively against war crimes for the first time in nearly 50 years when the United Nations passed resolutions for the establishment of an International Criminal Tribunal for the Former Yugoslavia (ICTY), in 1993, and the International Criminal Tribunal for Rwanda (ICTR), in 1994. Former leaders of those nations, which were gripped in the early to mid-1990s by brutal civil war resulting from centuries-old ethnic conflicts, currently stand charged with numerous crimes against humanity, including genocide.

The president of the ICTY and the presiding judge of appeals for the ICTR is Theodor Meron, an author, professor, and prominent scholar of international humanitarian law whose writings were influential in both building support for and establishing those tribunals. He is the only American to hold chambers in both courts. Meron's vast knowledge comes not just from scholarship but also from personal experience: as a Holocaust survivor he has witnessed the horrors of genocide and crimes against humanity firsthand. "We live in a world of bloody conflict," he told Thomas Adcock for the *New York Law Journal* (April 18, 2003). "The work of [the international criminal tribunals] is hard. These are horrendous crimes. But we have some satisfaction in bringing some justice to the world. And we have broader social goals: reconciliation and reconstruction, universal justice and a reliable judicial record."

The son of Yhiel and Bluma Znamirowski, Theodor Meron was born on April 28, 1930 in Kalisz, Poland. As Jews, Meron and his family were subjected to privations and suffering at the hands of the Nazis. In his youth he spent four years in Czestochowa, a Nazi labor camp in Poland, an experience that Meron does not like to speak about. "After a childhood spent in ghettos and labor camps, and the loss of so many loved ones, including my mother and brother, I find it best not to dwell on the past," he told Michael D. Goldhaber for the *American Lawyer* (August 2001). "It is best to build a better future in which such events can be avoided." The hardships and abuses Meron witnessed and endured in his youth have clearly given his life its direction and purpose. "From age 9 to 15, I did not go to school at all. There were tremendous gaps in my education. It gave me a great hun-

ger for learning, and I dreamed that one day I could go to school," he told Marlise Simons for the *New York Times* (January 3, 2004). "It is of course even more poignant that someone with my background can become a judge here"—the Hague, Netherlands, where the ICTY is based—"and even president of this body. I find it daunting."

Long before he arrived in the Hague, Meron had built a career as a leading scholar in the then "esoteric area," as he has described it, of international law, specializing in the history and application of the laws of war. He moved to Israel after World War II and received his first legal training at the University of Jerusalem. He continued his studies at Harvard University, in Cambridge, Massachusetts, earning a master of laws (LL.M.) degree in 1955 and a doctorate in juridical science (S.J.D.) in 1957. That same year Meron attended Cambridge University, in England, on a prestigious Humanitarian Trust Fellowship in International Law. He then joined the Israeli Foreign Service as a counselor to the Israeli Mission to the United Nations in New York. From 1967 to 1971 he served as a legal adviser to the Israeli Foreign Ministry. (In 1971 Meron also passed the bar exam in Israel.) He was then appointed Israel's ambassador to Canada, a post he held until 1975, and he later served as Israel's permanent representative to the United Nations in Geneva. He left the Israeli Foreign Service in 1977 and accepted an offer from New York University (NYU) to join its faculty as a professor of law. He settled permanently in the United States and became a naturalized citizen in 1984. That same year Meron, with the support of the International Committee of the Red Cross (ICRC), organized at NYU the first Seminar Program for Diplomats on International Humanitarian Law. Bringing together U.N. diplomats, scholars, and legal advisers to consider the fundamentals of humanitarian law, the laws of war, the Geneva Conventions, and other related topics, the ICRC-NYU Law Seminar Program for Diplomats has been held every year since. More than 1,000 U.N. ambassadors and representatives from around the world have participated in the program. As part of the seminar held in early March 2003, Meron gave a talk entitled "Re-Reading the Geneva Conventions." Since 1994 Meron has held the Charles L. Denison Chair at NYU Law School. Concurrently with his teaching at NYU, from 1991 to 1995 he held the post of professor of international law at the Graduate Institute of International Studies in Geneva and, from 1993 to 1998, served as co-editor in chief of the *American Journal of International Law*. (He remains an honorary editor of the publication.)

In 1998 Meron was a U.S. delegate to the diplomatic conference in Rome, Italy, that led to the establishment of the International Criminal Court (ICC). Based in the Hague, the ICC is the "first ever permanent, treaty based, international criminal court established to promote the rule of law and to ensure that the gravest international crimes do not go unpunished," as the official ICC Web site states.

(The ICC should not be confused with the International Court of Justice, which was established by the U.N. and is often called the World Court. Whereas the International Court of Justice adjudicates cases between countries, the ICC is empowered to bring individual defendants to trial. The two judicial bodies have formalized their cooperative relationship.) As of January 2005 the Rome Statute of the ICC had been signed by 139 countries and ratified by 97. (Conspicuously, the United States is not one of them. The administration of President George W. Bush is opposed to the ICC and has declined to sign the statute; among other reasons, it has expressed its concern that politically motivated cases may be brought against American citizens abroad, including military personnel.) The ICC would render ad-hoc courts such as the ICTY unnecessary in the future. Meron helped to draft the court's provisions on war crimes and crimes against humanity. In the summer of 2004, the chief prosecutor of the ICC, Luis Moreno-Ocampo, opened the court's first investigation, one concerning allegations of rape, torture, forced displacement, and the illegal use of child soldiers in the Democratic Republic of Congo since mid-2002. (The ICC has the jurisdiction to consider only those crimes committed after July 1, 2002, the date on which the Rome Statute came into force.)

Meron served as a counselor on international law to the U.S. State Department from 2000 to 2001. After President George W. Bush took office, in early 2001, Secretary of State Colin Powell nominated Meron to become the American representative among the 14 permanent judges at the ICTY. In March 2001 the U.N. approved Meron for a four-year term at the tribunal, and he took a leave of absence from NYU to become the third American to sit on the ICTY since it convened in May 1996. Meron was assigned to the court's appeals chamber, where he has heard cases from both the ICTY and the ICTR. According to the ICTY's official Web site, the court was established by the U.N. Security Council "in the face of serious violations of international law committed in the territory of the former Yugoslavia since 1991, and as a response to the threat to international peace and security posed by those serious violations." The late-20th-century events referred to in this mandate are deeply rooted in the history of the Slavic region known as the Balkans, an area between the Black and Adriatic Seas that now includes the independent nations or federations of Slovenia, Croatia, Bosnia and Herzegovina, and Serbia and Montenegro. In the first decades of the 20th century, a pan-Slavic unification movement led by Serbia reached its pinnacle and contributed to the start of World War I, when Archduke Franz Ferdinand of Austria was assassinated by a Serbian nationalist in 1914. The linguistically similar but culturally disparate territories were subsequently thrown together in an uncomfortable, loose confederation during the Paris Peace Conference, which formally ended World War I. In 1929 the region was renamed Yugoslavia, within which Serbs, Croats, Slovenes, Macedonians, and Montenegrins coexisted, along with Bosnian Muslims and Albanian and Hungarian minorities. The troubled confederacy managed to survive despite tremendous internal political and social strife. After World War II the Communist dictator Josip Broz, known as Tito, took control of Yugoslavia and exerted tight control until his death, in 1980. The political vacuum that ensued caused economic problems that heightened the nation's ethnic divisions. The disintegration of Yugoslavia had begun.

Slobodan Milosevic, a nationalist who envisioned a Greater Serbia, rose to the Communist Party leadership in Serbia in 1987 and was elected Serbian president two years later. Motivated by political and ethnic differences, Slovenia and Croatia separately declared independence in mid-1991, followed by Bosnia and Herzegovina in the spring of 1992. The Serbian-dominated Yugoslav army attempted to rally ethnic Serbs across the region and immediately mobilized against the breakaway provinces. Milosevic's Serbian forces specifically targeted Bosnian Muslims and other non-Serbs. Tens of thousands of people were killed; the rape and murder of civilians was common. Peace talks held in Dayton, Ohio, in 1995 led to an accord that ended the Balkan conflict. In the late 1990s, however, after a decade of being repressed by their Serbian rulers, ethnic Albanians in the southern Serbian province of Kosovo began a guerrilla war. Milosevic, then president of Serbia and Montenegro, sent in troops to crush the rebellion and purge ethnic Albanians from the province. The ensuing conflict did not cease until bombing raids organized by member nations of the North American Treaty Organization (NATO) drove Milosevic's forces out of Kosovo. Milosevic lost his bid for reelection in 2000 and was arrested the following year. He was then sent to the ICTY as the first head of state to be charged, while still in office (the indictment was levied on May 24, 1999), with war crimes and crimes against humanity. (In regard to his role in the conflict in Kosovo, Milosevic was initially charged, along with four other Serb officials, with the forced deportation from Kosovo of more than 70,000 ethnic Albanians and 340 counts of murder in seven separate incidents.)

The ICTY has indicted and prosecuted dozens of leaders accused of having committed atrocities during the violence that ravaged the former Yugoslavia in the 1990s. For example, in 2001 the ICTY found Radislav Krstic, a former commander in the Bosnian Serb Army, guilty of planning and leading the notorious 1995 massacre of more than 7,000 Bosnian Muslim boys and men in the town of Srebrenica; he was sentenced to 35 years in prison. (Meron was the presiding judge in Krstic's appeal.) The ICTY Web site lists what it terms the tribunal's "five core achievements": "spearheading the shift from impunity to accountability; establishing the facts; bringing justice to thousands of victims and giving them a voice; the accomplishments in international law; strengthening the rule of law." The Web site explains that "thanks to the ICTY, the question is no longer *whether* leaders should be held accountable, but rather *how* they can be called to account." In addition, as a result of the tribunal's work, "important elements of a historical record of the conflicts in the former Yugoslavia in the 1990's have emerged. Facts once subject to dispute have been established beyond a reasonable doubt." The more than 3,500 witnesses to the horrors of the war that have testified before the court have contributed to that historical record. Other important achievements of the tribunal concern the legal treatment and punishment of sexual violence in wartime, the identification of specific elements of the crime of genocide, and the clarification and expansion of international humanitarian law.

Despite its unprecedented legal achievements, the ICTY—and Meron's oversight of the entire tribunal's docket, which dates from 2003—will be judged (unfairly, in the opinion of some people) by how successfully it pursues its case against Slobodan Milosevic. Given the number of charges against Milosevic (66 counts of war crimes in Bosnia, Croatia, and Kosovo), the evidence required for conviction, and the fact that evidence must be gathered from war-torn countries whose current governments are reluctant to revisit the shameful and painful past, the tribunal's task is immensely difficult. Broadly stated, Milosevic's alleged crimes can be categorized as crimes against humanity, grave breaches of the Geneva Conventions, and violations of the accepted customs or laws of war. In addition, as Krstic's commander in chief, he also stands accused of genocide in the Srebrenica massacre. Predictably, the trial has moved slowly. It took the prosecution nearly three years to amass and present its case against the Serbian leader. Furthermore, Milosevic, a trained lawyer who chose to represent himself, has proven a cunning strategist in court. Using lengthy and incisive cross-examinations of key prosecution witnesses, as well as such courtroom tactics as procedural appeals, Milosevic has been able to a large degree to dictate the pace of the trial and to unsettle the prosecution.

Following a four-month adjournment of the trial in 2004 to allow Milosevic time to organize his defense, the former Serbian leader suffered several setbacks. His health worsened, and the court ruled that he may no longer represent himself. Milosevic decried the decision, but the court held firm. Since then Milosevic has been uncooperative with his defense team, who have been able to secure only a few of the roughly 1,600 witnesses (among them Prime Minister Tony Blair of Great Britain and former U.S. president Bill Clinton) that he wishes to call to the stand in his defense. The pace of this landmark trial slowed further when the tribunal announced that hearings in Milosevic's trial scheduled for the first week of February 2005 would be cancelled due to the defendant's poor health. The trial resumed two months later; as of October 2005

it was in its fourth year and was not expected to end before mid-2007.

In the appeals chamber Meron has also presided over trials involving the horrific violence that swept the small African nation of Rwanda in 1994. Rwanda had long been a hotbed of unrest between the Hutu and Tutsi peoples who inhabit the region. Each group has ruled Rwanda at different times, causing the other to suffer. In 1994 the Hutu controlled the government, while a Tutsi-dominated rebel group called the Rwandan Patriotic Front (RPF) sought to unseat them. As in Yugoslavia, economic distress further fueled tensions. Beginning in the spring of 1994, roaming bands of Hutu marauders, assisted and goaded on by the Hutu-controlled media and government, butchered an estimated 800,000 Tutsis and moderate Hutus in the span of 100 days. The killing did not stop until the U.N. Security Council authorized French troops to enter Rwanda, and the RPF entered the capital, Kigali, driving out the Hutu government.

The ICTR convened in Arusha, Tanzania, in 1995 and logged its first eight indictments in November of that year. The tribunal's first trial began in 1997. More than 50 suspects have been indicted for their involvement in the 1994 massacre. As reported on the official ICTR Web site, as of January 2005 the court has reached 17 judgments involving 23 accused—among them the former Hutu government's prime minister, Jean Kambanda; the former ministers of culture and education, information, and foreign affairs; and several Hutu journalists. Another 25 suspects are still on trial. Kambanda's case set an enormous precedent as it represented the first time a head of state has been convicted of the crime of genocide. As presiding judge of appeals for the ICTR, work he administers largely from the Hague, Meron acts as an interpreter of legal principles, an arbiter of in-trial procedural rulings to which defense attorneys have objected, and a final reviewer of verdicts and sentences that the defense deems unjust.

Both the ICTY and the ICTR have been under increased scrutiny in recent years. Given the scale of the crimes they try, the number of suspects and witnesses they must handle, and the volume of documents involved, the courts' work has taken a long time. "One of the problems American lawyers would find difficult to understand is our slow pace," Meron told Thomas Adcock. "Prosecution involves entire military campaigns over several years' time, and in several geographic regions. There is the difficulty of obtaining witnesses—and often, less than full cooperation of governments." Furthermore, the tribunals' efforts demand tremendous resources. The ICTY alone employs more than 1,200 people, and its budget for 2004–05 exceeded $271 million. U.N. funds have been insufficient, and in order to defray mounting costs, the courts have relied on direct contributions from individual nations, including the United States. In response to these pressures, the U.N. Security Council has urged both tribunals to complete all investigations by 2005, all trials by 2008, and all appeals by 2010. This, in turn, has forced both tribunals to focus their energies on those cases that are deemed to be the most important or that may yield the greatest measure of justice in light of the atrocities that were committed. Worthwhile but lower-priority cases will be transferred for trials in national courts that have agreed to accept them. In November 2004 the U.N. General Assembly elected Meron to another four-year term at the ICTY.

Meron has published many articles on international humanitarian law and related topics in scholarly and academic journals and has written more than eight books, among them *Human Rights Law-Making in the United Nations: A Critique of Instruments and Process* (1986), which was awarded a certificate of merit by the American Society of International Law; *Human Rights and Humanitarian Norms as Customary Law* (1989); *War Crimes Law Comes of Age* (1998), a collection of essays; and *International Law In the Age of Human Rights* (2004). In two other highly acclaimed books, Meron combined his professional expertise with a personal passion for the works of Shakespeare: *Henry's Wars and Shakespeare's Laws: Perspectives on the Law of War in the Later Middle Ages* (1993) and *Bloody Constraint: War and Chivalry in Shakespeare* (1998). In the first book he examined King Henry V's Ordinances of War, especially in light of the king's actions at the Battle of Agincourt in 1415. Despite being heavily outnumbered by French forces, Henry led his English troops to a famously swift and decisive victory in the muddy countryside outside the French town of Agincourt. During the battle Henry violated the chivalric code by ordering his men to kill the French soldiers they had taken prisoner, an event that Shakespeare later depicted to great effect in his play *Henry V*. In *Bloody Constraint* Meron focused on the broad system of chivalry found in Shakespeare's plays and explored the values that sustained and altered the customs of war in the Middle Ages and the Renaissance. Those values, Meron made clear, continue to affect the laws and practices of war today. "The fact is that before this tribunal [ICTY] we see the same type of age-old human tendency, of leaders and commanders washing their hands," Meron told Marlise Simons. "It was already of great concern in Shakespeare's time, and it remains at the very center of war crimes today. Shakespeare's dialogues that touch on the moral and legal duties of leaders, their accountability, their attempt to evade blame, will resonate in the ears of anyone who listens to the major trials going on here."

Meron sits on the board of editors of the *Yearbook of International Humanitarian Law*. He is a member of the Council on Foreign Relations, the American Society of International Law, the French Society of International Law, the American Branch of the International Law Association, and the Bar of the State of New York. In addition, he has served on advisory committees or boards of several human rights organizations, among them Americas

Watch and the International League for Human Rights.

Meron has been a fellow or lecturer at many universities and institutions around the world, including the International Institute of Human Rights, in Strasbourg, France; the Hague Academy of International Law; the Rockefeller Foundation, in New York; the Max Planck Institute, in Heidelberg, Germany; and the University of Cambridge and All Souls College, in England.

As is usual for a judge, Meron is not at liberty to comment publicly in any detail on his work in the ICTY and ICTR. He lives in the Hague.

—T.J.F.

Suggested Reading: *American Lawyer* p65+ Aug. 2001; International Criminal Tribunal for Rwanda Web site; International Criminal Tribunal for the Former Yugoslavia Web site; *New York Law Journal* p16 Apr. 18, 2003; *New York Times* A p4 Jan. 3, 2004, with photo; United Nations Web site

Selected Books: *Investment Insurance in International Law*, 1976; *The United Nations Secretariat*, 1977; *Human Rights in International Law*, 1984; *Human Rights Law-Making in the United Nations*, 1986; *Human Rights in Internal Strife: Their International Protection*, 1987; *Human Rights and Humanitarian Norms as Customary Law*, 1989; *Henry's Wars and Shakespeare's Laws*, 1993; *Bloody Constraint: War and Chivalry in Shakespeare*, 1998; *War Crimes Law Comes of Age: Essays*, 1998; *International Law In the Age of Human Rights*, 2004

Millionaire, Tony

1959– Cartoonist; illustrator

Address: c/o Fantagraphics Books, 7563 Lake City Way NE, Seattle, WA 98115

The illustrator and syndicated cartoonist Tony Millionaire is best known for his dark, absurdist weekly comic strip, *Maakies*, which has become a staple in alternative papers around the country, been published in three successful collections, and appeared in an animated form on the long-running television program *Saturday Night Live*. "Millionaire is the great master of the old-time freewheeling comic strip," a reviewer of one of his collections wrote for *Publishers Weekly* (February 10, 2003), "and [his] work takes full advantage of every last bit of the medium. It combines the comical seafaring tales of Drinky Crow (yes, a drunk crow) and Uncle Gabby (a monkey of questionable morals) with nonsense strips and the occasional foray into something utterly unconnected. . . . Millionaire

Courtesy of Tony Millionaire

Tony Millionaire at home with his daughters

offers transporting, irreverent and unique comics, all beautifully drawn." A recipient of some of the most prestigious awards in the comics industry, Millionaire has been highly praised for his virtuosity as a draftsman. In *Maakies* and in his popular *Sock Monkey* comic series, Millionaire juxtaposes his beautiful landscapes with the brutality and existential malaise of his ill-behaved menagerie. Describing *Sock Monkey* for the *Washington Times* (October 14, 2000), Joseph Szadkowski wrote that the "brilliance of the series comes in its careful balance between beautiful illustrations, storybook elegance and life's harsh realities."

The comics artist was born in Boston, Massachusetts, in 1959. Though some sources suggest that he was born with the last name Richardson, he maintains in interviews that "Millionaire" is indeed his real last name. "It's French, comes from my French grandmother," he told *Current Biography*. "The family disowned Grandfather Richardson after some family matters came to light in 1997. Seriously. I've always taken my grandmother's name because I liked her; turns out I was also wise." Millionaire was raised in Gloucester, Massachusetts, in a family of artists: his mother, Priscilla, taught art at a junior high school; his father, Howard, worked in advertising and design; and his maternal grandparents were painters. The earliest influences on his own art were the turn-of-the-century illustrators who drew the characters in his favorite children's books—Beatrix Potter's books featuring Peter Rabbit and other animals, Johnny Gruelle's *Raggedy Ann* series, and particularly A. A. Milne's *Winnie the Pooh* volumes, with art by Ernest H. Shepard. "The illustrations of Ernest Shepard made such a glorious dent in my head,"

Millionaire told an interviewer for *Westfield Comics* (December 2000, on-line), "I remember looking at them when I was a kid, just holding them close, looking at the way he drew the grass under that bear's foot. I fell in love with pen and ink looking at those pictures."

Millionaire's mother encouraged his interest in art and refused to let him, his sister, and three brothers have any coloring books. If they wanted to color, she told them, they had to draw the pictures first. "I told my Mom when I was ten years old that I wanted to be a commercial artist when I grew up. She said, 'What, you want to draw pork chops on the sides of cardboard boxes?'" Millionaire wrote to Spence D. in an E-mail interview for *IGN for Men* (January 28, 2000, on-line). "She convinced me to pursue the Fine Arts, one of which is pen and ink drawing, according to her. She was very pleased when I started cartooning, because that's what my illustrator grandfather always wanted to do." Millionaire's maternal grandfather worked with pen and ink and also owned a collection of old Sunday comics. "I remembered [lying] on the floor opening up these huge pages of color comics . . . ," he told John F. Kelly for *Comics Journal* (#215). "I loved the memory of those. That's why I draw comics now."

At the age of 10, Millionaire started drawing his first comic strip, "Zero-Man." "It was about a little egg-shaped superhero with a zero on his chest who was a loser, like Charlie Brown. Flew around proclaiming how great he was, and then crashing into trees," he told Kelly. "My parents sent me to a psychiatrist when they started seeing those." In high school, Millionaire recalled, he was a tall, nerdy boy who spent most of his time with his equally alienated best friend. "I smoked pot every day," he said to Kelly, "and I had a comic strip character in high school called 'Reefer Man'. . . . It was about a guy who smoked pot. He had a T-shirt with pictures of his lungs on the T-shirt with a star in each lung."

When he was 16 Millionaire began illustrating professionally, and after high school he attended the Massachusetts College of Art, in Boston. He was asked to leave after three and three-quarter years because he was not attending classes. "They threw in . . . psychology and English lit classes for some kind of funding reasons, the teachers were terrible High School rejects, so I just didn't go," he told a reporter for the Brooklyn, New York–based publication *Free Williamsburg* (April 2002). "I had my hands full with the excellent drawing and painting courses, not to mention earning a living, so I just eliminated the time-wasting courses. When they kicked me out I was relieved. An artist doesn't need a degree, unless he wants to teach, so I jumped for joy and left."

After leaving school Millionaire lived in the Mission Hills neighborhood of Boston and drew pictures of houses for a living. "I'd go out to fancy neighborhoods, drop cards in mailboxes with a little picture of a house on them, and they'd call me to draw their house," he told Kelly. Millionaire traveled throughout the United States and Europe, selling his drawings to support himself. He had settled in Berlin, Germany, where he lived in a squat for a few years, when he realized that he was tired of drawing houses. In the early 1990s he moved to Brooklyn, where he started drawing *Batty*, a strip about an alcoholic baseball player, for Spike Vrusho's baseball zine, *Murtaugh*. He also drew a regular strip for *Waterfront Week*, a one-page, daily zine distributed in bars and stores throughout Brooklyn. "I had a strip in there called *Medea's Weekend*, where I for a year or two years, maybe, learned how to draw comics. And how to meet deadlines. Having the discipline of having to draw a comic, no matter if you're in the mood to do it or not, you've got to get it done every week, if you've got a hangover, you're sick, it doesn't matter, you've got to have it done. Even if it's going to just be photocopied and put it in a storefront," he told Kelly. "It . . . pretty much changed my life."

None of those strips brought in enough money to cover Millionaire's bills, and in 1993 he found himself on hard times when his girlfriend kicked him out of her home on a harsh winter night. The bartender at one of Millionaire's favorite drinking spots, noticing that he was down on his luck, offered him a free beer for every comic strip he drew. "And since I was pretty broke at the time . . . I started drawing a cartoon about a little bird who drank booze and blew his brains out all the time," he told Kelly. The bartender made photocopies of the strips and included them in the establishment's newsletter. Millionaire made larger versions of the strips and submitted them successfully to *Murtaugh* and Selwyn Harris's fanzine *Happy-*

land. Eventually an editor at the *New York Press*, an alternative weekly paper in New York City, saw his comics and offered him a job drawing a regular strip.

Millionaire's weekly strip, *Maakies*, which began publication in 1994, pairs Drinky Crow with the rum-loving ape Uncle Gabby (named for Gabby Glaser of the rock band Luscious Jackson). Together, when not guzzling alcohol or chasing women, they serve on the crew of the *Maak*, an 18th-century warship, taking on their enemies—crocodiles with French accents wearing braided Napoleonic uniforms and German turtles in World War I–style U-boats. Though Uncle Gabby and Drinky Crow struggle with weighty existential issues, the strip is peppered with bathroom humor and jokes about sex and sexual dysfunction. The strips also feature a great deal of violence. "It is the perfect blend of ethereal wine and the rank liquid of the world's many gutters," James Norton wrote for *Flak Magazine* (October 15, 2000, on-line). "*Maakies* poses as a comic strip, but it's really a shorthand for the misery and squalor of the world, laced with an incredibly warped and robust vein of black humor and, occasionally, arcing poetic insight." Millionaire explained to Susan Carpenter for the *Los Angeles Times* (November 14, 2002), "*Maakies* is about the horror of being alive. It's not always about funny." Critics have often noted that the strip, in all its depravity, is set against the backdrop of Millionaire's beautifully rendered seascapes; they have particularly praised his finely detailed drawings of ships.

Maakies quickly became one of the most popular strips in the U.S. Alternative papers from across the country picked it up, and in 1997 the *Village Voice* tried to woo Millionaire away from the *New York Press*, offering to pay him four times as much. He disapproved of the way the *Village Voice* had treated other cartoonists, however, and he initially turned the offer down. Millionaire also created, with the help of the animator Mark Alt, six short *Maakies* cartoons for *Saturday Night Live*; two of them aired during the 1998 season. Despite the popularity of *Maakies*, the *New York Press* refused to pay Millionaire more than the $50 per strip he had been earning since 1994, so in 2003 he signed a contract with the *Village Voice*.

Fantagraphics Books has released three collections of Millionaire's weekly strips. *Maakies* (2000), containing 260 strips, features an introduction by the actor Andy Dick and a cover format by the noted graphic designer Chip Kidd, who chose an elongated, 12-by-14-inch trim size that was also used for the old collections of the classic *Mutt & Jeff* comics. Kidd also designed the covers for the collections that followed, *House at Maakies Corner* (2003), *When We Were Very Maakies* (2004)—which features an introduction by the novelist and memoirist Dave Eggers—and the forthcoming *Der Struwwelmaakies*. (The titles of the 2003 and 2004 collections were inspired by those of two of Milne's *Winnie the Pooh* books.) Reviewing *When*

We Were Very Maakies for *Booklist* (August 2004), Ray Olson noted that the comics are often "gory, violent, revolting, and, above all, absurd." He continued: "In them society is a dunghill; people are witless, faithless sadists; and life is nasty, brutal, and, alas, inescapable (witness the main characters' repeated suicides—and resurrections). But the rolling seas and towering clouds, the three-masted ships that sail on the one and beneath the other, the gardens and butterflies, the sweeping landscapes—all gorgeously drawn—amid which the maladventures of Drinky Crow and Uncle Gabby, Millionaire's alcoholic antiheroes, frequently unfold, betray a romantic sensibility of heartbreaking intensity."

Starting in 1998 Millionaire began drawing the *Sock Monkey* series of comic books, which are published sporadically by Dark Horse Comics. Its main character, also named Uncle Gabby, was inspired in part by the stuffed monkey that Millionaire's grandmother had made for him from an old sock when he was a boy. The Uncle Gabby of *Sock Monkey* belongs to Anne Louise, a little blond girl who resides in a grand Victorian house much like the home Millionaire's grandparents owned in Newton Lower Falls, Massachusetts. "It was a big, very old house with beautiful smells of plaster, old waxed wood and tollhouse cookies," he told the interviewer for *Westfield Comics*. "My cousin Anne Louise lived there, she was a few years older than my siblings and me, and she told us about this little tiny man that lived in the closet. She would leave cookie crumbs for him and the next day they would be gone. We really believed her and were kind of scared, but I remember how much more magical that house seemed than the Deck House we lived in."

Like his predecessor in the *Maakies* strips, Uncle Gabby is paired with a crow—in this case Mr. Crow, who is made of cloth and has button eyes. "They run around the old house trying to find beauty and poetry in the things they see (in the first book they think that a chandelier is a castle in heaven) but are constantly tripped up by crunching reality," Millionaire told the *Westfield Comics* interviewer. "Fire, rabid bats, weird things in the study like guns, booze and shrunken heads have a way of ruining their idealistic view of things." In *Sock Monkey, Vol. 3, No. 2*, Uncle Gabby accidentally knocks a baby bird from its nest. He is so distraught when he realizes that he has killed the bird that he wanders off into the wilderness. Unable to bear the guilt, he attempts to commit suicide by cutting his head off with a pair of sewing scissors. To his dismay he realizes that as a stuffed animal he cannot die. Anne Louise retrieves him by the end of the story and sews him back together. When Uncle Gabby asks her how she can love a murderer, Anne Louise replies, "How can I not love you? You're my sock monkey . . ." Assessing the comic-book series for *Time* (February 16, 2001, on-line), Andrew D. Arnold wrote, "Tony Millionaire's *Sock Monkey* disturbs me for all the right rea-

sons. . . . The stories read like original Grimm's fairy tales—the ones where Cinderella's stepsisters hack away at their feet with an ax so they will fit the glass slipper. They have a romantic, quaint naiveté mixed with moments of modern existential horror."

Many issues of the *Sock Monkey* series sold out, and Dark Horse Comics issued two collections in book format: *The Adventures of Sock Monkey* (2000) and *The Collected Works of Tony Millionaire's Sock Monkey* (2004). After the birth of his first daughter, Millionaire was inspired to write children's books featuring Uncle Gabby and Mr. Crow. *Sock Monkey: A Children's Book* was published in 2001, followed by *Sock Monkey: The Glass Doorknob* (2002) and *Tony Millionaire's Sock Monkey: Uncle Gabby* (2004). *That Darn Yarn*, a book intended for all ages, appeared in May 2005.

A year earlier Fantagraphics Books had published Millionaire's 32-page objet d'art *Mighty Mite: The Earmite*. The left-hand pages of the book tell the story of Gabby, an ape who has fled the circus and must scrounge for sustenance in a strange city. The right-hand pages feature the travels of the wandering earmite, Mighty Mite. The illustrations for Uncle Gabby's tale are drawn with somber grays, while Mighty Mite's are in full color. The reader does not discover until the final page of this four-by-four-inch book how the story lines intertwine.

Millionaire is the recipient of four Will Eisner Comics Industry Awards and two Harvey Awards, for *Sock Monkey* and *Maakies*. He has illustrated articles for the *New Yorker*, *New York* magazine, the *Wall Street Journal*, *Screw*, the *Boston Phoenix*, and many other publications. He has also illustrated walking-tour maps for the Ephemera Press and album covers for the music groups They Might Be Giants and the Morning Shakes. His work appears in numerous anthologies, including *The Dark Horse Book of Witchcraft*, *Bizarro World*, *9-11: Emergency Relief*, *Sin City: Dame to Kill For*, and *Legal Action Comics, Vol. 2*.

In 1999 Millionaire moved to California with his wife, the actress Becky Thyre. The couple have two preschool-age daughters. "It's getting harder to write comics about the themes of depression and darkness now that I live in Pasadena surrounded by flowers and babies," Millionaire told Carpenter. "I have to rely on my memory."

—J.C.

Suggested Reading: maakies.com; *Comics Journal* p94+ (#215); *Los Angeles Magazine* p32 May 1, 2000; *Los Angeles Times* p24 Nov. 14, 2002; *Time* (on-line) Feb. 16, 2001; *Westfield Comics* (on-line) Dec. 2000

Selected Books: *Maakies*, 2000; *The Adventures of Sock Monkey*, 2000; *Sock Monkey: A Children's Book*, 2001; *Sock Monkey: The Glass Doorknob*, 2002; *House at Maakies Corner*, 2003;

When We Were Very Maakies, 2004; *Mighty Mite: The Earmite*, 2004; *The Collected Works of Tony Millionaire's Sock Monkey*, 2004; *Tony Millionaire's Sock Monkey: Uncle Gabby*, 2004; *That Darn Yarn*, 2005

Evan Agostini/Getty Images

Mitchell, Pat

Jan. 20, 1943– President and CEO, Public Broadcasting Service

Address: PBS, 1320 Braddock Pl., Alexandria, VA 22314

"We're not making programming to appease the greatest number of eyeballs for advertisers. We're making programming to serve the public," Pat Mitchell told David Bauder for the Associated Press (February 7, 2000), on the day the Public Broadcasting Service (PBS) announced her appointment as its president and chief executive officer (CEO). When she stepped into that position, Mitchell already had a three-decade-long career in commercial television, as a journalist, network correspondent, talk-show host, award-winning producer, and executive. Her employers have ranged from local Boston and Washington, D.C., TV stations, in the 1970s, to NBC and CBS, in the 1980s, to the company that formed when Time Warner Inc. merged with the Turner Broadcasting System Inc., in the 1990s. Also in the 1990s, as the founder of her own business, she produced such documentaries as *Women in War: Voices from the Front Lines*, for the A&E television network, and *Shattered Lullabies*, for the Lifetime channel. "When I

was running my own little independent company and struggling to produce documentaries, I looked at PBS as a model," she told Philip Kennicott for the *Washington Post* (November 22, 2002).

Mitchell is the first woman and the first producer to lead PBS, which is the only noncommercial television service in the U.S. PBS was created in 1969 by the Corporation for Public Broadcasting (CPB), which came into being following the passage of the Public Broadcasting Act of 1967. That legislation states, "It is in the public interest to encourage the growth and development of public radio and television broadcasting, including the use of such media for instructional, educational, and cultural purposes." When President Lyndon B. Johnson signed the bill into law, he said, according to the CPB Web site, "The Corporation will assist stations and producers who aim for the best in broadcasting good music, . . . exciting plays, and . . . reports on the whole fascinating range of human activity. It will try to prove that what educates can also be exciting. It will get part of its support from our Government. But it will be carefully guarded from Government or from party control. It will be free, and it will be independent—and it will belong to all of our people." Thus, although the federal government provides all the financing for the CPB, the CPB is not a government agency; it is a private, nonprofit corporation. It does not produce, acquire, or distribute programs; rather, it provides funding—about 15 percent of the total—for public-television and -radio programming.

PBS, whose programs debuted on television in 1970, is also a private, nonprofit corporation. Currently, it issues licenses to about 170 noncommercial, educational entities (community organizations, colleges and universities, state authorities, and local or municipal authorities) that operate some 350 PBS member stations, which exist in all 50 states, Puerto Rico, the U.S. Virgin Islands, Guam, and American Samoa. In contrast to the CPB, PBS acquires and distributes programs, for use by its member stations. Its National Programming Service provides the stations with a package of "children's, cultural, educational, history, nature, news, public affairs, science and skills programming," as explained on the Web site pbs.org. Its other activities include the promotion of programs; efforts in support of member stations' fund raising; engineering and technology development—including, prominently and most recently, expansion of Internet services; services related to education, among them the distribution of materials for teachers, including free lesson plans in connection with many PBS programs and other guides for teachers as well as materials for parents who home-school their children; and marketing of PBS videos. In the 2004 fiscal year, 47 percent of its operating revenues came from assessments paid by member stations (an average of 50 percent of whose funds are contributions from viewers); 24 percent from the CPB and federal grants, principally from the U.S. Department of Education; 12 percent from sales of educational products; and the rest from such sources as royalties and investments.

Since its inception in the U.S., many people have questioned the legitimacy of publicly funded broadcasting, and some have complained that public radio and public television display a bias toward liberal, leftist, or secular principles and values. Some congressmen have repeatedly called for big cuts in the CPB's budget or for the elimination of government funding altogether. Like her predecessors, Mitchell has repeatedly responded with strong defenses of public radio and television. "I think it's really imperative in a democratic society that we have at least one public media enterprise that is not driven and determined by marketplace factors alone," she told a reporter for WorldScreen.com (April 2001). In a speech given in December 2004 at the University of Chicago, during a conference on the arts and humanities in public life, Mitchell said, "There is plenty of evidence . . . that a strong democracy depends on an informed and engaged public, and a strong and independent media best assures that result. Why else would shutting down such media enterprises be the first act of a dictator and open and free media usually the first casualty in any attack on freedom? And there is plenty of evidence that a strong public service media institution does inform and educate and engage citizens in ways that strengthen a country and indeed a world that has never needed such citizens more."

In the same speech, as quoted on the Web site of the university's Cultural Policy Center, Mitchell reported that "even in a 300 channel universe, every single week, 82 million Americans tune in to PBS"—nearly 28 percent of the U.S. population. In November 2004, she continued, "140 million people watched PBS. . . . For all the resources being spent against us on programming and promotion, on average, our audiences are twice as high on any given night as Discovery, A&E, or the History Channel, and are twice as high as many of the other cable companies, including CNN. All told, PBS audiences rank eighth among all national channels." Mitchell told Rick Steelhammer for the Charleston (West Virginia) Gazette (February 2, 2003), "We're still the No.1 source of video materials in all of America's classrooms."

In January 2005 PBS became the center of much media attention, when Mitchell made the controversial decision to drop from its package of programs an installment of the children's series Postcards from Buster that showed a lesbian couple with their children. At the same time, Margaret Spellings, the newly appointed secretary of the U.S. Department of Education, a source of PBS's funding, sent PBS a strongly worded complaint about the same episode. Less than three weeks later, Mitchell revealed publicly that she would not renew her second three-year contract with PBS, which ends in 2006.

The daughter of James Otis Edenfield and Bernice Tucker Edenfield, Mitchell was born Patricia Edenfield in Swainsboro, Georgia, on January 20, 1943, when the TV industry was in its infancy. (In 1947, according to Douglas Gomery in the Journal of Popular Film and Television [Fall 2001], there were only six TV stations and only 20,000 TV sets in use in the entire U.S.) Mitchell attended the University of Georgia, in Athens, where she earned a B.A. degree, magna cum laude, in 1964. The following year she received a master's degree in English literature from the same school. From 1965 to 1969 she taught English at the University of Georgia; from 1969 to 1970 she taught drama as well as English at Virginia Commonwealth University, in Richmond. Briefly in 1970 she worked in New York City as a writer and researcher for Look, a popular general-interest magazine. Later that year she was hired as a speechwriter by Garth Associates, a political-consulting firm.

Mitchell got her first job in television in 1971, at WBZ-TV in Boston, Massachusetts. During the half-dozen years she worked there, she produced the program Impact News Specials; she also served as a news anchor, a reporter, and the host of a women's show. In 1977 she moved to Washington, D.C., where she became the host of a live two-hour news and interview program called Panorama on WTTG-TV. Her work on Panorama earned her an Emmy Award. In 1983, in Los Angeles, California, she set up her own production company and, with Mary Muldoon, created what is said to be the first all-female talk show, Woman to Woman. Cohosted by Mitchell and Muldoon, Woman to Woman made its debut in September 1983 and was syndicated to more than 100 stations. It presented a roundtable discussion group made up of about a dozen women, who talked about marriage, family, raising children, and social, economic, and political issues. In 1984 Woman to Woman won an Emmy Award for most outstanding talk program. Nevertheless, according to Zina Klapper in Ms. (November 1984), it did not attract a large audience, and it was cancelled in 1984. Beginning in that year until 1989, while living in New York City, Mitchell was a correspondent for the NBC-TV morning show Today; sometimes she substituted for Today's co-anchor Jane Pauley. From 1989 to 1990 she held the job of arts correspondent at the weekly CBS-TV show Sunday Morning. In addition, during the 1980s Mitchell and Muldoon developed and co-hosted a program called Hour Magazine, which aired on Group W television, and toward the latter part of that decade, Mitchell worked for ABC's Home show as a producer and reporter. In about 1989 she also helped to found VU Productions, the nonfiction division of UBU Productions (which is known for the TV series Family Ties and Spin City). Among the reality series, specials, and documentaries for cable and broadcast television that she created and developed were Women in War: Voices from the Front Lines (1990), which focused on women in El Salvador, Israel, and Northern Ireland, and *Shattered Lullabies* (1992), a documentary on high infant mortality rates in the U.S.

In 1992 Mitchell joined Time Warner, with the title of executive vice president of TBS Productions. (Since the merger in 1996 of Time Warner Inc. and the Turner Broadcasting System Inc., owned by Ted Turner, Time Warner has sometimes been referred to as Turner/Time Warner.) In 1995 Mitchell was promoted to president of Turner Original Productions, a new division; its name later became CNN Productions. (Some sources give somewhat different titles for her.) At various times she had responsibility for commissioning, developing, and supervising the production of original nonfiction projects for CNN, TBS Superstation, and other Turner or Time Warner holdings; she was also expected to oversee the creation of television spin-offs of Time Inc. magazines and other products. Some 88 hours per year of natural-history programs and 400 hours' worth of documentaries and specials came to fruition under her leadership. Prominent among them were installments of *National Geographic Explorer*; the three-part, Emmy Award–winning series *A Century of Women* (1994), about influential 20th-century women; the 1995 Emmy winners *Hank Aaron: Chasing the Dream* and *Moon Shot*, a two-part special commemorating the 25th anniversary of the first moon landing; the TV special *Survivors of the Holocaust* and the six-part series *The Private Life of Plants*, written and hosted by David Attenborough, both of which won Emmy Awards in 1996; *The Coming Plague* (1997), a four-hour film, based on a book by Laurie Garrett, about epidemics of familiar diseases and outbreaks of ones previously unknown; the 24-part series *Cold War*, which covered the power struggle (extending from 1945 to 1991) between the Soviet bloc countries (the Soviet Union and its close Communist allies, among them Poland, East Germany, and Romania) and the Western democracies, and consequences of that struggle within both factions; and the 10-hour *Millennium: A Thousand Years of History* (1999), which documented notable events of the past 1,000 years. Mitchell worked with the renowned British documentarian Jeremy Isaacs on both *Millennium* and *Cold War*, the latter of which won a Peabody Award. Mitchell was also the executive producer of the weekly documentary series *CNN Perspectives.*

On February 7, 2000 came the announcement that Mitchell would become the new president and CEO of PBS. She succeeded Ervin Duggan, who had resigned after five and a half years in the job. Wayne Godwin, PBS's executive vice president, told Karen Everhart Bedford for *Current* (February 7, 2000, on-line) that Mitchell was "seen as a synergy-builder [who] listens remarkably well, and places a high value . . . on member stations and their relationships to local communities." In her first year Mitchell focused on the contents of PBS's lineup, with the goal of delivering more relevent

and compelling programs. She set up a five-member team to evaluate the 3,000 to 4,000 programming proposals submitted each year, and she helped to make the evaluation, approval, and financing of projects more efficient. Programming, she told an interviewer for worldscreen.com (April 2001, on-line), "begins with a mission, with the fact that we are commissioning and scheduling programming not to sell products but to really inform and inspire. I think it's our responsibility to make sure that we are doing more than just a television broadcast, and we are. Our programs are looked at in terms of impact on a community instead of ratings." "We are not going to measure any program by the size of its audience, the amount of its underwriting or what demographic it attracts," Mitchell told a *Pittsburgh Post-Gazette* (July 31, 2002) interviewer. WGBH-TV, in Boston, KQED, in San Francisco, and WNET, in New York, are three of the seven member stations that produce a significant number of PBS's programs.

Under Mitchell's direction, in 2002 PBS launched the dramatic series *American Family: Journey of Dreams*, whose characters are Hispanic and are portrayed by Hispanic actors and actresses, among them Edward James Olmos and Sonia Braga; *Ken Burns American Stories*, which features some of Burns's previously broadcast documentaries; and *Frontier House*, in which three contemporary American families are shown living under conditions that prevailed in the U.S. West in the 19th century. In an example of a new approach to a longtime PBS favorite, on November 24, 2002 the series *Mystery!* offered an episode based not on British material but on *Skinwalkers*, a Tony Hillerman novel that is set on an Indian reservation in the American Southwest. "The commercial guys won't take a chance on something they don't see as mainstream," Mitchell said to Rick Steelhammer for the *Charleston (West Virginia) Gazette* (February 2, 2003). "We saw *Skinwalkers* as a great way to modernize . . . *Mystery!* . . . and reach a broader audience." The "Skinwalkers" installment of *Mystery!* drew one of PBS's highest Nielsen ratings.

Parts of PBS's audience are often ignored by the commercial television industry: very young viewers and people who are middle-aged and older, especially those who have completed college. Among parents of preschoolers, PBS children's shows are favorites. "Parents know our children's programming to be nonviolent, pro-social and education-based," Mitchell said to Rick Steelhammer. The PBS lineup includes two dozen shows for youngsters. Among them are such animated series as *Barney*; *Jay Jay the Jet Plane*; *Teletubbies*; *Adventures from the Book of Virtues*, which offers Greek myths, Asian fables, African folktales, European fairy tales, Native American stories, and other classic narratives that seek to illuminate the nature of loyalty, integrity, and other admirable qualities; *Anne of Green Gables*, based on a famous novel by L. M. Montgomery, which, according to pbs.org, focuses on "respect for family and friends, the importance of collaboration, self-control, compassion for others, and taking responsibility for one's actions"; and *Clifford*, about a dog who has 10 "big ideas," among them "Be kind," "Believe in yourself," "Work together," and "Play fair." Others among PBS's programs for children are *Sesame Street*, *Reading Rainbow*, *Between the Lions*, *ZOOM*, and *Postcards from Buster*.

Postcards from Buster is produced jointly by WGBH, Cookie Jar Entertainment, and Marc Brown Studios; the show is part of PBS's "Ready to Learn" series, which receives a portion of its funds from the U.S. Department of Education. Buster is an animated rabbit who travels around the U.S. with his father meeting real children and their families and learning about their traditions and activities. (He has also visited Canada, Mexico, and Puerto Rico.) Buster's parents are divorced; the "postcards" are for his mother, with whom he lives most of the year. According to pbs.org, one of the "key educational goals" of *Postcards from Buster* is "to build awareness and appreciation of the many cultures in America." In various installments, Buster meets Native American, Inuit, Pentecostal Christian, Mormon, Muslim, and Orthodox Jewish families, as well as children whose parents immigrated to the U.S. from such countries as Lebanon, Cuba, and Greece. In the "Sugartime!" episode, which was to air in January 2005, Buster travels to Vermont, where he learns how maple syrup is made. The parents of the two sisters he meets are a lesbian couple, who remain mostly in the background. According to Mitchell, representatives from PBS, WGBH, and the Department of Education approved the proposal for the episode, which described the visit to the gay women and their children, and a PBS spokesperson, Lee Sloan, told Suzanne C. Ryan for the *Boston Globe* (January 22, 2005) that Mitchell felt "comfortable" with the complete version. Mitchell herself, however, has maintained that when she saw "Sugartime!" in its final form, she felt that aspects of it jeopardized PBS's "trusted position as a safe haven for parents," as she explained to Karen Everhart and Steve Behrens for *Current* (February 14, 2005, on-line). A "safe haven," she said, is "a place where parents can actually leave their children and not worry that they will be bombarded with commercial sales pitches, violence or antisocial behavior or issues that parents may or may not want to tackle with their children, or if they do want to, they would prefer to handle in their own time and not because a PBS program forced them to." After she and others at PBS consulted with a total of 100 member stations, producers, and others, PBS removed "Sugartime!" from its national schedule. Shortly afterward, according to Mitchell—or shortly before, according to some sources—Secretary of Education Margaret Spellings, on her second day on the job, sent Mitchell a publicly distributed letter that stated, as posted on the Department of Education's Web site (January 2005, on-line), "Many parents would not want their young children exposed to the life-styles portrayed in this episode. Congress' and the Department's purpose in funding this programming certainly was not to introduce this kind of subject matter to children, particularly through the powerful and intimate medium of television." Spellings demanded that if the program aired, all references to the Department of Education be deleted from the broadcast and from promotional materials about it; she also asked PBS to alert its member stations as to the contents of the show. Then she added, "We believe you should strongly consider refunding to the Department the Federal education funds that were used for the episode."

Not surprisingly, socially and politically conservative groups and commentators, such as the Fox News Channel's Bill O'Reilly, condemned the content of "Sugarland!" and applauded Spellings's stand, while those holding liberal views decried the actions of Mitchell as well as Spellings. Among the latter was the group Affirmation: United Methodists for Lesbian, Gay, Bisexual & Transgender Concerns, which, in an open letter to Mitchell posted on its Web site (January 25, 2005), declared, "Clearly this is censorship, and it is wrong. What happened to our basic civil rights and freedoms? What happened to parents being able to choose what their children watch on TV? . . . There is much on TV that we, as Christian mothers, have to protect our children from. We shield them from exposure to violence. We try to prevent them from hearing language that is not used in our homes. Now we must protect our children from those who would take away our civil rights. We must protect our children from narrow-mindedness and prejudice. We must protect our children from those who would restrict their growth and education regarding the wondrous cultural diversity that is ours to share as members of the American family." WGBH continued to offer "Sugarland!" to PBS member stations, some of whom aired it. In Minneapolis, Minnesota, on March 23, 2005, a nonprofit organization called aMaze arranged to have "Sugarland!" shown in a theater; 700 adults and children attended the event, at which the city's mayor, R. T. Rybak, proclaimed the day "Welcoming Buster Day."

On February 15, 2005 Mitchell announced that she would leave her post at PBS when her contract expires, in 2006. She maintained that her decision to resign was not connected to the controversy surrounding the "Sugarland!" episode. That statement notwithstanding, many observers linked the news of her forthcoming departure with the outcry surrounding *Postcards from Buster*. They also noted the onerousness of Mitchell's unabating struggle to obtain sufficient funding for PBS's programs in the face of repeated attacks on public television from members of Congress. Indeed, in June the House Appropriations Committee recommended a cut of $100 million in CPB's 2006 budget and $102.4 million for specific public-broadcasting programs; after widespread public protests, the full House voted to restore the former cut but not the latter. In addition, in June the media learned that the new chairman of the CPB, Kenneth Tomlinson, a Republican, had secretly hired Frederick Mann, who has ties to conservative groups, to record the frequency with which guests on public radio and television programs made comments critical or supportive of President George W. Bush and his administration's policies. Pointing to Mann's findings, Tomlinson accused public radio and television of having a liberal bias and of being unbalanced. Earlier, during a speech before the National Press Club on May 24, 2005, as posted on pbs.org, Mitchell said, "It is clear that PBS does not belong to any single constituency, no one political party or activist group or foundation or funder" and that it does not serve "an agenda of any kind. Our editorial standards ensure this and public opinion polls verify it."

In September 2005 Sun Microsystems announced that Mitchell would be joining its 10-member board of directors and its eight-person panel of independent directors. The appointments drew criticism from the media-watchdog group Center for Digital Democracy, whose executive director, Jeffrey Chester, maintained that an inherent conflict of interest was created when an executive of a public noncommercial entity also serves on the board of a for-profit organization. In response, a

PBS spokesperson, speaking to a reporter for *Communications Daily* (September 14, 2005), pointed out, "It's not unusual for heads of nonprofits and universities to serve on for-profit, noncompetitive boards."

From her six-year marriage to Jay Addison Mitchell, which ended in divorce in 1970, Mitchell has one son, Mark. In 2001 she married Scott O. Seydel, an Atlanta businessman whose companies create products from recycled materials; Seydel is also the chairman of the board of the conservation organization Global Green USA. One of Seydel's five children, his son Rutherford, is married to Ted Turner's daughter Laura.

—L.J.

Suggested Reading: *Charleston (West Virginia) Gazette* B p3 Feb 2, 2003; *Current* (on-line) Feb. 7, 2000, Feb. 14, 2005; pbs.org; *Pittsburgh Post Gazette* E p4 July 31, 2000; *Washington Post* C p1 Nov. 22, 2002, C p1 Feb 17, 2005

Selected TV Series or Documentaries: as producer—*Women in War: Voices from the Front Lines*, 1990; as executive producer—*A Century of Women*, 1994; *CNN Perspectives*, 1998; *Tattoos: Women of the Ink*, 1998

Morris, Butch

Feb. 10, 1947– Jazz musician and composer

Address: c/o Vittorio Albani, Pannonica Music, 27 via Guncina, 39100 Bolzano, Italy

"The contemporary artist capable of [Butch] Morris's visionary beauty is rare indeed," Bobby Hill wrote for the *Washington Post* (January 14, 1996). Morris, a jazz cornetist, composer, and conductor, is the inventor of conduction, a way of creating an improvised performance in which a conductor signals a group of musicians on whim to change rhythm, meter, and dynamics. "The idea is not to totally control the improvisation, but to put people in different psychological sound-states," Morris told Jon Pareles for the *New York Times* (July 26, 1985). "It maneuvers them; an improviser can be working in a particular structure and I'll change the structure, and all of a sudden they'll find themselves in another tonality or another form, and they'll have to work their way through it or work their way out of it." Morris has formed conduction ensembles—known as "skyscrapers"—around the world. Although Morris's background is in jazz, his ensembles consist of classical, folk, and avant-garde artists as well as jazz musicians. "This is not music they can take home and learn and so that places a demand on them they've never had," Morris told Gary Booth for the London *Financial Times*

Courtesy of Rebecca Meek

(November 4, 1997). "They know what Beethoven's Seventh sounds like, but we don't know what we're going to do until it happens, on the night." Writing for the *New York Sun* (February 11, 2005), Will Friedwald commented, "Morris's music is clearly a product of both American and European traditions of orchestral music. The solo breaks are essentially cadenzas, and the piece on the whole could be characterized as a suite: a series of distinct melodies. The difference is that, in Mr. Morris's music, the individual movements run in and out of each other organically. There's never a point where one melody simply stops, the orchestra pauses, and the next part begins."

Although each of the conduction performances (which totaled 141 as of late 2004) is unique, Morris conducts by using signs that all the musicians in his ensembles must learn. "As a musician goes about the job of improvising, Mr. Morris will look at him and give a signal: left hand extended, palm up means 'sustain a tone,'" Ben Ratliff wrote for the *New York Times* (April 3, 1998). "Left hand to temple and one finger in the air means 'Memory One (Remember That Phrase, Because Later I'll Call for It From You).' A minute later, he might establish 'Memory Two' from the same musician. Pointing to his left ear, then pointing to another player, he might ask a guitarist to mimic a pianist. Holding the baton upside-down and parallel to his body, moving it sideways in a certain direction, he orders a panning effect from the group. Meanwhile, he might gesture time and tempo to the drummer, producing a six-beat rhythm to lie under the music." The worst mistake a musician can make in one of Morris's ensembles is to play a line in unison with another performer. "People naturally gravitate towards playing together but I see 'copying' as a weakness, it is no better than playing notated music," Morris told Booth. "I may start in the middle of a piece, or extract parts to repeat them," he told Peter Watrous for the *New York Times* (April 30, 1991). "I'm not interested in doing the same thing every night, to sound the same. Music should be flexible on a daily basis, so that it doesn't stagnate. I want to get the audience involved—take the attention—and one way of doing it is by improvising."

Lawrence Douglas "Butch" Morris was born on February 10, 1947 in Long Beach, California, near Los Angeles. His father was a career navy officer, his mother a homemaker. Morris comes from a musical family; his eldest brother, Joe, and youngest, Michael, played clarinet; his sister, Marceline, played piano; and his brother Wilber is a recorded bassist and bandleader. When Butch was eight years old, Wilber gave him his jazz record collection, the largest in the neighborhood. During his time at public school, Morris tried his hand at several instruments, including piano, trombone, French horn, bass, and flute, eventually settling on the trumpet. He studied music theory, harmony, and composition in high school and also performed in the school's marching band, orchestra, and studio band. After school Morris worked in a music shop, where part of his job was to copy the arrangements—known as charts—for big bands, which gave him the opportunity to analyze the way that different arrangers approached the same song. After graduating he often played music with the

bassist George Morrow and saxophonist J. R. Montrose at local jam sessions and with small jazz bands that performed music written by such jazz luminaries as Horace Silver, Jackie McLean, Miles Davis, and Thelonious Monk.

In 1966, during the Vietnam War, Morris began a tour of duty with the U.S. Navy (some sources say army) as an ambulance driver. During the periods he spent alone during that time, he practiced playing music and began, as he told Hill, to "question what all these musical laws were." When he left the military he studied prosthetics and orthotics to prepare for a career in health science. After he discovered the free-jazz scene in California in the late 1960s, however, his focus returned to music. He switched to the cornet, a brass instrument similar to the trumpet, and joined the pianist Horace Tapscott's big band. He also made the acquaintance of many free-jazz musicians, including David Murray, with whom he would later form a musical partnership. ("Free" jazz refers to jazz that is unrestricted by predetermined chord or tempo structures.)

Morris moved in 1971 from the Los Angeles area to Oakland, California, which had a small but dynamic free-jazz scene. There, he studied cornet and composition with Little Benny Harris and conducting with Jackie Hairston. He also met the drummer Charles Moffett, who influenced Morris through the ensemble improvisations he led. "Moffett had certain things that he did, and the band knew what to do," Morris told Hill. "It might be the way he scoots his piano chair back or taps out rhythm on the piano." "My conducting teacher told me what couldn't be done," Morris said, according to the Pannonica Music Web site. "Charles Moffett taught me what could be done."

In 1976 Morris, like many other California musicians of the era, moved to New York City to take advantage of the low rents for large loft spaces, where they could live and practice and perform their music. He reunited there with his old friends David Murray and Frank Lowe, the latter of whom he had met in the San Francisco area in the early 1970s. In the fall of 1976, Morris and Lowe toured Europe, where Morris performed his first recorded music, on Lowe's album *The Other Side*. He also taught ensemble improvisation in Holland and Belgium. Returning to New York, Morris began to perform with Murray's octet and also took on the responsibility of conducting Murray's big band orchestra. Morris changed arrangements from performance to performance; in the first set of a 1978 concert, for example, he directed the band's flautist to play an unaccompanied solo, and in the next set he directed four saxophonists to accompany the flautist, creating, according to Hollie I. West in the *Washington Post* (July 4, 1978), "a shimmering and irresistible sound quality." A 1977 concert he performed with Murray's Low Class Conspiracy band in Amsterdam, Holland, was recorded and released in 1978 as *Volume Two: Holy Siege on Intrigue*. Reviewing the record for All Music Guide (on-line), Eugene Chadbourne found much to criticize but wrote that Morris's performance was a standout, "making passages subtle and beckoning," and that "it is this player's movements that carry the day." In 1978 Morris performed on Murray's album *Interboogieology*, for which he composed two of the album's four tracks. "The results are stimulating if not essential; a lesser but still interesting effort," Scott Yanow wrote for All Music Guide. In the early 1980s Murray's big band and octet were regular attractions at Sweet Basil, a jazz club in Greenwich Village. The octet can be heard on such albums as *Murray's Steps* (1982), and the big band played on albums including the two volumes of *Live at Sweet Basil* (1984). In the *New York Times* (June 2, 1985), Don Palmer wrote, "The band has coalesced into a powerful force that swings with a vengeance either at full tilt or at a whisper, and it is an extension of both Mr. Murray's tenor voice and Mr. Morris's off-center humor."

Morris opened the 1983 Kool Jazz Festival's New Music at Soundcape series in New York City, leading a group that included two violins, electric guitar, vibraphone, piano, and drums, in addition to his cornet. Reviewing the show for the *New York Times* (June 27, 1983), Robert Palmer wrote, "Some jazz composers are more concerned with melodic and rhythmic ideas than with instrumental color, but the feelings Mr. Morris was expressing . . . seemed to demand the richly allusive instrumental combinations he employed. Even the music's strong melodic and rhythmic shapes tended to sound inseparable from the instrumentation. The violins carried long, sighing melodies, and there were herky-jerky, where-did-the-beat-go rhythmic abstractions that a different sort of rhythm section would not have negotiated so effectively."

In 1985 Morris released *Current Trends in Racism in Modern America*, his first album of conduction music, recorded live at the Kitchen in New York. For the improvisational performance Morris assembled a 10-piece band, evenly divided between jazz musicians and those from the experimental New York "downtown" music scene, including John Zorn, Tom Cora, and Christian Marclay. Hill called the record "a daring and cacophonous blending of diverse musical instrumentation—reeds, harp, cello, turntables, etc.—that evokes the dark, brooding moods suggested by its title."

During the late 1980s and for several years in the 1990s, Morris continued to conduct the David Murray Big Band, which Peter Watrous referred to in the *New York Times* (May 21, 1992) as "one of the most exciting groups working in jazz, in part because of Mr. Morris's ability to draw jagged riffs and sleek backgrounds from it." "Butch Morris is the weirdest person on the planet," Murray told Watrous for the *New York Times* (April 30, 1991), "and that alone makes the band original. He can stretch out the band, make us go in all sorts of directions. He's brilliant, he's eccentric, and it comes out in the music." The 1991 recording *David Mur-*

ray Big Band Conducted by Lawrence "Butch" Morris was given a good review in the *Washington Post* (September 25, 1992) by Ruben Jackson, who wrote, "This will probably disappoint those lucky enough to have seen these longtime collaborators in concert settings, but it is still difficult not to be impressed by the aggregation's relaxed yet fervent updating of the big-band tradition." In addition to his work with Murray, Morris conducted his own ensemble and Jemeel Moondoc's Jes Grew Orchestra during that period.

Meanwhile, in 1986 Morris had collaborated on the album *Nine Below Zero* with the keyboardist Wayne Horvitz and the pianist Robert Previte. Also that year Morris led nine musicians and two singers in an hour of improvised music, while Willem Brugman read occasionally from a text by Sekou Sundiata, in the performance piece *The Image of None* at the Performing Garage in New York. Writing for the *New York Times* (March 30, 1986), Jon Pareles called the work "a flux of textures, improvisations and short motives. At times, it has a romantic sweep; at times, it is prickly and pointillistic. There are surging crescendos, areas of dappled stillness or delicate rhythmic eddies, as sections blur and dissolve into one another with no clear divisions. Minimalist repetition melts into improvisation, which coalesces into composed melody; the performers work like jazz soloists at one juncture and chamber players the next." Nonetheless Pareles also noted that "the parts were more impressive than the whole. . . . *The Image of None* needs editing, in both its text and music, and it needs a way of generating momentum."

In 1987 Morris released the album *Homeing*. The Medicine Show Theater Ensemble also premiered his music-theater work *Fire*. According to its presenters, as quoted by Jon Pareles for the *New York Times* (March 22, 1987), the piece "chronicles the serio-comic odyssey of a man toward quasi-psychedelic enlightenment through encounters with various life styles." In 1989 Morris led several of his conductions at the New Music America festival at the Brooklyn Academy of Music, where he also premiered his more conventional piece, "Dust to Dust."

Morris collaborated in 1990 with the musician-improvisers Martin Schutz, Hans Koch, and Hans Reichel on the album *X-Communication*, which consists of two pieces, totaling 70 minutes. "This is a group that looks for freedom at every turn, every window, and every pace," Thom Jurek wrote for All Music Guide. "They look to turn each musician loose from the ensemble to explore with the support of the ensemble whatever it is she or he feels compelled to journey toward. . . . The sounds, tones, textures, and timbral relationships encountered here are unique to this band; they have not been touched on before, and they will not be encountered again. These colors, so many shades of the dark, are beautiful to hear, to feel, and internalize." Also in 1990 Morris released the recorded version of *Dust to Dust*, an album of conduction using traditional jazz instruments, classical instruments, and two electronic samplers. "It is one of the few true jazz records I've heard in which the composition takes precedence over the soloists, and comes out capable of facing the competition," Steve Pick wrote for the St. Louis Post-Dispatch (July 19, 1991). In the following year Morris collaborated on the well-received album When the Sun Is Out You Don't See Stars with the bassist Peter Kowald, the saxophonist Werner Lüdi, and the vocalist Sainkho Namtchylak.

In 1993, with the percussionist Lê Quan Ninh and the flautist and trombonist J. A. Deane, Morris recorded Burning Cloud, a three-movement composition intended as a statement about the environment. That was followed two years later by Testament: A Conduction Collection, a boxed set of 10 compact discs containing recordings of many of his conductions. (Since the 25th conduction he had recorded them all.) Morris told Hill that the collection was "a celebration of the artist as a creative contributor to the overall art form, as opposed to any individual search for stardom or notoriety." Among the conductions were nos. 25 and 26, which featured traditional Turkish musicians and instruments, and no. 28, which featured traditional Japanese musicians and instruments. "I might work with Japanese Kabuki Theatre musicians who have relatively little knowledge of jazz but their culture makes them great improvisers. I'm after the individual craving of the improviser. What they really care about musically," Morris told John Fordham for the London Guardian (October 31, 1997). All of the discs were later released as separate albums.

Because learning to work within a conduction ensemble often takes musicians a long time, Morris has established skyscraper ensembles in New York, Berlin, Tokyo, London, and Istanbul, so that he can perform with a group versed in his style whenever he is in a given region. "I see what I do with conduction and the Skyscraper projects, as something music needs that music thinks it doesn't need," he told Fordham. "Some free improvisers who think they should just be left alone see what I do as authoritarian—telling them when to stop or start, play loud or soft or whatever, controlling the dynamics—but it isn't. I'm doing the same thing as a symphonic composer with my music, but the difference is that I don't tell the players what to do in the same way." In 1998 Morris released Conduction #70: Tit for Tat, which was recorded with 15 musicians in an abandoned watch factory in Zurich, Switzerland, and Conducts Berlin Skyscraper '95, which featured mostly classical musicians.

Although Morris holds both jazz and classical music in high esteem, he feels that both genres are in danger of stagnation. "I think a lot of contemporary music is in trouble, personally," he told Fordham in 1997. "The classical music institutions around the world, except maybe in Tokyo and Vienna, aren't teaching young players to think, just

how to take older players' jobs, and by the time they're ready a lot of the jobs probably won't even be there. Jazz music is being institutionalized too, following the European classical tradition. I did a gig once with a lot of the so-called young lions of jazz, and first of all they had no idea what to do with my methods, then when they did get an inkling of what it was about, they refused to do it. A chance for musicians who believe they're improvisers, to do something that will never be duplicated, and they wouldn't do it. I call that bad education and bad upbringing. Louis Armstrong, after all, wanted to play like King Oliver, who'd come before him. But look . . . what he did with it."

That comment notwithstanding, Morris participated in more conventional projects in the 1990s. He served as musical director for Robert Altman's movie Kansas City (1996), working with jazz musicians to re-create the spontaneity and musical stylings of 1930s jazz. The music from the film was released on two albums. In 1995 he played cornet on the mainstream jazz vocalist Cassandra Wilson's record New Moon Daughter, which topped Billboard magazine's jazz album chart.

In 2000 Morris was heard on Diego Cortez's album Stuzzicadenti 1997–99, and in the following year he conducted a septet on "Bien-Hoa Blues," a track on Billy Bang's record Vietnam: The Aftermath. In 2004 Morris conducted 22 trumpeters at a concert at Tonic in New York City. In his review for the New York Times (August 7, 2004), Ben Ratliff wrote that listening to the trumpeters was "like hearing nature: birds in the trees, crickets in a field, frogs on a lake, tidewater on a calm shore, in the strangely orchestrated ways that those elements sound. With downstrokes pointed in particular directions, Mr. Morris forcefully indicated how the notes should fall and from which players. With other gestures he brought forth ripples and squiggles and panning effects, leading the players gradually into ferment." In February 2005, in celebration of the 20th anniversary of his Conduction no. 1, Morris led conduction ensembles every night in New York City.

Morris lives in New York. In addition to his work with the skyscraper ensembles, he is the musical director of Folding Space, an 11-piece ensemble in New York that performs vocal music. He was nominated at the 1999 Bell Atlantic Jazz Awards for "composer of the year" and "creative musician of the year." He has worked on interdisciplinary projects with choreographers including Min Tanaka, visual artists such as David Hammons, writers such as Ntozake Shange, and dance and theater artists, among them the Wooster Group and the Dayton Contemporary Dance Company. He has received grants from the National Endowment for the Arts and the Mary Flagler Cary Trust and has been a fellow of the DAAD (the acronym for the name in German of the German Academic Exchange Service), in Berlin, and of Civitella Ranieri, in Umbertide, Italy. Morris has received commissions from several institutions, including the Venice Biennale and the Whitney Museum of American Art at Phillip Morris, and has been composer in residence for more than 20 institutions, including Tufts University, in Medford, Massachusetts, and Istanbul Bilgi University, in Istanbul, Turkey. He has arranged and supervised music for television programs, including the series *A Man Called Hawk*, and theater productions, including the writer-musician Greg Tate's production of *My Darling Gremlins*. Morris rarely plays the cornet in public anymore. "I like to constantly restructure and expand upon things that I've done," Morris told Pareles in July 1985. "In your life, you're always rethinking, seeing how your values change; there's a constant re-evaluation of who you are."

—G.O.

Suggested Reading: All Music Guide (on-line); (London) *Financial Times* p17 Nov. 4, 1997; (London) *Guardian* p24 Oct. 31, 1997; *New York*

Times C p19 July 26, 1985, E p28 Apr. 3, 1998; *St. Louis Post-Dispatch* F p4 July 19, 1991; *Washington Post* G p4 Jan. 14, 1996

Selected Recordings: *Current Trends in Racism in Modern America*, 1985; *Homeing*, 1987; *Dust to Dust*, 1990; *Testament: A Conduction Collection*, 1995; Conduction #70: *Tit for Tat*, 1998; *Conducts Berlin Skyscraper '95*, 1998; with David Murray—*Interboogieology*, 1978; *Live at Sweet Basil*, 1984; *David Murray Big Band Conducted by Lawrence "Butch" Morris*, 1991; with Hans Koch, Hans Reichel, and Martin Schutz—*X-Commmunication*, 1990; with Lê Quan Ninh & J.A. Deane—*Burning Cloud*, 1993; with Peter Kowald, Werner Lüdi, Sainkho Namtchylak—*When the Sun Is Out You Don't See Stars*, 1991; with Robert Previte and Wayne Horvitz—*Nine Below Zero*, 1986

Chung Sung-Jun/Getty Images

Morris, James T.

Apr. 18, 1943– Executive director of the United Nations World Food Program

Address: World Food Programme, Via C.G. Viola 68, Parco dei Medici, 00148 Rome, Italy

According to the World Food Program (WFP), the single largest agency under the umbrella of the United Nations, 10 million deaths each year result from hunger and malnutrition—that is, more than 27,000 people die every day from a basic lack of

food. Described on its official Web site as the U.N.'s "frontline agency in the fight against global hunger," the WFP has been supplying food aid to the world's most desperate regions since 1962. In 2002 James T. Morris, a former businessman and public servant, took a lead role in that humanitarian fight, becoming the WFP's 10th executive director. Speaking to Scott Olsen for the *Indianapolis (Indiana) Business Journal* (March 24, 2004), Peter Beering, a former business colleague of Morris's, praised him for his "coalition-building skills" and his "overall knowledge and appreciation of the world in which we live. He views the World Food Program as a calling." An editorial in the *Indianapolis Star* (July 3, 2004) stated that Morris had seized his role at the WFP "with the zeal of an evangelist and has brought new visibility and stature to the office." Concurrently with his duties at the helm of the WFP, Morris has served as U.N. secretary general Kofi Annan's special envoy for humanitarian needs in Africa since July 2002.

The WFP is the largest humanitarian agency in the world. As reported on the program's Web site, on any given day the WFP has 20 planes in the air; 5,000 trucks on the road; and 40 ships at sea delivering food aid to the world's hungry and poor. (Common forms of WFP food aid are sugar, salt, bread, beans, wheat, and rice. Ninety percent of WFP food aid is delivered to target areas by ship.) In the last 40 years the program has fed more than 1.2 billion people. Following the U.S.-led invasion of Iraq in 2003, Morris helped coordinate the WFP's feeding of an estimated 26 million Iraqis, the largest humanitarian operation in history. Including its mission in Iraq, in 2004 the WFP fed more than 110 million people—mostly refugees and others displaced by war—in 80 countries by delivering 5.1 million metric tons (5.6 million tons, in U.S. measure) of food.

In late 2004 and into 2005 the WFP grappled with another humanitarian crisis of immense proportions—the December 26 Indian Ocean earthquake, which struck off the northwest coast of Sumatra and generated powerful tsunamis that inflicted devastation to numerous regions along the rim of the Indian Ocean. The disaster left an estimated 250,000 dead and more than one million displaced. The WFP has been one of the major suppliers of relief to the region. By July 2005 the organization had distributed 123,000 metric tons (136,000 U.S. tons) of food to more than two million people, and had begun a series of projects designed to help the many areas affected by the disaster to make a successful long-term recovery. As Morris pointed out not long after the disaster hit, the strength of the WFP's response was partially a result of how swiftly it was able to act. At the World Conference on Disaster Reduction in Kobe, Japan, on January 19, 2005, Morris told the audience, as reprinted on the WFP Web site, "We have already reached most of the people in the most critical need, giving them a ration sufficient for two weeks. No tsunami survivor should die from hunger or malnutrition. We can be proud of that."

A major difficulty facing Morris and the WFP is that world hunger cannot be eradicated simply with more food; it is inextricably tied to other scourges, such as poverty, disease, and political and economic despotism. Indeed, failed economic policies, natural disasters, political and ethnic violence, and AIDS and other diseases are continually creating new populations without enough to eat. Trying to battle such deleterious forces, the WFP finds itself underfunded and unable to help all those in need. "We are losing the battle against hunger," Morris stated in his testimony before the U.S. Senate Foreign Relations Committee on February 25, 2003. "Never before have we had to contend with potential starvation on the scale we face today. . . . The greatest threat to life remains what it was a hundred years ago, five hundred years ago, a thousand years ago—it is hunger."

The only child of Kathlyne (née Gastes) and Howard James Morris, James T. Morris was born in Terre Haute, Indiana, on April 18, 1943. He received a B.A. in political science from Indiana University, in Bloomington, in 1965, and an M.B.A. from Butler University, in Indianapolis, in 1970. In 1968 he entered the public sector, becoming chief of staff to then-mayor of Indianapolis Richard Lugar, who is now a member of the U.S. Senate and the current chairman of the Senate Foreign Relations Committee. In 1973 Morris became the director of community development for the Lilly Endowment Inc., one of the largest charitable organizations in the world. The Lilly foundation was established by members of the Lilly family—known for the large pharmaceutical business Eli Lilly and Co.—as a private philanthropic foundation in Indianapolis in 1937. It is dedicated to fostering community development and to enriching the religious lives of Christians—mostly through the edu-

cation and support of young pastors—in the city of Indianapolis and beyond. In the more than 15 years he spent with the foundation, Morris held a series of ascending positions, including vice president for community development, executive vice president, and president, in which capacity he served the Lilly Endowment from 1985 to 1989.

Morris then became chairman and chief executive officer of IWC Resources Corp., which is in the water-utility services industry, and their primary subsidiary, the Indianapolis Water Co. With Morris guiding it, the IWC grew into a multimillion-dollar holding company with 2,500 employees. He attempted to diversify the company's personnel and increase educational opportunities for employees. He stepped down from his position in 2002, the year he took over for Catherine Bertini as the executive director of the WFP. (The U.N. secretary general and the director general of the U.N. Food and Agricultural Organization [FAO] jointly appoint the WFP executive director to a term of five years. The executive director is the head of the secretariat of the agency.) The WFP is headquartered in Rome, Italy. As the WFP head, Morris has met with many foreign leaders and has often spoken to both houses of the U.S. Congress on issues relating to world hunger.

Established in 1961 as a limited-term experimental program scheduled to begin work in 1963, the WFP was thrown into humanitarian action in 1962, earlier than planned, by natural disasters in Thailand and Iran and by the plight of millions of refugees settling in Algeria after it had achieved independence from France. Among its other humanitarian achievements in recent history, the WFP helped to save the lives of 18 million people in southern Africa following terrible droughts in 1992; saved 19 million flood victims in Bangladesh in 1998; and delivered then-record amounts of food to Ethiopia, Sudan, and other East African nations suffering from the effects of a severe drought in 2000. For funding, the agency relies almost entirely on voluntary contributions of cash, food, and supplies for growing, storing, or preparing food. Dozens of governments give money to the WFP every year; the United States is by far the largest donor, regularly accounting for around half of the organization's total annual contributions. In 2004 the WFP employed almost 11,000 people, 90 percent of whom worked in the field, delivering food and monitoring its allocation and use. The WFP has the largest budget of any U.N. agency or program but the lowest operational overhead.

The official WFP Web site lists a series of "hunger facts," which include the following bleak statistics: despite global production of enough food to nourish the world's entire human population, more than 800 million people do not have enough to eat; one of every three people in sub-Saharan Africa is hungry; about 520 million of the world's hungry live in Asia and the South Pacific; while the average American family spends 10 percent of its income on food, poor people spend more than

70 percent; 54 countries do not produce enough food to feed their own people; and hunger and malnutrition are the biggest threats to global health—they kill more people every year than HIV, malaria, and tuberculosis combined.

As a result of the World Food Program's work in Iraq, which has been ravaged by the U.S.-led invasion, begun in March 2003, and the subsequent rebel insurgency, the agency's funding and operations expanded considerably. It mounted the largest humanitarian operation in history, feeding 26 million Iraqis by distributing more than two million tons of food over a seven-month period. Also in 2003, the WFP's aid program to North Korea—which has been in place since 1995, following a famine that killed an estimated two million people—was suspended due to the North Korean government's refusal to allow donor nations to monitor how the WFP food aid was being dispersed. In June 2004 Morris visited several African nations, including Malawi, Mozambique, and Namibia, where he witnessed firsthand the widespread deprivation of millions of Africans who lack sufficient food or money and suffer from HIV infection. "What is happening in southern Africa absolutely represents the most serious humanitarian crisis in the world today," Morris told Craig Timberg for the *Washington Post* (June 23, 2004). As a prime example of the obstacles Morris and the WFP often face in their attempts to feed needy populations, the government of the southern African nation of Zimbabwe, led by President Robert Mugabe, has declined to meet with Morris, refuses to acknowledge the country's worsening food shortage, and will not accept WFP assistance. In June 2004 Morris also visited the Sudan, where marauding Arab militias have been attacking black African populations in the western region of Darfur. It is estimated that more than 1.8 million people have been displaced within the Sudan, and that more than 200,000 Sudanese have fled across the border into neighboring Chad. The situation for these refugees and displaced Sudanese is dire, as disease, the elements, and food shortages have decimated their ranks. In October 2004 the World Health Organization estimated that more than 70,000 Sudandese had died, mostly through starvation and disease, between March and October 2004. To gather evidence of the wide-scale suffering, Morris kept a journal in Darfur; parts of it appeared in the *Indianapolis Star* (June 6, 2004). Morris wrote, "We had been just two brief days in Darfur, but it was more than enough to show us something was desperately wrong. . . . The need for an immediate and dramatic reinforcement of the humanitarian effort was as clear as the starlit desert sky. . . . We owe it to our humanity not to leave these people to the militias, to the elements, to what for many will be a death sentence. We must act, and fast." Though there has been some degree of outcry against what is occurring in Darfur, the plight of the refugees has continued and the international community has done comparatively little to alleviate it.

Food shortages in sub-Saharan Africa are also greatly affected by AIDS; the disease, which is rampant in the region, is killing off adult food-providing members of society, leaving millions of hungry orphaned children. (Timberg reported that there are 11 million AIDS orphans in the region.) Morris has often addressed the links between disease and hunger and the need to combat the spread of HIV/AIDS in Africa—a continent of special concern to him because he also serves as the U.N. special envoy for humanitarian needs in Africa. "When you see a country in southern Africa where a third of the adult population is infected by HIV/AIDS, these are things you just don't forget," Morris told Scott Olsen. (As Morris told the *Washington Times* [January 12, 2004], there are approximately 30 million HIV/AIDS cases in Africa.)

The 2004 Indian Ocean earthquake, which struck off the coast of Aceh Province, on the Indonesian island of Sumatra, set off a series of tsunamis in the region that wreaked devastation on scores of Indian Ocean coastal communities; some tsunamis traveled as far as the eastern coast of Africa. The combined damage from the earthquake and tsunamis made the event one of the deadliest disasters in modern history. In the immediate aftermath of the disaster, the WFP was able to provide food from stocks already in place in Indonesia and Sri Lanka, as well as bring in new supplies by air, land, and sea. With help from governments, corporations, and individuals, the WFP distributed more than 4,000 metric tons (4,400 tons) of food within the first month—primarily rice, fortified biscuits, and noodles—in the hard-hit regions of Indonesia, the Maldives, and Sri Lanka, among others. The organization quickly drafted a six-month plan to bring aid to two million people, at a cost of $256 million. Early estimates held that some 169,000 metric tons (185,900 tons) of food would be needed for crucial assistance. In a January 6, 2005, press release, Morris remarked, "WFP food will help with the immediate needs of those who have lost family members, houses and livelihoods. But as they gradually get back on their feet, this six-month operation will shift its focus from ending their immediate hunger to sustaining families while they revive their farmland, repair their fishing boats and communities. We can give them the chance to provide for their future once again."

In his speech at the World Conference on Disaster Reduction, Morris outlined the agency's plans to improve its emergency response system. About 80 percent of the WFP's efforts go to responding to emergencies; about half of that, or 40 percent of the total, go toward helping those affected by natural disasters. Morris took the opportunity to praise the generous outpouring of contributions from the international community after the tsunamis: "This tremendous disaster," he explained, "has ignited the single element that has been missing from past humanitarian relief efforts: empathy. For the first time, the mass media, international travel and the internet—three accessories of globalization—

converged to make this a truly global crisis, in which we all shared." He added, however, that for the WFP, which plans to assist some 73 million people in 2005, the survivors of the terrible damage of the 2004 tsunami constitute only a portion of those in need. "Let me issue one word of warning. Emergencies seize our attention. We get swept up in the whirlwind of the media coverage. . . . But the truth is that those who die of hunger or HIV/AIDS rarely die in these kinds of emergencies. They die quietly in poor communities devastated by poverty in Bangladesh, Peru, and southern Africa. Every week, hunger claims as many lives as have been lost in the Indian Ocean tsunami. The chronic hunger and malnutrition that afflicts 300 million children worldwide does not create the dramatic media coverage of a tsunami, but it causes far greater suffering. We cannot afford to lose sight of that fact."

In the second half of 2005, the WFP was again grappling with a major food crisis brought on by a natural disaster, this time a massive earthquake in South Asia on October 8 that, as of a few weeks later, was estimated to have killed 78,000 people and to have left an estimated 3.3 million people homeless. Like the crisis that followed the tsunami, the earthquake crossed national borders, affecting parts of Pakistan, Afghanistan, India, and the disputed region of Kashmir; unlike the earlier disaster, the earthquake affected many areas that were extremely remote, making the humanitarian relief efforts of the WFP and other organizations much more difficult. "We had never ever had [a] logistical challenge like this," Morris told a group of reporters, according to Chisaki Watanabe for the Associated Press (October 25, 2005). "People are so difficult to reach. People are so far away from accessibility."

In addition to his work with the WFP, Morris has volunteered his services as treasurer to the United States Olympic Committee and chairman of its audit and ethics committee, and as a member of the board of governors of the American Red Cross. Morris has worked with many other nonprofit and educational organizations and institutions, including Butler University; Christian Theological Seminary, in Indianapolis; the Haskell Indiana College Foundation; Indiana State University, in Terre Haute; the Indiana Pacer Foundation; the NCAA Foundation; the Rose Hulman Institute of Technology, in Terre Haute; and the United Way of Central Indiana. His considerable contributions and dedication to his home state include service as president of the board of trustees at Indiana University and co-chairman of the Indianapolis Campaign for Healthy Babies. Morris also founded the Indiana Sports Corporation and Youthlinks Indiana.

Morris and his wife, Jacqueline Harrell Morris, have three children and six grandchildren. After his first year with the WFP Morris told Olsen, "What I am doing right now is very fulfilling. I suspect I've had the greatest year of personal growth in my life."

—C.F.T.

Suggested Reading: *Indianapolis Star* E p3 June 6, 2004, E p3 June 13, 2004; United Nations Web site; U.S. Senate Web site; *Washington Post* A p17 June 23, 2004; *Washington Times* A p19 Jan. 12, 2004; World Food Program Web site

---

Mos Def

(mohz def)

Dec. 11, 1973– Musician; actor

Address: c/o Geffen Records, 2220 Colorado Ave., Santa Monica, CA 90404

Mos Def is as adept at acting as he is at making music. He has earned plaudits for his performances on the Broadway stage, television, and the big screen, in the theatrical dramas *Topdog/Underdog* and *F_ _ _ _ _ g A,* the TV movie *Something the Lord Made,* and the independent film *The Woodsman.* A Grammy-nominated rap and hip-hop artist, he has made several critically successful, popular albums, among them *Mos Def and Talib Kweli Are . . . Black Star, Black on Both Sides,* and *The New Danger.* Mos Def has said that it is impossible for him to choose one form of artistic expression over the other. As he told Nekesa Mumbi Moody for the Associated Press (April 17, 2002), as posted on mosdefinitely.com (a Web site that was unavailable in late October 2005), "I'm able to use my art in different ways, and the fact that they're completely different is what I like about them."

Mos Def was born Dante Terrell Smith (Dante Beze, according to some sources) on December 11, 1973 in the New York City borough of Brooklyn. The oldest of 12 siblings, he was raised by his mother, Sheron, in the tough Brooklyn neighborhoods of Bedford Stuyvesant and East Flatbush; his father, Abdul Rahman, lived in nearby New Jersey. Mos Def (whose moniker is derived from one of his favorite phrases, "most definitely") began rapping as a way to distinguish himself in a sometimes violent urban environment. "I could play a little ball, but I was small," he told Daniel Fierman for *Entertainment Weekly* (April 12, 2002). "I could fight, but I wasn't really a fighter. . . . So I had to do somethin' to be able to just survive around my neighbors." His role in a play during fifth grade sparked his interest in acting. He later attended Julia Richmond High School, a performing-arts magnet institution in Brooklyn.

Kevin Winter/Getty Images

Mos Def

Mos Def appeared in an ABC movie of the week when he was in ninth grade. At age 16 he secured a part in *You Take the Kids*, a short-lived sitcom starring the comedian Nell Carter, which was filmed in Los Angeles, California. He acted in commercials and small roles for several years, then in 1994 landed a supporting role in another short-lived TV program, *The Cosby Mysteries*, starring Bill Cosby. Despite accruing some acting credits (often under the name Dante Beze), he earned little money. "The pay was so horrifically bad that I just couldn't [continue]," he told Kelefa Sanneh for the *New York Times* (March 31, 2002). In desperation, he decided to tap his other proven talent. "I was like, If I can write a rhyme, and somebody will put me on their record, that's $200 or $300. How long does it take me—an hour or two?"

In 1994 Mos Def formed the group Urban Thermo Dynamics with one of his brothers and a sister. Their album, made for a local label called Payday, marked his recording debut; it was not released until a decade later, however. He went on to make contributions to several other songs, including the Bush Babees' "Love Song" and De La Soul's "Big Brother Beat." He released his own single, "Universal Magnetic," in 1997, and in 1998 he sang on the single "Body Rock" with Q-Tip, a member of the band A Tribe Called Quest.

Later in 1998 Mos Def joined forces with his friend Talib Kweli to form Black Star, and the duo released *Mos Def and Talib Kweli Are . . . Black Star*. "I'd like to think of us as the modern-day hip-hop equivalent of Steely Dan," he told Oliver Wang for Sonicnet (March 11, 1999), as quoted on mostdefinitely.com, referring to a jazz-tinged rock duo with a large cult following. "Our music is a little

more challenging and has a little more texture and structure to it—but it's still accessible." *Mos Def and Talib Kweli Are . . . Black Star* was a critical and commercial success. "In an era when most rap has stormed pop's main stage only through lowest-common-denominator content, Black Star take an intelligent, articulate approach, reflecting more of the barbed poetics of influential black writers Amiri Baraka . . . and Langston Hughes than standard hip-hop calls to 'get jiggy with it,'" Wang wrote.

The choice to embrace more serious topics and avoid stereotypes reflected Mos Def's and Kweli's priorities. The friends co-own Nkiru Books, an Afrocentric bookstore in Brooklyn, where as teens they used to hang out and read. (The store is now managed by the rappers' mothers and functions as a neighborhood cultural center.) "These things that me and Kweli say on certain records are coming out of our love for our tradition and indigenous people in this country," Mos Def told Oliver Wang for the *San Francisco Bay Guardian* (September 16, 1998). "[It's] about the resilience of the spirit to move forward. I'm proud to be who I am—my history and heritage are rich. My ancestors were incredibly formidable people who survived things in history that killed others. . . . People made sacrifices for me to be who I am today, and I can't live my life not in their presence. Without them, things would be different for me. That's what it's really based on."

In 1998 Mos Def sang "Rock Rock Y'All" for A Tribe Called Quest's album *The Love Movement*. The following year he released his solo debut, *Black on Both Sides*. The album, which is now considered an important part of the hip-hop genre, met with nearly universal acclaim. "He astounded us with his debut album, . . . easily melding rap with rock, paying proper tribute to both genres' origins," Rickey Kim wrote for *Evil Monito* magazine (Spring 2002, on-line). "As Mos Def has moved toward the center of the hip-hop stage, he has consistently flipped the script, breathing much-needed life into a seemingly suffocating genre. With *Black on Both Sides* . . . Mos makes his auspicious arrival in the spotlight, and he's got a mouthful for his captive audience," Eric Demby wrote for the CD Now Web site. "From the record's outset . . . Mos lets you know that you're not in for some run-of-the-mill, market-driven, cameo-laden puff package." Mos Def told Demby, "This record is a very clear and fair representation of who I am and what I'm about, artistically and personally. What I wanted to do is exhibit that there exists a dimension in the realm of black thought and expression [and] that the common idea today—that the only things important to young black people today are sex, money and violence—is just not true. That it's possible and available to any artist to be himself or herself on their own terms, to be accepted and embraced by black people."

Mos Def has explained that the title *Black on Both Sides* refers to the fact that most forms of American popular music have roots in African-American culture and that black artists should not worry about being labeled "sellouts" if they incorporate styles currently regarded as "white." "Blues, jazz, rock and roll, all of those forms of music started out being popular forms of music among old ghetto people," he told Rickey Kim. "It wasn't like some super academic thing . . . it was poor black people singing about their lives, their experiences, their aspirations."

After making his solo recording, Mos Def resumed contributing to other artists' efforts. He joined the brother and sister with whom he had formed Urban Thermo Dynamics (who were now both with the group Medina Green) for the song "Crosstown Beef" on the *Soundbombing II* compilation album, released in 1999. In 2000 he contributed to the Tupac Shakur tribute album *The Rose That Grew from Concrete*, and his voice can be heard on the *Soundbombing III* album, released in 2002. He has performed with the Lyricist Lounge tour, a showcase for up-and-coming hip-hop acts, and his songs have been included on compilation albums from the tour.

In May 2001 Mos Def put together a new band, Black Jack Johnson (named after boxing's first African-American heavyweight champion), which featured the bassist Doug Wimbish and the drummer Will Calhoun, both from the band Living Colour; the guitarist Gary "Dr. Know" Miller of the punk group Bad Brains; and ex-Parliament-Funkadelic keyboard player Bernie Worrell. "This could be like a real exchange, not for just the mediums but for the audience, and furthermore show that hip-hop is an extension of that rock 'n' roll and blues tradition, not an alien element that's being imported from some other galaxy," he told Richard Harrington for the *Washington Post* (January 11, 2002). Reactions to the group, which fused rap and rock music, were mixed. "It's like [Bob] Dylan going electric," Mos Def told Jonathan Cohen for the Nude as the News Web site (May 21, 2001). "Some people were not happy with me at all. . . . I don't want what I do as an artist to be the property of people's expectations. I'm trying to speak as sincerely as I possibly can. . . . I was really moved to do the rock project." He continued, "[Combining rap and rock] raises a lot of social issues [because] music is a metaphor for . . . a lot of racial issues. . . . I'm not just challenging the audience, I'm challenging myself as well."

While he pursued his musical interests, Mos Def remained devoted to his acting career. He appeared in the obscure films *Where's Marlowe* (1998) and *Island of the Dead* (2000) before landing the part of the rapper Julius/Big Black Africa in Spike Lee's *Bamboozled* (2000). He was excited to get the chance to work with Lee, whom he had long admired. Mos Def next acted in *Carmen: A Hip Hopera*, a hip-hop retelling of Bizet's opera *Carmen* that aired on MTV in 2001, and he had small roles

in *Monster's Ball* (2001), which starred Halle Berry and Billy Bob Thornton, and the Eddie Murphy–Robert DeNiro comedic thriller *Showtime* (2002). He also made guest television appearances on *NYPD Blue*, *Spin City*, and *Oz*, among other shows. In December 2001 he hosted and served as executive producer of HBO's multipart special *Def Poetry Jam*, which showcased original material by contemporary poets and well-known music and comedy performers.

Mos Def made his Broadway debut on April 7, 2002, as Booth, one of two brothers in the Pulitzer Prize–winning drama *Topdog/Underdog*, by Suzan-Lori Parks. The two-character play also starred Jeffrey Wright and was directed by George C. Wolfe. "Actors would give their eyeteeth to work with people of this level," Mos Def told Robin Finn for the *New York Times* (April 19, 2002). "And here I am. This is a major, major, major turning point, not just for me, but for the culture. Not to sound too grand about it, but this is one of those rare instances where something of a high artistic order is like at ground level, at street level, where . . . kids are coming to Broadway to watch this play." In the drama Wright portrayed a former three-card-monte con man who has reformed and now makes a living as an Abraham Lincoln impersonator, getting shot at with blanks in a game at a video arcade. Mos Def portrayed Booth, the younger, more insecure brother, now trying to build his own career as a con man. "It's a very real human play about two brothers and their relationship to each other, their rivalry, their need for each other, their history," Mos Def told Richard Harrington. "It's a modern play about two young black men in modern times and the universal issues of family and abandonment, the human condition."

Mos Def had seen the production five times during its Off-Broadway run, during which Wright had co-starred with Don Cheadle. "I was a huge fan of the show," he told Mark Binelli for *Rolling Stone* (May 1, 2002). "To me, it was like hearing [John Coltrane's album] *A Love Supreme* for the first time, or [jazz composer and bassist Charles] Mingus, or [rock guitarist Jimi] Hendrix. But I had no idea I would ever be in the show. When I heard it was going to Broadway, the only thing I wanted to be in was the opening-night crowd." When scheduling conflicts prevented Cheadle from performing the role of Booth on Broadway, Wolfe asked Mos Def to read for the part; Mos Def had auditioned for Wolfe several years before, for a film version of the Broadway hit *Jelly's Last Jam*, which was never produced. "He has extraordinary charisma," Wolfe told Nekesa Mumbi Moody. "I think he's very hard working. I think he has a very large heart and a goodness. And I think those things come across on stage in a very strong way. And I think he has an incredible emotional reserve."

Most critics agreed. "Mos Def . . . is a true find," Wilson Morales wrote for the BET Web site (April 17, 2002). "From the moment he appears on stage . . . he brings credibility and conviction in his role." In a review for the Associated Press (April 7, 2002), the drama critic Michael Kuchwara wrote, "Mos Def's Booth is all jittery bravado, a cockiness laced with charm and a bit of petulance. The performer . . . is not as polished or as vocally adept as his co-star, but he projects a vulnerability that lends Booth considerable appeal." Ben Brantley wrote for the *New York Times* (April 8, 2002), "Mos Def, best known as a rap artist, finds both the delightful innocence and the harrowing brutality in the role of a little brother who never grew up." Of his experience on Broadway, Mos Def told Moody, "It was challenging, and I enjoy the challenge, because challenge is growth. It is a difficult piece, physically, emotionally, mentally, and it's worthwhile doing it. The most challenging thing is . . . being in command of the rhythm of the play as an actor, because it's a slippery kind of piece, and it has a naturalism to it, but it also has an abstraction to it. . . . From a mental standpoint, you really have to negotiate and be very pointed about what you do."

In 2003 George Wolfe directed Mos Def again, in the premiere production of Suzan Lori Parks's *F_ _ _ _ _ g A*, at the Off-Broadway Public Theatre. In that play, described as "direct, visceral, compelling, [and] ultimately extremely moving" by Gerald Rabkin in a review for culturevulture.net (March 20, 2003), he was cast as the son of an abortionist, Hester Smith (played by S. Epatha Merkerson); the son has spent the last 20 years in prison, for the crime of stealing a piece of meat during his youth. Tragedy ensues after the son escapes and Hester is told, erroneously, that he is dead. According to Rabkin, Mos Def "has an uncanny ability to simultaneously project sweetness and threat, sadistic anger and vulnerability, qualities that are essential to his complex character," and he described the actor's last scene as a "tour de force."

On the big screen, Mos Def had supporting roles in the romantic comedy *Brown Sugar* (2002) and the crime adventure *The Italian Job* (2003). In 2004 he played a cynical policeman in *The Woodsman*, a controversial film starring Kevin Bacon as a pedophile. Also that year he appeared to near-universal acclaim in *Something the Lord Made*, a television movie about Alfred Blalock, a pioneering white surgeon, and Vivien Thomas, the black surgical and research assistant who is now credited as an equal partner in Blalock's work. For his portrayal of Thomas, Mos Def was nominated for both an Emmy Award and an NAACP Image Award.

On January 31, 2005 Mos Def appeared in a benefit performance of the one-act play *Escape: 6 Ways to Get Away*. Later that year he played the part of a bandleader in the well-regarded television movie *Lackawanna Blues*; in the big-screen adaptation of Douglas Adams's comic science-fiction novel *The Hitchhiker's Guide to the Galaxy*, he was cast as Ford Prefect, an alien who, on Earth, pretends to be an out-of-work actor. Mos Def has roles in the upcoming films *16 Blocks*, *Journey to the End of the Night*, and *The Brazilian Job*, all of which were scheduled for 2006 release.

Earlier, in late 2004, Mos Def's long-awaited second solo album, *The New Danger*, was released. It quickly sold almost 100,000 copies and arrived on the *Billboard* album chart in fifth place. Tom Moon wrote for *Rolling Stone* (October 28, 2004, on-line), "It's all part of the Mos Def master plan to, as he explains on the gritty [song] 'Life is Real,' 'Reach the world but touch the street first.' The fed-up rhymes and sweetly sung refrains of *The New Danger* do exactly that, broadening the hip-hop palette without sacrificing, or selling out, its core ideals." The album was named one of the top 50 of 2004 by the editors of *Rolling Stone*, and a single from the recording, "Sex, Love & Money," was nominated for a Grammy Award for best urban/alternative performance.

Mos Def has often displayed a passion for social activism. In 2001 he participated in the Hip-Hop for Consciousness benefit for Imam Jamil al-Amin (the former Black Panther H. Rap Brown), who, in a highly controversial case, had been jailed since the previous year on charges of murder. (Despite the efforts of Mos Def and other supporters, in 2002 al-Amin was sentenced to life in prison.) Mos Def has also performed at benefits for breast-cancer awareness and has been vocal in protests against police brutality and cuts in public-school funding. His commitment to social activism stems in part, he has said, from his Muslim faith. He was first exposed to the religion at age 13, when his father taught him "how to make wudhu"—the ritual ablution Muslims perform before prayer, as he recalled to Ali Asadullah for the BeliefNet Web site. Six years later he took his shahada, the Muslim declaration of faith. "Mos Def . . . represents arguably the first time that an artist, solidly wedded to the orthodoxy of the religion, has stepped into mainstream popularity with a complete, well-articulated Islamic message as part and parcel of that popularity," Asadullah wrote. Mos Def has always incorporated his faith into his music. The first words on *Black on Both Sides* are "*Bismillah ar-Rahman ar-Raheem*," meaning "In the name of God, the most gracious, the most merciful," and many of his other lyrics are peppered with references to Allah and Islam. "You're not gonna get through life without being worshipful or devoted to something," he told Asadullah. "You're either devoted to your job, or to your desires. So the best way to spend your life is to try to be devoted to prayer, to Allah." His beliefs have led him to ban alcohol sales at his concerts.

Mos Def's mother and father and many of his siblings work for and with him. "My parents have been vocal and influential in all the decisions I made in my life," he told Asadullah. "It made sense to me to include [my father] officially and to include my mother officially 'cause she'd been there from the beginning. You need to have that synergy—because who really cares the most about you?" His parents handle everything from media relations to general management and corporate strategy, and one of his brothers tackles technical matters in the studio.

The single father of at least two children, Mos Def lives in a waterfront loft in Brooklyn. For a time he was romantically linked with the singer/songwriter Beyoncé (who, when she was known as Beyoncé Knowles, co-founded the trio Destiny's Child and played the title role in *Carmen: A Hip Hopera*). By his own account, he plans to continue to experiment as both an actor and a musician. "I'm not really playing by anybody else's rules or trying to live up to anyone's expectations but mine. . . . I'm not gonna twist my back into pretzels and question marks to get accolades from the buying public," he told Demby. "I'm a man. I'm not a trained seal."

—K.E.D.

Suggested Reading: *Entertainment Weekly* p32+ Apr. 12, 2002; *Evil Monito* (on-line) Spring 2002; *New York Times* B p12 Aug. 4, 2001, E p1 Apr. 8, 2002, II p10 May 19, 2002; *Washington Post* W p6 Jan. 11, 2002

Selected Recordings: *Mos Def and Talib Kweli Are . . . Black Star*, 1998; *Black on Both Sides*, 1999; *The New Danger*, 2004

Selected Films or TV Movies: *Bamboozled*, 2000; *Brown Sugar*, 2002; *The Woodsman*, 2004; *Something the Lord Made*, 2004; *Lackawanna Blues*, 2005; *The Hitchhiker's Guide to the Galaxy*, 2005

Selected Plays: *Topdog/Underdog*, 2002; *F _ _ _ _ _ _ A*, 2003; *Escape: 6 Ways to Get Away*, 2005

Myers, Joel N.

Nov. 3, 1939– Founder and CEO of AccuWeather Inc.

Address: AccuWeather, 385 Science Park Rd., State College, PA 16801-3751

Not so long ago, people relied on old sayings to predict the weather—"Red sky in morning, sailor take warning," for example. These days professional forecasters have Doppler radar and satellite images at their disposal, and predicting the weather has become a profitable business. Joel N. Myers, the founder and CEO of AccuWeather, is one of the leaders in the industry. Myers started his company in 1962, as a graduate student at Pennsylvania State University, at a time when weather forecasting in the United States was primarily the domain of the federal government. He has revolutionized the forecasting industry by providing accurate and localized weather forecasts to businesses and government agencies that require more than generalized reports; today his company serves more than 15,000 clients worldwide, including more than one-third of Fortune 500 companies. AccuWeather's 400 employees, among them 100 full-time meteorologists, also supply weather forecasts to domestic and international media outlets, including more than 750 newspapers, 250 radio stations, and 200 local television stations, as well as such major channels as CNN. In 1994 AccuWeather began providing free weather reports on its own Web site, AccuWeather.com; as of June 2004 the site was drawing some 3.4 million unique users a month, according to Dave Gussow in the *St. Petersburg Times* (August 13, 2004). In addition, the company supplies weather reports to major news Web sites, among them those of the *New York Times* and the *Washington Post*. Recently Myers's

company pioneered the "RealFeel" temperature gauge, which some industry analysts believe will ultimately replace the wind-chill factor as a more accurate representation of how cold outside air feels.

Although countless people disparage weather forecasters for having spotty records when it comes to accuracy of predictions, the science of weather forecasting improved greatly during the second half of the 20th century, since the development of mathematical models and the first computer-aided weather forecasts in the 1950s. Today meteorologists say that the five-day forecast is about as reliable as the three-day forecast was 15 years ago. AccuWeather faces heavy competition—from the Weather Channel, which exerts a powerful presence through its cable channel and the Internet; from the more than 100 small firms that, like AccuWeather, offer specialized forecasts for paying clients; and from the National Weather Service, the federal agency that produces most of the raw data that is used and interpreted by the other commercial weather companies. Despite the presence of such competitors, AccuWeather enjoys a strong reputation and continues to grow. For Myers, who spent years teaching meteorology at Pennsylvania State University, weather forecasting is an art as much as it is a science. "Warren Buffet beats the S&P virtually every year," he told Fred Guterl for *Newsweek* (September 30, 2002), referring to the noted investor Warren Buffet's ability to produce higher returns than the Standard & Poor 500 stock-market index. "It's the same thing with weather forecasters. You have some who can and some who can't. It's a matter of skill and talent."

Joel Norman Myers was born on November 3, 1939 in Philadelphia, Pennsylvania, the son of Martin Henry Myers and the former Doris A. Schwartz. His fascination with the weather began at an early age; by five or six he was already keeping a daily weather diary. "I remember being awe-

Courtesy of AccuWeather Inc.
Joel N. Myers (standing) at the headquarters of AccuWeather Inc.

struck around the age of five when it snowed," Myers recalled to William Ecenbarger for the *Chicago Tribune* (January 11, 1987). "When I was 11, I concluded that the weather affected every facet of life and got the idea to sell forecasts. Then on Oct. 15, 1954, Hurricane Hazel hit. That was something. I was in a constant state of excitement for 36 hours. We had a barometer [an instrument that measures atmospheric pressure] at Central High School, and I watched it drop all day long. I called the weather bureau every hour. While I was delivering my newspapers, I saw a screen door blow off a house. That evening I stood on the front porch with my father and brother, watching the wind and the trees bending to touch the house. I was mesmerized by the *weather!*"

In his early teens Myers received as a gift from his father a 20-year-old barograph (a recording barometer) that cost about $60—a considerable sum in the early 1950s. "It was a big deal to get," Myers recalled in an article edited by Kimbra Cutlip for *Weatherwise* (July/August 2001). "It had an eight-day clock, and I ran it regularly for years." At about the same time, Myers set up his own small-scale station to measure and record the weather. After he graduated from high school, he entered Pennsylvania State University (Penn State), then one of the few schools in the country with a meteorology program. He earned a B.A. degree in the field in 1962, after which he entered the university's graduate program in the same discipline.

Myers was spurred into starting his forecasting business in 1962, when a local gas utility company contacted Penn State during a search for a meteorologist to predict the weather for the approaching winter, which would allow the firm to gauge likely consumer demand. The head of the meteorology department referred them to Myers. In November 1962 Myers founded one of the first commercial weather-forecasting companies in the country. (According to some reports, Myers, lacking an office at first, had to report his earliest forecasts from a phone booth.) The company acquired its present name, AccuWeather, in 1971.

For a while Myers had trouble persuading businesses to purchase forecasts from him when they could obtain free forecasts from the radio and television reports delivered by the National Weather Service (NWS). The NWS is an agency of the U.S. government that monitors climatological data and issues daily weather forecasts and severe-weather warnings. It traces its roots back to 1870, when President Ulysses S. Grant authorized military stations to relay storm warnings; the Department of Agriculture assumed control of the growing operation in 1890. Today the NWS uses complex computer systems to amalgamate and report on information received from satellite images and Doppler radar as well as a network of more than 10,000 volunteers across the country who make daily weather measurements, monitoring such variables as temperature, humidity, wind speed, and barometric pressure.

Myers secured his first 100 clients by phoning some 25,000 businesses and giving them free trials of the AccuWeather service. He carved a niche for himself by providing not only more-accurate forecasts than the NWS, but detailed, localized reports as well. His first customers included a Penn State football coach and area ski resorts. The latter would prove to be among Myers's more important early clients, as they depended heavily on accurate reports so as to anticipate when they would need to use their snow-making equipment.

As AccuWeather began to build a customer base, Myers continued to earn his credentials as a meteorologist. He received a master's degree and Ph.D in meteorology from Penn State in 1963 and 1971, respectively, and worked as a weather broadcaster on television and radio between 1962 and 1985. In addition, he taught at Penn State between 1965 and 1981, as an assistant professor of meteorology.

In 1971 Myers decided to broaden the sale of AccuWeather's forecasts to media outlets. In a successful strategy, he got one television and one radio station in each major American metropolitan market to buy his forecasts; then, just as he had hoped, the stations started heavily promoting their "exclusive" AccuWeather forecasts to distinguish themselves from their competitors. Myers's company thus gained free publicity and, before long, additional customers. By 1983 AccuWeather's client list had swelled to 500 and included some 40 television stations as well as 120 radio stations and many newspapers. Also in 1983 AccuWeather began operating internationally, providing tailored forecasts for key crop-growing areas around the world.

For AccuWeather clients not connected with the media, specific weather predictions are important for various reasons. Investors and corporations, for example, refer to weather forecasts when deciding to buy or sell products, particularly crops and commodities. If a speculator knows that storms at sea will affect the transport of oil to the United States or other parts of the world, for instance, he or she can then surmise that the price of oil will go up. In 1977 AccuWeather's forecasters predicted a cold front that threatened to bring freezing temperatures to the citrus-producing regions of Florida. The forecasters pooled $5,000 of their own money and that of their fellow office workers and invested in frozen orange juice, assuming correctly that the cold front would prove devastating to that year's citrus crop. In two weeks their investment generated $40,000 in earnings for them. Other clients who depend on AccuWeather's predictions include school-district administrators, in anticipating school closings in the event of snowstorms; city-management officials, in order to prepare for snow removal; trucking companies, in planning transportation routes; construction companies, when laying concrete or erecting skyscrapers; and department stores, because weather can significantly affect consumer behavior.

In AccuWeather's early days, Myers was fond of telling reporters, "Long-range forecasting is witch-craft"—an assessment with which those in the industry would readily agree at that time. As computer models, radar, and satellite-imaging technologies have improved, however, AccuWeather's team of meteorologists have grown confident enough to say that the current five-day forecast is as accurate as the three-day forecast had been in previous decades. In addition, Myers told Fred Guterl that AccuWeather meteorologists are able to make 15-day forecasts "with some skill," although predicting the movements of storms is notoriously difficult. In the late 1990s AccuWeather began offering custom forecasts for businesses up to a month in advance. Though not as reliable as five-day forecasts, those predictions have become a necessity for many companies, which often pay up to $15,000 a month for AccuWeather's services.

By 1987 there were about 100 private firms offering the kinds of weather-forecasting services AccuWeather had pioneered. AccuWeather, like its rivals, relies heavily on raw data from the NWS, which it then filters through its own computer models and interprets for its clients. Many weather models are available, and accuracy depends upon using the right one. But just as important, meteorologists must be able to look beyond computer models and study weather patterns everywhere on Earth for developments that could affect conditions in North America several weeks in the future. "The thing is, a lot of meteorologists are lazy," Myers told Guterl. "They rely too much on the models. Very few look far beyond the United States." AccuWeather scientists examine data not only from the NWS but also from the World Meteorological Or-

ganisation and national weather services in Europe, Japan, and Canada. In 1999 AccuWeather's meteorologists astutely relied on data from Europe during Hurricane Floyd, which struck the Bahamas and southeastern United States, allowing them to predict the storm's trajectory better than the Weather Channel.

In 1994 Myers established AccuWeather.com, an on-line service providing free streaming-video forecasts, weather maps, and related information. (Paying subscribers receive access to additional features.) The site is popular, as Myers explained to Karen Brown for *Broadband Weekly* (June 4, 2001), because, for example, "if you are traveling to San Francisco or New York or whatever, what you can do is get on and get the five-day forecast with a talking head presenting it . . . just like you would see the weather in those cities."

Though the company faces more competition than ever before, AccuWeather has maintained a solid customer base, with a customer-renewal rate of 98 percent, according to Myers. In addition, although Weather.com, the Web site of the Weather Channel, is ranked as the most popular single source of information about weather on the Web, AccuWeather provides material to more than 1,200 other Internet sites, which in total, according to the AccuWeather Web site, draw an estimated 70 million unique users each month.

Myers is forging ahead with new weather forecasting technologies, including the patent-pending "RealFeel" temperature gauge, which the company introduced in 2000. In the past meteorologists have tried to present a more accurate evocation of an individual's experience of temperature by calculating for such factors as wind chill and humidity. The RealFeel formula, by contrast, takes into account multiple parameters, including temperature, wind, humidity, sunshine intensity, cloud cover, time of day, precipitation, and elevation. Myers, who spent years developing the formula with other meteorologists at AccuWeather, has said that once RealFeel is patented, he will publish the system for other scientists and weather researchers to study. The company's other technological innovations include a state-of-the-art meteorological database, begun in 1979, and On-Line with AccuWeather, an award-winning educational tool. The company has also developed a service for wireless customers that sends streaming video directly to cell phones and other wireless devices.

Joel N. Myers has three children: Daniel Martin, Sharon Annetta, and Erika Ann. He is a member of the American Meteorological Society, Sigma Xi, Phi Kappa Phi, Rho Tau Sigma, and Sigma Gamma Epsilon. He has written many articles and has appeared on such television shows as *Larry King Live*. Since 1981 he has been a trustee of Pennsylvania State University. In 2004 he received the National Weather Association's Operational Achievement Individual Award for his pioneering efforts in the field of meteorology.

Myers's leisure-time activities include collecting antique barometers. According to the *Weatherwise* article, Myers has acquired more than 220 barometers, most of which still work; they line the walls of his home and office and range from one-and-a-half-inch-diameter barometers from the early 1900s to ships' barometers to an angle barometer from 1774. Banjo barometers, so-named because they resemble the size and shape of a banjo, are among his favorites; some "that have real large faces . . . 15 inches across are just magnificient," he told *Weatherwise*. "The combination of the wood and the instrumentation, that's what makes them a thing of beauty."

—C.M.

Suggested Reading: AccuWeather.com; *Broadband Week* p42 June 4, 2001; *Chicago Tribune* V p1+ Jan. 11, 1987, with photo; *Editor & Publisher* June 23, 2003; *Forbes* p90 June 14, 1999; *Newsweek* p48 Sep. 30, 2002; *Weatherwise* p10 July/Aug. 2001, with photo

---

Nelson, Keith and Monseu, Stephanie

Founders of the Bindlestiff Family Cirkus

Nelson, Keith
May 10, 1970– Circus founder; performer

Monseu, Stephanie
Apr. 23, 1968– Circus founder; performer

Address: Bindlestiff Family Variety Arts Inc., P.O. Box 1917, New York, NY 10009

The Bindlestiff Family Cirkus, a theater troupe founded by Keith Nelson and Stephanie Monseu, has little in common with the three-ring extravaganzas associated with traditional circuses. In addition to reviving such vaudevillian forms of entertainment as sword swallowing, fire eating, and precision whip cracking, the pair have given such acts a modern and often bawdy cast. "[Their] success . . . lies in the tongue-in-cheek, half-insane tone of it all . . . ," a reviewer for *Backstage* (March 12, 2004, on-line) wrote. "The Bindlestiffs present irony piled atop irony, with a bit of underlying menace and lewdness to make everyone edgy." Nevertheless, Nelson and Monseu's performances do not mock classic forms of live entertainment so much as revel in them. The duo want to elicit gasps of astonishment from their audiences and feel that only live entertainment—with its attendant danger and excitement—can make people truly experience a sense of wonder. When asked by Stephen Lemons for the *Los Angeles Times* (September 19, 1999) to comment on the appeal of the Bindlestiff Family Cirkus, Monseu said, "There's more of an appreciation for a style of entertainment inclusive of many

disciplines—the variety show, burlesque and the sideshow circus. All of these things are very popular right now. TV and computers have isolated people to the point that they want to go back out and become members of a [live] audience."

Keith Nelson was born on May 10, 1970 in Holden, Massachusetts. As a joke, he told some interviewers that his parents were rodeo performers; in reality, they were high-school teachers. When Nelson was three months of age, he and his family moved to Winston-Salem, North Carolina; 10 years later they settled in the more rural North Carolina town of Advance. "Childhood was fine," Nelson told *Current Biography*. "[I was an] Eagle Scout, spent time hanging around airports [because] dad was a pilot. I started driving a school bus when I was 16 and a half."

Stephanie Monseu was born on April 23, 1968 in the Jamaica section of the New York City borough of Queens. Her father's family fled Poland and settled in New York just after World War II; her mother's family emigrated from Italy to the U.S. in about 1910. In early publicity interviews Monseu often joked that she hailed from a long line of circus performers, belly dancers, and tarot readers. (In actuality, she and her sister, Lorraine, are the first professional performers in their family.) Monseu recalled for *Current Biography*, "As kids in Queens we were always making little shows with cardboard sets for the backyard. At eight I recreated the bridge of the Starship *Enterprise* (I had a now-embarrassing crush on William Shatner) in the living room. When I was 10 and Lorraine was nine, my family bought a Catskills resort and moved us upstate, where we were amazed by the fresh air, wild critters, and homogeneity of the local populace. Once we moved upstate, [our] playmaking was in earnest because we got only one TV channel. My sister and I discovered the joys of making audio cassette plays and recorded trashy little country tunes." She continued, "Parallel to this imaginary cultural outlet was a lifelong addiction to adrenaline—I was very involved in track and field from first grade. In the country I'd ride my bike the five miles to town to see friends. I learned to ski and became an instructor at the age of 15, and was a member of the ski team at school. I joined the Drama Society, sang in the school and community choruses, and played alto clarinet in the marching band. I was always making things—drawings, jewelry, crafty cloth things, sewing. My pop's European and instilled a sense of thrift and a disdain for throwaway culture in us."

In his interview with *Current Biography*, Nelson traced his interest in performing arts to his days as a Boy Scout. "I was the Vice Chief of Ceremonies for the order of the Arrow; it is there that I learned a bit about how to make torches and create pageantry," he recalled. There were other influences as well. When Nelson was about 10 years old, he went with his family to a small circus that featured an "elephant dog," which could be viewed for a quarter. The attraction turned out to be an ordinary

Maike Schulz, courtesy of Bindlestiff Family Cirkus
Bindlestiff Family Cirkus co-founders Keith Nelson (left) and Stephanie Monseu

dog that had been shaved. The scam, he said, "helped create [my] foundation [for] understanding show biz." He was further inspired by the Emmett Kelly ventriloquist doll he was given at around the same time. (Nelson has an image of Kelly, a seminal figure in the world of circus arts, tattooed on his arm.)

Nelson attended Davie High School, in Mocksville, North Carolina, and then entered Hampshire College, in Amherst, Massachusetts. (Hampshire is part of a five-college consortium that also includes the University of Massachusetts, Mount Holyoke, Smith, and Amherst.) As he recalled for *Current Biography*, "My concentration of studies was Anarchist Theory. This left me with a B.A. in social science. Luckily, while at Hampshire, I learned to eat fire and juggle, the only two marketable skills I acquired at school. So I would say the combination of a useless degree and my two new skills led me to a life of circus."

"I didn't decide to go to college until I was 23," Monseu told *Current Biography*. "I had been interested in making jewelry and so chose the Fashion Institute of Technology on 27th Street in Manhattan for their Fine Arts Metals program. . . . Working with torches and kilns and molten metals definitely sparked an interest in fire. At school I learned techniques for metal fabrication that later informed some [of my] prop-making. But it was really an accident in May of 1993 that left me with a broken wrist, an unfinished final project, and a lot of time away from my jewelry tools that led to Bindlestiff's creation." She continued, "I had to get a job to pay off hospital bills, back rent, and student loans. I got a waitering job and met Keith and that's where the story takes a turn for the better."

Monseu's job was at Around the Clock, an all-night diner on Third Avenue and Ninth Street in Manhattan. When she learned that Nelson was a fire eater, she asked him to teach her the art. "When I learned how to eat fire," Monseu recalled to Emily Nussbaum for *Verve* (March/April 2001), "Keith and I were in the alley at three a.m., out behind the restaurant where I worked, and the snow was coming down all around us. There's just something about taking fire into your body like that—it's the primal fear, getting past those boundaries, the fear that it will get out of control. . . . It was like a dream. Magic. Everything stood still."

Nelson had come to New York City in 1991, as an undergraduate, to serve as an intern at Autonomedia, a radical-book publisher in the Williamsburg section of Brooklyn. The following year, after he had graduated, he moved into a corner of the book warehouse and began to dream of driving a bookmobile of radical literature across the country—and juggling, eating fire, and passing the hat for gas money. "When we met and got serious about performing, this dream looked more like a reality," Monseu told *Current Biography*. In their first act together, they performed as a fire-eating duo in clubs on the Lower East Side of Manhattan. "We called ourselves Fireplay and enacted weird flaming vignettes using metal props and leather costumes we'd make ourselves," she said. "We designed a logo, started making little flyers for our shows, started writing down ideas for bigger staging."

While performing at such alternative New York City clubs as the Blue Angel, Trip, and Mother, Nelson and Monseu began meeting other performers—magicians, escape artists, jugglers, and contortionists. Some among them later joined the Bindlestiff Family Cirkus. ("Bindle stiff" is a slang term for "hobo"; "bindle" refers to the bundle that such wanderers typically carried.) Bindlestiff, formed in 1995 under the umbrella organization of Bindlestiff Family Variety Arts Inc., sought not only to entertain modern audiences but also to increase their knowledge and appreciation of the traditional vaudeville, circus, burlesque, and sideshow acts that, for the most part, had faded from public consciousness with the rise of movies and then television.

The first official Bindlestiff performance took place at an Anarchist Scholars Conference in Montague, Massachusetts. "Keith and I loaded a handtruck with four cases of books, two suitcases with flammable liquids and some clown makeup onto a Greyhound bus and we were off," Monseu recalled to *Current Biography*. They also performed, among other sites, on the streets of New Orleans, Louisiana, during Mardi Gras and at Burning Man, an annual alternative-arts festival held in the Black Rock Desert, in Nevada. They began appearing frequently at the Charleston Bar and Grill in Williamsburg, an area that has since become popular with young artists and hipsters. Performing under the names Mr. Pennygaff (Nelson) and Philomena Bindlestiff (Monseu), the duo served as the emcees for a unique group of performers, and their act became an integral part of the neighborhood's performing-arts revival, in which older types of live entertainment were given a modern, often ribald, edge.

Speaking to *Current Biography* of Bindlestiff's earliest performances, Nelson recalled "the raw passion that drove us. We were willing to drive 15 hours at a time to play some of the most dilapidated venues imaginable. We slept on floors, ate bad food, and went months at a time without seeing a bed and clean laundry." They felt "a real sense of Do It Yourself-ism," as Monseu put it: "a closeness with the audience, a sense that we were discovering something really special together. An awareness that the audience was at every moment shaping the outcome of the show as much as we performers were. A sense of recklessness and invincibility, which is now tempered by age, experience, and liability insurance."

As Bindlestiff grew in popularity, Nelson, Monseu, and a changing roster of additional performers began touring the United States six months a year in a bus that doubled as a bookmobile. The troupe has occasionally tailored their most bawdy acts to comply with local laws, and there have been few complaints about their performances. "Circuses are an American tradition," Nelson told Steven Kotler for *Details* (January 2000). "So it's not just art hounds who come to see us. When we play the Midwest, our audience is a huge mix of ages, and it's the older folks who are the least shocked by our risque antics—they remember the adults-only hoochie tent [which typically featured scantily clad dancers] from carnivals of their youth." In *Verve*, Emily Nussbaum noted that while Nelson and Monseu "may be explicitly influenced by some rather headache-y cultural studies theories about spectacle—the notion that carnival tomfoolery can disrupt society's ideas of what normal really is—they consider themselves primarily entertainers, reviving lost arts. Their role models are [the political radicals] Abbie Hoffman and Emma Goldman, but also [the comedian] Carol Burnett."

As the Bindlestiff Family Cirkus's talent pool grew, with additions of new musicians, actors, clowns, dancers, and other circus performers and sideshow acts, their fan base expanded as well. In 2001 they had an eight-week, 24-performance run at the Present Company Theatorium, in New York City. Their national tour that same year, in which 91 performers participated, drew an estimated total of 20,000 people in 58 towns. In 2002 their winter show, "Buckaroo Bindlestiff's Wild West Jamboree," ran for 15 weeks at the historic Mazer Theater on the Lower East Side.

Despite their success as a touring show, both Nelson and Monseu wanted to create a permanent home for their productions. In August 2002 they opened the Palace of Variety and Free Museum of Times Square at Chashama, an arts center in the heart of New York City's theater district. Through an agreement with Anita Durst, an admirer of experimental theater and a member of the real-estate dynasty that owned the building where the Palace was housed, Bindlestiff began entertaining New Yorkers and tourists alike with a brand of vaudeville entertainment that had not existed in the area for more than 70 years. The theater housed an auditorium with a new façade and a ceiling rigged for aerial stunts, along with a museum devoted to the history of live entertainment. Nelson and Monseu also collected memorabilia and photos that chronicled Times Square's history—from its early days as a rural outpost, to its years as a vaudeville and theater center, to its seedier period as a center of pornography, to its most recent incarnation, as a sanitized tourist destination. There are compelling reasons to preserve traditional variety acts, Nelson told *Current Biography*: "For one, [they] are a major part of American history. Two, people need social environments and live entertainment. A life of only watching TV, sitting at computers, and never having a 'real' experience will not allow for a healthy society." Monseu added, "The historical context in which vaudeville and sideshows thrived is gone forever, but as Folk Art and an intrinsic piece of our cultural history, these forms should be studied and acknowledged. To see a historically accurate re-creation of vaudeville might only be interesting to a few fanatics like me, but to see live, socially relevant, affordable entertainment is exciting for everybody!"

The Bindlestiff Family Cirkus presented up to seven shows a day at the Palace of Variety. Hoping to attract new fans, the group planned daytime shows that offered family-friendly acts, while the late-night shows emphasized adult-oriented entertainment. In a review of a Palace of Variety show, Douglas Martin wrote for the *New York Times* (November 24, 2002), "What could be new about acts as ancient as jugglers brilliant at bumbling? The answer is attitude. Today's performers are clearly younger, the intellectual riffs on seemingly old-fashioned acts are green-apple fresh and, in some instances, shows are longer, deeper and more thoughtful."

The Palace of Variety was forced to close in late 2004, when the Durst family announced that office towers would rise at the site of the theater. Despite that setback, Monseu told *Current Biography*, "our goal for this next decade is to establish a permanent Palace of Variety here in New York City—a purpose-fitted building suited to aerial acts, variety arts, jugglers, physical comedy, sideshow, circus, and related arts. We want to offer space to our community to create, rehearse, perform and preserve their work. Our private library of books, video footage, circus posters, prints, and programs is the start for a research archive." In early 2005 Bindlestiff mounted a production called *From the Gutter to the Glitter* at the Theater for the New City, an Off-Off-Broadway venue in Manhattan.

As they look for a permanent home, Nelson and Monseu will continue to tour the country; on average the Bindlestiff Family Cirkus plans to visit 50 to 70 cities a year. Although the Bindlestiffs love touring, Monseu noted in her interview with *Current Biography*, "As we grow older and less enamored of the ol' punk rock style of van and couch touring, [we] seek longer runs in cities where we will be produced, paid, and hosted well." Nelson and Monseu have taught circus arts to inner-city children in cooperation with the New York City Housing Authority, and they have lectured at several colleges and universities. They hope to present a summertime Wild West show in New York City parks in 2005 and are currently developing a winter show, called "Cirque Noir."

—C.M.

Suggested Reading: *Backstage* p1+ Aug. 9–15, 2002; *Backstage* (on-line) Mar. 12, 2004; bindlestiff.org; *Details* p58 Jan. 2000, with photos; *New York Times* XIV p8 Feb. 1, 1998, with photo, Nov. 24, 2002, with photos; *Paper* p36 May 1996; *Time Out New York* p139+ Aug. 8–15, 2002, with photo

Frederick M. Brown/Getty Images

Nelson, Stanley

June 7, 1951– Documentary filmmaker

Address: Firelight Media, 324 Convent Ave., New York, NY 10031

"I love to do documentaries because you are there with the real people," the filmmaker Stanley Nelson told Bob Longino for the *Atlanta Journal-Constitution* (January 12, 2003). "You're telling a real story. It's important what real people really say. And you never have to think about adding somebody in a skimpy outfit just to get attention." According to a PBS Web site, Nelson's production company, Firelight Media—which he co-founded in 1998 with his wife, the writer Marcia Smith—is "dedicated to telling stories of people, places, cultures and issues that are underrepresented in the mainstream media." With that goal in mind, and serving as director, producer, and sometimes co-writer, he has made such documentaries as *Two Dollars and a Dream: The Story of Madame C. J. Walker and A'Lelia Walker*; *The Black Press: Soldiers Without Swords*; *Marcus Garvey: Look for Me in the Whirlwind*; and *The Murder of Emmett Till*. In 2003 the Museum of Modern Art (MoMA), in New York City, showed those four films in an exhibition entitled "Stanley Nelson: The Art of Making People Think."

In a blurb that appeared on MoMA's Web site, Jytte Jensen, an associate curator in the museum's Department of Film and Media, wrote, "For three decades, Stanley Nelson's documentaries have made audiences, distributors, and television commissioners alike sit up and take notice. With interviews, photographic stills, and found footage, the filmmaker's eloquent works combine historical research and current issues to provide a uniquely intelligent perspective. Nelson's exceedingly well-researched and balanced films are informative as well as entertaining, dealing with issues from past and present African American history and shedding light on current events. Commitment, clarity, and compassion distinguish Nelson's conscientious productions, which have garnered multiple awards and nominations, most recently, a MacArthur Fellowship."

"I never thought I craved recognition, but I have to admit, it feels real good," Nelson told Robin Finn for the *New York Times* (October 8, 2002, on-line), after learning that he had won the $500,000 MacArthur grant. "As an independent anything, you deal with a lot of insecurity; when you make documentaries, it's like going downstream on a river on an ice floe, never on solid ground, just jumping from one project to the next, hoping each time that the chunk of ice you land on is bigger than the last one." Among Nelson's most recent films are *Running: The Campaign for City Council* (2002), which focuses on races for elective office in New York City in 2001, and *Sweet Honey in the Rock: Raise Your Voice* (2005), about an internationally renowned group of African-American a capella singers. He and his wife were the executive producers for the PBS documentary *Beyond Brown:*

Pursuing the Promise (2004), which marked the 50th anniversary of the historic U.S. Supreme Court ruling that banned sanctioned segregation of local school systems.

The second of the four children of Stanley E. Nelson, a dentist, and the former A'Lelia "Liel" Ransom, a librarian, Stanley Nelson was born on June 7, 1951 in New York City. His parents divorced when he was 16. His maternal grandfather, F. B. Ransom, was a lawyer and the manager of Madame C. J. Walker, a pioneering entrepreneur who developed beauty products for black women. (Nelson's mother was named for Madame Walker's only child.) Nelson's younger sister, Jill Nelson, is a writer, editor, and college teacher; her book *Volunteer Slavery: My Authentic Negro Experience* won an American Book Award. His younger brother, Ralph, is a guitarist, vocalist, and bandleader. Nelson and his siblings grew up on Riverside Drive and 148th Street, on the Upper West Side of the New York City borough of Manhattan. The artistically minded Nelsons owned a summer home in Oak Bluffs, a resort town on the island of Martha's Vineyard, in Massachusetts, where many African-American professionals vacationed. Their close-knit community is the subject of Nelson's 2004 documentary, *A Place of Our Own* (broadcast as an installment of the PBS television series *Independent Lens*), which Joe Leydon, writing for *Variety* (January 19, 2004, on-line), described as "by turns celebratory and melancholy," "heartfelt and deeply personal," and "bittersweet."

As a child, Nelson recalled in an interview with *Current Biography*, "I wasn't any more interested in film . . . than anybody else. I think that when I was in college I realized I really wanted to do something artistic, something creative, and that's when I gravitated toward filmmaking." In the six years after his graduation from high school, Nelson attended five colleges: Beloit College, in Wisconsin; Atlanta University, in Georgia; and New York University, Hunter College, and City College, in New York City. He earned a B.F.A. degree in film from the Leonard Davis Film School at City College in 1976. After he tried in vain to get work connected with the making of feature films, he landed a job with William Greaves, who is now recognized as one of the nation's leading documentary filmmakers. Under the tutelage of Greaves, an African-American, he grew to love the art and craft of making documentaries. By the 1980s he was producing motion pictures for the United Methodist Church's film service, on both church-related subjects and other topics. Speaking of the latter, he told *Current Biography*, "When you saw them you wouldn't think, 'Oh this is a film by the Methodist Church.'" *Puerto Rico: Our Right to Decide* (1981), in which Puerto Rican students, teachers, farmers, fishermen, and church workers discussed the island's economic and social problems and voiced their preferences for statehood or independence, won a CINE Golden Eagle, an award that recognizes excellence in nontheatrical movies and videos. Also during the 1980s Nelson produced *Mandela*, about Nelson Mandela, who spent nearly three decades in a South African prison before becoming the first black president of that country, in 1994. In making that film, which also focuses on Mandela's former wife, Winnie, to whom he was married from 1958 to 1996, Nelson traveled in South Africa and witnessed firsthand the brutal oppression and racial segregation institutionalized by the nation's white minority through apartheid laws.

In 1987 Nelson won another CINE Golden Eagle, for his first truly independent film, *Two Dollars and a Dream: The Story of Madame C. J. Walker and A'Lelia Walker*. The elder Walker, who was born in 1867 to former slaves, has been identified as the country's first self-made female millionaire. After being widowed, at age 20, with a two-year-old daughter, Walker supported herself as a laundress. Her phenomenal success in business began in the early 1900s, with sales of a pomade that she concocted herself. While Walker and her daughter enjoyed the trappings of wealth, they also generously supported many endeavors of other blacks. According to a blurb posted on various Web sites, *Two Dollars and a Dream* "ties together social, political, and economic history, offering a well-rounded view of African American life from 1867 through the 1930s." The film won a 1988 Journalism Award for Documentary from the National Association of Black Journalists and was named both best production of 1988 and best production of the 1980s by the Black Filmmaker Foundation.

In the 1990s Nelson produced several PBS specials: *Freedom Bags* (1991), about the migration of black domestic workers from the South to the North during the early 1900s, which won first place for nonfiction at the 1991 Black Independent Film, Video, and Screenplay Competition; *Methadone: Curse or Cure* (1996), which was named best cultural-affairs documentary by the 1997 National Black Programming Consortium; and *Shattering the Silences: The Case for Minority Faculty* (1998), in which eight college teachers—an Asian American, three Latinos, three African-Americans, and a Native American—talked about their work experiences. Nelson has produced many PBS series as well, among them *Listening to America with Bill Moyers* and *What Can We Do About Violence? With Bill Moyers*. He also developed and filmed a number of documentaries for the Smithsonian Institution. Those include *Climbing Jacob's Ladder* (1991), a 30-minute documentary about the history of black churches in the U.S., and *Free Within Ourselves* (1993), a portrait of four African-American artists, which won a CINE Golden Eagle.

His various honors notwithstanding, Nelson received little mainstream attention until 1999, when his documentary *The Black Press: Soldiers Without Swords* debuted. To make the 90-minute film, which was funded by the National Endowment for the Arts, the Corporation for Public Broadcasting, and the Ford Foundation, among other supporters, Nelson and his team sifted through a hundred years' worth of microfilmed newspapers—literally thousands of editions—in every major American city. "If I was looking through the *Chicago Defender* from 1923 for a certain article, I would find that I would just be fascinated by the paper itself, so instead of looking for the article I was looking for I would just start reading the paper," Nelson told *Current Biography*, referring to a newspaper that spurred the mass migration of blacks from the Deep South to northern cities and that was, arguably, once the most influential black newspaper in the U.S. "It's just incredible. It's like this window into this whole world. . . . The ads are fascinating, the cartoons are fascinating, the pictures, the way they're laid out, the whole thing is just really fascinating." *The Black Press* chronicles the rise of black newspapers in the U.S., beginning with *Freedom's Journal* (1827–29), the first newspaper published by and for African-Americans, to the 40 such newspapers available at the time of the Civil War (1861–65), to periodicals in existence during the Jim Crow era and those that helped to energize the civil rights movement of the 1950s and 1960s. The film also profiled such pioneering black journalists as Ida B. Wells, a fearless anti-lynching crusader, suffragist, and women's-rights advocate, and Abie Robinson, who earned $5 a week writing and editing for the *California Eagle*, where he also assisted the pressmen and even cleaned the bathrooms. In addition, Nelson noted that the black press was the only place where most African-Americans could read works by W.E.B. DuBois and Marcus Garvey or learn about the accomplishments of black ballplayers.

The Black Press received universal praise. As Nelson told *Current Biography*, it "was the kind of film that was very hard to do, and I think a lot of people recognized that. If I say to you, 'I'm doing a film on the history of black newspapers,' most people couldn't understand how that film would look, what that film would be, and most people couldn't understand how that could be an entertaining film. But I think that it turned out to be a fun film, an entertaining film for people. It's not [just] a history lesson." In a representative review of the documentary for *Black Issues in Higher Education* (August 6, 1998), Jamilah Evelyn wrote, "Combining striking stills that capture the essence of the time and the comments of sagacious scholars who put the movement in perspective, Nelson creates a dynamic documentary and tribute to our publishing progenitors. . . . With candid interviews from former staffers and incredible photographs that reincarnate the times, Nelson uses his crisp filmmaking skills to transport us back to the days when the Black press flourished with a monopoly on the Black reading market." The film won the Freedom of Expression Award at the 1999 Sundance Film Festival, the National Association of Black Journalists' 1999 Journalism Award for outstanding coverage of black conditions, the 1999 Golden Gate Award at the San Francisco International Film Festival, and a first-place jury award for documentary at the 1999 Hollywood Black Film Festival. In addition, in 2000 Nelson earned a Silver Baton, an Alfred I. duPont–Columbia University award that honors overall excellence in broadcast journalism.

By his own account, while researching material for *The Black Press*, Nelson became intrigued by the popular weekly newspaper *Negro World* (1918–33), published by Marcus Garvey, (1887–1940), who founded the first black-nationalist movement. As Nelson told Lee Hubbard for Africana.com (March 30, 2001), "As I began to look into Garvey, I thought it was a great story and that it was time that we saw a film about Garvey." Nelson presented that story in his 90-minute documentary *Marcus Garvey: Look for Me in the Whirlwind* (2001), which he wrote, produced, and directed. In 1914 Garvey, an immigrant to the U.S. from Jamaica, founded the Universal Negro Improvement Association, whose goals were to encourage racial pride and a feeling of unity among all blacks and to urge black people to resist racism through any means necessary. Opposed to racial integration and convinced that blacks could never gain equal rights in a nation in which they were a minority, he launched a "back to Africa" movement, with the idea that blacks would set up an independent state in Africa. Regarded by many blacks as a prophet and redeemer, he organized a month-long conference in New York City in 1920 that attracted delegates from all over the world. His fame and popularity aroused the suspicions of the U.S. Department of Justice and other federal agencies, and he was convicted—unjustly, in the view of many of his supporters then and now—of mail fraud. Ultimately, the government's continued hounding, attacks by such African-American leaders as W.E.B. DuBois and A. Philip Randolph, and his egomania led to Garvey's downfall. He died in London in 1940 at the age of 53.

"Here was a guy who would do something that was something of incredible genius, and then the very next step was something that seemed like it was just so dumb," Nelson told *Current Biography*. "[I thought] what a great film character he was because he's complicated. He's larger than life. And also I think for me he's still, all and all, a hero. . . . Heroes usually are not saints. They have their good and bad. It almost takes somebody who's larger than life to have this dream that's larger than life. You have to kind of be half-crazy to have the kind of dreams and visions that Marcus Garvey had." In one of many complimentary reviews of the film, Geoffrey Jacques wrote for *Cineaste* (Fall 2001), "Through archival footage and stills of Garvey, his movement, and his times, as well as through interviews—with people like his two sons, Marcus Jr. and Julius Garvey, several elderly Garveyites, and with an array of historians—Nelson has constructed an affectionate, but critical, picture of this controversial, if legendary, leader." Joe Leydon, writing for *Variety* (February 12–18, 2001), agreed:

"Nelson has fashioned a meticulously balanced portrait, indicating [that] . . . Garvey accelerated his own downfall through egocentric excesses, ill-informed business decisions and an iron-willed refusal to accept criticism. . . . At the same time . . . [the film] also underscores Garvey's invaluable influence as one of the first and most important black leaders of the 20th century." The Black Filmmakers' Hall of Fame chose *Marcus Garvey* as its First Place Overall Winner in 2001, and at the Black International Cinema Festival, held in Berlin, Germany, in 2002, it was named best film/video documentary production of 2001.

In *The Murder of Emmett Till* (2002), Nelson documented the story of Till, a 14-year-old African-American from Chicago, who, in 1955, during a visit to relatives in Mississippi, was fatally beaten and shot for purportedly speaking to and/or whistling at a white woman. His mutilated, bloated corpse surfaced several days later in a river, where the killers had thrown it after attaching a heavy fan to the neck with barbed wire. Till's mother, Mamie Till Mobley, insisted that her son's casket remain open at the wake, where the thousands of people who paid their respects saw how brutally he had been battered. The national outrage and shock that the case triggered increased when a photo of Till in his casket appeared in *Jet* magazine; it grew more when an all-white jury, after a little more than an hour of deliberations, acquitted J. W. Milam and Roy Bryant, the two men accused of the murder. It escalated further when *Look* magazine, after paying Milam and Bryant $4,000, published an account in which the men described the killing—and even bragged about what they had done. "What we wanted to get across in *Emmett Till* [was] the story of these people who were what I call everyday heroes," Nelson told *Current Biography*, referring to, among others, Till's mother and two of her relatives who had testified in court for the prosecution. "They're what the civil rights movement was really made up of. We remember Martin Luther King and Malcolm X and those kind of larger-than-life people, but we forget that behind Martin Luther King on every march were thousands of these people who had to live in these towns after Martin Luther King left. They were really heroes and were what made the civil rights movement a movement. . . . What [Mamie Till Mobley] did was incredible. It's incredible in the history of lynching because that's not what was done. People were cut down from the tree or wherever and it was hidden away. But Mamie Till Mobley was different."

Nelson's wife, Marcia Smith, has written or cowritten several of Nelson's documentaries, among them *The Black Press*, *The Murder of Emmett Till*, *A Place of Our Own*, and *Sweet Honey in the Rock*. In an interview with Susan DeCarava for the Writers Guild of America, East (October/November 2004, on-line), Smith talked about the couple's modus operandi: "I usually write a very detailed treatment laying out that this is the story, this is how it's going to unfold—really a narrative treatment. Stan will then look at that and think about the visual elements. We'll kick around an idea for an extended time and then I'll work on the treatment, first, and then Stan works on it and we go back and forth until we go into production with this roadmap that we've both weighed in on. Once you go into production, however, all bets are off! Mostly because in most of our films, we both want as much of the story as possible to be told by people who actually lived it."

Nelson lives in the historic Hamilton Heights section of Harlem, in New York City, with Smith, their twin daughters, Kay and Nola, and Nelson's daughter, Olivia, from a previous relationship. Their brownstone houses their company, Firelight Productions. Nelson has taught courses in film production at Howard University and at the University of California at San Diego. He has won fellowships from Columbia University, the American Film Institute, the New York Foundation for the Arts, and the Washington, D.C., Commission for the Arts. In 2002 he served as a juror for the documentary competitions at the Sundance Film Festival and the Independent Feature Project. In his interview with *Current Biography*, he offered advice for aspiring young filmmakers: "Hang in there and make films. With video equipment becoming smaller, lighter and cheaper, there's more opportunity out there than ever. . . . I think there's always room for people who are doing new stuff. . . . You've got to figure out how to tell your own stories and how to tell them in a way that's different and exciting."

—C.M.

Suggested Reading: *All Movie Guide* (on-line); *Atlanta Journal-Constitution* M p1 Jan. 12, 2003; *Black Issues in Higher Education* p42+ Aug. 6, 1998; *Cineaste* p76+ Fall 2001; Internet Movie Database (on-line); *Jet* p14 Oct. 14, 2002; *New York Times* (on-line) Oct. 8, 2002, with photo; *Newsday* B p6 Jan. 20, 2003; *Village Voice* p53 Oct. 13, 1998, p43 Feb. 12–18, 2001

Selected Films: *Two Dollars and a Dream*, 1987; *The Black Press: Soldiers Without Swords*, 1999; *Marcus Garvey: Look for Me in the Whirlwind*, 2001; *The Murder of Emmett Till*, 2002; *A Place of Our Own*, 2004; *Sweet Honey in the Rock: Raise Your Voice*, 2005

orangephotography.com

Newmark, Craig

Dec. 6, 1952– Founder and chairman of craigslist.org

Address: craigslist, 1381 Ninth Ave., San Francisco, CA 94122-2308

"When you grow up a nerd, you feel like an outsider," Craig Newmark told Idelle Davidson for the *Los Angeles Times* (June 13, 2004, on-line). For a self-described outsider, Newmark is remarkably in the know; he is the founder of craigslist.org, a Web site through which users can buy and sell goods, find apartments and jobs, place personal ads, keep abreast of local events, and meet with others for activities. The site, which began as a simple E-mail list of events that Newmark sent to a handful of friends in an attempt to socialize more, now attracts a reported eight million visitors a month, posts approximately 100,000 new listings per day, and generates gross revenues of between $7 million and $10 million a year, by charging businesses for posting employment ads. (All other services are free). It currently serves 100 cities around the world and will likely continue to expand. "We're restricted to the planetary surface," Newmark told a reporter for *American Way Magazine* (February 1, 2004, on-line), "but for people [in any location] who want one, our goal is to get them a craigslist." As it turns out, Newmark may have been wrong about an earthly restriction; on March 11, 2005 more than 100,000 postings from craigslist.org were beamed into space by a Cape Canaveral–based company called Deep Space Communications Network, in the first intentional interstellar commercial transmission. (Radio and television signals are sometimes transmitted inadvertently.) "It's very fitting that the first [commercial] transmission into space is by a community Web site like craigslist," Jim Lewis, the vice president of Deep Space Communications Network, told Ker Than for CNN.com (March 24, 2005), "because it represents a wide cross section of society."

Craig Newmark was born on December 6, 1952 to Lee Newmark, an insurance salesman, and his wife, Joyce, a bookkeeper. The family, which also included Craig's younger brother, Jeff, lived in a house on Early Street in Morristown, New Jersey, a bucolic suburb less than 40 miles from New York City. Shortly after Craig's bar mitzvah (a rite of passage that typically occurs when a Jewish male turns 13), Lee Newmark died of lung cancer, and his family relocated to a Morristown apartment. "It was an extraordinarily difficult time for me, for us," Joyce Newmark told Navid Iqbal for the Morris County *Daily Record* (June 26, 2004, on-line). "But [Craig] always had a deep sense of responsibility. After my husband died, Craig helped me take care of my parents and my aunt, who were very ill. He was helping out all the time."

As quoted by Idelle Davidson, Newmark called himself "academically intelligent [but] socially retarded." A shy, awkward student, he wore the pocket protector and taped-together eyeglasses of the stereotypical nerd. His sixth-grade teacher was so worried about his absence of social skills that she sent Newmark to the school counselor; the counselor had little useful advice and instead taught Newmark to play chess. Nonetheless, when Newmark entered Morristown High School, he began participating in a variety of school activities, including the debate club, the Honor Society, the physics club, and the school radio station, WJSV-FM. He enjoyed the writings of the Objectivist author Ayn Rand, was an avid photographer, and eagerly engaged in discussions about politics and cinema. Newmark planned to become either a theoretical physicist or a computer engineer.

After he graduated from high school, in 1971, Newmark enrolled at Case Western Reserve University, in Cleveland, Ohio, where he earned B.S. and M.S. degrees in computer science in 1975 and 1977, respectively. Earlier, in 1976, Newmark had begun working at IBM as a senior associate programmer in Boca Raton, Florida; when he became an advisory systems engineer for IBM, in 1982, he relocated to Detroit, Michigan. From 1992 to 1993 he served as an advisory open-systems specialist for the company in Pittsburgh, Pennsylvania. In 1993 Newmark moved to San Francisco, California, to work as a system-security architect and general consultant for the investment firm Charles Schwab and Co., a position that he held for two years. After he left Schwab he remained in San Francisco and took a variety of consulting jobs for such companies as Xircom, Bank of America, NetGuide Live, JustInTime Solutions, Encanto Networks, Sun Microsystems, E-Forex, and Continuity Solutions.

In March 1995 Newmark attempted to broaden his social horizons by compiling a free E-mail list to alert friends to upcoming events in the Bay Area; he sent it to about a dozen people. Its enthusiastic reception inspired him to expand it into an on-line bulletin board featuring not only events but also apartment rentals, job opportunities, personal ads, and items for sale. He wrote software that could automatically add E-mail postings, and soon both friends and strangers were sending in listings. Newmark wanted to call the on-line list sf-events (for San Francisco), but his friends—who had already nicknamed the site "Craig's list"—suggested he stick to that simple title to emphasize the personal, straightforward nature of the site. (The notoriously bashful Newmark prefers to use a lowercase "C" to avoid drawing unnecessary attention to his own name.) Increasing numbers of Internet users began posting items on the site, and even as the dot-com industry crumbled, craigslist became one of the most often-visited sites in the U.S. On the heels of his success in San Francisco, Newmark created versions of the site for New York, Los Angeles, and other cities.

By 2005 site traffic had reached eight million visitors a month and approximately 100,000 new listings per day. As of October 2005, craigslist served more than 100 locales—in Europe, Canada, Australia, New Zealand, Africa, Asia, and South America as well as the U.S. Users maintain the lists by contributing messages or ads, flagging those they find offensive or dishonest, and voting for their favorites. (Newmark has involved himself only in cases of blatant abuse, such as when unscrupulous apartment brokers list falsified rates for rentals or stolen items are offered for sale.) The site is text-oriented and spare, with no flashy graphics or banner ads. Charlene Li, an analyst for Forrester Research, told Pete Barlas for *Investor's Business Daily* (May 15, 2003, on-line), "It's easy to use and there's a lack of a commercial feel, so people trust it." Newmark told Josh McHugh for *Wired* (September 2004, on-line): "Just by being good guys, we've created a culture of trust and fairness. The site makes it easier for people to get everyday stuff done, like selling things and finding an apartment. Then there's another aspect—it has helped people who have a hard time meeting other people. They're using the site and becoming friends, lovers, and every possible twist on those two situations." Newmark has been approached repeatedly about running banner ads on the site; despite the revenue ads would generate, he has thus far declined to do so. (In 2002 he played an April Fool's Day joke on craigslist users by briefly featuring specious ads for soy-based cat food, caffeinated cigarettes, and other nonsensical products.)

In 1999 Newmark realized that operating craigslist was more than a mere hobby, and he quit his job to devote more time to maintaining the site. In order to support himself, he began charging employers to post job listings. (Each job listing currently costs between $25 and $75.) The site's other services remain free. In 2004 the site earned approximately $7 million, and as of early 2005 craigslist employed some 18 staff members in its modest San Francisco office.

In 2000, after recognizing that he was trying to handle too much responsibility himself, Newmark promoted Jim Buckmaster, a staff member, to replace him as chief executive officer. (Newmark remained chairman and owns approximately 50 percent of craigslist.) Although he has received dozens of buyout offers, he has refused to sell craigslist, mainly because he believes that, in the hands of a large company, the site would lose its simplicity and spirit of democracy. "I admit that when I think of the money one could make from all this, I get a little twinge," he confessed to Josh McHugh. "But I'm pretty happy with nerd values: Get yourself a comfortable living, then do a little something to change the world." In late 2004 the Internet-auction giant eBay acquired a 25 percent stake in craigslist from a former employee of Newmark's who had been given the shares as a gift when the company was young. (The stocks had been virtually worthless at the time; details of the transaction were not made public, but some reports have estimated that the anonymous former employee pocketed several million dollars.) Despite fears from users that eBay's involvement would mean the end of craigslist as they knew it, the acquisition has had little effect on the site. Executives at eBay "have no interest in asking us to change [our mission] in any way," Buckmaster told Nick Wingfield for the *Wall Street Journal* (August 13, 2004, on-line). "They're happy with us having our full autonomy. They recognize us as experts in what we do." Industry observers have speculated that eBay wanted to keep the shares out of a competitor's hands and was eager for a potential advantage if Newmark ever changed his mind and decided to sell additional shares.

In 2001 craigslist won a Webby Award for best community site. (Newmark's entire acceptance speech reportedly consisted of the words, "Hey, mom, I love you!") Established in 1996, the Webby Awards are given by the International Academy of Digital Arts and Sciences in recognition of "excellence in Web design, creativity, usability and functionality," according to the academy's Web site. "What Craig does is the Web at its best," Tiffany Shlain, founder of the Webbys, told Jane Ganahl for the *San Francisco Chronicle* (July 29, 2001, on-line). "He took the intimacy of a community coffeehouse and put it online, and made the world a smaller place." Newmark has said that he is determined to keep craigslist community-oriented and user-friendly; craigslist's corporate motto is "Give people a break." He told Navid Iqbal, "On our site, there are a million acts of kindness every day. The world should be like that."

As an on-line April Fool's Day joke, Newmark, who has described himself as fiscally conservative and socially liberal, once launched a faux campaign for mayor of San Francisco. He publicly backed the unsuccessful Democratic presidential campaigns of former Vermont governor Howard Dean, who is now the chairman of the Democratic National Committee, and Senator John Kerry of Massachusetts, the 2004 nominee. At the invitation of San Francisco's mayor, Gavin Newsom, he sat on a public board that accepted complaints about city services.

Newmark has recently become intrigued by the idea of "community" or "open-source" journalism. Bemoaning the mainstream media's lack of credibility, he envisions building a team of talented nonprofessionals to investigate and report on government activities, corporate scandals, and other news and to fact check and edit the resulting articles. According to *Editor & Publisher* (May 6, 2005, on-line), he hopes his plan will become reality in time to provide readers with trustworthy political reports (to be posted daily on craigslist and other sites) by the 2006 midterm elections.

Newmark, who once took a ballet class in order to meet women—and landed in the hospital with a hernia—was named one of the top 10 bachelors of Silicon Valley by Women.com in 2000. In his free time he enjoys watching such TV shows as *The Simpsons* and *South Park*. He is frequently called upon to attend functions in support of the many charitable organizations with which he is involved, among them the Haight-Ashbury Food Program. In 2001 he established the Craigslist Foundation, which helps fledgling nonprofit groups.

—K.J.E.

Suggested Reading: cnewmark.com; *Investor's Business Daily* (on-line) May 15, 2003; (Morris County, New Jersey) *Daily Record* (on-line) June 26, 2004; *Newsweek* p94 Jan. 3, 2005, with photo; *PC World* p32 Nov. 2004, with photo; *San Francisco Chronicle* (on-line) July 29, 2001; *Sunset* (national edition) p168 Nov. 2004; *U.S. News & World Report* p62 Aug. 9, 2004, with photo; *Wired* (on-line) Sep. 2004

Nugent, Ted

Dec. 13, 1948– Musician; hunting advocate; radio and television host; magazine publisher; writer

Address: 4008 W. Michigan Ave., Jackson, MI 49202

From his octane-fueled music career, first as the lead guitarist for the Amboy Dukes, then as a solo artist, to his passion for hunting and the outdoors, Ted Nugent has spent his professional life pushing the limits. His propensity for performing on stage either while wearing a loincloth or only animal pelts and his well-publicized right-wing positions on such hot-button topics as gun control, abortion, and the death penalty have earned Nugent the nickname "Motor City Madman"—a reference to Detroit, Michigan, Nugent's hometown, which is the historical home of the automobile industry. They have also earned him a reputation as a colorful, unrepentant extremist. After landing a smash hit with the song "Journey to the Center of the Mind" with the Amboy Dukes in the late 1960s, Nugent split from the band and pursued a solo career. During the 1970s and 1980s, he recorded several more highly successful singles, including the now-classic "Wango Tango" and "Cat Scratch Fever." All told, Nugent has sold more than 30 million albums and is one of the top-grossing live musical acts of all time.

Nugent is also an avid hunter and outdoorsman. He is the editor and publisher of *Ted Nugent Adventure Outdoors* magazine, the president of Ted Nugent United Sportsmen of America, and the founder of Ted Nugent's Kamp for Kids, and in all

Ethan Miller/Getty Images

those capacities, he advocates hunting as both a way to commune with nature and a purer, healthier source of meat than the processed products derived from domesticated livestock. His outspoken views of those subjects have drawn criticism from animal-rights activists. Nugent has dismissed their arguments and has maintained that, far from simply killing animals and drawing resources from the land, he works harder than most environmentalists to preserve the natural world. "We have the figures back," he told Amy Benfer for *Salon* (June 11, 2002, on-line), "and they say that by the spring of '99, my Kamp for Kids and other hunting, sporting and conservation groups were responsible for planting over 10 million trees. So I'd like to ask my critics: How many trees have you planted? How many acres of wildlife habitat have you restored?"

In addition to his Kamp for Kids—which provides archery instruction, gun-safety lessons, and other hunting-related activities for youngsters— Nugent sponsors the organizations Hunters for the Hungry, which encourages hunters to provide surplus meat for the needy; Sunrize Safaris, which offers individuals the chance to hunt and camp with Nugent as their guide; and Hunt of a Lifetime, which gives terminally ill children the chance to hunt in the U.S. and overseas. He has also supported many local and national law-enforcement organizations and has long been a vocal critic of drug and alcohol abuse, serving as a national anti-drugs spokesman and working with programs dedicated to keeping young people sober and drug-free. For his charitable work and efforts within his community and in the outdoors, Nugent was honored on the floor of the U.S. Senate in 1994 and named Michigan conservationist of the year in 1999. "Some people with small minds call me an extremist," he wrote in an essay for chicago-scene.com (July 2001). "It is weird, extremely weird, to be given such a compliment by such an obviously uncomplimentary source. After all, when those who do nothing in the face of disaster condemn our progressive activism, it is living proof that we are on a True North track. Compared to my apathetic, lame critics, I am extremely proud to be an extremist."

Ted Nugent was born on December 13, 1948 in Detroit, Michigan. According to some sources, he first picked up a bow and arrow, supplied by his father, when he was five years old. When he was nine he began learning to play the guitar. He has traced his passion for hunting and the outdoors to about that time. "My first kill ever was with a Whammo slingshot," Nugent told Steve Miller for the *Washington Times* (May 2002). "I was 10 years old, and it was in a park near Redford Township in Michigan. I killed [a wild turkey] with a marble, and I took it home, and my mom and dad showed me how to dress it and cook it. There was definitely some cause and effect there." By the time he was a teenager, Nugent had formed his first rock band, the Royal Highboys. Soon afterward he formed the Lourds, with whom he won a Battle of the Bands contest, finishing the performance by playing a guitar solo atop the judges' table. Following that victory the Lourds became an opening act for such well-known groups as the Supremes and the Beau Brummels. However, hunting was the source of Nugent's greatest pleasure. "The family took annual fall excursions [to northern Michigan] for an extended weekend along the Titabawasee River . . . ," he wrote in an editorial for huntingdi-gest.com. "Dad and I rambled around the Ogemaw State Forest, bows in hand, for absolutely thrilling

adventure. He didn't push me by any means, but rather just exposed me to the thrill of the wild and taught me a little along the way."

In 1967 Nugent formed the Amboy Dukes, a Detroit-based version of a band he had led during the two years he and his family had lived in Chicago. Made up of Nugent, the former Lourds vocalist John Drake, Bill White on bass, Steve Farmer on rhythm guitarist, and Dave Palmer on drums, the Amboy Dukes released an eponymous debut album that year. The band quickly became a fixture in Detroit's club scene. Infused with a strong work ethic and a rough-and-tumble attitude, the Amboy Dukes were examples of the fast and furious Motor City sound that was becoming popular in the late 1960s. Such bands as the Stooges, MC5, and Mitch Ryder and the Detroit Wheels took conventional rock music and intensified it, creating a sound that made the Motor City distinct from other burgeoning music centers in the U.S. Nugent himself became known for his idiosyncratic diction.

In 1968 the Amboy Dukes released a hit single, "Journey to the Center of the Mind," the title track from the group's second album. Many people assumed that the song was about drug use, although the lyrics contain no references to artificial stimulants. Nugent, who maintains a rigid anti-drug stance, told Allan Vorda for *Psychedelic Psounds* (February 24, 1988, on-line), "When we put out 'Journey to the Center of the Mind' . . . it had that [image of a] pipe collection on the front cover and I didn't have the faintest idea what those pipes were all about! Everybody else was getting stoned and trying every drug known to mankind. I was meeting women, playing rock and roll. . . . I didn't have the faintest idea about dope. I didn't know anything about this cosmic inner probe. I thought 'Journey to the Center of the Mind' meant look inside yourself, use your head, and move forward in life." He also told Vorda, "I watched incredible musicians fumble, drool, and not be able to tune their instruments [because of drug or alcohol use]. It was easier to say no than to say, 'Hey, gosh, that's for me.' I've also seen my fellow musicians die. It was so obvious. The same reason you don't run across certain highways during peak rush hours." Nugent has maintained that he was never troubled about his lack of popularity with people in the music scene, some of whom ridiculed him because of his disapproval of drugs.

During the last years of the 1960s and the early 1970s, the Amboy Dukes released a series of well-received albums, including *Migration* (1969) and *Marriage on the Rocks* (1970). At the same time, Nugent was growing increasingly irritated by his bandmates' attitudes and their continued drug use. He fired Drake and Palmer, and afterward the band's lineups changed often. Renamed Ted Nugent & the Amboy Dukes, the group released the albums *Call of the Wild* (1973) and *Tooth, Fang & Claw* (1974), but Nugent found that managing the band was becoming intolerably stressful. "I was so upset internally with the amount of effort I was putting out with the constant human battering I was doing with the musicians," he recalled to Vorda. "I was bailing [a band member] out of jail in Montgomery, Alabama for breaking into a Coke machine. Or getting someone else out of jail because he got caught with a joint. . . . I also acted as a road manager. I used to book the band. I used to maintain all the equipment. I used to change the oil in the cars. I used to drive the truck and set it up. I handled all the hotels. I kept all the ledger books. I did everything. . . . So for the first time in my life I took a year off."

Nugent now focused his attention on carving out a solo career. After spending some time hunting deer in Colorado, he returned to the recording studio and soon released his first solo album, *Ted Nugent* (1975), to which Derek St. Holmes contributed rhythm guitar and vocals. In the *All Music Guide* (on-line), Greg Prato called the album "a prime slice of testosterone-heavy, raging, unapologetic rock & roll." Offering such classics as "Hey Baby," "Just What the Doctor Ordered," and "Motor City Madhouse," the album achieved platinum status (with more than one million copies sold).

With the then-unknown singer Meat Loaf replacing St. Holmes during the latter's brief absence, the band next released *Free-for-All* (1976). Popular singles from that album included "Hammerdown" and "Turn it Up." St. Holmes traveled with the band on its subsequent tour and collaborated on its follow-up album, *Cat Scratch Fever* (1977). Featuring the tracks "Cat Scratch Fever" and "Dog Eat Dog," songs that are still ranked among Nugent's best, the album proved to be Nugent's breakthrough effort, selling more than two million copies. "For sheer jubilant ferocity in recent hard rock," Ken Tucker wrote for *Rolling Stone* (July 28, 1977, on-line), "Ted Nugent has only himself to top, and he does it on *Cat Scratch Fever*." Tucker described Nugent's guitar playing as an "amalgam of innumerable heavy-metal quotations raised to fascination by the speed and cunning with which he runs through them."

Nugent's live album *Double Live Gonzo* (1978) sold extremely well. "As exciting as they were, Ted Nugent's first three albums lacked the sonic punch in the gut of his outrageous live performances, something readily proved by 1978's classic *Double Live Gonzo*," Ed Rivadavia wrote for the *All Music Guide* (on-line). On the band's extensive tours, Nugent's unrestrained stage shows made him the number-one-grossing musical act in 1977, 1978, and 1979. His subsequent recordings included *Scream Dream* (1980), *Intensities in 10 Cities* (1981), and *If You Can't Lick 'Em . . . Lick 'Em* (1988). These albums contained some of Nugent's most famous songs, including "Wango Tango," "Spread Your Wings," and "Terminus Eldorado."

In 1990 Nugent, along with the former Styx guitarist Tommy Shaw and Night Ranger bassist Jack Blades, formed Damn Yankees. A supergroup designed to challenge some of the "disposable" pop-metal acts of that era, the musicians released their debut album, *Damn Yankees*, in 1990. Propelled by the success of the first single, the ballad "High Enough," the record climbed to number 13 on *Billboard* magazine's album charts and achieved platinum status. The group's second effort, *Don't Tread* (1992), did not fare as well, and Damn Yankees disbanded in 1993. Nugent resumed his solo career with *Spirit of the Wild* (1995), an album that celebrated his passion for hunting and the wilderness. Critics praised the record as a restrained and mature effort. "*Spirit of the Wild* ranks as one of Ted Nugent's finest moments because it cuts away the filler and keeps the wildman's tendency for indulgence in check," Stephen Thomas Erlewine wrote for the *All Music Guide* (on-line). In 1996 Nugent released *Motor City Madness*.

In the late 1990s Nugent continued to tour extensively, averaging more than 100 shows a year. In 2000 he performed on a tour with the legendary rock band Kiss, which became the top-grossing concert act of the year. Nugent's live album *Full Bluntal Nugity* (2001) is a 12-track recording of a show Nugent played on New Year's Eve 2000 in Detroit. In 2002 he released *Craveman*, his first studio album in seven years. He told Benfer, "I crave the American dream. The American dream is about optimal partying. Not puking and dying—that's not a party. . . . My point is that *Craveman . . .* is a huge shout from the top of the top mountain. Mankind: A quality of life upgrade is available to each and every one of you . . . which means no drugs, no alcohol, no fast food—unless, of course, it's a mallard." The record received postive reviews. "Ted Nugent—gonzo guitarist, unabashed American patriot, shameless meat-eater/hunter—[has] cranked out a sure-to-become-classic with *Craveman*," Michael Paoletta wrote for *Billboard* (October 5, 2002, on-line). "The album is full bluntal nugity: over-the-top, sex-fueled lyrics and anthemic compositions featuring bluesy undercurrents that have guitars roaring with rock'n'roll fury."

While pursuing his musical career, Nugent has always made time for his other passions. Among them are the Ted Nugent Kamp for Kids; founded in 1990, the camp teaches children hunting and survival skills and wildlife conservation, in classes ranging from archery to compass reading to first aid. (Nugent is a certified hunting-safety instructor and an International Bowhunter Education Foundation instructor.) In 1989 Nugent established Hunters for the Hungry, which encourages hunters and meat processors to distribute game meat to people without enough to eat. To date, the organization has helped to deliver more than one million pounds of meat to the needy. Nugent himself is often on hand at soup kitchens, serving such dishes as venison stew. In 1994 his efforts in education and conservation led then-governor John Engler of Michigan to appoint him to the state's International Year of the Family council. Nugent has also served as director of the state's Hunting and Fishing Heritage Task Force and as an appointee to the

Michigan State Parks Foundation. He has been honored as Michigan's Recreation and Parks Association man of the year.

Gun control is chief among the topics about which Nugent is outspoken. A member of the board of directors of the National Rifle Association, he staunchly supports the view that the Second Amendment of the U.S. Constitution, which reads, "A well-regulated militia being necessary to the security of a free State, the right of the people to keep and bear arms shall not be infringed," means that even in the absence of a militia, people have the right to bear arms. He believes that most Americans are more "pro-gun" than they might admit. "Even those that claim to be against gun ownership . . . have made a big deal out of wishing for more law enforcement personnel on the streets of America," he said in an on-line chat on the ABC News Web site (August 3, 2000), "when in fact, in those jurisdictions where law abiding citizens have a higher rate of concealed weapons permits, they have for all practical purposes performed the very duties in stopping and deterring crime that armed law enforcement personnel have."

In response to animal-rights activists who have painted him as a bloodthirsty butcher, Nugent has insisted that he is interested in the overall ecology of the world. He and his family raise many animals and plant trees on their land. "In 2002, it is irrefutably documented that there are more deer, more turkey, more Canadian geese, more mountain lion, more bear than ever in recorded history in North America," he told Benfer. (Many scientists would dispute that assertion.) He continued, "There's not a farmer in America that if approached by a reasonably groomed, decent, courteous family wouldn't be pleased as punch to have you come in and help reduce the damned deer population! Or the mountain lion, or the elk—there's more elk, there's more moose, there's more buffalo than in over 150 years." " I don't even want to hear about animals being equal to human beings," he told Steve Walters for the Fort Lauderdale, Florida, *Sun-Sentinel* (March 13, 1993). "I don't even want to hear their rhetoric and their lies. I have on file with law enforcement agencies threats to kill my [four] children because we eat pheasants. They want to kill me, they want to take our lives because I hunt. We're talking evil, out-of-whack scum who have completely lost respect for life itself." He has also drawn fire from a number of animal-rights celebrities, among them the former Beatle Paul McCartney. "When McCartney says he won't eat anything with a face, I ask 'What are you saying to millions of Americans barbecuing chicken on the Fourth of July?' I think Paul should just shut up and sing. . . . I'm proud to be a hunter because it's as pure a function as giving birth. There's this vicious misrepresentation of hunting, a lie repeated so often people believe it: That I weigh 350 pounds, inbred, shooting Bambi and stop signs and the occasional nephew in the leg. Hunters are mothers and fathers . . . we understand how we fit in."

In 1990 Nugent published his first book, *Bloodtrails: The Truth about Bowhunting.* His second, the essay collection *God, Guns, & Rock 'N' Roll* (2000), offers autobiographical material along with discussions of social and political issues. The title of the book refers to what Nugent considers to be his greatest influences. "I'm 52 years clean and sober and I attribute that discipline in my life to the fact that I've been surrounded for 52 years by God, lots of guns and outrageous rock and roll," he told Geoff Metcalf for Metcalf's Web site. "It has been a good regimen for me. My parents raised me in a very loving, very disciplined—there's the key word—a disciplined environment to teach me self-discipline. And, as a hunter, I can't deny the incredible gifts of the Creator." *God, Guns, & Rock 'N' Roll* landed on the *New York Times* best-seller list, where it remained for several weeks. Nugent wrote his third book, *Kill It and Grill It: A Guide to Preparing and Cooking Wild Game and Fish* (2002), with his wife, Shemane. In addition to some of Nugent's exotic recipes (sweet-and-sticky rabbit, big-game meat cakes, and wild-boar chops, for example), it offers hunting stories and tips for inexperienced hunters and trappers. Nugent dedicated the book to "the great American families who celebrate hands-on environmental awareness in the grand and honorable culture of hunting, fishing, and trapping, thereby guaranteeing balanced biodiversity." In the book Nugent also explains why a diet of meat that one has killed oneself is better for health than meat sold in stores. "Pure, perfect-quality protein is available to everyone who wants to flex their natural instinct to be self-sufficient, independent, more honestly in tune with the source of their sustenance," he told Benfer. "There's plenty of critters to go around, plenty of land to go around. . . . Kill 'em and grill 'em! That's not just a clever title. I really mean it! If you want your body to be healthier, get off the salmonella, e-coli, mad cow, assembly-line toxic hell train! . . . What I do is pure." Articles by Nugent have appeared in many publications, including his magazine, *Ted Nugent Adventure Outdoors.*

Nugent has mentioned that he is considering running for governor of Michigan in 2010. He has served as a national spokesman for the conservative radio talk-show host Rush Limbaugh and such organizations as Mothers Against Drunk Driving, Big Brothers/Big Sisters, and the Drug Abuse Resistance Education law-enforcement program. He hosts the *Ted Nugent Morning Show* on WWBR in Detroit. He hosts the *Ted Nugent Morning Show* on WWBR in Detroit. In 2004 he joined the ranks of reality-TV personalities with *Surviving Nugent,* a VH1 series in which a dozen contestants competed against one another in wilderness activities on Nugent's Texas ranch. "One critic dubbed the series 'plain awful,'" Tony Allen-Mills reported in the London *Sunday Times* (May 16, 2004); the show was canceled after one season. Nevertheless, Nugent was hired to star in another reality show, *Wanted: Ted or Alive.* Scheduled to premiere on

November 5, 2005 on the Outdoor Life Network, the show puts five "city slickers" in the wilderness and presents them with challenges, such as killing and skinning a boar.

Nugent lives and often hunts on his 800-acre ranch in Jackson, Michigan. He opens the ranch each year to a few select hunters and accompanies them in the wild. He has two sons and two daughters. The children from his first marriage, which ended in divorce in 1976 after six years, are Toby and Sasha. The children from his union with his second wife, the former Shemane Deziel, whom he married in 1989, are Starr and Rocco. Shemane, a certified fitness instructor, helps her husband to write, edit, and produce *Ted Nugent's Spirit of the Wild* television series for the Public Broadcasting System and writes for *Ted Nugent Adventure Outdoors* magazine. His younger son's school once named him father of the year. "I always stop working in September," he told an Associated Press reporter (December 26, 1986), "because as a father I want to be more than a visitor." He hunts with his children and stresses to other parents the importance of getting their children involved in wildlife education or other activities that foster parent-child interactions and communication. In an essay on his official Web site, Nugent wrote, "If your kid spends more than 30 minutes a day in front of the TV set, watching programs or playing zombie inducing video games, you are asking for trouble. If you can't remember the last Saturday you took the family to a wild place, early and long, you are asking for trouble. If you can't talk with your kids because they have headphones glued to their ears, you are out of their loop, and may I dare say, a failing parent."

In an interview in 2000 with Classic Rock Revisited (on-line), Nugent said, "The reason I'm able to [accomplish what I have is that] my wife, Shemane, my four wonderful children, and the people I surround myself with, are working hard, playing hard, American families. We put our heart and soul into everything."

—J.K.B.

Suggested Reading: *Chicago Tribune* O p1+ July 29, 1994, with photos; *Field & Stream* p589 July 2003; *Orange County (New Jersey) Register* F p2 May 4, 1994, with photo; *People* p604+ Jan. 10, 1994, with photo; *Salon* (on-line) June 11, 2002, with photo; tnugent.com; Nugent, Ted. *God, Guns, & Rock 'N' Roll*, 2000

Selected Recordings: with the Amboy Dukes— *The Amboy Dukes*, 1967; *Journey to the Center of the Mind*, 1968; *Migration*, 1969; *Marriage on the Rocks/Rock Bottom*, 1970; *Survival of the Fittest: Live*, 1971; *Call of the Wild*, 1973; *Tooth, Fang & Claw*, 1974; as soloist—*Ted Nugent*, 1975; *Free-for-All*, 1976; *Cat Scratch Fever*, 1977; *Double Live Gonzo*, 1978; *Weekend Warriors*, 1978; *State of Shock*, 1979; *Scream Dream*, 1980; *Intensities in 10 Cities*, 1981; *Nugent*, 1982;

Penetrator, 1984; *Little Miss Dangerous*, 1986; *If You Can't Lick 'Em . . . Lick 'Em*, 1988; *Spirit of the Wild*, 1995; *Full Bluntal Nugity*, 2001; *Craveman*, 2002; with Damn Yankees—*Damn Yankees*, 1990; *Don't Tread*, 1992

Selected Books: *Bloodtrails: The Truth about Bowhunting*, 1990; *God, Guns, & Rock 'N' Roll*, 2000; *Kill It and Grill It: A Guide to Preparing and Cooking Wild Game and Fish* (with Shemane Nugent), 2002

Selected Television Shows: *Surviving Nugent*, 2004; *Wanted: Ted or Alive*, 2005

Matthew Cavanaugh/Getty Images

Obama, Barack

(oh-BAHM-uh, ba-RAHK)

Aug. 4, 1961– U.S. senator from Illinois (Democrat)

Address: 713 Hart Senate Office Bldg., Washington, DC 20510

Barack Obama emerged from a hard-fought March 2004 primary campaign to become the Democrats' choice to fill the Illinois U.S. Senate seat being vacated by retiring Republican Peter Fitzgerald. That victory pegged Obama, then an Illinois state senator, as a rising star in the party, to be sure. But few other than political insiders and the residents of his home state knew much about Obama, which is why the decision to make him the keynote speaker on the second day of the 2004 Democratic National Convention, held July 26–29 in Boston, Massachusetts, was met with curiosity. "Tonight is a particular honor for me because—let's face it—my presence on this stage is pretty unlikely," he admitted in the opening of his address, referring not only to his relative obscurity but to his background and upbringing. The product of the marriage between a black man from Kenya and a white woman from Kansas, Obama proceeded to talk about his family, calling theirs "a common dream, born of two continents." "I stand here today, grateful for the diversity of my heritage . . . ," he continued. "I stand here knowing that my story is part of the larger American story, that I owe a debt to all those who came before me, and that, in no other country on earth, is my story even possible."

The defining characteristic of the contentious 2004 presidential campaign had been (and continued to be) the division between so-called "Red" and "Blue" America: red being the pundits' blanket signifier for the allegedly Republican, conservative, and religious denizens of southern and midwestern states, and blue connoting the supposedly Democratic, liberal, secular population of the Northeast and West Coast. Amid this talk of red and blue, Obama delivered a message of shared values that crossed all color lines, racial and electoral. "Now even as we speak, there are those who are preparing to divide us, the spin masters, the negative ad peddlers who embrace the politics of anything goes," he declared to an energized crowd. "Well, I say to them tonight, there is not a liberal America and a conservative America—there is the United States of America. There is not a Black America and a White America and Latin America and Asian America—there's the United States of America. . . . We worship an awesome God in the Blue States, and we don't like federal agents poking around in our libraries in the Red States. We coach Little League in the Blue States and yes, we've got some gay friends in the Red States. There are patriots who opposed the war in Iraq and there are patriots who supported the war in Iraq. . . . In the end, that's what this election is about. Do we participate in a politics of cynicism or do we participate in a politics of hope?"

Obama's speech immediately made him the political equivalent of a rock star. "Here's a guy who hasn't served a day in the [U.S.] Senate, and I just saw an 'Obama '08' [for President] button," David Axelrod, Obama's media consultant, told Shira Boss-Bicak for *Columbia College Today* (January 2005). "It's out of control." The self-described "skinny kid with a funny name" also became fodder for pop culture: possible mispronunciations of his name, for example, was the topic of one of David Letterman's "Top 10" lists on *The Late Show*. Carried on a wave of good will and media attention, Obama went on to trounce his Republican opponent, Alan Keyes, with 70 percent of the vote, to become the fifth African-American to serve in the U.S. Senate, and only the third to do so since Re-

construction. Obama is also the first male African-American Democrat to be elected to the Senate. In the first few months of his freshman term, Obama has responded to the media attention with hard work, humility, and a purposeful avoidance of the spotlight. "I don't think humility is contradictory with ambition," he told Jeff Zeleny for the *Chicago Tribune* (March 20, 2005). "I feel very humble about what I don't know. But I'm plain ambitious in terms of wanting to actually deliver some benefit for the people of Illinois."

Barack H. Obama was born on August 4, 1961 in Honolulu, Hawaii. His father, also named Barack, which means "blessed" in Swahili, was born in the town of Alego along the Kenyan shore of Lake Victoria. A member of the Luo tribe—a nomadic people who had originated in the Sudan along the White Nile and migrated to Kenya—the elder Obama proved to be a gifted student. He won a scholarship to study in Nairobi, Kenya's capital, before being selected for a government sponsorship to go, in 1959 at age 23, to study econometrics at the University of Hawaii. The school's first African student, he established himself among its intellectual and social leaders, serving as the first president of the International Students Association, which he helped organize, and graduating at the head of his class in only three years. In 1959 he took a Russian class, in which he met an 18-year-old, female, Kansas-born anthropology major, Stanley Ann Dunham, known as Ann. The two fell in love soon after they met and married in 1960.

The elder Barack Obama received a scholarship to pursue a Ph.D. at Harvard University, in Cambridge, Massachusetts; the scholarship covered only his own expenses, however, and he left Hawaii alone when his son was two. He and his wife later divorced, and young Barack would see his father only once more, at age 10. When the younger Obama was six, his mother remarried, this time to a man named Lolo, an Indonesian-born fellow student at the University of Hawaii. The family moved to Jakarta, the capital city of Indonesia, where Obama's sister Maya was born. Ann taught English to Indonesian businessmen at the U.S. Embassy, while Lolo ascended from government surveyor to executive with an American oil company. When Ann and Lolo's relationship—which eventually ended in divorce—began to dissolve, Ann sent Obama back to Honolulu to live with her parents, who enrolled him in the prestigious Punahau Academy, a college-preparatory school attended by the islands' elite.

One of a handful of black students in the academy, Obama grew more conscious there of issues regarding race and identity. While his skin color and hair texture set him apart from the vast majority of his schoolmates, his home life made him socially, if not economically, similar to his classmates, as he had been raised by a white mother and grandparents in a middle-class environment. He sought black role models from among the men he played basketball with on the local public courts and his grandfather's poker buddies. "I learned to slip back and forth between my black and white worlds, understanding that each possessed its own language and customs and structures of meaning, convinced that with a bit of translation on my part the two worlds would eventually cohere," Obama wrote in his memoir, *Dreams from My Father*, published in 1995 and in different form in 2004. In the book he recalled sensing that his race affected the way others responded to him: "The feeling that something wasn't quite right stayed with me, a warning that sounded whenever a white girl mentioned in the middle of conversation how much she liked Stevie Wonder; or when a woman in the supermarket asked me if I played basketball; or when the school principal told me I was cool. I did like Stevie Wonder, I did love basketball, and I tried my best to be cool at all times. So why did such comments always set me on edge?" "I engaged in self-destructive behavior," he told Sandy Banks for the *Los Angeles Times* (March 13, 2005). "Sometimes I lashed out at white people and sometimes I lashed out at black people."

Amid his confusion Obama experimented with drugs and alcohol and let his grades slip. He nonetheless managed to graduate from Punahau, in 1979, and later that year he enrolled at Occidental College, in Los Angeles, California. After two years he transferred to Columbia University, in New York City, to study political science with a specialization in international relations. "Mostly, my years at Columbia were an intense period of study," Obama told Boss-Bicak. "When I transferred, I decided to buckle down and get serious. I spent a lot of time in the library. I didn't socialize that much. I was like a monk." One morning during his first semester at Columbia, in November 1982, he received a call from Nairobi, informing him that his father had been killed in a car accident. "At the time of his death, my father remained a myth to me, both more and less than a man," he wrote in his memoir.

In the period leading up to his graduation from Columbia, in 1983, Obama sought work as a community organizer, writing letters of application to progressive grass-roots organizations across the nation. His letters went unanswered, however, so he took a job as a research analyst for a financial consulting company. He was soon promoted to financial writer. "I had my own office, my own secretary, money in the bank," Obama wrote in *Dreams from My Father*. "Sometimes, coming out of an interview with Japanese financiers or German bond traders, I would catch my reflection in the elevator doors—see myself in a suit and tie, a briefcase in my hand—and for a split second I would imagine myself as a captain of industry, barking out orders, closing the deal, before I remembered who it was I had told myself I wanted to be and felt pangs of guilt for my lack of resolve." He quit his job and worked on a campaign to promote recycling in New York City, while sending out a second round of letters in search of community work. He eventu-

ally landed a job with the Developing Communities Project, a nonprofit coalition of secular and church groups on the South Side of Chicago. For three years he canvassed the neighborhood door-to-door and met with local business and political leaders in efforts to save manufacturing jobs, launch job-training programs, and improve city services in South Side housing projects. Along the way he acquired the skills and experiences that formed the foundation for his future political career.

During Obama's time in Chicago, his older sister Auma, the product of his father's first marriage (to a Kenyan woman) and one of seven half-siblings with whom he shares a father, came to the United States for an extended visit—during which she told Obama some of the details of his father's life. In the mid-1980s, when Obama was working as a community organizer and preparing to attend law school, he decided to travel to Kenya to see his father's homeland. "There, he managed to fully embrace a heritage and a family he'd never fully known and come to terms with his father, whom he'd long regarded as an august foreign prince, but now realized was a human being burdened by his own illusions and vulnerabilities," the lawyer and novelist Scott Turow, who is a friend and political supporter of Obama's, wrote for *Salon* (March 30, 2004, on-line).

In 1988 Obama entered Harvard Law School, where he gained national attention in 1990 as the first African-American to be elected president of the *Harvard Law Review*, the nation's most prestigious legal academic journal. "The fact that I've been elected shows a lot of progress. It's encouraging," he told Fox Butterfield for the *New York Times* (February 6, 1990). "But it's important that stories like mine aren't used to say that everything is O.K. for blacks. You have to remember that for every one of me, there are hundreds or thousands of black students with at least equal talent who don't get a chance." He earned his J.D. degree, magna cum laude, in 1991. While in school he had worked as a summer associate in a Chicago firm; Michelle Robinson, an associate attorney who had graduated from Harvard Law the year before, supervised him. The two married in 1992.

That year Obama led a voter-registration drive on Chicago's South Side that added approximately 150,000 new people to the rolls and helped the Democrat Bill Clinton to win Illinois in the 1992 presidential election. He turned down an offer to clerk for Abner Mikva, then chief judge of the U.S. Court of Appeals for the D.C. circuit, to accept a position at the Chicago firm of Miner, Barnhill & Galland. There, he focused on civil rights law, representing victims of housing and employment discrimination and working on behalf of voters' rights. Shortly thereafter, he began lecturing part-time on constitutional law at the University of Chicago Law School. "Teaching keeps you sharp," Obama told William Finnegan for the *New Yorker* (May 31, 2004). "The great thing about teaching constitutional law is that all the tough questions land in your lap: abortion, gay rights, affirmative action. And you need to be able to argue both sides. I have to be able to argue the other side as well as [the Supreme Court justice Antonin] Scalia does. I think that's good for one's politics."

All the while, Obama had ambitions to run for political office. In 1996 the Illinois Democrat Alice Palmer decided to give up her seat in the Illinois state Senate to run for Congress. Seeing his opportunity, Obama sought and secured Palmer's blessing to run for her seat, which represents Chicago's 13th District, covering the South Side, Hyde Park, and the University of Chicago. Palmer lost her bid for Congress and asked Obama to step aside so that she could run for reelection in the Illinois Legislature. Obama refused and, without a Republican opponent, easily won the election. He quickly gained a reputation as an effective legislator, skilled at working with the Republican majority. He sponsored and passed a bill requiring Illinois to share its data on its welfare program with researchers, and he helped to push through the first campaign-finance-reform legislation to pass in his state in a quarter-century.

Despite his fast start, Obama suffered two major political setbacks in 1999. A year-end vote on a controversial gun-control bill was coming to the floor of the state Legislature. The bill, forged in a bipartisan coalition between Chicago's Democratic mayor, Richard M. Daley, and the Republican Illinois governor, George Ryan, faced intense opposition from the Nation Rifle Association, one of the nation's most powerful lobbies, and the state Senate's Republican majority leader. Obama, who supported the measure, was visiting his family in Hawaii. Despite pleas to return, he was absent for the vote. The bill was defeated, and the local press and his Senate colleagues excoriated Obama. Around the same time, Obama made an ill-advised run for the U.S. House of Representatives against fellow Democrat Bobby Rush. Obama thought Rush an ineffectual lawmaker, but the four-term representative and former leader of the local Black Panther Party was very popular. In the 2000 Democratic primary, Rush defeated Obama by a two-to-one margin.

Obama bounced back emphatically in the following years. When Democrats took control of the Illinois state Senate in 2003, he successfully ushered 26 bills through the Legislature, including a large tax credit for the working poor and expanded health-care benefits for uninsured children and adults. Perhaps his greatest achievements were in criminal-justice reform. He co-sponsored landmark legislation to curtail racial profiling by requiring all police departments to record the race of every person stopped for questioning. He also sponsored a bill that made Illinois the first state to require its police to videotape interrogations in capital crime cases. Obama attained support from the police and state prosecutors by arguing that videotaping would cut down not only on coerced confessions but also on claims of police brutality. In addition, the videos are admissible in court, thus facilitating prosecution.

In entering the 2004 race to become the junior U.S. senator from Illinois, Obama joined a crowded field. The Democratic candidates alone included six others, among them Dan Hynes, the state comptroller and an Illinois Democratic Party favorite, and Blair Hull, a popular and wealthy businessman who invested $29 million of his own money in the primary. Obama's campaign was able to raise $6 million, enough to get him some television airtime and spread his populist message to a base beyond Chicago. Running a disciplined campaign, Obama was able to stay solidly in second place—just ahead of Hynes but behind Hull—and he began to gain ground among white liberals. As the primary approached, it was revealed that Hull, whose expenditures had built a 10-point lead in the polls, had abused his ex-wife. His campaign crumbled, and Obama surged ahead, capturing 53 percent of the vote and the Democratic nomination, in March 2004.

In the campaign preceding the general election, Obama faced—at first—another popular and wealthy businessman, the Republican nominee, Jack Ryan. A former partner at the prestigious financial-services company Goldman Sachs, Ryan presented an image as polished as Obama's: he, too, had a Harvard pedigree, having earned both his J.D. and M.B.A. degrees there. Ryan's pro-life, pro-gun, anti-gay, and anti-tax platform placed him firmly on the political right and diametrically opposite Obama, which promised, at the very least, some spirited debate. In June 2004, however, Ryan withdrew from the race, after the public release of testimony from his divorce case, which stated that he had forced his ex-wife to engage in sexual acts she found distasteful. After a scramble that lasted over a month—through Obama's Democratic National Convention address and the resulting surge in his popularity—the Republican Party settled on a new nominee for the Senate race: the former United Nations ambassador and presidential candidate Alan Keyes. A Maryland resident who had once famously labeled Hillary Clinton a carpetbagger, because the former first lady had declared her intention to run for a U.S. Senate seat representing New York shortly after she had moved there, the pugnacious Keyes was now the object of similar derision. Keyes, who is African-American, immediately went on the offensive. After Obama announced that he would not engage Keyes in six debates, as he had agreed to do with Ryan, the GOP candidate said that his opponent was afraid of facing him. The agreement with Ryan "was a special for in-state residents," Obama quipped in response to Keyes's attack, according to Scott Fornek in the *Chicago Sun-Times* (August 10, 2004, on-line).

In the end, Keyes's bluster took little toll on Obama's campaign, which built for Obama so comfortable a lead in the polls that he was able to take time to stump for Democratic candidates in Wisconsin,

Colorado, South Carolina, and other states, thus increasing his national profile and garnering favor among fellow Democrats. He also contributed $150,000 of his $14.3 million war chest to the Democratic Senatorial Campaign Committee, as well as $245,000 to Democrats in closer races in other states. His campaign clearly had no need for the extra money: in November 2004 Obama captured 70 percent of the vote, handily defeating Keyes.

Since he took office, in January 2005, Obama has deliberately kept a low profile, focusing on learning the procedures of the Senate and carefully choosing his public appearances. He has responded to high expectations and questions about his future political ambitions with a "first-things-first" attitude and with jokes about "sharpening pencils and scrubbing floors" for his more senior colleagues. "There's a large gap between the power that I'll wield in Washington and the enormous needs that I see in Illinois, such as healthcare, lack of well-paying jobs and need for educational reform," he said, according to Shira Boss-Bicak. "What I do expect to be able to accomplish is where there are issues that everyone agrees need to be worked on, I'll be able to insinuate myself into the debate and see that voices that otherwise would be left behind are introduced into those negotiations." Obama was appointed to three top Senate panels: the Environment and Public Works Committee, which provides oversight of the Department of Transportation and the Environmental Protection Agency; the Veterans Affairs Committee, which has jurisdiction over compensation, pensions, and medical treatment for veterans of the U.S. military; and the Foreign Relations Committee, which has responsibility for U.S. foreign policy, including treaties with foreign governments and diplomatic nominations.

So far, Obama has insinuated himself into several key debates before the Senate in the 109th Congress and shown an independent streak that sometimes defies party lines. Stating that President George W. Bush should be allowed some latitude in the appointment of his Cabinet, Obama contributed a "yes" vote toward the Senate confirmation of Condoleezza Rice as secretary of state. However, Alberto Gonzales's role as White House counsel in setting guidelines for the treatment of suspected terrorists held in U.S. military prisons—which were seen by many as overly harsh and, therefore, illegal—led Obama to register a minority vote of "no" in the confirmation of Gonzales as U.S. attorney general. Obama voted for a lawsuit-reform measure that changed the rules of class-action lawsuits in such a way as to reduce large-dollar judgments; the measure passed in the Senate. He opposed legislation to reform bankruptcy law to make it more difficult for consumers to avoid debt repayment, and he came out against a proposal to allow oil drilling in the Arctic National Wildlife Reserve, in Alaska. The Senate passed both bills.

Most surprising to Democrats was Obama's support of congressional intervention to grant the right of federal court review to the parents of Terri Schiavo, a Florida woman in a 15-year persistent vegetative state who had become the object of a protracted legal dispute between her parents and her husband over her right to die. Her husband, whose legal right to determine what was best for his wife in the absence of her own ability to do so was backed by the courts, asserted that his wife had declared while still cognizant that she did not want to be kept alive artificially; he wanted her feeding tube removed, which would result in her painless (as her doctors agreed) death from starvation. Terri Schiavo's parents, on the other hand, wanted her kept alive and fought for the right to determine her care. The public and political battle that erupted around the family's legal rights fell, for the most part, along party lines—with conservatives in favor of the parents and liberals behind the husband. "There's nothing unconstitutional about having a little more due process than was due," Obama said in defense of his decision, as reported by Rick Pearson in the Chicago Tribune (March 27, 2005). "Do I like the fact that Congress acts in rash fashion as opposed to deliberative fashion on this or any number of situations but fails to act on crises like the Medicare situation? No. But I have been there for only 3 1/2 months. What troubled me at the margins was not sufficient to raise an objection and shut down the Senate."

In late August 2004 Obama made his first trip overseas as a U.S. senator, accompanying the chairman of the Senate Foreign Relations Committee, Senator Richard Lugar of Indiana, to Russia, Ukraine, and Azerbaijan. On August 30, 2005, as a result of that mission, the U.S. and Ukraine signed an agreement placing safeguards on the storage or transport of potentially lethal pathogens and other such materials, whose existence dated back to Soviet-era biological weapons programs. "This agreement will help Ukraine improve its ability to diagnose, detect and respond to public health risks," Obama told Jeff Zeleny for the Chicago Tribune (August 30, 2005). "When it comes to issues of security against terrorist threats and security against infectious diseases, these problems know no borders." In a later interview with Zeleny for the Chicago Tribune (September 2,3 2005), Obama said, "You realize as a senator there are so many issues out there tugging on people, you've got to make things vivid for them in order to capture people's attention."

In the introduction to his memoir, Dreams from My Father: A Story of Race and Inheritance, Obama wrote, "The opportunity to write it first arose while I was still in law school, after my election as the first black president of the Harvard Law Review. . . . A few publishers called, and I, imagining myself to have something original to say about the current state of race relations, agreed to take off a year after graduation and put my thoughts to paper." The book received middling reviews. "At a young age and without much experience as a writer, Barack Obama has bravely tackled the complexities of his remarkable upbringing," Paul Watkins wrote for the *New York Times Book Review* (August 6, 1995). "But what would he have us learn? That people of mixed backgrounds must choose only one culture in which to make a spiritual home? That it is not possible to be both black and white, Old World and New? If this is indeed true, as Mr. Obama tells it, then the idea of America taking pride in itself as a nation derived of many different races seems strangely mocked." In a more complimentary assessment, a critic wrote for *Kirkus Reviews* (April 15, 1995): "At its best, despite an occasional lack of analysis, this affecting study of self-definition perceptively reminds us that the dilemmas of race generally express themselves in terms of individual human struggles." The book quickly fell out of print. However, following his electrifying Democratic National Convention address and the attendant upswing in public interest in Obama, copies of the memoir began appearing on the Internet auction site eBay, where they sold for several hundred dollars each. The memoir was then reissued in paperback, with an updated preface and a copy of the convention speech in the back; the book was otherwise unchanged. As of mid-May 2005, the 2004 edition of *Dreams from My Father* had spent 36 weeks on the *New York Times* paperback nonfiction best-seller list. In February 2005 Obama signed a $1.9 million, three-book deal with Random House. The first volume to be published is a children's picture book about his childhood, tentatively scheduled to appear in 2006.

Barack Obama's honors include the *Crain's Chicago Business* "40 Under 40" Award, 1993; the Monarch Award for Outstanding Public Service, 1994; the Legal Eagle Award for litigation leading to Illinois's compliance with national "Motor Voter" Legislation, 1995; the Best Freshman Legislator Award from the Independent Voters of Illinois/Independent Precinct Organizations, 1997; the Outstanding Legislator Award from the Campaign for Better Health Care and Illinois Primary Health Care Association, 1998; and in 2005, the NAACP Image Award and the Newsmaker of the Year Award from the National Newspaper Publishers Association. Also in 2005 *Time* magazine named him one of the most influential people of the year. In Kogelo Village, Siaya District, Kenya, a school has been renamed the Senator Barack Obama Secondary School, and locals there have begun referring to a popular beer called Senator as "Senator Obama" (a dubious honor, given that Obama does not drink). He now divides his time between Washington, D.C., and Chicago, where his wife, Michelle, the executive director of community affairs at the University of Chicago, and two young daughters, Malia Ann and Natasha, reside. Michelle told Jonathan Alter for *Newsweek* (December 27, 2004) that her husband "is not a politician first and foremost. He's a community activist exploring the

viability of politics to make change."

—T.J.F.

Suggested Reading: *Atlantic Monthly* p30 Sep. 1, 2004; *Black Issues in Higher Education* p17+ Oct. 7, 2004; *Chicago Tribune* C p1 Mar. 20, 2005, with photos; *Columbia College Today* p14+ Jan. 2005, with photos; *Ebony* p196 Nov. 2004, with photos; *Jet* p4 Aug. 16, 2004, with photos; *New Republic* p21 May 31, 2004; *New Yorker* p32+ May 31, 2004; *Newsweek* p74 Dec. 27, 2004, with photos; *Salon* (on-line) Mar. 30, 2004, with photo; *Time* p74 Nov. 15, 2004, with photos; *Washington Monthly* (on-line) Nov. 2004; *Washington Post* C p1 Feb. 24, 2005

Selected Books: *Dreams from My Father: A Story of Race and Inheritance*, 1995, reissued 2004

Koichi Kamoshida/Getty Images

Ortiz, David

(or-TEEZ)

Nov. 18, 1975– Baseball player

Address: Boston Red Sox, 4 Yawkey Way, Boston, MA, 02215-3496

The Boston Red Sox–New York Yankees rivalry dates back to the First World War. The year after the Red Sox won the 1918 World Series, the team's management decided to trade their star player, Babe Ruth, who would be remembered as one of the greatest baseball players in history, to the Yankees for a cash payment. Between 1919 and 2000 the Yankees won 26 world championships and the Red Sox won none, a disparity in team fortunes so vast that many fans and sportswriters speculated that the Red Sox had been "cursed" for selling Ruth. However, the curse, if indeed there was one, was lifted in 2004—and much of the lifting was done by the Red Sox's large-framed designated hitter David Ortiz. Having completed his second consecutive regular season of career-high numbers as a batsman—including an American League–leading 91 extra-base hits—Ortiz slugged three home runs, averaged .387 at the plate, and drove in 11 runs to help Boston defeat the Yankees in seven games in the 2004 American League Championship Series (ALCS). After being named the most valuable player of the ALCS, he continued his torrid hitting pace against the St. Louis Cardinals, hitting .308 with one home run and four runs batted in (RBIs) to lead the Red Sox to their first World Series title in 86 years. Though he is positioned at the heart of one of the most feared batting lineups in all of baseball, the six-foot four-inch, 230-pound slugger, known widely among his teammates and fans as Big Papi, is valued equally for his good humor and affable, upbeat manner. "Beyond his numbers, David is a huge clubhouse presence," the outfielder Gabe Kapler told Albert Chen for *Sports Illustrated* (August 2, 2004). "He knows exactly the right thing to say or do at the right time to fire us up and get us going again."

David Americo Ortiz was born on November 18, 1975 in Santo Domingo, in the Dominican Republic, where he grew up idolizing emerging Dominican baseball stars, such as the pitchers Ramon and Pedro Martinez. (Years later Ortiz and Pedro Martinez would become teammates on the Boston Red Sox.) A tall and athletic teenager, Ortiz excelled at both basketball and baseball at Estudia Espallat High School. Ten days after his 17th birthday, he was signed to a contract by the Seattle Mariners as an undrafted free agent. His first two seasons in the minor leagues, 1994 and 1995, were spent in Peoria, Arizona, playing as a first baseman for the Mariners' rookie-league affiliate. He showed his potential as a hitter, leading the league in 1994 in doubles. The following season he managed a 19-game hitting streak, in which he totalled 27 hits in 74 appearances at the plate. That same season he was named Peoria's Most Valuable Player by the Seattle Mariners development department. Ortiz's rapid progress earned him a promotion in 1996 to Seattle's Single-A affiliate, the Wisconsin Timber Rattlers, where he batted .322 with 18 home runs and 93 RBIs over 129 games; he led his club in batting average, hits, home runs, and RBIs. *Baseball America* named him the Most Exciting Player, Best Defensive First Baseman, and sixth-best overall prospect in the Midwest League. On August 29, 1996 the Mariners traded him to the Minnesota Twins for the infielder Dave Hollins.

Ortiz started the 1997 season playing Single-A ball in Fort Meyers, Florida, where he launched another hitting streak over 11 games, batting .432 in

that time with five homers and 22 RBIs. His early and continued success enabled him to move quickly through the ranks of the Twins' organization that season; he was promoted to the Double-A New Britain Rock Cats on June 7 and to the Triple-A Salt Lake Buzz (which have since been renamed the Salt Lake Stingers and are now the Triple-A affiliate of the Los Angeles Angels of Anaheim) on August 21. On September 2 he was called up to the Major Leagues and made his debut for the Twins as a pinch hitter against the Chicago Cubs. Though he did not get a hit in his only at-bat in that game, the next day he hit a double off Mark Pisciotta of the Cubs for his first Major League hit. On September 14 he hit his first and only home run of his brief inaugural big-league season, off Julio Santana of the Texas Rangers. Though Ortiz had played in only 15 games for the Twins by the end of the 1997 season, he hit .327 with a homer and six RBIs. He also received the Sherry Robertson Award as the Twins Minor League Player of the Year.

In 1998 Ortiz opened his first full season in the majors, during which he alternated as designated hitter and first baseman, with a seven-game hitting streak—before fracturing the hook hamate bone in his right wrist on May 10, which forced him onto the disabled list for two months. He began his rehabilitation playing 11 games with the Salt Lake Buzz before returning to the Twins' roster on July 11, when he hit a home run in each of his first two games back. For the season, playing in 86 out of 162 games, Ortiz had a .277 average with nine home runs and 46 RBIs—solid numbers, most sportswriters agreed, that would have increased with more playing time.

Ortiz returned to the minor leagues in Salt Lake for most of 1999. The young defensive specialist Doug Mientkiewicz had secured the starting spot at first base for the Twins, and the organization sent Ortiz down to work further on his defensive skills and at-bat discipline. He was recalled to the Twins on September 13. The 10 games he played in the majors that season were marred by difficulties at the plate: he had no hits and struck out 12 times in 20 plate appearances. Returning to the Twins in the 2000 season, however, Ortiz lived up to the potential he had shown in the minor leagues, hitting a solid .282 with 10 home runs (fourth in the club) and 63 RBIs (fifth in the club). The season held a number of highlights for Ortiz, including a game-winning RBI single in the ninth inning against the Tampa Bay Devil Rays, on April 4, and his first career grand slam, off Ramon Martinez of the Boston Red Sox, on September 7. He proved particularly effective against left-handed pitchers throughout the season, battering them for 33 hits in 78 at-bats and a .423 average.

During the 2001 season—after again fracturing his right wrist, an injury that demanded surgery and limited his play to only 89 games—Ortiz posted only a .234 batting average with 18 homers and 48 RBIs. He improved on those numbers during the 2002 season, hitting .272 with 20 home runs and

75 RBIs, but again found himself on the disabled list between April 19 and May 13, when he underwent surgery to remove bone chips from his left knee. Later that season he got his first taste of the play-offs, though after surging past the Oakland Athletics in the American League Division Series (ALDS), the Twins lost to the eventual World Series champions, the Angels, in the ALCS.

Following the 2002 season Ortiz became a free agent and was dropped from the roster by the Twins, who were looking to cut costs. A month after his release, he signed a one-year contract with the Boston Red Sox. Despite Ortiz's having a good reputation as a dependable teammate and positive clubhouse presence, the Red Sox's management was not willing to give him an extended contract because of what was perceived around the league as his erratic hitting. "When he first came up with Minnesota, he had some holes in his swing you could exploit," Ken Macha, the Oakland Athletics' manager, told Albert Chen. "You could throw the ball in hard on his hands, speed it up against him, then change speeds. Since then, he's closed the holes with a lot of hard work."

During his first season with Boston, Ortiz came into his own as a hitter. He posted career-high numbers, including a .288 average, 31 home runs, and 101 RBIs over 128 games. He averaged an RBI every 4.4 at-bats, the second-best ratio in the American League, while his average of a home run every 14.5 at-bats was fifth-best. Throughout the season he tallied 16 game-winning RBIs, one fewer than American League leaders Hideki Matsui and Eric Chávez, who played for the New York Yankees and the Athletics, respectively. At the end of the season he was named Baseball's Outstanding Designated Hitter and finished fifth in the American League Most Valuable Player voting. He also enjoyed another postseason run with the Red Sox, who lost to their longtime rivals, the Yankees, in the ALCS. (The Yankees went on to lose to the Florida Marlins in the 2003 World Series.)

At the end of the 2003 season, the Red Sox signed Ortiz to a two-year, $12.5 million contract. He responded in 2004 by posting his second consecutive season of career-best numbers, including a .301 batting average, 41 home runs, and 139 RBIs. He was named to his first All-Star team and hit a home run in the game (played in Houston), helping the American League to a 9–4 victory over the National League. Throughout the season the Red Sox and the Yankees battled for dominance in the Eastern Division of the American League. By early August the Red Sox had fallen to $9^1/_2$ games behind the first-place Yankees and were struggling to contend for the American League wild-card slot (given to the second-place team in each league with the best win–loss record). After pulling within three games of the Yankees, however, they clinched the wild-card position.

In the first round of the play-offs, the American League Division Series (ALDS), Boston faced the Angels. The Red Sox dominated the best-of-five series, sweeping the Angels in three straight games. In 11 plate appearances, Ortiz averaged .545 and drove in four runs. His only home run of the series came in the 10th inning of Game Three. With the teams tied at six runs apiece, Ortiz came to the plate and smacked the first pitch from the Angels' reliever Jarrod Washburn over Fenway Park's famed left-field wall, the "Green Monster," for a two-run homer. In the next round of the play-offs, the ALCS, the Red Sox faced their most hated rival and chief nemesis, the Yankees.

Throughout the first three games of that series, the Yankees lineup dominated Red Sox pitching, including a 19–8 Game Three drubbing at Fenway Park, in Boston. In the fourth game of the series, down 4–3 in the bottom of the ninth inning and three outs from elimination, the Red Sox rallied to tie the game. In the 12th inning Ortiz hit a walk-off two-run home run to seal a 6–4 Red Sox victory. Ortiz repeated his heroics in Game Five, hitting a single to score his teammate Johnny Damon and give the Sox a 5–4 win, this time in the bottom of the 14th inning. (Game Five set a record for the longest postseason game; it lasted five hours and 49 minutes.) A gritty performance by Curt Schilling, who pitched on a severely injured right ankle, secured a sixth-game victory for the Red Sox to tie the series at three wins apiece. In the seventh and deciding game, Boston scored six runs early on, including a two-run homer from the bat of Ortiz, en route to a 10–3 victory. In all of baseball's prior history, no team had ever lost the first three games of a best-of-seven series and won the series. The Red Sox were headed to their first World Series since 1986.

Most sportswriters and fans agreed that once the Red Sox had defeated the Yankees, a World Series championship seemed all but inevitable. Boston next faced the St. Louis Cardinals, a tough power-hitting club that the Red Sox pitchers were able to control, even as Boston's formidable lineup, anchored by Ortiz's .308 series average, wore down the Cardinals' pitching. St. Louis barely offered resistance as the Boston Red Sox swept them in four games to become World Series champions for the first time since Woodrow Wilson was president of the United States. They also became the first team to win eight consecutive games in a postseason, and only the fourth to win four consecutive games in the World Series without ever trailing. What perhaps made Boston's run even sweeter was that they conquered two teams that had confounded their championship quests so often in the past; between them, the Yankees and Cardinals had eliminated the Red Sox from the play-offs six times: 1946, 1949, 1967, 1978, 1999, and 2003.

Ortiz finished fourth in the 2004 American League Most Valuable Player voting, behind the Angels' Vladimir Guerrero, who finished first, Gary Sheffield of the Yankees, and Ortiz's teammate Manny Ramirez. No designated hitter has ever been named MVP for a season, in part because sportswriters prefer to consider all-around ballplayers, those who also field; Ortiz's high placement in the voting thus speaks to his relative importance to Boston and the dominance of his performance at the plate. Ortiz won the Edgar Martinez Award for the American League's best designated hitter, as voted by the national media, in addition to the Silver Slugger Award, given by the manufacturer of Louisville Slugger bats, as the best offensive player at his position.

Ortiz ended the 2005 season with a .300 batting average, 47 home runs (20 of which either tied the game for the Red Sox or gave them the lead), and 148 RBIs—numbers that again placed him in contention for the American League's Most Valuable Player award. His home-run total was second only to that of Alex Rodriguez (48) in the American League. Ortiz also led the league in RBIs.

Ortiz sees his exceptional run production and clutch hitting as merely part of his job. Talking to Judy Battista for the *New York Times* (October 19, 2004), shortly after belting the game-winning home run in Game Four of the ALCS, Ortiz noted, "That's all I do, hit, I don't go in the field. Whenever I get the chance, I've got to get it done. I'm the guy coming off the bench to hit every at-bat. I've got to do something for this ball club every time I come to the plate."

—C.M.

Suggested Reading: *Boston Herald* p98 Nov. 17, 2004; *New York Times* D p3 Oct. 9, 2004, D p2 Oct. 9, 2004, VIII p1 Oct. 24, 2004; *Sports Illustrated* p149 Aug. 2, 2004, p44 Oct. 25, 2004, p40 Nov. 10, 2004

Vince Bucci/Getty Images

Osborne, Barrie M.

1944(?)– Film producer

Address: Company Films, 2629 Main St., Ste. 167, Santa Monica, CA 90405

"Barrie Osborne would never be cast as a Hollywood producer," Joel Hoekstra observed in a profile of Osborne for the Carleton College *Voice* (Winter 2002). "Neither screechy nor demanding, without ego or swarming lackeys, he fits none of Tinseltown's stereotypes." Yet Osborne is indeed one of Hollywood's most respected producers, having worked on such blockbuster films as *The Matrix*, directed by Andy and Larry Wachowski, and the

Lord of the Rings trilogy, directed by Peter Jackson. Shooting *The Lord of the Rings* was a project of unprecedented proportions: not only was it the first time in history that three films have been made simultaneously, but it involved more than 100 speaking roles; almost two-dozen marquee actors; about 1,500 costumes; a film crew of 2,400; and more than 48,000 pieces of armor, weapons, prosthetics, and special-effects models. Osborne spent five years working on the trilogy, managing a budget of more than $300 million. "My role was keeping the film on track, helping with casting, overseeing the incredibly [complex] logistics, and working with the studio," he told Hoekstra. "I spent all of my time on the set and often I felt more like I was running a studio than running a movie." Osborne has earned a reputation in the industry for being an organizational wizard with an ability to keep budgets balanced. "With seeming ease and dexterity, he navigates the perilous shoals of the business: needy stars, egomaniacal directors, tightfisted studio execs," Hoekstra wrote. "Rumor has it that he once kept a picture on budget by getting a director to pay for an expensive battle scene with his own money."

Osborne, who began his career as an entry-level worker in the creation of television commercials, worked his way up in Hollywood to become an executive producer on such notable films as *Peggy Sue Got Married* (1986) and *Dick Tracy* (1990). In 1999 he served as an executive producer of *The Matrix*, one of the most successful and influential action films of the 1990s. While film budgets have swelled dramatically in recent years, Osborne explained to an interviewer for the New Zealand Press Association, as reprinted in the Wellington, New Zealand, *Dominion* (May 2, 2000), "so has audience expectation. If you're going to compete you have to have state-of-the-art technology." However, while making sure that an epic film has the special effects necessary to wow an audience, Osborne never loses sight of the staples of a good film: capable actors, a skilled director, and a strong story. "What attracts me to pictures is the personality of the people that I am going to be working with, and the screenplay," he told an interviewer for the official Web site for *The Matrix*.

Barrie M. Osborne was born in New York in about 1944. His father was a jeweler. Osborne was raised in New Rochelle, a suburb of New York City, and attended New Rochelle High School, where he excelled in math. After he graduated, in 1962, he attended Carleton College, a liberal-arts school in Northfield, Minnesota, where he majored in sociology. He played hockey and was a bassist in a student band. "I remember Barrie as a lamb, not a lion," Bill Dietrich, who roomed with Osborne at Carleton, told Joel Hoekstra. "He was kind, soft-spoken, noncompetitive, and artistic—sort of a sheep among the howling intellectual wolves that prowled Carleton." After he earned a bachelor's degree, in 1966, Osborne was drafted by the U.S. Army and sent to South Korea, where he worked with the Army Corps of Engineers. He helped to build roads and bridges and rose to the rank of first lieutenant. After his military service ended, in 1970, Osborne returned to the United States and got involved in the movie industry, having been inspired by the film work of some of his friends in college. He landed a job with a studio in New York that made TV commercials, spending his time "getting people coffee and running the Address-o-graph machine," as Osborne recalled to Hoekstra. His boss liked him. "He used to let me do budgets. I knew he would take my budgets and throw them in the waste can, but it was an outstanding chance for me to learn."

Osborne soon gained admission into the prestigious Assistant Directors Training Program (also known as the Producer Training Plan) of the Directors Guild of America, in California. Under the tutelage of such noted filmmakers as Francis Ford Coppola, Sydney Pollack, and Alan Pakula, Osborne learned to handle managerial and administrative tasks, and honed his interpersonal skills, while working on several projects, including *The Godfather: Part II* (1974), *Three Days of the Condor* (1975), and *All the President's Men* (1976). In addition, he served for a time as a unit production manager (someone who is responsible for scheduling and arranging production elements and the disbursement of production funds) for the television detective drama *Kojak*, starring Telly Savalas. After aiding in the production of *Sorcerer* (1977), Floyd Mutrux's rock-and-roll film *American Hot Wax* (1978), and James Bridges's drama *The China Syndrome* (1979), he was chosen to be the fourth and final production manager for Francis Ford Coppola's critically acclaimed *Apocalypse Now* (1979). Osborne worked on the film for about six months; because of his late arrival, he was spared some of the onerous filming conditions suffered by others in the cast and crew.

During the early 1980s Osborne held a variety of jobs connected with several motion pictures. He was a unit production manager on *Cutter's Way* (1981), starring Jeff Bridges; *The Escape Artist* (1982), starring Raul Julia; the box-office hit *The Big Chill* (1983), whose large ensemble cast included Tom Berenger, Kevin Kline, Glenn Close, Jeff Goldblum, and William Hurt; and *Fandango* (1985), starring Kevin Costner. He was also an associate producer for *Cutter's Way*, *The Big Chill*, and *Fandango*. In 1983 he was the production manager for the James Bond film *Octopussy*, starring Roger Moore, and in 1984 he was a line producer for *The Cotton Club*. For *Peggy Sue Got Married* (1986), directed by Coppola, Osborne served for the first time as executive producer. Starring Kathleen Turner as a woman who faints at a high-school reunion and wakes up during her senior year of high school, the film became a hit at the box office and received three Academy Award nominations.

During the mid-1980s Osborne served as vice president for feature production at Walt Disney Pictures. He oversaw the production of more than a dozen films, among them *Ruthless People* (1986), *The Color of Money* (1986), *Tough Guys* (1986), *Tin Men* (1987), *Three Men and a Baby* (1987), *Outrageous Fortune* (1987), *Good Morning Vietnam* (1987), and *Who Framed Roger Rabbit?* (1988). He was the executive producer for the cult horror hit *Child's Play* (1988) and for the lavish *Dick Tracy* (1990). The latter film, an adaptation of the classic detective comic strip that originated in 1931, was directed by Warren Beatty, who also played the title role. *Dick Tracy* grossed about $103 million in the United States and won three of the seven Academy Awards for which it was nominated. In 1992 Osborne was the executive producer for the German drama *Kinderspiele*. In 1994 he produced *China Moon*, a detective drama starring Ed Harris and Madeleine Stowe, and was also the executive producer for *Rapa Nui*, a movie about a civil war between two tribes on Easter Island, which was filmed primarily on location. In 1996 he was an executive producer for *The Fan*, a thriller starring Robert De Niro and Wesley Snipes. The following year he was a producer for the action film *Face/Off*, directed by John Woo and starring John Travolta and Nicolas Cage; the film grossed $112 million in the United States.

Osborne's work with the special-effects–laden *Face/Off* led to an invitation to work as an executive producer for *The Matrix* (1999), directed by Larry Wachowski and Andy Wachowski. In that film, the actor Keanu Reeves played a computer hacker named Neo, who learns that his perceived reality is actually a computer-generated simulation known as the Matrix. After a rebel named Orpheus (portrayed by Laurence Fishburne) reveals to Neo that the real world has been taken over by intelligent machines who keep humans plugged into the Matrix in order to harvest their energy, Neo joins the rebels in their fight against the machines. "The first step was the screenplay, which I really enjoyed," Osborne told Spencer Lamm in an interview for the official Web site for *The Matrix*, explaining what drew him to the project. "I thought it was a very original piece of work and liked the message. . . . Then I met Larry and Andy, and I thought they'd be great guys to work with. When I saw the storyboards, I realized it would be a really cool picture to do, so everything clicked for me from that point."

The Matrix was highly praised for its cutting-edge special effects and its original plot. It grossed over $171 million in the U.S. and won four Academy Awards. In Osborne's interview with Lamm, which took place before the film was released, the producer explained, "My role in *The Matrix* is to try to deliver the film that Larry and Andy have envisioned, within the confines of the budget and schedule that the studios have agreed to. When you come into conflict with this, or the vision has changed, or something is different on the set, I try to convey that to the studio in a convincing manner. This is so we can get their support to be able to continue in the manner that we want to, so we can complete the film in the manner that supports the vision. It all really comes out of the initial design and the script—the story boards as well— what they started out with a long, long time ago." Osborne also explained to Lamm the ways in which the approach to the special effects in *The Matrix* differed from that taken in *Face/Off*. Regarding the latter, and referring to a process in which actors are filmed in front of a green screen and backdrops are added later, he said, "[The filmmakers] originally wanted to do a lot of green screen stuff—the fight on the deck of the boat, the airplane going down the runway—and I felt that it would be supporting the story, the realism, if that was done practically. To actually make it a process on a real boat. But on [*The Matrix*] I found we argued a different point. We had to argue and convince Larry and Andy that they would actually accomplish [a rooftop chase scene] better on stage than they could have on real roof tops. Originally they had wanted to [do] the chase on real roof tops because the story is saying it is reality. But in actuality there is something altered—different—[and] it really supported doing some of this work on stage."

After the completion of *The Matrix*, Osborne signed on as a producer for Peter Jackson's epic adaptation of J.R.R. Tolkien's fantasy saga, *The Lord of the Rings*. "I was working on *The Matrix* when I got a call from a friend of mine to say that they were doing *The Lord of the Rings* in New Zealand," Osborne told an interviewer for the Film New Zealand Web site. "I was excited about that idea because I had worked in New Zealand before and loved it down there." Osborne met with Jackson, who wanted to shoot some of the scenes in majestic, remote locations; Osborne agreed, although the extra effort and expense would be significant. "We decided to film everywhere from volcanic islands like White Island, to the wonderful Fjords of the South Island to Lake Wakatipu, and I agreed with [Jackson] that the investment of logistics would pay off." Osborne was drawn to the movie right from the start: "When you're going to make a movie that you know will be a tough haul, you think, 'Is this someone I'm going to enjoy working alongside?'" Osborne explained to Marshall Fine for the Westchester County *Journal News* (January 27, 2004). "But I was reassured by Peter. He and I had a similar take on the material. He was already building Hobbitton. And I saw the elven armor and was blown away by the amount of detail. I knew it would be special."

At Jackson's urging, Osborne and the film's other producers agreed that the three *Lord of the Rings* films—*The Fellowship of the Ring* (2001); *The Two Towers* (2002); and *The Return of the King* (2003)— should be filmed at the same time. "A benefit of doing three at once is that you have a continuity of cast," Osborne told an interviewer for About.com. "The casts are going to look the same throughout all three movies. They go on this journey that took 15 months to film which is not too far different from the journey they go on in the course of the movie. There's a shorthand in the camaraderie that develops by working together for such a long period of time and they were such a great group of people that they truly became a fellowship. It took a lot of stamina to shoot for such a long time. [That] would be the only drawback but we built in some breaks in our production schedule so people would get a rest. However, there were times when we had five hours of rushes [also known as dailies, or rough prints of the day's footage] a night, which after a long day's work is a lot to watch." Osborne suggested that the films be released at six-month intervals, but he was voted down in favor of a yearly release schedule. "I'm glad I lost that argument," he was quoted as saying in an interview for TheOneRing.net. "We would have been dead."

Making three films at once was a large gamble for the studio, New Line Cinema, and although the cast and crew were enthusiastic, various gnawing doubts did not dissipate until Jackson screened 20 minutes of the still-incomplete first movie at the Cannes Film Festival in 2001. "There was such a great buzz after that—I felt pretty encouraged that we had something of great appeal," Osborne told Marshall Fine. "You can judge a story and whether you cast it right, whether it feels as though the elements come together—but you never really know. This was so widely appreciated by the public and the critics that it exceeded all expectations."

The Fellowship of the Ring opened to excellent reviews and immense public interest; it grossed $313 million domestically and $870 million worldwide, earning a near-record 13 Academy Award nominations in the process (of which it won four: for best cinematography, best visual effects, best makeup, and best original score). Osborne received a British Academy of Film and Television Arts (BAFTA) Award for best film and an AFI Movie of the Year Award (which he shared with Jackson as well as two other producers on the film, Frances Walsh and Tim Sanders). The following two *Ring* films were released on schedule and both drew large audiences and elicited high praise; in all, the trilogy has grossed more than $3 billion worldwide. "Peter never rested on the fact that the first one was a success," Osborne told Fine. "Peter pushed to get the most out of each film. The second film was a struggle, trying to figure out the place to cut from one story to the other without destroying the momentum. On the last film, there was so much rich material that we had to home in on what the central story was." *The Return of the King* won 11 Oscars (in every category for which it was nominated), tying the all-time record, held by both *Ben-Hur* (1959) and *Titanic* (1997). In addition, its best-picture award was the first in that category given to a fantasy film. It was also Osborne's first Academy Award; he shared the honor with Jackson and Frances Walsh.

Because of the great length of time and the commitment involved in shooting the trilogy, the cast and filmmakers became very close; in fact, after the cast all got tattoos of the elven number nine (in reference to the nine members of the fellowship), they made arrangements to have Jackson, Osborne, and Mark Ordesky (another producer who was very involved with the film) tattooed with the number 10, as a sign of their appreciation and affection. In his interview with Marshall Fine, Osborne described the deep sense of accomplishment that everyone shared after the filming was complete: "I remember early on, there was an Australian gaffer on the film, whose comment was, 'This project will separate the men from the boys—and I'm finishing as a man.' And that's what we all felt we'd done. It was this incredible challenge, the kind you never get to do—and will probably never be done again."

For Osborne's next project, he will team up with Shekhar Kapur, an Indian director whose credits include *Elizabeth* (1998), to shoot a major film in India. Heralded as a synthesis of Hollywood and Bollywood (a nickname for the Indian film industry), the movie, tentatively titled "Water," will meld romance, science fiction, politics, and Bollywood-style song and dance. The press has dubbed it "India's answer to China's *Crouching Tiger Hidden Dragon*," the 2000 martial-arts epic that became a huge success worldwide. "Water," which is about a scarcity of that resource and is set 15 to 20 years in the future, will have a budget of about $20 million (high for Bollywood films, which even at their most expensive seldom cost more than $10 million to produce), and will be made in both Hindi and English. "I'm so happy, I'm so proud, that I could convince Barrie to do this," Kapur remarked at a press conference, as quoted by an Associated Press (May 21, 2004) reporter. "We're hoping by the fusion of some of the best technicians and producers from India and Hollywood, that each can learn from the other, and therefore become much more international."

Osborne has also signed on to produce "Beggars Inc.," a movie written by Bob and Dick Kalich, about a Harvard Business School graduate who, unable to support himself, develops a scheme with panhandlers in his neighborhood to increase their daily earnings.

Osborne lives in Wellington, New Zealand, with his partner, Carol Kim, who has worked in production on many films, including the *Lord of the Rings* trilogy; the couple share a mansion, overlooking Wellington Harbour, that Osborne purchased to serve as his home base for the filming of the trilogy. He has a daughter, Danielle.

Osborne is liked and admired among those with whom he has worked. Tim Nielson, a sound editor for *The Lord of the Rings*, told Colin Covert, "Barrie has an incredible résumé, and there's no pretense about him, none of the bad Hollywood attitude that you encounter so often. He's just a regular guy who'll sit down and chat with you about anything." Regarding advice for aspiring producers, Osborne told Hoekstra: "You have to have a lot of perseverance. It's extremely hard to get into the business and you'll get a lot of rejection. But if you really want to get into it and you're committed and interested and love the business, you can succeed. I started from the very bottom and had only two things to offer people—dependability and enthusiasm."

—G.O.

Suggested Reading: (Carleton College) *Voice* Winter 2002; Film New Zealand Web site; (Minneapolis–St. Paul) *Star Tribune* (on-line) Dec. 15, 2002; *The Matrix* Web site; (Wellington, New Zealand) *Dominion* p23 May 2, 2000; (Westchester County, New York) *Journal News* E p1 Jan. 27, 2004

Selected Films: *Cutter's Way*, 1981; *The Big Chill*, 1983; *The Cotton Club*, 1984; *Fandango*, 1985; *Peggy Sue Got Married*, 1986; *Child's Play*, 1988; *Dick Tracy*, 1990; *China Moon*, 1994; *Rapa Nui*, 1994; *The Fan*, 1996; *Face/Off*, 1997; *The Matrix*, 1999; *The Lord of the Rings: The Fellowship of the Ring*, 2001; *The Lord of the Rings: The Two Towers*, 2002; *The Lord of the Rings: The Return of the King*, 2003

Paltrow, Gwyneth

Sep. 28, 1972– Actress

Address: c/o Stephen Huvane, PMK/HBH, 650 Fifth Ave., 33d Fl., New York, NY 10019

During the early years of her film career, Gwyneth Paltrow seemed to be better known for her connections than for her body of work. Her parents, the actress Blythe Danner and the producer Bruce Pal-

Junko Kimura/Getty Images

Gwyneth Paltrow

trow, were well-established in the film industry, and her high-profile relationships with the actors Brad Pitt and Ben Affleck had received more press than any of her performances. Though she received many good notices for her early work, the general impression given in the media was that she had little more to offer than an impeccable sense of style and a pretty face. Then came her highly regarded turn as Jane Austen's famous heroine in *Emma* (1996), a performance that led critics and filmgoers alike to reassess their initial impressions of Paltrow. In 1998 she played the lover of the young William Shakespeare in *Shakespeare in Love*, the role that won her an Academy Award and cemented her place as one of the most celebrated actresses of her generation. She has since taken on a broad range of parts, in such films as *Duets* (2000), which showcased her singing ability, and *The Royal Tenenbaums* (2001), in which she displayed a flair for dark comedy. Her recent films include *Sylvia* (2003), *Sky Captain and the World of Tomorrow* (2004), and *Proof* (2005).

Gwyneth Kate Paltrow was born on September 28, 1972 in Los Angeles, California. Her mother was first noted for her Tony Award–winning performance in *Butterflies Are Free* (1969) and has since been seen in numerous movie and television roles. Her father was a television producer whose credits included the series *The White Shadow* (1978-81) and *St. Elsewhere* (1982-88). During her grammar-school years, Paltrow and her family, which included her younger brother, Jake, lived in Santa Monica, California. When she was 11 they moved to the Upper East Side of Manhattan, in New York City. She enrolled at the Spence School, a prestigious, private school for girls. The students

there "were so advanced," Paltrow recalled to Charles Gandee for *Vogue* (August 1996). "You cannot believe the classes—law and physics in the seventh grade! I was at sea. I mean, I would have had an easier time trying to translate Hebrew. I'm not kidding. It was hard." Paltrow spent many of her summers during her childhood watching her mother rehearse and act in plays at the Williamstown Theater Festival, in Williamstown, Massachusetts. At the age of five, Paltrow was given a walk-on part on stage, and eventually she worked her way up to small speaking roles. In an effort to protect her from future rejection and to widen her interests, her parents tried to discourage her from pursuing her interest in performing, but Paltrow was not easily dissuaded. "Maybe it has something to do with my mother, but as far back as I can remember, acting is the only thing I ever wanted to do," she told Gandee.

After an ugly-duckling stage in her early teens, Paltrow blossomed into a beauty whose penchant for socializing at parties and clubs drove her parents to distraction. "I used to be so bad, I had a curfew of noon," she remarked to Georgia Dullea for the *New York Times* (August 1, 1994). She added that she would often sneak out at night, leaving notes that were variations on, "Dear Mom and Dad, I didn't run away. I haven't been kidnaped. I'm out at the clubs. You can punish me in the morning." Because of her erratic grades, she had trouble getting into a top college; she was finally accepted at the University of California at Santa Barbara after the actor Michael Douglas, an alumnus, spoke to an admissions officer on her behalf. Once in college, she had trouble concentrating on her classes, because, as she admitted to Gandee, she was often busy socializing and auditioning for parts in Los Angeles. (She landed a small role in the 1991 film *Shout.*)

The summer after her freshman year, Paltrow was cast in a revival of the William Inge play *Picnic* at the Williamstown festival. She played Millie Owens, a 16-year-old tomboy, acting opposite her mother, who portrayed Rosemary Sydney, an unmarried older woman. "After the opening, my father came to the dressing room and said, 'I don't think you should go back to college,'" Paltrow told Jeff Giles for *Newsweek* (July 29, 1996). "It was amazing. I think it was the first time he thought, 'She has the goods.'" She followed his advice, renting an apartment in Los Angeles after the theater season was over. Because her parents insisted that she support herself, Paltrow took a job as a hostess at a local restaurant.

In the same year, 1991, Paltrow was cast by the director Steven Spielberg, a family friend, as the young Wendy in *Hook* (a "grownup" sequel to *Peter Pan*). Her first major role was in the 1992 television miniseries *Cruel Doubt*. After landing the part of the daughter in that drama about murder in a family, she went to Europe on a vacation, then learned upon returning that Blythe Danner had been tapped for the part of the mother. Paltrow admitted to Georgia Dullea that she had been upset that people would think she had earned the role through nepotism: "This was my first job, and I wanted to make my mark." Both women got good reviews for their performances.

In 1993 Paltrow appeared as a doomed college student in the film *Malice*, a thriller that starred Alec Baldwin and Nicole Kidman. She had a larger supporting role in the drama *Flesh and Bone* (1993), playing Ginnie, a young thief who has a relationship with a mass murderer (James Caan). Her performance generated some excellent reviews, among them one by Janet Maslin of the *New York Times* (November 5, 1993), who wrote, "Ginnie is played with startling aplomb by the scene-stealing Gwyneth Paltrow, who is Blythe Danner's daughter and has her mother's way of making a camera fall in love with her." She also appeared that year in the made-for-television movie *Deadly Relations*, a violent story about a father (Robert Urich) who kills his two sons-in-law (Paltrow portrayed one of his daughters). In the summer of 1994, she was cast as Nina, an aspiring actress, in a Williamstown production of *The Sea Gull*, acting opposite her mother, who played Arkadina, an older, more famous performer. (Twenty years earlier, as a two-year-old, Paltrow had watched Danner play Nina.)

For the next several years, Paltrow appeared in a series of small character roles in movies. She portrayed a Bohemian actress in *Mrs. Parker and the Vicious Circle* (1994), a movie about the writer Dorothy Parker and her salon of the 1920s and 1930s, which met regularly at the Algonquin Hotel in New York City. In *Moonlight and Valentino* (1995), she played the neurotic, chain-smoking sister of a college professor (Elizabeth Perkins) coping with the death of her husband. Her portrayal of Patsy, Thomas Jefferson's possessive daughter, in *Jefferson in Paris* (1995) won praise from several critics, including Todd McCarthy, who wrote in *Variety* (March 27–April 2, 1995), "Paltrow is captivating as one of the story's most intriguing figures." For the horror-thriller *Seven* (1995), she was cast as the wife of a police detective (Brad Pitt), and in *Hard Eight* (1996), a film about the casino world in Reno, Nevada, she played a cocktail waitress. Other than *Seven*, none of the aforementioned films were particularly successful at the box office.

Paltrow has said that for several years she deliberately avoided opportunities for leading film roles. "I was in no rush to be the star of a movie, because there is so much responsibility placed on your shoulders," she remarked to Margy Rochlin for the *New York Times* (July 28, 1996). "I wanted to learn, to do smaller parts, really diverse things, things that are the opposite from the last role you've done." She changed her mind when the screenwriter and director Doug McGrath asked her to audition for the title character in *Emma*, a role she very much wanted to play. McGrath had seen her in *Flesh and Bone* and "thought she was mesmerizing," as he recalled to Charles Gandee. "She had a perfect Texas accent—a perfect regional Tex-

as accent. And I grew up in Texas, so I know. And that made me think, if she can do that, she can do an English accent. Plus, she was charming, intoxicatingly pretty, and intelligent—all of which the character needs." At Paltrow's reading, he was similarly impressed: "The minute Gwyneth started speaking, I felt like I was looking at the perfect Emma."

McGrath was sold on Paltrow, but executives at Miramax Studios equivocated about making the picture, relenting only when she agreed to star first in *The Pallbearer* (1996). In that film she played a woman who meets an old friend (David Schwimmer) at a funeral and discovers that he has been infatuated with her for years. *The Pallbearer* was a financial and critical failure, although a few reviewers singled out Paltrow for praise. By that time, filming on *Emma* was underway, and when it was released, most critics were charmed by her interpretation of Austen's headstrong character. One admirer, Michael Wilmington of the *Chicago Tribune* (August 9, 1996), averred, "Gwyneth Paltrow, with a smile as bemusedly fond as a contented cat's, eyes that sparkle like warm promises, and a head bobbing like a regal swan's, makes us love Emma all over again." Janet Maslin of the *New York Times* (August 29, 1996) wrote, "Gwyneth Paltrow makes a resplendent Emma, gliding through the film with an elegance and patrician wit that brings the young Katharine Hepburn to mind."

Following her critically praised performance in *Emma*, Paltrow suddenly found herself an in-demand leading actress in Hollywood. She used her newfound status to take on several diverse roles: as an Englishwoman whose life will follow one of two courses—determined by whether or not she catches a train—in *Sliding Doors* (1998); as the aloof Estella in a modern-day version of the classic Charles Dickens novel *Great Expectations* (1998); and as the cheating wife of a millionaire in *A Perfect Murder* (1998), the remake of Alfred Hitchcock's *Dial M for Murder*. Though none of these films proved to be a box-office hit, Paltrow received enough critical acclaim from those performances (as well as her turn as Emma) to enable her to land the coveted role of Viola in *Shakespeare in Love* (1998).

In the film the young playwright William Shakespeare's life is full of troubles. He suffers from romantic problems, constant debt, and writer's block—all while trying to complete his latest play, *Romeo and Ethel the Pirate's Daughter*. Meanwhile, Viola, a wealthy young woman and a great admirer of Shakespeare's work, dreams of becoming an actress. As women were not allowed on stage in the 16th century, Viola disguises herself as a young man and wins the part of Romeo. Before long she and Shakespeare begin a romance, one that is forbidden, as she is about to be married to the Lord Wessex. Critics heaped praise on the film—which went on to win the Oscar for best picture at the Academy Awards ceremony in early 1999—and on Paltrow, whose performance also won an Oscar. In a review for *Entertainment Weekly* (December 11, 1998), Owen Gleiberman proclaimed: "Best of all is Gwyneth Paltrow, who, at long last, has a movie to star in that's as radiant as she is. Her Viola is truly Shakespeare's match: ardent in a contemplative, almost sacramental way, her emotions so luminous they seem to be shining right through her skin."

Paltrow's next notable part was in *Duets* (2000), a comic/dramatic look at the karaoke bar scene. In it, she portrayed a young woman who pursues her long-lost father across the country, eventually becoming his singing partner. The film was directed by Paltrow's father, Bruce, who at the time of filming was recovering from a bout with throat cancer. Bruce Paltrow completed the film before succumbing to complications from the disease, in October 2002. "I was trying so hard to be strong for him [during the filming], but it was very difficult," Gwyneth Paltrow said during an interview with Eric Harrison published in the *Chicago Tribune* (September 16, 2000). "He was very, very sick and not himself. My biggest challenge was to just be professional and grown up and not be a scared daughter and just try to make his life as easy as possible."

In 2001 Paltrow received rave reviews for her portrayal of Margot, one of three siblings who are former child prodigies, in Wes Anderson's comedy *The Royal Tenenbaums*. Margot Tenenbaum became a playwright in the ninth grade; her brother Chas (played by Ben Stiller) was a scientist and business whiz as early as the sixth grade; and their brother, Richie (played by Luke Wilson), earned his reputation as a tennis pro in the third grade. Since their parents' divorce, the children have all seen their fortunes decline; their lives begin to improve only when, as adults, they move back into their parents' townhouse in Manhattan, following their father's announcement that he has terminal cancer. Paltrow's performance was singled out by many reviewers, including Anthony Lane, who wrote in the *New Yorker* (December 17, 2001): "Gwyneth Paltrow gives Margot the faraway haze of a spent force; with her eyes so rich in mascara that she must have been taking tips from a panda, and with the sad, swish perfection of her Fendi mink, she seems smaller and more defenseless than her earlier self, whom we glimpse in a flurry of flashbacks. Paltrow, like others in the cast, bites hard into this role, as if starved by most of the work she's been getting lately."

Paltrow has also had major or starring roles in such films as *Hush* (1998), *The Talented Mr. Ripley* (1999), *Bounce* (2000), *The Anniversary Party* (2001), *Shallow Hal* (2001), *Possession* (2002), and *View from the Top* (2003). In 2003 she starred in *Sylvia* as the poet and novelist Sylvia Plath, who killed herself at the age of 30, in 1963. Plath was married to the British poet Ted Hughes, whom many feminist scholars have blamed for her death. Instead of providing an overview of her life (which included bouts of depression and previous suicide attempts), the film looks at the intensely passionate and difficult relationship between Plath and Hughes. In a review for the *Chicago Sun-Times* (October 24, 2003), Roger Ebert wrote of Paltrow's performance: "Paltrow's great feat is to underplay her character's death wish. There was madness in Sylvia Plath, but of a sad, interior sort, and one of the film's accomplishments is to show in a subtle way how it was so difficult for Hughes to live with her." In the following year she played an intrepid journalist, opposite Jude Law as an adventurous newspaper reporter, in *Sky Captain and the World of Tomorrow*. Paltrow appears in the film adaptation of David Auburn's *Proof* (2005), in which she played the daughter of a brilliant mathematician who suffered from dementia before his death; the daughter, also a mathematician, fears that she herself is going mad. She will have a role in *Have You Heard?*, scheduled for a 2006 premiere.

After a series of high-profile romances, including those with her fellow actors Brad Pitt and Ben Affleck, Gwyneth Paltrow married Chris Martin of the rock band Coldplay in December 2003. Their daughter, Apple Blythe Alison Martin, was born on May 14, 2004.

—C.M.

Suggested Reading: *Chicago Sun-Times* (on-line) Oct. 24, 2003; *Chicago Tribune* p27 Sep. 16, 2000; *Biography* p57+ Oct. 2000, with photos; *Entertainment Weekly* p43 Dec. 11, 1998, p35 Mar. 1, 1999, p43 Mar. 17, 2000, p42 Nov. 28, 2003; *Internet Movie Database* (on-line); *Interview* p118+ Sep. 1995, with photos; *Los Angeles Times* Calendar p8+ July 21, 1996, with photos; *New York Times* II p11+ July 28, 1996, with photos, II p1 Oct. 19, 2003; *New Yorker* p97 Dec. 17, 2001; *Newsweek* p66+ July 29, 1996, with photos, p49 Aug. 20, 2001; *Vanity Fair* p98+ Feb. 2004, with photos; *Vogue* p206+ Aug. 1996, with photos

Selected Films: *Hook*, 1991; *Shout*, 1991; *Flesh and Bone*, 1993; *Malice*, 1993; *Mrs. Parker and the Vicious Circle*, 1994; *Moonlight and Valentino*, 1995; *Seven*, 1995; *Jefferson in Paris*, 1995; *Emma*, 1996; *Hard Eight*, 1996; *The Pallbearer*, 1996; *Sliding Doors*, 1998; *Great Expectations*, 1998; *A Perfect Murder*, 1998; *Shakespeare in Love*, 1998; *Duets*, 2000; *The Royal Tenenbaums*, 2001; *Sylvia*, 2003; *Sky Captain and the World of Tomorrow*, 2004; *Proof*, 2005

Courtesy of the *Wine Advocate*

Parker, Robert M.

June 23, 1947– Wine expert; author

Address: Wine Advocate, *P.O. Box 311, Monkton, MD 21111*

The wine expert Robert M. Parker Jr. is often referred to as one of the most powerful critics in the world. The assessments published in his bimonthly magazine, the *Wine Advocate*, and in his books not only make or break vintages but also influence the way vintners produce wine. In a controversial innovation, Parker revolutionized wine criticism by introducing a 100-point rating scale that is used by vineyards, retailers, and importers to tout their wares. Buyers frequently avoid any wine Parker has scored below 85, and vineyards reexamine their winemaking processes after receiving a low score. He is trusted not only for his palate but also his integrity: to ensure, and demonstrate, its freedom from pressures from the wine industry, the *Wine Advocate* does not accept any advertising. With his operations completely funded by subscriptions, Parker need not fear the loss of revenue from a disgruntled advertiser and can be totally honest in his reviews, which often feature higher or lower rankings than those of his competitors. "Parker has a perfect nose, a perfect palate and a perfect memory," the owner of Beaune, a small Burgundy vineyard, told John Henley for the *London Observer*, as quoted in the *Cleveland Plain Dealer* (July 14, 1999). "No matter how much you dislike him, you have to hand it to him—he can taste 80 different wines from 8 a.m. to 6 p.m., then go to a blind tasting of 30 wines and be able to state the vineyard and the vintage of 22 of them correctly. He's a computer."

Robert M. Parker Jr. was born on June 23, 1947 in Baltimore, Maryland. His father was a businessman who owned a small oil company; his mother was a homemaker. The first wine Parker remembers drinking was Cold Duck sparkling wine, at his then-girlfriend Patricia's 18th-birthday party. "I got so drunk her father had to drive me home," he told David Shaw for the *Los Angeles Times* (February 23, 1999). In 1967 he took a six-week trip to Europe to visit Patricia, who was studying at the University of Strasbourg, in France. At a restaurant where the couple went for dinner shortly after his arrival, Parker wanted to order a Coca-Cola, but he considered the price to be too high. Instead, he ordered a glass of table wine, encountering the beverage for only the second time in his life. "I adored the wine," he told Andrew Jefford for *Waitrose Food Illustrated* (April 2004, on-line). "For the first time in my life I had an alcoholic beverage that did not bloat me (as did beer), or blind me (as did liquor). Moreover, it deliciously complemented the food." Parker drank wine every night for the rest of his vacation as he and Patricia traveled through France and Germany.

After Parker returned to the United States, he started a wine-tasting group at the University of Maryland, in College Park, where he later received a B.A. in history, with a minor in art history. In 1969 he and Patricia married, and every summer afterward the couple vacationed in Europe, planning their itineraries around the great winegrowing regions. In 1973 Parker graduated from the University of Maryland Law School. "In law school they called me the phantom," Parker told Betsy Pisik for the *Washington Times* (October 1, 1990). "I would forget a [legal] case before I could get it back to my desk. But wine . . . . When I smell a wine I can remember when I drank it and with whom. Nothing in my life is as fascinating." Upon graduating from law school, Parker was hired as an attorney by the Farm Credit Banks of Baltimore. In time the bank promoted him to senior attorney and, by the early 1980s, to assistant general counsel.

Meanwhile, Parker had become increasingly enthralled by wine, and in his leisure time he read as much as he could on the subject, while tasting frequently. He had difficulty finding reliable information on wine quality and saw the need for a consumer's magazine for oenophiles (also spelled "enophiles"), or wine lovers. "There was a lot of grotesquely flawed wine being made, but no one was really saying that," he told Shaw. When Parker told his friends and family that he was thinking of launching such a publication, they tried to dissuade him, because they felt it would be unprofitable. Parker was determined, however, and in 1978 he borrowed $2,000 from his mother to begin the *Baltimore-Washington Wine Advocate*, which was later renamed the *Wine Advocate*. In late summer of that year, he sent the first issue free to thousands of wine drinkers whose names appeared on mailing lists that he had purchased from major wine retailers. Parker attracted fewer than 600 initial subscribers, just enough to cover his publishing expenses.

Beyond the demands of his daytime job, Parker spent between 20 to 30 hours a week tasting wine and writing about it. Having decided against having advertising and because he bought all the wines he wrote about with his own money, he subsidized his income from subscriptions and by organizing paid wine tastings. In 1981 he began writing a wine column for the *Washington Post*, earning $150 per article. The number of *Wine Advocate* subscribers rose quickly in 1983, after Parker wrote an enthusiastic piece about the 1982 vintage of Bordeaux wines before any other critics assessed them. As quoted by Frank J. Prial in the *New York Times* (December 6, 1989), Parker wrote in an issue of the *Wine Advocate* that 1982 "is a vintage of legendary proportions for all levels of the Bordeaux hierarchy. In short it is a vintage which has produced the most perfect wines in the post–World War II era." Parker's positive reviews led to a rush to purchase the wines before they were even bottled. Some wine critics questioned his conclusions, as they believed the vintage did not have enough acid and tannin to allow it to improve with age. Nevertheless, increasing numbers of laypeople and others apparently trusted his judgment. By March 1984 the *Wine Advocate* was generating sufficient income from subscriptions to enable Parker to resign from Farm Credit Banks to devote himself entirely to writing about wine. Three years later the *Wine Advocate* had approximately 20,000 subscribers. "There's a pretty even split between men and women," Parker said to William Rice for the *Chicago Tribune* (May 20, 1998), regarding his subscription base, which had reached 35,000 at the time of the interview. "A good many are retired military personnel and they tend to live on the East or West Coast, though circulation is climbing in the South. They seem to share a sense of adventure and love of travel as well as disposable income." Currently, a 90-day subscription costs $29; for a year, the price is $99.

Although there were several wine magazines on the market in the 1980s, Parker's was unique in several ways. Eschewing the complex, esoteric, flowery terms wine journals commonly use to describe wines, Parker wrote his critiques in succinct and concrete prose. In the *Chicago Tribune* (October 16, 1986), William Rice described Parker's approach as "stalwart and direct, John Wayne with a corkscrew in his hand instead of a six-gun." Parker also disagreed with the many critics who believed a wine had to taste bad at first in order for it to age gracefully into a fine wine. "A great wine will get better later, sure," he told Shaw, "but it should taste good even when it's young." The *Wine Advocate* became best known for Parker's 100-point rating scale, easily recognizable to any American who has ever taken a test in which 100 is a perfect score and anything below 60 is a failing grade. In Parker's system a wine that rates above 85 is very good

or excellent; any wine rated above 90 is outstanding. As of October 2004 he had given perfect scores to only 127 vintages (wines produced in particular years), or a 10th of 1 percent of the wines he has tasted. Before Parker introduced his system, wine critics had often used 20-point scales in which every wine started with a score of 20 and lost points for each flaw. On his Web site, Parker wrote that 20-point systems "do not provide enough flexibility and often result in compressed and inflated wine ratings. . . . I would prefer to underestimate the wine's quality than to overestimate it." In Parker's system each wine begins with a score of 50 and is given more points for positive attributes such as color, aroma, flavor, finish (a measure of the flavors and sensation that linger on the tongue after the wine is swallowed), and potential for improvement with age.

Parker's scoring system has stirred controversy since its inception. Although several of his competitors have since adapted the 100-point scale, many others have criticized it for taking the romance out of wine and applying a number to a subjective taste. In response, Parker declared on his Web site, "Wine is no different from any consumer product. There are specific standards of quality that full-time wine professionals recognize, and there are benchmark wines against which others can be judged." He also stated, "The numerical ratings are utilized only to enhance and complement the thorough tasting notes, which are my primary means of communicating my judgments to you." That caveat notwithstanding, his critics argue that consumers and retailers will make purchasing decisions based on one- or two-point differences in scores that actually indicate only tiny differences in quality. Some have also faulted Parker for not creating a separate score for a wine's aging potential. Parker has said he is occasionally mistaken about a wine's potential, but over time his scores for individual wines rarely vary by more than three points. In an acknowledgement of the merits of both positions, the food and wine writer David Rosengarten wrote for *Newsday* (July 31, 1991), "To give a wine a 95 is to create the appearance of scientific objectivity, where none can possibly exist. That understood, however, a consumer can use the ratings of a critic to his or her advantage if the consumer knows something about the palate that's doing the rating."

Most of Parker's tasting is done at his Maryland home, where he samples upwards of 100 wines a day and as many as 10,000 to 15,000 bottles every year. (He does not swallow what he is sampling for professional purposes.) "There may be other people who can taste as well as I can," he told Shaw, "and there sure are people who write better than I do, but no one works as hard as I do." He tastes some wines blind—that is, without seeing the vintner's name—and has been criticized for not doing the same for all wines. Parker has countered that complaint by noting that if he is unfamiliar with a vineyard, its name is irrelevant to him. He purchases about 70 percent of the wines he tastes (at a cost of about $150,000 a year) and does not solicit free samples (although he receives many). Parker rarely attends wine-industry tastings, so as to maintain his independence from the industry he writes about, and to make sure that his tastings are handled according to his standards. He drinks a little over a bottle of wine a day purely for pleasure.

If Parker's first sip of a wine tells him that it is not worth 80 points, he will not try it again. However, he will take two or three sips of higher-ranking wines in an attempt to discover nuances. Between samples Parker sips sparkling water to maintain a neutral palate. He also uses a small can of saline spray to keep his nasal passages moist and clear. Every year he has his nose, tongue, mouth, and lips examined by a top otolaryngologist (ear, nose, and throat doctor). "Probably 80 percent of anyone's appreciation of a wine is really olfactory . . . even though we perceive it as taste," he told Shaw. "Taste is actually a very crude instrument. Sure, you have to be able to taste the texture and the weight and harmony in a wine, the purity of the fruit and the equilibrium, but every wine I've ever given 100 points to, I could sense it was worth that the second I smelled it. And with a lot of the bargain wines I try, one sniff tells me they're so pathetic I don't even taste them; they never touch my lips."

In addition to his home tastings, Parker spends about three months each year tasting wines in vineyards in France and California. On his trips he sometimes samples as many as 500 wines a day. "It's a pretty boring lifestyle," he said during a televised interview for the *Charlie Rose Show* (February 14, 2005). "I mean, it sounds great and . . . people think it's romantic. And I love what I do. But . . . I work. I get up in the morning and I start working at 7:30 or 8:00, and I finish . . . between 6:00 and 7:00 p.m. I go back to my hotel, order several bottles of mineral water and a salad . . . and then I will just literally decompress by taking a few good books to read." During his working hours, Parker avoids foods that affect his palate, among them watercress, coffee, chocolate, and spicy dishes. "I'm a taster—and tasting is a matter of focus, of mental discipline," he told Shaw. "When a wine is in my mouth, I can taste it and smell it in all its dimensions—the full range of flower, plant, vegetable and earth, or red and black fruits."

In 1985 Simon & Schuster published Parker's first book, *Bordeaux*, which provided ratings and commentary on vintages from France's Bordeaux region, which most connoisseurs believe to be the world's finest wine-producing area. In the *Washington Post* (January 5, 1986), James Conaway praised *Bordeaux* for its "energy, focus and sheer weight of fact." Within five years Parker wrote the first editions of three more books: *Parker's Wine Buyer's Guide* (1987); *Wines of the Rhone Valley and Provence* (1988); and *Burgundy: A Comprehensive Guide to the Producers, Appellations, and Wines* (1990). With the exception of his most recent work, *The World's Greatest Wine Estates: A Modern Perspective* (2005), Parker has revised and expanded each of his books, some more than once, and they have been published in many languages abroad, where they have been received enthusiastically. *Bordeaux* was awarded England's 1987 Glenfiddich Award for the best book about alcoholic beverages; the 1992 International Association of Cooking Professionals (IACP) Award, as the best wine book of the year; and the 1993 Goldene Feder, Germany's most prestigious prize for books on wine and gastronomy. *Wines of the Rhone Valley and Provence* won the 1989 Tastemaker Award (now known as the James Beard Foundation Kitchen Aid Book Award), as the best wine book published in America, and the Wine Guild's 1989 Wine Book of the Year, in Britain. The wine and spirits manufacturer Moët-Hennessey presented Parker with its 1993 Wine and Vine Communication Award for the French editions of *Bordeaux* and *Burgundy*.

As Parker's status as a wine critic increased, many distributors began to buy primarily his higher-scoring wines, and merchants advertised their wines using his scores. The growth of Parker's influence led critics to charge that too many wine neophytes were making purchases solely on the basis of his rankings. Some merchants complained that no one would buy wines that Parker rated below 85. One anonymous wine journalist told Rice that Parker's system was "wine by the numbers. Retailers love the sensationalism of it. After a 90 rating, a wine, even an obscure one, will fly off the shelf. The system gets results, and Parker's reputation as a man who can move wine is enhanced." Parker himself has expressed frustration about what he considers misguided uses of his scoring system. "Often a wine with a lower score that has a good price and is ready to drink is a better bet than an expensive wine rated 90 that I say not to drink for five years," he told Rice. Parker has also been criticized for preferring robust, fruity wines that are full-bodied and rich, as opposed to lighter, more elegant wines—a charge he has denied. His critics argue that buyers' tastes have adjusted to duplicate Parker's, thus forcing good vineyards to change the types of wine they make. "There are wine makers all over the world who are making their wines for Robert Parker's palate," the *Baltimore Evening Sun* wine columnist Michael Hill told Shaw for the *Los Angeles Times* (August 24, 1987). Some vineyards whose vintages are poor in a particular year have even been known to set their prices high before Parker reviews their wines, so that they can earn greater-than-warranted profits. *The Emperor of Wine: The Rise of Robert M. Parker Jr. and the Reign of American Taste* (2005), an unauthorized biography by Elin McCoy, his editor at the magazine *Food & Wine* in the early 1980s, repeats the criticism that Parker's influence has become too great in the wine industry. In addition, it suggests that Parker has ceased to be a consumer advocate and has become, instead, an advocate for those who can afford high-priced wines. Earlier, Jonathan Nossiter's documentary about the wine industry, *Mondovino* (2004), suggested that Parker was participating, perhaps unconsciously, in a conspiracy with Michel Roland, a consultant to wineries, and the Mondavi family, Californian winemakers who have expanded their grasp all over the world, to homogenize the wine industry. "Some criticism has some justification," Parker told Linda Murphy for the *San Francisco Chronicle* (October 21, 2004), "but I've never sought power. I don't like it and I don't embrace it. I'm doing something that I truly love and I've made a good living at it. If a wine gets a great review that helps sell the wine, that's fine, but I don't go out and seek that."

Although Parker has his share of detractors, many vintners have praised him for stirring them to improve their craft. After Alain Raynaud—the proprietor of two vineyards in Bordeaux—received a 77 from Parker for one of his wines, he began to taste other vintages from the region that Parker had rated highly. "That forced me to change many, many things in my vineyards and in vinification [winemaking]," he told Shaw in 1999. "Most Bordeaux winemakers have changed the way of vinification. We in Bordeaux must thank Mr. Parker for forcing us to a greater quality than we had before." Parker's critiques have also led some large-scale producers, including the legendary California enologist Robert Mondavi, to avoid filtering and various other industrial techniques in favor of more-natural winemaking processes. Parker's opposition to industrial winemaking stems from his belief that it creates, at best, technically perfect wines that have no distinction in taste or variation from year to year or vineyard to vineyard. "Soon a wine made in Piedmont tastes like one from Bordeaux," Parker told Rice. "It may not be a bad wine, but it doesn't inspire you. The appeal of wine to me is that in each region and in each vintage it tastes different." Parker believes in the importance of what the French call *terroir*—the combination of microclimate, drainage, elevation, sunlight, and history that makes each vintage and each vineyard unique. Parker's praise of small winemakers who use natural techniques to grow and process their wines has helped them to compete with large, state-of-the-art vineyards.

In addition to writing and publishing the *Wine Advocate*, which currently has a subscription base of more than 50,000, Parker is a contributing editor of *Food and Wine Magazine*. He has written for the British magazine the *Field* and is the first non-Frenchman to serve as the wine critic of *L'Express*, a French magazine. In 1996, burdened by the rapidly growing demands on his time, Parker hired the wine merchant Pierre-Antoine Rovani to taste and write about more than half of the world's wine-producing regions; Rovani's reviews appear in the *Wine Advocate* and *Parker's Wine Buyer's Guide*. In 2003 the wine writer Daniel Thomases joined the *Wine Advocate* to cover Italian wines.

Parker has said that he cannot imagine retiring. "It's like you're forever a student," he told Charlie Rose. "No matter how much you know with each vintage, you go back to school. There are going to be surprises, there are going to be disappointments. There are going to be new stars and there are going to be stars that you thought were going to do it that fall on their face. And I love that aspect of it." He also feels a duty toward wine drinkers. "The more people you can educate and point in the direction of good-value wines," he told Jerry Shriver for *USA Today* (September 3, 1999), "the more educated their palates become, and it raises the level of wine appreciation. It truly is Mother Nature's gift to mankind."

Parker has received many honors. Chateauneuf du Pape, the most important wine village in France's Rhone Valley, named him an honorary citizen. (Only two other people have received that honor: the poet and Nobel laureate Frederic Mistral and the novelist, playwright, and filmmaker Marcel Pagnol.) Parker is also one of the few foreign recipients of France's two highest presidential honors: in 1993 President François Mitterrand named him a knight in the National Order of Merit, and in 1999 President Jacques Chirac named him a knight in the Legion of Honor. Parker has also been named a commander in Italy's National Order of Merit. Loyola College in Maryland selected him as the 1992 Marylander of the Year. He was deemed the Wine and Spirits Professional of 1997 at that year's James Beard Awards. In 2000 he was awarded the first Andre Simon Wine Writer's Award by the Florida Winefest & Auction.

Parker lives in Monkton, Maryland, with his wife, Patricia, and their adopted daughter, in the house in which Patricia grew up. The building has been remodeled over the years to include three wine cellars, Parker's office, and a tasting room. Patricia has edited the *Wine Advocate* since its inception, often softening Parker's more caustic criticisms. Perhaps not surprisingly in light of his nearly unsurpassed power as a critic in any field of endeavor, one of his assessments drew an anonymous death threat, and another triggered a libel suit.

—G.O.

Suggested Reading: *Chicago Tribune* N p6 May 20, 1998, with photo; *Cleveland Plain Dealer* F p4 July 14, 1999; *eRobertParker.com*; *Los Angeles Times* A p1 Feb. 23, 1999, with photos; *New York Times* C p1 Dec. 6, 1998, with photo; *Newsday* p65 Oct. 16, 1986; *San Francisco Chronicle* F p5 Oct. 21, 2004; *USA Today* D p7 Sep. 3, 1999, with photos; *Washington Times* E p1 Oct. 11, 1990, with photo

Selected Books: *Bordeaux*, 1985; *Parker's Wine Buyer's Guide*, 1987; *Wines of the Rhone Valley and Provence*, 1988; *Burgundy*, 1990; *The World's Greatest Wine Estates: A Modern Perspective*, 2005

Frazer Harrison/Getty Images

Patrick, Danica

Mar. 25, 1982– Racecar driver

Address: c/o Indy Racing League, 4565 W. 16th St., Indianapolis, IN 46222

The racecar driver Danica Patrick "is a slick, 5-foot-1, 100-pound package of talent and charisma," Bob Sansevere enthused in an article for the *Saint Paul (Minnesota) Pioneer Press* (June 4, 2005). "She also is extremely photogenic, which will only fuel her marketability and help heighten awareness that women—at least one woman, anyway—can compete with the best male drivers." On May 29, 2005 the 23-year-old Patrick became only the fourth woman ever to compete in the famous Indianapolis 500 race and the first woman to hold the lead during that competition; in addition, by finishing in fourth place, she achieved the best result yet attained by a female driver in the race, and—coincidentally or not—the Indy 500 event in which she competed drew more television viewers than any other in over a decade. While Patrick's activities have garnered much media attention due to her gender and good looks, she is seen by racing-industry insiders not as a mere novelty but as one with the skills necessary to become a champion. "If there's one great thing I think that's happened over the years [it] is that women are being accepted into a man's world in all different areas, whether it's flying a plane or driving a racecar," Patrick told Michael Vega for the *Boston Globe* (May 29, 2005). "I think it's much more accepting, and people are actually excited for it and they'd like to see something new and something fresh and something they've never seen before."

Patrick's parents, T.J. and Bev Patrick, met in the 1970s, while T.J. was racing snowmobiles and Bev worked as a mechanic for a female snowmobile driver. The older of their two children, Danica Sue Patrick was born on March 25, 1982 in Beloit, Wisconsin; her sister, Brooke, was born two years later. The family settled in Roscoe, Illinois, where they owned a plate-glass company and the Java Hut coffee shop. When Brooke was about eight years old, she wanted to try go-kart racing, and with their background in snowmobile racing, her parents were enthusiastic. After crashing four times in one race, Brooke decided that she was not meant to be a racer, but Danica, who had begun racing because of her sister's influence, soon became hooked. The 10-year-old began competing in go-kart races organized by the World Karting Association, and by the conclusion of the 1992 season (her first), she had finished second in points out of 20 drivers in her age group. "In my first race in go-karts, I was lapped within six laps by the competition," Patrick told an AutoRacing1.com (April 1, 2002) interviewer. "I knew I would have to concentrate, improve and be determined. But racing is something I wanted to do once I drove that kart for the first time." Patrick entered more events in the following years, winning her first Grand National Championship by the age of 12. In her progression from younger to more advanced categories of racing, she amassed two more national titles and 10 regional crowns, and in 1996 she dominated her class, winning 39 of 49 feature races. She also began attending a driving school run by Lyn St. James, a former participant in the Indianapolis 500. St. James recognized Patrick's talent and groomed her as a racer, making sure to introduce her young protégé to influential figures in the racing world. She even took Patrick with her to the 1997 Indy 500 to watch the race and make more connections. "Out of 200 that have gone through my program, no more than 10 set themselves apart that I've gone out of my way to help behind the scenes," St. James said in an interview with the *San Jose (California) Mercury News* (May 29, 2005). "They have to be exceptional. It's not good enough to just be good. The reality is you have to be extraordinary. I saw Danica as extraordinary."

As Patrick rose through the ranks of the youth go-kart circuit, she attracted the attention of racing officials who suggested that she switch from karts to racecars and relocate to England to polish her skills in the British developmental-racing series. Her family supported her endeavors, and with the aid of some sponsorships, Patrick went to England. (Patrick, who had attended Hononegah Community High School, in Rockton, Illinois, left at age 16 and later earned her GED.) "If you want to be the best lawyer, you go to Harvard," Bev Patrick explained for AutoRacing1.com. "If you want to be the best driver, you go to England." Patrick made her racing debut in England in 1998, when she competed in the Formula Vauxhall Winter Series. She raced in England for the whole of the following season, placing ninth in the Formula Vauxhall Championship. Then, in 2000, Patrick switched to the British Zetek Formula Ford Series, which is known for being extremely competitive and difficult. In placing second at the Formula Ford Festival, Patrick earned the highest-ever finish by either a woman or an American in the English event. In England "there were times it was tough on the soul, not being close to your family and friends," Patrick told Bill Center for the San Diego Union-Tribune (May 29, 2005). "But I learned in England and got tougher. I grew up over there very quickly. I learned about life as much as cars." In 2001 she returned to the United States, quickly winning the Gorsline Scholarship Award for the top up-and-coming young driver in U.S. road racing. "After racing in Europe, I received a lot of experience that can help me get to the top of the sport," Patrick told AutoRacing1.com. "I just need the chance to show my abilities."

Patrick soon got that chance. While in England managing the Jaguar Formula One team, the racing-team owner Bobby Rahal saw Patrick perform and was favorably impressed. In 2002 he signed her to a multiyear contract with Rahal Letterman, the prominent team he co-owns with the talk-show host David Letterman. Rahal designated Patrick as a driver for the next year's Toyota Atlantic Series; when she placed third in the series, Patrick became the first woman to occupy a spot on the winners' podium. She raced in the same event in 2004 and not only placed third but came within the top five in 10 out of 12 races. In 2003 Patrick drew attention—not all of it positive—for appearing scantily clad in the men's magazine FHM. In her own defense, Patrick told Terry Blount for the Dallas Morning News (May 29, 2005), "Anything that brings more attention to the sport is good."

At a news conference in May 2004, Rahal announced his decision that his increasingly popular new driver was ready to participate in the Indy Racing League (IRL), a series of races throughout the U.S. and Japan, the highlight of which is the famous Indianapolis 500 Mile Race. As Bill Center reported, Patrick herself expressed surprise: "I had no idea Bobby was going to say that. . . . It was one of those moments when you pinch yourself to make sure you heard what you just heard. It was my dream come true." The decision would make Patrick only the fourth woman ever to compete in the IRL; the first was Janet Guthrie (who raced in the event from 1977 to 1979), followed by Lyn St. James (from 1992 to 2000), and Sarah Fisher (from 2000 to 2004). Though Patrick would be a rookie in the race, Rahal expressed his faith in her. "Believe me, I never would have put her in this car if I thought she was going to make a fool out of herself or us," Rahal told Terry Blount. "She's under a lot of pressure here, but she can handle it." She also had to handle objections from some male drivers, who implied that Patrick's 100-pound frame gave her an unfair advantage by making her car lighter than theirs. The IRL president, Brian Barnhart, dis-

agreed, telling Dave Caldwell for the New York Times (May 31, 2005) that Patrick's weight "had a . . . minimal effect on the competition." Although she crashed in the first race of the 2005 IRL series and placed only 15th and 12th, respectively, in the next two, Patrick impressed even Rahal with her fourth-place performance in the fourth race, in Motegi, Japan. In the qualifying race for the Indianapolis 500, Patrick nearly crashed again, but instead drew kudos for her skillful handling of the near-miss. "That was one heck of a save," her fellow racer Tony Kanaan told the San Jose (California) Mercury News. "A lot of drivers would have wound up in the wall on that one. It was pretty impressive. She's got a lot of talent."

The Indianapolis 500 Mile Race, often referred to as the Indy 500, is one of the oldest and most prestigious events in car racing. It was first held over Memorial Day weekend in 1911 at the then-new Indianapolis Motor Speedway in Speedway, Indiana. Since then it has become a cherished tradition for both drivers and racing enthusiasts. Although the technology involved has developed and the rules have been refined over the years, the race remains a 500-mile-long course to be completed in 200 laps. With participants moving at an average speed of approximately 160 miles per hour (157.603 mph in the 2005 race), recent events have lasted between two and a half and three and a half hours (three hours, 10 minutes, and 21 seconds in 2005).

On May 29, 2005 Patrick became the first woman to take the lead during the Indianapolis 500, holding it for 19 laps before Tom Wheldon overtook her. She finished fourth, ahead of 29 others in the race, the best showing ever by a female driver at the Indy 500 and a highly respectable finish for any first-time competitor in the event. "She's the real deal . . . ," Lyn St. James told Michael Vega about Patrick, adding, "I think she will be a future winner." Patrick herself told Jim Gintonio for the Arizona Republic (June 8, 2005), "It's so early in my career, and I never thought I'd be a role model this early. It caught me off-guard, but it says a lot about how I was brought up, what my values have been and how my parents raised me. It's very flattering that being myself is enough to be a role model."

To continue being a role model, many observers have noted, Patrick must keep performing well. "She has to establish she belongs because she's good, not just because she's female . . . ," Mary Jo Kane, a professor of sports sociology at the University of Minnesota and director of the Tucker Center for Research on Girls and Women in Sport, explained to Bob Sansevere. "At the end of the day, you're judged on if you win or lose. Not whether you're male or female, not whether you're black or white, not whether you're rich or poor. Do you win?" Patrick's father, T.J., made a similar statement to Michael Vega: "My main concern is that if they try to do too much PR or keep [Patrick] too busy that she forgets about racing. She has to focus on racing, that's the key. The results will bring the people. She wants to be in here for the long haul. She's here to show everybody that she can race first, then she can pull her helmet off and let her long hair fall out." Patrick, too, apparently understands the need to stay at the top of her field. The abundance of press about her is "magnified because I'm a rookie and a woman. And because I drive for Rahal and David Letterman," she told Bill Center. "I understand why [the media attention is] all here. I just hope I give everyone more stories to write." By the end of the 2005 IRL season, Patrick had been awarded both the Indy 500 Rookie of the Year and the IRL IndyCar Series Rookie of the Year awards.

Patrick is engaged to Paul Hospenthal, the physical therapist who treated her in 2002, after she injured her hip while practicing yoga. The couple planned to marry in November 2005. They current-

ly share a home (along with Patrick's miniature schnauzer, Billy) in Scottsdale, Arizona, where Hospenthal runs the Desert Institute of Physical Therapy. In addition to yoga, Patrick stays in shape through running and weight training. She is also "kind of a TV junkie," as Hospenthal told *People* (June 6, 2005). For the same article, Bobby Rahal said about her, "Danica shakes your hand and, crunch, it's like a truck driver. That's the yin and yang of Danica. The exterior is nice and pretty—and underneath she is as tough as steel."

—K.J.E.

Suggested Reading: *Boston Globe* C p1 May 29, 2005; *Dallas Morning News* C p1 May 29, 2005; danicaracing.com; *People* p126 June 6, 2005, with photos; *San Diego Union-Tribune* C p1 May 29, 2005; *San Jose (California) Mercury News* p1 May 29, 2005

Frederick M. Brown/Getty Images

Perry, Tyler

Sep. 13, 1969– Playwright; screenwriter; producer; director; actor

Address: c/o Charles King, William Morris Agency, One William Morris Pl., Beverly Hills, CA 90212

Homeless and penniless as recently as seven years ago, the playwright, director, producer, and actor Tyler Perry has become one of the most popular and successful figures in contemporary black entertainment. Perry is among the central figures in

the revival of urban theater: traveling stage shows that are rooted in the African-American experience and cater primarily to blacks. Containing elements of gospel, or inspirational, theater, Perry's shows are primarily comedies. The main character of four of his eight plays is an outspoken grandmother called Madea, whose accessories include two Saturday night specials. To date, his productions of his plays—among them *I Know I've Been Changed, I Can Do Bad All by Myself, Diary of a Mad Black Woman, Madea's Family Reunion,* and *Meet the Browns*—have grossed more than $75 million in theater-ticket and DVD sales. The Hollywood film adaptation of *Diary of a Mad Black Woman* exceeded industry analysts' expectations by grossing over $44 million during its theatrical run, nearly nine times what it cost to produce. Lions Gate Films, which distributed the movie, plans to turn Perry's work into a major franchise.

Tyler Perry was born Emmitt Perry Jr. on September 13, 1969 in New Orleans, Louisiana, to Willie Maxine Perry and Emmitt Perry Sr. He has two older sisters and a younger brother. While he was growing up, he suffered a great deal of physical abuse at the hands of his father. Once, when he was in his early teens, he even attempted suicide, by slashing his wrists. "It was a cry for attention," he told Margenia A. Christian for *Jet* (December 1, 2003). "I was pretty young and totally frustrated." His rage toward his father led him, at age 16, to change his first name. As a youth he attempted to mask his pain by becoming the class clown; at home he sought refuge in reading, writing, and drawing. He earned a GED (the equivalent of a high-school diploma) and became a carpenter. Meanwhile, his memories of his father's cruelty toward him continued to torment him; he harbored resentment toward his mother as well. "I was unhappy and miserable for the first 28 years of my life," Perry told Zondra Hughes for *Ebony* (January

2004). "The things that I went through as a kid were horrendous. And I carried that into my adult life. I didn't have a catharsis for my childhood pain, most of us don't, and until I learned how to forgive those people and let it go, I was unhappy."

One day, while watching an installment of Oprah Winfrey's daytime television talk show, Perry learned that many people who have suffered terrible physical or mental abuse have found solace through writing. Soon, Perry began writing letters to himself in a journal. Those letters formed the basis for his first gospel musical, *I Know I've Been Changed*, about victims of childhood abuse who as adults confront their abusers. He set about to produce the musical himself, and in 1992, with about $12,000 in savings, he rented a theater. During the opening weekend, only 30 people showed up to see it. Perry was left penniless, and although he felt frustrated and angry, he refused to give up. Over the next six years, while working at odd jobs, he mounted the play several more times, with financial backing from others. The show failed each time, and he repeatedly found himself homeless; he often lived out of his car or temporarily in cheap hotels.

Perry's mother urged him to abandon thoughts of a career in theater and instead look for steady employment elsewhere, but Perry remained certain that playwriting was his calling. Although, by his own admission, he often had doubts about God's intentions, his faith sustained him through that difficult period. He has also credited his faith with giving him the courage to telephone his parents one day and tell them how he felt about the pain inflicted on him during his childhood. By the end of the call, he realized that he had forgiven his parents. He felt elated. On his official Web site, as quoted by Christine Miner Minderovic in *Contemporary Black Biography* (2003), he recalled, "Victims always feel as if they did things to themselves or something to 'deserve it.' The moment was so genuine and real that I knew something was about to change, but I didn't know what."

In March 1998, after having secured new financial backing, Perry mounted another production of *I Know I've Been Changed*, this time at the House of Blues in Atlanta, Georgia. By then he had nearly reached the limit of his tolerance for rejection and for living hand to mouth, so he vowed that the production in Atlanta would be his last if it did not succeed. On the frustration-filled opening night (the heating system in the theater would not work, among other problems), Perry happened to look out a window shortly before the curtain was scheduled to rise and, to his amazement, saw curling around the block a line of people waiting to see the show. That performance and the next eight sold out. Two weeks later he produced another mounting of *I Know I've Been Changed*, at the Fox Theater; its entire run sold out as well. Suddenly, Perry found himself being flooded with offers from producers who wanted to book *I Know I've Been Changed*—including some who had rejected his show earlier.

Among those who attended the show in Atlanta was the televangelist T. D. Jakes. What he saw inspired Jakes to propose to Perry that he produce a stage adaptation for Jakes's best-selling novel *Woman, Thou Art Loosed*. After reading the script, Perry told Jakes that he would do so, but only if he was allowed complete artistic control, including not only the direction and production of the work but also the freedom to rewrite the script. Jakes agreed. *Woman, Thou Art Loosed* opened in 1999 to critical and commercial acclaim; during its five-month run it grossed some $5 million. (In 2000 Perry adapted another of Jakes's works, *Behind Closed Doors*. It, too, debuted in Atlanta and became a big hit.) Soon, Perry was the darling of the urban theater circuit—once known as the "chitlin circuit"—an unofficial network of black-friendly performance venues.

During the past two decades several other producers have also entered the urban theater circuit, among them Shelly Garrett, with his shows *Beauty Shop* and its successors, *Beauty Shop Part 2* and *Beauty Shop: Under New Management*, and David E. Talbert, whose plays include *He Say . . . She Say . . . But What Does God Say?* and *The Fabric of a Man*. Perry has become the most successful among them, in part because, as he told Zondra Hughes, "with my shows, I try to build a bridge that marries what's deemed 'legitimate' theater and so-called 'chitlin' circuit theater,' and I think I've done pretty well with that, in bringing people in to enjoy a more elevated level of theater." Indeed, Perry's shows have drawn some 16,000 to 25,000 people per week. As of early 2004 Perry had earned more than $50 million through writing and producing his own shows.

Earlier, having felt a desire to move away from serious topical issues, Perry wrote *I Can Do Bad All by Myself* (2000), which features the character Mable "Madea" Simmons, a gun-toting, 68-year-old grandmother who wears glasses with cat's-eye frames, carries an oversized purse, and utters sassy one-liners and homespun wisdom in even doses. The name "Madea" comes from "Ma'dear," a contraction of "mother" and "dear" that, for some blacks, is an affectionate way of addressing a mother or grandmother. Based on the playwright's mother and Aunt Maeola (a "feisty minister," as Perry described her to Coles), and played on stage by Perry himself, Madea has become more famous than her creator. According to Perry, people are drawn to Madea because she is a product of a bygone era. "Everyone knows her," he explained to Margenia Christian. "We watch with nostalgia when we think about this type of grandmother. . . . She's not around anymore. When she was around, everybody's kid belonged to her. She kept the entire neighborhood straight. Now we're in a different time and different age where grandmothers are in their early and late 30s. People are looking for this Madea, the 68-year-old who doesn't care about being politically correct. She doesn't care what you think about her. She's going to tell the truth." In 2001 Perry was nominated for the Helen Hayes Award for outstanding lead actor for his role as Madea. (The Helen Hayes Awards honor achievement in professional theater in Washington, D.C.)

Perry made Madea a central character in his next three plays, *Diary of a Mad Black Woman* (2001), *Madea's Family Reunion* (2002), and *Madea's Class Reunion* (2003). He also branched out into the field of direct-to-video DVD sales by filming his Madea plays. Each of the Madea shows played to sold-out audiences, and Perry reportedly had difficulty keeping up with the demand for the DVDs. (As of March 2005 some $30 million worth of the DVDs had sold through small distributors.) In hopes of adapting the comedies for the silver screen, Perry attempted to strike a deal with a Hollywood studio. By his own account, he encountered a great deal of resistance from studio executives. Some insisted that he make changes to his plays; a few rejected his proposal outright, claiming that black people typically did not attend movies. Then Steve Pasternak, president of production at Lions Gate Films, received a Perry video and script from the William Morris Agency (which represents Perry), along with a memo "saying something like Tyler has done 57 gazillion dollars in sales, something outrageous for someone I never heard of," as Pasternak recalled to Mark Olsen for the *Los Angeles Times* (February 24, 2004). "It wasn't like we were tracking Tyler's activities," he explained. "He did so much from a grass-roots level, through his website, through the church, through word of mouth, that he completely slipped under the radar of the film industry." When he brought the video and script to a Lions Gate management conference, he discovered that none of the participants knew of Perry. "Then I started to ask African American people I know, or employees here, and they all knew who he was," he told Olsen. "I thought, 'We're not in on this secret.'"

Perry and Lions Gate agreed to make a motion picture of *Diary of a Mad Black Woman* for $5.5 million, of which Perry contributed half. The deal also allowed Perry to maintain considerable creative control over the project as both screenwriter and producer. In the film version, directed by Darren Grant, Helen (played by Kimberly Elise) believes she has it all—a husband, Charles (Steve Harris), who earns a substantial salary, and a beautiful mansion. On the eve of their 18th anniversary, Charles reveals to Helen that he is in love with another woman and wants a divorce. After Helen is thrown out of her own home, she moves in with Madea (Perry) and learns to rebuild her life, first by getting a job as a waitress and later by again testing the waters of romance, this time with a factory worker, Orlando (played by Shemar Moore). The story, which emphasizes the power of faith, forgiveness, and redemption, resonated with the film's primarily African-American audience; in its opening weekend (Friday, February 25–Sunday, February 27, 2005), its box-office receipts totaled

nearly $22 million. Despite decidedly mixed reviews, by mid-March 2005 *Diary of a Mad Black Woman* had grossed some $44 million, nearly nine times what it cost to make. The box-office total later reached about $50 million.

Shortly after the premiere of *Diary of a Mad Black Woman*, Lions Gate announced its plans to produce a second Perry film, *Madea's Family Reunion*, for release in February 2006. Beginning in the summer of 2005, Lions Gate will issue seven Perry DVDs, including the film version of *Diary*. "I've been talking to retailers ever since *Diary* opened, and we expect to sell a ton," Steve Beeks, president of Lions Gate Entertainment, told Elaine Dutka for the *Los Angeles Times* (March 15, 2005). "We're developing Tyler Perry as a brand, not unlike James Bond. Lions Gate is all about finding niches—and the faith-based one is easily defined, easy to reach." The DVD of *Diary* sold 2.4 million copies within one week of its release.

Perry's play *Meet the Browns*, a spinoff of *Madea's Family Reunion*, debuted in 2004; in 2005 the production was scheduled to appear in theaters in two dozen cities. His most recent play, *Madea Goes to Jail*, in which Perry stars, began touring in March 2005. Perry's other projects include a film version of his as-yet-unreleased play *A Jazz Man's Blues*, which focuses on the love life of a jazz singer.

Tyler Perry is unmarried. As the owner of a multimillion-dollar, 12-acre estate outside Atlanta, he has expressed the concern that many potential mates might be more interested in his fortune than in him and that they might not appreciate his struggles to climb out of poverty. Nevertheless, he has said that he would like to have a family. "I've put my private life on hold for too long because I wanted success; I wanted something to offer to my woman and my children," he told Zondra Hughes. "Now that I'm at the point where I feel like I have a little bit to offer, I'm ready to be a good husband and a good father. I know I can do it."

—C.M.

Suggested Reading: CNN.com (on-line) Mar. 2, 2005, with photo; *Black Enterprise* p113 Mar. 2001, with photo; *Ebony* p86+ Jan. 2004, with photos; Internet Movie Database; *Jet* p60+ Dec. 1, 2003, with photos, p51 Dec. 8, 2003, with photo, p51 Feb. 28, 2005; *Los Angeles Times* E p16 Feb. 24, 2005, E p4 Feb. 25, 2005, A p12 Mar. 7, 2005, E p1 Mar. 15, 2005; *New York Times* E p3 May 5, 2005, with photo; *People* p102+ Aug. 9, 2004; TylerPerry.com; *Contemporary Black Biography*, 2004

Selected Works: as playwright and actor—*I Know I've Been Changed*, 1998; *Woman, Thou Art Loosed*, 1999; *I Can Do Bad All by Myself*, 2000; *Diary of a Mad Black Woman*, 2001; *Madea's Family Reunion*, 2002; *Madea's Class Reunion*, 2003; *Madea Goes to Jail*, 2005; as playwright—*Meet the Browns*, 2004; as screenwriter and actor—*Diary of a Mad Black Woman*, 2005

Catherine Opie, courtesy of Regen Projects, Los Angeles

Pettibon, Raymond

June 16, 1957– Artist

Address: c/o David Zwirner, 525 W. 19th St., New York, NY 10011

A cult celebrity in the Los Angeles, California, punk scene during the late 1970s and early 1980s, the artist Raymond Pettibon has become internationally renowned for his creation of drawings that juxtapose comic-book–style imagery and evocative text fragments. Rendered mostly in black ink and inspired by a large assortment of literary and visual sources, Pettibon's images are characterized by an eclecticism that reveals the artist's wide-ranging interests. A "mild-mannered colossus roaming freely through the worlds of literature, dime-store novels, religion, sex, philosophy, and art history," as Cathy Curtis wrote for the *Los Angeles Times* (July 15, 1991), Pettibon is a master of non sequiturs, creating images that rely on incongruities and dissonances to create surprising effects. "It's more about an understanding of the physical way the mind works, an association, or a fluency of thoughts, rather [than] an expression of an idea," Pettibon told Elana Roston for the *New Times Los Angeles* (September 7, 2000). "The root of Pettibon's success," Lance Carlson wrote for *Artweek* (December 2003/January 2004), "resides in his combination of apposite form with countervailing content . . . ," that is, his use of imagery that at first seems to have little or nothing to do with the words that accompany it. "The combination of text and image acquires a significance that transcends either element, and this interplay is perhaps the most riveting aspect of Pettibon's work."

While some critics have accused Pettibon of poor draftsmanship, a shortcoming to which the artist has readily admitted, others have praised the facility and self-assurance of his drawings. Michael Kimmelman, writing for the *New York Times* (January 31, 2003), described Pettibon's style as "a certain underground comic book messiness that is really graphic virtuosity in disguise." Often reminiscent of the comics and advertisements of the 1940s, '50s, and '60s, Pettibon's imagery derives largely from cartoons and American popular culture. Baseball players, surfers, Jesus Christ, Charles Manson, light bulbs, the Bible, and trains are all recurring elements in his work, along with two cartoon characters who serve as the artist's alter-egos: Vavoom, a minor character from the television version of the comic strip *Felix the Cat*, and Gumby, the hero of the 1950s claymation television show of the same name. Vavoom, a small, cloaked figure with an enormous, gaping mouth that emits only a single word, his name, is a "one-note oracle with an earth-shattering voice [who] serves as a kind of reductive parody of Pettibon's role as an oddball bard," Michael Duncan wrote for *Art in America* (March 1, 1999). Gumby has the ability to enter books and participate in their stories; like him, Pettibon regards reading as an act not only of consumption but also of creation, in which he refashions existing narratives to suit his own purposes. In a conversation with Hunter Drohojowska for the *Los Angeles Times* (June 16, 1991), Pettibon described his approach to books as "a dialectic of reading," in which elements from texts find their way, often in altered form, into his art. "Gumby is a kind of metaphor for how I work," he explained during an interview for the Public Broadcasting Service (PBS) Art:21 Web site. "He actually goes into the book, goes into a biography or historical book, and interacts with real figures from the past and he becomes a part of it. He brings it to another direction."

An avid reader, Pettibon punctuates nearly all of his images with text lifted from or, more often, inspired by a wide variety of literary sources, ranging in style from "the formal syntax of the 19th century [to] the staccato parlance of the detective story," according to Hunter Drohojowska-Philp in the *Los Angeles Times* (September 26, 1999). The artist's muses include the Irish playwright Samuel Beckett, the American writer and critic Henry James, the French novelist Marcel Proust, the British writer and art critic John Ruskin, the American mystery writer Mickey Spillane, and the Austrian-born British philosopher Ludwig Wittgenstein, among many others. Describing Pettibon's work in a review for the *New York Times* (July 5, 1991), Roberta Smith wrote, "If [the mystery writers] Raymond Chandler [and] Dashiell Hammett had drawn pictures, they might have looked something like this." Indeed, Pettibon has admitted to spending more time reading and writing than drawing. "If I were to judge my own work in strictly literary and visual terms, personally I think that they're developed further on the literary level than on the visual," he told Kevin M. Williams for the *Chicago Sun-Times* (October 4, 1998).

Despite their formal similarity to comic strips and other popular entertainments, Pettibon's drawings are far from frivolous, deriving their seriousness from subtle interactions between image and text. In the *Los Angeles Times* (September 21, 1995), David Pagel wrote, "Pettibon's highly intelligent, low-brow drawings offer a nuanced, often moving meditation on aimlessness, indecision and missed opportunities." While Pettibon's objects and characters are drawn from popular culture and are therefore often familiar to viewers, their decontextualization transforms them, rendering them simultaneously foreign and pathetic. Heroes, recast as antiheroes, are juxtaposed with texts that allude to failures, misunderstandings, and rifts created by time and distance. As Jessica Lack wrote for the London *Guardian* (December 13, 2003), in Pettibon's work, "pin-up girls, athletes and high-school dropouts are all given a big dose of existential angst." Pettibon himself has cited this mournful quality as one of the defining features of his work, telling the interviewer for PBS, "I think it's work that is best when there isn't any final resolution. When you don't finally arrive. . . . There probably is more failure depicted in my work than there is success."

The tone of Pettibon's drawings ranges from the ironic to the elegiac, most often tending toward humor with undercurrents of melancholy and outrage. "Sometimes subtle, sometimes outrageous, sometimes plainly silly disconnections between text and image [provide] dollops of crude humor or gnomic comedy that [provoke] not laughter but something just shy of it," Michael Kimmelman wrote of the drawings. Clare Manchester, in a review for *Art Monthly* (October 2001), echoed Kimmelman's assessment, writing, "The hypocrisy and baseness of humanity are cloaked in a humour so black it is almost not funny." In one of Pettibon's drawings, a Boy Scout stands beside the phrase "that they might become clear and sunlit, too," prompting viewers to consider the plight of the ambiguous "they." In another drawing two figures, gazing soulfully into each other's eyes, are accompanied by the words, "I shall retain not your name, but your story." Pettibon's work, characterized by a sense of disjuncture, obliges viewers to recognize the gaps that divide them from other people.

Although Pettibon does not consider himself a political artist, many of his drawings involve such famous political figures as former president Ronald Reagan and former secretary of state Henry Kissinger or are based on political themes. "It's a way of making nothing sacrosanct and above comedy," he told the PBS interviewer, "[and] for once not to assume someone like the President automatically has a claim on anyone's respect, to follow him or to take him seriously." The equalizing instinct that has led Pettibon to create scathing images of politicians stems from the artist's belief that everything is worthy of consideration, regardless of its provenance. In Pettibon's art, Felix the Cat, Jesus Christ, baseball players, trains, and Marcel Proust all co-exist peacefully, each rendered with the same care and respect (or disrespect) as the others. As Pettibon explained during the PBS interview, "All I'm really asking is for you to look at [Gumby] with the same kind of respect that you would if it was some important historical figure or Greek statue." Nevertheless, he has repeatedly refused to ascribe an overarching purpose to his work, which, he insists, reflects very little of his personality. "[My] work is a lot more impersonal than most people give it credit for," he told the PBS interviewer. "It's a mistake to assume about any of my work that it's my own voice."

Raymond Pettibon was born Raymond Ginn on June 16, 1957 in Tucson, Arizona. His father, Regis Ginn, an English teacher and spy novelist, often called him by the French term of endearment "Petit Bon" (literally, "Small Good Thing"), a nickname that the artist later modified and adopted as his pen name. Pettibon's mother, Oie Ginn, often read to him when he was a child, an activity to which Pettibon has attributed his deep-seated appreciation for the rhythms and nuanced meanings of language. The fourth of five children, Pettibon was a quiet child who spent much of his time reading. At the age of 13, he became interested in anarchist politics, and he has considered himself an anarchist ever since.

Pettibon attended the University of California at Los Angeles (UCLA), where he drew political cartoons for the campus newspaper, the *Daily Bruin*. After he graduated, in 1977, with a bachelor's degree in economics, he worked briefly as a high-school mathematics teacher in Los Angeles's public-school system. Around the same time he began to assemble his drawings into photocopied booklets that would now be called fanzines or zines, which he sold for one or two dollars each. Inspired by the "do-it-yourself" aesthetic of the punk movement, which by then had taken hold in Los Angeles, the zines, usually consisting of 28 pages, featured black-and-white cartoons drawn in a raw, hard-edged style. In 1978 Pettibon assembled his first substantial collection of drawings into a self-published, 64-page, black-and-white comic book called *Captive Chains*.

Pettibon's older brother, Greg Ginn, was the lead guitarist of the influential punk band Black Flag and the founder of SST Records, an important punk record label. During the late 1970s Ginn began to include drawings by Pettibon on Black Flag's flyers and album covers; another well-known SST band, Minutemen, did so as well. Pettibon soon became something of a cult figure among underground-music devotees, who began to associate his unique drawing style with punk rock. Pettibon's loose association with the music industry persisted over the course of the next decade. In 1990 he drew the cover art for the rock band Sonic Youth's major-label debut album, *Goo*. Although many music fans and reviewers have regarded Pettibon as the punk scene's artist-in-residence, he has made repeated attempts during interviews to distance himself from both the music industry and the punk movement, neither of which he considers particularly relevant to his work.

Throughout the 1980s Pettibon continued to self-publish his drawings in the form of photocopied pamphlets. Between 1981 and 1988 he published 11 issues of his only serialized zine, *Tripping Corpse*, a critical portrayal of the hippie counterculture of the 1960s. During that period he began to show his work in fine-art galleries. He landed his first solo exhibition in 1986, at Semaphore Gallery in New York City. In 1988 Illiterati Press published a book of his drawings entitled *Meandering on a Riff*. The following year Pettibon had his second solo show, also in New York City, at Feature Gallery. In 1990 he was given his first solo exhibition in Los Angeles, at the Richard/Bennett Gallery, and since then he has exhibited extensively at prominent galleries in New York, Los Angeles, and other cities in the United States and Europe.

During the late 1980s Pettibon began writing, directing, and producing a series of deliberately crude, low-technology videos that offered tales of the West Coast's radical subcultures. His videos from that period include *The Whole World Is Watching: Weathermen '69* (1989), a mock documentary about the Weather Underground, a radical far-left political organization; *Sir Drone* (1989), a comedy about two musicians trying haplessly to form a punk band; *Judgement Day Theater: The Book of Manson* (1989), a film about the notorious cult leader and murderer Charles Manson; and *Citizen Tania* (1989), a dramatization of the 1974 kidnapping of the publishing heiress Patty Hearst by the Symbionese Liberation Army, a guerrilla group. (Pettibone's mother appeared in the last-named work.) The highly ironic, deadpan tone of those videos echoes that of Pettibon's drawings, as does their emphasis on language. (The logo that Pettibon chose to represent the series was an image of the word "Listen!" on a television screen.) Furthermore, just as Pettibon's drawings are based on his subjective reimagination of literature, so the videos are based on his subjective reimagination of history. In *Judgement Day Theater*, for example, Pettibon portrayed Manson as a Christ-like figure who has conversations with the writer Norman Mailer, the film director Roman Polanski (whose wife Sharon Tate was murdered by Manson and his gang), and the rock musician Jimi Hendrix. During an interview with Anny Ballardini for the Poetry-bay Web site, Pettibon explained, "I do not feel constrained to fit to what history has been. I rely on witness by other people, what I read about." Pettibon's most recent video, *Red Tide Rising: Venice and Mars* (2001), is about Jim Morrison, the lead singer of the Doors, who died in 1971 at the age of 27.

While most of Pettibon's drawings of the 1980s employ a straightforward, linear style and brief captions that evoke the tone of comics and film noir, the artist's more recent images are looser but denser and more complex. Since the early 1990s Pettibon has used soft, sinuous brushstrokes and occasional touches of color, in conjunction with the more graphic elements that have always characterized his work, to create painterly drawings in which images and words appear to flow seamlessly together. Instead of brief, gnomic phrases, the text often consists of long, poetic passages that fill the blank spaces between images. Many drawings include several areas of text, with each passage rendered in a different style, suggesting multiple voices.

In 1991 Pettibon was one of 23 American artists to receive a Louis Comfort Tiffany Foundation award, a biennial grant given to promising artists whose work has not yet received widespread critical or commercial recognition. In 1992 several of his drawings were featured in "Helter-Skelter: L.A. Art in the '90s," a major exhibition at the Los Angeles Museum of Contemporary Art (MOCA). The exhibition, which also featured works by the Los Angeles–based sculptor and performance artist Mike Kelley and the multimedia artist Paul McCarthy, among others, earned Pettibon his first major critical attention, marking the artist's full emergence from underground circles into the contemporary art scene. In 1993 several of Pettibon's drawings were included in the prestigious Whitney Biennial exhibition at the Whitney Museum of American Art, in New York City, further cementing his reputation.

During the late 1990s, expanding his scope beyond the boundaries of page-size paper, Pettibon began to create elaborate, wall-size drawings and collages, including site-specific installations at the Whitechapel Gallery, in London, England (2001), and Documenta XI, in Kassel, Germany (2002). Between September 1998 and January 2000, a traveling mid-career retrospective of Pettibon's work, comprising about 500 drawings (from a complete oeuvre of more than 7,000), was mounted successively at the Renaissance Society at the University of Chicago, in Illinois; the Drawing Center, in New York City; the Philadelphia Museum of Art, in Pennsylvania; and the Los Angeles MOCA. Suzanne Ghez, the director of the Renaissance Society, and Ann Temkin, a curator of 20th-century art at the Philadelphia Museum, organized the show, arranging Pettibon's drawings in groups according to the private and institutional collections to which they belonged, rather than chronologically or thematically. The unconventional presentation was meant to highlight the flexibility of meaning in Pettibon's art, demonstrating how the particular selections made by a collector often reflect the collector's own interests and preoccupations. Instead of a traditional museum catalog, the exhibition was accompanied by excerpts from texts selected by Pettibon, including works by Jorge Luis Borges,

Henry James, Ring Lardner, Marcel Proust, and Mickey Spillane, among others, collected under the title *Raymond Pettibon: A Reader.*

Pettibon's first major show in the United Kingdom, comprising more than 300 works on paper, was mounted at the Whitechapel Art Gallery, in London, England, in the fall of 2000. In addition to drawings, the exhibition featured examples of Pettibon's video work, underground comics, record covers, and book projects dating from the 1970s and early 1980s. Also on view were several handmade books and site-specific wall drawings, which Pettibon created especially for Whitechapel. In 2002 a similarly eclectic exhibition of Pettibon's work, "Plots Laid Thick," was organized by the Barcelona Museum of Contemporary Art, in Spain. After its appearance there, the show traveled to the Tokyo Opera City Art Gallery, in Japan, and the Hague Municipal Museum, in the Netherlands.

In recognition of Pettibon's body of work, which now includes more than 10,000 drawings, and his contribution to American art, the Whitney Museum honored the artist with its 2004 Bucksbaum Award. Presented once every two years to an artist featured in the Whitney Biennial, the Bucksbaum comes with a prize of $100,000 (the world's largest cash award for a visual artist) and a two-year artist-in-residency at the Whitney. In conjunction with the award, a solo exhibition of Pettibon's work was scheduled to take place at the Whitney in late 2005 or early 2006; a new hardcover book, *Raymond Pettibon*, containing a collection of images of his recent work, was scheduled for publication in March 2006. His works are in the permanent collections of the Museum of Modern Art, in New York City; the San Francisco Museum of Modern Art; the Philadelphia Museum of Art; and the Art Institute of Chicago.

Pettibon's art has been compared repeatedly to that of Mike Kelley, who, like Pettibon, makes frequent use of the visual and literary conventions of American subcultures and was tangentially involved in the punk movement. Benjamin H. D. Buchloh, in *October* (Spring 2000), drew parallels between Pettibon's work and that of the conceptual artist Jenny Holzer, who, like Pettibon, "adheres strictly to a nonjudging and nonselective arrangement of quotations." Other critics have suggested similarities between Pettibon's work and that of the 18th-century British poet and artist William Blake, whose evocations of epiphanic, visionary ecstasy, in his poetry and in his art, are echoed in some of Pettibon's drawings (for example, a picture of a baseball player accompanied by the words "What magnificences in a single day!"). The most frequent comparison that critics and journalists have made when discussing Pettibon has been to other contemporary graphic and comic-book artists, notably Robert Crumb (also known professionally as R. Crumb), in whose work Pettibon has claimed to have no particular interest.

Raymond Pettibon shares a house with his parents in Hermosa Beach, California.

— L.W.

Suggested Reading: *Art in America* p106+ Mar. 1, 1999; *Chicago Sun-Times* p21+ Oct. 4, 1998; *Los Angeles Times* p90+ June 16, 1991; *New York Times* E p40+ Feb. 26, 1999; *New York Times Magazine* p38+ Oct. 9, 2005, with photos; *October* p36+ Spring 2000; *Village Voice* p91+ Nov. 11, 1997; Hapkemeyer, Andreas and Luca Beatrice, editors. *Raymond Pettibon: The Pages Which Contain Truth Are Blank*, 2005

Selected Books: *Raymond Pettibon: A Reader*, 1998; *Thinking of You*, 1999; *Raymond Pettibon: The Books 1978–1998* (with Roberto Ohrt and Uwe Koch), 2006; *Traue deinen Augen* (Trust Your Eyes, with Otto Dix, Hans-Werner Schmidt, Ingebord Kahler, and Ulrike Rudiger), 2001; *Plots Laid Thick*, 2002

Peyroux, Madeleine

(PAY-roo)

1973– Singer, guitarist, and songwriter

Address: c/o Rounder Records, 1 Camp St., Cambridge, MA 02140

"Jazz really does try to include everything. It's always been popular music," the singer, songwriter, and guitarist Madeleine Peyroux asserted in an interview with Todd Leopold for CNN.com (January 12, 2005). "But the wonderful thing about jazz is its willingness to take chances." Peyroux might be said to have taken some chances herself, having dropped out of high school, performed as a teenager on the streets of Paris, and toured Europe and the U.S. with a band before bursting onto the music scene with the release of her debut album, *Dreamland* (1996). That record earned glowing reviews and led many critics to compare her voice to that of Billie Holiday—a reception that made the young singer's subsequent disappearance from the public eye all the more surprising. Eight years later Peyroux returned to the recording studio, to make an album that most critics have found to be even stronger than her debut work. On *Careless Love*, Peyroux covered not only jazz standards but the work of such contemporary artists as Bob Dylan and Elliott Smith.

Madeleine Peyroux was born in Athens, Georgia, in 1973. Her mother, Deidre, a French teacher, and her father, Adrian, a New Orleans–born drama professor, moved the family around quite a bit, relocating from Georgia to Hollywood, California, before Peyroux had turned two and from Hollywood to Brooklyn, New York, when Peyroux was six. While she "grew up on a rich musical diet—from Fats Waller and Johnny Cash to Peter, Paul and Mary," as Jane Cornwell reported in the London *Evening Standard* (March 18, 2005), Peyroux did not anticipate that she would become involved in

Rafa Rivas/AFP/Getty Images

Madeleine Peyroux

music full-time at an early age. "Back then, I had this idea that I was going to finish high school, go to college, and get a degree—both of my parents had, and that was my idea of the future," she said to a writer for the Lilith Fair Web site. "I didn't really question it, although I didn't want to do it that much." The events of her life played out a bit differently. Her parents divorced when Peyroux was 13; her mother accepted a job at an international bank in Paris, France, and Peyroux was sent to a girls' boarding school in England. Unhappy with the school's strictness, she soon ran away to join her mother and younger brother in Paris. "Moving to France was hard, because we had to learn the language," Peyroux admitted to Yoshi Kato for the California-based *Mercury News* (April 1, 1997, online). "But I was about the right age, I guess. Thirteen is a good age to go out and explore." Peyroux, who had recently begun playing the guitar and had learned songs by the Beatles and Simon and Garfunkel, was particularly interested in the Parisian music scene. At the age of 15, she began exploring the Latin Quarter of Paris, the center of a thriving culture of jazz musicians and others who performed on the street. By 1989 she had dropped out of high school (she later earned her GED) and begun to work for a group of busking musicians called the Riverboat Shufflers, passing the hat for tips from audiences and keeping a small portion of the money for herself. She soon persuaded the band to let her sing with them, beginning her busking career with the only song in her repertoire, "Georgia on My Mind." Shortly thereafter she performed an impromptu audition for another group, the Lost Wandering Blues & Jazz Band. After listening to the 16-year-old Peyroux's a cappella rendi-

tion of "Jeepers Creepers," the bandleader promptly accepted her into the group, with which she spent the next three years touring Europe in a brown Mercedes and also performing in the U.S. "There was so much stuff in that car," Peyroux recollected for the Lilith Fair Web site. "There were four or five of us plus a wash tub, mouse amps, a trumpet, two guitars, and all the duffel bags and sleeping bags." With the band, which customarily played a range of music from the 1930s, Peyroux played the washtub bass and sang. But, Peyroux told Lynell George for the *Los Angeles Times* (November 14, 2004), "by the time I was 18 I was done" with traveling in a cramped car, spending nights on friends' couches and floors, and playing for very little money. Instead, "I wanted to pursue things of more of a literary nature." She even turned down repeated offers of a recording contract from the producer Yves Beauvais, who had heard her sing in New York—until, as she said to George, "I got to the point where I didn't see why not." Peyroux then signed with Atlantic Records, where Beauvais was a producer.

Dreamland, Peyroux's debut album, was released in October 1996 to general acclaim. While the record was made up mainly of standards, such as Edith Piaf's "La Vie en Rose" and the Patsy Kline/Alan Block song "Walkin' After Midnight," it also featured three of Peyroux's original compositions. Acknowledging the similarity between the themes in her own songs and those addressed by the older material, Peyroux told Norman Provencher for the *Ottawa Citizen* (October 23, 1997): "I think good music will always show you how little things really change. The same problems that existed 50 years ago exist today. That's comforting in some ways." With the album, "the goal was to make [the music] sound convincing by turning it over again, because it's already had its day," she explained to Yoshi Kato. The resulting record was, according to Lynell George, "a sultry, sepia-toned set of songs that gave listeners pause—it was a grab-bag mix of styles and moods merging originals with nostalgia." "Madeleine Peyroux is a time traveler, a singer who can re-create an era of relative innocence and grace when music was much more than a marketable commodity," Calvin Wilson raved in the *(Kansas and Missouri) Kansas City Star* (August 14, 1997). Her voice, he wrote, is "part silk, part grit," and she "puts over jazz with sufficient exuberance to instantly disarm any skeptics." "It takes an awful lot of chutzpah for a 23-year-old woman to tackle such venerable source material," Stephen Thompson wrote for the *(Madison) Wisconsin State Journal* (February 20, 1997), "yet the results are marvelous all the way through."

The young singer had a mixed reaction to her newfound fame. Still in her early 20s, she felt overwhelmed by all the attention and its accompanying pressure to meet others' expectations of her. (She had also strained her vocal cords through extensive touring and developed a cyst that had to be surgically removed.) "On one side, you want people to hear you and to like you. On the other, you don't want to surrender your whole personal life," she lamented to Katherine Monk for the *Vancouver Sun* (June 26, 1997). In addition, she was bothered by the frequency with which critics compared her to Billie Holiday; while the late jazz singer was an idol of hers, Peyroux wanted to cultivate a sound that was distinctly her own. Unable to square others' reactions to her work with her own desires, Peyroux "spent some time trying to hide," as she told Jane Cornwell. She traveled across the country, stayed with her family, and lived for a year in a Christian community in Nashville, Tennessee, searching for a grounding in spirituality. She eventually returned to New York, where she worked for a short time as a waitress to support herself. She also began busking again, because, as she explained to Jane Cornwell, "I realised that music is so soothing, so healing, it would be a shame not to share it." (On one occasion she was arrested on a "quality of life" charge for singing on the street a few blocks from her Manhattan apartment.)

During her eight-year absence from recording studios, Peyroux met the guitarist, singer, and harmonica player William Galison, who heard her sing in a bar in New York City in 2002 and asked if he could accompany her on the harmonica. She agreed, and the two began performing together on a regular basis, becoming romantically involved as they played gigs in New York, Philadelphia, and, ultimately, Europe. Even after their romance fizzled, in 2003, Galison and Peyroux continued to perform together, and they recorded a seven-song EP, which they sold at their shows. Then, having signed a deal with Rounder Records, Peyroux ended her involvement with Galison. (After Galison

finished and released *Got You on My Mind*, the album he had begun with Peyroux, in September 2004, Rounder Records threatened him with a lawsuit. They later dropped the suit; Galison is suing Peyroux and Rounder for allegedly attempting to block the distribution of his CD by urging certain vendors to refrain from stocking the album. Peyroux has not commented on the lawsuit, telling Jane Cornwell only that she stopped working with Galison "for personal reasons. The recordings he's released are not very good." The suit is still pending.)

In September 2004 Rounder Records released Peyroux's second album, *Careless Love*. On it Peyroux covered songs by artists ranging from Bob Dylan and Hank Williams to Elliott Smith and Leonard Cohen. "Those writers have penned more than a few wonderful songs. They have a lifetime of quality work. It's daunting, it's scary, it's a dream come true to cover their songs," she told Nui Te Koha for the Melbourne, Australia, *Herald Sun* (April 16, 2005). Reviewers seemed to approve of Peyroux's decision to cover a range of songs, including some that were unusual choices for a jazz and blues artist. According to a review for the *Express* (January 21, 2005), an English publication, *Careless Love* "is the perfect showcase for [Peyroux's] smoke-and-honey vocals, while her choice of covers on the record is simply inspired." Lynell George enthused, "*Careless Love* seems to take up naturally where she left off [with *Dreamland*]—Peyroux's voice still burnished and deeply grooved, brimming with seen-it-all languor." Clive Davis, writing for the London *Times Online* (April 12, 2005) about a 2005 live performance by Peyroux, praised the singer as "a fascinating, and sometimes perplexing mixture of old and new. . . . What makes her so beguiling is the near-flawless choice of material and the exemplary arrangements—an elegant combination of restrained swing and an uptown blues format that used to be the private property of the late, great Charles Brown."

"I think the industry forgot me a lot quicker than my fans did," Peyroux told Mark Brown for the Denver, Colorado, *Rocky Mountain News* (February 1, 2005). "What was really humbling was to find that people who saw me eight years ago would come out and see me again." Most recently, Peyroux contributed a song to the compilation *Sweetheart 2005: Love Songs*, an album sold only in Starbucks coffee shops. Peyroux lives in Brooklyn and enjoys touring. "I have every reason to get far away from what I see here," the singer told Diana Simmons for the Sydney, Australia, *Sunday Telegraph* (December 5, 2004), referring to the re-election of President George W. Bush.

—K.J.E.

Suggested Reading: *Boston Herald* p40 Mar. 9, 2005, with photo; CNN.com Jan. 12, 2005; *(Melbourne, Australia) Herald Sun* W p3 Apr. 16, 2005; madeleinepeyroux.org; *Ottawa Citizen* C p6 Oct. 23, 1997

Selected Recordings: *Dreamland*, 1996; *Careless Love*, 2004

Courtesy of Common Cause

Pingree, Chellie

(SHEL-ee)

Apr. 2, 1955– President and CEO of Common Cause

Address: Common Cause, 1250 Connecticut Ave., N.W., #600, Washington, DC 20036

In February 2003 Chellie Pingree—whose former occupations include farmer, small-business owner, chairperson of a local school board, and Maine state senator, and who in 2002 ran unsuccessfully as a Democrat for one of Maine's seats in the U.S. Senate—was elected president and chief executive officer (CEO) of Common Cause. A nonpartisan, nonprofit citizens' watchdog organization based in Washington, D.C., Common Cause was founded in 1970 by John Gardner; earlier, while serving in the Cabinet of President Lyndon B. Johnson and then as the chairperson of the National Urban Coalition Action Council, Gardner had concluded that ordinary U.S. citizens lacked a collective voice in the nation's capital. "Everybody's organized but the people," Gardner once said, "everybody" referring to the thousands of industries and other special-interest groups whose lobbyists influence federal legislation, regulations, and policies. According to its Web site, Common Cause is "a vehicle for citizens to make their voices heard in the political process and to hold their elected leaders accountable

to the public interest." It is "committed to honest, open and accountable government" and to "encouraging citizen participation in democracy." Pingree began to gain an intimate familiarity with the political process and its strengths and weaknesses three decades ago, when she became involved in community affairs in the small Maine community in which she ran her farm and knitting-goods business and raised her three children. Among the high points of her highly effective, eight-year career in the Maine state Senate, in which for four years she served as the majority leader, were the passage of unprecedented health-care and prescription-drug bills that benefitted thousands of Maine residents who had no medical coverage and/or had very low incomes. In 2001 the national nonprofit organization Families USA, which is dedicated to making high-quality, affordable health care available to all Americans, named Pingree "consumer-health advocate of the year." As the head of Common Cause, she is working to enhance the transparency of government at all levels; strengthen and extend campaign-finance reform and promote increased public financing of political campaigns; implement changes in states' systems of electoral districting, which currently allow rampant gerrymandering in favor of one party or another; and limit the increasing control that a small number of giant corporations exert over the media. One of her prime goals is to convince people everywhere in the U.S. that each person can make a difference in the political process, whether by discussing issues with friends and relatives, writing letters or E-mail messages to or phoning legislators, attending public meetings, voting, or seeking election to public office in their communities, towns, cities, or states.

Rochelle Marie Pingree, known universally as Chellie, was born in Minneapolis, Minnesota, on April 2, 1955. As a 17-year-old new high-school graduate, she moved to North Haven, an island 12 miles off the coast of Maine, in Penobscot Bay. Pingree attended the College of the Atlantic, in Bar Harbor, Maine, where she studied human ecology, a discipline concerned in part with the consequences of human actions on the natural and man-made environments. After she graduated, with a B.A. degree, in 1976, Pingree bought a two-acre farm in North Haven. For a dozen years beginning that year, she raised sheep, chickens, cows, and vegetables on the farm, which eventually covered 90 acres. Concurrently, in 1981, she established North Island Yarn, a retail store that sold products hand-knitted by Pingree and her employees. Later, after renaming the business North Island Designs, she also marketed knitting kits and books of knitting patterns to some 1,200 retail outlets nationwide, along with the mail-order houses L. L. Bean and Lands' End. She wrote or co-wrote, with Debby Anderson, four books of knitting patterns, among them *Maine Island Classics: Knitting on a Maine Island* (1988), and she joined the National Writers Union, which is affiliated with the United Automobile, Aerospace, and Agricultural Implement Workers of America (familiarly known as the UAW), one of the nation's largest and most diverse labor organizations. North Island Designs continued operating until 1993.

Meanwhile, in 1975, while still an undergraduate, Pingree had married. During the next decade she became the mother of two daughters (Cecily and Hannah) and a son (Asa) and became involved in North Haven affairs. In the February 5, 2002 installment of an occasional "diary" that appeared in the UAW's on-line publication *Solidarity*, she wrote that in North Haven, she "learned what it is to be part of a community. On an island of 350, almost everyone serves on a board or committee at some time, or is an active volunteer or just involved in the morning conversations over coffee down at the store." According to Chris Mooney in *American Prospect* (October 7, 2002), North Haven is still a place where "people leave their keys in their cars so neighbors can borrow them." Its year-round population includes many lobstermen and other rugged individuals with whom Pingree "rub-[bed] shoulders" regularly, in Mooney's words. In the *Solidarity* piece, Pingree described the first time she stood up and spoke at a North Haven town meeting as "one of the scarier public speaking moments of my life." She soon became braver and, as she recalled, "found that being involved in small-town politics was very rewarding and quite an education." During the 1980s she served on the North Haven Planning Board, as a tax assessor, and on the local school board, the last of which she chaired for some time. (School-board chair, according to Pingree, is "the hardest job in politics.") "One thing that distinguishes local politics and makes it such a model for the way I believe policy should be made at all levels of government is accountability . . . ," she wrote for *Solidarity*. In a town as small as North Haven, "almost every decision you make will be discussed on the ferry, at the store over coffee and at the next baked bean supper. And, because most issues affect everyone's lives, community members feel an obligation to do their part when it comes to making decisions."

In 1992 Pingree won election to the Maine state Senate as a Democrat in District 21, a strongly Republican area that encompassed North Haven and other Penobscot Bay islands and more than a dozen municipalities in Knox County, on the mainland. She was reelected to three additional two-year terms in the Senate; because of reapportionment in Maine, she represented what had become District 12 during those three terms. Pingree quickly distinguished herself among Senate lawmakers through her ability to find creative solutions to problems and to build bipartisan consensus around issues. A poll conducted in 1995 by the now-defunct *Maine Times* newspaper named Pingree the state's favorite legislator. The following year she was elected majority leader of the state Senate. She was only the second woman in Maine history to win that position, which she held until

2000. As a Maine lawmaker she sponsored legislation that created the Parents as Scholars program, a student-aid service that helped low-income parents to pursue two- or four-year college degrees. During the mid-1990s she served as co-chair of both Maine's Committee on Housing and Economic Development and the Maine Economic Growth Council. In recognition of her efforts to expand opportunities for small-business owners, she was named the Economic Development Council's legislator of the year in 1994. According to Mooney, Pingree's experience in those legislative and advisory bodies was instrumental in her successful fight to establish a law that requires corporations that do business in Maine to report state-tax breaks and how they use subsidies given by the state. Pingree also served as chairperson of Maine Citizens Against Handgun Violence and the Maine Women's Vote Project, the latter of which works to increase voter turnouts for state elections. Her priorities also included advocating for increased public access to public land.

As a state senator Pingree was best known for her efforts regarding health care. As Senate majority leader she successfully led the fight to extend health care to 10,000 low-wage Maine families and reduce their prescription-drug costs. (With one of the highest percentages of senior citizens of all 50 states and as a state bordering Canada, where drug prices are regulated and often considerably lower than in the U.S., Maine has long been on the frontline of the national debate regarding the high costs of prescription drugs and the pharmaceutical industry's role in keeping prices high.) Pingree spearheaded the passage, in 2000, of Maine Rx, an unprecedented piece of legislation that requires pharmaceutical companies to negotiate the prices of drugs with the state government in order to keep drug costs low for state residents who do not have health insurance or whose salaries or wages are significantly lower than average. In drawing up the law, Pingree was aided by the Center for Policy Alternatives (the country's "leading nonpartisan progressive public policy organization serving state legislators," according to its Web site). More than 250,000 uninsured Maine residents became eligible to enroll for discounts on prescription drugs after Maine Rx went into effect. The program served as a model for prescription-drug programs instituted in Hawaii and Illinois, and Legislatures in other states are considering similar measures. "We shouldn't have to pass this bill in Maine, then in New Hampshire, then in Virginia," Pingree declared to Robin Toner for the *New York Times* (May 11, 2002). "[The federal government] ought to have a Medicare prescription drug benefit, and they ought to negotiate a really good price. . . . If we could do this in Maine, we can do it in Washington"—meaning that such reforms should be nationwide and not limited to individual states. The Pharmaceutical Research and Manufacturers of America unsuccessfully challenged Maine Rx before the U.S. Supreme Court as an unconstitutional regulation of interstate commerce.

Thanks to Pingree's achievements in the Maine state Senate, in 1997 she earned an Eisenhower International Exchange Program fellowship, which enabled her to travel in Hungary to observe that country's continuing transition from Communist rule to open democracy. While in Hungary Pingree also met with female business leaders and women involved in the country's politics. In 1998 Pingree was a member of a special White House delegation that oversaw the democratic elections in Bosnia and Herzegovina, which took place after years of ethnic and religious bloodshed there. In 1999 she interacted with female political leaders in Northern Ireland as a member of another U.S. delegation. Also during the 1990s Pingree traveled in India with a group organized by the Global Peace Initiative.

Because of term-limits regulations, Pingree was not permitted to seek reelection in 2001. That same year she was named a senior fellow at the Center for Policy Alternatives, in Washington, D.C. In 2002, after ruling out a run for the state governorship, Pingree campaigned for a seat in the U.S. Senate against the popular incumbent Maine Republican Susan Collins.(Maine's other senator, Olympia Snow, is also a woman and a Republican.) During her campaign, Chris Mooney wrote, "In her political ads and rapid-fire stump speeches, Pingree hones in on pocketbook issues, especially prescription drugs and corporate accountability. But she often approaches them not so much as an outraged corporate watchdog but from the folksy perspective of a small businessperson trying to keep the island's only general store running." The race was watched unusually closely nationwide, because some political observers believed that a Pingree victory was essential for the Democrats to hold onto their party's majority in the Senate. Senate Majority Leader Tom Daschle appeared with Pingree at several events during her campaign, and *Time* (June 10, 2002) ran a photo of Daschle and Pingree together. In an August 2002 entry for her UAW *Solidarity* "diary," Pingree wrote that the Maine Senate race began attracting further national press attention when it became public that the White House had conducted an "electronic slide show" revealing that the administration of Republican president George W. Bush considered "Maine's Senate seat to be one of a few in which a Democrat could unseat a Republican incumbent." In part because Senator Collins and the Maine Republican Party also come out in favor of health-care reforms, diminishing the selling power of Pingree's proposals, Collins defeated Pingree on Election Day, November 5, 2002, by 16 percentage points.

Pingree's record as a highly effective advocate of corporate responsibility and measures that would aid average, working-class citizens led the national governing board of Common Cause (chaired by Derek Bok, president emeritus of Harvard University) to elect her president and CEO of the organization on February 11, 2003. In a "public letter" to potential members issued in 1970, when Common Cause was launched, John Gardner stated, "The first thing Common Cause will do is to assist you to speak and act in behalf of legislation designed to solve the nation's problems. We are going to build a true 'citizens' lobby—a lobby concerned not with the advancement of special interests but with the well-being of the nation. We will keep you up-to-date on crucial issues before Congress. We will suggest when and where to bring pressure to bear. . . . We want public officials to have literally millions of American citizens looking over their shoulders at every move they make. We want phones to ring in Washington and state capitols and town halls. We want people watching and influencing every move that government makes." In addition to Gardner, Common Cause's previous presidents were Archibald Cox, a former solicitor general of the United States, who was most famous as a special prosecutor during the Watergate investigations, which led to the resignation of President Richard Nixon, and Pingree's immediate predecessor, Scott Harshbarger, a former Massachusetts attorney general. During its first 34 years, Common Cause was instrumental in the establishment of "sunshine" laws that promote transparency in regard to the activities of the U.S. Congress; a ban that prohibits members of Congress from accepting gifts from special-interest groups; the demise of the so-called grandfather clause that in the past allowed senior members of Congress to pocket their remaining campaign funds when they retired; the enactment of tough financial disclosure laws for members of Congress; the blocking of the federal government's expansion of weapon systems such as "Star Wars" (the missile defense shield); and, in 2002, the passage of the Bipartisan Campaign Reform Act.

Currently, Common Cause has about 300,000 members and supporters (the latter of whom receive the organization's E-mail messages). Some four dozen employees work at its Washington, D.C., headquarters, aided by about 100 volunteers. As president and CEO Pingree oversees Common Cause's finances, public communications, and programs; she is the public face of the organization's mission to mobilize citizens to take stands and speak out on issues regarding civil rights, corporate accountability, and ethical practices in government. On its Web site Common Cause urges citizens to "take action" by contacting their local U.S. senators and representatives about current issues; to visit Causenet, the organization's on-line issues and news-alert network; and to "become an activist" by talking with Common Cause volunteers to find out what sorts of actions Common Cause recommends in local communities. In October 2005, according to its Web site, the top goals of Common Cause were to "increase the diversity of voices and ownership in media; make media more responsive to the needs of citizens in a democracy and to protect the editorial independence of public broadcasting; advance campaign reforms that make people and ideas more important than money; make certain that government is open, ethical and accountable; remove barriers to voting and ensure that our voting systems are accurate and accessible; increase participation in the political process; [and] make certain that our government is held accountable for the costs, in lives and money, for the invasion of Iraq."

"It's hard not to think about raising carrots when you're trying to solve tricky issues in Washington," Pingree told Bill McConnell for Broadcasting & Cable (November 1, 2004, on-line). Among her other honors, in 1996 Pingree earned the Center for Policy Alternatives' Flemming Fellow Leadership Award. In 2004 the Maine state Legislature honored her with a Distinguished Achievement Award. Pingree contributed to the book *Sustaining Island Communities: The Story of the Economy and Life of Maine's Year-Round Islands* (1998). Since she assumed her post at Common Cause, she has become a resident of Washington, D.C. Her marriage, to Charles F. Pingree, ended in divorce in about 1990. In an on-line announcement re-

leased by the organizers of the Future of Music Policy conference, held in 2004, which addressed the issue of the increasing control of the nation's media by a decreasing number of megacorporations, Pingree (who spoke at that meeting) was quoted as saying that her son is an aspiring actor, and one of her daughters (Cecily) is building a career as an independent documentary filmmaker. Her other daughter, Hannah, is currently serving in the Maine House of Representatives, for a district that includes North Haven; at 27, she is the youngest member of the state House. Earlier, Hannah Pingree developed iVillage's Election 2000 Web site.
—C.F.T.

Suggested Reading: *American Prospect* Vol. 13, Issue 18, Oct. 7, 2002; Center for Policy Alternatives Web site; Common Cause Web site; Maine State Legislature Web site; National Conference of State Legislatures Web site; *New York Times* A p1+ May 11, 2002, with photos, A p11 June 1, 2002; *Time* p29 June 10, 2002, with photo

Prince-Hughes, Dawn

Jan. 31, 1964– Anthropologist; writer

Address: Dept. of Anthropology, Western Washington University, Arntzen Hall 315, 516 High St., Bellingham, WA 98225

"I always felt like I was meant to do something meaningful in the world, to help other people, to even someday be embraced by the human world that I had for so long rejected," Dawn Prince-Hughes said in an on-line interview for Random House, which published her memoir, *Songs of the Gorilla Nation: My Journey Through Autism*. Prince-Hughes has Asperger's syndrome, a little-known, little-understood form of autism whose symptoms usually manifest themselves during the first years of life. Asperger's often goes undiagnosed, because victims have more or less normal cognitive abilities and speech and, despite their extreme discomfort in most social situations and extreme sensory sensitivity, can appear to function normally. Hans Asperger, a Viennese physician, first described the syndrome in a paper published in 1944; 50 years passed before the American Psychiatric Association included it in its *Diagnostic and Statistical Manual of Mental Disorders*, one of the main reference tools of mental-health professionals in the United States. Prince-Hughes turned 30 the year that the fourth edition of the manual, which contains a reference to Asperger's syndrome, was published. By her own account, it was not until she was 36 that she was formally diagnosed and learned that the emotional and social problems that had plagued her all her

Courtesy of Western Washington University

life were symptoms of a condition that could be eased by medication and other means.

After dropping out of high school, Prince-Hughes endured several years of homelessness, then spent several years as a performer in a club that featured nude dancing. During a visit to the Woodland Park Zoo, in Seattle, Washington, when she was in her early 20s, Prince-Hughes felt an intense kinship with the zoo's gorillas, and she soon embarked on a careful study of the animals that has continued to this day. She resumed her education and earned both a master's degree and a doctoral degree in interdisciplinary anthropology. Meanwhile, through her interactions with the gorillas, she slowly became better able to deal with her condition and engage in conventional social intercourse. "When I speak of emerging from the darkness of autism," she wrote in *Songs of the Gorilla Nation*, "I do not mean that I offer a success story neatly wrapped and finished with a 'cure.' I and the others who are autistic do not want to be cured. What I mean when I say 'emergence' is that my soul was lifted from the context of my earlier autism and became autistic in another context, one filled with wonder and discovery and full of the feelings that so poetically inform each human life." Prince-Hughes is also the author of *Adam*, a novel, and of *Gorillas Among Us: A Primate Ethnographer's Book of Days*, which contains a foreword by the world-renowned primatologist and conservationist Jane Goodall. Prince-Hughes has taught at Western Washington University.

Prince-Hughes was born Kimberly Dawn Prince on January 31, 1964 to Ron Prince, an air-conditioning and heating repairman, and Joyce Prince, a homemaker. Her parents raised her and her sister, Davina, in Carbondale, Illinois, until Dawn was about 10. In her memoir Prince-Hughes wrote that she can trace her memories back to the moment she entered the world, aided by a doctor dressed in light blue and wearing black-framed eyeglasses. She began to experience symptoms of Asperger's at an early age. "I had an unusually strong reaction to bright lights and loud noises, . . . and I did not like to be held," she wrote in her memoir. "When people tried to cuddle me I would stiffen and push away from them, feeling like I was drowning. It was worse when they tried to kiss me." Unlike the vast majority of babies, she recalled, she never sucked or chewed on toys or other objects, and she learned to walk "without going through a crawling stage." "I didn't like the feel of the carpet or floor under my hands," she explained. Repetition and ritual dominated her waking hours. As a toddler, she would endlessly repeat words new to her, while racing around the rooms and hallways of her home or her maternal grandparents' home in a particular progression from which she never deviated; this was her favorite "game." In another symptom of what has been described as obsessive-compulsive behavior, which is common among Asperger's patients, she would sing commercial jingles "without surcease until my mother would inform me that I was driving her crazy," as she wrote in her memoir. When she was taken to places in her neighborhood, she "would insist on going the same way every single time." As a youngster she would listen to a phonograph record again and again, for a set number of times; if, when trying to catch lightning bugs at night, she failed to reach the particular quota she had set for herself, "the day would be ruined." "My sensory problems were also symptomatic of Asperger's,"

she wrote. "For instance, I held my hands in tight balls because I could not cope with the possibility of getting dirt on my palms. I developed a trick of picking things up using my thumb and the side of my index finger so that I wouldn't have to uncurl my hands. . . . Dust between my toes was enough to send me into a full-blown rage."

Despite her obvious intelligence, in school Prince-Hughes performed poorly, especially in mathematics. Most of her teachers, unaware of her true condition, considered her willfully difficult and uncooperative. One exception was her fifth-grade teacher, Kay Eckiss, who "seemed to understand my problems," as Prince-Hughes wrote in her memoir. Eckiss let Dawn choose for herself what she wanted to read and did not insist that the girl do more than a minimum of math. "Best of all, she did not make me go outside for recess and play with the other children"; instead, teacher and student would discuss a wide range of topics. "The times when . . . [Eckiss] disagree[d] with me, she gave me *reasons*. Logical and well-thought-out ones. This separated her from almost everyone else I had ever known. She made me want to understand." At the end of that year, Prince-Hughes's parents sold their house and nearly all their possessions and traveled west to find a new place to live. Thus, all at once, Prince-Hughes had to leave her childhood home, her beloved grandparents, and nearly all of her belongings to settle in a totally new location—changes difficult for the average child and immensely more difficult for a child with Asperger's. "I still think of this turn of events as the most traumatic in my life," she wrote in her memoir.

The trailer in which the Prince family settled abutted a large uninhabited space in which a herd of once-domesticated horses roamed wild. Through patience, careful observation of their behavior, and her intuitive understanding of the horses, Prince-Hughes gained their acceptance of her presence; one of them even allowed her to lie on his back. "My relationship with them and the emotional sustenance it gave me was a foreshadowing of the closeness I later had with the gorillas," she wrote. Her experiences in school and relationships with her peers, by contrast, were almost uniformly distressing. When she was in seventh grade, she began drinking alcohol habitually, having persuaded one of her mother's friends to provide her with a steady supply. After she entered high school, the public revelation that she was a lesbian, compounded with her self-acknowledged strangeness, led other students, both male and female, to torment her. "People would corner me in the bathroom and force my head into the toilet, slam me into my locker, and throw trash at me in the hall," she wrote in *Songs of the Gorilla Nation*. "They hit me in the head with books and spit on me. They defaced my locker. They took my food away. Once some senior students made a sign with a derogatory word on it and hung it around my neck." Because she "believed in pacifism," in her words, she responded to her attackers neither physically nor verbally except once, and on that occasion she was expelled for three days. One day when she was 16, another student made an inflammatory remark to her as Prince-Hughes was standing in front of her locker. "With slow deliberation I took my things back out of my locker and walked out of the school," she wrote in her autobiography; she never returned.

Her parents, according to Prince-Hughes, had always wanted what was best for her, but at that point they no longer knew how to help her. So they agreed to contribute toward the fees for a tiny room in an inexpensive, vermin-infested hotel, where she lived alone and became increasingly dependent on alcohol and drugs. Unable to pay for the room, she became homeless and began drifting around the country, sleeping in doorways or parks or in the houses of strangers who were kind enough to take her in for a few nights.

In the mid-1980s Prince-Hughes found herself in Seattle, where she took a job as a dancer in an establishment where clients paid by the minute to watch scantily clad dancers. Although exceedingly tiring, the dancing comforted her, because it enabled her to transport herself mentally to a fantasy world. "Dressed in animal skins and body paint . . . I would take huge leaps across the stage," she wrote in her memoir, "screaming in midair, and come down into a banging crouch in front of some horrified man who hadn't seen me launching toward him. Just as quickly I would leap away to grab the wooden railings situated all around the stage and hang suspended from them, swinging around with all my might. . . . I was called into the office many times and warned not to run amok in this way, but I just couldn't seem to help it."

During that period Prince-Hughes visited the Woodland Park Zoo, in Seattle, and became fascinated with a 275-pound gorilla named Nina. For the first time in her life, she felt a sense of kinship with another being. The gorilla's slow gestures, deliberate movements, and unwillingness to make eye contact led Prince-Hughes to believe that she had finally found a creature like herself. (She generally refers to the animals as "gorilla people.") For the next month, Prince-Hughes visited the gorillas every day. "In so many ways, large and small, I saw the best and worst of myself in the gorillas," she wrote in her memoir. "But they had accomplished what I had not: the ability to remain open and communicate with others of their kind in a way that made them feel whole." She also wrote, "These gorillas, so sensitive and so trapped, were mirrors for my soul as it struggled behind bars, gawked at by the distorted faces of my world, taken out of a context that was meaningful and embracing. . . . Gorillas, like autistic people, are misunderstood. They are seen as ugly, as caricatures of fully formed humanity, as unfinished or trapped in an anachronistic world that has no value."

After some time, her comfort with the gorillas enabled Prince-Hughes to approach researchers at the zoo and to feel increasingly at ease around them. "I had begun to find ways to make it known to them that I cared for them and had good intentions," she wrote. "I cared about them as people, and after years of watching gorillas, I was learning how to tell them that." The zoo provided her not only with a research setting but also a modest living, after she secured a low-level job there. She enrolled in an individualized animal-studies program at a local school where there were few traditional classes.

In 1994 Prince-Hughes began dating Tara Hughes, an English teacher who had one son and had recently divorced. The two fell in love and began living together. A few years later one of Prince-Hughes's relatives was diagnosed with Asperger's syndrome. Learning about the malady deeply disturbed Prince-Hughes. She began falling into violent rages for what appeared to be no reason; often, she directed her anger at her partner. When Tara felt she could no longer tolerate Prince-Hughes's behavior, she warned Prince-Hughes that she would leave her if she did not seek psychiatric help. In 2000 Prince-Hughes consulted a psychiatrist and was formally diagnosed with Asperger's syndrome. "I felt an immense wave of relief wash over me as everything suddenly made sense," she wrote in her memoir. "I looked back over my life, perhaps the way people do before they die, and thought of all the painful memories that could now be explained."

Meanwhile, Prince-Hughes had begun applying to Ph.D. programs. She matriculated at the Universität Herisau in Switzerland, which accepted her on the strength of her well-documented studies of the Woodland Park gorillas and essays written at the request of university examiners. She earned an M.A. degree and a Ph.D. degree in interdisciplinary anthropology by means of correspondence with Universität Herisau professors and advisers. Her doctoral dissertation was published in 2000 with the title *The Archetype of the Ape-Man: The Phenomenological Archaeology of a Relic Hominid Ancestor*. A description of the book on the Barnes & Noble Web site states, "Utilizing concepts in the fields of cultural and physical anthropology, ethology, psychology, and philosophy, this dissertation asserts as its conclusion that the archetype of the ape-man is a result of accreted and enacted collective memories, and reflects an important phenomenon integral to human thought and form." Also in 2000 Prince-Hughes became an adjunct professor at Western Washington University, in Bellingham.

The year 2001 saw the publication of two books by Prince-Hughes. In *Gorillas Among Us: A Primate Ethnographer's Book of Days*, she described the daily rituals, diet, and behaviors of the Woodland Park Zoo's gorillas, including the many ways in which they communicated with one another and with her. *"Gorillas Among Us* is a wonderful book that delights the mind and touches the heart . . . ," Jane Goodall wrote in her foreword. "It is the author's empathy with her subjects, her obvious love of gorillas, that makes this book so special." In Prince-Hughes's novel, *Adam*, the title character agrees to live for seven years in a large outdoor enclosure, without running water, modern conveniences, clothing, or other humans; in exchange, the wealthy man who owns the property promises that, at the end of the allotted time, he will support Adam financially for as long as he lives. Unable to maintain himself in that natural environment, Adam becomes malnourished and begins to hallucinate. He is saved from death by a humanlike apparition, who teaches him survival skills and also introduces him to ancient rites.

In *Songs of the Gorilla Nation* (2004), Prince-Hughes vividly recalled her many painful experiences as a social outsider and the ways in which Woodland Park's gorillas helped her to build a satisfying life for herself. In an assessment for the *New York Times Book Review* (March 21, 2004), the science writer Natalie Angier characterized the book as an "unsettling, lyrical, sometimes self-pitying but ultimately redemptive memoir." Arthur Salm, in a review for the *San Diego Union-Tribune* (May 9, 2004), criticized what he labeled Prince-Hughes's "unchecked anthropomorphism" of the gorillas. "*Songs of the Gorilla Nation* becomes a sad but invaluable document, recapitulating ways

in which people with Asperger's Syndrome have difficulty communicating," Salm wrote.

Prince-Hughes is the editor of *Aquamarine Blue 5: Personal Stories of College Students with Autism* (2002). She is on the advisory board of the nonprofit organization ApeNet, which, according to its Web site, is "a consortium of foundations and individuals who support interconnecting great apes with each other, as well as with humans, through enculturation and technology." In about 1999 she became the parent of a son, Teryk, whose biological mother is Tara Prince-Hughes. In helping to choose their anonymous sperm donor, Prince-Hughes ruled out any men who had not indicated in their descriptions of themselves a love of animals.

—C.M./R.E.

Suggested Reading: *New York Times Book Review* p12 Mar. 21, 2004; *People* p121+ June 14, 2004; Prince-Hughes, Dawn. *Songs of the Gorilla Nation: My Journey Through Autism*, 2004

Selected Books: fiction—*Adam*, 2001; nonfiction—*Gorillas Among Us: A Primate Ethnographer's Book of Days*, 2001; *Songs of the Gorilla Nation: My Journey Through Autism*, 2004; as editor—*Aquamarine Blue 5*, 2002

Prosper, Pierre-Richard

1963– Former U.S. ambassador-at-large for war-crime issues

Address: Prosper for Attorney General, 520 S. Grand Ave., Suite 700, Los Ángeles, CA 90071

One of the most horrific events of recent memory took place in the spring of 1994 in the central African nation of Rwanda, which is roughly the size of the state of New Hampshire. Over a period of about 100 days, more than 800,000 people were slaughtered, and approximately 250,000 women raped, by members of Rwanda's majority ethnic group, the Hutus, whose acts were intended to eliminate the country's primary minority ethnic group, the Tutsis. The violence between the two groups, which began in 1990 and was rooted in nearly a century of disagreements, had escalated on April 6, 1994, when an airplane carrying the Rwandan president, Juvenal Habyarimana, a Hutu, was shot down above the Kigali airport. The attack killed Habyarimana and several others aboard the plane, including Cyprian Ntayamira, the president of Burundi, a nation south of Rwanda. When the fighting ceased, nearly one million Tutsis and moderate Hutus—or 10 percent of the nation's population—had been killed, and approximately 300,000 were homeless.

R. D. Ward, courtesy of the U.S. Department of Defense

During the attacks, members of the Hutu militia—known as the Interahamwe, or "those who work together"—encountered a provincial mayor,

Jean-Paul Akayesu, in the village of Taba. After initially resisting the Interahamwe, Akayesu, a former teacher and school inspector, was persuaded by the group to become an abettor of the genocide. For his part in the devastation, Akayesu was later charged with 15 counts of genocide, torture, rape, murder, and crimes against humanity. (He pleaded "not guilty.") In September 1998, after a 14-month trial at the United Nations International Criminal Tribunal for Rwanda (ICTR), held in Arusha, in the bordering nation of Tanzania, Akayesu was convicted of nine of the charges. He thus became the first person convicted of genocide under the code established at the 1948 International Genocide Convention, which took place in the wake of World War II. The ICTR case against Akayesu was historic for another reason, as well: it established rape in a time of conflict as an act of genocide and a crime against humanity. Akayesu received three life sentences, to be served concurrently, and an additional 80 years in prison.

The lead prosecutor for the United Nations in the case against Akayesu was Pierre-Richard Prosper, the ambassador-at-large for war-crime issues at the U.S. State Department from July 2001 through October 2005 and the second person to hold the post. As ambassador Prosper traveled worldwide, meeting with heads of state to build bilateral and international support for U.S. policies related to the prosecution of war crimes, and he directly advised the U.S. secretary of state, Condoleezza Rice, on such matters. In early October 2005 Prosper left his post to seek the Republican Party's nomination for attorney general of California. A political neophyte, Prosper hoped to build on the reputation he had forged as a prosecutor in the United States attorney's office in Los Angeles.

Prior to his work at the State Department, Prosper built a reputation as a prosecutor of gang-related criminals in the Los Angeles, California, area. Many of Prosper's colleagues have said that he is unusually skilled in winning the confidence of potential prosecution witnesses, a strength he put to use during his 1996 visit to Rwanda, where he interviewed victims of sexual abuse and other survivors of the civil war to build evidence for the charges brought against Akayesu. For his part, Prosper has said that his effectiveness at his work can be attributed in part to the genuine compassion he shows toward the victims of crimes and potential witnesses. He told Ann M. Simmons for the Los Angeles Times (October 3, 1998), "You have to understand their fear, their concern, their pain. If you do, then it opens up the door."

The son of Jacques Prosper and Jeanine Prosper, physicians who had immigrated to the U.S. from the Republic of Haiti, Pierre-Richard Prosper was born in Denver, Colorado, in 1963. Following the family's brief return to Haiti, Prosper's parents completed their medical residencies in the United States, settling in Saratoga County, New York, where Prosper was raised. As a boy Prosper spent his summers visiting his relatives in Haiti's capital,

Port-au-Prince. The country was then under the oppressive rule of President François Duvalier (also known as "Papa Doc"); at his ambassadorial hearing before the U.S. Senate Foreign Relations Committee on June 27, 2001, Prosper recalled his early introduction to political repression: "Basic human dignity, which we today take for granted, was denied [in Haiti]. Individual life had little value," he said, as quoted on the U.S. Department of State Web site. "Freedom of speech was non-existent and movement was controlled. State-sponsored killings and disappearances became the norm. . . . This story is a sober reminder to me of a life that could have been and a life that should not be."

After graduating from Shenendehowa High School in Saratoga County in 1981, Prosper enrolled at Boston College, in Massachusetts, where he earned a B.A. degree in Romance languages and was also a member of the varsity lacrosse team. Afterward he attended Pepperdine University's School of Law, in Malibu, California, receiving his law degree in 1989.

Prosper had originally intended to become a corporate lawyer but found criminal law to be more interesting. He began prosecuting what he has described as "senseless killing" as a deputy district attorney for Los Angeles County from 1989 to 1994, a period when he was assigned mostly to cases of gang-related homicides. Prosper recalled to the New York Times (November 1, 1998), "I remember one day having 22 cases on my desk, all homicides and double homicides." While handling cases for the Compton and Inglewood areas of Los Angeles, he brought in life sentences for more than a dozen criminals. During his last two years as a deputy district attorney, Prosper succeeded in getting a life sentence for the driver in a gang-related drive-by shooting in which two teenagers were killed in front of a bus stop. From 1994 to 1996 Prosper was assigned as a federal prosecutor for the narcotics division of the Central District of California in Los Angeles. As an assistant U.S. attorney, he investigated and prosecuted major international drug cartels from such countries as Mexico and Colombia, working in conjunction with the U.S.'s Organized Crime Drug Enforcement Task Force.

It was during this time that Prosper's colleague Steve Mansfield, who had just returned from a U.S. State Department mission to Africa, presented him with graphic evidence of the genocide in Rwanda. According to some sources, Mansfield showed Prosper slides depicting the acts committed against the Tutsi, which were rooted in nearly a century of civil strife between the Tutsi and the Hutu, Rwanda's two major ethnic groups, and were exacerbated when an airplane carrying the Rwandan president, Juvenal Habyarimana, a Hutu, was shot down above the Kigali airport. Hutu politicians and people controlling a prominent local radio station promptly attributed the president's death to activities of Tutsi rebels. Within hours the Hutu militia, called the Interahamwe, began killing

Tutsis at a furious pace. The slaughter lasted 100 days, during which more than 800,000 Rwandans and moderate Hutus—or roughly 10 percent of the nation's population—were killed. At Mansfield's urging Prosper joined the International Criminal Tribunal for Rwanda. Soon afterward he visited that country, meeting with survivors of the atrocity. "I stood above mass-graves that contained the remains of hundreds of bodies. I quickly learned that what I was seeing was not only a crime against Rwandans, but truly a crime against all of humanity," he said in his Capitol Hill testimony before the Senate Foreign Relations Committee. Shortly following his arrival in Rwanda, Prosper was appointed lead prosecutor for the case, joining a team of prosecutors and judges from around the world. "It was really shocking and sobering," he told Simmons. "I had never seen anything like that before. I didn't know that human beings had the ability to do that kind of thing. It really woke me up. The feeling I had was that something had to be done; someone had to do something."

Many of the Rwandan women whose testimonies were vital to the prosecution's case were fearful of traveling from their rural villages to the neighboring country of Tanzania, where the tribunal was to be held. Members of the prosecution suggested that a female attorney be appointed to question the rape victims, who, it was thought, would feel more comfortable in the presence of a woman; the witnesses, however, insisted that Prosper be in charge of their court testimonies. His fluency in French proved to be crucial at that stage of the investigation, as many Rwandans speak French as a native language. One of his most challenging duties was to convince 24 witnesses, who feared reprisals for their testimony, that their names would not be used publicly; he also had to promise those witnesses transportation, under cover of darkness, to the tribunal in Tanzania. In addition, Prosper worked to convince skeptical Rwandans that the tribunal, which had met with criticism for what were thought to be its slow pace and disorganization, could render justice.

At the United Nations International Criminal Tribunal for Rwanda, Prosper sought seven life sentences for the former Rwandan provincial mayor Jean-Paul Akayesu. Prosper told Toby Harnden for the London *Daily Telegraph* (April 21, 2003), "This was someone articulate and intelligent, who was making a calculated decision to commit genocide—rather than a raw, passionate one. I realised that there could be a sophistication behind evil." In September 1998 Akayesu was convicted on nine of the 15 charges of genocide, torture, rape, and crimes against humanity leveled against him. (Prosper also played a minor role in the prosecution of another case at the tribunal.) Prosper later visited Akayesu in his prison cell; he had begun the practice of visiting criminals he had recently prosecuted while working as an attorney in Los Angeles. "I always say 'good luck' because they have to wake up every day of their lives in the con-

fines of a prison, remembering what they did to their victims and what they did to their own lives," Prosper told Peter Slevin for the *Washington Post* (October 30, 2002). "What we can't forget as the prosecutors or policymakers is that this is a human issue. Sometimes it requires talking straight to the affected person or their families to get a sense of what is necessary."

Prosper also visited the village of Taba, to tell the people there of the court's verdict. The villagers responded with cheers, and according to the *New York Times* (November 1, 1998), one woman brought him a message that read, "Even if you go, we will say that you have never left us." Prosper told Jimmie Briggs for *Crisis* magazine (July/August 2004): "In regard to Rwanda, [the U.S. and other countries] should have engaged immediately at the first warning sign. Even if neighboring states hadn't said something, we could have done something sooner. You can't look away and hope the problem goes away."

In 1999 Prosper served in the U.S. Justice Department as a special assistant to the assistant attorney general for the Criminal Division. From 1999 to 2001 he worked as the special counsel and policy adviser to David J. Scheffer, then the ambassador for war-crime issues. In that position Prosper traveled frequently to Europe, Asia, and Africa in an effort to build coalitions in support of U.S. government policies.

On July 13, 2001 Prosper was sworn in as ambassador-at-large for war-crime issues, having been confirmed by the U.S. Senate after President George W. Bush nominated him, on May 16, 2001. Prosper was the second ambassador for war crimes in United States history. Among the high-profile matters with which he dealt was the proposed ratification of a treaty that would establish an International Criminal Court (ICC) to be based in The Hague, in the Netherlands. As president, Bill Clinton signed the treaty, in December 2000, but did not submit it to the U.S. Senate for ratification. The Bush administration, by contrast, was vehemently opposed to such a treaty—so much so that the U.S. threatened to cut military aid to governments that ratified it. On behalf of the Bush administration, Prosper told reporters that the U.S. did not believe there were adequate safeguards within the treaty that would prevent Americans performing peacekeeping duties around the world from being subjected to unwarranted, "politicized" prosecution. "On any given day, there are people who would like to come after the United States and use any tool at their disposal," Prosper told Danish reporters, as quoted by the *Washington Post* (August 27, 2002). "And we truly believe that this is a process that is exploitable and can be politicized." Regarding the slaughter of more than 200,000 people by government-supported militias in Darfur, in the African nation of Sudan, the Bush administration recommended in early 2005 that the perpetrators be prosecuted by a new tribunal overseen jointly by the African Union and the U.N., rather than by the ICC. "We don't want to be party to legitimizing the I.C.C.," Prosper said, as quoted by the *New York Times* (February 1, 2005).

Prosper was believed to be a counterbalancing force within the Bush administration with regard to the international war criminal Charles Taylor, the former president of the West African nation of Liberia. During his tenure and earlier, Taylor was responsible for the violent deaths of innocent people in his country and fueled wars with other nations. Taylor is "the only indicted mass murderer in the world who lives freely and openly," in the words of Ryan Lizza in the *New Republic* (April 25, 2005); he was granted asylum in the African nation of Nigeria and has been living there since 2003, after swearing that he would not meddle in Liberian politics. Some members of the Bush administration's foreign-policy team were believed to be content with keeping Taylor in Nigeria. Others in the international community have urged that Taylor be brought to trial before a special international tribunal known as the Special Court for Sierra Leone (a country that borders Liberia to the east). Prosper supported bringing Taylor to trial as quickly as possible. He told Congress, as quoted by Ryan Lizza, "It is U.S. policy that Taylor must be held accountable and must appear before the Court."

In May 2005 Prosper visited Cambodia, in Southeast Asia, to look into whether the U.S. should provide financial support for a tribunal that the country set up in an agreement with the United Nations in June 2003. The tribunal would try former members of Cambodia's Communist government, known as the Khmer Rouge, which slaughtered an estimated 1.7 million of its citizens during its rule, from 1975 to 1979. Prosper told reporters in Cambodia that the U.S. would be willing to support an ad hoc tribunal to prosecute members of the Khmer Rouge for genocide and crimes against humanity if the process was free from corruption and political influence.

Prosper was responsible for overseeing the treatment and adjudication of war criminals at the U.S. military base in Guantanamo Bay, in Cuba, and was also responsible for forming policy for the prosecution of Iraqi war crimes. The prison camp at Guantanamo Bay, where Iraqi and Afghan soldiers, among others, have been detained since 2001, has been the subject of controversy; since January 2004 reports of abuse and torture of prisoners there have prompted demands from United Nations officials to inspect the camp. As of October 2005 only delegates of the International Committee of the Red Cross have been permitted to see the prisoners at Guantanamo and examine conditions there. According to the New York Times (June 24, 2005), Prosper "said the United States had been unable to meet the [U.N.] fact-finders' deadline to answer its request but intended to keep the matter open." In April 2003 the Bush administration announced that if any of the former leaders of Saddam Hussein's regime in Iraq, including Hussein himself, were to be captured, they would be tried

in their own country. Prosper told Toby Harnden for the London *Daily Telegraph* (April, 21, 2003): "If [justice] is delivered by a third party, Iraqis will dismiss it as being imperialist or politically motivated justice. If you put it in the hands of an international organization, the domestic participation is minimised and you have people who come in and will be the ones calling the shots rather than the Iraqis." (Hussein was captured in December 2003, following the start of the U.S.-led war against Iraq earlier that year. His trial started in Baghdad on October 19, 2005; it was confined to the charge of Hussein's role in the torture and killing of 148 Shiite males in the town of Dujail, Iraq, in 1982. After only three hours, the trial was adjourned until November 28, 2005.)

In October 2005 Prosper resigned from his State Department post and announced that he intended to seek the Republican nomination for state attorney general in California in 2006.

In addition to English and French, Prosper has a working knowledge of Italian and Spanish. He stays in shape by running and is known to enjoy playing pick-up basketball games. He is single and currently lives in Los Angeles, California.

—D.F.

Suggested Reading: *Crisis* p42+ July/Aug. 2004, with photos; (London) *Daily Telegraph* p12 Apr. 21, 2003; *Los Angeles Times* A p1 Oct. 3, 1998, with photos; *Miami Herald* A p11 May 9, 2002; *New York Times* I p13 Nov. 1, 1998; *San Francisco Chronicle* B p4 Oct. 5, 2005; U.S. Department of State Web site; *Washington Post* A p21 Oct. 30, 2002

Quinn, Aidan

Mar. 8, 1959– Actor

Address: c/o William Morris Agency, 1325 Ave. of the Americas, New York, NY 10019

"You know, I'm an outsider in an insider's game," the actor Aidan Quinn told Jim Schembri for the *Age* (March 9, 2001, on-line). "I do some mainstream movies occasionally, but even in those I'm an outsider. Then I do a lot of independent films, but I don't do the popular independent films!" Although he has appeared in more than 45 movies since his big-screen debut, in 1984, performing alongside such famous stars as Meryl Streep, Julia Roberts, Anthony Hopkins, and Johnny Depp, most of Quinn's appearances have been in supporting roles in films that did not garner great attention. "I'm always slightly annoyed with young people who come up to me and ask for advice," he told Jamie Painter for *Back Stage West* (May 6, 1999), "and when I sincerely question them, what I find out is that they're really asking me, 'Give me some

Aidan Quinn

Peter Kramer/Getty Images

advice on how to get famous,' which is not something I would know how to give anyone advice on, number one. Number two, it's not something I particularly have any interest in or respect for." Quinn has always been more interested in rich, plot-driven vehicles than in blockbuster movies that might boost his status in Hollywood. "I want to make sure we don't lose touch with the tradition of sitting around the fire and listening to stories," he told Bart Mills for *Biography* magazine (July 1999). "Let's not become people who warm themselves by the light of the TV." Quinn, who has also acted frequently on the stage, explained to Painter that he is inspired by the "harshness, the horror, and the beauty of human beings" and by the chance afforded an actor—"a kind of a sacred opportunity sometimes—to try to do those parts of us and [our] journeys justice."

The second of five children, Aidan Quinn was born in Chicago, Illinois, on March 8, 1959. His parents, Theresa and Michael Quinn, a homemaker and literature professor, respectively, had immigrated to the United States from Ireland shortly before Aidan was born. Four of the five Quinn siblings are involved in the movie industry: Aidan's older brother, Declan, is a cinematographer; his younger brother Paul is a screenwriter and director; and his younger sister, Marian, is an actress. Aidan's younger brother Robert is a landscaper in Los Angeles. The family's fortunes fluctuated during Quinn's childhood. "Our family life was really weird," Quinn told Mills. "I remember being on welfare when I was young. Then we went through a period when we lived in a big middle-class house, then we were broke again." The Quinn family moved back and forth between Ireland, where

they lived on a farm in Birr, County Offaly, and Illinois, where they resided primarily in the city of Rockford. Among Quinn's fondest childhood memories are those of outings to Chicago Cubs baseball games at Wrigley Field, in Chicago, and swimming trips to Lake Michigan.

Quinn had his first acting experience at age eight, when he filled the role of the little boy in a production of Samuel Beckett's play *Waiting for Godot* at Rockford College, where his father was teaching at the time. "All I wanted to do then was go outside and play," Quinn told Marion E. Kabaker for the *Chicago Tribune* (August 23, 1992). "I couldn't understand [*Waiting for Godot*], but once rehearsals started, I had the best time of my life. All the college kids in the cast were wonderful to me. I got to wear furs and paint and makeup. It was incredible." In his teens he attended high school both in Illinois and Belfast, in Northern Ireland. Quinn told Brendan Lemon for *Interview* (November 1990), "I was in love with [the Russian writer Fyodor] Dostoyevsky—in high school Raskolnikov and the Underground Man [disillusioned, antisocial Dostoyevsky characters] were my heroes! But I had a wonderful time being shocking, weird. Wearing clogs and women's bracelets." He added that despite those curious habits he was still "considered a kind of a tough character, so the jocks didn't know what to do with me. And I was good in sports, so I loved testing all the limits and playing with the social norms." Although he skipped many classes, he graduated from Rockford West High School, in Illinois.

While trying to land theater roles in Dublin, Ireland, in his late teenage years, Quinn supported himself by working as a hot-tar roofer. At age 19 he returned to Chicago, where he continued to work as a roofer. "I remember sitting on top of a high-rise building looking over Lake Michigan," he told Mills. "I loved my job. I'd dangle my feet over the edge 27 floors up. I was on the job at 7 a.m., and someone passed me a bottle of whisky and a joint. 'Oh, no,' I said to myself. 'This is not a good way to start the day. These guys are great, but they're all alcoholics. What am I going to do with my life?'" Quinn's first response to that question was to enroll in acting classes taught by the Chicago theater legend Byrne Piven at his Piven Theatre Workshop, in Evanston, Illinois. Quinn was hesitant, however, to commit himself fully to acting and attended the workshop only sporadically while earning his living by turns as a roofer, carpenter, library janitor, dishwasher, and bus boy. "I did about one play a year," he recalled to Mills, "partly because I couldn't get [a lot of acting] work and partly because I was lazy and insecure." He was also particular about the kind of work he would accept, turning down modeling and voice-over jobs. "I really am indebted to the Pivens—Byrne and his wife, Joyce—for being so supportive," Quinn told Kabaker. "They took me under their wing, gave me jobs fixing up their house when I didn't have any money. They even let me slide and not pay for acting classes."

Quinn made his stage debut in Chicago, under Piven's direction, in *The Man in 605*. In 1983 he made his New York City debut, performing Off-Broadway in Sam Shepard's *A Fool for Love*, which centers on a pair of former lovers who meet in a rundown motel near the Mojave Desert. The following year he appeared in a production of *Scheherazade*. Quinn's theater performances in 1985 included a turn in a modern interpretation of *Hamlet*—as the brooding prince of the title, he wore contemporary clothes, and instead of declaiming the famous line, "To be or not to be," he spray painted it on a wall—and roles in *The Irish Hebrew Lesson*, staged in Chicago, and in an Off-Broadway production of Sam Shepard's play *A Lie of the Mind*, which won a New York Drama Critics Circle Award. He made his debut as a director with *The Worker's Life*, presented as part of the New York City–based Ensemble Studio Theatre's Marathon '86. That same year he played a young man who returns home disillusioned after having fought in World War II in a mounting of Arthur Miller's *All My Sons*. The production was filmed and later televised as part of Public Broadcasting Service's *Great Performances* series. In a review for the *New York Times* (January 19, 1987), John J. O'Connor described Quinn as "especially impressive, displaying once again the special combination of tenderness and strength that once was the almost exclusive trademark of Montgomery Clift." In 1988 Quinn tackled the role of Stanley Kowalski—a part that Marlon Brando had made famous years earlier—in a Broadway revival of Tennessee Williams's *A Streetcar Named Desire*. The critical response to his performance was tepid. Michael Kimmelman, for example, in a *New York Times* (May 1, 1988) review, wrote that the audience "could perceive the intelligence and sweetness in Mr. Quinn's character. . . . Yet to place that figure in the midst of *Streetcar* is to undo the play's shattering climax: With Mr. Quinn in the scene, the final confrontation with Blanche lost its sickening punch and Stella's rejection of Stanley became tenuous and odd."

In Chicago Quinn often appeared on stage at the prestigious Goodman and Steppenwolf Theatres. Though he focused more on his movie career during the 1990s, Quinn remained fond of the stage and never entirely abandoned it. In 2002, for example, he appeared Off-Broadway in the play *The Exonerated*, which presented commentary from former death-row convicts who had been found to be innocent. (The stage drama was filmed and broadcast on Court TV in early 2005.) The following year Quinn took a brief turn in the starring role of the play *Trumbo*, about Dalton Trumbo, a screenwriter who was blacklisted and imprisoned during the anti-Communist hysteria of the Joseph McCarthy era, in the 1950s.

Quinn made his movie debut in 1984, playing a rebellious teenager from a poor family who falls in love with a cheerleader (Daryl Hannah) in *Reckless*. In 1985 he had a small part in the popular movie *Desperately Seeking Susan*, which starred Madonna and Rosanna Arquette. That same year his performance as a gay lawyer with AIDS in the made-for-television movie *An Early Frost*—one of the first movies ever to address the deadly disease—earned Quinn an Emmy Award nomination and the attention of critics. A reviewer for *New York* (November 18, 1985) described Quinn's performance as "superb, defiant, scared." In 1986 Quinn had a small role in *The Mission*, about Spanish Jesuit priests trying to protect a remote South American tribe from conquest by pro-slavery Portugal in the mid-18th century. Although *The Mission*, which starred Robert De Niro and Jeremy Irons, received decidedly mixed critical reviews, it was nominated for seven Academy Awards.

In *Stakeout* (1987), a lighthearted thriller starring Richard Dreyfuss and Emilio Estevez that did well at the box office, Quinn played a violent convict. In 1989 he traveled to the Seychelles Islands, in the Indian Ocean, to play the title character, a shipwrecked slave trader, in the film *Crusoe*, an adaptation of Daniel Defoe's classic 18th-century novel *Robinson Crusoe*. Roger Ebert, in the *Chicago Sun-Times* (April 21, 1989), praised the movie for having a "few important things to say and a magnificent way of saying them." Not all reviewers were as enthusiastic. In the *Washington Post* (April 21, 1989), Rita Kempley wrote that Quinn, "a skinny, sincere sort, gives a performance in which primitive meets yuppie. It's 'tarzansomething.' Mostly he builds fires, eats bugs, hunts, gardens and fishes."

Quinn continued to land regular work in movies in the 1990s. He played Nick, the main character's lover, in the big-screen adaptation of Margaret Atwood's best-selling novel *The Handmaid's Tale*. The movie, released in 1990, co-starred Robert Duvall, Faye Dunaway, and Natasha Richardson and conjured a bleak futuristic world. That same year Quinn co-starred in the writer and director Barry Levinson's *Avalon*, an autobiographical movie about a Russian Jewish family that has settled in the United States. In the made-for-television movie *Lies of the Twins* (1991), Quinn starred in the roles of Jonathan and James, identical-twin psychiatrists, one morally upstanding, the other evil. Both become entangled with a beautiful client (Isabella Rossellini). "Mr. Quinn, although a little flat as Jonathan, has fun putting a twinkle in the eye and a spin on the words of the unscrupulous James," Walter Goodman wrote in his review of *Lies of the Twins* for the *New York Times* (August 21, 1991). The actor returned to the jungles of South America to play the part of an earnest but naïve missionary in *At Play in the Fields of the Lord* (1991), which was based on the Peter Matthiessen novel of the same name.

Quinn next had a relatively high-profile role in the whimsical movie *Benny & Joon* (1993), as the long-suffering and overprotective brother of a mentally unstable woman (Mary Stuart Masterson) who falls in love with a quirky dreamer (Johnny

Depp). In general, the movie did not impress critics, though James Berardinelli, on the ReelViews Web site, thought that "Aidan Quinn, playing the 'straight man,' does a credible job—so credible, in fact, that he upstages his co-stars, which was obviously not the film makers' original intent."

Quinn had a small part in the actor and director Kenneth Branagh's remake of the classic monster tale *Frankenstein* (1994) and played Brad Pitt's responsible, ambitious older brother in *Legends of the Fall* (1994), which told the story of a father (Anthony Hopkins) and his three sons (Henry Thomas played the youngest brother) who live in the wilds of Montana in the early 1900s. *Legends of the Fall* earned a respectable $66 million at the box office. Quinn next portrayed the Irish Republican Army terrorist Harry Boland in *Michael Collins* (1996); in *Commandments* (1997) he starred as a doctor who—after being struck by lightening and losing his pregnant wife, his job, and his home—decides to systematically break each of the biblical Ten Commandments. While Quinn was praised for that performance, the movie was seen less favorably. "What might have made an elegant and even trenchant *Atlantic Monthly* short story becomes a strained, slight movie in this feature debut by writer-director Daniel Taplitz," Lisa Schwarzbaum wrote for *Entertainment Weekly* (May 16, 1997). "Quinn is a nice choice—he's got the difficult task of making Seth . . . moral and immoral at the same time, and he manages well." Also that year Quinn portrayed the explorer and war correspondent Henry Morton Stanley in the National Geographic Society's television movie *Forbidden Territory: Stanley's Search for Livingstone* (1997), which was filmed in Kenya and portrayed Stanley's search for and friendship with David Livingstone, a legendary missionary and explorer.

The movie *This Is My Father* (1998) was a family affair. Quinn's brother Paul wrote and directed; his brother Declan filmed it; and both Quinn, who also served as the film's executive producer, and his sister, Marian, appeared in it. The brothers were inspired to make the movie by a story their mother had told them when they were children. In the film James Caan plays a teacher who travels to Ireland to learn about his unknown father (played by Quinn in flashbacks), a farmer who fell in love with a young girl from a rich family in Ireland in 1939. In the *Village Voice* (May 11, 1999), Michael Atkinson described *This Is My Father* as a "generational saga born of equal parts career-building indie guile and heartfelt tribal bonding." "The results are lackluster and tame . . . ," he wrote, "[and] Quinn's brogue is decidedly shaky." In a more positive assessment, Leah Rozen, in *People* (May 17, 1999), called the movie "a powerful drama about a doomed romance and class differences." According to Rozen, "Quinn, who has been giving quietly superior performances for years, has never been better." Among his movie credits, Quinn has cited *This Is My Father* as one of his favorites. He was nominated for an Irish Film and Television Academy Award for his performance.

Quinn was cast as a detective who becomes the love interest of a young witch (Sandra Bullock) in *Practical Magic* (1998). The following year he appeared in the thriller *In Dreams* and also played the boyfriend of Meryl Streep's character in the drama *Music of the Heart*. He next appeared in the critically lauded but little-seen *Songcatcher* (2000). In that film, set in the Appalachian Mountains in 1907, he depicted a man who initially resists the efforts of a musicologist (Janet McTeer) to record the music of his isolated rural community. In a conversation with an interviewer for *USA Today* (June 4, 2002), Leonard Maltin, a senior film correspondent for *Entertainment Tonight*, described *Songcatcher* as a "wonderful movie that won a major award at Sundance [Film Festival] and then barely got released to theaters. This is an Oscar-caliber film. More people ought to know about it." A reviewer for *People* (June 25, 2001) wrote that while *Songcatcher* "gets a mite melodramatic later on," it is a "lyrical, thoughtful movie that's blessed with astute performances by McTeer . . . and Quinn." Also in 2000 Quinn portrayed the musician and former Beatle Paul McCartney in the well-received television movie *Two of Us*, which was a fictionalized version of the reconciliation that occurred between McCartney and his former bandmate John Lennon in the 1970s. Quinn appeared in two other television movies that year: *See You in My Dreams*, which was co-written by Sam Shepard, and an adaptation of Mark Twain's *The Prince and the Pauper*.

In 2002, in the movie *Stolen Summer*, Quinn portrayed an Irish-American firefighter who begins to question his beliefs when his youngest child befriends a Jewish boy. The film was a product of Project Greenlight, a televised competition for first-time filmmakers that was the brainchild of the actors Ben Affleck and Matt Damon and the film producer Chris Moore; it thus received more attention that it might have otherwise, though it failed to impress critics or audiences. Lisa Schwarzbaum described the movie for *Entertainment Weekly* (March 29, 2002) as a "tremulous first step by writer-director Pete Jones, a square tale of uplift. . . . The adult actors are gracious, but trapped by their roles as position-holders rather than people." In *Evelyn* (2002), which told the true tale of a father (Pierce Brosnan) who in 1953 fought a groundbreaking court case in Ireland to regain custody of his children, Quinn played an American lawyer. (His sister also had a small role.) Eddie Cockrell, writing for *Variety* (September 30, 2002), called Quinn "particularly relaxed and appealing as the Yank ambulance chaser." Quinn portrayed the man known as one of America's greatest traitors in *Benedict Arnold: A Question of Honor*, which premiered on the A&E cable-television network in January 2003. "The film will hold you because passion, intrigue and betrayal are never out of date," Terry Kelleher wrote in his review of *Benedict Arnold* for *People* (January 13, 2003). "Quinn, in a stops-out performance, plays Arnold as an impetuous, egotistical warrior who feels ill-paid for his courage in the patriots' cause."

In 2004 Quinn appeared in six films: *Cavedweller* (for which he was nominated for an Independent Spirit Award); *Return to Sender*; *Miracle Run*; *Shadow of Fear*; *Plainsong*; and *Bobby Jones, Stroke of Genius* (about the legendary golfer). He had a small role in *Nine Lives*, which was shown at the Sundance Film Festival in January 2005. A drama that explores the lives of individuals trapped by circumstances and relationships, *Nine Lives* features an ensemble cast, among them, in addition to Quinn, Glenn Close, Dakota Fanning, Holly Hunter, and Sissy Spacek. In 2005 Quinn appeared in a television adaptation of Richard Russo's best-selling novel *Empire Falls*, about residents of an economically depressed mill town. According to the Internet Movie Database, Quinn will also be seen in the upcoming drama "32A" and in "Location," an adaptation of Jack Kerouac's novel *On the Road* (1957), slated for release in 2006.

While Quinn has sometimes expressed his frustrations with the film industry—criticizing, for example, the way that box-office concerns impinge upon creative choices, including casting decisions—he has also maintained that being a movie star has never been one of his goals. He told Schembri, "It takes a lot of effort to stay on being a movie star, and I guess, because of the things that have happened in my life and in my work, in my in-built existential spiritual detachment from the absurdity of that yearning, I would say that it wasn't as important to me." However, as he told Painter, "I do love [acting] and I feel very grateful and fortunate. I don't know what else I would do."

Quinn's other big-screen film credits include *The Playboys* (1992), *Blink* (1994), *The Stars Fell on Henrietta* (1995), *Looking for Richard* (1996), *The Assignment* (1997), and *Song for a Raggy Boy* (2003). Other television movies in which Quinn has appeared include *Perfect Witness* (1989), *A Private Matter* (1992), and *Miracle Run* (2004). In 2004 Quinn appeared on several episodes of the popular television series *Third Watch*, and he is currently filming the pilot of a new NBC drama, "Book of Daniel," in the role of an unconventional priest who is addicted to prescription drugs and talks with Jesus Christ. A dozen episodes of the show have already been scheduled to air after its debut, in the middle of the 2005–06 season.

Quinn co-narrated the television documentary *Out of Ireland*, in 1995, and narrated the History Channel series *The Irish in America*, in 1997. In 2000 he narrated *The Messiah XXI*, a filmed performance of George Frideric Handel's famous oratorio (a Christmastime perennial) featuring the Irish Philharmonic Orchestra, the Irish Philharmonic Chorus, and the Visual Ministry Gospel Choir, along with a host of popular solo performers.

An avid nature lover and environmentalist who practices yoga and meditation, Quinn has been married to the actress Elizabeth Bracco since 1987. The couple have two daughters, Ava Eileen (born in 1989) and Mia (born in 1998). They have homes in New Jersey and upstate New York.

—K.E.D.

Suggested Reading: *Age* (on-line) Mar. 9, 2001; *Back Stage West* May 6, 1999; *Biography* p 44+ July 1999, with photos; *Detour* Mar. 1993; Internet Movie Database

Selected Plays: *The Man in 605*, 1983; *A Fool for Love*, 1983; *Scheherazade*, 1984; *Hamlet*, 1985; *The Irish Hebrew Lesson*, 1985; *A Lie of the Mind*, 1985; *The Worker's Life*, 1986; *A Streetcar Named Desire*, 1988; *The Exonerated*, 2002

Selected Films (including TV movies): *Reckless*, 1984; *Desperately Seeking Susan*, 1985; *An Early Frost*, 1985; *The Mission*, 1986; *Stakeout*, 1987; *Crusoe*, 1989; *The Handmaid's Tale*, 1990; *Avalon*, 1990; *Lies of the Twins*, 1991; *At Play in the Fields of the Lord*, 1991; *The Playboys*, 1992; *A Private Matter*, 1992; *Benny & Joon*, 1993; *Frankenstein*, 1994; *Legends of the Fall*, 1994; *The Stars Fell on Henrietta*, 1995; *Michael Collins*, 1996; *Commandments*, 1997; *Forbidden Territory: Stanley's Search for Livingstone*, 1997; *This Is My Father*, 1998; *Practical Magic*, 1998; *In Dreams*, 1999; *Songcatcher*, 2000; *Two of Us*, 2000; *Stolen Summer*, 2002; *Evelyn*, 2002; *Benedict Arnold: A Question of Honor*, 2003; *Song for a Raggy Boy*, 2003; *Plainsong*, 2004; *Return to Sender*, 2004; *Nine Lives*, 2005

Rabassa, Gregory

Mar. 9, 1922– Translator of literature

Address: Dept. of Hispanic Languages and Literatures, Queens College, 65-30 Kissena Blvd., Flushing, NY 11367

Gregory Rabassa has translated into English some of the most beloved and best-known Latin American literary works, and he is widely regarded as one of the most important translators of 20th-century literature. Since he entered that field, in the 1960s, Rabassa has translated more than three dozen books from Spanish and Portuguese into English, among them the works of the Nobel laureates Gabriel García Márquez, Octavio Paz, and Miguel Angel Asturias. It is thanks to Rabassa that the English-reading world has a translation of the Colombian García Márquez's masterpiece *One Hundred Years of Solitude* (1970), a magical-realist novel that sparked worldwide interest in Latin American literature and is considered one of the greatest novels of the 20th century. As quoted by Lucas Rivera for *OP Magazine* (July/August 2003, on-line), García Márquez himself, with customary flair and irony, called Rabassa the "best Latin American writer

Mario Ruiz/Time Life Pictures/Getty Images

Gregory Rabassa

in the English language." Dan Simon, the founder of Seven Stories Press, which has published some of Rabassa's work, told Andrew Bast for the *New York Times* (May 25, 2004) that Rabassa's greatest talent is his ability "to find the music in English that is true to the language of a wide range of writers in Spanish." Commenting on Rabassa's impressive intellectual accomplishments—including his mastery of five languages—and his indispensable contributions to literature, Simon added, "Had Rabassa become a diplomat or brain surgeon, we could easily imagine not having readable translations of [Julio] Cortázar and García Márquez."

Translating is an exacting yet inexact craft. It is often difficult, if not impossible, to convey the precise and full meanings of certain words, phrases, or expressions from one language to another, or to re-create the rhythm of one language in another tongue. In addition, the work of translators often goes unrecognized. As Simon explained to Bast, translators' names are often left off the covers of the books that they have made accessible to new readers, and yet, at the same time, "a poor translation of a text kills it in the market." Rabassa addressed such difficulties in his first full-length, original work, *If This Be Treason: Translation and Its Dyscontents*; a look back at his life and an apologia for the task of the translator, the book was published in 2005 to generally positive reviews. Rabassa told Bast that his thesis in the book is that "translation is impossible. People expect reproduction, but you can't turn a baby chick into a duckling. The best you can do is get close to it." Rabassa holds the title of Distinguished Professor of Hispanic Languages and Literatures at Queens College, in New York City, where he has taught for many years.

The youngest of three sons, Gregory Rabassa was born on March 9, 1922 in Yonkers, in Westchester County, New York. His father, Miguel Rabassa, originally from Cuba, worked as a sugar broker; his mother, Clara (Macfarland) Rabassa, was born in the U.S. Within a year of his birth, the family suffered financial setbacks and moved to New Hampshire, where they converted a farm into an inn. Rabassa attended a public high school, where he studied French and Latin. At Dartmouth College, in New Hampshire, he began "collecting languages," as he told Bast, learning German, Russian, and Portuguese. In 1942, the year after the U.S. entered World War II, Rabassa volunteered for service in the U.S. Army. He was stationed in North Africa and Italy, where his language skills made him a useful member of the Office of Strategic Studies, the precursor of the Central Intelligence Agency; his duties as a staff sergeant included breaking secret military codes and conducting interrogations. "That's where my translating career started," Rabassa told Rivera. As Edwin McDowell reported in *Americas* (July/August 1986), in his spare time during his army years, Rabassa translated Dante's *Divine Comedy* from the original Italian into English. "I was just passing the time," he told McDowell. "In those days I wanted to write more than anything else."

When Rabassa was discharged from the army, "all I wanted to do was go to college, because after the war I didn't want to work that hard anymore," he recalled to Rivera. Upon returning to the U.S., Rabassa took up residence in the Greenwich Village section of Manhattan, in New York City, an area famous for its music, art, and bohemian atmosphere. There, he wrote poetry and enjoyed live performances by such jazz musicians as the legendary saxophonist Charlie Parker. Rabassa attended Columbia University, in New York City, receiving his master's degree in Spanish literature in 1947. Next, while teaching at Columbia, he began working toward his Ph.D. in Portuguese, earning the degree from Columbia in 1954. His dissertation was titled "The Negro in Brazilian Fiction Since 1888." Rabassa's later travels in Mexico, Peru, Puerto Rico, and Brazil helped him to refine his knowledge of Spanish and Portuguese. Those travels had been inspired in part by one of his Spanish professors at Columbia. Rabassa recalled to McDowell, "It wasn't that long after the Spanish Civil War, and he said that Spain was finished—Latin America was where the future was."

After completing graduate school Rabassa worked as an editor for *Odyssey Review*, a literary magazine that featured new work from Europe and Latin America. In the mid-1960s an editor at the publishing company Pantheon noticed several of the translations Rabassa had done for *Odyssey Review*. Favorably impressed, the editor asked Rabassa to translate from Spanish to English the experimental novel *Rayuela*, by the Argentine novelist Julio Cortázar. *Rayuela* centers on the adventures of a writer, first in Paris, where he is surrounded by a bohemian clique, then back in his native Argentina, where he works a series of odd jobs, including attendant in an asylum for the insane. Without having previously read the book, Rabassa translated Cortázar's work word by word into English. "I read it as I translated it," he recalled to McDowell. "I do that with many books because it's more fun that way, and because translation should be the closest possible reading of the work anyway." (As McDowell pointed out, such an approach differs from that of many other translators, who read books from beginning to end before starting the work of translation.) Rabassa's translation of *Rayuela*, titled *Hopscotch*, published in 1967, won the first National Book Award for Translation. As quoted on amazon.com, the *New Republic* called *Hopscotch* the "most powerful encyclopedia of emotion and visions to emerge from the postwar generation of international writers." In the wake of the book's success, in both Spanish- and English-reading communities, Rabassa was in demand as a translator among publishers interested in Latin American literature. In the four years following the publication of *Hopscotch*, Rabassa translated seven other books from Spanish or Portuguese into English, including *The Green House*, an epic novel about life in Peru by the esteemed Peruvian writer Mario Vargas Llosa; *Mulata*, a story by the Guatemalan writer Miguel Angel Asturias about a poor farmer who becomes involved with an assortment of demons, witches, and fantastic beings; and the nonfiction book *An Introduction to Literature in Brazil*, by Afranio Coutinho.

To translate a writer's work successfully, Rabassa studies his or her phrasing and diction and pores over the metaphors on the page "like an anthropologist looking for lost artifacts," as Rivera wrote. Rabassa explained to Rivera that when he translates from Spanish or Portuguese to English, he translates not just a writer's words but his mind: "You can tell when a writer's voice is authentic," Rabassa told Rivera. "Good translations allow readers to get to know good writers." Explaining how he approached the works of García Márquez, Rabassa told Bast, "The English is hiding behind his Spanish. That's what a good translation is: you have to think if García Márquez had been born speaking English, that's how a translation should sound." Though he seeks to be technically precise, Rabassa often relies on his instincts, as well. "You just have to hit it right. I'm never sure whether something is right," he told Bast, "but I know damn well when something is wrong." He explained to McDowell: "The translator with a tin ear is as deadly as a tone-deaf musician. . . . If a work sings in the original and not in the translation, then the translation is little more than a linear glossary. But if it sings and is grossly inaccurate, then it perpetuates a fraud. Literary translation is always a balancing act between trying to be faithful to giving the readers the best book possible by an author, and trying to satisfy the demands of scholarship. I try to resolve it by staying as close as I can to the original while making it sound readable."

In several cases Rabassa has become friends with the writers whose work he translated. After translating a book by Luis Rafael Sanchez, Rabassa spent time with the writer on the beaches of his native Puerto Rico. A painting by the Ecuadorian writer Demetrio Aguilera Malta, whose novel *Seven Serpents and Seven Moons* (1979) Rabassa translated into English, hangs on Rabassa's apartment wall. After meeting Cortázar while translating *Rayuela*, Rabassa became good friends with the novelist. Speaking to Rivera, Rabassa called Cortázar "very experimental and particularly gifted and bright. I got along with him really well. He was a translator and a teacher like me. We both liked jazz, and he played the trumpet. He tried new things in his work, and he was a visionary in his writing." It was Cortázar who recommended that Rabassa translate García Márquez's internationally beloved novel *One Hundred Years of Solitude*, published originally in Argentina as *Cien Anos de Soledad*, in 1967.

The book, which led to García Márquez's's winning the Nobel Prize in Literature in 1982, covers events over a 100-year period in the fictitious South American town of Macondo, and tells a dizzying array of stories about many members, and different generations, of the Buendía family. Renowned as one of the most important works in the magical-realist style, which has been explored extensively in Latin American literature, *One Hundred Years of Solitude* blends realism—such as accounts of love affairs and wars—with tales of fantastical, often paranormal events: for example, an entire town becomes afflicted with insomnia; a woman ascends to heaven while hanging her laundry; and ghosts visit the houses of the living. The novel begins with a sentence, translated by Rabassa, that remains well-known in the Spanish-speaking world: "Many years later, as he faced the firing squad, Colonel Aureliano Buendía was to remember that distant afternoon when his father took him to discover ice." Rabassa's English-language translation was published in 1970 to wide popular and critical acclaim. Paul West wrote in a review of the novel for *Book World* (February 22, 1970), "Rabassa's translation is a triumph of fluent, gravid momentum, all stylishness and commonsensical virtuosity." "That's his greatest book," Rabassa told Rivera, with regard to García Márquez and *One Hundred Years of Solitude*. "I don't think he'll ever match the success of that book." Andrew Bast reported that García Márquez has gone so far as to say that Rabassa's translation of *One Hundred Years of Solitude* improved upon the original version. Others of Rabassa's translations of García Márquez's work include *Leaf Storm and Other Stories* (1979), *In Evil Hour* (1979), and *Chronicle of a Death Foretold* (1983).

Other Latin American literary works translated by Rabassa include *Marks of Identity* (1969), by the Spaniard Juan Goytisolo; *Sea of Death* (1984) and *Captains of the Sands* (1988), by the Brazilian writer Jorge Amado; and *Taratuta and Still Life with*

Pipe: Two Novellas (1993), by the Chilean Jose Donoso. Rabassa's honors include, in addition to the National Book Award, the translation prize (1977) from the writers' organization PEN for his work on García Márquez's The Autumn of the Patriarch; the Gulbenkian Award (1981), given by PEN, for best translation from Portuguese (for Osman Lins's Avalovara); the Alexander Gode Award from the American Translators Association (1980); and the first PEN medal in translation (1982).

Despite the critical success of many of the books Rabassa translated, he did not make much money from them. "If you live like a hermit, you could live off the money you make as a translator," he said to Rivera. "But you'd have to have your bowl of thin gruel every day." Rabassa is a Distinguished Professor of Hispanic Languages and Literatures at Queens College, in New York City. He still teaches the freshman course Hispanic Literature in Translation, as he has for many years. Recalling his younger days, the white-haired Rabassa remarked to Bast, "When I began teaching, I was the same age as my students, and I still labor in the delusion. So it's a good, youthful operation." He told Rivera that it is the "teaching of young minds that keeps me sharp. I believe I still have a lot more writing and translating in me."

In 2005 Rabassa published If This Be Treason: Translation and Its Dyscontents, his first book as an author. Part memoir and part disquisition on the craft of translation, the book met with positive reviews from most critics, who praised Rabassa's openness and his obvious love of his work. "In this easygoing ramble through a distinguished career," Michael Dirda wrote for the Washington Post (April 24, 2005), Rabassa "comes across as a charming (if somewhat garrulous) old coot. His style is loose and conversational, utterly without airs. He prefers digression to exposition, makes terrible puns and drops in repeated references to old jazz songs and even older movie stars. Rabassa also writes with striking honesty about his disdain for the New York publishing industry and his dislike for academic literary criticism."

Rabassa's daughter Kate is the product of his first marriage, to Roney Edelstein, which ended in 1966. On May 29 of that year he married Clementine Christos, a teacher and writer, with whom he has another daughter, Clara. The couple live in New York City.

— C.F.T.

Suggested Reading: Americas p36+ July/Aug. 1986, with photos; Library of Congress Web site; New York Times E p1 May 25, 2004, with photo; opmagazine.com; Queens College Web site

Selected Books: If This Be Treason: Translation and Its Dyscontents, 2005; as translator— Aguilera Malta, Demetrio. Seven Serpents and Seven Moons; Amado, Jorge. Captain of the Sands; Sea of Death; The War of the Saints; Antunes, António Lobo. The Return of the Caravels. Asturias, Miguel Angel. Mulata; Carvalho, Mário de. A God Strolling in the Cool of the Evening; Cortázar, Julio. Hopscotch; A Manual for Manuel; Sixty-Two: A Model Kit; Coutinho, Afranio. An Introduction to Literature in Brazil; Franco Ramos, Jorge. Rosario Tijeras; Donoso, Jose. Taratuta and Still Life with Pipe: Two Novellas; García Márquez, Gabriel. The Autumn of the Patriarch; Collected Novellas; In Evil Hour; Innocent Eréndira and Other Stories; Leaf Storm and Other Stories; One Hundred Years of Solitude; Goytisolo, Juan. Marks of Identity; Lins, Osman. Avalovara; Machado de Assis, Joaquim Maria. Quincas Borba; The Posthumous Memoirs of Brás Cubas; Melo, João de. My World Is Not of This Kingdom; Ribeiro, Darcy. The Brazilian People: The Formation and Meaning of Brazil; Sánchez, Luis Rafael. Macho Camacho's Beat; Torres, Ana Teresa. Doña Inés vs. Oblivion; Vargas Llosa, Mario. The Green House; Zárate Moreno, Jesús. Jail

Jed Jacobsohn/Getty Images

Randolph, Willie

July 6, 1954– Manager of the New York Mets

Address: New York Mets, Shea Stadium, 123-01 Roosevelt Ave., Flushing, NY 11368-1699

When the New York Mets introduced Willie Randolph on November 4, 2004 as the 18th manager in the history of the franchise, many expressed the view that Randolph's assumption of a professional baseball team's top post was long overdue. Beginning in the mid-1990s, as a bench coach and third-base coach, Randolph contributed to one of the storied New York Yankees' most successful periods: the team appeared in the World Series six times and qualified for postseason play in 10 consecutive years. As a player with the Yankees and other major-league teams, from 1975 to 1993, Randolph posted solid offensive numbers and was particularly adept as a second baseman. After a slow start in 2005, he led the Mets to a respectable win–loss record of 83–79. The team won 12 of its final 16 games, reversing a tendency the franchise exhibited under its previous manager, Art Howe, in which it collapsed in the final days of baseball's regular season. In taking the post of manager, Randolph became the first African-American manager of a major-league baseball team in New York's history.

The oldest of five children, Willie Larry Randolph Jr. was born on July 6, 1954 in Holly Hill, South Carolina, to Willie and Minnie Randolph, who worked as sharecroppers. His brother Terry played briefly in the National Football League, for the New York Jets and the Green Bay Packers. Soon after Willie Randolph was born, his family moved to the Brownsville section of the New York City borough of Brooklyn, settling in a project on Dumont Avenue. His father then worked in construction and moonlighted as a cabdriver. As far back as most people close to Randolph can remember, the activity that interested him most was playing baseball. Devoting his energy to the sport kept Randolph away from the rougher elements of his neighborhood. "He never had a mind to do anything bad," his father recalled to Kevin McAuliffe for *Sport* (October 1976), "but Willie was the type of guy who would do what *he* wanted to do. And we had a little problem 'cause [baseball] was the *only* thing he would do." In the public-housing area, Randolph started off playing stickball—an urban variation of baseball, played on concrete or asphalt with a ball called a spaldeen and a broom handle serving as a bat. When he was about 10 years old, a coach in the area, Galileo Gonzalez, recruited Randolph to play baseball on the neighborhood sandlot teams. Randolph later moved on to more organized baseball, run by the Cummings Brothers American Legion Post, and came under the tutelage of Frank Tepedino, the uncle of a former professional baseball player with the same name. By the time he began attending Tilden High School in Brooklyn, Randolph had developed superior fielding skills. His two most prominent athletic gifts—his "soft" hands (or manual dexterity) and foot speed—became his trademarks in his position as shortstop. In addition, Randolph displayed uncommon leadership skills at an early age. The manager of his high-school team, Herb Abramowitz, recalled to Joe Donnelly for *New York Newsday* (June 20, 1976): "His head was screwed on right from the moment I met him. . . . I trusted him with the equipment locker keys. He was the only student I ever did."

In June 1972 Randolph was picked by the Pittsburgh Pirates in the seventh round of the free-agent draft. After negotiating a modest signing bonus on his own, Randolph traveled to Bradenton, Florida, to play in rookie camp. For the next three years he played in the minor leagues of the Pirates' organization, beginning with a Class A team in Charleston, South Carolina, and progressing to Class AA ball in Thetford Mines, Ontario, and then to a Class AAA club in Charleston, West Virginia. During that period Randolph learned to play second base. He suffered a prolonged batting slump while in Thetford Mines in 1974 but had rebounded by late July of the following season to lead the triple-A International League in batting average.

In 1975 Randolph made his major-league debut for the Pirates, playing in 30 games. That year he collected only 10 hits in 61 at bats, compiling a mediocre overall batting average of .164. The Pirates, who already had a regular second baseman, Rennie Stennett, traded Randolph on December 11, 1975, along with the pitchers Ken Brett and Dock Ellis, to the Yankees in return for the pitcher George "Doc" Medich. Randolph's first season with the Yankees, in 1976, was a successful one. Playing on a team with such veterans as Thurman Munson, Greg Nettles, Lou Piniella, and Roy White, Randolph displayed his defensive talents at second base and an unusual patience at the plate, striking out just 39 times in 430 at bats; his ratio of 14.7 at bats per strikeout was fifth-best in the American League. (The improvement may have been due to the fact that his former team, the Pirates, favored the practice of swinging at many pitches; as a player for the Yankees, Randolph was able to be a patient batter, taking as many pitches as possible.) Hitting a respectable .267, he stole 37 bases (ninth-best in the American League), drove in 40 base runners, and scored 59 times. Despite being slowed by a nagging knee injury, which occurred in the middle of the 1976 season, Randolph was selected to appear in the All-Star Game as a rookie; he was unable to play, however, due to the torn cartilage in his knee. During that period Randolph began receiving compliments from baseball veterans. "He's quick with his hands, he covers the bag good," Randolph's manager, Billy Martin, told Dave Anderson for the *New York Times* (May 25, 1976). "He doesn't leave the air for balls to his right. He's got a good arm, good range. And he's really poised for his age. Very aggressive but quiet aggressive."

By winning 97 games in 1976, the highest number in the American League, the Yankees finished first in the Eastern Division, earning the right to appear in the play-offs for the first time in 12 seasons. After splitting the first four games of the best-of-five 1976 American League Championship Series (ALCS) with the Kansas City Royals, the team won the deciding fifth game at Yankee Stadium, advancing to the World Series—where they were swept in four games by the Cincinnati Reds. In the play-offs and World Series, Randolph's statistics tapered considerably; he collected just three hits in

33 at bats in the postseason and scored only one run. Randolph nonetheless won the James P. Dawson Award and was named to the Topps All-Rookie team for 1976, a year that also saw him tie the major-league record (13) for most assists by a second baseman.

In the 1977 season Randolph emerged as one of baseball's brightest young stars. Moved to the lead-off position in the Yankees' batting order, he scored 91 runs, hitting in front of sluggers Munson, Nettles, and Reggie Jackson. Of Randolph's 151 hits that season, 43 were extra-base hits, a career high. Randolph also set a career high in doubles that season, with 28. In October of that year, the Yankees beat the Kansas City Royals in a rematch of the 1976 ALCS to advance to the World Series against the Los Angeles Dodgers. The first game of that series, held at Yankee Stadium, may have been Randolph's finest as a player. In the sixth inning he hit his first World Series home run, against the pitcher Don Sutton, tying the score at 2–2. The game advanced into extra innings with the teams tied at three runs apiece. Randolph started the 12th inning with a double off the reliever Rick Rhoden and scored the winning run in that inning, on a single hit by Paul Blair. The Yankees went on to defeat the Dodgers in the 1977 World Series, four games to two.

Over the course of the next three seasons, Randolph continued to generate solid offensive statistics. He scored 87, 98, and 99 runs, respectively, leading the team in the runs-scored category in each of those seasons. (Nursing a pulled hamstring, however, he missed the 1978 play-offs, including the World Series against the Dodgers, which the Yankees won four games to two.) He posted high walk totals and low strikeout totals during that period. In 1980 he led the major leagues in walks (119) and was second in on-base percentage (.427).

After losing the 1981 World Series to the Los Angeles Dodgers, the Yankees uncharacteristically finished the decade without returning to the play-offs. Randolph nonetheless continued to post strong offensive numbers. On March 4, 1986 he was named the team's co-captain, along with the pitcher Don Guidry. In the following year he drove in a career-high 67 runners and achieved a .305 batting average, also a career high. Unlike many of the successful players of that era, Randolph gained a reputation for reticence and humility.

Nineteen-eighty-eight was Randolph's 13th and final season as a Yankee; he had played more games at second base with the team (1,788) than any other Yankee in history. His last four seasons as a player found him with four different teams: the Los Angeles Dodgers, the Oakland Athletics, the Milwaukee Brewers, and, in his final season, 1993, the Mets. In 1990, after being traded by the Dodgers to the Athletics for Stan Javier on May 13, Randolph helped Oakland get to the World Series, where the team was swept by the Cincinnati Reds in four games. Randolph finished his career with 2,210 hits, 1,239 runs scored, 316 doubles, 271

stolen bases, and a lifetime .276 batting average. He also amassed 1,243 walks against 675 strikeouts, which helped generate a strong lifetime on-base percentage of .373. In the field, his 1,547 double plays rank him third of all time, behind Bill Mazeroski (1,706) and Nellie Fox (1,619). He also finished his career with a solid fielding percentage of .980. Randolph was selected to play in six All-Star Games, in 1976, 1977, 1980, 1981, 1987, and 1989.

In 1993 Randolph took a job as an assistant general manager with the Yankees. The next season he became the Yankees' third-base coach, working under manager Buck Showalter. He served in that role for the next decade, surviving Showalter's departure and Joe Torre's arrival, in late 1995. Coaching some of the game's most consistent postseason performers, such as the shortstop Derek Jeter and the outfielders Bernie Williams and Paul O'Neill, Randolph helped the Yankees to return to form as a dominant force in baseball. In 2000 the Yankees won their third consecutive World Series title—their fourth in five seasons—by defeating the Mets, four games to one.

Interviewing more than 10 times between 1997 and 2004 for teams with managerial vacancies, Randolph became one of the busiest skipper candidates in the game. "I'm not going to get down and be defeated by anything," he told Murray Chass for the *New York Times* (October 30, 2002) after a series of unsuccessful interviews. "I'm going to believe in myself. I take one interview at a time. . . . When you're rejected time after time, it can't feel too good, but I'm tougher than that." Adding to Randolph's frustration was speculation that teams were meeting with him merely to satisfy a directive that baseball's commissioner, Bud Selig, had given to the league's owners in the late 1990s: that any major-league club with an opening for a manager or any other position vital to the team's operation must consider at least one minority candidate before filling the job. "Sometimes he'd go in knowing who the guy was they wanted to hire, and that they want him there for lip service. Because they needed a minority candidate," Roy White, a former teammate and close friend of Randolph's, told T. J. Quinn for the New York *Daily News* (November 5, 2004.) (As of October 2005, in Major League Baseball's 30 franchises, five members of minority groups served as managers. In addition to Randolph, the list included the San Francisco Giants' Felipe Alou, the Chicago White Sox's Ozzie Guillen, the Washington Nationals' Frank Robinson, and the Chicago Cubs' Dusty Baker. A sixth, the Pittsburgh Pirates' Lloyd McClendon, was fired on September 6, 2005.)

Following the 2004 baseball season, having been given free rein to choose a new manager for his underachieving team, the Mets' new general manager of baseball operations, Omar Minaya, named Randolph to replace the recently fired Art Howe. Minaya's interest in Randolph seemed to be partially rooted in the latter's history with New

York City, as well as in his solid record as a player and coach. Minaya believed that Randolph could meet the high expectations of most New York City baseball fans and would be comfortable dealing with the burden of media scrutiny. "Managing in New York is not only about baseball," Minaya said at the press conference at which Randolph's appointment was announced. "Managing in New York is about understanding the New York fan base, understanding the media, understanding the beat of the city. When you do the job on a daily basis, I think the fact that you're a New Yorker matters." Signed to a three-year contract worth $1.8 million, Randolph became the first black manager in New York baseball history.

It was hoped that Randolph and the Mets' other new hires, the budding star outfielder Carlos Beltran and the celebrated pitcher Pedro Martinez, could help rejuvenate a franchise whose record over the previous three seasons was 212–272 (.438). After beginning the 2005 season with five straight losses (their worst start in 42 years), the team quickly rebounded to win six consecutive games. The Mets concluded the 2005 season with a record of 83–79, finishing in a tie for third place with the Florida Marlins in the National League East division. (Both the Marlins and the Mets finished the season seven games in the standings behind the Atlanta Braves.) The Mets' final rank in their division provided evidence of their marked improvement over the previous two seasons: the team finished with the fifth-best overall record in the National League, behind the Braves, the Philadelphia Phillies, the St. Louis Cardinals, and the Houston Astros. "All teams go through a certain progression, and certain teams go to a point where you might not get it done this year but you learn from that experience," Randolph told Brian Mahoney for the Associated Press (October 3, 2005). "Our hitters are not there yet as far as how to execute in pressure situations," he said. "With our team, with the way we were as far as the collective style of how we played and the youth of our team, in some cases we just didn't seize the opportunity. And a lot of that has to do with experience."

Several Mets players have noted that Randolph has brought a steadying influence to the team. "He's calm and unflappable," the Mets' third baseman David Wright told Albert Chen for *Sports Illustrated* (April 25, 2005). "The confidence that this team had even when we were losing all trickled down from him. He was the same when we were 0–5 as he was after we won six in a row. He never panicked." For his part, Randolph said to John Harper for the New York *Daily News* (February 27, 2005) about the Mets, "We've got talent here but I've been around a lot of teams with talent. It's how guys play the game and playing for each other that matters. And you need the mind-set that you're going to go kick somebody's butt every day."

Randolph and the former Gretchen Foster married on February 1, 1975. The two grew up in the same building in Brooklyn. "From the time I got up

in the morning and looked out the window," his wife recalled to Donnelly, "he'd be playing stickball. And he'd be there at night. He would go up and come down with a handful of cookies. That's about all the time he took to eat between morning and night." As a boy Randolph once hit a ball that crashed into his future wife's back. He told Donnelly, "I don't think she thought it was funny that day, but we do get a kick out of it now." He and his wife live in New Jersey and have four children: Taniesha, Chantre, Andre, and Ciara.

—D.F.

Suggested Reading: *Inside Sport* p84+ Oct. 1989, with photos; New York *Daily News* p90 Nov. 5, 2004, with photos; *New York Times* p29 May 25, 1976; *Newsday* S p8+ June 20, 1976, with photos; *Sport* p51+ Oct. 1976, with photos; *Village Voice* p19+ Aug. 19, 1986, with photos

Scott Gries/Getty Images

Ray, Rachael

Aug. 25, 1968– Chef; writer; television host

Address: Food Network, 75 Ninth Ave., New York, NY 10011

As the host of four popular television shows and the author of more than a dozen cookbooks, Rachael Ray has become the undisputed queen of the Food Network cable station. Such accomplishments are impressive for any chef and are particularly so for one who, like Ray, had no formal culinary training—only the lessons learned as the daughter of restaurant owners. "My first vivid memory is watching Mom in a restaurant kitchen," Ray recalled for the Food Network Web site. "She was flipping something with a spatula. I tried to copy her and ended up grilling my right thumb!" Such mishaps (which, she has admitted, are common occurrences for her even today) have not dampened Ray's fondness for preparing food; her contagious enthusiasm, in fact, has contributed to the success of her shows *30 Minute Meals* and *Inside Dish with Rachael Ray*, through which she attempts to demonstrate that cooking need not be as laborious and time-consuming as many people think. "All I'm trying to do with my shows and books is to make cooking accessible," she explained to Jae-Ha Kim for the *Chicago Sun-Times* (June 11, 2003). The focus of her programs *$40 a Day* and *Rachael Ray's Tasty Travels* is on dining out inexpensively. Ray's many fans reportedly watch her shows not merely for the recipes and restaurant tips but for a dose of her upbeat, talkative, endearingly klutzy manner. Chris McNamara summed up her appeal when he wrote for the *Chicago Tribune* (December 8, 2004), "She's a dish— cute as a button, sharp as a tack and quick as a whisk in the kitchen."

Rachael Domenica Ray was born on August 25, 1968 on Cape Cod, Massachusetts. Her mother, Elsa Scuderi, who came from Sicily, and her father, a native of Louisiana, both worked in the restaurant business: her mother spent 40 years as a supervisor in a variety of restaurants, and her parents once owned a chain of restaurants, called the Carvery, in Cape Cod. Ray has an older sister, Maria, and a younger brother, Emmanuel. "All of us have big tempers and love spicy food," Ray told Madeleine Marr for the *Macon (Georgia) Telegraph* (May 18, 2005). She explained to Candy Sagon for the *Washington Post* (January 14, 2004) that because her mother "doesn't like strangers watching her children," Ray and her siblings "were literally brought up in a kitchen." When Ray was in first grade, the family moved to upstate New York; there, too, her parents owned a restaurant, and Ray worked in it. In an interview with D. Mason for the *Ventura County (California) Star* (October 30, 2004), she called her mother "the head chef of the only cooking school I've ever attended." Ray graduated from Lake George High School, in Lake George, New York. She reportedly moved to New York City after completing college, in about 1990. (Readily available sources do not identify the college.)

Ray followed her mother's career path, working at local restaurants and for caterers in upstate New York. In the early 1990s she found work at Macy's Marketplace in New York City, beginning at the candy counter and rising in the company to become the manager of the fresh-foods department. After spending two years at Macy's, she was hired as a store manager and buyer for an Upper East Side gourmet grocer, Agata & Valentina. Tiring of urban life, and wishing to leave behind her the nasty breakup of a romantic relationship, a mugging, and the hardships ensuing from a broken ankle, Ray moved to the cabin that her mother rented near the Adirondack Mountains, in New York State, close to where she was born. To earn a living, she managed pubs and restaurants at the Sagamore resort on Lake George. Soon afterward Ray secured a position as a buyer for Cowan & Lobel, a gourmet market in Albany, New York. "Through a series of accidents, I kept ending up in jobs I was completely unqualified for," Ray told Madeleine Marr.

While at Cowan & Lobel, Ray realized that many people were not buying the foods available there simply because they did not have enough time to cook or did not want to spend a lot of time cooking. Ray understood how they felt, as she told Linda Giuca for the *Hartford (Connecticut) Courant* (February 5, 2004): "I'm an intensely impatient person. That's why I'm a 30-minute cook and why I don't like baking." In order to boost sales, Ray began offering a cooking class, which she called 30-Minute Meals. The class was designed, she told Jessica Leshnoff for the *Washington Times* (November 26, 2004), "to keep it simple, keep it fun and deliver food in as much time as [customers] were willing to give to Domino's Pizza." To further simplify the cooking process, Ray focused on teaching her students such time- and energy-saving tips as estimating amounts of ingredients rather than measuring them and cooking meals with ingredients that most people already had in their kitchens. (Ray has since come under fire from critics for her use of frozen whipped topping, cornbread mix, and other such "convenience" products.) The class was a success, attracting everyone from retirees to Girl Scouts, and a local television station offered Ray her own weekly segment, which was nominated for two regional Emmy Awards. A companion cookbook, *30-Minute Meals* (1999), written with Dan Dinicola, sold 10,000 copies in 10 days.

In the winter of 2001, Al Roker, who reports on the weather and handles other assignments for the NBC morning program *Today*, called Ray with a request that she host a cooking segment on the show. Ray's appearance on the *Today* show was so successful that it attracted the attention of executives from the Food Network, who set up a meeting with her. "At the first meeting I said, 'I don't know what I'm doing here, really,'" Ray told Jon Tevlin for the Minneapolis, Minnesota, *Star Tribune* (November 8, 2003). "I am beer out of a bottle in a champagne world." The Food Network executives clearly disagreed and offered Ray her own show. "My life has been a total accident, a very happy, wonderful accident that I didn't and couldn't have planned," Ray told Chris McNamara.

30 Minute Meals first aired on the Food Network on November 17, 2002 and quickly became one of the most popular shows on the station—despite Ray's initial nervousness, which led to her slicing her finger just prior to the filming of the first episode. Ray's modus operandi, making cooking easy and fun, seemed to strike a chord with viewers. As she explained to Jessica Leshnoff, "I don't wear a chef's coat. I don't want anything on my show to remind you that you're watching a cooking show. I want it to feel like it's your neighbor, it's your kitchen. Can-do cooking is what I'm trying to do with that show." Soon after the debut of *30 Minute Meals*, the Food Network gave Ray the opportunity to host a second show, *$40 a Day*, which shows her traveling to different areas of the country and sampling foods from a variety of local restaurants on the budget indicated by the title. The second series, too, has proven to be popular with viewers. The year 2004 saw the premiere of *Inside Dish with Rachael Ray*, for which Ray has interviewed such celebrities as Tony Danza, Morgan Freeman, Mariel Hemingway, and Cheech Marin, among others, and persuaded them to share some of their own favorite recipes. In 2005 Ray began hosting another show, *Rachael Ray's Tasty Travels*, for which she journeys throughout the U.S., dispensing travel tips and dining suggestions. (*Tasty Travels* has a larger production budget than *$40 a Day*.)

Ray's success has been attributed to a combination of factors. Ray is "normal, she's cute, and she's fun," Jessica Leshnoff wrote. "She could be your sister or your favorite neighbor." Ray's interviewers and fans often pepper their descriptions of her with adjectives including "bubbly," "perky," "enthusiastic," "adorable," and "chatty." The habitually modest Ray said in an interview with Dan MacDonald for the Jacksonville *Florida Times-Union* (July 3, 2003), "I don't think there is anything sexy about me at all. I am the goofiest. I think of sexy as . . . very pretty women, in very nice clothing, doing pretty things. I'm a big goof." (Such humility notwithstanding, Ray participated in a photo shoot for the men's magazine *FHM*, in which she posed, scantily clad, by a stove.)

Ray's shows, particularly *30-Minute Meals*, have found an audience not only among adults pressed for time but among children, as well. "I guess I'm just goofy enough to seem like a cartoon," Ray told D. Mason. "I have this goofy laugh and wave my hands around a lot." She has stressed the value of exposing children to cooking. "Food should be fun. Cooking can give kids a wonderful sense of accomplishment," she told Natalie Haughton for the *Chattanooga (Tennessee) Times Free Press* (January 19, 2005). "Food teaches about sharing and math skills and is an ego- and confidence-booster for kids." In keeping with that view, Ray has given cooking demonstrations at camps and schools. "If kids are making a meal everyone wants to eat," Ray told Doug Blackburn for the *Monterey County Herald* (April 10, 2005), "there's a real emotional payoff for them."

Ray writes every night, concocting about 600 new recipes every year. She has penned numerous cookbooks, including *Rachael Ray's Open House Cookbook* (2000); *Comfort Foods: Rachael Ray's 30-Minute Meals* (2001); *Veggie Meals: Rachael Ray's 30-Minute Meals* (2001); *30-Minute Meals 2* (2003); *Get Togethers: Rachael Ray 30-Minute Meals* (2003); *$40 a Day: Best Eats in Town* (2004);

Rachael Ray's 30-Minute Meals for Kids: Cooking Rocks! (2004); *Cooking 'Round the Clock: Rachael Ray's 30-Minute Meals* (2004); *Rachael Ray's 30-Minute Get Real Meals: Eat Healthy Without Going to Extremes* (2005); and *Rachael Ray 365: No Repeats: A New 30-Minute Meal for Every Day of the Year*. Several books were scheduled for publication in November 2005: *Comfort Food: Rachael Ray's Top 30 30-Minute Meals*; *Guy Food: Rachael Ray's Top 30 30-Minute Meals*; and *Kid Food: Rachael Ray's Top 30 30-Minute Meals*. Another volume, *Rachael Ray Express Lane Meals: Great Dinners from the Pantry and Your Market's Express Lane*, was due to reach bookstores in 2006.

Ray also serves as editor in chief of *Every Day with Rachael Ray*, a new lifestyle magazine produced by the Reader's Digest Association. Her motivation for helming a magazine devoted to both cooking and lifestyle advice is simple, as she told Lia Miller for the *New York Times* (April 25, 2005). "I want to see legitimately useful information: here are shoes you can cook in and party in," she explained. "This is more about customer service. I grew up working in resort-town restaurants. In my mind I'm a waitress. I want to give the people what they want." She has also recently endorsed a line of cookware by the Meyer Corp., cutlery by Furi-technics, and electric kitchen appliances by Salton.

Ray divides her time between her cabin in the Adirondacks and an apartment in the Greenwich Village section of New York City. She is married to John Cusimano, an entertainment lawyer and member of the band The Cringe. Ray and her programs have sparked numerous Web sites, and thousands of fans show up for each of her book-signing events. "I don't know if anyone could deserve such warm, loving feelings from people," she said to Jessica Leshnoff, "but I certainly do enjoy it, and it's a lovely experience to have."

— K.J.E.

Suggested Reading: *Chicago Tribune* p5 Dec. 8, 2004; Food Network Web site; *Macon (Georgia) Telegraph* (on-line) May 18, 2005; *Ventura County (California) Star* (on-line) Oct. 30, 2004; *Washington Times* D p1 Nov. 26, 2004

Selected Television Shows: *30 Minute Meals*, 2002– ; *$40 a Day*, 2002– ; *Inside Dish with Rachael Ray*, 2004– ; *Rachael Ray's Tasty Travels*, 2005–

Selected Books: *30-Minute Meals* (with Dan Dinicola), 1999; *Rachael Ray's Open House Cookbook*, 2000; *Comfort Foods: Rachael Ray's 30-Minute Meals*, 2001; *Veggie Meals: Rachael Ray's 30-Minute Meals*, 2001; *30-Minute Meals 2*, 2003; *Get Togethers: Rachael Ray 30-Minute Meals*, 2003; *$40 a Day: Best Eats in Town*, 2004; *Rachael Ray's 30-Minute Meals for Kids: Cooking Rocks!*, 2004; *Cooking 'Round the Clock: Rachael Ray's 30-Minute Meals*, 2004; *Rachael Ray's 30-*

Minute Get Real Meals: Eat Healthy Without Going to Extremes, 2005; *Rachael Ray 365: No Repeats: A New 30-Minute Meal for Every Day of the Year*, 2005

Gary Dineen, courtesy of NBAE

Redd, Michael

Aug. 24, 1979– Basketball player

Address: Milwaukee Bucks, 1001 N. Fourth St., Milwaukee, WI 53203

Each year in June about 100 of the world's best basketball players apply for the National Basketball Association (NBA) draft. With two draft rounds and 30 teams in the league, 60 players are selected. The rest are left to either try to make it onto a team as a rare unsigned walk-on; play in the American developmental professional leagues, which are similar to baseball's minor leagues; play in a professional league abroad; or finish school without playing for their institution any more, because of eligibility rules governing college basketball. Even if a player is picked, he has no guarantee of an NBA career. About a quarter of the draftees each year are cut from their teams before the season, leaving them the same options as those who were not drafted. Declaring oneself eligible for the NBA draft before finishing college, therefore, is a major risk. Increasingly, young players are willing to take that risk. In 2001 alone, 75 underclassmen declared early eligibility for the draft, including six high-school players. The payoff for a player, if he is drafted and makes the team, can be worth millions of dollars, particularly if he is selected in the first 10 picks.

Listed by some prognosticators as a potential top-10 pick, the shooting guard Michael Redd entered the 2000 NBA draft following his junior year at Ohio State University (OSU). Using his size, strength, and athleticism to slash a path for himself to the basket, he had been a valuable member of OSU's men's basketball team, the Buckeyes. Redd's ability to dribble past defenders and finish plays made him a prolific scorer and a probable lock for the pros. Pro teams, however, had some reservations about him. The six-foot six-inch Redd was tall and athletic for a shooting guard, but his 235-pound body was deemed too heavy and soft for the demands of the NBA, where the talent level is so high that even perennial benchwarmers are great athletes. Moreover, NBA teams take the name of Redd's position quite literally: shooting guards have to be able to shoot from the outside to succeed in the pros. Redd's three-point field-goal average in college—where the arc is 19 feet, nine inches from the basket, exactly four feet shorter than the NBA's—was only 31.9 percent. Consequently, Redd's value slipped in the draft; when the Milwaukee Bucks selected him, he was in the 43d position, where he had slid about midway through the second round. "Was I disappointed? Very—for about five minutes. Then I began to look at it as a positive," Redd told Tom Kertes for *Basketball Digest* (February 2004). "I said to myself, 'Dude, you're in the NBA now. Stop sulking and rise to the challenge.'" After sitting out most of his rookie season with the talent-laden Bucks, Redd spent the summer working with his father and former high-school coach to improve his long-distance shot and to trim his physique. Redd came into training camp the following season 20 pounds lighter (having reduced his body fat from 14 to 9 percent) and with an improved shooting stroke. He had thereby begun his transformation into a rare and valuable asset in the NBA: a long-range threat. Three seasons—and three more summers of hard work—later, he returned to camp an NBA All-Star, following his breakthrough year, in which he ranked fifth in scoring among all players.

The son of James and Haji Redd, Michael Redd was born on August 24, 1979. He grew up 15 minutes from the OSU campus. He has traced his love of basketball to his father. "He was my first hero, my first role model," Redd told Kertes. "He was a pastor, very humble but also very passionate about his faith. He was the guy who first taught me to play basketball. And the first thing I remember him telling me is 'Be involved!'" For Michael the lessons started early, when he was too small to handle a basketball. Using balled-up socks and a trashcan, James Redd challenged his son to a shooting contest every night. "I'd always let it get to 9–9, and then I'd be sure to make the 10th one to win," James Redd told Chris Ballard for *Sports Illustrated* (February 23, 2004). "Would he get mad! He'd run down the hall, hitting stuff. He'd call me a cheater. I wanted to see his competitive spirit. That let me know he had one." Once he grew big enough to play with a real ball, Michael practiced whenever he could. If it was raining, he would dribble on the porch or in the basement. He "always ended up hitting the furnace," Haji Redd, a schoolteacher, told Ballard.

Redd attended West High School in Columbus, Ohio, where his father had once made a name for himself on the court. "Before Michael came along, I was the only All-American to come out of that high school. When he first went to West, I told him, 'This is my house.' He said, 'Dad, before I leave, it's going to be my house,'" James recalled to Gary D'Amato for the *Milwaukee Journal Sentinel* (January 22, 2003). "Well, it's his house now . . . and his basement, and his garage." Indeed, Michael Redd entered his senior year at West rated the second-best college prospect in the state by *Ohio Round-ball Prep* magazine and the 33d best high-school player in the nation at the Nike Supercamp. His senior season averages backed up those assessments: 25.7 points, 9.4 rebounds, and 3.4 steals per game. He was widely sought after by colleges across the country, among them the University of Michigan, whose basketball program is recognized as one of the nation's best. "At first, I wanted to go to Michigan for basketball," Redd told a reporter for *Sporting News* (November 24, 2003), "but by my senior year of high school, I felt it was more important to stick to Ohio State and help rebuild that program."

Redd started all 30 games for the Buckeyes in his first season (1997–98) and became the first true freshman to lead the Big-10 Conference in scoring. (Ohioans of all stripes traditionally refer to themselves as Buckeyes, a name that refers to a species of plant that thrives where many other can not.) The Buckeyes, however, experienced their fifth consecutive losing season, winning only eight games. "My friends used to call us the Suckeyes," Redd told Seth Davis for *Sports Illustrated* (November 15, 1999). "It was tough going to games knowing you were going to lose."

Ohio State, piloted by the backcourt tandem of Redd and Scoonie Penn, a point guard, turned its fortunes around dramatically in the 1998–99 season. The Buckeyes posted a 27–9 record, led by Redd's team-best average of 19.5 points per game, and finished the season as the nation's fourth-ranked team following a Final Four performance in the National Collegiate Athletic Association (NCAA) championships, during which they lost to the eventual champions, the University of Connecticut Huskies. With both Redd and Penn returning, along with a third starter from the Final Four team, expectations for the Buckeyes were high heading into the 1999–2000 season. But as the Ohio State coach Jim O'Brien noted to Seth Davis, "Things don't automatically carry over to the next season." Though the Buckeyes completed a 23–7 season with a share of first place in the Big-10 Conference, they were bounced in the second round of the NCAA Tournament by the University of Miami and finished the season ranked 17th. Soon afterward, Michael Redd declared his eligibility for the 2000 NBA draft and was chosen by the Bucks. (The name of the team, according to its official Web site, was suggested in 1968 by a fan who pointed out that the players, like male deer, are fast, agile jumpers.)

"It wasn't a mistake to come out of college early," Redd told Chris Tomasson for the *Akron Beacon Journal* (March 2, 2002). "It was the best move I ever made. I had one year to practice and learn the NBA game. It was like a redshirt year." (A redshirt year is one in which a college athlete elects not to play but maintains his eligibility for the team.) He appeared in only six Bucks games and scored only 13 points, none from behind the three-point arc. "It was very difficult at first," he explained to Kertes. "But then I adjusted. I had to. I did that by working hard off the court—and I was an animal in practice. I decided to treat practices as games." He thereby saw clearly exactly what he lacked. "I didn't have too much confidence in my shot," he told Chris Ballard for *Sports Illustrated* (February 25, 2002). "My legs would get tired, and I'd put up line drives. I knew I needed to work on it to play in the league." The summer after his rookie year, Redd set to work with his father and his high-school coach, Keith Neal, to put more arc in his shot and more spring in his legs. He made 400 to 500 jump shots every morning, followed by a series of sprints. After his lunch he would shoot for another hour before working out with weights, and then completed his regimen with another half hour of jump shots. The effort and conditioning began to pay dividends in Redd's practice intensity and performance, which immediately drew Bucks coach George Karl's attention. In his second season Redd played in 67 of 82 games, averaging 21.1 minutes and 11.4 points per game. He also set the NBA record for the most three-pointers in a single period, with eight in the fourth quarter in a game against the Houston Rockets on February 20, 2002. He became a valuable commodity off the bench when he became a restricted free agent. Milwaukee was slow to re-sign him, and Redd held out through the 2002–03 preseason camp. Ultimately, the Bucks' hand was forced by the Dallas Mavericks, who offered Redd a four-year, $12 million deal. Because Redd's free agency was restricted, league rules permitted Milwaukee to match Dallas's offer to retain him, and the Bucks' executives did so.

In the opinion of most observers, Redd has paid back Milwaukee's investment in full on the court. Coming into his third season, he worked hard to blend the two aspects of his game—as slasher and as shooter—more effectively. His ball-handling skills allowed him to either dribble past an opponent toward the basket or quickly pull up for a jumper, which he could now sink consistently. His advantages in size and strength compared with other shooting guards also made him a rebounding threat, a rare commodity in a guard, and he continued to progress as a defender. In 2002–03 Redd came off the bench as the Bucks' "sixth man," playing an average of 28.2 minutes in all 82 games, scoring 15.1 points per game, and finishing with 43.8 percent accuracy in three-point shooting—second best in the NBA that season. He placed second to the Sacramento Kings point guard Bobby Jackson for that season's NBA Sixth Man Award, which recognizes the top player in a reserve role and is among the league's most prestigious honors.

During the 2003–04 season, Redd made the final step in his transition from low-round draftee to star. Salary considerations and free agency had depleted the once veteran- and talent-rich Bucks, and Redd was one of only a few legitimate scoring threats left for its new head coach, the former NBA star Terry Porter. Rather than focus on improving his team's scoring options, Porter started with the fundamentals of defense. "Coach came in and said, 'Look guys, we have no big contracts or superstars on this team. So you either play [defense] as hard as humanly possible, or you'll sit right next to me on the bench,'" Redd recalled to Kertes. Redd followed Porter's advice, improving his one-on-one and team defensive skills and thus earning the starting shooting-guard job. Because of his efforts to become a better defender, Redd also gained more game time. He finished the season as the Bucks' leading scorer, with an average of 21.7 points per game. (He also contributed an average of five rebounds per game.) That year NBA coaches voted him to the Eastern Conference's All-Star team.

The Bucks, who were not expected to crack 20 wins, much less make the 2004 play-offs, ended the regular season with a 41–41 record, which earned them the sixth seed in the Eastern Conference play-offs. In the first round they played the third-place Detroit Pistons. The defensive-minded Pistons had targeted Redd as the Bucks' chief scorer and at times assigned two or even three players to stop him from getting a good look at the basket. Redd turned over the ball seven times and scored only 11 points, while the Pistons set a play-off record for team steals with 14 en route to a 108–82 trouncing of the Bucks. Milwaukee rebounded the following night to claim game two behind a 26-point performance from Redd. Detroit took the next three games—and the best-of-seven series—on their way to the NBA championship.

Following the 2004–05 season, the Milwaukee Bucks officially re-signed Redd (who had also been wooed by the Cleveland Cavaliers); his six-year contract is reportedly worth just under $91 million, making it the most lucrative deal in the franchise's history (and, according to some sources, the most financially rewarding for any athlete in Wisconsin's history).

Michael Redd has proven himself valuable off the court as well as on, through his work ethic and quiet leadership. "Michael is about the nicest guy," his teammate Damon Jones told Kertes. "He kids around and he's a friend, sure. But ballplaying-wise, he never says peep, just goes about his business. He has no pretension, no attitude, requires no 'look at me' props. He's God-fearing, humble, and

hungry." Another teammate, Desmond Mason, described Redd to Chris Ballard in 2004 as "one of the true gentlemen of this game." Redd does not drink or smoke; in his spare time he reads spiritual books, and he leads the team's Bible study group. "The values we instilled in him were to put God first in your life and family second. Treat people nice. Doesn't matter what color they are, black, white, whatever. Treat people the way you want to be treated," James Redd told Gary D'Amato. "What I'm most proud of is that he's a gentleman off the court and he never says anything negative about anyone, ever."

—T.J.F.

Suggested Reading: *Basketball Digest* p46 Feb. 2004, with photos; Milwaukee Bucks Web site; *Milwaukee Journal Sentinel* C p1 Jan. 22, 2003; *Sports Illustrated* p77+ Feb 25, 2002, p52+ Feb. 23, 2004, with photos

Eric Solomon, courtesy of the George Washington University

Reich, Walter

July 6, 1943– Psychiatrist; writer; educator

Address: Elliott School of International Affairs, George Washington University, 1957 E St., N.W., Washington, DC 20052

In a career spanning more than three decades, the psychiatrist and author Walter Reich has contributed tirelessly to the cause of human rights, both as a champion of the ethical practice of medicine and in his condemnation of crimes against humanity. As a young psychiatrist he led the fight at a 1977 meeting of the World Psychiatric Association to condemn the Soviet Union for misusing the practice of psychiatry to control dissidents; over the course of the following two decades, through his work with the Holocaust Memorial Museum in Washington, D.C., he sought to educate the general public about the horrors of the Holocaust in the hopes of preventing another such genocide. Reich has written extensively on subjects ranging from the struggle between Jews and Palestinians in the West Bank to the origins of terrorism and the psychological effects of terrorism on individuals and populations. In 2003 he was honored with the Scientific Freedom and Responsibility Award, given by the American Association for the Advancement of Science (AAAS) to those members of the scientific community "whose exemplary actions, often taken at significant personal cost, have served to foster scientific freedom and responsibility." In 2004 Reich received the American Psychiatric Association's Human Rights Award for having "inspired and fostered the effort to protect human rights not only in his prominent public writings but also through his leadership of organizations and institutions." Since 1995 he has been a cochair of the Committee of Concerned Scientists, which is devoted to the protection of the human rights of scientists, physicians, engineers, and other professionals.

The son of Simon Reich and the former Anna Nussbaum, Walter Reich was born in Rzeszów, Poland, on July 6, 1943, during World War II. As Jews trying to evade the Nazis, who had invaded Poland four years earlier, the Reich family spent much of the war in hiding. After the war they found themselves in a displaced-persons' camp in Berlin, Germany. In 1947, when Reich was three years old, the family immigrated to the United States.

After he completed high school, Reich enrolled at Columbia University, in New York City, where he received a bachelor's degree in philosophy and literature in 1965. He studied philosophy as a graduate student at Columbia before entering the New York University School of Medicine, from which he earned an M.D. degree in 1970. While in medical school he served as a research fellow in neuropsychology at the Laboratory of Psychology and Psychopathology of the National Institute of Mental Health (NIMH), in Bethesda, Maryland, in 1969. In 1970, in London, England, also while in medical school, he was a clinical fellow in neurology at the National Hospital for Neurological Diseases of the National Hospital, a visiting fellow at the Tavistock Centre for Human Relations, and a visiting fellow at the Hampstead Child-Therapy Clinic, where he studied with Anna Freud. After an internship in internal medicine at the Jackson Memorial Hospital and the University of Miami, in Miami, Florida, from 1970 to 1971, he completed his psychiatric residency at Yale University, in New Haven, Connecticut, from 1971 to 1973.

In 1973 Reich accepted an appointment as a research psychiatrist at the NIMH, where he studied the genetics of schizophrenia. At the same time he investigated psychiatric abuses occurring inside the USSR. In 1971 he had become aware that political dissenters in the Soviet Union were frequently diagnosed with mental illness and forced into special hospitals, often so that they would be unable to express their opinions publicly; Reich's research uncovered evidence that that practice had existed at least since the 1960s. His findings, based on interviews with Soviet dissidents, shocked the medical community. In the New York Times (January 30, 1983), Reich wrote: "Once in psychiatric hospitals, usually special institutions for the criminally insane, the dissidents were said to be treated with particular cruelty—for example, given injections that caused abscesses, convulsions and torpor, or wrapped in wet canvas that shrank tightly upon drying." In an earlier article for the New York Times Magazine (May 13, 1979), Reich had described the case of General Pyotr Grigorenko, a Soviet Army war hero who, in the 1960s, joined the dissident movement on behalf of the Crimean Tatars, an ethnic group expelled by the Soviet leader Josef Stalin from their native lands to Central Asia because of alleged disloyalty during World War II. Grigorenko was subsequently arrested and sent to psychiatric hospitals. When he came to the United States in 1978, he was examined in Boston, Massachusetts, New Haven, Connecticut, and New York City by a team of medical specialists, led by Reich. Those experts, from Harvard, Yale, and Columbia Universities, included psychiatrists, a neurologist, and a neuropsychologist; none of the doctors could find any evidence of mental illness in Grigorenko, and each was confident that the Soviet émigré had never suffered from such a disorder, even at the time of his arrest.

In 1971, outraged by findings in earlier, similar cases, Western psychiatrists had demanded action. At that year's meeting of the World Psychiatric Association, in Mexico City, Mexico, they attempted to censure their Soviet counterparts, only to be rebuffed by the Soviets, who accused them of Cold War politicking. Six years later, while serving as director of advanced studies at NIMH (a post he had assumed in 1976), Reich led the charge at the meeting of the World Psychiatric Association in Hawaii to censure the Soviet Union for its practice of punishing dissenters on the basis of purposely skewed mental diagnoses. This time, the censure motion passed by a narrow majority.

In a communication sent to Current Biography, Reich wrote that his "investigation of Soviet psychiatric theories and practices, including interviews with leading Soviet psychiatrists, taught me that while many practitioners in that country were cynically using the system to stifle dissent, others actually believed that anyone who disagreed with the Soviet government and economic and social systems must be mentally ill. Dissenters were often diagnosed as suffering from 'sluggish schizophrenia,' an illness not recognized by physicians in any other country. That abuse of psychiatry allowed the Soviet government to hospitalize dissidents, thus avoiding embarrassing public trials. Understanding that of all of the medical specialties, psychiatry is perhaps most at risk for this type of misuse, I also examined diagnostic practices in the United States to ensure that similar abuses would not occur. This examination led me to the conclusion that in this country, aberrant and unacceptable behavior is increasingly excused by attaching a psychiatric label to it, thereby undermining the concept of personal responsibility for one's behavior."

In 1984 Reich published *A Stranger in My House*, a study of the lives of Jews and Arabs in the West Bank—a territory annexed by Jordan in 1948, captured by Israel during the Six-Day War of 1967, and occupied by Israel afterward. Though populated by Palestinian Arabs when it was captured, the West Bank, as Reich wrote to *Current Biography*, "had been the center of the land of Israel during biblical times and attracted Jewish settlers, many of whom wanted to return to their people's geographical roots and holy places, such as Hebron and Shiloh." Through interviews with people on both sides, Reich provided a narrative of intolerance, religious nationalism, and violence and also evoked the deep passions and commitments to the land felt by both Arabs and Jews. He also conveyed the sense on the part of individuals on each side that those on the other side were in a way strangers in that place. In an assessment for the *New York Times Book Review* (October 28, 1984), David K. Shipler called Reich's book "a fine primer on the conflict over that small, kidney-shaped tract of territory that begins at the western bank of the Jordan River and stretches at points to within a few miles of the Mediterranean. . . . Dr. Reich's purpose is not to move into all the depths and subtleties of the issue—and especially not to dwell on the diplomatic dimension—but to offer a series of sharply-etched portraits of some of the principal Arab and Jewish actors, blending the human, religious and political ingredients into a creditable overview of the conflict."

In 1990 Reich edited *Origins of Terrorism: Psychologies, Ideologies, Theologies, States of Mind*, a collection of 15 essays by scholars, exploring the types and motivations of terrorism throughout history. At a conference held by the Woodrow Wilson International Center for Scholars in Washington, D.C., as quoted in the *Los Angeles Times* (March 24, 1987) by Robert C. Toth, Reich said, "There are many different kinds of persons and groups who end up turning to what we call terrorism. We may call them 'they,' but if we attempt to predict future actions, we must disaggregate the 'they.'" Reviewing Reich's book for the *Washington Post Book World* (October 7, 1990), a critic wrote: "Clearly, terrorists have always been a fact of life—think only of the Zealots of Judea, the Assassins of 13th-century Islam and the People's Will of 19th-

century Russia. More contemporary-minded readers will welcome the discussion here of the Weathermen of the United States, the Red Brigades of Italy and Northern Ireland's Provisional IRA. Tentative in their conclusions, these essays nevertheless sift through a fascinating amount of information."

Although Reich and his parents survived the Holocaust—the systematic murder by Nazi Germany, during World War II, of an estimated six million European Jews—the vast majority of his relatives, Polish Jews, were killed, most of them in the gas chambers of the Belzec death camp in Poland. Growing up among Holocaust survivors, Reich developed a deep interest—personal as well as scholarly—in the Holocaust and in Holocaust memorialization. He maintained that interest as he pursued his medical, scientific, institutional, and human-rights work. In the 1980s he served as a consultant in the planning of the United States Holocaust Memorial Museum, which opened in 1993 as the nation's official memorial to the victims of the Holocaust. In 1995 he was named the museum's second director, succeeding Jeshayahu Weinberg, its founding director. Under Reich's leadership the museum (which is an agency of the U.S. federal government, located adjacent to the national mall in Washington, D.C.) became one of the most-visited museums in the nation's capital, receiving some two million visitors each year. In addition, the museum collected a vast trove of archival material on the Holocaust, established the Center for Advanced Holocaust Studies, and created the Committee on Conscience to warn about the emergence of new genocides around the world.

Also during his tenure, which lasted until 1998, Reich fought a public battle with Miles Lerman, the chairman of the museum's presidentially appointed board of trustees, known as the United States Holocaust Memorial Council, as well as with the State Department and the White House—because, as he wrote to *Current Biography*, they "attempted to use the museum for political and diplomatic purposes." The conflict began in January 1998, when Lerman (who had been appointed to the board of trustees by President Bill Clinton), together with State Department and White House officials, invited the Palestinian leader Yasir Arafat to tour the Holocaust Museum without Reich's knowledge. Reich wrote to *Current Biography*, "Arafat had been scheduled to arrive in Washington later that month for meetings with President Clinton, and the administration, recognizing that many American Jews, as well as other Americans, doubted Arafat's peaceful intentions toward Israel, felt that, if Arafat could be shown to be touring the museum's exhibit about the murder of Europe's Jews and laying a wreath in their honor at the museum's eternal flame, those doubters would be persuaded that Arafat felt the pain of the Jews, cared about the Jewish tragedy during the Holocaust, and could be trusted with the fate of the Jewish state." When Reich learned about the invitation, he wrote to *Current Biography*, he "concluded that it had been a nakedly political act and said publicly that the museum must never be used for such a photoop and that it was wrong to use either the museum or the Holocaust to achieve political or diplomatic ends." He continued, "Lerman then had Arafat disinvited. In response to the disinvitation, Secretary of State Madeleine K. Albright, appearing on [the TV show] *Meet the Press*, said [as quoted in a report posted on the Web site of the U.S. Embassy in Israel] it was 'too bad' that Arafat had been disinvited, adding that 'it would have been appropriate to have him treated as a VIP.' Lerman then reinvited Arafat, and he and the council's executive committee asked me to escort the Palestinian leader on the VIP tour." Reich refused and then resigned; as he wrote in an opinion piece for the *Washington Post* (August 28, 1999), "It was a matter of conscience in a museum of conscience." Arafat did not show up at the museum that day, most likely, according to the *Weekly Standard* (August 30/September 6, 1999) and other publications, because of breaking news of the sex scandal involving Clinton and the former White House intern Monica Lewinsky.

The Jewish community in the United States was divided on the Arafat invitation. Some believed that it might be worthwhile to have the Palestinian leader visit the museum and gain a better understanding of the Holocaust. Others objected, noting that Arafat had ties to terrorists who denied that the Holocaust ever occurred. After Reich resigned his post, Katharine Q. Seelye reported for the *New York Times* (February 19, 1998), that "several friends" of Reich's suggested that the incident involving Arafat "was such a public relations debacle that top museum officials needed a scapegoat." In its "Notebook" section, a reporter for the *New Republic* (March 2, 1998) wrote, "We wonder how Lerman got the museum into this mess; . . . and how it is that Lerman has previously made the museum available to the political convenience of the administration, as in the inauguration last year? The issue is not just Arafat. The issue is also the character of the museum and its operation."

Shortly afterward, a U.S. House Appropriations subcommittee commissioned the National Academy of Public Administration (NAPA) to look into the matter. The resulting NAPA report noted that 55 of the 65 voting members of the U.S. Holocaust Memorial Council (many of whom were also State Department officials) had been appointed by the president, and that they should be kept out of the museum's day-to-day operations in order to keep it from being politicized. The report also warned that "federal institutions, especially one that carries the moral weight of the Holocaust, are vulnerable to political pressure from the executive branch or the Congress" and that the museum "should not be used as a tool to achieve particular political purposes," as it had in the Arafat matter. A commentator for the *Weekly Standard* (August 30–September 6, 1999) observed that the subcommittee's "findings vindicate Walter Reich, the museum director who resigned rather than lend himself to the Arafat

caper. Congress should write into law institutional arrangements that put the museum where, as Reich notes, it always should have been: 'off limits to any diplomatic manipulation.'"

In addition to writing books, Reich has contributed numerous opinion pieces over the years to various periodicals, including the *New York Times*, the *Washington Post*, the *Los Angeles Times*, the *Atlantic Monthly*, *Harper's*, the *Wall Street Journal*, and the *New Republic*. In recent years, for example, he has commented on the impact of terrorism—particularly the attacks of September 11, 2001—on the American psyche; suggested that Mel Gibson's 2004 film, *The Passion of the Christ*, would incite anti-Semitism; and, on the 60th anniversary of the liberation of the Auschwitz concentration camp, in January 2005, harshly criticized as lip service to the prevention of future genocide the various commemorations that were taking place—while at the same time stressing that, if carried out in way that educates the public about what actually happened during the Holocaust, such commemorations are valuable.

Reich was director of advanced studies at NIMH until 1986 and served as a senior research psychiatrist there until 1994. Since 1986 he has been a professor of psychiatry at the Uniformed Services University of Health Sciences, in Bethesda, Maryland. In 1985 he began his association with the Woodrow Wilson International Center for Scholars, in Washington, D.C., where he has served as a fellow and senior scholar as well as director of the project on health, science, and public policy. Since 1995 he has been a professor of psychiatry and behavioral sciences at George Washington University, in Washington, D.C., and since 1998, following his departure from the Holocaust Museum, he has been the Yitzhak Rabin Memorial Professor of International Affairs, Ethics and Human Behavior at the university's Elliott School of International Affairs. He is a distinguished fellow of the American Psychiatric Association.

Reich has received numerous awards for his contributions to the understanding of human rights issues in medical matters. In 1982 and 1983 he was a fellow at the Kennan Institute for Advanced Russian Studies at the Woodrow Wilson International Center for Scholars, and in 1984 he was named the Lustman fellow at Davenport College at Yale University and the David J. Fish memorial lecturer at Brown University. In 1978 he received an award for meritorious achievement from the Alcohol, Drug Abuse, and Mental Health Administration. From the United States Army he received the Order of Military Medical Merit (1991), and from the Uniformed Services University of the Health Sciences, he received the Outstanding Service Medal (1992). In 1994 he received the Solomon A. Berson Medical Alumni Achievement Award in Health Science from the New York University School of Medicine, and in 1998 he earned a special presidential commendation from the American Psychiatric Association "in recognition of his distinguished leadership and scholarship as director of the U.S. Holocaust Memorial Museum in Washington, DC, and of his being a renowned champion of human rights." He was given the Holocaust Humanitarian Award by the Holocaust Memorial Committee of Brooklyn, New York, in 1999. In 2003 he received the prestigious Scientific Freedom and Responsibility Award from the AAAS. In the following year he was presented with the Human Rights Award from the American Psychiatric Association.

Walter Reich has been married to Tova Rachel Weiss, a novelist, since June 10, 1965. The couple live in Chevy Chase, Maryland, and have three grown children: Daniel, David, and Rebecca.

—C.M.

Suggested Reading: AAAS.org; *Christian Century* p225+ Mar. 11, 1998; Elliott School of International Affairs Web site; *Los Angeles Times* I p22 Mar. 24, 1987, B p13 Feb. 25, 2004; *New York Sun* p8 Jan. 27, 2005; *New York Times* VI p21 Jan. 30, 1983, C p15 May 25, 1995, A p10 Feb. 19, 1998; *New York Times Book Review* p18 Oct. 28, 1984; *U.S. News & World Report* p48 Sep. 24, 2001, p52 Nov. 5, 2001; *Weekly Standard* p2 Mar. 2, 1998, p2 Aug. 30–Sep. 6, 1999;*Washington Post Book World* p13 Oct. 7, 1990; *Who's Who in the East*, 2001

Selected Books: *The Enemies of Memory*, 1982; *A Stranger in My House*, 1984; as editor—*Origins of Terrorism: Psychologies, Ideologies, Theologies, States of Mind*, 1990

Peter Read Miller/Courtesy of *Sports Illustrated*

Reilly, Rick

Feb. 3, 1958– Sportswriter

Address: Sports Illustrated, *135 W. 50th St., New York, NY 10020*

Rick Reilly "may be America's most widely read sportswriter—and the most entertaining," Mark Hyman wrote for *BusinessWeek* (April 22, 2002). "His 'Life of Reilly' column, which closes every issue of *Sports Illustrated*, alternately makes for the funniest and most poignant reading in the sports weekly." "Life of Reilly"—a play on *Life of Riley*, the name of a popular 1940s and '50s radio show and 1950s TV series—is the first bylined weekly opinion column in *Sports Illustrated*'s 40-year history. Known for his penchant for penning unique but apt metaphors and cliché-bending phrases, Reilly has in his 19 years' writing for *Sports Illustrated* become one of the profession's most decorated practitioners. The National Sportscasters and Sportswriters Association has named Reilly sportswriter of the year eight times. In his adventuresome and somewhat charmed career, Reilly has flown 600 miles per hour in an F-14 fighter plane; driven a stock car more than 140 miles per hour; accompanied models to exotic locations on several occasions for the photographing of the annual *Sports Illustrated* swimsuit issue; played golf with President Bill Clinton; and competed against 107 women for a spot in the Women's National Basketball Association. He has helped to write the autobiographies of such legendary sports figures as Wayne Gretzky, Charles Barkley, and Marv Albert and is the author of two comic novels, *Missing Links* (1996) and *Slo-Mo: My Untrue Story* (1999). A collection of his magazine pieces, *The Life of Reilly: The Best of Sports Illustrated's Rick Reilly* (2000), was a *New York Times* best-seller.

Rick Reilly was born in Boulder, Colorado, on February 3, 1958. He began his career in 1979, when, as a sophomore journalism major at the University of Colorado, he took a job recording phoned-in high-school volleyball scores for one of his hometown papers, the *Daily Camera*. In an interview for the *Denver Post* (May 11, 2003), he recalled for Adam Schefter that one of his journalism professors, upon learning that Reilly was writing about sports for the *Camera*, told him, "Don't do sports. You're better than sports." Reilly added, "And every now and then I look at one of my pay stubs [from *Sports Illustrated*] and just want to say to that professor, 'Uh, no I'm not!'" (When his contract with *Sports Illustrated* expired in the fall of 2002, Reilly was courted by the upstart magazine *ESPN*. There was speculation that Reilly, who was already earning a reported $750,000 per year, might become the first million-dollar-a-year print journalist. When he renewed his contract with *Sports Illustrated*, his new salary was not released.) Reilly graduated from the university in 1981, the same year his relationship with the *Camera* ended. He then wrote for two years for the *Denver Post*, where he covered mainly the Denver Broncos of the National Football League. For two years after that, he wrote for the *Los Angeles Times*.

In 1985 *Sports Illustrated* hired Reilly, who had had a long relationship with the magazine as a fan. In one piece for *Sports Illustrated* (February 7, 1989), he likened the magazine's iconic swimsuit issue to "the kitchen wall your parents used to mark your height against each year." "For instance, when I was 10," Reilly wrote later in that article, "the swimsuit issue meant about as much to me as a plate of liver and onions. It ruined one Thursday a year. . . . But when I was 13, something changed. . . . Looking back on it, it seems to me that was the day I banged my nose into adolescence." Without knowing what his future held in store, as a 12-year-old Reilly even inadvertently performed some freelance work for the publication: after he sneaked into a University of Colorado football game, he crossed paths with the *Sports Illustrated* photographer Walter Iooss, who got the adolescent a field pass so he could help carry camera equipment. "Iooss walked away with a cover shot (Oct. 5, 1970), and Reilly walked away with $9," Robert L. Miller wrote for *Sports Illustrated* (June 3, 1985).

Reilly's first story for *Sports Illustrated* was a profile of the major-league baseball star Dale Murphy. He soon gained a reputation for producing trenchant portraits of sports luminaries' lives. In one example of his insightful reportage and tenacity, he traveled to East Berlin in 1985 to profile the Olympic figure skater Katarina Witt. At the time, Witt—young, beautiful, and preternaturally gifted on ice—was Communist East Germany's brightest athletic commodity. Reilly's access to her was strictly limited. Through perseverance he gained time alone with the skater. "It was then that I decided she was another Gidget," Reilly told Donald J. Barr for *Sports Illustrated* (January 20, 1986), referring to a 1950s and '60s film and television character. "She was like an American teenager. She has her sports car and her girlfriend. She's bubbly, sharing inside jokes, giggling and blushing. She's a girl becoming a woman." Reilly's dogged pursuit of the person behind the persona resulted in a memorable profile.

Several of Reilly's popular books are memoirs of famous athletes or figures in the world of sports that he penned in collaboration with their subjects. They include *The Boz: Confessions of a Modern Anti-Hero* (1988), about the outspoken Oklahoma University linebacker Brian Bosworth; *Gretzky* (1990), about Wayne Gretzky, a former member of the Edmonton Oilers and the Los Angeles Kings hockey teams, whom many regard as the game's greatest-ever player; *I'd Love To but I Have a Game:*

27 Years without a Life (1993), about the well-known sports announcer Marv Albert; and *Sir Charles: The Wit and Wisdom of Charles Barkley* (1994), whose subject was known, especially during his days as a National Basketball Association (NBA) player, for his voluble and often humorous comments to the press. Reilly's novel *Missing Links* (1996) is a humorous romance with golf as a backdrop. A reviewer for the *New York Times*, as quoted on the *Sports Illustrated* Web site, opined that the book gave a reader "three laughs per page." Reilly's next book, *Slo-Mo: My Untrue Story* (1999), a farce centered on an imaginary NBA player, received similar assessments for its combination of wit and an insider's look at professional basketball. In keeping with the author's winking approach to the book, the playful byline for *Slo-Mo* reads "by Slo-Mo Finsternick as told to Rick Reilly."

The Life of Reilly: The Best of Sports Illustrated's Rick Reilly (2000) contains Reilly's best work on a wide variety of sports, capturing moments of both frivolity and poignancy. In a review of the book for Amazon.com, Jeff Silverman wrote, "As entertaining, clever, witty, and, at times, irate as his rants and raves at the end of each week's issue can be, it's the sheer talent and bravura he displays in the features he's penned for the magazine that best exhibit why he's considered one of the finest sportswriters of our time. If his columns have a way of constantly poking you in the ribs, the longer pieces can sometimes take your breath away." Reilly's latest book, *Who's Your Caddy?* (2003), relates many humorous situations in which Reilly found himself as he carried golf bags for such celebrities as the legendary golfer Jack Nicklaus and the real-estate mogul Donald Trump. He also carried the bags of lesser-known characters (such as a gambler who bet $50,000 on a single hole), as he recalled in some of the funniest stories in the book. Reviewing *Who's Your Caddy?* for Bookreporter.com, Stuart Shiffman wrote, "Get ready for an entertaining account of golfers, caddies and the truly unique relationship that exists between them."

Explaining his approach to writing, Reilly told Adam Schefter that his "all-time hero" was the sportswriter Jim Murray, who exemplified Reilly's motto, taken from an exhortation by Oscar Wilde, which Reilly recalled to Schefter as "Never write a sentence that's already been read." In addition to his varied journalism and book projects, Reilly has co-written a screenplay, "Leatherheads," a romantic comedy about the 1927 Duluth Eskimos, which belonged to the then-fledgling National Football League. He is reportedly at work on another screenplay.

An active and endlessly curious man, Reilly has tried his hand at magic, piano, mountain biking, scuba diving, basketball, skiing, and snowboarding. He is an avid and capable golfer. He married his high-school sweetheart, Linda Campbell, in 1983. They have three children: two sons—Kellen, who is named after the Football Hall of Fame tight end Kellen Winslow, and Jake—and a Korean-born daughter, Rae, whom they adopted in 1989. "Linda and I believe that we should only replace ourselves, but we also wanted more kids," he told Bill Colson for *Sports Illustrated* (October 25, 1999). "We had two boys, and we just had to have a girl." The family lives in Denver, Colorado; according to the *Sports Illustrated* biography of Reilly, the Reillys keep many pets, including fish, an eel, a rabbit, and a bird.

—C.F.T.

Suggested Reading: *Denver Post* (on-line) May 11, 2003; *Sports Illustrated* Web site, with photos

Selected Books: as author—*Missing Links*, 1996; *Slo-Mo: My Untrue Story*, 1999; *The Life of Reilly: The Best of Sports Illustrated's Rick Reilly*, 2000; *Who's Your Caddy?*, 2003; as co-author—*The Boz: Confessions of a Modern AntiHero*, 1988; *Gretzky*, 1990; *I'd Love to but I Have a Game: 27 Years without a Life*, 1993; *Sir Charles: The Wit and Wisdom of Charles Barkley*, 1994

Courtesy of Governor M. Jodi Rell

Rell, M. Jodi

June 16, 1946– Governor of Connecticut (Republican)

Address: Executive Office of the Governor, State Capitol, 210 Capitol Ave., Hartford, CT 06106

M. Jodi Rell's rise to prominence as a nonpartisan, genteel, but forthright politician has rescued her state government's once heavily damaged reputation. She became Connecticut's 87th governor on July 1, 2004, amidst federal probes into alleged corruption on the part of her predecessor, John Rowland. Rell had remained "above the political fray" during her nine years as lieutenant governor under Rowland, according to Avi Salzman in the *New York Times* (January 25, 2004), embracing important but noncontroversial causes such as improved technology in schools and libraries and the fight

against breast cancer. As governor since Rowland's resignation, Rell has continued her work in non-divisive areas, taking on the job, for example, of restructuring Connecticut's much-criticized State Ethics Commission, while also making her stand clear on a number of "hot-button" issues. She signed landmark legislation setting aside funds for embryonic stem-cell research and signed into law a measure that will afford Connecticut's same-sex couples many of the same rights and privileges as married heterosexual couples. Rell, a Republican who served as a representative in Connecticut's state Legislature from 1984 to 1994, is her state's second female governor; her term will expire in 2006. Rell told reporters at a press conference nearly a year after she took office, as quoted by Christopher Keating for the *Hartford Courant* (June 22, 2005), "A man said to me recently: 'I have to tell you that I'm proud to say that I'm from Connecticut again.' And I truly feel good about that." With her approval ratings reaching as high as 80 percent in some polls, in October 2005 Rell announced that she would seek to retain her office as a candidate in the 2006 gubernatorial election. "The public is so attuned to her goodness and her truth-telling that you'd need an atom bomb to loosen them from her," Lewis B. Rome, the state's Republican gubernatorial candidate in 1982, told William Yardley and Stacey Stowe for the *New York Times* (October 15, 2005).

The youngest of five children, Rell was born Mary Carolyn Reavis on June 16, 1946 in Norfolk, Virginia. Her father, Ben, worked for the federal government at a local naval base. When she was seven years old, her mother, Foy, died of congestive heart failure at the age of 43. Soon afterward Rell's father married a woman named Dorothy, whom Rell has since referred to as her mother. Dorothy Reavis played a large role in raising Rell; it was Dorothy who asked Rell not to permanently discard her first name, Mary, when friends and family started referring to her as "Jodi" later in her life. "That's why I sign things M. Jodi Rell," she explained to Marian Gail Brown for the *Connecticut Post* (January 25, 2004). "My mom loved the name Mary. So I kept the M for her."

According to Brown, "Rell's childhood home was a happy place that bustled with activity." Her grandparents, who lived on nearby Chesapeake Bay, visited frequently. Rell has recalled that politics was rarely discussed in her home but that both her father, a conservative southern Democrat, and her stepmother, a Republican, voted when elections were held. Rell told M. S. Sims for *Fairfield County Woman* (August 31, 1999), "My mother used to tell us kids to never say no to an opportunity. If it is something you want to do and you think you could do . . . then don't say no to an opportunity. She used to call it the 'woulda, coulda, shoulda' syndrome. You never want to look back and say I would have been a really good Lieutenant Governor; I should have run for that; I could have won that."

With the intention of becoming a grammar-school English teacher, Rell attended Old Dominion University, in Norfolk. It was during that time that she met Louis Robert Rell, a pilot who was stationed at the nearby naval base. The two married when M. Jodi Rell was 20. Soon afterward Louis Rell became a pilot for Trans World Airlines (TWA), and when he was assigned to New York City, the couple moved to nearby Parsippany, New Jersey. There, M. Jodi Rell worked as a clerk at the local YMCA. When a friend suggested to the couple that they move to Connecticut to escape the congestion of their area, Rell and her husband visited a town there called Brookfield. At the time Brookfield was known for having only two traffic lights, and local residents informed them that on one of the town's more frequently used roads, drivers often had to wait for herds of cattle to cross. Rell and her husband so adored the town upon making their first visit that they purchased a colonial-style home that had been built there in 1843.

Before the birth of her two children, in the early 1970s, Rell worked as an office clerk for an investment firm located in Danbury, Connecticut. According to several sources, politics did not initially interest her. Indeed, Avi Salzman quoted her as saying in the 1990s, "I'm an ordinary person who enjoys what she's doing, who loves people and loves to be involved with government. It's the political side I hate. I just want to do the job, not think to say the right thing to the right people," and as adding in 2004, "I don't consider myself a politician. I consider myself a person first and a government leader, not a politician." Rell's introduction to politics came when she accepted an invitation from a neighbor to attend an afternoon tea, which was being sponsored by the Brookfield Republican Women's Club. According to Marian Gail Brown, at the time of the event, she asked a local legislator a question for which he did not then have an answer. "A short time later, I heard from him," she explained to Brown. "He said, I researched your question and this is what I've found out. And I thought this is what government should be about, public service, constituent service, getting people answers to the questions they have." Soon after-

ward Rell became involved in local Republican Party politics, beginning with such mundane clerical tasks as bookkeeping and filling and sealing envelopes. She later began raising money locally for Republican candidates. By 1984 Rell had taken a position as the treasurer for state representative David Smith, who represented the state's 107th Assembly District, which encompassed Brookfield and the neighboring town of Bethel. Smith told Mark Pazniokas for the *Hartford Courant* (January 2, 2005): "She kept the books well. Very conscientious. Attended every staff meeting we had. Made good suggestions. She liked to do the work, but never wanted to be out front." In a move that surprised her, Smith chose Rell to succeed him when he decided in 1984 not to seek reelection. After initially resisting the idea, Rell ran for Smith's seat and won, receiving 64 percent of the vote. (As a consequence, she discontinued her studies at Western Connecticut State University, where she had gone to complete her undergraduate degree.)

As Brookfield's representative in the state Legislature from 1984 to 1994, Rell earned a reputation for being nonpartisan; according to some sources, she was often the lawmaker on whom fellow Republicans would rely to broker deals with Democrats. At the same time, she also became known for fighting to pass legislation in support of such traditional Republican causes as tax cuts. "It was something that our freshman class [of legislators] joked about," Representative Robert M. Ward, a Republican, told Avi Salzman. "When it appeared that most of us were supporting something that was good for the state, a good Republican issue, and say 90 percent of us were behind it, she knew if she could get us to 100 percent we'd be a more effective voice. That became known as 'Rell's Rule.'" By urging Republicans to vote together rather than allowing individual viewpoints to split votes, she earned a reputation as a consensus-builder and rose through the ranks, serving as an assistant minority leader in the state House, then as deputy minority leader.

By 1994 Rell's record in the state Legislature had attracted the attention of John Rowland, who had served for six years as a U.S. representative from the Fifth Congressional District of Connecticut. Rowland chose Rell as his running mate in that year's gubernatorial election, believing that her experience in state government would help him at the polls. Rowland won the election, becoming, at 37, the youngest governor in the state's history. He won reelection in 1998, defeating former U.S. congresswoman Barbara Bailey Kennelly, and in 2002, in a victory over former state comptroller Billy Curry.

One of Rell's first acts as lieutenant governor, in 1995, was to form the ad-hoc Commission on Mandate Reduction. The commission, which was made up of 11 state and local officials, was formed to help the state "steer clear of overblown promises and regulations," according to Cynthia Wolfe Boynton, writing for the *New York Times* Connecticut Weekly Supplement (June 4, 1995). To discuss issues with representatives from each of the state's 169 municipalities, she traveled to 101 town halls across Connecticut. She told Boynton: "Do you know how many people have said to me, 'Gee, we've never had a lieutenant governor come to our town hall'? Every town, every person is special. I want them to know that I'm a normal person, too, with two dogs, two kids and mud tracked into the house. I care about people, and I care about how people judge government." In 1998 she led a panel charged with overseeing development in downtown Hartford, Connecticut, which included the development of the Connecticut Convention Center at Adriaen's Landing. Also in her time as lieutenant governor, she pressured the state Legislature to make improvements in technology in schools and libraries a priority across the state. She insisted that public-school classrooms from kindergarten through 12th grades be equipped with Internet access, securing more than $30 million for the project. One result of her work was the creation of the Connecticut Education Network, which connected all state colleges, libraries, and schools. A goal of the network is to ensure that students are "cyber-ready" by the sixth grade, according to Rell's official Web site.

Early in Rowland's third term as governor, rumors began to circulate that contractors who had done business with the state had made improvements to Rowland's lakeside cottage for free. In addition, Rowland was accused of several other improprieties, including having taken partial ownership of businesses immediately before they were granted contracts from the state. The accusations led to federal investigations and then to indictments of some of the governor's closest aides. In December 2003, after he had denied the allegations, Rowland appeared on television, admitting that work had been completed on his cottage free of charge and that his earlier statements had not been true. An official investigation into the charges of corruption, and meetings to determine whether Rowland should face impeachment, began in January 2004. On June 18, 2004 the Connecticut Supreme Court ordered Rowland to appear before an investigative panel seeking his testimony in connection with his impeachment; three days later Rowland announced his resignation. On March 18, 2005, after accepting a plea bargain, Rowland was sentenced to one year and one day in prison and four months of house arrest.

Meanwhile, it was left to Rell, as Rowland's successor, to rescue the state's damaged reputation. In polls taken by Quinnipiac University, in Connecticut, days before she assumed the governorship, it was revealed that 59 percent of registered voters in the state did not know enough about Rell to express an opinion. "I was the governor's partner in policy; I wasn't his personal partner," Rell explained to the Boston Globe (June 23, 2004). "The day-to-day operations of his office are completely different from mine. I was not involved in those day-to-day operations. Policy decisions when asked, I gave advice. . . . If I had known [of the governor's misdeeds], I can assure you that I would have spoken up and they would not have gotten this far." Upon becoming governor, Rell immediately took steps to revive public trust in government. One of her first actions was to appoint a Special Counsel for Ethics Compliance to advise her on the activities of all state agencies, departments, and boards. In July 2004 she nominated Leonard C. Boyle, a widely respected federal prosecutor who was involved with the investigation into Rowland, to head Connecticut's new Department of Public Safety, whose annual budget is about $130 million. She also called for a review of contracting practices, introduced harsh penalties for ethics breaches, and fired four state commissioners. In November 2004, a Quinnipiac poll showed that Rell's approval rating had reached 80 percent. "Statistically speaking, practically no one dislikes Rell," Mark Pazniokas wrote in early 2005.

On June 15, 2004 Rell signed legislation that set aside $100 million for stem-cell research in the state of Connecticut over a 10-year period. The law requires fertility clinics to give people undergoing treatment information about donating embryos, but prohibit them from receiving payment for the donation of eggs or sperm. (The controversy surrounding the issue is rooted in the fact that the stem cells most adaptable and useful for research into the treatment of disease are those from human embryos, which die when the stem cells are removed. Many antiabortionists vehemently oppose the creation of test-tube embryos as stem-cell suppliers and the "killing" of the embryos.) Many believe that the law puts Connecticut in a position to compete with other states in the emerging scientific field. Rell told reporters, as quoted by the Associated Press (June 15, 2005): "Stem cells hold a huge amount of hope for the future of medicine. This is really a day of great promise. I don't think I can say that enough."

In late December 2004 Rell underwent surgery to remove a cancerous lump that had been detected on her breast; the surgeons performed a mastectomy and reconstructive surgery. Because the cancer was detected early and had not spread to her lymph nodes, no radiation treatment or chemotherapy was needed to augment the breast-removal surgery. At a breast-cancer walk in New Britain, Connecticut, on Mother's Day 2005, Rell made the following remarks, as quoted by the Hartford Courant (on-line): "We have to let people know that 1) it can happen to everybody. It doesn't care how old you are, color you are. I've been preaching the message for years, and, lo and behold, who gets breast cancer? I came to learn how really wonderful the people of Connecticut are. I am not exaggerating, I received at least 1,500 cards, letters and e-mails, and at least half of them said my mother had this, my sister, my wife, I did. We are working hard but we have a lot more to do. We are going to someday find a cure for this disease."

In April 2005 Rell signed into law a measure that will afford Connecticut's same-sex couples many of the rights and privileges of married couples, making the state the second (after Vermont) to legalize the civil union of same-sex couples and the first to do so without a ruling by a court. Opponents of the civil union law, which will go into effect in October 2005, have called it immoral and charged that Rell should support an amendment to the state constitution that would define marriage as the union of a man and a woman. "I want you to know that I have said all along that I believe in no discrimination of any kind," Rell said, as quoted by the *Connecticut Post* (April 21, 2005). "And I think that this bill accomplishes that, while at the same time preserving the traditional language that a marriage is between a man and a woman."

On May 13, 2005 Rell presided over the execution by lethal injection of Michael Bruce Ross, a convicted serial killer, at the Osborn Correctional Institution in Somers, Connecticut. Ross was the first person to be executed in New England in nearly 50 years. The case ignited debate about the death penalty in New England, where a majority of the states do not have facilities to carry out capital punishment. On the eve of Ross's death, hundreds of people who oppose the death penalty staged a vigil outside the facility. Ross had insisted that he deserved to die for the murders of eight young women in New York and Connecticut in the 1980s. For her part, Rell said, as quoted by the *Los Angeles Times* (May 14, 2005): "Michael Ross alone is responsible for his fate. He alone committed these despicable crimes, and he alone is responsible for the consequences of those actions."

In early June 2005 Rell riled some of her Republican colleagues in the state Legislature when, during negotiations surrounding the adoption of a new two-year state budget, she agreed to the restoration of an estate tax. Believed to have been a concession made to the Democrat-controlled Legislature, the tax "virtually assured swift passage of her first budget since she took office last July," according to William Yardley in the *New York Times* (June 8, 2005). Rell and other state officials defended the estate tax as a way to help close projected budget deficits for 2006 and 2007.

In a move that signaled to some that she was still attempting to rid her governorship of any connection to Rowland, Rell announced, in early August 2005, the closing of Connecticut's Juvenile Training School (CJTS), located in Middletown and believed to be a "symbol—and hard evidence—of the folly and corruption that eventually put her predecessor in prison," as William Yardley wrote for the *New York Times* (August 2, 2005). Rell denied claims that the closing had a political impetus, explaining that she had acted on the basis of an unsatisfactory report conducted by Connecticut's Department of Children and Families, in which it was revealed that the detention center's juvenile rehabilitation methods were "out of step with evolving approaches." The school "was intended to give the young men the tools that they needed to succeed when they returned home," Rell told Yardley, "to strengthen the connections to home, to family and to community and to help them succeed in school and in life." However, she continued, "it became apparent all too soon that it simply wasn't working . . . There was too little programming and little opportunity and too much of a prisonlike atmosphere and far too much recidivism. You couldn't help but be terribly saddened by the failure of C.J.T.S. to fulfill its promise." Rell said that the school should be phased out by 2008 and replaced by three smaller facilities, which, by their nature, would be less restrictive and place a greater emphasis on education.

On October 14, 2005 Rell announced that she would seek a full term as the governor of Connecticut in 2006. Her two most likely Democratic challengers are John DeStafano Jr. and Daniel P. Malloy, the mayors of the cities of New Haven and Stamford, respectively. In planning her campaign, Rell has vowed to follow self-imposed fund-raising restrictions, in keeping with her intention to portray herself as a reformer. She declared in a written statement, as quoted in the *New York Times* (October 25, 2005), that neither she nor her campaign workers will "solicit donations from lobbyists or their spouses, or PACs, or permit them to solicit donations" in her behalf. "The campaign will also bar contributions from persons with direct managerial responsibility for soliciting, developing, executing or signing a state contract on behalf of a corporation."

Rell received an honorary law doctorate from the University of Hartford in 2001 and another from the University of New Haven in 2004. In 1995 she was one of three women to receive the National Order of Women Legislators Leadership Award, along with Helen Thomas, who at the time was with United Press International, and Diane Sawyer of ABC News. Rell is known to be a meticulous list-maker; she sometimes wakes up at 3 or 4 a.m. to prepare for the workday. According to some sources, she demands extensive data from her staff members when pressed to make crucial decisions. (Mark Pazniokas paraphrased her as saying that she "understands the difference between deliberate and indecisive.") Rell's friends and colleagues have remarked that when she becomes uncomfortable in social situations—for example, when she must speak before a large crowd—she flushes red. "The redness starts somewhere on her torso, then rises like a thermometer, up her neck and into public view," Pazniokas wrote. "It is why scarves are a favorite accessory." An avid reader, she enjoys novels by John Grisham as well as biographies; she has also been known to listen to books on tape while taking walks. Rell "comes across as the kindly principal whose correct behavior and patient tone make students want to sit up straight," according to Stacey Stowe, writing in the *New York Times* (August 11, 2004). In a related comment, Pazniokas quoted Rell's chief of staff as referring to "'the Rell look,' a cold stare over her reading glasses" when she is displeased; another of Rell's acquaintances told Pazniokas that the governor "projects a maternal image." When she is not at her executive quarters in Hartford, Rell lives in Brookfield with her husband, Louis, in the white clapboard farmhouse they purchased in 1968. She and her husband also recently purchased a three-bedroom home in Florida. They have two grown children: Meredith O'Connor, who lives in Denver, Colorado, and whom Rell calls "Missy," and Michael Rell. "The nicest compliment I get all the time is, 'Hey, you know what? You're just normal, aren't you?'," Rell

told the *Hartford Courant* (January 2, 2005). "They feel comfortable asking to take my picture."

—D.F.

Suiggested Reading: *Fairfield County Woman* p37 Aug. 31, 1999, with photo; *Governing* p18 Sep. 2004, with photo; *Hartford Courant* Northeast p3 Jan. 2, 2005, with photos; *New York Times* XIV p1 Jan. 25, 2004, with photos, B p1+ June 8, 2005, B p1+ Aug. 2, 2005, with photo, B p4 Oct. 25, 2005, with photo; www.ct.gov

Peter Kramer/Getty Images

Rhodes, Randi

Jan. 28, 1958– Radio talk-show host

Address: c/o Tim Allan Walker, 3 Park Ave., 40th Fl., New York, NY 10016

When Air America Radio was launched, in March 2004, to combat the dominance of conservative commentators on the airwaves, the *Randi Rhodes Show* quickly became one of its most popular and talked-about programs. Rhodes's blending of a no-holds-barred delivery and an informed, progressive political sensibility has drawn the praise of liberals and the ire of conservatives. "A chain-smoking bottle blond, Rhodes is part Joan Rivers, part shock jock Howard Stern, part *Saturday Night Live*'s 'Coffee Talk Lady,'" Elinor J. Brecher wrote for the *Miami Herald* (January 31, 1993). "But

mostly, she's her rude, crude, loud, brazen, gleefully scatological self."

Randi Rhodes was born on January 28, 1958 in the New York City borough of Brooklyn; later, her family moved to the borough of Queens. "Rhodes" is not her real surname; to maintain her privacy, she does not reveal her real last name publicly. Her parents, Loretta and Norman, divorced when she was young. "I was a really bad kid," Rhodes told Brecher. "Such a handful. I really think a big part of my family's problems was me." Rhodes's mother told Brecher that Randi was outspoken from the time she could talk; in one example, when the girl was only five years old, she approached a woman wearing a coat with a fur collar and said, "I'll give you my gum if you give me that dog around your neck." Ten years later Rhodes moved to California with her father, who is a retired vice president of Technicolor (a manufacturer of motion-picture film, videocassettes, CDs, and DVDs). She had attended school sporadically for years, and her father tried to bribe her to finish her education by giving her a Corvette, a popular sportscar. His tactic proved ineffective; Rhodes never completed high school. She later passed an equivalency exam.

In 1976 Rhodes landed her first media job, as a reporter for a Mississippi newspaper. While she held that position, Rhodes, who is Jewish, told Brecher, "The Ku Klux Klan took me to lunch. . . . They sat me down and said, 'We don't take kindly to your type. The next visit we make to your house won't be so friendly.'" Soon afterward, she joined the U.S. Air Force in an attempt to gain more direction in her life. She became one of the air force's first three female flight engineers and was voted its "Most Outstanding Woman" in 1979. After she earned an honorable discharge, later that year, she secured her first radio job, at a small country-music station in Seminole, Texas. From there she moved to a rock station in Mobile, Alabama, then settled in New York, where she spun rock records for WAPP (now known as HOT-97). She chose the surname Rhodes as a homophonic tribute to Ozzy Osbourne's legendary guitarist, Randy Rhodes, who died in 1982.

At WAPP, many of Rhodes's colleagues were involved with illegal drugs. "It was the decadent '80s. I drank pretty good, but I was very much on the outside. The peer pressure really got me," Rhodes told Brecher. "I gave in and became a raging coke fiend. . . . [My show] was getting totally deranged. And the more deranged, the better the ratings got! Thank God it was only one year out of my life." Within a year of her arrival, the station was sold. Although the new owners told her that they intended to keep her on, she overslept the first day under their watch and was fired.

Rhodes returned to Texas, this time for a job in Dallas; six weeks after she began there, she lost that position, too, because of her drug use. A program director at another station in Dallas, Kevin Metheny (whom Howard Stern nicknamed "Pig Virus" when they worked together at the New York radio station WNBC), gave Rhodes another chance. "Pig Virus said, 'I know what your problems are. If you promise you'll go to this [rehabilitation] program, I'll hire you,'" Rhodes recalled to Brecher. "I agreed. Valentine's Day 1986 was the last time I ever did drugs." After about two years with Metheny's station, Rhodes teamed up with a shock jock for a program emanating from Milwaukee, Wisconsin. Again, she was fired after six weeks, this time because her partner made on-air comments that were perceived to be homophobic, and the station's gay listeners mounted an effective boycott of the show's sponsors. Less than a week later, Rhodes fell ill from the effects of a tubal pregnancy (one in which the embryo becomes implanted in a fallopian tube; such pregnancies must be terminated, usually surgically). Because she had no health insurance, she briefly drove an 18-wheeler between Milwaukee and Texas to earn enough to pay off her large medical bills.

In 1987 Rhodes moved to Broward County, Florida, to care for her ailing mother. There she broadcast during the Saturday overnight slot at the FM rock station WSHE. She quit in 1991, after several confrontations with her program director. During the next year she handled public-relations work in offices and helped her fiancé, Jim Robertson, manage a rock band. (She and Robertson married in 1996 and divorced in 2004.)

In September 1992 Rhodes signed a contract with WIOD in south Florida to host a show that filled the radio station's weeknight slot. Her first purchase after signing on at WIOD was a waterbed, from which she broadcast one installment. Another aired from the studio ladies' room. (Rhodes suffers from bowel trouble before every show, because of stage fright.) Rhodes's unscripted format—a four-hour brew of personal anecdotes, banter with call-in listeners, commentary on news headlines, scatological humor, and gonzo antics (the last of which have become less frequent) boosted her program to the number-one rating in her time slot among men 35 to 44 years old, the single most desirable demographic for radio advertisers. Rhodes began referring to herself as the Goddess, and she soon became a cash cow for WIOD.

Banking on the attractiveness of Rhodes's hard-hitting persona, the promotional department at WIOD began airing ads that referred to her as a bitch. "I told them I wanted it to stop [but] they said it would get people to pay attention," Rhodes told Lois Solomon for the *Palm Beach Post* (October 11, 1994). "I never called myself a bitch. I call myself a goddess." The station's refusal to change the ads led her to resign, in June 1994. That summer she acted in the film *Where in the Hell Is Robin Goodfellow*, an indie takeoff on Shakespeare's play *A Midsummer Night's Dream*; it was never released.

Rhodes next began what would become a 10-year stint at WJNO, an AM station in West Palm Beach. The *Randi Rhodes Show* aired in WJNO's weeknight slot before switching to the 3:00–7:00 p.m. drive-time slot, which attracts a wider audience and greater advertising revenues. In her daily comments on items in the news, Rhodes offered not only simple comic banter but pointed observations as well, and her listeners began asking her to talk more about politics. As she added a greater measure of political discussion to her personalized free-form mix, the *Randi Rhodes Show* became Palm Beach County's highest-rated radio talk show, beating such nationally syndicated stalwarts as Rush Limbaugh in that part of the country. "I've often told Randi that if she ever decided to run for [office in] the congressional district I represent, I'd just quit," Robert Wexler, a Democrat from Delray Beach, told Charles Passy for the *Palm Beach Post* (July 19, 2004).

As her show increased in popularity, Rhodes set her sights higher; she often expressed interest in national syndication or a television or film career. When she broached these ideas to agents, they ruled out such possibilities, because of her physical appearance. Rhodes herself was unhappy with how she looked. At promotional events fans sometimes commented that the "Goddess" moniker did not fit her, or that she had a "face for radio." "I'd laugh it off and I'd have a comeback," Rhodes told Christine Keating for the *Palm Beach Post* (October 22, 1995). "But after signing 200 autographs . . . I'd cry all the way home." In August 1995 Rhodes underwent six surgical procedures that altered her forehead, eyelids, nose, chin, ears, and neck. Accompanied by "before" and "after" photos, Keating's *Palm Beach Post* article documented Rhodes's surgery, as well as procedures performed on two other women by another doctor. During a broadcast following its publication, Rhodes questioned the handiwork of the other patients' surgeon, Schuyler Metlis. In response Metlis sued Rhodes, WJNO, and the station's owner for defamation, claiming that Rhodes's on-air comments had damaged his reputation and business. Four years later, in April 2000, when the suit came to trial, Circuit Judge Catherine Brunson dismissed it after only two days of testimony from the plaintiff, ruling that Metlis had failed to prove his case.

Rhodes received the syndication contract she had long desired when Air America Radio asked her to be its first evening drive-time host. Air America was created as an antidote to politically conservative radio stations. According to the widely quoted results of a survey conducted in 2003 by AnShell Media (a group that has financially supported Democratic politicians), 45 top-rated talk-radio stations devoted 310 weekly airtime hours to conservative programs, while liberal programs (not counting those on public and community radio outlets, such as National Public Radio) accounted for only five hours each week. Liberals have long bemoaned this imbalance, and media theorists have tried to explain it. One popular hypothesis is that conservative talk is more compelling to listeners. Another posits that the political left is a more fractious and diffuse population, and its factions' agendas do not overlap; thus, no single radio talk show could satisfy each of them. More conspiracy-minded theorists see a right-wing plot among media conglomerates, which, they say, give preference to conservative talk-show hosts. Rhodes herself believes that international corporations advertise as a way of controlling the contents of media offerings. As she said to a writer for the Web site BuzzFlash (January 3, 2003), "Ask yourself, why does [Archer Daniels Midland] advertise? Do they want to sell you a soybean? Why does Boeing advertise? Are you gonna buy aircraft? Aircraft parts? . . . They're buying content. Millions and millions of advertising dollars do affect the message you get. It controls the news that is reported and the news that is not." The enormous influence of the conservative talk-show host Rush Limbaugh must also be taken into account. Loud, arrogant, and argumentative, Limbaugh offered impassioned criticisms of liberals and defenses of right-wing ideology of a sort rarely heard since the mid- to late 1930s, when the so-called radio priest, Charles E. Coughlin, broadcast virulently anti-Semitic sermons to audiences that numbered in the millions. Limbaugh's show, once confined to the airwaves of Sacramento, California, and syndicated nationally in 1988, is currently carried on approximately 600 stations, and a reported 14.5 million people tune in to it. Its success spurred many industry executives to launch talk shows hosted by comparable conservatives.

Air Radio America began airing on March 31, 2004. The network has allied itself with such longtime liberal spokespeople as the satirist Al Franken and the actress and comedian Janeane Garofalo, whose wry, insular shows contrast sharply with that of Rhodes, a veteran radio populist. Beginning with her first Air America broadcast, Rhodes showed that liberals could be loud and arrogant, too. Her debut Air America discussion, with the consumer-rights advocate Ralph Nader via telephone, devolved into a heated exchange. Many Democrats still blame Nader, who ran for president in 2000, for taking votes that might have put Al Gore (the vice president under Bill Clinton) in the White House in 2001. They feared he would do the same to the presidential candidate John Kerry in the 2004 election. According to Robert Kolker in New York (April 12, 2004, on-line), Rhodes screamed at Nader, "I am mad at you—don't you understand?! You screwed up the last election, and now you're going to screw up this one!" Nader accused Rhodes of ruining Air America's first day, called her "a terrible interviewer," and hung up.

Behind the scenes, Air America has had many problems. The network, which was rushed into production, ran into technical difficulties in its first broadcasts and experienced financial problems within weeks of its launch. It lost affiliates in Chicago and Los Angeles, both of which are among radio's top markets, because of billing disputes, and its coffers at one point did not have enough to cover its payroll, forcing Rhodes to pay her producer out of her own pocket. In addition, its corporate board and executive staff underwent wholesale changes six weeks after the network went on the air. Operating entirely out of offices in New York City, Air America has yet to generate the collegial atmosphere and unity of vision evident at many news outlets. "I'd like to tell you everything's wonderful and we're all one big happy family, a big comedy troupe, but we're not," Rhodes told Kolker. "Al is Al and Janeane is Janeane—they're movie stars and TV stars. I'm a radio person. Radio on the show-business totem pole is where the dog lifts his leg." (Specifically, Rhodes has complained about the lack of promotional support from the network and her more famous colleagues.)

As of early November 2005, Air America had 70 national affiliates. Whatever the network's fortunes, Rhodes's show will likely stay in syndication. In any event, Rhodes has a standing job offer from the market manager of WJNO, which has an agreement with Air America to broadcast her show. Such offers are rare in radio. The market manager "gave me a safety net," Rhodes told Passey. "That was amazing to me."

In November 2005 Rhodes and John Scher, a New York concert promoter, were reportedly engaged in early negotiations regarding a touring show in 2006 that would combine comedy, music, and political discussion. In addition to emcee duties, Rhodes, along with Air America writers and political satirists including Barry Crimmins and Bruce Cherry, would perform before live audiences in some of the markets that Air America reaches. She explained in an on-line interview with Mediaweek that she looked forward to entertaining audiences "in a big way and a different way than they get from me on the radio. I'm so excited to do it."

Rhodes has been honored by the organization American Women in Radio and Television. She is said to be much quieter and more introspective in person than she is on the radio. She lives on Park Avenue in New York City and is raising her deceased sister's teenage daughter.

—T.J.F.

Suggested Reading: *Miami Herald* J p1 Jan. 31, 1993; *New Republic* p19 Feb. 16, 2004; *New York* (on-line) Apr. 12, 2004; *Palm Beach Post* D p1 Oct. 11, 1994, with photo, D p1 Mar. 31, 2004, with photo

Courtesy of Kirk Murray

Robinson, Marilynne

Nov. 26, 1943– Writer

Address: co/ Farrar, Straus & Giroux, 19 Union Sq. W., New York, NY 10003-3304

Like such writers as Henry Roth and Ralph Ellison before her, Marilynne Robinson made a celebrated fiction debut, whetting her readers' appetites for a second novel that would not appear for decades. Her first book, *Housekeeping* (1980), the story of two girls left in the care of their unconventional aunt, "is a nearly perfect work, still as singular and eery as when it was published . . . ," in the words of Mona Simpson, writing for the *Atlantic Monthly* (December 2004). "The book . . . found its place in that category of cherished marvels that happen only once in a lifetime, like certain comets." Robinson followed up *Housekeeping* with two works of nonfiction: *Mother Country* (1989), a diatribe against the British coverup of contamination of the Irish Sea with nuclear waste from a plutonium reprocessing plant, and *The Death of Adam: Essays on Modern Thought* (1998), an examination of where received ideas, such as Darwinism, Freudianism, and mistaken beliefs about the theology of John Calvin, have led society. Twenty-four years after her first book appeared, Robinson caused a

stir in the literary community with the publication of her second novel, *Gilead*, which takes the form of a letter from an aged father to his very young son. Paul Bailey, observing in the London *Guardian* (May 3, 2003) that the narrator of *Housekeeping* "walks . . . among the lost," added in a comment that might apply equally to *Gilead*, "It is Robinson's gift to convey what it is like to be in that peculiar, yet familiar, condition of loneliness." In the *Los Angeles Times* (December 12, 2004), Merle Rubin described Robinson as "a consummate artist, a scrupulous scholar, a believing Christian and a genuinely radical thinker" and wrote that she "approaches whatever she undertakes with the kind of gravitas one seldom encounters today. In place of the buzzwords and half-baked ideas that pass for conventional wisdom, she offers something truly unconventional and certainly much closer to wisdom." *Gilead* won both the 2004 Pulitzer Prize and the 2005 National Book Critics Circle Award for fiction.

The writer was born Marilynne Summers on November 26, 1943 in Sandpoint, Idaho, to John J. Summers, who worked for lumber companies, and Ellen (Harris) Summers, a homemaker. Robinson and her brother, David, an art professor at the University of Virginia, represented her family's fourth generation of Idahoans and lived in several towns in Idaho and Washington State during their formative years. In her essay "My Western Roots," included in the 1993 volume *Old West—New West: Centennial Essays* and available on the University of Washington Web site, Robinson wrote about the "lonesome" quality—a word she used in a positive way—of the areas where she grew up: "I remember when I was a child . . . walking into the woods by myself and feeling the solitude around me build like electricity and pass through my body with a jolt that made my hair prickle. I remember . . . thinking, there is only one thing wrong here, which is my own presence, and that is the slightest imaginable intrusion—feeling that my solitude, my loneliness made me almost acceptable in so sacred a place."

Robinson read a great deal as a child. "I find that the hardest work in the world—it may in fact be impossible—is to persuade easterners that growing up in the West is not intellectually crippling," she wrote in "My Western Roots." She added that some people, on learning that she is from Idaho, have asked questions to the effect of, "Then how were you able to write a book?" In fact, Robinson and her fellow students at Coeur d'Alene High School were made familiar with classical literature. Her Latin teacher, Mrs. Bloomburg, "trudged us through Cicero's vast sentences, clause depending from clause, the whole cantilevered with subjunctives and weighted with a culminating irony. . . . And at the end of it all, I think anyone can see that my style is considerably more in debt to Cicero than to Hemingway." (She added, "I admire Hemingway.") Robinson has often declared, as she did in the *New York Times Book Review* (May 13, 1984), that as a writer she was "influenced most deeply by the 19th century Americans—Dickinson, Melville, Thoreau, Whitman, Emerson and Poe. Nothing in literature appeals to me more than the rigor with which they fasten on problems of language, of consciousness—bending form to their purposes, ransacking ordinary speech and common experience, rummaging through the exotic and recondite, setting Promethean doubts to hymn tunes . . . always, to borrow a phrase from Wallace Stevens, in the act of finding what will suffice."

Robinson attended Brown University, in Providence, Rhode Island, where her brother was a senior when she was a freshman; she studied American literature, particularly that of the 19th century, and took creative writing courses taught by the novelist John Hawkes. After graduating, in 1966, Robinson returned west to enroll at the University of Washington, where she earned a Ph.D. degree in English in 1977. Her dissertation was an examination of Shakespeare's *Henry VI, Part II*. She went next to France, where she taught at the Université de Haute Bretagne, in Rennes, until 1979. Robinson has also taught in such institutions as Amherst College, the University of Massachusetts, Skidmore College, and the University of Kent in England (as a visiting professor in 1983–84). In 1991 she moved to Iowa City to join the faculty of the University of Iowa Writers' Workshop. She is currently on sabbatical leave.

Meanwhile, Robinson continued to work on the novel she had begun as a graduate student. That book, which appeared in 1981 as *Housekeeping*, soon came to be considered a 20th-century American classic. *Housekeeping* is narrated by Ruth, who describes how she and her sister, Lucille, left orphans by the suicide of their mother, come under the guidance of their deeply eccentric aunt Sylvie. Sylvie's behavior leads Lucille to seek refuge in the home of one of her teachers, after which she lives a conventional life in the town and has no contact with her sister or aunt. Ruth, meanwhile, is drawn to Sylvie and accompanies her on an odyssey into the wilderness. "Set in the Pacific Northwest, the novel is steeped in images of mountains, lakes and forests . . . ," Lisa Durose wrote for *ANQ* (Winter 1997). "Much of the haunting lyricism of Robinson's prose stems directly from the powerful and mysterious landscape she vividly describes."

Reviewers unanimously praised *Housekeeping*. Anatole Broyard noted in the *New York Times* (January 7, 1981), "It's as if in writing it, [Robinson] broke through the ordinary human condition with all its dissatisfactions, and achieved a kind of transfiguration. You can feel in the book a gathering voluptuous release of confidence, a delighted surprise at the unexpected capacities of language, a close, careful fondness for people that we thought only saints felt." Broyard concluded that Robinson "works with light, dark, water, heat, cold, textures, sounds and smells. She is like the Impressionists, taking apart the landscape to remind us that we are surrounded by elements, that we are separated from one another, and from our past and future, by such influences. . . . She knocks off the false elevation, the pretentiousness, of our current fiction. Though her ambition is tall, she remains down to earth, where the best novels happen." The *Time* (February 2, 1981) critic, Paul Gray, observed that *Housekeeping* "brilliantly portrays the impermanence of all things, especially beauty and happiness, and the struggle to keep what can never be owned." In the years after its publication, *Housekeeping* became the subject of many academic studies and dissertations; some viewed it as a feminist text, since it focuses on women living in and making their way through the wilderness without male companionship. The novel was nominated for the Pulitzer Prize for fiction and the P.E.N./Faulkner fiction award. It won the P.E.N./Hemingway award as well as the Richard and Hinda Rosenthal Award, given by the American Academy and Institute for Arts and Letters. *Housekeeping* was made into a 1987 film by Bill Forsyth.

The impact of Robinson's fiction debut was such that readers and critics eagerly awaited a follow-up novel. The writer turned, however, to nonfiction. She explained in an interview with Margo Hammond for the *St. Petersburg (Florida) Times* (November 7, 2004), "Fiction writing is just my mental life, or my spiritual life, but I have to put together an adequate mind, in a sense, to be able to write fiction. And the way that I do that is by writing other things." She was inspired to write her second book, *Mother Country: Britain, the Welfare State and Nuclear Pollution* (1989), after reading an article in England, where she was then teaching, about the risks of exposure to nuclear waste. Robinson then investigated the contamination of the Irish Sea and its surroundings by Britain's nuclear-industrial complex at Sellafield. There, nuclear waste was received from other countries, plutonium was extracted from it, and the detritus was dumped into the environment, causing widespread ecological damage. "To understand Sellafield," Jason Sherman wrote for the *Toronto Star* (February 24, 1990), Robinson "realized that she'd have to place Britain's social and economic history under the microscope." That involved an attempt to "re-educate" herself, as she told Jason Sherman, by re-examining the works of British thinkers she had always believed to be critics of the social and economic status quo, such as George Orwell and George Bernard Shaw—whom she now found to be "defenders of the very structures they apparently want to dismantle," as Sherman phrased it. In *Mother Country*, an indictment of the British government, Robinson wrote, "I am angry to the depths of my soul that the Earth has been so injured while we were all bemused by supposed monuments of value and intellect, vaults of bogus cultural riches. . . . The grief borne home to others while I and my kind have been thus occupied lies on my conscience like a crime."

After delving into 600 years of British history, Robinson concluded—according to Susan Slocum Hinerfield, writing for the *Los Angeles Times Book Review* (July 23, 1989)—that "beneath the famous civility the British have always wasted lives and credited the idea of human surplus" and that in Great Britain, "there is a lack 'of positive substantive personal and political rights.'" Merle Rubin, writing for the *Los Angeles Times Book Review* (December 12, 2004), agreed that the "heartfelt and disturbing" book was about "how a country like Britain, long regarded as a bastion of liberty, fair play, decency and democracy, could allow the welfare of its citizens to be gravely endangered by the plutonium at Sellafield (formerly called Windscale)." Peter Gorner wrote for the *Chicago Tribune* (July 12, 1989), "Frightened and furious, [Robinson] has written a venomous essay in the tradition of 19th century novelists, and it is a chilling and poignant scream of outrage." Some scientists, however, such as Max Perutz, a Nobel Prize–winning chemist, writing for the *New York Review of Books* (November 23, 1989), condemned *Mother Country* as presenting "monstrous exaggerations of the dangers presented by Sellafield." Robinson's book was banned in Great Britain but named a finalist for the National Book Award in the United States.

In *The Death of Adam: Essays on Modern Thought*, published in 1998, Robinson explored the works and ideas of past thinkers, including the 19th-century German political philosopher Karl Marx and the 19th-century British naturalist Charles Darwin, as a way of examining contemporary social attitudes—in which she found an over-reliance on received viewpoints and what might be called knee-jerk cynicism. In particular, she sought to defend the ideas—often misrepresented, in her view—of the 16th-century theologian John Calvin. Merle Rubin wrote for the *Christian Science Monitor* (January 14, 1999) that *The Death of Adam* "is both original and somber, brimming with fresh insights and perspectives that could well help to elevate the level of our public discourse," and in *Magill Book Reviews* (1999), Lois A. Marchino found Robinson "particularly adept at making connections between attitudes and events and between the myths society clings to and the realities of survival that are at stake if these myths are not re-examined. . . . The humanitarian vision which shapes each of the essays makes this a profound work at both the levels of individual self-understanding and of understanding contemporary culture."

Robinson's long-awaited second novel, *Gilead*, appeared in 2004. Its protagonist, John Ames, is a 76-year-old pastor in the small town of Gilead, Iowa; the novel takes the form of a letter he writes to his seven-year-old son, to be read after Ames's death. In recounting his own life, Ames describes his grandfather, also a preacher, who held services during the Civil War era while wearing a pistol, and his father, who rebelled against the grandfather by becoming a pacifist. *Gilead* addresses the theme of fathers and sons, in both the human and Christian senses; its plot hinges on the return to town of a fellow minister's prodigal son. James Wood wrote for the *New York Times Book Review* (November 28, 2004), "There is . . . something remarkable about the writing in *Gilead*. . . . Robinson's words have a spiritual force that's very rare in contemporary fiction." Philip Connors, writing for *Newsday* (November 21, 2004), observed, "[Ames's] yearning to understand the mysteries of the human heart, and his awareness that those mysteries would hardly be more clear were he allowed another hundred years to ponder them, give his letter, in the end, an almost unbearable poignancy. Imagining his son reading the letter in adulthood grants us the pleasure of extending the life of this austere, beautiful novel long beyond the last page."

Robinson has two adult sons from her marriage, which ended in divorce. She has described herself as a Congregationalist Christian.

—S.Y.

Suggested Reading: *ANQ* p31+ Winter 1997; *Atlantic Monthly* p135+ Dec. 2004; *Chicago Tribune* C p5 July 12, 1989; *Christian Science Monitor* p20 Jan. 14, 1999; *Critique* p95+ Winter 1989; (London) *Guardian* p37 May 3, 2003, p31 Sep. 25, 2004; New York *Newsday* II p6 July 26, 1989; *New York Times* C p18 Jan. 7, 1981, C p11 Nov. 25, 1987; *New York Times Book Review* p14 Feb. 8, 1981, p7+ May 13, 1984, p14 Feb. 7, 1999, p1 Nov. 28, 2004 with photo; *New York Times Magazine* p63+ Oct. 24, 2004 with photo; *Toronto Star* M p17 Feb. 24, 1990

Selected Books: fiction—*Housekeeping*, 1980; *Gilead*, 2004; nonfiction—*Mother Country: Britain, the Welfare State and Nuclear Pollution*, 1989; *The Death of Adam: Essays on Modern Thought*, 1998

Rusesabagina, Paul

(roo-suss-uh-bag-EE-na)

June 15, 1954– Rwandan humanitarian; inspiration for the film Hotel Rwanda

Address: c/o Amnesty International, 5 Penn Plaza, 14th Fl., New York, NY 10001

A hero, Paul Rusesabagina told Bob Nesti for the *Boston-Bay State Banner* (January 13, 2005, online), "is not someone who performs his duties and obligations. I didn't save people, I helped people; and that's the crucial difference. I did not save. I helped people to go through. Being a hero is something different than helping people." Regardless of those sentiments, there are almost certainly at least 1,268 people who consider Rusesabagina a hero:

Carlo Allegri/Getty Images

Paul Rusesabagina

the individuals he sheltered during the 1994 Rwandan genocide, when he was the manager of a luxury hotel in Kigali, the capital of Rwanda. The filmmaker Terry George dramatized the genocide and Rusesabagina's humanitarian response to it in a critically acclaimed motion picture, *Hotel Rwanda*, released in 2004. Largely due to the success of *Hotel Rwanda*, people around the world are now comparing Rusesabagina to Oskar Schindler, the German businessman who saved more than 1,000 Jews during the Nazi Holocaust and whose actions were immortalized in *Schindler's List* (1993), a film by Steven Spielberg. In December 2004 the organization Amnesty International, which is helping to promote *Hotel Rwanda* in order to educate the public about ongoing atrocities in such regions as the Sudan and the Congo, presented Rusesabagina with its Enduring Spirit Award, one of a host of human-rights honors he has received over the last decade.

In the early 1990s the population of Rwanda, a nation in Central Africa south of Uganda, west of Tanzania, and north of Burundi, consisted mostly of ethnic Hutus; more than four out of five Rwandans were Hutus, who have traditionally been farmers. The Tutsi ethnic group, traditionally cattle herders, comprised 15 percent of the population, and about 1 percent of Rwandans were members of the Twa, a subgroup of African Pygmies. Despite their common culture and language, the Hutus and the Tutsis had long been at odds. Belgian colonists, who had arrived in the region in 1916, considered the taller, thinner, fairer Tutsi superior to the shorter, stockier, darker Hutus and issued identification cards to differentiate between the groups. The colonists' favoritism toward Tutsis

on matters of power and influence bred resentment in many Hutus. In 1959, three years before Rwanda gained independence from Belgium, the Hutus rebelled, killing the Tutsi king and assuming control of the state. Over the ensuing years, thousands of Tutsis were killed or driven into exile. In 1990 a civil war began among the Hutus and a rebel Tutsi group called the Rwandan Patriotic Front (RPF). The conflict escalated after the airplane carrying the Rwandan president, Juvénal Habyarimana, a Hutu, was shot down above the Kigali airport, on April 6, 1994. The crash also killed the president of Burundi, Cyprian Ntayamira, who, with Habyarimana, had just attended a meeting of African leaders to discuss ways to allay the ethnic tensions in the region. Many observers have theorized that the plane was shot down by Hutu extremists unhappy with Habyarimana's moderate politics. Some Hutu politicians, along with people controlling a prominent local radio station, however, promptly blamed the deaths on Tutsi rebels; within hours, the Hutu militia—called the *Interahamwe*, or "those who work together"—began slaying Tutsis at a breakneck pace. They first killed Tutsis of prominence in business or politics, then turned on ordinary citizens. The militia instructed civilian Hutus to kill their Tutsi neighbors, friends, and relatives; the killers included some of Rusesabagina's best friends, among them some who resisted the Hutus' orders until they realized that many of those who refused to kill others were put to death themselves. The slaughter lasted 100 days, during which more than 800,000 Rwandans— roughly 10 percent of the nation's population— were murdered.

Not all Hutus and Tutsis had regarded one another as enemies. Indeed, many families included members of both ethnic groups. Paul Rusesabagina's was among them. Rusesabagina was born into a farming family on June 15, 1954 at Murama-Gitarama, in the south of Rwanda. He was one of nine children of a Hutu father and a Tutsi mother, and thus, according to the patrilineal system in place, was classified as a Hutu. In 1962 Rusesabagina entered the Seventh Day Adventist College of Gitwe, a primary and secondary school run by missionaries. From 1975 to 1978 he attended the Faculty of Theology, in Cameroon. In 1979 the Sabena hotel chain hired him as the manager of a newly opened hotel in the Akagera National Park. Realizing he had a talent in that field, from 1980 to 1984 he studied hotel management at Kenya Utalii College, in Nairobi. (A portion of his course work was done in Switzerland.) He then moved to Kigali, where he became the assistant manager of the elegant Hôtel des Milles Collines, another Sabena facility. He remained there until 1993, when he was promoted to the top spot at the nearby Hôtel Diplomats. Meanwhile, he had married a Tutsi woman named Tatiana and had four children with her.

One day in April 1994, Rusesabagina, Tatiana, their children, and many of their neighbors, most of them Tutsis, were rounded up by armed militants. The militants forced them out of their houses and onto a bus, where one of the militiamen handed Rusesabagina a gun. "Their leader told me to kill all the cockroaches [Tutsis]," Rusesabagina told Kyle Smith, Dietland Lerner, and Michael Fleeman for *People* (January 24, 2005). Horrified at the thought of murdering his friends and family, Rusesabagina thought quickly. "I showed [the leader] an old man and said, 'Do you really believe this old man is the enemy you are fighting against? Are you sure your enemy is that baby? Take me to the hotel, and I will give you some money. But I am the only one with a key, and if you kill me, you will not have the money." The bribe succeeded, and, after paying off the gunmen with money from the safe at the Hôtel Diplomats, Rusesabagina promptly drove the group to the Hôtel des Mille Collines, a five-story building that had also been left in his care by its fleeing Belgium owners.

Once Rusesabagina established the Hôtel des Mille Collines as a refuge, its reputation spread quickly, attracting frightened Tutsis from across Rwanda. Though the hotel was designed to house 200 occupants, it was soon crowded with more than 1,200 people, who slept in rooms, corridors, and even the snack bar. "People came to the hotel raped, injured, bleeding," Rusesabagina told Anne-Marie O'Connor for the *Los Angeles Times* (December 28, 2004). Relief agencies dropped off orphans, some Hutu military officers brought their Tutsi wives, and a local priest, Father Wenceslas, deposited his Tutsi mother at the hotel, knowing that she would be safer there than in his own church. (Later, Rusesabagina watched helplessly from the roof of the hotel as machete-wielding Hutus attacked people hiding in the church.) Rusesabagina and his wife made a pact with each other: rather than be butchered, she would jump off the roof of the hotel with their children if the militia invaded.

Soon the militia cut off the hotel's electricity, water, and switchboard lines; Rusesabagina doled out water twice daily from the hotel pool and made use of one remaining phone line that the militia had missed. Via that one line, he made calls "like a madman," as he told O'Connor, dialing everyone he could think of who might be able to help, including employees of the French government and the White House. Few of Rusesabagina's frantic calls were fruitful. The United Nations withdrew forces after some of its peacekeepers were killed, and no one in the international community sent troops. (Both Bill Clinton, during his second term as U.S. president, and U.N. secretary-general Kofi Annan have publicly apologized for their inaction.) The militia regularly attempted to infiltrate the hotel and remove its temporary inhabitants; Rusesabagina managed to stall them repeatedly by bribing them with Scotch, cigars, and money—and by using all the connections he had made

as a hotelier to call in favors from high-ranking officials. Once, his wife and children hid in a bathtub while he arranged to have the militia ordered out of the hotel. In the midst of widespread slaughter, Rusesabagina managed to protect everyone within the hotel.

Only when the approach of Tutsi guerrillas was imminent did the Hutu militia retreat, thus making it possible for Rusesabagina and the others to drive to a refugee camp near the Tanzanian border. Rusesabagina described the terrible journey to O'Connor: "There were no human beings; just dogs eating dead bodies," he recalled. "The whole country reeked. I never realized that all these people had been butchered. I felt like someone in a dream." At the refugee camp the Rusesabaginas found two nieces whose parents had been killed (along with most of Tatiana's family and some of Paul's relatives); Paul and Tatiana later adopted the girls.

After he left the camp, Rusesabagina returned to Kigali to resume his work as a hotel manager, but he found that the new Tutsi authorities viewed Hutu survivors with distrust, so he and his family moved to Belgium. He now lives in Brussels with Tatiana; their children, Lys, Diane, Roger, and Treasure (some sources spell the name "Tresor"); and their adopted nieces, Carine and Anaise (sometimes spelled "Karine" and "Anais"). He spends much of his time in Zambia (a nation southwest of Tanzania), where he runs a transport company. Rusesabagina told Anne-Marie O'Connor, "I never imagined so many people would join the killing mobs. That's why I don't trust people anymore. I know there are good people. But I'm always suspicious. I have completely changed."

In the aftermath of the genocide, many journalists, authors, documentarians, and filmmakers interviewed Rusesabagina in the vain hope of telling his story. After the director Terry George approached him, Rusesabagina watched films that George had either written or directed, including *In the Name of the Father* (1993), about a man accused of a terrorist bombing in England, and *Some Mother's Son* (1996), about a hunger strike among members of the Irish Republican Army in a British prison. Rusesabagina liked George's sensitivity and handling of politically charged issues and agreed to collaborate on the project. In early 2002 Rusesabagina spent several days with George and the writer Kier Pearson, recounting stories for them as they mapped out the script for *Hotel Rwanda*. George wanted the actor Don Cheadle to play Rusesabagina but feared that, in order to secure funding for the film, he might be forced to recruit an actor with proven box-office appeal, such as Will Smith or Denzel Washington. Then the producer Alex Kitman Ho joined the project and independently raised the needed funds, thus giving the filmmakers the freedom to hire Cheadle. Some critics have suggested that the reason why arranging both funding and studio distribution was difficult was that few in Hollywood cared about what had happened in Africa. "Ask anybody what was happening in '94, they probably remember [the former football star] O.J. Simpson [and his murder trial]," Ho told Justin Chang for *Variety* (January 3–9, 2005). "That was the big headline in this country."

Cheadle spent a week with Rusesabagina while preparing for the role, and Rusesabagina traveled to Johannesburg, South Africa, where the picture was being made, to lend support and supervise, when needed, during the filming. "When I met [Rusesabagina] I was struck that he wasn't 10 feet tall, he didn't swagger. He didn't cut an amazing path when he walked," Cheadle told Anne-Marie O'Connor. "He was just a man who did an extraordinary thing in an extraordinary circumstance. . . . The script really did a great job of not making him this huge heroic figure, but making him this common man who applied everything he knew as a hotel manager to survive." Cheadle continued, "He had to know how to talk to people, how to persuade, how to cajole, when to be forceful and when to back off. He applied that to save those lives, thinking every day was going to be his last day on Earth."

Ho told Justin Chang that the filmmakers "made a conscious effort to keep the slaughter [depicted onscreen] minimal." George explained further, "This has to be one of the most savage wars in a hundred years—just the enormity of the physical violence . . . people macheted to death. There's no way [to convey that] unless you use horror film tactics and prosthetics and all that stuff, and I didn't want to." Because of its relative lack of on-screen carnage, the movie secured a PG-13 rating. *Hotel Rwanda* premiered at the 2004 Toronto Film Festival. Although Rusesabagina has expressed his satisfaction at the depiction of his experiences, he found the film difficult to watch, as he still has nightmares about the genocide. Tatiana cried the first time she watched the picture, and some of their children have yet to see it. After the release of *Hotel Rwanda*, Rusesabagina and his wife decided that it was time to tell their nieces that they were adopted. (The girls were too young at the time of the genocide to comprehend or remember what had occurred.) "We did not want our children to learn their history from other people," he told O'Connor.

Hotel Rwanda was nominated for several Golden Globe Awards, and Cheadle was nominated for an Academy Award as best actor. Such acclaim is important to Rusesabagina only to the extent that it has brought the film and its message to the public. "The message of our movie is to say—look, this happened in Rwanda 10 years ago," he told a writer for collegenews.org (February 10, 2005). "The people of the world were not informed. Now today you are informed and again it is happening—are you not going to take action? Please do take action because it is happening in Sudan. It has been happening in the Congo for the last eight years—about [three and a half] million people have been killed. The world does not start and end in America and

Europe. It goes beyond." He added, "The politicians keep saying, 'Never again, never again.' Those two words are the most abused words in the world."

Rusesabagina has won, among other honors, the Peace Abbey Courage of Conscience Award (shared with his wife) and the Immortal Chaplains Foundation Prize for Humanity. He launched the Rusesabagina Foundation to aid survivors of the Rwandan genocide. He has spoken at the White House and continues to give talks frequently in many other places around the world.

—K.J.E.

Suggested Reading: Amnesty International Web site; *Boston-Bay State Banner* (on-line) Jan. 13, 2005; *Los Angeles Times* E p1 Dec. 28, 2004; *People* p113 Jan. 24, 2005; *Variety* p12 Jan. 3–9, 2005

Courtesy of Royce Carlton

Rutan, Burt

(roo-TAN)

June 17, 1943– Aeronautical engineer

Address: Scaled Composites, 1624 Flight Line, Mojave, CA 93501

Since April 21, 1961, when the Soviet cosmonaut Yuri Gagarin completed the world's first manned spaceflight around Earth, the history of human space exploration has been punctuated by a string of other noteworthy firsts. For example, on July 20, 1969 Neil Armstrong became the first man to walk on the surface of the moon. On April 12, 1981 the space shuttle *Columbia* became the first reusable winged vehicle to orbit Earth. The latest milestone in human space travel occurred on June 21, 2004, when *SpaceShipOne* (*SS1*), designed and built without military or government backing, became the world's first reusable spacecraft to be piloted beyond Earth's atmosphere by a civilian astronaut. Twice more that year, *SS1* flew to an altitude above 100 kilometers (62 miles), making it the winner of the $10 million Ansari X Prize, in a contest modeled after early–20th-century aviation competitions, which spurred the development of airplane design. *SSI* was the brainchild of Burt Rutan, a groundbreaking aeronautical designer and engineer who first gained widespread attention when his airship *Voyager* made an unprecedented around-the-world flight without refueling, in December 1986. Some observers believe that *SS1*'s high-concept, low-cost launch and reentry schemes, which stand in marked contrast to the expensive and elaborate systems devised by the National Aeronautics and Space Administration (NASA), qualify as works of genius. Rutan's design and technology were funded predominantly by Microsoft's co-founder Paul Allen and licensed by Richard Branson, the founder of Virgin Atlantic Airways, who plans to fund the construction of five more such airships and hopes to have the fleet ready to take tourists into space by 2007. Such tourism may be the first step in the conquest of space by entrepreneurs, and thus Rutan, by proving that space exploration need no longer be solely the domain of governments, may have ushered in a new era in the history of human spaceflight. In March 2005, in another first, the *Virgin Atlantic GlobalFlyer*, a custom-built jet that Rutan designed, completed the fastest nonstop aerial circumnavigation of the planet.

Born on June 17, 1943 in Portland, Oregon, to George Rutan, a dentist, and Irene Rutan, Elbert L. Rutan was raised in Dinuba, California. As a child his older brother, Dick, was an avid builder of model aircraft; he later became a military pilot and flew 325 combat missions during the Vietnam War. At age 11, Burt, as he was nicknamed, expressed an interest in building model planes. His father recalled to David F. Salisbury for the *Christian Science Monitor* (July 12, 1984) that he told his wife "to take him to the store and get him one of the simplest kits, because I didn't want him to get discouraged." But young Burt did not want a prefabricated kit, so his parents bought him the necessary materials to build a plane from scratch. He then designed and built an exact scale replica of a Boeing 707. Throughout his youth Burt won prizes for the remote-control planes he built.

George Rutan took flying lessons while his boys were young, earned a pilot's license, and purchased a small plane for recreation. "When I became a weekend pilot," he told Salisbury, "I never dreamed we would turn into such an aviation family." Burt learned to fly when he was 16, completing his first solo flight after only five and a half hours of instruction. He studied aeronautical engineering at California Polytechnic University, in San Luis Obispo, where he graduated third in his class, in 1965. Next he took a job with the U.S. Air Force as a civilian test-project engineer at Edwards Air Force Base, about 50 miles north of Los Angeles, California, in the Mojave Desert. Between 1965 and 1972 he oversaw 15 flight-test programs on various aircraft, ranging from fighter jets to the experimental XC-142 VSTOL tilt-wing troop and cargo transport craft, whose wings could rotate, so that it could hover like a helicopter or fly like a conventional plane.

In 1972 Rutan accepted a position with the Bede Test Center for Bede Aircraft in Newton, Kansas. James Bede, the company's owner, was then developing affordably priced, full-scale aircrafts that could be assembled from kits and flown by civilian aviation enthusiasts. Although he knew that Bede was having trouble earning a profit, the idea of designing and building kits for enthusiasts inspired Rutan. In June 1974 he struck out on his own and set up the Rutan Aircraft Factory in the Mojave Desert, whose clear skies, topography, and remoteness make it suitable for testing planes. The first kit Rutan manufactured, a delta-winged craft (that is, the wing was triangular), did not sell well, not least because it was difficult to assemble. Unwilling to give up his unique design, Rutan opted for foam and fiberglass parts instead of metal, as he had originally used. The result was the VariEze, a single-seat plane powered by a Volkswagen engine capable of propelling the craft at 170 miles per hour. Between 1976 and 1984 Rutan's company sold approximately 4,200 sets of VariEze plans. That plane's successor, the slightly larger LongEze, became available in 1980; approximately 4,000 sets of LongEze plans sold within four years. Each kit cost between $6,000 and $20,000, making it about as affordable as a new car at the time.

Rutan's designs proved extremely popular for two reasons: his pioneering use of lightweight building materials and his commitment to safety. All of Rutan's kit planes were designed with canards, small wings placed near the nose of the plane that acted as horizontal stabilizers and prevented stalling by keeping the nose elevated. Many airplane designers, including the brothers Wilbur and Orville Wright (who are credited with inventing the first motorized airplane capable of sustained flight), have included canards in their designs, but none as extensively as Rutan. By 1982 Rutan had designed 97 planes, some with such unusual designs that a few people who saw them in flight reported sighting UFOs. "With extremely few exceptions, maybe none, there is always a performance requirement," Rutan explained in an undated on-line interview with Diane Tedeschi for *AIR&SPACE/Smithsonian*. "It's how much it has to lift, how far it has to go, how fast it must be, that sort of a thing. So I start with the basic physics of an airplane that can get those requirements, and that pretty much sizes an airplane: how long its wings need to be, how much wing area, roughly. Then I look at the functionality: how the airplane is to be used, what kind of payload it has, what kind of access it needs, any special things that it needs to do. . . . And then I try a lot of different configurations to meet that, and then justify one at a time, throwing them out. . . . But I like to experiment, certainly. I like to see if there's other ways to provide the utility."

In 1982 Rutan, backed by investors, founded a second company, Scaled Composites, devoted to building prototype scale models of airplanes for other companies. The firm, which currently has approximately 145 employees, is capable of juggling more than a dozen different projects simultaneously. When Scaled Composites was founded, Dick Rutan had recently retired from the air force, and he and his friend Jeana Yeager had discussed making an attempt to set an aviation record. They settled on one of the few aeronautical feats yet to be accomplished: making a continuous circumnavigation of the globe without refueling. The standing overall distance record for a nonstop plane flight had been set in 1962 by a specially modified B-52 bomber, which flew over 12,000 miles, from Okinawa, Japan, to Madrid, Spain. His brother and Yeager's idea intrigued Burt, who concluded that it would be possible to build a plane capable of such a 25,000-mile flight.

Dick Rutan and Jeana Yeager founded the Voyager Corp. soon afterward, sinking $200,000 of their own money into the project. With Burt designing the craft and other companies donating parts and equipment, the *Voyager* airplane was built on a shoestring budget. When completed, the *Voyager* proved to be one of Burt Rutan's most astonishing designs: the airplane had a 111-foot wingspan—equal to a Boeing 727's—but weighed only 1,858 pounds, no more than a small car. Graphite composites, the synthetic material used in expensive tennis rackets, took the place of the standard aluminum airplane parts and accounted for the craft's dramatic lack of heft. Despite its frail appearance, the *Voyager* carried about 7,000 pounds of fuel and cruised at a top airspeed of 150 knots (about 172.5 statute, or land, miles per hour). The plane had two propellers, one in the nose for takeoffs and landings and one in the rear, for most of the flying at altitude. And like so many of Rutan's designs, the *Voyager* sported canards for added stability.

With Dick and Jeana on board, the *Voyager* took off from Edwards Air Force Base on December 14, 1986 and returned to the same spot nine days, three minutes, and 44 seconds later. The trip was generally problem free, except for a rear-engine failure seven and a half hours before landing. The crew solved the problem by turning on the front engine, which in turn restarted the rear engine. When it touched ground, on December 23, with only five gallons of fuel remaining in its 16 tanks, *Voyager* was greeted by more than 23,000 specta-

tors. For their accomplishment Rutan and the crew received the Presidential Citizens Medal from U.S. president Ronald Reagan, and the *Voyager* was shipped to the Smithsonian Institution, in Washington, D.C., where it is exhibited with other historic aircraft, including Charles Lindbergh's *Spirit of St. Louis*, which made the first solo flight across the Atlantic Ocean, in 1927.

Throughout the late 1980s and early 1990s, Burt Rutan phased out his kit-airplane business in favor of prototype construction, as lawsuits over accidents involving his home-built planes began to mount. "The interesting thing is, I was never sued by a person who bought a set of plans from me. Never sued by a customer. . . . The guys that I was at risk to—and still am—are people that buy an airplane someone else has built, and the relatives of whoever he may take for a ride," he told Diane Tedeschi. "And the case that went to a three- or four-week trial was [brought by] the relatives of a mistress in the backseat of a guy's airplane. [The pilot] was also killed in the accident, who would never have sued me. And the fact that he was three times the legal [intoxication] limit and had not put his airplane together properly after he took his wings off, and was doing aerobatics—even [all of] that didn't keep me out of spending hundreds of thousands of dollars to protect myself." During that period Rutan designed the *Starship*, an executive turboprop plane put into production by Beech Aircraft, and the unmanned *Raptor*, used as a missile interceptor by the U.S. government. He also designed the wings for the *Pegasus*, a rocket launched from a converted L-1011 airliner, built for the privately owned Orbital Sciences Corp., a satellite and small-rocket manufacturer.

In an interview with Andy Meisler for the *New York Times* (August 3, 1995), Rutan hinted at the direction in which his aviation design was taking him: "You know, many people look back and say, 'Gee, this is a really boring time, compared to the 60's, when we went so quickly to the moon from first orbit.' But I've got a theory that this is just a kind of gentle pause. There's going to be a renaissance, a super renaissance, in the next 15 years." Fascinated with space travel since his teens, he secretly began designing his own space vehicle, one that could send civilians into space regularly. His clandestine efforts gained further impetus when the St. Louis–based X Prize Foundation announced, in 1997, that it would award a $10 million prize to the first privately funded team that could put a ship into orbit twice in two weeks. The name of the award was changed to the Ansari X Prize in 2004, after two Iranian entrepreneurs, Anousheh and Amir Ansari, gave a multimillion-dollar contribution to the foundation. With 26 teams from seven countries competing, the prize effectively ignited a new space race reminiscent of the struggle in the late 1960s between the U.S. and the Soviet Union to be the first country to land a human on the moon. This time, the competition involved entrepreneurs and industrialists, not nations.

Rutan enlisted the help of the billionaire Microsoft co-founder Paul Allen, who contributed significantly to the project's estimated $20 million budget. The costliest aspects of spaceflight by far are connected with liftoff and reentry. Each time a space shuttle is launched, NASA employs an expendable, one-use-only booster-rocket system that costs about $300 million. During the shuttle's reentry, friction from the atmosphere (beginning at about 400,000 feet, or about 75 miles above Earth's surface) generates temperatures in excess of 2,000 degrees Fahrenheit. The heat is absorbed and dissipated by 24,000 specially constructed ceramic tiles that cover the shuttle's shell. Each tile costs about $2,000; the tiles crack when struck by the slightest debris, and damaged tiles cannot be reused. The cost to NASA of replacing the tiles between flights has averaged about $350,000. To keep expenses as low as possible during launchings, Rutan constructed a high-altitude aircraft, called the *White Knight*, that would carry *SS1* under its belly to an altitude of 48,000 feet and then release it. *SS1* would then fire its main engine, which would be fueled with a compound of nitrous oxide and rubber, and soar to the edge of space (arbitrarily defined as 100 kilometers, or about 62 miles or 327,360 feet above Earth), where it was to remain for three minutes. To protect the spacecraft's graphite-composite shell on reentry, Rutan designed a tail and wings that could tilt at a 65-degree angle, which would stabilize *SS1* at a certain velocity as it glided belly-first through the atmosphere, thus avoiding the far higher temperatures of a high-speed dive.

On April 4, 2004 the FAA (Federal Aviation Agency) granted Rutan's ship a license for a manned suborbital flight—the first ever for a civilian spacecraft. (Orbital flight requires far greater velocities than suborbital flight, and occurs at much greater distances above sea level.) On June 21, 2004, after three unmanned tests, which proved that *SpaceShipOne* was capable of high-altitude supersonic flight, Mike Mevill, its pilot, guided the ship into a 55-second vertical climb and reached a height of 211,400 feet, thus becoming the first civilian to pilot a ship out of Earth's atmosphere. However, in order to win the X Prize, Rutan's team had to send *SS1* twice within two weeks to an altitude of 328,000 feet. During its first qualifying 90-minute flight, on September 29, 2004, *SpaceShipOne* reached an altitude of 367,000 feet; on October 4, 2004 the craft matched its previous effort, capturing the Ansari X Prize. "The Boeings and Lockheeds of the world probably thought we were a bunch of home builders," Rutan said, referring to two major American aerospace manufacturers, moments after Mevill landed, as quoted by Christopher Palmeri in *BusinessWeek* (October 5, 2004, on-line). "I think they're looking at each other right now and thinking, 'We're screwed!'" In an interview with the BBC News (October 4, 2004, on-line), Ann Karagozian, head of the Combustion Research Laboratory at the University of California at Los Angeles, said of *SpaceShipOne*'s remarkable stability: "It is really unheard of in my opinion. . . . This could well be the technological concept that pushes us over the edge into the low-cost space travel arena."

That is precisely what the adventurer and entrepreneur Richard Branson is banking on. Two days before *SS1*'s first qualifying launch, Branson, a billionaire, who owns the Virgin Group of companies (among them Virgin Atlantic airline), announced that he had signed a deal with Burt Rutan to build a fleet of five commercial spaceships based on Rutan's design, to be flown under the new Virgin Galactic logo. The Virgin Group will spend roughly $100 million on the project, with plans to launch the first Virgin Galactic craft—named the *Enterprise* after the fictional starship on the 1960s television program *Star Trek*—by 2007. Virgin has also commissioned Rutan to build a new launcher and to outfit each of the five spaceships for five passengers. Rutan and Branson will occupy two of the five seats on the *Enterprise*'s maiden voyage. Each seat will probably cost $200,000. According to Branson, 13,000 people worldwide have already paid a deposit through Virgin Galactic's Web site, among them the rock musician Dave Navarro and the actor William Shatner, who played the captain of the *Enterprise* on *Star Trek*. Virgin Galactic need only fill 5,000 seats over the next five years in order to turn a profit, according to Branson, who also expects that the price of an average ticket will come down as more people sign up for flights. "This isn't just a pipe dream," Branson was quoted as saying by Chris Taylor and Kristina Dell in *Time* (November 29, 2004), which voted *SpaceShipOne* the "Coolest Invention of 2004." "We will get this to the point where thousands of people can go into space."

As an encore to his aerospace triumph, Rutan teamed up with Branson and the businessman, pilot, and adventurer Steve Fossett for a challenge to two aviation records: those for the fastest nonstop, non-refueled aerial circumnavigation of the world and the first ever by a solo pilot. Rutan designed a single-engine jet, the *Virgin Atlantic GlobalFlyer*, to carry about 18,000 pounds of fuel, which would equal 80 percent of the aircraft's total weight. Despite mysteriously losing 2,600 pounds of fuel in midflight, in March 2005 Fossett broke both records, piloting the *GlobalFlyer* around the globe in 67 hours.

Among many other honors, Rutan received the Rave Award in industrial design from *Wired* magazine in 2005. He was named Innovator of the Year by *R&D Magazine* in 2004 and listed among the 100 most influential people of 2005 by *Time*. He spends most weekday work hours on administrative duties for his company; on weeknights and weekends he designs aircraft. He has been married four times and has two children and four grandchildren.

—C.M.

Suggested Reading: *AIR&SPACE Smithsonian* magazine (on-line); BBC News (on-line) Oct. 4, 2004; *Bulletin of the Atomic Scientists* p6+ July/Aug. 2004, with photos; *BusinessWeek* (on-line) Oct. 5, 2004; *Chicago Tribune* I p7+ July 4, 1982, with photos; *Christian Science Monitor* p1+ July 12, 1984, with photos; *Economist* Dec. 18, 2004; *New York Times* A p1+ Dec. 23, 1986, A p1+ Dec. 24, 1986, with photo, C p1+ Aug. 3, 1995, with photos; *Newsweek* p63 July 16, 1984, with photos; Scaled Composites, LLC, Web site; *Time* p64 Nov. 29, 2004; *Washington Post* A p7 Dec. 24, 1986

Courtesy of Carl Safina

Safina, Carl

May 23, 1955– Marine conservationist; president of the Blue Ocean Institute

Address: Blue Ocean Institute, 250 Lawrence Hill Rd., Cold Spring Harbor, NY 11724

Carl Safina is a prominent ecologist and marine conservationist and president of the Blue Ocean Institute, an environmental organization based in Cold Spring Harbor, New York. He has also been a recreational fisherman since childhood. "I love the hunt and know the thrill of the kill," Safina told William J. Broad for the *New York Times* (September 22, 1998). "But I'm not sure we should be doing it. They [the fish] need a break." After reaching the conclusion that, if overfishing were to continue at the current rate, entire populations of fish might cease to exist, Safina became an advocate for the very creatures he grew up hunting. The winner of both a prestigious Pew Fellowship and a MacArthur Fellowship, Safina has written or co-written three books—*Song for the Blue Ocean: Encounters Along the World's Coasts and Beneath the Seas*; *Seafood Lover's Almanac*; and *Eye of the Albatross: Visions of Hope and Survival*.

Carl Safina was born on May 23, 1955 into a middle-class Italian American family in the Ridgewood section of the New York City borough of Brooklyn. His father, a schoolteacher, raised canaries, and in second grade, Safina began breeding pigeons in the family's backyard. When he was 10 the Safinas moved to Syosset, New York, a short distance from Long Island Sound, off the north shore of the island, where Carl and his father often went fishing for bass. As a teenager Safina played the drums in various jazz and rock bands. (He worked his way through college by entertaining at private parties and weddings in the New York metropolitan area.) When a classmate from Syosset High School recruited him to help with a bird-banding survey on Fire Island, off the south shore of Long Island, Safina's love for wild birds, or "living jewels," as he has called them, was ignited. He attended the State University of New York (SUNY) at Purchase, where he earned a B.A. degree in environmental science in 1977. He then trained hawks and worked briefly with falcons for the Peregrine Fund, a nonprofit organization. He also investigated suspected illegal toxic dumping sites for the New Jersey Department of Environmental Protection. He next entered a graduate program in ecology at Rutgers University in New Brunswick, New Jersey; he received M.S. and Ph.D. degrees in ecology in 1981 and 1987, respectively.

Beginning in 1979 Safina had also worked for the National Audubon Society, primarily studying hawks and seabirds. While observing foraging terns in the waters around Long Island for his doctoral degree, he noticed declines in creatures that shared the terns' realm—striped bass, tuna, marlin, sharks, and other fish, as well as sea turtles. Safina began to think that fish needed just as much protection as the birds he had been studying. "People never thought of fish as wildlife," he told Joe Haberstroh for *Newsday* (June 19, 2002). "They just thought fish was something that wound up in the fish store, or on a plate in a restaurant." One day in 1989, while he was fishing in the Atlantic Ocean about 50 miles off the coast of Fire Island, he noticed some fishermen catching "ridiculous amounts" of bluefin tuna, as he recalled to William J. Broad. "Somebody got on the radio and said, 'Guys, maybe we should leave some for tomorrow,'" he told Broad. "Another guy came on and said, 'Hey, they didn't leave any buffalo for me.'" That offhand comment affected Safina profoundly: he realized that, through overfishing, entire species of fish could literally vanish. He began referring to global overfishing as "the last buffalo hunt."

In 1990 Safina founded the Living Oceans Program at the National Audubon Society, where he served for a decade as vice president for ocean conservation. Concurrently, from 1991 to 1994, he served on the Mid-Atlantic Fisheries Management Council of the U.S. Department of Commerce, to which he was appointed by the secretary of commerce. In 2003 he co-founded and became president of the Blue Ocean Institute, an organization dedicated to inspiring among humans a closer relationship with the sea and helping more people realize its power and beauty. The Institute is designed to inspire, rather than demand, conservation by using science, art, and literature to build a "sea ethic" and a greater appreciation for the oceans and their inhabitants.

Safina's first book, *Song for the Blue Ocean: Encounters Along the World's Coasts and Beneath the Seas*, was published in 1998 to rave reviews. In it Safina described his travels with high-seas fish and fishermen; in the salmon rivers, forests, and coasts of North America's Northwest; and among the coral reefs of the tropical Western Pacific Ocean. He also recounted his experiences with individuals whose work might destroy or preserve those locales. The book was praised for its readability, poetic descriptions of the sea, and heartfelt pleas for conservation. It was named a *New York Times* Notable Book of the Year and a *Library Journal* Best Science Book, and won a *Los Angeles Times* award for nonfiction and the Lannan Literary Award for nonfiction. According to *Contemporary Authors* (1999), Richard Ellis characterized Safina for the *Los Angeles Times Book Review* as "an ecologist with the soul of a poet" and *Song for the Blue Ocean* "a frightening, important book."

In 2000 Safina co-wrote (with Mercedes Lee and Suzanne Iudicello) *Seafood Lover's Almanac*, a guide for those who love to eat seafood but are concerned about depleting fish and shellfish populations. The volume includes tips on recipes, suggestions for healthful eating, and information on nutritional values, along with alternatives to eating overfished species. Many reviewers lauded the book for educating readers about how to balance a seafood diet with a conservationist sensibility. The volume won the Renewable Natural Resources Foundation's outstanding achievement award.

Despite the attention he devoted to fish in his previous two books, Safina did not forget his first love, birds. In an article for *Time* magazine's Earth Day edition (April/May 2000), he considered the plight of the albatross, writing, "Like the albatross, we need the seas more than the seas need us. Will we understand this well enough to reap all the riches a little restraint, cooperation, and compassion will bring?" His next book, *Eye of the Albatross: Visions of Hope and Survival* (2002), followed a Laysan albatross, which he named Amelia, throughout one breeding season, detailing both the dangers Amelia and her kin faced and the remarkable feats they accomplished, such as living for up to 60 years and flying, as individuals, millions of miles in total. In a review for *American Scientist* (July 1, 2002), David Blockstein called the book "an honest first-person account of field biology in ac-

tion." "Thought-provoking, witty and beautifully written," Blockstein wrote, "the book recounts dramatic adventures (both human and avian), philosophically explores life and death, and chronicles the relationship between humans and nature." In 2003 *Eye of the Albatross* won the John Burroughs Medal, which has been awarded annually since 1926 to works that combine scientific accuracy, descriptions of fieldwork, and creative natural-history writing. *Eye of the Albatross* also garnered the inaugural National Academies Communication Award for explaining a scientific topic to the general public better than any other book published that year.

Safina has engaged in many successful conservation efforts. He has helped ban high-seas drift-nets and overhaul federal fisheries laws in the U.S., and has persuaded fishermen to call for and abide by international agreements to restore depleted populations of tuna, sharks, and other fish, as well as creatures that constitute bycatch or bykill (marine life unintentionally captured by fishermen), such as dolphins and sea turtles. In 1995 he was a force behind the passage of a new fisheries treaty through the United Nations, and in 1996 the U.S. Congress incorporated some of his ideas in the Sustainable Fisheries Act, which required rebuilding of marine-life populations depleted by fishing. In the late 1990s Safina also raised awareness of declining shark populations, and by 1998, in the absence of an official recovery plan, he and other activists had succeeded in persuading several prominent restaurateurs in Boston, New York, and Washington, D.C., to remove swordfish from their menus. "Everyone has to be part of the solution. There's little use in commercial and recreational fishers pointing fingers at each other," Safina said in an article for AScribe Newswire (August 26, 2004). "Commercial fishing is not all bad and recreational fishing is not all good. A fish doesn't care if you are a commercial or a recreational fisherman. It only cares if it surrounded by water—or on ice."

In 2000 Safina won a John D. and Catherine T. MacArthur Foundation Fellowship, popularly known as the "genius" grant. He has been using the prize money, which is distributed over the course of five years, to fund his research and the travel it entails. His other honors include the International Game Fish Association Conservation Award, the Pew Charitable Trust's Scholar's Award in Conservation and the Environment, the American Fisheries Society's Carl R. Sullivan Conservation Award, and recognition from Rutgers University as the most distinguished alumnus to graduate from the ecology and evolution program. He has received honorary doctorates from Long Island University and SUNY. *Audubon* magazine named him one of the top 100 conservationists of the 20th century, and the World Wildlife Fund named him a senior fellow in its Marine Conservation Program. Safina is a visiting fellow at Yale University, an adjunct professor at SUNY–Stony Brook, and an elected member of the Explorers Club. In addition to his books, Safina has written upwards of 100 articles for scientific and popular journals. Seizing every opportunity to enlighten the public about the continuing dangers to marine wildlife, he also lectures. He appeared on the Bill Moyers PBS special *Earth on the Edge* (2002). "I predict that over the next few years," he wrote in *Science and Technology* (Summer 2003), "consumer education will become the largest area of growth and change in the toolbox of ocean conservation strategy."

Safina is greatly concerned, as he told *Current Biography*, with the "embattlement of reason and science." He believes "that information must be conveyed in the context of values, and that we must reinvigorate veneration of reason and fuse it with a renewed quest toward truly traditional values of peace, compassion, generosity of spirit, and love." Although he is not religious in the conventional sense, he finds spirituality in nature and the creatures he studies.

Safina lives in Amagansett, on Long Island, with Patricia Paladines and her daughter Alexandra. They have several pets, including a rescue dog, a king snake, a rose-haired tarantula, a rabbit, and a goldfish. Like his work, Safina's leisure activities take him outdoors; besides fishing, he enjoys snorkeling, scuba diving, clamming, kayaking, and bird watching. His next book will focus on his travels with sea turtles.

—K.J.E.

Suggested Reading: *American Scientist* p378 July 1, 2002; AScribe Newswire Aug. 26, 2004; blueoceaninstitute.org; *New York Times* F p1 Sep. 22, 1998

Selected Books: *Song for the Blue Ocean: Encounters Along the World's Coasts and Beneath the Seas*, 1998; *Seafood Lover's Almanac* (with Mercedes Lee and Suzanne Iudicello), 2000; *Eye of the Albatross: Visions of Hope and Survival*, 2002

Scaturro, Pasquale V.

1954– Geophysicist; mountaineer; adventurer

Address: Exploration Specialists International, 1680 Hoyt St., Lakewood, CO 80215

Among other daring feats that have taken him around the world, the geophysicist, businessman, and adventurer Pasquale V. Scaturro has scaled Mount Everest, the world's highest mountain; served as a guide for the first blind person ever to reach that mountain's peak; and—in a perilous journey documented in a 2005 IMAX film—led the first known expedition from the base of the Nile River to its junction with the Mediterranean Sea. Scaturro began his career as a researcher for oil firms before founding his own company, to provide seismic data for the industry. His travels in that line of work, which often proved to be dangerous in themselves, seemed to have heightened, rather than quelled, his appetite for risk. "He was born 100 years too late," Scaturro's wife, Kim Scaturro, told James B. Meadow for the *Rocky Mountain News* (September 11, 2004). "He's an explorer. He'd never say this, but if he died doing something nobody had done, it would be OK." Scaturro himself said to Meadow, "If the adventure is big and the athletic challenge is there, that's what I want. Something different, something that's never been done before."

Pasquale V. Scaturro was born in 1954 in Southern California (Hollywood, according to Meadow), the second of the five sons of Vincent Scaturro, an immigrant from Sicily, and Audrey (Bolton) Scaturro. Each of the boys was given the first name Vincent; Pasquale and his brothers reversed their middle and first names to distinguish themselves from one another. Their parents' relationship was volatile, with police coming frequently in response to reports of domestic violence and sometimes arresting Pasquale's father. When Pasquale was 11 his mother began to exhibit symptoms of paranoid schizophrenia, and she was later institutionalized. Vincent Scaturro then moved his sons to Thousand Oaks, California, while he stayed behind to work in his restaurant. From that time on the boys were mostly on their own, with Pasquale assuming much of the responsibility for taking care of his brothers.

One positive experience in Pasquale Scaturro's childhood occurred when he was eight years old. One of his teachers paid for him to attend a YMCA summer camp housed in the mountains; Scaturro persuaded one of the counselors to let him tag along with a group of other counselors and campers who were attempting to climb the 11,502-foot Mount San Gorgonio, one of the tallest mountains in Southern California. As others—counselors and campers alike—gave up, Scaturro and one adult pressed on. Scaturro fought through his exhaustion to reach the top, where he felt elated and triumphant.

In high school, despite his family's turmoil, Scaturro earned good grades, shone as an athlete, and was popular with other students. He worked nights at a gas station during those years. He married at 18 and fathered a child the next year. Craving adventure, as well as a means of supporting his new family, Scaturro joined the U.S. Air Force. According to the Web site of the American Association of Petroleum Geologists (AAPG), he was stationed in England and began to study geology there. After he completed his tour of duty, with the rank of staff

Pasquale Scaturro (right) and Gordon Brown

Amro Maraghi/AFP/Getty

sergeant, Scaturro moved with his family to Flagstaff, Arizona, where he enrolled at Northern Arizona University. He graduated with a B.S. degree in geology and geophysics. Next he landed a job with the oil company Amoco, doing seismic research—or research into earthquakes and other land vibrations—and land exploration. In 1986 he founded his own company, Seismic Specialists Inc., which was devoted to gathering seismic data for the oil and gas industries. Scaturro's work took him around the world, as he researched and surveyed land, searched for potential sites of new oil wells, and evaluated and rejuvenated existing wells. Those journeys were often dangerous; in Somalia, for example, he was forced to dodge hand grenades in the midst of a war zone, and in several other countries he found himself held at gunpoint by bandits or rebel militias. In his interview with James B. Meadow, Scaturro explained that he was "not uncomfortable when there are people around me with guns. Usually I can negotiate my way out of any trouble."

As his company became successful, Scaturro began seeking out adventures for their own sake. In 1984 he and a group of friends took a rafting trip into the Bio-Bio region in Chile, known for its extremely rough whitewater rapids and towering volcanoes. The Bio Bio River was the first of many rivers he would successfully navigate. Not all of Scaturro's adventures have ended well, however. Soon after the 1984 river trip, Scaturro began scaling mountains; in 1993, while he was part of an expedition to climb the Himalayan peak Pumori, in Nepal, one of his teammates, Gregory Gordon, fell thousands of feet to his death while Scaturro watched helplessly. In the same year, on a rafting

trip on the Canadian rapids, a woman in his team was killed when their boat capsized and her head struck a rock.

Those experiences nearly led Scaturro to give up his adventures. In 1995, however, his love of excitement and novelty overcame his reservations, and he made his first attempt to scale Mount Everest, in southern Asia, which, at 29,028 feet, is the highest peak in the world. The first two people known to have reached the peak, in 1953, were Edmund Hillary, a native of New Zealand, and Tenzing Norgay, a Sherpa from Nepal. Thousands have since climbed to the summit, and hundreds have died in failed attempts. During the course of Scaturro's climb, he suffered an attack of malaria (which he had contracted years earlier, in Africa), and he reluctantly turned back. In December of that year, tragedy again befell Scaturro, when his son became paralyzed after roughhousing with fellow members of his high-school football team. "There's nothing in life that will make you want to kill yourself like the sight of your son taped to a board in an emergency room with his neck broken and a neurologist telling you he won't walk for the rest of his life . . . ," Scaturro told James B. Meadow. "That was, by far, the worst time of my life. I remember going outside and just weeping."

In 1998 Scaturro returned to Mount Everest, this time becoming the first Westerner ever to reach the mountain's summit. That Everest expedition was one of the most successful ever, bringing 19 people of the 21 in the party (or 12 of the total, according to the AAPG Web site) to the peak without serious injuries or fatalities. Scaturro's paralyzed son had accompanied him to the base camp of the expedition and was waiting for him when he returned.

In May 2001 Scaturro attempted an even more ambitious journey to the top of the same mountain, when he served as the guide and assistant for Erik Weihenmayer, a 32-year-old schoolteacher from Phoenix, Arizona, who wanted to become the first blind person ever to reach the peak of Mount Everest. The two undertook the adventure against the advice of many. "When he decided to lead our expedition to Mount Everest, I got a sense that he liked to defy the odds," Weihenmayer told James B. Meadow of Scaturro, whose friends call him PV. "I think PV gets a perverse kick doing things people say can't be done." In the weeks leading up to the trip, Scaturro was frequently asked if Weihenmayer was qualified for the challenge. "He's ultra-prepared," Scaturro told J. Michael Kennedy for the *Los Angeles Times* (January 5, 2001). "Everest is no technical challenge for this guy." (Everest did not represent Weihenmayer's first attempt to climb a daunting mountain; he had reached the highest peaks in both North and South America. Everest was simply the next step for Weihenmayer in his quest to scale each of the Seven Summits—the highest mountains in the world.) In an interview for the *Today* show (March 16, 2001, on-line) prior to the trek, Matt Lauer asked Scaturro if he had any doubts related to Weihenmayer's blindness. "There is a little more risk . . . ," Scaturro said. "On a regular expedition—a private expedition—you hate to say every man's for himself when the going gets dangerous, when you're up high and there's bad weather. . . . With Erik, we're his eyes. So we [the 19 others in the party] have to pay attention to the fact that we can't leave him. But at the same time, knowing that, Erik is better than 80 percent of the climbers that will ever climb Mount Everest . . . he's not a burden to us except that we have to be his eyes." On May 25, 2001 Weihenmayer stood at the top of Everest. (Scaturro was not with him, having fallen ill during the climb.)

In 2004 Scaturro again set out to do what no one had done before, when he and the filmmaker Gordon Brown set out to travel the entire length of the Nile River. (Gordon shot footage for a documentary about the trip.) The Nile is made up of two rivers—known as the White Nile and the Blue Nile—that join in Khartoum, Sudan, and flow into the Mediterranean Sea. It has long been a source of curiosity and intrigue for adventurers and explorers; in the 19th century the discovery of the source of the Nile was referred to as "the Great Prize." It was not until 1937 that the German explorer Bruckhart Waidekker proved that the main source of the massive, tortuous Blue Nile, with its treacherous rapids, was in Ethiopia, which has since been considered the true source of the river as a whole. In Ethiopia, as Scaturro told Alex Chadwick for the National Pubic Radio program *Day to Day* (April 28, 2004, on-line), the Nile begins as "a small but powerful white-water river, and then it dumps into Sudan where it becomes a big huge river that . . . is very remote, very long, very difficult to do."

On Christmas Day 2003 Scaturro, Brown, and their team set out on their quest, which they began on foot. Scaturro believed that the true source of the Nile was the Spring of Gish Abay, in the highlands of a small village called Sakala. Because the water there was too narrow and shallow to navigate by boat, the team walked for about five days until they reached Lake Tana, where they were able to begin rafting down the Nile. During the trip Scaturro kept a journal, whose entries were posted on his Web site, pvsnet.com. In his entry from January 9, 2004, he described what he considered to be a relatively calm day: "Had a couple of rock attacks today by both some Ethiopians hiding up above the cliffs and several troops of angry baboons. Also had a scare from a startled crocodile a few feet from Michel. Fortunately that was all of the excitement for today."

The group regularly faced attacks from hippopotamuses, crocodiles, and armed bandits who would fire rifle shots at them from the shore of the river. "I didn't know it before this trip," Gordon Brown said, according to James B. Meadow, "but one of my least favorite things is to be shot at." However, as Scaturro has told several interviewers, the greatest challenge of the journey turned out not to be crocodiles, bandits, or rapids but bureaucracy. Scaturro and his party were arrested by the Egyptian police for trying to take their boat across Lake Nasser, one of the world's most heavily guarded bodies of water. "They'd been waiting for us for four days. They knew we were coming," Scaturro said to Jordan Rane for the *Los Angeles Times* (May 11, 2004). "The moment we crossed the 20th parallel, they started up their motors, came right toward us, and one guy goes, 'Welcome to Egypt. Get out of your boat.' They took us straight to the army base and told us we were either turning right around and going back to Sudan or going to jail." The team acquiesced to the authorities' demand that they abandon their rafts and cross the Nasser in the ferry that carried tourists across the lake once a week. Scaturro then flew to Egypt, where, with the help of the U.S. Embassy, he contacted representatives at many levels of the Egyptian government, trying to get permission to cross the Nasser. After permission was granted, the team spent three days crossing the lake on their rafts and continued toward their ultimate destination. On April 28, 2004, over four months after they had begun their journey, Scaturro and Brown entered the Mediterranean Sea in their raft, becoming the first people in history to navigate the entire length of the Nile River. "I thought I would be elated when I finished," Scaturro said in an interview with the Associated Press (April 28, 2004) shortly afterward, "but I am just relieved that no one on the expedition died or suffered major injuries because we had so many obstacles thrown in our way."

Scaturro was quoted in PR Newswire (April 28, 2004) as saying, "The Nile is the most magnificent river in the world. It has rapids, waterfalls, jungle, canyons, deserts, hippos, crocs, long flat beautiful sections, huge beautiful sandbars. There is no other river in the world that can compare. And no other river in the world is as closely associated with a particular culture and society as is the Nile. Without the Nile there would be no Egypt, no pharaohs, no pyramids. The history of the western world is inextricably tied to the Nile." On February 25, 2005, with the release of the IMAX film *Mystery of the Nile*, the footage that Brown took on the expedition was made available to the public. As reviewers pointed out, the footage showcased land and water that had scarcely been seen before by human eyes, let alone on film. "Whatever style points the production team lose for their unoriginal title and very conventional river-journey story," Roger Moore wrote for the *Orlando (Florida) Sentinel* (February 18, 2005), "the movie itself . . . is most striking, taking us places we've never been before."

In 1995 Scaturro founded Tricon Geophysics, a seismic-research company with which he is no longer associated. He is still actively involved with Seismic Specialists and also runs Exploration Specialists International, which leads private mountain-climbing and rafting expeditions all over the world. Scaturro plans to continue his treks. After returning home from the Nile, he traveled by foot, car, raft, and bicycle on or along the entire Missouri River, in the United States, and planned several more trips to Africa to explore rivers, mountains, and deserts. He lives in Lakewood, Colorado, with his second wife, Kim, whom he married in 1998.
—R.E.

Suggested Reading: *Los Angeles Times* F p4 May 11, 2004; *Rocky Mountain News* A p25 Sep. 11, 2004

Selected Films: *Mystery of the Nile*, 2005

Courtesy of Standard Insurance Co.

Scdoris, Rachael

(suh-DORE-iss)

Feb. 1, 1985– Dogsled racer

Address: c/o Sports Unlimited, 1991 N.W. Upshur, Suite B, Portland, OR 97209

"I really wish people wouldn't think of me as the blind musher, but I know they always will," the dogsled racer Rachael Scdoris said to a reporter for the Salem, Oregon, *Statesman Journal* (December 24, 2004). "It is what it is." Scdoris was still an infant when she was diagnosed with congenital achromatopsia, a deficiency in the rods and cones in the retina, which control depth perception and the eyes' processing of light and color; as a result, she has 20/200 vision and is nearsighted, farsighted, and color-blind. She has nonetheless competed in sled-dog races since she was 12 years old. Scdoris races with the assistance of a visual interpreter, or V.I., who usually rides ahead of her on trails on a snowmobile to alert her by radio to impending obstacles.

Scdoris is best known for competing in the 33d Iditarod Trail Sled Dog Race, in March 2005. Often called "The Last Great Race on Earth," the Iditarod crosses Alaska, from Anchorage to Nome, a distance of more than 1,150 miles. The first Iditarod took place as part of Alaska's centennial celebration, in 1967. (In a purchase that became known as "Seward's Folly," in 1867 William H. Seward, the U.S. secretary of state, had acquired the territory from Russia for 2.5 cents per acre. Alaska attained statehood in 1959.) The race was conceived as a tribute to the historic Iditarod trail and its role in Alaskan history. The trail began, according to the official Iditarod Web site, as a dog-sled route between the coast and the mining towns in the state's interior; mail and supplies were sent in, and gold was brought out. A portion of the trail was used during the legendary Serum Run of 1925; when a diphtheria epidemic struck in Nome that year, 18 mushers and their dog teams relayed vaccine to the remote town, thus saving hundreds of lives, and those heroic efforts have become an inextricable part of Iditarod lore. The race starts on the first Saturday of March and takes the competitors across two mountain ranges, along the Yukon River, and over the frozen Norton Sound. The route alternates every year, going north from Ophir through Cripple, Ruby, and Galena in even-numbered years and south, from Ophir through Iditarod, Shageluk, and Anvik, in odd-numbered years. Scdoris had traveled the southern route before she withdrew from the race at the Eagle Island checkpoint, because her dogs had contracted a viral infection. She nonetheless made history, as the Iditarod's first legally blind competitor. Scdoris has signed up to compete in the 2006 Iditarod, with the veteran Iditarod musher Tim Osmar slated to serve as her visual interpreter.

Rachael Scdoris was born on February 1, 1985 in Oregon. An only child, she was raised by her father, Jerry Scdoris, who has bred sled dogs for more than 30 years and owns a sled-dog tour company. She grew up playing with the puppies in her father's kennel and often tagged along when her father rode his dogsled, traveling either in his sled with him or towed in a sled by herself. She made her first solo dogsled ride when she was only 11, pulled by two dogs, Coyote and Shane, both veteran Iditarod racers. One year later Scdoris competed in her first dogsled race, coming in fourth in the three-dog novice division at the Frog Lake Race in Mt. Hood, Oregon. During that time Scdoris was already preparing for the Iditarod. "She camped outside on the roof of [her family's] house for a year when she was 12 because that's basically what the Iditarod is, a really long camping trip with food drops," Becki Timson, a member of Scdoris's dog-handling team at the Iditarod, said to the *Statesman Journal* (December 24, 2004). "This is something she's wanted forever."

While Scdoris was growing up, other children teased her because of her disability. Being colorblind, Scdoris sometimes wore mismatched clothes, and her poor vision often caused her to trip or bump into things. "Then things changed all of a sudden in eighth grade. She had become such a beautiful athlete," Jerry Scdoris told the *Statesman Journal*. In high school Rachael Scdoris became a runner, earning a varsity letter in cross-country running as a freshman and another in track the following spring. She went on to become the track team's captain. When she was 15 Scdoris was invited by the U.S. Association of Blind Athletes to compete in an exhibition event—a 400-meter race in the Olympic trials, in which she came in third. "I saw her back when she was running cross country in high school," Rick Steber, the author of Scdoris's biography *No End in Sight* (2005) and a family friend, said to George Bryson for the *Anchorage Daily News* (February 27, 2005). "I've seen her trip on rocks, and I've seen her walk into guy wires, but she's never given up." Scdoris graduated from Redmond High School with a 3.5 grade-point average in 2003.

Scdoris turned 16 while competing in the International Pedigree Stage Stop Sled Dog Race, founded in 1996 by Frank Teasley to make dogsled racing more accessible to the general public. Competing at the race in Jackson Hole, Wyoming, Scdoris earned the distinction of being the youngest mush-

er—and first legally blind person—to finish a 500-mile sled-dog race.

In 2002 Scdoris requested, and was denied, use of a V.I. and other special accommodations that would make safe competition in the Iditarod possible for her. After her second rejection, in 2003, Scdoris traveled to Anchorage to make her request in person. The Iditarod Trail Committe's board of directors then voted unanimously to allow Scdoris to use a radio-enabled V.I., who would travel ahead of her with a team of dogs and inform Scdoris of trail conditions. In December 2003 Scdoris withdrew from the 2004 race, due to lack of money and preparation time, planning instead to race in the 2005 Iditarod. In the following February she competed in the first of her qualifying races for the Iditarod, finishing 11th out of the 14 who completed the 350-mile Race to the Sky in Montana. (Held every February, Race to the Sky is the longest continuous sled-dog race held in the lower 48 states and draws teams from the Pacific Northwest, Canada, and the Midwest.) In March she competed in the John Beargrease Mid-distance Marathon, in Minnesota; she came in sixth in that 400-mile race. (According to the John Beargrease Sled Dog Marathon Web site, the race is meant to honor "the spirit of frontier adventurism established at the turn of the century by John Beargrease, along with a host of other North Shore mail carriers. Beargrease and his fellow carriers were a colorful, boisterous breed whose ingenuity and determination helped ensure the tradition of continued mail delivery, even under adverse conditions.") The Atta Boy 300 Oregon World Cup served as pre-Iditarod training for Scdoris's sled dogs in January 2005. Founded by Jerry Scdoris in 2003, the Atta Boy is a 10-day event held in daily stages. There are two main racing events: a six-dog, mid-distance championship that is run during the first two days and the eight- to 12-dog mid-distance run that takes place over the following eight days. Rachael Scdoris competed in both events and finished 18th overall, on January 14, 2005. For most of the 47.7-mile course, Scdoris ran alongside or behind her team. Also known as the Race for Vision, the 2005 Atta Boy raised $40,000 for ophthalmology research and advancement.

On January 29, 2005 Scdoris began her last race before the Iditarod, the Tustumena 200 in Kasilof, Alaska. The two-day race took place in the Caribou Hills of Alaska's Kenai Peninsula. "I loved it—it was great," Scdoris said to George Bryson. "Everyone was telling me how tough it was, how dreadful the trails were, and I just went out there and had a great time." The Tustumena 200 (T200) dogsled race was begun in 1984 by Iditarod champion Dean Osmar as a way for his son to accumulate the racing miles he needed to qualify for the Junior Iditarod. It was considered a local race until the T200 Sled Dog Race Association reorganized it, in 1994; since then it has developed a reputation as one of the best Iditarod qualifiers because of the similarities in rules and equipment requirements between the two races. Tyrell Seavey was Scdoris's visual interpreter for the race, with responsibility for reporting obstacles to Scdoris at about the same time that they would be perceived by a person with 20/20 vision. Scdoris received no other assistance. She recalled to Bryson, "Tyrell yelled back once that there was a creek coming, and I was like, 'What? . . .' And the next thing you know my foot was in a creek. And I'm like, 'Oh, OK, creek!' But it was just like 2 ½ feet wide, and it wasn't a big deal." Scdoris placed 26th out of 30 competing mushers.

While training for the 33d Iditarod Trail Sled Dog Race, Scdoris and her visual interpreter Paul Ellering spent February with a host family in Willow, Alaska. With 16 dogs each on their sled teams, Scdoris and Ellering confronted what was considered to be one of the harshest trails in the race's history. Some sections were covered in deep, soft snow, and the winds blew at 40 to 50 miles per hour at the Yukon River. "There are times when I'm out there and I think, man . . . I wish I could see what's going on around here. But, you know, I don't know any different and . . . this is what I have so I'm gonna use it," Scdoris said when interviewed on ABC's World News Tonight with Peter Jennings on March 11, 2005, the date she was named as that program's Person of the Week.

Of the 79 competitors who started the Iditarod, Scdoris was the 14th musher to withdraw, leaving the race at the Eagle Island checkpoint—402 miles from the finish line in Nome, Alaska—after 118 hours and 14 minutes on the trail. "I was so disappointed and shed a lot of tears," Scdoris said, as quoted by the Associated Press State & Local Wire (March 18, 2005). According to Roy Gault, writing for the Statesman Journal (March 18, 2005), Scdoris told her agent, Paul Herschell, "It definitely hurts to have come so far not to reach Nome, but my dogs showed signs of getting sick, I knew we shouldn't go on. But this is only the beginning, definitely not the end. One day I will pass under the burled arch of Nome." Scdoris had left several sick dogs behind at prior checkpoints before reaching Eagle Island. Infection is one of the dangers of being toward the back of the pack in a dogsled race; as many as 1,200 dogs may have passed through an area in just a few hours or days, sometimes leaving those at the end exposed to high risk of infection. Scdoris's dogs "were showing signs of sickness, diarrhea, not wanting to take any food, and with that are some concerns about dehydration," as Amber Lindsey, a spokesperson for Scdoris's main sponsor, Standard Insurance, said to Roy Gault. "After careful consideration, Rachael made the difficult decision to scratch based on the well-being of her dogs, putting their needs before her own personal ambitions." Robert Sørlie of Norway had already claimed first place in the Iditarod a little over three hours before Scdoris's withdrawal from the race; Scdoris's team placed 66th. Reflecting later on her performance, Scdoris told a reporter for the Associated Press (June 24, 2005), "I made it through the tough stuff."

In addition to running and dogsledding, Rachael Scdoris has worked as a model (her image has appeared on packages of Atta Boy dog food) and public speaker. She sings with her church choir. "Rachael is wise beyond her years, very fun, very optimistic about life, and she certainly could have a much different attitude," Becki Timson said to the Statesman Journal. "She doesn't consider what she has to be a disability or a handicap. She considers being normally sighted rather overrated." Scdoris's hectic schedule keeps her too busy for dating. "Dad doesn't have to worry about keeping the boys away from me. I don't have time," Scdoris told the Statesman Journal. "I've always been one of those girls who have a lot of friends who are guys, but not guys who are boy friends." The Women's Sports Foundation, based in New York City, twice named Scdoris among the top female athletes in the U.S.

—L.J.

Suggested Reading: Anchorage Daily News D p1 Feb. 27, 2005; Associated Press State & Local Wire Mar. 18, 2005; (Salem, Oregon) Statesman Journal A p1 Mar 18, 2005; Steber, Rick. No End in Sight, 2005

Schjeldahl, Peter

(shell-doll)

Mar. 20, 1942– Art critic

Address: The New Yorker, 4 Times Sq., New York, NY 10036-6592

"If there is a genuinely influential voice in art criticism in America today, it would almost certainly be that of Peter Schjeldahl," David Clemmer wrote for the Santa Fe New Mexican (August 20, 2004). Schjeldahl, who has written about art for a variety of publications for over three decades and has been the New Yorker's art critic since 1998, is known for being an anti-academic, a self-educated enthusiast who believes that art is not the domain of the elite but a potential source of enjoyment and inspiration for all. He has often expressed his disdain for what he considers dry academic writing and tries to make his own reviews comprehensible and engaging. "I don't regard myself as in some way special among people who look at art," Schjeldahl told Mary Flinn, Susan Glasser, and Howard Risatti for Blackbird magazine (Spring 2004, on-line). "I'm special in that I remember my experience and can analyze and express it. That's my professional specialty, and if everybody could do that I wouldn't get paid nearly as much as I do. But in general I think I'm just another art lover with more time and leisure." That he has been able to make a living as an art critic is, Schjeldahl told Flinn, Glasser, and Risatti, "a great luxury and a stroke of luck."

Courtesy of Ada Calhoun

Peter Schjeldahl

Peter Schjeldahl was born on March 20, 1942 in Fargo, North Dakota. His family moved frequently, and he was raised in a succession of small towns in Minnesota. He attended Carlton College, in Northfield, Minnesota, leaving without earning a degree and working his way east as a reporter. He later enrolled at the New School, in New York City, from which he did not graduate; he has since described himself as a quintessential 1960s college dropout. In 1964 he traveled to Paris, France, where he hoped to earn a reputation as a surrealist poet—only to discover that the movement had peaked decades earlier. Still, he benefited from his time abroad, receiving an informal education and experiencing an epiphany with regard to the direction he wanted his life to take. Later, as a young man in New York, Schjeldahl "got to hang around artists and drink with artists and eat with artists and sleep with artists," as he explained to George Plimpton for the *New Yorker* (June 3, 2002, online). "I think I became a critic just because I was in awe of artists, and I wanted to worship at their shrine." Schjeldahl recalled that after seeing a painting by the Italian Renaissance artist Piero della Francesca in Italy and a show by the American artist Andy Warhol at the Sonnabend Gallery in Paris, he realized that art was the most important thing in his life and that he wanted always to be associated with it.

In 1965 Schjeldahl returned to New York City, where he has lived since. There, he wrote art criticism for publications including *ArtForum*, the *New York Times*, *Art in America*, *Vogue*, and *Vanity Fair*. (In the early 1970s, he briefly wrote movie reviews for the *New York Times*.) In 1980 he was hired as an art critic for the *Village Voice*, where

he remained for 18 years. During that time he also contributed criticism to *Seven Days* magazine. In October 1998, after leaving the *Voice*, he became a staff writer and regular art critic for the *New Yorker*. When he began his career as a critic, Schjeldahl said to George Plimpton, he would contact each artist he wrote about, to learn about his or her background, "but then I realized that the only good that did was to prove to me that those things were finally irrelevant, or just in the nature of guidelines. The work has to stand on its own."

Schjeldahl has said that he does not try to force his own opinions about art onto readers; neither does he advocate elitist attitudes toward art appreciation. "I regard opinions as, in a way, the least interesting aspect of criticism but one of the most essential," he told David Clemmer. "You want a judgment when you read a great criticism, not just someone showing how cute and clever they are. That's part of the social contract. . . . You read good critics to get a voice in your head to argue with or agree with and discuss with." Moreover, Schjeldahl is unafraid of changing his own opinion about artists or their works, as he told George Plimpton. He recently admitted, for instance, that he has begun to like some paintings by Lucian Freud, in spite of having previously dismissed Freud with a "pretty thorough hatchet job," as he said to Plimpton. (In the same interview, he said, "Taste is the residue of our previous experience, and if we are presented with something that doesn't fit we immediately try to reject it.") As Schjeldahl explained to Flinn, Glasser, and Risatti, he keeps his readers foremost in his mind while writing: "I have a one hundred percent responsibility to readers. That is, that they know that they're getting the straight stuff from me—that I don't have an agenda, or if I do that it's spelled out at the top of the piece."

Despite the fact that Schjeldahl is a frequent lecturer and has taught courses at Harvard University, in Cambridge, Massachusetts, where he is a faculty member in the Department of Visual and Environmental Studies, he has long expressed a disdain for academia. Whereas he sees criticism as a journey, often discovering that his opinions have changed just in the course of writing a review, Schjeldahl told Flinn, Glasser, and Risatti, "I think the definition of the academic . . . is that you start from the answer and work back and frame the question. Academic anything devotes all of its energy to secondary matters. The primary matters are already assumed, established, and then it becomes a quibble about secondary things. It's like an academic painting—the foot is drawn great, but you're not interested in the person with the foot." In his conversation with David Clemmer, he further clarified his distaste for what he deemed "academic art," saying, "Academic art shifts emphasis from what is being done to how it's being done. . . . I think of academic art as answers that have forgotten their questions." Schjeldahl, for his part, attempts to write in a style that is accessible and appealing. "If people don't want to read me, I starve—there are no rewards in being obscure or abstruse or over-bearing for me," he told Flinn, Glasser, and Risatti.

While Schjeldahl is not known for writing scath-ing reviews, he has displayed no reservations about attacking particular practices in art of which he disapproves. In his interview with Flinn, Glasser, and Risatti, he expressed relief that what he called the "P.C. [politically correct] juggernaut" of the 1990s has passed and that museum curators seem to have decreased their efforts to make exhib-its educational; such exhibits, he said, were "di-rected to what I think of as the I.S.V., the incredibly stupid viewer." Other sources of annoyance for Schjeldahl are museum installations that are inad-equately constructed (for example, those in which paintings are not properly lit or are hung too high) or overly elaborate (packed with distracting com-ponents or obstructed by labels and information cards).

Schjeldahl himself was given the opportunity to curate the 10th annual Navy Pier Walk sculpture installation in Chicago, Illinois. He selected the works for inclusion in the May 2004 event and su-pervised their placement, aiming to incorporate a variety of pieces that were surprising and struck him with their "crowd-friendliness," as he told Kevin Nance for the *Chicago Sun-Times* (May 4, 2004). Each sculpture he chose was, he felt, "some-thing that anticipates being looked at, something that encourages an approach, rather than some-thing that stands off to be beheld. . . . Certainly I don't want stuff up on pedestals. That's for court-houses." The experience was an unusual and en-joyable one for Schjeldahl. "I've been pretty strict-ly a critic, but darn, I love to play with the stuff," he told Mike Ramsey for Copley News Service (May 5, 2004). "I envy curators who get to say, 'Put that there.' It's fun." Schjeldahl curated the 2005 Navy Pier Walk sculpture exhibit, too. He told Doug George for the *Chicago Tribune* (June 17, 2005) that in choosing works for the show, he looked for those that were "fun to look at," in George's words, and sturdy enough to remain standing in high winds. "There's no secret agen-da," Schjeldahl told George. "Does art need to 'im-prove' people? No, I don't think it does."

In addition to writing reviews, lecturing, and teaching seminars at Harvard, Schjeldahl has penned a number of books, including *White Coun-try: Poems* (1968); *Since 1964: New and Selected Poems* (1978); *Erich Fischl* (1989); *De Kooning and Dubuffet: The Late Works* (1993); and *Columns and Catalogues* (1994). He has co-authored or co-edited several other volumes, among them *The Hydrogen Jukebox: Selected Writings of Peter Schjeldahl, 1978-1990* (with Malin Wilson, 1991); *Myths & Magical Fantasies* (with Reesey Shaw, 1996); and *The Inward Eye: Transcendence in Contemporary Art* (with Lynn M. Herbert and Klaus Ottman, 2002). Schjeldahl has received the Frank Jewett Mather Award of the College Art Association for Excellence in Art Criticism as well as a grant from the John Simon Guggenheim Memorial Founda-tion.

Schjeldahl is married to Brooke Alderson, a for-mer actress and the owner of Brooke's Variety, an antiques shop in Andes, New York. In another ex-ample of Schjeldahl's willingness to amend his opinions, he has recalled that when he and Alder-son met, they disliked each other instantly. They have now been married for more than 30 years. The couple have a daughter, Ada Calhoun, a writer and associate editor of the Web site Nerve.com. When pressed, Schjeldahl has named Rembrandt and Di-ego Velázquez as his favorite artists.

—K.J.E.

Suggested Reading: *Blackbird* (on-line) Spring 2004; Copley News Service May 5, 2004; *New Yorker* (on-line) June 3, 2002; *Santa Fe New Mexican* P p50 Aug. 20, 2004

Selected Books: Poetry—*White Country: Poems*, 1968; *An Adventure of the Thought Police*, 1971; *Since 1964: New and Selected Poems*, 1978; Nonfiction—*Richard Deacon*, 1983; *Art of Our Time (Saatchi Collection)* (with Hilton Kramer, Robert Rosenblum, and Robert Rosemblum), 1984; *Salle*, 1987; *Erich Fischl*, 1989; *The Seven Days Art Columns 1988-1990*, 1990; *The Hydrogen Jukebox: Selected Writings of Peter Schjeldahl, 1978-1990* (with Malin Wilson), 1991; *The Books of Anselm Kiefer 1969-1990* (with Gotz Adriani, Zdenik Felix, and Tony Stooss), 1991; *De Kooning and Dubuffet: The Late Works*, 1993; *Jean Dubuffet 1943-1963: Paintings Sculptures Assemblages* (with James T. Demetrion, Susan J. Cooke, and Jean Planque), 1993; *Columns and Catalogues*, 1994; *Myths & Magical Fantasies* (with Reesey Shaw), 1996; *The Symbolist Prints of Edvard Munch: The Vivian and David Campbell Collection* (with Elizabeth Prelinger and Michael Parke-Taylor), 1996; *Liza Lou: Essays by Peter Schjeldahl & Marcia Tucker* (with Noriko Gamblin), 1997; *Willem De Kooning: Drawings and Sculpture*, 1999; *Same Body, Different Day* (with Gary Stephan), 1999; *The Inward Eye: Transcendence in Contemporary Art* (with Lynn M. Herbert and Klaus Ottman), 2002; *Shards: Garth Clark on Ceramic Art* (with Garth Clark, John Pagliaro, and Ed Lebow), 2003

Schoenberg, Loren

July 23, 1958– Saxophonist; jazz historian

Address: c/o National Jazz Museum in Harlem, 104 E. 126th St., Suite 2D, New York, NY 10035

"Some people say to me, 'You should have been born fifty years earlier,'" the jazz historian and sax-ophonist Loren Schoenberg told John Robert Brown in an interview posted on the Web site of

Courtesy of Loren Schoenberg/The Jazz Museum in Harlem

Loren Schoenberg

the National Jazz Museum in Harlem. "Of course I would have grown up to the great music of Benny Goodman and Artie Shaw. And I'd have probably spent my life interviewing the widow of Scott Joplin!" Schoenberg has become a fixture in the jazz world because of his encyclopedic knowledge of the genre and passion for preserving its past. During the popular resurgence of jazz in the 1990s, Schoenberg played a significant role in reintroducing the public to the classic jazz music of the 1930s, '40s, and '50s. In addition to his activities as a performer, conductor, teacher, and writer, Schoenberg is the executive director of the National Jazz Museum in Harlem, which does not yet have a permanent home.

The youngest of three brothers, Loren Schoenberg was born on July 23, 1958 in Fairlawn, New Jersey. His father worked for the New York Telephone Co., which later merged with AT&T. His mother, a children's librarian, began teaching Loren the piano when he was three. A year later she hired a neighborhood piano teacher to take her son beyond the simple scales he had readily mastered. In an interview for the Jerry Jazz Musician Web site (September 9, 2002), Schoenberg recalled hearing Louis Armstrong perform on television, on *The Ed Sullivan Show*, when he was five or six years old. He also enjoyed listening to his father's Al Jolson records. Jolson (1888–1950), who made his name by singing in blackface, was the star of *The Jazz Singer* (1927), the first major film to have sound. "I didn't know anything about blackface or Jolson," Schoenberg told the Jerry Jazz Musician interviewer, "all I knew is that my father loved these records. I used to alternately play them and use them as frisbees. The records, as a result, didn't last long."

While growing up, Schoenberg loved old movies; he particularly enjoyed those featuring the legendary clarinetist Benny Goodman. Goodman (1909–86) was one of the first significant white jazz performers and bandleaders. (The genre originated with African-American musicians.) As a white man, Goodman was perfectly placed to bring the style into the American mainstream without the hindrance of racism. As a result of his musical fame, Goodman appeared in several films in the 1930s and '40s (among them *Hollywood Hotel*, *The Powers Girl*, *Stage Door Canteen*, and *The Gang's All Here*) that many aficionados remember mainly for their soundtracks rather than their overall quality. While watching those movies during the 1970s, Schoenberg became enamored of the music. Jazz's heyday as a popular form was over by then; while Schoenberg was borrowing from his local library and collecting classic 78 rpm records by such jazz originators as Louis Armstrong, Jelly Roll Morton, and Thomas "Fats" Waller, most of his peers were listening to rock music. "I never did like what was known as 'rock and roll,'" he said during his interview for the Jerry Jazz Musician Web site. "My relationship with it ended in 1961, when at age three, I won a Twist contest on my block. That was it."

Jazz, a largely improvisational musical style that evolved from blues, gospel, and ragtime music in the 1910s, surged to mainstream popularity in the 1930s, becoming an American institution and an international phenomenon. Scholars disagree about how to define the genre. In his book, *The NPR Curious Listener's Guide to Jazz* (2002), Schoenberg wrote: "What makes Jazz music different from country, classical, rock, and other well-known genres is its basic malleability. . . . The great majority of it is not, as many believe, spun out of the air, but is rather a highly organized and (hopefully) spontaneous set of theme and variations." In its classic form, jazz pieces alternate between sections in which ensembles play, and improvised solos that elaborate on the theme. Beginning in the 1950s, increasingly avant-garde experimentation spawned countless styles and variations that are now difficult to classify and distinguish.

By the time Schoenberg discovered jazz, many of its greatest practitioners had fallen from the spotlight and were struggling to get gigs. Consequently, he had opportunities to attend performances given by those musicians in humble venues near his home. He talked to the performers afterward and was occasionally invited to demonstrate his own pianistic skills for his idols, who were impressed that someone as young as Schoenberg was interested in jazz. In that way Schoenberg received informal piano lessons from Teddy Wilson and Hank Jones, master jazz pianists. Wilson at one point brought his young protégé to a jazz performance at the Waldorf-Astoria hotel, where Schoenberg met Benny Goodman.

In 1972 Schoenberg began volunteering at the now-defunct Jazz Museum in New York City; he thereby met more musicians and grew increasingly involved in the jazz scene. As a volunteer, Schoenberg, at the urging of the cornetist Ruby Braff, met the respected piano and music-theory teacher Sanford Gold, who strengthened and broadened Schoenberg's musical foundations through his lessons. The teenager met Benny Goodman again while working on a Goodman exhibit mounted at the museum. Later, two producers from the radio station WBAI who were researching an upcoming show on jazz were referred to Schoenberg as the local jazz expert. They brought Schoenberg on the air for an interview, and he enjoyed the experience so much that he produced two more shows for WBAI, in which he interviewed several well-known jazz musicians. At 15, inspired by the jazz saxophonist Lester Young, he began to teach himself how to play the saxophone.

In 1976 Schoenberg gained admittance to the prestigious Manhattan School of Music, in New York City, as a music-theory major, with a minor in piano. While he was a student there, Schoenberg got a job playing the saxophone in Eddie Durham's jazz quartet. "I'd been jamming, sitting in and waiting for an opportunity," Schoenberg told *Current Biography*. "I was the only young guy interested in these great old jazz players at the time. . . . They were happy to have somebody who knew all the old songs." His collaboration with Durham, one of the original members of the Count Basie Band, led to opportunities for Schoenberg to meet and work with such jazz musicians as the guitarist Al Casey, the saxophonist and clarinetist Eddie Barefield, and the drummers Jo Jones and Panama Francis. After two years at the Manhattan School of Music, Schoenberg switched his major to saxophone. That year he produced a Charlie Parker and Lester Young tribute at Carnegie Hall, in New York City, arranging the songs and gathering and performing with the musicians. "I got my first review in the *New York Times* with that concert," he told *Current Biography*.

In 1980 Schoenberg received an unexpected call from Benny Goodman, who told him that he intended to donate his collection of jazz arrangements to the New York Public Library. Schoenberg, known around the jazz world as a history buff and an expert on Goodman's music, seemed the logical choice to assemble the archive and write whatever explanatory material was necessary. Schoenberg left the Manhattan School of Music to work on the collection, which was to be given to the library in yearly installments. Goodman discontinued the donations after a few years; meanwhile, he had hired Schoenberg as his assistant. Later, Schoenberg became his personal and business manager.

Schoenberg had by then formed the Loren Schoenberg Big Band, a group devoted to performing the more obscure classics of the 1930s, '40s, and '50s. (The band later performed new works as well.) Big bands, the jazz equivalent of a symphony orchestra, had fallen out of favor in the 1950s and '60s due to the high cost of maintaining so many musicians. Schoenberg faced the same problem, and the situation was compounded because jazz was far less popular than it had been in the heyday of big bands. "It was difficult to keep the guys together because there was really no work," he told Stuart Troup for *Newsday* (May 26, 1989). "We would spend ten months rehearsing and have a one-night gig." Eventually, the skill of the performers and the quality of the arrangements enabled the group to overcome some obstacles, and Schoenberg's band began to find work. The group won over jazz critics with its musicality and deft handling of the classics. Years later the jazz critic Peter Watrous wrote for the *New York Times* (July 14, 1994), in a review of a performance by Schoenberg's band at the Village Vanguard, in New York City, "Mr. Schoenberg . . . knows exactly how to calibrate his orchestra. . . . The band crackled with energy and intelligence and never once raised its voice without reason." The band also performed at many other notable venues, including Blue Note, Michael's Pub, and Carnegie Hall.

For about eight years beginning in 1982, Schoenberg hosted a weekly radio show on WKCR, playing old jazz recordings, interviewing musicians, producing documentary specials, and broadcasting live performances. In 1984 he became a co-host of *Jazz from the Archives*, a radio program on WBGO emanating from the Institute of Jazz Studies at Rutgers University, in New Jersey; he continues to participate occasionally as one of several hosts on the program. Also in 1984 the Loren Schoenberg Big Band released its first album, *That's the Way It Goes*. The band went on to release *Time Waits for No One* (1987), *Solid Ground* (1988), *Just A-Settin' and A-Rockin'* (1989), *Manhattan Work Song* (1992), and *Out of This World* (1999). Schoenberg recorded *S'posin'* in 1990 with a quartet and has recorded with many other jazz musicians, among them the pianist John Lewis and the saxophonists Benny Carter and Jimmy Heath.

In 1985 Schoenberg's band formed an association with the New York Swing Dance Society and began playing at the organization's dance events all over New York City. Until then Benny Goodman had shown little interest in hearing the Loren Schoenberg Big Band. "It was frustrating," Schoenberg told John McDonough for the *Chicago Tribune* (April 2, 1989). "He didn't think of me as a working musician." Despite frequent hinting by Schoenberg, Goodman had never asked to attend a rehearsal or listen to the band's first record. Then, to Schoenberg's surprise and delight, Goodman asked the band to perform with him on a 1985 PBS television special, *Let's Dance*, which turned out to be Goodman's last televised performance. In describing the group's first rehearsal with Goodman, Schoenberg told McDonough that his knees shook when his mentor walked through the door at RCA carrying his clarinet. "Benny Goodman was going to play with my band," he recalled. "He could have had any band in the world he wanted, with any players. Money was no object. But this was the band he picked. I had to sit down."

Goodman died on June 13, 1986; his will stipulated that all his remaining jazz arrangements and recordings be donated to Yale University, in New Haven, Connecticut. Schoenberg appraised the Goodman Archives, and Yale later hired him to help curate the collection and to compile a 10-CD set of never-before-released Goodman recordings. Also in 1986 Schoenberg joined the American Jazz Orchestra, with which he remained until 1992, playing tenor sax and later acting as its musical director. Besides the American Jazz Orchestra, he has conducted the Lincoln Center Jazz Orchestra and the Smithsonian Jazz Masterworks Orchestra. In 1988 and 1989 Schoenberg conducted the West German Radio Orchestra for performances of works by George Gershwin and Duke Ellington in a concert series for audiences in Cologne, Germany. Also during that period, with the drummer and band leader Mel Lewis, he led a band organized by the third-stream jazz great Gunther Schuller in Japan. (Third-stream jazz, pioneered by Schuller, sought to meld jazz with classical music; in *The NPR Curious Listener's Guide*, Schoenberg identified it as an important precursor to world music.)

Schoenberg was the musical director for the 1993 International Duke Ellington Conference. In 1994, together with Dan Morgenstern, he won a Grammy Award for best album notes for the text accompanying *Louis Armstrong: Portrait of the Artist as a Young Man 1923–1934*, a boxed set of rare and essential Armstrong recordings. In 1997 the cabaret legend Bobby Short hired Schoenberg as his musical director and saxophonist; since then Schoenberg has performed with Short and his band 19 or 20 weeks out of the year at the Carlyle Hotel, in New York City. In September 1998, during the presidency of Bill Clinton, Schoenberg participated in a televised jazz special filmed at the White House, along with the trumpeter Wynton Marsalis, the pianists Marian McPartland and Billy Taylor, and the multi-instrumentalist David N. Baker Jr. Schoenberg played his sax and spoke about the long history of jazz. (Clinton is an amateur saxophone player; he played the instrument solo on TV, on the *Arsenio Hall Show,* during his 1992 presidential campaign.)

In 2001 the well-known documentary filmmaker Ken Burns recruited Schoenberg as an adviser for his ambitious Jazz Project, which culminated in a 10-installment series about the genre that aired to general acclaim on public television; the series later became available as a 10-DVD boxed set. Also that year Schoenberg became a host on Swing, a station broadcast on the fee-for-service Sirius satellite radio. Schoenberg records weekly segments for the station.

In 2002 Schoenberg was appointed executive director of the proposed National Jazz Museum in Harlem. "It's very clear that this is an idea whose time has come," he told John Robert Brown in an interview posted on the museum's Web site. "It's long overdue. America does not have a first class jazz museum in a major city." Leonard Garment, an adviser to President Richard Nixon and now president of the museum's board of directors, secured for the project a $1 million grant from the U.S. Congress in 2000, but much more money will be needed before the museum can become a reality. "The museum must be deeply rooted in the Harlem community," Schoenberg told Brown. "A museum like this will only succeed if there is a perception that it comes from the community and it receives support from the community leaders, and all the others in the locality, who have everything to gain from this. Harlem has been an incredible cradle for jazz. Importantly, it continues to be." In June 2003 Schoenberg and his National Jazz Museum in Harlem All-Stars band performed at the White House to raise awareness of the museum project. The band's guest performer was the 92-year-old baritone Herb Jeffries, an original member of the Duke Ellington Orchestra. After the performance, President George W. Bush declared June to be Black Music Month.

Schoenberg's big band continues to perform occasionally, though merely as "a labor of love," as Schoenberg told *Current Biography*. Schoenberg is on the faculty of the Institute for Jazz Studies at the Juilliard School of Music, in New York City; the Juilliard Evening School; Jazz at Lincoln Center's Jazz 101 series; and the Essentially Ellington Band Director Academy in Snowmass, Colorado. Schoenberg is also the program director of the Jazz Aspen Snowmass Academy Summer Session. He has taught at the New School, in New York City, and the Manhattan School of Music. In addition, he has given lectures at the Metropolitan Museum of Art and at Lincoln Center.

Schoenberg has written widely on jazz. His articles have appeared in the *New York Times*, *The Lester Young Reader*, and *The Oxford Companion to Jazz*, among other publications. Schoenberg's book, *The NPR Curious Listener's Guide to Jazz*, contains an introduction by Wynton Marsalis.

When the Jerry Jazz Musician interviewer asked him, "As consumption of jazz music continues to fade, how does it remain relevant to the culture?," Schoenberg responded, "That's a good question. I think I have a good answer. I teach, and one of the best things about teaching is that I come in contact with many of the best young players who migrate to New York, and I encounter players from other places too. These young players are making jazz relevant. . . . There is an alto saxophone player named Kris Bauman, and another, Dayna Stephens, both of whom are among the most thrilling improvisers I have ever heard in person. So yes, jazz will remain relevant. Is it ever going to be what it was? No. It may be something better, it may be something worse." In response to the interviewer's question, "If you could choose an event in jazz history that you could have attended, what would it be?," Schoenberg answered, "I guess if there was one place I could be it would be at the famous jam session in Kansas City in late 1933 with Coleman Hawkins and Lester Young. That is where I would want to go, because, first of all, we don't know what Lester Young sounded like as a young man. He didn't make his first record until he was 28, and I would love to have heard him at 20 or 24, to see how he evolved. To hear him play that night, through the night and into the morning, exhausting himself with Coleman Hawkins, is where I would wish to be."

Schoenberg lives in Riverdale, a section of the New York City borough of the Bronx.

—D.M.

Suggested Reading: *Chicago Tribune* p22 Apr. 22, 1989; Loren Schoenberg Web site; *New York Times* C p2 Sep. 14, 1988, C p12 July 14, 1994; *Newsday* p12 May 26, 1989

Selected Recordings: *That's the Way It Goes*, 1984; *Time Waits for No One*, 1987; *Solid Ground*, 1988; *Just A-Settin' and A-Rockin'*, 1989; *S'Posin'*, 1990; *Manhattan Work Song*, 1992; *Out of This World*, 1999

Selected Books: *The NPR Curious Listener's Guide to Jazz*, 2002

Todd Webster, courtesy of *The Ed Schultz Show*

Schultz, Ed

Jan. 1955– Radio talk-show host

Address: c/o Jones International Ltd., 9697 E. Mineral Ave., Centennial, CO 80112

As quoted by Roberta T. Vowell in the Norfolk *Virginian-Pilot* (March 13, 2004), the radio host Ed Schultz has described himself as a "gun-totin', red-meat-eatin' liberal." Schultz also opposes abortion and has been known to criticize his fellow Democrats, primarily for what he sees as their inability to connect with common folk. Given those stances, it is perhaps unsurprising that the former football player and sportscaster was once an outspoken, conservative Republican. It was after meeting the woman who would become his wife, the former

Wendy Noack, a psychiatric nurse and the operator of a shelter for the homeless, that Schultz reconsidered some of his opinions and began to refer to himself as a populist and a progressive. However one chooses to label him, the more than 15 million listeners of his talk-radio program, *The Ed Schultz Show*, seem to appreciate his message. "Ed is a rare talent who has tremendous appeal to all Americans," Tim Athans, the chief executive of the nonprofit group Democracy Radio, told a reporter for PR Newswire (January 7, 2005). "Americans got sick and tired of the same stale diet of right-wing malcontents who used to dominate radio. Ed Schultz represents a new dawn for progressive talk radio." "My listener is the working stiff," Schultz himself explained in his 2004 book, *Straight Talk from the Heartland*, as quoted on the American Progress Action Fund Web site. "Joe Six Pack. The mother who scrounges loose change because, when gas rises above $2 and milk is over four, she's in a pinch. Life on Wall Street is great, but it's life on Main Street that people are concerned about. My people have grease on their hands, sweat on their backs, and damn little to show for it."

The son of George and Mary Schultz, Ed Schultz was born in January 1955 and grew up in the Larchmont district of Norfolk, Virginia. He attended Larchmont Elementary School, Blair Junior High School, and Maury High School, from which he graduated in 1972. A large, muscular redhead, Schultz soon earned the nicknames Big Ed and Big Eddie. While in high school Schultz decided that his future lay in football, and by his senior year, he had become quarterback and captain of Maury's team, the Commodores. One of his high-school friends, Roy Gibbs, recalled to Roberta T. Vowell that Schultz "was not a natural athlete, but he was a grinder. He was real driven. He always had an idea he was going to be somebody, and he'd work as hard as it took to get there." Even as a teen, Schultz clearly had a mind of his own. "He wanted to wear white shoes, like [the legendary New York Jets quarterback] Joe Namath," another friend, Mark Ballard, told Vowell. "But [the] coach allowed only black high-top cleats. So Eddie covered his black cleats with white tape. He was the kind of a guy who wanted to march to his own beat, no matter what anybody thought." Schultz attended Moorhead State University (now Minnesota State University at Moorhead), where, as a quarterback, he was the passing champion in the National Collegiate Athletic Association's Division II in 1977. Schultz was then drafted as a free agent by the Oakland Raiders. He also played half a season with the Winnipeg Blue Bombers of Canada's professional football league and, later, earned a chance to try out for the New York Jets. To his disappointment, he did not make the team.

Schultz turned next to radio. He began his career in the late 1970s in Fargo, North Dakota, then relocated briefly to Texas before returning north, to become what Stephanie Simon described in the *Los Angeles Times* (February 5, 2004) as a "much-loved (and much-hated) sportscaster famed for his raucous play-by-play of North Dakota college football." During his 15 years in that capacity, Schultz was known for both his enthusiasm and his belligerence; one on occasion, after a rowdy fan at a 1988 football game threw a whiskey bottle into the broadcast booth, Schultz, enraged and cursing, pushed through the crowd, nearly starting a fight. (Following "The Bottle Incident," as it became known, Schultz was suspended.)

In 1992, feeling the need for a change, Schultz launched a daily two-and-a-half-hour regional talk show, *News and Views*, on station KFGO. For the first couple of years, Schultz's show had a decidedly conservative bent; as he explained to Stephanie Simon, "I lined up with the Republicans because they were antitax, and I wanted to make a lot of money." As host, Schultz frequently berated the three Democrats who represented his state in Congress, dubbing them the Three Stooges, and as Stephanie Simon reported, he even chided the homeless for complaining about the cold, saying, "How about getting a job?" Then, in 1998, he met a psychiatric nurse, Wendy Noack, at a party. Schultz promptly asked Noack on a lunch date, which she accepted, on one condition: they would have to meet at the Salvation Army cafeteria next to the homeless shelter where she worked. "You should have seen [Schultz's] face as he was moving along the line with his tray, getting his bologna sandwich and his cup of Campbell's soup. He was appalled," Noack recalled to Stephanie Simon. One of the homeless men at the cafeteria recognized Schultz from a televised sportscast and struck up a conversation. Schultz, who had entered the cafeteria feeling pleased with himself, having recently signed a 10-year contract with Clear Channel Radio, "left feeling pretty small . . . ," as he wrote in his book, *Straight Talk from the Heartland.* "More than once on the air I'd lambasted the homeless as lazy and the unemployed as freeloaders. In that moment [at the cafeteria], guilt swamped me. I got a lump in my throat, and it wasn't the baloney." When some of the homeless

men in the cafeteria began praising his radio show, "their adulation embarrassed me further," Schultz wrote. "I didn't see it then, but that Big Eddie was fading away. A baloney sandwich, a lovely blonde with wise eyes, and a group of straggly-haired homeless men: This reality check changed everything." Over the course of their next few dates, Schultz and Noack discussed the homeless people at the shelter, and Schultz reconsidered his attitudes, which began to seem to him overly simplistic.

After Schultz and Noack married, they took a road trip in their 38-foot Winnebago (nicknamed "the Big Eddie Cruiser"), with Schultz broadcasting his radio show from small towns and ranches across North Dakota. During that 2001 trip Schultz had numerous opportunities to talk with small-town residents, encounters that exposed him further to poverty and suffering and gave him a new perspective on life in the U.S. "I heard about what people are really concerned about," he told Roberta T. Vowell. "The kitchen table issues: the struggle on family farms; the under-funding of schools; the lack of support for [veterans], which leads to homelessness; the risks of being uninsured; and the rising costs of health insurance for those who can even get insurance." At around the same time, he got first-hand experience with the difficulties of dealing with the Medicare system, as his mother succumbed to Alzheimer's disease. Schultz decided that he had a new message to convey on the radio, one that would focus attention on "the little guys," the ordinary men and women who, he felt, had been alternately ignored and misrepresented by prominent right-wing figures—including himself. Feeling that the Democratic Party had more to offer the average person, Schultz switched his political affiliation. He explained his decision in a nationally televised interview for the show *Topic A with Tina Brown* (January 23, 2005): "I think that to have a strong country, you've got to have four strong pillars. You've got to defend the country, you've got to educate the country, you've got to feed the country, and you've got to have strong fiscal policy. And I think that the neocon agenda in America has shaken the foundation of this country. All four of those pillars have been shaken by this hard right move that this country's taken."

While Schultz now leans to the left of center rather than to the right, he considers himself a moderate liberal. He is opposed to abortion, though he refrains from discussing that topic on the air; he is an unapologetic gun owner and hunter; and he publicly stated his opinion that U.S. senator John Kerry of Massachusetts was a terrible choice as the 2004 Democratic presidential nominee, in part for reasons he mentioned during an interview with Howard Kurtz for the *Washington Post* (January 10, 2005). "The righties connect with Joe Beercan better than the Democrats do," Schultz said—that is, Republicans have gotten their message across to average citizens more effectively than have Democrats. His criticism of his new party, he maintains, is constructive—and delivered with a sense of humor, which, he has suggested, more liberals should cultivate.

The nationally syndicated, daily radio program *The Ed Schultz Show* debuted on January 5, 2004. The show was developed with the help of $1.8 million from Democracy Radio, a New York–based nonprofit group headed by Tom Athans, the husband of Democratic U.S. senator Debbie Stabenow of Michigan. Though the program was initially broadcast to only a handful of stations (different sources report the number as low as two and as high as 30), Schultz quickly increased his listenership, including among his first guests such prominent liberals as former U.S. Senate minority leader Tom Daschle of South Dakota and Senator Dianne Feinstein of California. By the end of the year, 80 stations had begun carrying *The Ed Schultz Show.* "A year ago they were laughing at us," Schultz told Howard Kurtz. "I knew I had the talent and could get the job done. I didn't believe what the industry was saying, that liberal talk radio couldn't make it." Schultz maintained in his interview with Tina Brown that political content alone did not account for his show's success: "Well, you can't run a radio show based on ideology. It has to have all the elements of a good show. It's got to be entertaining, it's got to have pace, it's got to have personality, activity, communication, entertainment. You lose any of those elements, you're not going to have a good radio show. It just so happens that I'm a progressive and a liberal and my point of view is attracting a whole new listenership to commercial talk radio, and that's the mission and we're finding a niche." According to Joel Connelly, writing for the *Seattle Post-Intelligencer* (February 2, 2005), Schultz has succeeded because, "unlike some super-serious liberals, Schultz has a sense of humor, and knows how to inform *and* entertain." For the same article, the radio host John Carlson offered another explanation for Schultz's prominence in the field: "Schultz is the most interesting of the liberal talkers because he's a former Republican and is running against the trend of left-of-center people moving rightward as they (and their kids) age." Schultz told Dick Kreck for the *Denver Post* (February 14, 2005), "I don't screen my calls. I don't run manufactured radio. People appreciate that they can get in, despite what their take might be."

Also in 2004 Schultz's book, *Straight Talk from the Heartland*, was published to primarily positive reviews. In an assessment for the *Grand Forks Herald* (November 21, 2004), Mike Jacobs, who admitted to not getting along with Schultz personally, praised the book as "an incisive analysis of what's wrong with the Bush administration's approach to public policy. And it's not a pointy-headed attack, either. It's delivered in hard-hitting, easy to understand segments."

In January 2005, after Schultz's show debuted on the Washington, D.C., station WRC, Schultz decided to broadcast alternately from the nation's capital and Fargo. Later in 2005 Schultz found himself butting heads with the American Forces Radio and Television Service network, which he claimed had agreed to broadcast his show to soldiers stationed overseas beginning in mid-October. Then, on October 17, Schultz's producer learned from Allison Barber, a deputy assistant secretary of defense, that the military's plan to broadcast the show to servicepeople had been abandoned. A week earlier Schultz had criticized Barber on the air, alleging that Barber had coached a group of U.S. soldiers in Iraq before their participation in a teleconference with President Bush; Pentagon officials had denied the charge, maintaining that Barber merely prepared the soldiers and did not tell them what to say. On his show Schultz voiced his suspicion that his criticism and the cancellation of the broadcasts by the Pentagon were connected, but the Pentagon asserted that the incident stemmed from "an unfortunate misinterpretation," as Dave Kolpack reported for the Associated Press (October 18, 2005, on-line). Schultz said to Kolpack, "It's censorship, that's what it is."

Schultz and his wife (who also serves as his producer) divide their time between their rented apartment in Washington and the home they are currently building in Detroit Lakes, Minnesota, about 45 miles east of Fargo. From his first marriage, Schultz has one son, David, an All-American golfer at Texas Christian University. He also has five stepchildren. In his free time he enjoys fishing, hunting, and golfing with his son. During his tenure at KFGO, in Fargo, Schultz helped to bring the station numerous honors, including the Marconi and Peabody Awards, both in 1997, and two Eric Sevareid Awards, in 2002 and 2003.

—K.J.E.

Suggested Reading: American Progress Action Fund Web site; bigeddieradio.com; *Los Angeles Times* Feb. 5, 2004; (Norfolk) *Virginian-Pilot* E p1 Mar. 13, 2004; *Washington Post* C p1 Jan. 10, 2005

Selected Radio Shows: *News and Views*, 1992–2004; *The Ed Schultz Show*, 2004–

Selected Books: *Straight Talk from the Heartland*, 2004

Courtesy of Jennifer Shahade

Shahade, Jennifer

(sha-HAH-dee)

Dec. 31, 1980– Chess player

Address: c/o Chess-in-the-Schools, 520 Eighth Ave., Fl. 2, New York, NY 10018

"People sometimes ask me if chess is fun," Jennifer Shahade said to Paul Hoffman for *Smithsonian* magazine (August 2003). "'Fun' is not the word I'd use. Of course I enjoy it, or I wouldn't play. But tournament chess is not relaxing. It's stressful, even if you win. The game demands total concentration. If your mind wanders for a moment, with one bad move you can throw away everything you've painstakingly built up." Shahade was the United States Women's Chess Champion in 2002 and 2004 and is already, at the age of 24, "the strongest American-born female chess player in history," according to Paul Hoffman. In February 2005 she was rated sixth out of 100 United States women competitors (a number of whom are foreign-born), according to U.S. Chess Online, the Web site of the U.S. Chess Federation. She has been praised for her bold tactical maneuvers, and her fierce play reflects her perception of chess. "The way that I play it competitively, it's mostly a sport. . . . I like to run and play basketball, but I'm actually more exhausted after the end of a chess game," Shahade said to a writer for *New York Times Upfront* (January 10, 2005), a publication of Scholastic Inc. On three occasions Shahade has represented the U.S. in the women's division at the Chess Olympiad, chess's equivalent of the Olympic Games: in Istanbul, Turkey, in 2000, she helped

her team achieve a tie for the 12th-place showing among 86 nations; in Bled, Slovenia, in 2002, she contributed to a ninth-place finish, among 89 other countries, for the U.S., and in 2004 she helped her country capture the silver medal. In 2002 she became only the second U.S. woman to earn her International Master (IM) norm, and in January 2003 she won her second IM title and a more prestigious Women's Grand Master (WGM) title, both awarded by the Federation Internationale de Echecs (International Chess Federation, or FIDE). (A "norm" is the number of points a player must achieve in international competition to qualify for FIDE titles.) Shahade teaches chess at the not-for-profit Chess-in-the-Schools program, in New York City, in which, according to Paul Hoffman, she tells her students to "play like girls!" and teaches them chess moves from famous games by strong women players. She is the author of *Chess Bitch: Women in the Ultimate Intellectual Sport* (2005).

Jennifer Shahade was born in Philadelphia, Pennsylvania, on December 31, 1980. Her father, Michael Shahade, is a four-time chess champion of Pennsylvania, and her mother, a chemistry professor at Drexel University, enjoyed the game as well. (Telling Paul Hoffman that women "are usually discouraged from pursuing chess and other intellectual activities that require time-consuming devotion," Jennifer Shahade said, "I was fortunate to have a mother who succeeded in the traditionally male field of chemistry" and who thus served as a role model.) Her father began teaching her to play chess when she was about seven years old. Shahade was not instantly captivated by the game. "For a long time I tagged along to tournaments with my brother and father, who were both master players," she said in an interview for the Jeremy Silman Web site, which is devoted to chess and film, among other subjects. "I was more interested in staying at nice hotels than in the actual chess." That changed when, at about 13, she attended the U.S. Chess Open in Chicago, Illinois. "Things started to click and I began to see more tactics, and beat experts and masters in blitz games," she said. "I gained a lot of confidence from that tournament, and had increased motivation to study and play." "By comparison I play like a real wuss," Michael Shahade said to Paul Hoffman about his daughter. "My style is more positional, accumulating tiny advantages until I win in the endgame. She goes for the jugular immediately and reaches positions that are so complicated they give me a headache to look at. I don't know how she does it." Referring to Jennifer Shahade's brother, who became a chess Grand Master when he was 14, Michael Shahade added, "Even Greg, whose play is much sharper than mine, doesn't take the kind of risks Jen does."

Shahade became a certified national master at the age of 15, in the 1996 Insanity Tournament at Marshall Chess Club, in the Greenwich Village section of New York City. "It's a crazy event," Shahade said to Paul Hoffman. "You play, I think, nine games. You play all night with the rounds starting at odd times like 2:11 a.m. and 4:23 a.m. . . . I managed to get it together and do well with no sleep." Shahade came in first in the tournament. In 1998 she became the U.S. Junior Open Champion, and in 2000 she represented the United States at the 34th Chess Olympiad, in Istanbul, Turkey. She won her first U.S. Championship in Seattle, Washington, in 2002, gaining the title National Women's Champion and earning her first International Master norm in the process. That occasion marked the first time in the history of the 157-year-old tournament that men and women had competed with each other, though there were still men's and women's titles. Shahade, who played only against men at the tournament, won the women's title by achieving the highest score of any woman present. Also in 2002 she competed again at the Chess Olympiad, this time in Bled, Slovenia. Shahade has recalled realizing in Bled that she lacked stamina. "I won five of my first six games, but then, sadly, I had a big slump so that I ended up with six wins and five losses," she told Paul Hoffman. "I'm used to American weekend tournaments in which four or five rounds are crammed into two or three days. The Olympiad lasted two weeks. I can play chess 12 hours a day for a weekend on sheer adrenaline and then crash, but I can't sit at the board with peak concentration for days at a time." (To increase her stamina, she began running, lifting weights, and shooting baskets.) She secured her second IM norm and a WGM norm the following year, at the U.S. Championship, in Seattle. After 10 days of play, involving 56 other competitors, Shahade was tied for the women's title with two immigrants, the Ukrainian-born Irina Krush and Anna Hahn, from Latvia. Shahade lost to Krush before Hahn, the underdog, beat them both to claim that year's title. In the following month Shahade graduated from New York University with a B.A. degree in comparative literature. She won her second U.S. Women's Championship in 2004, and in October of that year, the U.S. team—which included Shahade, Krush, Anna Zatonskih, and Susan Polgar—captured the silver medal at the Chess Olympiad in Calvia, Spain, the first medal in chess won by the U.S.

When asked in 2003 about her future plans, Shahade explained to Paul Hoffman, "I'm struggling right now with how much I want to make the game the focus of my life. I love chess, but it's the height of decadence. The positions you reach in a well-played game are beautiful, but the beauty is inaccessible to those who haven't mastered the game. There are many good reasons to teach kids chess—it helps them learn to concentrate, to think ahead, to see that their actions have consequences, to cope with defeat, and to be gracious in winning—but the game itself doesn't have a lot of social purpose. You can understand if someone is spending 16 hours a day trying to cure a disease or to write a novel, but to play better chess?" In defense of the game, Shahade said for the Jeremy Silman site, "Chess teaches you a lot about passion.

There are moments in chess analysis and play in which you feel tingles from the beauty of a certain move. This is the real thing, and sometimes I feel this in reading or looking at art or in a conversation. Without chess, I don't know if I would be able to recognize and appreciate this feeling as well."

Shahade currently supports herself by writing about, playing, and teaching chess. "This was not a conscious decision, but just an easy and enjoyable way to make money without working 9–5," Shahade said in her interview for the Jeremy Silman Web site. She teaches in the Girls Academy, part of the Chess-in-the-Schools program. "I think girls are less encouraged in the sport and there are fewer role models," Shahade said to the reporter for *New York Times Upfront*. "So I'm trying to change that." At Girls Academy, she said, "We get a bunch of girls together, all the most talented ones from the programs in the city, and I try to show them a lot of great female game." While more girls than ever before are learning chess, the game is still male-dominated. Of the approximately 1,200 members of the U.S. Chess Federation who ranked as masters or higher as of 2003, only 14 were female. Women were excluded from chess clubs in the U.S. and Europe until the mid-1880s and did not play in international tournaments until 1887, in London, England. Prejudices regarding female chess players remain, with Bobby Fischer, perhaps the world's most famous chess player, calling them "weakies," and another chess luminary, Garry Kasparov, once saying, according to Paul Hoffman, "[Chess is] a mixture of sport, psychological warfare, science and art. When you look at all these components, man dominates. Every single component of chess belongs to the areas of male domination." Kasparov's comments do not discourage Shahade. "You have to laugh," Shahade told Paul Hoffman. "You don't know whether he really believes what he is saying, or doing his usual thing of trying to get people riled up. And in a sense, who cares? All I know is that the chess world has accepted and encouraged me. I've never personally experienced any kind of discrimination or roadblock because I was a woman."

The widely continued practice of having separate tournaments for men and women is a controversial issue in the chess world. "Personally, I am not against women's only tournaments, because I think to play in such events from time to time is not necessarily an admission of inferiority," Shahade said for the Jeremy Silman Web site. "When I see an all women's tournament or training squad, it makes me happy because I see women competing and cooperating in a positive way."

Shahade enjoys photography, painting, and writing. Her book, *Chess Bitch: Women in the Ultimate Intellectual Sport*, is described on her Web site as an "eye-opening account of how young female chess players are successfully knocking down the doors to this traditionally male game and giving the phrase 'play like a girl' a whole new meaning." (In chess the queen, the most powerful piece on the board, is sometimes referred to informally as a "bitch.") In the book Shahade catalogues the largely unknown history of female chess players, up to the recent emergence of the 22-year-old Russian champion Alexandra Kosteniuk, who has been compared to the Russian-born tennis player Anna Kournikova for her willingness to promote her sport by calling attention to her good looks. In a review of *Chess Bitch* for the *Buffalo News* (September 11, 2005), Amy Moritz wrote, "The book is filled with interesting anecdotes about former and current players, including several who have a penchant for partying during tournaments. [Shahade's] examination of chess in Georgia, China and the Soviet Union among other countries lends a credible world view of the game." Moritz also wrote, "In the end, Shahade concludes that while the sport is gender-neutral, the governance structures and culture are not."

Shahade has also created a series of photographic self-portraits that are meant to challenge traditional attitudes about women's involvement in chess and intellectual pursuits in general. In one photo she wears a pink wig and pink gloves and glances over her shoulder while holding a book on chess. The photos are intended to demonstrate that women can be simultaneously sexy and intellectual.

Shahade's current goal is to obtain her third International Master norm. She also plays basketball, air hockey, and Ms. Pacman and is learning Spanish and yoga. She collects wigs and high-heeled shoes. Shahade's other interests include performance art, cultural theory, and travel. She lives in a loft in the Williamsburg section of Brooklyn, in New York City.

—L.J.

Suggested Reading: Jennifer Shahade Web site; Jeremy Silman Web site; *Smithsonian* p72+ Aug. 2003, with photos

Selected Books: *Chess Bitch—Women in the Ultimate Intellectual Sport*, 2005

Shields, Mark

May 25, 1937– Political analyst; syndicated columnist

Address: c/o Public Broadcasting Service, 1320 Braddock Pl., Suite 200, Alexandria, VA 22314-1649

One of the "wittiest political journalists in America," according to the *Wall Street Journal*, Mark Shields has also been described as a "walking almanac of American politics" by the *Washington Post*. Shields has written a weekly column for the *Washington Post* since 1980; it has been syndicated nationally since 1981. Once a week he appears on the PBS television series *The NewsHour with Jim Lehrer*, and he serves as moderator of CNN's *The Capital Gang*. He has provided thoughtful political analysis for more than 20 years, during which he has covered five presidential elections. "Known as one of our . . . funniest and fairest political pundits, Mark Shields is never at a loss for words," Linda Marx wrote for the *Orlando (Florida) Sentinel* (May 11, 1997). Before he began his career as a commentator, Shields was actively involved in politics, for many years as an adviser to candidates for public office. In 1968 he served as a campaign worker for Robert F. Kennedy, during the senator's bid to become the 1968 Democratic presidential nominee. He later worked on campaigns in more than 38 states. The civic-minded Shields, who advocates for greater social equity, is unshakably optimistic about the political process. "Politics is important," he told Leslie Milk and Ellen Ryan for the *Washingtonian* (January 2004). "It is nothing less than the peaceful resolution of conflict among competing interests. It works."

Courtesy of PBS

Mark Shields was born into a devout Irish Catholic family on May 25, 1937 in Weymouth, Massachusetts. His mother was a teacher; his father, a paper salesman, became the first Catholic elected to the local school board. His parents were both deeply interested in politics; they read five newspapers and discussed politics daily. The first time Shields saw his mother cry was the day that Adlai Stevenson, a Democratic senator from Illinois, lost a presidential election. (Stevenson ran twice against Dwight D. Eisenhower, in 1952 and 1956.) Shields kicked off his own political career at the age of six, collecting signatures on a petition for a hometown candidate. "Being involved in politics was considered to be an important civic duty and an important occupation where I grew up," Shields told the editors of *U.S. Catholic* (October 2004). "Like a lot of people of my era, I was born a Democrat and baptized a Catholic. If you were Catholic, especially a Pope Leo XIII Catholic, you believed in workers' rights and you recognized that the free market was the greatest creator of wealth but a severely flawed distributor of resources and wealth. The Democrats' political philosophy was the one we seemed naturally at home with."

Shields attended the University of Notre Dame, in South Bend, Indiana, majoring in philosophy with a minor in history. After he graduated, in 1959, he volunteered for the Marine Corps, inspired by his hero, then–Senator John F. Kennedy of Massachusetts, who had also joined the armed services as a young man. When Kennedy, who was Catholic, ran for president in 1960, he was embraced by the Catholic community. "I was in Marine Corps boot camp at [Parris] Island, South Carolina when I filled out my absentee ballot for Kennedy," Shields told *U.S. Catholic*. "In boot camp at that time, you were cut off from the world for 13 weeks. You didn't have television, radio, or newspapers. I didn't find out that Kennedy won until the Thursday after the election when my drill sergeant, a white Southern Baptist, put his hand behind my neck and said, 'Your goddamn mackerel snapper won.' Mackerel snapper was derogatory slang for Catholic back then." Shields did not like military life; he left the Marines in 1961. "I will not romanticize the Marine Corps," he wrote in one of his *Washington Post* (October 28, 1983) columns. "Surely there must have been more important moments in my life, but very few happier than the one when, after completing 13 weeks of boot camp . . . , I finally boarded the train north."

Shields next moved to Hollywood, California, where he briefly worked as a recruiter of studio audiences for television shows. In 1964 he relocated to Washington, D.C., to pursue a career in politics. For a while he was employed at the North Capitol Street post office. According to Leslie Milk and Ellen Ryan, his supervisor told him, "Shields, you have no future in the parcel post." Shields landed his first political job in 1965, as a legislative assistant (legislative director, according to some sources) for Senator William Proxmire, a Wisconsin Democrat. He next worked on a series of political campaigns. The first major one in which he participated was that of Senator Robert F. Kennedy of New York, who made a bid for the White House in 1968. Years later Shields told Curtis Wilkie for the *Boston Globe* (May 30, 1993) that Kennedy was "the first, last and only plausible presidential candidate who was truly antiestablishment." Shields worked as a field coordinator, organizing Kennedy's campaign for the California primary (some sources state that Shields also worked on the Ore-

gon and Nebraska primaries). On June 4, 1968 Kennedy achieved a narrow victory in California. That night his campaign came to a sudden and shocking end: while walking from a victory party to a press conference, Kennedy was shot by an assassin in the kitchen of the Ambassador Hotel in Los Angeles. He died the next morning. "I'll go to my grave believing that Robert Kennedy would have been the best President of my lifetime," Shields told Elizabeth Kolbert for the *New York Times* (July 14, 1993).

Shields went on to manage John J. Gilligan's successful bid for the governor's office in Ohio in 1970 and the unsuccessful campaign of Senator Edmund S. Muskie of Maine for the Democratic presidential nomination in 1972. Later in 1972 Shields worked for R. Sargent Shriver, a Kennedy family in-law and former head of the Peace Corps, who had been nominated for vice president on the ticket of Senator George S. McGovern of South Dakota. With more than half a million U.S. troops stationed in Vietnam, President Richard Nixon was running a reelection campaign based on flag-waving patriotism. The chances of unseating Nixon looked bleak, but Shields believed that the McGovern campaign held a trump card: McGovern was a bona fide war hero. As a bomber pilot in World War II, McGovern flew 35 missions over Europe and was awarded the Distinguished Flying Cross. Shields suggested that the McGovern camp film a television commercial showing members of McGovern's Army Air Corps crew reminiscing about their former leader's heroism. McGovern's advisers rejected that proposal, however, for fear that, in light of widespread anti-military sentiments associated with the Vietnam War, such an ad would be counterproductive. On Election Day McGovern lost to Nixon by one of the largest margins in the history of American presidential elections.

Shields worked on a slew of campaigns of other Democrats, among them Congressman Morris Udall of Arizona, who made an unsuccessful bid for the presidential nomination in 1976, and the congressional campaigns of Max Heller, Les AuCoin, and Phil Snowden. Shields delighted in that work. "The chance to do that which you feel morally obliged to do, that which you enjoy doing and do well, how many times in life do you get a chance like that? It's a marvelous, marvelous thing," Shields told Lynn Darling for the *Washington Post* (November 6, 1978). "A campaign is unlike anything else in people's lives. It's pressured, it's chaotic, it's complex, and always, always you know whether you won or lost." Most of Shields's candidates lost; he has often joked that he holds the record for writing concession speeches. "You have to figure that if you're a liberal Democrat and [Boston] Red Sox fan, life is bound to break your heart," he told Darling.

In 1979 Shields retired from campaign work and joined the *Washington Post* as a writer of political editorials. Within a year he was given his own column. In 1981 his column went national, when it was picked up by the Chicago Tribune–New York News syndicate. Around that time Shields began making radio and television appearances regularly; he had a nightly segment on *Look at Today* on ABC Radio in Washington, D.C., and frequently provided political analysis for NBC and the CBS program *Face the Nation*.

For about three years starting in 1980, Shields hosted a weekly half-hour talk show, *Inside Washington*, which aired on 77 public-television stations. The program examined everything from the intricacies of political speechwriting to politicians' seeming addiction to sports metaphors. *Inside Washington* was considered unique for its informality and was a big hit among both Democrats and Republicans on Capitol Hill. Fans of the show included Senator Robert J. Dole, Speaker of the House Thomas P. "Tip" O'Neill Jr., and Representative Thomas S. Foley. Senator Alan K. Simpson told Tom Shales for the *Washington Post* (June 30, 1983) that with *Inside Washington* Shields brought "a real breath of fresh air" to political commentary. "He's a dragon-slayer," Simpson told Shales, "and he has a spirited, light, pungent, wry kind of humor." Nevertheless, after the 1983 season the Maryland Center for Public Television, the show's producer, cancelled the program, because it had failed to attract a sufficiently large audience in the general population. Ironically, the show was pulled just as Lawrence K. Grossman, then the president of PBS, was considering it for national distribution. "We did some good stuff that I feel awfully good about," Shields told Shales. "We were trying to show that politics is a human business. It's taken a lot of knocks, but it's important in the long run, and most of the really crucial things about the future—war, peace, the environment—will be determined by politics."

In 1985 Shields published *On the Campaign Trail*, a collection of his *Washington Post* columns about President Ronald Reagan's successful 1984 reelection campaign. A reviewer for the *Washington Post* (March 24, 1985) wrote that Shields's book offers "a perceptive, and often amusing, look at American political geography and trenchant analysis of why it has changed."

In 1987 Shields started working as an on-air analyst for *The MacNeil/Lehrer NewsHour* (known as *The NewsHour with Jim Lehrer* since 1995, when Robert MacNeil retired). *NewsHour*, watched by millions of viewers each weeknight, provides in-depth analyses of current events through a news summary, live studio interviews, discussions, and on-site reporting. In 1988 Shields was paired with David Gergen, an editor at large for the conservative newsweekly *U.S. News & World Report*, to provide commentary on that year's presidential-election campaign. Gergen and Shields proved to be a strong team; many journalists cited their analyses of the campaign as superior to all others, and the 1989 *Political Almanac* named them the 1988 election season's best television pundits. The *Mac-*

Neil/Lehrer NewsHour won the prestigious Peabody Award in 1988 for its "extensive and exhaustive" coverage of the election and its "exceptional in-depth analysis of the electoral process."

The chemistry between Gergen and Shields was so potent that the pair continued their segments after the election, appearing every Friday. Insiders in Washington and members of the press corps started referring to Gergen and Shields as the "Bert and Ernie" of the Beltway, a reference to the famous puppet duo from the popular PBS show *Sesame Street*. Gergen played the straight man, much like Bert, and the more-animated Shields was pegged as Ernie. Whereas most pundits were known for their bluster and ability to lob biting insults at their opponents, Gergen and Shields never shouted at or insulted each other—and they often did not stick to party lines. "Neither of us ever felt that he was an apologist for a party or a point of view," Shields told Kolbert. For example, Shields, the resident Democrat, was sometimes tougher on President Bill Clinton than was Gergen, the Republican. "Gergen and Shields choose consensus-building over one-upmanship," Frazier Moore wrote for the Associated Press (July 13, 1992). "They are generally willing to set aside partisanship and talk turkey about the business of politics, building on each other's observations rather than undermining them."

In 1993 Gergen left *NewsHour* to work as a White House counselor in the Clinton administration. "David's been an absolute delight to work with the past six years," Shields told reporters, as quoted in the Cleveland, Ohio, *Plain Dealer* (June 3, 1993). "He's fair, he's thoughtful, he's reflective. And he laughs at my jokes. I'll miss him. I'll be like Dean Martin after he split with Jerry Lewis. Or maybe it was the other way around." *NewsHour* producers conducted an exhaustive, 10-month search for Gergen's replacement. Many prominent Republicans vied for the chance to match wits with Shields, among them the *Washington Times* columnist Suzanne Fields, the former White House press secretary Marlin Fitzwater, and the *Wall Street Journal* columnist Paul Gigot, among others. "We want somebody who's conservative," *NewsHour*'s political producer Peggy Robinson told the Associated Press (September 13, 1993) reporter Jill Lawrence. "But we don't want to have a brickbat contest where people scream and yell at each other."

In looking for someone whose style would complement Shields's leisurely, genteel approach to punditry, the producers ruled out candidates who tended to speak too quickly, interrupt, or stick to their party's line. "Political commentary is largely the province of bullies and bigshots, like George Will and John McLaughlin. Mr. Shields, in contrast, comes across as just a guy who likes to argue about current events at the barbershop—the pundit next door," Kolbert wrote. "On the air, he often introduces his remarks by saying he would like to make two points, then forgets to make the second.

He quotes lots of obscure politicians, needles his adversaries in a good-humored way and absolutely cannot resist a one-liner." In March 1994 producers at the *NewsHour* announced that Gigot would fill Gergen's old slot. Gigot stayed until the fall of 2001; he was succeeded by David Brooks, a senior editor at the *Weekly Standard* and the author of *Bobos in Paradise: The New Upper Class and How They Got There.* (Brooks is currently an op-ed columnist for the *New York Times.*)

Shields was among the original panelists of *The Capital Gang*, which premiered in 1988. The award-winning political roundtable airs every Saturday on CNN. Other panelists in the line-up included the syndicated columnist Robert Novak, former presidential adviser Pat Buchanan, *Time*'s White House correspondent Margaret Carlson, and the syndicated columnist Mona Charen (who was later replaced by the Washington editor of the *National Review*, Kate O'Beirne). Buchanan, the moderator, left the show in 1991 to run for president and was replaced by Al Hunt, executive Washington editor of the *Wall Street Journal.* On March 12, 1994 Shields replaced Hunt as the moderator. In 1998 Shields also joined Novak on CNN's weekly interview show *Evans & Novak*, which the syndicated columnist Rowland Evans and Novak had co-hosted for more than a decade. With the addition of Shields and fellow *Capital Gang* panelist Hunt, the show was renamed *Evans, Novak, Hunt & Shields.* After Evans died, in 2001, it became *Novak, Hunt & Shields.* The show was cancelled in 2002.

Shields describes himself as a liberal, and his on-air commentary and columns have supported policies that protect the poor, minorities, prisoners, organized labor, and the infirm. He does not always toe the Democratic Party line, though, and is staunchly pro-life. "As an admitted and non-recovering American liberal, I've generally believed the following: Every individual has the right to live free from fear and discrimination and the right to a share of earthly goods, including food, shelter, clothing, education and, yes, health care. Each person has the right to decent and productive work at fair wages, and every individual has the corresponding duty to work for the community good and to respect the rights of others . . . ," Shields wrote in one of his columns for the *Washington Post* (August 10, 1994). "But extend that belief in dignity, equality and sanctity of human life to include—as well as protection of the widow, the orphan and the elderly lonely—the unborn child, and you court excommunication from the ever-shrinking American liberal fellowship. . . . You actually can be simultaneously liberal and pro-life. It's just lonesome."

Shields regularly emcees charity events and has made frequent appearances at the National Press Club to roast his friends and colleagues. In a speech delivered on March 6, 2002 at Canisius College's Carol & Carl Montante Cultural Center, according to Anthony Cardinale in the *Buffalo News*

(March 7, 2002), Shields referred to Robert Novak as "the prince of darkness" and said that Pat Buchanan was absent from the event because he was receiving an award "from the Friendly Sons of the Spanish Inquisition." Shields then named "three great American presidents—Washington, who couldn't tell a lie; Nixon, who couldn't tell the truth; and Clinton, who couldn't tell the difference."

"Sharp-witted but never sharp-tongued, Shields has earned a reputation as one of Washington's good guys," Leslie Milk and Ellen Ryan wrote. They reported that he was a longtime supporter of So Others Might Eat, a nonprofit organization that helps the poor and homeless in Washington, D.C., and of efforts to assist "aging nuns whose orders need help." Shields has also aided a school in Boston that provides education and enrichment opportunities to children living in housing projects. In addition, he is involved in Project Children, a program that tries to break down barriers between Catholic and Protestant children from Northern Ireland by bringing them to the U.S. to live and work together.

Shields has taught classes on American politics and the press at Harvard University, in Cambridge, Massachusetts, and the Wharton School of Business at the University of Pennsylvania, in Philadelphia. He was named a Washingtonian of the Year for 2003 by the *Washingtonian*. He has received honorary degrees from Stonehill College, in North Easton, Massachusetts; Clark University, in Worcester, Massachusetts; and Hobart and William Smith Colleges, in Geneva, New York.

Shields lives in Chevy Chase, Maryland, with his wife, Anne, who worked for the Department of the Interior before her retirement. They have a married daughter, Amy.

—J.C.

Suggested Reading: CNN.com; *New York Times* C p1 July 14, 1993; PBS.org; *U.S. Catholic* p12+ Oct. 2004; *Washington Post* B p1+ Nov. 6, 1978

Selected Books: *On the Campaign Trail*, 1985

Shriver, Lionel

May 18, 1957– Writer

Address: c/o Kathy Anderson, Scovil, Chicak, Galen, 12 W. 19th St., New York, NY 10016

Until recently, the work of the novelist Lionel Shriver was critically acclaimed but unknown to the vast majority of the book-buying public. Her prominence rose significantly in 2004, when she received the Orange Prize, given in England to women who write in English, for her 2003 work *We Need to Talk About Kevin*. The narrator of that nov-

Terri Gelenian-Wood

Lionel Shriver

el is a woman, Eva, whose teenage son has murdered seven of his classmates as well as a teacher; the novel raised some eyebrows in the literary establishment, due less to the violence described in the story than to Eva's openly negative attitude toward motherhood. *We Need to Talk About Kevin* is not the first of Shriver's works to explore controversial views on the part of her protagonists; *Game Control* (1994), for example, features a character whose beliefs about human population control warrant the label "extremist." "If you don't allow yourself to write characters who do disagreeable things—if you only allow yourself to write about what you would be glad for your readers to imitate in real life—then you're pretty much constrained to characters who help little old ladies across the street and rescue cats from trees," Shriver told Andrew Lawless for the Three Monkeys Online Web site. Shriver's other novels are *The Female of the Species* (1987), *Checker and the Derailleurs* (1988), *The Bleeding Heart* (1990), *A Perfectly Good Family* (1996), and *Double Fault* (1997).

The writer was born Margaret Ann Shriver on May 18, 1957 in Gastonia, North Carolina, the second of the three children—and the only daughter—of Donald W. Shriver, a Presbyterian theologian who later became associated with Union Theological Seminary, in New York, and Peggy (Leu) Shriver, who became an administrator for the National Council of Churches. Shriver was raised mainly in Raleigh, North Carolina, and in New York City. She has described her parents as "Adlai Stevenson Democrats"; in an interview with Rachel Cusk for the London *Guardian* (October 4, 2003), she gave her mother and father credit for "the fact that I'm very engaged with moral matters, though that al-

ways sounds, if nothing else, unentertaining. So I come at these issues with a certain perversity, always looking at the hard case." Shriver decided at age seven that she would be a writer. At eight she rejected her feminine name because, as many sources have reported, she felt that men had an easier time in the world; she called herself Tony before adopting, at 15, the name Lionel. "I felt alienated from femininity—I've always had a sense of myself as fundamentally androgynous," she said, as quoted by Luke Leitch in the London *Evening Standard* (June 8, 2005). Also at eight, already reflecting on one of the themes that would inform *We Need to Talk About Kevin*, Shriver "foreswore motherhood," as she wrote in an essay that appears on the Reading Group Guides Web site. She and her brothers, she added, "were annoying. We were loud and sneaky and broke things. At eight, maybe I was simply horrified by the prospect of being saddled with myself."

In an interview posted on the Barnes & Noble Web site, Shriver identified Joseph Heller's novel *Catch-22*, about characters in World War II, as the work that has most influenced her as a writer. The "first 'grown-up' novel I ever read," *Catch-22* "convinced me that fiction for adults needn't be humorless, or laborious to read," she said. She recalled reading the book at 12 and having read it "eight times by the time I hit the tenth grade," explaining that there is "an amoral, anarchic quality to Heller's satire that struck a chord." Shriver attended Columbia University, in New York, receiving her B.A. degree in creative writing in 1978 and her M.F.A., in the same specialty, in 1982. During her lengthy talk with Robert Birnbaum for the Web site *identitytheory.com* (July 24, 2003), Shriver said that she chose Columbia because, thanks to her father's association with Union Theological Seminary, "I didn't have to pay for it." As for the decision to pursue a degree in writing, she admitted, "It's not a very difficult degree to earn. There is no science to creative writing and it feels very self-indulgent. I have always been aware that most of the great writers of the past didn't go to workshops. It's always seemed a little embarrassing to me. On the other hand, I did want to get published. I badly needed some connections, which is why most people go to these programs. It's not to learn to write finer sentences."

After graduating from Columbia Shriver taught English in several colleges in New York. Then, in 1985, she began to lead the life of an expatriate and world traveler. She spent six months touring Western Europe and another half-year living on a kibbutz in Israel before going to Belfast, Northern Ireland, where she intended to stay for nine months to research a book. (It was eventually published as the novel *The Bleeding Heart*.) As it turned out, she lived there for 12 years, during which she made visits of as long as a year to Nairobi, Kenya; New York; Bangkok, Thailand; and Vietnam. She reported from all of those places for the *Wall Street Journal*, the *Economist*, the *Philadelphia Inquirer*, the *Jerusalem Post*, and the *Guardian*, as well as other media outlets. Living abroad, she told Robert Birnbaum, "gives you a different perspective."

Shriver's first novel, *The Female of the Species* (1987), is set in Kenya. The main character, Gray Kaiser, is an anthropologist who encountered an isolated tribe in 1948 and has returned on the eve of her 60th birthday to make a film about her discoveries. The story is narrated mainly by Errol, Gray's assistant, who watches as Gray becomes obsessed in Kenya by Raphael, a 24-year-old whose manipulative, dominating behavior evokes Gray's memories of another man she once knew. In the *New York Times Book Review* (July 19, 1987), Katherine Bouton wrote that *The Female of the Species* was unusual for a first novel in that it was not apparently autobiographical but "totally imagined. . . . That fictive quality is both the novel's weakness and its promise. . . . It is . . . hard not to admire the breadth and consistency of Lionel Shriver's inventiveness and the exuberance of her imagination."

The New York City borough of Queens is the setting of Shriver's 1988 novel, *Checker and the Derailleurs*. Checker, a 19-year-old, charismatic drummer in a rock band, is in love with the 29-year-old Syria, a glassblower, but has arranged her marriage to the band's saxophonist, an illegal immigrant. The critic for the *Magill Book Reviews* (on-line) noted that the novel's "premise of loss and renewed life is well developed," and Ethan Bumas remarked in *Library Journal* (May 15, 1988) that the novel "is at its best funny, clever, and touching."

Shriver's next novel was *The Bleeding Heart* (1990, published in Great Britain in 1992 as *Ordinary Decent Criminals*). Its 30ish protagonist, Estrin, like Shriver herself, has gone to live in Belfast amid violent conflict between Unionists, who want Northern Ireland to remain part of Great Britain, and Republicans, who want the region to join the rest of the Irish Republic. Estrin meets Farrell, a former bomb dismantler for both sides who becomes a conciliator at political conferences between the two factions. The *Publishers Weekly* (July 20, 1990) reviewer found the novel to be "ultimately tragic, . . . woven through with threads of Irish politics and the anguish of people whose lives can take meaning only from external cues. Shriver's writing is outstandingly lucid and bright, with an original blend of American and Irish whimsical irony." Margaret Walters noted in the London *Independent* (June 21, 1992) that the novel is "a love story, and a surprisingly moving one. But Shriver's edgy, accurate wit, her ear for rhetorical inflation and self-deception, and her refusal to be conned by personal or political platitudes expand her novel: its real subject is the seductiveness and the sadness of Belfast itself."

Shriver noted in the *New Statesman* (June 10, 2002) that in "demographic terms, for more than a century westerners have seemed unable to decide what they fear most. The precipitous drop in Euro-pean fertility rates has produced anxiety about numerical dwindling. . . . Yet the sixfold increase in worldwide population during the same period has prompted a contrary fear of crushing biological overload. Given the emotive nature of these opposing horrors—'we are about to disappear!' v 'we are being overrun!'—it is less surprising that population issues have filtered into the western literary canon than that their direct treatment in mainstream literature is rare." Shriver published *Game Control* (1994) to address the issue in a fictional format. Noting that most literature about the population problem is futuristic and that, in it, the feared swarms of humanity have not yet arrived, she wrote, "By contrast, my own more mainstream *Game Control* is set in modern-day Nairobi," and its "irascible protagonist is . . . convinced that we are reproducing ourselves into extinction, and is therefore researching a pathogen that would neatly decimate a third of the world's population overnight." The character Calvin, a demographer, was once concerned with conserving elephants on a game preserve; now, his "game" is the human animal. He and two other characters exemplify approaches to the population problem: Eleanor, a liberal social worker distributing birth-control materials to people who do not use them properly, falls in love with Calvin, whose solution to both elephant and human overpopulation involves culling. Wallace, a retired population worker, has come to feel that humans are the solution to their own problems and that, therefore, the more people the better.

"The three are not so much people as opportunities for argument, certainly in the first half of the book, as the impressive arrays of theories and statistics are laid out," Sylvia Brownrigg wrote for the *Guardian* (May 3, 1994). "In the second, the rather overwrought plot takes over and they each take on the looming presence of characters in a science fiction drama." Marek Kohn, who reviewed *Game Control* for the *Independent* (April 10, 1994), felt that the satire in Shriver's novel had fallen short. "To believe that [Eleanor] would fall in with [Calvin's] schemes, even conditionally," he wrote, "demands that we both accept the terms of the problem and grasp the horror contained within it. If those requirements were met, we'd be seduced, like [Eleanor], into thinking the unthinkable, and the potential for a monstrous comedy could be unleashed. . . . The trouble with *Game Control* is that it's funny, but not appallingly so."

The central character in *A Perfectly Good Family*, Shriver's 1996 novel, is Corlis McCrea, who, like Shriver herself, is the middle child between two brothers. Upon the death of their mother, the McCrea children return to North Carolina to settle her estate. The assets are to be divided four ways, not three, with the fourth share going to the American Civil Liberties Union, which the liberal parents supported. For the siblings to get possession of the family mansion, their old home, two of them must form an alliance; Corlis is torn between her brothers, the elder a wild and promiscuous drinker, the younger a repressed conservative. "Shriver cleverly contrives to precipitate her characters into a traumatic free-for-all, an obstacle course of horribly loaded preferences," Alex Clark noted in the *Guardian* (March 29, 1996). "For children brought up in a world of moral imperatives, this gift of self-determination, immediately qualified by the need for co-operative action, is a distinctly double-edged sword. . . . Choice, Shriver underlines, is enslavement as well as liberation, and *A Perfectly Good Family* is a fine illustration of that point." Fanny Blake, reviewing the novel for the *Independent* (May 5, 1996), was equally positive: "Often funny and always intelligent, this is a sharply observed history of the redoubtable McCrea family, shot through with sardonic wit and black comedy."

Double Fault (1997) is a story of the marriage of two professional tennis players. After Willy, once an up-and-coming star in the sport, is eclipsed by her husband, Eric, and sidelined by injury, she can scarcely bear the thought of his victories. The book received mixed notices. The *Publishers Weekly* (June 30, 1997) reviewer complained of Shriver's seeming didacticism, commenting that the novelist "stacks the deck against Willy, whose defeatist family and embittered coach have filled her with mean-spirited insecurities, so that her final sacrifice for Eric (equally cocky but more individualized and just plain nicer) is also, unfortunately, her only really instinctive, unprogrammed gesture in the book." Louise Redd, by contrast, wrote for the *Dallas Morning News* (September 21, 1997), "Though *Double Fault* is crammed with Willy's failures, her final tragedy has the effect of turning up the volume just a notch on all her previous angst. Ms. Shriver throws out no false note of hope, no hoopla about the resiliency of the good ol' human spirit. . . . She has written a gorgeous, compelling tragedy in which she stays with her game every step of the way."

Although most reviewers of her work had placed Shriver in the top rank of contemporary literary novelists, that assessment was not reflected in sales figures of her books. That changed in 2004, when she won the Orange Prize for her novel *We Need to Talk About Kevin*, published in the previous year. (Ironically, given Shriver's stated attitude about femininity, the Orange Prize is presented only to women.) Shriver explained in her essay on the Reading Group Guides Web site that two factors had moved her to write the novel: her new ambivalence about her longstanding refusal to have children, now that she was in her early 40s and facing "the imminent closure of the reproductive window"; and news stories about shootings of teens by their classmates, in particular the highly publicized 1999 murders in Columbine, Colorado. Those incidents added to her fear about parenthood the possibility that her child "might turn out to be a killer." The narrator of *We Need to Talk About Kevin* is Eva, who reveals in letters to her husband, from whom she is separated, her negative feelings about parenthood. Her son, Kevin, at the age of 15, massacred seven of his schoolmates and a teacher. Has Eva's dislike of her son contributed to Kevin's amorality, or has his innate criminality caused her to turn away from him? "I think *Kevin* has attracted an audience," Shriver wrote in a piece for the *Guardian* (February 18, 2005, online), "because my narrator, Eva, allows herself to say all those things that mothers are not supposed to say."

The *Publishers Weekly* (March 24, 2003) reviewer called Shriver's "the most triumphantly accomplished" of a number of fictional works inspired by real-life shootings. The reviewer added that *We Need to Talk About Kevin* is "a harrowing, psychologically astute, sometimes even darkly humorous novel, with a clear-eyed, hard-won ending and a tough-minded sense of the difficult, often painful human enterprise." For Zoe Green, writing in the *Observer* (February 27, 2005), the "novel is an elegant psychological and philosophical investigation of culpability with a brilliant denouement. . . . Eva's voice carries this novel, which is as much a psychological study of her as it is of Kevin and, although her reliability as a narrator becomes increasingly questionable as she oscillates between anger, self-pity and regret, her search for answers becomes just as compulsive for the reader."

Lionel Shriver is married to a jazz drummer and divides her time between London, England, and New York City.

—S.Y.

Suggested Reading: *Dallas Morning News* p91 Sep. 21, 1997; (Glasgow) *Herald* p6 July 24, 1993; Identity Theory (on-line) July 24, 2003; *Jerusalem Post* B p9 May 10, 2002; *Library Journal* p94 May 15, 1988; (London) *Guardian* p13 May 3, 1994, T p17 Mar. 29, 1996; (London) *Independent* p36 June 21, 1992, p28 Apr. 30, 1994, p36 May 6, 1996; (London) *Observer* p16 Feb. 27, 2005; *Magill Book Reviews* (on-line); *New Statesman* p38+ June 10, 2002; *New York Times Book Review* p13 July 19, 1987; *Publishers Weekly* p52 July 20, 1990, p65 June 30, 1997, p55 Mar. 24, 2003; *Washington Post* D p3 June 30, 1987, E p3 Nov. 20, 1990

Selected Books: *The Female of the Species*, 1987; *Checker and the Derailleurs*, 1988; *The Bleeding Heart*, 1990; *Game Control*, 1994; *A Perfectly Good Family*, 1996; *Double Fault*, 1997; *We Need to Talk About Kevin*, 2003

Courtesy of Jack Alterman

Siddons, Anne Rivers

Jan. 9, 1936– Novelist; former journalist

*Address: c/o Author Mail, HarperCollins, 10 E.
53d St., New York, NY 10022-5244*

"Sometimes, I can feel in my bones a woman who's been dead 100 years wagging her finger at me, telling me that a lady doesn't make waves, a lady doesn't confront," the writer Anne Rivers Siddons told Cynthia Ganz and Gail Cameron Wescott for *People* (September 16, 1991). "Sometimes I find myself deferring to some old gentleman with no sense at all. It's not easy to escape." Siddons is the author of *Heartbreak Hotel*, *Peachtree Road*, *Colony*, *Downtown*, *Low Country*, and 11 other novels whose heroines, like her, are natives of the United States South. While her "commitment" to the South is "absolute," in her words, she has strived to escape the mindset associated with the stereotypical southern belle and with the romanticized notions about the South that have long manifested themselves in popular culture. Because she believes that she depicts the South "as it really is," as she told Ganz and Wescott, Siddons has rejected comparisons of any of her novels to Margaret Mitchell's Pulitzer Prize–winning Civil War epic *Gone with the Wind* (1936), but like that immensely popular book, many of hers have become bestsellers. "What's intriguing about Siddons is how much she transcends the usual parameters of fluff fiction, both in terms of literary finesse and penetrating intelligence," the literary critic and essayist Donna Seaman wrote for *Booklist* (May 15, 1994). Siddons began her professional life as a designer and layout artist for advertising firms; she later pre-

pared copy for ads as well. In the early 1960s she was an editor at *Atlanta* magazine; her nonfiction pieces have appeared in that magazine and others, among them *Gentlemen's Quarterly*, *Redbook*, *Georgia*, *House Beautiful*, *Lear's*, *Goodlife*, and *Southern Living*. She has also published a collection of essays and the travel guide *Go Straight on Peachtree: A McDonald City Guide to Atlanta* (1978).

The only child of Marvin Rivers, a prosperous lawyer, and the former Katherine Kitchens, a high-school secretary, the writer was born Sybil Anne Rivers on January 9, 1936 in Atlanta, Georgia. Like six generations of her ancestors, she was raised in the nearby town of Fairburn. By her own account, her parents expected her to become something of a southern belle; her goals, therefore, were supposed to be marriage and homemaking rather than a career outside the home. In high school she earned top grades, served on the cheerleading squad, and was selected homecoming queen. In her senior year she was named Centennial Queen of Fairburn. She also wrote occasional pieces for the local Fairburn newspaper.

After her high-school graduation, in 1954, Siddons enrolled at Auburn University, in Alabama. She studied architecture before changing her major to illustration. As an undergraduate she joined a sorority and and "did the things I thought I should," as she told a HarperCollins interviewer a few years ago, as quoted on fantasticfiction.co.uk and bookfinder.us. "I dated the right guys. I did the right activities." Her extracurricular pursuits included writing for the campus newspaper, the *Auburn Plainsman*. One year, when she held the post of *Plainsman* editor, she wrote what she described to the HarperCollins interviewer as "an innocuous, almost sophomoric column" for the paper in support of racial integration. The piece took the form of an editorial in response to events in the burgeoning civil rights movement, such as the Montgomery, Alabama, bus boycott (which extended from December 1955 to January 1957), launched by African-Americans in an ultimately successful effort to desegregate that city's public buses. Auburn University administrators asked her not to print the editorial, but she did so anyway; when it was published, a statement appeared alongside it in which the administrators declared that the college did not support integration. After a similar editorial by her appeared in a later issue of the *Plainsman*, Auburn administrators stripped her of her editorship.

After Siddons received a B.A.A. (bachelor of applied arts) degree, in 1958, she attended a few classes at the Atlanta School of Art. According to *Contemporary Authors* (1999), in about 1959 she began working in the advertising department of the Retail Credit Corp., where she prepared ad designs and layouts. From 1961 to 1963 she held a similar position with Citizens & Southern National Bank; there, her responsibilities grew to include copywriting, and she gained a newfound appreciation of her talents as a writer. Before that time, she told the HarperCollins interviewer, "writing came so naturally that I didn't value it. I never even thought that it might be a livelihood, or a source of great satisfaction. Southern girls, remember, were taught to look for security."

In 1963 Siddons quit her job at the bank to join the staff of *Atlanta*, then edited by Jim Townsend, whom *Time* once dubbed "the father of city magazines." Founded two years earlier by the Atlanta Chamber of Commerce, *Atlanta* is among the oldest of American city magazines. As *Atlanta*'s city editor, Siddons covered many events connected with the civil rights movement. Decades later, writing for *Atlanta* (May 2001), she recalled that she and her colleagues "knew, with pride, . . . that Atlanta was the epicenter of the civil rights movement, and that its great hero and master spirit, Dr. Martin Luther King, Jr., was one of our own. Many of us at the magazine knew personally some of Dr. King's lieutenants, ridiculously young men who had stared impassively down gun barrels and been clubbed and hosed and dogged in a half dozen cities across the wounded South. They were our heroes. They still are mine."

In 1966 Siddons married Heyward L. Siddons, a business executive, and became stepmother to his four young sons (Lee, Kemble, Rick, and David) from his previous marriage. The next year she left *Atlanta* to work at Burke-Dowling Adams, an advertising agency. In 1969 she was hired by Burton Campbell Advertising, where she remained until 1974. During that time she received a letter from Larry Ashmead, an editor at Doubleday, who had admired some of her *Atlanta* articles and wondered whether she might be interested in writing a book. Assuming the letter to be a prank by someone who had swiped some Doubleday stationery, Siddons tossed the letter away. Several weeks later Ashmead tracked her down, and soon afterward she signed a contract with Doubleday for a collection of essays and a novel. The former, *John Chancellor Makes Me Cry*, was published in 1975; the latter, *Heartbreak Hotel*, in 1976.

The essays in *John Chancellor Makes Me Cry* (most of which appeared earlier in *Atlanta*, *Georgia*, or *House Beautiful*) are devoted to such subjects as Siddons's memories of one of her grandfathers; her reactions to the evening news on TV; her husband's and her work in advertising; her stint as her husband's nurse during his bout with the flu; a trip she took to New York City; a stray cat that she adopted; and her experiences while on jury duty. In a review for *Library Journal* (June 15, 1975), Patricia Goodfellow cheered: "These random essays . . . show great variety, wit, and a lively, polished style. Some of the domestic vignettes rival [those of the humorist] Erma Bombeck. . . . A few of these selections are a shade too trendy and . . . may date rapidly; but on the whole, [it is] a stylish, enjoyable collection." Bombeck herself wrote for the *New York Times Book Review* (April 13, 1975) that Siddons's essays "combine humor, intimacy and insight into a marriage." The one "that gives readers the most insight" into Siddons, in Bombeck's view, describes a month in which Siddons experienced several painful emotional blows in succession.

The heroine of Siddons's semiautobiographical novel *Heartbreak Hotel*, Maggie Deloach, is a beautiful, popular 1950s college student whose life takes an unexpected turn after she writes a pro-integration article for her campus newspaper. In the *New York Times Book Review* (September 12, 1976), Katha Pollitt wrote, "This is a marvelously detailed record of a South as gone with the wind as Scarlett O'Hara's."

The House Next Door (1978), Siddons's third book, is a horror novel that Stephen King, known worldwide for his own horror novels, praised in his nonfiction book *Danse Macabre* (1981), a critique of such tales; indeed, he ranked it with Shirley Jackson's classic, harrowing 1959 novel *The Haunting of Hill House*. Writing *The House Next Door*, Siddons told Bob Summer for *Publishers Weekly* (November 18, 1988), was "something of a lark. It's different from anything I've ever written, or probably ever will. But I like to read occult, supernatural stories. Some of the world's great writers have written them, and I guess I wanted to see what I could do with the genre."

Siddons next published her travel guide, *Go Straight on Peachtree* (1978), and her novel *Fox's Earth* (1981). The plot of her next novel, *Homeplace* (1987), centers on Micah Winship, a successful journalist, who returns to her childhood home in a small Georgia town after an absence of more than 20 years. A previously scheduled break from her job and her daughter's visit with Micah's ex-husband have made it possible for Micah to help care for her dying father, to whom she feels no sense of duty. Against her will, she finds herself becoming involved with the happenings of her town. In a *Washington Post* (August 3, 1987) review, Alice Digilio wrote, "Siddons is a fine teller of tales. . . . And by the time we've turned the last page and the hammock has ceased to rock, some of the old wisdom about human nature and love has been reaffirmed. In Siddons' world the genuine triumphs over the sham; the trivial falls down before the significant. And needless to say, love conquers all. Of course, that's why we escaped to read in the hammock in the first place."

Siddons's first resounding commercial success came with *Peachtree Road* (1988). That novel is set in Atlanta and spans four decades, beginning during the early days of World War II, when James Bondurant deserts his wife and three children. Mother and children find a home with Bondurant's brother and sister-in-law, who have a seven-year-old son named Shep. The boy soon bonds with his younger cousin Lucy, who later creates havoc in the lives of people close to her. In the *Washington Post* (October 14, 1998), the novelist Ellen Feldman noted that while Siddons was sometimes guilty of overwriting, *Peachtree Road* "is also a carefully wrought [novel] that somehow manages to retain the grace and delicacy of the world it mourns. More important, it is a compulsively readable book. Siddons is a born teller of tales. Just when we think we know the story of Lucy and Shep Bondurant, the author pulls us up with a double-twisted ending that recasts everything that has gone before. Like the gracious old houses that line it, *Peachtree Road* is a world we live in and carry with us long after we leave it." Currently, almost a million copies of *Peachtree Road* are in print.

Siddons followed *Peachtree Road* with *King's Oak* (1990), *Outer Banks* (1991), *Colony* (1992), and *Hill Towns* (1993). In 1992 she had signed a three-book contract with HarperCollins worth about $3.25 million, and in 1994 she inked a deal with them totaling $13 million. *Colony* is about a southern native named Maude, who beginning in 1922 spends every summer with her disapproving mother-in-law and other members of her husband's clan in an old, wealthy coastal enclave in Maine. The *Virginia Quarterly Review* (Autumn 1992, on-line) described *Colony* as a "beautifully crafted novel" with a "roomy narrative"; in an abstract of a *New York Times* (August 2, 1992, on-line) assessment, Joan Mooney wrote of Siddons's "absorbing multigenerational novel," as she put it, "We are hooked from the moment we meet Maude . . . as a 17-year-old tomboy running wild in the South Carolina countryside." Siddons's next novel, *Downtown* (1994), is about the coming-of-age of Maureen "Smoky" O'Donnell in mid-1960s Atlanta. After a sheltered childhood, Smoky becomes a journalist for the city's newest magazine, *Downtown*, and comes in contact with a rich aristocrat, a free-spirited photographer, and participants in the civil rights movement, among others. In a *Library Journal* (June 15, 1994) review, Joyce Smothers wrote, referring to a best-selling contemporary American novelist and one of the greatest American playwrights of the 20th century, respectively, "Echoes of Pat Conroy and Tennessee Williams can be heard in half a dozen apocalyptic scenes, keeping us flipping through the last 200 pages of this hefty chronicle of Atlanta in the Sixties. . . . Siddons . . . has drawn on memory to create a satisfying historical romance spiced with wry humor." Donna Seaman, in *Booklist* (May 15, 1994), wrote of the story, "It's 1966, and change is in the air, especially in the newly glamorous mecca of Atlanta. . . . Siddons devotes a lot of ink to describing the conflicting dynamics of this time and place and often seems overwhelmed by material we sense is close to her heart. In fact, for the first 100 pages or so, she seems to be driving with the brakes on. When she does let loose, she treats us to some irresistible romance as well as an unusual, if cursory, dramatization of the struggle between the Black Panthers and followers of Martin Luther King, Jr." She concluded that *Downtown* is a "rewarding" page-turner.

Merrit Fowler, the main character in Siddons's *Fault Lines* (1995), is "a self-sacrificing housewife who is tempted to walk away from her old life," as Joanne Wilkinson described her in *Booklist* (September 1, 1995). Married to a workaholic and emotionally depleted by the burdens of caring for her sickly mother-in-law, Merrit follows her daughter to her sister's home in California. In the aftermath of a devastating earthquake, the three women reevaluate their lives and ambitions. *Fault Lines* reminded Wilkinson of both Robert Waller's *Bridges of Madison County* (1992) and Anne Tyler's *Ladder of Years*. "It's apparent from the get go, though," she noted, "that Siddons is working more along the lines of Waller's melodrama than Tyler's wry sendup. . . . There's enough Sturm und Drang in this one to register 8.0 on the Richter scale, and Siddons pumps up every scene with overly lush prose and strangled dialogue. . . . Hollywood glam, a natural disaster, anorexia—everything, in fact, but the kitchen sink. . . . Read it and weep." Shannon Dekle, in *Library Journal* (September 15, 1995), agreed: "Siddons has produced another heart-wrenching drama of Southern women. . . . As in *Downtown*, Siddons deliciously portrays the story of three women who have failed to find internal happiness . . . [and] keeps readers absorbed until the climactic ending."

As Siddons's novel *Up Island* (1997) opens, the protagonist, Molly Redwine, is grappling with the death of her mother, her father's resulting depression, her husband's desertion, and her son's imminent departure from home. In hopes of making a fresh start, Redwine uproots herself from her native Atlanta and settles in Martha's Vineyard, in Massachusetts, where, among other activities, she ministers to both a cancer patient and a pair of swans. In a review for *People* (June 9, 1997), Kim Hubbard wrote, "Siddons manages to make Molly's island interlude, which might easily feel contrived, come across as just the step this particular sort of strong-willed woman would take. The action drags in places; obviously smitten with the Vineyard's rolling landscape, the author seems determined to catalog its every delight. Yet Molly's journey to healing, and her discovery that families come in more forms than she could ever have imagined, make *Up Island* an affecting read." *Up Island* and its successors *Low Country* (1998) and *Nora, Nora* (2000) appeared on many best-seller lists.

Siddons's novel *Islands* (2004) also examines the idea that families are what we make of them. In *Islands*, four friends meet once a year on one or another of the three barrier islands near Charleston, South Carolina, to share, with the intimacy of blood relations, their losses, joys, and challenges. "As always, Siddons writes with a graceful lushness, evoking the wild salt marshes of the coast and Charleston's candlelit drawing rooms with equal ease," Nancy Pate wrote for the *Chicago Tribune* (May 13, 2004). "*Islands* doesn't have the depth of *Colony*—perhaps her best book—but it will have readers longing for sandy beaches and carefree days spent with good friends who feel like family." A number of Siddons's books are available on audiocassettes.

Siddons's most recent novel, *Sweetwater Creek* (2005), spent 15 weeks on the *New York Times* best-seller list. In it the author described the coming-of-age of a 12-year-old named Emily Parmenter. In the opinion of Claudia Smith Brinson, writing for the *Chicago Tribune* (September 28, 2005), it is Siddons's "best work."

In the early 1980s, according to Cynthia Sanz and Gail Cameron Wescott, Siddons's growing renown led to strains in her marriage. "But we got some counseling," her husband, Heyward Siddons, who is 11 years her senior, told the *People* reporters, "and it made me grow up, and the jealousy turned to admiration and greater love." At the time of that conversation, every evening the couple would read aloud whatever Anne Siddons had written that day, as part of the editing process. In 1998 Siddons and her husband moved their primary residence from Atlanta to Charleston, South Carolina. She writes in a separate building in the yard of their house, which was built in the 18th century. She also maintains a condo in an Atlanta high-rise and spends summers with her husband in their house in Brooklin, Maine, where many of his ancestors lived.

—C.M.

Suggested Reading: *Atlanta Magazine* p100+ May 2001, with photos; *Booklist* p1645 May 15, 1994, p7 Sep. 1, 1995; *Chicago Tribune* p4 May 13, 2004; *People* p33 June 9, 1997, p41 July 31, 2000; *Publishers Weekly* p55+ Nov. 18, 1988; *Southern Living* p100+ Sep. 1994, with photos; *Washington Post* B p3 Oct. 14, 1988; Matuz, Roger, ed. *Contemporary Southern Writers*, 1999; Walsh, William J. *Speak, So I Shall Know Thee: Interviews with Southern Writers*, 1993

Selected Books: nonfiction—*John Chancellor Makes Me Cry*, 1975; *Go Straight on Peachtree: A McDonald City Guide to Atlanta*, 1978; fiction—*Heartbreak Hotel*, 1976; *The House Next Door*, 1978; *Fox's Earth*, 1981; *Homeplace*, 1987; *Peachtree Road*, 1988; *King's Oak*, 1990; *Outer Banks*, 1991; *Colony*, 1992; *Hill Towns*, 1993; *Downtown*, 1994; *Fault Lines*, 1995; *Up Island*, 1997; *Low Country*, 1998; *Nora, Nora*, 2000; *Islands*, 2004; *Sweetwater Creek*, 2005

Singer, Bryan

Sep. 17, 1965– Film director

Address: c/o Warner Bros., 4000 Warner Blvd., Burbank CA 91522

With the release of his intricately plotted thriller *The Usual Suspects* (1995), Bryan Singer was hailed as one of Hollywood's most exciting young directors. In his second feature, *Apt Pupil* (1998), Singer showed that he had the ability not only to adapt well-regarded sources (in this case a Stephen King novella of the same name) but also to plumb the depths of human nature and convincingly portray the impressionability of a young mind. In 2000 he explored prejudice and paranoia in the film version of the long-running comic book *X-Men*, in which superpowered beings representing the next phase of human evolution try to survive in a world dominated by ordinary Homo sapiens. *X-Men* became one of the biggest hits of that summer and inspired a Singer-directed sequel, *X2: X-Men United* (2003), a worldwide smash hit. Thanks to Singer's proven track record in bringing comic-book heroes to life on the big screen, Warner Bros. has signed him to direct the next Superman film, *Superman Returns*, due for release in the summer of 2006.

Bryan Singer was born on September 17, 1965 in New York City. He was raised by his adoptive parents in a Jewish household in southern New Jersey, where he attended West Windsor–Plainsboro High School. After his graduation he enrolled at

Kevin Winter/Getty Images

the School of Visual Arts, in New York City, to study filmmaking. He soon transferred to the University of Southern California's School of Cinema-Television; he graduated in 1989. Around that time Singer wrote and directed *Lion's Den*, a short film about a group of friends who reunite a few years after high school only to discover how little they now have in common. Filmed at a cost of $16,000, the movie starred the actor Ethan Hawke, a childhood friend of Singer's. The 25-minute film garnered the budding director enough attention to enable him to mount a feature-length production for his next project. That motion picture, *Public Access* (1993), Singer's first collaboration with the screenwriter Christopher McQuarrie, looked at how the sensibilities of the residents of Brewster, a small town, are warped by the influences of mass media. The flashpoint occurs when a stranger to Brewster lands a job as the host of a local call-in show and, while on the air, asks, "What's wrong with Brewster?" As complaints pour into the show, he becomes an arbiter of public opinion, attracting the attention of local politicians who seek to use his influence to their own advantage. The film won the Grand Jury Prize at the 1993 Sundance Film Festival.

Singer's next film and second collaboration with McQuarrie, *The Usual Suspects*, became one of the most talked-about independent films of 1995. Starring a powerhouse cast—including Gabriel Byrne, Benicio Del Toro, Chazz Palminteri, and Kevin Spacey—the film is a convoluted thriller told in flashback and centers on a near-mythical criminal mastermind named Keyser Söze and the fates of five thieves who perform a heist at his bidding. Spacey and McQuarrie won Academy Awards for their work on the film, which received mostly positive reviews. Janet Maslin, a *New York Times* (August 16, 1995) critic, wrote that *The Usual Suspects* "has been made to be seen twice, with a plot guaranteed to create minor bewilderment the first time around. Mr. Singer and the screenwriter . . . include a great many hints and nuances that won't be noticeable until you know which suspect bears the most watching. Suffice it to say that this film's trickiest role is handled with supreme slyness. And that acting of that caliber, plus a whopper of an ending, compensates for some inevitable head-scratching on the way home." In an assessment for the *Washington Post* (August 18, 1995), by contrast, Desson Howe complained, "Most of the action involving the five suspects occurs in flashback while Spacey is grilled by U.S. Customs agent Chazz Palminteri. . . . The Spacey interrogation becomes the main event. But although the character matchup is interesting (the bullying inspector versus the unreliable creep), you miss those other engaging lowlifes; the movie's flashback-happy, time-bouncing structure feels like a long-winded interruption. . . . After following the beckoning twists and turns, you're left trapped and more than a little disappointed for getting in so deep."

According to various sources, as a boy Singer formed a "Nazi Club" with a group of friends who, like him, were fascinated by World War II; his mother found out about the club and put a stop to it. One of the main characters in *Apt Pupil* (1998), which Singer directed, is similarly fascinated by the war. In *Apt Pupil* (1998), an adaptation of a Stephen King novella, Todd, a suburban teenager

(played by Brad Renfro), discovers that Kurt, one of his elderly neighbors (portrayed by the noted Shakespearian actor Ian McKellen), is a Nazi fugitive living incognito. Todd and Kurt strike a deal: if the old man tells him about the horrors of the war, Todd will not reveal his identity to the authorities. The film received mixed reviews, and was considered a box-office failure. In his critique for *Newsweek* (October 12, 1998), David Ansen wrote, "Director Singer and screenwriter Brandon Boyce are playing a dangerous game themselves, mixing weighty historical themes with bald melodrama. In the end, artifice overwhelms art. *Apt Pupil* is too serious to work as a genre movie, and too contrived to be taken seriously." Lisa Schwarzbaum, on the other hand, suggested in an article for *Entertainment Weekly* (October 23, 1998) that viewers "absorb *Apt Pupil* as a student-teacher parable, a shaping-of-character tale about an unusual Nazi suspect and an alienated kid as American as apple strudel, and you're in for a start more disturbing than anything Keyser Soze could provide."

For his next project Singer was asked by Tom DeSanto, his co-producer on *Apt Pupil,* to direct a film version of the extremely popular *X-Men* comic books, which have been published monthly by Marvel Comics since 1963. Singer, who had never read the comics growing up, said no to the project—twice. "I had no interest in it because I didn't know what it was," Singer explained in an interview with Jeff Jensen for *Entertainment Weekly* (July 21, 2000). "It was just a comic book." When DeSanto pressed Singer a third time to look at some *X-Men* comics, the director reluctantly agreed. He found that the series consisted of more than simply stories of superheroes beating up on super-villains; it offered a thoughtful meditation on prejudice and isolation. According to the *X-Men*'s storyline, the world is split into two groups: genetically ordinary human beings and mutants, a subset of humanity with extraordinary mental or physical abilities. The mutants themselves are divided into two groups, one led by Professor Charles Xavier, the telepathic founder of the X-Men, who believes that mutants must work together to integrate themselves into ordinary society to show that they pose no threat. The other group is led by Magneto, the self-styled "master of magnetism," who believes that a war is coming that will decide which race will inherit the earth. Among the most powerful mutants, Magneto plans not only to spearhead the campaign against humanity but also to lead the mutants after the fall of the old order.

After four decades of story development, the team of X-Men has grown from five to dozens of characters, and the comic's mythology has become complex. In order to bring *X-Men* to the screen, Singer and his writers decided to use only the key characters from the comic. In addition to Professor Xavier, the "good guys" in the film include Cyclops, the team leader who has the ability to fire pulverizing blasts of energy from his eyes; Wolverine, an amnesiac with ultrafast healing powers that allowed someone in his unremembered past to graft metal to his skeleton and retractable claws to his forearms; Storm, who can control the weather; and Jean Grey, who has telekinetic and limited telepathic abilities. On Magneto's side, known as the Brotherhood of Mutants, are Toad, who is abnormally agile and can crawl up walls; Sabertooth, a strongman with powers similar to Wolverine's; and Mystique, a shape shifter. In the film version, both sides try to recruit a young girl named Rogue, whose ability to absorb other people's attributes through physical contact makes her key to Magneto's plan for world dominance.

Though 20th Century Fox had doubts about the potential appeal of the film—and, for that reason, limited Singer's budget to $75 million—*X-Men* grossed more than $150 million domestically and almost $300 million worldwide, placing it among the top-grossing hits of 2000. While most critical responses were positive, some reviewers found the film muddled. In a critique for the *Chicago Sun-Times* (July 14, 2000), Roger Ebert wrote, "I started out liking this movie, while waiting for something really interesting to happen. When nothing did, I still didn't dislike it; I assume the X-Men will further develop their personalities if there is a sequel, and maybe find time to get involved in a story. No doubt fans of the comics will understand subtle allusions and fine points of behavior; they should linger in the lobby after each screening to answer questions." Similarly, Andrew O'Hehir wrote for *Salon* (July 14, 2000, on-line), "With supreme confidence (or perhaps hubris), director Bryan Singer and his team of writers have . . . made *X-Men* the opening chapter in a saga; its plot structure is closer to that of a TV-series pilot episode than a film epic meant to stand on its own. Despite these peculiarities—or maybe because of them—*X-Men* is a distinctively absorbing entertainment, offering just enough popcorn thrills for mass audiences and just enough chewiness for hardcore sci-fi fans."

Singer's next film was the sequel to *X-Men*, *X2: X-Men United* (2003), in which the war between mutants and humans anticipated by Magneto has begun. Following an attempted assassination on the president of the United States by a mutant, a military scientist named William Stryker, acting covertly, attacks the school Professor Xavier runs in Westchester County, New York, and captures a number of the younger mutants. Meanwhile, the X-Men search for the mutant who tried to kill the president as well as the mastermind who put him up to it. Aiding them is Magneto, who forms an unlikely alliance with the X-Men to stop Stryker.

Like its predecessor *X2* received varied critical responses, though fans generally praised it; the film earned approximately $215 million in the United States alone. In his review for the *Chicago Sun-Times* (May 2, 2003), Roger Ebert gave the film three out of four stars, but objected that it "lacks a beginning, a middle and an end, and exists more as a self-renewing loop. In that it is faithful to comic books themselves, which month after month and

year after year seem frozen in the same fictional universe. Yes, there are comics in which the characters age and their worlds change, but the X-Men seem likely to continue forever, demonstrating their superpowers in one showcase scene after another. Perhaps in the next generation a mutant will appear named Scribbler, who can write a better screenplay for them." Lisa Schwarzbaum, writing for *Entertainment Weekly* (May 9, 2003), declared that, though she knew little about the X-Men, she "fell completely and happily under the sway of this new and improved sequel."

In interviews Singer has often said that he expected to direct a trilogy of X-Men films and has given many indications that he feels great affection for that universe of characters. Thus many were surprised when an announcement revealed that he would not be participating in the making of the next X-Men film. According to information made public in April 2004, he and the *X2* screenwriters Dan Harris and Mike Dougherty are scheduled to write 12 issues of *Ultimate X-Men* for Marvel Comics. Singer has signed with Warner Bros. to direct the new Superman film, *Superman Returns*, which is currently in production in Australia. He reportedly has provided the story for the upcoming remake of the 1976 sci-fi film classic *Logan's Run*.
—C.M.

Suggested Reading: All Movie Guide (on-line); *Chicago Sun-Times* (on-line); *Entertainment Weekly* p48 Oct. 23, 1998, p27+ July 21, 2000, with photos, p49+ May 9, 2003, with photo; *New York Times* (on-line) Aug. 16, 1995; *Newsweek* p88 Oct. 12, 1998; *Salon* (on-line) July 14, 2000; *Variety* p20 Jan. 24–30, 1994; *Washington Post* (on-line) Aug. 18, 1995

Selected Films: *Lion's Den*, 1988; *Public Access*, 1993; *The Usual Suspects*, 1995; *Apt Pupil*, 1998; *X-Men*, 2000; *X2: X-Men United*, 2003

Smith, Amy

Nov. 3, 1962– Mechanical engineer; inventor; educator

Address: Edgerton Center, MIT, 77 Massachusetts Ave., D-Labs, Cambridge, MA 02139

"Problem solving has always been in my blood," the mechanical engineer and inventor Amy Smith told Elizabeth Karagianis for the Massachusetts Institute of Technology (MIT) publication *Spectrum* (Spring 2000, on-line). "I'm the kind of person who will walk into a restroom, see a broken sink and fix it instead of complaining that someone else should do it." Far from confining herself to improvements of plumbing or anything else in common use in the United States, Smith has devoted her extraordi-

Courtesy of Amy Smith

Amy Smith in Haiti, explaining her method for making charcoal briquettes from discarded sugar-cane stalks

nary ingenuity and energy not to advancing technologies but, as Kari Lynn Dean wrote for *Wired News* (October 11, 2004, on-line), to "using old technology in fresh ways," with the goal of improving the lives of thousands of poor people in the most impoverished places on Earth. Indeed, thousands of people have already benefited from her three most widely known inventions: a relatively inexpensive, easy-to-repair portable mill for grinding grain into flour; a nonelectrical device called a phase-change incubator, for identifying potentially harmful microorganisms in drinking water; and an oil-drum "kiln" for converting waste sugarcane stalks (stalks previously pressed for their juice) into charcoal—a fuel that is vitally needed in parts of the world where people still cook over wood fires but where supplies of firewood are rapidly dwindling. "Looking at things from a more basic level, you can come up with a more direct solution, and a lot of people go well, duh, that's really obvious!" Smith said to Dean. "But that's what you want: people saying it should have been done that way all along. It may sound small in theory, but in practice, it can change entire economies." She also told Dean, "A lot of people look at where technology is right now and start from there. . . . If you go back to the most basic principles, you can eliminate complexity. The stuff I do is just very simple solutions to things, which is critical when you are developing applications for the third world." A former Peace Corps volunteer who now teaches at MIT, Smith has won several prestigious awards for her work, most notable among them the remunerative MacArthur Fellowship. In an interview with a reporter for PR Newswire (February 9, 2000), she

observed, "Necessity is the mother of invention, but it has often struck me that the most needy are often the least empowered to invent." Referring to her MacArthur grant, she said to Dean, "I've always wanted to have funding to help the people with good ideas who I see and think, 'If only they had the resources, they could do this cool project.' I'd like to use a significant portion of the money to enable people who have the potential to make a significant impact in places like Haiti and India, the ability to just say, 'Hey, that sounds good, lets do it.'"

The second of four children, Amy Smith was born on November 3, 1962 in Lexington, Massachusetts, where she grew up. Her mother was a junior-high-school math teacher; Smith has said that her mother always taught her, as Elizabeth Karagianis paraphrased Smith's words, "If you see a problem, do something about it." Smith's father, Arthur C. Smith, is a professor of electrical engineering at MIT; for five years he served there as the dean for undergraduate education and student affairs, and for two years, he was chairman of the faculty. Smith's older sister, Abby Smith, teaches marine science at the University of Otago, in New Zealand. Smith also has a younger sister and a younger brother. In interviews she has recalled that her family had stimulating conversations at mealtimes, on such subjects as ways to prove the Pythagorean theorem (a proposition fundamental to Euclidean geometry). During the year that she would have spent as a second-grader, Smith attended a village school for boys in northwestern India, where her family lived while her father taught at an Indian technical institute. (Classes in the boys' school, but not the girls', were taught in English.) That experience "set a lot of things in motion for her," as her father remarked to a reporter for the *Boston Business Journal* (February 25, 2000). "It's very different from growing up in a Boston suburb." Her father described Smith as having "always had a different view of what was important in the world." For seven years after she became old enough to babysit, Smith contributed half her earnings to UNICEF.

At Lexington High School Smith devoted much time to musical pursuits, as a member of the band, the orchestra, the chorus, the consort choir, and the madrigals group. She also participated in many activities at the Unitarian-Universalist Follen Community Church, in Lexington. After she completed high school, in 1980, she enrolled at MIT. As an undergraduate she played on the campus basketball, water polo, and volleyball teams. She earned a B.S. degree in mechanical engineering in 1984. During the next two years, she held a part-time engineering-design job; she also volunteered at a food bank and a soup kitchen, coached Special Olympics hopefuls, and tutored students in inner-city high schools.

In 1986 Smith joined the Peace Corps for a four-year stint—twice the normal commitment. She was assigned to work in Botswana, a land-locked nation in south-central Africa. For two years she served as a teacher of math, science, and English at Itekeng Community Junior Secondary School, in the city of Ghanzi. "It's clear that the algebra I taught kids there isn't going to change the whole world," she told Elizabeth Karagianis. "But the fact that the students knew I cared about them made it possible for many of them to continue their educations." For the next two years, as a Ministry of Agriculture regional beekeeping officer, Smith trained farmers in raising bees for honey. In 1988 she was named the JFK Peace Corps Volunteer of the Year in Africa (an honor named for John F. Kennedy, who as president launched the corps). "In the Peace Corps, the people are your social life," Smith told Karagianis. "You don't go to movies. You don't go to concerts. You go to people's houses and you talk to them. The big thing I learned is that people are the most important thing in the world." That sentiment was reinforced when, while Smith was overseas, her mother died. Her death, Smith said, "made me realize you must do what you can to help people. You never know when it will be too late." When she returned briefly to the U.S. to attend her mother's funeral, she was thrust from one of the world's poorest countries to an affluent American community in the U.S., where entire aisles of the local supermarket offered variations on a single product. The jolt she felt at the contrast contributed to her later decision to continue her education and use her engineering skills for the benefit of those living in impoverished parts of the world.

In the early 1990s Smith enrolled in the graduate program in mechanical engineering at MIT. While in Botswana she had occasionally ground grain into flour, using her own muscle power to pound it, as countless women in Third World nations have done for millennia. Producing flour in that way "is one of the most labor-intensive tasks performed by women in rural areas of developing countries," as Smith noted on her MIT Web site; the work often consumes four hours or more each day. In a small fraction of the time and with far less effort, the same job can be accomplished with a commercially produced, motorized appliance called the hammermill. A hammermill is relatively costly, however, and the steel screen that separates the flour from unground particles is its most fragile part; replacements for broken screens "cannot be produced locally," as Smith explained, and they, too, are expensive. As an alternative (and as her master's-degree project) Smith devised a mill that, in her words, "take[s] advantage of the differences in the aerodynamic properties of the particles" to separate the flour from larger particles; there is no screen, and any part that breaks can be repaired locally. The cost of producing the mill is approximately a quarter of that of manufacturing the traditional hammermill, and its operation requires only 30 percent as much energy. Moreover, as she observed when she tested it in a village in Senegal, in West Africa, her mill produces flour 10 times faster than manual grinding, and the flour it produces has been deemed superior to what emerges from a hammermill. Smith earned an M.S. degree in mechanical engineering from MIT in 1995. As a student in MIT's Technology and Policy Program, she received a second master's degree, in 2001.

Earlier, Smith had also invented what is known as the phase-change incubator. The idea for it came to her in 1997, after a visit to Uganda, where she had gone specifically to find "appropriate design problems" for an undergraduate course she was teaching, as Denise Brehm reported in an MIT press release (November 24, 1999, on-line). In Uganda, Smith had met a volunteer working for the African Community Technical Service who was testing for the presence of bacteria in local water supplies. In large parts of Uganda, as in vast areas of other parts of the developing world, virtually all available drinking water is contaminated with bacteria. In order to destroy them with the proper chemicals, the type or types of bacteria must be identified, by placing a sample of the water in question on a growth medium (a substance that stimulates bacteria to multiply rapidly), which must remain at a specific elevated temperature for at least 24 hours. For decades, testers had relied on equipment powered by electricity (from a generator or batteries) to raise the temperature and keep it at the proper level. But sources of electricity do not exist in many of the places that lack clean drinking water.

To fabricate a new type of incubator, Smith looked for a substance that could be heated over a wood or coal fire to a specific temperature and then, with proper insulation, retain the heat for the requisite 24 hours. She found it by trolling an 855-page chemical-supply catalog for materials that were neither poisonous nor expensive and that changed from the liquid phase to the solid phase at that particular temperature (about 111 degrees Fahrenheit, or 44 degrees Celcius)—the "phase-change" temperature. Just as the temperature of water that is turning to ice remains at 32 degrees F. (0 degrees C.) during the transition, the wax-like substance that Smith selected for the incubator remains at about 111 degrees F. during its transformation from liquid back to solid—a process that takes about 24 hours. The components of Smith's incubator, which is about one cubic foot in volume, are a rigid container thickly lined with poly-urethane insulation, into which fits an aluminum cylinder filled with the wax-like substance and capped by an aluminum holder for test tubes or petri dishes. The water sample to be tested is placed on a growing medium in the test tube or petri dish. To test it for bacteria, the user first heats the filled cylinder over a fire. When the wax-like substance melts, the cylinder, with the holder at its top, is placed inside the box. After 24 hours, all bacteria present will have reproduced sufficiently to form visible colonies, thus enabling the user to identify their species. According to Brehm, "A liquid-crystal top that changes color with the temperature fluctuation will probably be used to alert workers that the chemical compound has reached the appropriate temperature and/or cooled again to room temperature." In a television interview with Beverly Schuch and Lauren Thierry for the CNNfn program Business Unusual (May 25, 2000), Smith mentioned other possible applications for the phase-change incubator, such as transporting vaccines and incubating blood samples or tissue cultures.

In 1999 Smith's phase-change incubator won the B. F. Goodrich Collegiate Inventors Award, which carried a stipend of $20,000. The next year Smith won the Lemelson-MIT Student Prize for Inventiveness for her development of the grain mill and the incubator. As quoted by the Associated Press and Local Wire (February 9, 2000), Lester Thurow, chairman of the Lemelson-MIT Awards Program, said upon announcing Smith's receipt of the honor, "While technology is often seen as increasing the 'digital divide,' technology is also needed to decrease that divide. Amy Smith is the perfect example of an inventor-innovator who's using technology to close that gap." Smith planned to invest the $30,000 prize money in marketing her inventions, first to small community-development organizations and later to such major relief agencies as the Red Cross and the World Health Organization.

Also in 2000 Smith joined the faculty of MIT as an instructor at the university's Edgerton Center, in Cambridge, Massachusetts. In collaboration with the MIT Public Service Center, she created Public Service Design Seminars, in which students identify technological problems in developing countries and then work both on site and in MIT design laboratories to come up with solutions. She also founded the MIT IDEAS Competition (the acronym stands for "Innovation, Development, Enterprise, Action, and Service"), which, according to an MIT Web site, "encourages teams to develop and implement projects that make a positive change in the world." Judges evaluate entries as to their originality, feasibility, sustainability, and value to the community for which they have been designed. Winning entries in recent years include a computerized system for assisting blind or visually impaired pedestrians; a community-based telephone service that helps non–English-speaking immigrants; and a more-effective system for anticipating floods and warning those in areas that may be affected. Relevant travel expenses of competitors is paid or partially covered by MIT Public Service Fellowships or through another avenue at MIT.

In September 2004 Smith learned that she had won a MacArthur Fellowship, better known as a "genius grant," not only for what she had already invented but also in recognition of her potential for continuing to help developing areas technologically. The fellowship carries a stipend of $500,000, to be delivered in five yearly installments with no strings attached; that is, Smith has the freedom to use it in any way she wants, and she does not have to reveal how it is spent. She told various interviewers that she intended to use much of the money to supplement the funding she was already receiving for her work.

In one of her most recent projects, Smith and her co-workers found a way to create charcoal from agricultural waste, for use as a fuel in Haiti, the poorest country in the Western Hemisphere. Hundreds of years ago Haiti's lush forests provided a seemingly boundless supply of wood for fuel. Beginning in the 1600s French settlers denuded huge tracts to create plantations, mostly for growing sugar cane, with African slaves providing the manpower. During the 20th century Haiti's human population rose exponentially, creating an ever-growing demand for wood and a jump in logging operations. During hurricanes, the deforestation and the resulting soil erosion led to far more severe flooding and far greater destruction of remaining trees than in past centuries. Currently, forests remain on only 2–3 percent of the land. Reforestation efforts have so far proved futile in Haiti because of people's never-ending need for fuel. Thus, there was a pressing need for an alternative fuel. Smith and her students devised a way of producing charcoal from stalks of sugarcane, which are discarded after all the juice has been squeezed out. As described in "Fuel from the Fields: A Guide to Converting Agricultural Waste into Charcoal Briquettes Fuel," co-authored by Smith and posted on an Edgerton Center Web site, the materials and equipment needed are unwanted canes (called bagasse), which have been completely dried and, preferably, chopped up; an empty oil drum, slightly modified with a chisel or other tool; a few bricks; cassava flour; water; and the makings of a small fire. Stripped to its essentials, the process entails briefly heating the bagasse and then depriving it of oxygen in a completely sealed oil drum, where after 24 hours or so it turns into pieces of charcoal, each no bigger than about 1/10th inch on a side. After the charcoal is cooled, it is mixed with a paste consisting of cassava flour and water and then formed into briquettes, either by hand or with a tool. A major benefit of the charcoal, in addition to the ease and minimal cost of its manufacture, is that, unlike materials for traditional wood fires, it does not produce smoke when burned. In Haiti and many other places around the world, the smoke from indoor wood-burning cooking fires often causes respiratory diseases in babies and children; indeed, untold thousands of children die from such diseases every year.

While not working in the field, Smith devotes much of her time to her church; she has taught Sunday school, led programs that provide food for the hungry in Boston, and worked in a high-school exchange program on Hopi and Navajo reservations. In her leisure time she enjoys playing musical instruments, including the penny whistle, guitar, tenor saxophone, and Navajo flute.

—C.M.

Suggested Reading: Amy Smith's MIT Web page; Ascribe Newswire Sep. 28, 2004; Associated Press State and Local Wire Feb. 9, 2000; *Boston Business Journal* p3 Feb. 25, 2000; *Boston Globe* D p9 Feb. 10, 2000, B p1+ Sep. 28, 2004; (MIT) *Spectrum* (on-line) Spring 2000, with photo; Nevada Inventors Web site Feb. 9, 2000; *New York Times Magazine* p86+ Nov. 30, 2003, with photos; PR Newswire Feb. 9, 2000; *Who's Who in Science and Engineering*, 2005; *Wired News* (on-line) Oct. 11, 2004

Smith, Kiki

Jan. 18, 1954– Sculptor; printmaker

Address: c/o PaceWildenstein, 32 E. 57th St., 2d floor, New York, NY 10022

"More than many other artists of her place and time, Kiki Smith casts spells," the art critic Paul Richard wrote for the *Washington Post* (March 21, 1998). Known primarily as a figural sculptor, Smith has been a leading figure in the New York art scene for over 20 years, creating works whose peculiar magic ranges from a dark, unsettling potency to a mystical air of enchantment. Through her evocative and often eerie sculptures, drawings, and prints, Smith has explored issues of femininity, spirituality, and mortality, presenting the human body as a locus of spiritual and narrative meaning. In the *New York Times* (November 18, 1994), Holland Cotter defined Smith's subject as "the human body, seen as a fragmented, near-immaterial organism, sexually and pathologically fraught." Smith's works, which comprise representations of internal organs, isolated appendages, and figures in the round, incorporate an array of materials, including bronze, paper, plaster, wax, glass, fabric, and ceramic. Simultaneously beautiful and disquieting, many of them suggest vulnerability, sickness, and pain, eliciting from viewers a mixture of aesthetic appreciation and revulsion. In the *Boston Herald* (January 23, 1994), Mary Sherman noted Smith's expertise at "transforming the typically unpleasant—entrails, body organs and mangled bodies—into aesthetic reveries" and characterized her art as "beauty tinged with a hint of terror."

Scott Wintrow/Getty Images

Although Smith is best known for her life-size female nudes in wax and bronze, many of which radiate an "unsettling combination of the macabre and the transcendent," in the words of Holland Cotter, her recent work has also included images of animals, stars, and elements culled from folktales and classical mythology. Considerably less fraught with troubling emotion than her representations of the naked body, these new elements suggest Smith's growing interest in spirituality and the natural world, as well as her fascination with the decorative arts, in which astrological, mythological, and animal imagery have figured heavily.

In addition to wax and bronze, Smith has often used delicate materials, such as paper and fabric, and turned to crafts traditionally regarded as feminine, such as embroidery and sewing. "I really like making things delicate," she told Carlo McCormick for the *Journal of Contemporary Art* (on-line). "I guess you could call them 'girls' materials'; but they're just things that are associated with girls: soft materials like papier-mache. . . . I like that quality of fragility." While many critics have expressed admiration for Smith's "intensely emotional, defiantly feminine art," as Kristine McKenna described it in the *Los Angeles Times* (March 13, 1994), others have faulted her for what they perceive to be an overly sentimental and girlish aesthetic. "There's more than a hint of the fey and twee and the self-regardingly sensitive about her approach, which I find annoying," Adrian Searle wrote in a review for the London *Guardian* (August 17, 1999). Smith has acknowledged her penchant for effeminate, romantic imagery, telling Kristine McKenna, "I'm just a hippie, and the work I make is totally sentimental and schlocky." During an interview with Christine Temin for the *Boston Globe* (June 9, 1996), she added, "I'm always on the brink of kitsch."

The eldest of three daughters, Kiki Smith was born on January 18, 1954 in Nuremberg, Germany. Her father was the celebrated minimalist sculptor Tony Smith; her mother, Jane Lawrence, was an opera singer and actress. Smith grew up in South Orange, New Jersey, where her interest in art and her taste for both the macabre and the decorative blossomed. As a child the artist mummified small animals, wrapping them in cloth and adorning them with artificial jewels before burying them in the backyard. Along with her sisters—the twins Seton, who is also a visual artist, and Beatrice (nicknamed Bebe), who died of AIDS in 1988—she often helped her father make cardboard models for his geometric sculptures. "[Art] was never separated out from life—it was just part of it," Smith recalled to Kristine McKenna. Another important part of life for the Smith family was their Catholicism, which has served as a major source of inspiration for Kiki Smith's art.

In 1973, shortly after graduating from high school, Smith moved to San Francisco, California, where she lived communally with the members of the Tubes, a rock band. The following year she enrolled at the Hartford Art School, in West Hartford, Connecticut, where she studied film for a year and a half before dropping out and moving to New York City, in 1976. For the next several years, she supported herself by means of a series of odd jobs, among them bartender, short-order cook, electrician's assistant, surveyor, and commercial airbrusher in the textile industry. During this period she befriended several members of Collaborative Projects Inc. (Colab), an artists' collective known for mounting experimental exhibitions in unconventional venues. In 1979 Smith joined Colab and began to participate in its group shows, along with such artists as Charles Ahearn, Jenny Holzer, Cara Perlman, Tom Otterness, and Robin Winters. In 1980, the year her father died, Smith took part in Colab's legendary "Times Square Show," an exhibition mounted in an abandoned four-story building that had once housed a massage parlor and a bus depot. Smith's contribution was a series of paintings based on anatomical designs. The show featured the work of hundreds of then-unknown artists, a "souvenir shop" where low-price copies of artworks were for sale, and nightly performances. It was an instant success, attracting the attention of journalists and curious visitors alike. Impressed with the ambition and originality of the exhibition, the art dealer and critic Jeffrey Deitch wrote a review of it for the prestigious magazine *Art in America*, thus further boosting Colab's reputation—and, by association, Smith's.

Over the next several years, Smith's burgeoning interest in human biology led her to create many objects and drawings based on cellular forms, organs, severed appendages, and organic systems, particularly those involving reproduction and digestion. In 1985 she studied glasswork at the New York Experimental Glass Workshop, where she created a transparent sculpture of a human stomach. The piece impressed representatives of the antacid maker Pepto-Bismol, and the company commissioned her to make another glass stomach for a television advertisement. Also in 1985 Smith spent three months training as an emergency medical technician (EMT) at Interfaith Hospital, in Brooklyn, New York, with the aim of learning more about the workings of the human body. Although gaping wounds and other injuries fascinated her, she gave up her work at the hospital. "What I discovered was that I basically wasn't interested in the physical healing of things," she explained to Kristine McKenna.

By the time Smith had her first solo exhibition, in 1988, at the Fawbush Gallery, in the SoHo section of New York City, the human body had emerged fully as the dominant theme of her work. Drawings of uteri, a terracotta sculpture of a human rib cage, an installation involving X-rays, and other pieces based on internal organs and systems abounded in her show. One construction consisted of 12 large bottles of mirrored glass, each of which bore in Gothic letters the German word for a bodily fluid. A year later Smith was honored with two solo museum exhibitions: "Concentrations 20: Kiki Smith," at the Dallas Museum of Art, in Texas, and "Kiki Smith," at the Center for the Arts at Wesleyan University, in Middletown, Connecticut.

Smith's work of the late 1980s is literally visceral, rife with allusions to the functions and experiences of the body, from conception and gestation to digestion and excretion to death and decay. By representing or evoking the body's internal organs and fluids, Smith sought to compel viewers to contemplate their own physical existence. "Smith transforms the buried consciousness of mortality into an open wound," Susan Kandel wrote for the *Los Angeles Times* (December 17, 1992). During the 1990s—which the art critic Michael Kimmelman, in the *New York Times* (August 16, 1992), described as "the decade of the human body as political battleground"—debates concerning AIDS and abortion began to dominate the public dialogue. Having gained a sudden topical relevance, Smith's body-oriented work attracted unprecedented attention from critics and the press and catapulted the artist to international art stardom. Smith has cited AIDS and her sister's death from the disease as an important subject of her work of that period, much of which deals with mortality and the physical deterioration of the body. "I think AIDS has had a lot to do with people's consciousness of the body as a political and social weapon or landscape . . . ," she told Carlo McCormick. "We've become aware of the body as a social organism that is very much manipulated by different venues and different agendas." Abandoning her previous fascination with the parts and functions of the body, Smith began to make works based on the human body as a whole. It was a bold departure for the artist, who had focused on organs and interiors because she wanted to create archetypes with which a wide range of viewers could identify rather than portraits, whose specificity she feared would be limiting. "I don't like personality," Smith explained to Carlo McCormick. "I just want to talk about the generic experience of the body without it becoming specific to specific people."

Smith's shift in thematic focus entailed adjustments in tone as well as materials. In contrast to her early pieces in glass and paper, which are lyrical and poetic despite their fleshly subject matter, her work from the early to mid-1990s, most of it life-size sculptures of female nudes in wax and bronze, is both literally and figuratively darker. Some of the figures appear flayed, with muscles and veins exposed. Others urinate, trail excrement, or drip breast milk, menstrual blood, or semen. For *Blood Pool* (1992) Smith created a blood-red body curled in a fetal position on the floor, its spinal column—a strip of gleaming, white vertabrae—laid bare. Simultaneously disconcerting and pitiable, the sculpture engages viewers by first horrifying them and then demanding their sympathy. "This work is many things," Susan Kandel wrote, "but most of all it is a plea for mercy."

Smith has also made many sculptures based on biblical stories. As with her other figures, she has chosen mostly female subjects, placing emphasis on their corporeality as a narrative element. "It's one of my loose theories that Catholicism and art have gone well together," she commented during an interview for the Public Broadcasting System's Art:21 Web site, "because both believe in the physical manifestation of the spiritual world, that it's through the physical world that you have spiritual life, that you have to be here physically in a body."

A life-size bronze sculpture of a nude, flayed Virgin Mary (1993) suggests Mary's sufferings as the mother of Christ by confronting viewers with a stark image of physical pain. A sculpture of Mary Magdalene (1994), naked but covered in hair and shackled at the ankle, endows its subject with an animalistic sexuality, suggesting her early vocation as a prostitute. *Lot's Wife* (1993), a plaster column mixed with salt, alludes to the biblical story in which a woman is turned into a salt pillar after she disobeys her husband's orders. Similarly, *Lilith* (1994), a cast-bronze figure of a crouching, naked woman that hangs improbably on the wall, takes as its subject the mythological first wife of Adam, who left her husband after he refused to treat her as an equal. The strange position of the sculpture on the wall and its realistic glass eyes, which gaze directly at the viewer, are unsettling, suggesting both Lilith's defiant power and the mistrust with which rebellious women have traditionally been regarded.

In 1994, reportedly on the advice of her astrologer, Smith left the Fawbush Gallery, her dealer of 10 years, and acquired representation at PaceWildenstein, a prestigious gallery on the Upper East Side of Manhattan. She debuted at PaceWildenstein that fall with an exhibition called "Drawings," which, despite its title, also included prints, reliefs, collages, and sculptures. Holland Cotter wrote of the works that Smith presented at that show, "Breast and genital shapes made of tissue-fine paper swell out in rounded reliefs; images of flayed hands and feet done with reddish paint have the desiccated look of autumn leaves, and hollow portrait heads of the artist dangle from strings like punching bags."

In the late 1990s Smith turned her attention to animals and astronomical bodies, subjects that she felt had been largely overlooked by contemporary artists. In particular, she became fascinated with birds, whose prevalence in various mythologies appealed to her mystical sensibilities. She began to make drawings of the bird specimens on display at the Peabody Museum of Archaeology and Ethnology at Harvard University, in Cambridge, Massachusetts, then later transformed the sketches into prints or made sculptures based on them. Portrayals of stags and bats also began to figure heavily in Smith's sculptures and prints.

Recently, Smith has channeled her interest in enchantment and spirituality into images and objects based on fairy tales and mythology. In 2001 the International Center of Photography, in New York City, mounted an exhibition of her work, entitled "Kiki Smith: Telling Tales," which Sarah Boxer, in the *New York Times* (April 27, 2001), described as "a multimedia mythology." The show, which included sculptures, drawings, videos, and paper puppets as well as photographs, combined imagery from the stories of Snow White (apples and witches) and Little Red Riding Hood (wolves and young girls) with imagery related to Smith's meditations on sexuality, danger, and vulnerability. Although not as disconcerting as the flayed and excreting figures of the 1990s, the new works were considerably less tame than Smith's glass animal and star sculptures.

In 2002 the Whitney Museum of American Art, in New York City, commissioned Smith to create a site-specific work in Central Park for the 2002 Whitney Biennial exhibition. The result was *Sirens and Harpies*, a set of 20 bronze figures based on Greek mythology, each with the head of a woman and the body of a bird. From December 2003 to March 2004, the Museum of Modern Art, also in New York City, mounted a major retrospective of Smith's prints and multiples, entitled "Kiki Smith: Prints, Books, and Things." The exhibition, which included prints created with a wide variety of techniques, from etching and lithography to rubber-stamping and photocopying, treated the themes of anatomy, nature, and femininity. Mysterious pictures of young girls, animals, and body parts danced among images of stars and butterflies; their naïve, labored style and "atmosphere of studied inexpertise," in the words of Holland Cotter, contributed to the effect of innocence and magic that characterizes much of Smith's recent work. According to Cotter, Smith's prints conjured "the affecting image of a precocious child straining against the limits of materials in order to articulate certain intensely felt ideas." Smith herself has discussed the spiritual aspect of printmaking, which she has likened to repetitive devotional activities, such as the Catholic practice of saying rosaries (in which each bead represents a prayer).

Smith's interest in women's bodies influenced her piece *Near* (2005), a large-scale, cast bronze, structure that resembles an unfolded cardboard box or a box kite; it incorporates two gilt and copper-leaf female figures—Smith's reinterpretations of the female subjects in the early-American painting *David, Joanna and Abigail Mason* (attributed to the so-called Freake-Gibbs Painter, 1670). Adjacent to the bronze sculpture is one composed of 250 hand-blown glass teardrops. The unconventional piece was commissioned by the M. H. de Young Memorial Museum, in San Francisco; the first large-scale sculpture by Smith to join the museum's permanent collection, it hangs above the entry to the institution's Contemporary Arts and Crafts Gallery.

Kiki Smith lives and works in New York City. Inspirations for her recent work include 19th-century Victorian life and Russian folklore. She has been honored with a Skowhegan Medal for Sculpture (2000), from the Skowhegan School of Painting and Sculpture, in Maine. Her work is in the permanent collections of many prominent museums, among them the Solomon R. Guggenheim Museum and the Metropolitan Museum of Art, in New York City, and the Museum of Contemporary Art, in Los Angeles.

—L.W.

Suggested Reading: *Boston Globe* B p21+ June 9, 1996; (London) *Guardian* T p10+ Mar. 7, 1995; *Los Angeles Times* p74+ July 7, 1991, p5+ Mar. 13, 1994; *New York Times* H p23+ Aug. 16, 1992, C p11+ Nov. 9, 1994, with photo, C p1+ Nov. 15, 1996, E p41+ Dec. 5, 2003; *San Francisco Chronicle* E p1+ May 21, 2005; *Washington Post* C p1+ Mar. 21, 1998

Carlye Calvin, courtesy of NOAA

Solomon, Susan

Jan. 1956– Atmospheric scientist

Address: c/o NOAA Public Affairs, 14th St. & Constitution Ave., N.W., Rm. 6217, Washington, DC 20230

"As a young student of chemistry in the late 1970s," the atmospheric scientist Susan Solomon wrote for the Web site of the University Corp. for Atmospheric Research, "I became intrigued with the notion that chemistry could be explored on a planet instead of in a test tube." Solomon embraced that idea in two journeys to Antarctica, in 1986 and 1987, that were critical in providing evidence of damage to the ozone layer, which has since been widely acknowledged as one of the most daunting threats to Earth's environment. For her work in revealing the effects of industrial chemicals on the ozone, Solomon was awarded the National Medal of Science, the highest honor presented to scientists by the United States government. Solomon has also been active in the study of global warming, the term for what many scientists believe to be the gradual heating of Earth's atmosphere by man-made pollutants. In addition, she is the author of *The Coldest March*, a nonfiction book about the ill-fated journey to Antarctica by the explorer Robert Falcon Scott.

Susan Solomon was born in January 1956 in Chicago, Illinois. Her father was an insurance salesman; her mother was a fourth-grade schoolteacher. Solomon has felt an inclination toward the sciences "since I was about 10 years old and I watched [the undersea explorer] Jacques Cousteau on TV," as she told Julie Hutchinson for the *Chicago Tribune* (May 24, 1992). She excelled in chemistry in high school and majored in that subject at the Illinois Institute of Technology, in Chicago. She graduated with a B.S. degree in 1977 and spent that summer working at the National Center for Atmospheric Research (NCAR). She received a Ph.D. degree in chemistry from the University of California at Berkeley in 1981. That same year she began working as a research chemist for the U.S. government's National Oceanic and Atmospheric Administration (NOAA), where she has spent more than 20 years investigating the causes of the depletion of the ozone layer.

Often referred to as a "natural sunscreen," the ozone layer lies in Earth's stratosphere (between 10 and 50 kilometers, or between six and 30 miles, above the surface). Ozone (O_3) forms when ultraviolet radiation from the sun splits oxygen molecules (O_2) into atomic oxygen (single oxygen atoms, O); the atomic oxygen combines with O_2 to form O_3. The ozone layer blocks certain components of the sun's rays, such as ultraviolet rays, which can cause skin cancer in humans. In 1973 Sherwood Rowland and Mario Molina, chemists at the University of California at Irvine, began to test the influence of chlorofluorocarbons (CFCs), industrial chemicals used, for example, in refrigerators, air conditioners, and aerosol spray cans, on the stratosphere. Over time they formed the theory that CFCs might be causing the ozone layer to thin, allowing more of the sun's ultraviolet rays to seep through the atmosphere. Rowland immediately spoke out about his discovery, calling for a ban on all CFCs; he was met largely with skepticism and ridicule, in part because he and Molina lacked hard evidence of what they suspected. In 1984 Anne Burford, the head of the Environmental Protection Agency during President Ronald Reagan's administration, called the claims of ozone depletion a "scare issue"; several years later that administration's secretary of the interior, Donald Hodel, suggested that any danger presented by a hole in the ozone layer was minimal, and that people could protect themselves simply by wearing sunglasses and sunscreen. In 1985, however, a team of British scientists discovered that the ozone layer over Antarctica had been depleted by about 30 percent in 10 years, which was far faster than anyone had thought, and that the hole in the layer was deepening each spring.

In 1986 Solomon, greatly interested in the findings of Rowland and Molina, took center stage on the issue. She presented a new theory, which was that while chlorofluorocarbons could be harmful to ozone, it was the intense cold of the Antarctic that was accelerating the process to such an extent. Since the deepening of the hole occurred in the spring, as British scientists discovered and Solomon's team confirmed, the researchers theorized that the damage was done in the late winter; studying this phenomenon meant heading into Antarctica, the planet's coldest region, during its coldest season. Solomon thus led a research team into the Antarctic in the heart of winter in an attempt to record data on how CFCs affect the ozone layer.

In an interview with Gabrielle Walker for *New Scientist* (October 13, 2001), Solomon explained that she had been excited to visit the cold, desolate region: "I loved it from the minute I stepped off the airplane," she said. "I loved the wildness of it. I loved the pristineness, the emptiness, the ferocity, the absolutely unforgiving nature of that environment. I love the things about nature that remind us how powerful it is and how puny we are, and Antarctica is as fierce and beautiful as you can get." Her work there proved to be difficult. "This is one of the most challenging things that we've ever come across in atmospheric chemistry," Solomon said to James Gleick for the *New York Times* (July 29, 1986) just before her trip. "Whatever the source [of the ozone depletion] is, we need to understand it because this is a change in the ozone that's of absolutely unprecedented proportions. We've just never seen anything like what we're experiencing in the Antarctic."

Solomon studied the way in which the Antarctic air absorbed moonlight during the long winter nights. To do so she set up a system of mirrors to reflect moonlight—and exposed herself to extremely harsh conditions. "The mirrors were on the roof of our laboratory about a mile from the main base," Solomon told Gabrielle Walker. "One night I was observing and about 3am it clouded over so I went to sleep. When I woke up in the morning a howling blizzard was under way." Solomon headed out into the intense winds to save the mirrors and continue the research. "I went up there and tried to get the things down, and the wind was gusting up and I was pushed several feet across the roof. I dropped down spreadeagled and crawled back and finally got the mirrors down."

The expedition, which extended from August to November 1986, was met with considerable interest from the media. Michael Parfit wrote for the *Los Angeles Times* (August 31, 1986), "The voices that come floating up from the bottom of the Earth will be using words like ozone and chlorofluorocarbons and stratosphere, but they will be talking about human survival." The experiments conducted by Solomon's team did not lead them to immediate conclusions about the causes of the ozone damage, and the scientists announced that it would be necessary to take another trip the following year. By the end of her 1987 trip, Solomon was more certain of her findings. "The evidence right now," she said in an interview for the CBS News program *West 57th*, as quoted by John Horn in the *Orange County Register* (July 4, 1987), "strongly suggests that [chlorofluorocarbons] are the most likely cause of the ozone hole."

In addition to supporting that belief, Solomon's experiments bolstered the theory that the ozone hole appeared over Antarctica because the intense cold accelerated the chemical reactions that took place due to the CFCs. She also asserted that the eruption of the volcano Mount Pinatubo, in the Philippines, in 1991 had contributed to the depletion of ozone over Antarctica. "Volcanic particles make chlorine from CFCs more effective at ozone destruction," Solomon said to Mark Steene for the *Advertiser* (October 1, 1998).

In 1987, fueled by rising evidence that CFCs were responsible for the life-threatening hole in the ozone layer, the United Nations Environment Program sponsored a gathering in Canada of 46 nations whose industries produced significant amounts of CFCs. At the meetings, collectively called the Montreal Protocol, the countries' representatives agreed to freeze CFC use at existing levels; the accords were revised and expanded in 1992, calling for progressive cuts in CFC use. Meanwhile, the ozone hole continued expanding; in 1998 it was measured at three times the size of Australia. Its growth was attributed largely to the prior buildup of CFCs, which take about 50 years to dissolve. "It's going to be several decades before we see the end of the Antarctic ozone hole," Solomon told Mark Steene. She expressed some optimism, however, noting that the decrease in CFC emissions would eventually lead to the closing of the hole, and adding, "If you had to have an ozone hole," the area above the uninhabited Antarctica was "probably the best place to have it."

For her role in identifying and legitimizing the notion of ozone depletion and identifying its causes, Solomon has received many accolades and awards. In 1994 a glacier in Antarctica was christened the Solomon Glacier, in her honor. In March 2000 she was awarded the United States' highest scientific honor when then-president Bill Clinton presented her with the National Medal of Science. Upon being named for the award, Solomon reacted with modesty. "I was in the right place in the right time with the kind of science opportunity that only happens very rarely, a once-in-a-scientific-lifetime," she said, as quoted by Ann Schrader in the *Denver Post* (February 1, 2000). William Daley, then secretary of commerce, called Solomon "one of the most important and influential researchers in atmospheric science during the past 15 years," as quoted by the Environment News Service (February 4, 2000).

In 2001 Solomon published *The Coldest March: Scott's Fatal Antarctic Expedition,* a book about the explorer Robert Falcon Scott, who in 1912 was in a race with Roald Amundsen to lead the first team to reach the South Pole. Amundsen beat Scott by a month; on Scott's return trip, he and his team of four men froze to death. Scott described the expedition in great detail in his diary, which was found on his body. In the years after his death, Scott was portrayed by later explorers and authors as an incompetent man whose mistakes were responsible for the tragedy. Solomon probed more deeply into the story of Scott, having come across his cabin in Antarctica during one of her trips there. After reading his diaries, she decided to look further into the atmospheric conditions that existed in Antarctica in the year he died, and her findings inspired her to write the book. Solomon sought to provide a more balanced view of Scott, claiming in the book that he and his team had encountered conditions no one could have survived. "No one could have predicted the persistent cold weather that Scott faced," she explained to Gabrielle Walker. "In 17 years of direct data from the area where he died, there's only been one year like that. George Simpson, Scott's meteorologist, was convinced that the weather was highly unusual, but he couldn't prove it and I could. That's when I knew I had to write this book." Solomon explained that during Scott's expedition, "the average daily low should have been around −30 degrees C in March. That feels toasty once you've acclimatized. But −40 degrees C is an entirely different matter. You feel as if your nostrils are being freeze-dried, and frost forms at the edge of your eyes. That kind of cold has really serious consequences for an expedition." In a review of the book for the *Spectator* (October 13, 2001), M. R. D. Foot wrote, "Over and over again, Solomon picks on the legends that have accumulated round Scott to his disadvantage, and disproves them." By the end of the book, according to Foot, Solomon has vindicated Scott and his team to the extent that "we can truly believe they were heroes."

In 2002 Solomon was selected to be a part of the Intergovernmental Panel on Climate Change (IPCC), an international group established by the World Meteorological Organization (WMO) and the United Nations Environment Program (UNEP) to examine changes in the atmosphere over time. Working with the IPCC, Solomon turned her attention toward another potentially fearsome phenomenon: global warming. Often confused with theories about the hole in the ozone layer, the global-warming theory holds that the burning of fossil fuels and other human-generated pollution are responsible for a slow and gradual warming of Earth's atmosphere. The issue of global warming is politically charged, and Solomon has been careful to provide balanced assessments of the dangers the phenomenon may pose. (In a controversial move, the United States refused to adopt the Kyoto Accords, through which more than 160 nations agreed to try to curb the production of greenhouse gases. In March 2001 President George W. Bush declared that lowering emissions of carbon dioxide as called for in the agreement would be too costly for American companies.) As quoted on the IPCC Web site, Solomon described the need for scientists to address the issue, saying, "I . . . don't think we want to go down in history as the generation that thought it might be causing the climate to start to change but just couldn't be bothered to try and figure out whether that was true or not." She said, as quoted by the Associated Press (June 23, 2004), "The serious debate that is ongoing now is how much global warming we will have if we continue to put CO_2 [carbon dioxide] into the atmosphere." On the other hand, she has also rejected claims that certain environmental disasters, such as a lethal heatwave in France in 2003, were due to global warming. "People who attributed France's heatwave last year to global warming have been left with egg on their faces," she said, as quoted by Colin Patterson in the Wellington, New Zealand, *Dominion Post* (September 4, 2004). "2004 has been cold and wet." Above all, she has stressed that with regard to such issues as global warming, science should not be mixed with politics. "I don't think

we should detract from the dignity of our science by making political statements," Solomon told *Current Biography*. "As scientists we have to be objective and focused, not political."

In June 2004 Solomon received the Blue Planet prize, a prestigious award (which includes $460,000) presented by the Asahi Glass Foundation of Japan to scientists dedicated to preserving the environment. Solomon lives in Boulder, Colorado, where she works for the NOAA and continues to research atmospheric phenomena. She is married and has one stepson.

—R.E.

Suggested Reading: *Orange County Register* G p1 June 5, 1988; *Time* p60 Feb 17, 1992; *Vancouver Sun* D p1 May 4, 1996; *New Scientist* p4646 Oct. 13, 2001

Selected Books: *The Coldest March: Scott's Fatal Antarctic Expedition*, 2001

Spellings, Margaret

Nov. 30, 1957– U.S. secretary of education

Address: U.S. Department of Education, 400 Maryland Ave., S.W., Washington, DC 20202

"The issue of education is close to my heart. And on this vital issue, there is no one I trust more than Margaret Spellings," George W. Bush said in nominating Spellings to be the second U.S. secretary of education of his presidency, as quoted by Maura Reynolds in the *Los Angeles Times* (November 18, 2004). During Bush's tenure as governor of Texas, Spellings served as his senior adviser on education, and later, as assistant to the president for domestic policy, she helped design one of the largest and most controversial overhauls of public education in recent history: the No Child Left Behind act. That legislation has made public schools accountable for performances of students in third through eighth grades on yearly tests and has allowed children in failing public schools to transfer to more successful public or charter institutions. At the time of her nomination to the post of education secretary, the senior presidential adviser Karl Rove called Spellings "the most influential woman in Washington that you've never heard of," according to Ben Feller, writing for the Associated Press (November 16, 2004), and Gail Russell Chaddock wrote for the *Christian Science Monitor* (November 18, 2004), "It is a studied art to be both influential and little known in official Washington, and Margaret Spellings . . . has mastered it well. Spellings couldn't be picked out of a lineup by most of the nation's teachers, yet has had more to do with the new mandates in their classrooms than anyone in

Paul Morse, courtesy of the White House

Washington." Since she was sworn in as education secretary, in January 2005, however, Spellings has had a much higher profile, working to solidify and expand the programs that make up the No Child Left Behind act. The eighth U.S. secretary of education, and the first to have children in school while serving in the post, Spellings called the issue of education "the optimistic, hopeful side of public policy," as quoted by Amy Goldstein in the *Washington Post* (March 28, 2001). "I can't think of anything that is more high impact."

The eldest of four daughters, Spellings was born Margaret Dudar on November 30, 1957 in Michigan, where both of her parents were students at the University of Michigan in Ann Arbor; her father, John Dudar, was studying for his doctorate in geology, while her mother, Peg Dudar, was working toward her master's degree in social work. When Margaret was in third grade, the Dudars moved to Houston, Texas, where John Dudar had found work in the oil business. Over the years there Peg Dudar worked for various social ministries. Spellings attended public school and in seventh grade became the first in her group of friends to host a dinner party, serving fondue from card tables. "I was a little Martha Stewart. I still have those leanings," she told Goldstein. Spellings attended Sharpstown High School, in Houston, and took a job at a local grocery store—Handy Andy—that she would hold through college. She was quickly promoted at the store to a position in the customer-service booth. "I loved it—the power surge of standing on an elevated platform with Plexiglas and a microphone," she told Goldstein.

Spellings graduated from high school in 1975 and began studies that fall at the University of Houston. At 21 she married and took the surname La Montagne. After earning a B.A. degree in political science and journalism, in 1979, she worked for former Texas governor John B. Connally in his unsuccessful attempt to secure the 1980 Republican presidential nomination. After the close of the campaign, Spellings moved to Austin, Texas, where she worked for Governor William P. Clements as well as for members of the Texas House of Representatives, Austin Community College, and the American Cancer Society. She also worked as a clerk for the state House Education Committee during the period leading up to the 1984 passage of school-reform legislation, which gave the state more authority over its schools. Despite that success, Spellings began to have doubts about the approach she had taken to education. She later joined the Texas Association of School Boards as government relations director. In that position, along with her friend and colleague Louann Martinez, she frequently battled teachers' unions, actions that led their opponents to dub them "princesses of darkness." (In response, the two purchased black capes.) Jay Levin, a lobbyist for the Texas State Teachers Association who frequently opposed Spellings on education issues, told Michael Dobbs for the *Washington Post* (November 18, 2004), "She was a worthy adversary. I admired her because of her tenacity and the intensity she brought to debating the issues."

In 1989 George W. Bush, then the owner of the Texas Rangers baseball club, began to consider making a run for the Texas governorship the following year. His colleague Karl Rove asked Spellings to brief Bush on education issues. Bush did not run for governor in 1990 but did so four years later, at which time, remembering Spellings's strong belief in local control of schools and her in-

depth knowledge of school finance, he chose her as the political director of his campaign. "One of the reasons he wanted her is she was clearly one of the best minds in Texas on education policy," Rove said, according to Robert Dodge, writing for the *Dallas Morning News* (November 18, 2004). After Bush won the election that fall, Spellings served in his administration as senior adviser for education policy. In that position she was instrumental in the creation in 1996 of the Texas Reading Initiative, which requires students to read at their own level or higher by the third grade. She also helped design the Safe Schools Act of 1995, which gives Texas teachers more power to remove violent or otherwise disruptive students from their classrooms. In 1999 the Texas legislature passed the Student Success Initiative, which Spellings helped to design; that legislation forbids schools to let third graders advance to fourth grade if they cannot pass the reading portion of the Texas Assessment of Academic Skills (TAAS). While such measures were controversial, Spellings earned praise from legislators and lobbyists on both sides of the political spectrum. "The neat thing about Margaret is that she was open to listening to any idea, as long as you weren't wasting her time," Gayle Fallon, president of the Houston Federation of Teachers, told Chaddock.

In the fall of 2000, during the final month of Bush's campaign for the presidency, Spellings split her time between the governor's office and the campaign trail, where she briefed reporters on Bush's stance regarding education. Bush had advocated national education reform similar to the changes enacted in Texas. "No other state has this kind of accountability system that can shine a light on performance like ours," Spellings was quoted as saying in the *Seattle Times* (March 30, 2000). Indeed, 1994 TAAS scores had risen dramatically, although the scores of Texas high-school students on college admissions tests had not. At the same time, other data emerged that indicated that the improvement in TAAS scores was not as significant as it had appeared, and some educators worried that public-school curriculum was now so focused on preparation for TAAS that subjects not covered by the test were being ignored. After Bush won the presidential election, the National Center for Public Policy and Education, a nonpartisan group, gave Texas poor to mediocre grades for its efforts to prepare high-school students for college. "I think it's credible," Spellings said about the rating to Ben Wear for the *Austin American-Statesman* (December 1, 2000). "Obviously, we're disappointed it didn't take into account the most recent data. But it shows us that we are working in the areas that we need to work."

In January 2001 Bush appointed Spellings assistant to the president for domestic policy. In that role she helped to shape the president's education policy—to a greater extent, some felt, than did Secretary of Education Rod Paige. She was also responsible for developing and implementing the president's policies on health, labor, transportation, the justice system, housing, welfare reform, and "faith-based" initiatives. During Bush's first term in office, Spellings worked diligently on crafting and lobbying for the No Child Left Behind act, Bush's education plan aimed at decreasing achievement gaps between students of different gender, ethnicity, or income level. The legislation requires public schools to test students in third through eighth grades in reading and math on an annual basis, and to test students at least once during high school. The information from the tests is given to educators, parents, and students in the form of annual report cards and is used to assess schools and teachers. The act allows low-income parents whose children are in public schools deemed to be failing to transfer the children to better public schools or to charter institutions. The No Child Left Behind act also raised qualification standards for teachers and set annual performance standards for schools in the teaching of certain subgroups of students, such as minorities and children of low-income families. After much debate, the bill won overwhelming congressional approval in December 2001 and was signed into law by President Bush in January 2002.

The No Child Left Behind act proved to be controversial. Officials in many states felt that the law took away too much of their authority and interfered with their own school-accountability systems, and that the program would cost too much to carry out successfully. Some also criticized the aspect of the legislation that allowed military recruiters access to schools and to contact information for all students. As the law began to be implemented, in 2003, many state legislatures adopted resolutions that were critical of it. Spellings sent an adviser from her office to the Department of Education and to some state capitals to help assuage fears regarding the new law. Although the administration succeeded in improving relations with state legislatures where the law was concerned, many Democrats who had supported the bill complained that the administration had underfunded its implementation. Others noted that the law removed funding for elective courses and after-school programs. Republicans countered by stating that money for the nation's poorest schools had now increased by 50 percent.

During Bush's first term Spellings helped to promote the Bush administration's $25 million effort to persuade parents to talk to their children about the dangers of using drugs. Spellings has also pushed the Bush administration's case for giving federal money for sex-education programs only to those that primarily promote abstinence.

After his election to a second term as president, Bush nominated Spellings to succeed Paige as U.S. secretary of education, a post in which she would oversee around 4,400 employees and a budget of over $56 billion. "She believes that every child can learn," Bush was quoted as saying by Diana Jean Schemo for the *New York Times* (November 18, 2004), "and that every school can succeed. And she knows the stakes are too high to tolerate failure." The nomination was greeted warmly by Democrats and Republicans alike, and on January 6, 2005 the Senate's Health and Education Committee approved Spellings unanimously for Senate confirmation. Spellings told the committee that while she was aware of the concerns regarding No Child Left Behind, she was committed to addressing them. She also informed the committee of the administration's plans to expand the legislation to affect high-school students. "With only 67 of every 100 ninth-graders graduating from high school on time and with the United States lagging in math . . . we must turn our attention to high schools and to math and science," Spellings said, as quoted by George Archibald for the *Washington Times* (January 7, 2005).

Before Spellings's confirmation could be brought to a vote on the Senate floor, it was revealed that the Department of Education had paid the television and radio commentator Armstrong Williams $240,000 to promote No Child Left Behind on the air. Spellings said she and her chief of staff did not learn about the deal until after the contract had been signed. Democratic senator Frank Lautenberg of New Jersey placed a hold on Spellings's nomination as a result of the disclosure but lifted it on January 19, after she promised to review the actions that led to the approval of payments to Williams. On January 20 the Senate voted to confirm Spellings as secretary of education, and she was sworn in on January 31. By early February the Department of Education ended its contract with Ketchum, the public-relations firm hired primarily to promote No Child Left Behind. (The $1.3 million contract with Ketchum included the money given to Williams.)

Meanwhile, Spellings's term as secretary had begun on a controversial note, when she criticized PBS on January 25 for spending public money to air an episode of an animated children's show that featured lesbian characters. The title character of *Postcards from Buster* is a talking rabbit who travels the country and meets families of different descriptions; in an episode that was scheduled to air that winter, Buster travels to Vermont, where he learns about farm life from two lesbian couples and their children. Responding to the criticism, officials at PBS decided not to distribute the show, but some affiliated stations aired it nonetheless. Spellings's stance brought her applause from social conservatives but derision from liberals, some of whom characterized her comments as bigoted. Spellings called that assessment inaccurate, explaining that she did not personally disapprove of gay lifestyles. She told Brian Friel for the *National Journal* (February 12, 2005), "When you turn on *Sesame Street* and you go take a shower . . . you don't necessarily think that that's going to provoke a debate or discussion in your family that you may or may not want to have with your 6-year-old. I think those issues—sexuality and human development and that sort of topic—are appropriate for parents to enter into in their own time and in their own way, and not at the discretion of the Department of Education, [using] federal tax dollars."

In February 2005 Bush unveiled his proposed budget for the 2006 fiscal year, which cuts the funding of the Department of Education by $56 million—Bush's first reduction of the department's resources. In total, Bush highlighted 48 education programs for elimination or reduction, including Upward Bound, Gear Up, and Talent Search, all of which are aimed at helping disadvantaged students prepare for college. He also proposed eliminating financing at the state level for the Safe and Drug-Free Schools programs. In addition, $4.7 billion would be redirected from 64 programs in order to finance other initiatives, primarily for high-school students, special education, and college-loan financing. Democratic senator Edward M. Kennedy of Massachusetts was quoted by Anne E. Kornblut for the New York Times (February 8, 2005) as saying that the proposal was "the most antistudent, antieducation budget since the Republicans tried to abolish the Department of Education." Spellings, for her part, played down the significance of many of the reductions, explaining that 15 of them amounted to cuts of $5 million or less per program. The budget would also set aside $269 million for math and science partnerships between public schools and "private entities" that are intended to improve the skills of children deemed to be at-risk, as well as $200 million to help high-school students with reading problems. In its effort to extend No Child Left Behind to high schools, the administration proposed spending $13.3 billion on high schools in low-income neighborhoods, an increase of 4.7 percent. The budget also included a $1.5 billion initiative to require literacy and math testing of students in ninth through eleventh grades. In addition, the president called for $64 million to subsidize the Advanced Placement (college-level courses and exams through which high-school students receive college credit) and the State Scholars program (rigorous courses designed to prepare high-school students for college and beyond). Spellings told George Archibald that in order for states to give high-school students incentives to take such courses, the president would ask Congress to approve $1,000 increases in Pell Grants for students' first two years of college; accordingly, in the budget Bush proposed a 45 percent increase for the grants.

Living up to expectations that she would be more flexible than her predecessor at the Department of Education, Spellings worked with state and local officials on controversial aspects of the No Child Left Behind act. In North Dakota the new regulations marked around 4,000 teachers, many of whom had been teaching for years, as unqualified. Spellings overturned the results and approved the qualifications of the teachers. She also assuaged controversy in New York by stating that school districts did not always have to allow students in low-

performing schools to transfer if such measures caused overcrowding. She said further that parents who had children in low-performing schools could also receive tutoring at federal expense if their students could not get into high-performance schools. Spellings told Sam Dillon for the New York Times (February 14, 2005) that she would continue to try to balance states' rights with the federal government's mission to improve education for poor and minority students. "That's the most important thing I'm going to do," she told Dillon, "to thread the needle of that balance."

In April 2005 Spellings announced that preferential treatment would be given to states that prove they are serious about raising students' achievement; specifically, states demonstrating either progress in, or a strong commitment to, improving their education systems will be given freedom to choose the manner in which they test students with mild disabilities, around three percent of all students. It was also reported that Spellings may allow a tripling of the number of special-education students provided with some form of accommodation in standardized tests—that is special versions of the tests. "This is a new day," she said according to Dillon in the New York Times (April 18, 2005). "States that show results and follow the principles of No Child Left Behind will be eligible for new tools to help you meet the law's goals."

Turning her attention to higher education, Spellings launched the Commission on the Future of Higher Education in October 2005. The commission, which is composed of academics, businesspeople, and government officials, will review U.S. colleges and attempt to forge a higher-education strategy for the nation. Its immediate goal is to produce, by August 2006, recommendations for making "colleges more accessible and affordable for families, accountable to policy-makers and competitive with peers worldwide," as Ben Feller explained for the Associated Press (October 17, 2005). The task is a difficult one. The kinds of data on primary and secondary schools that Spellings used to help the Bush administration develop the No Child Left Behind act are not available for colleges. Thus, as Spellings explained to Feller, there is "little good information about what's working and what's not, leading to 'the accidental way that we make policy.'" To gather the data it needs, the commission members will travel throughout the country for several months to research problems in universities and develop a more deliberate policy. Critics accused Spellings of forming the commission too late, since the Higher Education Act was to be reauthorized in 2006, before the commission would be ready to release its report.

Spellings has two children from her first marriage, which ended in divorce in 1997. Her second husband, Robert Spellings, an attorney, whom she married in September 2001, has two children from his first marriage. One of Spellings's daughters attended a private high school until she began college, in the fall of 2005. Some might think it unusual for a child of the secretary of education to attend a private rather than a public secondary school. "When we first moved [to Washington, D.C.], I tried public school for both of them," she explained to Patty Reinert for the *Houston Chronicle* (February 10, 2005). "We moved, obviously, cross-country, and in 9th grade with a teenager, and a girl, that's just a hard thing to do, and it was, I'd say, fairly traumatic. It wasn't the right setting for her at the time. That's why parents make decisions about their schools, and that's why I made that decision about my own child. That's why we're for school choice—because we think parents can make their own decisions about their children's education and they know best." In an interview with David Jackson for the *Dallas Morning News* (September 2, 2001), Spellings recalled that she had opted for natural childbirth for both of her children, and that she had nursed each of them for a long period.

"I'm kind of an earth-mother type of Republican," she told Jackson. She is also pro-choice with regard to abortion. Spellings is known as an accomplished pianist and gourmet cook and a passionate exerciser. She has also been described as having an impressive memory.

—G.O.

Suggested Reading: Associated Press Feb. 1, 2005; *Christian Science Monitor* USA p3 Nov. 18, 2004; Cox News Service Jan. 26, 2001; *Dallas Morning News* F p3 Sep. 2, 2001, A p2 Nov. 18, 2004, with photos; *National Journal* Feb. 12, 2005; *New York Times* A p1+ May 5, 2001, with photos, A p28 Nov. 18, 2004, with photo, A p18 Feb. 14, 2005, with photo, A p22 Apr. 8, 2005; *Slate* (on-line) Dec. 4, 2002; *Washington Post* A p21 Mar. 28, 2001; *Washington Times* A p3 Feb. 9, 2005

Office of Communications, Princeton University

Spergel, David

Mar. 25, 1961– Astrophysicist

Address: Princeton University, Dept. of Astrophysical Sciences, 132 Peyton Hall, Princeton, NJ 08544

"I love exploring the frontiers of science . . . ," the astrophysicist David Spergel told Michael D. Lemonick for *Time* magazine (2001, on-line). "I try to choose projects where the answers will be exciting not only for my colleagues but also for everybody else." Spergel made headlines in 1990 with his the-

ory, which has since been generally accepted, about the shape of the universe, and in 2001 *Time* named him one of the top scientists in the United States. In the same year he won a MacArthur Fellowship—often referred to as the "genius" grant—and watched as his creation for the National Aeronautics and Space Administration (NASA), the Wilkinson Microwave Anisotropy Probe (WMAP), was launched into space. Two years later, after analyzing data from the satellite, Spergel was able to announce to the world his confirmation of the validity of the big bang theory (which holds that the universe was created by a cosmic explosion), as well as his conclusive finding that the universe is 13.7 billion years old. As Michael D. Lemonick wrote, "Even in a field in which the most brilliant minds are inevitably compared with Albert Einstein, Spergel stands out." In addition to his accomplishments as a researcher, Spergel has won praise as a professor at Princeton University. As Scott Tremaine, chairman of the school's Department of Astrophysical Sciences, enthused for the Princeton University Web site, "The breadth of [Spergel's] research accomplishments is matched by his enthusiasm for teaching. He has taught—and taught well—almost every undergraduate and graduate course in the department and is one of our most successful and sought-after research supervisors." For the same Web site, Spergel himself explained: "I think that there is a public view that scientists—particularly those who win awards like the MacArthur—go off and work alone in hidden labs. . . . This is not so. I enjoy working together with students and colleagues. For me, the fun of science is working together to solve interesting questions." Complementing his theoretical work in the field of cosmology, Spergel has gained hands-on experience as a designer of instruments for locating previously undiscovered planets.

David Nathaniel Spergel was born on March 25, 1961 in Rochester, New York, to Martin Spergel, now a physics professor at York College of the City University of New York, and Rochelle Spergel, a lawyer, who is retired. David Spergel's brother, John, is a pediatric immunologist at the University of Pennsylvania, and his sister, Lauren, works in human resources in Lawrenceville, New Jersey. Interested in math, physics, and particularly astronomy even as a child, Spergel joked in an interview with *Current Biography* that he "went into the family business." He attended Princeton University, in Princeton, New Jersey, where he received his bachelor's degree in astronomy in 1982. He then enrolled at Harvard University, in Cambridge, Massachusetts, where he received his master's degree (1984) and his Ph.D. (1985), both in astronomy. While at Harvard, Spergel spent a year at Oxford University, in England, as a traveling scholar. After receiving his Ph.D., Spergel spent an additional year at Harvard as a postdoctoral fellow, serving during that time as a member of the university's Institute for Advanced Study. Meanwhile, in 1987, he returned to Princeton as a professor in the Department of Astrophysical Sciences. He is currently associate chair and director of graduate studies in that department; he is also an associate faculty member of the Department of Mechanical and Aerospace Engineering. Both his research and teaching skills have been lauded by the Princeton administration; the university's president, Shirley M. Tilghman, commented for the Princeton Web site (October 24, 2001, on-line), "From the time of his undergraduate years at Princeton, David Spergel has been an astonishingly bold and creative scholar. . . . He has tackled some of the most difficult and crucial problems in astrophysics and has achieved insights that continue to shape the research agenda in the field. He also has applied his tremendous energy and personal warmth to his teaching, which is greatly appreciated among undergraduates today."

While composing his Ph.D. thesis, "Astrophysical Implications of Weakly-Interacting Massive Particles," Spergel focused his attention on the subject of dark matter, which, according to a widely accepted theory, composes most of the mass in the universe. (Dark matter is matter that cannot be observed by emitted radiation; its gravitational effects on visible objects, such as stars and galaxies, indicates its existence.) This study resulted in his theory that dark matter produces a "wind" of particles that flows against Earth, thus allowing for predictions as to the levels of dark matter that may be detected at different times. (There should be a greater presence in June than in January, for instance.) This proposal is still being investigated by other scientists who specialize in dark matter.

Spergel told Michael Lemonick that he admires "people who tackle new problems" and who "don't just repeat their Ph.D. research forever." Spergel himself adheres to those standards, as demonstrated when, after his study of dark matter,

he attacked a new topic—the shape of the Milky Way. At the 1990 annual meeting of the American Astronomical Society, in Crystal City, Virginia, Spergel and his collaborator, Leo Blitz of the University of Maryland at College Park, presented their conclusions on the subject. Their finding was that the Milky Way, the galaxy that contains our solar system, is different from what had been previously believed. Contrary to the widely held belief that the galaxy was spiral-shaped, Blitz and Spergel contended that it is actually shaped like a bar with a spiral at either end. The galaxy contains millions of stars at the center, which are shaped, collectively, like a football, not a globe, as was previously thought. In presenting their findings, as Blitz told Philip J. Hilts for the *New York Times* (January 12, 1990), he and Spergel had found "something of a holy grail for astronomers who study the structure of the Milky Way." Spergel and Blitz's depiction of the galaxy is now the accepted model.

Spergel next focused on the question of cosmic structure—why galaxies form in clusters rather than spreading uniformly through space—a phenomenon that he and a Cambridge University professor, Neil Turok, had researched throughout the late 1980s and early 1990s. At that time they proposed that the clustering occurred because of knots of warped space-time, dubbed "topological defects," which, when questioned by *Current Biography*, Spergel compared to "bubbles in an ice cube. The energy associated with these 'crystal defects' curve and warp space-time." This inventive theory proved to be incorrect: observations from the ground and from satellites did not match the pattern of fluctuations Spergel and Turok had predicted. (Spergel has explained that while there were no errors in his calculations, the calculations were in the service of an erroneous speculation.) In what Michael Lemonick characterized as a "display of intellectual honesty," Spergel admitted that this observational data did not support his model.

At the 1997 American Astronomical Society conference, held in Toronto, Ontario, Canada, Spergel, Blitz (who had relocated to the University of California, Berkeley), Peter Teuben of the University of Maryland, Dap Hartmann of the Harvard-Smithsonian Center for Astrophysics in Cambridge, Massachusetts, and W. Butler Burton of the University of Leiden in the Netherlands presented their findings with regard to another astronomical phenomenon. The topic was the set of mysterious clouds traveling at a high speed across the Milky Way. Observed as early as the 1960s, the clouds have been an enigma for scientists ever since. The major obstacle to unraveling the mystery is that astronomers have been unable to determine the clouds' distance from Earth and, hence, their size. Spergel and his colleagues suggested at the convention that the clouds are more than a million light-years away from our galaxy and that their movement can be attributed to the gravity of the Andromeda galaxy and the Milky Way. They also proposed that the gas that composes the clouds is a remnant of the primordial gas that coalesced to form the entire Local Group of galaxies, the group that contains the Milky Way and the Andromeda galaxy, among other objects. This conclusion was supported by a computer simulation of the formation of the Local Group but was not accepted as a definitive resolution of the mystery surrounding the clouds. Spergel's theory is considered viable, but scientists are still pursuing other possible explanations as well. If the theory is correct, though, the presence of relic gases would sustain the present rate of star formation for billions of years to come.

His earlier display of ethics, Spergel has said, earned him an invitation in 1994 to work with scientists at NASA as the principal theorist on the design team for the Wilkinson Microwave Anisotropy Probe (WMAP). WMAP was designed to map the oldest radiation (or energy radiated in wave or particle form) in the universe by recording cosmic radio waves. Although, as a theoretical astrophysicist, Spergel had no previous practical experience in satellite creation, he threw himself into the work, often rising at seven in the morning and working until two in the morning. After eight years of labor, the 1,800-pound WMAP satellite was launched from Cape Canaveral, Florida, in June 2001. Following the transmission of the WMAP data, Spergel and his team revealed their findings in early 2003. The robotic probe had created the clearest pictures of radiation ever taken, which, when examined, allowed Spergel and his colleagues to fix the exact age of the universe at 13.7 billion years—a discovery that marked the first time ever that the age of the universe had been determined conclusively. These findings also provided clear evidence of the big bang, only a theory until confirmed by WMAP data, and determined that the big bang occurred 14 billion years ago. In addition, the data revealed that only four percent of the universe is made of atoms, whereas the other 96 percent is composed of invisible dark matter. Spergel commented to Ira Flatow on the National Public Radio program *Talk of the Nation* (February 21, 2003), "So as often happens in science, we answer some questions, and we raise and deepen others as our data improves." Spergel called his work on the WMAP one of the most satisfying experiences of his life.

Due largely to his contribution to WMAP, Spergel was awarded a 2001 MacArthur Fellowship by the John D. and Catherine T. MacArthur Foundation. The fellowships, which consist of no-strings-attached monetary awards distributed over a five-year period (Spergel received $500,000), are given to those individuals who, according to the MacArthur Foundation Web site (on-line), demonstrate "extraordinary originality and dedication in their creative pursuits and a marked capacity for self-direction" as well as "exceptional creativity, promise for important future advances based on a track record of significant accomplishment, and potential for the fellowship to facilitate subsequent creative work." "The MacArthur Fellowship is both a wonderful opportunity and honor," Spergel said for the Princeton University Web site (October 24, 2001). "The fellowship will help me juggle the challenges of research, teaching and three young children."

After the success of the WMAP satellite, Spergel again went to work for NASA on designing a second spacecraft intended to discover Earthlike planets in other solar systems. Spergel knew little about optics or telescope design when he began the project but, as he told Michael Lemonick, "I got a book and taught myself optics." He then proposed the creation of a telescope with an innovative lens design that could detect a dim planet by blocking the light of brighter stars. NASA hopes to launch the telescope, called the Terrestrial Planet Finder, in approximately 10 years.

Spergel has received a variety of awards during the course of his career and has published numerous articles in such publications as the *Astrophysical Journal*, *Nature*, and *Physics Letters*. He is currently chair of NASA's Origins Subcommittee, which oversees the Hubble Space Telescope, the James Webb Space Telescope, and NASA's program of searching for undiscovered planets. The committee advises NASA on long-term goals rather than technical aspects of space exploration.

Since August 26, 1990 Spergel has been married to Laura H. Kahn, a physician, with whom he has three children: Julian, Sarah, and Joshua. In his free time, Spergel is an avid skier and bicyclist. Currently, he is on sabbatical leave from Princeton.

—K.J.E.

Suggested Reading: David Spergel's Web site; National Public Radio (online) Feb. 21, 2003; *New York Times* A p22 Jan. 11, 1990; Princeton University Web site; *Time* (on-line) 2001

Staley, Dawn

May 4, 1970– Basketball player; coach

Address: Dawn Staley Foundation, P.O. Box 12950, Philadelphia, PA 19108

The point guard Dawn Staley is one of the nation's best-known and most successful female basketball players. Together with the center Lisa Leslie and the forward Sheryl Swoopes, she has also been among the most visible exemplars of professional women's basketball, leading the U.S. national team to victory in many international games since the mid-1980s. Over the course of her professional career, she has earned 10 international gold medals, including three at the Olympic Games (in 1996, 2000, and 2004) and two at the World Championships (in 1998 and 2002). Currently, Staley is the head coach of the women's basketball team at Tem-

Nick Laham/Getty Images

Dawn Staley

ple University, in Philadelphia, Pennsylvania, and a point guard for the Comets, a Houston, Texas–based team in the Women's National Basketball Association (WNBA). Before being traded to the Comets, she served as a point guard for the Charlotte Stings, in Charlotte, North Carolina. She began her sports career as a high-school basketball star in Philadelphia and went on to dazzle crowds with her performance as a college player at the University of Virginia (UVA) at Charlottesville. She embarked on her professional U.S. career as a point guard for the Philadelphia Rage, a team in the short-lived American Basketball League (ABL). Although other female basketball players tower above the five-foot six-inch Staley, the point guard has distinguished herself with her expert passing ability and her unselfish, team-oriented approach to the game. "I get more pleasure from a pass than from a basket," she told Douglas S. Looney for *Sports Illustrated* (November 19, 1990). Extraordinarily self-disciplined, Staley wears a rubber band on her right wrist to snap whenever she loses the ball. She is famed for her flashy style; indeed, the former Los Angeles Laker guard and basketball legend Magic Johnson described her to David Scott for *Sports Illustrated for Kids* (December 1997) as "a showstopper." "She's what it's all about," Johnson continued, referring to her skills on the court: "no-look, behind-the-back, through-the-legs." Lisa Boyer, the Rage's coach, echoed Johnson's appraisal, telling David Scott, "She seems to have eyes behind her head."

Dawn Michelle Staley was born on May 4, 1970 in Philadelphia, Pennsylvania, to Clarence Staley, a construction worker and part-time car mechanic, and Estelle Staley. The youngest of five children,

she grew up with three brothers (Lawrence, Anthony, and Eric) and a sister (Tracey) in the Raymond Rosen housing projects, in North Philadelphia, a neighborhood she described during an interview with Vic Dorr Jr. for the *Richmond Times Dispatch* (February 14, 2003) as "one of the roughest, if not the roughest, in town." A shy, quiet child, she came out of her shell during street basketball games played with her brothers and other boys from the area, among them Hank Gathers, who later became a college basketball legend at Loyola Marymount College, in Los Angeles, California. Often the only girl on the court, for a while Staley was greeted with sexist comments, such as "Go back to the kitchen." Before long she won her critics over with her quick, accurate passes, which gave the boys opportunities to shoot and score. "As long as they knew I wasn't shooting and was passing, they picked me," Staley recalled to Steve Jacobson for New York *Newsday* (July 22, 1996). Within a short time she had become a fixture in the boys' pick-up games, honing her skills among players twice her size and developing the speed and dexterity that would later make her one of the world's best female point guards. "My advice to girls," she told Douglas S. Looney, "is to play against the guys. That gave me the heart to play against anybody. I'm glad they were rough."

When Staley was in the seventh grade, Debbie Ryan, the women's basketball coach at UVA, learned of her aptitude for basketball and sent her a letter offering her a full sports scholarship when she completed high school. Over the next several years, Ryan sent Staley about 200 additional letters and called her on the telephone hundreds of times, urging her to consider attending UVA after high school. As an inner-city student with no way to pay for higher education, Staley realized that basketball was her ticket out of the ghetto. At the high school she attended, the Dobbins/Randolph Area Vocational Technical School (Dobbins Tech), she led the girls' basketball team, the Lady Mustangs, to three Philadelphia public-high-school championships. Averaging 33.1 points per game, Staley was named the national high-school player of the year by *USA Today*.

Among the several colleges that attempted to recruit her when her high-school basketball career took off, Staley felt especially drawn to UVA, in large part out of gratitude for the school's early expression of interest. In 1988 she enrolled at UVA on a basketball scholarship and joined the school's women's basketball team, the Cavaliers. That same year she became a member of the USA Junior World Championship Team, with which she averaged 10.8 points per game, the second-highest individual score on the team. Two years later, in 1990, she played for the USA Select Team, spending several weeks touring Italy and what was then Czechoslovakia.

As a college sophomore Staley suffered a double-knee injury, the first in a long series of knee problems. She also suffered personal losses: the deaths of one of her grandmothers and of Hank Gathers, who collapsed during a game at Loyola and died the same day, at age 23. Moreover, her relationship with her coach, Debbie Ryan, became strained due to minor individual differences. In general, however, Staley's college basketball career was marked by few problems and numerous successes. During her four years at UVA, she helped the Cavaliers to four National Collegiate Athletic Association (NCAA) tournaments, three appearances in the NCAA Final Four (in 1990, 1991, and 1992), and three Atlantic Coast Conference (ACC) tournament titles. In the 1991 NCAA championship, which UVA lost, 70–67, in overtime to the University of Tennessee, Staley scored an impressive 28 points. The NCAA named her the Final Four's most outstanding player, making her the first player in history from a losing team to win the honor. Also that year she received the Honda-Broderick Cup Award, the Honda Basketball Sports Award, and the *Sports Illustrated* Player-of-the-Year Award. In both 1991 and 1992, she was named the ACC player of the year and the national women's college basketball player of the year and honored with the Naismith Award, generally recognized as the most prestigious basketball honor in the United States.

Staley is still the ACC's career leader for total assists (729) and assists per game (5.6). She also holds the NCAA record for career steals (454) and is the Cavaliers' all-time leading scorer, with a total of 2,135 points over four seasons. Furthermore, she holds the UVA records for scoring average (16.3 points per game over the course of four years), free throws (505), most points in a game (37), most steals in a game (10), most free throws in a season (147 in 1989), and most assists in a season (235 in 1991) and overall (729). Staley earned a bachelor's degree, with a major in rhetoric and communication studies, in 1992, thereby becoming the first person in her family to finish college. When she graduated, UVA retired her jersey number—an honor that has been conferred on only two other athletes in the school's history. "Dawn is the one who really put [UVA's] women's [basketball] program on the map," the WNBA's current president, Val Ackerman, told Jamie Miller during an interview for the *UVA Alumni News* (Fall 2004, online). "She was the player."

Because women's professional basketball had not yet gained widespread popularity in the United States, Staley, like many other American female basketball players of her generation, spent the next several years playing overseas as a freelancer on international teams. She began her professional career in Segovia, Spain, where she played during the 1992–93 season. The following season she played with four different professional teams, in Italy, France, Spain, and Brazil, and the season after that she joined a team based in Tarbes, France.

In 1994 Staley joined the U.S. women's national team in order to train for the 1996 Olympics. That year she helped the U.S. win a bronze medal in the World Championships, where she averaged 11.6 points and 3.9 assists per game, and a gold medal at the Goodwill Games, where she averaged 9.3 points per game and attained a team high of 5.8 assists per game. Her strong performance at the Goodwill Games earned her the title of most valuable player, and that same year she was named the USA Basketball Female Athlete of the Year. She also finished eighth in the voting for the U.S. Olympic Committee's Sportswoman of the Year.

In the fall of 1995, Staley suffered an injury to her left knee that required surgery. She broke her right hand that December but continued to train with the U.S. team, averaging only five points a game but keeping her assist-to-turnover rate high. Also in 1995 the athletic-apparel company Nike signed Staley, Sheryl Swoopes, and Lisa Leslie to promotional contracts that included a television commercial, filmed by the director Spike Lee, in which the women were shown defeating three men in a three-on-three basketball game. Just before the 1996 Summer Olympic Games, held in Atlanta, Georgia, Nike commissioned a seven-story mural of Staley to be painted on the side of a building overlooking her childhood neighborhood. Among the many subjects for murals that the company had sponsored nationwide, Staley was the first woman in over a decade, and the first African-American woman ever, to be selected for the tribute.

The U.S. women's national basketball team had a tremendously successful season in 1995–96; it won all 60 of its international games and topped off its string of victories with a gold medal at the Olympics, after defeating Brazil, 111–87. In recognition of those accomplishments, both USA Basketball and the U.S. Olympic Committee named the U.S. women the team of the year. Staley gave her gold medal to her mother, whom she has cited as the biggest positive influence on her life. "She's been my constant," Staley told John Crumpacker for the *San Francisco Chronicle* (August 13, 2004). "She has been my rock."

The experience of winning an Olympic gold medal led Staley to contemplate the many obstacles that she had overcome on her way to professional success. As she told Jamie Miller, "I reflected on my upbringing, my environment, all of the opposing, negative things that pull you away from achieving your goals. And I know that somebody out there, some little kid, . . . is in the position I was in. Nobody would have believed I'd be an Olympian or a gold medalist." Inspired by the recognition of how lucky she was to have transcended the limiting circumstances of her childhood, Staley decided to set up a nonprofit organization to give underprivileged youths in North Philadelphia some of the opportunities that she herself had lacked. "I wanted somebody else to feel what I was feeling," she said, "some other young person to achieve that lifelong dream." In December 1996 she established the Dawn Staley Foundation, a nonprofit organization that sponsors after-school educational and recreational programs for middle-school children in Philadelphia. Two years later Staley was honored with an American Red Cross Spectrum Award for her volunteer work with the foundation. Her humanitarian work has also earned her a WNBA Entrepreneurial Spirit Award (1999) and a WNBA Hometown Hero Award (2001).

The fall of 1995 saw the founding of the ABL, the first women's professional basketball league in U.S. history. Staley, along with nine of her teammates from the national team, signed to the eight-team league. On June 19, 1996 she was assigned to the Rage, a Virginia-based team that played its home games in Richmond and spent the off-season in Philadelphia. When the Rage reached the 1997 ABL finals, the ABL decided to move the team from Richmond to Philadelphia as a concession to Staley, who wanted to spend more time on activities with her foundation.

Despite her professional and financial success with the Rage, Staley signed with the ABL's rival league, the WNBA, in 1998, because the WNBA's shorter season (30 games, as compared to 44 in the ABL) would be easier on her weak knees. "Longevity—basically, that's what it came down to," she told Vic Dorr Jr. for the *Richmond Times Dispatch* (September 1, 1998). "It definitely wasn't financial. That's not why I play. I play because I love this game, because I have a passion for it. That's what made the WNBA so attractive to me: I want to play for as long as I can, and I think the WNBA gives me the best chance to do that." In December 1998, less than four months after Staley had signed a three-year contract with the WNBA, the ABL folded, due to financial difficulties. Earlier, in June 1998, the U.S. women's national team won the world championship and was named the USA Basketball team of the year, largely due to Staley's 52 assists, an all-time record for the world championships.

On May 4, 1999 Staley was selected by the Charlotte Sting in the first round of the WNBA draft. That year she ranked second in the WNBA in free-throw percentage (93.4) and third in assists per game (5.5), and either ranked first or tied for the team lead in scoring in eight games and in assists in 25 games. On two separate occasions she scored 23 points in a game, her personal WNBA career high. During the 1999 play-offs she played in 157 of the 160 minutes that the Sting was on court. Her performance with the Sting that season earned her the 1999 WNBA Sportsmanship Award; she also won the 1999 WNBA Entrepreneurial Spirit Award for establishing the Dawn Staley Foundation.

In 2000 Staley replaced Kristen Foley as the head coach of Temple University's women's basketball team, the Owls. Under her leadership the Owls had their first winning season in over a decade, with 19 wins and 10 losses, a near reversal of the team's 10–18 record of the previous season. The Owls also earned a third seed in the 2001 Atlantic-10 (A-10) Basketball Conference championships. "Coach Staley and her staff just had us believing in ourselves," Natalia Isaac, a senior guard

at Temple, told Kathy Orton for the *Washington Post* (March 13, 2002). "They got us believing that we could compete with anybody in the country as long as we came out to play." In her second season with the Owls, Staley led the team to victory in the Atlantic-10 and then to its first NCAA Tournament appearance since 1989. Following these successes, Temple signed her to a five-year contract extension. In 2004 Staley led the Owls to a 14–2 record, which placed them at the top of the Atlantic-10 East standings. When Temple made it to the NCAA Tournament once again, she was named the Atlantic-10 coach of the year.

Around the same time that she began coaching, Staley was selected to compete with the U.S. national team at the Summer Olympic Games, held that year in Sydney, Australia. Prior to the 2000 Games, Staley helped the U.S. women achieve a record of 38 wins and only two losses, setting a successful precedent for the team's outstanding Olympic performance. Not only did Staley receive her second Olympic gold medal that year, but she also led the team in assists per game (3.6) and ranked fourth overall.

Staley's performance with the Sting in 2000 was no less impressive. She set a Sting record for assists, finishing the season with 190, or an average of 5.9 per game, third-best in the WNBA. She also finished sixth in the league in free-throw percentage and in total minutes played and ranked first or tied for the team lead in scoring in three games and in assists in 25 games. Her 2000 ratio of assists to turnovers was 2.09, the highest of her professional career and seventh-highest in the league that year.

In 2001 Staley represented the Charlotte Sting on the WNBA's Eastern Conference all-star team; she was so honored in 2002 and 2003 as well. She started in all eight of the Sting's 2001 play-off games and averaged 11.8 points, 4.4 assists, and 2.3 rebounds per game. Furthermore, she led the team or tied for first place in scoring nine times and in assists 28 times and finished second in the WNBA in total assists, third in assists average, and fifth in free-throw percentage and total minutes played. On July 9, 2001 she became the first woman in U.S. professional basketball history to achieve a total of 1,000 career assists, and on July 14 she scored the 2,000th point of her U.S. professional career.

In 2004 Staley was once again selected to represent the United States at the Summer Olympics, held that year in Athens, Greece. She was also chosen as the U.S. flag bearer for the opening ceremonies, an honor that has been conferred on only four other American women in Olympic history. For the third time in a row, the U.S. women carried home the Olympic gold, defeating the Australian team 74–63. Although normally more prominent in passing than in scoring, Staley scored 14 points, more than anyone else on the team except the forward Tina Thompson, who scored 18.

The final round of the 2004 Olympics marked the 205th and last game of Dawn Staley's international basketball career. Although Staley still plans to play as a point guard for the Houston Comets, whom she joined in August 2005, her most serious days as a professional athlete are behind her. "I carried the flag in, and the gold out," she told Sally Jenkins for the *Washington Post* (August 29, 2004). "Actually, it's a storybook ending." Staley intends to focus her energies on coaching. But before her planned retirement following the 2006 season, she is determined to chase the WNBA title that so far has eluded her. Because she has joined the Comets, Staley's chances of winning a championship have been significantly increased, in part because she has been reunited her with Comets head coach, Van Chancellor, who was also the head coach of the 2004 U.S. Women's Olympic basketball team, and with her Olympic teammates Sheryl Swoopes and Tina Thompson.

Staley is earning a master's degree in business administration at Pfeiffer University, in Charlotte, North Carolina. She recently completed a series of four inspirational books (as yet untitled) for pre-adolescent girls. "My job in life right now," she told Jamie Miller, "is to help our kids in the [Dawn Staley] foundation find some kind of success that will take them to a better time; and for our kids at Temple, to put them in a position to influence lives and to get the most out of life—to become successful and give it back to someone else."

—L.W.

Suggested Reading: (New York) *Newsday* A p49+ July 22, 1996; *New York Times* VIII p3+ Nov. 24, 1991; *Sports Illustrated* p112+ Nov. 19, 1990; *Washington Post* E p1+ Aug. 29, 2004

Jeff Karda/Getty Images

Stewart, James "Bubba"

Dec. 21, 1985– Motocross racer

Address: c/o AMA Pro Racing Headquarters, 13515 Yarmouth Dr., Pickerington, OH 43147

James "Bubba" Stewart is the first African-American to dominate the sport of motocross racing. After a decorated run as an amateur racer, Stewart turned professional in 2002 and soared, flipped, and motored his way to the American Motorcyclist Association (AMA) Chevrolet Motocross Championship. He took the title again in 2004. In its April 2003 issue, *Teen People* named Stewart one of "20 Teens Who Will Change the World,"

and in June 2004 *Sports Illustrated* listed Stewart two places ahead of the basketball legend Magic Johnson among the 101 most influential minority athletes.

Motocross—essentially motorcycle racing on dirt courses—is a niche sport with a thus-far limited appeal. As reported by Dan Steinberg for the *Washington Post* (July 23, 2004), in 2003 fewer than one million fans attended outdoor motocross and arena-based supercross motorcycle competitions of the kind in which Stewart participates; while those events are sometimes televised, often on tape delay, they tend to draw low ratings. By comparison, Steinberg noted, NASCAR (stock-car racing), the most popular motorsport in the U.S., draws consistently high television ratings, and NASCAR officials claim their sport has a fan base of 75 million people. Despite the fact that both the fans and athletes involved in motorsports remain overwhelmingly white, and that motocross racing, in particular, remains an "insular sport," in Steinberg's words, Stewart is fast becoming a "pop culture icon who could ultimately transform the face of motorsports while broadening the fan base beyond white America." When asked whether he was attempting to change motocross, in particular, and motorsports, in general, by opening them up more to minorities, Stewart told Steinberg, "I mean, I am, but I'm not. I'm just riding, you know?" Stewart told Steinberg that he has probably heard himself compared to Tiger Woods, the black golfer who dominated that traditionally white sport after bursting onto the scene in the late 1990s, close to 5,000 times. His goal, however, is to make his own mark, to be "the first James Stewart of motocross/supercross," as he told Steinberg.

The designations "motocross" and "supercross" refer to the venues in which the races take place. Motocross races are usually held in the spring and summer on hilly, winding dirt courses located in rural areas across the country. The more popular supercross races take place during the winter and spring on dirt courses built inside stadiums and arenas in big cities. Both types of races feature an assortment of topographical obstacles, such as hills and bumps, that the riders must navigate, often by making gravity-defying jumps. There are two main race divisions, which take their designations from the size and power of the bikes used in each: the 125-cc class and the 250-cc class. The former is considered the entry level of professional motocross and supercross racing, as the 125-cc motorbikes are smaller and less powerful that the 250-cc bikes.

James Stewart Jr. was born in Florida on December 21, 1985. According to the Web site kidzworld.com, Stewart's first ride on a motorcycle occurred with his father when the boy was just two days old. James Stewart Sr. had been a former professional motocross rider in central Florida. He gave James Jr. his first motorbike on the occasion of his son's fourth birthday. That same year James Jr. competed in his first race. Showing a preternatural ability on his motorbike, at age seven he won his first national amateur championship, earned his first official sponsorship, and was being featured in racing videos. When Stewart reached eight years of age, he became a fan of the motocross racer Jeff "Chicken" Matiasevich. Emulating his favorite rider, for a time Stewart called himself Baby Chicken. The nickname that stuck, however, was Bubba, which is reportedly a variation of Boogie, another of Stewart Jr.'s childhood pet names. Stewart's family traveled around the country in a motorhome so that he could compete in races. Stewart and his younger brother, Malcolm, were educated at home. (The family's current house, in Haines, Florida, reportedly boasts an outdoor motocross track in the backyard, along with a trampoline and air hockey and pool tables.)

Stewart quickly established himself as a fast rider, able to capture "big air," the sport's jargon for the ability to execute jumps of great heights. No rider so young had ever before displayed such abilities on a motorbike. The financial gains resulting from his success on the dirt tracks and his growing number of endorsement contracts allowed Stewart to begin collecting luxury cars when he was just 15 years old.

After winning 11 national amateur championships—and thus building, before he reached the age of 18, "the most impressive amateur career in American motocross history," as Steinberg described it—Stewart turned professional in 2002; that same year he won the AMA Chevrolet Motocross Championship, winning rookie-of-the-year honors in the process.

Stewart wears number 259 on his jersey in honor of one of his motocross heroes, Tony Haynes, who broke his neck while competing in 1993, leaving him paralyzed from the waist down. Accidents are common in the sport, and the physical toll on riders' knees, legs, and backs is substantial; many do not continue racing past their mid-20s. Stewart himself has suffered numerous injuries, including,

at various times, a dislocated knee and shoulder and a broken ankle and collarbone. Nevertheless, on a 125-cc motorbike he was considered nearly unbeatable. Kelly Smith, a veteran rider, told Steinberg, "He's so dominant, as long as he keeps [his bike] on two wheels [i.e. doesn't fall] he wins, there's no getting around that."

Not only has Stewart proven himself to be the best racer in the 125-cc class, but he has endeared himself to fans by being one of the most flamboyant riders. For example, he is known for running into the stands after victories or performing various idiosyncratic victory dances (some of which he has given names, including the sprinkler, the worm, and the bomb). He has contributed to the design of his colorful, sometimes florid, race uniforms, which usually sport the word "Bubbalicious" on the rear end. One of Stewart's signature stunts is his self-titled "Bubba Scrub," in which he turns his bike so that it is parallel and low to the ground while in the air off a jump; the move saves time and delights fans. Stewart told Steinberg, "I figure I see a lot of boring personalities out there [on the racing circuit], and I didn't want to be one of those guys."

Stewart has become a magnet for sponsors, including such companies as Gatorade (sports drinks), Kawasaki (motorcylces), and Oakley (sunglasses, apparel, and accessories). He has been approached by television producers interested in creating a reality television show based on his life and career; been called by the Academy Award–winning actor Tom Cruise—who is known to be fond of extreme-action sports—in regard to a possible movie deal; and seen his image on giant Oakley billboards in London, Toronto, and Montreal. His likeness can also be seen in the MX2002 game for Playstation. Stewart is said to earn between $3 million and $5 million a year from his winnings and endorsements, making him one of the two highest-paid motocross riders in the country. (The other is Carmichael.)

Stewart's last season on a 125-cc motorbike, in 2004, was a stunning success. Out of 12 races he entered that year, he won 11, bringing his career total of wins for professional 125-cc racing to 28, two more than that achieved by Ricky Carmichael, the reigning champion of the 250-cc class and for a long time the record holder among 125-cc riders. He also beat Carmichael by winning a total of four AMA national championships. Stewart's 2005 season, on the other hand, was disappointing and by far his most injury-prone yet. Though he went into it confident that he could handle the transition to a 250-cc motorbike, he placed only fifth in the first round in that year's Supercross 250 series. The following week, practicing in Phoenix, Arizona, for the second round, Stewart was thrown from his bike and broke his left arm. He missed nine races before finishing third in the 11th of the 16 rounds in the series. Two first-place wins in the following three rounds brought him back to the fore, but in May he broke his thumb in the second heat of the final round, leaving him with a 10th-place standing in Supercross that year. That summer's Motocross series proved even more disappointing for him. Stewart placed second in one race and third in two but never won a race. He suffered a concussion and a hip injury after a collision with Carmichael in New Berlin, New York, in July. There were also a number of races in which he was plagued by a stomach problem that was not properly diagnosed until after the season finished. In October Stewart announced on his Web site (jamesstewartonline.com) that doctors had determined that he had been suffering from a serious bacterial infection in his digestive tract—one that was exacerbated by stress and excitement. The condition was being treated by a regimen of antibiotics, Stewart said, and he was looking forward to competing in the 2006 season.

Stewart has considered hosting his own talk show or driving in NASCAR in the future. (The champion's business manager told Steinberg that several NASCAR teams have already approached him to express interest in Stewart's joining them.) Stewart counts among his friends such sports-world heavyweights as Michael Jordan, Tiger Woods, and the baseball player Ken Griffey Jr. He

has been introduced to numerous entertainment figures. He rode his motorbike in the hip-hop star David Banner's video for the track "Crank It Up." Banner and his fellow hip-hop star Lil' Kim performed at Stewart's 18th-birthday party.

Speaking of Stewart's appeal, Mark Fewell, the senior director of business development for Boost Mobile, a division of Nextel and one of Stewart's sponsors, said to Steinberg: "It's not simply the fact that he's African American; it's the fact that he's so good at what he does." For his part, Stewart told Steinberg that the color of his skin has never been a a matter of concern for him. When he started racing, he said, "I was so small and so young, I never really thought about it. And then once I realized everything—oh, there's not a whole lot of 'me' out there—I was already used to it."

—C.F.T.

Suggested Reading: AMA Chevrolet Motocross Championship Web site; jamesstewartonline.com; Transworld Motocross Web site; *Washington Post* A p1+ July 23, 2004, with photos

---

Stott, John

Apr. 27, 1921– Evangelical clergyman

Address: John Stott Ministries, 1050 Chestnut St., Suite 203, Menlo Park, CA 94025

Although many Americans may not recognize his name, John Stott is one of the nation's most influential evangelical preachers. "If evangelicals could elect a pope, Stott is the person they would likely choose," Michael Cromartie, who directs the Evangelicals in Civic Life Program at the Ethics and Public Policy Center, has said, as paraphrased by David Brooks in the *New York Times* (November 30, 2004, on-line). Stott has written dozens of books, many of which have been translated into a total of more than 70 languages, and his writings and preaching have influenced two generations of evangelicals and evangelists. Brooks described Stott's tone as "friendly, courteous and natural. It is humble and self-critical, but also confident, joyful and optimistic." As a pastor of a London church (All Souls), a missionary, and a chaplain to the queen of England, Stott has advocated the importance of developing a personal relationship with Jesus, spreading the Gospel, and doing good deeds. "Evangelism and social action went together in the ministry of Jesus. So they ought to go together in ours," Stott told Carol McGraw for the *Orange County (California) Register* (October 3, 1998). In his book *The Cross of Christ*, as quoted in *Christianity Today* (April 2, 2001, on-line), he wrote, "It is never enough to have pity on the victims of in-

Corey Widmer, courtesy of John Stott

justice if we do nothing to change the unjust situation itself." His emphasis on social work has made him something of a controversial figure among evangelicals who believe that nothing should distract them from their primary task of converting people to Christianity. Likewise, he has drawn the criticism of more-liberal theologians, such as those within the Episcopal Church, for his stances in favor of the death penalty and against abortion and homosexuality.

John Robert Walmsley Stott was born on April 27, 1921 in London, England, to Sir Arnold Stott, a well-known physician and an agnostic, and Lady Emily (Holland) Stott, whose family was Lutheran. As a child, Stott attended services and Sunday school with his mother and sisters at All Souls Church, an Anglican parish on Langham Place, near Oxford Circus, in London. He later wrote, as quoted by Peter J. Blackburn on the Testimonium Web site, that he went "more out of affectionate loyalty to [my mother] and out of routine, than as a personally meaningful discipline." He has said that one of his earliest memories is of sitting high up in the gallery of the church and dropping bits of paper onto the heads of the people seated below him.

Stott attended Rugby School, an elite boarding school in Rugby, England, where he became head boy—a top student-leadership position. In February 1938 he heard a talk by Eric Nash, an evangelist, at the school's Christian Union. In a biographical essay posted on his Web site, he recalled that the theme of Nash's lecture was "What then shall I do with Jesus, who is called the Christ?" Stott was riveted. "That I needed to do anything with Jesus was an entirely novel idea to me," he wrote, "for I had imagined that somehow He had done whatever needed to be done, and that my part was only to acquiesce."

Soon Stott began proselytizing, and he persuaded several of his schoolmates to lead actively Christian lives. In the fall of 1939, he began studying at Trinity College, a division of Cambridge University, in England, where he received a first degree (given to students with very high marks) in French and theology. At Trinity the 19-year-old Stott began to give public Bible readings. Having rejected his father's idea that he join the diplomatic service, in 1945 Stott was ordained in the Church of England. He immediately began serving as an assistant curate at All Souls, his childhood church. The rector of the church was in ill health, so Stott took on more responsibilities than was usual for an assistant curate. After the rector of All Souls had a third coronary operation, in 1950, the congregation petitioned King George VI—the then–titular head of the Church of England—to name Stott rector. Stott became the rector of All Souls before his 30th birthday. At the time, evangelicals did not have much influence in the Anglican Church, and Stott resolved to increase their impact. With that goal in mind, he revitalized the Eclectic Society, a discussion group founded by Anglican clergymen in 1783. Between 1960 and 1965 the membership of the society grew from about 20 to more than 1,000. In 1967 Stott chaired the first National Evangelical Anglican Congress (NEAC). In 1977 he chaired the second as well; the massive gatherings now occur at intervals of 10 to 15 years. The congresses have been credited with inspiring evangelical separatists to return to the Anglican Church. In recent years increasing numbers of evangelicals have been appointed to bishoprics in the church.

As rector of All Souls, Stott focused much of his energy on preaching, evangelism, and social welfare. He instituted a weekly training course in evangelism for his parishioners, as well as children's services, midweek lunchtime services, and services for the sick. He established a Christian community center, called the All Souls Clubhouse, and organized courses for new Christians in the homes of established churchgoers. His rousing, biblically based sermons were very popular, and church membership grew to such an extent that Stott asked prospective members of All Souls to consider joining other evangelical congregations in the area.

Basic Christianity, a guide to the fundamentals of the religion and arguably Stott's best-known work, was published in 1958. An estimated 2.5 million copies of the book are in print worldwide. In 1959 Stott was appointed a chaplain to Queen Elizabeth II; in 1991 he took on the title of extra chaplain. Meanwhile, he remained committed to helping the poor. He told Carol McGraw, "It's clear that with the great poverty and starvation in the world, that Christians cannot live in luxury and extravagance. We must simplify our economic lifestyle, not because we think it will solve the macroeconomic problems of the world, but out of solidarity with the poor. With empathy comes more desire to change society for the better."

In 1970 Stott began to lecture frequently at seminars overseas, particularly in the Third World, which he refers to as the "Majority World." The following year he formed the Langham Partnership, to teach pastors in those parts of the globe effective ways to preach and evangelize. The partnership sends dozens of future pastoral leaders to England and the United States to obtain advanced degrees in theology. Stott has "nurtured a whole cadre of Christian leaders in those countries where most of the growth in Christianity is today, so he's partly responsible for that growth," Ted Schroder, a pastor at Christ Church in San Antonio, Texas, told J. Michael Parker for the *San Antonio Express-News* (March 13, 1999). In the U.S. the organization is called John Stott Ministries. Sister movements are active in Australia, Canada, and Hong Kong, among other countries.

Despite the demands of his rectorship and missionary work, Stott wrote prolifically. In 1973 he published *Your Mind Matters: The Place of the Mind in Christian Life*, in which he tried to demonstrate that reason is vital to religion. As he wrote, "God's purpose is both [religious] zeal tempered by knowledge and knowledge fired by zeal." Earlier, he had written in *Christian Basics* (1969), as quoted on his Web site, "Christianity lays great emphasis on the importance of knowledge, rebukes anti-intellectualism for the negative, paralyzing thing it is, and traces many of our problems to our ignorance. Whenever the heart is full and the head is empty, dangerous fanaticisms arise."

Stott was one of the major architects of the Lausanne Covenant, which was signed by more than 2,300 evangelicals from 150 nations at the 1974 International Congress on World Evangelization, held in Lausanne, Switzerland. The covenant declared the core principles of world evangelism, and thanks to Stott's insistence, it contained several references to social responsibility. As quoted on Stott's Web site, the covenant states, "The message of salvation implies also a message of judgment upon every form of alienation, oppression and discrimination, and we should not be afraid to denounce evil and injustice wherever they exist."

In 1975, after 25 years of service, Stott retired as rector of All Souls and took on the title of rector emeritus. He remained busy with the Langham Partnership and continued to write. His many books include *Baptism and Fullness: The Work of the Holy Spirit Today* (1975); *Christian Mission in the Modern World* (1975); *Christian Counter-Culture: The Message of the Sermon on the Mount* (1978); *Focus on Christ* (1979); *God's New Society* (1979); *Understanding the Bible* (1979), which has been revised and reprinted several times; *Between Two Worlds: The Art of Preaching in the Twentieth Century* (1982); *God's Book for God's People* (1982); *Involvement* (1985); *The Cross of Christ* (1986), a meditation on the meaning of the cross; *Decisive Issues Facing Christians Today* (1990); *The Contemporary Christian: Applying God's Word to Today's World* (1992); *Acts: Seeing the Spirit at Work* (1998); *Evangelical Truth: A Personal Plea for Unity, Integrity, and Faithfulness* (1999; reissued in 2005); *Incomparable Christ* (2001); *Basic Christian Leadership: Biblical Models of Church, Gospel, and Ministry* (2002); *Favorite Psalms: Growing Closer to God* (2003); and *Life in Christ: A Guide for Daily Living* (2003). According to johnstott.org, "Such a prodigious literary output has been helped by unusual self-discipline and the unstinting support of Frances Whitehead, his secretary for nearly 50 years."

Stott's books are aimed at both laymen and members of the clergy, and most have been reviewed favorably in the religious and mainstream media. In an assessment for the *Dallas Morning News* (March 25, 1995) of *Romans: God's Good News for the World* (1995), a commentary on St. Paul's letters to the Romans, for example, Paul R. Buckley wrote, "Stott is well-acquainted with the theological giants who have scaled this Everest of Paul's letters, but he doesn't hesitate to depart from them when he believes the text demands it. . . . [He] writes popularly but with straight-to-the point erudition; his work is mercifully free of the lame anecdotes that drag so many popular evangelical books down." Buckley also thought well of *Guard the Truth: The Message of 1 Timothy & Titus* (1997); he wrote for the *Dallas Morning News* (May 17, 1997) that the book's strength "lies in sober, reflective, verse-by-verse exposition of the texts."

In 2003 Stott published *Why I Am a Christian*, a widely reviewed volume in which he argued for the primacy of the Christian faith over other religions. *Why I Am a Christian* explores Christianity in an age of pluralism, when many Westerners are skeptically examining their own beliefs, switching faiths, becoming agnostic, or embracing a multifaith outlook. "We should treat everyone with respect," Stott said to Carol McGraw. "But that doesn't mean we should treat their religion with the same respect. For example, Muslims say that Jesus was never crucified. [The crucifixion is] central to Christianity. So we can't say both are right. Of course, this goes against postmodernism that says there is no universal truth." Nancy K. Brown, in an undated critique for *Christian Book Previews* (on-line), wrote of *Why I Am a Christian*, "This is a book for every follower of Christ. The clear and rational reasoning it provides can be used by all believers who desire an answer to the question of why they, too, are Christians." A *Publishers Weekly* reviewer, as quoted on Amazon.com, wrote, "In a time when many Christian authors recommend the claims of Christian faith by descriptions of faith encounters and invitations to 'dance with the mystery,' Stott, author of many foundational apologetic works, offers a clear and compelling account of the theological basis for his own belief. . . . For those accustomed to arguments conducted by way of emotive stories, his reliance on logic may feel a bit dry. But readers of a more analytic temperament will find a compelling discussion of the claims of Christ in a remarkably readable, brief form. It's the sort of book that Christians who need a more reasoned, thoughtful approach to their faith will read and then pass along to skeptical friends."

While Stott is known for his humility and compassion, he is unmovable on certain issues: abortion, homosexuality, and the death penalty. His staunch positions led David Brooks to remark that discovering Stott's views after experiencing his gentle demeanor was "like being in *Mr. Rogers' Neighborhood*"—a reference to a popular children's television program hosted by the unusually gentle, softspoken Fred Rogers—"except he has a backbone of steel." John Shelby Spong, a retired liberal Episcopal Church bishop who has debated Stott, wrote for *Beliefnet* (on-line), "When challenged, Stott's pious smile disappears and his soft voice becomes edgy and rejecting. He suggests that anyone who disagrees with him disagrees with the revealed will of God."

Stott is firmly against abortion. "We have to learn to think of mother and unborn child as two human beings at different stages of development," he wrote in *Authentic Christianity* (1995). He continued, "Induced abortion is feticide, the deliberate destruction of an unborn child, the shedding of innocent blood." Stott is in favor of the death penalty, although he believes it should be used sparingly. "I personally believe that the state should retain the authority to take life or 'bear the sword' (Romans 13:4)," he wrote in *Christian Basics*, "as a witness to what murderers deserve, but that in many (even most) cases, when there are any mitigating circumstances, the sentence should be commuted to life imprisonment." He has also been outspoken in his views on homosexuality, telling Carol McGraw, "I have no doubt that homosexuality is forbidden in Scripture. It derives from the Christian teaching of marriage, in which a man shall leave his parents and cleave to his wife. That means monogamous and heterosexual. . . . But obviously we want to be welcoming to those who are homosexual, but urge them to lead a celibate life, as all single people should."

Such views have made Stott a figure of controversy within the Episcopal Church and other church bodies in the United States. Bishop Spong, for example, has called Stott to task for what he calls "outdated" views, including his opposition to divorce. James Karpen, the rector of St. Paul and St. Andrew Methodist Church in New York City, criticized Stott's stances in a letter to the *New York Times* (December 3, 2004): "Pro-death penalty?" Karpen wrote. "Can you get any further from the Christian message? And just where is the Gospel mandate against homosexuality? Jesus never mentions it. Evangelicalism ought to require a faithfulness to the Evangel, the Gospel, the message of Christ. I admire my conservative colleagues who stand up unapologetically for what they believe. But it pains me to see the great evangelical tradition sold out so cheaply to social conservatism masking as faith. And there is a difference between faithfulness and rigidity."

In 2005 *Time* magazine named Stott among the people its editors considered the world's most influential. Stott has been awarded honorary doctorates from several British, Canadian, and American colleges. In addition, he received a Lambeth degree in divinity. (Lambeth degrees are bestowed by the Archbishop of Canterbury in recognition of lifelong contributions to the church. They are awarded in the areas of divinity, law, arts, literature, medicine, and music.) Stott is the founder and honorary president of the London Institute for Contemporary Christianity, an evangelical organization whose mission, as stated on its Web site, is to "equip Christians to engage biblically, relevantly and vigorously with the issues they face."

Stott is the subject of an authorized two-volume biography by Timothy Dudley-Smith: *The Making of a Leader: John Stott: A Biography of the Early Years* (1999) and *A Global Ministry: John Stott: A Biography of the Later Years* (2001). Stott relaxes by engaging in bird watching and photography. When he travels, he brings his binoculars and camera with him; by his own account, he has seen roughly 2,500 species of birds. His book *The Birds Our Teachers: Biblical Lessons from a Lifelong Bird Watcher* (1999) includes his own photographs.

Stott has never married. Acccording to his Web site, "he came close to it on two occasions, and he acknowledges that with the responsibility of a family he could never have written, travelled and ministered in the way he has."

—G.O.

Suggested Reading: *Christianity Today* p24+ Jan. 8, 1996, p54+ Sep. 16, 1996, with photo, p60+ Apr. 2, 2001; John Stott Ministries Web site; *New York Times* (on-line) Nov. 30, 2004; *Orange County (California) Register* B p1 Oct. 3, 1998; *Time* p45 Feb. 7, 2005; Dudley-Smith, Timothy. *John Stott: A Comprehensive Bibliography*, 1995, *The Making of a Leader: John Stott: A Biography of the Early Years*, 1999, *A Global Ministry: John Stott: A Biography of the Later Years*, 2001; Stott, John. *Why I Am a Christian*, 2003

Selected Books: *Men with a Message*, 1954; *Fundamentalism and Evangelism*, 1956; *Basic Christianity*, 1958, 1971; *Your Confirmation*, 1958, 1991; *The Preacher's Portrait*, 1961; *Confess Your Sins*, 1964; *The Epistles of John*, 1964, 1988; *Baptism and Fullness: The Work of the Holy Spirit Today*, 1964, 1975; *The Canticles and Selected Psalms*, 1966; *Men Made New*, 1966; *Our Guilty Silence*, 1967; *The Message of Galatians: Only One Way*, 1968; *Christian Basics*, 1969; *One People*, 1969, 1982; *Christ the Controversialist*, 1970; *Your Mind Matters*, 1973; *The Message of 1 Timothy: Guard the Gospel*, 1973; *Balanced Christianity*, 1975; *Christian Mission in the Modern World*, 1977; *Understanding the Bible*, 1979; *Christian Counterculture: The Message of the Sermon on the Mount*, 1978; *The Message of Ephesians: God's New Society*, 1979; *Focus on Christ*, 1979; *Between Two Worlds: The Art of Preaching in the Twentieth Century*, 1982; *God's Book for God's People*, 1982; *The Bible Book for Today*, 1982; *I Believe in Preaching*, 1982; *Issues Facing Christians Today*, 1984, 1990; *The Authentic Jesus*, 1985; *Involvement*, 1985; *The Cross of Christ*, 1986; *The Message of Acts: To the Ends of the Earth*, 1990; *Decisive Issues Facing Christians Today*, 1990; *The Message of Thessalonians: Preparing for the Coming King*, 1991; *The Contemporary Christian: Applying God's Word to Today's World*, 1992; *Romans: God's Good News for the World*, 1995; *Authentic Christianity*, 1995; *Guard the Truth: The Message of 1 Timothy & Titus*, 1997; *Acts: Seeing the Spirit at Work*, 1998; *Evangelical Truth: A Personal Plea for Unity, Integrity, and Faithfulness*, 1999, 2005; *The Birds Our Teachers: Biblical Lessons from a Lifelong Bird Watcher*, 1999; *Incomparable Christ*, 2001; *Basic Christian Leadership: Biblical Models of Church, Gospel, and Ministry*, 2002; *Favorite Psalms: Growing Closer to God*, 2003; *Why I Am a Christian*, 2003; *Life in Christ: A Guide for Daily Living*, 2003

Courtesy of Drew Struzan

Struzan, Drew

(STREW-zan)

Mar. 18, 1947– Illustrator

Address: c/o XL Brand Inc., 3500 W. Burbank Blvd., First Fl., Burbank, CA 91505

"A [movie] poster becomes that one image that represents the entire film," Drew Struzan told John Kehe for the *Christian Science Monitor* (September 9, 1999). "If it is accurate and truthful and has good spirit, it resides with you forever." Struzan is one of the most prolific creators of movie posters in the history of film. He has produced advertisements for more than 150 films and is responsible for creating what have become the definitive depictions of Indiana Jones, the *Star Wars* characters, and the Muppets. He has also produced posters for such blockbusters as *Rambo: First Blood* (1982), *Back to the Future* (1985), and *Harry Potter and the Sorcerer's Stone* (2001). "People know my work worldwide, but they don't know there's one guy that did so much of it," Struzan told Shogo Hagiwara for the Tokyo *Daily Yomiuri* (November 13, 2003). Thanks to several recent exhibitions of Struzan's work and the publication in 2004 of two comprehensive books, *Drew Struzan: Oeuvre* and *The Movie Posters of Drew Struzan*, film fans are beginning to recognize his enormous contributions. "I'm not seeking fame and I'm not seeking any particular honor for [my work]," he told Hagiwara. "My reward is that I get to do it. . . . I make something with my hands, and that makes people happy. And that makes me valuable because they are happy. I like [it] that way and that's all I need."

Drew Struzan was born on March 18, 1947 in Oregon City, Oregon, and spent most of his formative years in California. An artistic prodigy, he began drawing before he could speak, and, by the age of six, he was reportedly churning out hundreds of drawings; he made them on toilet paper, because his family was too poor to buy drawing paper for hm. At about that time, he took part in a project conducted by researchers at Stanford University, in California, who studied him and his paintings. Later, when Struzan was in middle school, he drew portraits of his classmates to earn enough money to buy himself a bicycle and painting supplies. After he graduated from high school, Struzan, who had been diagnosed as dyslexic, attended the Art Center College of Design in Los Angeles, California. Given the choice of two majors, fine art or illustration, Struzan elected to study illustration, as it was a more likely source of steady income than fine art. He worked his way through college by selling his artwork whenever possible. When he was 19 years old, he was hospitalized briefly for the effects of malnutrition. Despite such travails he married in 1968 and graduated in 1970, earning a B.A. with great distinction, the Art Center's designation for graduating with high honors. He studied for a master's program from 1970 to 1972. Unlike many of his classmates who headed to New York to look for work, Struzan stayed in California, because he could not afford to make the trip east.

After a period of freelance work, Struzan found a job as a staff artist at the graphic-design firm Pacific Eye and Ear, and two years later he became a partner at Pencil Pushers Inc., both in Los Angeles. In those early positions Struzan illustrated album covers for musicians and groups, ranging from Glenn Miller to the Beach Boys to Black Sabbath, as well as for recordings of music by such composers as Johann Sebastian Bach. His album cover for Alice Cooper's *Welcome to My Nightmare* (1975), which depicted the rocker in a top hat and tails, was particularly popular and was named one of the top 100 album covers of all time by *Rolling Stone* magazine. In 1975 he also painted his first film poster, for *The Black Bird*, starring George Segal. He left agency work to resume his freelance career in 1982. "As I worked and built up a reputation, career and portfolio, the movie industry started to recognize the work I was doing and started to offer me jobs," he told Hagiwara. "I slowly worked my way into it. It wasn't that I was pursuing movies in particular. It just happened that way." Following his work on *The Black Bird*, Struzan illustrated posters for such films as *Return to Macon County* (1975), *Car Wash* and *Robin and Marian* (both 1976), and *Empire of the Ants* (1977). "Because I brought my particular taste and my particular education to it, and I wasn't trying to imitate things that came before me, I became kind of an innovator and a creator in the field," he told Hagiwara.

Struzan created posters primarily for low-budget movies until 1977. That year he received a call from Charles White III, a fellow Art Center graduate. White, primarily an airbrush artist, had been commissioned by George Lucas to create a poster for his film *Star Wars* and wanted help. (Later, the film became known as *Star Wars: Episode IV—A New Hope.*) White's specialty was depicting mechanical devices, not people, so he enlisted Struzan to paint the portraits of human characters, while he himself depicted the spaceships and robots. The resulting poster was designed to look like an advertisement for a film epic from the 1920s or '30s. Lucas, the writer, director, and producer of the *Star Wars* franchise, appreciated the effort, particularly the old-fashioned look of the piece, and he hired Struzan to create the poster for the third installment of the series, *Return of the Jedi*, in 1983. (That film was initially titled *Revenge of the Jedi*, but Lucas changed his mind at the last minute, and the posters printed with the original title were ordered destroyed. The few that survived are highly prized by collectors.)

At the suggestion of Lucas (who has several of Struzan's original paintings in his private collection), Bantam Books hired Struzan to create the covers for a series of *Star Wars* volumes. The commissions provided the artist with a steady source of work for many years. (According to Bantam's Web site, the company has published more than 40 original *Star Wars* titles; Struzan has made 24 of the covers.) When Lucas re-released the *Star Wars* trilogy in the late 1990s, he asked Struzan to create a commemorative poster. Struzan hit upon the idea of producing three posters that could be viewed individually or placed together to be viewed as a triptych. He was given three weeks to complete the job. "It took 20 years to get to this point and now I had three weeks to sum up the most successful trio of films of all time," he told an interviewer for TheForce.net, an unofficial *Star Wars* site. "There's pressure for you." He worked through weekends and holidays and met the deadline; the striking set of posters he painted is considered highly collectible today. His next project for Lucas was the poster for the long-awaited *Star Wars* prequel, *Episode I: The Phantom Menace*, in 1999. (Struzan was one of a select few individuals who saw a rough cut of the film before it was released.) He painted the posters for *Episode II: Attack of the Clones* (2002) and *Episode III: Revenge of the Sith* (2005) as well.

Lucas solicited Struzan for another notable series of films he produced (and Steven Spielberg directed), featuring an intrepid archaeologist named Indiana Jones. Struzan created the poster for *Raiders of the Lost Ark* (1981), which introduced Indiana Jones to audiences. To keep the plot a secret during the making of film, Struzan was given only a one-paragraph synopsis and a few still pictures from which to gain inspiration. Harrison Ford, who played the Indiana Jones character in the film, did not pose for Struzan; rather, Struzan painted an image of his own body and head but with the face of Ford (not an uncommon practice in the absence of an actual model). Ford, pleased with the results, later thanked Struzan for the depictions. Struzan

created three sample drawings, one of which was chosen and, with minor alterations, printed on the poster. Lucas and his co-producers chose a different artist to create the advertisement for the second film in the series, *Indiana Jones and the Temple of Doom* (1984); dissatisfied with the result, they asked Struzan to quickly come up with something else. He prepared three preliminary drawings in a single day; the executives approved one immediately, and he finished the painting within about four days. The illustration on the poster for *Indiana Jones and the Last Crusade* (1989) is also his, as is the art for more than a dozen *Indiana Jones* book covers, several *Indiana Jones* computer-game boxes, and the poster and logo for the Indiana Jones Adventure ride in Disneyland. As quoted in *Drew Struzan: Oeuvre*, Harrison Ford once said, "There's something exciting about seeing your picture on a movie poster, but it's an overwhelming feeling to be drawn on one, especially the way Drew does it. Because now you know you're not just a star—now you're art."

Steven Spielberg, who met Struzan through his work on *Raiders of the Lost Ark*, further helped the artist's career with commissions outside the *Indiana Jones* series. Struzan produced art for a number of productions in which Spielberg was involved in some capacity, including *E.T. the Extra-Terrestrial* (1982); *Back to the Future* and *The Goonies* (both 1985); *An American Tail* (1986); *Three O'Clock High* and **Batteries Not Included* (both 1987); *Back to the Future Parts II* and *III* (1989 and 1990, respectively); *Hook* (1991); and *The Flintstones* (1994). Struzan has expressed great respect for both Spielberg and Lucas, telling James Bradley for TheRaider.net, a Web site aimed at Indiana Jones fans, that his dealings with the two have been the "best working experiences of my career." Spielberg is quoted as saying in *Oeuvre* that the admiration is reciprocated: "Drew Struzan's artwork makes such a promise of grand entertainment that he puts tremendous pressure on all of us directors to keep that promise with our films."

Struzan has also created posters for, among other films, *The Muppet Movie* (1980), a Jim Henson production; *Return to Oz* (1984), a live-action fantasy; *Better Off Dead* (1985) and *Adventures in Babysitting* (1987), both teen comedies; *Newsies* (1992), a musical; and *Mallrats* (1995), an off-beat offering from the director Kevin Smith. Recently, Struzan painted a poster for the film *Hellboy* (2004), at the request of the director Guillermo del Toro. In 2004 Struzan also painted the 10-year anniversary poster for the popular film *The Shawshank Redemption*. In 2005 Struzan created the posters not only for the final installment of the Star Wars series but for also a Spanish-language film, *Torrente 3: El Protector*, and a short called *Blood Makes Noise*.

With the advent of increasingly sophisticated technology, film posters now frequently feature computer-modified photos rather than hand-painted images. Struzan told Robert Epstein for the

Los Angeles Times (March 19, 1993), "Computers don't enhance. They manipulate images. The computer can only do what it is told to do. Computers don't think, they don't feel. Art is about feelings." Struzan has turned increasingly to other outlets for his paintings. He has produced ads, created covers for *T.V. Guide* and *Sports Illustrated*, and painted designs for stamps for the U.S. Postal Service, featuring portraits of the comedian Lucille Ball; the actors Edward G. Robinson, Henry Fonda, and John Wayne; and the author Zora Neale Hurston. In 1995 Struzan illustrated the children's book *Traveling Again, Dad?*, by Michael Lorelli, and the following year he redesigned the box cover and playing cards for Milton Bradley's popular board game *Clue*. Struzan has also designed collectible items for the Franklin Mint, including more than 100 plates, playing cards depicting figures from the Old West, and a special collector's edition of *Clue*.

Struzan's art has appeared in several volumes, including *The Art of Drew Struzan: Star Wars Portfolio*, a CD-Rom released in 1999; *The Movie Posters of Drew Struzan* (2004); and *Drew Struzan: Oeuvre* (2004), which includes his album and book covers, film posters, and extensive biographical information. From 1995 to 2005 paintings by Struzan were exhibited in a series of one-man shows in Japan. In 1999 the Norman Rockwell Museum, in Stockbridge, Massachusetts, mounted an exhibit of more than 65 pieces of Struzan's work; additionally, he is the only living artist represented in the collection of the National Museum of American Illustration, in Newport, Rhode Island. In 2002 the Academy of Sci-Fi, Fantasy and Horror Films presented Struzan with a lifetime achievement award. Besides Lucas, Struzan's notable collectors include Spielberg, del Toro, the singer Bette Midler, the actor Eddie Murphy, and the filmmakers William Dear and Frank Darabont.

Struzan and his wife, Dylan, live in Pasadena, California. Struzan's studio is in a building in his backyard. The couple's son, Christian, trained by his father as an artist, periodically collaborates with Struzan on posters and has founded XL Laboratories, a small agency devoted to creating print advertising for the motion-picture industry. Struzan has often expressed satisfaction with his life's work. "I'm selling movies, yes," he told Tom Russo for *Entertainment Weekly* (May 28, 1999). "But if I can do it with art, with beauty, in a way that reaches people and touches them . . . that's what makes me happy."

—K.J.E.

Suggested Reading: *Boston Globe* p25 Nov. 29, 1988; DrewStruzan.com; TheForce.net; TheRaider.net; (Tokyo) *Daily Yomiuri* p13 Nov. 13, 2003

Selected Books: *Drew Struzan: Oeuvre*, 2004; *The Movie Posters of Drew Struzan*, 2004

Summitt, Pat

June 14, 1952– Basketball coach

Address: Lady Vols Media Relations Office, 117 Stokely Athletic Center, University of Tennessee, Knoxville, TN 37996-4610

On March 22, 2005 Pat Summitt, the coach of the University of Tennessee's women's basketball team, the Lady Volunteers, led her players to a 75–54 victory over the Purdue Boilermakers to earn her 880th career win; with that victory, she surpassed the record set by Dean Smith of the Carolina Tarheels for most wins of any coach in college-basketball history. As coach of the Lady Volunteers (usually referred to as the Lady Vols) since the 1974–75 season, Summitt has brought the team to six national championships and has reached the "Final Four" round of the play-offs on 16 occasions. Summitt's rise to prominence has in many ways paralleled that of women's college basketball itself, which has gone from drawing small crowds and commanding little media attention to enjoying a level of popularity that rivals that of the men's division. With her "steely blue eyes," which "sometimes seem like they could rip a hole through a player's heart," as they were described by Antonya English in the *St. Petersburg (Florida) Times* (March 9, 1999), Summitt employs methods of motivating her team that have sometimes been considered intense and harsh, and she has often been compared in that regard to Bobby Knight, the controversial coach of Indiana State's Hoosiers for 29 seasons. "Pat Summitt's not for everybody," Michelle Marciniak, who played for Summitt's 1996 championship team and later for the Women's National Basketball Association (WNBA), told Ed McGranahan for the *Greenville (South Carolina) News* (March 2, 2005). "She's so challenging to play for. She challenges you sometimes to the point of frustration and tears, but that is how she gets your attention."

Patricia Head Summitt was born in Henrietta, Tennessee, on June 14, 1952, the fourth of the five children of Hazel and Richard Head. Her father, a strict authoritarian, expected hard work from Summitt and the other children at the family's tobacco farm and grocery store. In her book *Reach for the Summit* (1998), co-authored with Sally Jenkins, she wrote, "My ideas about respect are severe. But then, they were formed by a severe man, my father, who whipped me. . . . My father demanded respect with his belt. We got regular whippings— hard ones." At night, after her chores were done, Summitt would play basketball with her three old-

Pat Summitt

er brothers; her father, aware of her talent and enthusiasm for the game, moved the family so that his daughter would be able to attend Cheatham County High School in Ashland City, Tennessee, which had a women's basketball program. Summitt went on to attend college at the University of Tennessee at Martin, where she played for the Lady Pacers, leading the team to a 64–29 record during her four-year tenure at the school. During that period, before universities were required to provide equal funding for male and female athletic programs, women's college basketball teams tended to have very limited resources. "When I went to college there were no scholarships . . . ," Summitt said to Jessica Hopp for the *Tennessean* (July 27, 2003). "We drove in vans. A lot of times we had four to the room sleeping and sometimes we slept on gym floors. We had to be careful where we went to eat because of the cost."

Summitt graduated with a bachelor's degree in physical education. Then, having gotten an invitation in 1972 to try out for the U.S. national women's basketball team, she was inspired to seek a berth in the 1976 Olympic Games, which would feature women's basketball for the first time. "It seemed to me that there was no greater mark of respect than to be an Olympian," she wrote in *Reach for the Summit*. "But also, I knew I wanted to make a difference for women. So I think that's when I found my real calling." Realizing that she wanted to stay involved with collegiate basketball, she enrolled in a master's-degree program in physical education at the University of Tennessee at Knoxville; the program would allow her to teach courses as well as serve as assistant coach of the school's women's basketball team, the Lady Volunteers.

When the team's head coach left unexpectedly before the start of the 1974–75 season, Summitt found herself head coach of the Lady Vols at 22 years of age. The program had existed since about 1903; the university "said 'yes' to women's basketball long before it was the popular thing to do," Summitt said, as quoted by Tom Sharp for the Associated Press (January 9, 1994). Still, women's college basketball was widely ignored at the national level until it was officially recognized by the National Collegiate Athletic Association (NCAA), in 1982. Summitt's first years as coach of the Lady Vols thus found her with almost no budget to build the team or recruit players. She was reduced to placing ads around the campus, seeking out young women who were interested in playing on the team. As Summitt told Steve Ballard for the *Indianapolis Star* (March 22, 2005), "At the first practice, there were about 65 kids, and about half of them decided not to come back. After running sprints, four of them went up the steps of the gym and out of the building."

In December 1974 Summitt lost the first game she coached, when Mercer University defeated the Lady Vols by one point. "I wasn't prepared . . . ," Summitt later told Lori Riley for the *Hartford Courant* (December 31, 2002). "Of course, we didn't have film back then, so I didn't get to look at all my mistakes. I'm sure I made a lot of them." According to Tom Sharp, she recalled about that time, "I was certainly not mature enough and certainly not qualified enough for the job. But they took a chance on me. . . . I wanted to survive a year, do a good job coaching, meet my academic requirements, and also train for the Olympic trials. My thoughts were very divided at the time, but I wasn't thinking that 'I'm going to build a national powerhouse at Tennessee.'" On January 10, 1975, in their second game under Summitt's leadership, the Lady Vols defeated Middle Tennessee State, 69–52, in front of 53 fans, according to the University of Tennessee Web site—giving Summitt her first victory as coach of the team.

In the following year Summitt achieved her goal of competing in the 1976 Olympic Games, overcoming a leg injury to serve as co-captain of the U.S. team. Though they were defeated soundly by the gold-medal–winning Soviet team, the Americans came in second, capturing the silver medal. With the Olympics over, Summitt continued to coach the Lady Vols. In 1979 the team celebrated its 100th victory under her leadership. Relatively early in her coaching career, Summitt earned a reputation for being a strict disciplinarian. One night in 1977, after hearing that her team had stayed out until 4:00 a.m. partying, Summitt planned an extremely hard practice for them the next day. She recalled in *Reach for the Summit*: "I dragged four plastic trash cans into the gym, and I placed them at the four corners of the court. . . . Then I made them practice—for four hours. . . . Every so often another young lady would limp over to the sideline and do some business."

In 1984 Summitt returned to the Olympics, this time as a coach, in Los Angeles, California. American spectators had eagerly awaited a showdown with the Soviet Union's women's team, and Summitt had been confident that the home-court advantage would bring her team a victory. That year, however, the Soviet Union boycotted the Olympic Games, and the U.S. team defeated South Korea to take the gold medal. The victory resulted in a great deal of publicity for women's basketball in the U.S.

By 1987, when the Lady Vols had had six appearances—and as many losses—in the Final Four, some spectators had begun to wonder why Summitt had not been able to snare a national title. Matters changed that year, when she led the Lady Vols to their first championship, a 67–44 victory over longtime rival Louisiana Tech. "The monkey's off my back," she said to the *Chicago Tribune* (March 31, 1987) after the game. "It was a long time getting here." Tennessee's star of the game was freshman Tonya Edwards, who scored 13 points with seven rebounds; she would again help Summitt's team to win a championship when the Lady Vols defeated Auburn University's Lady Tigers in 1989. The Lady Vols continued their streak of odd-year championships in 1991—their last national title for several years.

By the 1995–96 season Summitt's activities away from the court had begun to draw nearly as much media attention as her team's games. The press made much, for example, of Summitt's 1990 visit to the home of a prospective player, Michelle Marciniak, in Pennsylvania—at a time when Summitt was nine months pregnant. Going into labor during the meeting, Summitt flew immediately back to Tennessee, where she gave birth to a baby boy, Ross Tyler. Right afterward she returned to the business of trying to lure Marciniak to her basketball squad. (Marciniak enrolled at Notre Dame but transferred to Tennessee the next year. After sitting out a season as penalty, she began playing for the Lady Vols in the 1994–95 season.)

While the team lost to Connecticut at the conclusion of that year's Final Four, they regrouped in 1996 with a team that would begin a history-making series of championship victories. That year Summitt's team defeated Connecticut in the semifinals of the Final Four and went on to best Georgia's Lady Bulldogs for the national title. The 1996 team won largely on the strength of freshman Chamique Holdsclaw, who was quickly becoming a sensation in collegiate basketball. The championship represented a personal victory for Summitt, who said publicly on several occasions that it brought the first significant show of approval she had ever received from her father. She wrote in *Reach for the Summit*: "I was forty-three years old before my father hugged me for the first time. . . . I had said publicly over the years that he was a forbidding man, and that I'd never been able to win his approval. I guess he got tired of hearing about it. . . . He put his arms around me, and in his own awkward way, hugged me and kissed me. A few days later, he said, grudgingly, 'Now I don't want to hear any more about how I never hug you or tell you how proud I am.'" Summitt's father died in October 2005.

The 1996–97 season got off to a disappointing start, with the Lady Vols losing to teams that had not beaten them in years and dropping out of the 10 top-ranked squads for the first time in a decade. Summitt wrote in her book that that year's Lady Vols "were too quiet, they were listless, they had no attitude. I felt like a dentist pulling teeth." She worried that the team was depending too much on the talents of Chamique Holdsclaw. "Everybody had too much respect for Chamique Holdsclaw as a player," she wrote. "They all stood around, assuming Chamique would win games by herself." Holdsclaw said to Kelli Anderson for *Sports Illustrated* (April 17, 1997), "Pat was fed up. She told us to quit acting like babies. She also set game goals. For instance, if we made more than 15 turnovers or gave up too many rebounds, we'd have to run extra sprints. I think that really helped turn things around." That season the Lady Vols made one of the greatest comebacks in college basketball history, rocketing back into championship contention with win after win as the season neared its end. Chamique Holdsclaw scored 24 points and seven rebounds in the championship game against Old Dominion's Lady Monarchs to help bring the Lady Vols a 68–59 victory. The team was the first in NCAA history to win the title after suffering more than six losses during the regular season, and only the second ever to win back-to-back championships. They are the subject of the television documentary *A Cinderella Season: The 1997 Lady Vols Fight Back*, which aired on HBO in 1998. *Raise the Roof*, Summitt's book about the season, co-written with Sally Jenkins, was published in 1998.

The following season the Lady Vols continued their winning ways, entering the Final Four with a perfect record and defeating Louisiana Tech in the championships to cement a 39–0 record for the season—the most wins in women's basketball in a season with no defeats. While that win was the Lady Vols' last championship victory to date, the team has compiled winning records in the years since. On January 14, 2003 the Lady Vols defeated DePaul University's Blue Demons to hand Summitt her 800th win. In March 2005 basketball fans took note as Summitt quickly closed in on Dean Smith's record of 879 career wins. On March 20 she squared off against one of her former players, Kellie Harper (formerly known as Kellie Jolly), now the coach of Western Carolina's Lady Cats, winning the game 94–43 and tying Smith's record. "It's really not about a number," Summitt said to Elizabeth A. Davis for the Associated Press (March 21, 2005). "It's about people—the people here at the university, the administration, all the great assistant coaches I've had, the loyal people who have stuck by me for years, the people I work with in the office and certainly all the players." Two days later the Lady Vols defeated Purdue, 75–54, to make Summitt the most winning coach in college-basketball history. "Obviously, to be in the company with Coach Smith, to think about all the people that were a part of these wins, I never thought I'd live this long," Summitt said after the win, as quoted by Mel Greenberg in the *Lowell Sun* (March 29, 2005). Following Summitt's achievement, the University of Tennessee announced a new name for the basketball court at Thompson-Boling Arena, where the Lady Vols play, dubbing it "The Summitt." "It really touches me," Summitt said to Elizabeth A. Davis for the Associated Press (March 23, 2005) about the renaming in her honor. "I never even thought about anything like that ever. I don't think there could have been a better gift in terms of the feeling that I had and how much I love this university."

In 2000 Summitt was inducted into the Basketball Hall of Fame for her achievements with the Lady Vols; only the fourth woman coach to be inducted, Summitt called the honor "a great compliment to the growth of the women's game," as the *Memphis Commercial Appeal* (October 16, 2000) reported. Summitt is a much-sought-after motivational speaker, sharing insights on her winning ways with organizations as diverse as the CIA and Victoria's Secret.

Pat Summitt lives in Tennessee with her husband, R. B. Summitt, and their son, Ross Tyler. She has been approached on several occasions about coaching a professional team in the WNBA, but told Dick Patrick for *USA Today* (March 15, 2005), "I just love the college campus and college athletics. That's a place where you can teach and influence and impact lives. . . . I see so many pro athletes I think are spoiled individuals. And they're adults. I think that with fame and money, sometimes, somehow, people think that empowers them to be jerks. . . . I think I'd really struggle with my upbringing and my philosophy as a basketball coach in the pros. . . . I'm not saying I'd never go there. I will admit I thought long and hard about it." Others predict that she will continue to coach the Lady Vols. Michelle Marciniak said to Lynn Zinser for the *New York Times* (April 3, 2005) about Summitt, "We just talked on the phone, and I said, 'You'll still be coaching when you're 80 years old.' . . . She still has that fire. She'll put that number [of wins] way over 1,000. Definitely."

—R.E.

Suggested Reading: Associated Press Mar. 23, 2005; *Sports Illustrated* p40 Apr. 8, 1996, p42 Apr. 7, 1997; *St. Louis Post Dispatch* D p6 Mar. 28, 2003; *USA Today* C p1 Mar. 15, 2005; Summitt, Pat, and Sally Jenkins. *Reach for the Summit*, 1998

Selected Books: with Sally Jenkins—*Reach for the Summit*, 1998; *Raise the Roof*, 1998

Taintor, Anne

Aug. 16, 1953– Artist; entrepreneur

Address: P.O. Box 9, Youngsville, NM 87064

Although the name of the artist and entrepreneur Anne Taintor may not be widely known, her work is nearly inescapable. Her refrigerator magnets, which typically feature images of prim-looking women snipped from vintage advertisements accompanied by unexpected, often indecorous witticisms, adorn kitchens all over the U.S. and in many places overseas; her artwork and sassy sentiments are also featured on mugs, T-shirts, calendars, candles, cocktail napkins, soap wrappers, and an array of other items. In an article by Jane Mahoney for the *Albuquerque (New Mexico) Journal* (February 15, 2004), Taintor described the look of her products as "vintage revisited"—a style that has become increasingly popular since 1987, when she founded her small company, Anne Taintor Inc. Labeled a "master of the droll juxtaposition" by Melissa Dribben in the *Philadelphia Inquirer* (November 2, 2003), she has traced her sense of humor, which is often described as subversive, to her early years. "I really appreciate it that lots of people think I'm very funny, but the fact is I just talk like everyone else in my family," she said in an interview posted on the Bad Girls Press Web site. "I just hit on a way to cash in on our dinner table conversations."

Anne Taintor was born into a Roman Catholic family on August 16, 1953 in Lewiston, Maine. Her parents, Frederick and Jane Taintor, met while both were attending law school; after they earned their law degrees, they promptly married and started their family. Her father practiced law, while her mother stayed home, cooking, cleaning, and managing the household, which grew to include five children. In addition to Anne, the Taintor siblings are Rick, a community- and regional-planning consultant; Liz, a certified public accountant; Christopher, an attorney; and Ellen, who works for Anne's company in sales and marketing. (A photo on the company's Web site shows Ellen as a toddler on the beach.) "We definitely got the message on some level that [being a housewife] was a lousy deal," Taintor told Dribben.

For as long as she can remember, Taintor has regarded herself as an artist. "When I was a little kid, I always wanted to be famous, with a painting in the Louvre," she told Mahoney. During her teen years she painted a series of family sailboats with wildly colored flowers. The boats "were pretty ugly by the time I was done with them," she admitted to Dribben. Taintor attended Radcliffe College, a women's school in Cambridge, Massachusetts. (Closely associated with Harvard University, it is now known as the Radcliffe Institute for Advanced Study.) She earned a B.A. degree in visual and environmental studies in 1977.

domestically
disabled

she liked
imaginary
men
best of all

(Left) Anne Taintor in her studio; (right) details of two of her works

Soon afterward Taintor married, and in the early 1980s she gave birth to a daughter, Hannah; a few years later she and her husband divorced. Her life as a stay-at-home mother ended when she began working as a cartographer at DeLorme, an atlas and map company based in Yarmouth, Maine. As a single mother, however, she wanted a job that would allow her to work from home and spend more time with Hannah. She had been making jewelry during the weekends and evenings, and, encouraged by her father, she opted to quit her cartography job and pursue that line of work full-time. "I figured if Dad thought it was a good idea, it couldn't be completely foolhardy," she said in the Bad Girls Press Web site interview. Besides, she explained, "I was barely making enough money to pay for childcare anyway, so it wasn't a huge risk." She launched Anne Taintor Inc. in 1987 in South Portland, Maine.

Taintor scoured garage sales for vintage women's magazines, from which she clipped images to use in collages, which she fashioned into barrettes, pins, and earrings. She eked out a living selling her wares at craft shows. Then, as she recalled to Patricia Corrigan for the *St. Louis (Missouri) Post-Dispatch* (May 5, 2004), "a friend said I should make magnets, and I remember thinking that had to be the dumbest idea ever." Despite her misgivings, Taintor began to decorate magnets, superimposing cut-out words and phrases over vintage pictures. She enjoyed speculating about what the people in the old photos might actually have been thinking. "I look through old magazines and everyone looks very complacent and delighted with everything," Taintor told Sloane Stephens Cox for the *Pensacola (Florida) News Journal* (January 7,

2004). "[But] I think they were thinking something else at the time." In Taintor's imagination, those thoughts tended to be far different from—and often racier than—what the models' demure expressions might suggest. For example, a magnet that features a deadpan brunette staring fixedly outward bears the words "Maybe I *want* to look cheap." Another collage shows an apron-clad housewife beaming in front of her refrigerator and reads "I'm happy . . . yet aware of the ironic implications of my happiness." A picture of two career women in suits carries the line "We have nothing to fear but our mothers." A particularly popular design depicts a beaming woman cuddling a cherubic infant; its message is "Wow! I get to give birth *and* change diapers." Sometimes the models' expressions or poses inspire the text; the words in others are verbatim quotes from Taintor family conversations. "Everyone [in the family] is very verbally oriented and very ironic," the artist told Mahoney. "That's just how they talk." In total, the company's line currently consists of 250 different designs. Occasionally, older female customers recognize themselves as the models in photos Taintor has used.

Sold in an assortment of boutiques and other shops, the magnets were an instant hit. They were especially popular among women, particularly those of Taintor's generation and the previous one, who had been surrounded by such images as children or young adults. "People think [my work is] feminist. I dunno," Taintor said to Joseph Ditzler for the *Albuquerque (New Mexico) Journal* (June 9, 2003). "I'm not anti-male." As sales of her magnets began to soar, Taintor expanded her line, adding more designs and such items as coasters, greeting cards, framed prints, and notepads. Additionally, she has licensed select designs to companies that offer pajamas, T-shirts, mugs, tissues, soaps and lotions, candles, calendars, address books, and playing cards, among other products. In 2003 Chronicle Books released a collection of Taintor's images, entitled *I Can't Be Good All the Time*. Another compilation, *I'm Becoming My Mother*, was published in 2004.

As soon as Hannah graduated from high school in Maine, Taintor and her partner, Nathan Janoff, moved to Youngsville, New Mexico, a town with a population of 80. "I'm out here in the middle of nowhere—or rather it's the center of the universe [to me]," Taintor told Jane Mahoney. "I love the wide openness of New Mexico," she said in the Bad Girls Press interview. "I love living in a place without stores. But what clinched [the decision to move] was the Abiquiu reservoir right down the road, because I do need to swim!" The Taintor/Janoff house, which was custom-designed, is environmentally friendly.

Taintor creates her designs in her Youngsville studio. She owns a former warehouse in nearby Coyote, where some of her products are assembled. She currently employs nine women (all local women except for her sister Ellen, who lives in Massachusetts), which makes Anne Taintor Inc. the second-largest year-round employer in Coyote. (The United States Forest Service is the largest.) Because the Coyote facility can no longer keep up with demand, most of what she sells is produced in a factory in the New York City borough of Brooklyn. Anne Taintor products can be found at more than 2,000 retail outlets throughout the United States, as well as in Canada, Europe, Australia, and New Zealand, and on-line.

Taintor is said to be resourceful and frugal. Her source materials tend to be inexpensive, though they have increased in price since she began her enterprise. She now buys more vintage copies of *Ladies' Home Journal*, *Good Housekeeping*, and other women's magazines through eBay, the on-line auction house, than at yard sales.

To celebrate her 50th birthday, Taintor took a trip back to Maine for a family reunion and a wedding—her own, to Nathan Janoff, with whom she had lived for 12 years. "We did it on my birthday so we wouldn't forget our anniversary," she told Melissa Dribben. In her spare time, Taintor enjoys hiking, snorkeling, and yoga.

—K.J.E.

Suggested Reading: *Albuquerque (New Mexico) Journal* p1 June 9, 2003, p6 Feb. 15, 2004; annetaintor.com; Bad Girls Press Web site; *Pensacola (Florida) News Journal* B p1 Jan. 7, 2004; *Philadelphia Inquirer* M p4 Nov. 2, 2003; *St. Louis (Missouri) Post-Dispatch* E p1 May 5, 2004

Tangerine Dream

German music group

Froese, Edgar
(FROO-suh)
June 6, 1944– Electronic musician

Froese, Jerome
Nov. 24, 1970– Keyboardist

Address: *c/o TDI Music, P.O. Box 30 33 40, 10728 Berlin, Germany*

Over the course of its 35-year existence, the German-based rock group Tangerine Dream has influenced the development of electronic music, perhaps more so than any other music act. In the band's early years, their members drew inspiration from psychedelic rock and classical minimalism to produce a series of records that are still hailed as visionary and avant-garde. Even as the band became more mainstream, in the late 1970s and early 1980s, their work anticipated much of 1980s pop music, in its heavy reliance on synthesizers with sequencer rhythms. During that time the band members also began composing film soundtracks; to date they have completed more than 60 original film scores, including those for *Thief* (1981), *Risky Business* (1983), and *Legend* (1985). In doing so, Tangerine Dream helped push electronic music as an acceptable medium for film composition. "Some people think electronic music has to be cold and icy," the band's founder, Edgar Froese, told Robert Palmer for the *New York Times* (June 25, 1986), "but if you know how to use the instruments and put that particular human touch in it, it can sound beautiful." In the 1990s, as they became influenced by the very electronica artists they had inspired earlier, Tangerine Dream infused their increasingly produced sound with club rhythms. Remarking on this varied musical history, Froese, the only member of Tangerine Dream to have performed on all of the group's albums, told Ashley Franklin and Nick Willder for *SoundScapes* (online), "It's more like a long story which could be cut in different episodes. That was what Tangerine Dream was all about. Apart from the development in technology there is a kind of subjective personal diary. Whatever we went through as a band or as individuals can be seen in whatever we do on stage or record."

Edgar Froese was born on June 6, 1944 in Tilsit, East Prussia, which was then part of Poland. After Germany's defeat in World War II, Froese's family, like other German residents of East Prussia, were forced to relocate to Germany; Froese grew up in West Berlin. As a teenager he was taken with the

Courtesy of TDI Music

Tangerine Dream at present: Edgar Froese (left) and Jerome Froese

dadaist and surrealist movements in art, which stressed dreamlike and avant-garde images. He also enjoyed the writings of Gertrude Stein, Henry Miller, and Walt Whitman. In the mid-1960s Froese organized multimedia events at the home of the surrealist painter Salvador Dali in Spain. Inspired to work with music, Froese joined a rock band called the Ones, as a guitarist. The band released one single before breaking up in 1967. Froese then formed Tangerine Dream, whose first lineup included the bassist Kurt Herkenberg, the drummer Lanse Hapshash, the vocalist Charlie Prince, and the flutist Voker Hombach. Over the next two years the group played at a variety of student events in West Berlin, in a psychedelic-rock style that centered on Eastern and jazz-inflected guitar lines and drug-influenced lyrics and was similar in that way to the music of their American contemporaries the Grateful Dead and the Jefferson Airplane. After a time the group's work began to Froese to seem futile. As he said to Andy Gill for the British magazine *Mojo* (April 1997, on-line), "What can you do if you're in a position where you can run round in circles and still never catch up what is already there? That period of time was when [Eric] Clapton was big with Cream, and [Jimi] Hendrix was big—what did it mean for a German to take a guitar and start playing like that? It was ridiculous."

In an effort to create original sounds, Froese formed a new version of Tangerine Dream in 1969, with the drummer Klaus Schulze and Conrad Schitzler, the latter of whom played wind instruments. The group began jamming in an improvised manner similar to that of the British psychedelic

rockers Pink Floyd and the German avant-garde group Amon Düül. In 1969 Tangerine Dream recorded their debut single, "Ultima Thule," which featured both guitars and violins. After an unsuccessful trip to London, England, to recruit a lead singer for his new band, Froese returned to Berlin—"burned out and penniless," as he told Gill—to find a letter from the German record label Ohr. As Froese recalled to Gill, the letter said, "'We listened to your tape and it sounds great, we want to sign you!' I thought, What tape?" The music in question was on a collection of improvised demos Tangerine Dream had recorded in an abandoned warehouse but had not expected to release. During the recording of the music, the band had filtered keyboard, guitar, and bass lines—as well as music produced with found objects—through various effects processors to create a sparse, almost trance-inducing sound. Released as *Electronic Meditation* in June 1970, the band's first record has inspired a cult following with its raw sound. Klaus Schulze and Conrad Schitzler left for solo careers after the album was released. (Schulze would later become a founding member of the renowned German psychedelic group Ash Ra Tempel.) Following their departure, the organist Steve Schroyder and the keyboardist and drummer Christopher Franke joined the band. Not long after the lineup change, the band caused an outcry of protest when they appeared on television playing a piece written for guitar, cello, drums, and 12 pinball machines.

In 1971 Tangerine Dream released *Alpha Centauri*, on which the band increased their use of keyboards, relying less heavily on guitars. In particular they had drawn inspiration from the VCS3 synthesizer lent to them by a fellow music enthusiast. "We didn't know what it was about, we would just turn things right to left, left to right, get some sounds out of it, and put them straight on the record!," Froese told Gill. "It sounded as strange as we thought a sound could be at that time. That's all we could do on *Alpha Centauri*! So it's maybe a bit poor if you listen to it today, but back in '72 or '73 it sounded avant-garde!" Consisting of three slow-building pieces, *Alpha Centauri* helped pioneer the "space rock" sound, characterized by organ chords played slowly over gurgling synthesizers, improvised drumming, and flutes. Schroyder left the band after the album's release and was replaced by Peter Baumann. Baumann's first record with the group, *Zeit* (1972), pushed the boundaries of electronic music in a rock format, consisting as it does of one down-tempo composition in four movements, with no melody or drums and with such instruments as cellos and vibraphones thrown into the mix. That record has more in common with classical minimalist pieces by Steve Reich or Philip Glass than with the work of most rock acts. Remarking on the band's shift to mostly electronic instrumentation, Froese told Gill, "There was a gig somewhere in the South of Germany where we walked on-stage with the usual line-up and were playing some crazy free music with rock instruments, and all of a sudden we realised that if you do that for years you end up nowhere, with nowhere to go. Even though we were doing crazy things, the sound was pretty normal. We felt we had to make an absolute break, so after the gig we decided to sell everything we had in the way of normal instruments and do something completely new. At the same time, we were watching what was happening in the avant-garde community, where people were getting rid of harmonies and melody lines and so on. We knew we wouldn't make any money out of it, but we bought some little sine-wave generators and microphones which we put on different things like calculators and stuff, and produced sounds which we then sent through echo and reverb units. It sounded so stupid that we thought we'd get some attention, at least!"

The year 1973 brought Tangerine Dream's album *Atem*, a somewhat more accessible work than *Zeit*. Through *Atem*, the band came to the attention of an influential British deejay, John Peel, who called it the record of the year. At this time the band refused to record any more music for the Ohr label, due in large part to the actions of its owner, Rolf-Ulrich Kaiser, who among other tactics allegedly spiked musicians' drinks with LSD in secret and recorded the musical results for another of his labels. With growing interest in their music, Tangerine Dream signed a five-year contract with the fledgling Virgin Records, which had recently become a major player in the record industry thanks to their release of Mike Oldfield's all-electronic album *Tubular Bells*, used to sinister effect in the 1973 film *The Exorcist*. Tangerine Dream's own all-electronic approach, however, brought them criticism from rock-music purists. During one of the group's performances, at about the time that *Phaedra* (1974) was released on the Virgin label, the audience pelted the band with apples and bananas, forcing the group to leave after 10 minutes of performing. At a concert in Paris an audience member in the balcony threw a plastic bag full of marmalade onto the band's equipment, ending the band's show. Froese told Gill, "In those days people were not very polite about what we did. In a *Melody Maker* interview in '73 or '74 . . . I said, 'In about 10 years' time, everybody will play synthesizers'—the guy stopped his tape recorder, said, 'You're an idiot,' and walked out. They thought we were aliens just fooling them." Years later John Bush, writing for the *All Music Guide*, nonetheless called *Phaedra* "one of the most important, artistic and exciting works in the history of electronic music." The record's slow-moving, occasionally melodic synthesizer lines play over complex, arpeggiated sequencer patterns and other eerie effects. Although the record received mostly negative reviews from the mainstream press at the time it appeared, it made the Top 20 on the British charts and was certified gold, meaning that it sold at least 500,000 copies.

As a result of their newfound popularity, Tangerine Dream was invited to play at the Roman Catholic Reims Cathedral, in France, on December 13, 1974. After the crowd, expected to be 1,500 people, swelled to almost 6,000, large numbers of audience members found themselves packed into the pews and unable to get out to use the bathrooms. As a result, some in the audience urinated against the pillars of the cathedral, causing a great public outcry—which led to, among other things, the group's being officially banned by Pope Paul VI from playing in Roman Catholic churches. Nonetheless, they were invited in 1975 to perform at several cathedrals affiliated with the Church of England, including Coventry Cathedral, York Minster Cathedral, and Liverpool Cathedral. That year Tangerine Dream released *Rubycon*, which features one 35-minute epic piece, on which the band added treated (as well as untreated) pianos and organs to their all-electronic sound. Tangerine Dream followed up the live album *Ricochet* (1975) with *Stratosfear* (1976), for which they worked with more acoustic instruments, such as untreated piano, harpsichord, harmonica, and guitar. In addition the album's music showed a shift toward more conventional songwriting, with stronger melodies and rhythm.

In 1977 William Friedkin, the director of *The Exorcist*, asked the band to compose music for his upcoming film *Sorcerer* (1977). Without seeing any footage of the film, relying on a script alone, the band completed the score, which led to dozens of other film-scoring opportunities for the group. "Financially," Froese told Robert Palmer in 1986, "making sound tracks keeps us going independent of record companies. And artistically, seeing a vision and creating something in response to it is very much apart from sitting in front of a blank notebook not knowing what to do." After the live album *Encore* (1977), Baumann left Tangerine Dream for a solo career; he would later form Private Music, which became a major New Age label and featured such artists as Shadowfax, Yanni, and John Tesh. Replacing Baumann with Steve Jolliffe and adding the percussionist Klaus Kruger, Tangerine Dream put out *Cyclone* in 1978. The most controversial album of Tangerine Dream's career, *Cyclone* angered many of the band's fans with its addition of lyrics sung by Jolliffe and its general shift to a more mainstream sound. Jolliffe left the band after the record appeared, and the group returned to all-instrumental mode for *Force Majeure* (1979), albeit with more of a guitar-driven approach than on previous releases. After that record came out, Johannes Schmoelling joined the group on organ, while Klaus Kruger departed. Schmoelling's first concert with Tangerine Dream, at the Palast der Republik in East Berlin, was the first live performance by a Western rock group in a Communist nation in Eastern Europe. A recording of the performance was later released as the album *Pergamon* (1986). Schmoelling made his studio debut with Tangerine Dream on *Tangram* (1980), which found the band continuing to move in a more melodic and pop-friendly direction while still recording with mostly electronic instruments. "In the early '70s," Froese told Andy Gill, "we did 100 per cent improvised stuff, just sat down and started playing. . . . Then we moved on and started structuring things more, when technology became more reliable and flexible and you could store things and recall them better."

During the 1980s Tangerine Dream composed the music for more than 30 films, among them *Thief* (1981), the box-office smash *Risky Business* (1984), *The Keep* (1984), *Firestarter* (1984), *Vision Quest* (1985), *Legend* (1985), *Three O'Clock High* (1987), *Shy People* (1987), and *Deadly Care* (1987). Tangerine Dream's use of electronic instrumentation in their scores led many other film composers to experiment with synthesizers. Despite being seen as visionaries in some circles, the band was also derided for composing "by the numbers" when it came to their film scores. Writing about the band's score for the film *Legend*, for example, Fred Bayles of the Associated Press (July 30, 1986) noted, "Without a picture, the music is dull." Long-time fans also complained that the band's music was becoming watered down. The group's 1981 album, *Exit*, contains shorter, more self-contained pieces with pop instrumentation and dance-floor influences. Although thematically concerned with the topical issue of nuclear war, the music was a far cry from the experimentation of the band's previous work. Tangerine Dream's next record, *White Eagle* (1982), focused on environmental concerns while retaining much of the sound of *Exit*. The group followed with *Logos: Live at the Dominion* (1982), which comprises a diverse cross-section of Tangerine Dream's music, moving from minimalist-influenced material to their more recent, conventionally structured pieces.

In 1983 the band released their last studio album for Virgin, *Hyperboea*, for which they added Eastern-influenced melodies to their sound. The band's next studio album, *Le Parc* (1985), released on the Jive Electro label, contains short compositions representing different parks from around the world. *Le Parc* marked the first time the group had used sampling technology on a studio record. The group utilized meditative Native American sounds on the track "Yellowstone Park," while "Central Park" is, in contrast, more modern in tone and had a danceable beat. Both critics and fans hailed the effort as among the band's best in years. After the album's release Johannes Schmoelling left the band and was replaced by Paul Haslinger, who came from a classical-music background and brought a more structured feel to Tangerine Dream's music. His first record with the group was *Underwater Sunlight* (1986), the theme of which is the underwater world. The band followed with *Tyger* (1987), which features more vocals than any previous Tangerine Dream album—specifically, Jocelyn Bernadette Smith singing verse of the English poet William Blake. That year the group also released *Canyon Dreams*, which was composed for a video of the same name, about the Grand Canyon. Fusing the band's earlier, progressive styles and their more modern leanings of the 1980s, the album brought the group their first of seven Grammy nominations. In 1987, after 16 years with the band, Christoper Franke left to focus on a solo career. His last concert—the band's 750th—was taped and released as the live album *Livemiles* (1988). "I felt I needed a creative break," Franke said of his reasons for leaving the group, as quoted on the Web site Sound on Sound. "Because I think we started to repeat ourselves. We ended up with so much equipment that we took on a lot of jobs to pay for it, became overworked and did too many things at the same time. We did not have time to explore our minds for fresh ideas or explore the great computer instruments we had at our disposal. Kids with much more time than us, but less experience, began producing better sounds, and I began to feel our quality was dropping. This was a very bad feeling for a group who always wanted to be on the cutting edge of music." Responding to such assessments, Edgar Froese told Ashley Franklin and Nick Willder, "I agree absolutely . . . it's not the same band any more. . . . Specifically the style of music is somehow related strongly to your consciousness. If consciousness changes, what you do will change, because your daily working, thinking, behaving process are absolutely linked 100% to your consciousness. That's why there is a development. We are not the same people any more."

Optical Race (1988) was the group's first album to be released on their former bandmate Peter Baumann's label, Private Music Records. The album has been called one of Tangerine Dream's more accessible works. In 1990 Edgar Froese's son, Jerome Froese (born on November 24, 1970), joined Tangerine Dream as a keyboardist. The group's first album to feature his work is *Melrose* (1990), which consists of smooth yet technically complex music that, like a great deal of the band's more recent material, is often categorized as New Age—a designation with which Edgar Froese disagrees strongly. New Age music "is not the music we play," he told an interviewer for *Dream Collector* (June 1994), as quoted on the Voices in The Net Web site, "even if record dealers, music reviewers and listeners are always looking for a 'stylistic drawer' to put Tangerine Dream into. And, even more annoying than [New Age] music is the 'New Age' philosophy where everything is a caricature of a positive world. . . . 'New Age Music' is just the acoustical wallpaper for this world view, but this is exactly not the way we see the world around us. Tangerine Dream music is not the right choice for people who are still into baby food." Following the appearance of *Melrose*, Paul Haslinger left Tangerine Dream to compose film soundtracks; he would also form the Berlin Symphonic Film Orchestra and Sonic Images Records, one of the fastest-growing soundtrack labels in the world. Tangerine Dream's first album after his departure was *Rockoon* (1992), which features strong rhythms and was nominated for a Grammy Award. In 1993 the band collaborated with the actress Kathleen Turner on the album *Rumpelstiltskin*, on which Turner narrated the classic fairy tale of the title to musical accompaniment by Tangerine Dream. That year the band also released two live albums, *Dreaming on Danforth Avenue* and *220 Volt Live*, the latter of which was nominated for a Grammy Award. Those were followed by *Turn of the Tides* (1994), a concept album based on an excerpt from a story that Edgar Froese had written. In addition to the Froeses, the record features Linda Spa on saxophones and Zlatko Perica on guitar. *Turn of the Tides* opens with Tangerine Dream's interpretation of the Russian composer Modest Mussorgsky's *Pictures at an Exhibition*. The album as a whole was nominated for a Grammy Award. Less well-received was *The Dream Mixes* (1994), the first volume in a series of remixes of earlier work by Tangerine Dream. "It was a terrible thing," Froese told Franklin and Willder about the remixes. "I never ever had any desire to do it. It is something I'm really not interested in going through again. The reason is simply that if a band grows and becomes more and more popular, record companies have a commercial interest in releasing the back catalogue. So those companies said 'okay we want to release it.' I said 'great, but what and how?' And the answers I got were totally like scrambled eggs. They didn't know what to do, they didn't know how to do it. So I said, 'look, let's make an agreement: you have to support me in such and such a way, and I'll do it myself.' And that's the only reason I did it, otherwise the music would have been released in an almost crap direction."

In 1995 the band came out with the Grammy-nominated *Tyranny of Beauty*, which found them fusing heavily produced, ambient music with dance-club beats, an approach they repeated on *Goblins Club* (1996). In 1997 the band released the live record *Tournado*, which was intended as a musical description of the landscape of the American Southwest. The record represented Tangerine Dream's departure from the more club-oriented releases for which they were becoming known, and a return to the more ethereal sounds of their earlier material. In 1998 came *Ambient Monkeys*, which features a variety of sound effects produced by animals and machines, from monkeys to ocean creatures to trains. While not a groundbreaking work, in many ways it was the band's most experimental album in almost two decades. The following year Tangerine Dream brought out soundtracks to two documentaries—*Transsiberia: The Russian Express Railway Experience*, whose soundtrack prominently features electronic rhythms, and *What a Blast: Architecture in Motion*. At this time the band formed their own record label. "If you want to do what you like to do: try to be honest with your fans, your audiences," Edgar Froese told Franklin and Willder for *SoundScapes*. "That's why we set up our own label; our own pub-

lishing company. Now we can be more creative in terms of releasing material, which we couldn't have before because everything had to be agreed by the companies." Also in 1999 the group released *Mars Polaris* and *Dream Encores*, the latter of which consists of the band's encores from live shows from past years. In 2000 the band released *Great Wall of China*, the soundtrack to the same-titled documentary, which accentuated the band's techno influences. More ethereal was *The Seven Letters from Tibet* (2000), based on the mystical properties ascribed by some to the number seven. In 2002 the group came out with *Inferno* (2002), a concept album based on the 13th- and 14th-century poet Dante Alighieri's *Divine Comedy*. The album was recorded live in a European church with a small female choir and fuses progressive rock, electronica, classical music, and church music. A second Dante-inspired record is Tangerine Dream's *Purgatorio* (2004). The past couple of years have also seen releases of the group's live albums recorded in Germany, Canada, France, and Australia, respectively, as well as of the soundtrack album *Mota Atma* (2003). Reviewing that record for amazon.com, Jerry McCulley wrote, "This soundtrack (recorded in the fall of '02) . . . is a compelling summation of the band's various phases and enduring appeal. The brooding, sensuous textures of their expansive mid-'70s prime are often efficiently set here to the pulsing sequencer rhythms that propelled much of their film work from *Sorcerer* onwards, but deftly seasoned with samples and sparing uses of natural instruments that give it a deceptively transparent sense of the organic. Young Jerome Froese seems locked into his father's electro muse at the genetic level, producing one of T-Dream's most sonically elegant and rewarding modern albums."

The two current members of Tangerine Dream—Edgar Froese and Jerome Froese—both have solo careers. Jerome Froese has released several singles, while his father's solo efforts began with *Aqua* (1974), a collection of four free-form, tranquil pieces. Edgar followed in 1975 with *Epsilon in Malaysian Pale*, which mirrors Tangerine Dream's sound from that period. *Macula Transfer* (1976) consists of material written on airline flights, while *Stuntman* (1979) features a mix of short melodic pieces and all-electronic, ethereal sounds that pointed in the direction Tangerine Dream would take in the 1980s. *Kamikaze* (1982) and *Pinnacles* (1983) were followed two decades later by the five volumes in Froese's Ambient Highway series. Edgar Froese told Mark Naman for *STart Magazine* (October 1988) that when he formed Tangerine Dream he "had this crazy dream about using technology in the most advanced way possible. I'm still on that adventurous trip." Both Edgar and Jerome Froese currently live in Berlin, Germany. Edgar's wife (who is Jerome's mother) has provided photographs for the Froeses' respective solo records.

—G.O.

Suggested Reading: Associated Press July 30, 1986; *LiteraryMoose* (on-line); *Mojo* Apr. 1997; *New York Times* C p25 June 25, 1986, with photo; *Soundscapes* (on-line); *STart Magazine* p67+ Oct. 1988; *Voices in The Net* (on-line)

Selected Recordings: *Electronic Meditation*, 1970; *Alpha Centauri*, 1971; *Zeit*, 1972; *Atem*, 1973; *Phaedra*, 1974; *Rubycon*, 1975; *Ricochet*, 1975; *Stratosfear*, 1976; *Sorcerer*, 1977; *Encore*, 1977; *Cyclone*, 1978; *Force Majeure*, 1979; *Tangram*, 1980; *Thief*, 1981; *Exit*, 1981; *White Eagle*, 1982; *Logos: Live at the Dominion*, 1982; *Hyperborea*, 1983; *Risky Business*, 1984; *Firestarter*, 1984; *Flashpoint*, 1984; *Streethawk*, 1985; *Le Parc*, 1985; *Legend*, 1985; *Underwater Sunlight*, 1986; *Tyger*, 1987; *Canyon Dreams*, 1987; *Optical Race*, 1988; *Melrose*, 1990; *Rockoon*, 1992; *Rumpelstiltskin*, 1993; *Dreaming on Danforth Avenue*, 1993; *220 Volt Live*, 1993; *Turn of the Tides*, 1994; *Tyranny of Beauty*, 1995; *Goblins Club*, 1996; *Oasis*, 1997; *Ambient Monkeys*, 1998; *Transsiberia: The Russian Express Railway Experience*, 1999; *Mars Polaris*, 1999; *Great Wall of China*, 2000; *The Seven Letters from Tibet*, 2000; *Inferno*, 2002; *Purgatorio*, 2004

IFC, Getty Images

Taylor, Lili

Feb. 20, 1967– Actress

Address: c/o William Morris Agency, 151 El Camino Dr., Beverly Hills, CA 90212

"So many female roles in commercial movies are just devices, not a lot of energy, not a lot of fun," the actress Lili Taylor lamented to Charles Aaron for *Spin* (September 1996, on-line). "I always wanted to be the detective or the pirate, not just the girl by his side." Unlike the "A"-list Hollywood actresses with whom she has worked, such as Julia Roberts and Catherine Zeta-Jones, Taylor has not played lead roles in big-budget mainstream productions. She has won a great deal of praise, however, for the intelligence and empathy she has brought to her portrayals of secondary characters and of protagonists in independent films, includ-

ing the revenge-bent militant feminist Valerie Solanas in *I Shot Andy Warhol* and the reluctant bride Jojo Barboza in *Mystic Pizza*. Taylor also became familiar to cable-TV audiences in 2002 through her role as the nagging Lisa Kimmel Fisher on the HBO series *Six Feet Under*. "I can't play a woman who doesn't have integrity," Taylor told Lisa Kennedy for *Out Magazine* (August 1999, on-line), "who isn't written honestly. I can play a woman who has a lot of problems, who is negative, but if she's not written fully or if she comes from a point of view that's simple or misogynistic, then no. No." Toni Kalem, who directed Taylor in the film *A Slipping Down Life*, told Stephen Whitty for the Newhouse News Service (May 17, 2004), "Lili has these qualities of strength and vulnerability and spirituality that you can't act. . . . She has an honesty to her."

The fifth of the six children of Park and Marie Taylor, Lili Anne Taylor was born on February 20, 1967 and raised in the Chicago, Illinois, suburb of Glencoe. Taylor's grandfather had helped to found the town, which later became a well-to-do area—to such an extent that Lili Taylor's middle-class family found itself "pitted against this environment" of wealth, as the actress told Charles Aaron. "There was a lot of resentment [toward the wealthy] in my family, probably to make us feel better about ourselves," she explained. Much of that attitude came from her father. "He wanted to be a poet," Taylor told Aaron, "but he was trying to run a hardware store, and we didn't even have a hammer in the house. There was a bit of a clash there. He was a guy who, because of this family situation, had to go to work and abandon his dream." When it came to their children's dreams, however, Park and Marie Taylor offered plenty of encouragement, and their daughter Lili learned to pursue her desires regardless of obstacles. A tomboy, she won a place as the only girl on the local soccer team. She began acting in grade school; her first play was a fifth-grade production of *You're a Good Man, Charlie Brown*. Park Taylor recalled a performance his daughter gave in sixth grade, when she appeared in *Once Upon a Mattress*: "She just belted the number out, so the person in the very back row could hear her.

She brought down the house," he told Patrick Z. McGavin for the *Chicago Tribune* (May 16, 1996). "There was a guy with the Chicago Symphony [Orchestra] standing next to me and he said, 'That girl is going to have a future in show business.'" Park Taylor recalled to McGavin, "Even at a very early age, Lili had an incredible eye and ear for detail and assimilation," citing the time that the nine-year-old Lili adopted a Swedish accent after overhearing a Swedish couple chatting during dinner.

During her years as a student at New Trier High School, in Winnetka, Illinois, Taylor often felt depressed and angst-ridden, and she contemplated suicide. After seeing a therapist, she, like her father, was diagnosed as manic-depressive. Her therapist decided against medicating Taylor, however, feeling that her symptoms might disappear if she could find an outlet for her creative energies. That, Taylor later said, is exactly what happened: she became increasingly involved in theater, starring in her high school's 1984 production of *The Effect of Gamma Rays on Man-in-the-Moon Marigolds*. Beginning at age 14 she rode her bicycle to Evanston, Illinois, to attend classes at the Piven Theatre Workshop, where she starred in productions with fellow students John and Joan Cusack, Jeremy Piven, Lara Flynn Boyle, and Aidan Quinn, all of whom would go on to successful careers. Taylor had "enormous potential," the theater's co-founder Joyce Piven told Patrick Z. McGavin. "She was ferocious, passionate and intense. She was incredibly ambitious. She was somebody who had a mind of her own." After graduating from high school, in 1985, Taylor entered the Goodman School of Drama at DePaul University, in Chicago, but left the program following a dispute with the school's administrators. (Taylor sought paid acting jobs to help fund her studies, but the drama program did not permit its students to work professionally until after graduation.) She continued to act with the Piven company while looking for paid work. In 1988 she moved to New York City.

Meanwhile, Taylor had landed bit parts in the 1987 television movie *Night of Courage* and the 1988 John Hughes film *She's Having a Baby*. Also in 1988 Taylor was cast as the best friend of the sisters played by Julia Roberts and Annabeth Gish in the film *Mystic Pizza*. For that coming-of-age tale, in which the three Portuguese-American girls work in a pizza parlor in Mystic, Connecticut, Taylor portrayed Jojo Barboza, who loves her boyfriend but is reluctant to marry him. Although Jojo is largely a comic foil for the more serious characters played by Roberts and Gish, Taylor earned praise for injecting pathos and sincerity into her portrayal. Roger Ebert wrote for the *Chicago Sun-Times* (October 21, 1988, on-line), "I have a feeling that *Mystic Pizza* may someday become known for the movie stars it showcased back before they became stars." Indeed, the film launched the careers of both Roberts and Taylor. Taylor's next film, *Say Anything . . .* (1989), paired her with John Cusack. In it she played the small but memorable part of

Cusack's friend Corey, who has recently been jilted by her boyfriend, Joe. In what is commonly considered one of the funniest scenes in the film, Corey announces at a party, "I wrote 63 songs this year. They're all about Joe, and I'm going to play every single one of them tonight"—and then makes good on her promise. Taylor's next projects included roles in *Born on the Fourth of July* (1989) and the television movies *Family of Spies* and *Sensibility and Sense* (both 1990).

In 1991 Taylor found herself in an unusual situation. She had been cast as the female lead in the film *Bright Angel*, but the producers asked (in vain) that she be replaced, because they felt that she was not attractive enough for the part. On the other hand, when she appeared the same year in the film *Dogfight*, as a waitress whom a marine (played by River Phoenix) tricks into participating in an "ugly date" contest, critics complained that Taylor was too good-looking for the role. Throughout her career, in fact, Taylor has encountered mainstream filmmakers and producers who have considered her insufficiently seductive for lead roles and too attractive to be cast in "ugly girl" parts. Thus she has often been relegated to second-tier or character roles in major studio productions, such as *Arizona Dream* and *Watch It* (both 1993).

Taylor has blossomed, however, in independent productions. In 1993, for instance, she starred in the quirky *Household Saints*, a film by Nancy Savoca, who had directed Taylor in *Dogfight*. In *Household Saints*, about three generations of a family living in New York's Little Italy, Taylor played Teresa, a devout teenage Christian who has religious visions. According to Janet Maslin in the *New York Times* (September 15, 1993, on-line), "Ms. Taylor gives an eerie, radiant performance as the teen-age Teresa, who yearns to join a convent and is thwarted by her parents. Although Ms. Taylor doesn't appear until an hour and a quarter into the film, she dominates it the rest of the way." Taylor then appeared in smaller roles in the big-budget films *Rudy* and *Short Cuts* (both 1993), *Touch Base*, *Mrs. Parker and the Vicious Circle*, and *Prêt-à-Porter* (all 1994), and *Cold Fever* and *Four Rooms* (both 1995) before landing her next major role, in the 1995 picture *The Addiction*. Directed by Abel Ferrara, known for making gory thrillers, *The Addiction* featured Taylor as a graduate student of philosophy turned vampire; in the film vampirism serves as a metaphor for various evils, such as drug addiction, AIDS, and war atrocities. While the film as a whole received mixed reviews, Taylor's performance earned widespread praise. Desson Howe enthused in the *Washington Post* (October 27, 1995, on-line) that "you enjoy the presence of Taylor, whose intense, serene performance really makes its mark," and Caryn James wrote for the *New York Times* (October 4, 1995, on-line), "With lank hair, no make-up, and an extreme case of library pallor, Ms. Taylor gives a stunning performance as Kathleen Conklin, the philosophy student who finds herself caught in the eternal struggle between light and darkness."

Taylor's next role would become, along with her part in *Six Feet Under*, the one with which she is most closely identified. When the writer-director Mary Harron was making her feature debut, *I Shot Andy Warhol* (1996), she pursued Taylor for the role of the main character, the lesbian and radical feminist Valerie Solanas—because, as she told Betsy Sherman for *BPI Entertainment News Wire* (May 15, 1996), "I was convinced she could make Valerie credible. . . . And also that she could make Valerie sympathetic, which was important to me." Solanas, the founder and sole member of SCUM (the Society for Cutting Up Men) and author of the SCUM Manifesto, turned for support to the artist Warhol and the coterie of artists, addicts, and transvestites who hung out at his storied New York City studio, The Factory, but she was considered too outré even for them. When Warhol refused to produce her play, Solanas began to view him as the chief obstacle to her achieving financial success. On June 3, 1968 she shot Warhol three times. (He underwent a five-hour operation and survived.) Solanas was sentenced to three years in prison for reckless assault; after her release, she drifted in and out of mental hospitals, most likely supported her drug habit through prostitution, and died in obscurity, in 1988. Critics heaped praise on both *I Shot Andy Warhol* and its star. Janet Maslin raved in a review for the *New York Times* (April 5, 1996, online), "This film's extraordinary centerpiece is Lili Taylor, giving a great, funny, furiously alive performance that deserves to put her on the mainstream map. Ms. Taylor . . . finds a dream role in this film's tirelessly combative Valerie." For her performance as Solanas, Taylor won the first-ever Special Jury Award at the Sundance Film Festival.

The year 1996 was a productive one for Taylor; in addition to playing Valerie Solanas, she appeared in the films *Girls Town* (which she cowrote); *Killer: A Journal of Murder; Illtown; Cosas que nunca te dije* (released in the United States as *Things I Never Told You*); *Plain Pleasures;* and *Ransom.* The last-named film, a box-office blockbuster starring Mel Gibson and Rene Russo, was an unusual choice for Taylor; she was attracted to the project because the director, Ron Howard, having seen *The Addiction*, specifically requested that Taylor play the part of a kidnapper. Taylor next appeared in *Kicked in the Head*, the television movie *Subway Stories: Tales from the Underground* (both 1997), *O.K. Garage, The Impostors, Come to*, and *Pecker* (all 1998). The following year the director Jan de Bont cast her as Eleanor "Nell" Vance in the widely panned *The Haunting*, a remake of the 1963 movie of the same title (both based on Shirley Jackson's 1959 novel, *The Haunting of Hill House*). Also in 1999 Taylor starred in *A Slipping Down Life* (based on the Anne Tyler novel), which premiered at that year's Sundance Film Festival but, due to financing problems, was not distributed to theaters until 2004. Taylor next had a role in the movie *High Fidelity* (2000), adapted from the Nick Hornby novel and starring John Cusack; appeared

in the short-lived television series *Deadline* (2000–01); played the title character in *Julie Johnson* (2001); and had roles in *Gaudi Afternoon* (2001) and the television movies *Anne Frank: The Whole Story* (2001) and *Live from Baghdad* (2002).

When Taylor joined the cast of the HBO cable-television series *Six Feet Under*, in 2002, she introduced herself to a wider audience. Despite, or because of, its quirkiness—which it had in common with a number of other projects of Taylor's—the darkly comic drama about the Fishers, a family of morticians, has enjoyed considerable mainstream popularity. Taylor played Lisa Kimmel, the girlfriend of the eldest Fisher son, Nate. Upon learning of Lisa's pregnancy, the couple get married. Lisa is, as Bob Edwards called her on the National Public Radio program *Morning Edition* (March 29, 2004), "an archetype, the female nag." Taylor told Edwards that in order to avoid giving a clichéd performance, she thought a great deal about the psychology behind Lisa's personality. "She does not understand how she's impacting [Nate]," Taylor explained. "She doesn't understand how afraid she is and how she's living out that fear, and that . . . doing what she's doing is not gonna give her the result that she's hoping to get. Really, a lot of it just boils down to fear." With her insufferable priggishness, Lisa became the character whom *Six Feet Under* devotees loved to hate, even after she mysteriously died in the show's third season. (She returned as a ghost in season four.) Following her stint on *Six Feet Under,* Taylor lent her voice to an animated penguin in the television special *Penguins Behind Bars* (2003) and also appeared in the movie *Casa de los babys (*2003), playing one of six American women trying to adopt babies in South America. Taylor recently completed the filming of *Factotum* and *The Secret*, both scheduled for 2006 U.S. premieres. Another film in which Taylor has a role, *The Notorious Bettie Page*, opened to largely positive reviews at the 2005 Toronto Film Festival.

In preparing for parts, Taylor immerses herself in each character, not only reading, rereading, and taking notes on scripts, but referring to the *Diagnostic and Statistical Manual of Mental Disorders* to gain insights into some of her more complex or disturbed characters. "I have to put myself out of the way when I'm creating a character," Taylor told Stephen Whitty. "I have to clean the slate and open the channels, and let whatever the voice of that character is come through. I have to let her be who she is, not who I am or even who I want her to be. . . . It's really a kind of crash analysis, I guess, except I'm on both sides of the couch." Despite her deep involvement with each character, Taylor does not believe in taking her work home with her, as she explained to Whitty: "Acting is letting another person into your brain. Mental illness is letting them stay there."

While Taylor still cannot be considered a big box-office name, she has earned a reputation as the queen of independent cinema. She also remains deeply involved in theater. Her New York stage appearances include roles in *Brighton Beach Memoirs* (1986–87), *What Did He See?* (1988–89), *Aven U Boys* (1993), and *The Dead Eye Boy* (2001). She made her Broadway debut in a production of Chekhov's *Three Sisters* (co-starring Calista Flockhart and Amy Irving) in 1997. "To me, Lili is almost electric," Justin Theroux, who appeared with Taylor in *Three Sisters,* told Maureen Dezell in an interview for the *Boston Globe* (July 4, 2003). "There could be people juggling behind her and setting things on fire onstage, and people would be watching her, because of what's going on in her eyes." In 2003 she performed at the Williamstown (Massachusetts) Theatre Festival in a revival of the 1977 murder mystery/black comedy *Landscape of the Body,* which allowed her to fulfill her dream of working with John Guare, the author of the play. The following year she appeared as Lemon, a fragile, off-kilter young woman, in a Broadway revival of the actor/writer Wallace Shawn's provocative play *Aunt Dan and Lemon,* in which the characters espouse unpopular political viewpoints (Lemon embraces Nazism, for example). While the play often angered audiences, Taylor won an Obie Award for her performance. She was a member of the Naked Angels theater group, in New York City, until she, her former boyfriend, the actor Michael Imperioli, and the actor/playwright Tom Gilroy created their own theater company, Machine Full. Under the auspices of Machine Full, Taylor directed her first play, *Halcyon Days,* at the Workhouse Theater in New York City. Taylor also works with the 52nd Street Project, through which actors help children stage shows in the Hell's Kitchen area of New York City.

Over the course of her career, Taylor has amassed a variety of honors, including an Independent Spirit Award for best supporting actress in *Household Saints* (1993); a Sundance Film Festival Special Recognition Award for Acting for her work in *I Shot Andy Warhol* (1996); a Blockbuster Award for best supporting actress for *Ransom* (1997); and three Seattle Film Festival Awards, all for best actress, for *Cold Fever, I Shot Andy Warhol,* and *Girls Town.*

Taylor lives in New York City's West Village; she recently acquired a house in the country, where she goes to relax. Never married, she has been linked romantically with the actors John Cusack, Matthew Broderick, Eric Stoltz, Michael Imperioli, and Michael Rapaport. (At one point she filed charges against Rapaport for stalking her; he pleaded guilty and agreed to seek therapy.) Taylor, described in articles as humble and as an amiable but private person, is not often recognized on the street, which is to her liking. Still, she is reportedly gracious to those fans who recognize her. "It's easy for actors to lift their heads up into the clouds and lose touch with reality," she told Alison Lundgren for *Velocity* (August 1999, on-line). "You can see how people can get so self-important when 500 people a day are telling them they're great. But you have to stay grounded. If I get recognized by a fan

on the street, I realize it's not really about me. That person might be moved by my work, but I'm more of a messenger who has helped move them."

—K.J.E.

Suggested Reading: *Boston Globe* E p17 July 4, 2003; *BPI Entertainment News Wire* May 15, 1996; *Chicago Sun-Times* (on-line) Oct. 21, 1988, July 1, 1999; *Chicago Tribune* p1 May 16, 1996; Internet Movie Database (on-line); *New York Times* (on-line) Sep. 15, 1993, Oct. 4, 1995, Apr. 5, 1996, July 23, 1999; *Newhouse News Service* (on-line) May 17, 2004; *Spin* (on-line) Sep. 1996

Selected Films: *Mystic Pizza,* 1988; *Say Anything . . . ,* 1989; *Dogfight,* 1991; *Arizona Dream,* 1993; *Household Saints,* 1993; *Rudy,* 1993; *Short Cuts,* 1993; *Touch Base,* 1994; *Mrs. Parker and the Vicious Circle,* 1994; *Prêt-à-Porter,* 1994; *Cold Fever,* 1995; *Four Rooms,* 1995; *The Addiction,* 1995; *I Shot Andy Warhol,* 1996; *Girls Town,* 1996; *Ransom,* 1996; *Pecker,* 1998; *A Slipping Down Life,* 1999; *The Haunting,* 1999; *High Fidelity,* 2000; *Casa de los babys,* 2003; *The Notorious Bettie Page,* 2005

Selected Television Programs: movies—*Sensibility and Sense,* 1990; *Subway Stories: Tales from the Underground,* 1997; *Deadline,* 2000–01; *Anne Frank: The Whole Story,* 2001; *Live from Baghdad,* 2002; series—*Six Feet Under,* 2002–03

Selected Plays: *Brighton Beach Memoirs,* 1986-87; *What Did He See?,* 1988–89; *The Myth Project: A Festival of Competency,* 1989; *Aven U Boys,* 1993; *Three Sisters,* 1997; *The Dead Eye Boy,* 2001; *Landscape of the Body,* 2003; *Aunt Dan and Lemon,* 2004

Thompson, John W.

Apr. 24, 1949– CEO and chairman of Symantec Corp.

Address: Symantec Corp., 20330 Stevens Creek Blvd., Cupertino, CA 95014

As CEO and chairman of the board of Symantec, John W. Thompson has transformed that company into the largest Internet-security provider in the world. Currently, more than 100 million customers use Symantec products, among them almost all of the Fortune 500 companies and 95 percent of the Global 500 companies. Since Thompson's arrival, in 1999, Symantec's revenues have more than doubled, to nearly $2.5 billion annually—a figure that most analysts previously thought impossible for most software companies to reach. Known as gregarious and charming, Thompson is the first

Richard Ellis/Getty Images

John W. Thompson

African-American to head a major Silicon Valley company. He began his career as a new college graduate, in an entry-level sales position with IBM. Over the next 28 years, he worked his way steadily up through the ranks; his last title at IBM was that of general manager of sales for North America—the company's largest market. Richard A. Clarke, the chairman of Good Harbor Consulting, told Alan Hughes for *Black Enterprise* (September 2004) that Thompson has "the ability to make everybody like him and want to be with him in that sort of winning salesman personality. . . . But he combines that with a hard-nosed, make-it-happen determination and a real understanding of the detail and technology." Thompson himself told Anne Saita, a senior editor at *Information Security* (February 2003), "It's a combination of hard work and good support structure that helps to get you going, but it's determination along the way that keeps you moving along. I had enough of all those to get me where I am today."

John W. Thompson was born on April 24, 1949 in Fort Dix, New Jersey, where his father, John H. Thompson, was stationed as a soldier. The family lived at a series of army bases until his father's military discharge, after which they settled in a middle-class neighborhood in West Palm Beach, Florida. In Florida his father worked for the U.S. Postal Service; he also became a landlord. Thompson's mother, Eunice Thompson, taught in an elementary school; according to some sources, she was a school principal. "My mom and dad believed very much in the concepts of working hard for what you want and making sure you're properly prepared for what your pursuits are," Thompson told Anne Saita. "We were a loving bunch, but a very compet-

itive bunch. My sister was a smart lady and always pushed the envelope on grades."

Thompson began his schooling in West Palm Beach. As a youngster he mowed lawns in his neighborhood and accompanied his father on his rent-collection route. "I always had this aspiration of someday being a businessman," Thompson told Hughes. "Now, I didn't know what that meant, because back in those days—in the early to mid-60s—a business leader in the black community . . . ran the local grocery store [or] might very well have had a dry cleaning service. A business in the black community back then was fairly localized, not something that had national or global scale."

Thompson was something of a hellion in high school. He took little interest in his studies but learned to play the clarinet well enough to earn a scholarship to Lincoln University of Missouri. When he learned, as a freshman, that his scholarship required him to major in music, he transferred to Florida A&M, in Tallahassee, where he pursued a bachelor's degree in business. At 19, while still an undergraduate, Thompson married, and soon afterward he became a father. To support his family, he worked as a salesman in a stereo store.

IBM recruited Thompson while he was an undergraduate, and he accepted the entry-level sales position offered to him before he earned his degree, in 1971. He intended to enter law school after working for IBM for a couple of years, but to his surprise, he enjoyed being a part of the expanding computer industry. "I got hooked, like many young IBMers, on the excitement and success that you can have from a fast-paced career at what at the time was a very, very rapidly moving and growing company," he told Hughes. Thompson, who was the only black employee in his sales office, wore his hair in an Afro, and for a while he resisted conforming to the conservative dress code that prevailed among his co-workers, because he believed that his competence as a salesman, not his wardrobe or hairstyle, was what mattered most. But after he concluded that his appearance was adversely affecting his ability to close deals, he adopted more traditional business attire.

Thompson's skill as a salesperson caught the attention of IBM administrators, and he earned a series of promotions. He was appointed manager of the Atlanta, Georgia, sales office, then became the assistant to the regional manager in Boston, Massachusetts. He later oversaw marketing for the Boston area. His exceptional performance led IBM to pay for his tuition at the Sloan School of Management, at the Massachusetts Institute of Technology, where he earned a master's degree in management science in 1983.

In 1990 IBM named Thompson general manager of the firm's Midwest region, based in Chicago, Illinois. Revenues had been falling in that region for some time; in response, Thompson's predecessors had taken the tack of cutting part of the sales force each year. Determined to come up with a plan to boost sales, Thompson conducted exhaustive research at IBM operations around the globe. Combining the best practices he had observed, he reorganized the Midwest sales force into teams, in which the people who handled customer relations were supported by a group of product specialists. The new system led to lowered costs, reduced staff size, improved customer satisfaction, and stabilized revenues; indeed, it turned the Midwest into IBM's most profitable region. Thompson's strategy was so effective that it became the model for the entire company.

In 1994 Thompson was appointed the general manager of IBM's Personal Software Products division, with responsibility for overseeing the development of the OS/2 operating system. OS/2 was the first operating system to combine 32-bit power with a graphical user interface, and though critically acclaimed, it competed directly against the 16-bit operating system offered by Microsoft—a company notorious for shutting out its competition by cutting deals with distribution channels, software vendors, and equipment manufacturers. "People would say, 'Gee, what did you do wrong that you were punished and got that job?'" Thompson recalled to Clare Haney for *InfoWorld* (May 3, 1999). Thompson saw the folly in competing head-to-head with Microsoft on the consumer market and focused on marketing OS/2 to medium-to-large businesses that used technology in customer-service applications. "Our focus with OS/2 had been on trying to do it all for everyone—corporate, consumer, small business. We were running down dead-end streets," Thompson told Hal Karp for *Black Enterprise* (June 30, 1997). Recognizing the growing importance of networks to businesses, he repositioned OS/2 as "network-centric" and launched a new version that included voice recognition, a Web browser, and other features. While under his oversight, OS/2 and accompanying software generated $1 billion in sales for IBM. In December 1996 Thompson was promoted to general manager of IBM's North American sales and service group; the company's largest geographic unit, it had generated $32.5 billion in revenues in 1996.

His success at IBM notwithstanding, Thompson longed to direct a company as the chief executive officer. He set little store by rumors that he was on a short list of people to replace Louis Gerstner as IBM's CEO when Gerstner retired. "It was clear to me that the itch I had couldn't be satiated or scratched inside IBM," he told Hughes. "I was going to have to leave to go fulfill what had become my aspirations at that time." While on a business trip, Thompson met Robert S. "Steve" Miller, a former chairman of the board and CEO of Bethlehem Steel, who was on the board of directors of Symantec. At that time Symantec was the seventh-largest software company in Silicon Valley. Its popular software lines included Norton Anti-Virus and Norton Utilities. Miller was struck with Thompson's qualifications as well as his willingness to take risks, and he recruited him to succeed Gordon E. Eubanks, who had served as Symantec's CEO for

about 16 years and had announced his intention to retire..

On April 14, 1999 Symantec's board named Thompson president, CEO, and chairman—a triple crown that guaranteed that he would face little resistance as he reshaped the company. Following the announcement of his appointment, the value of Symantec stock jumped 11.5 percent. "Symantec is a good company that has the potential to become a great company," Thompson told a reporter for *JET* (May 24, 1999). "I'd love to be the guy to lead it towards that." In his new job, Thompson became one of the few members of minority groups and the only African-American to lead one of the top 150 companies in Silicon Valley. Shortly before Symantec hired Thompson, the Reverend Jesse Jackson had visited Silicon Valley to chastise the executives of high-tech companies for failing to employ and promote more people of color. (According to Carl Carman, whom Thompson succeeded as chairman of Symantec, Thompson's race had played no role in the company's selection.) "The world will watch and be curious if I am a leader who can bring this company to the forefront," Thompson told Cassandra Hayes for *Black Enterprise* (July 31, 1999). "This is a testament to where I have progressed in my career, not my race. If I'm prepared, we will do well."

When Thompson arrived at Symantec, the company held a significant share of the market for antivirus software, but many analysts believed that its acquisitions of such products as Java development tools and personal-contact management systems had resulted in unwieldy bloat. Thompson wanted to convert the company from a software vendor to the one-stop shop for all corporate security needs. He sold unrelated product lines and purchased companies that made products related to Internet security, such as firewalls and intrusion-detection software.

The antivirus business had traditionally been driven by the consumer retail market. In the late 1990s consumer spending was increasing by less than 10 percent a year. Corporate spending, by contrast, was rising 35 percent a year, as all types of businesses opened their networks to consumers and suppliers. Corporate sales comprised only 39 percent of Symantec's revenues in 1998. Thompson was determined to increase that figure to 70 percent. By December 31, 1999, when the third quarter of the fiscal year ended, it had grown to 46 percent.

Within one year of Thompson's appointment, the value of Symantec stock had risen sixfold. In a press release dated December 27, 2000, Thompson declared, "We have never been more confident in our future." As evidence of his firm's well-being and bright outlook, he mentioned that such industry giants as Oracle, Yahoo, and Earthlink were using Symantec's security technology and noted that with its acquisition, a few days earlier, of Axent Technologies, a maker of firewalls and other security products, Symantec had become the largest Internet-security company on earth. He also announced that according to the latest figures issued by PC Data, a service that tracked retail software sales in the U.S., seven Symantec products ranked among the top 20 of the best-selling business software, and Symantec's Norton AntiVirus 2001 ranked number one.

The high price that Symantec had paid to buy Axent Technologies—nearly $1 billion in Symantec stock—raised some eyebrows among industry observers, who pointed out that Axent's software was not among the best on the market. They also warned that Thompson was taking a risk in assuming that customers would choose one vendor to handle all their security needs rather than seek top-of-the-line products from whoever provided them. Two years later Thompson told Anne Saita, "Our approach is about delivering an integrated set of offerings that reduce the complexity and costs of securing the environment. We will either prove that is the right approach, or not. And I'm betting my personal reputation on the fact that we're right." Other companies, such as Symantec's competitor Network Associates, had tried packaging security products before, but without much success. Thompson was banking on the idea that as security threats became more complex, business would prefer working with a single security provider that could handle them on multiple fronts. "Probably the biggest challenge security companies face in today's climate is convincing customers of the need for comprehensive, integrated security [technology] at multiple tiers within the network," Thompson told Ben Hesket for CNET News.com (February 5, 2002). "Securing the perimeter alone is no longer enough to provide the necessary protection from today's blended threats like Code Red and Nimda."

According to the Cooperative Association for Internet Data Analysis (an organization known by its acronym, CAIDA), on July 19, 2001 Code Red infected more than 359,000 computers in less than 14 hours, and "at the peak of the infection frenzy, more than 2,000 new hosts were infected each minute." Nimda, which struck a few months later, infected many of Microsoft's operating systems. Such so-called blended threats presented a new challenge for Internet-security providers, because, as their name implies, they use multiple transmission and spreading techniques to infiltrate and disable networks. According to a survey of 300 companies in 25 countries conducted by Riptech, a leading provider of security services (which Symantec purchased in mid-2002), between July 2001 and December 2001, there was a 79 percent increase in attacks. This increase proved a boon to Symantec, and that December the company announced a two-for-one stock split—an unusual occurrence in a market where most technology stocks were struggling. "The Symantec brand, our people, our position in the industry, allowed us to do perhaps better than average in this tough economic environment," Thompson told an interviewer for the *Wall Street Transcript* (June 2002). Analysts used

to doubt that a software company like Symantec could earn more than $1 billion in revenues, but Symantec did so in 2002. Its revenues reached $2 billion in 2004. The firm's projected 2005 revenues are $2.57 billion.

In September 2002 President George W. Bush appointed Thompson to the National Infrastructure Advisory Committee, which recommends ways to secure critical cyber information systems. Thompson has suggested that the government launch a national awareness campaign, along the lines of the Smokey the Bear campaign (which aims to prevent forest fires), to encourage safe computing. "When we see a problem in the environment, in the past we have reacted. So the question for us as a country is whether we think the problem of the damage in productivity and the damage to the network is big enough that we should react," he told Robert Lemos for CNET News.com (March 12, 2002). "There is purported to be somewhere in the range of $12 billion to $13 billion in damage from malicious attacks last year alone."

Thompson remained head of Symantec after its merger, in 2005, with Veritask, a maker of data storage software. Thompson told Laurie J. Flynn for the *New York Times* (June 25, 2005) that the newly enlarged firm would be a "one-stop shop" allowing customers to meet their needs for both data-storage and computer-security software.

Thompson hopes that his success will encourage more people of color to pursue careers in business and technology. In part with that goal, he has lectured at two of Jesse Jackson's "Digital Connections" conferences, which were initiated to encourage greater diversity in the technology sector. He was named in *Time*'s Digital 50 in 1999 and in *Forbes* magazine's list of America's Most Powerful People in 2000; dubbed one of the 50 Most Important African-Americans in Technology by BlackEngineer.com in 2001; ranked 12th on *Fortune* magazine's list of Most Powerful Black Executives in 2002; listed as one of the nation's top managers by *BusinessWeek* in 2002, 2003, and 2004; and named Corporate Executive of the Year by *Black Enterprise* in 2004.

Thompson is a member of the board of directors of UPS, Nisource, and Seagate. He formerly served on the board of directors at Fortune Brands and the Northern Indiana Public Service Company (NIPSCO). He has also served as chairman of the Florida A&M University Cluster, the Illinois Governor's Human Resource Advisory Council, and the Silicon Valley Blue Ribbon Task Force on Aviation Security and Technology.

Thompson lives in Woodside, California, with his wife, Sandi, a tax lawyer. He has an adult son and daughter from a previous marriage. In his spare time he enjoys golfing, gourmet cooking, fishing, and hunting.

—J.C.

Suggested Reading: *Black Enterprise* p108+ Sep. 2004; *Information Security* p64 Feb. 2003; *New York Times* E p3 June 25, 2005; *San Jose Mercury News* A p1+ Apr. 15, 1999

Courtesy of the *New York Times*

Tierney, John

Mar. 25, 1953– Journalist; columnist

Address: New York Times, *229 West 43d St., New York, NY 10036*

"I don't like to make people angry for the sake of being angry, but I want to challenge people's assumptions," John Tierney told Howard Kurtz for the *Washington Post* (March 2, 2005, on-line) upon his appointment on March 1, 2005 as an op-ed columnist for the *New York Times*. A self-described libertarian with a reputation as a provocateur, Tierney fills the slot at the *Times* occupied for over three decades by the recently retired William Safire, who for years was the sole conservative voice on the newspaper's op-ed page. Tierney's appointment pleased the segment of the newspaper's readership eager to have a second conservative viewpoint alongside that of David Brooks, who began writing a *Times* op-ed column in September 2003. Tierney is "just a very interesting thinker," the *Times*'s editorial-page editor, Gail Collins, told Kurtz. "He thinks outside the box, has a very distinct worldview. . . . He'll be writing about stuff in ways that no one else on our team does."

Tierney brings to his new post nearly 30 years of experience as a journalist, the last 15 spent at the *Times*, where he wrote the column "The Big City"

for eight years beginning in 1994 and has covered national politics, foreign affairs, and a host of other topics. His freelance articles have appeared in such publications as the *Atlantic Monthly, Esquire, New York, Newsweek, Rolling Stone, Playboy, Reader's Digest, Vogue, Washington Monthly,* and the *Wall Street Journal.* Tierney is also the author of two books: the comic novel *God Is My Broker: A Monk-Tycoon Reveals the 7$^1/_2$ Laws of Spiritual and Financial Growth,* co-written with Christopher Buckley, and *The Best-Case Scenario Handbook,* a satire inspired by the popular *Worst-Case Scenario* nonfiction series by Joshua Piven and David Borgenicht.

The first child of John William and Patricia Anne Tierney, both academics, John Marion Tierney was born on March 25, 1953 in Elgin, Illinois, a suburb of Chicago, into a large Irish Catholic family. His brother Patrick, a research associate in Latin American studies at the University of Pittsburgh, is the author of the controversial book *Darkness in El Dorado: How Scientists and Journalists Devastated the Amazon.* Tierney's family moved often while he was growing up, living in other states, including Indiana and Minnesota, and outside the U.S., in South America and Spain, before settling in Pittsburgh, Pennsylvania. Tierney graduated from Central Catholic High School in Pittsburgh. In his youth he considered himself a liberal, but he underwent a change of attitude when he tried to land a job in one of Pittsburgh's steel mills and "was affronted early on by the featherbedding he saw in unions," as Buckley told Kurtz— "featherbedding" being the union practice of purposely hiring more workers than are needed for a given job, or of placing limits on workers' productivity.

Tierney received a B.A. degree in American studies from Yale University, in New Haven, Connecticut, in 1976. During his college years he landed summer internships as a reporter for the *Minneapolis Tribune,* the *Philadelphia Bulletin,* and the *Pittsburgh Press.* In addition, he worked as a part-time copy editor at the *New Haven Register* and as a stringer for the New York *Daily News.* In college he also served as the editor of the *Yale Daily News Magazine,* a campus publication, through which he met Buckley.

Tierney's first full-time position as a reporter after college was at the *Bergen Record,* in New Jersey, where he wrote about science and energy from 1976 to 1978. He next took a position as a general-assignment reporter on the metropolitan staff at the now-defunct *Washington Star,* from 1978 until 1980. While working at the *Star,* Tierney dated the future Pulitzer Prize–winning journalist and columnist Maureen Dowd, who also currently writes a twice-weekly op-ed column for the *New York Times.* (In a joint statement published in the New York *Daily News* [March 4, 2005] upon Tierney's appointment as an op-ed columnist, Tierney and Dowd wrote: "We have agreed not to publish any embarrassing revelations about each other, unless one of us gets really, really desperate for a column.") Tierney served as a staff writer for *Science* magazine from 1981 to 1985 and supported himself for the next several years as a freelance writer.

In 1990 Tierney joined the *New York Times* as a metropolitan reporter. That same year he turned his attention again to science, writing a widely referenced and reprinted article entitled "Betting the Planet," which ran in the December 2, 1990 issue of the *New York Times Magazine*. The article described a $1,000 wager between an ecologist, Paul R. Ehrlich, the author of books and articles warning of devastating effects of increases in human population, and an economist, Julian L. Simon, who had challenged Ehrlich's predictions of imminent food shortage, natural-resource depletion, and declining life expectancy. "Specifically, the bet was over the future price of five metals," Tierney wrote, "but at stake was much more—a view of the planet's ultimate limits, a vision of humanity's destiny." Referring, respectively, to the mythological prophet of terrible events and to an irrepressibly optimistic character in Voltaire's novel *Candide*, Tierney observed, "It was a bet between the Cassandra and the Dr. Pangloss of our era." Showing confidence in "human ingenuity" and a "flexible marketplace," as he phrased it in the article (a traditionally libertarian position), Tierney cast "Simon as a daring underdog and Ehrlich as the established purveyor of conventional wisdom," in the words of Chris Mooney. "This particular way of shaping a story—centering it on the exploits of a 'libertarian hero' figure—recurs in Tierney's writing." From 1994 to 2002 Tierney wrote "The Big City," a column about New York that ran once a week in the *Times Magazine* and then moved to the newspaper's Metro Section, where it appeared twice weekly.

What many readers seem to find most appealing about Tierney's writing is the impish sense of humor it reveals. During the years that he wrote "The Big City," he reported on quite a few of his own antics, such as his five successful attempts to hail cabs in front of banks while wearing a ski mask and carrying what resembled a money-filled bag; his giving tickets to pedestrians for antisocial behavior, such as littering, and rewarding others on the street with $20 each for keeping their pets leashed, as New York City law requires; and his famous impersonation of a homeless person loitering in front of the comedian and actress Rosie O'Donnell's mansion, after O'Donnell had criticized New York mayor Rudolph Giuliani for having the homeless removed from the streets. (A police officer quickly told Tierney to move on.) Calling Tierney's best columns "gleeful journeys of intellectual or comic discovery," Mooney wrote: "They're fueled by rhapsodic libertarian ideology, a faith in progress and human abilities that could be called naive—or far worse. But even this has its good side. As the former *Reason* editor Virginia Postrel observes, at least Tierney's not a cranky libertarian of the sort who's constantly griping about taxes and big government. It simply doesn't fit his temperament."

"Recycling Is Garbage," perhaps Tierney's best-known article, appeared in the *New York Times Magazine* on June 30, 1996. Nearly a decade before the piece was published, a barge, the *Mobro 4000*, unsuccessfully attempted to transport over 3,000 tons of waste from the town of Islip, New York, to North Carolina. When officials in North Carolina refused to accept the waste, the barge traveled 6,000 miles, along the eastern coast of the United States, into the Gulf of Mexico, and east to the islands of the Bahamas, having its cargo rejected in nine locations before returning to New York. The *Mobro 4000*'s voyage led many to conclude that the U.S. was creating trash faster than it could find room to dispose of it. In "Recycling Is Garbage" Tierney described the *Mobro 4000*'s circuitous voyage and its consequences, among which was a widespread call for more government-sponsored recycling programs. The article disparaged the practice of recycling, claiming that its benefits are small in comparison with its costs. Recycling programs "offer mainly short-term benefits to a few groups—politicians, public relations consultants, environmental organizations, waste-handling corporations—while diverting money from genuine social and environmental problems," Tierney wrote. "Recycling may be the most wasteful activity in modern America: a waste of time and money, a waste of human and natural resources." Tierney's article inspired an unusually high number of responses, including an 86-page rebuttal from the Natural Resources Defense Council.

In the mid-1990s Tierney brought his sense of humor to fiction writing. With Christopher Buckley, the founding editor of *Forbes FYI* magazine, he wrote *God Is My Broker: A Monk-Tycoon Reveals the 7½ Laws of Spiritual* and *Financial Growth* (1998), a parody of religious-themed self-help books. The novel tells the story of a former Wall Street trader turned Catholic monk, Brother Ty, who rescues his bankrupt monastery in upstate New York by cashing in on trading tips he believes are coming from God. The monastery acquires such vast wealth that it is transformed into a theme park. *Publishers Weekly* (March 30, 1998) called *God Is My Broker* "culturally savvy, yet as gleefully over the top as a college skit."

On the NBC morning program *Today* on December 4, 2002, Tierney said, "We're so surrounded by bad news, and we spend so much time preparing for the worst, that we're not ready when good stuff happens." In that spirit, he wrote *The Best-Case Scenario Handbook: A Parody* (2002), inspired by the best-selling *Worst-Case Scenario* series of books by Joshua Piven and David Borgenicht. Among other items, *The Best-Case Scenario Handbook* advises readers on how to accept an Oscar, what to do if named *Time* magazine's Person of the Year, and how to respond when an ATM, without prompting, suddenly starts dispensing piles of cash. The first piece of advice under "How to receive a divine visitation" reads, "Do not look directly into your Visitor's eyes. Some deities consider this 'not done,' and a few respond quite bad-ly."

For several months in 2003, assigned to the *Times*'s Baghdad bureau, Tierney filed reports from Iraq; otherwise, for three years prior to his appointment as an op-ed columnist, he was a correspondent in the newspaper's Washington bureau. During the 2004 presidential campaign, he wrote a weekly campaign-digest column called "Political Points." Since his appointment to the op-ed page, in March 2005, Tierney has continued to court controversy. His May 10, 2005 column, "Bombs Bursting on Air," contended that media representatives should "reconsider their . . . fondness for covering suicide bombings" in the Middle East. Tierney wrote, "I realize that we have a duty to report suicide bombings . . . especially when there's a spate as bad as in recent weeks. And I know the old rule of television: If it bleeds, it leads. But I'm still puzzled by our zeal in frantically competing to get gruesome pictures and details for broadcasts and front pages." Recalling his own dispatches from Baghdad during the summer of 2003, Tierney wondered if such zeal may have led to some terrorists' seeing the bombings as effective means of gaining publicity. In another recent column he supported President George W. Bush's extremely controversial call to privatize Social Security.

In a column entitled "Where Cronies Dwell" (October 11, 2005), Tierney lashed out at what he perceived to be a liberal bias among faculty members at American journalism and law schools that are widely described as "elite." Citing a study conducted by the conservative journalist David Horowitz, the president of the Center for the Study of Popular Culture (which publishes the on-line journal *FrontPage Magazine*), Tierney wrote, "Democrats outnumber Republicans by 8 to 1 at the law schools"; among journalism schools, the ratios are "4 to 1 at Northwestern and New York University, 13 to 1 at the University of Southern California, [and] 15 to 1 at Columbia." "The problem isn't so much the stories that appear as the ones that no one thinks to do," Tierney wrote. "Journalists naturally tend to pursue questions that interest them. So when you have a press corps that's heavily Democratic—more than 80 percent, according to some surveys of Washington journalists—they tend to do stories that reflect Democrats' interests."

Tierney received the 1998–99 Distinguished Column Writing Award from the New York Publishers Association. In 1988, for a *Newsweek* cover story he wrote entitled "The Search for Adam and Eve," he received the Westinghouse Science Journalism Award from the American Association for the Advancement of Science. Early in his career the American Institute of Physics presented him with the United States Steel Foundation Science Writing Award. During the 1993–94 academic year he worked as a fellow at the Freedom Forum Media Studies Center, in New York, where he researched the media's coverage of environmental issues.

Tierney is married to the former Dana Grose-close, a writer. The couple have a son, Luke.
—D.F.

Suggested Reading: *American Prospect* p28+ Sep. 10, 2001, with photos; *New York Times* Web site; *Publishers Weekly* p71 Mar. 30, 1998; *Washington Post* (on-line) Mar. 2, 2005

Selected Books: fiction—*God Is My Broker: A Monk-Tycoon Reveals the 7½ Laws of Spiritual and Financial Growth* (with Christopher Buckley), 1998; nonfiction—*The Best-Case Scenario Handbook: A Parody*, 2002

Courtesy of Namaste Publishing

Tolle, Eckhart

(TOH-lee, EK-hart)

1948(?)– Spiritual teacher; writer

Address: P.O. Box 93664, Nelson Park RPO, Vancouver, BC, Canada V6E 4L7

"All of life is a journey," the spiritual teacher and author Eckhart Tolle told Lloyd Robertson for the *CTV News* program (May 10, 2003), according to a transcript of the interview on the Web site of CTV Television, a Canadian broadcast network. "So why not enjoy this moment, you will never have anything else." The idea of embracing the present instead of hoping for future happiness and achievements is the central message of Tolle's book *The Power of Now* (1999). After *The Power of Now* became a best-seller, Tolle found himself much in demand as a speaker on the New Age lecture and reading circuit. The theme of his seminars and teachings is that, in order to become enlightened, an individual must stop listening to his or her inner voice, which concentrates on the past and the future rather than the present. Eckhart has said that before finding peace within himself and formulating his spiritual concepts, he lived in a state of suicidal depression and acute anxiety. Then, at age 29, he had a nighttime revelation that allowed him to let go of such negative feelings and focus instead on the joy of being alive. He eventually began teaching others how to enjoy the kind of inner peace he claimed to have found, describing his methods and recommendations in *The Power of Now*. "You have probably come across 'mad' people walking in the street incessantly talking or muttering to themselves," Eckhart wrote in the book, as quoted by a writer for the Victoria, British Columbia, *Times Colonist* (April 16, 2001). "Well, that's not too much different from what you and all other 'normal' people do, except that you don't do it out loud. The voice comments, speculates, judges, compares, complains, likes, dislikes and so on." According to Eckhart, whose ideas are closely aligned with those of Buddhism, this inner voice leads us to review the past and worry about the future, resulting in anxiety and fear; in order to reach inner peace and enlightenment, we must learn to block out that distracting voice.

Eckhart Tolle was born in Lunen, Germany, in about 1948. (His given name was Ullrich; he later changed it to Eckhart in honor of Meister Eckhart, a famous mystical Christian of the medieval era.) His family moved to England when he was 13. He graduated from the University of London and then became a research scholar in literature at Cambridge University, also in England. The deep depression, anxiety, and suicidal feelings Tolle had had since childhood ended when he experienced what he has described as a profound spiritual transformation. "One night, not long after my 29th birthday, I woke up in the early morning hours with a feeling of absolute dread," he recalled to Wendy Kale for the *Colorado Daily* (November 15, 2001). "This time it was more intense than ever before—everything felt so alien and hostile. However, the most loathsome thing to me was my existence. What was the point in continuing to live with this burden of misery? Then suddenly I became aware of repeating the thought—I cannot live with myself any longer. I became aware of what a peculiar thought it was. Am I one or two? If I cannot live with myself, there must be two of me: the 'I' and the 'self' that I cannot live with. Maybe only one of them is real." Eckhart has said that in that moment of realization he heard the words "resist nothing" and felt complete inner peace.

Following his revelation, Tolle left his job and became a vagrant. For two years he did little but roam London parks. "When the inner transformation happened . . . one could almost say a balance was lost," he told Andrew Cohen for *What Is Enlightenment?* magazine (Fall/Winter 2000, online). "It was so fulfilling and so blissful simply to *be* that I lost all interest in *doing* or interacting. For quite a few years, I got lost in Being." He added that he had "almost relinquished doing completely—just enough to keep myself alive and even that was miraculous. I had totally lost interest in the future. And then gradually a balance re-established itself." He eventually began telling others about his experience and how they, too, might gain peace and happiness. In 1999 Tolle published *The Power of Now: A Guide to Spiritual Enlightenment.* In the book he outlined his ideas on how to find peace and joy by living fully in each moment. While he has claimed that he is not an adherent of or affiliated with any particular religion, he has often quoted the words of Jesus, Buddha, and other religious and spiritual thinkers from ancient times to the present, and many of his ideas resemble Buddhist teachings. Tolle believes that by embracing the current moment, "the now," we can accept our lives and that this will lead us to inner peace. "That's the end of suffering," he told Robertson. "If you look at any spiritual practice, it ultimately points to that, a state of surrender to life." "The key to living in the moment is surrender," he told Kale. "Only someone who has surrendered can have true spiritual power. If you totally surrender you will be free in any situation. You have to feel the power of the moment, feel the fullness of being and feel your presence." Tolle has said that most people ignore the importance of the present in their rush toward the future. Referring to such individuals, he told Grania Litwin for the *Times Colonist* (May 27, 2001), "They think, when I have achieved this I will be OK. Then I can be in the now. But not now. Now is not good enough yet. Not complete enough yet. This is the deep-seated mind structure that pulls you continually to the future." When people surrender and accept life as it is, according to Tolle, the past ceases to have power over them, and they have no fear or anxiety about the future.

Tolle has said that he is not advising people to ignore or fail to plan for the future. "Transcending the world does not mean to withdraw from the world, to no longer take action, or to stop interacting with people," he told Cohen. "Transcendence of the world is to act and to interact without any self-seeking. In other words, it means to act without seeking to enhance one's sense of self through one's actions or one's interactions with people." Living in the now also does not absolve an individual from responsibility for improving society, in Tolle's view. "Action arises out of acceptance of what is. It is the basis of action," he told Litwin. "Saying 'yes' to the present moment means that no matter what is happening on the surface, you are aligned with life. Like a swimmer, the water carries you. You are no longer dependent upon certain things being a certain way." Tolle also stresses that life should be a journey of self-discovery. "Life is not designed to make you happy," he told Litwin. "It is designed to help raise your consciousness."

Part of raising one's consciousness is learning to deal with the "pain body," a part of our physical beings that, according to Tolle, feeds on pain for survival. "It feeds on negative emotions and thoughts, takes possession of your mind and others' around you, especially your partner's," he told Litwin. "To unplug the pain body, you bring presence and spaciousness to it. You watch it directly. It might be a fear, a heaviness, depression, pain, but it will gradually lose its energy charge if you watch it."

Tolle believes that the fundamental problem for every individual is identification with the mind, something that results in constant, compulsive thinking—what Tolle calls "mind noise." These distracting thoughts are focused on ourselves and our troubles, fears, desires, emotions, and pain. "Most people are totally identified with their own thoughts," he said at a presentation in Vancouver, British Columbia, Canada, in September 2002, as quoted by Douglas Todd in the *Vancouver Sun* (October 5, 2002). "Thought separates us. I don't mean you shouldn't think any more. But we need to end thinking as the main mode on this planet. We just shouldn't be so captivated by thoughts." If we can quiet our racing minds, Tolle explained to Todd, we "won't be so reactive. You'll be able to align yourself with the suchness of the moment." He told Cohen that he can sometimes "sit for two hours in a room with almost no thought. Just complete stillness. Sometimes when I go for walks, there's also complete stillness; there's no mental labeling of sense perceptions. There's simply a sense of awe or wonder or openness, and that's beautiful."

Printed in an initial run of only 3,000 copies, *The Power of Now* sold modestly at first. Sales surged after the media titan Oprah Winfrey, having learned about the book from the actress Meg Ryan, gave it a plug in the July/August 2000 issue of *O, The Oprah Magazine*. In 2002 Oprah gave Tolle's book another push when she discussed it during an episode of her eponymous television talk show, telling her large viewing audience that she had read *The Power of Now* eight times and kept it on her bedside table. (Many of the books Oprah has publicly recommended have subsequently rocketed onto best-seller lists.) *The Power of Now* was soon a hot topic in many book-club discussions and appeared on many recommended-reading lists. Thanks to its newfound fame, *The Power of Now* rose to number one on Amazon.com's sales list and spent 20 weeks on the *New York Times* best-seller list. According to Amazon.com, *The Power of Now* has been translated into more than 30 languages and has sold more than two million copies worldwide.

In a review of the audio version of *The Power of Now* for the Durham, North Carolina, *Herald-Sun* (February 2, 2003), Susie Wilde wrote, "New Age jargon always jars my listening, but what Tolle has to say is worth giving up prejudices [for]. His voice is gentle, and his carefully chosen words provide understanding. His concept of the false, thinking self makes sense, and his suggestions for avoiding its traps are useful. His premise suggests the same path most enlightened leaders propose, but somehow Tolle's everyday examples give a good sense of the here and now he urges listeners to seek." Andrea Sachs, writing for *Time* (April 21, 2003), disagreed, finding the book unhelpful for solving everyday problems. "What is Tolle telling readers that they seem so eager to hear? His Zen-like message, reminiscent of that of hippie guru Ram Dass, is that happiness is achieved by living in the present: 'In the Now, in the absence of time, all your problems dissolve.' But the book, awash in spiritual mumbo jumbo ('The good news is that you can free yourself from your mind'), will be unhelpful for those looking for practical advice."

Two years after *The Power of Now* went on sale, Tolle published *Practicing the Power of Now: Essential Teachings, Meditations, and Exercises from The Power of Now*, an instruction manual and companion guide. *Stillness Speaks*, Tolle's third book, appeared in August 2003. In it he examines the concept and practice of stillness in the teachings of Buddha and Jesus and in such spiritual texts as the *Tao Te Ching* and the Vedas and Upanishads of India. (Tolle has said that because his teachings do not belong to any single religious tradition, they are accessible to all people.) "Tolle describes stillness with eloquent economy," a reviewer for *Publishers Weekly* (August 11, 2003) stated. "Beautiful stand-alone paragraphs offer insight into the defensive nature of the ego versus what he sees as our true being, the attentive, receptive mind behind thought, the spaciousness and peace that blossoms inside when we accept what is, including death. 'Your unhappiness ultimately arises not from the circumstances of your life but from the conditioning of your mind.' No one will doubt that Tolle has freed himself from nagging thoughts and fears. But the rest of us?"

In October 2005 Tolle published *A New Earth: Awakening to Your Life's Purpose*. In a news release posted on his Web site (October 11, 2005), Tolle wrote that when he was writing that book, "people would sometimes ask me, 'What is the new book about?' And invariably, my answer would be, 'I only ever write or speak about one thing.' What is that one thing? Spiritual awakening." Like the *Power of Now*, *A New Earth* offers practical suggestions for freeing oneself from what Tolle, in a description of the book on his Web site, calls "egoic consciousness."

Before *The Power of Now* was published, Tolle had no savings, no health insurance, and no investments. "I was probably living below the poverty line," he told Todd. "But if people told me I was poor, I would have said, 'I didn't know that.'" He told Cohen, "For many years I was a recluse. But since the publication of [*The Power of Now*], my life has changed dramatically. I'm now very much involved in teaching and traveling. . . . Yet I still feel that inside nothing has changed. I still feel exactly the same as before. There is still a continuous sense of peace, and I am surrendered to the fact that on an external level there's been a total change." He told Todd that he enjoys the "relative abundance in my life. . . . But the enjoyment is the same. I used to travel in buses, but now I have my own car." Tolle lives in Vancouver, British Columbia, with his girlfriend and business partner, Kim Eng. In 2005 Eng was in the process of assuming some aspects of Eckhart's teaching, in classes, lectures, and one-on-one phone sessions to individuals and groups. Local groups dedicated to Eckhart's teachings have been organized in more than 20 countries, from Namibia to Singapore. According to Johnny Dodd, writing for *People* (March 21, 2005), Ekhart drives an SUV, occasionally drinks a glass of wine, and enjoys watching reruns of the television series *Seinfeld*. Eckhart also insisted to

Dodd that he was not a guru: "I always say the truth is not to be found within anybody else. It's in you."
—K.E.D.

Suggested Reading: Eckhart Tolle's Web site; *People* p115+ Mar. 21, 2005, with photos; *Vancouver (Canada) Sun* D p3 Oct. 5, 2002, with photos; (Victoria, Canada) *Times Colonist* A p10 May 27, 2001, with photo; *What Is Enlightenment?* (on-line) Fall/Winter 2000, with photos

Selected Books: *The Power of Now: A Guide to Spiritual Enlightenment,* 1999; *Practicing the Power of Now: Essential Teachings, Meditations, and Exercises from The Power of Now,* 2001; *Stillness Speaks,* 2003; *A New Earth: Awakening Your Life's Purpose,* 2005

Courtesy of General Electric

Trotter, Lloyd

Apr. 9, 1945– Business executive

Address: GE Consumer & Industrial, Appliance Park, Louisville, KY 40225

"A job isn't a job to me. It's a passion—something you love to work at," Lloyd Trotter said to Jan Goldberg for the *EEO Bimonthly Equal Employment Opportunity Career Journal* (February 28, 1995). In a career at General Electric (GE) that spans over three decades, Trotter has worked his way up from a field-service engineer to president and chief executive officer of the Consumer & In-

dustrial Division. GE was formed in 1892, through the merger of the Edison General Electric Co. (founded by Thomas A. Edison) and the Thomas-Houston Co. Currently, the firm manufactures electrical appliances and equipment, ranging from lightbulbs and refrigerators to airport scanners and aircraft engines. (GE also owns 80 percent of the media and entertainment conglomerate NBC Universal.) Consumer & Industrial is one of GE's 11 major businesses; its divisions manufacture appliances, lighting products, and so-called integrated industrial equipment, such as circuit breakers. Trotter has attributed his success to more than just job performance. "I think people come into a new environment and because they are so intent on proving they can do the job, they don't spend the time . . . looking around the organization and really learning what the business is all about," he said to Jan Goldberg. "This would make these individuals more effective in doing not only their jobs but in gaining a better and greater understanding of what the enterprise wants and needs in order to be strong. Success requires considerably more than being able to perform job functions. You must be able to add value to that company through your presence."

One of three children, Lloyd D. Trotter was born on April 9, 1945 in Cleveland, Ohio. His father, a clergyman, worked as a die setter at General Motors; his mother was a homemaker. His brother, Lee Trotter Jr., described young Lloyd Trotter as "a normal kid who enjoyed writing, public speaking, model trains and riding his motor scooter" and said that he "was a good student," as Mitch King paraphrased him for the Cleveland *Call and Post* (August 28, 2002). Lloyd Trotter also harbored a childhood love of sweets—in particular, black walnut ice cream and chocolate-chip cookies. "When I wanted to bribe him it was with chocolate chip cookies," his brother said to Mitch King.

Trotter graduated from John Adams High School in 1963. There, he had met the program director for the tool-and-die apprentice program at the Cleveland Twist Drill Co., and upon graduation he applied for the program. In doing so, he encountered discrimination because of his being African-American. "I saw the waiting room and the personnel office, and I thought, boy, anybody could walk in and pick up an application and talk to someone," Trotter was quoted as saying by Price M. Cobbs and Judith L. Turnock in *Cracking the Corporate Code* (2003). "But then a guard stopped me with, 'Can I help you?' And I said, 'I have an appointment. I'm here to fill out an application.' And he said, 'We don't have any jobs.' That was the answer. I gave him my explanation, and he said, 'Wait here.' I still didn't get into the waiting room. This company was making a conscious effort to do something about past discrimination, but I think they started doing it without a lot of planning or communication. So right away I was reminded of what I was getting ready to face." Trotter later received an apology from the company's president and was accepted into the apprentice program. He attended evening classes at Cleveland State University, taking the courses necessary for his apprenticeship. Before he had completed his bachelor's degree in business administration, in 1972, Trotter had been promoted to a job in product design and application engineering.

Meanwhile, in 1970, Trotter—who had been working with a distributor who sold the Twist Drill Co.'s cutting tools to General Electric—went with a GE engineer to examine the new tools. The equipment did not seem to Trotter to be working well, and he stated his opinion. "So [the GE representatives] asked me if I would help them," Trotter was quoted as saying by Price M. Cobbs and Judith L. Turnock. "I said, 'I don't live far from here. Why don't I come in every Monday? I'll give it my best shot. I'll tell you what I think, and you can decide what you want to do.' Well, that went on for about six months, and then we scheduled another qualifying run on the machine. I noticed there were a lot of people standing around, and this run was really successful. My contact there introduced me to his boss, who said, ' I want to get right to the point. Would it be a problem for you to come and work for us?' I told him I really had to think about it. Compared to Cleveland Twist Drill, that part of GE was really home-grown then. I said, 'I still have about two years of night school left, and I'm not planning on starting anyplace in a nonprofessional category.' They offered me a service engineering job, so I joined GE in 1970."

Trotter went to work as a field-service engineer with General Electric's High Intensity Quartz Lighting Department, in Nela Park, in East Cleveland. He has cited his confidence in himself and his abilities as helping him to find an important place at the company. "I worked with guys who were engineers, and I found I added value to their thought processes," Trotter said, according to Cobbs and Turnock. "Knowing I could do that kept me going. And people appreciated my ideas. I ran across individuals who didn't want me there, no question about that. But mostly I found if I could help them be successful, they were more than willing to let me do that."

In 1978 Trotter went to work at General Electric's Appliance Park, in Louisville, Kentucky, which houses GE's manufacturing facilities and National Sales and Service organizations. He was brought in to improve manufacturing efficiency; during his first two years in Louisville, he helped automate part of the dishwasher assembly lines, and in his last two years there, he was in charge of them. "I really enjoyed the challenges of large-scale manufacturing, so I sought out a broad-based career in that field," Trotter said to Robert Schoenberger for the Louisville *Courier-Journal* (February 22, 2004).

In 1990 Trotter became vice president and general manager of GE's Manufacturing for Electrical Distribution & Control (ED&C), based in Plainview, Connecticut. The ED&C makes products that distribute, control, and protect electrical power for commercial and residential use. The promotion made Trotter responsible for ED&C's entire manufacturing process and the supervision of 18,000 employees in North America, South America, Europe, and Southeast Asia. By using self-governed work teams, Trotter tripled production. "I understand how to take complex problems, distill them to issues, and then put very simple, clear directions around them. Then everyone is involved in the movement to resolve or at least improve the situation," Trotter was quoted as saying by Cobbs and Turnock. Within two years Trotter had been promoted to president and CEO of Electrical Distribution & Control and had supervisory responsibilities that extended to more than 40,000 employees worldwide.

Electrical Distribution & Control merged with GE Industrial Control Systems in 1998. Trotter was named a GE senior vice president and the president and CEO of the new Industrial Systems. "Career goals must be set and you must work aggressively toward them," Trotter said to Jan Goldberg. "In addition, you must continue to revise them as you go along. I never had a goal to be President or CEO of General Electric Company. Coming from a bluecollar family, when I graduated from college, my goal was to be a plant manager. Once I understood that a plant manager position was achievable, I recalibrated that goal, then set my next goal, and so on and so on and so on. I didn't have one goal—I had many."

The end of 2003 brought more success Trotter's way. In December he became president and chief executive officer of the new GE Consumer & Industrial Division, which combined the Consumer Products division and the Industrial Systems division. (Consumer Products included appliances and lighting, while Industrial Systems manufactured such products as circuit breakers and electric motors.) His new responsibilities included overseeing 75,000 employees worldwide, cutting costs, and improving profits. The promotion meant a move back to Louisville. According to Trotter, things had changed there in his absence. "Everything has gotten faster. The machine tools have gotten smarter. It takes more skill to operate them," Trotter said to Robert Schoenberger. "The whole manufacturing platform has been thrown up in the air and reconfigured."

The Louisville-based GE Foundation, a philanthropic offshoot of GE, announced in September 2005 that a grant of $25 million would be awarded to the Jefferson County Public School system, to be used for the development of ways to improve the achievements of students in math and science and to increase the number of students who apply to college. The grant is an outgrowth of the GE Foundation's College Bound initiative, which started in 1989. "This initiative represents the spirit of volunteering and giving back that is at the heart of our Company," Trotter said, as quoted in *Business Wire* (September 26, 2005). "GE volunteers here in Louisville are committed to helping the district graduate students who can compete in the global marketplace. We know that it will take all of us working together to make this happen but we look forward to bringing the expertise and leadership of our employees to help with this initiative."

Trotter has the distinction of having worked in every one of the divisions he manages at General Electric. "As I came up, I realized the common denominator among the top people was broad-based experiences, jobs that led to demonstrating broad-based skills and the ability to increase your sphere of influence. That was the key in building a career, expanding your learning and adding value along the way," Trotter said, according to Cobbs and Turnock. "Every job that looks like a promotion may not be a good job for you. I've seen people derail their careers with what I call 'chimney careers.' You go up very fast, but you're very narrow. Without intending to, you become a specialist. You are blocked, and there's no way to connect the dots to get back. I was lucky in this way. What was fun for me was to find a new job that was a new experience. If a job offered that, even though it was not up, I went for it. I did a lot of different things just because I thought they would be fun to do, and those turned out to be building blocks for broader skills and greater influence."

Trotter is the founder of the GE African American Forum, a group of black employees who meet to discuss career advancement issues and opportunities. The African American Forum has initiated the creation of other groups at General Electric and has inspired other large companies to encourage the formation of similar groups for discussion and career advancement. Trotter has been credited with starting several mentoring programs at General Electric, as well. Addressing the lack of diversity in management, those programs match lower-level employees with experienced managers, so that the former can receive guidance on career choices that lead to higher positions. In recent years General Electric has increased the diversity of its upper ranks, with more appointments of minority executives. "Overall, workplace situations are better than they used to be," Trotter said to Jan Goldberg about that issue, "but we still have a long way to go. This is partly because the equation is never the same. If in fact we are dealing with the same old set of issues that we were dealing with ten years ago, I'd say that there should be a lot of progress, but the issues have changed and the complexity is greater, meaning the changes and the creativity that we've got to apply to the answers must be different. Most companies are facing this—but as I said earlier, they still have a long way to go." As an example of issues that are relatively new to companies, Trotter referred to initiatives aimed at helping employees to balance work and family life.

Cleveland State University awarded Trotter the Alumni Special Achievement Award for 1999 and held an informal session in which Trotter discussed with students and staff members at the College of Business Administration the importance of education and his own pursuit of success. "You will be using every tool you ever learned just about anywhere you go in business," Trotter said, as reported by Kortney Stringer in the Cleveland *Plain Dealer* (June 22, 1999). "Your education really never stops, and whatever you learn just adds to it and makes it more robust." Students said that they found Trotter's advice helpful, and they appreciated the information he passed on to them. "Face it, there's not a lot of people in his position in a large corporation who sit and tell you this is how I did it and this is what I went through," Tonya Davis, a Cleveland State University graduate student, said to Kortney Stringer. "Having him here physically telling us about all the aspects of making it is very beneficial." In 2001 Cleveland State University awarded Trotter an honorary doctorate in business administration. In its July 2002 issue, *Fortune* magazine honored Trotter as one of the 50 "Most Powerful Black Executives," ranking him at number 11. Among the accomplishments that brought him that distinction was the $6 billion in revenues for Industrial Systems in 2001. The National Society of Black Engineers also recognized Trotter in 2002, presenting him with its Executive Leadership Award. In 2003 he received the Benjamin E. Mays Award, presented in memory of the late president of Morehouse College. (The award was given by the group A Better Chance, which identifies and recruits developing leaders among academically gifted students of color.)

Lloyd Trotter lives in the Cherokee Park neighborhood of Louisville with his wife, Teri. He has a collection of Harlem Renaissance art and also collects wine from around the world. "He is a real steady guy, a loyal person and a great individual with a dry sense of humor," Lee Trotter, Lloyd's brother, said to Mitch King. Trotter has three children and five grandchildren.

—L.J.

Suggested Reading: (Cleveland) *Call and Post* A p6 Aug. 28, 2002; (Cleveland) *Plain Dealer* C p2 June 22, 1999; *EEO BiMonthly Equal Employment Opportunity Career Journal* p27 Feb. 28, 1995; (Louisville) *Courier-Journal* E p1 Feb. 22, 2004; Cobbs, Price M. and Judith L. Turnock. *Cracking the Corporate Code,* 2003

Courtesy of Nina Subin

Urrea, Luis Alberto

(oo-RAY-ah, loo-EES al-BARE-toh)

Aug. 20, 1955– Writer

Address: c/o Author Mail, Little, Brown and Co., 1271 Ave. of the Americas, New York, NY 10020

In novels and short stories, books of nonfiction, and volumes of poetry, Luis Alberto Urrea has illuminated the experiences of impoverished Mexicans and those Mexican-born people who, like him, have crossed the border to live in the U.S. He is perhaps best known for his "border" trilogy, comprising the nonfiction works *Across the Wire: Life and Hard Times on the Mexican Border* (1993), *By the Lake of Sleeping Children: The Secret Life of the Mexican Border* (1996), and *Nobody's Son: Notes from an American Life* (1998), which describe the plight of the poor in Tijuana, Mexico, and Urrea's own difficult growing-up years. The writer continued his chronicle of the destitute of his native country with *The Devil's Highway* (2004), an account of the ill-fated journey of 26 Mexican men through the desert toward the Arizo-

na border. Urrea's poems have been collected in volumes including *The Fever of Being* (1994) and *Ghost Sickness* (1997), and he is the author of the fiction works *In Search of Snow* (1994), *Six Kinds of Sky* (2002), and *The Hummingbird's Daughter* (2005). In an observation that might be applied to Urrea's body of work as a whole, Jennifer Modenessi wrote in her review of *The Hummingbird's Daughter* for the *Contra Costa (California) Times* (July 3, 2005), "There's . . . an earthy dose of the everyday spiking Urrea's prose—mud, stink and death counterbalance some of Urrea's more otherworldly themes and keep the book firmly grounded in the loam."

One of six children, Luis Alberto Urrea was born on August 20, 1955 in Tijuana, Mexico. His father, Alberto, came from Sinaloa, Mexico, and traced his heritage to the Basque region of northern Spain; his mother, Phyllis, was a white woman from New York. "My mother was a New Yorker with a bohemian flair, but deeply conservative views," Urrea told Daniel Olivas during an interview for the Web site *The Elegant Variation* (June 2005). "My father was a Mexican military man and cop with a poet's soul." His father had had an important security post on the staff of the president of Mexico until about 1954, when he fell out of favor with his superiors. "One of the stories he always used to tell us," Urrea said to Ernie Grimm for the *San Diego Reader* (June 24, 2004, on-line), "was that he had been asked to perform a task he could not get himself to perform, and he had been paid $2000 in a check from the president of Mexico that he had never cashed. And after he had died, when I went through his papers, I found the check. . . . You can assume what it was; they must have wanted him to kill someone." After Urrea's father lost his position on the president's staff, the family fell on hard times; his parents commuted across the border to San Diego, California, where his father worked for a tuna cannery and his mother for a department store. Because Urrea was then left in the care of Mexican women, his first language was Spanish, and he has recalled thinking as a small boy that his mother was insane because she spoke English, which he did not understand. Urrea has described his parents' marriage as volatile and recalled that he himself was mistreated by members of his extended family. Such experiences, he has said, have informed the tragicomic nature of much of his writing. (He had health problems as well, contracting tuberculosis in Tijuana.) One source of solace during his boyhood was his relationship with his godparents, Abelino and Rosario García, who appear in fictional form in *In Search of Snow* and *The Fever of Being.*

When Urrea was three years old, his family moved to San Diego. They lived in the largely African-American neighborhood of Logan Heights before moving to the mostly white San Diego suburb of Clairemont when Urrea was in the fifth grade. In Clairemont, "far from being the athlete and army captain my father wanted, and even farther from being the crew-cut Ivy League lawyer my mother wanted, I was this post-beatnik art kid," Urrea told Daniel Olivas. He attended Clairemont High School, which later became known as the model for the 1982 film *Fast Times at Ridgemont High*. At the suggestion of a teacher, Urrea read a book of poems by Stephen Crane, which so impressed the teenager that he began trying to imitate Crane in writing his own poetry. He was also influenced by the lyrics of the songwriter Leonard Cohen. In about 1970 he bought a copy of the poetry volume *The Lords and the New Creatures*, by the rock-music icon Jim Morrison, "and that was it," as Urrea told Ernie Grimm. "I was hooked on poetry." Urrea was the first member of his family to attend college, majoring first in drama, then in writing, and earning a bachelor's degree from the University of California at San Diego in 1977. One of his teachers there was the writer Ursula Le Guin. Urrea wrote and illustrated *Frozen Moments*, a book of short stories and poetry, as his senior thesis; the university paid for a few copies of the work to be published in 1977.

"Once college was over, I hung out, dude," Urrea wrote for his Web site. "Me and my gang spent every night driving around with tankfuls of 35 cent gas." During that time he also wrote lyrics for a rock band, Harlequin, worked as a movie extra ("Don't ask—it's too humiliating," he wrote for his Web site), and wound up working in an all-night grocery store. He began to emerge from that seemingly aimless lifestyle when Ursula Le Guin included one of his stories in her anthology *Edges* in 1980. Then Cesar Gonzalez, whom Urrea has identified as an important figure in his life, got him a position as a teaching assistant in the Chicano Studies program at Mesa College, in San Diego. Urrea also began doing work with Spectrum Ministries, under E. G. Von Treutzchler III, who ministered to a group of people living in desperately poor conditions in a district called the Borderlands, in Tijuana, and who became an additional mentor for the young writer. In 1982 Urrea was tapped by Harvard University, in Cambridge, Massachusetts, to teach writing workshops. Meanwhile, he did graduate work at the University of Colorado, in Boulder, earning his M.F.A. degree in 1987, the year he became an associate professor at Massachusetts Bay Community College. He taught writing on a freelance basis from 1990 to 1996 and at the University of Southwestern Louisiana from 1996 to 1999. In the latter year he began teaching at the University of Illinois, in Chicago, where he now has tenure.

Urrea's first book to be issued by a major publisher, *Across the Wire: Life and Hard Times on the Mexican Border* (1993), is an account of the people living in almost subhuman squalor 20 minutes from downtown San Diego. Urrea wrote "with unflinching candor and raw clinical detail about the very worst manifestations of the disease, brutality and sexual degradation that afflict the men, women and children who live in the Borderlands," Jon-

athan Kirsch observed in the *Los Angeles Times* (February 10, 1993). "And if the reader is rendered sick at heart or sick to the stomach by the particulars of human misery, so be it. 'Poverty *is* personal: it smells and it shocks and it invades your space,' Urrea writes. 'You come home dirty when you get too close to the poor'. . . . But Urrea refuses to abandon the hope of redemption, no matter how remote it may seem, and so, curiously enough, *Across the Wire* is *not* a tale of unrelieved despair." Kirsch called the book "a work of investigative reporting that is also a bittersweet song of human anguish." David Unger, writing for the *New York Times Book Review* (February 21, 1993), hailed *Across the Wire* as "testimonial literature at its best."

In 1994 Urrea published his first collection of poetry, *The Fever of Being*, as well as his debut novel, *In Search of Snow*. The latter book is set in Arizona in the 1950s and follows Mike McGurk, a man in his late 20s, as he drifts through life in the company of his father, a mechanic and sometime bare-knuckle brawler. "Urrea wrests strange, beautiful poetry out of a mean, lean desert terrain . . . in this impressive first novel, a blend of deadpan humor, picaresque adventure and search for self," the *Publishers Weekly* (February 7, 1994) reviewer observed. Ray Gonzalez pointed out in the *Nation* (July 18, 1994) that *In Search of Snow*—along with other books then being published by Chicanos—represented a sign that Chicano literature was being fully integrated into the mainstream, since the book was not relegated to small-press publication or dependent on word-of-mouth sales efforts, as works by Mexican-American writers had been in the past. *In Search of Snow* "is a joy to read because Urrea is not sticking to the somber tone so common among other young Chicanos now writing," Gonzalez wrote, noting that Urrea "has a flair for creating strong characters and bringing them alive in a blend of drama, slapstick comedy and cinematic technique."

Urrea returned to nonfiction, and to the poor sections of Tijuana, for *By the Lake of Sleeping Children: The Secret Life of the Mexican Border* (1996). On the California side of the Tijuana/U.S. border, as Urrea observed, are luxurious houses and swimming pools; those are visible from the other side, where an enormous garbage dump provides the only livelihood for the wretchedly deprived population. "The politically constructed divide maps the geography of Urrea's bifurcated identity," Ronald Takaki remarked in the *Washington Post Book World* (December 15, 1996): "his Mexican father and American mother, his birth in Tijuana, and his growing up in San Diego." Takaki quoted Urrea as writing, "My father raised me to be 100 percent Mexican, often refusing to speak English to me, tirelessly patrolling the borders of my language. . . . And my mother raised me to be 100 percent American: she never spoke Spanish . . . If, as some have suggested lately, I am some sort of 'voice of the border,' it is because the border runs down the middle of me. I have a barbed-wire fence neatly bisecting my heart." Carolyn Alessio, who reviewed the book for the *Chicago Tribune* (December 15, 1996), found that Urrea had "portray[ed] the poverty and desperation of his native Tijuana in a language both truthful and improbably poetic."

In *Ghost Sickness* (1997), Urrea's second collection of poetry, the narrator of the poems travels by car through the desert of the American Southwest, driven by the ghost of his father in one section and taking the wheel himself in the later sections. "By the last stanza in this collection," Sharon Preiss noted in the *Tucson Weekly* (February 16, 1998), "the words and sounds—the feelings—are those of relief. At last we hear harmonious music, a voice that, having traveled through the discord of the abyss, is now clear and still. The ghost has been laid to rest, and peace envelops this difficult landscape of memory, image, word, and sound."

Nobody's Son: Notes from an American Life (1998) is the concluding volume of Urrea's border trilogy. It is both a memoir and a meditation on "la raza," the joys and sorrows of being a Mexican-American. Part of the sorrow, for Urrea, stemmed from the wealth of anti-Mexican sentiment he encountered—from people including his own mother, who asked him why, when he was teaching at Harvard, he could not call himself Louis instead of Luis. "You are not a Mexican!" she declared. "This is not, however, just a book about race," the *Publishers Weekly* (August 10, 1998) reviewer wrote. "In fact, it's just as much about writing, and at its best Urrea's staccato phrases build up to a vivid, often brutal image." Rebecca Martin, writing for *Library Journal* (October 1, 1998), noted the "energetic and darkly humorous" nature of Urrea's book, and added, "The essential tone, however, is of self-deprecating humor about the challenge of explaining a dual identity, a task he accomplishes with passion and understanding."

Vatos (2000) is a collaboration between Urrea and the photographer Jose Galvez, in which *vatos*, "street slang for dude, guy, pal, brother," are celebrated in photographs and Urrea's poem "Hymn to Vatos Who Will Never Be in a Poem." Tom Mayo, writing for the *Dallas Morning News* (October 1, 2000), called the book a "deeply rhythmic litany . . . that is by turns haunting and inspiring." *Wandering Time: Western Notebooks* (2000), written in sections corresponding to the seasons of the year, is an account of Urrea's travels through the western United States and of the people he encountered along the way. The book includes references to many writers who influenced his own takes on travel and nature—references that "are refreshing details in an otherwise bland piece," in the opinion of Cynde Bloom Lahey, writing for *Library Journal* (February 15, 1999). In *World Literature Today* (Summer 2000), however, Catharine E. Wall praised the book, writing, "Urrea has illustrated well one of his own adages, that 'a good writer must excel at two things: poking around and paying attention.'"

Urrea's second work of fiction, *Six Kinds of Sky* (2002), is a collection of short stories dealing with the grief-stricken, broken-down, and wretchedly poor—largely among Mexican-Americans—in the West. "Class struggle, official corruption, the remote distance of the U.S.A. and its concerns, perhaps stereotypical Mexican themes, are brought to life by the characters that populate this fiction and the gentle humor with which most of them are etched," Richard J. Murphy remarked in the *Review of Contemporary Fiction* (Fall 2002). Urrea, the *Publishers Weekly* (January 21, 2002) reviewer noted, "is a poetic writer who draws strong characters and wears his literary compassion on his sleeve, and he uses all of his gifts to full advantage here."

Urrea's book *The Devil's Highway* (2004) is the true story of 26 men who in May 2001 walked through the desert from Veracruz, Mexico, to the Arizona border, to try to get into the U.S. Fourteen of the men died on the way. Urrea told the story in novelistic fashion, concentrating on the men's emotions and on the horrifying details of what happens to those who almost literally burn to death in the desert. Emiliana Sandoval, writing for the *Detroit Free Press* (March 28, 2004), called *The Devil's Highway* "a beautiful book about a horrible trip." Chris Lehmann, writing for the *Washington Post Book World* (March 28, 2004), noted, "Urrea spares the reader none of the grisly details. He describes the six stages of hyperthermia—stress, fatigue, syncope, cramps, exhaustion and stroke—with a poet's practiced eye." After the publication of *The Devil's Highway*, Urrea was awarded the Lannan Foundation's literary prize for nonfiction in 2004. The book was nominated for a Pulitzer Prize.

The Hummingbird's Daughter, the novel Urrea published in 2005, took 20 years to write. It tells in a romantic and magical-realist fashion the story of his distant relative Teresita Urrea, who was born in 1873—in the time of the vicious dictator Porfirio Diaz—and who, because of her healing powers, was known as the Saint of Cabora. The illegitimate daughter of a wealthy rancher, Teresita was born to a young teenager her father seduced; eventually her father made her part of his household and had her educated. She was further trained by Huila, a medicine woman, and belief in her powers grew after she was raped and murdered (or so everyone thought) by a ranch hand, only to rise before the mourners at her own wake. Because of her revolutionary fervor, she was declared an enemy of Diaz. David Hiltbrand observed in the *Philadelphia Inquirer* (May 31, 2005, on-line) that *The Hummingbird's Daughter* is "an extraordinary example of what can transpire when a remarkable story is granted to a truly gifted writer," and called the novel "an epic as steeped in lore and magic, in beauty and suffering, in religion and passion, as old Mexico itself." "Poor, illegitimate, illiterate and despised, Teresita is the embodiment of the dictum that the last shall be first, and her ascension over the course of 500 pages is a myth that is also a charmingly written manifesto," Stacey D'Erasmo remarked in the *New York Times Book Review* (July 3, 2005). Urrea's "brilliant prose is saturated with the cadences and insights of Latin-American magical realism," the *Publishers Weekly* (April 18, 2005) reviewer wrote, noting that the book is "sweeping in its effect, employing the techniques of Catholic hagiography, Western fairy tale, Indian legend and everyday family folklore against the gritty historical realities of war, poverty, prejudice, lawlessness, torture and genocide. Urrea effortlessly links Teresita's supernatural calling to the turmoil of the times, concealing substantial intellectual content behind effervescent storytelling and considerable humor."

Urrea lives in Naperville, Illinois, with his second wife, Cindy, a journalist whom he calls Cinderella. The couple have three children: Eric, Megan, and Rosario. Urrea has at least one child from his previous marriage. He is an associate professor of writing and English at the University of Illinois. "My favorite place is Colorado. My favorite food is salad, though I'm a sucker for a good buffalo burger," Urrea announced on his Web site. "I don't drink and I don't smoke and I, like everybody else in America today, have diabetes. I hate diabetes, but I love being alive."

—S.Y.

Suggested Reading: *Boston Globe* D p8 Apr. 25, 2004; *Chicago Tribune* C p1 Dec. 15, 1996; *Contra Costa Times* July 3, 2005 online; *Dallas Morning News* C p11 Oct. 1, 2000; *Library Journal* p88 Oct. 1, 1998; *Los Angeles Times* E p6 Feb. 10, 1993, E p5 Sep. 5, 1994; *Los Angeles Times Book Review* p12 May 115, 2005; *Nation* p98+ July 18, 1994; *New York Times* E p2 Nov. 10, 2004; *New York Times Book Review* p9 Feb. 21, 1993, p8 July 3, 2005; *Philadelphia Inquirer* (on-line) May 31, 2005; *Publishers Weekly* p71 Feb. 7, 1994, p18 Aug. 10, 1998, p65 Jan. 21, 2002, p44 Apr. 18, 2005; *Washington Post Book World* p1 Dec. 15, 1996, p3 Mar. 28, 2004

Selected Books: nonfiction—*Across the Wire: Life and Hard Times on the Mexican Border*, 1993; *By the Lake of Sleeping Children: The Secret Life of the Mexican Border*, 1996; *Nobody's Son: Notes from an American Life*, 1998; *The Devil's Highway*, 2004; fiction—*In Search of Snow*, 1994; *Six Kinds of Sky*, 2002; *The Hummingbird's Daughter*, 2005; poetry—*The Fever of Being*, 1994; *Ghost Sickness*, 1997; *Vatos* (with Jose Galvez), 2000

Virilio, Paul

1932– French philosopher; architect

Address: c/o École Spéciale d'Architecture, 254 blvd. Raspail, 75014 Paris, France

According to the French philosopher and architect Paul Virilio, human history has been most profoundly shaped by two interconnected forces: technology and warfare. Through his writings Virilio has engaged in a sustained exploration of the destructive powers of technology as a whole and its military application in particular, focusing on the ways in which technological advancement has altered urban landscapes, social interactions, cultural production, and human perception. Taking the concept of speed as his starting point, he has argued that societal changes in general may be attributed to advances in speed technologies, from early forms of transportation, such as wagons, to modern computer and media networks that transmit information at almost the speed of light. Known as the first theorist to identify acceleration as a defining feature of contemporary civilization, Virilio has coined the word "dromology," based on the Greek word *dromos*, meaning "race," to describe the study of speed and its implications for cultural and political life.

In addition to speed technology, Virilio has demonstrated a particular interest in technologies that simulate or alter visual perception. Through

Courtesy of Semiotext(e), MIT Press

his investigations and analyses of such innovations as closed-circuit television (CCTV) systems, live television news coverage, and other vehicles of mediated imagery, he has explored the role of technology in artificially extending the ordinary range of human sight and bringing into view things that lie far beyond physical reach. Virilio has concluded that, while visual technologies have, in many ways, broadened human fields of vision, they have also resulted in a certain truncation and disembodiment of perspective. Surrounded by images of faraway sites, people have become detached from their own geographical locations, according to Virilio; the ability to be everywhere simultaneously has resulted in a sense of being nowhere at all. As Virilio explained to John Armitage during an interview for the on-line journal *Ctheory* (October 18, 2000), "Interactivity is the equivalent of radioactivity. For interactivity effects a kind of disintegration, a kind of *rupture*." Similarly, during an interview with Louise Wilson for *Ctheory* (October 21, 1994), Virilio proclaimed, "Virtuality will destroy reality."

Because of his pessimistic, at times apocalyptic vision of the future, Virilio is widely regarded as a bleak philosopher; indeed, one of his most widely quoted statements is "One day the day will come when the day will not come." Despite his dire pronouncements about a world that he believes has become dehumanized by technology and warfare, Virilio is a believer in human endurance in the face of imminent disaster. As he told Wilson, "This may sound like drama," but the situation he perceives "is not the end of the world: it is both sad and happy, nasty and kind. It is a lot of contradictory things at the same time. And it is complex. . . . I believe this is, all in the same time, a fantastic, a very scary and an extraordinary world." In an essay that appears on the University of Texas at Arlington's Critical Theory Web site, Douglas Kellner wrote, "Virilio denies the technological imperative and affirms the dignity and sovereignty of human beings over things."

Virilio's writings have been compared to those of the German philosopher Edmund Husserl, the French philosophers Michel Foucault and Jean Baudrillard, and especially the French existentialist philosopher and psychologist Maurice Merleau-Ponty, who was Virilio's mentor at one time. Elements of Virilio's work have also been identified with the Futurist writings of the Italian author Filippo Tommaso Marinetti, the technological and scientific analyses of the German-born physicist Albert Einstein, and the cultural and architectural criticism of the French architect Bernard Tschumi. Nevertheless, although Virilio is often discussed in terms of other theorists, his unique focus on themes of war, speed, technology, and perception have set him apart from his peers. In an article for the London *Guardian* (December 2, 2000), Steven Poole joked, "You too can make Virilio at home: mix equal parts Foucault, Baudrillard and [the American linguist Noam] Chomsky, add eight cloves of garlic, and blow up with two sticks of dynamite."

Paul Virilio was born in 1932 in Paris, France, to a Breton mother and an Italian Communist father. At the onset of World War II, in 1939, he was evacuated to the port of Nantes, in western France,

which his parents believed to be safer than Paris. Eventually, however, American and British forces began dropping bombs on Nantes to drive out the German troops who had invaded the city. Virilio, witnessing the extreme violence and destruction made possible by recent innovations in weaponry, was profoundly impressed by "the full power of technology," as he recalled to James Der Derian during a 1997 interview that appears on the University of California, Irvine, Web site. He has credited his later philosophical interests to his wartime experiences, telling Der Derian, "War was my university. Everything has proceeded from there."

Although war and technology have been his lifelong intellectual preoccupations, Virilio's early professional pursuits were in an unrelated field. As a young man he attended the École des Métiers d'Art, in Paris, where he became a skilled stained-glass artisan. He created windows for several churches, working alongside the French artists Henri Matisse and Georges Braque. In 1950, deeply impressed by a company of priests he had met through his work, he embraced Christianity, a religion whose tenets and guiding principles, according to some critics, have contributed to his philosophical outlook.

For a time during the Algerian war for independence from France (1954–62), Virilio was under military conscription to the French colonial army. At the end of his term of service, he enrolled as a philosophy student at the Sorbonne, in Paris, where he studied phenomenology under Maurice Merleau-Ponty. In 1958 Virilio embarked on a phenomenological inquiry into themes of territorial organization and military space, returning to the martial subjects that had captured his interest as a child in war-ravaged Nantes. He focused his investigation on the Atlantic Wall, a fortified barrier that the Germans had built along the Atlantic coast of Europe during the war in an effort to hold off British and American forces. After completing his studies at the Sorbonne, Virilio established an architectural practice in Paris, despite his lack of formal architectural training.

In 1963, in collaboration with the architect Claude Parent, the sculptor Morice Lipsi, and the painter Michel Carrade, Virilio co-founded Architecture Principe, an association of French architects and artists. He also became the president and editor of the group's eponymous magazine, which published architectural manifestos and essays. One of Architecture Principe's most well-known activities was its promotion of "oblique architecture," a formal system, based on slanted shapes, that sought to break free from the rigidly defined horizontal and vertical elements of contemporary architecture. From 1963 to 1966 Virilio and Parent collaborated on the design for the cathedral of Sainte-Bernadette du Banlay, at Nevers, a "bunker church" styled after military architecture. In 1969 the architects joined forces again to design the Thomson-Houston aerospace research center, in Villacoubly, outside Paris.

Virilio was an active participant in the historic uprising of students and workers that took place in Paris in May 1968. Later that year a panel of students nominated him for a full-time professorship at the École Spéciale d'Architecture (ÉSA), in Paris. Virilio accepted, becoming the ÉSA's director of studies in 1973, its general director in 1975, and its chairman of the board in 1989. Also in 1973 he became the editorial director of Espace Critique, a series of academic books published by Editions Galilée.

Virilio published a number of short essays and architectural drawings during the 1960s and early 1970s. His first major work was an exhaustive photographic and philosophical examination of the architecture of the Atlantic Wall, entitled *Bunker archéologie* (*Bunker Archeology*) and published in 1975. Toward the end of the 1970s, Virilio cofounded a free radio station, Radio Tomate (Tomato Radio), with the philosopher Felix Guattari.

In 1977 Virilio published *Vitesse et politique: essai de dromologie* (*Speed & Politics*), one of his most influential works. The book was Virilio's first sustained attempt to present speed as one of the defining concepts of contemporary civilization. In exploring the impact of technologies of motion on politics, economies, and cultures, he offered a unique "war model" for the growth of the modern city, claiming that military progress, not economic and social forces, catalyzed the disappearance of fortified cities after the feudal period. For Virilio, "war and the need for speed, rather than commerce and the urge for wealth, are the foundations of human society," according to an article about Virilio on the European Graduate School Web site.

Virilio's *Esthétique de la disparition* (*The Aesthetics of Disappearance*), an examination of the relationship between biological optics and technological simulations of sight, appeared in 1980. In 1983 he collaborated with the French theorist and critic Sylvère Lotringer to publish *Pure War*, the book that introduced his thinking to the United States. Virilio uses the term "pure war" to describe war that takes place in the electromagnetic sphere (between combating technologies) rather than on the ground (as physical conflict between human beings). As Ed Halter explained in an article for the *Village Voice* (November 19, 2002), pure war is "a dream of clean, surgical war between disembodied technologies that seeks to remove human casualty from the equation."

Virilio's writings from the early 1980s include *Guerre et cinéma* (*War and Cinema*, 1984), *L'espace critique* (*Lost Dimension*, 1984), and *L'horizon négatif* (*Negative Horizon*, 1985). In 1985 Virilio curated an exhibition called Les Immatériaux (The Immaterial), at the Centre Georges Pompidou, in Paris, that explored the connections between computer technology and contemporary architecture. Two years later he was awarded the Grand Prix National de la Critique Architecturale (Grand National Prize for Architectural Criticism).

With *La machine de vision* (*The Vision Machine*), published in 1988, Virilio presented a history of human perception and the technologies that have simulated and influenced it. In particular, he examined the automation of perception through the proliferation of CCTV systems and other surveillance technologies, as well as military developments, such as cruise missiles and "smart bombs," whose target-locating mechanisms simulate sight. According to Kenneth Baker in a review for the *San Francisco Chronicle* (August 28, 1994), Virilio's study demonstrated that "innovations in optics and visual representation, at least since the end of the 18th century, have developed in tandem with, and often for the sake of, the enhancement of warfare."

In 1989 Virilio became the director of the program of studies at the Collège International de Philosophie de Paris, which was then headed by the philosopher Jacques Derrida. That same year he contributed a short essay, entitled "The Last Vehicle," to *Looking Back on the End of the World*, an anthology of philosophical papers edited by Dietmar Kamper and Christoph Wulf.

In *L'inertie polaire* (*Polar Inertia*), published in 1990, Virilio examined the ways in which new technologies have altered traditional conceptions of space, territory, and the body. Building on themes he had introduced in earlier works, he argued that media and communications networks, by replacing physical reality with an instantaneous present in which everything happens without reference to the body, have transformed physical motion into an unnecessary and obsolete activity and made inertia the defining condition of modernity. He treated similar ideas in his 1995 book, *La vitesse de libération* (*Open Sky*), an exploration of the breakdown of collective and individual relationships to time, space, and movement in a global society shaped by electronic media. Lamenting the dissolution of the significance of geographical locations and intimacy, Virilio claimed that the real spaces and communal affiliations of the past have been replaced by an abstract informational sphere in which people have become disassociated from one another and their immediate surroundings.

Virilio collaborated with the Fondation Cartier on a 1991 exhibition called La Vitesse (Speed), at Jouy-en-Josas, near Paris. That same year he published *L'écran du desert* (*Desert Screen*), an essay about the 1991 Gulf War and the mass media's treatment of it. Emphasizing the extent to which live media coverage had shaped people's perceptions of that war, Virilio argued that the television screen had become a kind of transnational battlefield, complete with victories and defeats. As he explained to Der Derian, "The Gulf War . . . was a local war in comparison with the Second World War, with regard to its battlefield. But it was a worldwide war on the temporal level of representation, on the level of media, thanks to the satellite acquisition of targets, thanks to the tele-command of the war. . . . For the first time, as opposed to the

Vietnam War, it was a war rendered live, worldwide—with, of course, the special effects, all the information processing organized by the Pentagon and the censorship by the major states. In fact, it is a war that took place in the artifice of television, much more than in the reality of the field of battle, in the sense that real time prevailed over real space." "War occurred in Kuwait," Virilio told Wilson, "but it also occurred on the screens of the entire world. The site of defeat or victory was not the ground, but the screen."

In 1992 Virilio became a member of the High Committee for the Housing of the Disadvantaged, a French organization dedicated to helping the homeless. The following year he published *L'art du moteur* (*The Art of the Motor*), an investigation of the implications of technology and war for the cultural realm. According to Virilio, advances in speed and war technologies have created a modern aesthetic based on kinetic rather than formal properties. "For instance," he told Wilson, "when I take the TGV [Train à Grande Vitesse] in France, I love watching the landscape: this landscape, as well as works by [the Spanish artist Pablo] Picasso or [the Swiss artist Paul] Klee, is art. The engine makes the art of the engine. . . . Now all we have to do to enter the realm of art is to take a car."

In 1996 Philippe Petit conducted an interview of Virilio that was published under the title *Cybermonde: la politique du pire* (*Politics of the Very Worst*). Also in 1996 Virilio published *Un paysage d'événements* (*A Landscape of Events*), a collection of 13 essays dating from 1984 to 1996. The essays, which focused on various cultural events of the 1980s and 1990s, treated themes ranging from urban rioting and lawlessness to media coverage of the Gulf War.

Virilio next published *La bombe informatique* (*The Information Bomb*, 1999), an examination of information and communication technologies and the potential threats that they pose to human society. *Stratégie de la déception* (*Strategy of Deception*), a collection of essays about the role of technological innovations in the 1999 war in Kosovo, appeared in the same year. Noting the relatively limited amount of ground combat and the extensive air bombing that that war entailed, he told Armitage, "What is so astonishing about the war in Kosovo for me is that it was a war that totally bypassed territorial space. It was a war that took place almost entirely in the air." Virilio also explored the connection between global telesurveillance and destructive weapons, suggesting that information and arms technologies have become increasingly interrelated.

In 2000 Virilio published *La Procedure Silence* (*Art and Fear*), containing two essays about 20th-century art. In the first, "A Pitiless Art," he interrogated the motives and methods of avant-garde artists, suggesting that the cold acceptance of human suffering in Dadaist and Futurist art, among other schools, demonstrates a lack of pity. He further argued that, in its pitilessness, avant-garde art had

much in common with the use of deadly weapons in modern warfare. As Andrew Hussey wrote for the *New Statesman* (April 14, 2003), Virilio sought to show that "the avant-garde movements of the 20th century set in motion the project of 'smashing humanism to smithereens'" by creating "art shaped by a suicidal form of thinking, art that is attracted to horror and has no real moral content or value."

In late 2002, about a year after the September 11, 2001 terrorist attacks on the World Trade Center, in New York City, Virilio published the book *Ground Zero*, which presented a characteristically pessimistic analysis of contemporary social, political, and cultural values. Touching on a wide range of topics, he suggested that technological progress and warfare have transformed the world into a self-destructive, morally bankrupt dystopia. That same year Virilio published *Crepuscular Dawn*, a collection of conversations with Sylvère Lotringer about speed, war, and architecture.

Also in 2002 Virilio curated an exhibition at the Fondation Cartier entitled Ce qui arrive (Unknown Quantity), for which he wrote a catalog of the same title. The exhibition, which closed in March 2003, was devoted to images of disaster, a "museum of accidents" reflecting Virilio's longstanding belief that progress and catastrophe are inextricably linked. "To invent the train," Virilio told Der Derian, "is to invent derailment; to invent the ship is to invent the shipwreck." The exhibition included a sculpture made from the wreckage of airplane parts, several installation pieces, and photographs and video projections of natural disasters, train derailings, explosions, nuclear accidents, and bombings. It also featured a real-time video made at the site of the World Trade Center, where a crane was being used to sift through smoldering wreckage.

In 2003 Virilio published *Ville Panique* (*City of Panic*), an examination of suicide terrorism and its basis in rootlessness and speed. According to an article by Alan Riding for the *New York Times* (September 3, 2003), Virilio identified the suicide terrorist as a new kind of soldier who "acts without declaration of war, without a flag, without a name and without a genuine battle."

Paul Virilio lives in the city of La Rochelle, France. An emeritus professor at the ÉSA, he spends his time writing philosophical and critical works and collaborating with private organizations dedicated to housing the homeless.

—L.W.

Suggested Reading: *Ctheory* (on-line) Oct. 18, 2000; University of California, Irvine, Web site; *Queen's Quarterly* p329+ Sep. 2001; *New Statesman* (on-line) Apr. 14, 2003

Selected Books: *Speed & Politics*, 1977; *The Aesthetics of Disappearance*, 1980; *Pure War*, 1983; *Lost Dimension*, 1984; *The Vision Machine*, 1988; *The Art of the Motor*, 1993; *Open

Sky, 1995; *The Information Bomb*, 1999; *Strategy of Deception*, 1999; *Art and Fear*, 2000; *Ground Zero*, 2002; *Unknown Quantity*, 2002; *City of Panic*, 2003

Rich Arden/ESPN

Vitale, Dick

(vih-TAHL)

June 9, 1939– Sports commentator and columnist

Address: ESPN Television, ESPN Plaza, Bristol, CT 06010

"Awesome, baby!," the trademark exclamation of Dick Vitale, college basketball's top broadcast analyst and an icon of the sport, captures succinctly this commentator's effusive passion and enthusiasm for the game. Vitale began his career as a coach of high-school and college basketball in his native New Jersey; he next worked as a coach for a professional team, the Detroit Pistons of the National Basketball Association (NBA). He became a college basketball analyst for the ESPN cable sports channel in 1979, the year that network was launched. Every year since then he has been highly prominent on the sports channel during the college-basketball season, which extends from November through March, providing analyses of games, hosting his own weekly basketball program, and writing for *ESPN The Magazine* and the network's Web site. Vitale's contract with ESPN extends through 2012. Concurrently with those jobs, Vitale has served as a college-basketball analyst for ABC Sports since 1988. He has co-authored seven

books, including *Time Out, Baby!* (1991), an account of his dizzying schedule during the 1990–91 college-basketball season, and *Holding Court: Reflections on the Game I Love* (1995). In addition, Vitale issues a highly respected college-basketball review, *Dick Vitale's College Basketball Magazine*, before the start of every season.

Vitale is best known for what are sometimes called "Vitale-isms," his on-air wordplay and coining of original phrases related to basketball: for example, he refers to young star players as "diaper dandies"; a "PTPer" is a prime-time player, or one who performs well in important games; "Maalox time" (a reference to an over-the-counter medicine for intestinal upsets) identifies the tension-filled final minutes of a close game; and an "All-Windex performer" (the brand name is that of a household product for cleaning glass) denotes a player who is an outstanding rebounder (because the backboard against which the basket rests, and off which errant shots often bounce, is made of and often referred to as "the glass"). "If Dick Vitale were a punctuation mark, he'd be an exclamation point," Hal Bock wrote for the Associated Press (December 6, 2003), "a big bold one, dancing around, celebrating a dunk or a dribble, a block or a basket." Along with many other honors, for his work as a basketball analyst Vitale has been nominated for eight CableAce Awards and won two, in 1994 and 1995, respectively, and has been elected to seven halls of fame, among them the National Italian Sports Hall of Fame, the University of Detroit Hall of Fame, and the Florida Sports Hall of Fame. In 1998 Vitale was awarded the Basketball Hall of Fame's Curt Gowdy Media Award, the hall's highest tribute to a journalist (other than enshrinement). Honored as much for his philanthropy as for his work, Vitale was named man of the year in 1996 by the Suffolk County, New York, branch of the Make-A-Wish Foundation, which fulfills the dreams of terminally ill children. He sits on the board of directors of the Jimmy V Foundation, a nonprofit organization dedicated to finding a cure for cancer. Having become something of an icon in American sports (and one of the most imitated broadcasters working today), Vitale is also an experienced corporate endorser and a motivational speaker, and he has appeared in motion pictures. "I'm living the American dream," Vitale has said, according to the ESPN Web site. "I learned from my mom and dad, who didn't have a formal education but had doctorates of love. They told me that if you gave 110 percent all the time, a lot of beautiful things will happen. I may not always be right, but no one can ever accuse me of not having a genuine love and passion for whatever I do." "My soul has always been in basketball," he told Curry Kirkpatrick for *Sports Illustrated* (November 19, 1986). "I will die in the game."

Richard Vitale was born in East Rutherford, New Jersey, on June 9, 1939. His father, who worked in a factory, and his mother, who sewed coats to supplement her husband's earnings, instilled in their son a strong work ethic, telling him that if he worked hard, he could achieve the proverbial American dream. During a book signing at a Barnes & Noble store, Texassports.com reported, Vitale told his audience that his mother "always told me to never believe in the word 'can't.'" As a child Vitale would narrate aloud the play-by-play of his own shots and movements as he pretended to play basketball with rolled-up socks at home. As a student at East Rutherford High School, according to some sources, he played on the school's basketball team. The worsening of damage to his left eye—as a child he had accidentally poked the eye with a pencil—ended any hopes Vitale had of an athletic career. He received a B.S. degree in business administration from Seton Hall University, in South Orange, New Jersey, in 1962, and then a master's degree in education from William Paterson College (now known as William Paterson University), in Wayne, New Jersey. (According to the biography of Vitale on the ESPN Web site, he has also earned 32 graduate-school credits in education.)

Vitale and his friends in New Jersey, who called him "Richie," immersed themselves in watching basketball, both high-school games in their region and the college game played all over the country. New Jersey was a rich breeding ground for coaches and players, among them Rollie Massimino, Hubie Brown, and Mike Fratello, to name but a few, who went on to careers in the college and professional basketball ranks. In high school and college, when sitting with friends in the stands at games, Vitale would often regale his companions by detailing aloud every on-court move.

While studying for his master's degree, Vitale took a job teaching at Mark Twain Elementary School in Garfield, New Jersey. In 1963 he began coaching basketball at Garfield High School, where he stayed for one year. He then signed on to coach the basketball team at his alma mater, East Rutherford High School. During his seven seasons there (1964–70), the East Rutherford team achieved great success: they won four state sectional championships and two consecutive state championships and in one year had a 35-game winning streak. Next, from 1970 to 1972, Vitale served as an assistant basketball coach at Rutgers University, also in New Jersey, where he helped to recruit to the team Phil Sellers and Mike Dabney, both of whom later played significant roles in advancing Rutgers' men's basketball team to the Final Four in the 1976 National Collegiate Athletic Association (NCAA) tournament. (In the annual NCAA college basketball tournament, one of the more exciting events in sports, 64 teams selected from around the country play single-elimination games in a series of rounds until one team, the national champion, remains; surviving until the Final Four, the round in which four teams remain, is a notable accomplishment. The tournament, held in March, is often referred to as March Madness.)

From 1973 to 1977 Vitale coached at the University of Detroit, in Michigan, where his team compiled an impressive five-season winning percentage (.722) and enjoyed a 21-game winning streak during the 1976–77 season. In one of those 21 games, his team beat that year's eventual national champion, Marquette. Due to the strain and tension of coaching, and perhaps his inborn intensity, Vitale developed stomach ulcers; sometimes he would drink milk during games to ease his pain. In 1976 the University of Detroit made Vitale an honorary alumnus. In 1977 he was named the school's athletic director and chosen as man of the year by the Detroit Athletic Club. The next year he was named head coach of the NBA's Detroit Pistons. Hampered by a shifting roster of players, the Pistons compiled a poor record (30–52) under Vitale during the 1978–79 season. Several weeks into the next year, with the Pistons again playing mediocre basketball, Vitale was dismissed as head coach. Later that same year Vitale joined ESPN as an analyst. Despite his lack of success as a coach at the professional level, the former Piston and NBA star Bob Lanier once told Kirkpatrick that Vitale has a "brilliant basketball mind."

On December 5, 1979 Vitale called the play-by-play action of ESPN's first-ever television broadcast of an NCAA game, between Wisconsin and DePaul. Since then he has provided his highly informed, colorful analyses during upwards of a thousand televised games. In the early 1980s Vitale worked at ESPN alongside the Hall of Fame broadcaster Jim Simpson, whom Vitale has credited with helping him to develop his knowledge of basketball and his broadcast acumen and style. Today, in addition to providing analyses of televised games during the college basketball season, Vitale provides commentary on his weekly segment, "Dick Vitale's Fast Break," which airs as part of ESPN's program *SportsCenter*. He also serves as an analyst for ESPN Radio each Monday during the college-basketball season, on the *Mike & Mike in the Morning* show (hosted by Mike Golic and Mike Greenberg). Vitale often writes about basketball as well. He is a regular contributor to *ESPN The Magazine*, and his weekly column is one of the most popular features on the ESPN Web site. Since he joined ABC Sports as a college-basketball analyst, in 1988, Vitale has called many games televised on the network and has also covered the NBA finals and the 1992 Summer Olympic Games for ABC Radio.

Anyone who has ever watched a college basketball game has probably heard one of Vitale's patented locutions. In Vitale-speak, an "M-and-Mer" (pronounced "Em-and-Em-er") refers to the mismatch of a smaller player guarding a bigger one, which creates an exploitable advantage for the latter's team; a "doughnut offense" is one with no viable player to fill the center position in the middle of the court; and a "Dow Joneser," a reference to the stock market index, is a player whose performances fluctuate from bad to good. His sayings have taken on a life of their own, being repeated, as mockery or otherwise, by other broadcasters, and they have spread beyond the realm of basketball.

Some critics and basketball observers have characterized Vitale as more of an entertainer than an analyst and his voice and unflagging enthusiasm as grating. Vitale has been compared to the legendary sports broadcaster Howard Cosell, who often seemed to divide audiences into two camps: those who loved him and those who loathed him. Soon after Vitale launched his career on ESPN, William Taaffe described him in *Sports Illustrated* (May 14, 1984) as the "loudest, most verbose, most opinionated basketball broadcaster yet produced by Western Civilization." But Taaffe qualified his criticism: "Still, Vitale's enthusiasm is so full of good cheer that it's hard to dislike the guy." Several years later, in *Sports Illustrated* (February 1, 1988), Jack McCallum, too, offered a mixed appraisal of him: "Dick Vitale is a hot item these days, and isn't it nice that a guy with a balding pate, bulging eyes, a chalk-on-the-blackboard voice and preternatural enthusiasm has made the grade? But while giving Vitale points for not being the typical network smoothie, let's not ignore the fact that the ego of college basketball's frog prince is out of control and that his self-importance is starting to get in the way of his often perceptive commentary."

Well aware that his broadcast style irritates some listeners, Vitale told Fritz Quindt for the *Sporting News* (November 17, 2003), "Sure, I'm a loudmouth, a hot dog! [But] lots of people like hot dogs! . . . No critic ever said I've come to a game unprepared. You don't last 25 seasons only saying, 'Awesome, baby!'" In *Sports Illustrated* (March 7, 1994), Rick Reilly wrote, "Basically, Vitale is a former C-plus student with a very large mouth and an even larger heart who swallowed a microphone and therefore cannot be turned off. And Vitale knows it." Vitale responded to Reilly's complaint by saying, "I break all the rules. I never went to broadcasting school. I'm not blond and good-looking. I'm ugly. I'm not polished, and I talk too much. But I must be doing something right, baby, because the phone rings off the hook. Knock wood." Indeed, he remains one of the most recognized and well-known television sports broadcasters. By most accounts Vitale is extremely popular with college-basketball fans and the players themselves, who often ask him for autographs, sometimes repeating his pet phrases back to him or rubbing his bald head affectionately.

Reilly reported that, in the early 1990s, when a Syracuse University communications professor asked his class to name the one sports announcer about whom they would like to write, 70 percent of the students chose Vitale. What made that result even more remarkable is that Syracuse University is the alma mater of Bob Costas, Marv Albert, and Dick Stockton, all of whom are famous sports broadcasters in their own rights. Over the years Vitale has often been asked to compare college basketball with the version of the game played professionally in the NBA and to explain his evident preference for the former. Referring to the fact that college athletes play mostly for the glory of their schools and are not paid to play, whereas many of those in the professional ranks earn huge salaries, leading apparently to more egocentrism and a focus on individual players, Vitale told Bock, "In college, it's all about the [school's] name on the front of the jersey. The NBA game is about [an individual player's] name on the back of the jersey." Questioned about the relative frequency of sordid scandals and infractions of NCAA rules in college basketball, involving such offenses as fraud, academic cheating, and, in some cases, players' lawbreaking, Vitale told Bock that coaches, with good intentions, often take their chances with potentially or actually difficult but athletically talented teenagers. "Every coach believes he can change every kid. I did, too. But these [troubled] kids never proved they wanted to be on a college campus."

Vitale has co-written seven books about his life in basketball. With Curry Kirkpatrick he wrote an autobiography, *Vitale: Just Your Average Bald, One-Eyed Basketball Wacko Who Beat the Ziggy and Became a PTP'er* (1988; "the Ziggy" refers to his being fired from his coaching job with the Detroit Pistons). That book was followed by *Time Out, Baby!* (1991, written with Dick Weiss); *Tourney Time: It's Awesome Baby* (1993, with Mike Douchant); *Dickie V's Top 40 All-Everything Teams* (1994, with Charlie Parker and Jim Angresano); and—all with Dick Weiss—*Holding Court: Reflections on the Game I Love* (1995), *Campus Chaos: Why the Game I Love Is Breaking My Heart* (1999), and *Living a Dream: Reflections on 25 Years Sitting in the Best Seat in the House* (2003). Vitale has served as a columnist for *Basketball Times* and a guest columnist for *USA Today*. To capture in writing his speaking style, Vitale, working from notes and extemporizing, dictates his articles to editors at both publications. ESPN has released several home videos featuring Vitale, among them *Time Out, Baby!*, *Dick Vitale's All-Time College Hoops Superstars*, and *Dick Vitale's Dreamtime, Baby*, and has televised two Dick Vitale specials, *The Game of Life* (1991) and *Game Plan for Life* (1994), both of which are video recordings of motivational speeches Vitale gave to high-school players at basketball camps. ESPN's CD *Jock Jams*, which contains recordings of Vitale and others, has sold several million copies. On the Web site Dickvitaleonline.com, Vitale sells shirts, hats, bobblehead dolls, and other merchandise featuring his likeness or trademark phrases.

Notable for his generosity, Vitale has often awarded as many as five scholarships a year to the Sarasota (Florida) Boys and Girls Club. At the 1999 Dick Vitale Sports Night, an annual banquet, he helped to raise more than $600,000 for the club; that figure has since risen to $1 million. The following year the club announced plans to begin construction of the Dick Vitale Physical Education and Health Training Center, and in 2001 it elected Vitale to its hall of fame. In 2002 *Sarasota Magazine* named him one of the area's most influential citizens. At Notre Dame University, Vitale has set up an endowment, the Dick Vitale Family Scholarship, which is awarded annually to an undergraduate of Irish descent who participates in athletics or other extracurricular activities and does not receive financial aid. Vitale is a board member of the Jimmy V Foundation, which was co-founded by ESPN and the former North Carolina State University basketball coach Jim Valvano, a close friend of Vitale's who died of cancer in 1993; along with Duke University men's basketball coach Mike Krzyzewski and ESPN/ABC analyst John Saunders, Vitale co-chairs the V Foundation Golf Classic, one of several annual events the foundation holds to raise funds for cancer research. Vitale sits on the advisory boards of the Harlem Globetrotters and the Henry Iba Citizen Awards and is a member of the selection committees for the Naismith and Wooden Awards, college basketball's highest honors; he is also a member of the Associated Press voting panel that annually selects the top 25 college basketball players in the country.

Vitale has given motivational speeches to large corporations and organizations across the country. He has been on the roster of the Washington Speakers Bureau since 1987. He has made cameo appearances as himself in the movies *Hoop Dreams* (1994), *Blue Chips* (1994), *The Sixth Man* (1997), *He Got Game* (1998), and *Love and Basketball* (2000), and as fictional characters in *The Naked Gun: From the Files of Police Squad* (1988) and *Jury Duty* (1995). In 2005 Vitale filmed a segment for another movie, an upcoming drama about high-school basketball, starring Haley Joel Osment and tentatively titled "Home of the Giants." On the small screen, he appeared along with Jim Valvano as a furniture mover on a 1992 episode of the hit series *The Cosby Show*. In 1996 he was the subject of a "Top 10 List" segment on *Late Show with David Letterman*—"Top Ten Signs Dick Vitale Is Nuts!" Vitale himself appeared on the show to read the list, which included such "signs" of craziness as "I've referred to everything as baby, except an actual baby." He also appeared, in archival footage of his broadcasts, in the television movie *A Season on the Brink* (2002). Vitale has been profiled on the HBO program *Real Sports* and by such national magazines as *Playboy, Travel & Leisure, Sports Illustrated, Sport,* and *People*.

Vitale has earned many honors, for both his television work and his altruism. In 1977 United Fund named him Detroit man of the year. In 1978 the Hartford Insurance Co. gave him the Greater Detroit Community Award. *Basketball Times* named him one of the sport's five most influential personalities in 1983. He was elected to the East Rutherford Hall of Fame in 1985. In 1988 he received an Honorary Citizens Award from Father Flanagan of Boystown. The following year the American Sportscasters Association named Vitale sports personality of the year, as did the National Invitation Tournament Metropolitan Media in 1991. In 1995 the ex-NBA great Magic Johnson's Roundball Classic, an annual charity event, honored Vitale for his outstanding contributions to youth. That same year Vitale received the John Domino Award for Professional Services from St. Bonaventure University and the Empire Sports Network. In 1997 he received an honorary degree from Notre Dame University. He earned a lifetime achievement award from the Sons of Italy in 1999; the next year he was honored with the Cliff Wells Appreciation Award for outstanding service to the college basketball coaching community and the sport in general. In 2001 the College Sports Information Directors of America gave Vitale the Jake Wade Award for his contributions to college athletics. In addition, Vitale has received the Phil Rizzuto "Scooter Award," given to the most caring broadcaster in the New York City metropolitan area, and the Black Coaches Association award for dedication to youth. He has also been elected to the Elmwood Park, New Jersey, Hall of Fame.

In two of the many entertaining anecdotes told about Vitale, he once stood on his head in the ESPN studio after pledging to do just that if the underdog Austin Peay State University team defeated the heavily favored and more talented Illinois University team in the NCAA tournament, and on another occasion he allowed himself to be passed through the stands on the raised arms of dozens of Duke University fans during a game.

Vitale and his wife, Lorraine, live in Florida. The couple have two daughters, Terri and Sherri, both of whom attended Notre Dame University on tennis scholarships and earned master's degrees in business administration. At all times Vitale carries in his pocket a picture of St. Jude, the Catholic saint associated with miracles.

—C.F.T.

Suggested Reading: basketballtimes.com; dickvitale.com; ESPN Web site; *Sporting News* p7 Mar. 12, 2001; *Sports Illustrated* p68 May 14, 1984, with photo, p114+ Nov. 19, 1986, with photos, p69 Feb. 1, 1988, with photo

Selected Books: with Curry Kirkpatrick—*Vitale: Just Your Average Bald, One-Eyed Basketball Wacko Who Beat the Ziggy and Became a PTP'er,* 1988; with Mike Douchant—*Tourney Time: It's Awesome Baby,* 1993; with Charlie Parker and Jim Angresano—*Dickie V's Top 40 All-Everything Teams,* 1994; with Dick Weiss—*Time Out, Baby!,* 1991; *Holding Court: Reflections on the Game I Love,* 1995; *Campus Chaos: Why the Game I Love Is Breaking My Heart,* 1999; *Living a Dream: Reflections on 25 Years Sitting in the Best Seat in the House,* 2003

Stephen Zusy/Getty Images

Walker, Olene S.

Nov. 15, 1930– Former governor of Utah (Republican)

Address: 3135 Jacob Hamblin Dr., Saint George, UT 84790

Olene S. Walker was the mother of seven children, a veteran officer of several parent-teacher organizations, and a doctoral-degree candidate in educational administration when, in 1980, less than two weeks short of her 50th birthday, she won an elective office in government for the first time, in a contest for a seat in the Utah House of Representatives. She served eight years as a state lawmaker, losing her bid for reelection to a fifth term in 1988; during her last term she was her party's majority whip. In 1992 Walker ended a campaign for a seat in the U.S. House of Representatives to join Mike Leavitt's ticket in his successful bid for the governorship. After she had served as the lieutenant governor of Utah for nearly 11 years, she succeeded Leavitt as the state's governor, when he left that post to become head of the federal Environmental Protection Agency. Known for her grandmotherly charm, kindness, approachability, and seemingly inexhaustible energy, Walker was the oldest governor in the nation. A Republican, she was the first woman to serve as either lieutenant governor or governor of Utah and was the 15th governor since Utah joined the Union, in 1896. In her various offices Walker developed a reputation as a moderate who championed such issues as improved and better-funded public education, greater availability of low-cost housing, and affordable health care for more Utahns. Walker's attempt to win election as

governor in her own right in 2004 failed when delegates at a state Republican convention voted in favor of more-conservative candidates. Nevertheless, Walker remains one of Utah's most popular public figures, and observers believe she will be remembered among the state's most accomplished civil servants. "Win or lose," Walker told Mark Sappenfield for the *Christian Science Monitor* (April 28, 2004) shortly before her defeat at the state GOP convention, "I think I'm leaving a stepping stone to show that any individual has the ability to become governor."

A daughter of Thomas Ole "T.O." Smith and the former Nina Hadley, Olene Walker was born Olene Smith on November 15, 1930 in Ogden, Utah. Walker's parents were both educators: her mother taught in a grammar school, and her father served for over two decades as superintendent of the Ogden school district. Walker and her four siblings were raised on a farm outside Ogden, in what is now West Haven. Her early years coincided with those of the Great Depression, which began with the stock-market crash of October 1929 and ended in about 1941, after the U.S. entered World War II. Her experiences during those difficult economic times and her many farm chores, among them milking cows, thinning sugar-beet plants, and hauling hay, taught Walker to "understand the value of hard work," as she explained to Sappenfield. Popular with her classmates, Walker was elected student-body president of Wilson Junior High School in Ogden.

After completing high school, Walker entered Brigham Young University (BYU), in Provo, Utah, where she served as vice president of the student body and as a homecoming-queen attendant. She graduated with a B.A. degree in political science and a minor in history in 1954. To assuage her father's doubts about the potential usefulness of a political-science degree, Walker also earned a teaching certificate. She then enrolled at Stanford University, in Palo Alto, California, where she obtained a master's degree in political theory in 1954. While at Stanford, Walker maintained a long-distance relationship with her future husband, Myron Walker, whom she had met at BYU and who was serving in the army. She planned to travel to Italy on an academic scholarship prior to entering a doctoral program, with the goal of making a career in academia; instead, she got married, after Myron Walker was discharged from the military.

Over the next decade or so, Walker gave birth to four sons and three daughters; during the same period, the family moved over a dozen times. With the exception of a brief stint as a high-school teacher, in 1961, she devoted herself to homemaking and child care and also to working as a volunteer in whatever community her family found itself. "I was the PTA [Parent-Teacher Association] chair at every school because when you have seven children, that's what you do," Walker told Sappenfield. In 1968 the Walkers moved to the Avenues section of Salt Lake City, Utah, where they have maintained a home ever since. (Among the oldest neighborhoods in the city's downtown, the Avenues was designated a historic district in 1978. It contains primarily specialty shops and private homes.) In 1962 Myron Walker had become the vice chairman and general manager of the Nelson Ricks Creamery. In 1969 he left that position and purchased Country Crisp Foods (a potato-chip business), where he held the titles of chairman and CEO until 1996; Olene Walker served as vice president from 1969 to 1992. Meanwhile, during the 1970s, Olene Walker worked for the Salt Lake School District while pursuing a doctorate in educational administration at the University of Utah; she would work on her dissertation between the hours of 11:00 p.m. and 3:00 a.m. Walker has said that she is able to function on little sleep and has described herself as a "night person," so juggling homemaking, a full-time job, and a heavy load of schoolwork, much of which she tackled in the wee hours, did not faze her. She earned a Ph.D. degree in 1986.

Earlier, in 1980, some of Walker's neighbors had encouraged her to run for the Avenues district's seat in the Utah House of Representatives, whose 75 members serve two-year terms. (The other portion of the Utah State Legislature is the Senate, whose 29 members serve four-year terms.) Campaigning as a Republican, the party that her parents had always supported, Walker won the race to become one of only six female representatives and senators in the Legislature. In 1980 Utah's population was approximately 1,461,000; Walker represented about 19,500 of the total. She had many uncomfortable moments during her first term, which began in 1981. When legislative aides distributed printed material, for example, they sometimes overlooked Walker, apparently because they assumed that she was a secretary. Once, during a discussion of budget matters in a committee meeting, as Walker recalled to Linda Fantin for the Salt Lake Tribune (August 18, 2003), a male politician asked her rhetorically, "What's a nice woman like you doing worrying about money?" "I almost laid him low," Walker told Fantin. "But I saw a third of the men ducking their heads, so I just said, 'With what you're presenting, some of us nice women have to worry about money.'" During her first two years in office, tragedy struck her family, when her father and two of her three brothers, along with their wives, were killed in a plane crash.

Walker ran for reelection to the state House successfully three times. During her eight years as a state representative, she developed a reputation as a political moderate whose calm and soothing demeanor coexisted with uncommon energy and drive. With her strong interest in education, she worked hard to secure as much money as possible for Utah's public schools and for various literacy programs. She also championed affordable housing, to the extent that the Legislature created what is called the Olene Walker Housing Trust Fund; according to a Utah government Web site, "The fund

is comprised of state and federal funds that assist in the construction, rehabilitation, and purchase of multifamily and single-family housing throughout Utah. . . . Utahns served by the fund include those with low incomes, first-time home buyers, and residents with special needs such as the elderly, the mentally and physically disabled, victims of domestic abuse, and Native Americans." Walker also pushed successfully for the creation of a special "rainy-day" account in which the state government sets aside surplus revenues for use in the event of economic downturns. Rising through the ranks of the Republican legislative leadership, she served as the party's majority whip during her fourth term (1987–89). As she campaigned for a fifth term, in 1988, Walker hoped to become the first female speaker of the state House. During her years in the Legislature, however, her district (number 24) had increasingly voted Democratic. Partly for that reason, she lost a spirited race to her Democratic opponent, Paula Julander. Walker attributed her defeat to Julander's enthusiastic campaign; as she told Judy Fahys for the Salt Lake Tribune (February 14, 2000), "I walked the district once. She walked it three times."

After she left the Legislature, Walker remained committed to public service. She directed the Utah Division of Community and Economic Development and served on several state commissions, among them the Governor's Commission on Child Care, the Constitutional Revision Commission, and the Commission on Criminal and Juvenile Justice. In 1992 Walker began campaigning for the seat for Utah's Second Congressional District in the U.S. House of Representatives, with the goal of getting her name on the Republican primary-election ballot. Not long afterward Michael O. "Mike" Leavitt, a Republican candidate for governor, invited her to be his running mate. "That was an agonizing decision," Camille Anthony, one of Walker's campaign workers, recalled to Rebecca Walsh for the Salt Lake Tribune (November 2, 2003). "[Walker] was in the lead [in the congressional race]. But she decided she would be a more effective tool and public servant at the state level than back in Congress." In November 1992, with only 42 percent of the vote, Leavitt defeated the Democratic Party candidate, Stuart Hanson (whose running mate was Paula Julander), and a third-party hopeful. The following January Walker was sworn in as the first female lieutenant governor in Utah history. Leavitt and Walker won reelection in 1996 and 2000.

The first white settlers of Utah were members of the Mormon Church (known officially as the Church of Jesus Christ of Latter-Day Saints), who arrived there in the mid-1800s, when the territory was owned by Mexico. In area, Utah is the 11th largest state. According to the 2000 census, that year approximately 2,233,000 people lived there, placing Utah 34th among the 50 states in population; in population density, it ranked 41st. From 1990 to 2000 the population grew by almost 30 percent. In 2000 about 85 percent of Utahns identified themselves as non-Hispanic whites; 9 percent as Hispanics; 1.7 percent as Asians; 1.3 percent as Native Americans; and 0.8 percent as African-Americans. The average age of Utahns is about 27, making it the "youngest" state. (The average age of the nation's population as a whole is over 35.) According to various sources, from 50 percent to 70 percent of the residents are Mormons. Utah's main industries, in terms of the gross state product (which totaled $70.4 billion in 2001, or less than 1 percent of the total gross national product of the U.S.), are services (in such areas as finance, insurance, real estate, and private health care), government (including military installations), manufacturing (including aerospace products and chemicals), retail trade, transportation and public utilities, construction, wholesale trade, mining (copper, gold, magnesium, beryllium, molybdenum, and uranium, among other elements), and agriculture (mainly ranching), forestry, and fishing. The state's information-technology industry ranks among the nation's largest, and the tourism industry has been growing rapidly.

Though many of her duties as lieutenant governor were ceremonial, Walker wielded considerable influence in the Leavitt administration and helped to formulate substantive policy initiatives, particularly in the areas of education, literacy, low-income housing, Medicaid, and penalties for drunk drivers. During her first term she led the Healthcare Reform Task Force, whose work resulted in the formation of the Children's Health Insurance Program. She later chaired the Workforce Task Force, whose proposals led to the formation of the Utah Department of Workforce Services, which, according to its Web site, "provides comprehensive employment-related information and support services to meet the needs of employers, job seekers, and the community." During the 2002 Winter Olympics, held in Salt Lake City, Walker "needed to have two security details assigned to her," according to Sappenfield, because she worked about 19 hours a day.

In August 1996 the GOP's presidential candidate, Senator Robert Dole of Kansas, named Walker chair of the Republican National Convention's platform subcommittee on individual rights and personal safety. The subcommittee was charged with writing the party's official position on the exceedingly controversial matter of abortion. "I'm taking this as an honor, although it's difficult to see it as that," Walker quipped to Bob Bernick Jr. for the *Deseret News* (July 31, 1996). Angered by Dole's selection of Walker, who was perceived as a moderate on abortion issues, Congressman Henry Hyde of Illinois filled the subcommittee with ardent opponents of abortion who favored an uncompromising stance. The group produced a plank that advocated amending the Constitution to ban abortion but that also recognized the existence of some diversity of opinion among Republicans.

In August 2003 President George W. Bush nominated Mike Leavitt to head the Environmental Protection Agency. Anticipating, correctly, that the U.S. Senate would confirm his nomination and that he would therefore resign from the governorship before the scheduled end of his third term, some conservative Utah Republicans suggested that his successor—Walker—be designated "acting governor" rather than "governor" after his departure. The state attorney general ruled, however, that Walker's title should be "governor." Walker was sworn in as governor on November 5, 2003, along with her chosen lieutenant governor, Gayle McKeachnie, a lawyer. During her inaugural address she promised to concentrate on improving education in Utah but was otherwise vague about her plans for the state, which faced a fiscal crisis caused by increasing education and Medicaid costs. During her first days in office, she concluded that raising taxes to finance education would be impossible during a year in which state legislators were running for reelection. She instead suggested cutting departmental budgets, raising state fees, floating bonds, and shifting money from the state's Centennial Highway fund. Walker also voiced her opposition to a proposal that called for the depositing of nuclear waste in Utah.

In January 2004, after naming a commission to analyze Utah's tax structure, Walker unveiled her budget for 2005. The plan, which called for $8 billion in expenditures (3.4 percent more than the total in the 2004 budget), was drawn largely from proposals made earlier by Leavitt. Among other measures, it proposed a shift to public-school allocations of $116 million previously earmarked for roads and water subsidies—a step that the Legislature turned down. The lawmakers also gutted Walker's early-reading-readiness initiative and voted for a 1 percent raise in the salaries of state employees rather than the 2 percent raise that Walker had asked for. In last-minute negotiations in late February, Walker and the Legislature compromised. The reading program received $30 million in funding, and state employees a 1 percent raise and a one-time, $300 bonus. Reflecting on the final budget, Walker told Bob Bernick Jr. for the *Deseret Morning News* (March 4, 2004), "My priorities have been met, for the most part. We've struck a balance [on taxation], bonding is within a range I can accept. There's more one-time money than I'd like in ongoing programs, but it's OK, and we've put a small amount into the Rainy Day Fund." Earlier, Walker had announced her opposition to Utah's use of the firing squad in carrying out the death penalty, arguing that lethal injection was a more humane method of execution. In March 2004 the state outlawed the use of the firing squad, except for inmates on death row who had already expressed their preference for it over the use of a lethal injection.

On March 6, 2004 Walker announced that she intended to run for the governorship in the November election. "I have thoroughly enjoyed being governor for the last four months, but I've concluded there is still much to do," she said, according to Dan Harrie in the *Salt Lake Tribune* (March 7, 2004). Despite her position as the incumbent governor and her overall popularity with the electorate, Walker faced an uphill battle. There was already a crowded field of Republican candidates vying for the party's nomination. In addition, the 3,500 delegates to the Utah Republican Party convention, who, in May, were to choose two candidates to run in the Republican primary for the office of governor (as well as candidates for state attorney general and congressional seats), were significantly more conservative than the average voter.

Walker clashed with the Legislature in the months leading up to the convention, further threatening her nomination prospects. In particular, she vetoed two bills that had been supported by conservatives: one that provided private-school vouchers to special-needs students and one that protected parents of "mature minors" from medical-neglect charges. In the first debate between Republican gubernatorial candidates, held on March 25, 2004, Walker was roundly criticized for those and other vetoes, and the following month, over Walker's objections, Republicans in the Legislature scheduled an "override" session. The lawmakers ultimately overrode two of Walker's vetoes.

At the Utah Republican Convention, held on May 8, 2004, Nolan Karras, a businessman with legislative experience, and Jon Huntsman Jr., an entrepreneur who had served as U.S. ambassador to Singapore under President George H. W. Bush, each won more of the delegates' votes than Walker. The loss effectively ended Walker's political career. "I would have loved to be governor for four more years," she told Rebecca Walsh for the *Salt Lake Tribune* (May 9, 2004). "But I'll go back and be the best governor I can. We'll continue to work on the projects we were working on. I'm delighted to be governor for a few more months."

A prolonged drought led Walker, on August 4, 2004, to declare Utah an agricultural disaster area and request federal assistance for farmers. Later that month she announced that she was undecided as to whether to support an amendment to the state constitution that would ban same-sex marriages, arguing that though she felt marriage applied only to a man and a woman, the language in the suggested proposal might raise legal issues. Walker also presented her spending plan for 2005–06, which totaled $8.6 billion and was based on a projected 10.1 percent growth in tax revenues. This plan, which featured no tax increases yet proposed increased spending on education, state salaries, construction, and other public projects, was met with skepticism by some state Democrats. Walker nevertheless called it "a solid footprint" upon which the incoming administration could build, according to Bob Bernick Jr. and Lisa Riley Roche in the *Deseret Morning News* (December 11, 2004). At her last official news conference, in December 2004, Walker

sounded philosophical about her departure from office. "Governors are like relay runners," she said, as reported by Rebecca Walsh in the *Salt Lake Tribune* (December 17, 2004). "You run the baton for a while. And then your obligation is to get off the track."

Olene and Myron Walker, who are Mormons, have seven children (Stephen, David, Bryan, Lori, Mylene, Nina, and Thomas) and, as of mid-2004, 25 grandchildren. The couple maintain homes in Salt Lake City and in St. George, in the southwestern corner of the state. According to Mark Sappenfield, Walker "exudes a grits-and-cornbread charm that explains why legislative colleagues called her 'Aunt Bea'"—a reference to a lovable character from a 1960s TV sitcom. After her chances of remaining in the governor's office past January 2005 vanished, Walker told Bob Bernick Jr. and Jerry D. Spangler for the *Deseret Morning News* (May 11, 2004), "I'll just be a grandmother, go down to St. George and play some golf." That statement notwithstanding, in May 2005, along with her husband, she was named a U.N. missionary for the Church of Jesus Christ of Latter-Day Saints. In that capacity she spent part of the summer of 2005 in New York City, where she spoke to ambassadors from countries that have barred Mormons from entering their territory, with the aim of persuading those officials to try to reverse their nations' stance. Also in May 2005 she was elected to the board of trustees of the National Parks Conservation Association, whose mission, according to its Web site, is "to protect and enhance America's national park system for present and future generations."

Walker received the Athena Award at the annual American Express Women & Business Conference in 2004. In 2005 she earned the Distinguished Utahn Award from the Salt Lake and Utah Valley chapters of the Brigham Young University Management Society. Also in 2005 she became the first woman to be inducted into the Hinckley Institute of Politics Hall of Fame, which is associated with the University of Utah. Her other honors include an honorary doctoral degree from Westminster College, in Salt Lake City.

—P.B.M.

Suggested Reading: *Christian Science Monitor* p1 Apr. 28, 2004; (Salt Lake City, Utah) *Deseret News* B p1 Jan. 28, 2000; (Salt Lake City, Utah) *Deseret Morning News* A p1 Aug. 12, 2003, A p1 Aug. 14, 2003; *Salt Lake Tribune* B p1 Oct. 30, 2000, with photo, A p1 Aug. 12, 2003, with photo, A p1 Aug. 18, 2003, with photo

Alex Wong/Getty Images

Wallis, Jim

June 4, 1948– Evangelical minister; social activist

Address: Sojourners Fellowship, 2401 15th St., N.W., Washington, DC 20009

"Whoever wins the battle over values is going to win the American political future," Jim Wallis told Jason White for the Religion News Service (January 27, 2005). "The Republicans are comfortable with the language of moral values, but then they narrow it to one or two issues, albeit important issues, like abortion and gay marriage and family issues. A serious moral values conversation will challenge an economic agenda that rewards wealth over work and favors the rich over the poor and sees war as the first resort not the last resort." Espousing a mixture of left-leaning politics and conservative values, Wallis is among the few evangelical Christian leaders who speak out about social injustice. He is the founder of the Sojourners Fellowship, a group based in a poor, urban area of Washington, D.C., and serves as the editor in chief of the fellowship's magazine, *Sojourners*, which focuses on such issues as the environment, nuclear disarmament, poverty, and government policies.

Wallis told Wen Stephenson for the *Boston Globe* (January 23, 2005) that he agrees with right-wing Evangelicals that political decisions should be made on the basis of moral and religious values, "but then you've got to make an argument for the common good, you've got to persuade your fellow citizens that this is best for the country, that these are good things for all of us." Nonetheless, Wallis does not completely identify with liberals, who he feels are scared of talking about faith and provide

more lip service than action on social issues. "I am from the progressive world, I am from the left but I will say . . . there is no progressive, economic agenda that will [alleviate] poverty in our neighborhoods unless we begin to reweave the fabric of family and community," he said at a conference of social activists, as reported by Bob von Sternberg for the Minneapolis, Minnesota, *Star Tribune* (May 2, 1996). He explained to Gayle White for the *Atlanta Journal-Constitution* (January 19, 2002), "What you don't have is a really powerful movement drawn from liberals and conservatives who want to eradicate poverty and help people move out of poverty into dignity and self-sufficiency. . . . We need to change both the structural barriers and the cultural barriers that keep people stuck in poverty." Wallis has attempted to fill that vacuum by forming the ecumenical Call to Renewal, a group of churches and faith-based organizations across the theological spectrum that have agreed to work together to combat poverty. "Most of the world's religions believe in this concept . . . that the value of each person is the same," he told Howard Kohn for the *Los Angeles Times* (November 6, 1994). "A rich person's life is no more sacred than a poor person's. If we could only adopt this simple concept in our lives, how might the world be transformed?" In fighting for dramatic social change, Wallis is attempting to revitalize the religiously conservative but socially liberal movements that helped lead to some of the greatest social advancements in American history. "Many of the most progressive social movements in American history—anti-slavery, women's suffrage, the fight for child labor laws, and the civil rights movement—had overt religious roots and motivations," Wallis told Stephenson.

John Wallis was born on June 4, 1948 in Detroit, Michigan. He is the son of James E. and Phyllis Wallis, members of a Baptist church who raised their children as evangelical Christians. As a teenager Wallis questioned why his church was racially segregated and why the community did not do more to help the poor. As a result of his questioning, he was ostracized; even his parents had difficulty understanding their son. "To them," he told Kohn, "faith was a personal act. They didn't relate it to people's suffering on the larger scale of war or racism. But I kept asking, why do we live in this nice little white, middle-class enclave, while a mile away, black people are living in slums?" Wallis began to attend African-American churches in inner-city Detroit and later became a civil rights activist. As a student at Michigan State University, in East Lansing, he also protested the Vietnam War. He came to the conclusion that no activism could be complete without ministry to the poor. "I was not on drugs or strung out," he told Megan Rosenfeld for the *Washington Post* (August 24, 1980), "it was a spiritual process, a pilgrimage. It was a political and intellectual conversion as well as personal." After earning a B.S. degree, in 1970, he began studies at Trinity Evangelical Divinity School, in

Deerfield, Illinois. There, he continued to organize protests as he had in East Lansing, actions that led some of the school's alumni to call for his expulsion. In one memorable exercise while he was in divinity school, Wallis cut out every reference to the poor in a copy of the Bible, leaving dozens of holes in the pages. In 1971 Wallis and several other divinity students created *Sojourners* magazine, which focused on the Christian mission to pursue social justice.

Wallis left divinity school in 1972 without a degree. That year, in Chicago, Illinois, he formed the Sojourners Fellowship, an ecumenical, live-in community of Christians devoted to social justice. In 1975 he moved the fellowship to an inner-city neighborhood in Washington, D.C., 20 blocks north of the White House. In their new location the approximately 45 members of the community helped residents of the neighborhood with landlord-tenant issues through the fellowship's Southern Colonial Heights Tenants Union. They also ran a food bank and education programs for adults and teens and operated an all-purpose community center. Each fellowship member received less than $20 a month for personal expenses. "I would like our life style not to make people gasp," Wallis told Rosenfeld. "We don't want people to think we're either crazy or admirable. We're not a commune; this is not a place where people sleep around. Nor do we live a monastic existence; we're not suffering. We're trying to show that you can establish a new way of life. We can live on less than we ever thought we could."

In 1979 Wallis's work with Sojourners led the editors of *Time* to name him one of their "50 Faces for America's Future." By 1980 *Sojourners* had a subscription rate of 45,000, and Wallis was spending about half of each year traveling around the country, to provide people with an alternative to such right-wing preachers as Jerry Falwell and Jimmy Swaggart. Wallis frequently discussed the growing gulf between rich and poor and the nuclear-arms race, both of which he found inconsistent with biblical teachings. While he criticized right-wing Evangelicals for not having enough compassion and for believing in God-ordained American power, he also attacked President Jimmy Carter, a Democrat, for not following his moral convictions with regard to nuclear disarmament, human rights, and U.S. support of military dictatorships. In 1981 Wallis, along with the leaders of four other church groups, wrote the New Abolitionist Covenant, which included, among other items, a promise to bear witness against the existence of nuclear weapons. In 1983 he and hundreds of others were jailed for demonstrating against nuclear weapons in the rotunda of the U.S. Capitol. "Opposition [to] nuclear weapons is a matter of obedience to Jesus Christ," he said, as reported by Stan W. Metzler for United Press International (May 29, 1983). He also commented that Christians "cannot simultaneously love [their] enemies and plot their annihilation." Wallis was arrested again the following April at the U.S. Defense Department's test-ban site near Las Vegas, Nevada, along with 14 other people who were demonstrating to call attention to continuing underground testing of nuclear weapons. The members of the Sojourners Fellowship also arranged to follow a train that carried nuclear weapons so that it could be greeted with vigils and demonstrations as it reached various locations. In the mid-1980s the fellowship began its Witness for Peace program, in which groups of 15 to 20 activists went to Nicaragua to rebuild schools and hospitals and to help the local populace after U.S.–backed rebel attacks. Ultimately, more than 1,000 people took part in the program. "All life is sacred for us," Wallis told George E. Curry for the *Chicago Tribune* (June 11, 1985). "We want to defend life whenever and wherever it is threatened, from the beginning of the life cycle to the end, whether it be women or the unborn, or those oppressed in Central America, or workers and children in South Africa, or people of Afghanistan, suffering under Soviet invasion or whether it be on death row or whether it be all of us under the shadows of nuclear war."

Wallis's actions often brought him into conflict with conservative Evangelicals. Pat Robertson, according to Curry, has called Wallis a "socialist"; Jerry Falwell deems him and others like him "pseudoevangelicals." For his part, Wallis told Curry that the right-wing evangelical movement "is more American than Christian. The gospel it preaches is much more an American gospel than it is the message of the Bible. Many leaders of that movement are kind of religious coconspirators with established power, and they've become court chaplains."

During the lead-up to the U.S.-led Gulf War, fought in response to Iraq's occupation of Kuwait in 1990, Wallis vocally opposed the actions of President George H. W. Bush. "Are we finally ready to make the critical choices to opt for energy conservation and the shift to safer, more reliable and renewable sources of fuel for the sake of the Earth and our children? Or are we prepared to bomb the children of Baghdad if necessary to protect 'our oil?'" he wrote in an op-ed piece for the *Washington Post* (October 30, 1990). Although he was cautiously optimistic after Bill Clinton's election to the presidency in 1992, Wallis quickly became discouraged with what he saw as Clinton's failure to follow through fully on his promises. Wallis told Robert Marquand for the *Christian Science Monitor* (January 26, 1995), "Clinton makes good speeches . . . but it isn't followed with a coherent vision that includes action that means something. We need a new politics with spiritual values." Wallis was later critical of President Clinton's having lied to a grand jury about his extramarital sexual relations with Monica Lewinsky, a former White House intern. He told Cathy Lynn Grossman for *USA Today* (January 26, 1998), "There is a connection between personal morality and social morality, between personal integrity and public trust." He stopped short of completely condemning the president, however. "You can't only focus on someone's personal morality," he told Grossman. "Is he faithful to his spouse, a good parent and all the rest. [You must] look at his public morality—how he treats the poor, how he treats his enemies."

Despite his demanding work with the Sojourners Fellowship and his hectic lecture schedule, Wallis found time to write or edit many books. He had published his first, *Agenda for Biblical People*, in 1976. In *Call to Conversion* (1981), he criticized churches for failing to heed Jesus's call to help all people. Wallis next edited the books *Waging Peace: A Handbook for the Struggle to Abolish Nuclear Weapons* (1982) and *Peacemakers, Christian Voices from the New Abolitionist Movement* (1983). That year he also published *Revive Us Again: A Sojourner's Story*. In 1987 he edited *Rise of Christian Conscience: The Emergence of a Dramatic Renewal Movement in the Church Today*. He co-edited (with Joyce Hollyday) both *Crucible of Fire: The Church Confronts Apartheid* (1989) and *Cloud of Witnesses* (1991). In *Soul of Politics: A Practical and Prophetic Vision for Change* (1994), Wallis wrote of the need for the U.S. to confront the ongoing effects of its racist past. In a review of the book for the *Pittsburgh Post-Gazette* (January 29, 1995), Tony Norman described it as "equal parts political biography and spiritual tract, with Wallis expertly knitting together the disparate skeins of secular and theological thought that make him one of our most fascinating and unlikely political radicals." Other critics praised the book but criticized Wallis for not offering in-depth solutions to the problems he identified. In the *Washington Post* (January 22, 1995), for example, Jim Naughton wrote that Wallis "offers a romanticized view of the oppressed and an uninformed analysis of the middle-class. He is strident in his denunciation of our 'predatory' economic system but silent when faced with articulating an alternative."

In May 1995 Wallis was instrumental in forming Call to Renewal, a national ecumenical federation of approximately 80 churches and faith-based organizations that put their differences aside to work to overcome poverty. The organization hosts annual Roundtables on Poverty for national religious leaders and meetings about poverty that are attended by hundreds of people from many religious and secular organizations. The group also signed a declaration that stated its disagreement with such right-wing religious groups as the Christian Coalition and Focus on the Family. The declaration, as printed in the *Orlando Sentinel* (May 27, 1995), states, "The almost total identification of the religious right with the new Republican majority in Washington is a dangerous liaison of religion with political power." At the time the group estimated that as many as one-third of the total evangelical population could be considered progressive. "The public perception of a right-wing evangelical juggernaut is a false impression that we would like to

correct," Wallis told a reporter for the *Wisconsin State Journal* (May 28, 1995). In December of that year, Wallis and 54 evangelical leaders associated with Call to Renewal were arrested in the Capitol rotunda for protesting Congress's lack of action to help the poor. "The poor don't have a voice here," Wallis told Francis X. Clines for the *New York Times* (December 8, 1995). "The poor don't have clout. They don't have the special interest."

Wallis was highly critical of the welfare-reform law passed by the U.S. Congress in 1996, which made it more difficult for recipients of aid to stay on welfare rolls. He vocally challenged conservative churches to enter into relationships with poor people on more than a symbolic level and for liberal churches to turn their words of compassion into action. In 1999 Call to Renewal sponsored the National Summit on the Church and Welfare Reform. In 2000 Wallis helped spearhead Call to Renewal's "Covenant to Overcome Poverty," a petition signed by a reported one million Christians. The petition stated in part that biblical precepts and Christian obligation demand that all people have access to affordable housing and health care, be able to live in safe neighborhoods and earn a living wage for responsible work, and have equal educational opportunities. "It has become fashionable to deny poverty's existence based on the generalized assumption that we are all in the midst of good economic times," Wallis told Ira J. Hadnot for the *Dallas Morning News* (June 18, 2000). "Only yachts are rising in this tide of economic prosperity. Poor people are being left behind in record numbers." While the presidential candidates George W. Bush and Al Gore focused part of their 2000 campaigns at wooing middle-class "soccer moms," Wallis told Hadnot that no one was talking about the woman working "at the drive-in window of a Burger King" who "keeps running back and forth to a small table in the back. It is 4 p.m., and she is trying to help her children with their homework while working this window. She cannot afford after-school care or health benefits."

In December 2000 Wallis, who had voted for Gore in the previous month's election, and 20 other religious leaders met with President-elect Bush. He has since met with Bush on other occasions. In Wallis's view, the president's religious faith is sincere but incomplete. Wallis disagreed with Bush on the need for military action in Afghanistan, and in 2003 he led a delegation of religious leaders to visit with Prime Minister Tony Blair of Great Britain—a proponent of war against Iraq—to try to persuade him to change course. "Any war on terrorism that doesn't fundamentally target the eradication of global poverty is in fact doomed to failure," Wallis told Gayle White. Despite his disagreements with President Bush on military matters, he was enthusiastic about Bush's controversial plan to support faith-based charities with federal funds. In an op-ed piece for the *New York Times* (February 3, 2001), he wrote, "I don't believe such an office [the White House Office of Faith-Based and Community Initiatives] threatens the principle of church-state separation. Why not forge partnerships with the most effective non-profits, whether they are religious or secular? And why discriminate against non-profits just because they are religious?" In 2000 Wallis published *Faith Works: Lessons from the Life of an Activist Preacher.* "With an idealism firmly rooted in practicality," Marilyn Gardner wrote for the *Christian Science Monitor* (March 23, 2000), "Wallis's book, like his life work, serves as an eloquent reminder of the importance of reaching out."

More recently, Wallis wrote in an editorial for *Sojourners* (July/August 2003, on-line) that the faith-based initiative effort "is fast becoming a hollow program that merely provides equal access for religious groups to the crumbs falling from the federal table." Wallis was also disenchanted with other aspects of the Bush administration, and he found the Democrats equally frustrating. "How a candidate deals with poverty is a religious issue, and the Bush administration's failure to support poor working families should be named as a religious failure," he wrote in an op-ed piece for the *New York Times* (December 28, 2003). "Neglect of the environment is a religious issue. Fighting preemptive and unilateral wars based on false claims is a religious issue. . . . Such issues could pose problems for the Bush administration among religious and nonreligious people alike—if someone were to define them in moral terms. The failure of the Democrats to do so is not just a political miscalculation. It shows they do not appreciate the contributions of religion to American life."

During the 2004 presidential campaign, Wallis tried to convince Evangelicals that, contrary to what many of their leaders said, Bush was not the only acceptable candidate for Christians. He helped introduce a petition—signed by more than 40 Christian leaders and 40,000 laypeople—that criticized the belief that Christians could vote in good conscience for Bush only. The petition appeared in a full-page ad in the *New York Times* that was paid for by supporters of *Sojourners*. "Good Christians can vote for President Bush; I have no problem with that," Wallis said during a sermon, according to Jean Torkelson in the *Rocky Mountain News* (September 13, 2004). "But you can't ordain one candidate as God's candidate and you can't be single-issue voters." Many political observers believed that the Democratic presidential nominee, Senator John F. Kerry of Massachusetts, lost his bid for the presidency because he could not connect to citizens with deep evangelical faith. After the election Wallis became a sought-after adviser for the Democratic Party; he has since spoken before the Democratic members of both the House of Representatives and Congress.

In early 2005 Wallis published *God's Politics: Why the Right Gets It Wrong and the Left Doesn't Get It.* The book berates conservatives for not fighting for peace, the environment, and the eradication of poverty and criticizes liberals for failing to take

concrete action on those issues and to recognize the importance of faith and moral values in a healthy society. "The real theological problem in America today," he wrote in the book, as quoted by Sandi Dolbee in the *San Diego Union-Tribune* (March 3, 2005), "is no longer the religious right, but the nationalist religion of the Bush administration, one that confuses the identity of the nation with the church, and God's purposes with the mission of American empire." *God's Politics* peaked at number two on the Amazon.com sales chart and reached sixth place and fifth place on the bestseller lists of the *New York Times* and the *Washington Post*, respectively. Wallis's other books include *Who Speaks for God?: An Alternative to the Religious Right—A New Politics of Compassion, Community and Civility* (1996).

Wallis is married to Joy Carroll Wallis, an Anglican priest who is a native of England. (She reportedly served as the inspiration for a British television comedy series called *The Vicar of Dibley*.) The couple have two children and live as part of the Sojourners Fellowship. Although their Washington, D.C., neighborhood is slowly gentrifying, it is still plagued by poverty and crime. "For me, living in that kind of place was a spiritual discipline as much as prayer," he told Jason White. "Because it forced me to be conscious of what it means to live in a poor and violent neighborhood, even if in one sense I am never fully a part of it because of my options and choices. So when I am having conversations at these national levels about these issues, I know this stuff at a feeling level, at a friendship level, at a painful level."

From 1998 to 1999 Wallis taught at the John F. Kennedy School of Government at Harvard University, in Cambridge, Massachusetts. He currently speaks at more than 200 events a year and struggles to find funding for his magazine and his community. "Sojourners falls between the cracks. We are anathema to both sides," he told Howard Kohn. "The Christian Right will not help us because we talk about racial and economic justice and are opposed to war; the liberal-funding world is remarkably biased against religion." Nevertheless, Wallis retains hope. "Whenever we feel helpless and hopeless," he wrote in *The Soul of Politics*, as quoted by Tom Roberts in the *National Catholic Reporter* (November 18, 1994), "we need to understand that our situation is never as static as it may appear to be. Hope always involves the breaking open of new possibilities from seemingly hopeless circumstances. In fact, at the heart of our best spiritual traditions is the wisdom of believing that life will arise out of death."

—G.O.

Suggested Reading: *Boston Globe* E p1 Jan. 23, 2005, with photo; (Madison, Wisconsin) *Capital Times* C p1 Dec. 19, 1994, with photo; *Dallas (Texas) Morning News* J p1 June 18, 2000, with photo; *Los Angeles Times Magazine* p16 Nov. 6, 1994, with photo; *National Catholic Reporter* p25 Nov. 18, 1994; *New York Times* p9 Dec. 28, 2003; Religion News Service Jan. 27, 2005; Sojourners Fellowship Web site; (Minneapolis, Minnesota) *Star Tribune* A p24 May 2, 1996, B p7 June 3, 2000, with photo; *USA Today* D p5 Jan. 26, 1998, with photos; *Washington Post* H p1 Aug. 24, 1980, with photo

Selected Books: as writer—*Agenda for Biblical People*, 1976; *Call to Conversion*, 1981; *Revive Us Again: A Sojourner's Story*, 1983; *Soul of Politics: A Practical and Prophetic Vision for Change*, 1994; *Who Speaks for God?: An Alternative to the Religious Right—A New Politics of Compassion, Community and Civility*, 1996; *Faith Works: Lessons from the Life of an Activist Preacher*, 2000; *God's Politics: Why the Right Gets It Wrong and the Left Doesn't Get It*, 2005; as editor or co-editor—*Peacemakers, Christian Voices from the New Abolitionist Movement*, 1983; *Rise of Christian Conscience*, 1987; *Crucible of Fire: The Church Confronts Apartheid*, 1989; *Cloud of Witnesses*, 1991

Jamal Aruri/AFTP/Getty Images

Ward, William E.

1949(?)– U.S. Army general

Address: European Command Office HQ, Patch Barracks, 70569 Stuttgart, Germany

On February 7, 2005 U.S. secretary of state Condoleezza Rice announced that Lieutenant General William E. Ward, a 34-year veteran of the United States Army, was being appointed as the United States' new security coordinator in the Middle East. The assignment made him a key figure in helping to establish stable relations between Israelis and Palestinians, who have been locked in a cycle of retaliatory violence since peace talks between the two groups broke down in 2000. Ward's appointment reflects his extensive previous experience as a peacekeeper; he was stationed in Somalia during the United Nations' intervention in that country's civil war and was also the commander of an international stabilization force in Bosnia and Herzegovina, in the former Yugoslavia, in 2002. At the Sharm el-Sheikh Peace Summit, held in Egypt in February 2005, Israeli prime minister Ariel Sharon and the chairman of the Palestinian Authority, Mahmoud Abbas, pledged their dedication to ending their conflict, with the Israelis agreeing to withdraw from some of the areas they occupied and the Palestinians promising to crack down on the militant groups that carried out guerrilla attacks on Israelis; Ward has been charged with helping to ensure a smooth transition to Palestinian rule in the wake of the withdrawals. "Disengagement remains our immediate focus . . . ," Ward said of his assignment, in his testimony before the Senate Foreign Relations Committee, as quoted in *FDCH Political Transcripts* (June 30, 2005). "Disengagement success will be a function of the actions taken by both sides leading up to, during and after. . . . Both the Israelis and the Palestinians must take action to do what they stated they would do, irrespective of what the other side is doing or not doing."

William E. Ward was born in about 1949 in Baltimore, Maryland, and raised in nearby Ruxton. His father, who had served in World War II, was the manager of an apartment complex. Ward received a bachelor's degree in political science from Morgan State University, in Baltimore, in 1971, the year he was commissioned as a second lieutenant in the U.S. Army and stationed at Fort Bragg, North Carolina. He went on to earn a master's degree in political science from Pennsylvania State University in 1979 and to graduate from the U.S. Army Command and General Staff College in 1983 and from the U.S. Army War College in 1992. Meanwhile, he rose through the ranks of the military, serving as a rifle platoon leader in South Korea from 1974 to 1976 and as an instructor, and later assistant professor, at the Military Academy at West Point, in New York, from 1978 to 1982. He was the United States Army Military Community's executive officer in Aschaffenburg, Germany, in 1985 and 1986. In 1992 and 1993 he served as a commander in Operation Restore Hope in Mogadishu, Somalia, where United States forces had intervened in a civil war that had resulted in a famine and the starvation of thousands of Somalis. (The intervention saw a bloody battle in Mogadishu between U.S. soldiers and the forces of General Ali Aidid, one of several rival warlords fighting for control of Somalia; the warlords had been hijacking food and supplies intended as humanitarian aid to desperate Somali citizens. During the combat 18 American soldiers were killed.)

From 1996 to 1998 Ward was assistant divisional commander of the 82d Airborne Division, at Fort Bragg, and in 1998 he became chief of the Office of Military Cooperation in Cairo, Egypt. In the following year he was appointed as the commander of the 25th Infantry Division (Light) and as the top U.S. Army official in Hawaii; in that position he was responsible for more than 15,000 active-duty military personnel. (The "light" designation refers to the fact that the division must "[depend] on its feet instead of armored vehicles such as tanks" and must be "ready to go on as little as 18 hours' notice," as Mike Gordon reported in the October 18, 1999 edition of the *Honolulu Advertiser*.) By the time of his appointment, Ward had gained a reputation for being close to his troops, even participating in exercise drills with them. In an interview with Mike Gordon, Ward said, "I might be asking these soldiers to go somewhere where they'll die. If I am that impersonal that I don't know them, then shame on me." Colonel John Carmichael, who had served with Ward in Cairo, said to Gordon, "I think [Ward] likes to focus on mission first and people always. I think that sums up his perspective. He places a high priority on the mission, as we all do, but he takes care of the people while he does it." While in Honolulu Ward was charged with putting several Hollywood stars through basic training to help them prepare for their roles in the 2002 film *Pearl Harbor*. After working with the actors Ben Affleck and Josh Hartnett, Ward said, as quoted in *FDCH Federal Department and Agency Documents* (April 13, 2000),"These actors became ambassadors for our Army. They will tell others of their experience. As the actors portray those soldiers in the Army Air Corps in the World War II era, they will do so with honesty and respect because they gained knowledge of what it means to be a soldier."

In 2002 Ward became the commander of the Stabilization Force in Bosnia and Herzegovina (SFOR), an international task force that had been established to enforce the 1995 Dayton Peace Accords, which ended the civil war that had ravaged the former republic of Yugoslavia in the early 1990s. "I challenge the leadership of the new government to work hand in hand with the multinational and international community to take the difficult and sometimes unpopular decisions that will make Bosnia-Herzegovina a place dominated by democratic institutions, the rule of law and sound economic reforms," Ward said, as quoted by the Agence France Presse (October 8, 2002). Ward's work with SFOR also involved protecting American interests in the region in the aftermath of the September 11, 2001 terrorist attacks against the United States. "Since the 11th of September 2001, terrorism has taken on a priority for deployed forces around the world, and it is certainly a concern for the Stabilization Forces here," Ward told Guy Taylor for the *Washington Times* (December 14, 2002). "Our force-protection posture reflects it, our situational awareness reflects it, our contacts with local officials who are also involved in this process all reflect that."

Ward served with SFOR until October 2003, when he was appointed the deputy commander of the U.S. Army in Europe. While retaining that position, in February 2005—in light of the peacekeeping abilities he had demonstrated in Somalia and Bosnia—he was appointed as a special envoy between the Israelis and Palestinians in their attempts to negotiate a peace settlement after years of conflict. For decades that conflict has plagued the Middle East, beginning with disputes over the land of Palestine and then, after Israel was proclaimed an independent country, on May 14, 1948, centering on the 7,992 square miles that constitute Israel. The conflict erupted into full-scale armed combat on the day that Israel was proclaimed a state and again in 1956, 1967, and 1973. Factions of Palestinians have continually waged military, guerrilla, and political war against Israel, with the goal of forming a Palestinian state and, in the case of some extremists, eradicating Israel. Israel, in turn, has for many years—unlike many other countries—refused to recognize an official Palestinian governmental entity. The governing body known as the Palestinian National Authority (PNA) was formed in May 1994, in accordance with the terms of the Declaration of Principles, to represent Palestinians in the occupied territories. At the 2005 Sharm el-Sheikh Peace Summit, Israel had promised to give up some of the territories it had occupied, beginning with the Gaza Strip, in exchange for assurances from the recently elected chairman of the Palestinian Authority, Mahmoud Abbas, that Israel would be spared any acts of violence from Palestinian extremists. Ward's initial task was to help coordinate Palestinian security forces, which were in a state of disarray, so that they would be prepared to keep order in their own territory following the withdrawals. In announcing Ward's new assignment, U.S. secretary of state Condoleezza Rice said that Ward would "provide a focal point for training, equipping, helping the Palestinians build their forces," and keeping track of efforts to prevent violence, according to the Agence France Presse (February 16, 2005). Abbas welcomed Ward's assistance, telling Glenn Kessler for the *Washington Post* (May 28, 2005), "We have noticed and felt an American commitment, and perhaps this commitment manifests itself through the mandate of General Ward, which will expand."

In May Abbas began urging the United States to allow Ward to function as an intermediary between the Palestinians and the Israelis; Israel initially disagreed, citing the failure of previous such liaisons, specifically George Tenet, the former director of the CIA, and the retired general Anthony Zinni before him. U.S. president George W. Bush agreed to Abbas's request, however, and Ward began helping the Palestinians and the Israelis coordinate the demolition of the homes of Israeli settlers who had abandoned their territory in Gaza as part of the peace negotiations.

On June 30, 2005, after an initial trip to the Middle East, Ward gave a report to the Senate Foreign Relations Committee on the state of Palestinian readiness to police their own territory. He had found that while the Palestinians had shown eagerness to rebuild their security forces, they were far from ready to begin policing themselves. "It will take a resourcing, a training regimen," he told the committee, as quoted in *FDCH Political Transcripts.* "It will take a training program that includes discipline, that includes causing a situation where you have loyalty attributed to individuals as opposed to the institutions—the legitimate institutions—of the government." Ward told the committee that this process "will occur over time. That transformation will take time. And it does not currently exist."

Ward also addressed skepticism from some American politicians as to whether both sides were earnest in their desire for peace. "They have done things with respect to expressing their commitment to this process, but they must follow through on those commitments," he told the Senate Foreign Relations Committee about the Palestinians. "The requirement for both sides to compromise and to develop a sense of trust and cooperation remains an ongoing challenge. Most accounts of these bilateral meetings that do occur, however, are positive. And I get that from both parties."

In late July 2005 Ward told a hearing of the Export Financing and Related Programs Subcommittee of the House Appropriations Committee, as quoted in the Federal News Service (July 26, 2005), "The Palestinian security sector is attempting to emerge from a fractured, corrupt and dysfunctional structure, with separate fiefdoms and power centers, with no clear lines of control, and unresponsive to a central authority." He continued, "Our focus is to assist the Palestinians in developing a security sector that is based on the rule of law, good governance, with clear lines of authority, and responsive and responsible to the elected political leadership and to the Palestinian people." He later added, "Both sides need to honor the commitments and understandings agreed to at Sharm el-Sheikh, which are critical in creating an atmosphere conducive to furtherance of the process." In August 2005 between 6,000 and 8,000 Israeli settlers began withdrawing from Gaza, after 38 years of Israeli presence in the region; the process was completed on August 23. In testimony before the Middle East and Central Asia Subcommittee of the House International Relations Committee, Ward said, as quoted in by the Federal News Service (September 21, 2005), "Disengagement did occur, and I think we should all take note of the fact that it occurred in an organized manner and very substantially not under fire as many feared that it would." Ward continues to work with the Palestinians and the Israelis in their efforts toward peace. "It's not an overnight affair," he told the House Appropriations Committee about building up the Palestinian forces. "It is a long-term proposition. But

steps are being taken. . . . Ongoing progress is occurring to get there. But . . . it does not happen overnight."

In August 2005 Ward was appointed as deputy commander, U.S. European Command (EUCOM), Stuttgart, Germany. EUCOM, according to its Web site, is "a unified combatant command whose mission is to maintain ready forces to conduct the full spectrum of military operations unilaterally or in concert with the coalition partners; to enhance transatlantic security through support to NATO; to promote regional stability; and advance U.S. interests in Europe, Africa, and the Middle East." Ward's appointment brought with it the rank of four-star general.

Ward's numerous medals and commendations include the Meritorious Service Medal with six oak leaf clusters, the Joint Service Commendation Medal, the Army Commendation Medal with three oak leaf clusters, the Army Achievement Medal with oak leaf cluster, and the Legion of Merit with two oak leaf clusters. Ward (who is nicknamed "Kip") and his wife, Joyce, have two children.

—R.E.

Suggested Reading: *Boston Globe* A p7 Feb. 9, 2005; *Honolulu Advertiser* A p1 Oct. 18, 1999; *New York Times* p24 Dec. 26, 2002; *Washington Post* A p17 May 28, 2005; *Washington Times* A p1 Dec. 14, 2002

Weyrich, Paul

(WY-rik)

Oct. 7, 1942– Conservative pundit; founder of the Free Congress Foundation

Address: Free Congress Foundation, 717 Second St., N.E., Washington, DC 20002

One of the most influential strategists in contemporary American politics, Paul Weyrich is a key architect of cultural conservatism, a philosophy based on the idea that the United States has strayed from, and must return to, the principles of its Judeo-Christian roots. Weyrich has helped form several political action committees (PACs) and think tanks to combat what he perceives as the moral decay of American society and the scourge of political correctness. A conservative Christian, Weyrich left the Roman Catholic Church because he felt that it had become too liberal in the wake of the Vatican II reforms of the early 1960s. He has focused on such goals as the restriction of abortion rights, the prevention of gay marriage, and the promotion of religiously based social programs. He is the founding president of the Heritage Foundation, a conservative group whose self-stated mission is "to formulate and promote conservative public policies based on the principles of free enterprise,

Cynthia Johnson/Getty Images

Paul Weyrich

limited government, individual freedom, traditional American values, and a strong national defense." He is currently the chairman and CEO of the Free Congress Research and Education Foundation (more commonly known as the Free Congress Foundation, or FCF), an organization he founded in 1977 to battle what has been termed the "culture war" between religious traditionalists on the right and left-leaning secularists.

Paul Michael Weyrich was born in Racine, Wisconsin, on October 7, 1942 to Ignatius A. Weyrich and the former Virginia M. Wickstrom. His father had been a farmhand in post–World War I Germany, a country then so crippled by spiraling inflation that a month's wages could scarcely buy a glass of beer. When a priest from his village, who had moved to the United States, offered to pay his passage to the U.S., the elder Weyrich eagerly accepted the opportunity. The same priest helped him to get a job stoking the furnace at a Catholic hospital in Racine, a position he held for the next 50 years.

Surrounded by a sea of immigrant families in a working-class area—Italians, Slovaks, Czechs, and Ukrainians who generally voted for Democratic candidates—the Weyrichs found themselves among the few Republicans in the neighborhood. Paul Weyrich considered becoming a priest but ultimately decided against doing so. He explained in an interview with James Conaway for the *Washington Post* (March 22, 1983), "It would be misunderstood [now] if I said the Lord spoke to me. I didn't hear a voice. But the compulsion from within was not to do it. . . . I think the Lord was trying to save me from what was coming in the church [the reforms of Vatican II], which I never could have put up with."

In high school Weyrich gained a reputation as a fierce debater. His rhetorical skills brought him to the attention of Gordon Walker, a local businessman with Republican Party connections; Walker frequently helped Weyrich raise funds to pay for trips to regional debating contests. Weyrich honed his skills, in part, by speaking out on conservative issues to certain members of his mother's family, who were affiliated with labor unions and tended to vote for Democratic Party candidates. More often than not, Weyrich has said in interviews, his debate opponents found themselves agreeing with him.

Following his high-school graduation, Weyrich enrolled at the University of Wisconsin and supported himself by working at WLIP, a Kenosha radio station. He earned an associate's degree in 1962. On July 6, 1963 he married Joyce Anne Smigun and—with a wife to support—embarked upon a series of jobs. He spent about a year as a reporter at the *Milwaukee Sentinel* and then returned to broadcast journalism as a political reporter and newscaster for CBS in Milwaukee, where he remained until 1965. In 1966 he became a news director at Station KQXI in Denver, Colorado.

During the 1966 midterm elections (in the middle of Lyndon B. Johnson's only full term as president), Weyrich met Gordon Allot, a Republican candidate for a seat in the U.S. Senate from Colorado. Allot won the Senate race and, having seen potential in the conservative young reporter, asked Weyrich to become a member of his Washington, D.C., staff. Weyrich readily agreed, and between 1967 and 1973 he served as Allot's assistant. From 1973 to 1977 he served as an assistant to Carl T. Curtis, a Republican senator from Nebraska.

Earlier, after he had arrived in the nation's capital, Weyrich had begun to form a plan to promote and disseminate conservative ideology. In 1973 he approached the beer magnate Joseph Coors, known for his support of conservative causes, for financial aid in setting up a public-policy think tank capable of making quick responses to any government initiatives. He envisioned it as a counterpart to the Brookings Institution, which is considered liberal or centrist. Coors wrote a check for $250,000, and Weyrich started the Heritage Foundation, which advocated small government, school prayer, an end to legalized abortion, and a restriction of welfare benefits.

Weyrich was unwilling to simply respond to public-policy issues through his new foundation; he wanted to actively aid conservative political candidates. In 1974 he created a PAC called the Committee for the Survival of a Free Congress, the precursor of the FCF. With only $5,000 in seed money provided by Coors, he and his fellow conservatives began a letter-writing campaign that raised approximately $500,000 for conservative candidates during the 1974 midterm elections.

In the 1970s the United States was still struggling to recover from the consequences of the assassination of President John F. Kennedy, in 1963;

the killings of Robert F. Kennedy and Martin Luther King Jr., in 1968; and the bitter divisions in the American public over civil rights and the Vietnam War. Against this backdrop, television-based evangelism began to gain in popularity. Evangelical shows typically featured charismatic preachers who denounced the permissiveness of contemporary American society and exhorted their viewers to embrace fundamental Christian values. The audiences for those programs soon numbered in the millions. Although many viewers had previously been apolitical, they became the core membership of the modern conservative movement.

Until that time, conservatives had typically been individuals who greatly valued prudence in economic matters but otherwise sought compromise on a broad range of social issues. The new, religiously motivated conservatives, by contrast, exhibited a staunch unwillingness to compromise on what they considered key issues: they were against the Equal Rights Amendment, school busing, and abortion, for example, and favored school prayers and little regulation of certain individual liberties, including the right to bear arms. This newly politicized group (which was now being called the New Right) thus often felt themselves at odds not only with liberals, but with traditional conservatives as well. Weyrich himself frequently noted, as quoted by Dennis Farney in the *Wall Street Journal* (September 11, 1980), "We are no longer working to preserve the status quo. We are radicals, working to overturn the present power structure in this country."

Weyrich spent the rest of the 1970s working with various PACs to ensure the election to Congress of Republican conservatives, such as Newt Gingrich of Georgia. He was credited with coining the term "moral majority," which was then used as the name of an influential (but now-defunct) political action group founded by the Reverend Jerry Falwell in 1979. In 1980 Weyrich turned his attention to presidential politics and the election of Ronald Reagan to the presidency. Despite Weyrich's fiercely dogmatic personality and far-right political views, his advocacy and organizational skills enabled him and a group of fellow conservatives, among them Falwell, Howard Phillips, and Phyllis Schlafly, to arrange a meeting with Reagan. During the meeting they urged Reagan (in vain, as it turned out) not to choose George H. W. Bush as his running mate in 1980, on the grounds that he was too liberal. That such a meeting took place illustrates the growing power of the religious right at that time.

The New Right did not greet Reagan's ascent with unanimous approval, in part because its members felt that his brand of Republicanism was too closely associated with the more moderate politics of California, where Reagan had been governor. Weyrich noted in his interview with Conaway, "The problem with Republicans is that most of them in leadership positions never had to work for a living. Those people in the [Reagan] White House who have clout are from the upper crust. If you wear a certain kind of . . . fur, if you are a Hollywood star, or David Rockefeller, or one of the biggies from California, you're welcome. But if you're the average guy, who've you got speaking for you?"

Though Weyrich supported the Reagan administration's aggressive stance against the Soviet Union (which Weyrich characterized as a model of godless oppression), he was critical of Reagan's unwillingness to vigorously address such social issues as abortion. Additionally, he believed that the economic boom that was occurring was fostering the creation of a materialistic society, one in which people valued the accumulation of wealth above all else. In 1987, as president of the FCF, he spearheaded the drafting of a manifesto, "Cultural Conservatism: Towards a New National Agenda," that urged compassion toward the needy. (This ideology, which became known as "compassionate conservatism," was later embraced by a number of politicians, most notably George W. Bush, who made a similar philosophy the centerpiece of his run for the White House in 2000.) Weyrich argued that service toward others—in particular, helping poor people become self-reliant home owners—is an obligation for conservatives. The document also recommended, according to E. J. Dionne Jr. in the *New York Times* (November 30, 1987), "a substantial toughening of divorce laws, an end to legal abortion, a voucher program to strengthen private and parochial schools and a reversal of court decisions that fail to 'recognize that a general encouragement of religion does not violate the principle of separation of church and state.'" "It is implicitly critical of homosexuality," Dionne added, "although it avoids strident language." The document also made an effort to bridge the widening gap between conservatives and liberals by stressing that, as quoted by Dionne, "both liberals and conservatives have been disturbed by America's cultural drift. Both realize that a moral vacuum is dangerous to a nation. The absence of a moral base breeds a 'me first' ethic of greed and ostentation and a loss of the concept of the common good."

In 1989, during George H. W. Bush's administration, Weyrich made headlines by publicly condemning John G. Tower, the president's first choice for secretary of defense. In public testimony Weyrich declared that he had seen Tower drink excessively on a number of occasions and that he had observed him behaving inappropriately with women. Although his testimony caused a furor among Republicans, Weyrich remained unapologetic about revealing what he had about Tower. In an unsigned *New York Times* (March 2, 1989) piece, he was quoted as saying, "I myself have learned the hard way that it serves no good, either for the individual or the community, to overlook or conceal the immorality of public figures. In every case where I thought it best to remain silent so as to avoid division or scandal, subsequent events forced me to rue my decision. Such things have a way of making themselves known, and time only serves to exacerbate the situation." Soon afterward the Senate rejected the nomination of Tower by a vote of 53–47, and the Bush administration offered Richard B. "Dick" Cheney's name for consideration instead. Cheney was ultimately sworn in as secretary of defense.

With the collapse of communism in Eastern Europe in 1989 and the dissolution of the Soviet Union in 1991, the conservatives in the United States lost one of the lynchpins of their hold on political power: strong anti-communism. Even the most fervent anti-communists found much to admire in the new era of glasnost (openness) that had dawned in the Soviet Union under the leadership of Mikhail Gorbachev. Following a visit to the USSR in 1989, Weyrich accepted the reality of Soviet reform, having witnessed firsthand the new religious freedoms in that country. As Eloise Salholz wrote for Newsweek (December 18, 1989), "The emergence of democratic values throughout the Soviet bloc has brought American conservatives a measure of vindication. After a half century of opposition, anti-communists feel pleased to see the people rising to repudiate the system erected in their name. And they believe that it was Reagan's hard line on [the missile defense system] Star Wars and his insistence on a strategic presence in Europe that finally helped to persuade the Soviets to relinquish their expansionist aims."

When Bill Clinton, a moderate Democrat, entered the White House, in January 1993, the religious right found a new target. During the 1992 presidential campaign, Clinton had had to grapple with charges of adultery and draft dodging. His support of abortion rights made him a natural enemy in the eyes of Weyrich and his associates. Their efforts helped the Republicans, led by Newt Gingrich, to win control of Congress in the 1994 midterm elections. Weyrich used the National Empowerment Network (NEN), a public-affairs cable channel he had set up in early 1991, as a bully pulpit to attack Clinton's programs, notably the president's efforts to tighten gun control. Weyrich's lobbying had a considerable impact on the Republican members of Congress, who quickly pushed through bills to reform welfare, cut taxes, create a line-item veto, and prevent national recognition of homosexual marriages. Nevertheless, Weyrich remained unhappy, because Republican members of Congress were forced to compromise with their Democratic colleagues and a Democratic president in order to get these bills signed into law. He mounted numerous letter-writing campaigns and used NEN as a platform to denounce Republicans who compromised on any key conservative issue. Such Republicans included Senator Orrin G. Hatch of Utah, whom Weyrich characterized as traitorous for backing several Clinton judicial nominees, and Representative Trent Lott of Mississippi, whom he criticized for favoring a chemical-weapons treaty. David Grann wrote for the New Republic (October 27, 1997), "If Weyrich were the only conservative purging Republicans, he would be no more than an interesting character—a minor, albeit compelling, player in the history of the conservative movement. Yet he has become, in many respects, a case study of the conservative mind—a metaphor for the right's deep-seated inability to accept the compromising nature of power."

Weyrich's power waned somewhat in the late 1990s, as his cable channel collapsed and some Republican politicians began to avoid him because of his growing intransigence. He began suggesting to his fellow conservatives that they had lost the "culture war," and declared, "We need to drop out of this culture, and find places, even if it is where we physically are right now, where we can live godly, righteous and sober lives," as quoted by Alain Epp Weaver in the Christian Century (March 17, 1999). Nancy Gibbs, writing for Time (April 5, 1999), thought that such a declaration of defeat was odd: she wrote, "By so many measures, the state of the union is so sound that you have to wonder why conservatives don't just declare victory and go home. Crime is down, divorce is down, likewise abortion, teen pregnancy, drunk driving and welfare rolls. . . . We are more charitable and churchgoing than we were in the hallowed 1950s. Yes, there is sewage in the culture, but [conservative writer William J.] Bennett's books are best sellers too."

In any event, Weyrich has remained a driving force in Washington. He has criticized the administration of President George W. Bush, particularly in areas pertaining to civil liberties. In an unlikely union of the left and right, Weyrich and other conservatives joined forces with the liberal American Civil Liberties Union to criticize Attorney General John Ashcroft and the Justice Department for its Operation TIPS program, which encouraged utility workers, Postal Service employees, and trucking-company workers to contact the government if they noticed any suspicious activity. Both groups were also critical of the government's attempts to fight terrorism by having the Federal Bureau of Investigation monitor people's Internet use, church affiliations, and library records. Weyrich, who had supported Ashcroft when Ashcroft had represented Missouri in the Senate, lashed out against the attorney general's efforts to monitor citizens' activities as an example of the dangers of unchecked government power. "[Ashcroft] gave quite an excellent speech when the Clinton administration was trying to set it up to read people's e-mail, and he objected very vociferously to it and said this wasn't acceptable under the Fourth Amendment, and now he turns around and more or less advocates the same thing," Weyrich told Libby Quaid, an Associated Press writer, on August 19, 2002. In 2005 he was among the large number of conservatives who—along with an even greater number of people deemed more or less liberal—criticized President Bush's nomination of Bush's White House counsel, Harriet Miers, for a seat on the Supreme Court. (Miers withdrew from consideration in October of that year.)

Weyrich is currently a member of the Melkite Greek Eparchy, a conservative Catholic church; he was ordained as a deacon in 1990. He frequently appears on television as a promoter of conservative principles and serves as a member of the boards of several organizations. He has received many awards for his work, beginning in 1960 with the Youth of the Year Award from the Racine Optimist Club; in 2003 he was presented with the Patriot of the Year Award from the Leadership Institute. Weyrich has held various transportation-industry posts, among them the chairmanship of Dulles International Airport, in Washington, D.C., and board member of the National Railroad Passenger Corp. (Amtrak).

Weyrich and his wife, Joyce, are the parents of five: Dawn, Peter, Diana, Stephen, and Andrew. They have 10 grandchildren.

—C.M.

Suggested Reading: *Christian Century* p300+ Mar. 17, 1999; Free Congress Foundation Web site; *New Republic* p20+ Oct. 27, 1997; *New York Times* B p7 Aug. 18, 1980, with photos, B p12 Nov. 30, 1987, with photo, B p12 Mar. 2, 1989, B p10 Mar. 6, 1989, B p12 Mar. 16, 1989, with photo; *Newsweek* p25 Dec. 18, 1989, p36 Jan. 30, 1995; *Time* p47 Apr. 5, 1999, p68 Feb. 21, 2000; *Wall Street Journal* p1+ Sep. 11, 1980; *Washington Post* D p1+ Mar. 22, 1983, with photos, C p9 Apr. 3, 1991, A p13 May 2, 1993, with photos

Evan Agostini/Getty Images

Wilson, Luke

Sep. 21, 1971– Actor

Address: c/o Francis Powers & Co., 501 S. Beverly Dr., Beverly Hills, CA 90212

The actor Luke Wilson, who has starred in such films as *Legally Blonde* (2001), *The Royal Tenenbaums* (2001), and *Old School* (2003), thinks of himself as "somewhat of a hothead," as quoted by Michele Orecklin in *Time* (June 30, 2003, on-line). That self-assessment notwithstanding, colleagues of Wilson's describe him as easy to work with and endearing. His *Charlie's Angels* co-star Cameron Diaz called him "quiet and kind of shy but very

much a gentleman," according to a *People* (May 13, 2002, on-line) writer. Rob Reiner, who directed Wilson in *Alex & Emma* (2003), told Orecklin that Wilson is "graceful and easy. . . . He's what I call an unsweaty actor. He doesn't push things too hard." The director of *Charlie's Angels*, Joseph McGinty Nichol (better known as McG), asserted to Elaine Dutka for the *Los Angeles Times* (June 29, 2003, on-line), "Luke is the ultimate Texas gentleman—the antidote to your notion of a pretentious leading man. . . . He'd never allow a lady to enter an elevator after him, which is part of his charm. He reminds me of a Cary Grant or a Gregory Peck, guys who speak softly and carry a big stick."

Wilson's real-life charm seems to have spilled over into his acting career, as he often finds himself playing the suitors of characters portrayed by such stars as Reese Witherspoon, Kate Hudson, and Gwyneth Paltrow, as well as Cameron Diaz. "He has established a comfortable niche as the male ingenue: a solid, supportive guy, unfazed by high-octane women in higher heels," Orecklin observed. "He's just handsome enough to be believable as a love interest but not so pretty that he outshines his co-stars." Wilson is the brother of the actor and screenwriter Owen Wilson, who is well known for his comedic performances in such films as *Zoolander* (2001) and *Meet the Parents* (2000), and for his work alongside Luke in *The Royal Tenenbaums* and *Bottle Rocket* (1996). In the *Washington Post* (November 30, 2001), Michael O'Sullivan wrote of Owen Wilson, "With his slight but scrappy physique, broken-looking nose, perpetual smirk and that smart but devilish glint in his almost-too-pretty cornflower-blue eyes, the actor is more like the half-crazy boy next door than Rambo." While fans may debate which of the two is the better-looking or more talented actor, the brothers deny any personal rivalry; they work well together and have remained best friends as they have adjusted to their status as Hollywood heartthrobs. Until recently, they shared a house in Los Angeles. "When

I'm working on Owen's film, he's the boss," Wilson said after the completion of *The Royal Tenenbaums*, as quoted by Miki Turner for the *Seattle Times* (January 2002, on-line).

Luke Cunningham Wilson was born on September 21, 1971 in Dallas, Texas. He is the third son of Robert Wilson, who managed the local public-television station and later became an advertising executive and writer, and Laura Wilson, a photographer. He was raised with his older siblings, Andrew (born in 1964) and Owen (born in 1968). Shy and athletic as a youngster, Wilson, like his brothers, attended the all-boys St. Mark's School of Texas, in Dallas. (Owen Wilson was expelled from the school after cheating on a geometry test and was sent to a military academy.) He briefly attended a private high school in New England before leaving because of homesickness. After high school Wilson attended several colleges in succession: Texas Christian University, in Fort Worth; Southern Methodist University, in Dallas; and Occidental College, in Los Angeles. "I wasn't one of those guys who knew what he wanted to do or even thought about it," he recalled, as quoted by Michelle Tauber in *People* (March 10, 2003). His interest in sports, primarily track and field, lessened after he took a drama course at Occidental. He was especially inspired by works by the Pulitzer Prize–winning playwright Sam Shepard, who is known for such frank, character-driven dramas as *Curse of the Starving Class*, *Buried Child*, and *True West*.

In 1993 Owen Wilson and a college friend of his, Wes Anderson, wrote a short film entitled *Bottle Rocket*, about a crew of inept wannabe criminals in central Texas; they offered Luke Wilson one of the lead roles opposite Owen. "Acting came at the right time," Luke told Michele Orecklin. "It gave me something to focus on." Anderson directed the 13-minute short, and with some help from the screenwriter L. M. Kit Carson, a Wilson family friend, the novice crew entered the film in the Sundance Film Festival. Their movie caught the attention of the producer James L. Brooks, who was so impressed that he flew to Dallas to visit Anderson and the Wilsons and offered to turn it into a feature film. Brooks recalled to David Kronke for the *Los Angeles Times* that the three Wilson brothers, Anderson, and Bob Musgrave, who had also acted in the film, "were all living in this same one room. . . . Everyone who walked in was either working on [the film] or in the cast. I loved the way they were living together. You want guys living together like that to do a movie together. It was amazing to find all this new talent in this one room, in this one movie." Luke Wilson explained to Kronke that there were advantages to working so closely with his siblings and friends: "You don't have to worry about a brother's feelings, 'cause they don't have any," he joked. "It has always helped, because we didn't have to talk about stuff. It just felt natural." One subject that did require discussion was *Bottle Rocket*'s subplot involving Wilson's character, Anthony, and Inez, the motel maid with whom

he falls in love. Wilson told Kronke that when they were filming the full-length version of the picture he began "hearing these murmurs: 'You gotta deliver the romance!'" He recalled, "Owen sat me down, he talked to me about true love, and Wes had a talk about it, and I heard [the producer] Polly Platt ask Wes, 'Has he even ever had a girlfriend?' . . . I had the flu at the time and I can hear Polly outside my room on the cellular phone: 'I don't know, he seems really out of it.' And I have to go out that night and Deliver the Romance." With some pointers from Owen—"Lean forward. . . . Whenever you say anything or she says anything, be sure to lean forward. And keep your eyes really big"—Wilson soon gained skill in that aspect of acting. Although test screenings of *Bottle Rocket* proved to be disappointing (there were times when half the audience walked out), and it was not widely seen, critics wrote highly of it, praising its offbeat humor and fresh voice.

In 1997 Wilson was a cast member of several movies. He had a supporting role in *Telling Lies in America*, with Brad Renfro and Kevin Bacon, which received mixed reviews. He next appeared in *Best Men*, which was almost universally panned. In that motion picture he played a man who, upon his release from prison, rushes off to marry the woman (Drew Barrymore) who has been waiting for him. En route to the wedding, he unwittingly becomes an accomplice in a bank robbery that goes comically awry. Wilson also had a part in *Scream 2* (alternately known as *Scream Again* or *Scream Louder*), a sequel to the 1996 horror/comedy picture that enjoyed great popularity among teens. Meanwhile, *Bottle Rocket* had attracted the interest of the chairman of Walt Disney Studios, Joe Roth, who provided generous funding for *Rushmore* (1998), which Anderson and Owen Wilson co-wrote and which Anderson directed. Luke Wilson mentioned to Edward Burns for *Interview* (December 2001, on-line) that he contributed "about two pages of what Wes and Owen considered corny jokes—but they were all gold." Wilson had only a small role in *Rushmore*, which is centered on Max, a precocious 15-year-old scholarship student at the fictional prep-school Rushmore. Also in 1998 Wilson appeared in the forgettable films *Dog Park*, a romantic comedy set for the most part in the dog run of a large park; *Bongwater*, in which he played an aspiring artist who woos a young woman who is often high on drugs; and the black comedy *Home Fries*, in which he was cast as Dorian Montier, who accidentally kills his stepfather and winds up dating the older man's pregnant girlfriend (Drew Barrymore). *Home Fries* drew a lukewarm reception, but it brought more attention to Wilson than he had attracted before (mainly because he had become Barrymore's real-life boyfriend).

In 1999 Wilson co-starred, with Joshua Malina, in *Kill the Man*, a film about the travails of the proprietor of a small business that is competing with a large photocopying franchise. Also that year he appeared in *Blue Streak*, alongside the comedian Martin Lawrence, who is known for his riffs on urban life. In *Blue Streak* a jewel thief (Lawrence) stashes a massive diamond in the air duct of a building under construction right before the law catches up with him. When he emerges from prison years later and seeks to retrieve the jewel, he discovers that the building is a police station. With the aim of gaining access to the premises, he impersonates a police officer and is teamed with Wilson's character, a naive rookie who has no idea that his partner is really a crook. Wilson was especially busy in 2000: he played Heather Graham's wandering husband in *Committed* and received excellent reviews as Dink Jenkins in *My Dog Skip*, a family-oriented film set in the 1940s. Based on a best-selling memoir, *My Dog Skip* follows the maturation of a young boy against the backdrop of his close relationship with a terrier pup. Wilson also appeared as Cameron Diaz's goofy but lovable boyfriend in the box-office hit *Charlie's Angels*. (The film—featuring three female detectives who solve crimes by using a combination of martial arts, intuition, and sex appeal—was based on the 1970s television drama of the same name.) In 2001 Wilson played the boyfriend of yet another famous blond, Reese Witherspoon, in *Legally Blonde*. In that successful comedy, Witherspoon was cast as Elle Woods, an ostensibly bubble-headed sorority sister who enters law school to win back her college boyfriend. Wilson fared less well in John Carpenter's horror flick *Soul Survivors* and the virtually unnoticed films *The Third Wheel*, with Ben Affleck and Denise Richards, and *Bad Seed*.

Also in 2001 Wilson appeared in what was lauded as his best role since that of *Bottle Rocket*'s Anthony: that of Richie Tenenbaum, a former tennis champ who is tormented by his love for his adopted sister, Margot (Gwyneth Paltrow), in *The Royal Tenenbaums*. The film, which also stars Owen Wilson, Gene Hackman, Anjelica Huston, Danny Glover, Ben Stiller, and Bill Murray, was co-written by Owen Wilson and Wes Anderson and directed by Anderson. Both Owen and Luke had been slated to play the brothers Virgil and Turk in *Ocean's Eleven* (a remake of the 1960 buddy picture that featured Frank Sinatra, Dean Martin, Sammy Davis Jr., and Peter Lawford), but they dropped out of the project in favor of *The Royal Tenenbaums*. "Luke had to grow this beard for his part, so he couldn't really take any other work," Anderson told Jessica Winter for the *Village Voice* (December 18, 2001). Winter wrote, "Wilson's Richie—with his shaggy, doleful [appearance]—is the broken heart of *The Royal Tenenbaums*," and she quoted Anderson as saying, "Luke is so hidden away behind his beard and his glasses and his long hair, and he wears that headband for the whole movie—he seems kind of wounded and gentle." Wilson was pleased to portray a tennis champ (whose appearance was modeled on that of the real-life tennis player Bjorn Borg) because it reminded him of his childhood. He recalled to a writer for *Tennis* (June 2003), "My brothers and I would have spirited doubles matches, the three of us and my dad. . . . Sometimes racquets were thrown, but it was fun." To prepare for the film, Wilson brushed up on his tennis by practicing with the actor Sean Penn and the producer Barry Mendel. "[Mendel] worked me hard," he told the *Tennis* interviewer. "I finally complained, 'Ah, Barry, you know I don't have to even play tennis well in the movie. Richie plays while he's having a breakdown.'" Lucas Hilderbrand, in a review for Popmatters.com, described Richie's on-court meltdown as a "deliriously funny sequence," and Jessica Winter dubbed it "the film's tragicomic peak." The movie earned excellent reviews and received an Academy Award nomination for best screenplay.

In 2003 Wilson appeared in *Masked and Anonymous*, a film starring the musician Bob Dylan; *Old School*, a popular comedy with Vince Vaughn and Will Ferrell; *Alex & Emma*, a romantic comedy, starring Kate Hudson, that was roundly dismissed by critics; and two successful sequels: *Charlie's Angels: Full Throttle* and *Legally Blonde 2: Red, White & Blonde*. He and Owen Wilson appeared together in *Around the World in 80 Days* (2004), an unconventional take on the Jules Verne novel of the same name. In *Around the World in 80 Days*, the two Wilsons played the brothers Orville and Wilbur Wright (who are credited with designing and flying the first effective airplane); Jackie Chan, Steve Coogan, and Arnold Schwarzenegger also appeared in the film. Wilson also had a small part in *Anchorman: The Legend of Ron Burgundy* (2004), a comedy starring Will Ferrell and Christina Applegate. Wilson's projects in 2004 included the straight-to-DVD film *Wake Up, Ron Burgundy: The Lost Movie*, and *The Wendell Baker Story*, in which his character is an ex-convict working at a nursing home. Released in 2005, *The Wendell Baker Story* marked two firsts for Wilson: he co-wrote the script (with his brother Owen) and co-directed the film (with his brother Andrew). Also in 2005, Wilson was to appear in the films *Idiocracy*, *The Family Stone*, and *Mini's First Time* (none of which had reached theaters as of late October). According to the Internet Movie Database, he is currently filming *Hoot* and *Super Ex-Girlfriend*, both of which are tentatively scheduled for 2006 release.

The frequent comparisons between Wilson and his brother Owen notwithstanding, the two are very close (and are close to their brother Andrew). Wilson said to Elaine Dutka, "It bothers me when people ask if Owen and I are competitive. . . . It's not like 'my rentals are higher, but you're beating me at the box office.' . . . We love each other. I wouldn't be doing what I'm doing if it weren't for him." When David A. Keeps, writing for *Details* (March 1999), asked both men who was the finer actor and would become the bigger star, each brother pointed to the other. Luke said, "I think Owen. He's the triple threat: actor, accomplished writer, and producer. . . . This little guy puts Stanislavsky to shame," to which Owen responded, "But this guy's got the rugged good looks of Stanislavsky"—references to the Russian-born actor, director, and producer Constantin Sergeyevich Stanislavsky (1863–1938), who developed what became known as the Method, a system for training actors. The brothers' camaraderie is evident in virtually every interview. Luke was about 31 when he moved out of the Los Angeles home that he shared with Owen; the Wilson brothers and Anderson had continued living together when they moved to Los Angeles after filming *Bottle Rocket.* "Now that we're getting older, though, it's harder to sustain the team," Wilson told Elaine Dutka. "Wes went to New York and after 10 years of living in the same place, Owen encouraged me to find lodging elsewhere. I was dragging my feet, the last to let go."

Wilson shares his new home, which is only a few miles from Owen's, with a chocolate Labrador retriever named Ted and a mixed-breed dog called Brother. His romantic relationship with Drew Barrymore ended, as did a subsequent one with Gwyneth Paltrow. He said to Dutka, "At my age, my father had three sons, and I've always wanted my own family. . . . Though my characters in *Alex &*

Emma and *Old School* are commitment-phobic, I'm not. I told Rob [Reiner], 'I'm a family man without a family.'"

—K.J.E.

Suggested Reading: *Details* p76+ Mar. 1999, with photos; *Los Angeles Times* p23 Feb. 4, 1996, p12 June 29, 2003; *People* p71+ Mar. 10, 2003; www.wilson-brothers.com

Selected Films: *Bottle Rocket,* 1996; *Telling Lies in America,* 1997; *Best Men,* 1997; *Scream 2,* 1997; *Bongwater,* 1998; *Dog Park,* 1998; *Home Fries,* 1998; *Rushmore,* 1998; *Kill the Man,* 1999; *Blue Streak,* 1999; *My Dog Skip,* 2000; *Committed,* 2000; *Charlie's Angels,* 2000; *Legally Blonde,* 2001; *Soul Survivors,* 2001; *The Royal Tenenbaums,* 2001; *The Third Wheel,* 2002; *Masked and Anonymous,* 2003; *Old School,* 2003; *Alex & Emma,* 2003; *Charlie's Angels: Full Throttle,* 2003; *Legally Blonde 2: Red, White & Blonde,* 2003; *Around the World in 80 Days,* 2004; *Anchorman: The Legend of Ron Burgundy,* 2004; *Wake Up, Ron Burgundy: The Lost Movie,* 2004; *The Wendell Baker Story,* 2005

Wolfe, Art

Sep. 13, 1951– Photographer

Address: 1944 First Ave. S., Seattle, WA 98134

The internationally renowned photographer Art Wolfe has made the natural world his specialty. Wolfe has traversed the globe dozens of times with the aim of capturing images that will inspire people and encourage them to work toward protecting and preserving the biosphere and biocultural diversity: Earth's plant and animal species and ecosystems and human cultural traditions. In a typical year he shoots 2,000 rolls of film (and now uses a digital camera as well); since the mid-1970s he has taken more than a million pictures. Thousands of them have been published—in magazines, on calendars, posters, and greeting cards, and, counting translations, in five dozen books (including several for which he also wrote the text). Many have also been sold as museum-quality prints. According to Lori Linenberger in the *Wichita (Kansas) Eagle* (April 27, 2001), William G. Conway, a former director of the Wildlife Conservation Society, once called Wolfe "the most prolific and sensitive recorder of a rapidly vanishing natural world." "Wolfe can imbue even a three-toed tree sloth with a natural beauty; what he accomplishes with a lion and its cub or with a bald eagle approaches genius," Ann Lloyd Merriman wrote for the *Richmond (Virginia) Times-Dispatch* (December 17, 2000).

Courtesy of Art Wolfe

"Whether it's cultural tribes or landscapes or wildlife, I try to make [each photograph] very clean and strong," Wolfe told Laura Cassidy for the *Seattle (Washington) Weekly* (April 30, 2003). "Even if it's a very complex tapestry, it's still a clean, complex tapestry. There aren't a lot of extraneous details. There's no confusion. You look through a body of my work, whether you like it or not, there's no doubt about what the picture is about." While his work requires in-depth knowledge of species and habitats, Wolfe—a trained artist—approaches his subjects with the eye of a painter rather than a scientist. "I think he's as interested in color and pattern and light as the subject," Gary Luke, the editorial director of Sasquatch Books, which published Wolfe's book *Alaska*, told Donna Freedman for the *Anchorage (Alaska) Daily News* (June 11, 2000). "He's not just trying to document something. He's looking for composition." In addition to wild places, animals, and people in far-off cultures, Wolfe is attracted to what he calls "intimate landscapes," such as bulls'-eye designs created by iron deposits on stones in Wrangell–St. Elias National Park and Preserve, in Alaska, and the corpse of an eyeless salmon covered by a thin layer of snow. In 2003 he told Laura Cassidy, "The very last pictures I took were aerials over the Colorado estuary as it enters the Sea of Cortez in Mexico. I was just as excited to see those results as I was 30 years ago looking at my first results. That excitement of seeing has never diminished." Wolfe has rejected the complaints of conservationists who have faulted him for not aiming his lens at evidence of environmental devastation. As he told Patricia Corrigan for the *St. Louis (Missouri) Post-Dispatch* (October 15, 2003), "I prefer to motivate through the positive, to win support for issues like environmental protection with positive images, by focusing on what's beautiful on the Earth."

Wolfe regularly gives workshops in wildlife photography. He has produced three video programs—*On Location with Art Wolfe*, *Techniques of the Masters*, and *The Living Wild*—and he served as the host of *American Photo's Safari* (the title refers to the magazine *American Photo*) on ESPN from 1993 to 1995. His commitment to preserving wild lands, wildlife, and indigenous cultures extends beyond photography. He is on the board of the Wildlife Conservation Society and has often provided free photographs to environmental organizations for use during particular campaigns. He has also given talks to such groups without charge. "It really is a tiny planet," he told Brent Stovall for *PhotoMigrations* (2003, on-line). "In the last few decades, we started viewing Earth from space, and we saw how little a globe it is. There are still some wild areas left, and some fairly reasonable sized pieces of land. Just because some of these places are remote does not mean they are protected. We as a species need to take better care of the planet we are on."

Arthur Richard Wolfe was born in Seattle, Washington, on September 13, 1951. He has a brother and a sister. His mother, Ellinor Wolfe, was a commercial artist; his father, Richard Wolfe, worked as a photographer for the U.S. Navy and later as a wedding photographer. Wolfe has loved the outdoors since his childhood. His earliest memories are of hiking, camping, and fishing in the North Cascades Range. He grew up in West Se-

attle, a suburb of the city, which was still fairly rural in the 1950s; a ravine near his home is now a city park. "There were a lot of woods there," Wolfe told Bob Keefer for Keefer's Web site, bkpix.com (February 23, 2003). "Everybody had chickens and ducks and horses and sheep. There was an immediate connection with wildlife and animals. I was always one of those kids out in the ravine, investigating." The young Wolfe would bring home birds' eggs, insects, and other collectibles from the natural world. He took his first nature photos, with a plastic Brownie Fiesta camera, while he was in junior high school. "I was hooked," he told Bill Marvel for the *Dallas Morning News* (May 18, 2001). After he graduated from high school, Wolfe took a course in mountain climbing; he would bring an old 35mm camera with him on his hikes, both to record images for nostalgia and to show his friends. "It wasn't long before my focus changed," he told Tom Foust for the *Arizona Daily Star* (March 24, 1994). "Pretty soon the climbing became secondary; it became a means of taking pictures." Curious to see whether there would be any interest in his photos, Wolfe persuaded the manager of the North Face outdoor-equipment outlet in Seattle to hang some enlargements on the walls of the store. Soon, customers were asking where they could purchase the photos.

Wolfe attended the University of Washington at Seattle, where he majored in art (concentrating in painting) and minored in art education. He had no intention of making photography a career—few people earned a living as nature photographers then—and he took no photography courses. But, increasingly, he became more interested in photography than in painting. "I bristled at sitting down and painting, and then waiting for oil paint to dry," he told Corrigan. "I liked the spontaneity of photos, the ability to shoot a lot in a short time." Wolfe graduated in 1975, with a bachelor's degree in fine arts. His first magazine assignment, in 1977, entailed photographing bears on Kodiak Island for *Alaska* magazine. *Indian Baskets of the Northwest* (1978), by his friend Allan Lobb, was the first book to feature his photographs. In July 1979 "Wild Beach," a photo essay by Wolfe about Washington's Olympic Peninsula, appeared in the National Audubon Society's magazine *Audubon*. Also in the late 1970s, the U.S. Army Corps of Engineers hired him to spend six months recording on film images of the animal species living in the valley that would be flooded after the scheduled building of a new dam. Within five years of his completing college, Wolfe received an assignment from *National Geographic* to photograph long-eared owls (so-named because of the two prominent tufts of feathers atop their heads); the results appeared in the January 1980 issue. The following year the Frye Art Museum, in Seattle, mounted an exhibition of his watercolor paintings and photos. (The Frye held shows of his work in 1983, 1988, and 2003, too.) In 1985 a collection of his photos was published as the book *The Imagery of Art Wolfe*, with text by Charles Bergman. His photographs illustrated *Vanishing Arctic: Alaska's National Wildlife Refuge* (1988), by T. H. (Thomas Henry) Watkins, the longtime editor of the Wilderness Society's magazine. The next year others among his photos of Alaska appeared in *Alakshak: The Great Country*, with text by Art Davidson. During the first year of Bill Clinton's presidency, the White House chose Wolfe's next collaborative effort with Davidson, *Light on the Land* (1991), as a "gift of state," to be presented to select visiting dignitaries. Wolfe's first published collection of landscape photos, *Light on the Land* includes Davidson's retellings of myths and legends.

During his three-decade-long career, Wolfe has traveled roughly nine months each year, sometimes to areas considered dangerous for geographic, political, or other reasons. He prepares for his expeditions by carefully researching the places he plans to visit and their resident wildlife (and, in some cases, the cultures of human inhabitants). By his own account, he attempts to visualize his photographs before he reaches his destinations, so he has some idea of what he will be looking for; at the same time, he keeps an eye out for the unexpected. While on his trips he works from before dawn until dark. Wolfe's agent, Patrick Donehue, currently vice president of photographer relations at Corbis, a stock-photography provider, told Darlene Pfister for the Minneapolis, Minnesota, *Star Tribune* (October 18, 1998), "What sets Arthur apart is that he is absolutely relentless in the pursuit of the imagery he wants to make. Once he decides he wants a certain image, he won't give up on it. For this type of work, that means you have to wait for the right light, the right climatic conditions, and with wildlife, for the right action to happen in front of you. That takes patience and determination, and Art has that, particularly the determination." Waiting for suitable conditions or the right moment may take 10 days or more. Since Wolfe's travel expenses usually consume about half of whatever advance he receives for a proposed book, he works on five or six books concurrently. "That's a point most aspiring photographers miss," he told Glenn Giffin for the *Denver Post* (May 25, 1997). "They think there's lots of money in fine art books, but there's NO money in art books."

Lack of financial gain notwithstanding, in the 1990s Wolfe provided all the photos for two dozen books in addition to *Light on the Land*. For *The Kingdom: Wildlife in North America* (1990), with text by the Montana-based biologist Douglas Chadwick, he concentrated on endangered and threatened species. *Owls: Their Life and Behavior: A Photographic Study of the North American Species* (1990), which has text by Julio de la Torre, led Mark Wilson to write for the *Boston Globe* (December 16, 1990), "Pictures just don't get any better." *Chameleons: Dragons in the Trees* (1991), *Masters of Disguise: A Natural History of Chameleons* (1992), and *Hiding Out: Camouflage in the Wild* (1994) contain text by James Martin. Wolfe collabo-

rated with William Ashworth for *Bears, Their Life and Behavior: A Photographic Study of the North American Species* (1992) and *Penguins, Puffins and Auks: Their Lives and Behavior: A Photographic Study of the North American and Antarctic Species* (1993). Of the latter book, T. H. Watkins wrote for the *Washington Post* (December 5, 1993), "If there is a better introduction to the special wonder of 'the birds that walk like us'. . . it is hard to imagine what it could be."

Wolfe collaborated with Art Davidson on *Endangered Peoples* (1993), which illustrates the difficulties indigenous people face because of globalization and other outside pressures; its foreword is by the Nobel Peace Prize laureate Rigoberta Menchú Tum of Guatemala. The term "indigenous" refers to people who live where many generations of their ancestors dwelled; whose culture and society distinguish them from others in their regions; and, as explained at terralingua.org, whose customs, traditions, or special laws or rules wholly or partially regulate their status. *Endangered Peoples* offers photos (by John Isaac as well as Wolfe) of members of such far-flung peoples as the Cree Indians in Canada, the Kelabit tribespeople of Malaysia, and the Mauber of East Timor. "I was after a strong style of photograph," Wolfe told John Marshall for the *Seattle Post-Intelligencer* (November 22, 1993), "one that would make you connect with their faces. I wanted to challenge you to look at indigenous people closely, really look into their eyes. Because nobody wants to hear more about the ozone layer or look at another starving child. So you have to connect—you have to make them want to get involved." According to Marshall, *Endangered Peoples* "manages to mingle outrage and compassion, wrenching personal stories and dispiriting statistics." The proceeds of the book went to organizations that help indigenous peoples. Wolfe's pictures of indigenous peoples also illustrate his book *Tribes* (1997).

Wolfe worked with Martha Hill, a former photo editor for *Audubon* magazine, on *The Art of Photographing Nature* (1994), a guide for both novice and advanced photographers. Writing for the Associated Press (August 19, 1994), Rick Sammon called it "an easy-to-read and inspiring book, one that can expand the photographic horizons of even seasoned photographers." The year 1994 also saw the publication of *Migrations: Wildlife in Motion*, with text by the science writer Barbara Sleeper. *Migrations*, which Wolfe has claimed was intended more as a work of art than simply a record of reality, includes photos that he and his staff digitally altered to create stronger patterns—for instance, by filling in gaps in pictures of herds by duplicating images of individual animals that appear elsewhere in the photo. Wolfe informed readers in the book's introduction that some of the photos had been digitally altered, but he did not specify which photos or in what ways—an omission that he later described as a mistake. In 1996 Galen Rowell, a renowned outdoor photographer who disapproved of such manipulations, sent the *Denver Post* examples from Wolfe's book; subsequently, the newspaper reported that Wolfe had changed one-third of the photos in *Migrations*. That revelation sparked controversy among nature photographers, with purists complaining that Wolfe had damaged the trust between photographers and readers, who believe that what they are seeing on the page is exactly what the photographer saw through the viewfinder; after all, bookstores shelved *Migrations* in their nature sections, not their art sections. Others pointed out that manipulation of images has occurred virtually since the birth of photography, when photographers developed their own black-and-white prints in chemical baths. "People are still debating with me that this is a biology book, that it's not art," Wolfe told M. L. Lyke for the *Seattle Post-Intelligencer* (April 22, 1996). "Can you imagine that? Somebody debating with the artists whether a book is art or nature? I find it presumptuous." He also said that he believed some of the criticism grew out of jealousy and that all photographers distort reality in subtle ways with double exposures, wide-angle lenses, density filters, or false lighting. "I want the freedom to push the limits of my craft, to embrace the latest technology, to take chances, to challenge myself in new ways," he told Lyke.

Wolfe shot most of the photos in *Wild Cats of the World* (1995) in zoos and animal sanctuaries. "I don't have enough years in my life to go out and shoot all these tiny cats in jungles," he told M. L. Lyke. "It would be a herculean effort. It would take 25 years, and you still wouldn't get them all." For *In the Presence of Wolves* (1996), he again digitally altered some photos for artistic purposes. "I wanted to make the images more like paintings, to create something not photographically obtainable, like a pack of wolves winding through a mysterious forest," he told Lyke. In photographing the images published in *Rhythms from the Wild* (1997), he used very long exposure times to capture creatures in motion; many of the intentionally blurry images show only one animal in focus. He joined with Donald F. Bruning, the Bronx Zoo's longtime curator of birds, to produce *Bald Eagles: Their Life and Behavior in North America* (1997), and with Ghillean Prance, who directed the Royal Botanic Garden, at Kew, England, from 1988 to 1999, on *Rainforests of the World: Water, Fires, Earth & Air* (1998). In 2000, for the first time, Wolfe self-published a book. Titled *The Living Wild*, it "look[s] at wildlife worldwide in the last three years of the millennium,"as he told Mark Edward Harris for *Outdoor Photographer* (on-line). "The intent of the book is for it to be a retrospective view of the state of wildlife." Among the 140 animal species pictured is the Bornean bay cat, which had never been captured on film before, and the notoriously elusive giant panda, whose population in the wild is believed to total no more than 1,000. The zoologists Richard Dawkins and George B. Schaller, the primatologist Jane Goodall, the conserva-

tionist John C. Sawhill, and William Conway wrote essays for the book, whose theme is the conservation of animal species and their environments. *The Living Wild* was named one of the year's top 10 books by the Independent Book Publishers Association; it won a National Outdoor Book Award and a Western U.S. Book Design Award.

Wolfe's press, Wildlands, published his book *Africa*, with a foreword by Jane Goodall and text by Michelle A. Gilders, in 2001, and *One World, One Vision: The Photographs of Art Wolfe* in 2003, in conjunction with an exhibit of his work at the Frye Art Museum. His fourth self-published book, *Edge of the Earth, Corner of the Sky* (2003), is a collection of landscapes. "This one is a personal book," Wolfe told Corrigan. "It took a lot of time and energy, and I'm really proud of it. I love to inspire people, and I hope this book affects people." *Edge of the Earth, Corner of the Sky* received an Independent Book Publishers Association award, the Benjamin Franklin Book Award from the Publishers Marketing Association, and an International Photography Award, among other honors. Wolfe's most recent books, published in 2004, include *Northwest Wild* and *Alaska Wild*, both subtitled *Celebrating Our Natural Heritage*; *Elements: Earth, Air, Fire, Water*; and *Cats: Smithsonian Answer Book*. *Vanishing Act*, with text by Barbara Sleeper, was scheduled for publication in late 2005. His photos illustrate the children's books *O Is for Orca: A Pacific Northwest Alphabet Book* (1995), *1, 2, 3 Moose: A Pacific Northwest Counting Book* (1996), *Animal Action ABC* (1996), and *C Is for Coyote: A Southwest Alphabet Book* (2002).

Wolfe lives by himself in Seattle. Currently, he has nine employees; an intern from a local school helps out, too. He has set up a nonprofit foundation that, in the event of his untimely demise, would further his interests in conservation through the administration of his body of work. The prestigious graphics and design magazine *Graphis* included his books *Light on the Land* and *Migrations* on its list of the 100 best books published worldwide in the 1990s. Wolfe was named Photographer of the Year by *PhotoMedia* magazine in 1996 and Outstanding Nature Photographer of the Year in 1998 by the North American Nature Photography Association. The National Audubon Society awarded him its inaugural Rachel Carson Award, in 1998, for his work in support of the national wildlife-refuge system. The Columbia University School of Journalism honored him in 2000 with its Alfred Eisenstaedt Magazine Photography Award, named for one of the 20th century's premier photographers.

—G.O.

Suggested Reading: *Anchorage Daily News* K p1 Feb. 23, 1997; artwolfe.com; *Denver Post* D p7 May 25, 1997, with photo, I p8 June 8, 1997; (Minneapolis, Minnesota) Star Tribune E p1 Oct. 18, 1998, with photos; *Outdoor Photographer* (on-line), with photo; *PhotoMedia Magazine* (on-line) Spring/Summer 2003; *Seattle Post-Intelligencer* C p1 Apr. 22, 1996, with photos; *Seattle Times* J p1 Nov. 17, 1991, with photos; *Seattle Weekly* p74 Apr. 30, 2003, with photos; *St. Louis Post-Dispatch* E p1 Oct. 15, 2003, with photos

Selected Books: *The Imagery of Art Wolfe*, 1985; *Rhythms from the Wild*, 1997; *Tribes*, 1997; *The Living Wild*, 2000; *One World, One Vision*, 2003; with Allan Lobb—*Indian Baskets of the Northwest*, 1978; with Art Davidson—*Alakshak: The Great Country*, 1989, *Light of the Land*, 1991, *Endangered Peoples*, 1993; with Barbara Sleeper—*Migrations*, 1994, *Wild Cats of the World*, 1995, *Primates*, 1997; with Barbara Wilson—*Icebergs and Glaciers: Life at the Frozen Edge*, 1995; with Brenda Peterson—*Pacific Northwest*, 1998; with Chris Childs—*Colorado*,

2000, *Elements*, 2004; with Donald Bruning—*Bald Eagles: Their Life and Behavior in North America*, 1997; with Douglas Chadwick—*Kingdom: Wildlife in North America*, 1990; with Eric S. Grace—*Natures of Lions*, 2001; with Ghillean T. Prance—*Rainforests of the World*, 1998: with Gregory McNamee—*In the Presence of Wolves*, 1995; with James Martin—*Masters of Disguise: A Natural History of Chameleons*, 1992, *Hiding Out: Camouflage in the Wild*, 1994, *Frogs*, 1997; with Julio de la Torre—*Owls: Their Life and Behavior*, 1990; with Mark Brazil—*Wild Asian Primates*, 2000; with Michelle A. Gilders—*Africa*, 2001; with Nick Jans—*Alaska*, 2000; with Peter Jensen—*California*, 2001; with Peter Potterfield—*The High Himalaya*, 2001; with William Ashworth—*Bears, Their Life and Behavior*, 1992, *Penguins, Puffins and Auks*, 1993

Chris Brown/Courtesy of Wolfram Research Inc.

Wolfram, Stephen

Aug. 29, 1959– Physicist; software executive

Address: Wolfram Research Inc., 100 Trade Centre Dr., Champaign, IL 61820-7237

"I've been lucky enough to do quite a few different kinds of things," the physicist and computer-software entrepreneur Stephen Wolfram told Tim Studt for *R&D Magazine* (November 1, 2002, online), "and the reason I do science is simple: I really like it. I like discovering things, and particularly I like building new intellectual structures. My busi-

ness enterprises have been successful enough that I have the financial freedom to pursue whatever I want, and what I want is to do science." Wolfram published his first scientific paper in 1975 at age 15. During the next 15 years, he wrote dozens of articles, alone or with others, for prestigious journals on topics related to particle physics, cosmology, mathematics, computation theory, technical computing, and cellular automata. He was among the first group of people to win a MacArthur Foundation Fellowship, in 1981; he remains the youngest person ever to win that honor, popularly known as the "genius grant." After brief stints at the California Institute of Technology, the Institute for Advanced Study, and the University of Illinois at Urbana-Champaign, he left academia to found Wolfram Research, whose main product has been Mathematica, an innovative mathematical software program. The proceeds from his company freed him to pursue his research independently. Wolfram—whom the renowned physicist Richard Feynman once called "astonishing"—has concluded that science has been proceeding in the wrong direction for the past 300 years. He maintains that, despite remarkable advances, science has been unable to solve many of the great mysteries of the universe because of a fundamental error in methodology. Instead of using mathematics to try to calculate laws of nature, Wolfram believes that scientists ought to think of the universe as a giant computer generating the great complexity of nature by running programs based on simple rules. To that end, he spent more than a decade in seclusion, conducting computer experiments to see if he could approximate some of the processes of nature. In 2002 he reemerged, having completed his 1,192-page book, *A New Kind of Science*. In it he wrote, as quoted by Steven Levy in *Wired* (June 2002, online), "I have little doubt that within a matter of a few decades what I have done will have led to some dramatic changes in the foundations of technology—and in our basic ability to take what the universe provides and apply it for our own human purposes." Wolfram's friend Terrence Sejnowski, a computational neurobiologist, told Michael S. Malone for *Forbes* (November 27, 2000, on-line), "Steve Wolfram is the smartest scientist on the planet, and if anyone is capable of creating a new science, he is the one."

Stephen Wolfram was born in London, England, on August 29, 1959. His brother, Conrad Wolfram, who is about 10 years younger, lives in Great Britain, where he currently serves as the director of strategic and international development of Wolfram Research. His father, Hugo Wolfram, is a textile manufacturer; he has also written at least two novels. His mother, Sybil Wolfram, now deceased, taught philosophy at Oxford University; she was also a cultural anthropologist. Her writings include the books *In-laws and Outlaws: Kinship and Marriage in England* (1987) and *Philosophical Logic: An Introduction* (1989). By his own account, Wolfram was a difficult boy, one whose babysitters seldom worked for the family for long. "I was viewed as a hopeless, crazy child," he told G. A. Taubes for *Fortune* (April 11, 1988). "My parents concluded that I was 'impossibly psychologically confused and would never get anywhere in life.'"

At age 10 Wolfram decided he wanted to be a scientist and began reading scientific journals. From 1967 to 1972 he attended the Dragon School, a famous preparatory school in Oxford. At 13 he won a scholarship to Eton College, one of England's most exclusive boarding schools (equivalent, in terms of the ages of students, to an American high school); he attended as a so-called King's Scholar. He received prizes in various subjects at Eton and earned money while there by doing other students' homework and designing computer games for them. By age 14 he had written a book (which was never published) on particle physics. According to a timeline on his Web site, in 1973 he constructed his first computer programs, using an Elliott 903C, a commercial computer that was still a rarity, especially in schools; also that year he conducted his "first scientific computer experiments," in his words. In 1975 the 15-year-old Wolfram published his first paper, in the *Australian Journal of Physics*. Feeling bored at school, he left Eton after four years, and, at age 17, won a scholarship to Oxford University. In 1976, before he entered St. John's College (one of Oxford's 39 colleges), he worked in the theory division of the Rutherford Appleton Laboratory, in Oxfordshire. Also in 1976 he published his second scientific paper, "Neutral Weak Interactions and Particle Decays," in the journal *Nuclear Physics*. In the summer of 1977, Wolfram worked with the Theoretical High-Energy Physics Group at the Argonne National Laboratory, operated by the University of Chicago, in Illinois. (The Argonne lab later became a facility of the U.S. Department of Energy.) While there he co-wrote, with two others, a pa-

per titled "Quantum-Chromodynamic Estimates for Heavy-Particle Production"; published in 1978 in *Physical Review*, it is considered a seminal work in the field. During that period he also began to link particle physics and cosmology; he revealed his findings in "Heavy-Particle Production by Cosmic Rays" and "Abundances of New Stable Particles Produced in the Early Universe," both published in *Physics Letters* in early 1979.

Wolfram had not yet earned a degree from Oxford when, in 1978, he accepted an invitation from Murray Gell-Mann, who had won the Nobel Prize in physics in 1969 for his work on the theory of elementary particles, to enter the graduate program in physics at the California Institute of Technology (Caltech), in Pasadena. In collaboration with Geoffrey C. Fox, in 1978 he invented what are known as Fox-Wolfram variables, which have been widely used in particle-physics experiments as a means of characterizing the overall "shapes" of particle-interaction events. He also discovered what was labeled the Politzer-Wolfram upper bound on the mass of quarks. (H. David Politzer, another Caltech researcher, earned the Nobel Prize in physics in 2004.) In addition, he began developing SMP (Symbolic Manipulation Program), a computer program for doing algebra. (For a description of it, see his 1981 article "SMP: A Symbolic Manipulation Program," which appears on Wolfram's Web site.)

Also during this extremely productive period, according to his timeline, Wolfram developed the standard quantum chromodynamical (QCD) approach to the simulation of events involving subatomic particles (QCD being the theory of how two kinds of subatomic particles, quarks and gluons, interact with themselves and one another); described the "basic phenomenon of inflationary cosmology" (a theory associated with Alan H. Guth, then at Stanford University, that offers a description of events during a fraction of the first second of the creation of the universe); and "carried out [the] first complete calculation" of the generation of matter-antimatter asymmetry. The quality of Wolfram's work so impressed professors at Caltech that the university awarded him a Ph.D. in theoretical physics in 1979, when he was 20 years old. In 1980 he joined the school's faculty.

Wolfram earned a MacArthur Foundation grant in 1981, the first year that those fellowships were distributed; his award totaled $128,000. According to the MacArthur Foundation Web site, the grants reward people of "exceptional creativity" who have shown "promise for important future advances based on a track record of significant accomplishment, and potential for the fellowship to facilitate subsequent creative work." Kenneth W. Hope, an administrator of the fellowship, described Wolfram to Robert Lee Hotz for the MIT publication *Technology Review* (October 1997) as "so remarkably smart. He dazzled a lot of people."

By the early 1980s Wolfram had begun to feel dissatisfied with theoretical physics and with mathematics-based science in general. Whereas Isaac Newton and Albert Einstein, respectively, had discovered mathematical equations to formulate a law of gravity and to show the equivalence between energy and matter, mathematics had proved less useful in explaining complex phenomena. The gravitational interaction of two bodies in space could be expressed mathematically, but when three or more bodies were involved, the mathematics became prohibitively complex. Instead of the mathematical models science has relied upon since Newton, Wolfram wondered if computational models, in which a set of relatively simple initial rules produces complex results, might explain natural phenomena better. Perhaps, understanding the universe required only the discovery of those rules, rather than the devising of complex equations. He wondered, in other words, if natural phenomena behaved like computers.

In 1981 Wolfram started delving into the field of cellular automata (CAs), which originated with the eminent mathematicians John von Neumann and Stanislaw Ulam. CAs are dynamic systems that affect squares, or cells, according to a programmed rule. The most famous example of a cellular automaton is the Game of Life, created by the Cambridge mathematician John Horton Conway. Cellular automata consist of a collection of identical units called "cells" and a simple rule for assigning a color to each cell. The cells can be arranged in any uniform way, such as in a line, square, or cube, so long as each cell has the same shape neighborhood as all the others. In each step, each cell updates its own color just by taking the colors in its neighborhood and applying the rule. In the very simplest two-color cellular automata, each cell depends on its immediate left and right neighbors. This means that there are eight combinations of possible colors in its neighborhood, and therefore there are 2^8 (256) different possible rules for updating the colors of the cells. Inspired by the idea of complexity arising from simplicity, Wolfram began enumerating all cases of CA rules and examining patterns that resulted.

In 1982, after quarreling with Caltech administrators over the rights to SMP, Wolfram left Caltech for the Institute for Advanced Study, an independent, private facility in Princeton, New Jersey, where he continued to pursue his work with computers. That year he published the scientific paper "Cellular Automata as Simple Self-Organizing Systems." For some months he felt disappointed that his CA programs were not generating complexity on a par with that found in nature. Then, in June 1984, he discovered Rule 30, a simple CA capable of generating great complexity and apparent randomness. "It took me several years to absorb how important this was," Wolfram said, as Michael Malone reported. "But in the end, I realized that this one picture contains the clue to what's perhaps the most long-standing mystery in all of science:

where . . . the complexity of the natural world comes from." Wolfram's work with CAs was influential; it has been cited in more than 10,000 articles and gave rise to the field of complexity theory. However, Wolfram felt that most other researchers were missing the point of his studies, including his colleagues at the Institute for Advanced Study.

In 1986 Wolfram left Princeton for the University of Illinois at Urbana-Champaign, where he established his own institute, the Center for Complex Systems Research. That year he began working on Mathematica, a programming language building on the ideas of SMP. Developed by Wolfram and his assistants over the course of two years, Mathematica was not only capable of performing applied algebra and calculus; it also calculated complex equations almost instantaneously and generated three-dimensional models that enabled users to visualize problems. Wolfram packaged the language into a software application, also called Mathematica.

In 1988 Wolfram left the University of Illinois and started Wolfram Research to market the product. One of his objectives was to free himself financially to pursue his research outside the confines of academia and government agencies. "This business about begging for money from the government is for the birds," Wolfram told Taubes. "Personally, if I'm going to go out and raise money for my research, I much prefer to deal with smart business people who run venture capital firms than with the bozos the government employs to administer funds." With more than two million users, Mathematica has become the most widely used mathematics program—and it has made Wolfram wealthy. By 1991 he was running Wolfram Research mainly from home, via phone and E-mail. The rest of his time, from the evenings to the early morning hours, he spent in his soundproofed office working on his computational model of the universe. "He dropped totally out of the scene in every sense of the word," Terrence Sejnowski told Steven Levy in 2002. "He hasn't published a word, he doesn't go to meetings. He's in a self-made isolation center." Tucked away in his office and surrounded by such monumental scientific treatises as Newton's *Philosophiae Naturalis Principia Mathematica* and Charles Darwin's *On the Origin of Species*, Wolfram set out to complete his own masterpiece.

In 2002, after more than 10 years of work and—by his own account—100 million keystrokes, Wolfram self-published his opus, *A New Kind of Science*. Because of the many high-definition graphics it contains, he did not trust the book to established publishers. The theme of the book is that computation is better than mathematics for revealing the simplicity underlying nature's complex phenomena. Wolfram began the book with these words: "Three centuries ago science was transformed by the dramatic new idea that rules based on mathematical equations could be used to describe the natural world. My purpose in this book is to initiate another such transformation, and to introduce a new kind of science that is based on the much more general types of rules that can be embodied in simple computer programs." Wolfram postulated the theory of computational equivalence, which states that beyond a certain amount of complexity, all natural phenomena—from the workings of the human brain to the creation of weather patterns— are in essence equally complex. "The aphorism that weather has a mind of its own may be less silly than you might assume," Wolfram told Michael Arndt for *BusinessWeek* (May 27, 2002). "The weather represents computations as sophisticated as anything in our brains." Other things that Wolfram sought to explain using his new computational science are time's forward-only direction; stock-market patterns (Wolfram's theories in this area are already being applied by some brokerage firms); the possibility of building computers at the atomic level; and the shapes of natural objects. Among the evidence that he cited in support of his theory was the resemblance of some of his CA programs to patterns in nature. Pictures of one of his CAs, for example, look exactly like a textile cone shell belonging to a mollusk that lives in deep mud. Wolfram maintains that the patterns that develop from nature's algorithms are more of a limiting factor on the variety of life than is natural selection. "I've come to believe," he told Malone, "that natural selection is not all that important."

A New Kind of Science was one of the most highly anticipated science books in years. It quickly became a top seller on Amazon.com; the 50,000 copies in its first printing sold almost immediately, and a second printing soon went on sale. Reviews were mixed, though most experts agree that it will take a long time before Wolfram's book can be properly evaluated. In *Nature* John L. Casti, a mathematician with the Santa Fe Institute, in New Mexico, gave *A New Kind of Science* a ringing endorsement, as did Gregory J. Chaitin, an IBM math guru, and Terrence Sejnowski. However, Freeman Dyson, a respected physicist with the Institute for Advanced Study, pronounced it "worthless!," as John Cornwell reported in the London *Sunday Times* (June 2, 2002). In *New Scientist* (July 6, 2002), Robert Matthews accused Wolfram of attempting to tear down the foundations of science without offering anything substantial to replace it. "Wolfram has seen what he thinks is a surprising degree of complexity arising from simple rules," Matthews wrote, "and believes this might tell us about some set of simple causes behind our complex world. But he doesn't provide much more to go on than that." As an example, Matthews cited Wolfram's discussion of turbulence in fluids, a deceptively complex scientific riddle that Einstein maintained was an important challenge for science. Wolfram devised a simple algorithm for turbulence that produces results similar to but not exactly like real turbulence, which, Matthews contended, is no better than what other scientists have accomplished using mathematics. Furthermore,

many scientists have accused Wolfram of neglecting to give credit to others for their ideas. In the *Boston Globe* (June 19, 2002), Gareth Cook noted that Wolfram's central premise of complexity arising from simplicity was elaborated upon by Alan Turing in 1936, when he proposed that a theoretical machine following a simple "definite method" (essentially an algorithm) consisting of elementary operations on paper tape could solve any mathematical or logical problem. "The ideas are good ideas, and I am in sympathy with them," Seth Lloyd, a physicist at the Massachusetts Institute of Technology (MIT), told Cook. "But most of them were thought of by other people over the last 50 or 100 years." Conversely, George Johnson wrote for the *New York Times* (June 9, 2002, on-line), "No one has contributed more seminally to this new way of thinking about the world. Certainly no one has worked so hard to produce such a beautiful book. It's too bad that more science isn't delivered this way."

Since the publication of his book, Wolfram and his family have moved from Chicago to the Boston area. He and his wife, who is a mathematician, have four children. Wolfram has said that he will likely continue to pursue the basic algorithm that he believes is at the foundation of the universe. He told Levy, "I think there will be a time when one will sort of hold those lines of code in one's hand, and that is the universe. And what does that mean? . . . In a sense, that is a very unsatisfying conclusion, that sort of everything that's going on, everything out there, is all just five lines of code we're running." Levy wrote, "If he is right, his book indeed belongs to history. Either way, the world is about to reckon with a scientist who's making the biggest leap imaginable: remaking science itself, with only his computer and his brain."

—P.G.H./T.J.F.

Suggested Reading: *Boston Globe* A p1 June 19, 2001; *BusinessWeek* p120D Nov. 14, 1988; *Forbes* (on-line) Nov. 27, 2000; *Fortune* p90+ Apr. 11, 1988, with photos; (London) *Sunday Times* June 2, 2002; *New Scientist* p46+ Aug. 25, 2001, p46+ July 6, 2002; *New York Times* p26 May 21, 1981, F p1 June 11, 2002; *Technology Review* p22+ Oct. 1997; *Wired* (on-line) June 2002; wolfram.com

Selected Books: *A First Look at Mathematica*, 1996; *A New Kind of Science*, 2002; *Cellular Automata and Complexity*, 2003; *The Mathematica Book* (fifth edition), 2003

Eliot Schechter/Getty Images

Wood, Kerry

June 16, 1977– Baseball player

Address: Chicago Cubs, Wrigley Field, 1060 W. Addison, Chicago, IL 60613

On May 6, 1998, in his fifth major-league start, the 20-year-old Chicago Cubs rookie pitcher Kerry Wood tied a major-league record by striking out 20 batters in a single game. The resulting media frenzy catapulted the young Texan, who is known for his blistering fastball, to stardom. Despite an injury he suffered toward the end of that season, Wood captured the National League's rookie-of-the-year award, earning comparisons to his fellow Texas pitching greats Nolan Ryan and Roger Clemens. However, further damage to his sore right elbow—his pitching arm—in a 1999 spring-training game threatened his career. He underwent Tommy John surgery (a procedure developed by Frank Jobe in 1974 that is named for the first major-league pitcher on whom Jobe performed it) to replace a ligament in his elbow with one from his forearm. Whether he would return to his rookie form—indeed, whether he would ever pitch professionally again—after a year's recuperation remained in doubt. But Wood recovered, returning to the Cubs' pitching rotation early in the 2000 season. In the four years since, Wood has reestablished himself as one of the premier pitchers in baseball. "Woody's a tough guy and a great competitor," the Cubs' manager, Dusty Baker, told Dan McGrath for the *Chicago Tribune* (September 7, 2003). "He's a once-in-a-lifetime talent."

At six feet five inches and 225 pounds, Wood is an intimidating presence on the mound. His fastball, which has reached 100 miles per hour, is his best pitch and the one he uses to set up the rest of his pitching repertoire. Prior to surgery Wood threw a "slurve," a hybrid between a slider and a curve ball; the ligament damage in his elbow was blamed in part on that pitch. After his recovery Wood deployed a deceptive change-up, which he has continued to develop, and he altered the delivery of his "slurve" to be more mechanically sound, like a traditional slider. As of the end of the 2004 season, Wood had started a total of 164 games for the Cubs, recording 67 wins and 50 losses. His career earned-run average (ERA) stands at 3.63; he has struck out 1,209 batters while yielding 512 walks. Wood has pitched in five play-off games for the Cubs, one in 1998 and four in 2003, winning two and losing two; his postseason ERA is 3.94. Wood started the deciding game of the 2003 National League Championship Series, taking the loss as the Florida Marlins outscored the Cubs and won the right to represent the National League in the World Series.

Kerry Lee Wood was born on June 16, 1977 in Irving, Texas, a suburb of Dallas. His father, Garry Wood, worked as a quality-control operator for a publishing company; his mother, Terry Wood, was employed as an insurance underwriter. A gifted athlete, Garry Wood fielded the shortstop position for his high-school baseball team and taught his son how to play the game. "My dad was like my pitching coach growing up, and when he worked with me in the back yard we tried to emulate Nolan Ryan's mechanics," Wood told McGrath. "[My dad] didn't know a whole lot about pitching, but we knew Nolan Ryan must have pretty good mechanics to throw as hard as he did for as long as he did." Ryan, whose number, 34, Wood wears for the Cubs, "was one of my idols," he continued. "When he takes the mound he gives off the attitude that you're not going to beat me—it's my mound, it's my plate, it's my game. I just like the way he goes about it. I admire his whole pitching demeanor." Like many young athletes in Texas, Wood also played football, but when he was nine years old, he decided to concentrate solely on baseball. "I was tiny," he explained to Paul Sullivan for the *Chicago Tribune* (April 16, 1998). "I was one of the smallest guys on my Little League team. I was a fast guy, always had a pretty good arm. I played short and third and pitched occasionally, but I wasn't one of the [regular] pitchers."

The summer before he entered MacArthur High School, in Irving, Wood injured his throwing arm while practicing his curve ball; after giving his arm a rest, the velocity of his throws increased. Wood made MacArthur's varsity baseball squad in his sophomore year, at which point he decided he wanted to be a pitcher. Between his sophomore and junior years, however, he grew six inches, which ruined his coordination. "I had to start over," he said to Claire Smith for the *New York*

Times (May 18, 1998). Thanks to mild winters where he lived, Wood could practice all year, and his coordination improved. Prior to his senior year, in a controversial move, Wood transferred to Grand Prairie High School, in a nearby town, which had a highly regarded baseball program. At Grand Prairie, Wood compiled a record of 14 victories, including two no-hitters, and no losses during the 1994–95 season. In 81.1 innings he struck out 152 batters and notched a minuscule 0.77 ERA. (In baseball statistics, when speaking of numbers of innings, .1 indicates a third of an inning and .2 indicates two-thirds.) Wood was named a high-school all-American and Texas's 5-A Division player of the year. Recalling his time at Grand Prairie, Wood told McGrath, "Our practices were like major league spring training—work stations, individual instruction, everything organized to the minute. I really made a lot of progress my senior year. That's when the scouts started coming around." "We didn't have to do a whole lot of coaching [with Wood]," Randy Heisig, who was an assistant coach at Grand Prairie, told Smith. "He had a fluid motion and all the mechanics. His work ethic was incredible."

Wood entered the amateur draft in early June 1995. The Chicago Cubs selected him with the fourth overall pick and signed him to a contract, which included a $1.265 million signing bonus. Wood made his professional debut later that year, pitching in a total of 7.1 innings in three games for two of the Cubs' Class A farm teams: Fort Myers of the Florida State League and Williamsport of the New York–Penn League. He played his first full professional season in 1996, with the Daytona Cubs of the Florida State League, with whom he quickly lived up to expectations. In 22 starts he compiled an impressive 2.91 ERA on the way to 10 victories and two defeats. He averaged more than one strikeout per inning, striking out 136 batters in 114.1 innings while holding opposing hitters to a .179 batting average. Wood was also among minor-league leaders in strikeouts per nine innings, with 10.7. *Baseball America* ranked Wood the top prospect in the Florida State League and declared him the Cub organization's player of the year. Based on his performance in 1996, Wood was promoted to the Cubs' Class AA affiliate in Orlando, Florida, to begin the 1997 campaign. He pitched well and in midseason was again promoted, to the organization's AAA team, the Iowa Cubs of the Pacific Coast League. In total Wood started 29 games in 1997, striking out 186 batters in 151.2 innings. He registered an ERA of 4.57 and held his opponents to a .181 batting average. While many Cubs fans were eager to see the blue-chip prospect pitch for the big-league club, Wood expressed some trepidation during the off-season, telling reporters that he was not sure he was ready to join the Cubs and might prefer to start the season in Iowa to work on his mechanics. He was invited to the Cubs' spring-training camp in Mesa, Arizona, where he acquitted himself well, but the Cubs management did not

want to rush the young pitcher. He spent the first weeks of the 1998 season in Iowa before being called up to the majors, on April 10.

Wood started for the Chicago Cubs on April 12, 1998, pitching a game against the Expos in Montreal. He threw for 4.2 innings, striking out seven batters while yielding four runs on three hits and three walks in a 4–1 loss. "I'm not disappointed," Wood said of his first big-league outing to Paul Sullivan for the *Chicago Tribune* (April 13, 1998). "I'm not pleased with it, but I'm not going to dwell on it. I got a loss. It's my first one and I'm glad it's out of the way." Six days later Wood debuted at the Cubs' home ballpark, Wrigley Field, pitching five shut-out innings against the Los Angeles Dodgers to claim his first major-league victory. He allowed four hits and struck out seven players. Afterward he told Ken Daley for the *Dallas Morning News* (April 19, 1998), "I was like a little kid out there today. I was nervous the first four innings. Hopefully, there will be a lot more wins for me." After his first four starts, Wood's record stood at two wins and two losses with a 5.89 ERA. In his fifth game Wood gave one of the best pitching performances in baseball history. Facing the Houston Astros at Wrigley Field, Wood struck out 20 batters, setting the National League record and tying the major-league mark held by Roger Clemens. He yielded one hit over nine innings, completely shutting down the Houston hitters. "It's the best game I've ever seen pitched," then–Cubs manager Jim Riggleman told Rick Morrissey for the *Chicago Tribune* (May 7, 1998). Wood remained modest despite such praise, telling Morrissey, "I'm going to give most of the credit to the fans. They were in it the whole game." He also refused to appear on late-night television, turning down invitations from both David Letterman and Jay Leno, remarking, according to Ken Daley for the *Dallas Morning News* (May 29, 1998), "I don't like being on the front page of the paper. I don't like seeing myself on TV. That's just not me. It's not going to be by my choice to go on and do that stuff." In his next start Wood struck out 13 Arizona Diamondbacks over seven innings, setting the major-league record for strikeouts in consecutive starts, with 33, and earning his fourth win. Wood was subsequently declared Major League Baseball's player of the week for May 4–10. "There's a special buzz around the ballpark when he pitches," Ed Lynch told Tom Verducci for *Sports Illustrated* (June 8, 1998). "It's like a carnival, a happening. The players sense it. Everyone knows it when they come to the park—Kerry's pitching today." "I was very uncomfortable," Wood recalled to Daniel G. Habib for *Sports Illustrated* (July 7, 2003). "The attention I had generated in high school, in the minors, was nothing like what I got after I struck out 20. I wasn't ready for it. It was just my fifth game, and I was still getting acclimated to the big leagues." The Cubs advanced to the play-offs despite losing Wood for the final month of the season because of his sore right elbow. Wood pitched the third game of the National

League Division Series against the Atlanta Braves in early October. The prolonged layoff did not hamper his performance: he gave up just one run and three hits over five innings, though the Cubs fell 6–2 and were eliminated from the play-offs. Based on Wood's 13–6 record, 3.40 ERA, and 233 strikeouts, the third-most in the National League and a new record for a Cubs rookie, the Baseball Writers Association of America selected him for National League rookie-of-the-year honors.

In the off-season Wood developed pneumonia and various other respiratory ailments. Tests indicated that he suffered from an atrial septal defect (ASD), a small hole in his heart. The condition was treatable and described as unlikely to affect his pitching or his overall health. However, another malady soon developed and threatened to derail Wood's promising major-league career. Pitching in a spring-training contest on March 13, 1999, Wood threw 1.1 innings before leaving the game. The next day he reported a swollen elbow, and an MRI revealed a torn ulnar collateral ligament, reparable only by season-ending surgery. He was expected to miss at least a year, and there was a possibility he would never pitch again. During his recovery Wood traveled with the Cubs and spent a great deal of time fishing. In December 1999 he threw while on a mound, and by March 2000 his fastball was once again measuring 97 miles per hour. Wood made three starts in the minor leagues in April 2000, before returning to pitch in an 11–1 victory for the Cubs over the Houston Astros on May 2. He gave up one run on three hits and four walks while striking out four batters. He also revealed a new pitch, a changeup, which is a deceptive pitch that is delivered with the same arm velocity as a fastball but that travels much slower because of the way the ball was gripped, and he helped the Cubs with his bat by swatting a two-run homer. "It felt great to be back out there," Wood told Teddy Greenstein for the *Chicago Tribune* (May 3, 2000). "From day one after surgery, I never had any doubt that I'd get back to the level of where I was." Wood's control was fitful in the first months after his return, as he gave up a number of walks to opposing batters. At the end of the 2000 season, his record stood at 8–7. He had pitched 137 innings in 23 games started, notched 132 strikeouts, and held opposing batters to a .226 average.

According to conventional baseball wisdom, pitchers who have successfully undergone the Tommy John procedure generally do not return to presurgery form until their second season back. The same held true for Wood. During a vastly improved 2001 campaign, Wood started 28 games, winning 12 and losing six. His ERA was 3.36, and he held opposing hitters to a .202 batting average, the best in the major leagues that year. In 174.1 innings Wood compiled 217 strikeouts, the fifth-most in baseball that season. Over nine innings his mean number of strikeouts was 11.2, the second-highest in the major leagues that year. On May 25, in one of his more dominating performances,

Wood pitched a one-hit shutout against the Milwaukee Brewers, striking out 14 batters and walking four. Toward the end of the season, he was forced to go on the disabled list for several weeks due to shoulder tendonitis. With another 217 strikeouts in 2002, Wood became the first Cubs pitcher since Ferguson Jenkins, who recorded more than 200 strikeouts per season for the Cubs from 1968 to 1971, to record two consecutive 200-strikeout seasons. Wood started 33 games, completing four of them, and threw 213.2 innings, compiling a 3.66 ERA. He pitched far better than his 12–11 record indicated: Cubs batters offered little run support, averaging fewer than two runs per game in each of Wood's defeats, while the Cubs bullpen often lost the lead after he left the game. In seven of his starts, Wood reached double digits in strikeouts. Overall, he held opponents to a .221 batting average, one of the lowest marks in the league, and, once again, he was among the National League leaders in strikeouts and strikeouts per nine innings. He also hit 16 batters, earning him a reputation as a pitcher willing to actively discourage hitters from crowding the plate. Among the highlights of his season was a May 7, 2002 contest against the Cubs' division rival, the St. Louis Cardinals, in which Wood threw a complete-game shutout, striking out nine batters and allowing only two walks and four hits.

The 2003 season featured a number of milestones for Wood. In addition to being named the opening-day starter for the first time—an honor reserved for a staff's ace—he earned a spot on the National League All-Star Team and led the major leagues in strikeouts, with 266, becoming the first Cub to claim the honor since Ferguson Jenkins did so in 1969. Wood's strikeout mark was the third-best in Cubs history. He won a career-best 14 games, with 11 losses, and his 3.20 ERA was eighth-best in the league. In 211 total innings, he held opposing batters to a .203 average. During interleague play Wood outdueled his fellow Texan and boyhood idol Roger Clemens, who was pitching for the New York Yankees, in a 5–2 Cubs victory on June 7, frustrating Clemens's bid for his 300th victory. In his first All-Star Game appearance, Wood pitched a scoreless fourth inning. Later that summer he became the youngest pitcher in history to reach 1,000 strikeouts. In his final six starts, he earned three wins against one defeat while posting a 0.84 ERA, a closing performance that helped propel the Cubs to their first play-off berth since 1998. Pitching against the Atlanta Braves on September 30, 2003, in the opening game of the first round of the National League play-offs, Wood struck out 11 batters over eight innings and belted a two-run double to lead the Cubs to a 4–2 victory. He notched another victory later in the series as the Cubs advanced to the National League Championship Series (NLCS) against the Florida Marlins. In the third game of the NLCS, he pitched 6.2 innings and struck out seven batters, yielding three runs on seven hits and three walks en route to a Cubs win in extra innings. With the series tied three games apiece, Wood took the mound for the Cubs in the deciding seventh game. Despite aiding his own cause by hitting a home run, he was not at his best on the mound, giving up seven runs over 5.2 innings to earn the season-ending loss.

Wood signed a three-year, $32.5 million contract with the Cubs prior to opening day in 2004. The season was difficult for him. He started 22 games, winning eight and losing nine. He missed more than two months between May and July, due to tendonitis in one of his triceps. In 140.1 innings he struck out 144 batters, walked 51, and posted a 3.72 ERA. In August he was suspended for five games for arguing with an umpire and was ejected from his first game following his suspension after hitting three batters in a tense matchup with the Houston Astros, the Cubs' rival for the National League wild-card berth to the play-offs, which the Astros ultimately captured.

The 2005 season was equally disappointing for Wood. Suffering from a shoulder strain early in the season, he missed 10 weeks prior to September, when he underwent season-ending surgery. Pitching for 66 innings, Woods started only 10 games,

losing four and winning three. He served as a relief pitcher in another 11 games and ended the season with a 4.23 ERA, having struck out 77 batters and walked 26. His hopes are now pinned on doing well in 2006, and, by his own account, he is glad that he elected to receive surgery during the 2005 season. By the time spring training begins in 2006, he told a reporter for the Associated Press (September 6, 2005), "we should be ready . . . , and ready to go."

Wood married Sarah Pates in November 2003. The couple have homes in the Chicago area and Arizona. When not playing baseball, Wood enjoys fishing, playing golf, and bike riding. Asked by Rick Sorci for *Baseball Digest* (August 2000) what he would do if he was not a baseball player, Wood said, "This is it. This is all I ever wanted to do or be."

—P.B.M.

Suggested Reading: *Chicago Tribune* S p10 Apr. 16, 1998, with photo, C p13 Sep. 7, 2003, with photo; *New York Times* C p4 May 18, 1998, with photo; *Sports Illustrated* p48 May 18, 1998, with photo, p46 July 7, 2003, with photo

Obituaries

Written by Kieran Dugan

ALBERT, EDDIE Apr. 22, 1906–May 26, 2005 Actor; long after establishing himself solidly on stage and in motion pictures, chiefly as a character actor, gained his greatest popularity as Oliver Wendell Douglas, the big-city lawyer turned gentleman farmer in the television situation comedy *Green Acres* (1965–71); had first come to wide public attention as Bing Edwards, one of the three male leads—the other two were played by Ronald Reagan and Wayne Morris—in both the original Broadway production of *Brother Rat* (1936) and the screen adaptation (1938) of that comedy about cadets at the Virginia Military Institute; on Broadway, also created the role of the playwright from Oswego in the farce *Room Service* (1937), starred in the musicals *The Boys from Syracuse* (1938) and *Miss Liberty* (1949), and replaced Robert Preston in the lead of *The Music Man* (1960); while typically cast in amiable supporting parts on the big screen, turned in some of his best performances when playing against type, in such film roles as Captain Erskine Caldwell, the neurotic and cowardly army officer reckless of his men's safety in *Attack!* (1956), and Warden Hazen, a sadistic prison official, in *The Longest Yard* (1974); was nominated for Academy Awards for best supporting actor for his roles as Irving Radovich, the wisecracking photographer friend of the Gregory Peck character in *Roman Holiday* (1955), and as Mr. Corcoran, the comically disagreeable father-in-law of the Charles Grodin character in *The Heartbreak Kid* (1972); was also outstanding as Steve Nelson in *Smash-Up* (1947), the salesman Charles Drouet in *Carrie* (1952), the Persian peddler Ali Hakim in *Oklahoma!* (1955), Burt McGuire in *I'll Cry Tomorrow* (1955), and Captain McLean in *The Teahouse of the August Moon* (1956); was born Edward Albert Heimberger in Rock Island, Illinois; early in his career, hosted and sang on the radio in the Midwest and New York and was an aerialist with a one-ring circus in Mexico; after acting in summer stock, made his Broadway debut in a minor role in the flop *O Evening Star* in 1936; in Hollywood, reprised his stage role as Bing Edwards not only in the film version of *Brother Rat* but also in the sequel to that movie, *Brother Rat and a Baby* (1940); played the male leads in such films as *On Your Toes* (1939), *An Angel from Texas* (1940), *The Great Mr. Nobody* (1941), and *Ladies' Day* (1943), and supporting roles in *Out of the Fog* (1941), *Eagle Squadron* (1942), and *Bombardier* (1943), among other pictures; as a wartime U.S. Navy officer, saw heroic action on an amphibious transport ship in the South Pacific (1943) before his assignment to the navy's training-films branch (1944–45); after the war, formed Eddie Albert Productions, which made 16-millimeter educational films for children and young people and documentaries for industrial firms; back in Hollywood, starred in *Rendezvous with Annie* (1946), co-starred with James Stewart in *You Gotta Stay Happy* (1948), was one of several leading players in *Hit Parade of 1947*, and had supporting roles in *The Perfect Marriage* (1946), *Time Out of Mind* (1947), and *The Dude Goes West* (1948); co-starred with Lucille Ball in the slapstick comedy/mystery *The Fuller Brush Girl* (1950); subsequently, was cast as Elliott Atterbury in *The Gold Rush* (1955), Bill Gorton in *The Sun Also Rises* (1957), Colonel Thompson in *The Longest Day* (1962), and police captain Ed Kosterman in *McQ* (1974); accrued a total of 79 feature-film credits, including Max Wagner in *A Dispatch from Reuters* (1940), Dr. Clint Forrest in both *Four Wives* (1939) and *Four Mothers* (1941), Wacky Waters in *Ladies' Day* (1943), and police chief Maloney in *Brenda Starr* (1989); on the television adventure series *Switch* (1975–78), co-starred as Frank MacBride, an ex-cop who teams up with an ex-con (Robert Wagner) to form a private investigation agency; during part of the run of the prime-time television soap opera *Falcon Crest* in the 1980s, made semi-regular appearances as Carlton Travis; made some 100 appearances in other television dramatic formats, including miniseries and episodes of adventure series and situation comedies; was a prominent activist in environmental and humanitarian relief causes; was predeceased by his wife of 39 years, Margo, and survived by his son, Edward Albert Jr., and his adopted daughter, Maria; died at his home in Pacific Palisades, California. See *Current Biography* (1954).

Obituary *New York Times* C p14 May 28, 2005

ANGELES, VICTORIA DE LOS Nov. 1, 1923–Jan. 14, 2005 Spanish opera singer; a lyric soprano whose repertoire prominently included such roles as Mimi in *La Bohème*, Violetta in *La Traviata*, and the title roles in *Madama Butterfly* and *Carmen*; also included in her operatic repertoire *Don Giovanni*, *The Barber of Seville*, *Acis and Galatea*, *Pelleas et Melisande*, *Die Meistersinger*, *Lohengrin*, *Manon*, *I pagliacci*, *Cavalleria rusticana*, *Ariadne auf Naxos*, *Faust*, and *Simon Boccanegra*; was born in Barcelona, Spain; completed a six-year course at the Conservatorio de Liceo in Barcelona in only three years, at age 18, and graduated with full honors; made her debut in a recital in 1944 and her operatic debut, as the Countess in Mozart's *Le nozze di Figaro*, later that year, in Barcelona; won the Geneva International Singing Competition in 1947; first sang at the Paris Opera in 1948; made a concert tour of South America in 1949; early in 1950, toured Scandinavia, England, and Italy; in October 1950, made her American debut at Carnegie Hall, in New York City; in March 1951, began her tenure of nearly 10 years at the Metropolitan Opera in New York City; in 1961, opened the Bayreuth Festival in a new production of Tannhäuser; beginning that year, concentrated on recital work, specializing in German lieder and Spanish and French songs; made more than 80 records for EMI, among them 21 complete operas and more than two dozen solo recital albums; earned for her recordings an Edison Music Award, six Grands Prix du Disque, and eight Grammy Awards; was married and the mother of two children; died in Barcelona. See *Current Biography* (1955).

Obituary *New York Times* I p26 Jan. 16, 2005

ARAFAT, YASIR Aug. 4, 1929–Nov. 11, 2004 Chairman of the Palestine Liberation Organization (1969–2004); president of the Palestinian National Authority (1994–2004); co-founder (1959) and leader of the militant group Fatah; personified the cause of Palestinian nationalism for four decades, at first as a guerrilla chief seeking—in effect—modern Israel's displacement from the territory of historic Palestine (viewed by him as the rightful Palestinian Arab homeland) and in later years as a statesman and ostensible peacemaker; while admired by his supporters for his passionate leadership of his people's struggle for self-determination, was viewed by his detractors, especially those in Israel, as an unreconstructed terrorist at heart, inimical to peace in the Middle East; was deemed even by some Palestinian dissidents as more effectual in his striving for power than his exercise of it; was born in Cairo, Egypt, into a merchant family with ties to Jerusalem and Gaza; was raised in Cairo and among relatives in Jerusalem and Gaza; when he was a civil-engineering student at the University of Cairo (then King Fuad I University), joined the Muslim Brotherhood and headed the Union of Palestinian Students; after receiving his degree, in 1957, emigrated to Kuwait, where he became a successful construction contractor; in Kuwait in October 1959, joined with several other clandestine activists in founding Fatah (also called Al Fatah and al-Fatah), a movement dedicated to advancing armed struggle as a means of establishing an independent Palestinian homeland on the site of the historic Palestine; soon assumed the leadership of Fatah; led Fatah into the Palestine Liberation Organization (PLO) when that organization was created by the Arab League, in 1964; in the mid-1960s, began launching minor guerrilla raids into Israel, some from the West Bank; following the second Arab-Israeli war—the Six-Day War of 1967 (in which Israel captured the Golan Heights from Syria, the West Bank from Jordan, and the Gaza Strip from Egypt)—moved into Jordan, along with some 380,000 Palestinian refugees from the West Bank; continued to mount raids into Israel from Jordan; emerged as the preeminent Palestinian liberation leader when he repulsed an Israeli attack on his base in Karameh, Jordan, in 1968; the following year, was elected chairman of the Palestinian National Council by the PLO's parliament; meanwhile, was becoming persona non grata in Jordan, in part because of Fatah's threat to social order there and in part because King Hussein of Jordan was troubled by Fatah's alleged role in airliner hijackings and other international acts; in the early 1970s, was driven out of Jordan and into Lebanon, whence his commandos continued their raids into Israel; in November 1974, delivered a historic speech before the United Nations General Assembly in which he described himself as the bearer of "an olive branch" as well as "a freedom fighter's gun"; with that speech, won for the PLO observer status in the U.N. General Assembly and U.N. recognition of the Palestinians' right to self-determination; after a dozen years in Lebanon, was routed from that country by the combined attacks of Israeli, Syrian, Lebanese, and dissident Palestinian forces in the early 1980s; subsequently, operated out of exile in Tunisia for several years before finally moving back to the West Bank; gained stature in the Arab world and drew attention in the West when the Palestinian intifada (uprising) erupted in the West Bank and Gaza in 1987; following his negotiations with the Israeli leaders Yitzhak Rabin and Shimon Peres that led to the sealing of the Oslo peace accords, shared the 1994 Nobel Peace Prize with Rabin and Peres; also in 1994, pursuant to the signing of the Oslo accords and the concomitant establishment of the Palestinian Authority, became head of the latter; in one of the freest elections ever conducted in the Arab world, was popularly ratified as president of the Palestinian Authority with 88 percent of the votes cast in the West Bank and Gaza in January 1996; at the invitation of U.S. president Bill Clinton, engaged in peace negotiations with Israeli Prime Minister Ehud Barak at Camp David in August 2000; reportedly agreed with Barak on the borders of a future Palestinian state, but refused to sign off on the deal, partly, if not in large measure, because of disagreement over the partition of Jerusalem; meanwhile, became the target of criticism from a young guard of Palestinian nationalists in the West Bank and Gaza, associated with the militant group Hamas, that was seething with impatience for a resolution of the conflict and disappointment with Arafat not only for his failure in that regard but also with his failure to rid the Palestinian Authority of corruption and provide better governance; was blamed by Israeli prime minister Ariel Sharon, one of his archenemies, and others to have approved, in September 2000, Hamas's launching of a protracted campaign of violence (the second intifada), including an escalation of suicide bombings, that was directed against Israel but was also intended to weaken Arafat's administration; became isolated in his compound when, beginning in December 2001 and increasingly during 2002, the Israeli Defense Forces invaded the West Bank city of Ramallah, the seat of the Palestinian Authority, and using bulldozers in addition to weaponry, demolished much of the Mukataa, the governmental center of the Palestinian Authority; lived under virtual house arrest until his last days; after surviving scores of assassination attempts over the years, fell terminally ill with a blood disorder in the autumn of 2004; with the permission of Israeli authorities, was flown to France for medical treatment on October 26, 2004; died of multiple organ failure at Percy military hospital in suburban Paris; was survived by, among others, his second wife, Suha Tawil, and their daughter, Zahwa. See articles in *Current Biography 1994* and *Current Biography International Yearbook 2002.*

Obituary in *New York Times* B p10 Nov. 11, 2004

AVEDON, RICHARD May 15, 1923–Oct. 1, 2004 Photographer; one of the most influential tastemakers of his time; while he enjoyed earning his living by means of his groundbreaking fashion photography, in which he combined realism with fantasy, glamour, and casual theatricality, found, by his own account, "deeper pleasure" in what he considered his "deeper work"—portraiture; in that work, was a stark, unsparing minimalist, standing his subjects unposed against plain white backgrounds, with no distracting props or context, thus producing sometimes unflattering results; created a chiefly black-and-white gallery of extraordinary range, including, most famously, a virtual who's who of American celebrities—from the likes of Charlie Chaplin and Ezra Pound to Marilyn Monroe, Rose Kennedy, Hillary Rodham Clinton, Saul Bellow, and Christopher Reeve in a wheelchair—and also a variety of less celebrated subjects, including working-class types, drifters, and social activists; used an 8x10 Deardorf camera mounted on a tripod; stood, not behind the camera, but beside it, chatting with his subjects; was born into a Russian Jewish immigrant family in New York City (where he lived all his life), the son of a father who started a retail women's-clothing business that eventually became known as Avedon's Fifth Avenue; at nine, began photographing his sister, Louise, with a Kodak Box Brownie camera; was poet laureate at De Witt Clinton High School in the Bronx; dropped out of high school when he was 17; subsequently, took Columbia University extension courses in literature; contributed verse to the New York City newspapers Sun and Journal-American; was given a Rolleiflex camera as a going-away gift from his father when he joined the wartime Merchant Marine in 1942; served in the Merchant Marine's photography branch until 1944; back in New York City, took photography courses at the New School for Social Research (now the New School University) under Alexy Brodovitch, then the art director of Harper's Bazaar magazine; after doing some photographic work for Bonwit Teller, an upscale Manhattan department store, became staff photographer under Brodovitch at Harper's Bazaar in 1946; departing from the convention of the icy mannequin in his fashion shoots for Harper's Bazaar, took his models (including Dorian Leigh, Dorothy Horan, and Suzy Parker) out of the studio to such unlikely locations as the zoo, the circus, the NASA launching pads at Cape Kennedy, junkyards, the waterfront, and the Egyptian pyramids, and shot the women laughing, cavorting in the rain, dancing, and the like; was the inspiration for Dick Avery, the fashion photographer played by Fred Astaire in the Hollywood musical Funny Face (1957); in the early 1960s, photographed activists in the civil rights struggle; was with Harper's Bazaar until 1965 and with Vogue magazine from 1966 to 1970; in 1969, photographed the Chicago Seven, the anti–Vietnam War activists who were on trial for conspiracy; during the Vietnam War, traveled to Vietnam twice; shot portraits of napalm burn victims; in 1972, participated in an anti-war demonstration in Washington, D.C., and was arrested for civil disobedience; in 1975, was commissioned by Rolling Stone magazine to create a portfolio on America's "power elite" in politics, in business and finance, and on the culture fronts (the resulting set of 73 portraits, titled "The Family," filled most of a special issue of Rolling Stone in 1976, with one critic calling it "the photographic equivalent of

roadkill"); commissioned by the Amon Carter Museum in Fort Worth, Texas, spent five years (1979–84) creating the portfolio of portraits of ranch hands, miners, waitresses, and others published under the title In the American West (1985); during the 1980s, contributed to the outsized photo magazine Egoist a number of series of photographic documentaries, including one on the fall of the Berlin Wall; in 1992, became the New Yorker magazine's first staff photographer; found lucrative assignments with such advertising clients as Revlon cosmetics, Levi's jeans, Douglas Aircraft, Christian Dior clothes, and Calvin Klein's Obsession perfume; collected his photographs in books and exhibition catalogs, beginning with Observations (1959) and including Nothing Personal (1964), The Naked and the Dressed: Twenty Years of Versace (1998), and Portraits (2002); shared one book of photos, The Sixties (1999), with Diane Arbus; saw the publication of Evidence (1994), the catalog of a retrospective of his work from 1944 to 1994, in which Jane Livingston quoted one condemner of his oeuvre: "There is something cruel, even vicious, about posing a spastic mental patient, a crippled farmer, a one-armed knife-scarred prisoner, a pathetic alcoholic derelict, all for the sake of producing sensational portraits"; in 1993, published An Autobiography (1993); was married and divorced twice; in the last months of his life, worked on an election-year New Yorker project called "On Democracy," photographing politicians, convention delegates, and ordinary voters across the U.S.; was in the midst of that project when he suffered a cerebral hemorrhage in San Antonio, Texas; died at Methodist Hospital in San Antonio; was survived by a son (from his second marriage) and four grandchildren. See Current Biography (1975).

Obituary New York Times A p1+ Oct. 2, 2004

BACHER, ROBERT F. Aug. 31, 1905–Nov. 18, 2004 Nuclear physicist; professor emeritus, California Institute of Technology; helped to design the first atomic bomb; earned B.S. and Ph.D. degrees at the University of Michigan; did postdoctoral work at the University of Michigan, the California Institute of Technology (Caltech), and the Massachusetts Institute of Technology (MIT); was an instructor at Columbia University (1934–35); in 1935, joined the faculty of Cornell University, where he became a full professor of physics and director of the laboratory of nuclear studies; on leave from Cornell during World War II, worked on military-related projects at the radiation laboratory of MIT (1940–43) before his assignment to the Manhattan Project, the top-secret program for developing the first atomic bomb; at the project's laboratory at Los Alamos, New Mexico, headed the experimental-physics division (1943–44) and the bomb-physics division (1944–45); served on the U.S. Atomic Energy Commission from 1946 to 1949; joined the faculty of Caltech in 1949; chaired Caltech's division of physics, mathematics, and astronomy from 1949 to 1962; was provost of Caltech from 1962 to 1970; took emeritus status in 1976; was a member of the U.S. delegation to the nuclear-test-ban negotiations in 1958; served on many governmental advisory panels; was predeceased by his wife, Jean, and survived by a son, a daughter, and two grandchildren; died in Montecito, California. See *Current Biography* (1947).

Obituary *New York Times* A p25 Nov. 22, 2004

BANNISTER, CONSTANCE Feb. 11, 1913–Aug. 17, 2005 Photographer; reached an international audience with her tens of thousands of pictures of photogenic babies in newspapers, magazines, and other media; had a knack for capturing ranges of expressions on the faces of her infant subjects; in some instances, arranged the photos in humorous series, with captions matching the expressions, as in two satirical paperbacks she published in the 1950s, *Senator, I'm Glad You Asked Me That!* and *We Were Spies Behind the Iron Curtain*; was born Constance Gibbs in Ashland City, Tennessee; took the name Bannister from the first of her marriages, to Stephen Arthur Bannister; as a teenager in Ashland City, became interested in photography when a boyfriend gave her a camera; in 1937, moved to New York City, where she studied at the New York School of Applied Design, the School of Modern Photography, and the New York Institute of Photography; in her first job, was an Associated Press society photographer in Palm Beach, Florida, in 1938 and 1939; later, worked for the *Chicago Tribune*, photographed touring Broadway shows, and sold glamour photos to *Life* magazine; after returning to Manhattan, opened a studio on Central Park South; gradually concentrated on infant photography, at first shooting studio portraits of babies of affluent parents; during World War II, helped sell U.S. war bonds with her "Bannister Baby" posters; provided the photographs accompanying the verses of Ernest Claxton in *A Child's Grace* (1948); created a syndicated comic strip, "Baby Banters," that ran in some 50 newspapers for six years in the late 1940s and early 1950s; for Hollywood, made the short subjects *Bannister's Bantering Babies* (Warner Brothers), *Babies by Bannister* (Columbia Picturres), and *Babies in Bannisterland* (Harold Young Productions); designed realistic baby dolls marketed by the Sun Rubber Co.; saw her photos of babies grace the covers of such magazines as *Look*, *Woman's Day*, and *McCall's* and the labels of and advertisements for the products of Clapp's Baby Foods, Gerber Baby Foods, Beechnut, and other companies; made many television appearances with her photographs; was married three times and divorced twice; was survived by her third husband, Joseph H. Hatcher, and by two daughters and six grandchildren; died in Woodbury, New York. See *Current Biography* (1955).

Obituary *New York Times* C p16 Aug. 20, 2005

BEENE, GEOFFREY Aug. 30, 1927–Sep. 28, 2004 Fashion designer; "an artist who [chose] to work in cloth," as he was once described in the *New York Times*; was an innovative modernist who early on declared his independence from the international haute-couture pack and its commercially motivated fads; with deft bias-cutting and draping of jersey, tweed, velvet, crepe, lace, leather, and other fabrics, including synthetics—and a dash of playful imagination—created sophisticated, flattering, artfully simple dresses, gowns, boleros, jumpsuits, and trousers; had a muse in the journalist Amy Fine Collins,

who wore Beene-designed clothes exclusively beginning in the late 1980s, and thought, as Collins observed, not two-dimensionally, front and back, but "in the round, about the contortions of the body, the spiral of human movement. That's why his seams spiral"; said himself, as quoted in the *New York Times*, "Designing is an architectural problem. You are faced with a piece of crepe or wool, the flattest thing in the world, and you have to mold it to the shape you want. Clothing is nothing until it hits the body. The body gives it shape"; routinely worked with what might be called "found objects"; for example, incorporated heavy-duty industrial zippers in some otherwise fine garments and transformed Hudson's Bay blankets bought from L. L. Bean into evening coats trimmed with satin; won a record eight Cody Fashion Critics Awards and a place in the Cody Fashion Hall of Fame; was born and bred in Louisiana; under family pressure, aspired at first, briefly, to a career in medicine; as a premed student for three years at Tulane University, gained a three-dimensional familiarity with human anatomy that would help him to combine style with comfort in couture; was formatively inspired by the work of the Hollywood costume designer Adrian; studied at the Traphagen School of Fashion in New York City and the Académie Julian and L'École de la Chambre Syndicale in Paris; worked for eight years in Manhattan with the ready-to-wear house Hamay and for three years with Teal Traina's fashion firm before setting up shop under his own name, in 1963; over the following several years, became, as Jay Cocks observed in *Time* (October 10, 1988), "one of the country's best-known and most sought-after designers, specializing in a kind of overembellished chic"; in 1967, designed the wedding dress of Lynda Bird Johnson (Mrs. Charles S. Robb), the elder daughter of President Lyndon B. Johnson; in 1972, was stung by a fashion review in the *New Yorker* in which Kennedy Fraser criticized him for excessive indulgence in the fanciful and for dressing women in "concrete" constructions; in reaction, was moved, as he said, to "rethink clothing and change [his] career," in the direction of lighter and looser couture with whimsy still present but restrained; regarded as "probably the single most significant piece of clothing [he] ever designed" one of his 1983 creations, a long black wool coat with gold insets along its back and sleeves that Jay Cocks called "a masterly combination of grand luxe and offhand invention, a subtle experiment in enlarging the possibilities of wearable form"; in the 1990s, collaborated with the American Ballet Theatre and the choreographer Twyler Tharp, dressing dancers in garments "so delicate they looked as though they might fall to the floor with a breath," as Iain R. Webb wrote for the London *Independent* (October 7, 2004); in addition to his high-priced women's couture, offered several less-expensive lines of items for women, including Beene Bag sportswear, along with swimwear, jewelry, a women's fragrance, and a line of menswear; maintained two residences, an estate in Oyster Bay, Long Island, and a duplex on Manhattan's Upper East Side; died at his home in Manhattan; was survived by a sister, Barbara Ann. See *Current Biography* (1978).

Obituary *New York Times* A p23 Sep. 29, 2004

BEL GEDDES, BARBARA Oct. 31, 1922–Aug. 8, 2005 Stage, screen, and television actress; a winsome performer whose unconventional beauty was accented by her wistful visage and understated smile; typically projected a combination of high breeding and down-to-earth strength; reached high points in her career with her creations of the roles of Maggie, the antsy young wife of an inattentive husband in *Cat on a Hot Tin Roof* on Broadway, of Midge, the underappreciated loyal ally of the male protagonist in the motion picture *Vertigo*, and of Eleanor ("Miss Ellie") Southworth Ewing, the staunch, long-suffering matriarch of a powerful but fractious and dysfunctional oil-and-cattle-rich Texas family in the prime-time soap opera *Dallas*, arguably the most popular dramatic serial in the history of television; for her portrayal of Miss Ellie, won an Emmy Award in 1980; was a daughter of Norman Bel Geddes, a renowned theatrical and industrial designer; made her Broadway debut at age 18 as Dottie Colburn in the comedy *Out of the Frying Pan* (1941); had leading roles in the short-lived Broadway productions *Little Darling* (1942), *Nine Girls* (1943) and *Mrs. January and Mr. X* (1944); caught the attention of director Elia Kazan, who cast her as Genevra Langdon, the female lead in *Deep Are the Roots*, a drama, daring for its time and controversial, about an interracial love affair in the Jim Crow South, which became a hit of the 1945–46 Broadway season and brought her a Theatre World Award; made her feature-film debut starring with Henry Fonda and Vincent Price in *The Long Night* (1947); was nominated for an Academy Award for her portrayal of Katrin Hanson, the daughter/narrator in *I Remember Mama* (1948); starred with Robert Mitchum and Robert Preston in the grade-A Western *Blood on the Moon* (1948) and with Robert Ryan and James Mason in Max Orphul's film noir *Caught* (1949); was cast as Nancy Reed, the wife of the Public Health Service officer (Richard Widmark) racing the clock to prevent a plague, in Elia Kazan's thriller *Panic in the Streets* (1950) and as Virginia Foster, the girlfriend of the young man (Richard Basehart) threatening to jump off a skyscraper, in Henry Hathaway's high-tension quasi-documentary *Fourteen Hours* (1951); disappeared from the silver screen for seven years following her reluctance to "name names" in her testimony at U.S. House Un-American Activities Committee hearings into alleged Communist influence in the motion-picture industry; spent that hiatus back on Broadway; played Mordeen in the short run of *Burning Bright* in 1950; created the role of Patty O'Neill in the hit comedy *The Moon Is Blue*, which enjoyed an original Broadway run of 27 months (1951–53); played Rose in *The Living Room* for 22 performances in 1954; beginning in March 1955, created the role of Maggie, the "cat" who is agitated by sexual frustration and animated by greed in *Cat on a Hot Tin Roof*, Tennessee Williams's now classic drama about a decaying Old South family, which had an original Broadway run of 20 months; played Mary in *The Sleeping Prince* (1956) and Katherine (opposite Henry Fonda) in *Silent Night, Lonely Night* (1959–60); was nominated for a best-actress Tony Award for her creation of the role of Mary McKellaway in Jean Kerr's hit comedy *Mary, Mary* (1961–64); in 1966 replaced Anne Jackson in the role of Ellen Manville in

the long-running comedy *Luv*; in her final Broadway appearances, played Jenny in *Everything in the Garden* (1967–68) and Katy Cooper in Jean Kerr's comedy *Finishing Touches* (1973); meanwhile, had returned to Hollywood as the concerned ex-fiancée of the James Stewart character in Alfred Hitchcock's suspense drama *Vertigo* (1958); co-starred as the wife of the clarinetist Red Nichols (Danny Kaye) in the bio-picture *The Five Pennies* (1959); was cast as one of the five World War II–era female Yugoslav partisan guerrillas in *Five Branded Women* (1960); had the supporting role of Clarissa in the Peyton Place–like *By Love Possessed* (1961); in her last two feature films, played Ruth, the mother of the young man (Michael Douglas) killed in Vietnam in *Summertree* (1971) and Mrs. Todd, the mother of the serial killer (Richard F. Lyons) in *The Todd Killings* (1971); between 1950 and 1969 garnered 23 credits in network-television drama, including starring appearances in three episodes of *Alfred Hitchcock Presents*, the most memorable of which was "Lamb to the Slaughter," broadcast in April 1958; on that occasion, played Mary Maloney, a wife who bludgeons her philandering husband to death with a blunt object—a frozen leg of lamb—and disposes of the murder weapon by making it the entrée of a meal she shares with the police detectives investigating the case; after several years in retirement, returned to acting on network television out of financial necessity in 1976; during that year, appeared as Maggie in an episode of *Spencer's Pilots*; the following year, played Mrs. Webb in a special television production of the play *Our Town*; was a charter member of the cast of *Dallas*, which was launched on the CBS television network in 1978, achieved enormous worldwide popularity as well as first place (by a wide margin) in the domestic ratings by the early 1980s, and ran until 1991; played Miss Ellie through the entire run of *Dallas*'s Ewing family saga, save for sixth months in 1984–85, when she was sidelined by heart surgery and replaced by Donna Reed; also acted in regional theater, in plays produced by her second husband, Windsor Lewis, who died in 1972; had previously been married to and divorced from the engineer Carl Schreuer; in addition to acting, designed greeting cards and stationery and wrote and illustrated two children's books, *I Like to Be Me* (1963) and *So Do I* (1972); died at her home in Northeast Harbor, Maine; was survived by two daughters, one from each of her two marriages. See *Current Biography* (1948).

Obituary *New York Times* C p17 Aug. 11, 2005

BELLOW, SAUL June 10, 1915–Apr. 5, 2005 Author; arguably, the preeminent Jewish American novelist of his time; a virtuosic storyteller who won the National Book Award three times, for his novels *The Adventures of Augie March*, *Herzog*, and *Mr. Sammler's Planet*, and the Pulitzer Prize for *Humboldt's Gift*; received the Nobel Prize for Literature in 1976; wrote novels that had vividly limned protagonists and served as a canvas—and as comic relief—for his own struggles with, in his words, "the big-scale insanities of the twentieth century" and the "mess" of his own life; "wove memoir from his Jewish upbringing and his adult life in academia into what came to define America's post-war literature of opportunity," as Susan Goldenberg wrote for the London *Guardian* (April 6, 2005); mingled "high-flown intellectual bravado with racy, tough street Jewishness," as the critic Irving Howe noted; found "problematic" the 1940s American literary scene dominated by "Freud, French existentialism, and Hemingway's [macho stoicism]," as Gloria L. Cronin, professor of English at Brigham Young University and president of the Saul Bellow Society, wrote for *The Literary Encyclopedia* (on-line); according to Cronin, spent his career, after his early flirtation with the Flaubertian standard was behind him, "writing against the grain of what he called a destructive existentialism, alienation ethics, absurdism, nihilism, the loss of the unitary Romantic self, and fears of the imminent collapse of Western civilization"; was born to Russian Jewish immigrant parents in Lachine, Canada, and grew up in a Yiddish-speaking home in Montreal, Canada, and Chicago, Illinois, the latter of which is the setting for much of his fiction; earned a B.S. degree with honors in anthropology and sociology at Northwestern University; during World War II, was rejected by the military because of a hernia but performed some service in the Merchant Marine; served his literary "apprenticeship," as he said, with his first two novels: *Dangling Man* (1944), the fictional journal of a demoralized young man waiting to be drafted, and *The Victim* (1947), a story about anti-Semitism written, in his words, "under the spell of Dostoevsky's *The Eternal Husband*"; while living in Paris on a Guggenheim Fellowship (1948–50), moved beyond the morose modernism of those works and began writing *The Adventures of Augie March* (1953), a boisterously comic picaresque tale set in Depression-era Chicago; was inspired to create the character of Augie in part by his memory of a brash childhood friend of his, "a wild talker who was always announcing cheerfully that he had a super scheme" and was never disheartened by the schemes' failures; would never repeat that novel's wild exuberance, according to Gloria L. Cronin, "but . . . would continue to produce American optimists who repeatedly reject European despair"; published the popular short 1956 novel *Seize the Day* (which, judging by its sober tone and theme of alienation, seemed to date from before *The Adventures of Augie March*); next wrote *Henderson the Rain King* (1959), about an eccentric millionaire American pig farmer who travels to Africa for spiritual regeneration: a multi-level parody—a send-up of colonial racism, social-scientific theorizing, literary modernism, and Hemingwayesque adventurism; said that *Herzog* (1964), his masterwork and grandest commercial and critical success, was intended to be "about the mental condition of the country and its educated class"; invented as *Herzog*'s title character a Jewish "Everyman," a self-described "learned specialist in intellectual history," who is suffering both academic failure and cuckolding by his most recent wife and his best friend; explained that Herzog was "taken by an epistolary fit, and writes grieving, biting, ironic and rambunctious letters not only to his friends and acquaintances but also to the great men, the giants of thought, who formed his mind"; next published the polemical novel *Mr. Sammler's Planet* (1970), a com-

mentary on the radical movements and student and urban unrest of the late 1960s as voiced by Artur Sammler, a curmudgeonly Polish-born aristocrat and intellectual, a survivor of the Holocaust, living on Manhattan's Upper West Side; in *Humboldt's Gift* (1975), which the Saul Bellow Society described as "in part a serious religious discussion couched in a deflecting comic idiom," created as the protagonist Charlie Citrine, a Chicagoan who is trying to come to terms with the death of his mentor, the poet Von Humboldt Fleischer (a character based on Bellow's friend Delmore Schwartz, a self-destructive poet and critic) and the near loss of his own poetic gift and at the same time is involved in low sexual and gangland pursuits; produced in the protagonist of *The Dean's December* (1982) the Chicago academic Dean Albert Corde, a thinly disguised self-portrait; in *More Die of Heartbreak* (1987), his 11th novel, offered what the Saul Bellow Society judged to be "a Prufrockian lament about failed men and absent mermaids which is full of misogynous love-lore, comic characters, botched loves, fatal forays into the danger zones of sex and romance, farcical retreats, and serio-crackpot sexual philosophizing"; with *Ravelstein* (2000), according to that society, wrote a piece of "autoethnographic fiction, a memorial to Allan Bloom of the University of Chicago in which Bellow, ostensibly posing as a Boswell, is writing a Johnsonian tribute to his late friend"; published a total of 18 books of fiction, including the novellas *The Bellarosa Connection* (1989) and *The Theft* (1989) and three collections of short stories; in addition, published the books of essays *To Jerusalem and Back* (1976) and *It All Adds Up* (1994); also wrote several plays, including *The Last Analysis*, which flopped on Broadway in 1964; taught at a succession of colleges and universities, including Bard College and New York University; was a member of the Committee on Social Thought at the University of Chicago from 1962 to 1972, when he joined the faculty of Boston University; in growing older, became just as opposed to postmodernism as he had been to modernism; to the end, adhered to a traditionalist aesthetic, rooted in such sources as the Torah, Shakespeare, and the great 17th-century Russian novelists; was married five times and had numerous love affairs; was the father of three adult sons, one by each of his first three wives, and, by his fifth wife, Janis Freedman (who was more than 40 years his junior), a daughter, born when he was 84; died at his home in Brookline, Massachusetts. See *Current Biography* (1988).

Obituary *New York Times* A p1+ Apr. 6, 2005

BERMAN, LAZAR Feb. 26, 1930–Feb. 6, 2005 Russian-born pianist; a powerful virtuoso who combined emotional, often thunderous force with perfect technical control; a brilliant exponent of the Romantic repertoire, especially acclaimed for his interpretations of Liszt; was born to Jewish parents in Leningrad (now St. Petersburg) in what was then the Soviet Union; began to study the piano at age two under the tutelage of his musically gifted mother; at age three and a half, was enrolled in a special children's class at the Leningrad Conservatory; at four, made his concert debut; subsequently, studied at the Central Music School in Moscow; in 1940, at age 10, made his debut as an orchestral soloist, playing a Mozart concerto with the Moscow Philharmonic under the baton of Grigori Stolyarov; studied at the Moscow Conservatory from 1948 to 1953 and attended master classes there until 1957; in the meantime, won prizes in international competitions in East Berlin (1951), Brussels (1956), and Budapest (1956); beginning in 1957, toured the USSR constantly, giving scores of concerts a year in as many cities and towns; in 1957 was allowed by Soviet authorities to embark on a tour of Western Europe, in the course of which he recorded the Beethoven "Appassionata" and Liszt B minor sonatas in London; in 1959, following his marriage to a French woman, was recalled to Moscow; for more than a decade, performed only in the Soviet bloc; began performing in Italy in the early 1970s; made his American debut in a recital at Miami University in Oxford, Ohio, in January 1976; in New York City the following month, gave a recital at the 92d Street YMHA and followed that up with an appearance with the New Jersey Symphony at Carnegie Hall; again at Carnegie Hall, in November 1976 gave a recital consisting of Liszt's complete Transcendental Etudes and Schumann's Sonata in F sharp minor; while in the U.S., recorded the Tchaikovsky First Piano Concerto under the baton of Herbert von Karajan; performed the same concerto with an orchestra conducted by Antal Dorati; at Royal Festival Hall in London in December 1976, gave a recital of music by Prokofiev and Liszt; in London two years later, appeared with Klaus Tennstedt and the London Symphony Orchestra playing Liszt's A Major concerto; when Soviet authorities found banned American literature in his luggage in 1980, was again restricted to the Soviet concert circuit; later in the 1980s, as the Soviet Union began to dissolve, was allowed to travel abroad as he wished; in August 1990, left Russia to teach in Norway and Italy; in December 1990, began living in Italy, in Imola; four years later, took Italian citizenship; in 1995, settled in Florence, Italy; in 1997, went to the Musikhochschule in Weimar, Germany, to begin a two-term stint as a guest professor there; announced his retirement from the concert stage in January 2004; can be heard on a sizable discography of studio releases and recordings of live concerto performances; died in Florence, Italy; was survived by his second wife (third, according to some sources), Valentina Berman, a pianist, and by his son, Pavel Berman, a violinist with whom he sometimes collaborated in recitals and recordings. See *Current Biography* (1977).

Obituary *New York Times* C p19 Feb. 9, 2005

BERNHARD LEOPOLD, CONSORT OF JULIANA, QUEEN OF THE NETHERLANDS June 29, 1911–Dec. 1, 2004 German-born consort of Queen Juliana of the Netherlands; father of Queen Beatrix of the Netherlands; was born in Jena, Germany, into the princely family of Lippe, the titular rulers of the principality of Lippe-Biesterfeld; married Crown Princess Juliana in 1937; a dashing bon vivant who drove fast sports cars (and later took to wearing a white carnation in his lapel), he gained immediate popularity with the Dutch people; during World War II, was chief military commander with the Dutch government-in-exile in London, whence he headed the Dutch resistance to the Nazi occupation of his adopted land; while in England, trained as a pilot and was made an honorary wing commander with the Royal Air Force; after the war, became inspector general of the Dutch armed forces; with Crown Princess Juliana, led the work of postwar reconstruction in the Netherlands; made numerous goodwill missions to other countries; flew his own plane to the U.S. in 1950, two years after Queen Wilhelmina's abdication and Juliana's succession to the throne; used his myriad international connections in setting up the Bilderbergers, a rather secretive annual forum of influential Western politicians, businesspeople, and others; chaired that group from 1954 to 1976; cofounded the World Wildlife Fund, in 1961; was president of the fund until 1977; resigned his public offices following allegations that he had accepted bribes from the Lockheed Aircraft Corp. for helping to steer sales of Lockheed Starfighters to the Dutch Air Force; in a statement released after his death, admitted to having received a $1 million "sweetener" from Lockheed; was predeceased by his wife, Juliana (who abdicated in favor of her daughter Beatrix in 1980), and survived by their four daughters; died in Utrecht University Hospital, near Amsterdam, the Netherlands. See *Current Biography* (1950).

Obituary *New York Times* C p11 Dec. 2, 2004

BERTON, PIERRE July 12, 1920–Nov. 30, 2004 Canadian writer and broadcaster; widely read columnist; prominent television personality; prolific author; created his most enduring legacy in his best-selling books of popular Canadian history, especially the saga consisting of the four volumes *Klondike: The Life and Death of the Last Gold Rush* (1958), *The National Dream: The Great [Canadian Pacific] Railway, 1871-1881* (1970), *The Last Spike: The Great Railway 1881-1885* (1971), and *The Promised Land: Settling the West 1895-1914* (1984), which together became the basis for an eight-part television miniseries produced by the Canadian Broadcasting Corp.; was born in Canada's Yukon Territory; began working as a reporter for the Vancouver (British Columbia) *News Herald* while he was earning a B.A. degree at the University of British Columbia; became the newspaper's city editor when he was 21; after World War II service in the Canadian army, worked briefly as a features writer for the *Vancouver Sun* before joining *Maclean's* magazine as assistant editor, in 1947; was promoted to managing editor 10 years later; wrote more articles for *Maclean's* than most of the magazine's staff writers; in addition, moonlighted on radio shows; subsequently, moved on to television; hosted the nightly TV talk program *The Pierre Berton Show* (1962–73); also hosted the current-affairs show *The Great Debate* and the historical series *My Country* and was a panelist on the celebrity quiz show *Front Page Challenge*; in 1954, published his first book, *The Royal Family: The Story of the British Monarch from Victoria to Elizabeth*; in 1958, resigned from *Maclean's* and was hired to write a daily column for the *Toronto Star*; recycled some of his columns in *Adventures of a Columnist* (1960) and other books; devoted more time to the writing of books after quitting the *Toronto Star*, in 1962; turned out a spate of lesser books while researching and writing his more serious historical works; wrote some 50 books, including the memoir *Starting Out: 1920-1947* (1987), *The Dionne Years* (1977), *The Invasion of Canada, 1812-1813* (1980), *Flames Across the Border: The Canadian-American Tragedy* (1981), *The Arctic Grail* (1988), and *Niagara: A History of the Falls* (1997); in his last years was writing a column for the Toronto *Globe and Mail* newspaper; died in Toronto, Canada; was survived by his wife, Janet, and eight children. See *Current Biography* (1991).

Obituary *New York Times* A p27 Dec. 3, 2004

BETHE, HANS July 23, 1906–Mar. 6, 2005 German-born American theoretical nuclear physicist; astrophysicist; astronomer; professor emeritus, Cornell University; was awarded the 1967 Nobel Prize in physics for "his contributions to the theory of nuclear reactions, especially his discoveries concerning the energy production in stars"; in addition to his solo achievements, developed with others the quantum mechanical theory of bremsstrahlung (German for "braking radiation") in relativistic electrons, the theory of electron and proton showers in cosmic rays, the theory of the nucleus of the deuteron, and the alpha-beta-gamma theory of the primordial origin of the chemical elements; during World War II, was an ambivalent participant in the Manhattan Project, which developed the first atomic bomb; later, became a leading voice for nuclear-arms control and nonproliferation; was born to a Jewish mother and a non-Jewish father in Strasbourg, Germany (now Strasbourg, France); earned doctorates in medicine as well as physics; as a Ph.D. candidate at the University of Munich, applied the then-new system of quantum mechanics to explain the Davisson effect of electron diffraction and refraction in crystals; became interested in the passage of fast particles through matter, a problem to which he would return throughout his career; taught at several German universities before leaving the country when Hitler assumed power, in 1933; taught at universities in England from 1933 to 1935; in the U.K., studied the emission of radiation by high-energy particles when deflected by an electromagnetic field; in 1935, immigrated to the U.S. and joined the faculty of Cornell University as an assistant professor; became a full professor in 1937; between 1935 and 1938, did studies in nuclear reactions that enabled him to build on Niels Bohr's theory of the compound nucleus; subsequently, did studies explaining energy generation in all types of main-sequence stars through a series of nuclear reactions; in 1938, worked out details of the so-called Critchfield proton-proton chain to account for energy production in stars smaller than the sun; in the same year, independently of similar work done by C. F. Weizsacker, used the carbon-nitrogen cycle to explain how the more massive stars generate their energy; as head of the theoretical physics department at the Los Alamos atomic laboratory during World War II, provided the theoretical calculations indicating that an explosion of an atom bomb would not spark a chain reaction that might destroy the world; in returning to Cornell after the war, brought back with him from Los Alamos several of his collaborating atomic scientists, including Richard Feynman; in 1947, collaborated with Feynman in calculating the so-called Lamb Shift in the levels of energy of hydrogen, paving the way for the quantum-electrodynamic revolution; in the same year, with Robert Marshak, anticipated the discovery of the pi meson; later, worked on solid-state theory, the splitting of atomic energy when an atom is inserted in a crystal, neutron stars, and the theory of metals, especially that of order and disorder in alloys; was a scientific adviser to three U.S. presidents (1956–64) and to the U.S. mission to the Geneva Conference on the Discontinuance of Nuclear Weapons Tests in 1958; was a founder of the Federation of Atomic Scientists; after his formal retirement at Cornell University, in 1975, continued his studies of thermonuclear processes, shock waves, and neutrinos; spent his last years at the Interferometer Gravitational Wave Observatory, predicting the rate of collapse in stars; published numerous papers and, among other books, *The Road from Los Alamos* (1991) and *Selected Works, with Commentary* (1997); co-wrote the textbook *Intermediate Quantum Mechanics* (third edition, 1997); had a son and a daughter by his wife, the former Rose Ewald; died at his home in Ithaca, New York. See *Current Biography* (1950).

Obituary *New York Times* A p1+ Mar.8, 2005

BROOKS, DONALD Jan. 10, 1928–Aug. 1, 2005 Fashion and costume designer; between the late 1950s and mid-1970s, helped to establish the so-called American look in women's wear with his "subtle kind of clothes"—as he described them—including "dresses that are not too tightly fitted but are not sloppy and that are feminine and soft but not covered with ribbons and bows"; in his couture and boutique collections offered items (gowns, coats, sportswear, and lounging wear as well as day dresses) marked by simplicity of line, striking colors, fine detailing, and distinctively patterned fabrics, many of them of his own design; in his custom designing, boasted a list of celebrity clients that included Jacqueline Kennedy Onassis, Claudette Colbert, Ethel Merman, and Carol Channing; was also an esteemed designer of costumes for theater, film, and television; was born Donald Marc Bloomberg; grew up in New Haven, Connecticut, and New York City; studied at Syracuse University's School of Fine Arts and, in New York City, the Fashion Institute of Technology and the Parsons School of Design; in 1950, began his career at Lord & Taylor, an upscale Manhattan department store, where he advanced from advertising and display to sketching for ready-to-wear sportswear collections; went on to do fashion designing for a succession of Seventh Avenue firms; in January 1959, became the chief fashion designer at Townley Frocks Inc., where he was given full artistic freedom; while with Townley Frocks, began custom-designing clothes for affluent customers at Henri Bendel, a Manhattan specialty shop; in 1962, received a Coty American Fashion Critics Award (the first of several) for the "broad scope of his designing talent, from clothes at a moderate price to custom-order perfectionism, to the most fabulous stage costumes, and including the creation of his own print patterns, which frequently set trends in the fashion world"; from 1965 to 1973, designed four collections a year under his own signature label; began designing for the theater with his award-winning costumes for Diahann Carroll in the Broadway musical *No Strings* (1962); went on to design the costumes for, in all, a score of New York stage productions, including the Broadway shows *Barefoot in the Park, Flora, The Red Menace, On a Clear Day You Can See Forever, Fade Out, Fade In*, and *The Last of the Red Hot Lovers*; was nominated for Academy Awards for the costumes he designed for the motion pictures *The Cardinal* (1963), *Star* (1968), and *Darling Lili* (1970); later, designed costumes for the film *The Bell Jar* (1979); designed the costumes for a number of television films and miniseries; won an Emmy Award for the costumes he designed for Lee Remick in the made-for-TV movie *The Letter* (1982); at the Parsons School of Design in October 2003, was honored with a retrospective exhibition titled Donald Brooks: Designer for All Seasons, which included among his creations a pair of crepe de chine pajamas bearing a print of chickens against a cloudy white-and-blue background and evening wear including a multi-tiered crepe black dress, a halter dress trimmed with gold thread, and a Navajo-print gown; died at Stony Brook University Hospital on Long Island, New York; was survived by his sister, Kay Blick. See *Current Biography* (1972).

Obituary *New York Times* C p17 Aug. 3, 2005

CALLAGHAN, JAMES Mar. 27, 1912–Mar. 26, 2005 British statesman; Labour Party leader; former prime minister; a pragmatist who sought consensus in his parliamentary career and the several cabinet positions he held; as prime minister (1976–79), positioned himself to the right of his party's center; maintained power only with the cooperation of the Liberal Party and the Scottish and Welsh Nationalists and the Ulster Unionists; in coping with an economic crisis in which inflation peaked at 26 percent and was destroying the currency, was forced in 1978 to approve the issuance of a White Paper calling for a 5 percent limit on pay increases and sanctions against employers who exceeded it, thus sparking the 1978–79 "winter of discontent," during which organized labor closed much of the country down with strikes by hospital supervisors, ancillary National Health Service staffers, tanker drivers, teachers, sewage workers, janitors, water and electricity workers, trash collectors, and gravediggers; was unable to prevent a no-confidence vote, which his government lost by one vote (311–310) in Parliament, following which, in the general election in May 1979, his party lost to the Conservatives under the leadership of Margaret Thatcher, Britain's first female prime minister; entered civil service in 1928 as a tax officer with Inland Revenue; in 1936, left civil service and began working full-time as assistant secretary of the union representing Inland Revenue; served in the British navy in World War II; won election to Parliament as a Labour member in 1945; as chancellor of the exchequer (1964–67), introduced a corporation tax, a capital gains tax, and a selective employment tax; as home secretary (1967–70), was faced with difficult issues in immigration, police corruption, student unrest, and, above all, a flare-up of sectarian violence in Northern Ireland; helped to quiet the situation in Ulster by enabling Terence O'Neill, the prime minister there, to dissolve the B Specials, the unpaid, part-time force of Protestant police volunteers, hated by the Catholic community since its creation in 1920, which was still being employed to guard power stations; sent to Northern Ireland a force of British army troops large enough to replace the B Specials in that security task; as foreign secretary (1974–76), renegotiated the terms of Britain's membership in the European Union (then the European Economic Community); could do little about the Turkish occupation of northern Cyprus; succeeded Harold Wilson as leader of the Labour Party and prime minister in April 1976; after the fall of his government, in May 1979, remained leader of the Labour Party until a year later, when the party's left wing, which viewed him as a traitor to socialism, forced him to resign; remained in Parliament until 1987; was created Baron Callaghan of Cardiff in 1987; died at his home in Ringmer, East Sussex, England, 11 days after the death of his wife, the former Audrey Moulton; was survived by a son and two daughters. See *Current Biography* (1968).

Obituary *New York Times* B p6 Mar. 27, 2005

CARMINES, AL July 25, 1936–Aug. 9, 2005 Interdenominational Protestant clergyman; avant-garde theatrical impresario, composer, and performer; a major force in the flowering of Off-Off-Broadway theater; as a minister at the politically and artistically progressive Judson Memorial Church in Manhattan's Greenwich Village in the 1960s and 1970s, was brashly instrumental in transforming the sanctuary into a venue for experimental theater—notably musical productions—liberated from commercial and other constraints prevailing on Broadway and even to some degree Off-Broadway; helped pioneer, in the view of Michael Bronski (writing in the homosexual-oriented newspaper *Bay Windows*, September 1, 2005), an acceptance in popular culture of a "queer sensibility" that "rejected traditional dramatic forms, was highly critical of accepted sexual and gender norms, and drew heavily upon 'camp'—that elusive gay male style and sense of humor that ridiculed and mocked traditional ways of being in the world"; collaborated as a composer with Lawrence Kornfield, Judson's director in residence, on a number of productions based on plays and other texts by Gertrude Stein, including *Listen to Me* and *Doctor Faustus Lights the Light*; had a one-man cabaret act in addition to his work in theater; began playing the piano, tap dancing, and singing at public functions when he was a child growing up in Hampton, Virginia; was influenced by both his father's atheism and his mother's strict Protestant faith; after earning a B.A. degree in English and philosophy at Swarthmore College, matriculated (with some ambivalence) at Union Theological Seminary; in 1961, received his bachelor of divinity degree and was ordained a minister; received a master's degree in sacred theology; at the suggestion of Lawrence Kornfield, began contributing music (including the score for five pages of lines by Gertrude Stein in the one-act play *What Happened?*) to productions of the Judson Poets' Theater when he was an assistant minister at Judson Memorial Church (1961–64); after becoming an associate minister at the church, in 1964, assumed a more prominent role in the Judson Poets' Theater, ultimately restructured the troupe and renamed it the Judson Musical Theater; realized his first major success with Rosalyn Drexler's wicked spoof *Home Movies*, for which he composed the music and in which he was cast in the irreverent role of Father Shenanigan, in a production, launched at Judson early in 1964, that moved to the Off-Broadway Provincetown Playhouse in May of the same year and brought Carmines the first of his five Obie Awards, for composition; received Vernon Rice Awards for both composition (of a score to a text by Gertrude Stein) and performance (as singer and pianist) with a subsequent hit of his, the McLuanesque, nonlinear *In Circles* (1967–68), a tour de force of musical styles, from jazz to tango, waltz, and opera, that played Off-Broadway at the Cherry Lane and Gramercy Arts theaters after its run at Judson; won a Drama Desk Award for best composer of 1968–69 for his score for *Peace*, the lyricist Timothy Reynolds's adaptation of Aristophanes to a minstrel-show setting, which moved to the Astor Place Theater after its Judson run; wrote the score for Maria Irene Fornes's *Promenade*, the hit of Judson's 1969–70 season, a satirical view of contemporary culture from the point of view of convicts; swept the credits—as librettist, composer, lyricist, actor, and director—with *Joan* (the story of Joan of Arc transplanted to the East Village) and with the 1973 musical *The Faggot*, which moved from Judson into a long run at the Truck and Warehouse Theater; wrote for Broadway *W.C.*, a musical about W.C. Fields starring Mickey Rooney and Bernadette Peters, which failed out of town in its pre-Broadway tryout in 1971; never fully recovered from a cerebral aneurysm that he suffered in 1977; resigned his position at Judson Memorial Church in 1981; the following year, founded the Rauschenbusch Memorial Church, a congregation affiliated with the United Church of Christ; remained pastor of that church, on West 57th Street in Manhattan, until his death; died at St. Vincent's Hospital in Greenwich Village; was survived by his companion, Paul Rounsaville. See *Current Biography* (1972).

Obituary *New York Times* B p7 Aug. 13, 2005

CARSON, JOHNNY Oct. 23, 1925–Jan. 23, 2005
Television personality; comedian; one of the most popular entertainers in the annals of American show business; succeeded Jack Paar as host of the NBC television network's *Tonight Show* in 1962; emceed that late-night talk/variety program (known as the *Tonight Show Starring Johnny Carson* during his tenure) for 30 years, until 1992; built the show's average audience to 15 million, made it the biggest money-maker in NBC history, and personally set a record for durability in TV hosting; off the air, was reputed to be almost painfully shy; on the air, had an assured, understated rapport with the camera, projecting a charmingly puckish persona that combined heartland innocence (communicated by disarming boyish grins and wide-eyed double-takes) with cosmopolitan sophistication; delivered the jokes in his opening monologue—a commentary on

people and events in the day's news that he prepared in collaboration with his staff—with seamless ease and masterly timing; displayed deft wit in the celebrity banter that transpired in the course of the show; in recurring skits on the program, played such characters as Art Fern, a sleazy automobile salesman, and Carnac the Magnificent, a turbaned clairvoyant who divined not the answers to questions but the questions to answers; among his guests were numerous performers, especially young comedians, who traced their ascent in show business to their appearances on the show; was born in Iowa and grew up there and in Nebraska; after navy service in World War II, began working in local radio while earning a B.A. degree at the University of Nebraska; got a job as a staff announcer at television station KNXT in Los Angeles in 1951; on Sunday afternoons at KNXT, presented a half-hour comedy show, *Carson's Cellar*; in 1952, was hired as a writer for the *Red Skelton Show*, then on the NBC television network; remained with that show after it moved to CBS in 1953; briefly substituted as emcee when Skelton was sidelined with an injury in 1954; emceed the CBS prime-time game show *Earn Your Vacation* for 10 weeks in 1954; hosted the *Johnny Carson Show*, a half-hour CBS variety program that ran at night for nine months in 1955–56 and in the daytime for four additional months; on the ABC network, hosted the game show *Who Do You Trust?* from 1957 to 1962; meanwhile, sat in for Jack Paar on the *Tonight Show* in the spring of 1958; after succeeding Paar, in 1962, made few appearances outside of the weeknight hour-plus *Tonight Show Starring Johnny Carson* except for some performances in Las Vegas and the emceeing of some television specials, including five Academy Award ceremonies (1979–82 and 1984); was married four times and had three sons, including one who predeceased him; died in Los Angeles. See *Current Biography* (1982).

Obituary *New York Times* A p1+ Jan. 24, 2005

CHISHOLM, SHIRLEY Nov. 30, 1924–Jan. 1, 2005
Former Democratic congresswoman; former New York State assemblywoman; a staunchly independent trailblazer for women in politics; for seven terms over a period of 14 years (1969–83) in the U.S. House of Representatives, held the seat for New York's 12th Congressional District, centered in the impoverished Bedford-Stuyvesant neighborhood in Brooklyn, New York City; was the first black woman to serve in Congress; was also the first black woman to seek (in 1972, unsuccessfully) a major party's presidential nomination; before entering politics, became an expert in early-childhood education; was born with the surname St. Hill; acquired the name Chisholm from the first of her two marriages; was born in Brooklyn; grew up there and in the island country of Barbados in the West Indies, her mother's birthplace; received a B.A. degree in sociology from Brooklyn College in 1948 and an M.A. degree in elementary education from Columbia University in 1952; while earning the degrees, taught at the Mount Calvary Child Care Center in Harlem and then the Friends Day Nursery School in the Brownsville section of Brooklyn; was associated with Hamilton-Madison House, a settlement house in the Two

Bridges/Chinatown neighborhood on Manhattan's Lower East Side, for 40 years, first as a nursery-school teacher (1953–59) and then as a board member; was an educational consultant to the day-care division of New York City's Bureau of Child Welfare from 1959 to 1964; in 1964, was elected to the New York State Assembly, where she represented her home district (the 55th Assembly District) until 1968, when she ran successfully for the first of her terms in Congress; the next year, broke ranks with the Democratic Party by supporting John V. Lindsay, who was running (successfully) for a second term as mayor of New York as a Liberal-Independent; in her own congressional campaign, had used the slogan "Fighting Shirley Chisholm—Unbought and Unbossed"; lived up to those words from the beginning of her tenure in Congress, which she found to be, at that time, a club "ruled by a small group of old men"; initially, was relegated to the House Agriculture Committee, an assignment ludicrously irrelevant to the concerns of her urban constituency; refusing to "be a good soldier," as she was asked, broke protocol by complaining, and gained assignment to the Veterans Affairs Committee and later to Education and Labor, committees in which she could more effectively serve as an advocate for poor communities, including those in inner cities, and for women's rights, including abortion rights; pushed for legislation increasing federal funding of child-care facilities; cosponsored the Adequate Income Act of 1971; strongly opposed the Vietnam War; was sometimes at odds with her male peers in the Congressional Black Caucus, as when she voted for Hale Boggs, who was white, for House majority leader, over John Conyers, a caucus member, and when she sought the Democratic presidential nomination, despite the opinion of many caucus members, voiced privately, that her doing so would cause more harm than good; recalled that black people in her community "crucified" her when she made a hospital visit to George C. Wallace, the Alabama governor and one-time segregationist, after he was severely injured in an assassination attempt in 1972; chose not to run for an eighth term in Congress in 1982; at that time told a reporter, "I've always met more discrimination being a woman than being a black"; wrote the memoirs *Unbought and Unbossed* (1970) and *The Good Fight* (1973); after leaving Congress, in January 1983, taught for four years at Mount Holyoke College, in Massachusetts; was much in demand on the lecture circuit; said that her "greatest political asset" was her "mouth, which professional politicians fear[ed]"; moved to Florida in 1991; died at her home in Ormond Beach, Florida. See *Current Biography* (1969).

Obituary *New York Times* B p9 Jan. 3, 2005

CLARK, KENNETH B. July 24, 1914–May 1, 2005 Psychologist; college professor; civil rights activist; in 1946, in partnership with his wife, the psychologist Mamie Phipps Clark, founded the Northside Center for Child Development (originally called the Northside Testing and Consultation Center), a guidance clinic for troubled children and young people in the Harlem section of New York City; decisively influenced the U.S. Supreme Court's 1954 decision declaring racial segregation in public education un-

constitutional, in the case of Brown v. Board of Education; was born in the Panama Canal Zone and raised by his mother in Harlem; after receiving B.A. and M.S. degrees at Howard University, earned a Ph.D. in experimental psychology at Columbia University; taught psychology at Howard University (1937–38) and Hampton Institute (1940–41); contributed to the research for the Carnegie Corp. project (1938–43) headed by the Swedish economist and social reformer Gunnar Myrdal, which resulted in Myrdal's book *An American Dilemma: The Negro Problem and Modern Democracy*; as an assistant social-science analyst on the research staff of the U.S. Office of War Information, spent a year (1941–42) traveling around the country compiling information on the morale of the African-American population; in 1942, joined the faculty of the Psychology Department of the City College of New York; was the first black to become a tenured instructor at City College and the first to be elected to the New York State Board of Regents, on which he served from 1966 to 1986; in the early 1950s, volunteered his and his wife's research to the service of the team of NAACP lawyers who were preparing to bring before the U.S. Supreme Court their case against racial discrimination and segregation in public education, in which the plaintiffs' key argument was that "separate but equal" education was self-contradictory, that segregated schooling resulted in inferior education for black children; in the report that was appended to the NAACP's successful brief, testified that segregated schooling not only contributed to negative self-perception and emotional instability among black children but was psychologically damaging to white children as well; subsequently, founded Harlem Youth Opportunities Unlimited, or HARYOU, an education-oriented organization that qualified for $110 million in federal funding for its part in President Lyndon B. Johnson's "war on poverty" and which, under pressure from Harlem congressman Adam Clayton Powell, was merged with the Powell-sponsored Associated Community Teams (ACT) to form HARYOU-ACT; retired as a professor in the CUNY system in 1975; wrote *Dark Ghetto: Dilemmas of Social Power* (1965) and *Pathos of Power* (1974); saw the history of the still thriving and influential Northside Center (which is now interracial) told in the book *Children, Race, and Power* (1996), by Gerald Markowitz and David Rosner; was predeceased by his wife, Mamie, and survived by a daughter, a son, three grandchildren, and five great-grandchildren; died at his home in Hastings-on-Hudson, New York. See *Current Biography* (1964).

Obituary *New York Times* A p1+ May 2, 2005

COCHRAN, JOHNNIE L. JR. Oct. 2, 1937–Mar. 29, 2005 Attorney; civil libertarian; a brilliant legal strategist and masterly trial lawyer, elegant in style and gifted in low-key but powerful courtroom eloquence, accented with pithy phraseology; founded and headed a firm that grew to include offices across the U.S. and won awards of hundreds of millions of dollars in torts, including personal-injury suits against such major corporations as Coca-Cola and the Walt Disney Co.; was best known for his work in criminal cases and in particular his defense of clients—from common folk to black celebrities—many of whom were perceived to be victims of unjust law enforcement; achieved legal superstardom when he emerged as the outstanding member of the "dream team" that successfully defended the former football star, television sports commentator, and actor O. J. Simpson when he was on trial for the murders of his ex-wife and one of her acquaintances—a trial that began in Los Angeles in January 1995 and went on for eight and a half months, during which it was covered extensively on national TV; countered seemingly overwhelming evidence against Simpson, including DNA and blood samples, by presenting to the largely black jury his scenario of a frame-up by racist white police, notably including the detective Mark Fuhrman, who had found a bloody glove on Simpson's property on the night of the murders; referring to a crucial point in the trial—when Simpson was asked to try the glove on and seemed to have difficulty fitting his hand into it—uttered in his closing argument his most famous courtroom aphorism: "If it doesn't fit, you must acquit"; summoned the memory of the genocidal racism of Adolf Hitler for comparison with Fuhrman's wanting, in Cochran's words, "to take all black people now and burn them or bomb them"; asked the jury to "send them [the powers that be] a message"; was victorious on October 3, 1995, when the jury returned a verdict of not guilty on both murder counts; after passing the California bar in 1963, worked for two years as a Los Angeles city deputy attorney; in 1965, entered private practice in Los Angeles; soon became known in the black community for handling cases involving alleged police misconduct; said years later, "Those were extremely difficult cases to win in those days, but [the] issue of police abuse really galvanized the minority community. . . . These cases could really get attention"; in 1970, went to court in defense of Elmer "Geronimo" Pratt, a former Black Panther who was accused of murder; lost the case, after which Pratt spent 27 years in prison before Cochran helped him win his freedom, in 1997; to try "to make changes from the inside," joined the Los Angeles County district attorney's office as assistant DA and number-three prosecutor in 1978; returned to private practice in the early 1980s; earned praise of a sort from Gregory Moore, the managing editor of the *San Antonio Informer*, who believed that "the one sports legacy that [Cochran] should be remembered for" was his successful representation of the family of the black college football player Ron Settles in their wrongful-death suit against the police in the Los Angeles suburb of Signal Hill, California, in whose custody Settles died in 1981; in that case, won a pretrial settlement of $760,000 in 1983; went on to win an estimated total of $42 million from various California municipalities and police districts; in 1985, won the dropping of rape and assault charges against the black football Hall of Famer Jim Brown; in 1989 and 1990, won acquittal for the black TV actor Todd Bridges on charges including attempted murder with a deadly weapon; sued the city of Los Angeles in behalf of Reginald Denny, the white truck driver beaten by a black mob in 1991; representing Michael Jackson in the pop-music star's first defense against child-molestation charges, arranged an out-of-court settlement and withdrawal of the charges in 1993; representing Snoop Doggy Dogg in 1996, won the acquittal of that "gangsta" rapper on murder charges and the dropping of manslaughter charges against him; in 1997, helped to settle for $8.75 million the civil case of the Haitian immigrant Abner Louima against the Brooklyn police officers accused of torturing him; in 2001, with Benjamin Brafman, defended the rap musician Sean "P. Diddy" Combs in a weapons and robbery case; in the late 1990s, participated in a daily show on the Court cable TV network; in 1999, merged his law firm with a major Manhattan-based personal-injury law firm to form the Cochran Firm/Schneider, Kleinick, Weitz, Damashek & Schoot; wrote two autobiographical books: *Journey to Justice* (1996), with Tim Rutten, and *A Lawyer's Life* (2002), with David Fisher; died at his home in Los Angeles; was survived by his second wife, the former Dale Mason, by two daughters from his first marriage, and by a son from his relationship with Patricia Sikora, his erstwhile mistress. See *Current Biography* (1999).

Obituary *New York Times* A p15 Mar. 30, 2005

COLEMAN, CY June 14, 1929–Nov. 18, 2004 Composer; pianist; a major creator of jazz-influenced show tunes; won three Tony Awards for his Broadway scores; composed such hit songs as "Witchcraft," "Hey, Look Me Over," and "Big Spender"; was born in the New York City borough of the Bronx to Jewish immigrant parents; a child prodigy, began playing the piano at four and made his Carnegie Hall debut before he was nine; was grounded in classical piano by his local teacher in the Bronx, at the High School of Music and Art (now the Fiorello H. LaGuardia School of Music and Art and Performing Arts) in Manhattan, and at the New York College of Music; outside of academia, gravitated to jazz as a teenager and young man; early in his career, played the piano in cocktail lounges and society-music and jazz clubs and on several television shows; also composed music for television; in his first popular-song collaboration, joined the lyricist Joseph A. McCarthy in writing the hit "Why Try to Change Me Now?" (1952), among other songs; after a brief collaboration with the lyricist Bob Hilliard, in the late 1950s began a five-year collaboration with the lyricist Carolyn Leigh that yielded the scores for the Broadway musicals *Wildcat* and *Little Me* and some 20 published songs, including the hits "Witchcraft," "Firefly," "I've Got Your Number," "Hey, Look Me Over," "The Best Is Yet to Come," "Rules of the Road," and "Real Live Girl"; collaborated with Dorothy Fields on the Broadway musicals *Sweet Charity* (1966)—which included the hits "Big Spender" and "If My Friends Could See Me Now"–and *Seesaw* (1973) and with Michael Stewart on *I Love My Wife* (1977); teamed with the lyricists Betty Comden and Adolf Green on the musical *On the Twentieth Century* (1978) and with Michael Stewart on *Barnum* (1979); in addition to composing the music and co-writing the lyrics, co-produced the musical *Welcome to the Club* (1989), a commercial flop; was much more successful with *City of Angels* (1989), a Tony winner for which David Zippel wrote the lyrics; again collaborated with Comden and Green on *The Will Rogers Follies*, which won the awards for best musical and best original score at the Tony ceremonies in June 1991; in collaboration with the lyricist Ira Gasman, scored his last Broadway musical, *The Life* (1997); scored the motion picture *Father Goose* (1964), which included the song "Pass Me By," and The Heartbreak Kid (1972); when *Sweet Charity* was adapted for the screen (1969), was nominated for the Academy Award for best musical score (1970); conceived and co-wrote Shirley MacLaine's television special *If They Could See Me Now* (1974), for which he won two Emmy Awards; produced the 1975 Shirley MacLaine television special *Gypsy in My Soul*, which won the Emmy for best television musical show of the year; was survived by his wife, Shelby, and a daughter; died in Manhattan. See *Current Biography* 1990.

Obituary *New York Times* A p17 Nov. 20, 2004

CREELEY, ROBERT May 21, 1926–Mar. 30, 2005 Poet; fiction writer; essayist; taught for many years at New York State University at Buffalo; was a minimalist poet generally categorized as a modernist in the anti-academic, natural-speech tradition of Ezra Pound and William Carlos Williams; at the beginning of his career, in the 1950s, was identified with the Black Mountain school of open, "projective" verse, described by the poet and critic Charles Olson, that school's leader, as a "high energy construct" transmitted to the reader as directly as "the breathing of the man who writes"; for his part, shared his sense of energy with improvisational jazz musicians and abstract-expressionist painters; attracted wider attention after his poems began appearing in *Poetry* magazine in 1957; established himself as an important poet with the publication in 1962 of *For Love: Poems 1950–1960*, a collection of verse (including "Ballad of a Despairing Husband") chiefly on themes relating to marriage, marital difficulties, infidelity, and loneliness, among other autobiographical subjects; striving to give shape to what he called "who I know myself to be, for that instant," continued to experiment with bursts of truncated lines in volatile and often anguished poems of love and intimate relations in such books as *Words* (1967) and *Pieces* (1968); as he aged, became increasingly fragmented in his verse, until his last years, when he settled into relative tranquility in his personal life and became less colloquial and more darkly reflective in his poems; in his fiction—including the novel *The Island* (1963) and the short stories collected in *The Gold Diggers* (1965)—as in his poetry, relied on autobiographical subject matter and rejected formal conventions; published a total of some 60 books, including eight volumes of his correspondence with Charles Olson (1980–87), *Collected Poems* (1982), *Collected Prose* (1984), *Autobiography* (1990), and *Loops: Ten Poems* (1995); won the Bollingen Prize in 1999; was an American Field Service ambulance driver in Burma and India during World War II; dropped out of Harvard University in 1947; later received a B.A. degree at Black Mountain College, a short-lived (1933–56) experimental arts college in North Carolina, and an M.A. at the University of New Mexico; in January 1950, gave a reading of his poems on *This Is Poetry*, a Boston radio program hosted by Sidney "Cid" Corman, who began publishing Creeley's poetry and

short fiction in his magazine, *Origin*; meanwhile, had begun corresponding with Ezra Pound and William Carlos Williams and such second-generation modernists as Charles Olson and the poet Louis Zukofsky; with his first wife, Ann McKinnon, and their two sons and one daughter, lived in southern France (1951–52) and on the island of Majorca, Spain (1952–54); with McKinnon, founded the Divers Press to publish his work and that of other writers ignored by the literary establishment; at the request of Charles Olson, who had become rector of Black Mountain College, taught at the college for two semesters, in 1954 and 1955; edited the *Black Mountain Review*, a literary magazine that had a duration of seven issues (1955–57); after his chaotic marriage was dissolved, in mid-1955, spent some time in San Francisco, becoming acquainted with Kenneth Rexroth and other leaders of the literary renaissance there that ushered in the Beat Generation of writers; in 1956, took a teaching job at a boys' high school in Albuquerque, New Mexico; in Albuquerque, met and married (in January 1957) his second wife, Bobbie Louise Hall (aka Hoeck, aka Hawkins); by her, had two daughters in addition to two stepdaughters from her previous marriage; became an instructor at the University of New Mexico in 1961; subsequently, taught at the University of British Columbia and San Francisco State University; became David Gray Professor of Poetry and Letters at the State University of New York at Buffalo in 1978; later, taught briefly at Brown University; following the dissolution of his second marriage, in 1976, married Penelope Highton, in 1977; by that third and final marriage, had a son and a daughter; was survived by all three of his wives and by eight children; in his final days, was in residence at the Lannan Foundation's writers' retreat in Marfa, Texas; died in Odessa, Texas. See *Current Biography* (1988).

Obituary *New York Times* C p13 Apr. 1, 2005

CUNHAL, ÁLVARO Nov. 10, 1913–June 13, 2005 Portuguese Communist leader; lawyer; author; artist; a brilliant intellectual with a charismatic personality whose influence in public affairs in 20th-century Portugal was powerful; in politics, was an unreconstructed Stalinist; at first working largely in clandestinity, because the Pardida Comunista Portugues (PCP), or Portuguese Communist Party, was then outlawed, built that party into the strongest opponent of the right-wing dictatorship of Antonio Salazar (1932–68) and Marcello Caetano (1968–74); joined the PCP when he 17 and a freshman at the University of Lisbon; was elected head of the party's youth division in 1935; at about the time he received his doctorate in law (1940), became the de facto leader of the PCP; was elected general secretary in 1961; spent much of his time living underground, in exile, or in prison until April 1974, when Premier Caetano's government was overthrown in a bloodless military coup; was appointed minister without portfolio in the new regime's first cabinet; held that position from May 14, 1974 until July 1975; was highly respected for his influential writings on political subjects, including the history of the class struggle in Potugal; published the book *Discursos Políticos* in 1988; wrote four best-selling novels with political slants under the pseudonym Manuel Tiago; created drawings, paintings, engravings, and sculptures under the name António Vale; resigned as general secretary of the PCP in 1992; died in Lisbon; was survived by his wife, Fernanda Barroso, and by a daughter, Ana Maria, from a previous liaison with Isaura Dias. See *Current Biography* (1975).

Obituary *New York Times* A p21 June 14, 2005

DANCER, STANLEY July 25, 1927–Sep. 8, 2005 Harness-racing driver; owner; breeder; a shrewd discoverer of equine talent, and an uncanny trainer; was born into a farming and harness-racing family in West Windsor, New Jersey, and raised on the family farm in New Egypt, New Jersey; dropped out of school after the eighth grade; was introduced to harness racing at Freehold Raceway in New Jersey; later became a groom at Roosevelt Raceway in Westbury, Long Island, New York; began riding the sulky at Roosevelt Raceway in 1947; drove several winners for other owners before starting his own stable, by buying a supposedly superannuated gelding named Candor for $250; with loving care and training, revived Candor's vitality; over a period of three years (1949–51), won $13,000 driving Candor; subsequently, discovered, trained, and drove his second winner, Volo Chief; soon was training and driving some two dozen horses and was in demand as a finder and buyer of horses for others; became the top driver at Yonkers Raceway during the 1950s; won the Yonkers Trot a record six times, beginning in 1959; led Grand Circuit drivers in purses in 1961, 1962, 1964 (when he became the first to win $1 million), and 1966; drove Cardigan Bay to that pacer's career total of $1 million in winnings, a first for a horse; was named driver of the year on the circuit in 1968; during the 1960s, found and trained many of the major prize-winning horses in harness racing, including some for other owners; trained and drove the trotter Su Mac Lad, who was named Horse of the Year in 1962; drove his trotter Noble Victory to a record time of one minute and 55 and $3/_5$ seconds in a mile race in 1966; was the only driver to win three triple crowns for three-year-olds, with his trotter Nevele Pride in 1966, with the trotter Super Bowl (whom he had bought for his first wife, Rachel, and Mrs. Hilda Silverstein) in 1972, and with his pacer Most Happy Fella in 1970; set records in winning the Cane Pace/Futurity four times between 1964 and 1976 and the Hambletonian five times between 1974 and 1983; when his horse Dancer's Crown, a conspicuous favorite, died shortly before the Hambletonian in 1983, agreed to enter the race with a little-known filly named Duena instead, and drove that long shot to victory; trained and drove seven horses of the year, including the pacer Albatrross in 1971 and 1972 and the pacer Keystone Ore in 1976; was inducted into the Harness Racing Hall of Fame in 1969; drove his last winning race in 1996, ending with a career total of $28,002,426 in winnings; in 1985, following his divorce from Rachel Young in 1983, married Jody O'Connor, who survived him, along with his two sons, two daughters, seven grandchildren, and four great-grandchildren; died in Pompano Beach, Florida. See *Current Biography* (1973).

Obituary *New York Times* Sep. 9, 2005

DANGERFIELD, RODNEY Nov. 11, 1921–Oct. 5, 2004 Comedian; an old-style stand-up comic who told one-line jokes and whose distinctive shtick was that of a luckless schlemiel who complained of getting "no respect"; was a potbellied man with bulbous eyes who fidgeted nervously with his tie as he delivered such one-liners as "I told my psychiatrist that everyone hates me. He told me I was being ridiculous—everyone hadn't met me yet"; was born Jacob Cohen in Babylon, Long Island, New York; after his father, a womanizing vaudeville comedian, abandoned the family, was raised by his mother in Kew Gardens, Queens, New York City; when he was 19, began entertaining in B-level venues in and around New York under the name Jack Roy, wearing a funny hat, doing some dance steps, and delivering undistinguished jokes; after nine years, all but terminated that act, following what has been described as a "particularly humiliating experience" during an engagement at a Catskills resort hotel; settled into his first marriage, with Joyce Indig, a singer, by whom he had two children, Brian and Melanie; during the 1950s, sometimes performed in clubs on weekends while supporting himself and his family full-time by selling paint and aluminum siding; returned to show business full-time in the early 1960s with a new name, Rodney Dangerfield, and a sad-sack persona whose slogan was "Nothing goes right"; refined that mantra into "I don't get no respect" in the early 1970s (seemingly a reference to the Mafia dons in the motion picture *The Godfather* [1972], who talk about the importance of getting respect); meanwhile, was transcending the limited club circuit through appearances on television; began attracting national attention on *The Ed Sullivan Show*; secured that attention with 97 performances on the *Tonight Show Starring Johnny Carson* over the following two decades; had his own niche on the *Dean Martin Show* (1972-73); hosted *Saturday Night Live* in 1975; on cable television, had five specials on Home Box Office; spent five years presenting his routine at the MGM Grand Hotel in Las Vegas; in 1969, opened his own comedy club, Dangerfield's, in Manhattan; in his club, on his HBO specials, and in his Vegas act, showcased such young comedic talents as Roseanne Barr, Jerry Seinfeld, and Jim Carrey; made his screen debut in a featured role in *The Projectionist* (1971); clinched his fame with his role as Al Czervik, a nouveau-riche boor behaving obnoxiously in an elite golf club, in *Caddyshack* (1980); later starred in the screen comedies *Easy Money* (1983) and *Back to School* (1986); had a straight supporting role in the film *Natural Born Killers* (1994); recorded several albums, including the Grammy Award–winning *No Respect* (1980); wrote the autobiography *It's Not Easy Bein' Me: A Lifetime of No Respect but Plenty of Sex and Drugs* (2004); married Joyce Indig twice and was divorced from her twice, in 1962 and 1970; married Joan Child in 1993; died in Los Angeles.

Obituary *New York Times* A p27 Oct. 6, 2004

DAVIS, GLENN Dec. 26, 1924–Mar. 9, 2005 Former football player; at the U.S. Military Academy at West Point, New York, in the mid-1940s, teamed with Doc Blanchard to form one of the most celebrated backfields in college football; after winning 13 letters in four sports in high school in La Verne, California, entered West Point in 1943; as a freshman fullback, gained 1,028 yards in 144 attempts; moved to halfback when Blanchard joined the team as fullback in 1944; with Blanchard, became known as the "touchdown twins" in the sports press; with his breakaway lightning speed and ability to make end runs, was dubbed "Mr. Outside" while the more burly Blanchard, whose specialty was plunging through the line, was called "Mr. Inside"; with Blanchard, paced Army (as the Military Academy team is popularly known) to National Collegiate Athletic Association championships in 1944 and 1945 and to a tie with Notre Dame for the championship in 1946 (over those three seasons, Army had a record of 27 wins, no losses, and one tie, with Notre Dame); was runner-up to Blanchard for the Heisman Trophy in 1944, and won the Heisman in 1945; was a consensus first-team All American three times (1944, 1945, and 1946); led the nation in touchdowns in 1944, with 20, and in average yards per carry in rushing in 1944 and 1945, with 11.5; attained college career totals that included 2,957 yards rushing, 855 yards passing, and 59 touchdowns and an average of 8.26 yards per carry rushing that as of 2005 still stood as an NCAA record; in combination with Blanchard, set NCAA records for touchdowns (97) and points scored (585) by teammates in a college career; achieved his college stats at a time when, as defensive back, he was limited to 58 minutes per game; off the gridiron, set school records in track and field and earned varsity letters in baseball and basketball; as a center fielder on the Army baseball team, was a top major-league prospect; on leave from the military, played himself (with Blanchard as himself) in the motion picture *Spirit of West Point* (1947); in an accident during filming, tore cartilage and ligaments in his right knee, which failed to heal properly; in 1950, following three years of military service in Korea, joined the Los Angeles Rams, a professioanl team then in the Natioanl Conference of the National Football League; as the Rams' leading running back in 1950, traveled 416 yards and scored three touchdowns; as a receiver, ran an additional 592 yards and scored four touchdowns; helped the Rams to achieve a win–loss record of 9–3; defeated the Chicago Bears in the conference play-offs, only to lose to the Cleveland Browns in the NFL championship game; in 1951, when the Rams won the NFL championship, declined in performance (largely because of his damaged knee), registering only 200 yards and one touchdown rushing and 90 yards rushing and one touchdown receiving; retired from football at the end of the 1951 season; following his retirement, worked for nearly three decades as a special-events director for the *Los Angeles Times* newspaper; was married briefly to his first wife, the movie actress Terry Moore, and for many years to his second wife, Ellen Harriet Lancaster Slack, until her death, in 1995; was survived by his third wife, the former Yvonne Ameche, and a stepson, John S. Slack II, among others; died at his home in La Quinta, California. See *Current Biography* (1946).

Obituary *New York Times* A p25 Mar. 10, 2005

DAVIS, NATHANAEL V. June 26, 1915–Mar. 22, 2005 Aluminum-company executive; philanthropist; was the nephew of Arthur Vining Davis, who founded the Aluminum Co. of America (Alcoa) in 1886, and the son of Edward K. Davis, who in 1928 organized an offshoot of Alcoa called Aluminium Ltd., the holding company for Alcan (Aluminum Co. of Canada), among other subsidiaries, until 1951, when it became a fully independent entity; was president and chief executive officer of Alcan Inc. from 1947 to 1979 and chairman of the board of that company from 1972 to 1986; by building hydroelectric generators in Quebec and British Columbia, provided the Canadian company with its own power sources; made Alcan the second-largest producer of primary aluminum in the world; majored in international law and economics at Harvard University and did graduate work at the London School of Economics; was an intelligence officer with the U.S. Navy during World War II; chaired for 30 years the Arthur Vining Davis Foundations, a multifaceted philanthropy; died at his home in Boca Grande, Florida; was survived by his wife, Lois, a son and a daughter, seven grandchildren, and a great-grandchild. See *Current Biography* (1959).

Obituary *New York Times* C p13 Apr. 1, 2005

DAVIS, OSSIE Dec. 18, 1917–Feb. 4, 2005 Actor; playwright; producer; director; a tall and deep-voiced performer who consistently projected dignity in his scores of character portrayals on stage, screen, and television; an activist for actors' rights, civil rights, and civil liberties; was eulogized by the film critic Roger Ebert as a "legendary figure, who combined militancy with grace and humor"; with Ruby Dee, comprised one of the entertainment world's most prominent marital partnerships, about whom the director Spike Lee observed, "They were strong and brave at a time when many Negro entertainers stood on the sidelines. They were with Dr. King in Birmingham, Selma, and the March on Washington, and never worried about the negative impact it might have on their careers"; in a distinguished career spanning more than half a century, scored his most famous triumph as playwright and actor with his play *Purlie Victorious*, in which he combined folk comedy with social satire in lampooning the segregationist mores of the Jim Crow South; starred in that play on Broadway (heading a cast that included Ruby Dee) in 1960–61 and in the film version bearing the title *Gone Are the Days* (1963); also wrote the libretto for *Purlie* (1970), the hit Broadway musical based on the play; among other memorable credits, replaced Cleavon Little as Midge in the Broadway play *I'm Not Rappaport* (1986–87), another hit, and later starred opposite Walter Matthau in the movie version (1996) of that play; among his more than 30 feature-film roles were those of Chuck in the comedy *Grumpy Old Men* (1993), Coach Odom in Spike Lee's *School Daze* (1988), the wise neighborhood alcoholic who gives the advice echoed in the title of Lee's *Do the Right Thing* (1989), and the minister father of the Wesley Snipes character in Lee's *Jungle Fever* (1991); after graduating from high school in Waycross, Georgia, and studying drama at Howard University, in Washington, D.C., joined the Rose McLendon Players, a small theatrical troupe in Harlem; was a medic with the U.S. Army in World War II; in 1946, made his Broadway debut in the title role in *Jeb*, a short-lived production about a black war hero's ungrateful welcome back home in the old segregated South; met Ruby Dee when she was a member of the cast of *Jeb*; subsequently, toured with her in the national company of the American Negro Theater's production of *Anna Lucasta*; married Dee in 1948; beginning in the late 1940s and continuing into the 1950s, was engaged in protesting the political oppression occurring at that time under the aegis of what was generally known as McCarthyism, including the blacklisting of the "Hollywood Ten" and others (Paul Robeson, for example) accused of "subversive" affiliations or sympathies; early on as a playwright, wrote the short work *Alice in Wonder* (1953), an attack on McCarthyism produced at a little theater in Harlem; later expanded that play into *The Big Deal*; on Broadway, played Trem in *The Leading Lady* (1948), Stewart in *The Smile of the World* (1949), Jacques in *The Wisteria Trees* (1950), the Angel Gabriel in a revival of *The Green Pastures* (1951), Jo in *The Royal Family* (1951), Al Clinton in *Remains to Be Seen* (1951), Dr. Joseph Clay in *Touchstone* (1953), and Cicero in the hit musical *Jamaica* (1957–59), among other roles; in October 1959, replaced Sidney Poitier as Walter Lee Younger in the original Broadway production of *Raisin in the Sun* (1959–60), in which Ruby Dee was already cast as Ruth Younger; was subsequently cast in *Ballet for Bimshire* (1963) and *The Zulu and the Zayda* (1965); also performed in *A Celebration of Paul Robeson* (1988); delivered the eulogy at the funeral of Malcolm X, in 1965, and was a leader in raising funds for the support of Malcolm's widow and children; in an uncredited role, with Ruby Dee, made his motion-picture debut in *No Way Out* (1950); went on to play roles in such feature films as *The Joe Louis Story* (1954), *The Cardinal* (1963), *The Hill* (1964), *The Scalphunters* (1968), *The Client* (1994), *Dr. Dolittle* (1998), and Spike Lee's films *Get on the Bus* (1996) and *She Hate Me* (2004); wrote and directed the feature films *Cotton Comes to Harlem* (1970) and *Countdown at Kusini* (1976); co-produced the latter with Ruby Dee; also directed the feature films *Black Girl* (1972) and *Gordon's War* (1973); had roles in many TV dramas (including the lead in a 1955 production of *The Emperor Jones*), made-for-TV movies (including *Twelve Angry Men*, 1997), situation comedies, and other series, including the miniseries *Roots: The Next Generation* (1979), in which Ruby Dee was also cast; with Ruby Dee, hosted a storytelling show on public television during the 1980–81 season; published the dual autobiography *With Ossie and Ruby: In This Life Together* (1998); was a co-recipient with Dee of Kennedy Center Honors in December 2004, when they were cited for "work that has touched us all" and for the "courage and tenacity" with which they "have thrown open many a door previously shut tight to African American artists and planted the seed for the flowering of America's multicultural humanity"; died in Miami Beach, Florida, where he was making a motion picture titled *Retirement*; was eulogized at his funeral service, in Riverside Church in Manhattan, by Harry Belafonte, who said that he had used his gifts, especially his mastery

of language, "to articulate our deepest hope for the fulfillment of our oneness with all humanity" and for "his fervent dedication to justice," to "defending the causes of the poor, the humiliated, the oppressed"; survived by Dee as well as a son, two daughters, and seven grandchildren. See *Current Biography* (1969).

Obituary *New York Times* A p14 Feb. 5, 2005

DELOREAN, JOHN Z. Jan. 6, 1925–Mar. 19, 2005 Automotive executive; engineer; designer; entrepreneur; a dashing visionary in the development of personalized passenger cars from the 1950s to the 1980s; after contributing for many years to what *Motor Trends* magazine honored as "styling and engineering leadership" at the General Motors Corp. (chiefly, GM's Pontiac division), founded the DeLorean Motor Co. and began manufacturing his dream car, the DMC-12, a futuristic stainless-steel sports coupe with gull-wing doors, in December 1980; during its short, troubled history—which included criminal charges that DeLorean resorted to drug-related money-raising and money-laundering in trying to keep his operation afloat—oversaw the company's manufacture of approximately 9,200 DeLoreans (as the cars were popularly known) in two calendar years (through 1982) and three model years (1981–83) and saw them become prized vintage items among automobile collectors, as are the GTOs he created at Pontiac; also provided the time-travel vehicle driven by the Michael J. Fox character in the *Back to the Future* movie comedies; earned master's degrees in industrial engineering and business administration; after working as an engineer with the Chrysler Corp. for four years, became chief of research and development for the Packard Motor Co. in 1952; moved to the General Motors Corp. in 1956 as director of advanced engineering in the Pontiac division; conceived the high-powered, wide-track Catalina and Bonneville cars and such innovations as the bumper for the Endura and the drive chain for the Tempest, Pontiac's first compact car; helped boost Pontiac from sixth to third place among American car manufacturers; obtained patents for the recessed windshield wiper and the overhead-cam engine; as chief engineer (1961–65), introduced his sporty GTO, Pontiac's first "muscle car," a modified Tempest with a V-8 engine, 31,000 of which were sold within a year, with sales nearly tripling within two years; as general manager of the Pontiac division (1965–69), approved a number of innovations, including cockpit-like interiors; between 1964 and 1968, enjoyed the satisfaction of seeing sales of Tempest and Grand Prix cars contribute to a rise in annual Pontiac sales from 688,000 to 877,000; in 1969, was named general manager of GM's foundering Chevrolet division; through sweeping organizational changes and product innovations, turned operations around to the point where, in 1969, the Chevrolet division accounted for about half of GM's corporate volume; was group executive in charge of GM's North American car and truck operations from 1972 until his resignation from GM the following year; served a year's term (1973–74) as president of the National Association of Businessmen, a private organization devoted to providing job training and placement for the chronically unemployed; in 1974, formed the DeLorean Motor Co. for the purpose of manufacturing his DMC-12, or DeLorean; spent more than three years securing seed money and looking for a manufacturing base; finally reached an agreement with the United Kingdom's Northern Ireland Development Agency for an investment package in return for his creation of jobs in an area of high unemployment; completed construction of his production plant in Dunmurry, County Cavan, in 1980; within months after the Deloreans began rolling off the assembly lines, experienced enormous financial difficulties, as a result of which the DeLorean Motor Co. became insolvent in January 1982, went into receivership the following month, and closed down in October 1982; arranged for the assemblage of the last DeLoreans on the assembly lines (marketed as 1983 models) to be completed by another company, Consolidated (later known as KAPAC); meanwhile, in October 1982, just before the closure of his plant, was indicted in an American court on charges of selling cocaine to undercover police in Los Angeles and conspiring in money laundering; was acquitted of both charges on grounds of entrapment in 1984; retreated to his ranch in Somerset, New Jersey; declared bankruptcy in 1999; a year later, lost his ranch, when it was sold under court order for $15.25 million, which was distributed to his creditors; was married four times (the second time to the fashion model Cristina Ferrare) and divorced three times; was survived by, among others, his fourth wife, Sally Baldwin, and a son and two daughters from his first marriage; died in Summit, New Jersey. See *Current Biography* (1976).

Obituary *New York Times* B p7 Mar. 21, 2005

DERRIDA, JACQUES July 15, 1930–Oct. 8, 2004 French philosopher of language and literature; an epistemological subversive, responsible for the creation of the critical technique called deconstruction, which questions and throws in doubt the meaning of any and every given text, analyzing it in search of hidden or unconscious agenda, including political and cultural biases; was born in Algeria to Sephardic Jewish parents; was educated at lycées in Algiers and Paris and at the École Normal Supérieure in Paris; attended Harvard University on a grant for one year (1956–57); taught French and English to schoolchildren in Kolea, Algeria, from 1957 to 1959; taught philosophy and logic at the University of Paris from 1960 to 1964; for some dozen years was associated with the young intellectuals who published the Marxist journal *Tel Quel*; left that group over disagreement with its increasingly Maoist orientation; was a founding member of GREPH (Groupe de recherches sur l'enseignement philosophique); taught the history of philosophy at the École Normal Supérieure from 1965 to 1984; lectured regularly at universities in England and the U.S., especially Yale and Cornell; launched his attack on absolute certainty in meaningful language in general and on Western epistemology in particular in his introduction to *L'Origine de la géométrie* (1962), a translation from the German of the phenomenologist Edmund Husserl that was in turn translated into English as *Edmund Husserl's Origin of Geometry* (1978); carried forward that attack in early essays in *Tel Quel* and in a number of books, including three definitive works published in 1967: *La Voix et la phénomène*, *L'Écriture et la différence*, and *De La grammatologie* (translated as *Of Grammatology*, 1976); published a total of some 40 books, including studies of Socrates, Condillac, Marx, Freud, Artaud, Nietzsche, Heidegger, and Genet, among others, and books translated into English, among them *Margins of Philosophy* (1982), *Memoires: For Paul de Man* (1989), and *Without Alibi* (2002); also published, among other books translated into English, a conversation with John D. Caputo titled *Deconstruction in a Nutshell* (1997) and the collections of interviews *Points* (1995) and *Negotiations* (1995); lived in the Paris suburb of Ris-Orangis with his wife, the psychoanalyst Marguerite Aucouturier, by whom he had two sons; had another son outside of marriage; died in a hospital in Paris. See *Current Biography* (1993).

Obituary *New York Times* A p1+ Oct. 10, 2004

DIAMOND, DAVID July 9, 1915–June 13, 2005 Composer; a classical traditionalist whose large canon of highly structured and melodic music—including 11 symphonies, 11 quintets, numerous concertos, and sonatas and varied other compositions for voice as well as orchestra and solo instruments—was not fully appreciated during the hegemony of atonal serialism; was born into a Jewish family of modest means in Rochester, New York; taught himself to play the violin in childhood; later mastered the piano; studied successively at the Cleveland Institute of Music, the Eastman School of Music in Rochester, and the New Music School in New York City, and with Nadia Boulanger in Paris; for many years, was financially supported by scholarships, grants, and awards or supported himself at odd jobs, the best of which were stints on radio as a violinist with the *Hit Parade* and the *Carnegie Hall Radio Show* orchestras and on Broadway with the pit orchestras of musicals; in 1941, composed his First Symphony and First String Quartet; the following year, composed his well-known Second Symphony, a long neo-Romantic work that was not given its world premiere until October 1944, when it was performed by the Boston Symphony Orchestra under Serge Koussevitsky; in 1943, composed one of his most popular works, Rounds for String Orchestra, first performed by the Minneapolis Symphony under Dimitri Mitropoulos in November 1944; wrote both his Third Symphony and his Fourth Symphony in 1945; also composed during the 1940s such works as his Quartet for Piano and String Trio in E Minor, Third String Quartet, Sonata for Violin and Orchestra, Second Concerto for Violin and Orchestra, and Chaconne for Violin and Piano; in addition, wrote scores for motion pictures, notably *Anna Lucasta* (1949), some ballet music, and some incidental music, including two suites for *Romeo and Juliet* (1947 and 1951); described his life in the U.S. at that time as "miserable," in part because of the ascendancy of unmelodic 12-tone music but in larger measure because his outspoken profession of his homosexuality, unfashionable at that time, exacerbated his admitted notoriety as "a kind of bohemian character" with a volatile temper; was admonished by his friend Serge Koussevitzky, "You must be more discreet! You must not talk about those things in public!"; unable to obtain a university position in the U.S., moved to Italy in 1951; after spending a year as a Fulbright professor at the University of Rome, settled in Florence on a Guggenheim fellowship (his third); lived in Florence for more than a dozen years except for occasional visits to the U.S.; during his Florentine years, wrote, among other works, his Sixth Symphony, Seventh Symphony, Eighth Symphony, Night Music for Accordion and String Quartet, Elegy for English Horn and Strings, and Elegy for Flute and Strings; temporarily made a transition from the Romantic and diatonic to the more chromatic and complex; in such works as *The World of Paul Klee* (1957), experimented with the 12-tone scheme but did so in a flexible manner so that the expressive content was not impaired; also composed during the 1950s a Concerto for Piano and Orchestra, a Quintet for Clarinet, Two Violas, and Two Cellos, a Fourth String Quartet, and a song cycle for baritone titled *The Midnight Meditation*; after it again became popular to write accessible music, composed such works as his Piano Quintet (1972) and Violin Sonata No. 2 (1981); worked for 20 years on his Ninth Symphony, which had its premiere under the baton of Leonard Bernstein in 1985; two years later, in collaboration with Elie Wiesel, completed *A Song of Hope*, a Torah-based composition for eight voices; meanwhile, in temporary returns to the U.S., taught at the University of Buffalo in 1961 and 1963; after returning to the U.S. permanently, in 1966, taught at the Manhattan School of Music and the University of Colorado; was on the faculty of the Juilliard School of Music from 1973 until 1986 and composer in residence at the 92nd Street YMHA-WA in Manhattan from 1991 to 1994; lived out his last years in Rochester, New York; died in Rochester. See *Current Biography* (1966).

Obituary *New York Times* C p20 June 15, 2005

DWORKIN, ANDREA Sep. 26, 1946–Apr. 9, 2005 Writer; a self-professed radical feminist who "brilliantly deconstructed the culture of misogyny," as Carol Sternhell has observed; ferociously crusaded for women's rights and against pornography, causes she viewed as inextricably interlinked; was born into a Jewish family in Camden, New Jersey; after graduating from Bennington (Vermont) College with a degree in literature in 1968, traveled in Greece and the Netherlands; lived for five years in the Netherlands, where she endured a three-year abusive marriage to a Dutch anarchist; back in the U.S., supported herself for many years by working at a variety of occupations, including teacher, waitress, sales clerk, receptionist, and prostitute; finally, became assistant to the poet Muriel Rukeyser, who encourged her writing aspirations; while still working for Rukeyser, published her first book, *Woman Hating: A Radical Look at Sexuality* (1974), whose stated purpose was "to destroy patriarchal power at its source, the family, and in its most hideous form, the nation-state, . . . to destroy the structure of culture as we know it"; itemized such female-subjugating practices as foot-binding in China, witch-hunting in Europe and colonial America, and the propagation of sex-role mythology in both fairy tales and pornography: in

her next major work, *Pornography: Men Possessing Women* (1981), argued that the eroticization of violence in much of pornography incites men to violence against women in real life; in her most controversial book, *Intercourse* (1987), asserted that even consensual heterosexual sex is an "expression of men's contempt for women," that "the woman in intercourse is a space inhabited, a literal territory occupied literally, occupied even if there has been no resistance, no force"; saw that book widely dismissed as historico-sociological nonsense by reviewers, including Caroll Sternhell, who wrote for the *New York Times*: "I'm a feminist too—that's why this nonsense disturbs me so much"; reiterated the theme of *Intercourse* on later occasions, including passages in *Letters from a War Zone: Writings, 1976-1989* (1989), in which she described marriage as "a legal license to rape" at one point and at another compared marriage to prostitution ("One of the differences between marriage and prostitution is that in marriage you only have to make a deal with one man"); with the legal scholar Catharine A. MacKinnon, drafted a piece of legislation defining pornography as a violation of women's civil rights, thus allowing women to sue for damages—a position adopted in ordinances in several American cities, all of which were defeated in the courts; saw such governmental measures polarize feminists, many of whom were concerned that such legislation threatened free speech and/or reinforced the "porn made me do it" excuse for rapists and batterers; shared her insights and research with the activists who launched the Campaign Against Pornography in the United Kingdom in 1986; in addition to her nonfiction, wrote two semi-autobiographical books, the novel *Ice and Fire and Mercy* (1991) and *The New Woman's Broken Heart* (1980), a collection of short stories; published a total of a dozen books, including *Our Blood: Prophecies and Discourses on Sexual Politics* (1976), *Right-Wing Women* (1983), *Life and Death: Unapologetic Writings on the Continuing War Against Women* (1996), and *Scapegoat: The Jews, Israel, and Women's Liberation* (2000); contributed to the anthology *Take Back the Night* (1980); with Catharine A. MacKinnon, wrote *The Reasons Why: Essays on the New Civil Rights Law Recognizing Pornography as Sex Discrimination* (1985) and *Pornography and Civil Rights: A New Day for Women's Equality* (1988); in 2002, published the autobiography *Heartbreak: The Political Memoir of a Feminist Militant*; a professed lesbian, found her "life companion" in the male pro-feminist activist John Stoltenberg, a professed homosexual, whom she married in 1998, after living with him for 24 years; died at their home in Washington, D.C. See *Current Biography* (1994).

Obituary *New York Times* B p7 Apr. 12, 2005

EBERHART, RICHARD Apr. 5, 1904–June 9, 2005 Poet; professor emeritus of English, Dartmouth College; "essentially a visionary [poet] for whom the sensory world [was] wonderfully vivid," as his fellow poet Jean Garrigue observed; was "characteristically . . . intellectual and abstract, but his driving conceptions [were] emotionally ignited by a visionary intensity," according to the poet and critic M. L. Rosenthal; was "a lyric poet who took on the great subjects," in the words of Cleopatra Mathis, the director of Dartmouth's creative-writing program, those subjects including the tension between mind and matter and between animality and spirituality, the loss of innocence, and, above all, the longevity of art despite the brevity of life; viewed poems, as he said, as "in a way . . . spells against death," attempts to "draw the possibility of pleasure from the general suffering which is the mortal state"; often, as in the poem "Seals, Terns, Time," wrote in the context of the natural world; in one of his most quoted poems, "The Groundhog," recorded his changing attitudes toward death as he observed the stages of decay in a dead animal; wrote "Cover Me Over" as if from his own grave; typically, wrote verse characterized by short lines, infrequent rhymes, and irregular rhythms; with his "good grainy language," as Hayden Carruth noted, had "the ability to hit sometimes upon the perfect image, startling and simple"; was raised in privilege on Burr Oaks, his family's 40-acre estate in rural Austin, Minnesota; earned a B.A. degree at Dartmouth College and an additional B.A. degree and an M.A. degree at Cambridge University; published his first book of verse, *A Bravery of Earth*, in 1930, his second, *Reading the Spirit*, in 1937, and his third, *Song and Idea*, in 1942; served as an officer with the U.S. Navy in World War II; after the war, was assistant manager of his wife's family's business, the Butcher Polish Co., for six years; in his book *Poems, New and Selected* (1945), included his well-known World War II poems, the most famous of which is "The Fury of Aerial Bombardment"; published *Burr Oaks* in 1947 and *Brotherhood of Men* in 1949; was poet in residence at the University of Washington in Seattle during the scholastic year 1952–53, professor of English at the University of Connecticut in 1953–54, poet in residence and professor of English at Wheaton College in 1954–55, and resident fellow in creative writing at Princeton University in 1955–56; became professor of English and poet in residence at Dartmouth College in 1956; took a leave of absence from Dartmouth to serve two one-year terms as consultant in poetry in English at the Library of Congress (1959–60, 1960–61), a position tantamount to national poet laureate; published the book of verse *Undercliff* in 1953, the volume *Great Praises* in 1957, *The Quarry* in 1964, *Shifts of Being* in 1968, and *Fields of Grace* in 1972; won a Pulitzer Prize for *Selected Poems, 1930–1965* (1965) and a National Book Award for *Collected Poems, 1930–1976* (1976); published *Ways of Light: Poems, 1972–1980* in 1980, *The Long Reach: New and Uncollected Poems, 1948–1984* in 1984, *Collected Poems, 1930–1986* in 1988, *Maine Poems* in 1989, and *New and Selected Poems, 1930–1990* in 1990; also wrote several verse plays, published in *Collected Verse Plays* (1962); shared the Bollingen Prize with John Hall Wheelock in 1962 and the Frost Medal of the Poetry Society of America with Alan Ginsberg in 1986; resigned as poet in residence at Dartmouth College in 1968; became emeritus professor in 1970; died at his home in Hanover, New Hampshire; was predeceased by his wife, Helen, and survived by a son, a daughter, and six grandchildren. See *Current Biography* (1961).

Obituary *New York Times* A p21 June 14, 2005

EISNER, WILL Mar. 6, 1917–Jan. 2, 2005 Artist; a strip cartoonist, or, as he preferred to be called, sequential artist; was a major figure in the golden age of the comic book; was also, arguably, the inventor of the "graphic novel"; coined the name of that genre; contemporaneously with several other artists (most notably Bob Kane, the creator of Batman), but with less gimmickry and greater intellectuality, developed the comic strip from a juvenile entertainment into a medium for sophisticated visual storytelling; with imaginative plotting and masterly draftsmanship, sometimes reflecting his whimsical spirit and sense of humor, wrote and drew adventure sequences that look like film noir storyboards raised to a fine craft; once explained that his "intention was to do short stories" in the comics medium; is best known as the creator of *The Spirit* strip, the eponymous protagonist of which is Denny Colt, "a middle-class crime fighter" who, unlike such comic-book heroes as Superman and Captain Marvel, plies his vigilantism without benefit of supernatural powers; was born into an immigrant Jewish family in the borough of Brooklyn, New York City; grew up there and in the borough of the Bronx; was encouraged in perfecting his artistic hand by his father, a scenery painter in a Yiddish theater; sold his first comic feature to a magazine when he was 19; turned out strip after strip for comic books in the late 1930s, when that format was originating in the pulp-magazine industry; in 1939, was hired by the Register and Tribune newspaper syndicate to put together a weekly comics insert consisting of several stories spread over some 16 pages; while editing the whole insert—a Sunday supplement read by five million readers of 20 newspapers—wrote and drew some of the stories himself; on June 2, 1940, introduced his character called the Spirit, aka Denny Colt, a private investigator who operates out of a cemetery crypt in a metropolis called Central City; feigning death, Colt is able, in Eisner's words, to "go after criminals the law cannot touch"; during World War II, was drafted into the U.S. Army and had *The Spirit* produced by others; for the army, edited and drew for the journal *Firepower* and contributed to *Army Motors*; created a cartoon character named Joe Dope, a klutz whose mishaps were intended to instruct soldiers in safety, especially in equipment maintenance; after discontinuing *The Spirit*, in 1952, founded the American Visuals Corp. and the Educational Supplements Corp.; produced comics for businesses, the federal government, the military, and schools; during the 1960s, headed two newspaper syndicates; in 1976, published his first graphic novel, *A Contract with God*, actually a collection of four short stories about Jewish tenement dwellers in the Bronx (and on vacation in the Catskills in one of the stories), the title story focusing on a slumlord who experiences a crisis of religious faith; went on to publish more than 10 graphic novels, including *Life on Another Planet*, *Big City*, *A Life Force*, *The Dreamer*, and *The Building*; published a graphic version of *Robert's Rules of Order* and his graphic autobiography, *To the Heart of the Storm*; placed his archives under the custodianship of Kitchen Sink until 2000, when DC Comics signed a commitment to keep the entire Will Eisner Library, including the graphic novels, in print; saw the issuing, in June 2000 by DC Comics, of a hardcover edition of *The Spirit*, which will total 26 volumes when the run is completed; died in Fort Lauderdale, Florida; was predeceased by his daughter, Alice, and survived by his wife, Ann, and his son, John. See *Current Biography* (1994).

Obituary *New York Times* C p14 Jan. 5, 2005

EXON, J. JAMES Aug. 9, 1921–June 10, 2005 Three-term Democratic U.S. senator from Nebraska (1979–97); two-term governor of Nebraska (1971–79); a social and fiscal conservative who could be stubbornly independent when not building coalitions across party lines; before entering politics, founded Exon's Inc., an office-supply company in Lincoln, Nebraska; headed that company for 16 years (1954–70); served with the U.S. Army Signal Corps in the Pacific theater in World War II; won his first election as governor in 1970 by a modest margin, on a platform promising smaller government and lower taxes; proceeded to keep that promise, vetoing the state legislature's spending plans an average of 20 times a year; with his frugal fiscal policies, became immensely popular with Republican as well as Democratic voters and won reelection by a comfortable margin in 1974; as governor, sought federal subsidies, tax credits, and emergency funding for Nebraska's farmers (as he would continue to do in Washington), but otherwise looked to federal spending programs only as a last resort; in the U.S. Senate, was a member of the budget and armed services committees; in his first term, supported the tax and spending cuts in the legislative agenda of President Ronald Reagan but was appalled at the president's indifference to looming budget deficits; while a staunch believer in a strong defense, also believed that frugality should be applied in some measure to military as well as social programs; in 1983, voted for prayer in public schools; during his second term, co-sponsored the Exon-Florio Act, giving the president the authority to review attempts by foreign corporations to acquire American companies, especially military contractors, and to take action against those takeovers deemed threatening to national security; voted against federal funding for abortions in 1993 and against safeguarding access to abortion clinics the following year; introduced the Senate versions of balanced-budget amendments in 1991, 1993, and 1995; saw the House version of the amendment pass in 1995 but the Senate version fail to pass by one vote that year; in February 1995 introduced the Communications Decency Act, designed to protect children from both pornography and pedophiles on the Internet (which, in revised form, became an amendment to the Telecommunications Act of 1996, which was signed into law by President Bill Clinton in February 1996 but in June 1997 was ruled unconstitutional by the the U.S. Supreme Court); in 1996, introduced a bill placing a moratorium on underground nuclear tests; in his last two years in the Senate, chaired the Budget Committee; did not seek reelection to the Senate in 1996; after leaving the Senate, served on a committee (headed by the former CIA director John M. Deutch) created by Congress to study the threat of the use of biological and nuclear weapons by terrorists, and contributed to the committee's report, issued in 1999, recommending the creation of

a federal agency along the lines of the subsequently created Department of Homeland Security; died in Lincoln, Nebraska; was survived by his wife, Patricia, three children, and numerous grandchildren and great-grandchildren. See *Current Biography* (1996).

Obituary *New York Times* B p8 June 13, 2005

EYADÉMA, GNASSINGBÉ Dec. 26, 1937–Feb. 5, 2005 President of the Republic of Togo (1967–2005), a small former French colony on Africa's west coast; while casting himself with some justification as a regional peacemaker, was domestically a ruthless dictator, maintaining through military force—including an elite guard composed of fellow members of his Kaybe tribe, a relatively poor group in northern Togo—a repressive regime serving only his interests and those of his loyal soldiers and his tribe; in 1953, crossed the border into Dahomey (now Benin) and joined the French army there; served with the French army in Indochina, Algeria, and Niger; returned to Togo in 1962, two years after the country gained its full independence from France; in 1963, took part in a rebellion of French army veterans, the majority from the Kaybe tribe, who had grievances against Sylvanus Olympio, Togo's first democratically elected president, a member of a well-known family in southern Togo's Ewe tribe; assassinated Olympio; saw a civilian president, Nicolas Grunitzky, installed, while he himself became the Togo army's chief of staff; in January 1967 led a bloodless coup that drove Grunitzky into exile in the Côte d'Ivoire, where Grunitzky was killed in an automobile accident two years later; in April 1967, declared himself president and minister of defense; suspended the national constitution; outlawed all political parties save for his own Rally of the Togo People (RPT); enjoyed the unwavering patronage of a succession of French governments, because of his value to them in U.N. voting and the like; was condemned by other Western governments for his violations of human rights and failure to pursue democratic reform; succumbing to international pressure, ostensibly legalized opposition parties in 1993; won the putatively democratic election that year; suffered the imposition of economic sanctions (effective until 2004) by the European Union because of allegations that his security forces had massacred 20 democratic activists; when the voting began to go against him in the election in 1998, stopped the process and declared himself the winner; was subsequently accused by Amnesty International of a consistent pattern of arbitrary arrests, torture, killings, and disappearances; was reelected in 2003; died in Lomé, Togo, just before he was to fly to France for medical treatment; was succeeded by his son, Faure Gnassingbé, who won a popular election in April 2005. See *Current Biography* (2002).

FAHD, KING OF SAUDI ARABIA 1922(?)–Aug. 1, 2005 The fifth ruler in a line of succession going back through three of his 36 brothers to their father, Abdul Aziz (Ibn Saud), the founder of the Saud dynasty; as such, headed the world's most oil-rich nation and exerted great influence among the Arab states of the Persian Gulf region; following the death of King

Abdul Aziz, in 1952, served as minister of education (1953–62) and minister of the interior (beginning in 1962) in the government of King Saud; following the royal house's deposition of King Saud in 1964, remained minister of the interior under King Faisal until 1975, when Faisal was assassinated and replaced by another of Fahd's older brothers, Khalid; as crown prince to Khalid, a weak king, Fahd was the de facto ruler, and his authority became de jure when he ascended the throne upon Khalid's death in 1982; was a relatively progressive sovereign; domestically, had limited success in his effort to modernize Islamic tradition; similarly, in his foreign policy, fueled the fanaticism of the jihadist "holy warriors" (led most prominently by the wealthy Saudi-born Islamist radical Osama bin Laden) with his pursuit of close relations with the U.S., especially when it included the stationing of American military forces on Saudi soil; in 1995 was incapacitated by a stroke and forced to turn the affairs of state over to his half brother Crown Prince Abdullah; died in the King Faisal Specialist Hospital in Riyadh, Saudi Arabia; was succeeded on the throne by the 81-year-old Abdullah; had six sons (five of whom survived him) and a number of daughters from at least four marriages. See *Current Biography* (1979).

Obituary *New York Times* C p16 Aug. 2, 2005

FAIRCLOUGH, ELLEN Jan. 28, 1905–Nov. 13, 2004 Former Canadian secretary of state; first female federal cabinet minister in Canadian history; early in her career, was an accountant in a stockbrokerage firm; when her employer went out of business, in 1935, hung out a shingle as an independent certified public accountant and auditor in Hamilton, Ontario; built her practice into the firm of Hamilton Office Service Ltd.; inspired by her husband's interest in politics, joined him as a member of Ontario's Young Conservative Association; running on the Progressive Conservative ticket, was elected a member of the Hamilton City Council in 1946 and Hamilton city controller three years later; was elected to the Canadian House of Commons in a by-election in Ontario's Hamilton West Riding in 1950; was reelected in 1954 and 1957; on June 21, 1957 was named secretary of state and nominal custodian of the Great Seal in Prime Minister John G. Diefenbaker's Progressive Conservative minority government; in that position, served chiefly as the official channel of communications between the Canadian federal government and both the British Crown and the Canadian provincial governments; also oversaw the administration of various business laws, the issuance of letters patent, the translation of documents, and the arrangement of welcome and hospitality for official visitors; following the massive victory of the Progressive Conservatives in the elections of 1958, became minister of citizenship and immigration in Diefenbaker's new, majority government; was named postmaster general in 1962; lost her parliamentary seat in the elections of 1963, when the Progressive Conservative Party was voted out of power; was predeceased by her husband, Gordon, and her son, Howard; died in Hamilton, Ontario. See *Current Biography* (1957).

Obituary *New York Times* A p25 Nov. 16, 2004

FEIFEL, HERMAN Nov. 4, 1915–Jan. 18, 2003 Psychologist; the founder of contemporary death psychology; professor emeritus, University of Southern California School of Medicine, Los Angeles; a psychologist with the U.S. Veterans Administration for 42 years; with his work in thanatology, broke societal taboos surrounding the discussion of death; made dying and bereavement legitimate subjects of scientific and scholarly study; laid the foundation for the work of Elisabeth Kübler-Ross and others and for the death-awareness and hospice movements; earned his Ph.D. degree in psychology at Columbia University; was a psychologist with the U.S. Army Air Corps during World War II; subsequently, taught in succession at Brooklyn College, American University, the Menninger School of Psychiatry in Topeka, Kansas, and the University of California before joining the faculty of the University of Southern California in 1958; began his work as a psychologist with the Veterans Administration at Winter General Hospital in Topeka in 1950; moved to Los Angeles as a research and clinical psychologist at the V.A. Mental Hygiene Clinic there in 1954; six years later, was appointed chief psychologist at the V.A. Outpatient Clinic in Los Angeles; organized and chaired a symposium called "The Concept of Death and Its Relation to Behavior" at the 1956 meeting of the American Psychological Association, the first such symposium ever convened; inspired by the wide-ranging discussion that took place on that occasion, began collecting essays for a book that would be as broad in its range; in 1959 published that groundbreaking book, *The Meaning of Death*; edited a second book, *New Meanings of Death* (1977); published more than 100 articles; never married; died at his home in Los Angeles. See *Current Biography* (1994).

Obituary *Newsday* A p49 Jan. 24, 2003

FITZGERALD, GERALDINE Nov. 24, 1913–July 17, 2005 Stage and screen actress; at the age of 25, with her classic Irish beauty and a voice once described as "soft and low and lilting and round"—and armed with impressive Anglo-Irish ingénue credits—began her Hollywood career auspiciously, with her moving portrayal of Ann King, the confidante of the dying woman (Bette Davis, her real-life friend and mentor) in *Dark Victory* (1939) and with her Oscar-nominated supporting performance as Isabella Linton, the woman whom the vengeful Heathcliff (Laurence Olivier) marries just to make her miserable, in *Wuthering Heights* (1939); as Isabella, "shone with a youthful spirited freshness that well matched Laurence Olivier's glowering, impossibly glamorous Heathcliff," as Bernard Adams observed in the London *Independent*, and, as Olivier himself acknowledged in retrospect, provided the only reason "a bloody awful film . . . still holds up"; did not realize her full potential in motion pictures because her independent and strong-willed temperament clashed with Hollywood's studio system; under contract to Warner Brothers for seven years, fought constantly over the roles assigned to her by studio executives, who penalized her with long suspensions; nevertheless, established a substantial filmography in addition to her varied work in the legitimate theater (her first love) and on television; was born in Ireland into a family distinguished in theater and the law; was the niece of the celebrated Irish actress Shelah Kathleen Richards; in 1932, made her professional stage debut at Dublin's Gate Theatre, where Orson Welles had made his debut about a year before; moving to England, made her motion-picture debut as Jill in *Open All Night* (1934); next was cast as Peggy Summers in *Blind Justice* (1934); drew greater notice in such movie roles as that of Ruth Fosdyck in *Turn of the Tide* (1935), the Yorkshire fishing-village romance that launched Yorkshireman J. Arthur Rank into his career as a movie mogul, and that of Maggie Tulliver in *The Mill on the Floss* (1937); in 1938, married Edward Lindsay-Hogg, a horse breeder and songwriter; in 1938, moved with him to New York City, where he hoped to further his songwriting career; partly for financial reasons, contacted Orson Welles, who had co-founded the Mercury Theater troupe in Manhattan; playing Ellie Dunn in a Mercury Theater production of George Bernard Shaw's *Heartbreak House* in 1938, attracted the notice of the motion-picture producer Hal Wallace, who signed her to the contract that launched her Hollywood career; under that contract, was cast in 14 roles, including that of the pregnant convicted murderer in *A Child Is Born* (1939), one of the three siblings in *The Gay Sisters* (1942), Marthe de Brancovis in *Watch on the Rhine* (1943), Edith Galt Wilson, President Woodrow Wilson's second wife, in *Wilson* (1944), Gladys Halvorsen in the film noir *Nobody Lives Forever* (1946), and one of the three holders of a single winning sweepstakes ticket in *Three Strangers* (1946); after her contract with Warner Brothers expired, was cast as Susan Courtney, a victim of larceny, in the British feature film *So Evil My Love* (1948), and as Elizabeth Grahame, the female half of the adulterous couple suspected of murdering the male half's wife, in *The Late Edwina Black* (1951; aka *Obsessed*), also a British production; returned to American film as the wife who goads her husband (Gary Cooper) into a successful political career for selfish reasons, with boomerang effect, in *Ten North Frederick* (1958); had the major supporting roles of the social worker Marilyn Birchfield in *The Pawnbroker* (1964) and the Reverend Wood in *Rachel, Rachel;* was cast as Mrs. Jackson in *The Last American Hero* (1973) and Jessie Stone in *Harrry and Tonto* (1974); had roles in a total of some 40 feature films, including *Café Mascot* (1936), *The Strange Affair of Uncle Harry* (1945), *O.S.S.* (1946), *The Mango Tree* (1977), *Arthur* (1981), *Easy Money* (1983), and *Poltergeist II* (1986); meanwhile, had continued pursuing her career in the legitimate theater, on Broadway, Off-Broadway, and in regional theater; on Broadway, created the roles of Rebecca Tadlock in *Sons and Soldiers* (1943), of Ann Richards in *Hide and Seek* (1957), and of Felicity in *The Shadow Box* (1977); also on Broadway, played Essie Miller in a revival of Eugene O'Neill's *Ah, Wilderness* (1975) and Nora Melody in a revival of the same playwright's *A Touch of the Poet* (1977–78); in revivals elsewhere, played Jennifer Dubedat in *The Doctor's Dilemma* (1955), Goderil in *King Lear* (1956), Gertrude in *Hamlet* (1958), the Queen in *The Cave Dwellers* (1961), and Juno Boyle in *Juno and the Paycock* (1975); with special éclat, played Mary Tyrone in an Off-Broadway production of O'Neill's *Long Day's*

Journey into Night in 1971; as a producer and director, co-founded in 1971 the Everyman Company, which engaged hundreds of children in New York City neighborhoods in participation in street-theater productions; coordinated the Lincoln Center Community Street Theater Festival in 1972; put together a cabaret act called "Songs of the Street" (later shortened to "Street Songs"), a mixture of song (including folk song) and theater (including autobiographical material) that she performed in supper clubs and took to Broadway in a production titled *Geraldine Fitzgerald in Songs of the Street* in 1976; was nominated for a Tony Award for her direction on Broadway in 1982 of the original play *Mass Appeal*; on television, was cast in numerous dramatic productions and series or episodes in series and made guest appearances on situation comedies; played Rose Kennedy in the miniseries *Kennedy* (1983); was nominated for an Emmy Award for a guest role on the situation comedy *The Golden Girls* in 1989; in 1946, divorced Edward Lindsay-Hogg and married Stuart Scheftel, her husband until his death, in 1994; was survived by a son from her first marriage, the stage, screen, and television director Michael Lindsay-Hogg, a daughter from her second marriage, the clinical psychologist Susan Scheftel, and the actress Tara Fitzgerald, her great-niece; died at her home in Manhattan. See *Current Biography* (1976).

Obituary *New York Times* B p7 July 19, 2005

FLETCHER, ARTHUR Dec. 22, 1924–July 12, 2005 An extraordinarily effective activist in the cause of equal economic opportunity for minorities; U.S. government official; a liberal African-American Republican; as assistant secretary for wage and labor standards in the Department of Labor under President Richard M. Nixon from 1969 to 1971, implemented the so-called revised Philadelphia Plan, in which affirmative action was adopted as a federal mandate for companies with federal contracts and for labor unions whose members are involved in such contracts; subsequently, served as President Gerald R. Ford's deputy assistant for urban affairs; chaired the U.S. Civil Rights Commission (1990–93) under President George H. W. Bush; with the U.S. Army, was wounded in combat in France during World War II; while earning a B.A. degree in political science at Washburn University, in Topeka, Kansas, after the war, was a star rushing back on the university's football team; after his graduation, in 1950, played professionally as a defensive end for a brief time, with, in quick succession, the Los Angeles Rams, the Baltimore Colts, and the Hamilton (Ontario) Rams; entered Republican Party politics as a minority organizer in the successful gubernatorial campaign of Fred Hall, a liberal Republican, in Kansas; was assistant public-relations director with the Kansas Highway Commission from 1954 to 1957 and vice chairman of the Kansas State Republican Central Committee from 1954 to 1956; helped to raise funds for the *Brown v. Topeka Board of Education* desegregation lawsuit, which eventually was successfully fought up to the U.S. Supreme Court; was assistant football coach at Washburn University in 1957; in the following years, was engaged in various business enterprises; taught at Burbank Junior High School in

Berkeley, California, from 1960 to 1965; helped to desegregate the Berkeley school system; at the invitation of YMCA officials, in 1965 moved to East Pasco, a small black ghetto on the outskirts of Pasco, Washington, where he directed a federally funded employment training project and organized the East Pasco Self-Help Cooperative Association; through his work in East Pasco, caught the attention of the national Republican Party organization; in 1968, when invited to address the party's platform committee, expressed ideas that provided the basis for the "black capitalism" program endorsed by the Republican National Convention in Miami that summer; lost his race for the lieutenant governorship of Washington in November 1968 by a narrow margin; was executive director of the United Negro College Fund from 1971 to 1973; in the 1980s, declined an offer of employment at the Reagan White House but agreed to give advice to President Ronald Reagan when asked; recalled, as quoted in *Ebony* (July 1, 1991), "I advised him [President Reagan]; he just didn't take my advice"; regarded President Reagan, a fellow Republican, as "the worst president for civil rights in his century"; in his later years, headed Fletcher's Learning Systems, a company devoted to the creation and marketing of books and audiotapes and videotapes designed to help businesses comply with affirmative action guidelines; was predeceased by his first wife, Mary, and survived by his second wife, Bernyce Hassan-Fletcher, several children, and many grandchildren and great-grandchildren. See *Current Biography* (1971)

Obituary *New York Times* C p17 July 14, 2005

FOOTE, SHELBY Nov. 17, 1916–June 27, 2005 Civil War historian; novelist; before 1958, as John Herbert Roper observed in the *Journal of Southern History* (August 1, 2004), "moved in the second rank of the Southern literary renaissance then in full-force march" with the novels in which he "described feelingly and believably the race relations, class tensions, poverty, old money, and gender strains" in his native Mississippi Delta; in 1958, published *Fort Sumter to Perryville* (1958), the first volume of *The Civil War: A Narrative*, the nonfiction trilogy that brought him acclaim and on which his reputation securely rests; in writing that volume and its two sequels—*Fredericksburg to Meridian* (1963) and *Red River to Appomattox* (1974)—adhered, in his words, to "the historian's standards without his paraphernalia" and "employed the novelist's methods without his license" to create a finely detailed but eminently readable account of the war between the states, vivid in imagery and strong in characterization; left out footnotes, believing that "they would detract from the book's narrative quality by intermittently shattering the illusion that the observer is not so much reading a book as sharing an experience"; concentrated strictly on the military history of the war, avoiding reference to its economic, social, and political aspects; was born in Greenville, Mississippi, the great-grandson of Captain Hezekiah William Foote, who fought for the Confederacy at Shiloh; in his youth, was most profoundly influenced by William Alexander Percy, a local author and the uncle and guardian of Walker Percy, his best friend, who

became a successful novelist; was introduced to the world of books through Will Percy's private library; enrolled at the University of North Carolina at Chapel Hill in 1935; left college in 1937 without earning a degree; as an army captain stationed in Ireland in World War II, was court-martialed and dismissed from army service in 1944 for being absent without leave to be with an Irish girlfriend in Belfast (Tess Lavery, who became his first wife, briefly, until their divorce); in 1945, served for a short time in the Marine Corps; after the war, made his first sale of a short story, to the *Saturday Evening Post* in 1946; the following year, published the short-story collection *The Merchant of Bristol*; in 1949, published *Tournament*, the first of his novels set in fictional Jordan County, Mississippi; subsequently, published *Follow Me Down* (1950), *Love in a Dry Season* (1951), and *Jordan County: A Landscape in Narrative* (1954); adapted the last mentioned into the play *Jordan County: A Landscape in the Round* (1964); abandoned the setting of the Mississippi Delta to write the Civil War novel *Shiloh* (1952) and *September, September* (1978), a novel about a gang of three white people who conspire to kidnap a black child for ransom in Memphis in 1957; revealed his sage and gentlemanly personality to millions of American television viewers when, speaking in his luxuriant Mississippi Delta drawl, he made 89 on-screen appearances as a commentator (in addition to being an off-screen consultant) in Ken Burns's 11-hour PBS documentary *The Civil War*, originally aired on five consecutive nights in September 1990; was described, along with his work, by John Herbert Roper in a review for the *Journal of Southern History* of C. Stuart Chapman's biography *Shelby Foote: A Writer's Life*: "Contradictions, especially of the individual self, emerge as a theme not only in Foote's novels and essays but in Foote himself and his life experiences. There is [for example] his simultaneous hatred of racism and longing for the old-style Southern gentry [and] his Jewish heritage [apparently through his maternal ancestors], accepted in the famously bigoted Delta but rejected in liberal Chapel Hill. . . . Chapman demonstrates that Foote's liberal ideas about race relations were rejected so thoroughly as to cause Foote to retreat . . . into a private world of art. Chapman assesses these contradictions as the reason Foote never completed his last literary work, *Two Gates to the City*"—a novel about a Mississippi Delta family set in 1948, with flashbacks to the Reconstruction era and flash-forwards to the 1960s; died in Memphis, Tennessee, where he had lived since 1953; was divorced from his second wife, Peggy DeSommes, and survived by his daughter with DeSommes, Margaret, and by his third wife, the former Gwyn Rainer, and their son, Huger Lee. See *Current Biography* (1991).

Obituary *New York Times* B p8 June 29, 2005

FREEMAN, LUCY Dec. 13, 1916–Dec. 29, 2004 Author; journalist; published books chiefly concerned with psychoanalysis and related subjects; was born Lucy Greenbaum; acquired her professional surname from the first of her two marriages; after earning a degree in social studies at Bennington College, in 1938, worked briefly at newspapers in Tuckahoe and Mamaroneck, New York, before joining the *New York Times* as assistant fashion editor; went on to do general news, feature stories, and book reviews at the *Times*; beginning in the late 1940s, specialized in mental-health and social-welfare stories; related her personal experience undergoing psychoanalysis in her first book, *Fight Against Fears* (1951), a best-seller; subsequently, published *Children Who Never Had a Chance* (1952), *Hope for the Troubled* (1953), a guide to available aid, including guidance by social workers, to those with mental, emotional, or interpersonal problems, and *Before I Kill More* (1955), an account of the crimes of William Heirens and an analysis of his emotional and moral development; wrote a total of well over a score of books in the same or related veins, including *The Dream* (1971), *The Hurt and the Fury: Overcoming Hurt and Loss from Childhood to Old Age* (1978), and *What Do Women Want?* (1978); also wrote some murder novels and the memoir *The Beloved Prison: A Journey into the Unknown Self* (1989); died at the Hebrew Home for the Aged in Riverdale, the Bronx, New York City. See *Current Biography* (1953).

Obituary *New York Times* B p6 Jan. 3, 2005

FRY, CHRISTOPHER Dec. 18, 1907–June 30, 2005 British playwright; was in the forefront of the neo-Elizabethan renaissance of English verse drama that flourished between the end of World War II and the ascendancy of the "kitchen sink" school of dramaturgy led by the "angry young man" John Osbourne in the mid-1950s; was "a product of the religious drama movement which launched T. S. Eliot [his mentor and friend] as a dramatist," as an anonymous obituary writer for the London *Telegraph* (July 4, 2005) observed; had a particular Christian background, heavily proto-Quaker and pacifist, which was more overtly reflected in his earlier works but contributed to the ebullience and sanguinity of the dazzling contemplative comedies that made him famous: plays, as the *Telegraph* writer noted, that "conveyed an optimism about humanity and a sense of divine providence that were of great comfort in a world coming to terms with the newly revealed horrors of the Holocaust and the atom bomb" and that, in the words of Kenneth Tynan, "gave us access into imagined worlds in which rationing and the rest of austerity's paraphernalia could be forgotten"; emerged from relative obscurity with *A Phoenix Too Frequent*, a comedy derived from a story by Petronius that opened at the private Arts Theatre Club in London in March 1946 and moved to the West End in a production starring Paul Scofield the following November; achieved fame three years later with the full-length work *The Lady's Not for Burning*, his masterpiece, a clever comedy shaded with dark undertones—a verse play (written for the most part in elegiac pentameter), set circa 1400, about the love that mutually saves Thomas Mendip, a life-weary demobilized soldier just back from the Hundred Years' War, and Jennet Jourdemayne, a young woman whose exceptional scientific expertise, mistaken for witchcraft, makes her a candidate for burning at the stake; saw the play premiere at the Arts Theatre Club in March 1948 and, after a tour of the provinces, enjoy an eight-month run at the Globe Theatre in the West End (May 1948–January 1950), with John Gielgud and Pamela Brown playing the protagonists and Richard Burton and Claire Bloom in supporting roles; with Gielgud and Brown reprising their roles, saw the play move in November 1950 to Broadway, where it ran for 151 performances and was critically hailed as "a poetic fantasy of rare splendor and delight," with "wit and radiance and bite" in its language and "a beautiful balance between scenes of sheerest nonsense and extremely moving passages"; meanwhile, beginning in January 1950, scored his second West End hit with *Venus Observed*, a tale about a widowed nobleman, Hereward, Duke of Altair, who asks his son to choose a stepmother from among the Duke's three paramours (Laurence Olivier starred as Hereward in the West End production and went on to direct Rex Harrison in the role on Broadway in 1952); wrote *The Lady's Not for Burning* ("Spring") and *Venus Observed* ("Autumn") as the first two works in a planned quartet celebrating the salutary seasons in life and the survivability of the human spirit; completed the quartet with *The Dark Is Light Enough* ("Winter," 1954) and *A Yard of Sun* ("Summer," 1970); before becoming prominent, co-founded the Tunbridge Wells Repertory Players and was director of the Oxford Playhouse; during the 1930s, wrote the religious pageants The Boy with a Cart: Cuthman, Saint of Sussex, The Tower, and *Thursday's Child* and began writing *The Firstborn* (not produced until 1946); later wrote the plays *Thor, with Angels* (1948), *A Sleep of Prisoners* (1951), *Curtmantle* (1961), *One Thing More, or Caedmon Construed* (1985), and *A Ringing of Bells* (2000); in addition, wrote plays for radio and television and translations of plays by Jean Anouilh, Jean Giradoux, Henrik Ibsen, and Edmond Rostand; co-wrote the scenarios for the motion pictures *Ben-Hur* (1959), *Barabbas* (1962), and *The Bible* (1966); wrote the Fry family history *Can You Find Me?* (1978); died in Chichester, West Sussex, England; was predeceased by his wife, Phyllis, and survived by his son, Tam. See *Current Biography* (1951).

Obituary *New York Times* B p7 July 5, 2005

GIULINI, CARLO MARIA May 9, 1914–June 14, 2005 Italian musician; a self-effacing and perfectionistic conductor who achieved international renown with his precise and elegant directing in both concert halls and opera houses; in the latter, concentrated chiefly on the operas of Verdi and Mozart; in the former, was best known for his meticulous and lyrically warm versions of the classical German and Viennese Romantics, from Beethoven through Bruckner to Mahler, his own favorite being Brahms, with whose Fourth Symphony, as he interpreted it, he was closely associated; was born in Barletta, Italy, and raised in Bolzano in the formerly Austrian South Tyrol, where he became fluent in German and began absorbing the Austro-German culture, including the music; learned to play the violin in childhood; attended a local music school until he was 16, when he went to Rome to study with Remy Principe; at Principe's suggestion, took up the viola; in Rome, matriculated at the Accademia di Santa Cecilia, where his studies included composition with Alessandro Bustini; later, studied conducting with

Bernadino Molinari; in 1934, won a national competition to fill a vacancy in the viola section of the orchestra of Rome's Teatro Augusteo; made his public debut as a conductor directing a concert in Rome in 1944, at the Teatro Augusteo, according to some sources, or at the Teatro Adriana, according to others; was second conductor of Radio Italiana in Rome from 1944 to 1950, when he became the founding director of the radio orchestra in Milan; in the latter position, with a broadcast of Haydn's *Il Mondo della luna* in 1951, attracted the attention of the venerable conductor Arturo Toscanini, who became a friend and mentor; also in 1951 (1950, according to some), made his debut as an opera conductor directing *La Traviata* at the Bergamo Festival; subsequently, conducted Manuel de Falla's *La Vida Breve* at La Scala in Milan; became principal conductor at La Scala in 1953; at La Scala, began to collaborate with the stage and screen director Luchino Visconti; left La Scala in 1955 to become principal conductor of the Teatro dell'Opera in Rome; in the same year, made his debut in the United Kingdom, conducting *Falstaff* at the Edinburgh Festival; directed Luchino Visconti's productions of *Don Carlo* at Covent Garden in 1958 and of *Il Trovatore* in the same London venue in 1963; felt that his most successful collaboration with Visconti was the production of *The Marriage of Figaro* that was first staged in Rome in 1964 and which became the highlight of the Rome opera company's visit to the Metropolitan Opera in New York City in 1968—the occasion of Giulini's first operatic appearance in the U.S. but not his American conducting debut, which had occurred in 1955, at the podium of the Chicago Symphony Orchestra; had a 23-year, on-and-off relationship with the Chicago Symphony, culminating in a nine-year engagement (1969–78) as principal guest conductor; was principal conductor of the Vienna Symphony Orchestra from 1973 to 1976 and of the Los Angeles Philharmonic from 1978 to 1984; showed little attraction for the classical-music world's "new music," although he did conduct performances of Webern's works; conducted the first performances of works by the contemporary composers Giorgio Federico Ghedini, Boris Blacher, Gottfried von Einem, Ezra Ladermann, Goffredo Petrassi, and Mario Zafred; in rare returns to opera, conducted Ronald Eyre's production of *Falstaff* in Los Angeles in 1982 and subsequently in Covent Garden and Florence; left a rich discography, including Bach's Mass in B Minor, Stravinsky's *Firebird*, the Beethoven and Brahms symphonies, selected Dvořák, Franck, and Schubert symphonies, and various works by Schumann, Rossini, Ravel, Britten, and Debussy; died in Brescia, Italy; was predeceased by his wife, Marcella, and survived by three sons. See *Current Biography* (1978).

Obituary *New York Times* B p11 June 16, 2005

GLASS, H. BENTLEY Jan. 17, 1906–Jan. 16, 2005 Biologist; geneticist; university professor; a provocative progressive theorist in such fields as the biology of race, nuclear danger, and "brave new world" genetics; was distinguished professor of biology and vice chairman in charge of academic affairs at the State University of New York at Stony Brook from 1965 to 1971; while on the faculty of Johns Hopkins University (1948–65), began his research on the "genetic drift" between racially different populations; concluded that "the races are in fact disappearing, although the process will require thousands of years at present rates"; thus, incidentally, provided counterarguments to the propaganda of white racists when the Baltimore public schools were integrated; in 1955–56, chaired a special committee of the American Association of University Professors (AAUP) that recommended the censuring of several colleges and universities for violating academic freedom in their dismissals of faculty members with alleged subversive associations in their backgrounds; as president of the AAUP in 1958, protested the loyalty-oath clause in the National Defense Education Act; in 1960, was appointed to Maryland's Radiation Control Advisory Board but refused to sign the loyalty affidavit required for that post; from 1955 to 1963, was a member of the U.S. Atomic Energy Commission's advisory committee on biology and medicine; warned against the radiation peril posed by some medical technologies, by possible accidents in the peaceful uses of nuclear energy, and by fallout from nuclear-weapons testing in the atmosphere; deplored the "colossal ignorance" over the full extent of genetic damage that radioactive fallout might cause; warned against international "H-bomb snowballing"; was frighteningly graphic in describing the probable the effects of a full-scale nuclear war, when "the cockroach . . . will take over the habitats of the foolish humans and compete only with other insects or bacteria"; beginning in the late 1960s, issued a series of predictions envisioning a separation of sexual activity from laboratory-controlled human reproduction; declared, "No parents in that future time will have the right to burden society with a malformed or mentally incompetent child"; published a number of books, including *Genes and the Man* (1943), *Science and Liberal Education* (1960), and some biology textbooks for secondary schools; contributed several hundred articles to professional and general periodicals, including the *Quarterly Review of Biology*, which he edited from 1958 to 1965, and *Science*, the publication of the American Association for the Advancement of Science (AAAS); held several offices with the AAAS, including its presidency (1969); died in Boulder, Colorado. See *Current Biography* (1966).

Obituary *New York Times* B p9 Jan. 20, 2005

GOODPASTER, ANDREW J. Feb. 12, 1915–May 16, 2005 U.S. Army general, retired; former commander, Supreme Headquarters, Allied Powers Europe (SHAPE), the military arm of NATO; former superintendent, the U.S. Military Academy at West Point; graduated from West Point in 1939; in World War II, commanded an engineering battalion in North Africa and Italy; after twice being wounded in combat, spent the last year of the war on the general staff of the War Department; after the war, earned graduate degrees in engineering and international relations at Princeton University; in Brussels, Belgium, in the early 1950s, was assistant to General Alfred Gruenther, the chief of staff to General Dwight D. Eisenhower, then the commander of SHAPE; under President Eisenhower in the White House from 1954 to 1961, was staff secretary in a military-style chain of command working under and in constant collaboration with the president's chief of staff; between 1962 and 1967, held a succession of top positions with the Joint Chiefs of Staff; in 1967, was named senior U.S. Army member of the United Nations Military Staff Committee; was commandant of the National War College (1967–68); in 1968, was deputy to General Creighton Abrams, commander of the U.S. Military Assistance Command in Vietnam; in the same year, was the third-ranking member of the U.S. delegation to peace negotiations with the North Vietnamese in Paris; at the completion of his assignment as commander of SHAPE (1969–74), retired as a four-star general; in retirement, was a senior fellow at the Woodrow Wilson International Center for Scholars at the Smithsonian Institution; giving up one of his stars, came out of retirement to serve as superintendent at West Point in the rank of lieutenant general (1977–81); subsequently, was a senior fellow at the Eisenhower Institute; in addition to his two Purple Hearts, won a Distinguished Service Cross, a Silver Star, and the Medal of Freedom; died at Walter Reed Army Medical Center in Washington, D.C. See *Current Biography* (1969).

Obituary *New York Times* D p8 May 17, 2005

GRAY, L. PATRICK July 18, 1916–July 6, 2005 U.S. government official; a lawyer and former U.S. Navy commander who as acting director of the Federal Bureau of Investigation (May 1972–April 1973) under the Republican presidency of Richard M. Nixon was—in the words of Gordon Hodgson in the London *Guardian* (July 9, 2005)—"too straight and naïve to survive in the shark pool that was President Nixon's Washington" and thus became "the ultimate fall guy" in the scandal that drove Nixon to resign from office, in August 1974; was an assistant attorney general when that scandal—the political conspiracy called Watergate—began to come to light, with the burglary (instigated by Nixon reelection campaign officials) of the Democratic National Committee headquarters in the Watergate building complex in Washington, D.C., in June 1972; was in that position when the scandal, which included the White House's multifaceted cover-up of its connection to that break-in, was brought toward full exposure through the persistent investigative work of the *Washington Post* reporters Bob Woodward and Carl Bernstein, abetted by information leaked to Woodward clandestinely from the outset by Gray's associate director at the FBI, W. Mark Felt (identified only as "Deep Throat" by Woodward for three decades, until his true identity was revealed in May 2005); saw the cover-up begin to fall apart when he (Gray) appeared before the Senate Judiciary Committee for confirmation of his nomination as permanent director of the FBI in late February and early March 1973; during the Senate hearings, volunteered the information that he had for seven months been handing over the FBI's internal files on Watergate to White House counsel John W. Dean 3d through Attorney General Richard G. Kleindienst and that he had discussed Watergate privately with John Ehrlichman, Nixon's domestic affairs adviser, "on maybe half a dozen occasions"; also revealed that he had destroyed some files (apparently related to political "dirty tricks" but not to Watergate itself) at the request of the White House; electrified Washington with his revelations, and angered Nixon and his aides, who made the decision that Gray would be left to "twist slowly, slowly in the wind," as Ehrlichman put it; experienced the Nixon administration's withdrawal of his nomination for permanent FBI director and resigned as acting director on April 27, 1973; upon his graduation from the U.S. Naval Academy at Annapolis in 1940, had been commissioned an ensign in the navy; served aboard the submarine *Steelhead* in the Pacific during World War II; as a navy postgraduate student after the war, earned a J.D. degree at the George Washington University School of Law; in the rank of captain, served in the Korean War; after that war, was stationed for several years at the navy's School of Naval Justice; for two years beginning in 1958, was military assistant to the chairman of the Joint Chiefs of Staff and special assistant to the secretary of defense for legal and legislative affairs; in June 1960, left the navy to become an aide to Robert Finch, the director of Richard M. Nixon's campaign as the Republican candidate for the U.S. presidency that year; after Nixon's defeat by the Democratic candidate, John F. Kennedy, in November 1960, practiced general law in New London, Connecticut, for nine years; also, established a small business-investment company, which grew into Capital for Investment Inc.; at the same time, continued to raise funds for the Republican Party and to maintain contact with Nixon and his campaign managers; following Nixon's election to the presidency in 1968, served as executive assistant to Robert Finch, then the secretary of the Department of Health, Education, and Welfare (now the Department of Health and Human Services), for one year (January 1969–January 1970); while back in law practice during 1970, continued to serve the Nixon administration as a public-school desegregation consultant; in December 1970, returned to government as assistant attorney general in charge of the civil division in the U.S. Department of Justice; while in that position, was nominated by President Nixon in February 1972 for the post of deputy attorney general, a nomination that was still pending at the time of the death on May 2, 1972 of J. Edgar Hoover, the director (since 1924) of the FBI; on May 3, 1972 had his nomination as deputy attorney general withdrawn by President Nixon, who—passing over W. Mark Felt, Hoover's close protégé for decades and his heir expectant—appointed him acting director of the FBI; following his 11 very difficult months in that position, returned to the practice of law in Groton and New London, Connecticut; in 1978, was indicted for having approved illegal break-ins of homes during the FBI's manhunt for suspected members of the Weather Underground, a violent radical movement; succeeded in pleading for the dismissal of the charges, but had to sell his house and cash in his insurance policies to pay his lawyers' fees; was survived by his wife, two sons, two stepsons, and several grandchildren; died at his home in Atlantic Beach, Florida. See *Current Biography* (1972).

Obituary *New York Times* B p11 July 7, 2005

HAILEY, ARTHUR Apr. 5, 1920–Nov. 24 or 25, 2004 British-born novelist; one of the most commercially successful authors of his time; as a painstaking researcher and natural storyteller, appealed to a mass market with a formula that was scorned by some in the critical establishment; combined authenticity of background detail with engrossing and suspenseful narrative lines tracing the intersecting or overlapping routes of myriad characters drawn from real life; thus created fictional documentaries in which readers were embedded in specific panoramic ambiances, from grand hotel, hospital, or airport, for example, to the worlds of industry, finance, foreign correspondence, and law enforcement; saw some of his best-selling novels made into popular motion pictures, including *Hotel*, *The Final Diagnosis*, and the box-office smash hit *Airport*; had first made his mark as a writer of teleplays during the golden age of live television drama; was a Royal Air Force pilot during World War II; immigrated to Canada in 1947; during his early years in Canada, successively edited *Bus and Truck Transport* magazine, managed sales promotion and advertising for a manufacturer of tractor trailers, and ran his own advertising agency; in 1956, wrote his first teleplay, *Flight into Danger*, a suspenseful drama about an airline passenger (a former fighter pilot) who takes over the controls when the two pilots of the airliner become incapacitated; drew unprecedented audience responses with that drama when it was presented live on the CBC network in Canada and on NBC's *Alcoa Hour* in the U.S.; in quick succession, turned out 14 more plays for such TV dramatic showcases as *Studio One*, *U.S. Steel Hour*, and *Kraft Television Theatre*; won an Emmy for the hospital drama *No Deadly Medicine* (1957); made the latter the basis for *The Final Diagnosis* (1959), his first novel, which was followed by *In High Places* (1962), a story of international politics and diplomacy; was on the best-seller lists for a year with *Hotel* (1965), a tale consisting of slices of life during five days in an elegant old New Orleans hotel, and more than a year with *Airport* (1968), which takes place in single night in an international airport in the Midwest; set *Wheels* (1971) in Detroit's automobile industry; crafted *Overload* (1979) around the subject of an energy crisis; saw both *The Moneychangers* (1975) and *Strong Medicine* made into television miniseries; announced his retirement after the publication of *The Evening News* (1990), in researching which he spent time with rebel guerrillas in the jungles of Peru; emerged from retirement to write *Detective* (1997), about a Miami cop pursuing a serial killer; wrote a total of 11 books published in 40 countries and translated into 38 languages; had 170 million books in print; since 1969, lived in the Bahamas with his second wife, Sheila, by whom he had a son and two daughters; also had two sons from his first marriage (dissolved in 1950); died in Lyford Cay, New Providence Island, the Bahamas. See *Current Biography* (1972).

Obituary *New York Times* C p6 Nov. 26, 2004

HALLAREN, MARY A. May 4, 1907–Feb. 13, 2005 Army officer, retired; was a commander in the U.S. Women's Army Corps during World War II, when the newly formed WACs (as they were popularly

known) were an auxiliary to the U.S. Army; after the war, in the rank of reserve lieutenant colonel, became director of the WACs; was commissioned a regular army colonel in 1948, when the WACs became a component of the U.S. Army (remaining a separate component in the U.S. Army until 1978, when the corps was dissolved and women were integrated alongside men into all the military services, 18 years after her retirement); before launching her military career, taught at the Lowell (Massachusetts) Junior High School for 15 years; during vacations, backpacked extensively in North America, South America, Europe, and the Near East; in July 1942, seven months after the U.S. entered World War II, enrolled in the Officer Candidate School of the Women's Army Corps (then called the Women's Auxiliary Army Corps) at Fort Des Moines, Iowa; served as a battalion commander stateside from August 1942 to July 1943, when she became commander of the first battalion of WACs to be sent overseas, to England, for noncombat duty with the Eighth and Ninth Army Air Forces; led that battalion across the English Channel to continental Europe in the wake of the Normandy invasion of France by the Allies in 1944; in March 1945, was appointed WAC director for the European Theater of Operations (ETO), in command of more than 9,000 WACs in England, France, Belgium, Germany, and Austria; following the Allied victory in Europe, was coordinator of the ETO's policies dealing with civilian employees, their accommodations, and their morale; returned to the U.S. in 1946 with many decorations, including the Bronze Star, the Legion of Merit with Oak Leaf Cluster, and the Croix de Guerre avec Vermeil; became deputy director of the WACs in June 1946 and director in May 1947; was among those instrumental in persuading Congress to pass the 1948 Women's Army Services Integration Act, making the Women's Army Corps a component of the U.S. Army; directed the Women's Army Corps until 1953; retired from military service in 1960; from 1965 to 1978, was executive director of Women in Community Service (WICS), a national nonprofit organization which, in partnership with the U.S. Department of Labor, is devoted to assisting low-income women, families, and youths in making the transition from incarceration, welfare, homelessness, drug dependence, and the like to self-reliance and economic independence; died in McLean, Virginia. See *Current Biography* (1949).

Obituary *New York Times* A p23 Mar. 9, 2005

HARGIS, BILLY JAMES Aug. 3, 1925–Nov. 27, 2004 Christian clergyman; broadcast evangelist; a politically ultraconservative fundamentalist preacher in the rustic "bawl and jump" tradition; founder of the Church of the Christian Crusade and the Christian Crusade Ministries, dedicated to fighting "for Christ" and nationalism and against international "godless Communism" and its "godless allies" in the U.S., including liberals in government, the quasi-governmental Federal Reserve Bank, education, unions, entertainment, and the mainstream Protestant churches; at the height of his popularity during the Cold War, reached an audience of millions of "loyal patriots" over several hundred radio and television stations in the Bible Belt; in 1943, during a brief period of study at Ozark Bible College, an unaccredited school in Bentonville, Arkansas, was ordained a minister in the Disciples of Christ (who removed him from their roster two decades later); after serving for several years in a succession of pastorates in Missouri and Oklahoma, founded his Christian Crusade and turned to radio preaching, in the early 1950s; drew international attention in 1953, when he participated in the Rev. Carl McIntyre's Bible Balloon Project, in which tens of thousands of hydrogen balloons carrying quotations from the Bible were launched from West Germany eastward across the Iron Curtain "to succor the spiritually-starved captives of Communism"; completed the construction of his million-dollar Christian Crusade Cathedral in Tulsa, Oklahoma, in 1965; at the national convention of the Christian Crusade in Tulsa in 1969, mounted "an offensive against the religious heresy and degenerate Marxist political philosophy of the World Council of Churches/National Council of Churches"; in Tulsa in 1971, founded the American Christian College for the purpose of teaching "God, government, and Christian action"; in the mid-1970s, when numerous students, male and female, made sexual allegations (never legally confirmed) against him, resigned as president of the college, which closed down soon thereafter (in 1977); wrote numerous books that were published by the Christian Crusade's own press, including *The Far Left* (1964) and his autobiography, *My Great Mistake* (1985); in mid-2004, turned the leadership of the Christian Crusade over to his son, Billy James Hargis II; lived with his wife, Betty, on their Rose of Sharon Farm in Neosho, Missouri; died in a nursing home in Tulsa, Oklahoma; in addition to his wife and several children, was survived by many grandchildren and great-grandchildren. See *Current Biography* (1972).

Obituary *New York Times* B p6 Nov. 29, 2004

HEATH, EDWARD July 9, 1916–July 17, 2005 British politician and statesman; member of Parliament (1950–2001); leader of the Conservative Party (1965–75); prime minister (1970–74); was the most European-oriented of Conservative leaders; as prime minister, signed the Treaty of Rome, taking the United Kingdom into the European Economic Community (now the European Union) in 1973; thus fulfilled a long-frustrated ambition of his, but added little to his popularity at home, which desperately needed a boost; was beset by the troubles in Northern Ireland, where his efforts to ward off civil war ingratiated him neither with Unionists nor Catholic separatists and lost him the support of Ulster Unionist MPs that he needed in Westminster; more severely, was bedeviled by economic problems, in coping with which he was led into a politically fatal confrontation with trade unions; was born to working-class parents in Broadstairs, Kent; learned to play the piano and the organ in childhood; won an organ scholarship at Balliol College, Oxford University, where he studied the modern greats in philosophy, politics, and economics, played the organ in the college chapel and excelled in debating; was second in command of an artillery regiment in World War II; after the war, commanded a regiment in the Honourable Ar-

tillery Company and entered civil service as an administrator in the Ministry of Civil Aviation; was elected to represent the London suburb of Bexley in Parliament in 1950; became a government whip when the Conservatives returned to power in 1951; at that time, co-founded the One Nation group of Conservative MPs, dedicated to serving all social classes and vigilant against the return of the mass unemployment of the 1930s; was chief Conservative whip from 1955 to 1959 and minister of labor from October 1959 to July 1960; as lord privy seal in the early 1960s, was the chief negotiator in Britain's application for membership in the European Economic Community, which was vetoed by President Charles de Gaulle of France in January 1963; as secretary of state for industry, trade, and regional development and president of the board of trade in 1963, oversaw the abolition of retail price maintenance; in 1964, was elected the leader of the Conservative Party by his fellow Conservative MPs (then in opposition in the House of Commons) rather than in smoke-filled back rooms, the procedure up until then; succeeded Labourite Harold Wilson as prime minister upon the victory of the Conservatives in the general election of 1970; as prime minister, oversaw the arrest of hundreds of suspected members of the Irish Republican Army in 1971; the following January, authorized the dispatch of British paratroopers on a peacekeeping mission in Londonderry, the unintended outcome of which was the Bloody Sunday massacre of 14 civilians (13 of whom were Catholic civil rights demonstrators) and an exponential escalation of the violence in Ulster; subsequently, imposed direct rule of Northern Ireland from Westminster; alienated Ulster Unionists with his behind-the-scenes Sunningdale Agreement with some Northern Irish factions; meanwhile, experienced increasing problems with the economy, beginning with a growing rate of unemployment fraught with the threat of dire social consequences in depressed pockets of the population, to counter which he reversed his wonted stance and turned to government intervention in behalf of failing businesses and industries and other expansionist solutions; succeeded in increasing economic demand, but then was faced with balance-of-payment difficulties and escalating inflation; making another U-turn, imposed a statutory incomes policy, which was effective until the energy crisis of the autumn of 1973, when the British workweek was reduced to three days, garbage began piling up in the streets, and labor unions were emboldened to challenge the guidelines for wages; seeking a popular mandate when the National Union of Mineworkers voted for an all-out strike if denied a substantial wage increase in February 1974, called for a general election, in which, by a tiny margin, the Conservative Party polled more votes than the Labour Party (11,872,180 to 11,645,616) but suffered a loss in parliamentary seats because the nine Ulster Unionist MPs protesting Heath's Sunningdale Agreement threw their support to Labour, bringing the latter party's total to 301 seats, four more than the Conservative total; left 10 Downing Street on March 4, 1974, making way for Harold Wilson's return to the prime ministership and his retention of that post following the next general election, in October 1974, in which Wilson's minority government was confirmed with a majority of the vote, albeit by a razon-thin margin; became the focus of criticism emanating from the Centre for Policy Studies, formed between the two elections by some Conservative MPs, including Margaret Thatcher, who replaced Heath as party leader in 1975 and led the comeback of the Conservatives to power in 1979; snubbed for a cabinet position by Thatcher, withdrew to the sidelines; feeling not only that his record in office was being belittled but also that much of his agenda was being subverted, "sulked in [Thatcher's] long shadow," as Dennis Kavanagh wrote for the London *Independent* (July 18, 2005); on occasion, went public with criticisms of Thatcher's "monetarist" economic policies, her "Casino capitalism," and her opposition to the monetary integration of Europe (while she developed a warm relationship with U.S. president Ronald Reagan); was a champion yachtsman, skippering his crews to victory in the Sydney-to-Hobart race in 1969 and the Admiral's Cup in 1971 and 1979; was knighted in 1992; published his autobiography, *The Course of My Life*, in 1998; was a lifelong bachelor; died in his mansion in Salisbury, England. See *Current Biography* (1962).

Obituary *New York Times* A p17 July 18, 2005

HECHT, ANTHONY Jan. 16,1923–Oct. 20, 2004 Poet; a formalist steeped in the genteel tradition and a consummate master of technique, from the serious 10-syllable line to the double dactyl, a limerick-like humorous form of his own invention; in verse marked by irony and a richness of allusion, dealt, as he said, "sometimes with very terrible aspects of existence"; "wrote unabashedly in the the high style," as Dana Gioia, a poet and the chairman of the National Endowment for the Arts since 2003, observed, adding that he did so "with emotional force and exquisite musicality" and "found a way to take his tragic sense of life and make it so beautiful that we have to pay attention to its painful truth"; took on "society in the largest sense" without losing his "wonderful dark humor," in the words of Deborah Garrison, his editor at Alfred A. Knopf; produced his modest but finely wrought canon over a period of half a century, beginning with the baroque and exuberant verse of a *A Summoning of Stones* (1954); over the following years, progressed to the more direct and simple style of the poems collected in the Pulitzer Prize–winning 1967 volume, *The Hard Hours* (including "Halloween," reflecting his lifelong fascination with childhood as a subject), and the self-assured, sophisticated intricacy of narrative skill displayed in *The Venetian Vespers* (1979); in 2001, published *The Darkness and the Light*, which included the poem about death "Flight Among the Tombs," beginning with a 22-part sequence illustrated with wood engravings by Leonard Baskin and ending with "A Death in Winter," an elegy to Joseph Brodsky; in 2003, published *Collected Later Poems* (2003); after receiving a B.A. degree at Bard College, in 1944, was inducted into the U.S. Army; as an infantryman in Europe in the waning days of World War II, witnessed the liberation of a Nazi concentration camp near the Czech-German border; as a human being and as a Jew, was profoundly affected by that experience, which contributed to his sense of evil in the world and which

he would transmute into the images of the Holocaust that recur in his later works; after the war, studied under John Crowe Ransom at Kenyon College; later, earned an M.A. degree at Columbia University; won the Prix de Rome in 1950 and the Bollingen Prize in 1983; taught at several universities, chiefly the University of Rochester, where he was on the faculty from 1967 to 1985; was poetry consultant to the Library of Congress from 1982 to 1984; in addition to poetry, wrote essays in literary criticism, published in several collections, including *Obbligati* (1986); died at his home in Washington, D.C.; was survived by his second wife, Helen, three sons, and two grandchildren. See *Current Biography* (1986).

Obituary *New York Times* B p10 Oct. 22, 2004

HEILBRONER, ROBERT L. Mar. 24, 1919–Jan. 4, 2005 Economist; author; professor emeritus, the New School (a university); a professional economist who wrote lucidly and in a graceful, accessible style rare among practitioners of "the dismal science"; wrote his masterpiece and first book, *The Worldly Philosophers: The Lives, Times, and Ideas of the Great Economic Thinkers* (1953), a work that has sold well over two million copies, went into its seventh edition in 1999, and is surpassed in popularity among American books on economics only by Paul Samuelson's college text *Economics*; went on to write books exploring the "internal dynamics" of capitalism, which he viewed not simply as a matter of markets and exchange but, on a grander scale, as a socioeconomic system involving the acquisitive drive for wealth and the interdependence of the private and public sectors; over the years, modified his original Marxist-influenced democratic-socialist perspective, especially after the collapse of the Soviet system; told Mark Skousen in an interview for *Forbes* (May 27, 1991), "Just because socialism has lost does not mean that capitalism has won. . . . Capitalism is and always has been in crisis"; earned a B.A. degree in history at Harvard University and a Ph.D. degree in economics at the New School, where he held the Norman Thomas Chair in the graduate faculty; published more than a score of books, including *The Future As History* (1960), *The Limits of American Capitalism* (1966), *Between Capitalism and Socialism* (1970), *Marxism, For and Against* (1980), *The Nature and Logic of Capitalism* (1985), and books on macroeconomics, microeconomics, the U.S. credit system, the national debt and deficit, and the World Bank; was survived by his wife, Shirley, and his two sons, David and Peter. See *Current Biography* (1975).

Obituary *New York Times* A p19 Jan. 12, 2005

HELD, AL Oct. 12, 1928–July 26, 2005 Abstract artist; a painter of what he called "synthetic constructs," large-scale impastos (inspired in part by his interest in radio astronomy) of geometric shapes configured in what critics have variously described as a "dream world" and a "time-warp universe of space flight"; was born to Polish Jewish immigrants in the borough of Brooklyn, New York City; grew up there and in the borough of the Bronx; as a streetwise adolescent, dropped out of high school; after serving in the U.S. Navy (1945–47), became involved in leftist causes as a member of Folksay, a group of writers, artists, musicians, and labor-union activists; at the suggestion of friends, began to try his hand at art; took advantage of his right to educational funding under the federal Servicemen's Readjustment Act (better known as the G.I. Bill) to enroll at the Art Students League in Manhattan in 1948; painted figuratively, in a social-realist style, for several years before he fell in with the trend to abstract expressionism and began working in the painterly gestural style preeminently exemplified by the "action" painter Jackson Pollock, which would dominate the art world for two decades; sought unsuccessfully to go to Mexico to apprentice under the Marxist revolutionary muralist David Alfaro Siqueiro; instead, used the remainder of his G.I. Bill grant to study at the Académie de la Grande Chaumière in Paris, France (1950–53); in Paris in 1952, gave his first solo show, an exhibition indicating the beginning of his transition from representational works to abstractions aimed at reconciling Pollock's subjective dripped-paint expressionism with the objectivity of Piet Mondrian's geometrical compositions; after returning to New York, became identified with the internationally influential Tenth Street group of abstract expressionists; by the early 1960s, had become one of the schismatics known as the "post-painterly abstractionists" (a term coined by the critic Clement Greenberg), artists (including minimalists and color-field painters) who in varying ways reacted against subjective expressionism and sought to modify the abstract expressionist style in favor of greater discipline and objectivity; chose to reduce the gestural element and concentrate on relatively hard-edge geometric designs; using masking tape and multiple coats of paint (finally sanded down to eliminate or mute the evidence of the painting process and the painter's hand), created configurations of contiguous or overlapping circles, squares, triangles, and other simple shapes, precisely defined; over the years, developed his canvases and murals—richly colored except during one protracted black-and-white period—into more complex and fantastic designs, in which the circles became spheres, the squares became cubes, and the triangles became pyramids, and so forth, often floating like three-dimensional objects in seemingly infinite spatial perspectives, as in his *Solar Wind* series; in 1983, completed one of his largest pieces, the mural *Montegna's Edge*, 14 feet six inches by 52 feet 10 inches, which hangs in the entry of the Boca Raton (Florida) Museum; later executed, among other murals, one that adorns a wall in the New York City subway system, at 53d Street and Lexington Avenue; also painted watercolors; beginning in 2003, mounted a traveling exhibition of recent paintings and watercolors (the largest of which was nine feet square) titled Expanding Universe; taught at Yale University from 1962 to 1980; maintained homes in Briceville, New York, and Todi, Italy; was married and divorced four times; was survived by his companion, Pamela Gagliani, his daughter, Mara, from his third marriage, to the sculptor Sylvia Stone, and a grandchild; died at his home in Todi, Italy. See *Current Biography* (1986)

Obituary *New York Times* A p21 July 29, 2005

HILDEGARDE Feb. 1, 1906–July 29, 2005 American singer; pianist; legendary supper-club chanteuse; the most famous of the veterans of the heyday of cabaret and, incidentally, the first modern American entertainer to truncate her/his name, which she did early in her career at the suggestion of the songwriter and vaudeville impressario Gus Edwards; was billed as "The Incomparable Hildegarde," an epithet coined by the newspaper columnist Walter Winchell, who described her as "the girl who sings like Garbo looks"; appealed to smart-set audiences on both sides of the Atlantic with her chic but friendly persona, her humorous and sometimes risqué ad-libbing, and her sweet renditions—in an indefinable, vaguely European accent, often to her own piano accompaniment—of a repertoire that prominently included such songs as "I'll Be Seeing You," "Lili Marlene," "The Last Time I Saw Paris," and "Darling, Je Vous Aime Beaucoup," her signature song, which was written specifically for her by the songwriter Anna Sosenko, her business manager and housemate from 1933 until they broke up, in 1956; was born to German Catholic immigrant parents in Adell, Wisconsin, and christened Hildegarde Loretta Sell; began her career playing piano accompaniment for silent movies in Milwaukee when she was 16 and a student of music at Marquette University; later, toured the vaudeville circuit as a pianist with several musical acts; during a stopover in Camden, New Jersey, met and formed her partnership with Anna Sosenko, who proceeded to mastermind and/or supervise every detail of her transition to glamorous nightclub singer, including soigné grooming, couturier costuming including elbow-length opera gloves, dramatic lighting, and astute promotion; to become practiced in the art of cabaret at a time when opportunities in the U.S. were minimal, left for Europe in the autumn of 1933, accompanied by Sosenko; during a period of expatriation of more than three years, chiefly in France, won popularity with the upper-class patrons of such venues as the Club Casanova in Paris and the Ritz-Carlton and Savoy clubs in London; performed in several British movies and stage revues; began her recording career as well as her radio career, on BBC programs; back in the U.S., was a guest or regular singer on programs on the NBC and CBS radio networks; for three years beginning in 1944, starred in *The Raleigh Room*, a weekly NBC radio show that simulated the milieu of a supper club; meanwhile, beginning in 1939, was booked in cabaret rooms of Manhattan's Waldorf-Astoria, Ritz-Carlton, and Versailles hotels, among other venues; reached the top of her field in the 1940s, with a six-year engagement in the Persian Room of the Plaza Hotel and an income as high as $17,500 a week; in the 1940s and 1950s, had record sales in the hundreds of thousands; traveled the cabaret circuit with her own quartet, which was sometimes augmented by house orchestras: in engagements at the Cotillion Room of the Hotel Pierre in Manhattan in the 1950s, for example, had the musical support of both Stanley Melba's orchestra and the Cotillion Strings; at a ceremony hosted by Eleanor Roosevelt in 1961, received an award naming her "First Lady of the Supper Clubs"; soon afterward, was named a Lady of the Equestrian Order of the Holy Sepulchre of Jerusalem by the Vatican; made her Carnegie Hall debut in

1962; published her autobiography, *Over 50 . . . So What?*, in 1963; was one of the stars in the Broadway revue *Keep 'Em Laughing* in 1942; later, was in the touring companies of the musicals *Can-Can* and *Follies*; in 1980, toured in the nostalgia musical *The Big Broadcast of 1944*; appeared in a number of television specials; performed at the Algonquin Hotel in 1993; during the same year, was joined by Anna Sosenko (with whom she had reconciled) in a performance at the Russian Tea Room; participated in the annual Cabaret Convention at Town Hall in 1994; lectured at universities and other venues; performed at Carnegie Hall on the occasion of her 90th birthday, in 1996; was a contributor to various Catholic activities, including charities and such causes as the Blue Army of Our Lady of Fatima, which is devoted to the quest for world peace; lived in Manhattan; died at New York Presbyterian/Weill Cornell Hospital, in Manhattan. See *Current Biography* (1944).

Obituary *New York Times* I p31 July 31, 2005

HOUSTON, JAMES A. June 12, 1921–Apr. 17, 2005 Artist; author; a non-Eskimoid Canadian who lived with the Inuits of Canada's eastern Arctic for 14 years and was singularly responsible for introducing their art to the wider world; helped the Eskimo people immeasurably—"Ever since he came, the Eskimo people have been able to find work," the Inuit artist Pitseolak wrote in his book *Pitseolak: Pictures Out of My Life* (1971)—and in return, was given the knowledge of the indigenous people's lore and legend that would provide him with the inspiration for his work in design and filmmaking and for a score of books, including his four adult novels and the many tales he wrote and illustrated for children; was formatively influenced by the interest that his father, a businessman who traveled widely, had in the indigenous culture of Canada's Pacific Northwest; decided on a career in art when he was nine; after graduating from high school, studied at the Ontario College of Art for a year; following service with the Canadian army in World War II, studied art in Paris; in 1948, embarked on a painting and drawing expedition on the remote shores of upper Hudson Bay that turned into a complete and sustained immersion in the indigenous life there; with his first wife, settled in Cape Dorset, home of the Sikusalingmiut, where they raised their two sons as Inuits; early on, began delivering ivory, bone, and soapstone carvings created by the local people to the Canadian Handicraft Guild in Montreal; subsequently, taught the people how to make prints from their original stone cuts; became a Northern Service officer for the Canadian government in 1952; was named the first federal civil administrator of West Baffin Island in 1955; toured his 65,000-square-mile domain by dog sled, visiting 13 far-flung camps inhabited by a total of 343 Eskimos; oversaw the establishment of government-subsidized workshops, facilitating the development of sculpture and printmaking as cottage industries that made the people less dependent for a living on the hunting of caribou and on the declining fur trade; organized the West Baffin Eskimo Cooperative; in 1962, left Cape Dorset to accept a position as associate director of design with the Steuben Glass Co. in New York City; in Manhattan, met Margaret K. McElderry, the editor

of children's books at Harcourt, Brace publishers, who encouraged him to try his hand at writing and illustrating books, which he proceeded to do in his spare time; in 1971, resigned his full-time position at Steuben Glass; moved to the position of consultative director with the company, which allowed him to concentrate on his writing and illustrating of books; with his initial publication, *Tikta'Liktak: An Eskimo Legend* (1965), won the first of a number of awards from the Canadian Library Association; went on to write and illustrate many more Eskimo tales, including *The White Archer* (1967), *Wolf Run* (1971), *Spirit Wrestler* (1980), *Long Claws* (1981), *Eagle Song* (1983), and *The Falcon Bow* (1986); wrote such novels as *The Ice Master* (1997) and such memoirs as *Confessions of an Igloo Dweller* (1995) and *Zigzag* (1998); also edited, illustrated, or otherwise contributed to several volumes devoted to Canadian Eskimo art (and, to a lesser degree, Canadian Indian art); adapted his adult novel *The White Dawn* (1971) into a Paramount adventure feature film with the same title (1974); shared in many international film awards for his work as a producer, director, or technical adviser for a number of documentaries; in 1987 and again in 2002, was given major retrospective exhibitions of his crystal and metal designs for Steuben Glass, among the best known of which is "Arctic Fisherman," a sculpture of an Inuit spear fisherman within a block of glass; following his divorce from his first wife, the former Alma Georgina Bardon, married Alice Watson, who survived him; died in New London, Connecticut. See *Current Biography* (1987).

Obituary *New York Times* B p6 Apr. 22, 2005

HUNTER, EVAN Oct. 15, 1926–July 6, 2005 Novelist; under various names, wrote fast-paced and suspenseful best-sellers marked by realistic language and authentic settings; under the pseudonym Ed McBain, created his innovative 87th Precinct crime mysteries, set in the New York–like metropolis of Isola, in which he sought to make the protagonist not a single investigator, as in traditional detective fiction, but rather "a squad of cops . . . a conglomerate lead character," and thus created what became the basis for the NBC urban cop show *87th Precinct* (September 1961–September 1962) and the made-for-TV movie *Ed McBain's 87th Precinct* (NBC, 1995), the former of which helped inspire *Hill Street Blues* and other police-procedural series on TV; under his own name (legally changed from Salvatore Albert Lombino to Evan Hunter in 1952), realized the first of his many best-sellers with *The Blackboard Jungle* (1954), the story (based in part on his own brief experience with juvenile delinquents in the New York City public-school system) about the baptism of fire of an idealistic, fledgling New York high-school teacher, which was adapted for the popular motion picture *The Blackboard Jungle* (1955), scripted by its director, Richard Brooks; in *Second Ending* (1956), a story about drug addiction, used jazz jargon in creating a convincing musical background, probably derived in part from his memories of playing piano with a swing band; in *Strangers When We Meet* (1958), dealt with suburban infidelity; in *Buddwing*, told the story of an amnesiac; dealt with war in *Sons* (1969) and with the negative impact of the counterculture on family relations in *Love, Dad* (1981); as Evan Hunter, wrote a total of some 24 novels, including *Walk Proud* (1979) and *The Moment She Was Gone* (2002); was born in Manhattan and grew up in the Bronx, New York City; originally aspired to be an artist; attended classes at the Art Students League and the Cooper Union for the Advancement of Science and Art; began writing stories when serving in the U.S. Navy (1944–46); after receiving a B.A. degree in English at Hunter College in 1950, began selling science-fiction stories to pulp magazines while working for six months as a teacher of English in two New York City vocational high schools and for two years as an editor with the Scott Meredith Literary Agency; to educate himself in the authentic detail he brought to his Ed McBain novels, spent much time with New York Police Department homicide detectives, forensic experts, and other personnel, including cops on the beat; published *Cop Hater*, the first of the 87th Precinct novels, in 1956; followed it with some 56 more, including *Fuzz* (1968) and ending with *Findings* (2005); in addition to the 87th Precinct novels, used the pen name Ed McBain in writing 13 Matthew Hope mysteries; also wrote eight novels (including *Diehard*, 1958) under the pseudonym Curt Cannon, eight (including *Rocket to Luna*, 1953) under Richard Marsten, and six under other pseudonyms; wrote the screenplays for the motion-picture adaptations of his novels *Strangers When We Meet* (1960) and *Fuzz* (1972) and for Alfred Hitchcock's *The Birds* (1963); wrote the scripts for several television miniseries, including *The Chisholms* (1979–80), an adaptation of his *The Chisholms: A Novel of the Journey West* (1976); as Evan Hunter, wrote, in addition to novels, numerous short stories and two plays; also wrote the memoirs *Me and Hitch* (1997) and *Let's Talk* (2005), the latter was about his coping with the removal of his cancer-ridden larynx and the implanting of a prosthetic voice box; died at his home in Weston, Connecticut; before marrying Dragica Dimitrijevic (who survived him), was married to and divorced from Anita Melnick and then Mary Vann; had three sons from his first marriage and a stepdaughter from his second. See *Current Biography* (1956).

Obituary *New York Times* B p10 July 7, 2005

IAKOVOS, ARCHBISHOP July 29, 1911–Apr. 10, 2005 Primate of the Greek Orthodox Archdiocese of North and South America (1959–96), an ecclesiastical jurisdiction of the Ecumenical Patriarchate of Constantinople (Istanbul); in that position, was the religious leader of the largest Eastern Orthodox denomination in the Americas, comprising an estimated 1,300,000 communicants, including some 1,150,000 in 375 parishes in the U.S., with the combined Eastern Orthodox population—including Russian, Syrian, Coptic, and 15 other communions—in the Americas totaling about 2,600,000; as archbishop, championed religious unity, human rights, and civil rights; was proud of leading his immigrant flock out of its ethnic isolation and into acceptance "by the family of religions in the United States"; opened or widened dialogue with other Christian denominations and other religions and sought to unite the di-

verse Orthodox communions; was born Demetrios A. Coucouzis on the Turkish island of Imroz (Imbros or Imvros, according to various sources); in 1934, was ordained a deacon; in 1939, immigrated to the U.S. and joined the theological faculty of the Holy Cross Theological School, the seminary of the Greek Orthodox Archdiocese in the Americas, then located in Pomfret, Connecticut, and now located in Brookline, Massachusetts; took the name Iakovos when he was ordained a priest in Boston, in 1940; while serving as dean of the Cathedral of the Annunciation in Boston (1942–54), earned a master's degree in theology at the Harvard University School of Divinity (1945); became a U.S. citizen in 1950; was elevated to the rank of bishop in 1954; was the representative of the Greek Orthodox Ecumenical Patriarchate at the World Council of Churches' headquarters in Geneva, Switzerland, from 1955 until the Holy Synod of the Ecumenical Patriarchate elected him Archbishop of North and South America, in 1959; soon after his enthronement, became the the first Greek Orthodox archbishop to meet with a Roman Catholic pope (Pope John XXIII) in 350 years; marched with the Reverend Martin Luther King Jr. in Selma, Alabama, in 1965; was president of the World Council of Churches for several years; while a traditionalist in most matters, encouraged the use of English in the liturgy, especially for the benefit of younger people and converts not very familiar with Greek; was removed from office in 1996, according to an obituary of him by Felix Corley for the London *Independent* (April 23, 2005), most likely because of "his championing of the rights of Orthodox in the United States to their own Church. As head of the largest Orthodox jurisdiction, he had convened a meeting in 1994 to bring the ten ethnic churches in North America under one umbrella. Patriarch Bartholomew of Constantinople (Istanbul), senior cleric in the Orthodox world, had initially been supportive, but pulled the plug when he felt a united American Orthodox Church would seek to be independent"; died at a hospital in Stamford, Connecticut. See *Current Biography* (1960).

Obituary *New York Times* B p7 Apr. 12, 2005

JANEWAY, ELIZABETH Oct. 7, 1913–Jan. 15, 2005 Novelist and critic; in her fiction, focused on the psychological interplay of her characters, usually in family situations; in her nonfiction, pursued predominantly feminist themes; was born—in Brooklyn, New York—with the surname Hall; acquired the name Janeway from her marriage to Eliot Janeway, an economist and writer; won *Story* magazine's college short-story contest when she was a senior at Barnard College; developed what began as a short story into the well-received stream-of-consciousness novel *The Walsh Girls* (1943), about the relationship between two New England sisters reunited following the death of the husband of one of them in a Nazi concentration camp; related the life and loves of a successful career woman in her second novel, *Daisy Kenyon* (1945), which was made into a feature film; in *The Question of Gregory* (1949), examined the impact of a young man's death in wartime combat on his family; told the story of a Brooklyn family during the Depression years in *Leaving Home* (1953); followed the female protagonist of *The Third Choice* (1958) through her two marriages and a love affair; in her sixth novel, *Accident* (1964), presented the varying perspectives of several characters regarding a fatal car crash; began her nonfiction writing with juvenilia: *The Vikings* (1951) and *The Early Days of the Automobile* (1956); in 1971 published the first of her more serious works of nonfiction, *Man's World, Women's Place: A Study in Social Mythology*; brought together some of her essays in literary and social criticism in the volumes *Between Myth and Morning: Women Awakening* (1974) and *Cross Sections: From a Decade of Change* (1982); published *Powers of the Weak* in 1980 and *Improper Behavior* in 1987; with others, edited *Discovering Literature* (1968), *The Writer's World* (1969), and *Women: Their Changing Roles* (1973); died in Rye, New York; See *Current Biography* (1944).

Obituary *New York Times* I p26 Jan. 16, 2005

JENNINGS, PETER July 29, 1938–Aug. 7, 2005 Canadian-born broadcast journalist; during 41 years as a national reporter, foreign correspondent, and news anchor with the American Broadcasting Co. (ABC), brought to network radio and television in the U.S. a familiar presence, one of urbanity and unfailing poise; was the sole anchor and senior editor of ABC's *World News Tonight with Peter Jennings* for 22 years; led that program into first place in popularity among prime-time television-network news telecasts in the late 1980s and early 1990s; was born in Toronto, Ontario, Canada, one of the two children of Charles Jennings, a pioneering Canadian television journalist who became head of news programming with the Canadian Broadcasting Corp. (CBC); through his father's influence, had some childhood experience behind the microphone; dropped out of prep school to become an interviewer on radio station CFJR in Brockville, Ontario; subsequently, worked as a host or reporter in public affairs and news programming with the CBC; in 1962, joined the Canadian commercial television network CTV as co-anchor of the CTV National News; left CTV to join ABC News in New York City as a television reporter in September 1964; first anchored ABC's nightly national news telecast—unhappily that time around—for three years beginning in February 1965; returned to reportorial duties in January 1968 and began to establish his reputation as an award-winning foreign correspondent; following a posting in Rome, went to Beirut, Lebanon, to establish the first American television bureau in the Middle East; among other staff members in Beirut in the early 1970s, worked with the sound recordist Charles Glass, who has recalled—in the London *Independent* (August 8, 2005)—how Jennings seemed to be the archetype of the dashing foreign correspondent but worked hard "to play down his good looks and detested the name his more envious colleagues gave him: 'Stanley Stunning'"; "always filed more radio than television reports," as Glass recalled, and in his weekly radio commentary *Jennings' Journal* created "ABC News Radio's most popular and informative program"; at the end of 1974, returned to the U.S. to serve as ABC News's Washington correspondent; also, read the news on *A.M. America*, ABC's first early-morning effort (Jan-

uary–October 1975) to compete for the breakfast-hour viewership against NBC's *Today* show and the predecessor of ABC's *Good Morning America*, introduced in November 1975; also that November, was reassigned overseas as ABC's chief foreign correspondent, based in London; in that job, gained status for the London desk under the innovative aegis of Roone Arledge, the head of ABC Sports (who assumed in addition in 1977 the presidency of ABC News); was chief foreign correspondent in July 1978, when Arledge converted the network's daily prime-time newscast into *ABC World News Tonight*, a four-desk (later, three-desk) broadcast with Jennings serving as the London anchor; was a member of the triumvirate when Frank Reynolds, the Washington anchor, fell terminally ill, in 1983; replaced Reynolds in Washington in July 1983, and the following September, moved to New York City as the sole anchor of a revamped nightly newscast titled *World News Tonight with Peter Jennings*; saw ABC's nightly national news broadcast, which for decades had been trailing those of the NBC and CBS networks in popularity, gradually rise in the ratings, move into first place in 1989, and remain in the lead for eight years, until it was surpassed by NBC's *Nightly News*, anchored by Tom Brokaw, in the mid-1990s; at the peak of the popularity of *World News Tonight with Peter Jennings*, in the early 1990s, attracted an average viewership of nearly 14 million each weeknight; brought to the broadcast an international perspective that contributed to the allegations of "liberal bias" leveled against him by such conservative watchdog groups as the Media Research Center; became a naturalized American citizen in 2003 without relinquishing his Canadian citizenship; was married four times—the final time to Kayce Freed, his widow—and divorced three times; had a son and a daughter by his third wife, Kati Marton; made his last broadcast on April 5, 2005, when he announced that he had been diagnosed with late-term lung cancer; died at his home in Manhattan. See *Current Biography* (1977).

Obituary *New York Times* A p1+ Aug. 8, 2005

JENSEN, OLIVER O. Apr. 16, 1914–June 30, 2005 Historian; editor; co-founder of *American Heritage*, a bi-monthly publication devoted to the coverage of people and events in U.S. history in an accessible popular-magazine style and format; developed an interest in trolleys, railroads, and steamships when he was growing up in New London, Connecticut; after receiving a B.A. degree in government at Yale University, in 1936, was employed in New York City for several years as a writer first of radio scripts and then of advertising copy; was a staff writer with *Life* magazine from 1940 to 1942, when he took a leave of absence to do wartime service in the U.S. Navy; following destroyer convoy duty in the Atlantic, was transferred to navy aviation; in the summer of 1943, was sent to the Pacific to join Admiral Mark A. Mitscher's Task Force 58—a mighty flotilla of battleships, cruisers, destroyers, and above all, aircraft carriers—in the capacity of a navy historian who would record an epic sea-air offensive; from first-hand observation, supplemented by research and interviews, wrote a lively narrative tracing the history of Task

Force 58 from its first action in the Marcus Island raid of September 1, 1943 through the battles of Wake, Rabaul, the Gilbert and Marshall Islands, Truk, Palau, Hollandia, and the great battles of the Philippine sea—a narrative, originally prepared for the navy's Battle Report series under the auspices of the Council of Books in Wartime, that became a best-seller when published early in 1945 by Simon and Schuster and Pocket Books with the title *Carrier War*; after his discharge from the navy, in January 1946, with the rank of lieutenant, returned to *Life* magazine as a writer/editor for four years; with two *Life* colleagues, Joseph Thorndike and James Parton, founded Thorndike, Jensen & Parton, a custom publishing company, in 1950; four years later, with Thorndike, Parton, and the historian Bruce Catton, founded *American Heritage*, an ad-free, hardcover, general-interest magazine containing articles, art portfolios, photographs, diaries, and biographies relating to American history; succeeding Catton, was the editor of the magazine from 1959 to 1976; was chief of the division of prints and photographs at the Library of Congress from 1981 to 1983; published, among other books, *The Revolt of American Women: A Pictorial History* (1952), *The American Heritage History of Railroads in America* (1975), *America's Yesterdays: Images of Our Lost Past Discovdered in the Photographic Archives of the Library of Congress* (1978), and *America's Railroads* (1981); with other railroad buffs, bought a section of the old New Haven Railroad, a steam line, in the late 1960s and restored it, turning it into the Valley Railroad, a thriving tourist attraction based in Essex, Connecticut; was president of the Valley Railroad for many years and served on its board until his death; was married and divorced four times before his marriage in 1970 to the former Alison Pfeiffer Hargrove, who died in 2000; was survived by a stepdaughter, two stepsons, and four step-grandchildren; lived in Old Saybrook, Connecticut before moving into Aaron Manor, an assisted-living facility in Chester, Connecticut; died in Aaron Manor. See *Current Biography* (1945).

Obituary *New York Times* B p8 July 1, 2005

JOHANNESEN, GRANT July 30, 1921–Mar. 27, 2005 Utah-born concert pianist; recording artist; an internationally acclaimed virtuoso who during a career spanning more than half a century "preserved his individuality and [went] his own way," as the critic Harold Schonberg observed; while not ignoring the classical standards—he played the complete cycle of Beethoven piano concertos with extraordinary frequency, for example—preferred to seek out the more rarely performed piano pieces of the great masters (Mozart, Schubert, Liszt, Schumann, Chopin, Brahms, et al.), and concentrated on exploring modern veins of music, including the French repertoire, rare Russian repertoire, and selective byways in contemporary American music, such as the oeuvres of fellow Utahans and members of the Church of Latter Day Saints (LDS); was best known for his sensitive interpretations of works of such French composers of the early 20th century as Camille Saint-Saëns, Francis Poulenc, Darius Milhaud, Paul Dukas, and Gabriel Fauré; was the first pianist to record all of Fauré's compositions for piano; was born to Norwe-

gian immigrant parents in Salt Lake City; began playing the piano when he was five; studied piano under Mabel Borg-Jenkins in Salt Lake City before moving to the East Coast and studying under the pianists Robert Casadesus and Egon Petri and the composer Roger Sessions; also studied under Nadia Boulanger at her conservatory in Fontainebleau, France; made his Manhattan recital debut at Town Hall in 1944; gave the first of his many performances with the New York Philharmonic in 1947; beginning with a tour of Western Europe with that orchestra in 1949, regularly toured abroad; was especially well received in appearances in the Soviet Union in 1962, 1965, and 1970; was often a soloist with the Utah Symphony Orchestra and the Cleveland Orchestra; was director of the Cleveland Institute of Music from 1974 to 1985; through the 1990s, regularly gave recitals in such venues as Manhattan's Weill Hall and the New York Public Library; included in his American repertoire works of such composers as George Gershwin, Aaron Copland, Wallingford Rieger, Samuel Barber, Norman Dello Joio, Roy Harris, Peter Mennen, and such fellow Utahans as Crawford Gates and Helen Taylor, his first wife; in 2003, recorded the CD *Mormoniana*, a suite representing the collaboration of 16 composers who shared his LDS faith; was married to Helen Taylor from 1943 until her death in an automobile accident seven years later; in 1963, married the cellist Zara Nelsova, with whom he performed and recorded; was divorced from Nelsova in 1973; was survived by a son, David, from his first marriage, and two grandchildren; died in Germany. See *Current Biography* (1961).

Obituary *New York Times* D p8 Mar. 30, 2005

JOHN PAUL II May 18, 1920–Apr. 2, 2005 Supreme Pontiff of the Roman Catholic Church; Sovereign of the Vatican City State; the 263d successor (some historians say the 262d) to St. Peter as Bishop of Rome; the first non-Italian pope since the Dutch-born Adrian VI (1522–23); the third-longest-serving pontiff (1978–2005) in the history of the papacy; the most traveled pope in history; an iconic figure on the world stage, where, by dint of his charismatic personality, he was able to assert moral certitude in an age of secular relativism; was a complex spiritual leader, grounded in mysticism but committed to a busy international pastoral itinerary that took the papal mission out of the Vatican cloister; was soaring in his rhetoric against political, social, and economic injustice and extraordinarily ecumenical in his outreach to other religious traditions, most notably in his unprecedented, humble commitment to reconciliation with the Jews, "the people of the Covenant," his "older brothers" in the faith, in his words; condemned totalitarian regimes for their assaults "on the dignity of the human person"; encouraged the popular opposition that toppled such dictators as Ferdinand Marcos in the Philippines and Augusto Pinochet in Chile; with his quiet support for the Solidarity free-labor-union movement, contributed not only to the fall of the Soviet-backed Communist government in his native Poland but to the total collapse of communism in Eastern Europe; while suspicious of Marxism (in which he was learned) in whatever guise—"liberation theology" was one such manifestation, in his view—was also unsparing in his criticism of the excesses of capitalism and materialism and the "culture of death" in the industrialized West; deplored the inequities between rich and poor nations; in keeping with his general pro-life stance, doubted the justifiability of any modern war, and specifically opposed the American war in Iraq, launched in 2003; within the Catholic Church, was an orthodox hardliner; cut short the localization of authority and the permissiveness in doctrine and discipline that had ensued from Vatican Council II; while continuing the church's mission to protect the vulnerable of the world, stringently reaffirmed its restriction of the priesthood to a male, celibate clergy and its age-old stands against divorce, sex outside marriage, homosexual unions, abortion, and euthanasia; aroused displeasure among progressive Catholics with that conservative side of his agenda and with his seemingly limp response to the pedophilia scandal involving a few American priests and the bishops who enabled them; heard from moderate Catholics who agreed with his condemnation of abortion but did not see the sense of his equal denunciation of artificial contraception; often mollified critics with his warm, benign personal style; served as a strong spiritual father to the multitudes of faithful who cheered him at every turn in his international pilgrimages; especially appealed to young people; saw, under his pontificate, the Catholic populations of Europe and North America decline but those in Africa, Latin America, and Asia grow, with a resulting net increase of 41 percent worldwide, from 757 million in 1978 to more than a billion in 2005; with such achievements, led Father Richard John Neuhaus, a convert from the Lutheran ministry, to observe that the Roman Catholic Church had reached "a stronger position than it's been in since the Protestant division in the sixteenth century"; as the former Karol Józef Wojtyla of Poland, had been steeled in (and learned to be a cagey geopolitical statesman in) the crucible of totalitarian oppression, under the Nazis during World War II, as a young poet, actor, student of literature, linguistics, and philosophy, and a clandestine seminarian, and subsequently under the Soviet-backed Communist regime, as a priest, bishop, and cardinal; as a cardinal, participated in framing some of the reforms of Vatican Council II (1962–65), but repudiated the notion that the council had sanctioned the application of democratic procedures and cafeteria-style options to the expression of faith; as pope, began his international traveling with a tour of Latin America early in 1978; was greeted with a thunderous outpouring of religious and patriotic affection on his several visits to Poland, the first of which took place in June 1979; on May 13, 1981 (the 64th anniversary of the reported apparition of the Virgin Mary at Fatima, Portugal), was greeting a throng in St. Peter's Square while standing in the back of his Popemobile, a modified Mercedes-Benz off-road vehicle, when a young Turk named Mehmet Ali Agca attempted to assassinate him; suffered two bullet wounds, one of which was near fatal and from both of which he recovered fully; a devotee of the Virgin Mary since childhood, believed that she had intervened ("guided this bullet") to save his life; later, announced that he forgave Agca, and made a visit of reconciliation to him in his prison cell; thenceforth, was enclosed in a bulletproof glass box in the Popemobile (which was sometimes a modified Ford limousine); resumed his international journeys early in 1982; continued to tour the world until the summer of 2005; in addition to 146 pastoral visits within Italy, evangelized in 129 countries over the course of 104 trips to five continents, including a number to North America; abroad, attended many youth rallies organized during his visits, including one in Manila that drew a record attendance of some five million; was multilingual; at the Vatican, presided at the beatification of some 1,300 "blessed" persons (including Mother Teresa of Calcutta, whom he had met a number of times) and the canonization of more than 460 saints; created 231 cardinals; wrote five books: *Crossing the Threshold of Hope* (1994), *Gift and Mystery: On the Fiftieth Anniversary of My Priestly Ordination* (1996), *Roman Triptych: Meditations* (2003), *Rise, Let Us Be on Our Way* (2004), and *Memory and Identity* (2005); issued an extraordinary number of papal documents, including 14 encyclicals, among them three serving as frameworks for analysis of current sociopolitical questions, one each on the Virgin Mary, the Slavic saints Cyril and Methodius, the Holy Spirit, Divine mercy, Redemption, moral behavior, the relationship between faith and reason, the Eucharist, ecumenism, and evangelization; in the encyclical *Evangelium Vitae* (1995), explained the basis for the pro-life position in Scripture, in Christian tradition, and in natural law ("the dignity of every human person") and itemized aspects of what he meant by "the culture of death": "an endless series of wars and a continued taking of innocent human life," "violence against women, children, the poor, the weak," "a cultural context that does not accept suffering," "threats which . . . hang over the incurably ill and the dying," "the refusal to accept those who are weak and needy, or elderly, or those who have just been conceived," "the contraception mentality," "the use of human embryos in medical research; genocide; deliberate famines," "people who are rejected, marginalized, uprooted, and oppressed," and "the selfishness of the rich countries which exclude poorer countries from access to development"; regarding capital punishment, said, "If bloodless means are sufficient to defend human lives against an aggressor and to protect public order and the safety of persons, public authority must limit itself to such means"; oversaw the publication of a new Catechism of the Catholic Church; was a robust outdoorsman until disease began hobbling him in his later years; died in his apartment three stories above St. Peter's Square, after which six days of mourning culminated on April 8, 2005 in an open-air funeral mass in St. Peter's Square attended by millions (including a Who's Who of world leaders), certainly one of the largest and most impressive such gatherings in world history, and one seen by additional hundreds of millions worldwide on television; was laid to rest in a crypt below St. Peter's Basilica. See *Current Biography* (2000).

Obituary *New York Times* p1+ Apr. 3, 2005

JOHNSON, JOHN H. Jan. 19, 1918–Aug. 8, 2005 Publisher; founder and president of the Chicago-based, African-American–oriented Johnson Publishing Co.; beginning with a $500 loan in the 1940s, "built a media empire that sixty years later is still number one and still 100 percent black-owned," as Tavis Smiley noted in his euolgy at the funeral service for Johnson in the Rockefeller Memorial Chapel at the University of Chicago; published *Ebony*, the jewel in the crown of the Johnson empire, a slick monthly picture magazine patterned after *Life* and *Look* that survived the demise of those popular mainstream periodicals and continues to maintain a circulation of approximately 1.6 million and a healthy advertising base; was born in rural Arkansas City, Arkansas, where he voluntarily repeated the eighth grade in a racially segregated elementary school because there was no local high school for black children and he did not want to drop out of school; moved to Chicago with his mother and stepfather in 1933; at DuSable High School on Chicago's South Side, was president of his class and managing editor of the school paper; at a banquet honoring outstanding high-school students in 1936, caught the attention of Harry Pace, the president of the Supreme Life Insurance Co., who became his patron; at the insurance company, moved up the ranks from office boy to principal stockholder and board chairman; on the way up, edited the company's house organ, a task that inspired him in 1942 to begin publishing *Negro Digest*, a magazine similar to *Reader's Digest* in format; suspended publication of that magazine in 1951 but later reincarnated it as a nonprofit literary quarterly, a showcase for promising black writers of both fiction and nonfiction; meanwhile, founded *Ebony* in 1945; launched *Tan*, a women's general-interest magazine, in 1950 and *Jet*, a pocket-sized newsweekly with a sensational slant, in 1951; briefly in the early 1960s, published another magazine, *Hue*, resembling *Jet* but containing features rather than news; in 1973, branched out beyond magazine publishing (and some book publishing) to found Fashion Fair Cosmetics, a line of cosmetics for darker-skinned women; was a member of the board of directors of the Urban League and the board of trustees of Tuskegee Institute; with Lerone Bennett Jr. (who was executive editor of *Ebony* for many years), wrote his autobiography, *Succeeding Against the Odds*, published by Warner Books in 1989; was "an American original," as Bennett put it at the funeral service at the University of Chicago, at which former U.S. president Bill Clinton (who had presented the Medal of Freedom to Johnson in 1996) credited him with having "a vision of keeping hope alive by showing black people faces of hope" and went on to recall that Johnson had been part of the mass migration of African-Americans northward out of the Jim Crow South: "Out of this swarm of hardworking, family-loving men and women carving out their own version of the American dream," Clinton said, "[Johnson] stood out because his dream was bigger and he had a vision for how to achieve it"; was predeceased by his son, John Harold Johnson Jr., and survived by his wife of 64 years, Eunice, and his daughter, Linda Johnson Rice, who succeeded him as president of the Johnson Publishing Co.; died in Chicago. See *Current Biography* (1968).

Obituary *New York Times* A p16 Aug. 9, 2005

JOHNSON, PHILIP July 8, 1906–Jan. 25, 2005 Architect; historian of architecture; art patron; curator; a major, restless force in 20th-century American architecture and design; as an early protégé of Ludwig Mies van der Rohe, a founder of European Modernism (also known as the International Style, a term co-coined by Johnson), was instrumental in introducing that streamlined, highly functional school of architecture and design to America; in the homes and public buildings he himself designed, soon began breaking modernism's taboo against ornamentation; experimenting with abstracted versions of classical and other historical forms, including Renaissance, baroque, and German Expressionist elements, moved successively into postmodernism and deconstructivism without abandoning his commitment to a formalist aesthetic; achieved a succès de scandal with his design (in partnership with John Burgee) of Manhattan's revivalist AT&T skyscraper (1984), now called the Sony Building, a stunningly eclectic defiance of modernism; through an inheritance of Alcoa stock from his father, was independently wealthy; received a B.A. degree in philosophy at Harvard University in 1930 and a graduate degree in architecture there in 1943; at Harvard, studied under Walter Gropius and Marcel Breuer, both of whom had been associated with Mies van der Rohe at the Bauhaus, the avant-garde German school of design that was the fount of modernism; had visited the Bauhaus as a young man; played an important role in the founding of the Museum of Modern Art (MoMA) in New York City in the late 1920s; established MoMA's department of architecture and design and directed that department from 1930 to 1936 and again from 1946 to 1954; during the 1930s, went through a period of flirtation with fascist politics; during the following decade, began designing private residences, the best known of which is the Glass House (1949), his own home in New Canaan, Connecticut; contributed some of the design (notably the Seven Seasons Restaurant) for Mies van der Rohe's Seagram Building (1958), a trend-setting Manhattan skyscraper; in the late 1950s also began designing several additions to MoMA, including the Sculpture Garden; designed the Roofless Church (1960) in New Harmony, New York, and the Museum for Pre-Columbian Art (1963) at Dumbarton Oaks in Washington, D.C.; with Richard Foster, designed the New York State Theater (1964) at Lincoln Center in Manhattan and the Kline Science Center (1965) at Yale University in New Haven, Connecticut; in 1967 formed a a partnership with John Burgee that would last through the 1980s; in addition to the AT&T building, designed with Burgee the Investors Diversified Services Center (1973) in Minneapolis, the Pennzoil Place galleria (1976) in Houston, and the Crystal Cathedral (1980) in Garden Grove, California; also with Burgee, designed the Pittsburgh Plate Glass headquarters in Pittsburgh, International Place in Boston, the United Bank Center Tower in Denver, the Dade County Cultural Center in Miami, Momentum Place in Dallas, the First Republic Bank (now the Bank of America Center) in Houston, the 101 California building in San Francisco, the Century Center in South Bend, Indiana, and the revivalist building at 53d Street and Third Avenue in Manhattan; in his semi-retirement, remained a consultant to John Burgee Architects;

wrote the book *Architecture 1949–1965* (1966); co-wrote *The International Style: Architecture Since 1922* (1932), *Mies van der Rohe* (1947), and *Deconstructivist Architecture* (1988); lived alternately in his apartment in Museum Tower overlooking the Sculpture Garden he created at the Museum of Modern Art and in his Glass House compound in New Canaan, Connecticut, which he had enlarged incrementally in varying styles over the years; died in the Glass House compound; was survived by David Whitney, his companion of 45 years. See *Current Biography* (1991).

Obituary *New York Times* A p1+ Jan. 25, 2005

KENNAN, GEORGE F. Feb. 16, 1904–Mar. 17, 2005 Legendary U.S. career diplomat; scholar; author; conceived the cornerstone American Cold War policy of "containment" vis-à-vis the expansionist-prone Soviet Union; early on, foresaw the ultimate collapse of the USSR; helped to shape the Marshall Plan that made possible the revival of Western Europe in the years following World War II; in an interview with Jeff Trimble for *U.S. News & World Report* (March 11, 1996), recalled: "When I came back from Moscow [after World War II], I was appalled at the reaction when I told people that my view of the Soviet leadership was not very favorable. . . . I wanted to say . . . these people represent a very serious problem for us—but one that could be dealt with by means short of war. It was in this sense that I spoke of the need for 'containment.' But it was interpreted much more as though I had meant there was a military threat, that the Russians wanted to attack Western Europe. This fear was exaggerated. Their troops were exhausted, their supplies were exhausted, their country had been destroyed. They were in no position to start another war"; earned a B.A. degree in history at Princeton University and later received training in Russian language, literature, history, and political theory at the University of Berlin; entered the U.S. Foreign Service in 1927, a time when the U.S. did not have diplomatic relations with the USSR; over the following six years, was assigned to minor diplomatic positions in Geneva, Hamburg, Berlin, and "listening posts" around the USSR, in Tallin (Estonia), Riga (Latvia), and Kaunas (Lithuania); accompanied Ambassador William C. Bullitt to Moscow when the American Embassy reopened there in 1933; over the following dozen years, filled consular or embassy positions in Vienna, Prague, Lisbon, and Berlin as well as Moscow, where he was second secretary (1935–36) and minister-counselor (1944–46); in February 1946, sent to the State Department in Washington a historic cablegram in which he explained to policy planners trying to understand the inscrutable Josef Stalin that Moscow was "impervious to the logic of reason but highly sensitive to the logic of force"; in April 1946 was summoned to Washington, where he lectured at the National War College before Secretary of State George C. Marshall named him director of the State Department's policy-planning staff in April 1947; in an anonymous article in *Foreign Affairs* (July 1947), wrote, "Soviet pressure against the free institutions of the Western world is something that can be contained by the adroit and vigorous application of

counterforce"; remained a principal adviser to Dean Acheson when Acheson succeeded Marshall as secretary of state, in 1949; was ambassador to Moscow from May to October 1952, when the Soviets declared him persona non grata; in 1953, left the Foreign Service and joined the Institute for Advanced Study in Princeton, New Jersey; became a professor in the institute's School of Historical Studies in 1956; returned to the U.S. Foreign Service in the administration of President John F. Kennedy; served as ambassador to Yugoslavia from 1961 to 1963; on assignment from the State Department, met with Svetlana Alliluyeva, Josef Stalin's daughter, in Switzerland in 1967 and helped persuade her to immigrate to the U.S.; published numerous books on modern European and Russian history, international relations, and American foreign policy and diplomacy; also wrote two books of memoirs (1967, 1972), a Kennan family history, and several books of personal reflections; died in Princeton, New Jersey; was survived by his wife, Annelise, and three daughters and a son. See *Current Biography* (1959).

Obituary *New York Times* A p1+ Mar. 18, 2005

KEYS, ANCEL Jan. 26, 2004–Nov. 20, 2004 Physiologist; former professor, University of Minnesota; a foremost pioneer in the establishment of contemporary cardiovascular epidemiology; was a trailblazer in the application of mathematics to the objectively quantifiable measurement of such physiological processes as the effects of heat and cold and, especially, starvation on the human body; did landmark research in the relationship of nutrition to health and, most famously, the connection between diet and heart disease; earned Ph.D. degrees at both the University of California at La Jolla and Cambridge University in England; joined the faculty of the University of Minnesota in 1936; three years later, founded a laboratory of physiological hygiene that developed into the division of epidemiology in the university's School of Public Health; directed the division for thirty-three years; as a consultant to the U.S. Department of War in the early 1940s, created what the department named the K ration (the "K" apparently standing for "Keys"), the pocket-sized ready-to-eat emergency meal pack issued to combat troops in World War II; later in the war, with conscientious-objector volunteers at the University of Minnesota, conducted the first systematic experiments in human starvation and subsistence diets, the results of which proved beneficial in the rehabilitation of millions of nutrition-deprived survivors of the war in Europe; in a subsequent study involving 286 middle-aged Minneapolis-St. Paul businessmen, concluded that those who suffered coronary attacks generally had higher serum cholesterol levels; was convinced, however, that it was not cholesterol-rich foods that contributed to the increase in blood cholesterol; in studies conducted in foreign countries in addition to the U.S. over the following years, concluded that dietary fat was a crucial factor, that the eating of saturated fat tended to raise the blood cholesterol count—and thus to cause arterial blockage resulting in heart attacks—and the eating of unsaturated fats (as in many Mediterranean cuisines) tended to lower it; with his wife, Margaret, a biochemist, wrote three popular books: *Eat Well and Stay Well* (1959), *The Benevolent Bean* (1957), and *How to Eat Well and Stay Well the Mediterranean Way* (1975); with others, wrote *The Biology of Human Starvation* (1950) and *Seven Countries: A Multivariate Analysis of Death and Coronary Heart Disease* (1980); died in Minneapolis, Minnesota. See *Current Biography* (1966).

Obituary *New York Times* B p10 Nov. 23, 2004

LANGE, DAVID Aug. 4, 1942–Aug. 13, 2005 Prime minister of New Zealand (1984–89); lawyer; Methodist lay preacher; a moderately socialistic Labour Party leader who, as prime minister in Wellington, antagonized Washington by implementing his party's antinuclear policy; on the other hand, alienated much of his blue-collar constituency with the relative conservatism of his radical economic reforms, aimed at freeing New Zealand from its traditional stifling protectionism and enabling it to be more competitive in the international free market; held bachelor's and master's degrees in law; while employed by a reinsurance company during a sojourn in England (1967–68), devoted his free time to working with the poor in the West London Mission of the Methodist preacher Lord Soper; at that time, met his first wife, Naomi Joy Crampton, a volunteer at the mission; after returning to New Zealand, practiced law in large measure in behalf of downtrodden clients, including aboriginal Maori people; was elected to New Zealand's House of Representatives in 1977; became Labour Party leader in 1983; upon becoming prime minister, in 1984, immediately began applying the therapy of "Rogernomics" (named for his finance minister, Roger Douglas) to the country's ailing economy; loosened controls on interest rates, floated the New Zealand dollar, and corporatized government-owned businesses and industries; beginning in 1985, prohibited all nuclear-powered vessels and all ships carrying nuclear weapons from entering New Zealand ports, an action that resulted in the suspension of New Zealand from the ANZUS defense alliance in which the U.S., Australia, and New Zealand had been joined for four decades; also in 1985, entered into a prolonged confrontation with France, after French secret agents sabotaged and sank the converted trawler *Rainbow Warrior*, the flagship of the environmental group Greenpeace, which was moored in Auckland Harbor, New Zealand, preparing to lead a flotilla of yachts in a voyage to Mururoa Atoll in the Tuamotu Archipelago in French Polynesia, where the French were conducting nuclear-bomb trests; called the bombing (actually consisting of two explosions) "a sordid act of state-backed terrorism"; in 1986, in collaboration with U.N. secretary-general Javier Perez de Cuellar, negotiated a settlement that exacted financial compensation and an apology from France; regarding the French nuclear-bomb tests in Polynesia, said that if the tests were indeed as safe as France claimed, then France should "do them in Strasbourg"; after leaving the prime ministry, served as attorney general and minister of state (1989–90); was divorced from his first wife following disclosure of his affair with the speechwriter Margaret Pope; married Pope in 1992; had two sons and a daughter from his first marriage and a daughter from his sec-

ond; died in Auckland, New Zealand. See *Current Biography* (1985).

Obituary *New York Times* I p27 Aug. 14, 2005

LAPP, RALPH E. Aug. 24, 1917–Sep. 7, 2004 Physicist; author; consultant; an authority on radiation hazards, civil defense, and other issues relating to the military and industrial uses of nuclear power; had a resumé extending back to World War II, when, as a participant in the top-secret Manhattan Project, he helped to create the first atomic bombs; gained international fame and raised awareness of the dangers of atmospheric nuclear testing with his best-seller *The Voyage of the Lucky Dragon* (1958), the story of 23 Japanese fishermen who, along with their day's catch of tuna, were contaminated by a shower of radioactive fallout from a U.S. hydrogen-bomb test conducted 100 miles away, at Bikini Atoll in the Marshall Islands in the central Pacific—an instance of collateral contamination that shut down the Japanese seafood industry for a time in 1954; despite his deep concern about the dangers of atmospheric testing as well as the specter of nuclear war, thought that the nuclear-power industry had "an impressive radiation safety record," that occupational and airline exposure hazards were "minor," and that the negative health effects of natural background radiation, such as that from radon, were overstated; was earning his Ph.D. degree (with a concentration in the study of cosmic rays) at the University of Chicago when he joined the team at the Manhattan Project's pseudonymous "Metallurgical Laboratory" in 1942; while contributing to the creation of the first atomic bombs (originally intended to counter Germany's possible success in developing atomic weaponry), foresaw the dreadful long-term consequences of releasing the nuclear genie upon the world; was one of the 70 Manhattan Project scientists who signed a petition sent to President Harry S. Truman on July 17, 1945—three months after Germany's surrender and a month before the atomic attacks on Hiroshima and Nagasaki—pointing out to the president that, with the defeat of Germany, resort to the use of atomic bombs against Japan "could not be justified, at least not unless the terms [to] be imposed upon Japan have been made public in detail and Japan knowing these terms has refused to surrender" and urging him to consider the "moral responsibilities" involved; was assistant director of the Metallurgical Laboratory in Chicago from 1943 to 1945; after the war, was assistant director of the Argonne National Laboratory, operated by the University of Chicago for the newly created U.S. Atomic Energy Commission (and currently a n arm of the Department of Defense); was assigned as well to the Atomic Energy Commission's military liaison committee; in July 1946, led a group of 30 scientists in gathering and analyzing naval data at the first of the series of nuclear-bomb tests conducted at Bikini Atoll; subsequently, worked in research and development at the War Department (the predecessor of the Department of Defense); in that position, prepared the 1947 report "Atomic Bomb Explosions: Effects on an American City"; in 1949, became head of the nuclear-physics branch of the Office of Naval Research; after leaving government service in 1950, headed the Nuclear Science Service, a consulting firm; regularly contributed articles to the *Bulletin of the Atomic Scientists* and *Scientific American*; in 1949, published his first popular book, *Must We Hide?*, about civil defense; in that book, warned about the vulnerability of vertically populated (that is, ones in which many people live in high-rise buildings) American cities like New York to atomic attack but assured readers that protection against thermal radiation from such attacks could be "easily accomplished"; later published *The New Force* (1953), *Atoms and People* (1956), *Man and Space* (1961), *Kill and Overkill* (1962), *America's Energy* (1970), *Arms Beyond Man: The Tyranny of Weapons Technology* (1970), *The Logarithmic Century* (1973), and *My Life with Radiation: Hiroshima Plus Fifty Years* (1995); died in Alexandria, Virginia; was survived by his wife, Jeannette, and two sons. See *Current Biography* (1955).

Obituary *New York Times* C p10 Sep. 10, 2004

LAREDO, RUTH Nov. 20, 1937–May 25, 2005 Classical pianist; "America's first lady of the piano"; in her keyboard style, combined technical mastery with both dynamism and elegance; "performed with a signature blend of fiery emotion, assured technique, and refined intelligence," as Wes Phillips wrote for *Stereophile* (May 30, 2005, on-line), "and her concerts were always immensely rewarding. Among the public at large, she is perhaps best known for her Beethoven, Mozart, Rachmaninoff, and DeFalla, although it was always a treat to hear her Ravel, Stravinsky, Barber, and Rorem as well"; left a discography including, most remarkably, the complete solo piano works of Rachmaninoff and the complete piano sonatas and preludes of Scriabin; as one reviewer of her recordings of the Scriabin oeuvre observed, captured the composer's "mad and slightly evil quality" by means of her "sensuous, beautifully controlled playing"; was born Ruth Meckler in Detroit, Michigan; found her life decisively changed when at age eight she attended a piano recital by Vladimir Horowitz; wrote in an article for *Keynote* (April 1983), "My love for the piano and for Rachmaninoff, Scriabin, and Chopin really began on that day in Detroit"; studied piano first under her mother and then under Mischa Kottler and Edward Bredshall, who arranged for her to make her formal concert debut performing Beethoven's Piano Concerto no. 2 with the Detroit Symphony under Walter Poole when she was 10; during five years of study under Rudolf Serkin at the Curtis Institute of Music in Philadelphia (1955–60), was grounded in the standard German repertory and encouraged to explore her personal interests in other repertories, including the French and Russian, and to restrict interpretation to information within the musical scores; summers, performed at Serkin's Marlboro Festival, in Vermont; at the Curtis Institute, met and married a fellow student, the Brazilian-born violin prodigy Jaime Laredo; because of her marriage and her husband's sudden fame, experienced the unintended effect of having her emergence as a soloist and virtuoso in her own right delayed for a decade and a half; made her debut at Carnegie Hall with the American Symphony Orchestra under Leopold Stokowski in 1962, a landmark event that was a rarity for her then; generally, traveled the world with her husband, performing in the sublimated role of his accompanist (or at least she was perceived as such); in 1969, advanced to the clear status of co-soloist with him, and after their divorce, in the mid-1970s, saw her performing career begin to flourish; made her debut with the New York Philharmonic under Pierre Boulez in 1974; gave her first solo recital at Alice Tully Hall in 1976 and at Carnegie Hall five years later; in the mid-1970s, made her first tours of Western Europe and Japan; later, included Russia and the Ukraine in her international itineraries; performed with such American orchestras as the Boston, Detroit, and National symphonies and the Cleveland and Philadelphia orchestras; also performed chamber music regularly, with the Tokyo, Vermeer, Emerson, Guarneri, Muir, St. Lawrence, and Shanghai quartets, among other string ensembles; in a scene in Woody Allen's motion picture *Small Time Crooks* (2000), is seen as herself as a piano recitalist, playing Rachmaninoff; edited Rachmaninoff's scores for publication; was a columnist with *Piano Today*; published *The Ruth Laredo Becoming a Musician Book* (1992), a guide for young pianists; for 17 years, beginning in 1988, gave a series of sold-out concerts "with commentary" at the Metropolitan Museum of Art, in New York City; gave the last performance in that series at the Met on May 6, 2005, three weeks before her death, from ovarian cancer; died in her apartment in New York City; was survived by her daughter, Jennifer, her son-in-law, the British cellist Paul Watkins, and a granddaughter. See *Current Biography* (1987).

Obituary *New York Times* C p15 May 26, 2005

LING, JAMES J. Dec. 31, 1922–Dec. 17, 2004 Entrepreneur; pioneering conglomerate developer; in Dallas, Texas, in 1946, set up the Ling Electric Co.; with that small electrical-contracting firm as his base, began acquiring other enterprises; over a period of 14 years, built Ling-Temco-Vought Inc., also known as LTV, the first billion-dollar conglomerate in the U.S., a sprawling corporation with diversified holdings ranging from meat processing and sporting goods to steel, aerospace, electronics, and communications; following stock-market setbacks and the filing of an antitrust suit against the company by the U.S. Department of Justice, was forced to step down as chief executive officer and chairman of the board, in 1970; went on to found other companies, most notably Empiric Energy Inc. in Dallas; was predeceased by his wife, Dorothy. See *Current Biography* (1970).

Obituary I p50 *New York Times* Dec. 26, 2004

LINOWITZ, SOL M. Dec. 7, 1913–Mar. 18, 2005 U.S. diplomat; lawyer; former chairman of the Xerox Corp.; was ambassador to the Organization of American States during the administration of President Lyndon B. Johnson; later, was an international negotiator for President Jimmy Carter; began practicing law in Rochester, New York, in 1938; resumed that practice following his service on the legal staff of Secretary of the Navy James V. Forrestal during World War II; in the postwar years, served as president of the Rochester Institute of International Affairs and the Rochester Association of the United Nations; was involved in efforts to liberalize print and electronic media in Rochester, which he regarded as too conservative; at the Rochester City Club in 1947, met Joseph C. Wilson, the young president of the Haloid Co., a manufacturer of photographic supplies; for Wilson, did the legal work for obtaining from an industrial research organization in Ohio the rights to an experimental process of electrophotography invented by Chester Carlson—an electrostatic copying process, requiring no wet chemicals, that would become known as xerography, a word derived from the Greek terms for "dry writing"; was named a director of the Haloid Co. in 1949 and vice president in charge of the company's patents and licensing in 1951; set up the company's overseas operations and partnerships; in 1961, was made chairman of the board of the company, which was renamed the Xerox Corp. the following year; became chairman and chief executive officer of Xerox International in 1966, the year that saw Xerox's gross revenues reach approximately $500 million; meanwhile, was involved in such U.N. activities as advising the U.S. delegation to the U.N. Conference on the Applications of Science and Technology to the Developing Areas, and co-founded and chaired the executive committee of the International Executive Service Corps; in 1965, became a White House adviser on foreign-assistance programs; in 1966, was named by President Johnson to the twin posts of U.S. representative to the Organization of American States, with the rank of ambassador, and the U.S. representative on the Inter-American Committee for the Alliance for Progress; after being sworn in as ambassador to the OAS, relinquished his executive posts at Xerox and put his 35,000 shares of stock in trust; also relinquished his senior partnership in Harris, Beach, Wilcox, Dale & Linowitz, the law firm handling legal matters for Xerox; under President Carter in 1977, joined with Ellsworth Bunker in negotiating the transfer of the Panama Canal to Panama; in 1979, pursuant to the 1978 Camp David accords, represented President Carter in the Middle East, dealing with such issues as Palestinian autonomy; in 1969, joined the international law firm of Coudert Brothers as a partner; later, became general counsel with that firm; remained with the firm until 1994; wrote *The Making of a Public Man: A Memoir* (1985); with Martin Mayer, wrote *The Betrayed Profession: Lawyering at the End of the Twentieth Century* (1994); was prominently active in Jewish causes; died at his home in Washington, D.C.; was survived by his wife, Toni, with whom he had four daughters and eight grandchildren. See *Current Biography* (1967).

Obituary *New York Times* A p13 Mar. 19, 2005

MARKOVA, ALICIA Dec. 1, 1910–Dec. 2, 2004 British ballerina; ballet director; contributed to the development of Britain's first ballet troupes; co-founded the company that became today's English National Ballet; was a petite woman who projected as a dancer, in addition to exquisitely nuanced phrasing, seemingly effortless airborne movement that belied an underlying technique described by Agnes de Mille as "bolts of lightning and steel"; while admired in a repertory she inherited from Anna Pavlova—including Michail Fokine's *Les Sylphides* and *The Dying Swan*—and such 19th-century Romantic classics as *Giselle* (with which she was most closely associated), was also an original muse for modernity's vanguard, including the choreographers Ninette de Valois, Frederick Ashton, Antony Tudor, George Balanchine, Bronislava Nijinska, and Leonid Massine; inspired such roles as the Nightingale in *Le Chant du Rossignol*, written for her by Balanchine; was born in suburban London with the surname Marks; a child prodigy, made her professional debut at 10; found a patron in the impresario Sergei Diaghilev, the founder of the Ballets Russes, who Russianized her surname, made her a member of his corps de ballet, and began grooming her for principal roles; was taught by the composer Igor Stravinsky not to learn steps by rhythmic counts and beats but rather by dancing to melody; after Diaghilev's death, in 1929, alternated between engagements in music halls and cinema houses and performances of works by Ashton and Tudor with Marie Rambert's struggling Ballet Club; in 1932, became a charter guest artist with Ninette de Valois's Vic-Wells Ballet, the pioneer indigenous British ballet troupe, which would develop into the Royal Ballet; with Vic-Wells, became the first British ballerina to dance the title role in *Giselle*; in 1935, formed the Markova-Dolin Company with the Irish dancer Anton Dolin, the partner with whom she had become most closely associated and would so remain for 30 years; in 1938, left the Markova-Dolin Company to join Massine's newly formed Ballet Russe de Monte Carlo, where she was soon rejoined by Dolin; made her American debut as Giselle with the Ballet Russe de Monte Carlo in 1938; remained in the U.S. when World War II broke out in Europe, in 1939; with Dolin, spent the war years in the U.S. dancing with the Ballet Theatre (which became the American Ballet Theatre); during that period, created the roles of Juliet in Tudor's *Romeo and Juliet* and Zemphira in Massine's *Aleko*; after the war, toured internationally with Dolin; in London in 1950, founded the London Festival Ballet, the predecessor of the English National Ballet; during the 1950s, appeared as a guest dancer with companies on both sides of the Atlantic; gave concert tours with Milorad Miskovitch and Erik Bruhn; partnered with Miskovitch in her farewell performance, in L'Apres-midi d'un Faune with the London Festival Ballet in 1962; was named a Dame of the British Empire in 1963; from 1963 to 1969, was director of the Metropolitan Opera Ballet in New York; lectured at the University of Cincinnati's Conservatory of Music in the early 1970s; later, gave master classes for the Royal Ballet and other companies; also presided over dance festivals, conferences, and productions of ballets that included her most celebrated roles; wrote the autobiographies *Giselle and I* (1960) and *Markova Remembers* (1986); never married; died in Bath, England. See *Current Biography* (1943).

Obituary *New York Times* A p27 Dec. 3, 2004

MARTIN, AGNES Mar. 22, 1912–Dec. 16, 2004 Canadian-born American abstract painter; a so-called post-painterly modernist who emerged from Abstract Expressionism and anticipated Minimalism; most typically, created, on canvas, relatively small abstract grids traversed by horizontal and vertical stripes on pale, luminous fields; often drew penciled lines before or after applying acrylics, oils, or watercolors; insisted that her paintings "are not abstractions from nature" and "have neither objects, nor space, nor time—not anything, no forms"; earned degrees in art education from Columbia University and the University of New Mexico; was influenced by the Zen Buddhism of D. T. Suzuki and the philosophy of Jiddu Krishnamurti; from 1937 to 1952, taught in public schools in Delaware, Washington State, and New Mexico; in Taos, New Mexico, began exhibiting her paintings, which at that time were mostly conventional portraits and still lifes; started experimenting with semiabstract painting in 1954; three years later, responded to an invitation from the Manhattan gallery owner Betty Parsons and moved to New York City; in Lower Manhattan, became one of the informal group of painters known as the Coenties Slip Nine—among them Ellsworth Kelly, James Rosenquist, and Jack Youngerman—who were experimenting with breaks from the dominant Abstract Expressionism of such painters as Jackson Pollock and Barnet Newman; developed her abstract style during the next decade, as seen in works exhibited at the Betty Parsons Gallery and, later, the Robert Elkon Gallery; in addition to such paintings as *Orange Grove* (1965), created some collages, including *The Garden* (1958), consisting of found objects glued to canvases in orderly rows; in 1967, quit painting and moved to Cuba, New Mexico; over the following six years, concentrated on writing and lecturing; during that period, did no painting except for a suite of 30 serigraphs called *On a Clear Day*; after returning to painting in 1974, remained in New Mexico while exhibiting and selling her works through PaceWildenstein Galleries in New York; in her last years, abandoned the modernist grid of her previous work in favor of floating free-form rhomboid shapes described by a *New York Times* critic as "retro-geometric"; died in Taos, New Mexico; left no survivors. See *Current Biography* (1989).

Obituary *New York Times* C p9 Dec. 17, 2004

MATSUI, ROBERT T. Sep. 17, 1941–Jan. 1, 2005 Congressman; a Democrat who represented California's Fifth Congressional District in the U.S. House of Representatives from 1979 until his death; was born in Sacramento, California, to second-generation Japanese-American parents; spent three and a half of his earliest years in a World War II internment camp in Tuli Lake, Oregon; after earning degrees in political science and law at the University of California, practiced law in Sacramento; before going to Washington, served on the Sacramento City Council and as vice mayor of Sacramento; was elected to his first two-year term in Congress in 1978; was reelected 13 times, most recently in 2004; helped push through Congress the bill compensating 120,000 Japanese-Americans for their internment during World War II, enacted into law in 1988; at his death, was the third-ranking Democrat on the House Ways and Means Committee and the senior Democrat on the Social Security Subcommittee; vehemently opposed President George W. Bush's plan to partially privatize Social Security; died at the National Naval Medical

Center in Bethesda, Maryland. See *Current Biography* (1994).

Obituary *New York Times* B p6 Jan. 3, 2005

MAUCH, GENE Nov. 18, 1925–Aug. 8, 2005 Baseball manager; a master strategist and tactician nicknamed "the little general"; ranked fourth in major-league history in his duration as a manager (26 years), sixth in games managed (3,938), and 11th in games won (1,901—or 1,902, according to some sources—with 2,037 losses); began his professional baseball career as a utility infielder who was dependable but not outstanding at the plate; between 1943 and 1959, was traded among seven major-league teams (five National and two American League) and their farm systems; spent six years in the minor leagues, five of them as player/manager; during nine years and 304 games on the major-league level, had 176 hits (37 of them for extra bases) in 737 times at bat, for an average of .239, and drove in 62 runs; became manager of the National League's Philadelphia Phillies in 1960; was named National League manager of the year in 1962 and again in 1964, when the Phillies almost won the league pennant, finishing in second place; following the 1968 season (his ninth in Philadelphia), when the National League expanded from 10 teams to 12 and split into two divisions, signed on as manager of the Montreal Expos, a new franchise in the newly created National League East; was named National League manager of the year a third time in 1973; moved to the American League West as manager of the Minnesota Twins (1976–80); with the California Angels, also in the American League West, was manager (1981–82), personnel manager (1983–84), and dugout manager (1985–87); guided the Angels to two division titles, in 1982 and 1986; retired following the 1987 season; emerged from retirement to serve as a bench coach with the National League's Kansas City Royals in 1995; died in Rancho Mirage, California; was survived by his wife, Jodie, and a daughter, Leeane. See *Current Biography* (1974).

Obituary *New York Times* A p16 Aug. 9, 2005

MAYR, ERNST July 5, 1904–Feb. 3, 2005 German-born American zoologist; neo-Darwinian biologist; philosopher of science; professor emeritus, Harvard University; former curator of ornithology, American Museum of Natural History (AMNH); a principal architect of the "modern evolutionary synthesis," bringing together the perspectives of the laboratory geneticist and the field naturalist for the more effective study of evolution within the Darwinian framework; in 1940, in one of many papers based on his ornithological fieldwork and taxonomy, defined species as "groups of actually or potentially interbreeding natural populations which are reproductively isolated from other groups," a definition that became the centerpiece of the "new systematics"; in his book *Systematics and the Origin of Species* (1942), cogently argued his theory of alliotic speciation, according to which new species emerge over long periods of time and only in geographic isolation, not from individual mutations that could occur within a single generation; observed, "That geographic speciation is the prevailing process of speciation, at least in animals, was no longer questioned after this time"; later, introduced the concept of peripatric speciation, suggesting that the most physically distinct variations within a species occur in members living on the edge of the species range; was born into a family of physicians; was an ardent birdwatcher from childhood; while perfunctorily completing preclinical studies in medicine at the University of Greifswald, began working during summer vacations under the ornithologist Erwin Stresemann at the University of Berlin's Zoological Museum; after earning a Ph.D. in zoology from the University of Berlin, in 1926, was assistant curator at the Zoological Museum for six years, until 1932; during that period, met Walter Rothschild, the 2d Baron Rothschild, the world's leading collector of bird and butterfly specimens; was sent by Rothschild on a year-long ornithological expedition to Papua New Guinea in 1928; remained in the South Pacific until 1930 under the sponsorship of the University of Berlin and the AMNH; in New Guinea and the Solomon Islands, shot and killed some 3,000 birds of paradise and other exotic birds to obtain their feathered skins for his several sponsors; joined the staff of the AMNH in New York City as a Whitney research associate in ornithology in 1931; the next year, when Rothschild sold his unrivaled collection of 280,000 bird skins to the AMNH, was named associate curator of the museum's Whitney-Rothschild Collection; held that position until 1944, when he became curator of the collection; compiled *List of New Guinea Birds* (1941), his major taxonomic work; left the AMNH to join the faculty of Harvard University as Alexander Agassiz Professor of Zoology in 1953; became director of Harvard's Museum of Comparative Zoology seven years later; after his formal retirement, in 1975, maintained an office at Harvard but spent winters at Rollins College, in Winter Park, Florida; wrote some dozen books, including *Animal Species and Evolution* (1963), *Principles of Systematic Zoology* (1969), *The Growth of Biological Thought* (1982), *Toward a New Philosophy of Biology* (1988), *One Long Argument: Charles Darwin and the Genesis of Modern Evolutionary Thought* (1991), *This Is Biology* (1997), and *What Makes Biology Unique?* (2004); brought together a selection of his essays in *Evolution and the Diversity of Life* (1976); included a section arguing against creationism in his book *What Evolution Is* (2001); co-wrote and edited a score of books, including some field guides to birds; died in Bedford, Massachusetts; was predeceased by his wife, Margarete Simon, and survived by two daughters and their descendents. See *Current Biography* (1984).

Obituary *New York Times* A p15 Feb. 5, 2005

MCGHEE, GEORGE CREWS Mar. 10, 1912—July 4, 2005 U.S, diplomat; geophysicist; oil magnate; earned a B.S. degree in geology at the University of Oklahoma and a doctorate at Oxford University; early in his career, worked in seismology with the Continental Oil Co. in Oklahoma and served as vice president of the National Geophysical Co. in Dallas, Texas; in 1935, patented a new method for making dip determination of geological formations; in 1939, married Cecelia Jeanne De Golyer, daughter of the prominent Dallas oil producr Everette Lee De Golyer;

with the assistance of his father-in-law, organized a prospecting group that discovered and bought up oil fields in the Lake Charles region of Louisiana and elsewhere; as a result, was a millionaire before he was 30; in 1940, joined his father-in-law as a partner in the Dallas firm of De Golyer, MacNaughton and McGhee, consulting geologists; early in World War II, held senior positions on the U.S. War Production Board; later in the war, served with the U.S. Navy, as liaison officer to the U.S. Army Air Force's 21st bomber command; after the war, joined the U.S. Department of State as a special assistant for economic affairs; was coordinator for aid to Greece and Turkey from 1947 to 1949, special representative to the Near East on the Palestine refugee problem in 1949, assistant secretary of state for Near Eastern, South Asian, and African affairs from 1949 to 1951, and ambassador to Turkey from 1951 to 1953; as undersecretary of state for political affairs in the early 1960s, headed troubleshooting missions to the Congo and the Dominican Republic; wrote several memoirs and other books relating to his diplomatic career, including *Envoy to the Middle World: Adventures in Diplomacy* (1983), *On the Frontline in the Cold War* (1997), and (with his wife) *Life in Alanya: Turkish Delight* (1992); also wrote *The Dance of the Billions: A Novel About Texas, Houston and Oil* (1990); was predeceased by his wife; was survived by three daughters, a son, five grandchildren, and two great-grandsons; died in Leesburg, Virginia. See *Current Biography* (1950).

Obituary *New York Times* I p32 July 24, 2005

MERCHANT, ISMAIL Dec. 25, 1936–May 25, 2005 India-born filmmaker; co-founder (with the American director James Ivory) of Merchant Ivory Productions, one of the longest-lived among leading independent film companies; was primarily the company's producer, the fount of financial acumen behind the making of a trove of opulent cross-cultural films on relatively modest budgets; on several films, served as director; worked on films (usually written by Ruth Prawer Jhabvala) that at first, from the early 1960s into the 1970s, were recherché productions shot in India and concerned with the afterglow of the British Raj in that country; later, as an anonymous obituary writer for the *Economist* (June 2, 2005) observed, focused on works concerned with "the way non-conformists (in the literal sense) were affected by class distinction and prejudice in English and American literature"; in the 1980s and 1990s, saw Merchant Ivory's name on a string of box-office hits, lush adaptations of the novels of Henry James and E. M. Forster, among other literary works; after graduating from St. Xavier's College (an affiliate of the University of Bombay) in Mumbai (formerly Bombay), India, earned a master's degree in business administration at New York University; made his filmmaking debut as the executive producer of a short subject, *The Creation of Woman* (1960); in Manhattan in May 1961, met and formed his partnership with James Ivory, with the aim of making English-language motion pictures in India for international distribution; included prominently in his original plan the opportunity to finance his films with funds from the frozen Rupee accounts of major

American distributors, accounts that could be utilized only for films made in India; in November 1961, with Ivory, met the author Ruth Prawer Jhabvala, a German Jew who was educated in England and married to a citizen of India; persuaded her to join their enterprise as screenwriter; chose as their first joint effort *The Householder* (1963), a feature film based on Jhabvala's comic novel about a young man's coming of age; unlike his approach to most of their later feature films, had *The Householder* shot in black and white; next released *Shakespeare-Wallah* (1965), a bittersweet comment on a vanishing way of life, represented by the adventures of a minor itinerant Shakespearean acting troupe performing before dwindling audiences in post-colonial India; for the better part of two decades, made films on shoestring budgets and found appreciative audiences only in art cinemas; produced *Savages* (1972), an allegorical comedy-drama, about a group of primitive people who adapt to "civilized" life in a deserted mansion, that fared moderately well in Europe but flopped in the U.S.; after repeated commercial failures, finally reached a significant mainstream movie-house audience in the U.S. as well as Europe with the screen adaptation of Henry James's *The Europeans* (1979), which ushered in a new era for Merchant Ivory, one in which the company concentrated on painstakingly detailed period dramas on a large scale; surpassed the critical and financial success of *The Europeans* with *Heat and Dust* (1983), Jhabvala's screen adaptation of her novel consisting of parallel stories of two women discovering India, and with the Merchant Ivory adaptation of Henry James's *The Bostonians* (1984); saw Merchant Ivory attain financial security with the runaway commercial and critical success *A Room with a View* (1986), an exquisite adaptation of E. M. Forster's comedy of Edwardian manners and mores set in large measure in Florence, Italy, which won three Academy Awards, as did *Howard's End* (1992), an adaptation of Forster's novel about class distinction in England circa 1910; produced the controversial *Maurice* (1987), an explicit adaptation of Forster's long-sequestered novel about a male homosexual love affair, *The Remains of the Day* (1993), based on a novel by Kazuo Ishiguro, and *The Golden Bowl* (2000), based on a Henry James novel; directed the feature films *In Custody* (1993), *The Proprietor* (1996), *Cotton Mary* (1999), *The Mystic Masseur* (2002), and *The Goddess* (2005); with Ivory, made a total of more than 40 motion pictures, including documentaries and shorts and several made-for-television films, among them *Roseland* (1977), *Jefferson in Paris* (1995), and *Le Divorce* (2003); wrote a memoir, *My Passage from India* (2002), and several cookbooks; shared with Ivory an apartment in London, a townhouse in Manhattan, and a 14-room manor on an estate in Claverack, New York; died in London. See *Current Biography* (1993).

Obituary *New York Times* C p18 May 26, 2005

MERRILL, ROBERT June 4, 1917–Oct. 23, 2004 Opera singer; with his rich and powerful baritone voice, was a pillar of the Metropolitan Opera Company for three decades (1945–51 and 1952–76); was born Moishe Miller in the New York City borough of Brooklyn to Polish Orthodox Jewish immigrants; was grounded in harmony, theory, and sight-reading by his mother, who had performed as an operatic and concert singer in Poland; as a teenager, attended a singing studio at the William Fox Theater in Brooklyn, where he was taught "popular interpretation"—chiefly, crooning in the style of Bing Crosby; later studied under Samuel Margolis, one of the leading voice teachers in New York City; originally, was also drawn to baseball; pitched briefly for a semiprofessional team; at the beginning of his career as a singer, filled engagements in synagogues, at bar mitzvahs and weddings, in Yiddish theaters on Second Avenue on Manhattan's Lower East Side, and at resort hotels in the Catskills; signed a contract with the National Broadcasting Co. (after winning first prize on Major Bowes' *Original Amateur Hour* radio program, according to at least one source); on network radio, sang with the NBC Concert Orchestra and became a regular on the orchestra leader Phil Spitalny's program *Serenade to America*; was engaged for a nine-week season at Radio City Music Hall; meanwhile, in 1939, failed to reach the finals in the Metropolitan Opera's radio competition *Auditions of the Air*; in the early 1940s, had specialized coaching in opera; began singing opera during a multi-city tour booked by the National Concerts and Artists Corp. in 1944; on that tour, sang the elder Germont in *La Traviata*, Amonasro in *Aïda*, Valentine in *Faust*, Tonio in *I Pagliacci*, and Escamillo in *Carmen*; in 1944, again became a contestant in the Metropolitan Opera radio auditions, now titled *The Metropolitan Presents*; in the finals in 1945, tied for first place, winning a Metropolitan Opera contract; made his debut at the Met in December 1945 as the elder Germont; at the Met over the following five years, sang Escamillo, Figaro in *The Barber of Seville*, Sir Henry Ashton in *Lucia di Lammermoor*, the High Priest in *Samson and Dalila*, and Rodrigo in *Don Carlos*; in 1951, was unable to participate in the Met's annual spring tour because of conflict with a contract he had previously signed with Paramount Pictures; for breach of contract, was suspended from membership in the Met by Rudolph Bing, the general manager of the opera company; was reinstated in time for the 1952 spring tour and remained on the Met roster until his retirement, in 1976; returned to the Met stage on the occasion of the opera company's centennial, in 1983; performed a score of roles in more than 500 Met productions; sang Germont about 100 times and Escamillo about 75; included in his repertoire Rigoletto, Renato in *Un Ballo in Maschera*, Tchelakov in *Boris Godunov*, Silvio in *I Pagliacci,* Marcello in *La Bohème*, Malatesta in *Don Pasquale*, Don Carlo in *La Forza del Destino*, Gerard in *Andrea Chenier*, and Iago in *Otello*; sang often on radio and television and occasionally in nightclubs; appeared in several motion pictures, including the musical *Aaron Slick from Punkin Crick* (1952), in which he had a supporting role; was a fan of the New York Yankees baseball team; for many years, sang the National Anthem or was heard singing the song on a recording on opening day at Yankee Stadium; left a legacy of opera recordings on the RCA label; with Sandford Doby, wrote the autobiography *Once More from the Beginning* (1965); painted oil canvases, notably images of clowns; was married to the opera singer Roberta Peters for three months in 1952 and then, in 1954, married the pianist Marion Machno; had a son and a daughter with his second wife; died at his home in New Rochelle, New York. See *Current Biography* (1952).

Obituary *New York Times* C p19 Oct. 26. 2004

MESSICK, DALE Apr. 11, 1906–Apr. 5, 2005 Artist; pioneering female cartoonist; in 1940, broke the exclusive male proprietorship of the funny pages with her comic strip *Brenda Starr, Reporter*, chronicling the adventures of a glamorous and sassy female journalist with a metropolitan newspaper, a strip that, at the peak of its popularity, in the 1950s, was appearing in more than 250 newspapers nationwide (it is currently being written by Mary Schmich and drawn by June Brigman and distributed by Tribune Media Services); changed her first name from Dalia to Dale for ambiguity's sake, when she discovered that many newspaper editors were prejudiced against female artists; began to draw comic strips as a schoolgirl; studied one summer at the Art Institute of Chicago; was working as a designer of greeting cards for a company in New York when she began trying to break into the comic-strip market; with the help of Mollie Slott, a top aide to Joseph M. Patterson, the publisher of the New York *Daily News* and head of the Chicago Tribune–New York News Syndicate, successfully submitted the trial strip for *Brenda Starr, Reporter* to the syndicate via Patterson (who was biased against female artists and kept the strip out of the *Daily News* while allowing it to run in other syndicate newspapers beginning on Sunday, June 30, 1940); drew *Brenda Starr* as a Sunday strip (though it did not run in the *Daily News* until after Patterson's death, in 1946); inked the strip until 1985, when she turned it over to other hands; later, wrote and drew a single-panel cartoon called "Grammy Glamour" for a publication for the elderly in California; wrote an autobiography titled "Still Stripping at Ninety," which is yet to be published; died in Penngrove, California. See *Current Biography* (1961).

Obituary *New York Times* A p25 Apr. 8, 2005

MILLER, ARTHUR Oct. 17, 1915–Feb. 10, 2005 Playwright; the foremost exponent of expressionistic realism in the post–World War II American theater; a dramaturgical moralist with a Depression-forged leftist political perspective and a Jewish-bred social conscience, harsh in its judgment of injustice in the world and sensitive to the guilt and shame of personal ethical compromise with injustice; was described by Elia Kazan, the director most prominently associated with him professionally (and, with ambivalence, privately), as similar to Kazan himself in that they both "came out of the Group Theater tradition that every play should teach a lesson and make a thematic point"; made his points most powerfully in the climaxes of several plays about tortured interpersonal relations in outwardly normal but deeply dysfunctional middle-class American families of unspecified ethnicity (save European heritage), each similarly structured, even to the detail of two sons; in his first Broadway hit, *All My Sons* (1946–47), wrote about a son discovering that his father, an aeronautics manufacturer, had under economic pressure knowingly supplied fatally defective World War II

fighter-plane parts to the government and then shifted the blame to his innocent partner; in the second, his most celebrated work, the tragedy *Death of a Salesman* (1949–50), wrote about Willy Loman, an archetypal personification of the American dream gone awry, a traveling man who spends his life and loses his soul in the cause of selling his wares only to end up pathetically, shucked off by his employers and disgraced as a father (and husband) in a confrontation with his sons; saw that much-honored popular international classic enjoy several Broadway revivals, inspire a feature film (1951) and two television productions (1965 and 1986), and remain a favorite staple in repertory; in his later plays, most closely followed the same pattern in *The Price* (1968); in the quasi-autobiographical *After the Fall* (1964), apparently vented his feelings regarding his failed five-year marriage to the screen sex icon Marilyn Monroe and the betrayals committed by close colleagues of his (notably Kazan) when they turned informer against Communist and "fellow traveling" associates during the era of McCarthyism; wrote about the Salem witch trials in *The Crucible* (1953), in which his intention was to make an analogy between the religious hysteria of 1692 and the political hysteria of McCarthyism; saw *The Crucible* become second-most-popular of his works, if measured in terms of repertory; arrived at his universalism through his "struggle with Jewish identity . . . intertwined with his rejection of capitalism and American society," as Ami Eden observed in the *Forward* newspaper (July 30, 2004); in his autobiography, *Timebinds* (1987), recounted how the Wall Street crash of 1929 devastated his father's previously thriving New York City garment-manufacturing business and how his mother "endlessly and angrily" expressed her disappointment with her husband and his fellow "mean-spirited, money-mad 'cloakies' . . . who cared for nothing but business"; when working briefly in the family business, was dismayed to witness the contempt with which his father was treated by buyers; later, became familiar with the troubled interpersonal relations between a salesman uncle of his and the uncle's two sons, a trio who would became models for the central characters in *Death of a Salesman*; began to aspire to playwriting in the mid-1930s, when he saw a production of Clifford Odets's hugely successful exercise in Marxist agitprop *Waiting for Lefty* and read Kenneth T. Rowe's book *Write That Play*; later, was influenced by Greek tragedy and the dramatist Henrik Ibsen; studied drama under Rowe at the University of Michigan, where he received his B.A. degree in English in 1938; during and immediately after his college years, wrote several unproduced plays that reflected his rebellion against his family heritage and his then Marxist critique of politics and society; during World War II, wrote radio drama and, on a Hollywood assignment, did reportage on life in army camps, the best of which was collected in the book *Situation Normal* (1944); also in 1944, made his Broadway debut with *The Man Who Had All the Luck*, an instant flop; in 1945, published the novel *Focus*, about a Gentile personnel director who, through mistaken identity, becomes a victim of his company's subtle policy of anti-Semitism; in *A View from the Bridge* (1955), told the story of a Sicilian-American longshoreman in Brooklyn whose frustrated lust for his teenage niece devastates his life and his family; in 1957, was found guilty of contempt of Congress for refusing to cooperate with the Red-hunting House UnAmerican Activities Committee, a conviction that was later dismissed on appeal; for Marilyn Monroe, his wife at the time, wrote the screenplay for the motion picture *The Misfits* (1960); following his election to the presidency of PEN, in 1965, traveled the world in behalf of that association of writers for a number of years; in response to the Soviet treatment of dissident writers, wrote *The Archbishop's Ceiling* (1977); following *The American Clock* (1984), a collage of scenes evoking the political and social climate of the Depression, had no full-length play on Broadway until *Broken Glass* (1994), a poignant drama about the shattering psychological and psychosomatic impact that news of the Holocaust in Nazi Germany, beginning with Kristallnacht in 1938, had on an American Jewish husband and wife; wrote a total of some 25 plays, beginning with *Honors at Dawn* (1935) and including *The Creation of the World and Other Business* (1972), *The Ride Down Mount Morgan* (1991), *The Last Yankee* (1993), *Mr. Peters' Connections* (1998), *Resurrection Blues* (2002), and *Finishing the Picture* (2004); among his short stories—collected in *I Don't Need You Any More* (1967)—said he was proud of only one, "Monte Saint Angelo"; wrote the scenario for the controversial television movie *Playing for Time* (1981), about the women's orchestra at Ausch-witz; in his nonfiction book *On Politics and the Art of Acting* (2001), examined recent political cam-paigns and concluded that Americans are more im-pressed by a candidate's "personality, his acting, than by his proposals or his moral character"; sired two children in the first of his three marriages, to Mary Grace Slattery; after his divorce from Marilyn Monroe, was married for 40 years to the photogra-pher Inge Morath, who bore him a son, Daniel (who has Down syndrome and was institutionalized at birth), and a daughter, the writer Rebecca Miller; af-ter Morath's death, in 2002, lived with the painter Agnes Barley, who was 55 years his junior; died on his farm in Roxbury, Connecticut. See *Current Biog-raphy* (1973).

Obituary *New York Times* A p1+ Feb. 12, 2005

MILLS, JOHN Feb. 22, 1908–Apr. 23, 2005 English actor; one of the best loved and most durable stars of 20th-century British cinema; began his career on London's West End stage when he was 19; first came to international attention in the youthful role of Pe-ter Colley in the movie *Goodbye, Mr. Chips* (1939); became known to many American filmgoers when they viewed *In Which We Serve* (1942), the World War II morale booster written by Noël Coward and directed by Coward and David Lean; in that film, played the heroic Cockney seaman Shorty Blake, a role written specifically for him by Coward; was cast in the supporting role of Billy Mitchell in the Cow-ard/Lean film *This Happy Breed* (1944); played Pip in Lean's *Great Expectations* (1946) and Willie Mos-sop in the same director's *Hobson's Choice* (1954); starred with his daughter Hayley Mills in *Tiger Bay* (1959); won the Academy Award for best supporting actor for his portrayal of the mute Irish village idiot

Michael in Lean's *Ryan's Daughter* (1970); began his theatrical career as a song-and-dance man in the West End and on tour in 1929 and 1930; under the mentorship of Noël Coward, was cast in the lead of the comedy *Charlie's Aunt* (1930–31) and such re-vues as *Cavalcade* (1931), among other theatrical productions; played classical roles with the Old Vic Company in the late 1930s; was commissioned in the Royal Monmouthshire Rifles early in World War II; was discharged from military service for medical reasons in 1942; back on the London stage, was cast as Lew in *Men in Shadow* (1942), the first of a num-ber of plays written for him by his second wife, Mary Hayley Bell Mills; three years later, appeared as Ste-phen Cass in his wife's *Duet with Two Hands*; in the early 1950s, was cast as Candy in her *The Uninvited Guest* (1953); in a rare sojourn in the U.S., played Lawrence of Arabia in *Ross* on Broadway (1960–61); accrued more than 100 motion-picture credits, including those of William Wilberforce in *Mr. Pitt* (1942), Lt. Freddie Taylor in *We Dive at Dawn* (1943), Captain Robert Falcon Scott in *Scott of the Antarctic* (1948), Basset in *The Rocking Horse Win-ner* (1950), Albert Parkis in *The End of the Affair* (1955), Captain Anson in *Ice-Cold Alex* (1959), Cor-poral Tubby Bins in *Dunkirk* (1958), Lieutenant Col-onel Basil Barrow in *Tunes of Glory* (1960), Ezra Fit-ton in *The Family Way* (1966), General Kitchener in *Young Winston* (1972), Scudder in *The Thirty-nine Steps* (1978), the Viceroy in *Gandhi* (1982), and Montgomery Bell in *Who's That Girl?* (1987); on tele-vision, played, among other roles, Dundee in the se-ries *Dundee and the Culhane* (1967), Albert Collyer in the series *Young at Heart* (1980), Jarvis Lorry in the miniseries *A Tale of Two Cities* (1989), and Mr. Chuffey in the miniseries *Martin Chuzzlewit* (1994); was sometimes credited as Sir John Mills after he was knighted in 1976; before his marriage to Mary Hayley Bell, had been married to and divorced from Aileen Raymond; was survived by his wife Mary, his daughters Hayley and Juliet, both actresses, and his son Jonathan, a motion-picture scenarist and pro-ducer; died st his home in Dedham, Buckingham-shire. See *Current Biography* (1963).

Obituary *New York Times* B p7 Apr. 25, 2005

MORRISON, PHILIP Nov. 7, 1915–Apr. 22, 2005 Theoretical nuclear physicist; astrophysicist; profes-sor emeritus, Massachusetts Institute of Technology; an inventor of the atomic bomb who went on to be-come a campaigner for international civilian control of nuclear research and nuclear arms; a pioneer in the search for intelligent extraterrestrial life; a popu-larizer of science; at age four, contracted polio, which left him with a disabled leg; by age five, was building radios; at the University of California at Berkeley, did his doctoral work in theoretical phys-ics under J. Robert Oppenheimer; in 1942, joined the so-called Manhattan Project, the top-secret U.S. gov-ernment program for the development of the atomic bomb; following his initial assignment to the project's metallurgical laboratory at the University of Chicago, was transferred to the Los Alamos (New Mexico) Scientific Laboratory, headed by Oppenhei-mer; as a group leader at Los Alamos, supervised and monitored the testing of the first atomic bomb in the desert at Alamogordo, New Mexico, in July 1945; a few weeks after the successful test, traveled to Tinian Island in the Marianas to help assemble one of the two bombs that would be dropped on Japan in August 1945; following the Japanese surrender, on August 14, 1945, was a member of the team of scientists sent by the U.S. government to survey from the air the damage caused by the bombs; at Los Alamos, was a colleague of Hans Bethe, a theoretical nuclear physicist on leave from Cornell University; came to Cornell in 1946 along with Bethe, Richard Feynman, and several other Los Alamos collaborators; suspected of being a national security risk, was summoned to testify before the U.S. Senate Internal Security Subcommittee in 1953; while admitting once having had Communist sympathies, denied ever having been a Soviet agent; as an associate professor at Cornell, gradually shifted his interest to astrophysics and cosmology; estimating that there may be several billion planets in the universe capable of sustaining advanced life forms, proposed with the physicist Giuseppe Cocconi beginning "a discriminating search" for radio signals from intelligent extraterrestrial beings; with Cocconi, announced that project in the paper "Search for Interstellar Communication," published in the journal *Nature* (September 1959); in 1964, left Cornell and joined the faculty of the Massachusetts Institute of Technology, remaining there for four decades; in 1976, was named by the National Aeronautics and Space Administration to chair a group of scientists devoted to locating radio signals from outer space; in addition to serving as book-review editor for *Scientific American* and contributing papers to professional journals (including the *Bulletin of Atomic Scientists*), wrote for popular magazines; often in collaboration with his second wife, Phyllis Singer Morrison, was an innovative and influential popularizer of science through such projects as courses of study for primary and secondary schools, including the African Primary Science Project; with Phyllis, created *The Ring of Truth*, a six-part educational documentary series he hosted on the PBS network in 1987; also with her, wrote *Powers of Ten: A Book about the Relative Size of Things in the Universe and the Effect of Adding Another Zero* (1994); with others, wrote *Elementary Nuclear Theory* (1956), *My Father's Watch: Aspects of the Physical World* (1974), *The Price of Defense: A New Strategy for Military Spending* (1979), *Nuclear Weapons and Nuclear War* (1983), and *Reason Enough to Hope* (1998); co-edited *Search for the Universal Ancestors* (1985), among other books; collected 100 of his book reviews in his *Long Look at the Literature* (1990); was predeceased by his wife and survived by a stepson; died at his home in Cambridge, Massachusetts. See *Current Biography* (1981).

Obituary *New York Times* B p9 Apr. 26, 2005

NELSON, GAYLORD June 4, 1916–July 3, 2005 Two-term Democratic governor of Wisconsin (1959–63); three-term U.S. senator (1963–81); a foremost progenitor of the contemporary American environmental movement; founded Earth Day in 1970; was a catalyst in the creation of the U.S. Environmental Protection Agency by President Richard M. Nixon in

collaboration with Congress, also in 1970; as governor, created the Outdoor Recreation Acquisition Program, which enabled the Wisconsin state government to acquire and protect a million acres of state park land, wetlands, and open spaces with funding from a penny-a-pack tax on cigarettes; in the U.S. Senate, was an early and unrelenting opponent of the American military incursion in Vietnam and a promoter of progressive legislation in the areas of civil rights, drug safety, public health, and legal assistance for the poor; made his greatest impact with his campaign "to save the natural resources of America," an endeavor he announced in his first Senate speech, in March 1963; persuaded President John F. Kennedy to make an 11-state speaking tour promoting the conservation of natural resources in September 1963; was a co-sponsor or influential backer of such legislation as the Wilderness Act of 1963, which assured the conservation of millions of acres of federal land, of the Clean Air Act of 1963 and the 1970 revision of that act, of the Endangered Species Act of 1973, and of the Federal Water Pollution Control Act of 1972, which as amended in 1977 became known as the Clean Water Act; played an important role in steering through Congress the legislative proposal, emanating from the administration of President Lyndon B. Johnson, that became the Wild and Scenic Rivers Act of 1968, which created a National Wild and Scenic Rivers System in which "certain selected rivers of the nation which, with their immediate environments, possess outstandingly remarkable scenic, recreational, geologic, fish and wildlife, historic, cultural or other similar values, shall be preserved in free-flowing condition and that they and their immediate environments shall be protected for the benefit and enjoyment of present and future generations"; had a degree in philosophy and anthropology from San Jose College and a degree in law from the University of Wisconsin; following combat service as an army officer in World War II, practiced law in Madison, Wisconsin, for 13 years; was elected to three terms in the Wisconsin state Senate before becoming governor; after leaving the U.S. Senate, was involved with a wide range of land-preservation issues as counselor to the Wilderness Society; died in Kensington, Maryland; was survived by his wife, Carrie Lee, a son, a daughter, and three grandchildren. See *Current Biography* (1960).

Obituary *New York Times* B p6 July 4, 2005

NITZE, PAUL H. Jan. 16, 1907–Oct. 19, 2004 U.S. government official; expert in national-security affairs; strategic-arms negotiator; over a span of half a century, served under a succession of presidents, from Franklin D. Roosevelt to Ronald Reagan; was the major architect of the U.S. strategy of containment via-à-vis the Soviet Union during the Cold War; earned a B.A. degree in economics and finance at Harvard University in 1928; during the 1930s, despite the Depression, made a fortune as an investment banker on Wall Street; in 1937, switched from the Democratic to the Republican Party to protest President Franklin D. Roosevelt's effort to pack the Supreme Court with additional justices favorable to his New Deal policies; later, returned to the Democratic Party; in 1940, went to Washington as an assistant to Under Secretary of the Navy James V. Forestal; during World War II, held top positions in the Office of the Coordinator of Inter-American Affairs, the Board of Economic Warfare, and the Strategic Bombing Survey; after the war, as deputy director of the Office of International Trade Policy at the State Department, helped develop the European Recovery Program, better known as the Marshall Plan; in 1949, succeeded George V. Kennan as director of the State Department's policy-planning staff; in that position, directed the drafting of a document titled N.S.C.-68, a formative study in the development of the military aspect of the U.S.'s anti-Soviet strategy; said, years later, "I didn't think we should go to war with the Soviets and I don't think they wanted to go to war with us. But how do you conduct things so that the Soviets would be deterred from foreign expansion and be forced to look inward at their own problems?"; during the Republican administration of President Dwight D. Eisenhower (1953–61), worked outside of government as president of the Foreign Service Educational Foundation, a privately supported organization financially responsible for Johns Hopkins University's School of Advanced International Studies (which would be renamed for him in 1989); in the 1960s, was successively assistant secretary of defense for international-security affairs, secretary of the navy and deputy secretary of defense in the Democratic administrations of John F. Kennedy and Lyndon B. Johnson; in the early 1970s, was appointed to the U.S. delegation to the Strategic Arms Limitation Talks (SALT) with the Soviet Union; played an important role in negotiating the first Antiballistic Missile Treaty before resigning from the delegation, in 1974; when excluded from the Democratic administration of President Jimmy Carter later in the 1970s, organized opposition to Carter's 1979 SALT treaty on grounds that it would result in permanent American strategic inferiority; joined with other prominent conservative Democrats in forming the Committee on the Present Danger, which helped get out the vote for Republican presidential nominee Ronald Reagan in his successful race against Carter in 1980; the following year, was assigned by Reagan to head talks with the Soviet Union aimed at reducing intermediate-range missiles in Europe; in 1982, cutting through the bureaucratic protocol and acting independently of instructions from higher-ups, took a famous "walk in the woods" in the Jura Mountains near Geneva, Switzerland,with his Soviet counterpart, Yuli Kvitsinsky; on that occasion, achieved a breakthrough in the negotiations, but the agreement between him and Kvitsinsky was rejected by both the Soviet Union and Washington; during President Reagan's second term, tried unsuccessfully to negotiate a "grand compromise" with the Soviets, offering limitations on President Reagan's proposed Strategic Defense Initiative ("Star Wars") in exchange for reductions in the nuclear weaponry of both countries; refused to accept the seemingly ceremonial post of ambassador at large emeritus when it was offered to him by President George H. W. Bush; published many books, including *From Hiroshima to Glasnost; At the Center of Decision: A Memoir* (written with Ann M. Smith and Steven I. Reardon, 1989), *Tension Between Opposites: Reflections on the Practice and Theory of Politics* (1993), and other volumes (many of them collection of essays) on arms control, nuclear and space negotiations, foreign policy, and national security; working out of an office at the Paul H. Nitze School of Advanced International Studies in the 1990s, continued to turn out essays aimed at influencing public policy in his field of expertise; in April 2004, witnessed the christening of a U.S. Navy guided-missile destroyer named for him; was the subject of a biography by Strobe Talbott, *The Master of the Game: Paul Nitze and the Nuclear Peace* (1988); died at his home in Washington, D.C.; was predeceased by his first wife, Phyllis,and survived by his second wife, Elisabeth, two sons, two daughters, a stepdaughter, and many grandchildren and great-grandchildren. See *Current Biography* (1962).

Obituary *New York Tmes* B p9 Oct. 21, 2004

NORTON, ANDRE Feb. 17, 1912–Mar. 17, 2005 Author; was born Alice Mary Norton in Cleveland, Ohio; sometimes wrote under the pseudonym Andrew North; began her career as a writer of spy and historical fiction for juveniles and young adults; subsequently, attracted an adult readership with her science-fiction novels, often about alienated or oppressed protagonists who find personal fulfillment in the denouements of their galactic adventures; held and greatly increased that readership with her later fantasy fiction; was a staff member of the Cleveland Public Library from the early 1930s through the 1940s; in 1934, published her first novel, *The Prince Commands*, described by her as "a Graustarkian romance for teenagers"; in *The Sword Is Drawn* (1944), wove a fictional tale about the Dutch Underground in World War II; continued in the espionage vein in *Sword in Sheath* (1949) and *At Swords' Points* (1954); set her historical novels *Follow the Drum* (1942) and *Scarface* (1948) in Colonial Maryland and the West Indies, respectively; combined mythological lore with historical fiction in *Huon of the Horn* (1951), a tale of the "Duke of Bordeaux who came to sorrow at the hands of Charlemagne and yet won the favor of Oberon, the elf king"; wrote three more historical novels, *Yankee Privateer* (1955), *Stand to Horse* (1956), and *Shadow Hawk* (1960); meanwhile, had begun the second phase of her career, with the publication of her first science-fiction novel, *Star Man's Son 2250 AD* (1952), about a mutant rejected by society, who, following a nuclear war, embarks on a salutary space voyage; later wrote, among other science-fiction novels, *Shadow Rangers* (1953), *The Stars Are Ours!* (1954), *Star Guard* (1955), and *Star Born* (1957); in 1963, began the fantasy phase of her career, with *Witch World*, the first in a series of more than 30 interlocking tales set in a magical alternate universe of warring fiefdoms; began her "magic" sequence of stories with *Steel Magic* (1965); wrote more than 130 novels (some in collaboration with others), including *Ralestone Luck* (1938), *Voodoo Planet* (1956), *The Time Traders* (1958), *Storm Over Warlock* (1960), *The X Factor* (1965), *Octagon Magic* (1967), *Operation Time Search* (1967), *Dark Piper* (1968), *Fur Magic* (1968), *Postmarked the Stars* (1969), *Moon of Three Rings* (1969), *Ice Crown* (1970), *Dread Companion* (1970), *Exile to the Stars* (1971), *Red Hart Magic* (1976), *Tales of the Witch World* (1987–90), *Annals of the Witch World* (1994),

Lost Lands of the Witch World (2004), *Beast Master's Planet* (2005), and *Three Hands for Scorpio* (2005); wrote a score of short stories; edited a number of books, including a series of anthologies of fiction by others; with Martin H. Greenberg, wrote *Catfantastic: Nine Lives and Fifteen Tales* (1989) and four additional books in the "Catfantastic" series; from 1999 to 2004, operated "High Hallack," a retreat and research library for writers in Murfreesboro, Tennessee; died in Murfreesboro. See *Current Biography* (1957).

Obituary *New York Times* B p8 Mar. 18, 2005

ORBACH, JERRY Oct. 20, 1935–Dec. 28, 2004 Stage, screen, and television actor; a versatile and ingratiating performer who emerged from stardom in Broadway musicals and character parts in movies to become most closely identified with his major role on TV, that of Detective Lennie Briscoe in *Law and Order*, a weekly, hour-long NBC crime show filmed on location in New York City; played Briscoe, a streetsmart and world-weary New York Police Department homicide cop with a mordant wit (delivered deadpan), from 1992 to 2004, with an offhand, nononsense manner belying a humane heart; was born in the Bronx, New York City; grew up there and in Waukegan, Illinois; began his career in regional theater and summer stock; in 1955 moved back to New York City and became an understudy in a long-running Off-Broadway production of *The Threepenny Opera*; in that musical, took over the role of the Streetsinger in 1957 and the lead role of Macheath in 1958; still Off-Broadway, sang the dual role of the Narrator and the bandit El Gallo in *The Fantasticks* (1960–61); made his Broadway debut creating the role of Paul Berthalet in the musical *Carnival!* (1961–63); subsequently, toured in *Carnival!* and had roles in several revivals; played Harold Wonder, the neurotic antihero, in Bruce Jay Friedman's comedy *Scuba Duba* (1967–68), an Off-Broadway hit; for his performance as Chuck Baxter, the likable fall guy in the Neil Simon/Burt Bacharach/Hal David musical *Promises, Promises*, received the Tony Award for best starring actor in a musical in the 1968–69 Broadway season; again on Broadway, created the role of Billy Flynn, the slick, silver-tongued shyster in the original production of the musical *Chicago*, in 1975, and that of the tough-minded musical producer Julian Marsh in *42nd Street*, in 1980; meanwhile, was accruing dramatic credits on TV, including the title role of the Boston private detective in *The Law and Harry McGraw* (1987–88); was cast in *Law and Order* from the start of that series, in 1990, but was not promoted to the chief homicide-detective role until 1983; continued in the Lennie Briscoe role through the 2003–04 TV season; after that, began work in *Law and Order: Trial by Jury* (which began airing in March 2005), in which the job of his character changed from homicide detective to investigator for the district attorney's office; in films, was cast in such roles as Kid Sally Palumbo in *The Gang That Couldn't Shoot Straight* (1971), Gus Levy in *Prince of the City* (1981), Nicholas DeFranco in *F/X* (1986), and Jake Houseman in *Dirty Dancing* (1987); died in Manhattan; was survived by his wife, Elaine, and two sons from a previous marriage. See *Current Biography* (1970).

Obituary *New York Times* C p10 Dec. 30, 2004

PECK, M. SCOTT May 22, 1936–Sep. 25, 2005 Psychiatrist; author; wrote inspirational self-help books that realized combined sales of more than five million copies in North America alone and were translated into 20 languages; stressed the importance of recognizing that "life is difficult" and that depression is a natural human state, to be handled with self-discipline and community-mindedness; believed that "thinking we're here to be happy" and that problems are to be escaped from leads only to greater problems; was the son of David W. Peck, a Manhattan attorney and judge; although raised in a secular household, developed a strong interest in spirituality and religion; embraced both Zen Buddhism and a Christian faith; transferred from Phillips Exeter Academy to Friends Seminary, a Quaker day school in New York City; after receiving a B.A. degree at Harvard University and engaging in pre-med studies at Columbia University, earned his medical degree at Case-Western Reserve University; completed his internship and residency in psychiatry after serving in the U.S. Army in the 1960s; was chief of the department of psychology at the U.S. Army Medical Center in Okinawa, Japan, from 1967 to 1970 and assistant chief of psychiatry and neurology in the office of the U.S. surgeon general in Washington, D.C., from 1970 to 1972; practiced psychiatry in Preston, Connecticut, from 1972 to 1984; saw his first book, *The Road Less Traveled: A New Psychology of Love, Traditional Values, and Spiritual Growth* (1978), sell more than four million copies and remain on the *New York Times* best-seller list for eight years, a nonfiction record; later wrote *People of the Lie* (1983), *The Different Drum* (1987), *Further Along the Road Less Traveled* (1993), and *The Road Less Traveled and Beyond* (1997); also wrote the novel *A Bed by the Window* (1990); saw his books become recommended reading in Alcohics Anonymous and other 12-step recovery programs; following his divorce from his first wife, Lily Ho, married Kathleen Kline Yates, who survived him; was also survived by his and Kathleen's son and two daughters; died in Warren, Connecticut. See *Current Biography* (1991).

Obituary *New York Times* B p8 Sep. 28, 2005

PERDUE, FRANK May 9, 1920–Mar. 31, 2005 Poultry farmer; businessman; turned his family's erstwhile egg company, Perdue Farms, into one of the world's largest processors of brand-name fresh chicken—one that sold more than 52 million pounds of fresh chicken and turkey products each week in 2004—and was also a major producer of poultry feed; was a pioneer in transforming poultry into a branded product offered in diverse forms; became famous as the star of the folksy TV ads promoting his company; made innovations in production, marketing, and advertising that have been widely imitated by other poultry businesses; while growing up in Salisbury, Maryland, worked along with his parents on the farm his father had founded in 1920 to raise Leghorn chickens, primarily for egg production; dropped out of Salisbury State College after two years and returned to the farm, where, soon afterward, an infectious disease decimated the Perdues' 2,000 Leghorns; with his father, turned to the hardier breed of New Hampshire Reds and shifted from egg to broiler production; became president of Perdue Farms in 1952, when the company was averaging revenues of $6 million a year from sales of 2,600,000 broilers; in 1957, built a large facility in Salisbury, including a feed mill and hatcheries and saw annual revenues from sales exceed $35 million by 1967; in 1968, expanded into processing, buying machines capable of processing 14,000 broilers an hour; increasingly, concentrated on hatching and processing, contracting out the raising phase to other farms; in 1971, built a larger plant in Accomac, Virginia, capable of processing 28,000 birds an hour; in 1976, opened a hatchery and third processing plant in Lewiston, North Carolina; soon afterward, added a fourth broiler processing plant in Felton, Delaware, and a plant solely for the processing of roasters in Georgetown, Delaware; by that time, had well over 3,000 employees and some 900 contract growers; unlike some other processors, shipped his poultry to East Coast markets fresh, packed in ice, with every fowl or part thereof carrying a Perdue tag as a guarantee that it had been subjected to a second inspection by company graders after U.S. Department of Agriculture agents had passed it as Grade A; between 1971 and 1991, appeared in some 200 TV ads; was also heard on radio; remained on as chairman of the executive committee after his son, James, succeeded him as chairman; was survived by his third wife, Mitzi, four children, two stepchildren, and two grandchildren; died at his home in Salisbury, Maryland. See *Current Biography* (1979).

Obituary *New York Times* A p12 Apr. 2, 2005

PIEL, GERARD Mar. 1, 1915–Sep. 5, 2004 Science writer; publisher; one of the triumvirate who in the mid-20th century revived *Scientific American*—the country's longest continuously published periodical, founded in 1845 to report on the progress of the industrial revolution—and remade it into the leading nontechnical journal of the atomic age; was a scion of the Piel Brothers Brewery family; before receiving a B.A. degree in history at Harvard College in 1937, worked briefly as a cub reporter with the *Grand Forks (North Dakota) Herald*; afterward, became an editorial trainee at Time Inc.; within two years, was named science editor of *Life* magazine; after six years with *Life* (1939–45), worked as an assistant to Henry J. Kaiser at Kaiser's companies in Oakland, California, for a year and a half (1945–47); meanwhile, together with Dennis Flanagan, who was war and technology editor at *Life*, and Donald H. Miller, a management consultant, conceived the idea of a magazine that would serve as a forum in which scientists and other experts could write about current discoveries and inventions and discuss issues of moment for a general readership; in January 1948, after raising initial financial backing, purchased *Scientific American*, a magazine then in decline, with only 2,000 paying subscribers and virtually no advertisers; became the magazine's publisher, while Flanagan became editor and Miller general manager; gradually recruited a roster of contributors that

would ultimately include some 100 Nobel Prize winners; as Jeremy Bernstein recalled for *Commentary* (May 1997), being tapped by Piel or Flanagan "was like being admitted to an honor society"; by the 1960s, was attracting so many advertisers that some were being turned away; expanded *Scientific American* into a number of international editions and reached a total circulation of more than a million; promoted discussion of such issues as nuclear proliferation and the Cold War's prospect of "mutual assured destruction"; coined the phrase "thinking the unthinkable"; was publisher of *Scientific American* until 1984, when he became chairman of the board; as chairman, oversaw the sale of the magazine (which remained based in New York City) to the international conglomerate Verlagsgruppe Georg von Holtzbrinck in 1986; wrote the books *Science in the Cause of Man* (1962), *The Acceleration of History* (1972), *Only One World: Ours to Make and to Keep* (1992), and *The Age of Science: What Scientists Learned in the Twentieth Century* (2001); lived on Manhattan's Upper East Side; died in Mount Sinai Hospital in Queens, New York City; was survived by his second wife, Eleanor, a daughter and son, and numerous grandchildren and great-grandchildren. See *Current Biography* (1959).

Obituary *New York Times* C p11 Sep. 7, 2004

RAINIER III, PRINCE OF MONACO May 31, 1923– Apr. 6, 2005 31st hereditary ruler of Monaco, located on the Mediterranean Sea near the French-Italian border, a tiny, independent principality, famous for its gambling casino, in Monte Carlo, its oceanographical museum, and its annual Grand Prix auto race, with some 28,000 inhabitants living in three communes (La Condamine, Monte Carlo, and Monaco city, the capital) on an area of approximately 370 square acres; was born into the Genoese Grimaldi family, the dynasty that has controlled Monaco since the 10th century, through his maternal lineage; was educated in schools in England and France, including the University of Montpelier and the University of Paris; served as an officer in the French army early in World War II, until the defeat of the French by the Germans; ascended the throne in 1949, when the treasury of the principality (which has no income, inheritance, or capital-gains taxes) was almost empty, revenues from the Monte Carlo casino having declined drastically because the casino's traditional clientele, European aristocracy, had emerged from World War II financially injured, and casinos elsewhere in Europe were offering new competition in the postwar years; encouraged the strengthening of the country's cosmetics and pharmaceutical industries, promoted tourism and real estate development, and made Monaco more attractive as a tax haven and commercial center, while the gambling industry was ultimately revived with the help of investments from the Greek shipping magnate Aristotle Onassis; in addition, reformed Monaco's constitution, ending the autocratic power of the sovereign by introducing a National Council of 18 elected members; in 1956, married the American movie actress Grace Kelly, who died in an automobile accident in 1982; with Princess Grace, had three children: Princess Caroline, Prince Albert (who assumed the duties of regent when Rainier became incapacitated in March 2005, and who succeeded his father to the throne, with the title Prince Albert II, upon Rainier's death), and Princess Stéphanie; was survived by his daughters and seven grandchildren, all by his daughters; died in a hospital in Monaco. See *Current Biography* (1955).

Obituary *New York Times* B p11 Apr. 6, 2005

RAO, P. V. NARASIMHA June 28, 1921–Dec. 23, 2004 Prime minister of India (1991–96); Congress Party leader; scholar; linguist; as prime minister, set in motion the economic reforms that rescued India from Socialist bankruptcy and transformed it into an Asian free-market giant; before emerging on the Indian national scene, was a state legislator and government official in Andhra Pradesh, India; was first elected to the Lok Sabha, the lower house of India's parliament, in 1977; in the cabinet of Prime Minister Indira Gandhi, was minister of foreign affairs (1980–84) and home affairs (1984); following the assassination of Indira Gandhi, in 1985, held a succession of portfolios, including foreign affairs and human-resource development, under Mrs. Gandhi's son Rajiv, until the latter's assassination, in 1991; succeeded Rajiv Gandhi at a time when India was in a state of economic crisis, with $71 billion in foreign debt, dwindling foreign-exchange reserves, and a soaring inflation rate; authorized his finance minister, Manmohan Singh, to institute a series of reforms that liberated the Indian economy from stifling government control, invited foreign investment, and promoted exports; spent his last years under the shadow of a bribery scandal; combined autobiography with fiction in his book *The Insider* (1998); translated novels by others; died in New Delhi, India. See *Current Biography* (1992).

Obituary *New York Times* C p8 Dec. 24, 2004

RAWL, LAWRENCE May 4, 1928–Feb. 13, 2005 Petroleum engineer; business executive; former chief executive officer and chairman of the board of the Exxon Corp. (now Exxon Mobil Corp.), the world's largest petroleum company; after earning a B.S. degree in petroleum engineering at the University of Oklahoma, joined the Humble Oil & Refining Co., the predecessor to Exxon Co., USA, as an engineer in 1952; advanced up the ranks to become an executive vice president of Exxon USA in 1976; from 1978 to 1980, was executive vice president of London-based Esso Europe, which was overseeing Exxon's operations in Africa as well as Europe; returned to the U.S. as a senior vice president and a director of the Exxon Corp. in 1980; was elected president in 1985; as president, collaborated with CEO and board chairman Clifton C. Garvin Jr. in a massive corporate downsizing and reorganization that continued after he succeeded Garvin, in 1987; included in his program the merger of the six divisions that formerly handled international operations into one unit, Exxon Co. International, and the reduction of the corporation's research and development budget by 20 percent and its capital and exploration budget by 31 percent; conversely, expanded the corporation's chemical operations and increased its energy reserves; was little known outside the petroleum industry until March 1989, when the tanker *Exxon Valdez* struck

Bligh Reef in Prince William Sound, Alaska, spilling an estimated 11 million gallons of crude oil across 1,300 miles of coastline, creating one of the worst environmental catastrophes in American history and a public relations disaster for Exxon and Rawl himself; in addition to charges relating to the cause of the accident, suffered the wide excoriation of the corporation for its procrastination in containing the pollution and beginning a cleanup; drew fire for waiting six days before commenting in public on the accident and three weeks before visiting the site of the spill; when he did face the press, was perceived to be adversarial; on April 3, 2005, a week and a half after the event, published a statement saying "how sorry I am that this accident took place" and pledging to "meet our obligations to all who have suffered damage from the spill"; oversaw Exxon's expenditure of some $3 billion on the cleanup and related costs; resigned as chairman and CEO in 1993; among other philanthropic acts, established an engineering scholarship fund at the University of Oklahoma; in 1997, founded the LGR Foundation, devoted to advancing both the interests of children and youth in Texas and to issues relating to Alzheimer's disease; died in Fort Worth, Texas; was survived by his wife, Gail, and children and grandchildren. See *Current Biography* (1992).

Obituary *New York Times* B p9 Feb. 16, 2005

REEVE, CHRISTOPHER Sep. 25, 1952–Oct. 10, 2004 Actor; research activist; as an actor, was best known for his screen incarnation of the mythological comic-book hero Superman in a series of feature films (1979–87); in real life, was a national, if not international, inspiration for his brave coping with his permanent quadriplegia (total paralysis from the shoulders down, making life impossible without a respirator), dating from a horse-riding accident in May 1995, and for his tireless advocacy regarding issues concerning paralytics; chaired the Christopher Reeve Paralysis Foundation, which has raised tens of millions of dollars for stem-cell, spinal-cord, and other such biomedical research; as a schoolboy in Princeton, New Jersey, acted in school plays and began performing professionally at the McCarter Theater in suburban Princeton; by the age of 16, had become a member of Actors Equity; during the summer between the 10th and 11th grades, apprenticed at the Williamstown (Massachusetts) Theatre Festival; subsequently, acquired further experience in stock and regional theater; after studying English and music theory at Cornell University, enrolled in the drama division of the Juilliard School of Performing Arts; was cast for two years in the role of Ben Harper in the daily soap opera *Love of Life* on the CBS television network; concurrently, began performing Off-Broadway with such troupes as the Circle Repertory Company and the Manhattan Theatre Club; in 1976, made his Broadway debut, as the doting grandson of the character played by Katharine Hepburn in *A Matter of Gravity*; spent the summer of 1980 acting at the Williamstown Theatre; on Broadway in 1980–81, starred as Kenneth Talley Jr., an embittered Vietnam veteran who lost both his legs in the war, in *Fifth of July*; made his screen debut in a bit part in *Gray Lady Down* (1978); was propelled to celebrity with the huge success of *Superman: The Movie* (1978), in which he portrayed an alien from the planet Krypton who masquerades as the mild-mannered metropolitan newspaper reporter Clark Kent and assumes his true identity as the Caped Crusader/Man of Steel during societal crises whose solutions require the intervention of his superhuman physical powers; reprised that role in three sequels (1980, 1983, and 1987); deluged with screenplay offers, carefully considered which parts would best help him "escape the cape"; turned down $1,000,000 to star in *American Gigolo*, which he considered distasteful, to accept the lead in the modestly budgeted *Somewhere in Time* (1980), a love/fantasy story involving time travel; was attracted to *Somewhere in Time* because, as he said, it was "an absolutely honest attempt to create an old-fashioned romance . . . based on love rather than on sex or X-rated bedroom scenes"; later, turned down the lead in *The Running Man*; played the younger of the two playwrights involved in a deadly twisting and turning cat-and-mouse game in the film *Deathtrap* (1986); in one of his pet projects, the crime drama *Street Smart* (1987), starred in the role of Jonathan Fisher, an unscrupulous Manhattan magazine writer; co-starred with Kathleen Turner and Burt Reynolds in *Switching Channels* (1988); starred as Basil Ransome in the Merchant-Ivory production *The Bostonians* (1984); had the supporting role of Lewis in another esteemed Merchant-Ivory period drama, *The Remains of the Day* (1993); included among his other film credits the title roles in *Monsignor* (1982) and *The Aviator* (1985), the dual role of Frederick Dallas/Philip Brent in *Noises Off* (1992), and roles in a number of made-for-television movies, including Major John Dodge in *Great Escape II* (1988), Father Thomas Cusack in *Mortal Sins* (1992), Will Parker in *Morning Glory* (1993) and Alan Johnson in three *Black Fox* Westerns (1995); was a tall (six-foot four-inch) and athletic man whose recreational activities included skiing, sailplaning, and piloting airplanes in addition to horseback competition; ironically, in his last motion-picture role before his life-changing equestrian accident, starred as Dempsey Cain, a police detective who is paralyzed and confined to a wheelchair for life after being shot by a drug dealer; after his own accident, acted (chiefly with his face alone) the lead in a made-for-TV remake of *Rear Window* (ABC, 1998); won a Screen Actors Guild Award for that performance; for cable television, directed *In the Gloaming* (HBO, 1997), a drama about a young man dying of AIDS and those around him, including his mother (played by Glenn Close); also for cable, directed *The Brooke Ellison Story*, the real-life story of a girl stricken with quadriplegia at 11, who goes on to graduate from Harvard; in a speech at the 1996 Democratic National Convention, urged greater funding for medical research; with his wife, the actress and singer Dana (Morosi) Reeve, in 2002 founded in Short Hills, New Jersey, the Christopher and Dana Reeve Paralysis Resource Center, which houses the largest American collection of paralysis-related publications and is devoted to teaching paralyzed people to live with as much independence as possible; wrote two autobiographical books: *Still Me* (1998) and *Nothing Is Impossible* (2002); lived in Pound Ridge, New York; died in Northern Westches-

ter Hospital in Mount Kisko, New York, of a systemic infection stemming from pressure sores; in addition to other relatives, was survived by his wife, Dana, their son, Will, and his son, Matthew, and daughter, Alexandra, from a previous relationship, with Gae Exton. See *Current Biography* (1982).

Obituary *New York Times* A p1+ Oct. 12, 2004

REHNQUIST, WILLIAM H. Oct. 1, 1924–Sep. 3, 2005 Jurist; a juridical originalist and minimalist; the 16th chief justice of the United States (1986–2005); as such, presided over the U.S. Supreme Court, on which he had sat as an associate justice since 1972; quietly, gradually, with judicial restraint, led the court away from the activist liberal legacy bequeathed under Chief Justice Earl Warren (1953–69) and into a conservative ascendancy that carried with it a reaffirmation of states' rights in the American system of "dual federalism"; pursued the strict-constructionist implementation of James Madison's declaration that the U.S. Constitution was meant to delegate to the federal government certain enumerated powers, "few and defined," while leaving to the state governments "numerous and indefinite" powers; was named to the Supreme Court as an associate justice by President Richard M. Nixon, a Republican, and elevated to the position of chief justice by nomination of President Ronald Reagan, also a Republican; was himself a Republican in the tradition of Robert A. Taft and Barry Goldwater; was formatively and strongly influenced by his reading of the economist Friedrich Hayek's classic *The Road to Serfdom*; in the words of Nina Totenberg of National Public Radio, summing up his career, "went from being a lone conservative dissenter in his early days to a builder of conservative consensus as chief justice. In his last two terms as chief justice, however, the conservative bulwark that he had worked so hard to build has faced challenges on critical issues, ranging from affirmative action and gay rights to national security. Those cases followed an illustrious career for a justice who gained the respect of fellow justices of all ideologies, many of whom regarded him as a fair and efficient administrator of the court"; after service with the U.S. Army Air Forces in World War II—in part as a weather observer in North Africa—earned degrees in political science at Stanford University and Harvard University and an LL.B. degree at Stanford's law school, where he graduated first in his class; clerked at the Supreme Court for Justice Robert H. Jackson for 18 months in 1952 and 1953; practiced law in Phoenix, Arizona, from 1953 to 1969; during that time, became active in Republican Party politics; in 1964, served as a legal adviser in Barry Goldwater's presidential campaign; in 1969, joined the administration of President Nixon as assistant attorney general in charge of the office of legal counsel in the Department of Justice; in that position, promoted tough law-and-order policies; held the position until he was named to the Supreme Court; signaled his future trajectory on the court with his dissent in the *Roe v. Wade* case legalizing abortion nationwide in 1973; followed that up with votes in favor of leaving abortion law to the discretion of the states; voted against further government involvement in school desegregation and affirmative action; wrote the majority 5-to-4 opinion in *U.S. v. Lopez* (1995), which ruled that Congress, in attempting to regulate intrastate noncommercial activity (possession of firearms near local schools in that instance), exceeded its power to regulate interstate commercial activity under Article I, Section 8, Clause 3 of the Constitution; also wrote the majority 5-to-4 opinion in *Zelman v. Simmons-Harris* (2002), which approved a school-voucher plan that did not exclude parochial schools; in 2000, voted with the 5-to-4 majority in the controversial *Bush v. Gore* decision, which brought to an end the prolonged manual presidential vote recount in Florida and thus was perceived by some as deciding or helping to decide the winner of the election; in criminal law, voted in favor of police searches and seizures, the introduction of search results in trials, and wider police immunity from lawsuits; in and out of court, contributed to the removal of procedural obstacles blocking states from carrying out the death penalty; on the other hand, disappointed some of his law-and-order allies by voting for the upholding of Miranda rights in *Dickerson v. U.S.* (2000); disappointed libertarians with his votes against individual rights, such as in cases in which he sided with copyright and patent holdings; as chief justice, created a unique chevron for his black judicial robe, consisting of four golden bars on each sleeve; presided over the impeachment trial of President Bill Clinton in 1999; wrote the books *The Supreme Court: How It Was, How It Is* (1987), *Grand Inquest: The Historic Impeachments of Justice Samuel Chase and President Andrew Johnson* (1992), *All the Laws But One: Civil Liberties in Wartime* (1998), and *Centennial Crisis: The Disputed Election of 1876* (2004); died at his home in Arlington, Virginia; was predeceased by his wife, Nan, and survived by his three adult children. See *Current Biography* (2003).

Obituary *New York Times* p38 Sep. 4, 2005, A p16 Sep. 5, 2005

ROBINSON, ARTHUR H. Jan. 5, 1915–Oct. 10, 2004 Cartographer; geographer; professor emeritus, University of Wisconsin at Madison; the dean of American mapmakers; helped to establish cartography as a recognized academic discipline; designed the Robinson Projection, a truer flat-surface representation of Earth than the Mercator map that had been in use since the 16th century and the later projection designed by Alphons J. Van der Grinten; after receiving his B.A. degree at Miami University, in Oxford, Ohio, earned advanced degrees in geography at the University of Wisconsin and Ohio State University; during World War II, was chief of the map division of the U.S. Office of Strategic Services, the predecessor of the Central Intelligence Agency; in that position, oversaw the creation of some 5,000 maps of strategic or tactical importance in Allied military operations; immediately after the war, joined the University of Wisconsin's Department of Geography; was the driving force behind the establishment of the department's Cartographic Laboratory, a world-class research center, and its outstanding cartographic library, now known as the Arthur H. Robinson Library; remained an adviser to the library after his retirement, in 1980; early in his career, contributed

maps to geography book series published by Scott, Foresman and Co., Macmillan, and Harvard University Press (the American Foreign Policy Library series); published his first book, *The Look of Maps: An Examination of Cartographic Design*, in 1952; the following year, published the first edition of his *Elements of Cartography*, which became the most widely used textbook in the field; later wrote *Early Thematic Mapping in the History of Cartography* (1982); co-wrote books on the physical and cultural elements of geography, the fidelity of isopleth maps, and the influence of pattern on the perception of dot area symbols in cartography; on commission by the Rand McNally Co. in 1963, designed his innovative world map, a pseudo-cylindrical projection in which he worked out compromises between distortions in areas and distances to achieve a relatively natural visualization; explained: "The projection is kind of like a work of art. I was trying to get the best visual representation of the round Earth, to make it look as though it was rounded, with the best shapes and least distortion of area"; made the outline of his map nearly oval in order to suggest Earth's roundness; enjoyed such successes as having Rand McNally immediately begin using the Robinson Projection in its educational maps and in the *Rand McNally International Atlas*, having the projection gain wide acceptance by the Pentagon and other government agencies as well as the private sector, and seeing the National Geographic Society, the standard-setter in the field, use it in its world maps from 1988 to 1998, when it replaced it with the Winkel Tripel Projection; died in Madison, Wisconsin; was predeceased by his first wife, Elizabeth, and survived by his second wife, Martha, and several progeny. See *Current Biography* (1996).

Obituary *New York Times* B p9 Nov. 15, 2004

ROCHBERG, GEORGE July 5, 1918–May 29, 2005 Composer; pianist; the first postmodernist among American classical composers; an erstwhile leading exponent of serialism who, beginning in the mid-1960s, became the foremost apostate from the constricting hegemony of that rigidly 12-tone school of composition; while venomously derided by many of his former modernist colleagues for what they regarded as his backsliding to Romanticism and his "polystylistic machinations," earned the gratitude of a new generation and a posterity of composers by leading the liberation of their craft from the stranglehold of the dodecaphonic idiom and opening it to a range of musical languages (not excluding atonalism itself, it is important to note); in explaining his apostasy, said, "I saw that [exclusive] twelve-tone composition was another form of minimalism, a spiritual and psychological starvation. You reduce your palette, your scope, your variety. In the last fifty years we learned how not to be open or direct or simple. We hid behind complexity, what I call 'fancy footwork.' We were afraid that beneath the complexities there was nothing. Anyway, I was a singer. And serialism doesn't permit melody"; as a history major, worked his way through Montclair (New Jersey) State Teachers College by teaching piano and playing in jazz bands; subsequently, studied at the Mannes School (now College) of Music in New York City;

as a U.S. Army lieutenant in World War II, was seriously wounded at Normandy; after the war, earned a B.A. degree in music at the Curtis Institute of Music in Philadelphia and an M.A. degree in music at the University of Pennsylvania; later, studied at the American Academy in Rome; first attracted the attention of the music establishment with his impressionistic symphonic poem *Night Music* (1948), which became the second movement in the original version of his First Symphony (1949), a work showing the influence of Bartók, Stravinsky, and Hindemith; in the early 1950s, surrendered to the influence of Arnold Schoenberg, the inventor of the 12-tone system of musical composition, and of the dodecaphonic composer Luigi Dallapiccola; suppressing his natural lyricism and emotional vigor, began to compose in an atonal style; perfected his serial technique in such works as Chamber Symphony for nine instruments (1953), Second Symphony (1955–56), and Cheltenham Concerto for solo winds and string orchestra (1958); wrote the piano piece Twelve Bagatelles (1952), which was later adapted for full orchestra and renamed *Zodiac* (1964); with the death of his son, Paul, in 1964—widely viewed as a watershed in his career—began his apostasy from serialism; for a year following Paul's death, was unable to compose; upon returning to composition with *Contra Mortem et Tempus* (1965), found the atonal idiom inadequate for the expression of his bereavement; in violation of the modernist prohibition against any links with tradition or with "historical tonality," created such collages as the orchestral piece *Music for the Magic Theater* (1965) and the Third Symphony (1966-69), filling the latter with allusions to Schutz, Bach, Mahler, and Ives and the former with references to Mozart, Mahler, and Beethoven; in his String Quartet no. 3 (1972), simulated the styles of Beethoven, Brahms, Mahler, and Bartók; achieved his most resounding critical and popular success with the richly tonal Concerto for Violin and Orchestra (1975); demonstrated with his powerful Fifth Symphony (1984–85)—in which he combined explosions of atonality with tonal echoes of Stravinsky and Mahler—the fact that he had rejected exclusive dodecaphonism, not the option of using serialism simultaneously with other musical idioms; included flute-like bird calls in his melodic piece *To the Dark Wood* (1985); recruited his wife, Gene, to write the text for his *Phaedra* (1973–74), a monodrama for mezzo-soprano and orchestra, and the libretto for his opera *The Confidence Man* (1982); showed his interest in Japanese forms in *Ukiyo-e* (1995), a short piece for solo harp; left a catalogue of almost 100 works, including six symphonies, seven string quartets, several song cycles, and a concerto for oboe and another for clarinet; was music editor with the Thomas Presser Co., the music publishing house, from 1951 to 1960; taught at the Curtis Institute of Music from 1949 to 1954 and at the University of Pennsylvania from 1960 to 1983; headed the Music Department at the latter school from 1960 to 1968; was composer-in-residence at several music festivals; published *The Aesthetics of Survival: A Composer's View of Twentieth-Century Music* (1984), a collection of his essays edited by William Bolcom; at the time of his death, had been working on two books, an autobiography and a theoretical examina-

tion of chromaticism; lived in Newtown Square, Pennsylvania; died in Bryn Mawr Hospital in Bryn Mawr, Pennsylvania; was survived by his wife, Gene, and his daughter, Francesca. See *Current Biography* (1985).

Obituary *New York Times* B p9 June 1, 2005

RODINO, PETER W. June 7, 1909–May 7, 2005 Democratic U.S. representative from New Jersey (1949–89); lawyer; was the son of a blue-collar Italian immigrant father; spent 10 years working his way through the University of Newark and the New Jersey Law School (now the Rutgers School of Law, Newark); entered general law practice with the firm of Metro & Rodino in Newark in 1938; after combat service as an officer in the U.S. Army in World War II, ran for Congress unsuccessfully in 1946 from New Jersey's 10th Congressional District, where his base was Newark's then predominantly Italian-American North Ward; two years later, was elected to his first two-year term in the U.S. House of Representatives; was reelected 19 times in succession thereafter; in Congress, established a staunchly liberal record; was a champion of organized labor, civil rights, immigration reform, and fair housing; as a member of the House Judiciary Committee, wrote that committee's majority reports laying the groundwork for the civil rights bills of 1957, 1960, 1964, and 1968; also as a member of the committee, became expert in bankruptcy law; was instrumental in the House passage of the 1965 act doing away with quotas favoring immigration from Western Europe and of the 1966 fair-housing act as well as the declaration in 1968 of Columbus Day as a federal holiday to be celebrated on the second Monday in October; became chairman of the Judiciary Committee during the 93d Congress (1972–74); remained chairman of the committee through the rest of his tenure in Congress; gained national prominence in 1974, when, as chairman of the Judiciary Committee, he presided over the impeachment hearings of President Richard M. Nixon; co-sponsored the Immigration Reform and Control Act of 1986, also known as the Simpson-Rodino Act, which, signed into law by President Ronald Reagan, granted amnesty to millions of illegal aliens; helped to stifle proposals for constitutional amendments for prayer in schools and against abortion on demand and busing for the purpose of school integration; was one of the managers appointed by the House to conduct the impeachment hearings against Harry E. Claiborne, judge of the U.S. District Court for Nevada, in 1986 and those against Alcee Lamar Hastings, judge of the U.S. District Court for the Southern District of Florida, in 1988; chose not to run for reelection in 1988; after leaving Washington, joined his son's law firm in East Hanover, New Jersey, and taught at Seton Hall Law School,in Newark; died at his home in West Orange, New Jersey; was predeceased by his first wife, Marianna; was survived by his second wife, Joy, his daughter, his son, and several grandchildren and great-grandchildren. See *Current Biography* (1954).

Obituary *New York Times* I p30 May 8, 2005

ROTHSCHILD, MIRIAM Aug. 5, 1908–Jan. 20, 2005 British naturalist; a self-trained generalist who in some of her achievements surpassed even professional specialists in scientific fields ranging from entomology and parasitology to organic horticulture; fit her own description of George John Romanes, Darwin's protégé: "the epitome of . . . a certain type which has long since disappeared—the amateur scientist, the philosophical naturalist . . . who set up his own laboratory at home and devoted his life to an enthusiastic . . . quest for the truth"; was the world's leading authority on fleas; made groundbreaking discoveries regarding the plant-derived defense poisons of insects, especially in her research on butterflies (done in collaboration with Tadeus Reichstein); seeing the relationship of parasites to their hosts and of animals to plant life, was a pioneer in developing and promoting today's ecological, web-of-life approach to nature conservation; in her 90-acre garden at Aston Wold, the 1,000-plus-acre Rothschild estate in Polebrook near Oundle and Peterborough in Northamptonshire, cultivated a wildflower garden symbolizing, as she said, "the new sympathy with wildlife" (which included, at Aston Wold, such animals as rabbits, foxes, and hedgehogs); promoted a national movement for replacing lawns as well as desiccated landscapes with wildflower meadows; collected, propagated, and sold wildflower seeds; was the granddaughter of Nathan Meyer Rothschild, the first Lord Rothschild, the namesake of the founder of the British line of Rothschilds and the first observant Jew to be given peerage; was born at Aston Wold; from childhood, was inspired by the zoological work of her father, Nathaniel Charles Rothschild, a banker whose leisure time was spent gathering the world's largest collection of slide-mounted flea specimens, 30,000 in all, now in the possession of the British Natural History Museum; after her father's death, when she was 15, came under the influence of her uncle Lionel Walter Rothschild, the second Lord Rothschild, who was also a prodigious zoologist, the creator of a private zoological museum at Tring Park in Herefordshire; saw a total of 275 plant and animal genera and species named in her honor or that of her father or uncle; in the late 1920s, studied marine life in Naples, Italy; in the early 1930s, researched the bivalve Nucula and its parasites at the Marine Biological Station in Plymouth, England; later in the 1930s, concentrated on raising and studying gulls and other birds and bird parasites in her aviary at Aston Wold; after her uncle's death, edited *Novitates Zoologicae*, the Tring museum journal (1938–41); at different times during World War II, did research with wood pigeons for the Ministry of Agriculture and was a member of the large, diverse team assigned to the secret British military intelligence code-breaking project at Bletchley Park, Buckinghamshire; before, during, and after the war, strove, often in vain, to facilitate the influx into Britain of Jewish refugees from continental Europe; in the postwar years, continued her work on the biology of fleas and other parasites; spent decades cataloging—in collaboration with Harry Hopkins (not to be confused with the American public official)—her father's collection of slide-mounted flea specimens; published *An Illustrated Catalogue of the Rothschild Collection of Fleas (Siphonaptera) in the British Mu-* seum (Natural History), With Keys and Short Descriptions for the Identification of Families, Genera, Species, and Subspecies in six volumes between 1953 and 1983 and another edition in 1987; wrote or co-wrote, among other books, *Fleas, Flukes and Cuckoos* (1952), *Animals and Man* (1986), *The Butterfly Gardener* (1983), A *Color Atlas of Insect Tissue via the Flea* (1986), *Butterfly Cooing Like a Dove* (1991), *The Rothschild Gardens* (1996), and *Rothschild's Reserves, Time and Fragile Nature* (1997); wrote the memoir *Dear Lord Rothschild: Birds, Butterflies and History* (1983), essentially a biography of her uncle Lionel Walter Rothschild; in 1996 opened the National Dragonfly Museum at Aston Wold; won numerous awards for her research in entomology and parasitology and for the livestock she raised on her farm at Aston Wold as well as the plants she cultivated there; was named a Commander of the British Empire in 1982 and a Dame of the British Empire in 2000; from a 14-year marriage that was dissolved in 1957, had six children, two of whom were adopted; was predeceased by a son and a daughter and survived by a son and three daughters; died at Aston Wold. See *Current Biography* (1992).

Obituary *New York Times* C p17 Jan. 25, 2005

SAGAN, FRANCOISE June 21, 1935–Sep. 24, 2004 French author; in an exquisite classical French style, austere and epigrammatic, wrote eccentric romantic novels in which, typically, affluent characters (sometimes a young woman coupled with a father figure), occupationally idle and morally and philosophically vacuous, escape existentialist ennui in tenuous, often uncommitted love; in 1954, as a precocious 19-year-old, published the first of her small novels (close to novelettes in length), the phenomenal best-seller *Bonjour Tristesse* (translated into English with the same title, 1955), a wistful, tragic tale internationally viewed as the clarion testament of a cynical generation of French youth; soon came to be viewed as the leading exponent of the French incarnation of the Beat Generation; later tempered her "recounting [of] the rotting of a generation" (the phrasing of the writer of the entry on her in *Les Autuers de la Littérature Française* with touches of ironic humor and moral consciousness; the surname Sagan was a pseudonym; was born Françoise Quoirez into a prosperous bourgeois family in Cajarc, France; after attending convent schools in Paris, entered the University of Paris in 1952, when she was 17; spending her time partying and frequenting Latin Quarter cafés and cellars, listening to jazz and discussing Existentialist philosophy, skipped lectures at the Sorbonne and neglected her studies; during that period, began thinking about and making notes for what would become her first novel; when she failed her second-year examinations at the Sorbonne, in June 1953, began writing that novel, in part to placate her family for her academic failure; spent only one month finishing the novel, a story told from the point of view of Cecile, an amoral, sexually active 18-year old woman who lives relatively happily with her father, a philandering widower, tolerating his successive lovers as long as they do not seriously compete with her for his affection and thwarting his plan to remarry, driving his fiancée to suicide in the process; saw the book, published in 1954, enjoy not only critical and commercial success—within four years, it sold more than 800,000 copies in France, more than a million in the U.S., and was translated into 20 languages—but also a succès de scandale, which puzzled her until, years later, she came to understand that, at the time, "it was unconceivable that a young girl of seventeen or eighteen should make love without being in love with a boy of her own age and not be punished for it" and unheard of as well that a daughter "should know about her father's love affairs, discuss them with him, and thereby reach a kind of complicity with him on subjects that had until then been taboo between parents and children"; was unhappy with Otto Preminger's screen version of Bonjour Tristesse (1958); dealt with a love affair between a 20-year-old Sorbonne student and a married man twice her age in her second novel, Un Certain Sourire (1956; A Certain Smile, 1956), which sold 450,000 copies in France within a year and a half; traced transitory love affairs involving nine characters in Dans un mois, dans un an (1957; Those Without Shadows, 1957) and wrote of a love triangle in Aimez-vous Brahms? (1959; English translation under the same title, 1960; Ingmar Bergman's screen version was Goodbye Again, 1961); later wrote, among other novels, Les merveilleux nuages (1961; The Wonderful Clouds, 1962), La chamade (1966; Chamade, 1967), Le garde du coeur (1968; The Heart-Keeper, 1968), Un peu de soleil dans l'eau froide (1969; A Few Hours of Sunlight, 1971) Des bleus a l'ame (1972; Scars on the Soul, 1974), Des yeux de soie (1976; Silken Eyes, 1977), Le lit défait (1977; The Unmade Bed, 1978), Un orage immobile (1983; The Still Storm, 1986); and Un sang d'aquarelle (1987; Painting in Blood, 1988); dealt with life changes brought with illness in the novel Un chagrin de passage (1994; A Fleeting Sorrow, 1995); directed the film version of her novel Les fougères bleues, released in 1977; published a number of books of nonfiction, including the autobiography Réponses (1974; translated under same title, 1979), a collection of interviews, and two books devoted to personal reflections and memories of people she had known; wrote, among other plays, Châeau en Suède, La robe mauve de Valentine, Un piano dans l'herbe, and Il fait beau jour et nuit; for some years was written about in the international tabloid press because of a lifestyle that included high-stakes gambling, alcohol consumption, and driving fast sports cars; in 1957, barely survived the skull fracture and other injuries she suffered in a single-vehicle automobile accident; emerged from that experience with an addiction to morphine; was fined for breaching narcotic laws twice, in 1990 and 1995; was married and divorced twice; by the second marriage, had a son, Denis; died in Honfleur, France. See Current Biography (1960).

Obituary New York Times Sep. 25, 2004

SALINGER, PIERRE June 14, 1925–Oct. 16, 2004 Bilingual journalist; President John F. Kennedy's press secretary; U.S. senator (1964–65); was for many years an international correspondent with the ABC television network, based chiefly in Paris, France; was born in San Francisco to a Jewish American father and a Catholic French mother; grew up in a home where French was his first language; was decorated for service with the U.S. Navy in World War II; while earning a degree in history at the University of San Francisco after the war, worked nights as a cub reporter with the San Francisco Chronicle; became a full-time reporter in 1947; later, was promoted to night editor; with the Chronicle, gained prominence as a muckraking investigative reporter; at the same time, was active in Democratic Party politics; was press director and speech writer in the California campaigns of presidential candidate Adlai Stevenson in 1952 and 1956; left the Chronicle to become the West Coast editor of the weekly Collier's in 1955; for Collier's, wrote an exposé of corruption and racketeering in the teamsters union under the presidency of Dave Beck, headquartered in Seattle, Washington, including financial malfeasance and collusion with criminal elements to subvert and corrupt law enforcement; the magazine ceased publication before the article could be published, but it came to the attention of Robert F. Kennedy, who was at that time a U.S. Senate counsel; in 1957, when a Senate select labor-racketeering committee was formed with Kennedy as its chief counsel, was hired as a staff investigator; as such, contributed to hearings that led to the conviction and imprisonment of Beck; through his work with the Senate rackets committee, met Senator John F. Kennedy, Robert's older brother; joined John F. Kennedy's presidential campaign in 1960 and became White House press secretary when Kennedy took office, in January 1961; following the assassination of President Kennedy, in November 1963, reluctantly stayed on as President Lyndon B. Johnson's press secretary until March 1964; when U.S. senator Clair Engle of California died, the following summer, was appointed by California governor Edmund G. "Pat" Brown to complete the last few months of Engle's term; ran for a Senate term in his own right in November 1964; lost to the Republican candidate, George Murphy; spent the next three years working in the private sector, as a vice president of the National General Corp. and Continental Airlines, sucessively; left Continental Airlines in January 1968 to work in Robert F. Kennedy's campaign for the presidency; traumatized by Robert's assassination (which he witnessed), in June 1968, moved to Paris, France, as director of European operations with the Great America Management and Research Co.; returned briefly to the U.S. to work in George S. McGovern's unsuccessful presidential campaign in 1972; back in Paris, was hired by the popular newsweekly L'Express to write a column reporting on and interpreting the American scene; soon became a frequent presence on French radio and television; became the "American in Paris," more readily recognizable in France than he was in the U.S.; began working for the ABC television network in 1976; became a full-time European correspondent for ABC News in 1978 and head of ABC's Paris bureau in 1979; played a crucial behind-the-scenes role in arranging the negotiations that led to the release of 66 Americans held hostage in the U.S. embassy in Tehran, Iran, in January 1981; told the inside story of the hostage crisis and its resolution in the award-winning, three-hour ABC documentary America Held Hostage: The Secret Negotiations (1981) and a book of the same title (1981); as ABC

News's chief foreign correspondent from 1983 to 1993, spent much of his time in London as well as Paris; damaged his reputation by subscribing to the spurious theory, circulated on the Internet, that the crash of TWA Flight 600 airliner off the coast of Long Island, New York, in July 1996 was caused by a stray U.S. Navy test missile; had earlier floated an imaginative theory connecting the destruction of Pan American Flight 103 by a terrorist bomb over Lockerbie, Scotland, in 1988 to a U.S. Drug Enforcement Agency sting gone wrong; from 1993 to 1998, was a consultant with Bjurson-Marsteller, a communications consulting firm; after living in the U.S. for several years, resumed residence in France in protest against George W. Bush's becoming president pursuant to the election of 2000; wrote, among other books, the autobiographical volumes *With Kennedy* (1966), *Je suis un Americain* (I Am an American, 1975) and *P.S.: A Memoir* (1995), the novel *On Instructions of My Government* (1971), based on the Cuban missile crisis, and *Guerre du Golfe: le dossier secret* (1991; translated as *Secret Dossier: The Hidden Agenda Behind the Gulf War*, 1991); was married four times and divorced thrice; died in a hospital a few miles from his home in Le Thor, near Avignon, France, and was buried in Arlington National Cemetary; was survived by his French wife, Nicole, and two sons. See *Current Biography* (1987).

Obituary *New York Times* B p7 Oct. 18, 2004

SCHELL, MARIA Jan. 15, 1926–Apr. 26, 2005 Austrian-born actress; "one of the very few stars of postwar German-speaking cinema who had a lasting impact on the international film scene," as the Austrian film critic Alexander Horwath has observed; from early typecasting as a beautiful "blond angel" from the Alps, graduated to the emotionally intense, often lachrymose roles that typified her prime; was born in Vienna to a Swiss playwright father and a French-Austrian actress mother; with her parents and siblings (including her younger brother Maximilian, an actor), fled to Zurich, Switzerland, when Hitler's forces began occupying Austria in 1938; became a Swiss citizen; when she was 16, made her screen debut as Meiti in the Swiss film *Der Steinbruch* (1942); from 1946 to 1948, performed in repertory with the State Theater of Bern; later made appearances in the legitimate theater including a European tour opposite Albert Bassermann in a production of Goethe's *Faust*; with her portrayal of Selma in the Austrian film *Der Engel mit der Posaune* ("The Angel with the Trumpet," 1948), came to the attention of British filmmakers; made her debut in English-language pictures in the British remake, *The Angel with the Trumpet* (1950); under British producers and directors, was subsequently cast as Helena Friese-Greene in *The Magic Box* (1951), as Nicole in *So Little Time* (1952), and as Helen Rolt, the mistress of the protagonist in *The Heart of the Matter* (1953); in 1954, won the best-actress award at the Cannes Film Festival for her performance as Helga Reinbeck in *Die Letzte Brücke* ("The Last Bridge"); in 1956, won the Venice Festival prize for her portrayal of the title role of the long-suffering laundrywoman in René Clément's *Gervaise* (1956); played a woman suffering the absence of her lover and awaiting his return in Luchino

Visconti's *La Notti bianchi* (1957) and a wife trying to cope with her husband's infidelities in Alexandre Astruc's *Une Vie* (1958); made her Hollywood debut in an uncommonly extroverted portrayal of the lusty Grushenka in *The Brothers Karamazov* (1958), a role that had been sought by Marilyn Monroe; cited as her favorite among her roles that of Elizabeth Mahler in *The Hanging Tree* (1959); while still in Hollywood, starred opposite Glenn Ford in *Cimarron* (1960); in Britain, was cast as Ruth Leighton in *The Mark* (1963); following a tentative retirement of a half-dozen years, beginning in 1963, returned to the screen in character roles; accrued a total of more than 80 credits in motion pictures (including Frau Miller in *The Odessa File* and Mrs. Hauser in *Voyage of the Damned*) and on television (including Mrs. Speer in *Inside the Third Reich*); made her final public appearance at the premiere in February 2002 of the film *Meine Schwester Maria* (*My Sister Maria*), a poignant 90-minute documentary about her life produced, directed, and narrated by her brother Maximilian; was married and divorced twice; died in Preitenegg, Austria; was survived by a son and a daughter. See *Current Biography* (1961).

Obituary *New York Times* C p18 Apr. 28, 2005

SCHLEIN, MIRIAM June 6, 1926–Nov. 23, 2004 Author; wrote books for young and very young children that educated them entertainingly, in terms understandable to them, about such subjects as the concepts of space, time, weight, speed, and measure and, especially, the wide variety of life in the animal kingdom; after earning a degree in English and psychology at Brooklyn College, worked successively as secretary to a magazine publisher, assistant in a radio "continuity" department, writer of advertising copy, and secretary to a juvenile-book editor; began publishing her books in 1951; wrote almost 100 of them, including *Shapes* (1952), *Fast Is Not a Ladybug* (1953), *Heavy Is a Hippopotamus* (1954), *City Boy, Country Boy* (1955), *It's About Time* (1955), *The Bumblebee's Secret* (1958), *The Fisherman's Day* (1959), *The Way Mother's Are* (1963), *What's Wrong with Being a Skunk?* (1974), *Lucky Porcupine* (1980), *Billions of Bats* (1982), *The Dangerous Life of the Sea Horse* (1986), *I Sailed with Columbus* (1991), and *The Puzzle of the Dinosaurs* (1996); wrote three books that were named Junior Literary Guild selections: *The Four Little Foxes* (1953), *Elephant Herd* (1954), and *Amazing Mr. Pelgrew* (1957); wrote the Caldecott Medal winner *When Will the World Be Mine?*, first published in 1953, which earned the award when it was republished 20 years later; in one of her last books, *Hello, Hello!* (2002), wrote about the special ways in which different animal species—from lions and zebras to wolves and penguins—communicate with their kind; lived and died in New York City. See *Current Biography* (1959).

Obituary *New York Times* C p10 Dec. 2, 2004

SCHOLDER, FRITZ Oct. 6, 1937–Feb. 10, 2005 Painter; sculptor; according to Arizona Commission on the Arts (on-line), "blew open the doors of 'acceptable' Indian imagery, resulting in a furor that launched the New Indian Art Movement"; genetically, was three-quarters European and one-quarter

American Indian (the Southern California Luiseno tribe); was the son of a school administrator employed by the U.S. Bureau of Indian Affairs; in public high school in Pierre, South Dakota, took an art class with Oscar Howe, a noted Sioux painter who incorporated Cubism in his work; studied under Arthur Kruk, James Grittner, and Michael Gorski at the Wisconsin State University and, later, with the pop artist Wayne Thiebaud at Sacramento City College, in California, where he earned a B.A. degree in 1960; had his first show, organized with Thiebaud's help, in 1958; participated in the Rockefeller Indian Art Project at the University of Arizona in 1961; received an MFA at the University of Arizona in 1964; taught painting and art history at the Institute of American Indian Arts in Santa Fe, New Mexico, from 1964 to 1969; toured Europe and Africa in 1969; traveling under U.S. State Department auspices in the 1970, researched the vampire legend in Transylvania and made his first visit to Egypt; from the 1970s on, worked in his compound in Scottsdale, Arizona, in a studio standing separate form his adobe house; confined his teaching activities to "artist in residence" status at California universities, Dartmouth College, and the Oklahoma Summer Art Institute, among other schools; died in Phoenix, Arizona; was survived by his third wife, Lisa, a son and a grandson. See *Current Biography* (1985).

Obituary *New York Times* A p19 Feb. 14, 2004

SCHRIEVER, BERNARD Sep. 14, 1910–June 20, 2005 U.S. Air Force four-star general, retired; aeronautical engineer; a founding father of the air force's aerospace program, which began in the military context of the Cold War with the Soviet Union; as the general in charge of the Ballistic Missile Division of the Air Research and Development Command (ARDC) for 12 years in the 1950s and 1960s, oversaw the research, development, and production of the Atlas, Titan, Thor, and Minuteman intercontinental ballistic missiles; concurrently, was responsible for providing the launching sites, tracking facilities, and ground-support equipment necessary for those projects; was born in Bremen, Germany, to a German mother and father (an engineer with a German steamship line who was interned in the U.S. when the U.S. entered World War I, in 1917); after the war, with his family, joined the father in the German-American community of New Braunfels, Texas; became a naturalized U.S. citizen in 1923; received a B.S. degree in engineering at the Agricultural and Mechanical College of Texas (Texas A&M) in 1931; later, earned a master's degree in mechanical engineering at Stanford University; entering the Army Air Corps Reserve, won his pilot's wings in 1933; during World War II, advanced up the ranks from bomber pilot in the Pacific to commander of Advanced Headquarters, Far East Service Command; after the war, when the air force became a separate service, was assigned to the Pentagon; assumed command of ARDC's Ballistic Missile Division (then called the Western Development Division) in 1954; retired in 1966; after his retirement, worked as an industry consultant; was survived by his second wife, the singer Joni James, a son and two daughters from

his first marriage, and 11 grandchildren. See *Current Biography* (1957).

Obituary *New York Times* A p21 June 24, 2005

SCOTT, GEORGE Mar. 18, 1929–Mar. 9, 2005 Gospel singer; guitarist; a founding member of the famous Blind Boys of Alabama, a gospel group (ranging from quartet to septet over the years) composed of singers nearly all of whom have been at least legally blind; was totally blind from the time of his birth, in Notasulga, Alabama; learned Braille and received vocational training at the Talladega (Alabama) Institute for the Deaf and Blind; in the institute's glee club, sang alongside Clarence Fountain, Johnny Fields, and J. T. Sutton (the only one with sight), originally under the direction of Velma B. Taylor; in the late 1930s, along with Fountain, Fields, and Sutton, formed the Happyland Jubilee Singers, adding Olice Thomas soon afterward; later, with the other band members, inducted the Reverend Paul Exkano to replace Thomas after the latter died of an accidental gunshot; in late 1940s, began touring with the Happyland Jubilee Singers; in 1948, with the group, made such recordings as "Stand by Me" and "I Can See Everybody's Mother but I Can't See Mine"; at about that that time, joined with his bandmates to change their name to the Blind Boys of Georgia, in emulation of the Blind Boys of Mississippi; along with his bandmates, engaged in an epic rivalry with the Blind Boys of Mississippi; lived through personnel changes, including, in 1951, Exkano's replacement by Percell Perkins, a former Mississippi Blind Boy, and Perkins's replacement by Joe Watson, and Watson's replacement by Jimmy Carter, another former Mississippi Blind Boy; during the 1950s, made 11 LPs with the Blind Boys of Alabama, who, because they refused to follow the lead of gospel singers like Sam Cooke in compromising with the secular music industry, had little mainstream success until they performed in the musical *Gospel in Colonus* Off-Broadway in 1983 and subsequently on Broadway; thereafter, saw their popularity soar on the blues and folk touring circuits as well as in gospel's amen quarters; shared in the group's worldwide acclaim, triggered by the release of their album *Brought Him with Me* (1995), recorded live during three nights at the House of Blues in Hollywood; contributed to the band's crossover recordings *Holdin' On* (1997) and *Spirit of the Century* (2001); continued to tour internationally, along with longtime and new, younger members; died at his home in Durham, North Carolina. See *Current Biography* (2001).

Obituary *New York Times* C p11 Mar. 12, 2005

SHAW, ARTIE May 23, 1910–Dec. 30, 2004 Clarinetist; bandleader; composer; arranger; author; a great, albeit neurotic and erratic, rebel of the swing era; shared with Benny Goodman the claim to preeminence among the white big-band leaders of that era; broke the color line in swing music by including such black artists as the singer Billie Holiday and the trumpeter Roy Eldridge in his bands; was born Arthur Jacob Arshawsky; from the beginning, was torn between music and writing; as a musician, was grounded in jazz; when still a teenager, began playing with the bands of Jimmy Cavallaro and Austin

Whylie, among others; was also a sideman with recording-studio and radio-network orchestras; made his debut as an ensemble leader conducting a hastily assembled jazz chamber combo in a performance of his "Interlude in B Flat" at the Imperial Theater in New York City in May 1935; soon afterward, formed his first band, essentially an enlargement of the chamber ensemble, heavy on strings; in March 1937, began touring major ballrooms with his first full big band, a 14-piece contingent, playing swing arrangements of the music of such composers as Jerome Kern and Richard Rodgers as well as his own compositions; shot to stardom in the autumn of 1938, when his recording of Cole Porter's "Begin the Beguine" became a smash hit; two years later, formed a 31-piece studio band with which he recorded the hit "Frenesi" (1940); also recorded his Concerto for Clarinet and such hits as "Deep Purple," "I Cover the Waterfront," "Nightmare," and "Stardust" (widely regarded as the greatest clarinet solo of all time); meanwhile, toured with a band that included within itself the jazz quintet known as the Gramercy Five; appeared with his band in several movies; in the U.S. Navy during World War II, organized and led a service band, with which he performed under hazardous conditions in the South Pacific for 18 months; in the late 1940s and early 1950s, formed a succession of bands, including one influenced by bop music; in one of his several retreats from big-band activity, studied classical music for two years (1947–49); performed with symphony orchestras and chamber ensembles; announced his retirement in 1954; at that time, when McCarthyism was heating the political climate in the U.S., moved to Spain to avoid harassment by the U.S. House of Representatives' Un-American Activities Committee; lived in exile on Spain's Costa Brava for five years; in 1983 formed the Artie Shaw Orchestra, which for many years performed his old arrangements and some new music under the baton of (and featuring the clarinet and saxophone of) Dick Johnson; wrote the autobiography *The Trouble with Cinderella* (1952); later wrote the never published "The Education of Albie Snow," a mixture of fiction and autobiography; wrote two collections of short stories, *I Love You, I Hate You, Drop Dead!* (1965) and *The Best of Intentions* (1989); from the music he produced between 1937 and 1954, selected the contents of two collections of recordings released in 2001: *The Very Best of Artie Shaw*, an 18-track set, and *Self Portrait*, a five-CD collection; won a Grammy Award for lifetime achievement in 2004; was married eight times (to wives who included the glamorous movie stars Lana Turner and Ava Gardner); was the subject of a TV documentary produced by Ken Burns; died at his home in Newbury Park, California. See *Current Biography* (1941).

Obituary *New York Times* A p24 Dec. 31, 2004

SHORT, BOBBY Sep. 15, 1924–Mar. 21, 2005 Singer; pianist; a celebrated cabaret entertainer who specialized nostalgically in "the great American songbook" of the 1920s and 1930s; an elegant tuxedoed performer whose sophistication did not preclude an aspect of his persona variously described as that of a boyish "cherub" or "teddy bear"; sang with distinctive clear phrasing and accompanied himself with a keyboard style that was a cross between conventional society piano and rollicking stride; in the intimacy of such rooms as Manhattan's Café Carlyle (his gig for the last thirty-five years of his career), interpreted with joyous ebullience not only the vintage Broadway show tunes of such white composers as Cole Porter, Rodgers and Hart, Harold Arlen, Jerome Kern, Vernon Duke, and the Gershwins but also the songs of such black composers as Duke Ellington and Billy Strayhorn, Eubie Blake, James P. Johnson, and Fats Waller; also included in his repertoire gems from the hands of Noël Coward, Cy Coleman, and the playwright and cocktail pianist Ivor Norvello; was born in Danville, Illinois, to parents who were, in his words, "part of the great Negro migration that beat it out of Kentucky and points south"; taught himself to play the piano by ear in early childhood; while still a schoolboy, began performing under chaperonage in taverns and other venues, including vaudeville houses, first around Danville and then in Chicago, St. Louis, and other cities; dropped out of school in 1937 to seek his fortune in New York City, abortively; after a few months, returned to Danville and to school; following his graduation from high school in 1942, traveled nationally, doing gigs in clubs in Chicago, Milwaukee, New York, and Los Angeles; was a mainstay at the Café Gala in Los Angeles from 1948 until 1954, save for a year in Paris and London; over the following years, had extended engagements at a number of nightclubs and supper clubs, notably including the Manhattan boites L'Intrigue, the Blue Angel (co-owned by Lou Jacoby), and Le Caprice, a combination restaurant-nightclub on East Fifty-fourth Street that he and Jacoby opened in 1964 and that closed after little more than a year; during the 1965-66 Off-Broadway season, had a part in the New Cole Porter Revue; on May 19, 1968, gave a resoundingly successful concert at New York's Town Hall with the singer Mabel Mercer; returned to Town Hall with Mercer for a second even more successful concert the following year; in 1968, signed a contract to perform six nights a week, eight months a year in the Café Carlyle lounge at the up-scale Hotel Carlyle on Manhattan's Upper East Side; later reduced his schedule at the Carlyle to five or six nights during four-month stints; continued his engagement at the Café Carlyle through 2004; attracted a chic following of aficionados that included the rich and famous; played at the White House for presidents Nixon, Carter, Reagan, and Clinton; appeared as himself in Woody Allen's motion picture *Hannah and Her Sisters* (1986) and in episodes of several television situation comedies; left a legacy of recordings on the Atlantic and Telarc labels; was nominated for Grammy awards for the albums *Late Night at the Café Carlyle* (1993) and *You're the Tops: Love Songs of Cole Porter* (2002); wrote the autobiographies *Black and White Baby* (1971) and, with Robert G. Mackintosh, *The Life and Times of a Saloon Singer* (1995); was the founder and president of the Duke Ellington Memorial Fund, dedicated to creating a monument to Ellington at the northeast corner of Manhattan's Central Park; made the best-dressed lists with his natty custom-made wardrobe, from tuxedo-and-bow-tie to white tails and an ankle-length camel's hair coat; lived in a triplex apartment in the Carnegie Hall building in Manhattan; also had a home in southern

France; died in Manhattan; was survived by an adopted son, Ronald Bell. See *Current Biography* (1972).

Obituary *New York Times* C p17 Mar. 22, 2005

SIMON, CLAUDE Oct. 10, 1913–July 6, 2005 Author; Nobel laureate; is commonly identified, perhaps more closely than warranted, with the group of French avant-garde experimental writers most prominently represented by Alain Robbe-Grillet and known as the "new novelists," a group that, more elitist than popular in its appeal, began to come together under the aegis of Jérôme Lindon at the Paris publishing house of Éditions de Minuit in the 1950s and produced what was dubbed *le nouveau roman* ("the new novel") by Émile Henriot in the newspaper *Le Monde* on March 22, 1957 (and later, in a term coined by Jean-Paul Sartre, "the antinovel"); shared with the members of the group a determination to subvert the conventions of the traditional novel, including plot, narrative structure, chronology, character development, psychological analysis, and authorial subjectivity (as Jean Ricardou, one of their leading theorists, declared, the new novelists were not writing adventures but adventuring in writing); in accord with that dictum, viewed his work as writer as one of "discovery" rather than "expression"; also declared that he was "incapable of making up a story" and thus wrote "directly from real life"; produced what came to be considered the definitive Simon "novel," a sort of pell-mell memoir, a nonlinear outpouring of collective and personal memory in which unpunctuated sentences sometimes run on for pages and past is blurred with present; used as grist for his books his readings in ancient and modern military history, his family's history, his father's death in combat in World War I, and his own experiences as a child and during the Spanish Civil War and World War II, as a vineyardist in southern France and as a painter manqué; was born in Madagascar, then a French colony, where his father, a French army career officer, was stationed; grew up in Perpignan, in southern France, and in Paris, where he attended the Collège Stanislas; studied painting with André Lhote and tried his hand at photography; during the Spanish Civil War (1936–39), visited Spain as an observer sympathetic to the Republican side (with which he, like George Orwell, became disillusioned); serving with a cavalry regiment early in World War II, was one of the handful of French who survived the slaughter at the Battle of the Meuse (which, coincidentally, had been the site of his father's death 26 years before); subsequently, escaped from a German prisoner-of-war camp and joined the French Resistance; after the war, inherited some wine-growing property at Salses, near Perpignan; with the income from his vineyard, was able to support himself while continuing the writing career he had begun during the 1930s; early on, was influenced by William Faulkner, Marcel Proust, and Albert Camus; published his first book, the existentialist fable *Le Tricheur* (The Swindler), in 1945; followed that with *La Corde raide* (The Tightrope, 1947), a fairly straightforward account of the Spanish Civil War; indicated his interest in the "fog" of semiconscious impressions in the relatively conventional novels *Gulliver* (1952) and *Le Sacre du printemps* (The Rite of Spring, 1954); began accruing his "new novelist" credentials with his fragmentations of perception and distortions of chronology in *Le Vent* (1957; translated as *The Wind*, 1959) and *L'Herbe* (1958; *The Grass*, 1960); hit his stride in the genre with *La Route des Flandres* (1960; *The Flanders Road*, 1961), which is widely regarded as one of his two masterpieces, the other being *Les Géorgiques* (1981; *The Georgics*, 1989); in all, wrote a score of books, including *Le Palace* (1962; *The Palace*, 1963), *La Bataille de Pharsal* (1969; *The Battle of Pharsalus*, 1971), *Histoire* (1967; published in English under the same title, 1968), *Les Corps conducteurs* (1971; *Conducting Bodies*, 1974), *Leçon de choses* (1975; *The World About Us*, 1983), *L'Acacia* (1989; *The Acacia*, 1991); *Le Jardin des plantes* (1997; *The Jardin des Plantes*, 2002), and *Le Tramway* (2001; *The Tramway*, 2002); following his divorce from Yvonne Ducing, married Rhea Karavas in 1978; received the Nobel Prize in Literature in 1985; died in Paris. See *Current Biography* (1992).

Obituary *New York Times* p21 July 10, 2005

SIN, JAIME Aug. 31, 1928–June 21, 2005 Roman Catholic prelate; cardinal; as archbishop of Manila (1974–2003), was the leader of the Catholic Church in the Philippines, a nation whose population of 88 million is 85 percent Catholic; drew international attention when he used his influence to help rally the "people power" that brought down two Filipino presidents; was ordained a priest in 1954; served as the founding rector of St. Pius X Seminary in Roxas City from 1957 to 1967, when he was consecrated a bishop; was elevated to membership in the College of Cardinals in 1976; vis-à-vis the dictatorship of President Ferdinand Marcos, succeeded for more than a decade in maintaining an ambivalent stance, described by him as "critical collaboration" and by one reporter as a "near-perfect balancing act"; hardened his stance when Benigno Aquino, the leading political opponent of the increasingly oppressive Marcos regime, was assassinated in 1983, and played a central role in the nonviolent overthrow of Marcos three years later; threw his support behind a nationwide campaign of civil disobedience initiated by Corazon Aquino after Marcos declared himself victorious over Aquino, Benigno's widow, in a rigged presidential election held on February 7, 1986; over the Church-owned radio station, Radio Veritas, broadcast a message calling upon Filipinos to rally to the protection of two of Marcos's top military aides, Juan Ponce Enrile and Fidel Ramos, who defected to the Aquino side and barricaded themselves in the Defense Ministry building in Manila on February 22, 1986; was gratified when, in response, hundreds of thousands of people filled Epifanio de los Santos Avenue in Manila for three days, forming a human shield between the Defense Ministry building and the troops loyal to Marcos who were advancing toward it and who, unwilling to fire on the protesters, retreated; saw Marcos, under pressure from the U.S. government, concede the presidency to Corazon Aquino on Febraury 25, 1986; again felt compelled to use his influence in the political arena a dozen years later, out of disappointment with the presidency of Joseph Estrada, who was popularly elected in 1998 and then proceeded, allegedly, to show evidence of corruption in his government and less than exemplary behavior in his personal life; issued a pastoral letter criticizing Estrada in January 1999 and subsequently helped lead popular protests against him, forcing him to resign the presidency in 2001; retired as archbishop when he reached the mandatory retirement age of 75 in 2003; published a number of books, among them *The Christian Basis of Human Rights* (1978), *Slaughter of the Innocents* (1979), and the compilation of pastoral letters *On the Way of Truth* (1999), some of which focus on his concern for social justice and the plight of the poor and vulnerable in society; died in Manila. See *Current Biography* (1995).

Obituary *New York Times* A p19 June 21, 2005

SISCO, JOSEPH Oct. 31, 1919–Nov. 23, 2004 U.S. diplomat; a highly resourceful and energetic top negotiator and mediator with the U.S. State Department for a quarter of a century; at his most prominent, in the early and middle 1970s, was in constant motion conducting shuttle diplomacy in the Middle East, his arena of greatest expertise; following his service with the U.S. Army in World War II, earned a Ph.D. degree as a specialist in Soviet affairs at the University of Chicago; began his government service as an officer with the U.S. Central Intelligence Agency (1950–51); in 1951, joined the State Department, where he rose within a few years to the position of assistant secretary of state for international organization affairs; concurrently, served on the U.S. delegations to the United Nations from 1952 to 1968, when he became chief U.S. mediator in the Middle East; in January 1969, was appointed assistant secretary of state for Near Eastern and South Asian affairs by President Richard M. Nixon; wrote the paper that served as the template for Nixon's Middle East policy, which was concerned with, among other matters, containing the Soviet Union's influence in the area and persuading the Arab states that the U.S. administration was trying to be evenhanded in addressing the Arab-Israeli conflict; in the early 1970s, helped to quell violent confrontations between Israel and Egypt, Syria and Jordan, and India and Pakistan; as chief deputy to Secretary of State Henry Kissinger, resolved a flareup of the dispute over Cyprus between Greeks and Turks in 1974; in that year, was promoted to under secretary of state for political affairs; after leaving government, in 1976, was president (1976–80) and chancellor (1980–81) of American University; in 1981, became a partner in Sisco Associates, an international management and consulting firm founded two years earlier by his wife, Jean Head Sisco; as a consultant, specialized in political and economic analysis for American and foreign companies; in 2004, while recognizing that the administration of President George W. Bush had made mistakes, expressed approval of that administration's conduct of foreign policy, including the war in Iraq; was predeceased by his wife and survived by his two daughters; died at his home in Chevy Chase, Maryland. See *Current Biography* (1972).

Obituary *New York Times* B p11 Nov. 25, 2004

SONTAG, SUSAN Jan. 16, 1933–Dec. 27, 2004 Writer; novelist; essayist; cultural critic; a glamorous intellectual icon in 20th-century American letters; made her striking and provocative entrance into New York literary society in the early 1960s; at that time, was writing critical essays that were, in her words, "not criticism at all, strictly speaking, but case studies for . . . a theory of my own sensibility"—a purely aesthetic theory, which valued style over content and without reference to morality and conventional standards, in a "space of pleasure" where "low," even "awful" forms of popular art, including pornography, may be appreciated on their own terms; was born Susan Rosenblatt; took the surname (Sontag) of her widowed mother's second husband; received a B.S. degree at the University of Chicago in 1951, when she was 18, and M.A. degrees in English literature and philosophy at Harvard University in 1954 and 1955, respectively; later, studied briefly at Oxford University and the University of Paris; was strongly influenced by French avant-garde trends in art, film, literature, and critical theory; following a brief editorial stint at *Commentary* magazine, held several teaching positions, including one at Columbia University (1960–64); at the same time, was publishing essays (at first chiefly in the form of book and film reviews) in the *Nation* and other periodicals, especially the *New York Review of Books*; in those essays, took provocative positions on subjects ranging from the French anti-novel and New Wave cinema to American post-abstract painting, aleatory music, and outré underground films and "happenings"; became famous in 1964 with the publication in *Partisan Review* of her essay "Notes on 'Camp,'" in which she wrote with scholarly appreciation of "the essence of Camp . . . its love of the unnatural, of artifice and exaggeration" and rejoiced in "the triumph of the epicene style"; was a National Book Awards finalist with her first collection of essays, *Against Interpretation* (1966), which included "Notes on 'Camp'" along with other pieces that defied "bourgeois-rationalist" categories of meaning and value; wrote the experimental novels *The Benefactor* (1963) and *Death Kit* (1967); in her second collection of essays, *Styles of Radical Will* (1969), included her first expressly political piece, "Trip to Hanoi," an anti–Vietnam War diatribe written after she visited the capital of North Vietnam in 1968; from 1969 to 1976, lived in Europe, chiefly in Paris; during that sojourn, wrote and directed four films; modified her purely aesthetic sensibility slightly in some of the essays collected in *On Photography* (1977) and to a greater degree in "Fascinating Fascism," one of the pieces in *Under the Sun of Saturn* (1980); published a collection of short stories, *I, etcetera*, in 1978; at the time of the first of her several bouts with cancer, wrote *Illness as Metaphor* (1978), in which she explored the kinds of language used to describe illness, including that which sometimes tends to blame the sufferer; a decade later, pursued the same subject in *AIDS and Its Metaphors* (1988); as an activist on the radical democratic left, confessed (in 1982) that she "did not understand the essentially despotic nature of the Communist system" until the suppression of the Solidarity labor movement in Poland in 1981; in 2001 published the collection of essays *As the Stress Falls*; wrote the essay serving as the text for *Women* (1999), a book of photographs by Annie Leibovitz, her companion for a number of years; realized a best-seller with her third novel, *The Volcano Lover* (1992), about the romance between the British admiral Horatio Nelson and Emma Hamilton; won the National Book Award for fiction with her fourth novel, *In America* (2000), a fictionalized account of the Polish actress Helena Mojeska's journey to the U.S. and establishment of a utopian community; in 1993, placed her life in danger by going to Sarajevo, a beleaguered city in the then war-torn Bosnia and Herzegovina (in the former Yugoslavia), to stage a production (itself controversial) of Samuel Beckett's play *Waiting for Godot*; was inspired by that experience to write her last book, *Regarding the Pain of Others* (2003), about the difference between the reality of war and the imagery in war communiqués; died in Manhattan; was survived by David Rieff, her son from her marriage (1950–58) to Philip Rieff. See *Current Biography* (1992).

Obituary *New York Times* A p1+ Dec. 29, 2004

STUTZ, GERALDINE Aug. 5, 1924–Apr. 8, 2005 Business executive; publisher; fashion and retailing consultant; as president (1957–85) of Henri Bendel, a Manhattan women's specialty store, not only turned a failing business around but transformed a rather dowdy carriage-trade retailer into a chic and trend-setting fashion emporium modeled after her own sophisticated, au courant image and in accord with her "street of shops" merchandising vision; after earning a B.A. degree in journalism at Mundelein College, in Illinois, and working briefly for a public-relations firm in Chicago, moved to New York City; there, took on several jobs, including the editing of four movie magazines; was working for a magazine distributed by a hotel chain when, in 1947, she chanced to meet the editor in chief of *Glamour* magazine, who hired her as an associate fashion editor; with *Glamour*, earned a reputation as an authority on women's accessories, sportswear, French haute couture collections, and, above all, the shoe market; after seven years with *Glamour*, did a brief stint as fashion and publicity director for Mademoiselle Shoes; when the Genesco conglomerate (then the General Shoe Co.), purchased I. Miller, a noted shoe manufacturer, in 1954, was recruited by W. Maxey Jarman, Genesco's president, to serve as fashion coordinator of I. Miller's wholesale branch; the following year, was named by Jarman vice president and general manager of I. Miller's 17-store retail division, which she saved from near bankruptcy; in 1957, was installed as president of Henri Bendel, Genesco's latest acquisition, which was then running at a loss of almost $1 million a year; proceeded, as she later explained, to remodel Bendel into "an old-time specialty shop done in a contemporary style" and aimed at "a specific shopper—the big-city woman leading a sophisticated life who wanted clothes that were chic and elegant"; served as the prototype of that hypothetical shopper; was named on the lists of Best-Dressed Women in the Fashion Industry in 1959, 1953, and 1964 and elected to the industry's Hall of Fame in the best-dressed category for professionals in 1965; in her first action at Bendel, converted the store's vast ground-floor selling area into a "street"

of nine individual boutiques for accessories and gifts in a wide range of prices; oversaw the redecoration of the second floor, which housed the high-priced Paris couturier collections, to make it resemble a luxurious townhouse, and installed a modish beauty salon on an upper floor; introduced such innovations as limiting the stock of high-priced clothing to sizes two to 10, introducing unknown American and European avant-garde designers, and employing dramatic advertising and display techniques; was so successful that by 1980, Bendel was showing a pre-tax profit of $1.4 million on sales of $15 million; in 1980, with the backing of an anonymous Swiss-based investment consortium, purchased Henri Bendel for an estimated $7 million and became the managing partner in the ownership; in 1985, with her partners, sold the store to The Limited Inc.; was the publisher of Panache Press at Random House publishers from 1985 unitl 1993, when she became president of the GSG Group, a New York–based consulting firm for fashion and retail marketing; was also on the board of Hanover Direct Inc., which owns the San Francisco house-and-home store Gumps; was married to the British abstract painter David Gibbs for 12 years, until their divorce, in 1977; maintained homes in Manhattan and Roxbury Falls, Connecticut; died at her home in Manhattan. See *Current Biography* (1983).

Obituary *New York Times* B p9 Apr. 9, 2005

SUBANDRIO Sep. 15, 1914–July 3, 2004 Former deputy prime minister and foreign minister of Indonesia; physician; after earning his medical degree, in 1941, joined the Jakarta Central Hospital as a surgeon; because of his activity in the anti-Japanese underground, was forced to leave the hospital during Japan's wartime occupation of Indonesia; during that period (1942–45), ran a private clinic in the city of Semarang; when World War II ended, in August 1945, quit his medical practice to devote his energies to the radical nationalist movement of Sukarno, who assumed the presidency of Indonesia in October 1945 and declared an end to the long colonial rule of the Netherlands (which ceded sovereignty in 1949); was appointed secretary general of the information ministry in Sukarno's cabinet in 1946; was Indonesia's chargé d'affaires in London (1947–50), ambassador to the Court of St. James's (1951–54), and ambassador to the Soviet Union (1954–56); was named foreign minister by Sukarno in 1957 and deputy prime minister in 1963, when Sukarno gave himself the additional title of prime minister; was an adroit spokesman for and implementer of Sukarno's policies of domestic "guided democracy" and international nonalignment, save for a special close relationship with Communist China; increasingly, seemed to some in Indonesia's military to be complicit in the accelerating influx of Indonesian Communist Party (PKI) members into the government; was found guilty of crimes against the state (which he vehemently denied) and received a sentence of death (later changed to life in prison) after Major General Suharto crushed the PKI in September 1965 and led a military takeover that deprived Sukarno of all but nominal authority (and ultimately displaced him); was released from prison in 1995; died at his home in South Jakarta; was predeceased by his first wife and survived by his second wife and two sons. See *Current Biography* (1963).

Obituary *New York Times* C p23 Sep. 14, 2004

TANGE, KENZO Sep. 4, 1913–Mar. 22, 2005 Japanese architect; urban planner; theoretician of architecture; professor emeritus, University of Tokyo; was inspired both by traditional Japanese architecture and by the school of international modernism as represented by the French architect Le Corbusier; modified modernism's pure functionality and box-like forms by introducing "something to say to the human emotions," as he explained in his acceptance speech when he received the 1967 Pritzker Prize, international architecture's highest honor; said that the result of the modification was a postmodernist "mixture of aesthetic elements . . . that have already reached an impasse," and that he was trying to find "a way out of that impasse"; was influential in the founding of Japan's Metabolist movement, which rejected static form and function and concentrated on changeability of space and function in architecture and urban planning; strove for an architecture of open space, a bold idea in a densely populated small island nation; graduated from Tokyo University's architectural department in 1938; after working for four years in the Tokyo studio of the Le Corbusier–trained architect Kunio Mayekawa, returned to Tokyo University for graduate studies in urban planning; in 1946, joined the university faculty and organized the Tange Laboratory at the university and the Tanken Team of research students who would contribute to the rebuilding of war-devastated Japan, including the city of Hiroshima, which had been flattened by the first atomic bomb, and Tokyo, which had been similarly devastated by firebombing; in 1949, won the competition to build the Peace Center in Hiroshima (completed in 1955), which consists of a park and three buildings, including a Memorial Museum, and represented the first major use of reinforced concrete in building construction in Japan; designed the Shizuoka Convention Hall in Ehima (1953–54), the Kagawa Prefecture Building 1955–58), the Tokyo City Hall (1957), and the National Museum of Western Art in Ueno (1959); in 1959, received his doctoral degree at Tokyo University with the dissertation "Spatial Structure in a Large City," in which he presented a theory of urban planning allowing for future growth and functional changes; in 1960, with the Tanken Team, announced a "Plan for Tokyo" (which would have wide influence in the urban planning for Asia's first megacity), which envisioned the growth of the badly congested city center over Tokyo Bay by means of a narrow bridge of landfill he called a "civic axis" supporting a rapid-transit system, communications facilities, and office and residential megastructures built on floating platforms and connected by highways and pedestrian causeways to either side of the axis; for the Tokyo Olympics in 1964, designed the Yoyogi National Indoor Stadium; also in 1964, saw the completion of his design for Tokyo's St. Mary's Cathedral; presented his master plan for the Japan Expo in 1970 and his plans for a new Tokyo City Hall complex in 1987, the latter including an assembly hall, a plaza, two build-

ing towers, and a park; in 1991, replaced his previously constructed Tokyo City Hall with a new, larger building accommodating some 13,000 workers; also designed the Fuji Television Building (1996), consisting of two towers connected by earthquake-proof bridges, and the Japan Olivetti Technical Center; abroad, participated in the urban reconstruction of Skopje, Yugoslavia (1965) and designed the Kuwait International Airport (1979), the Saudi Arabia Royal Palace (1982), the Musée des Arts Asiatiques in Nice, France, and buildings in Italy, Nigeria, and Singapore; in the U.S., designed the Baltimore Inner Harbor project and the Minneapolis Art Museum expansion; retired from his professorship at the University of Tokyo in 1974; was married twice; had a daughter (who predeceased him) and a son; died at his home in Tokyo; was given funeral rites at St. Mary's Cathedral. See *Current Biography* (1987).

Obituary *New York Times* C p16 Mar. 23, 2005

TAYLOR, THEODORE July 11, 1925–Oct. 28, 2004 Theoretical physicist; a leading designer of nuclear weapons who went on to become an antinuclear activist after experiencing "a profound change of heart," as Ed Ayres, one of his protégées, wrote in *World Watch* (January 11, 2001): "As a young man working for the U.S. government [Taylor] had personally designed the largest-yield atomic bomb ever exploded by any government and he had also designed the smallest one—a suitcase-sized device that doubtless contributed to his subsequent thinking about how wrong that whole super-arms race had been. By the 1970s, Taylor was spending full time analyzing how terrorist groups or individuals could acquire nuclear materials and expertise and urgently trying to warn the world of their threat. . . . He developed scenarios of nuclear extortion, blackmail, and terrorist attack—just how they could happen. . . . What is most vivid in my memory of those scenarios is not the details but the passionate and unflagging belief of Ted Taylor that the building of such weapons had been a terrible mistake"; received a B.S. degree in physics in the U.S. Navy's V-12 officer-training program at the California Institute of Technology during World War II; later flunked out of the doctoral program at the University of California at Berkeley but went on to earn a Ph.D. degree at Cornell University; worked at the Los Alamos (New Mexico) Scientific Laboratory from 1949 to 1956; became the lab's leading designer of fission weapons; designed the "Super Oralloy," the largest and most powerful fission bomb ever made, but specialized in miniaturization; developed, among other small fission bombs, the "Davy Crockett," a 50-pound "suitcase" bomb more powerful than the 9,000-pound "Little Boy" that had obliterated Hiroshima, Japan, on August 6, 1945; in 1956, joined the General Atomic Division of General Dynamics Corp., where his initial work entailed collaboration on the design of "Triga," a safe reactor for the peaceful use of atomic energy; subsequently, managed Project Orion, the General Dynamics Corp.'s attempt to create an interplanetary spaceship powered by successive nuclear explosions rather than chemical fuel; over a period of seven years, worked in close collaboration with Freeman Dyson and other scientists on that project, which was hampered by domestic bureaucratic obstacles and brought to a halt by the 1963 treaty banning nuclear-weapons tests in the atmosphere and outer space as well as under water; from 1964 to 1966, was deputy director for scientific matters of the Defense Atomic Support Agency, which had been set up at the Pentagon to coordinate the activities of all branches of the armed forces in the management and direction of nuclear-weapons testing, nuclear-stockpiling surveillance, and related matters; it was in that position that he underwent his conversion, realizing that "the nuclear arms race had a force and a momentum [he] had never dreamed of": in 1967, founded the International Research and Technology Corp., a consulting firm concerned with the private monitoring of safeguards for nuclear weapons; spent two years in Vienna, Austria, observing the workings of the International Atomic Energy Agency, an 80-nation agency seeking "to accelerate and enlarge the contribution of atomic energy to peace, health, and prosperity throughout the world" and to set up and administer safeguards against the diversion to military purposes of the information and materials it provided; became concerned about the relative ease with which materials—especially plutonium from nuclear power plants—could be stolen, either on site or in transit; was appalled at the amounts of materials unaccounted for (MUF) appearing on the books of privately operated nuclear-power plants; repeatedly pointed out the ease with which a terrorist group or even an individual could build a crude nuclear device using nonclassified technology; to doubters, proposed that the U.S. government conduct an experiment proving that there could be a "simple-minded way to make something that would knock over the World Trade Center" using off-the-shelf technology; inspired a March 1975 Nova television documentary about the success of a college student in using publicly available information to design an A-bomb; meanwhile, had begun a positive pursuit of alternatives to both fossil-fuel energy and nuclear power; with Charles C. Humpstone, wrote *The Restoration of the Earth* (1973), in which they proposed an economical plan for converting solar energy into electrical power via hydroponic greenhouses for the cultivation of bumper crops and the burning of those crops to drive steam turbines; also co-wrote *Nuclear Theft: Risks and Safeguards* (1974) and *Nuclear Proliferation: Motivations, Capabilities, and Strategies* (1977); in 1980, founded Nova Inc., devoted to promoting alternative sources of energy, including solar and pneumatic; was the subject of the book *The Curve of Binding Energy: A Journey into the Awesome and Alarming World of Theodore B. Taylor* (1974), by John McPhee; lived for many years in Wellsville, New York; died in a nursing home in Silver Spring, Maryland. See *Current Biography* 1976.

Obituary *New York Times* A p29 Nov. 5, 2004

TEBALDI, RENATA Feb. 1, 1922–Dec. 19, 2004 Opera singer; an Italian lyric-spinto soprano with a rich legato and soaring pianissimo—what the conductor Arturo Toscanini called "the voice of an angel"; a tall and statuesque woman with a warm personality and a striking stage presence; had an exclusively Italian repertory, ranging from many Puccini interpretations, including Mimi in *La Bohème* and the title role in *Tosca*, to roles in the operas of Boito, Cilea, and Giordano; was most closely associated with Verdi roles, including Desdemona in *Otello*, Violetta in *La Traviata*, Alice Ford in *Falstaff*, and the title roles in *Aïda* and *Giovanna d'Arco*; made her professional debut at Rovigo, Italy, in 1944; two years later, participated in a concert conducted by Toscanini and broadcast throughout Europe on the occasion of the reopening of La Scala in Milan; soon became a favorite with operagoers in Rome, Naples, Florence, Venice, Turin, Bologna, and other Italian cities; during the 1950s, endured an ostensible rivalry with the singer Maria Callas that was fomented by her Italian fans and those of Callas and promoted by the press; meanwhile, toured France, Spain, England, and South America; in 1950, made her U.S. debut, with the San Francisco Opera Company; later became popular in Chicago; in 1955, began a 17-year tenure—not counting one year when she was sidelined with vocal problems—with the Metropolitan Opera Company in New York; gave her farewell performance at the Met in 1973; retired from singing in 1976; recorded much of her repertory on the Decca/London label; died in the Republic of San Marino. See *Current Biography* (1955).

Obituary *New York Times* A p1+ Dec. 20, 2004

TEBBEL, JOHN Nov. 16, 1912–Oct. 10, 2004 Author; journalist; educator; known for his highly readable popular histories, especially his chronicles of book and newspaper publishing, including his major work, the four-volume *A History of Book Publishing in the United States* (1972–81); held a B.A. degree from the Central Michigan College of Education (1935) and an M.S. degree from the Columbia University School of Journalism (1937); early in his career, had stints as a reporter or feature writer for several newspapers, as managing editor of the *American Mercury* magazine, and as a book editor at E. P. Dutton and Co.; taught in New York University's Journalism Department from 1949 to 1976; in his first book, *An American Dynasty* (1947), dealt candidly with the powerful Medill/Patterson/McCormick newspaper-owning family; also in 1947, published *The Marshall Fields: A Study in Wealth*; later wrote, among more than a score of other books, *George Horace Lorimer and the Saturday Evening Post* (1948), *The Life and Good Times of William Randolph Hearst* (1952), *The Inheritors: A Study of America's Great Fortunes and What Happened to Them* (1962), *David Sarnoff: Putting Electrons to Work* (1963), *The Compact History of the American Newspaper* (1963), *American Paperback Books: A Pocket History* (1964), *The American Magazine: A Compact History* (1969), *The Media in America* (1974), *Aging in America: Implications for the Mass Media* (1976), *Between Covers: The Rise and Transformation of Book Publishing in America* (1987), *Turning the World Upside Down: Inside the American Revolution* (1993), *America's Great Patriotic War with Spain: Mixed Motives, Lies, and Racism in Cuba and the Philippines, 1898-1915* (1996); co-wrote a number of books, including *Makers of Modern Journalism* (1952) and *The Press and the Presidency* (1986);

in addition to his nonfiction, wrote several historical novels, including *The Conquerer* (1951), set in colonial New York, and *Touched with Fire* (1952), a fictionalized account of the North American explorations of René-Robert Cavelier, Sieur de La Salle; died at his home in Durham, North Carolina; was survived by his wife, Kathryn, a daughter, a grandchild, and two great-grandchildren. See *Current Biography* (1953).

Obituary *New York Times* C p8 Oct. 15, 2004

THALER, WILLIAM J. Dec. 4, 1925–June 5, 2005 Physicist; professor emeritus, Georgetown University; achieved a measure of celebrity in the late 1950s, when, as a researcher for the U.S. Navy, he invented an over-the-horizon radar system for sensing nuclear bomb tests, missile firings, and satellite launchings worldwide; in 1951, received his Ph.D. degree at Catholic University and joined the acoustics branch of the Office of Naval Research; the following year, was transferred to that office's field-projects branch; in 1955, became chief of that branch; took part in all the nuclear weapons tests at Eniwetok Atoll and in Nevada from 1952 to 1960; supervised Project Argus, which measured the effect of the shell of radiation that enveloped the earth when three atomic bombs were detonated 300 miles over the South Atlantic in the summer of 1958; meanwhile, in the summer of 1957, conceived his idea for an electronic surveillance system that, unlike existing radar, would be able "see" over the curvature of the earth and detect the ionization from nuclear fireballs and rocket exhausts up to 5,000 miles away (the idea was simply to send out radio signals and then read the backscatter from their encounter with the electrically charged particles of ionspheric gases); under the code name Project Teepee he successfully tested his invention over the following two years; later invented a device for transmitting sound on a laser beam; in 1960, left the Office of Naval Research to join the faculty of Georgetown University; headed the Physics Department at Georgetown until 1975, when he became chief scientist in the Office of Telecommunications Policy in President Gerald R. Ford's White House; returned to Georgetown in 1978, when President Jimmy Carter disbanded the Office of Telecommunications Policy; taught and did research at Georgetown until his retirement, in 1996; died at his home in Virginia; was survived by his wife, Barbara, a daughter, three sons, and nine grandchildren. See *Current Biography* (1960).

Obituary *New York Times* A p11, June 18, 2005

THOMPSON, HUNTER S. July 18, 1939–Feb. 20, 2005 Writer; the hard-living and gun-packing self-crowned "mad-dog prince" of what he randomly designated as "Gonzo journalism," his outrageous contribution to the development of the "new journalism" pioneered by the likes of Tom Wolfe and Gay Talese, a first-person genre of fact reportage allowing for an admixture of fantasy; when serving in the U.S. Air Force (1956–58), covered sports for a base newspaper; after his discharge from military service, worked for several publications, lived in Big Sur, California, and investigated the Beatnik scene in San Francisco's North Beach; from 1961 to 1963, was a

correspondent in South America for the *National Observer* newspaper; back in San Francisco, wrote for various magazines about such subjects as student radicalism on the University of California's Berkeley campus and the hippie drug culture in Haight Ashbury; wrote an article on the notorious motorcycle gang Hell's Angels for *Rolling Stone* magazine, leading to his unflattering book *Hell's Angels: A Strange and Terrible Saga* (1967), published after he had ridden with the gang for a year (and been assaulted by some of its members); meanwhile, had moved to Aspen, Colorado; was politically radicalized when he saw "innocent people beaten senseless" in the clash of police with anti–Vietnam War demonstrators outside the Democratic National Convention in Chicago in 1968; became a founding leader of the "freak politics" movement in the Aspen area, devoted to resisting the despoiling of the area by the ski and real-estate industries, just as commercial interests had despoiled the Beatnik and hippie communities in San Francisco; traced the genesis of his Gonzo style to the time when he was writing a story on the 1970 Kentucky Derby for *Scanlon's Monthly*; said that he had "blown his mind, couldn't work," so he finally "just started tearing pages out of [his] notebook and numbering them and sending them to the printer"; was surprised when the published article was greeted as a "great breakthrough in journalism"; thought, as he later recalled, "If I can write like this and get away with it, why should I keep trying to write like the *New York Times*?"; inspired by an assignment for *Rollng Stone* magazine, wrote his book *Fear and Loathing in Las Vegas: A Savage Journey to the Heart of the American Dream* (1972), a nightmarish odyssey in which his alter ego, Raoul Duke, "bent and twisted" on alcohol and assorted chemicals (from LSD to "uppers, downers, screamers, laughers"), is pitted against the hustlers of a city of raw power and blatant wealth, against "the shark ethic," the extreme negation of the dream of the "flower children"; in covering the 1972 Democratic and Republican presidential campaigns for *Rolling Stone*, was candid in his partiality for the Democratic candidate, George McGovern, and his scorn for Richard M. Nixon ("the Werewolf in us, the bully, the shyster"); collected that series of articles in *Fear and Loathing on the Campaign Trail '72* (1973); brought together other articles he wrote for *Rolling Stone* and other magazines in *The Great Shark Attack: Strange Tales from a Strange Time* (1979); in *The Curse of Lono* (1980), illustrated by Ralph Steadman, wrote about Hawaii; collected columns of his originally published in the *San Francisco Examiner* in *Generation of Swine: Tales of Degradation in the '80s* (1988); published a total of some 15 books, including *Songs of the Doomed: More Notes on the Death of the American Dream* (1991), *Better Than Sex: Confessions of a Political Junkie* (1994), *Fear and Loathing in America: The Brutal Odyssey of an Outlaw Journalist 1968-1976* (2000), *The Kingdom of Fear: Loathsome Secrets of a Star-Crossed Child in the Final Days of the American Century* (2003), and several volumes of Gonzo Letters and Gonzo Papers; on the motion-picture screen, was played by Bill Murray in *Where the Buffalo Raom* (1980) and by Johnny Depp in *Fear and Loathing in Las Vegas* (1998); after his marriage to and divorce from Sandra Dawn (the mother of his son, Juan), married Anita Beymuk, who survived him; died from a self-inflicted gunshot wound on his farm in Woody Creek, Colorado, near Aspen. See *Current Biography* (1981).

Obituary *New York Times* B p9 Feb. 22, 2005

VAN DUYN, MONA May 9, 1921–Dec. 2, 2004 Iowa-born poet; first female poet laureate of the U.S.; wrote outside the loop of the American literary establishment, with elegance and subtlety but quotidian midwestern sensibility; rejected the sobriquet "domestic poet" with the explanation, "I use domestic imagery [including home canning] and I extend that imagery through the whole poem, but I'm not writing about that. It's simply used as a metaphor"; described one of her major themes as "the idea of time as a taking away of things and love and art as the holders and keepers of things"; ranged from free verse to formal poetic structures and experiments with those structures; following graduate work at the University of Iowa, taught English there from 1943 to 1946; along with her husband, Jarvis Thurston, taught at the University of Louisville from 1946 to 1950, when university officials objected to her promotion into the department where her husband taught on grounds of a "no nepotism" rule; with her husband, left the University of Louisville and moved to the faculty of Washington University in St. Louis; taught English at Washington University until 1967; published her first, slender book of poems, *Valentines to the Wide World*, in 1959; five years later published *A Time of Bees* (1964); won the Bollingen Prize and the National Book Award with her third collection, *To See, To Take* (1970); in *Bedtime Stories* (1972), brought together verses she wrote from the point of view of her grandmother, in a German-American dialect; followed that book with *Merciful Disguises* (1973) and *Letters from a Father, and Other Poems* (1982); won the Pulitzer Prize for poetry for *Near Changes* (1990); subsequently published *Firefall* (1993), *If It Be Not I: Collected Poems 1959–1982* (1993), and *Selected Poems* (2002); was named poet laureate, an annual appointment of the Library of Congress, in 1992; with her husband, founded and for many years edited the literary magazine *Perspective*; in her autobiographical submission to *World Authors* (1980), told of suffering, ever since "the incident at Louisville," intermittent bouts of depression, and undergoing shock treatments and months-long stays in psychiatric hospitals; however, "unlike Lowell, Berryman, Plath or Sexton," found the subjects for her poems not in her illness but in "the years of good health between depressions"; expressed regret at being "unable to have children"; was survived by her husband; died at her home in St. Louis, Missouri. See *Current Biography* (1998).

Obituary *New York Times* A p17 Dec. 4, 2004

VANDIVER, S. ERNEST July 3, 1918–Feb. 21, 2005 Democratic governor of Georgia (1959–63); lawyer; a watershed figure in modern Georgia history; in a turbulent time, put law and statesmanship above politics to restore honesty and competence to government in Georgia and to guide the state out of its Jim Crow past; on his way to the governor's mansion, served as mayor of Lavonia, Georgia (1946) and the state's adjutant general (1948–54); concurrently, was director of selective service (1948–54) and civil defense (1951–54); was elected to a four-year term as lieutenant governor in 1954; when campaigning for governor in 1958, at first promised that he would "use every legal means at my command to maintain segregation"; attacked by opponents as being "soft on segregation," was driven to more extreme rhetoric; made a pledge to white voters that he would later regret: "Neither my child nor yours will ever attend an integrated school in my administration"; as governor, successfully urged the Georgia General Assembly to pass legislation reforming the state mental-health system and reasserting the assembly's "constitutional right to control the public purse strings," to address the conflict of interests among state officials and limit the spending power of the governor in a state where "in the past quarter of a century nearly one dollar out of every four has been spent by executive decree"; oversaw the elimination of Georgia's county-unit system of statewide voting, which had enabled rural politicians to control the state for decades; dwarfed those accomplishments by his role in the ending of Jim Crow in Georgia—a role that included some clandestine actions that were little known for a long time; as governor-elect in 1958, at the behest of U.S. senator Herman Tallmadge, met secretly with 15 of the state's leading black citizens at Talmadge's home to, in his words, "begin looking for ways to get us out of the situation we were in"; during the Democratic candidate John F. Kennedy's (ultimately successful) campaign for the presidency in 1960, made a secret deal: in return for Kennedy's promise not to send federal troops to Georgia to desegregate the schools, announced his support for Kennedy's candidacy; subsequently, received a call from Kennedy asking for his help in securing the release of the civil rights leader Martin Luther King Jr. from an Atlanta jail; gave that help by contacting his brother-in-law Bob Russell, a nephew of Senator Richard Russell, who contacted George Stewart, the executive secretary of the Georgia Democratic Party, who in his turn contacted the segregationiost judge Oscar Mitchell, who ordered King's release (a result credited in the press at the time to President Kennedy's brother Robert, whose telephone call to Mitchell was actually the confirmation of a fait accompli); meanwhile, found himself caught between a series of federal court rulings ordering the racial integration first of Atlanta public schools and then of the University of Georgia on the one hand and, on the other, Georgia laws requiring the closing of schools rather than acceptance of their desegregation; in January 1961, persuaded the Georgia General Assembly to repeal those laws, making possible the entrance of two African-American students, Charlayne Hunter (now Charlayne Hunter-Gault) and Hamiton Holmes, to the University of Georgia; ran unsuccessfully for the U.S. Senate in 1972; after leaving politics, practiced law and farmed cattle; died at his home in Lavonia, Georgia; was survived by his wife, Betty, a son and two daughters, and four grandchildren. See *Current Biography* (1962).

Obituary *New York Times* C p19 Feb. 23, 2005

VANDROSS, LUTHER Apr. 20, 1951–July 1, 2005 Singer; songwriter; recording artist; record producer; a dominant vocalist on the rhythm-and-blues charts from 1981 into the new millennium; a soulful romantic balladeer who delivered his elegantly crafted songs about love—and sometimes loss—in a distinctive, supple tenor voice, one of the most sensual and seductive in popular music, at once silky smooth and capable of lush baroque harmonics and thrilling crescendos; with some 21 albums, including *Forever, For Always, For Love* (1982), *Busy Body* (1983), *The Night I Fell in Love* (1985), *Give Me the Reason* (1986), *Any Love* (1988), *The Best of Luther Vandross: The Best of Love* (1989), *Never Let Me Go* (1993), *Songs* (1994), *This Is Christmas* (1995), and *Luther Vandross* (2001), produced a string of hits that usually went platinum (with sales of at least one million); had total album sales estimated at or near 30 million; reached the Top 10 on the charts with such singles as "Don't Want to Be a Fool" and "Here and Now" and the Top 40 with "'Til My Baby Comes Home," "She Won't Talk to Me," "I Really Didn't Mean It," and "Stop to Love," among other singles; won the Grammy Award in the category of best male R&B vocal performance for "Here and Now" in 1991, for "Power of Love/Love Power" in 1992, and for "Dance with My Father" in 2004; also in 2004, shared with Beyoncé Knowles the Grammy for best R&B vocal duo for "The Closer I Get to You"; won additional Grammys as the co-writer (with Marcus Miller and Teddy Vann) of "Power of Love/Love Power" and for the album *Dance with My Father*; over the years, was nominated for a score of other Grammys, including those in the "male vocal" category for "Love the One You're With" (one of his rare crossover hits), "I Know," "Any Day Now," and "When You Call on Me/Baby That's When I Come Runnin'"; in the "vocal duo" category, shared the nomination for "Doctor's Orders" with Aretha Franklin (whose career he, as a producer, helped revive), for "The Best Things in Life Are Free" with Janet Jackson, and for "Endless Love" with Mariah Carey; in the "best composition" category, shared the nomination for the song "Give Me a Reason" with the composer Nat Adderly Jr., for "Your Secret Love" with Reed Verteney, and for "Dance with My Father" with Richard Marx; grew up in a musical family in Manhattan and the Bronx, New York City; was formatively influenced less by male pop singers than by black female singers and groups, from Dinah Washington to Dionne Warwick and including the Shirelles and the Supremes; once explained: "Women's interpretive values seem less restricted. The peaks and values are much wider than what men choose to do—not what men are capable of doing, but what they choose to do. Cissy Houston and the Sweet Inspirations behind Aretha [Franklin] taught me what thick, luscious harmony was all about"; saw his older sister Patricia sing backup with the male group the Crests (famous for their 1958 hit recording "Sixteen Candles"), who practiced in the Vandross home; in high school in the Bronx, began collaborating musically with his fellow student and guitarist Carlos Alomar; with Alomar, formed a group called the Shades of Jade, which evolved after high school into a 16-member ensemble called Listen My Brother; in 1974, after two miserable semesters at Western

Michigan University, was introduced by Alomar to the British rock superstar David Bowie, who was recording his album *Young Americans* in Philadelphia; contributed to the arrangements and backup vocals on that album and to the music on two Bowie tours of the U.S.; through Bowie, found work with the singer Bette Midler, and through Midler's producer, the Atlantic Records executive Arif Mardin, got regular work as an arranger and backup vocalist at Atlantic recording sessions with such artists as Carly Simon, Chaka Khan, Ringo Starr, Barbra Streisand, and Donna Summer; wrote the song "Everybody Rejoice," which was included in the musical *The Wiz* (Broadway, 1975; motion picture, 1978); during the 1970s, found his most lucrative livelihood singing voice-over jingles in television or radio commercials for Burger King, Pepsi-Cola, Miller Beer, Juicy Fruit Gum, AT&T, and the U.S. Army, among other advertisers; in the late 1970s, with the help of Arif Mardin, was signed to the Cotillion label, an Atlantic offshoot, as the lead singer of a group called Luther, which made two unsuccessful recordings; was also a prominent voice in recordings by Patti Austin and such groups as Chic and Change; did not come into his own until, with the encouragement of his friend Roberta Flack, he drew on his own savings to rent time at a 24-track studio and signed a solo contract with Epic Records that gave him creative control; under that contract, produced and recorded *Never Too Much* (1981), his first solo album and the first of his million-selling records; opening on tour for Roberta Flack about that time, introduced his inventive cover of Bacharach and David's "A House Is Not a Home," which remained the signature of his live shows for two decades; produced Dionne Warwick's album *How Many Times Can We Say Goodbye* (1983) and sang the title duet with her; toured with Anita Baker in 1988; toward the end of his contract with Epic Records, cut the albums *I Know* (1998), *Always and Forever* (1998), and *Greatest Hits* (1999); after 18 years with Epic, recorded one album (*Smooth Love*) on the Virgin label before signing with J Records, a new label launched by Clive Davis, in 2001; on the J label recorded, among other albums, *The Essential Luther Vandross* (2003) and *Live 2003 at Radio City Music Hall* (2003); in 2003 reached the number-one spot on the *Billboard* charts with the album *Dance with My Father* and the single of the same name; following a stroke in April 2003, never performed in public again and recorded only to a small extent; lived in Manhattan; died at the John F. Kennedy Medical Center in Edison, New Jersey. See *Current Biography* (1991).

Obituary *New York Times* C p16 July 2, 2005

VANE, JOHN R. Mar. 29, 1927–Nov. 19, 2004 British pharmacologist; research director; with the Swedish scientists Sune K. Bergstrom and Bengt I. Samuelson, shared the 1982 Nobel Prize in Medicine or Physiology for pioneering research in prostaglandins, unsaturated fatty acids involved in such bodily functions as the contraction of smooth muscle and the control of temperature; was in particular cited for having "discovered prostacyclin and, in addition, [having] made the fundamental discovery that anti-inflammatory compounds such as aspirin act by blocking the formation of prostaglandins"; in 1955, two years after receiving his Ph.D. degree in pharmacology at Oxford University, began advanced study and research at the Institute of Basic Medical Sciences of the University of London in the Royal College of Surgeons; remained at the Royal College for eighteen years, progressing from senior lecturer to professor of experimental pharmacology; with his group at the college, developed the cascade super fusion bioassay technique for dynamic and instantaneous measurement of the release and fate of vasoactive hormones in the circulation or perfusion fluid of isolated organs; in the mid-1960s, in collaboration with Priscilla Piper and other members of his research team, began focusing on prostaglandins; in 1971, announced his discovery that aspirin inhibited the conversion of arachidonic acid into prostaglandins that contribute to pain, swelling, and fever following bodily injury; in 1973, left academia to accept a position in the private pharmacological sector, that of group research and development director with the Wellcome Foundation Ltd.; took with him a nucleus of colleagues from the Royal College of Surgeons; with his discovery of prostacyclin in 1976, advanced medical knowledge of the body's capacity to control blood-clotting; helped to develop two widely used prescription drugs, the cyclooxygenase-2 inhibitors for pain and inflammation and the ACE (angiotension converting enzyme) inhibitors for high blood pressure, heart failure, and other circulatory diseases; was knighted in 1984; died in Farnborough, England; was survived by his wife, Daphne, and two daughters. See *Current Biography* (1986).

Obituary *New York Times* B p10 Nov. 23, 2004

WALWORTH, ARTHUR C. July 9, 1903–Jan. 10, 2005 Writer; won the 1958 Pulitzer Prize in the biography category for *Woodrow Wilson: American Prophet* (1958), the first of his two volumes on the 28th president of the U.S., the second volume of which was *Woodrow Wilson: World Prophet* (1958); also wrote *China's Story in Myth, Legend, and Annals* (1935), *School Histories at War: A Study of the Treatment of Our Wars in the Secondary School History Books* (1938), *Black Ships Off Japan: The Story of Commodore Perry's Expedition* (1946), and *America's Moment, 1918: American Diplomacy at the End of World War I* (1977); after graduating from Philips Andover Academy and Yale University (where he majored in English), briefly taught English and modern European history in China; before devoting himself to writing full-time, was employed in sales, advertising, and editorial work in the educational department of Houghton Mifflin publishers in Boston, from 1927 to 1943; died in Needham, Massachusetts; was survived by a sister. See *Current Biography* (1959).

Obituary *New York Times* B p9 Jan. 20, 2004

WEBER, DICK Dec. 23, 1929–Feb. 13, 2005 Bowler; was professional bowling's most recognizable figure for half a century; consistently ranked among the top three bowlers of his time; with his renown, was signally instrumental in spurring the rise in popularity of the sport; as the son of the manager of a bowling

alley in Indianapolis, Indiana, began bowling in childhood; in 1954, joined the Budweisers, a professional bowling team sponsored by the Budweiser Brewing Co. in St. Louis; had the best tournament average (214) in the American Bowling Congress in the four years beginning 1957; was among the charter members of the Professional Bowlers Association (PBA), which was formed in 1958 and launched its first tour in 1959; won 10 of the first 23 PBA tournaments; became one of bowling's first national stars through television broadcasts of PBA events on the ABC network on Saturdays during the 1960s and 1970s; then and later, made appearances on numerous other television shows, most notably those hosted by David Letterman; was voted bowler of the year by the Bowling Writers Association of America in 1961, 1963, and 1965; was named to the ABC All-America team by the same association 10 times as of 1969; won the Bowling Proprietors Association of America All-Star singles championships in 1962, 1963, 1965, and 1966; was inducted into the American Bowling Congress Hall of Fame in 1970 and the PBA Hall of Fame in 1975; between 1959 and 1992, won 26 PBA tour titles, placing him seventh in rank among competitors in the tours; also won six titles on the PBA senior tour; as of 1992, had career winnings of almost $900,000; won his 44th PBA title in September 2004; died in Florissant, Missouri; was survived by his wife, Juanita, and four children, including two outstanding bowlers, his sons Pete (who has become the second-leading money-winner in the history of professional bowling) and John. See *Current Biography* (1970).

Obituary *New York Times* B p9 Feb. 16, 2005

WEIZMAN, EZER June 15, 1924–Apr. 24, 2005 Israeli statesman; military leader; a founder of the Israel Air Force; former president of Israel; a pragmatic individualist who in the course of his career moved from the right to the left of the political spectrum, from hawk to dove; played a key role in forging peace with Egypt; was a native-born Israeli who came from one of the prominent Jewish families of the pre-state Palestinian yishuvim (settlements); was a nephew of Chaim Weizman, a pioneering Zionist statesman and Israel's first president; was born in Tel Aviv in what was then the British mandate of Palestine; flew with the British Royal Air Force as a fighter pilot in Egypt and India during World War II; back in Palestine after the war, fought as a member of two of the Jewish paramilitary organizations then engaged in anti-British operations; following a stint in sabotage with the Irgun Zvai Leumi, joined the Haganah as the leader of a squadron of nine pilots flying Piper Cub airplanes; flew supplies in to the besieged Jewish settlements in the Negev during the internal strife that preceded the creation of the state of Israel, in May 1948; oversaw the delivery of the second-hand Messerschmitts and Spitfires purchased from Czechoslovakia that became the initial core of Israel's air force; later, integrated the French Mirage fighter jet into the air force; flew daring missions in the Israeli air attack on Egypt during the War of Independence (1948–49); rose through the ranks to become commander of the Israel Air Force (1958–66) and deputy chief of staff of the Israel Defense Forces

(1966–69); in those positions, prepared for and executed Israel's successful preemptive strike against the Arab forces in the Six Day War of 1967; upon retiring from the military, in 1969, served as minister of transport in the coalition cabinet of Golda Meir (1969–70); in 1976, published his autobiography, *On Angels' Wings*; in 1977, successfully ran for the Knesset, Israel's parliament, as a member of Menachem Begin's conservative Likud Party; also successfully managed the general Likud campaign in that election, bringing Begin to power; was minister of defense in the Begin government (1977–80); through his rapport with President Anwar Sadat of Egypt, contributed indispensably to the success of the peace talks at Camp David, attended by Sadat, Begin, and U.S. president Jimmy Carter in 1978; in 1980, resigned from Begin's cabinet and formed the Likud Party's Yachad faction, which later merged with the Labour Party; was minister without portfolio from 1984 to 1988, when he became minister of science in the coalition government of Yitzhak Shamir; resigned from Shamir's cabinet in 1990, after it was discovered that he had engaged in illegal meetings with Palestine Liberation Organization (PLO) leaders; quit party politics at the end of his last term in the Knesset, in 1992; the following year, was elected president (a largely ceremonial post) by the Knesset; in 1996, in a peacemaking gesture, invited Yasir Arafat, the head of the PLO, to his home in Caesarea; in 1998, was elected to a second five-year term as president; in August 2000, resigned the presidency amidst allegations that when he was a cabinet member and lawmaker during the 1980s, he had accepted bribes valued at $300,000 from two businessmen, one French and the other Israeli; admitted receiving gifts but denied that they were bribes; was predeceased by his son, Shaul, and survived by his wife, Reuma, and a daughter; died in Caesarea, Israel. See *Current Biography* (1979).

Obituary *New York Times* B p8 Apr. 25, 2005

WESTMORELAND, WILLIAM C. Mar. 26, 1914– July 17, 2005 U.S. Army officer, retired; the four-star general whose fate it was, as he said, "to serve for over four years as senior American commander in the most unpopular war this country ever fought"— the American military expedition in Vietnam, which had begun as an "advisory" mission to what was then South Vietnam; upon his arrival as deputy to General Paul Harkins, the commander of MACV (Military Assistance Command Vietnam), in January 1964, found only 16,300 American Green Beret "advisers" on the scene, training and assisting South Vietnamese soldiers in "counterinsurgency" operations against the Vietcong, the South Vietnamese Communist guerrillas fighting for a united Vietnam under the aegis of what was then North Vietnam; was named to succeed General Harkins as commander of MACV early in the summer of 1964, after Washington's confidence in the South Vietnamese army had dwindled and the Vietcong had grown in strength and been reinforced increasingly by North Vietnamese army regulars; was chosen for the command post after U.S. president Lyndon B. Johnson (on the advice of his secretary of defense, Robert McNamara) decided that the situation was becoming a

test of his administration's resolve in containing communism globally and that the American presence in South Vietnam had to be escalated and moved into an overt combat mode; was in command when, at the beginning of August 1964, confused, ambiguous reports about the encounter of two U.S. destroyers and unfriendly North Vietnamese patrol boats in the Gulf of Tonkin provided President Johnson with the grounds (or the pretext, in the view of many historians) he needed for persuading Congress to grant him (in the Gulf of Tonkin Resolution, passed on August 7, 1964) virtually unrestricted power to wage undeclared war in Vietnam; tried to fight the war away from villages—where security was left to South Vietnamese troops—so as not to expose civilians to the massive firepower at his disposal; oversaw what was essentially a war of attrition, aimed at hurting the enemy at a faster pace than their casualties could be replaced; saw, as the war progressed, the American forces suffer tens of thousands of casualties while inflicting hundreds of thousands of losses on the enemy; in 1967, made two requests of President Johnson: first, that his troop strength, which then stood at 500,000, be augmented by another 200,000, and second, that he be allowed to seek and destroy enemy forces in their sanctuaries in North Vietnam, Cambodia, and Laos; was denied both requests by the White House—which had done an about-face regarding the war, now viewing it, in Robert McNamara's words, as "acquiring a momentum of its own that must be stopped"; led the beating back of the North Vietnamese and Vietcong's massive so-called Tet offensive, launched in late January 1968—which, though the Vietcong suffered a military failure, was psychologically a succès fou for the Vietcong, because the press coverage of the event turned public opinion in the U.S. decisively against the war; was recalled in March 1968 to Washington, where he served as army chief of staff until his retirement, in 1972; a graduate of the U.S. Military Academy at West Point, had been a highly decorated artillery battalion commander in World War II and commander of an airborne regimental team in the Korean War; subsequently, commanded the army's elite 101st Airborne Division (the Screaming Eagles); for several years preceding his Vietnam assignment, was superintendent of West Point; in 1976, published the memoir *A Soldier Reports*; with his wife, had one son and two daughters; died in Charleston, South Carolina. See *Current Biography* (1961).

Obituary *New York Times* A p1+ July 19, 2005

WHIPPLE, FRED L. Nov. 5, 1906–Aug. 30, 2004 Astronomer; professor emeritus, Harvard University; past director of the Harvard–Smithsonian Center for Astrophysics; revolutionized the study of the nature and behavior of comets; discovered six comets; ascertained cometary orbits; clarified the relationship between comets and meteors; began his career in astronomy at a time when comets were widely assumed to be not discrete bodies but flying collections of dust or gravel loosely held together by gravity; disputed that assumption in a paper he published in 1950; proposed a "dirty snowball" or "icy comet" model, picturing the comet as having a discrete nucleus of frozen water, methane, and other hydrogen compounds mixed with silicates and other substances and covered with a porous gravelly crust; theorized that when the orbiting comet approaches the sun, the nucleus begins to thaw, discharging gases that have a jet-propulsion effect; saw his hypothesis vindicated 36 years later by closeup photographs of Halley's Comet taken by the European Space Agency's *Giotto* spacecraft; for the U.S. military during World War II, helped invent the tactic of "confusion reflectors," shreds of aluminum foil dropped from Allied aircraft to confuse German radar; anticipating manned space flight by 15 years, in 1946 proposed the "Whipple shield," the metallic bumper used by NASA to protect its spacecraft from bombardment by high-speed meteoric particles; during the International Geophysical Year 1957–58, recruited a force of some 200 amateur volunteers who joined professionals at tracking stations monitoring the orbit of the Soviet satellite *Sputnik* at a time when the U.S. government refused to recognize that the Soviets had beaten the U.S. in the satellite-launching contest; after receiving a Ph.D. degree at the University of California at Berkeley in 1931, joined the staff of the observatory (then called the Harvard College Observatory) at Harvard University in Cambridge, Massachusetts; became an instructor in astronomy at Harvard in 1932, lecturer in 1938, associate professor in 1945, and professor in 1950; chaired the Department of Astronomy at Harvard for 28 years, beginning in 1949; in addition, directed the Smithsonian Astrophysics Observatory in Cambridge from 1955 to 1973, when it merged with the Harvard Observatory to become the Harvard–Smithsonian Center for Astrophysics; remained with the center in the position of senior scientist; was instrumental in establishing the Mount Hopkins Observatory (renamed the Fred Lawrence Whipple Observatory in 1982) near Tucson, Arizona, operated jointly by the Harvard–Smithsonian Center and the University of Arizona; retired from the Harvard faculty in 1977 but continued to report in at the Harvard–Smithsonian Center six days a week for two decades; became the oldest-ever member of a space-mission science team when NASA launched its Comet Nuclear Tour mission into outer space in 2002; in addition to the standard text *Earth, Moon, and Planets* (1941), published numerous papers in his field; died in Cambridge, Massachusetts; was married twice and was survived by his second wife, a son, and two daughters. See *Current Biography* (1952).

Obituary *New York Times* C p13 Aug. 31, 2004

WHITE, JOHN F. Oct. 11, 1917–Apr. 22, 2005 Television executive; educator; president emeritus of the Cooper Union for the Advancement of Science and Art; a pioneer in noncommercial television; from 1958 to 1969, was president of National Educational Television (originally the National Educational Television and Radio Center), the predecessor of the Public Broadcasting Service; oversaw the growth of NET into a network providing cultural and public-affairs programming to 161 affiliate stations across the U.S.; was instrumental in adding educational shows for children, among them *Mr. Rogers' Neighborhood* and *Sesame Street*; held degrees in political science;

before heading NET, was admissions counselor at Lawrence College (his alma mater), dean of students and director of development at the Illinois Institute of Technology, vice president of Case Western Reserve University, and general manager of WQED in Pittsburgh, the first community-owned television station in the country; as president of Cooper Union, from 1969 to 1980, led that college out of dire financial straits and through a period of physical makeover and academic reorganization; was a prodigious fundraiser; died in Virginia Beach, Virginia; was survived by his wife, Joan, a son, a daughter, and eight grandchildren. See *Current Biography* (1967).

Obituary *New York Times* A p21 Apr. 27, 2005

WHITE, REGGIE Dec. 19, 1961–Dec. 26, 2004 Professional football player; Evangelical Christian minister; a six-foot-five, 300-pound defensive end, nicknamed "the Minister of Defense," who ranked as one of the best defensive linemen in National Football League history; was also known for his spiritual influence on teammates and even some opponents and his work with inner-city youth; playing for the University of Tennessee, was named a consensus All-American in 1983; began his professional career with the Memphis Showboats of the short-lived U.S. Football League (1984–85); went on to play defensive end with the Philadelphia Eagles (1985–92), the Green Bay Packers (1993–98), and the Carolina Panthers (2000); during his 15 seasons in the NFL, made 198 tackles of opposing quarterbacks behind the line of scrimmage, a league career record for sacks that was surpassed by Bruce Smith in 2004; set a Super Bowl record of three sacks when the Packers defeated the New England Patriots in Super Bowl XXXII in 1997; was elected to the Pro Bowl 13 consecutive times (1986–98) and to the All-Pro team seven times; was named defensive player of the year twice, in 1987 and 1998; for a number of years was a minister at the Inner City Community Church in Knoxville, Tennessee; founded the Knoxville Community Development Bank in order "to tackle the roots of economic despair" by providing business and personal loans to borrowers considered "at risk" by other banks; with his wife, Sara, in 1991, founded Hope Palace, a residence for unwed pregnant women and new mothers on the Whites' 32-acre farm in Maryville, Tennessee; published *The Reggie White Touch Football Playbook* (1991); in March 1998, delivered a speech before the Wisconsin State Assembly in which he said of homosexuality: "We've allowed this sin to run rampant in our nation, and because it has run rampant in our nation, our nation is in the condition it is in today"; at the time he gave the speech, was being considered for a job on the CBS television network's NFL studio show, a position he was subsequently denied; founded Reggie White Motorsports, which, in collaboration with Joe Gibbs Racing, began fielding during 2004 a two-car short-track stock-car team as a way of opening NASCAR racing to drivers and mechanics who were members of minority groups; lived in Cornelius, North Carolina; died in Presbyterian Hospital in Huntersville, North Carolina; was survived by his wife and two children. See *Current Biography* (1995).

Obituary *New York Times* A p6 Dec. 27, 2004

WIESENTHAL, SIMON Dec. 31, 1908–Sep. 20, 2005 Founder and director (1961–2005) of the Jewish Documentation Center in Vienna, Austria; iconic Nazi hunter; "the conscience of the Holocaust"; a former architect who, after surviving incarceration and near death in a succession of concentration and extermination camps during World War II, dedicated his life to compiling dossiers on Hitler's genocidal henchmen and their agents and bringing to justice the fugitives among them still at large throughout the world; considered himself responsible for representing not only the millions of Jews (including 89 of his own relatives and in-laws) who perished in the Shoah but the totality of what he estimated to have been the 11 million "inferior" peoples and dissidents—including Gypsies, Poles, and Jehovah's Witnesses and their like—systematically consumed by the Nazi killing machine; at the same time, did not believe in collective guilt, because of the goodness of the several exceptional persons among his captors who secretly contributed to his survival; was born in Buchach in Polish Galicia, now the Lvov (Lwów, in Polish) Oblast subdivision of the Ukraine; after earning a degree in architectural engineering at the Technical University of Prague in Czechoslovakia, in 1932, opened an architectural office in the city of Lvov; specialized in designing private residences; married Cyla Müller in 1936; was forced to close his architectural practice and become a mechanic in a factory when the Soviets occupied Lvov Oblast and instituted a purge of "bourgeois" elements there at the beginning of World War II; after the Germans displaced the Russians in 1941, and his blond-haired wife escaped incarceration by assuming the false identity of a Polish Catholic ("Anna Kowalska"), began his harrowing forced excursion through several camps (some devoted to the dreadful "final solution") operated under the aegis of the Third Reich, beginning with Janowska, near Lvov, and ending with Mauthausen, in Austria; weighed 99 pounds and was barely alive when Mauthausen was liberated by American troops, in May 1945; was subsequently reunited with his wife; for two years after the war, worked with a U.S. Army unit in Austria gathering and preparing evidence for war crimes trials; in 1947, opened his own Jewish Historical Documentation Center in Linz, Austria; closed that center in 1954 and turned its files over to the Yad Vashem archives in Israel; opened his center in Vienna seven years later; compiled dossiers on hundreds of Nazis and agents of the Nazis; in 1963 ferreted out Karl Josef Silberbauer, the police inspector who had arrested Anne Frank and her family in Amsterdam, the Netherlands; was disappointed when prosecutors dropped that case on the grounds that Silberbauer was not responsible for deporting the Franks to the concentration camps where Anne, her mother, and her sister died; also in 1963, was appalled when an Austrian jury acquitted Franz Murer, "the Butcher of Vilna"; motivated by those disappointments, thereafter bolstered his work by vigorously promoting it in the international press; brought to justice such criminals as nine of the 16 SS officers tried in Stuttgart, Germany, in 1966, among them Franz Stangl, the commandant of the Treblinka and Sobibor death camps, sentenced to life in prison in 1970, Hermine Braun Steiner (aka Hermine Ryan), "the Stamping

Mare of Majdanek," given a life sentence in 1980, and Dinko Sakic, commander of the Jasenovac camp in Croatia, sentenced to 20 years in prison in 1999; laid claim to tracking down, among others, Eduard Roschmann, "the Butcher of Riga," Erich Rajakowitsch, the man in charge of the "death transports" in the Netherlands, and Josef Mengele, a physician called the "Angel of Death" at Auschwitz (who died before he could be captured—though Weisenthal did not believe that the man who died was actually Mengele); contrary to a common misconception (which he did little to discourage), played no role in the capture (by agents of the Mossad, the Israeli intelligence agency, in 1960), prosecution, and execution of Adolph Eichmann, the Gestapo technocrat who had supervised the implementation of the "final solution"; wrote, among other books, memoirs translated into English as *The Murderers Among Us* (1967) and *Justice, Not Vengeance* (1989); was portrayed by Ben Kingsley in the made-for-television movie *The Murderers Among Us* and was the inspiration for characters in the feature films *The Odessa File* and *The Boys from Brazil*; received, among other honors, the French Legion of Honor, the American Presidential Medal of Freedom and Congressional Medal of Honor, and a British knighthood; saw his legacy carried forward by the Simon Wiesenthal Center in Los Angeles, which is dedicated to "fighting anti-Semitism, Holocaust denial, terrorism, and hate around the world"; despite his achievements, drew criticism in some Jewish quarters for several of his positions, including his high estimate of the number of non-Jewish victims of the Holocaust and his benign assessment of the Nazi connections in the background of the Austrian statesman Kurt Waldheim; was predeceased by his wife, Cyla, and survived by his daughter, Pauline; died at his home in Vienna. See *Current Biography* (1975).

Obituary *New York Times* A p1+ Sep. 21, 2005

WILKINS, MAURICE H. F. Dec.15, 1916–Oct. 6, 2004 New Zealand–born British biophysicist; Nobel laureate; with his work in X-ray diffraction analysis, contributed to the discovery of the double-helix structure of deoxyribonucleic acid, or DNA, the genetic-code–carrying micromolecule within the chromosomes of all cellular life and that of some viruses; was educated in England from the age of six on; after receiving his B.A. degree in physics at St. John's College, Cambridge University, in 1938, joined the British Ministry of Home Security and Aircraft Production; was assigned by the ministry to do graduate work under Sir John T. Randall, who was conducting radar research at Birmingham University; under Randall, conducted studies on luminescence and phosphorescence that contributed to the improvement of wartime radar screens; after receiving his Ph.D. degree in physics, in 1940, was transferred to a team of physicists working under Sir Marcus Oliphant on the separation of uranium isotopes for atomic bombs, the first of which were then being developed; in 1944, was sent to the U.S. to participate in the Manhattan Project, the top-secret, successful American effort to build the first atomic bombs; with the Manhattan Project team at the University of California, Berkeley, conducted mass-spectrographic studies of the separation of uranium isotopes; "partly on account of the bomb," as he later explained, "lost some interest in physics"; partly influenced by reading Erwin Schrödinger's book *What Is Life?: The Physical Aspects of the Living Cell*, "got interested in going into the biology field"; when World War II ended, in 1945, accepted the invitation of Randall that he join the newly created Biophysics Unit at St. Andrew's University in Scotland as a lecturer; the following year, moved with Randall to the British Medical Research Council's Biophysics Unit at King's College, University of London, where Randall became director; at King's College, began his concentration on the physical structure of DNA, using ultrasonics and ultraviolet microscopy before turning to X-ray crystallography; obtained the first X-ray photo that clearly showed a helical form with the assistance of Raymond Gosling, a graduate student who was pursuing his Ph.D. degree under Wilkins's mentorship; became frustrated after Randall, in 1951, brought into the King's College unit Rosalind Franklin, an excellent crystallographer who improved on his X-ray photo but refused to collaborate closely with him; seeing that Franklin, while elaborating on the physical structure of DNA, failed to elucidate the structure's function, played a role in delivering her unpublished data without her permission to the biologists Francis Crick and James D. Watson, who were nearing a breakthrough in DNA research at Cambridge University's Cavendish Laboratory; in 1953, when Crick and Watson announced in the magazine *Nature* their revolutionary model of DNA's structure as a double helix and explained the structure's copying mechanism for genetic material, joined with Rosalind Franklin in publishing articles about the work done at King's College; in 1962 (four years after Franklin's death), shared the Nobel Prize in medicine or physiology with Crick and Watson; was deputy director of the Biophysics Unit at King's College from 1955 to 1970 and director of the unit from 1970 to 1972; was director of the Medical Research Council's Neurobiology Unit from 1972 to 1974 and head of the Cell Biophysics Unit from 1974 to 1980; was named professor emeritus at King's College in 1981; wrote the autobiography *The Third Man of the Double Helix* (2003); with his wife, Patricia, had two sons and two daughters; died in London. See *Current Biography* (1963).

Obituary *New York Times* B p10 Oct. 7, 2004

WRIGHT, TERESA Oct. 27, 1918–Mar. 6, 2005 Actress; on stage and screen, ranged from early fetching ingénue roles through years of eclipse to splendidly seasoned late-life character parts; is probably most fondly remembered by fans of her screen work for her role as the young niece who slowly, chillingly, realizes that her "good old" Uncle Charley (Joseph Cotton) is the Merry Widow serial killer, in the director Alfred Hitchcock's *Shadow of a Doubt* (1943), Hitchcock's own favorite among his movies; began her career on stage; apprenticed for two summers (1937, 1938) at the Wharf Theater in Provincetown, Massachusetts, where she worked as a stagehand and, looking far younger than her years, acted in juvenile roles; understudied as Emily Webb first under Martha Scott and then under Dorothy Maguire in the original Broadway production of *Our Town*, in 1938; subsequently, played Emily on the road; with the Tamworth, New Hampshire, Barnstormers in the summer of 1939, was again cast in juvenile roles; in the 1939–40 Broadway season, created the role of Mary Skinner in *Life with Father*; was witnessed playing that role by the imperious Hollywood producer Samuel Goldwyn, who was looking for a young woman who could "look sixteen, demure, and un-actressy and yet be enough of an actress to play dramatic scenes with Bette Davis" in his planned screen version of *The Little Foxes*; backstage, "looking for all the world like a little girl experimenting with her mother's cosmetics," she was found by Goldwyn, who was impressed with her "unaffected genuineness and appeal"; was signed to a screen contract by Goldwyn, in which she stipulated that she would not be required, as most starlets then were, to do demeaning publicity, including posing for sexually suggestive photographs; was nominated for Academy Awards for best supporting actress for her performances as Alexandra in *The Little Foxes* (1941) and as the daughter-in-law in *Mrs. Miniver* (1942); won the latter Oscar; was nominated for a best-actress Oscar for her first starring screen role, that of Eleanor Gehrig, the wife of Lou Gehrig (Gary Cooper), in *Pride of the Yankees* (1942); co-starred with Cooper again in the comedy *Casanova Brown* (1944); played a young woman who falls in love with a returning World War II veteran who is already married in William Wyler's classic *The Best Years of Our Lives* (1946), one of the highest-grossing pictures in screen history; was then slated to play in *The Bishop's Wife*, but was cut from the cast when she became pregnant after all her costumes had been made, a circumstance for which "Goldwyn never forgave me," as she later said; on loan from Goldwyn, made *Shadow of a Doubt* with Hitchcock; again on loan from Goldwyn, starred opposite Robert Mitchum in the director Raoul Walsh's Freudian Western *Pursued* (1947) and with Ray Milland in Lewis Allen's period melodrama *The Imperfect Lady* (1947); back at Metro-Goldwyn-Mayer, made the period romance *Enchantment* (1948); felt Goldwyn's disenchantment with her grow when she refused to cooperate in doing publicity for that film; was fired soon afterward, when she withdrew from the title role in *Roseanna McCoy* because of illness; returned to the motion-picture screen in a more worthy role, that of the fiancée of a paraplegic war veteran (Marlon Brando) who helps him cope with his condition, in *The Men* (1950), produced by Stanley Kramer and directed by Fred Zinneman; was married to Niven Busch, the father of her two children, who wrote and produced the Western *The Capture* (1950), in which she co-starred with Lew Ayres; starred opposite Cornel Wilde in another Western, *California Conquest* (1952), a Columbia release; in the following years, returned occasionally to the stage while raising her children; on Broadway, had a supporting role in *Mary, Mary* in 1962, played Alice in *I Never Sang for My Father* (written by her second husband, Robert W. Anderson) in 1968, and was cast as Linda Loman in a revival of *Death of a Salesman* in 1975; also had roles in revivals of *Mornings at Seven* (1980) and *On Borrowed Time* (1991); on television, was nominated for three Emmy Awards; back on the motion-picture screen, had character roles in *The Happy Ending* (1969), *Roseland* (1977), *Somewhere in Time* (1980), *The Good Mother* (1988), and *The Rainmaker* (1997); following the dissolution of her third marriage, to Carlos Pierre, remarried Anderson, then divorced him again but remained friends with him; died in New Haven, Connecticut; was survived by her son and daughter and two grandchildren. See *Current Biography* (1943).

Obituary *New York Times* A p21 Mar. 8, 2005

WRISTON, WALTER B. Aug. 3, 1919–Jan. 19, 2005 Banker; the most influential American banker of his time; with his aggressive policies of expansion and diversification and his innovations (including the first automatic-teller-machine network and the promotion of credit-card lending), built the holding company Citicorp (now Citigroup) and its banking arm, Citibank, into the most profitable international financial-services business; in so doing, galvanized the global banking industry and transformed the monetary habits of bank customers; was the son of Henry Merritt Wriston, a history professor and a president of Brown University; was himself lettered in history as well as international law; in 1946, after military service in World War II, joined First National City Bank—the New York City commercial bank that was the predecessor of Citibank—as a junior inspector in the controller's office; rose to the position of vice president in 1954, executive vice president in 1960, and president in 1967; in his first year as president, launched a massive corporate reorganization, including the creation of Citicorp, a holding company able to engage in varied financial activities normally forbidden to banks; became chairman and chief executive officer of both Citibank and Citicorp in 1970; oversaw Citicorp's growth in assets by 761 percent, to $150.6 billion (euro 115 billion), its net income by 764 percent, to $890 million, and its loans by 937 percent, to $102.7 billion; by the time he retired, in 1984, however, had seen Citicorp stiffed for hundreds of millions of dollars in unpaid loans to undeveloped and to developing countries; later saw the corporation recover from that loss partly through the merger with Travelers Group Inc., which resulted in the creation of Citigroup in 1998; chaired President Ronald Reagan's Economics Policy Advisory Board; received the U.S. Presidential Medal of Freedom in 2004; during his retirement, published the collection of essays *Risk and Other Four-Letter Words* (1986) and the book *The Twilight of Sover-*eignty: *How the Information Revolution Is Transforming the World* (1992); died in Manhattan. See *Current Biography* (1977).

Obituary *New York Times* A p20 Jan. 21, 2005

ZHAO ZIYANG Oct. 17, 1919–Jan. 17, 2005 Prime minister of the People's Republic of China (1980–87); general secretary of the Chinese Communist Party (1987–89); a pragmatic technocrat whose ideological flexibility, anathema to Marxist hard-liners, was crucial to the development of China's economic modernization; sacrificed his political career, and his freedom, by taking the pro-democratic side in the bloody Tiananmen Square massacre of 1989; as first secretary of the Communist Party in Guangdong Province, beginning in 1965, introduced a successful agricultural privatization program that would eventually serve as the national model; in the short run, however, was punished for his "revisionism"; during the Maoist "Cultural Revolution" of the late 1960s, was denounced as a "counterrevolutionary" capitalist stooge by the radical Red Guards, dismissed from his provincial post, and paraded through the streets of Guangzhou, the capital city of the province, in a dunce cap; was rehabilitated by Prime Minister Zhou Enlai in the early 1970s; as first secretary of the Communist Party in Sichuan Province from 1975 to 1980, restored the economy of that province, which had been on the brink of disaster, with his reforms; in April 1980, was called to Beijing, the Chinese capital, by Deng Xiaoping, who had assumed the de facto supreme leadership of China following the death of Mao Zedong; after working for five months as deputy prime minister in charge of the government's daily operations, became prime minister, in September 1980; as prime minister, supplied the ideas for the salutary market-minded national economic package for which Deng would largely be credited, including coastal development, greater self-management and incentives in industry, and a more liberal pricing system in addition to agricultural reform; was ousted from his position as general secretary of the Chinese Communist Party by the party's executive committee for supporting students demanding a more open society in demonstrations in Tiananmen Square, in Beijing, in late May and early June 1989, during which Chinese troops fired on the students, killing hundreds of them; lived under house arrest in Beijing for the remainder of his life; died in Beijing. See *Current Biography* (1984).

Obituary *New York Times* B p5 Jan. 17, 2005

CLASSIFICATION BY PROFESSION—2005

AGRICULTURE
  Pingree, Chellie

ANTHROPOLOGY
  Behar, Ruth
  Prince-Hughes, Dawn

ARCHAEOLOGY
  Hancock, Graham

ARCHITECTURE
  Mayne, Thom
  Virilio, Paul

ART
  Celmins, Vija
  Charles, Michael Ray
  Cometbus, Aaron
  Drake, James
  Gopnik, Adam
  Hawkinson, Tim
  Kidd, Chip
  Luckovich, Mike
  Mankoff, Robert
  Millionaire, Tony
  Pettibon, Raymond
  Schjeldahl, Peter
  Smith, Kiki
  Struzan, Drew
  Taintor, Anne
  Wolfe, Art

ASTRONAUTICS
  Gregory, Frederick D.
  Griffin, Michael
  Rutan, Burt
  Spergel, David

BUSINESS
  Anderson, Ray C.
  Aoki, Rocky
  Bittman, Mark
  Boulud, Daniel
  Cantwell, Maria
  Capa, Cornell
  Chapman, Duane
  Domini, Amy
  Donald, Arnold W.

Fields, Mark
Forsee, Gary D.
Fossett, Steve
Gordon, Bruce S.
Hamilton, Laird
Henry, Brad
Henry, John W.
Hobson, Mellody
Ilitch, Michael
Kenyon, Cynthia
Lampert, Edward S.
Mankoff, Robert
Martinez, Rueben
McCann, Renetta
Morris, James T.
Myers, Joel N.
Newmark, Craig
Pingree, Chellie
Rusesabagina, Paul
Rutan, Burt
Taintor, Anne
Thompson, John W.
Trotter, Lloyd
Walker, Olene S.
Wolfram, Stephen

CONSERVATION
  Anderson, Ray C.
  Safina, Carl
  Wolfe, Art

EDUCATION
  Behar, Ruth
  Benedict XVI
  Canada, Geoffrey
  Charles, Michael Ray
  de Branges, Louis
  Doudna, Jennifer
  Ehlers, Vernon J.
  Fausto-Sterling, Anne
  Graves, Florence George
  Hall, Tex G.
  Kusturica, Emir
  Lax, Peter D.
  Levine, Mel
  Martinez, Rueben
  Myers, Joel N.

Rabassa, Gregory
Reich, Walter
Shahade, Jennifer
Shields, Mark
Smith, Amy
Spellings, Margaret
Spergel, David
Summitt, Pat
Tolle, Eckhart

FASHION
  Coddington, Grace
  Diaz, Cameron

FILM
  Bateman, Jason
  Behar, Ruth
  Burstyn, Mike
  Clarkson, Patricia
  Cromwell, James
  Diaz, Cameron
  Everett, Rupert
  Foxx, Jamie
  Garofalo, Janeane
  Giamatti, Paul
  Hallström, Lasse
  Hamilton, Laird
  Harcourt, Nic
  Johansson, Scarlett
  Kaufman, Charlie
  Kusturica, Emir
  Leon, Kenny
  Lohan, Lindsay
  Lumet, Sidney
  Meiselas, Susan
  Mos Def
  Nelson, Stanley
  Osborne, Barrie M.
  Paltrow, Gwyneth
  Perry, Tyler
  Quinn, Aidan
  Rusesabagina, Paul
  Singer, Bryan
  Struzan, Drew
  Taylor, Lili
  Wilson, Luke

FINANCE
Domini, Amy
Lampert, Edward S.

GASTRONOMY
Boulud, Daniel
Jackson, Michael
Parker, Robert M.
Ray, Rachael

GOVERNMENT AND
  POLITICS, U.S.
Baldwin, Tammy
Cantwell, Maria
Chertoff, Michael
Ehlers, Vernon J.
Felt, W. Mark
Gregory, Frederick D.
Griffin, Michael
Hall, Tex G.
Henry, Brad
Huckabee, Mike
Langevin, Jim
Martin, Kevin J.
Martz, Judy
Obama, Barack
Pingree, Chellie
Prosper, Pierre-Richard
Rell, M. Jodi
Shields, Mark
Spellings, Margaret
Walker, Olene S.
Weyrich, Paul

JOURNALISM
Fadiman, Anne
Germond, Jack W.
Gladwell, Malcolm
Gopnik, Adam
Gordon, Ed
Graves, Florence George
Hancock, Graham
Ifill, Gwen
Jackson, Michael
Lelyveld, Joseph
Luckovich, Mike
Reilly, Rick
Schjeldahl, Peter
Shields, Mark
Shriver, Lionel
Tierney, John
Vitale, Dick

LAW
Chapman, Duane
Chertoff, Michael
Henry, Brad
Martin, Kevin J.
Meron, Theodor
Obama, Barack
Prosper, Pierre-Richard

LITERATURE
Behar, Ruth
Brynner, Rock
Busiek, Kurt
Colbert, Gregory
Cometbus, Aaron
Everett, Rupert
Fadiman, Anne
Jones, Sarah
Kidd, Chip
Knipfel, Jim
Lehane, Dennis
Perry, Tyler
Rabassa, Gregory
Robinson, Marilynne
Shriver, Lionel
Siddons, Anne Rivers
Tierney, John
Urrea, Luis Alberto

MATHEMATICS
de Branges, Louis
Lax, Peter D.
Wolfram, Stephen

MEDICINE
Angell, Marcia
Gawande, Atul
Levine, Mel
Reich, Walter

MILITARY
Gregory, Frederick D.
Ward, William E.

MUSIC
AC/DC
Branch, Michelle
Burstyn, Mike
Cave, Nick
Cometbus, Aaron
Elling, Kurt
Everett, Rupert
Fairport Convention
Foxx, Jamie

Graham, Susan
Green Day
Harcourt, Nic
Kusturica, Emir
Lohan, Lindsay
Los Lobos
McGrath, Judy
Morris, Butch
Mos Def
Nugent, Ted
Peyroux, Madeleine
Schoenberg, Loren
Tangerine Dream

NONFICTION
Anderson, Ray C.
Angell, Marcia
Arnold, Eve
Behar, Ruth
Benedict XVI
Bittman, Mark
Boulud, Daniel
Cometbus, Aaron
Ehlers, Vernon J.
Fadiman, Anne
Fausto-Sterling, Anne
Fortey, Richard
Gawande, Atul
Germond, Jack W.
Gladwell, Malcolm
Gopnik, Adam
Hancock, Graham
Hannity, Sean
Harcourt, Nic
Huckabee, Mike
Jackson, Michael
Lax, Peter D.
Lelyveld, Joseph
Levine, Mel
Nugent, Ted
Obama, Barack
Parker, Robert M.
Prince-Hughes, Dawn
Ray, Rachael
Reich, Walter
Robinson, Marilynne
Safina, Carl
Schjeldahl, Peter
Schoenberg, Loren
Shahade, Jennifer
Shields, Mark
Stott, John
Tolle, Eckhart
Virilio, Paul

Hannity, Sean
Harcourt, Nic
Huckabee, Mike
Ifill, Gwen
Kaufman, Charlie
Knievel, Robbie
Kusturica, Emir
Leon, Kenny
Lewis, Ananda
Lohan, Lindsay
Lumet, Sidney
McGrath, Judy
Mitchell, Pat
Mos Def

Myers, Joel N.
Nugent, Ted
Quinn, Aidan
Ray, Rachael
Shields, Mark
Taylor, Lili
Vitale, Dick
Wilson, Luke

THEATER
  Burstyn, Mike
  Clarkson, Patricia
  Cromwell, James
  Davidson, Gordon

Everett, Rupert
Giamatti, Paul
Jones, Sarah
Leon, Kenny
Lumet, Sidney
Mos Def
Nelson, Keith and Monseu,
  Stephanie
Paltrow, Gwyneth
Perry, Tyler
Quinn, Aidan
Taylor, Lili

2001–2005 Index

This is the index to the January 2001–November 2005 issues. It also lists obituaries that appear only in this or other yearbooks. For the index to the 1940–2000 biographies, see Current Biography: Cumulated Index 1940–2000.

Bilandic, Michael A. obit Apr 2002

Biller, Moe obit Yrbk 2004

Birendra Bir Bikram Shah Dev, King of Nepal obit Sep 2001

Bishop, Eric see Foxx, Jamie

Bittman, Mark Feb 2005

Björk Jul 2001

Black, Jack Feb 2002

Blackburn, Elizabeth H. Jul 2001

Blaine, David Apr 2001

Blakemore, Michael May 2001

Blass, Bill obit Nov 2002

Blind Boys of Alabama Oct 2001

blink-182 Aug 2002

Block, Herbert L. obit Jan 2002

Bloomberg, Michael R. Mar 2002

Blount, Winton Malcolm obit Jan 2003

Blur Nov 2003

Bocelli, Andrea Jan 2002

Boland, Edward P. obit Feb 2002

Bond, Julian Jul 2001

Boorstin, Daniel J. obit Yrbk 2004

Borge, Victor obit Mar 2001

Borodina, Olga Feb 2002

Borst, Lyle B. obit Yrbk 2002

Bosch, Juan obit Feb 2002

Boudreau, Lou obit Oct 2001

Boulud, Daniel Jan 2005

Bourdon, Rob see Linkin Park

Bowden, Mark Jan 2002

Boyd, John W. Feb 2001

Bracken, Eddie obit Feb 2003

Bragg, Rick Apr 2002

Branch, Michelle May 2005

Brando, Marlon obit Yrbk 2004

Breathitt, Edward T. obit Sep 2004

Brenly, Bob Apr 2002

Brier, Bob Sep 2002

Brier, Robert see Brier, Bob

Brin, Sergey and Page, Larry Oct 2001

Brinkley, David obit Sep 2003

Brodeur, Martin Nov 2002

Brody, Adrien Jul 2003

Broeg, Bob May 2002

Brokaw, Tom Nov 2002

Bronson, Charles obit Mar 2004

Brooks, Donald obit Yrbk 2005

Brooks, Gwendolyn obit Feb 2001

Brooks, Vincent Jun 2003

Brower, David obit Feb 2001

Brown, Aaron Mar 2003

Brown, Charles L. obit Sep 2004

Brown, Claude obit Apr 2002

Brown, Dee obit Mar 2003

Brown, J. Carter obit Yrbk 2002

Brown, Jesse obit Yrbk 2002

Brown, Kwame Feb 2002

Brown, Lee P. Sep 2002

Brown, Robert McAfee obit Nov 2001

Brown, Ronald K. May 2002

Browning, John obit Jun 2003

Brueggemann, Ingar Nov 2001

Brumel, Valery obit Jun 2003

Bryant, C. Farris obit Yrbk 2002

Brynner, Rock Mar 2005

Bryson, David see Counting Crows

Buchholz, Horst obit Aug 2003

Buckley, Priscilla L. Apr 2002

Budge, Hamer H. obit Yrbk 2003

Bundy, William P. obit Feb 2001

Bunim, Mary-Ellis see Bunim, Mary-Ellis, and Murray, Jonathan

Bunim, Mary-Ellis obit Yrbk 2004

Bunim, Mary-Ellis, and Murray, Jonathan May 2002

Burford, Anne Gorsuch see Gorsuch, Anne

Burgess, Carter L. obit Yrbk 2002

Burnett, Mark May 2001

Burrows, Stephen Nov 2003

Burstyn, Mike May 2005

Burtt, Ben May 2003

Bush, George W. Aug 2001

Bush, Laura Jun 2001

Bushnell, Candace Nov 2003

Busiek, Kurt Sep 2005

Butler, R. Paul see Marcy, Geoffrey W., and Butler, R. Paul

Caballero, Linda see La India

Cactus Jack see Foley, Mick

Calderón, Sila M. Nov 2001

Callaghan, James obit Yrbk 2005

Calle, Sophie May 2001

Camp, John see Sandford, John

Campbell, Viv see Def Leppard

Canada, Geoffrey Feb 2005

Canin, Ethan Aug 2001

Cannon, Howard W. obit Yrbk 2002

Cantwell, Maria Feb 2005

Canty, Brendan see Fugazi

Capa, Cornell Jul 2005

Capriati, Jennifer Nov 2001

Caras, Roger A. obit Jul 2001

Card, Andrew H. Jr. Nov 2003

Carlson, Margaret Nov 2003

Carmines, Al obit Yrbk 2005

Carmona, Richard Jan 2003

Carney, Art obit Yrbk 2004

Carroll-Abbing, J. Patrick obit Nov 2001

Carroll, Vinnette obit Feb 2003

Carson, Johnny obit Jul 2005

Carter, Benny obit Oct 2003

Carter, Jimmy see Blind Boys of Alabama

Carter, Regina Oct 2003

Carter, Shawn see Jay-Z

Carter, Vince Apr 2002

Cartier-Bresson, Henri obit Yrbk 2004

Cash, Johnny obit Jan 2004

Castle, Barbara obit Yrbk 2002

Castro, Fidel Jun 2001

Cattrall, Kim Jan 2003

Cavanagh, Tom Jun 2003

Cavanna, Betty obit Oct 2001

Cave, Nick Jun 2005

Cela, Camilo José obit Apr 2002

Celmins, Vija Jan 2005

Chaban-Delmas, Jacques obit Feb 2001

Chaikin, Joseph obit Yrbk 2003

Chandrasekhar, Sripati obit Sep 2001

Chao, Elaine L. May 2001

Chapman, Duane Mar 2005

Charles, Michael Ray Oct 2005

Charles, Ray obit Yrbk 2004

Chase, David Mar 2001

Chauncey, Henry obit Mar 2003

Cheney, Richard B. Jan 2002

Chertoff, Michael Oct 2005

Chiang Kai-shek, Mme. see Chiang Mei-Ling

Chiang Mei-Ling obit Mar 2004

Child, Julia obit Nov 2004

Chillida, Eduardo obit Yrbk 2002

Chisholm, Shirley obit Apr 2005
Churchland, Patricia S. May 2003
Claremont, Chris Sep 2003
Clark, Kenneth B. obit Sep 2005
Clarkson, Patricia Aug 2005
Clemens, Roger Aug 2003
Clinton, Hillary Rodham Jan 2002
Clooney, Rosemary obit Nov 2002
Clowes, Daniel Jan 2002
Clyburn, James E. Oct 2001
Coburn, James obit Feb 2003
Coca, Imogene obit Sep 2001
Cochran, Johnnie L. Jr. obit Oct 2005
Cochran, Thad Apr 2002
Coddington, Grace Apr 2005
Cohen, Rob Nov 2002
Cohn, Linda Aug 2002
Colbert, Edwin H. obit Feb 2002
Colbert, Gregory Sep 2005
Coleman, Cy obit Feb 2005
Collen, Phil see Def Leppard
Collier, Sophia Jul 2002
Collins, Jim Aug 2003
Collins, Patricia Hill Mar 2003
Columbus, Chris Nov 2001
Cometbus, Aaron Mar 2005
Como, Perry obit Jul 2001
Conable, Barber B. obit Sep 2004
Connelly, Jennifer Jun 2002
Conner, Nadine obit Aug 2003
Connor, John T. obit Feb 2001
Conway, Gerry see Fairport Convention
Conway, John Horton Sep 2003
Cook, Richard W. Jul 2003
Cooke, Alistair obit Oct 2004
Coontz, Stephanie Jul 2003
Coppola, Sofia Nov 2003
Corelli, Franco obit Mar 2004
Coulter, Ann Sep 2003
Counsell, Craig Sep 2002
Counting Crows Mar 2003
Cox, Archibald obit Yrbk 2004
Coyne, Wayne see Flaming Lips
Crain, Jeanne obit Sep 2004
Cranston, Alan obit Mar 2001
Creed May 2002
Creeley, Robert obit Yrbk 2005
Crick, Francis obit Yrbk 2004

Crittenden, Danielle Jul 2003
Cromwell, James Aug 2005
Cronyn, Hume obit Yrbk 2003
Crosby, John obit Yrbk 2003
Cruz, Celia obit Nov 2003
Cruz, Penelope Jul 2001
Cuban, Mark Mar 2001
Cunhal, Álvaro obit Yrbk 2005
Currie, Nancy June 2002

Dacre of Glanton, Baron see Trevor-Roper, H. R.
Daft, Douglas N. May 2001
Dancer, Stanley obit Yrbk 2005
D'Angelo May 2001
Dangerfield, Rodney obit Feb 2005
Darling, Sharon May 2003
Davidson, Gordon Apr 2005
Davis, Benjamin O. Jr. obit Yrbk 2002
Davis, Glenn obit Yrbk 2005
Davis, Nathanael V. obit Yrbk 2005
Davis, Ossie obit Yrbk 2005
Davis, Wade Jan 2003
de Branges, Louis Nov 2005
de Hartog, Jan obit Jan 2003
De Jong, Dola obit Sep 2004
de la Rúa, Fernando Apr 2001
de Meuron, Pierre see Herzog, Jacques, and de Meuron, Pierre
De Sapio, Carmine obit Yrbk 2004
De Valois, Ninette obit Aug 2001
de Varona, Donna Aug 2003
Deakins, Roger May 2001
Dean, Howard Oct 2002
DeBusschere, Dave obit Yrbk 2003
DeCarlo, Dan Aug 2001 obit Mar 2002
Deep Throat see Felt, W. Mark
Def Leppard Jan 2003
Del Toro, Benicio Sep 2001
Delilah Apr 2005
Dellinger, David obit Yrbk 2004
DeLonge, Tom see blink-182
DeLorean, John Z. obit Yrbk 2005
Delson, Brad see Linkin Park
DeMarcus, Jay see Rascal Flatts
DeMille, Nelson Oct 2002
Densen-Gerber, Judianne obit Jul 2003

Derrida, Jacques obit Mar 2005
Destiny's Child Aug 2001
Diamond, David obit Yrbk 2005
Diaz, Cameron Apr 2005
Dillon, C. Douglas obit May 2003
Dirnt, Mike see Green Day
Djerassi, Carl Oct 2001
Djukanovic, Milo Aug 2001
DMX Aug 2003
Domini, Amy Nov 2005
Donald, Arnold W. Nov 2005
Donaldson, William Jun 2003
Donovan, Carrie obit Feb 2002
Doubilet, David Mar 2003
Doudna, Jennifer Feb 2005
Douglas, Ashanti see Ashanti
Douglas, John E. Jul 2001
Drake, James Jul 2005
Drozd, Steven see Flaming Lips
Drucker, Eugene see Emerson String Quartet
Dude Love see Foley, Mick
Dugan, Alan obit Oct 2004
Dunlop, John T. obit Sep 2004
Dunne, John Gregory obit Yrbk 2004
Dunst, Kirsten Oct 2001
Duritz, Adam see Counting Crows
Dutton, Lawrence see Emerson String Quartet
Dworkin, Andrea obit Yrbk 2005

Eban, Abba obit Mar 2003
Eberhart, Richard obit Yrbk 2005
Ebsen, Buddy obit Yrbk 2003
Eckert, Robert A. Mar 2003
Eddins, William Feb 2002
Edwards, Bob Sep 2001
Egan, Edward M. Jul 2001
Egan, Jennifer Mar 2002
Eggleston, William Feb 2002
Ehlers, Vernon J. Jan 2005
Eiko see Eiko and Koma
Eiko and Koma May 2003
Eisner, Will obit May 2005
Elizabeth, Queen Mother of Great Britain obit Jun 2002
Elling, Kurt Jan 2005
Elliott, Joe see Def Leppard
Elliott, Sean Apr 2001
Emerson String Quartet Jul 2002
Eminem Jan 2001
Engibous, Thomas J. Oct 2003

Ensler, Eve Aug 2002
Epstein, Samuel S. Aug 2001
Ericsson-Jackson, Aprille J. Mar 2001
Estenssoro, Victor Paz *see* Paz Estenssoro, Victor
Etherington, Edwin D. obit Apr 2001
Eugenides, Jeffrey Oct 2003
Eustis, Oskar Oct 2002
Eustis, Paul Jefferson *see* Eustis, Oskar
Evanovich, Janet Apr 2001
Evans, Dale obit Apr 2001
Evans, Donald L. Nov 2001
Eve Jul 2003
Everett, Rupert Jan 2005
Exon, J. James obit Yrbk 2005
Eyadéma, Etienne Gnassingbé Apr 2002 obit Yrbk 2005
Eyre, Chris May 2003
Eytan, Walter obit Oct 2001

Faber, Sandra Apr 2002
Fadiman, Anne Aug 2005
Fahd, King of Saudi Arabia obit Yrbk 2005
Fahd, Prince of Saudi Arabia *see* Fahd, King of Saudi Arabia
Fairclough, Ellen obit Yrbk 2005
Fairport Convention Sep 2005
Fallon, Jimmy Jul 2002
Farhi, Nicole Nov 2001
Farrell, Dave *see* Linkin Park
Farrell, Eileen obit Jun 2002
Farrelly, Bobby *see* Farrelly, Peter and Bobby
Farrelly, Peter and Bobby Sep 2001
Fast, Howard obit Jul 2003
Fattah, Chaka Sep 2003
Faulk, Marshall Jan 2003
Fausto-Sterling, Anne Sep 2005
Fay, J. Michael Sep 2001
Feifel, Herman obit Yrbk 2005
Felt, W. Mark Sep 2005
Ferré, Luis A. obit Mar 2004
Ferrell, Will Feb 2003
Ferrer, Rafael Jul 2001
Ferris, Timothy Jan 2001
Fey, Tina Apr 2002
Fiedler, Leslie A. obit Yrbk 2003
Fields, Mark Apr 2005
Finckel, David *see* Emerson String Quartet
Fishman, Jon *see* Phish
Fitzgerald, Geraldine obit Yrbk 2005

Flaming Lips Oct 2002
Flanagan, Tommy obit Mar 2002
Fletcher, Arthur obit Yrbk 2005
Foer, Jonathan Safran Sep 2002
Foley, Mick Sep 2001
Fong, Hiram L. obit Yrbk 2004
Fong-Torres, Ben Aug 2001
Foote, Shelby obit Yrbk 2005
Forrest, Vernon Jul 2002
Forsberg, Peter Nov 2005
Forsee, Gary D. Oct 2005
Forsythe, William Feb 2003
Fortey, Richard Sep 2005
Foss, Joseph Jacob obit Yrbk 2003
Fossett, J. Stephen *see* Fossett, Steve
Fossett, Steve Apr 2005
Fountain, Clarence *see* Blind Boys of Alabama
Fox Quesada, Vicente May 2001
Foxx, Jamie May 2005
Francis, Arlene obit Sep 2001
Francisco, Don Feb 2001
Frankenheimer, John obit Oct 2002
Franklin, Shirley C. Aug 2002
Franks, Tommy R. Jan 2002
Franzen, Jonathan Sep 2003
Fraser, Brendan Feb 2001
Fredericks, Henry St. Clair *see* Mahal, Taj
Freeman, Lucy obit Yrbk 2005
Freeman, Orville L. obit Yrbk 2003
Freston, Tom Aug 2003
Friedman, Jane Mar 2001
Frist, Bill Nov 2002
Froese, Edgar *see* Tangerine Dream
Froese, Jerome *see* Tangerine Dream
Fry, Christopher obit Yrbk 2005
Fugazi Mar 2002
Fukuyama, Francis Jun 2001

Gades, Antonio obit Yrbk 2004
Galinsky, Ellen Oct 2003
Galloway, Joseph L. Sep 2003
Galtieri, Leopoldo obit Yrbk 2003
Gandy, Kim Oct 2001
Garcia, Sergio Mar 2001
Gardner, John W. obit May 2002

Garfield, Henry *see* Rollins, Henry
Garofalo, Janeane Mar 2005
Garrison, Deborah Jan 2001
Gary, Willie E. Apr 2001
Garza, Ed Jun 2002
Garzón, Baltasar Mar 2001
Gaskin, Ina May May 2001
Gaubatz, Lynn Feb 2001
Gawande, Atul Mar 2005
Gayle, Helene Jan 2002
Gebel-Williams, Gunther obit Oct 2001
Geis, Bernard obit Mar 2001
Gelb, Leslie H. Jan 2003
Gennaro, Peter obit Feb 2001
Germond, Jack W. Jul 2005
Gerson, Michael Feb 2002
Giamatti, Paul Sep 2005
Giannulli, Mossimo Feb 2003
Gibson, Althea obit Feb 2004
Gibson, Charles Sep 2002
Gibson, Mel Aug 2003
Gierek, Edward obit Oct 2001
Gilbreth, Frank B. Jr. obit Jul 2001
Gillingham, Charles *see* Counting Crows
Gillis, John *see* White Stripes
Gilmore, James S. III Jun 2001
Ginzberg, Eli obit Yrbk 2003
Giroud, Françoise obit Jul 2003
Giulini, Carlo Maria obit Yrbk 2005
Gladwell, Malcolm Jun 2005
Glass, H. Bentley obit Yrbk 2005
Goff, M. Lee Jun 2001
Gold, Thomas obit Yrbk 2004
Goldberg, Bill Apr 2001
Golden, Thelma Sep 2001
Goldman-Rakic, Patricia Feb 2003
Goldovsky, Boris obit Aug 2001
Goldsmith, Jerry obit Nov 2004
Goldsmith, Jerry May 2001
Goldstine, Herman Heine obit Yrbk 2004
Golub, Leon obit Yrbk 2004
Gonzales, Alberto R. Apr 2002
Gonzalez, Henry obit Feb 2001
Good, Mary L. Sep 2001
Good, Robert A. obit Yrbk 2003
Goodpaster, Andrew J. obit Yrbk 2005
Googoosh May 2001
Gopnik, Adam Apr 2005

Gordon, Bruce S. Oct 2005
Gordon, Cyrus H. obit Aug 2001
Gordon, Ed Jul 2005
Gordon, Edmund W. Jun 2003
Gordon, Mike *see* Phish
Gorman, R. C. Jan 2001
Gorsuch, Anne obit Yrbk 2004
Gorton, John Grey obit Yrbk 2002
Gottlieb, Melvin B. obit Mar 2001
Gould, Stephen Jay obit Aug 2002
Gourdji, Françoise *see* Giroud, Françoise
Gowers, Timothy Jan 2001
Gowers, William Timothy *see* Gowers, Timothy
Graham, Franklin May 2002
Graham, Katharine obit Oct 2001
Graham, Susan Oct 2005
Graham, Winston obit Yrbk 2003
Granholm, Jennifer M. Oct 2003
Grasso, Richard Oct 2002
Graves, Florence George May 2005
Graves, Morris obit Sep 2001
Gray, L. Patrick obit Yrbk 2005
Gray, Spalding obit Yrbk 2004
Greco, José obit Mar 2001
Green, Adolph obit Mar 2003
Green, Darrell Jan 2001
Green Day Aug 2005
Green, Tom Oct 2003
Greenberg, Jack M. Nov 2001
Greene, Wallace M. obit Aug 2003
Greenstein, Jesse L. obit Yrbk 2003
Greenwood, Colin *see* Radiohead
Greenwood, Jonny *see* Radiohead
Gregory, Frederick D. Oct 2005
Gregory, Wilton D. Mar 2002
Griffin, Michael Aug 2005
Griffiths, Martha W. obit Yrbk 2003
Grigg, John obit Apr 2002
Grohl, Dave May 2002
Gruber, Ruth Jun 2001
Grubin, David Aug 2002
Gudmundsdottir, Björk *see* Björk

Guerard, Albert J. obit Mar 2001
Gunn, Thom obit Yrbk 2004
Gursky, Andreas Jul 2001

Haas, Jonathan Jun 2003
Hacker *see* Hackett, Buddy
Hackett, Buddy obit Oct 2003
Hagen, Uta obit Yrbk 2004
Hahn, Hilary Sep 2002
Hahn, Joseph *see* Linkin Park
Hailey, Arthur obit Yrbk 2005
Hailsham of St. Marylebone, Quintin Hogg obit Feb 2002
Hair, Jay D. obit Jan 2003
Halaby, Najeeb E. obit Yrbk 2003
Halasz, Laszlo obit Feb 2002
Hall, Conrad L. obit May 2003
Hall, Deidre Nov 2002
Hall, Gus obit Jan 2001
Hall, Richard Melville *see* Moby
Hall, Steffie *see* Evanovich, Janet
Hall, Tex G. May 2005
Hallaren, Mary A. obit Yrbk 2005
Hallström, Lasse Feb 2005
Hamilton, Laird Aug 2005
Hammon, Becky Jan 2003
Hampton, Lionel obit Yrbk 2002
Hancock, Graham Feb 2005
Hanna, William obit Sep 2001
Hannity, Sean Apr 2005
Hansen, Liane May 2003
Harcourt, Nic Oct 2005
Harden, Marcia Gay Sep 2001
Hardin, Garrett obit Apr 2004
Hargis, Billy James obit Yrbk 2005
Hargrove, Marion obit Yrbk 2004
Harjo, Joy Aug 2001
Harris, Richard obit Yrbk 2003
Harrison, George obit Mar 2002
Harrison, Marvin Aug 2001
Harrison, William B. Jr. Mar 2002
Hartke, Vance obit Yrbk 2003
Hartmann, Heidi I. Apr 2003
Haskins, Caryl P. obit Feb 2002
Hass, Robert Feb 2001
Hassenfeld, Alan G. Jul 2003
Hauerwas, Stanley Jun 2003
Hawkinson, Tim Aug 2005
Hax, Carolyn Nov 2002
Hayes, Bob obit Jan 2003

Haynes, Cornell Jr. *see* Nelly
Haynes, Todd Jul 2003
Headley, Elizabeth *see* Cavanna, Betty
Heath, Edward obit Yrbk 2005
Heath, James R. Oct 2003
Hecht, Anthony obit Yrbk 2005
Heckart, Eileen obit Mar 2002
Heilbroner, Robert L. obit Yrbk 2005
Heilbrun, Carolyn G. obit Feb 2004
Heiskell, Andrew obit Yrbk 2003
Held, Al obit Yrbk 2005
Helms, Richard obit Yrbk 2003
Henderson, Donald A. Mar 2002
Henderson, Hazel Nov 2003
Henderson, Joe obit Oct 2001
Hendrickson, Sue Oct 2001
Henry, Brad Jan 2005
Henry, John W. May 2005
Hepburn, Katharine obit Nov 2003
Herblock *see* Block, Herbert L.
Herndon, J. Marvin Nov 2003
Herring, Pendleton obit Yrbk 2004
Herzog, Jacques *see* Herzog, Jacques, and de Meuron, Pierre
Herzog, Jacques, and de Meuron, Pierre Jun 2002
Hewitt, Lleyton Oct 2002
Hewlett, Sylvia Ann Sep 2002
Heyerdahl, Thor obit Yrbk 2002
Heym, Stefan obit Mar 2002
Hicks, Louise Day obit Jun 2004
Hidalgo, David *see* Los Lobos
Higgins, Chester Jr. Jun 2002
Hildegarde obit Yrbk 2005
Hill, Dulé Jul 2003
Hill, Faith Mar 2001
Hill, George Roy obit Jun 2003
Hill, Grant Jan 2002
Hill, Herbert obit Yrbk 2004
Hillenburg, Stephen Apr 2003
Hiller, Wendy obit Yrbk 2003
Hines, Gregory obit Yrbk 2003
Hines, Jerome obit Jun 2003
Hinojosa, Maria Feb 2001
Hirschfeld, Al obit Jul 2003
Hobson, Mellody Aug 2005
Hobson Pilot, Ann May 2003

Hoffman, Philip Seymour May 2001
Hogg, Quintin *see* Hailsham of St. Marylebone, Quintin Hogg
Holden, Betsy Jul 2003
Holland, Dave Mar 2003
Holm, Ian Mar 2002
Hong, Hei-Kyung Nov 2003
Hooker, John Lee obit Sep 2001
Hope, Bob obit Yrbk 2003
Hopkins, Bernard Apr 2002
Hopkins, Nancy May 2002
Hoppus, Mark *see* blink-182
Horwich, Frances obit Oct 2001
Hounsfield, Godfrey obit Yrbk 2004
Houston, Allan Nov 2003
Houston, James A. obit Yrbk 2005
Howard, Tim Sep 2005
Howe, Harold II obit Yrbk 2003
Hoyle, Fred obit Jan 2002
Huckabee, Mike Nov 2005
Hughes, Karen Oct 2001
Hull, Jane Dee Feb 2002
Hunter, Evan obit Yrbk 2005
Hunter, Kermit obit Sep 2001
Hunter, Kim obit Yrbk 2002

Iakovos, Archbishop obit Yrbk 2005
Ifill, Gwen Sep 2005
Ilitch, Michael Feb 2005
Illich, Ivan obit Yrbk 2003
India.Arie Feb 2002
Inkster, Juli Sep 2002
Isbin, Sharon Aug 2003
Istomin, Eugene obit Feb 2004
Ivins, Michael *see* Flaming Lips
Izetbegovic, Alija obit Jun 2004

Ja Rule Jul 2002
Jackman, Hugh Oct 2003
Jackson, Hal Oct 2002
Jackson, Lauren Jun 2003
Jackson, Maynard H. Jr. obit Yrbk 2003
Jackson, Michael Aug 2005
Jackson, Peter Jan 2002
Jackson, Thomas Penfield Jun 2001
Jakes, T.D. Jun 2001
James, Alex *see* Blur
James, Edgerrin Jan 2002
James, LeBron Nov 2005

Janeway, Elizabeth obit Yrbk 2005
Jarring, Gunnar obit Yrbk 2002
Jarvis, Erich D. May 2003
Jay-Z Aug 2002
Jeffers, Eve Jihan *see* Eve
Jeffords, James Sep 2001
Jenkins, Jerry B. *see* LaHaye, Tim and Jenkins, Jerry B.
Jenkins, Roy obit Yrbk 2003
Jennings, Peter obit Sep 2005
Jennings, Waylon obit Apr 2002
Jensen, Oliver O. obit Yrbk 2005
Jet *see* Urquidez, Benny
Jimenez, Marcos Perez *see* Pérez Jiménez, Marcos
Jobert, Michel obit Yrbk 2002
Johannesen, Grant obit Yrbk 2005
Johansson, Scarlett Mar 2005
John Paul II obit Jun 2005
Johnson, Brian *see* AC/DC
Johnson, Eddie Bernice Jul 2001
Johnson, Elizabeth A. Nov 2002
Johnson, John H. obit Yrbk 2005
Johnson, Philip obit Sep 2005
Jones, Bobby Jun 2002
Jones, Chipper May 2001
Jones, Chuck obit May 2002
Jones, Larry Wayne Jr. *see* Jones, Chipper
Jones, Norah May 2003
Jones, Sarah Jul 2005
Jonze, Spike Apr 2003
Joyner, Tom Sep 2002
Judd, Jackie Sep 2002
Judd, Jacqueline Dee *see* Judd, Jackie
Juliana Queen of the Netherlands obit Yrbk 2004

Kabila, Joseph Sep 2001
Kael, Pauline obit Nov 2001
Kainen, Jacob obit Aug 2001
Kamen, Dean Nov 2002
Kane, Joseph Nathan obit Nov 2002
Kani, John Jun 2001
Kann, Peter R. Mar 2003
Kaptur, Marcy Jan 2003
Karbo, Karen May 2001
Karle, Isabella Jan 2003
Karon, Jan Mar 2003
Karsh, Yousuf obit Nov 2002
Karzai, Hamid May 2002
Kase, Toshikazu obit Yrbk 2004

Kass, Leon R. Aug 2002
Katsav, Moshe Feb 2001
Kaufman, Charlie Jul 2005
Kazan, Elia obit Yrbk 2004
Kcho Aug 2001
Keener, Catherine Oct 2002
Keeshan, Bob obit Yrbk 2004
Kelleher, Herb Jan 2001
Keller, Bill Oct 2003
Kelman, Charles obit Yrbk 2004
Kennan, George F. obit Yrbk 2005
Kennedy, Randall Aug 2002
Kent, Jeff May 2003
Kentridge, William Oct 2001
Kenyon, Cynthia Jan 2005
Kepes, György obit Mar 2002
Kerr, Clark obit May 2004
Kerr, Jean obit May 2003
Kerr, Mrs. Walter F *see* Kerr, Jean
Kesey, Ken obit Feb 2002
Ketcham, Hank obit Sep 2001
Keys, Ancel obit Yrbk 2005
Keys, Charlene *see* Tweet
Kid Rock Oct 2001
Kidd, Chip Jul 2005
Kidd, Jason May 2002
Kiessling, Laura Aug 2003
King, Alan obit Yrbk 2004
Kittikachorn, Thanom obit Yrbk 2004
Klaus, Josef obit Oct 2001
Kleiber, Carlos obit Yrbk 2004
Klein, Naomi Aug 2003
Knievel, Robbie Mar 2005
Knipfel, Jim Mar 2005
Knowles, Beyoncé *see* Destiny's Child
Koch, Kenneth obit Yrbk 2002
Koizumi, Junichiro Jan 2002
Kolar, Jiri obit Yrbk 2002
Koma *see* Eiko and Koma
Konaré, Alpha Oumar Oct 2001
Koner, Pauline obit Apr 2001
Kopp, Wendy Mar 2003
Kostunica, Vojislav Jan 2001
Kott, Jan obit Mar 2002
Kournikova, Anna Jan 2002
Kramer, Stanley obit May 2001
Krause, David W. Feb 2002
Kreutzberger, Mario *see* Francisco, Don
Krugman, Paul Aug 2001
Kübler-Ross, Elisabeth obit Yrbk 2004
Kushner, Tony Jul 2002
Kusturica, Emir Nov 2005

Kyprianou, Spyros obit May 2002

La India May 2002
La Montagne, Margaret see Spellings, Margaret
La Russa, Tony Jul 2003
Lacy, Dan obit Nov 2001
LaDuke, Winona Jan 2003
Lagardère, Jean-Luc obit Aug 2003
LaHaye, Tim see LaHaye, Tim and Jenkins, Jerry B.
LaHaye, Tim and Jenkins, Jerry B. Jun 2003
Lally, Joe see Fugazi
Lampert, Edward S. Sep 2005
Landers, Ann obit Nov 2002
Lange, David obit Yrbk 2005
Langevin, Jim Aug 2005
Lapidus, Morris obit Apr 2001
Lapp, Ralph E. obit Feb 2005
Lara, Brian Feb 2001
Lardner, Ring Jr. obit Feb 2001
Laredo, Ruth obit Yrbk 2005
Lassaw, Ibram obit Yrbk 2004
Lauder, Estée obit Yrbk 2004
Lavigne, Avril Apr 2003
Law, Ty Oct 2002
Lax, Peter D. Oct 2005
Le Clercq, Tanaquil obit Mar 2001
Leakey, Meave Jun 2002
Lederer, Esther Pauline see Landers, Ann
Lee, Andrea Sep 2003
Lee, Geddy see Rush
Lee, Jeanette Oct 2002
Lee, Mrs. John G. see Lee, Percy Maxim
Lee, Peggy obit May 2002
Lee, Percy Maxim obit Jan 2003
Lee, Richard C. obit Jun 2003
LeFrak, Samuel J. obit Yrbk 2003
Lehane, Dennis Oct 2005
Leiter, Al Aug 2002
Lelyveld, Joseph Nov 2005
Lemmon, Jack obit Oct 2001
Leon, Kenny Nov 2005
Leonard see Hackett, Buddy
Leone, Giovanni obit Feb 2002
Leslie, Chris see Fairport Convention
LeSueur, Larry obit Jun 2003
Letterman, David Oct 2002
Levert, Gerald Oct 2003
Levine, Mel Nov 2005
LeVox, Gary see Rascal Flatts

Levy, Eugene Jan 2002
Lewis, Ananda Jun 2005
Lewis, David Levering May 2001
Lewis, David S. Jr. obit Yrbk 2004
Lewis, Flora obit Yrbk 2002
Lewis, John obit Jun 2001
Li, Jet Jun 2001
Li Lian Jie see Li, Jet
Libeskind, Daniel Jun 2003
Lifeson, Alex see Rush
Lilly, John C. obit Feb 2002
Lima do Amor, Sisleide see Sissi
Lincoln, Abbey Sep 2002
Lincoln, Blanche Lambert Mar 2002
Lindbergh, Anne Morrow obit Apr 2001
Lindgren, Astrid obit Apr 2002
Lindo, Delroy Mar 2001
Lindsay, John V. obit Mar 2001
Ling, James J. obit Yrbk 2005
Lingle, Linda Jun 2003
Link, O. Winston obit Apr 2001
Linkin Park Mar 2002
Linowitz, Sol M. obit Yrbk 2005
Lippold, Richard obit Yrbk 2002
Liu, Lucy Oct 2003
Lloyd, Charles Apr 2002
Locke, Gary Apr 2003
Lohan, Lindsay Nov 2005
Lomax, Alan obit Oct 2002
London, Julie obit Feb 2001
Long, Russell B. obit Yrbk 2003
López Portillo, José obit Yrbk 2004
Lord, Walter obit Yrbk 2002
Los Lobos Oct 2005
Loudon, Dorothy obit Yrbk 2004
Love, John A. obit Apr 2002
Lowell, Mike Sep 2003
Lozano, Conrad see Los Lobos
Lucas, George May 2002
Luckovich, Mike Jan 2005
Ludlum, Robert obit Jul 2001
Luke, Delilah Rene see Delilah
Lumet, Sidney Jun 2005
Luns, Joseph M. A. H. obit Yrbk 2002
Lupica, Mike Mar 2001
Lyng, Richard E. obit Jun 2003
Lynne, Shelby Jul 2001

Mac, Bernie Jun 2002
Machado, Alexis Leyva see Kcho
MacKaye, Ian see Fugazi
MacKenzie, Gisele obit Jul 2004
Maddox, Lester obit Yrbk 2003
Magloire, Paul E. obit Nov 2001
Maguire, Tobey Sep 2002
Mahal, Taj Nov 2001
Maki, Fumihiko Jul 2001
Malley, Matt see Counting Crows
Maloney, Carolyn B. Apr 2001
Manchester, William obit Yrbk 2004
Mankind see Foley, Mick
Mankoff, Robert May 2005
Mann, Emily Jun 2002
Mansfield, Michael J. see Mansfield, Mike
Mansfield, Mike obit Jan 2002
Marcinko, Richard Mar 2001
Marcus, Stanley obit Apr 2002
Marcy, Geoffrey W. see Marcy, Geoffrey W., and Butler, R. Paul
Marcy, Geoffrey W., and Butler, R. Paul Nov 2002
Margaret, Princess of Great Britain obit May 2002
Markova, Alicia obit Yrbk 2005
Marlette, Doug Jul 2002
Marshall, Burke obit Yrbk 2003
Marshall, Rob Jun 2003
Martin, A. J. P. see Martin, Archer
Martin, Agnes obit Apr 2005
Martin, Archer obit Yrbk 2002
Martin, James S. Jr. obit Yrbk 2002
Martin, Kenyon Jan 2005
Martin, Kevin J. Aug 2005
Martin, Mark Mar 2001
Martinez, Pedro Jun 2001
Martinez, Rueben Jun 2005
Martz, Judy Mar 2005
Mary Kay see Ash, Mary Kay
Masters, William H. obit May 2001
Mathers, Marshall see Eminem
Matsui, Connie L. Aug 2002
Matsui, Robert T. obit Apr 2005
Matta obit Yrbk 2003

Mauch, Gene obit Yrbk 2005
Mauldin, Bill obit Jul 2003
Mauldin, William Henry *see*
Mauldin, Bill
Mayne, Thom Oct 2005
Mayr, Ernst obit May 2005
Mays, L. Lowry Aug 2003
McCambridge, Mercedes obit
Yrbk 2004
McCann, Renetta May 2005
McCaw, Craig Sep 2001
McCloskey, Robert obit Yrbk
2003
McConnell, Page *see* Phish
McCrary, Tex obit Yrbk 2003
McCurry, Steve Nov 2005
McDonald, Gabrielle Kirk Oct
2001
McGhee, George Crews obit
Yrbk 2005
McGrady, Tracy Feb 2003
McGrath, Judy Feb 2005
McGraw, Eloise Jarvis obit
Mar 2001
McGraw, Phillip Jun 2002
McGraw, Tim Sep 2002
McGreal, Elizabeth *see* Yates,
Elizabeth
McGruder, Aaron Sep 2001
McGuire, Dorothy obit Nov
2001
McIntire, Carl obit Jun 2002
McIntosh, Millicent Carey
obit Mar 2001
McKinney, Robert obit Yrbk
2001
McLean, Jackie Mar 2001
McLean, John Lenwood *see*
McLean, Jackie
McLurkin, James Sep 2005
McMath, Sid obit Jan 2004
McNair, Steve Jan 2005
McNally, Andrew 3d obit Feb
2002
McQueen, Alexander Feb
2002
McWhirter, Norris D. obit
Yrbk 2004
McWhorter, John H. Feb 2003
Mechem, Edwin L. obit Yrbk
2003
Meiselas, Susan Feb 2005
Mendes, Sam Oct 2002
Menken, Alan Jan 2001
Merchant, Ismail obit Yrbk
2005
Merchant, Natalie Jan 2003
Meron, Theodor Mar 2005
Merrill, Robert obit Feb 2005
Merton, Robert K. obit Yrbk
2003
Messick, Dale obit Yrbk 2005
Messier, Jean-Marie May 2002

Messing, Debra Aug 2002
Meta, Ilir Feb 2002
Meyer, Cord Jr. obit Aug 2001
Meyer, Edgar Jun 2002
Meyers, Nancy Feb 2002
Michel, Sia Sep 2003
Mickelson, Phil Mar 2002
Middelhoff, Thomas Feb 2001
Miller, Ann obit Yrbk 2004
Miller, Arthur obit Jul 2005
Miller, J. Irwin obit Yrbk
2004
Miller, Jason obit Yrbk 2001
Miller, John Aug 2003
Miller, Neal obit Jun 2002
Millionaire, Tony Jul 2005
Millman, Dan Aug 2002
Mills, John obit Yrbk 2005
Milosz, Czeslaw obit Yrbk
2004
Mink, Patsy T. obit Jan 2003
Minner, Ruth Ann Aug 2001
Mirabal, Robert Aug 2002
Mitchell, Dean Aug 2002
Mitchell, Pat Aug 2005
Miyazaki, Hayao Apr 2001
Moby Apr 2001
Moiseiwitsch, Tanya obit Jul
2003
Monk, T. S. Feb 2002
Monseu, Stephanie *see*
Nelson, Keith and Monseu,
Stephanie
Montresor, Beni obit Feb
2002
Moore, Ann Aug 2003
Moore, Dudley obit Yrbk
2002
Moore, Elisabeth Luce obit
Yrbk 2002
Moore, Gordon E. Apr 2002
Moore, Paul Jr. obit Yrbk
2003
Moorer, Thomas H. obit Yrbk
2004
Morella, Constance A. Feb
2001
Morial, Marc Jan 2002
Morris, Butch Jul 2005
Morris, Errol Feb 2001
Morris, James T. Mar 2005
Morris, Lawrence *see* Morris,
Butch
Morrison, Philip obit Aug
2005
Mos Def Apr 2005
Moseka, Aminata *see*
Lincoln, Abbey
Moses, Bob *see* Moses,
Robert P.
Moses, Robert P. Apr 2002
Mosley, Sugar Shane Jan 2001

Mosley, Timothy *see*
Timbaland
Moss, Frank E. obit Jun 2003
Moten, Etta *see* Barnett, Etta
Moten
Moynihan, Daniel Patrick obit
Yrbk 2003
Mulcahy, Anne M. Nov 2002
Murkowski, Frank H. Jul 2003
Murray, Jonathan *see* Bunim,
Mary-Ellis, and Murray,
Jonathan
Murray, Jonathan *see* Bunim,
Mary-Ellis, and Murray,
Jonathan
Murray, Ty May 2002
Musharraf, Pervaiz *see*
Musharraf, Pervez
Musharraf, Pervez Mar 2001
Mydans, Carl M. obit Yrbk
2004
Mydans, Shelley Symith obit
Aug 2002
Myers, Joel N. Apr 2005
Myers, Richard B. Apr 2002

Nabrit, Samuel M. obit Yrbk
2004
Najimy, Kathy Oct 2002
Narayan, R. K. obit Jul 2001
Nash, Steve Mar 2003
Nason, John W. obit Feb 2002
Nasser, Jacques Apr 2001
Nathan, Robert R. obit Nov
2001
Ne Win obit Yrbk 2003
Neals, Otto Feb 2003
Neeleman, David Sep 2003
Negroponte, John Apr 2003
Nehru, B. K. obit Feb 2002
Nelly Oct 2002
Nelson, Gaylord obit Yrbk
2005
Nelson, Keith *see* Nelson,
Keith and Monseu,
Stephanie
Nelson, Keith and Monseu,
Stephanie Jun 2005
Nelson, Stanley May 2005
Neustadt, Richard E. obit
Yrbk 2004
Newman, J. Wilson obit Yrbk
2003
Newmark, Craig Jun 2005
Newton, Helmut obit Yrbk
2004
Nguyen Van Thieu *see* Thieu,
Nguyen Van
Nicol, Simon *see* Fairport
Convention
Nikolayev, Andrian obit Yrbk
2004
Nitze, Paul H. obit Mar 2005

Nixon, Agnes Apr 2001
Norton, Andre obit Yrbk 2005
Norton, Gale A. Jun 2001
Novacek, Michael J. Sep 2002
Nowitzki, Dirk Jun 2002
Nozick, Robert obit Apr 2002
Nugent, Ted Apr 2005

Obama, Barack Jul 2005
O'Brien, Ed see Radiohead
O'Connor, Carroll obit Sep 2001
O'Connor, Donald obit Apr 2004
O'Hair, Madalyn Murray obit Jun 2001
O'Keefe, Sean Jan 2003
Olin, Lena Jun 2003
Ollila, Jorma Aug 2002
O'Neal, Stanley May 2003
O'Neill, Paul H. Jul 2001
Orbach, Jerry obit Apr 2005
O'Reilly, Bill Oct 2003
Orlean, Susan Jun 2003
Orman, Suze May 2003
Ortiz, David Aug 2005
Ortner, Sherry B. Nov 2002
Osawa, Sandra Sunrising Jan 2001
Osborne, Barrie M. Feb 2005
Osbourne, Sharon Jan 2001
Oudolf, Piet Apr 2003
Oz, Mehmet C. Apr 2003

Paar, Jack obit Yrbk 2004
Page, Clarence Jan 2003
Page, Larry see Brin, Sergey, and Page, Larry
Paige, Roderick R. Jul 2001
Palmeiro, Rafael Aug 2001
Paltrow, Gwyneth Jan 2005
Park, Linda Sue Jun 2002
Park, Rosemary obit Yrbk 2004
Parker, Robert M. May 2005
Parsons, Richard D. Apr 2003
Pascal, Amy Mar 2002
Patchett, Ann Apr 2003
Patrick, Danica Oct 2005
Pau, Peter Feb 2002
Paulson, Henry M. Jr. Sep 2002
Payne, Alexander Feb 2003
Paz Estenssoro, Victor obit Sep 2001
Peart, Neil see Rush
Peck, Gregory obit Sep 2003
Peck, M. Scott obit Yrbk 2005
Pegg, Dave see Fairport Convention
Pelosi, Nancy Feb 2003
Pelzer, Dave Mar 2002

Perdue, Frank obit Oct 2005
Pérez Jiménez, Marcos obit Feb 2002
Pérez, Louie see Los Lobos
Perkins, Charles obit Feb 2001
Perle, Richard Jul 2003
Perry, Tyler Jun 2005
Person, Houston Jun 2003
Perutz, Max obit Apr 2002
Petersen, Wolfgang Jul 2001
Pettibon, Raymond Apr 2005
Peyroux, Madeleine Nov 2005
Phillips, Sam Apr 2001
Phillips, Scott see Creed
Phillips, William obit Yrbk 2002
Phish Jul 2003
Phoenix see Linkin Park
Piano, Renzo Apr 2001
Picciotto, Guy see Fugazi
Pickering, William H. obit Yrbk 2004
Piel, Gerard obit Feb 2005
Pierce, David Hyde Apr 2001
Pierce, John Robinson obit Jun 2002
Pierce, Paul Nov 2002
Pierce, Samuel R. Jr. obit Feb 2001
Pincay, Laffit Sep 2001
Pingree, Chellie Jan 2005
Pitt, Harvey Nov 2002
Plimpton, George obit Jan 2004
Plimpton, Martha Apr 2002
Poletti, Charles obit Yrbk 2002
Pollitt, Katha Oct 2002
Pomeroy, Wardell B. obit Yrbk 2001
Popeil, Ron Mar 2001
Posey, Parker Mar 2003
Potok, Chaim obit Yrbk 2002
Poujade, Pierre obit Yrbk 2004
Powell, Colin L. Nov 2001
Powell, Michael K. May 2003
Prigogine, Ilya obit Yrbk 2003
Prince-Hughes, Dawn Apr 2005
Prinze, Freddie Jr. Jan 2003
Prosper, Pierre-Richard Aug 2005
Pusey, Nathan M. obit Feb 2002

Queloz, Didier Feb 2002
Quine, W. V. obit Mar 2001
Quine, Willard Van Orman see Quine, W. V.
Quinn, Aidan Apr 2005

Quinn, Anthony obit Sep 2001

Rabassa, Gregory Jan 2005
Racette, Patricia Feb 2003
Radiohead Jun 2001
Raimi, Sam Jul 2002
Rainier III, Prince of Monaco obit Yrbk 2005
Rakic, Patricia Goldman see Goldman-Rakic, Patricia
Rall, Ted May 2002
Ralston, Joseph W. Jan 2001
Ramirez, Manny Jun 2002
Rampling, Charlotte Jun 2002
Randall, Tony obit Yrbk 2004
Randolph, Willie Sep 2005
Rania Feb 2001
Rao, P. V. Narasimha obit Yrbk 2005
Rascal Flatts Aug 2003
Ratzinger, Joseph see Benedict XVI
Rawl, Lawrence obit Yrbk 2005
Ray, Rachael Aug 2005
Reagan, Ronald obit Sep 2004
Redd, Michael Mar 2005
Redgrave, Vanessa Sep 2003
Reeve, Christopher obit Jan 2005
Reeves, Dan Oct 2001
Regan, Donald T. obit Yrbk 2003
Rehnquist, William H. Nov 2003 obit Yrbk 2005
Reich, Walter Aug 2005
Reid, Antonio see Reid, L. A.
Reid, Harry Mar 2003
Reid, L. A. Aug 2001
Reilly, Rick Feb 2005
Reitman, Ivan Mar 2001
Rell, M. Jodi Sep 2005
Ressler, Robert K. Feb 2002
Reuss, Henry S. obit Mar 2002
Reuther, Victor obit Yrbk 2004
Reynolds, John W. Jr. obit Mar 2002
Reynoso, Cruz Mar 2002
Rhodes, James A. obit Jul 2001
Rhodes, John J. obit Yrbk 2004
Rhodes, Randi Feb 2005
Rhyne, Charles S. obit Yrbk 2003
Rice, Condoleezza Apr 2001
Richler, Mordecai obit Oct 2001
Richter, Gerhard Jun 2002

Rickey, George W. obit Yrbk 2002
Ridge, Tom Feb 2001
Riefenstahl, Leni obit Yrbk 2004
Riesman, David obit Yrbk 2002
Riley, Terry Apr 2002
Rimm, Sylvia B. Feb 2002
Rimsza, Skip Jul 2002
Rines, Robert H. Jan 2003
Riopelle, Jean-Paul obit Yrbk 2002
Ripley, Alexander obit Yrbk 2004
Ripley, S. Dillon obit Aug 2001
Ritchie, Robert James see Kid Rock
Ritter, John obit Yrbk 2004
Rivers, Larry obit Nov 2002
Robards, Jason Jr. obit Mar 2001
Robb, J. D. see Roberts, Nora
Robbins, Anthony see Robbins, Tony
Robbins, Frederick C. obit Yrbk 2003
Robbins, Tony Jul 2001
Roberts, Nora Sep 2001
Robinson, Arthur H. obit Yrbk 2005
Robinson, Janet L. Mar 2003
Robinson, Marilynne Oct 2005
Rochberg, George obit Yrbk 2005
Roche, James M. obit Yrbk 2004
Rockefeller, Laurance S. obit Yrbk 2004
Rodino, Peter W. obit Yrbk 2005
Rodriguez, Alex Apr 2003
Rodriguez, Arturo Mar 2001
Rogers, Fred obit Jul 2003
Rogers, William P. obit Mar 2001
Rollins, Edward J. Mar 2001
Rollins, Henry Sep 2001
Romer, John Jul 2003
Romero, Anthony Jul 2002
Rooney, Joe Don see Rascal Flatts
Rosas, Cesar see Los Lobos
Rose, Jim Mar 2003
Ross, Herbert obit Feb 2002
Ross, Robert Oct 2002
Rostow, Eugene V. obit Yrbk 2003
Rostow, Walt W. obit Jul 2003
Rote, Kyle obit Yrbk 2002

Roth, William V. Jr. obit Yrbk 2004
Rothschild, Miriam obit Yrbk 2005
Rowan, Carl T. obit Jan 2001
Rowland, Kelly see Destiny's Child
Rowley, Janet D. Mar 2001
Rowntree, David see Blur
Rudd, Phil see AC/DC
Rule, Ja see Ja Rule
Rumsfeld, Donald H. Mar 2002
Rusesabagina, Paul May 2005
Rush Feb 2001
Russell, Harold obit Apr 2002
Rutan, Burt Jun 2005
Ryan, George H. Sep 2001
Ryder, Jonathan see Ludlum, Robert
Ryer, Jonathan see Ludlum, Robert

Safina, Carl Apr 2005
Sagan, Francoise obit Feb 2005
Said, Edward W. obit Feb 2004
Salinger, Pierre obit Feb 2005
Sánchez, David Nov 2001
Sanders, Ric see Fairport Convention
Sandford, John Mar 2002
Santos, José Nov 2003
Sapp, Warren Sep 2003
Saramago, José Jun 2002
Savage, Rick see Def Leppard
Savimbi, Jonas obit Jun 2002
Sayles Belton, Sharon Jan 2001
Scammon, Richard M. obit Sep 2001
Scaturro, Pasquale V. Oct 2005
Scavullo, Francesco obit Yrbk 2004
Scdoris, Rachael Jul 2005
Schaap, Phil Sep 2001
Schell, Maria obit Yrbk 2005
Schilling, Curt Oct 2001
Schindler, Alexander M. obit Feb 2001
Schjeldahl, Peter Oct 2005
Schlein, Miriam obit Yrbk 2005
Schlesinger, John obit Yrbk 2003
Schoenberg, Loren Feb 2005
Scholder, Fritz obit Yrbk 2005
Schott, Marge obit Yrbk 2004
Schriever, Bernard obit Yrbk 2005

Schultes, Richard Evans obit Sep 2001
Schultz, Ed Aug 2005
Scott, George obit Yrbk 2005
Scott, George see Blind Boys of Alabama
Scott, Jill Jan 2002
Scottoline, Lisa Jul 2001
Scully, Vin Oct 2001
Sears, Martha see Sears, William and Martha
Sears, William and Martha Aug 2001
Seau, Junior Sep 2001
Sedaris, Amy Apr 2002
Selway, Phil see Radiohead
Senghor, Léopold Sédar obit Mar 2002
Serrano Súñer, Ramón obit Yrbk 2004
Setzer, Philip see Emerson String Quartet
Seymour, Lesley Jane Nov 2001
Seymour, Stephanie Oct 2002
Shahade, Jennifer Sep 2005
Shaheen, Jeanne Jan 2001
Shalhoub, Tony Nov 2002
Shapiro, Irving S. obit Nov 2001
Shapiro, Neal May 2003
Shaw, Artie obit Apr 2005
Shawcross, Hartley obit Yrbk 2003
Shearer, Harry Jun 2001
Shepherd, Michael see Ludlum, Robert
Shields, Mark May 2005
Shinoda, Mike see Linkin Park
Shoemaker, Willie obit Apr 2004
Short, Bobby obit Nov 2005
Shriver, Lionel Sep 2005
Shyamalan, M. Night Mar 2003
Siddons, Anne Rivers Jan 2005
Silver, Joel Nov 2003
Simmons, Earl see DMX
Simon, Herbert A. obit May 2001
Simon, Paul obit Yrbk 2004
Simone, Nina obit Yrbk 2003
Sin, Jaime obit Yrbk 2005
Singer, Bryan Apr 2005
Sinopoli, Giuseppe obit Sep 2001
Sisco, Joseph obit Yrbk 2005
Sissi Jun 2001
Slater, Kelly Jul 2001
Slavenska, Mia obit Apr 2003
Smiley, Tavis Apr 2003

Smith, Amy Jun 2005
Smith, Chesterfield H. obit Yrbk 2003
Smith, Dante Terrell see Mos Def
Smith, Elinor Mar 2001
Smith, Howard K. obit Aug 2002
Smith, Jeff obit Yrbk 2004
Smith, Kiki Mar 2005
Smith, Maggie Jul 2002
Smith, Orin C. Nov 2003
Smylie, Robert E. obit Yrbk 2004
Snead, Sam obit Yrbk 2002
Snow, John Aug 2003
Soffer, Olga Jul 2002
Solomon, Susan Jul 2005
Sontag, Susan obit May 2005
Sothern, Ann obit Aug 2001
Souzay, Gérard obit Yrbk 2004
Spahn, Warren obit Yrbk 2004
Sparks, Nicholas Feb 2001
Spellings, Margaret Jun 2005
Spence, Hartzell obit Yrbk 2001
Spencer, John Jan 2001
Spencer, Scott Jul 2003
Spergel, David Jan 2005
Spitzer, Eliot Mar 2003
Sprewell, Latrell Feb 2001
St. John, Robert obit Yrbk 2003
Stackhouse, Jerry Nov 2001
Staley, Dawn Apr 2005
Stanfield, Robert Lorne obit Yrbk 2004
Stanley, Kim obit Jan 2002
Stanton, Bill May 2001
Stapp, Scott see Creed
Stargell, Willie obit Sep 2001
Stassen, Harold E. obit May 2001
Steele, Claude M. Feb 2001
Steig, William obit Apr 2004
Steiger, Rod obit Yrbk 2002
Stein, Benjamin J. Sep 2001
Steingraber, Sandra Sep 2003
Stern, Isaac obit Jan 2002
Stevens, Ted Oct 2001
Stewart, Alice obit Yrbk 2002
Stewart, James "Bubba" Feb 2005
Stoltenberg, Gerhard obit Mar 2002
Stone, W. Clement obit Yrbk 2002
Storr, Anthony obit Sep 2001
Stott, John May 2005
Straight, Michael obit Yrbk 2004

Stratton, William G. obit Aug 2001
Straus, Roger W. Jr. obit Yrbk 2004
Streb, Elizabeth Apr 2003
Stroman, Susan Jul 2002
Struzan, Drew Mar 2005
Stutz, Geraldine obit Yrbk 2005
Subandrio obit Apr 2005
Sucksdorff, Arne obit Sep 2001
Sugar, Bert Randolph Nov 2002
Sullivan, Daniel Feb 2003
Sullivan, Leon H. obit Sep 2001
Summers, Lawrence H. Jul 2002
Summitt, Pat Jun 2005
Sun Wen Apr 2001
Sutherland, Kiefer Mar 2002
Suzuki, Ichiro Jul 2002
Suzuki, Zenko obit Yrbk 2004
Sweeney, Anne Jun 2003
Swinton, Tilda Nov 2001
Syal, Meera Feb 2001

Taintor, Anne Jun 2005
Tajiri, Satoshi Nov 2001
Talley, André Leon Jul 2003
Talmadge, Herman E. obit Jun 2002
Tange, Kenzo obit Yrbk 2005
Tangerine Dream Jan 2005
Tarter, Jill Cornell Feb 2001
Tartt, Donna Feb 2003
Tauscher, Ellen O. Mar 2001
Taylor, John W. obit Apr 2002
Taylor, Koko Jul 2002
Taylor, Lili Jul 2005
Taylor, Theodore obit Feb 2005
Tebaldi, Renata obit Apr 2005
Tebbel, John obit Mar 2005
Tejada, Miguel Jun 2003
Teller, Edward obit Sep 2004
Thaler, William J. obit Yrbk 2005
Thieu, Nguyen Van obit Jan 2002
Thomas, Dave see Thomas, R. David
Thomas, R. David obit Apr 2002
Thompson, Hunter S. obit Yrbk 2005
Thompson, John W. Mar 2005
Thomson, James A. Nov 2001
Thomson, Meldrim Jr. obit Sep 2001

Thurmond, Strom obit Nov 2003
Thyssen-Bornemisza de Kaszan, Baron Hans Heinrich obit Yrbk 2002
Tice, George A. Nov 2003
Tierney, John Aug 2005
Tigerman, Stanley Feb 2001
Timbaland Mar 2003
Tisch, Laurence A. obit Yrbk 2004
Titov, Gherman obit Jan 2001
Tobin, James obit May 2002
Toledo, Alejandro Nov 2001
Toles, Thomas G. see Toles, Tom
Toles, Tom Nov 2002
Tolle, Eckhart Feb 2005
Tre Cool see Green Day
Tremonti, Mark see Creed
Trenet, Charles obit Sep 2001
Trenkler, Freddie obit Yrbk 2001
Trevor-Roper, H. R. obit Jul 2003
Trigère, Pauline obit Jul 2002
Trotter, Lloyd Jul 2005
Trout, Robert obit Jan 2001
Trudeau, Pierre Elliott obit Jan 2001
Truman, David B. obit Yrbk 2004
Tsui Hark Oct 2001
Tureck, Rosalyn obit Yrbk 2003
Turner, Mark Nov 2002
Turre, Steve Apr 2001
Tweet Nov 2002
Tyson, John H. Aug 2001

Unitas, Johnny obit Yrbk 2002
Uris, Leon obit Yrbk 2003
Urquidez, Benny Nov 2001
Urrea, Luis Alberto Nov 2005
Ustinov, Peter obit Aug 2004

Valentine, Bobby Jul 2001
Van den Haag, Ernest obit Jul 2002
Van Duyn, Mona obit Nov 2005
Van Exel, Nick Mar 2002
Van Gundy, Jeff May 2001
Vance, Cyrus R. obit Apr 2002
Vandiver, S. Ernest obit Yrbk 2005
Vandross, Luther obit Yrbk 2005
Vane, John R. obit Yrbk 2005

Varnedoe, Kirk obit Yrbk 2003
Verdon, Gwen obit Jan 2001
Vick, Michael Nov 2003
Vickrey, Dan see Counting Crows
Vieira, Meredith Apr 2002
Virilio, Paul Jul 2005
Viscardi, Henry Jr. obit Yrbk 2004
Vitale, Dick Jan 2005
Voulkos, Peter obit Aug 2002

Wachowski, Andy see Wachowski, Andy and Larry
Wachowski, Andy and Larry Sep 2003
Wachowski, Larry see Wachowski, Andy and Larry
Walker, Mort Feb 2002
Walker, Olene S. Apr 2005
Wall, Art obit Feb 2002
Wallis, Jim Jul 2005
Walsh, John Jul 2001
Walters, Barbara Feb 2003
Walters, Vernon A. obit Jul 2002
Walworth, Arthur C. obit Yrbk 2005
Ward, Benjamin obit Yrbk 2002
Ward, William E. Nov 2005
Ware, David S. Sep 2003
Warnke, Paul C. obit Feb 2002
Washington, Walter E. obit Yrbk 2004
Wasserman, Lew R. obit Yrbk 2002
Watkins, Donald Jan 2003
Watkins, Levi Jr. Mar 2003
Watson, Arthel Lane see Watson, Doc
Watson, Doc Feb 2003
Waugh, Auberon obit May 2001
Wayans, Marlon see Wayans, Shawn and Marlon
Wayans, Shawn and Marlon May 2001
Weaver, Pat obit Yrbk 2002
Weaver, Sylvester see Weaver, Pat
Webber, Chris May 2003
Weber, Dick obit Yrbk 2005
Weinrig, Gary Lee see Rush
Weiss, Paul obit Yrbk 2002
Weisskopf, Victor F. obit Yrbk 2002
Weitz, John obit Apr 2003
Weizman, Ezer obit Aug 2005

Wek, Alek Jun 2001
Wellstone, Paul D. obit Yrbk 2003
Welty, Eudora obit Nov 2001
Wesley, Valerie Wilson Jun 2002
Westmoreland, William C. obit Nov 2005
Wexler, Jerry Jan 2001
Weyrich, Paul Feb 2005
Whipple, Fred L. obit Yrbk 2005
Whitaker, Mark Aug 2003
White, Byron Raymond obit Jul 2002
White, Jack see White Stripes
White, John F. obit Yrbk 2005
White, Meg see White Stripes
White, Reggie obit Yrbk 2005
White Stripes Sep 2003
Whitehead, Colson Nov 2001
Whitford, Bradley Apr 2003
Whitson, Peggy Sep 2003
Wiesenthal, Simon obit Yrbk 2005
Wiggins, James Russell obit Mar 2001
Wilber, Ken Apr 2002
Wilder, Billy obit Yrbk 2002
Wilhelm, Hoyt obit Yrbk 2002
Wilkins, Maurice H. F. obit Yrbk 2005
Wilkins, Robert W. obit Yrbk 2003
Williams, Cliff see AC/DC
Williams, Harrison A. Jr. obit Mar 2002
Williams, Michelle see Destiny's Child
Williams, Serena see Williams, Venus and Williams, Serena
Williams, Ted obit Oct 2002
Williams, Venus see Williams, Venus and Williams, Serena
Williams, Venus and Williams, Serena Feb 2003
Willingham, Tyrone Nov 2002
Wilson, James Q. Aug 2002
Wilson, Kemmons obit Yrbk 2003
Wilson, Luke Feb 2005
Wilson, Owen Feb 2003
Wilson, Sloan obit Yrbk 2003
Winsor, Kathleen obit Yrbk 2003
Winston, Stan Jul 2002
Woese, Carl R. Jun 2003
Wojciechowska, Maia obit Yrbk 2002
Wolfe, Art Jun 2005

Wolfe, Julia Oct 2003
Wolff, Maritta M. obit Yrbk 2002
Wolfowitz, Paul Feb 2003
Wolfram, Stephen Feb 2005
Wong-Staal, Flossie Apr 2001
Wood, Elijah Aug 2002
Wood, Kerry May 2005
Woodcock, Leonard obit Apr 2001
Woods, Donald obit Nov 2001
Woodward, Robert F. obit Yrbk 2001
Wooldridge, Anna Marie see Lincoln, Abbey
Worth, Irene obit Aug 2002
Wright, Jeffrey May 2002
Wright, Steven May 2003
Wright, Teresa obit Yrbk 2005
Wriston, Walter B. obit Aug 2005
Wyman, Thomas obit Yrbk 2003

Xenakis, Iannis obit Jul 2001

Yashin, Aleksei see Yashin, Alexei
Yashin, Alexei Jan 2003
Yassin, Ahmed obit Yrbk 2004
Yates, Elizabeth obit Nov 2001
Yates, Sidney R. obit Jan 2001
Yokich, Stephen P. obit Yrbk 2002
Yorke, Thom see Radiohead
Young, Angus see AC/DC
Young, Malcolm see AC/DC

Zahn, Paula Feb 2002
Zaillian, Steven Oct 2001
Zambello, Francesca May 2003
Zatopek, Emil obit Feb 2001
Zerhouni, Elias Oct 2003
Zeta-Jones, Catherine Apr 2003
Zhao Ziyang obit Yrbk 2005
Zhu Rongji Jul 2001
Ziegler, Ronald L. obit Jul 2003
Zimmer, Hans Mar 2002
Zinni, Anthony C. May 2002
Zivojinovich, Alex see Rush
Zollar, Jawole Willa Jo Jul 2003
Zorina, Vera obit Yrbk 2003
Zucker, Jeff Jan 2002
Zukerman, Eugenia 2004